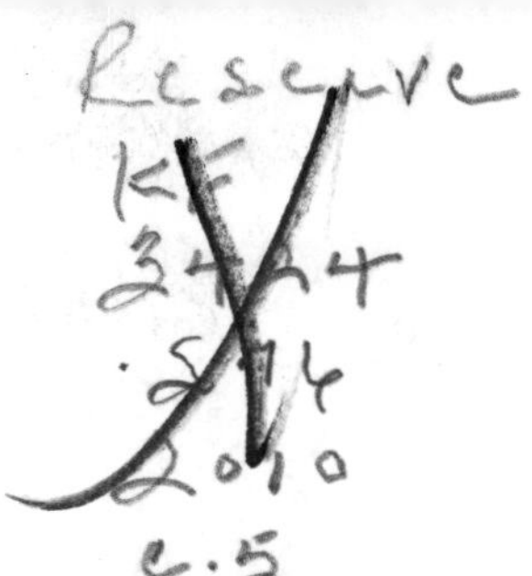

ARBITRATION LAW

SECOND EDITION

by

KATHERINE V.W. STONE
Professor of Law
University of California at Los Angeles School of Law

RICHARD A. BALES
Professor of Law
Northern Kentucky University, Salmon P. Chase College of Law

FOUNDATION PRESS
2010

195 Broadway, 9th Floor
New York, NY 10007
Phone Toll Free 1–877–888–1330
Fax (212) 367–6799
foundation–press.com

Printed in the United States of America

ISBN 978–1–59941–646–5

Mat #40833150

PREFACE TO SECOND EDITION

Arbitration has become an important aspect of the practice of law. Private agreements in many fields—commercial law, corporate law, employment, medical malpractice, real estate, family law, consumer law, private international law, and many others—routinely include arbitration clauses. When disputes arise, lawyers need to understand the legal significance of arbitration clauses and how to practice before an arbitration tribunal. Lawyers need to know whether and under what conditions arbitration clauses are enforceable, what kinds of defenses can be raised, what discovery is available, what procedures will be involved, and what remedies will be available in the arbitration forum. Lawyers who draft agreements also need to know the implications of including an arbitration clause and the options available to parties in designing arbitration clauses. Thus anyone practicing private law today needs to know the law of arbitration.

This book presents a comprehensive treatment of the legal issues involved in the use of arbitration. The first four chapters address issues that arise in private arbitration, that is, when arbitration is the product of an agreement between two contracting parties. The last chapter addresses issues that arise in court-ordered arbitration. Together the book gives the student a thorough understanding of arbitration law, and provides a solid foundation for legal practice, whether in alternative dispute resolution tribunals or in the civil justice system.

The Second Edition of Arbitration Law makes a number of changes from the previous edition of this book to reflect and incorporate changes in this dynamic area of law. Chapter 1 explores controversies that have arisen in the definition of arbitration and presents recent changes to the law of state versus federal jurisdiction. It also includes the recent Supreme Court case, *14 Penn Plaza v. Pyett*, that made a major change in the use of arbitration to address statutory claims in the labor-management setting. In Chapter 2, we have split the section on arbitrability into two subsections to delineate the analytically distinct issues of *what claims are arbitrable* and *who decides what claims are arbitrable*. We have also added a number of recent cases. In Chapter 3, we have subdivided the section on discovery into four subsections to reflect the diverse array of legal issues involved. A new section on class actions has been added. Several new cases have also been added to reflect development of the law. In Chapter 4, we have subdivided the section on judicial review into six subsections, and we have added a case concerning the enforceability of contractual damage-stripping clauses in arbitration agreements. Chapter 5 remains largely as it was in the First Edition, except the Introduction has been edited to reflect the decreasing prevalence of court-ordered arbitration.

We hope that this new edition of ARBITRATION LAW will provide law students with a thorough understanding of all the doctrinal and analytic tools needed to successfully practice law today. The cases revisit many issues that students encountered in their courses in contracts and civil procedure, but from a different perspective. Thus we also hope that by revisiting those subjects from a different perspective, students will gain a deeper understanding of the interaction between substantive law and the procedures available for addressing legal claims.

KATHERINE V.W. STONE
RICHARD A. BALES

ACKNOWLEDGMENTS

Foundation Press and the author gratefully acknowledge the authors and publishers that permitted us to reprint excerpts of copyrighted works. They are:

American Arbitration Association, *Commercial Arbitration Rules.* Permission granted by the American Arbitration Association.

Auerback, Jerold S., JUSTICE WITHOUT LAW? (1983). Permission granted by Oxford University Press.

Bernstein, Lisa E., *Understanding the Limits of Court-Connected ADR: A Critique of Federal Court-Annexed Arbitration Programs,* 141 U. Pa. L. Rev. 2169 (1993). Permission granted by Lisa E. Bernstein, University of Chicago Law School.

SUMMARY OF CONTENTS

TABLE OF CONTENTS

CHAPTER TWO Defenses to Arbitration 197

TABLE OF CASES

Principal cases are in bold type. Non-principal cases are in roman type. References are to Pages.

ARBITRATION LAW

CHAPTER ONE

THE AGREEMENT TO ARBITRATE

1. INTRODUCTION TO ARBITRATION

At first blush, a casebook called ARBITRATION LAW might sound like an oxymoron. After all, arbitration is usually considered an alternative to law, one of several forms of alternative dispute resolution that enable parties to avoid legal procedures and legal rules in resolving their disputes. If arbitration is an alternative to law, or simply outside the law, then how can there be a body of law about arbitration? The answer is that although arbitration is an alternative to formal judicial process, it also is a procedure embedded firmly within the legal system. Legal rules determine whether an agreement to arbitrate can be enforced against an unwilling party, and if so, what defenses can be raised to void an obligation to arbitrate. Legal rules also determine whether an award that results from arbitration will be binding, and whether the losing side has any rights of appeal. Beyond these foundational issues are secondary legal issues that arise in arbitration, such as what types of due process protections must be present for an arbitral award to be valid and judicially enforceable, what kinds of issues can be subject to arbitration, and under what circumstances an arbitration procedure is so biased, one-sided, or unfair as to be unenforceable. Legal rules also determine whether state or federal law applies to these and countless related issues that can arise in any particular arbitration procedure.

Arbitration is one of several forms of alternative dispute resolution (ADR) that have become major elements in legal practice. Arbitration, mediation, and other alternative dispute resolution mechanisms are commonly used today in such disparate fields as securities regulation, commercial law, employment law, family law, labor law, medical malpractice, construction law, insurance, and international private law. Parties and their lawyers increasingly seek to resolve their differences without resorting to litigation. In fact, it is difficult to practice law in any area today without encountering contractual provisions or institutional arrangements that mandate the use of alternative dispute resolution.

Of the alternative dispute resolution mechanisms in widespread usage, arbitration plays a unique role. Mediation, conciliation, mini-trials, and fact-finding are ultimately settlement enhancement devices—procedures designed to assist parties' own efforts to settle their disputes. All of these mechanisms attempt to move parties toward a mutually satisfactory settlement that can be represented in a consensual agreement. Arbitration, on the other hand, does not aim to achieve a consensual resolution of a dispute. Rather its aim is to have a neutral third party hear the facts of a dispute and issue a binding award. After a typical arbitration, unlike mediation and conciliation, there is a winner and a loser. This fact helps explain why there is so much more litigation about arbitration than about other forms of alternative dispute resolution. Parties who lose disputes often believe that they have been treated unfairly or the outcome is unjust, and when they do, they often seek another opportunity or another forum in which they can attempt to prevail.

To a greater extent than other forms of ADR, arbitration is framed by complex legal rules and arbitration practice is populated by lawyers. Lawyers typically draft the agreements that obligate parties to arbitrate their disputes. Lawyers also are called upon to enforce these agreements by obtaining judicial decrees to compel parties to honor their promises to arbitrate or to mediate. Lawyers participate in arbitration proceedings directly, either by presenting cases or advising from the sidelines. On occasion, lawyers are required to enforce the awards or the settlement agreements that result from arbitration procedures. If there is a dispute about the meaning or the scope of an agreement to use arbitration, lawyers are the ones who advocate their client's position. Lawyers also raise defenses and claim exceptions to the enforcement of such agreements to assist parties who want to avoid having their cases decided in alternative fora. Thus lawyers need to know what procedures apply, what evidentiary rules are possible, what remedies might be forthcoming, and what the standard of judicial review is in the highly varied types of arbitration tribunals.

Arbitration historically has been used to resolve disputes between contracting parties about the application, interpretation, or performance of their contractual obligations. In recent years, however, the Supreme Court has expanded the reach of arbitration agreements to apply not only to contractual issues such as contract formation, performance and breach, but also to disputes concerning statutory rights. In several seminal cases, the Supreme Court held that civil disputes concerning alleged violations of the antitrust laws, the securities laws, and the anti-discrimination laws are within the scope of parties' contractual promises to arbitrate. As a result, these and many other statutes are now interpreted and applied by arbitrators in private tribunals rather than by judges in courtrooms. At the same time, the use of arbitration has grown exponentially in consumer, employment, real estate, and many other areas. For example, in the employment area, more employees are currently subject to employment arbitration agreements than are covered by collective bargaining agreements. These arbitral fora are quickly replacing courts as the primary arbiters of the meaning of employment statutes. Thus, in order to understand the developments in regulatory laws, it is necessary to understand how such laws are applied in arbitral settings.

In addition to the growing use of arbitration by private parties, the state and federal courts have embraced arbitration as a means of conserving judicial resources. Some state trial courts and federal district courts require that civil actions below a specified jurisdictional amount go to nonbinding arbitration before they can be scheduled for trial. Court-ordered arbitration thus represents a major change in the civil justice system, and presents different issues than those that arise in private arbitration. For example, some have argued that requiring parties to arbitrate as a precondition to litigation so raises the cost of litigation that it effectively deprives parties of their constitutionally protected access to the courts. Others have suggested that court-ordered arbitration must include a full and unfettered right of appeal to preserve its constitutionality. Thus, any lawyer involved in litigation must know how to operate in an arbitral setting and know what are the legal rules that frame this form of dispute resolution.

This book presents a comprehensive treatment of the legal issues involved in the use of arbitration. The first four chapters address issues that arise in private arbitration, that is, arbitration that is the product of an agreement between two contracting parties. The last chapter addresses issues that arise in court-ordered arbitration. Together they will give the student a thorough understanding of arbitration law, and provide a solid foundation for legal practice whether in alternative dispute resolution fora or in the civil justice system.

A. Arbitration Agreements Are Everywhere

Today, arbitration agreements are *everywhere*—from consumer agreements to employment contracts, from mergers and acquisition deals to the routine sale of goods between merchants. Given that arbitration agreements are truly ubiquitous, practitioners increasingly encounter arbitration law issues in their daily practice. Over 13,000 firms and practitioners now list alternative dispute resolution ("ADR") as a practice area on Martindale Hubbel; over 6,000 list "arbitration law" specifically. Therefore, it is becoming more and more important for students and attorneys to learn this area of the law that is growing at an accelerated rate. Not only is this area of law important to study for purposes of legal practice, it is also becoming an important topic in American contemporary jurisprudence.

The two cases that follow illustrate how arbitration issues arise in the contemporary world.

* * *

Bragg v. Linden Research, Inc.

487 F.Supp.2d 593 (E.D. Pa. 2007).

■ Eduardo C. Robreno, District Judge.

This case is about virtual property maintained on a virtual world on the Internet. Plaintiff, March Bragg, Esq., claims an ownership interest in such virtual property. Bragg contends that Defendants, the operators of the virtual world, unlawfully confiscated his virtual property and denied him access to their virtual world. Ultimately at issue in this case are the novel questions of what rights and obligations grow out of the relationship between the owner and creator of a virtual world and its resident-customers. While the property and the world where it is found are "virtual," the dispute is real.

Presently before the Court are Defendants' Motion to Dismiss for Lack of Personal Jurisdiction and Motion to Compel Arbitration. For the reasons set forth below, the motions will be denied.

I. BACKGROUND

A. Second Life

The defendants in this case, Linden Research Inc. ("Linden") and its Chief Executive Officer, Philip Rosedale, operate a multiplayer role-playing game set in the virtual world known as "Second Life." Participants create avatars to represent themselves, and Second Life is populated by hundreds of thousands of avatars, whose interactions with one another are limited only by the human imagination. According to Plaintiff, many people "are now living large portions of their lives, forming friendships with others, building and acquiring virtual property, forming contracts, substantial business relationships and forming social organizations" in virtual worlds such as Second Life. Owning property in and having access to this virtual world is, moreover, apparently important to the plaintiff in this case.

B. Recognition of Property Rights

In November 2003, Linden announced that it would recognize participants' full intellectual property protection for the digital content they created or otherwise owned in Second Life. As a result, Second Life avatars may now buy, own, and sell virtual goods ranging "from cars to homes to slot machines." Most significantly for this case, avatars may purchase "virtual land," make improvements to that land, exclude other avatars from entering onto the land, rent the land, or sell the land to other avatars for a profit. Assertedly, by recognizing virtual property rights, Linden would distinguish itself from other virtual worlds available on the Internet and thus increase participation in Second Life.

Defendant Rosedale personally joined in efforts to publicize Linden's recognition of rights to virtual property. For example, in 2003, Rosedale stated in a press release made available on Second Life's website that:

> Until now, any content created by users for persistent state worlds, such as Everquest® or Star Wars Galaxies TM, has essentially become the property of the company developing and hosting the world.... We believe our new policy recognizes the fact that persistent world users are making significant contributions to building these worlds and should be able to both own the content they create and share in the value that is created. The preservation of users' property rights is a necessary step toward the emergence of genuinely real online worlds.

Press Release, Linden Lab, Linden Lab Preserves Real World Intellectual Property Rights of Users of its Second Life Online Services (Nov. 14, 2003). After this initial announcement, Rosedale continued to personally hype the ownership of virtual property on Second Life. In an interview in 2004, for example, Rosedale stated: "The idea of land ownership and the ease with which you can own land and do something with it ... is intoxicating.... Land ownership feels important and tangible. It's a real piece of the future." Michael Learmonth, Virtual Real Estate Boom Draws Real Dollars, USA Today, June 3, 2004. Rosedale recently gave an extended interview for Inc. magazine, where he appeared on the cover stating, "What you have in Second Life is real and it is yours. It doesn't belong to us. You can make money." Michael Fitzgerald, How Philip Rosedale Created Second Life, Inc., Feb. 2007.

Rosedale even created his own avatar and held virtual town hall meetings on Second Life where he made representations about the purchase of virtual land. Bragg "attended" such meetings and relied on the representations that Rosedale made therein.

C. Plaintiffs' Participation in Second Life

In 2005, Plaintiff Marc Bragg, Esq., signed up and paid Linden to participate in Second Life. Bragg claims that he was induced into "investing" in virtual land by representations made by Linden and Rosedale in press releases, interviews, and through the Second Life website. Bragg also paid Linden real money as "tax" on his land. By April 2006, Bragg had not only purchased numerous parcels of land in his Second Life, he had also digitally crafted "fireworks" that he was able to sell to other avatars for a profit. Bragg also acquired other virtual items from other avatars.

The dispute ultimately at issue in this case arose on April 30, 2006, when Bragg acquired a parcel of virtual land named "Taessot" for $300. Linden sent Bragg an email advising him that Taessot had been improperly purchased through an "exploit." Linden took Taesot away. It then froze Bragg's account, effectively confiscating all of the virtual property and currency that he maintained on his account with Second Life.

Bragg brought suit against Linden and Rosedale in the Court of Common Pleas of Chester County, Pennsylvania, on October 3, 2006. Linden and Rosedale removed the case to this Court and then, within a week, moved to compel arbitration....

III. MOTION TO COMPEL ARBITRATION

Defendants have filed a motion to compel arbitration that seeks to dismiss this action and compel Bragg to submit his claims to arbitration according to the Rules of the International Chamber of Commerce ("ICC") in San Francisco.

A. Relevant Facts

Before a person is permitted to participate in Second Life, she must accept the Terms of Service of Second Life (the "TOS") by clicking a button indicating acceptance of the TOS. Bragg concedes that he clicked the "accept" button before accessing Second Life. Included in the TOS are a California choice of law provision, an arbitration provision, and forum selection clause. Specifically, located in the fourteenth line of the thirteenth paragraph under the heading "GENERAL PROVISIONS," and following provisions regarding the applicability of export and import laws to Second Life, the following language appears:

> Any dispute or claim arising out of or in connection with this Agreement or the performance, breach or termination thereof, shall be finally settled by binding arbitration in San Francisco, California under the Rules of Arbitration of the International Chamber of Commerce by three arbitrators appointed in accordance with said rules.... Notwithstanding the foregoing, either party may apply to any court of competent jurisdiction for injunctive relief or enforcement of this arbitration provision without breach of this arbitration provision.

TOS ¶ 13.

B. Legal Standards

1. Federal Law Applies

The Federal Arbitration Act ("FAA") requires that the Court apply federal substantive law here because the arbitration agreement is connected to a transaction involving interstate commerce....

2. The Legal Standard Under the FAA

Under the FAA, on the motion of a party, a court must stay proceedings and order the parties to arbitrate the dispute if the court finds that the parties have agreed in writing to do so. 9 U.S.C. §§ 3, 4, 6. A party seeking to compel arbitration must show (1) that a valid agreement to arbitrate exists between the parties and (2) that the specific dispute falls within the scope of the agreement. Trippe Mfg. Co. v. Niles Audio Corp., 401 F.3d 529, 532 (3d Cir. 2005); PaineWebber, Inc. v. Hartmann, 921 F.2d 507, 511 (3d Cir. 1990).

C. Application

1. Unconscionabilty of the Arbitration Agreement

Bragg resists enforcement of the TOS's arbitration provision on the basis that it is "both procedurally and substantively unconscionable and is itself evidence of defendants' scheme to deprive Plaintiff (and others) of both their money and their day in court."

Section 2 of the FAA provides that written arbitration agreements "shall be valid, irrevocable, and enforceable, save upon such grounds as exist at law or in equity for the revocation of any contract." 9 U.S.C. § 2. Thus, "generally applicable contract defenses, such as fraud, duress, or unconscionability, may be applied to invalidate arbitration agreements without contravening § 2." Doctor's Assocs. v. Casarotto, 517 U.S. 681, 687, 116 S.Ct. 1652, 134 L.Ed.2d 902 (1996) (citations omitted). When determining whether such defenses might apply to any purported agreement to arbitrate the dispute in question, "courts generally ... should apply ordinary state-law principles that govern the formation of contracts." First Options of Chicago, Inc. v. Kaplan, 514 U.S. 938, 944, 115 S.Ct. 1920,

131 L.Ed.2d 985 (1995). Thus, the Court will apply California state law to determine whether the arbitration provision is unconscionable.

Under California law, unconscionability has both procedural and substantive components. Davis v. O'Melveny & Myers, 485 F.3d 1066, 1072–73 (9th Cir. 2007); Comb v. PayPal, Inc., 218 F.Supp.2d 1165, 1172 (N.D.Cal. 2002). The procedural component can be satisfied by showing (1) oppression through the existence of unequal bargaining positions or (2) surprise through hidden terms common in the context of adhesion contracts. The substantive component can be satisfied by showing overly harsh or one-sided results that "shock the conscience." The two elements operate on a sliding scale such that the more significant one is, the less significant the other need be. * * *

(a) Procedural Unconscionability

A contract or clause is procedurally unconscionable if it is a contract of adhesion. A contract of adhesion, in turn, is a "standardized contract, which, imposed and drafted by the party of superior bargaining strength, relegates to the subscribing party only the opportunity to adhere to the contract or reject it." *Comb,* 218 F.Supp.2d at 1172; *Armendariz,* 99 Cal.Rptr.2d 745, 6 P.3d at 690....

The TOS are a contract of adhesion. Linden presents the TOS on a take-it-or-leave-it basis. A potential participant can either click "assent" to the TOS, and then gain entrance to Second Life's virtual world, or refuse assent and be denied access. Linden also clearly has superior bargaining strength over Bragg. Although Bragg is an experienced attorney, who believes he is expert enough to comment on numerous industry standards and the "rights" of participants in virtual worlds, he was never presented with an opportunity to use his experience and lawyering skills to negotiate terms different from the TOS that Linden offered....

The procedural element of unconscionability also "focuses on ... surprise." ... Here, although the TOS are ubiquitous throughout Second Life, Linden buried the TOS's arbitration provision in a lengthy paragraph under the benign heading "GENERAL PROVISIONS." ... Linden also failed to make available the costs and rules of arbitration in the ICC by either setting them forth in the TOS or by providing a hyper-link to another page or website where they are available.

Comb [*v. PayPal, Inc.*, 218 F.Supp.2d 1165 (N.D.Cal. 2002)] is most instructive. In that case, the plaintiffs challenged an arbitration provision that was part of an agreement to which they had assented, in circumstances similar to this case, by clicking their assent on an online application page. 218 F.Supp.2d at 1169. The defendant, PayPal, was a large company with millions of individual online customers. Id. at 1165. The plaintiffs, with one exception, were all individual customers of PayPal. Id. Given the small amount of the average transaction with PayPal, the fact that most PayPal customers were private individuals, and that there was a "dispute as to whether PayPal's competitors offer their services without requiring customers to enter into arbitration agreements," the court concluded that the user agreement at issue "satisfie[d] the criteria for procedural unconscionability under California law." Id. at 1172–73. Here, as in *Comb*, procedural unconscionability is satisfied.

(b) Substantive Unconscionability

... Substantive unconscionability focuses on the one-sidedness of the contract terms. *Armendariz*, 99 Cal.Rptr.2d 745, 6 P.3d at 690; *Flores*, 113 Cal.Rptr.2d at 381–82. Here, a number of the TOS's elements lead the Court to conclude that Bragg has demonstrated that the TOS are substantively unconscionable.

(i) Mutuality

Under California law, substantive unconscionability has been found where an arbitration provision forces the weaker party to arbitrate claims but permits a choice of forums for the stronger party. See, e.g., Ticknor v. Choice Hotels Int'l, Inc., 265 F.3d 931, 940–41 (9th Cir. 2001); Mercuro v. Superior Court, 96 Cal.App.4th 167, 116 Cal.Rptr.2d 671, 675 (2002). In other words, the arbitration remedy must contain a "modicum of bilaterality." *Armendariz*, 99 Cal.Rptr.2d 745, 6 P.3d at 692. This principle has been extended to arbitration provisions that allow the stronger party a range of remedies before arbitrating a dispute, such as self-help, while relegating to the weaker party the sole remedy of arbitration.

In *Comb*, for example, the court found a lack of mutuality where the user agreement allowed PayPal "at its sole discretion" to restrict accounts, withhold funds, undertake its own investigation of a customer's financial records, close accounts, and procure ownership of all funds in dispute unless and until the customer is "later determined to be entitled to the funds in dispute." 218 F.Supp.2d at 1173–74. Also significant was the fact that the user agreement was "subject to change by PayPal without prior notice (unless prior notice is required by law), by posting of the revised Agreement on the PayPal website." Id.

Here, the TOS [is] substantively unconscionable for lack of mutuality. The TOS proclaim that "Linden has the right at any time for any reason or no reason to suspend or terminate your Account, terminate this Agreement, and/or refuse any and all current or future use of the Service without notice or liability to you." TOS ¶ 7.1. Whether or not a customer has breached the Agreement is "determined in Linden's sole discretion." Id. Linden also reserves the right to return no money at all based on mere "suspicions of fraud" or other violations of law. Id. Finally, the TOS state that "Linden may amend this Agreement ... at any time in its sole discretion by posting the amended Agreement [on its website]." TOS ¶ 1.2.

In effect, the TOS provide Linden with a variety of one-sided remedies to resolve disputes, while forcing its customers to arbitrate any disputes with Linden. This is precisely what occurred here. When a dispute arose, Linden exercised its option to use self-help by freezing Bragg's account, retaining funds that Linden alone determined were subject to dispute, and then telling Bragg that he could resolve the dispute by initiating a costly arbitration process. The TOS expressly authorized Linden to engage in such unilateral conduct....

(ii) Costs of Arbitration and Fee–Sharing

Bragg claims that the cost of an individual arbitration under the TOS is likely to exceed $13,540, with an estimated initiation cost of at least $10,000. He has also submitted a Declaration of Personal Financial Information stating that such arbitration would be cost-prohibitive for him (doc. no. 41). Linden disputes Bragg's calculations.... The Court's own calculations indicate that the costs of arbitration, excluding arbitration, would total $17,250. With a recovery of $75,000, the ICC's administrative expenses would be $2,625 (3.5% of $75,000). See ICC Rules at 28. In addition, arbitrator's fees could be set between 2.0% ($1,500) and 11.0% ($8,250) of the amount at issue per arbitrator. Id. If the ICC set the arbitrator's fees at the mid-point of this range, the arbitrator's fees would be $4,875 per arbitrator. Id. Here, however, the TOS requires that three arbitrators be used to resolve a dispute. TOS ¶ 13. Thus, the Court estimates the costs of arbitration with the ICC to be $17,250 ($2,625 + (3 × $4,875)), although they could reach as high as $27,375 ($2,625 + (3 × $8,250)).

These costs might not, on their own, support a finding of substantive unconscionability. However, the ICC Rules also provide that the costs and fees must be shared among the parties, and an estimate of those costs and fees must be advanced at the initiation of arbitration. See ICC Rules of Arbitration. California law has often been applied to declare arbitration fee-sharing schemes unenforceable. See Ting v. AT&T, 319 F.3d 1126, 1151 (9th Cir. 2003). Such schemes are unconscionable where they "impose[ ] on some consumers costs greater than those a complainant would bear if he or she would file the same complaint in court." Id.... Here, even taking Defendants characterization of the fees to be accurate, the total estimate of costs and fees would be $7,500, which would result in Bragg having to advance $3,750 at the outset of arbitration. The court's own estimates place the amount that Bragg would likely have to advance at $8,625, but they could reach as high as $13,687.50. Any of these figures are significantly greater than the costs that Bragg bears by filing his action in a state or federal court. Accordingly, the arbitration costs and fee-splitting scheme together also support a finding of unconscionability.

(iii) Venue

The TOS also require that any arbitration take place in San Francisco, California.... [T]he record in this case shows that Linden serves millions of customers across the United States and that the average transaction through or with Second Life involves a relatively small amount. In such circumstances, California law dictates that it is not "reasonable for individual consumers from throughout the country to travel to one locale to arbitrate claims involving such minimal sums." Indeed, "[l]imiting venue to [Linden's] backyard appears to be yet one more means by which the arbitration clause serves to shield [Linden] from liability instead of providing a neutral forum in which to arbitrate disputes."

(iv) Confidentiality Provision

Arbitration before the ICC, pursuant to the TOS, must be kept confidential pursuant to the ICC rules. Applying California law to an arbitration provision, the Ninth Circuit held that such confidentiality supports a finding that an arbitration clause was substantively unconscionable. *Ting*, 319 F.3d at 1152. The Ninth Circuit reasoned that if the company succeeds in imposing a gag order on arbitration proceedings, it places itself in a far superior legal posture by ensuring that none of its potential opponents have access to precedent while, at the same time, the company accumulates a wealth of knowledge on how to negotiate the terms of its own unilaterally crafted contract. Id. The unavailability of arbitral decisions could also prevent potential plaintiffs from obtaining the information needed to build a case of intentional misconduct against a company. See id.... Thus, the confidentiality of the arbitration scheme that Linden imposed also supports a finding that the arbitration clause is unconscionable....

(c) Conclusion

... Taken together, the lack of mutuality, the costs of arbitration, the forum selection clause, and the confidentiality provision that Linden unilaterally imposes through the TOS demonstrate that the arbitration clause is not designed to provide Second Life participants an effective means of resolving disputes with Linden. Rather, it is a one-sided means which tilts unfairly, in almost all situations, in Linden's favor. As in *Comb*, through the use of an arbitration clause, Linden "appears to be attempting to insulate itself contractually from any meaningful challenge to its alleged practices." 218 F.Supp.2d at 1176....

Finding that the arbitration clause is procedurally and substantively unconscionable, the Court will refuse to enforce it.

* * *

Questions

1. When reading a case about arbitration, be sure to note whether the case is (i) a consumer or employment contract in which one party is more sophisticated than the other, and where there is some element of adhesion (these are sometimes derisively called "cram-down" agreements), or (ii) a business contract arrived at between sophisticated parties bargaining at arms length. Courts are much more likely to enforce the latter than the former; courts in California and the Ninth Circuit in particular tend to scrutinize the former. Also note whether a given case involves a predispute agreement to arbitrate, as in *Bragg*, or a postdispute agreement to arbitrate. Are there special problems of fairness presented when arbitration agreements are part of contracts of adhesion? When they are presented before a dispute arises?

2. Arbitration law often raises important policy issues. For example, should courts enforce arbitration agreements signed by consumers and employees who have had little or no opportunity to bargain over the terms of arbitration? Should the law differentiate between these "agreements" and arm's-length agreements? Are cram-down arbitration agreements different from other standard-form agreements, such as shrink-wrap agreements on software, that courts routinely enforce? See the *Sotelo* case below.

3. Arbitration is "privatized" dispute resolution, and as such, the parties have considerable freedom to establish their own procedures. As *Bragg* demonstrates, however, the law imposes some limits on this freedom. How much freedom should parties have to craft any procedures they desire?

4. Litigation is conducted before a judge to whom the case is randomly assigned. In arbitration, the parties themselves choose, and pay for, the arbitrator(s). What are the advantages and disadvantages of each?

5. The *Bragg* court, in deciding the cost issue, focused only on whether the cost of *filing* for arbitration was commensurate with the cost of filing a lawsuit. Is this the proper comparison? How would you expect the overall costs of arbitration to compare to litigation? What factors might make arbitration more expensive? Less expensive?

Sotelo v. DirectRevenue, LLC

384 F.Supp.2d 1219 (N.D. Ill. 2005).

■ GETTLEMAN, DISTRICT JUDGE.

Plaintiff Stephen Sotelo filed a five-count putative class action complaint against defendants . . . alleging that, without his consent, defendants caused software known as "spyware" [or "adware"] to be downloaded onto his personal computer. Plaintiff alleges that Spyware tracked plaintiff's Internet use, invaded his privacy, and caused substantial damage to his computer. Plaintiff asserts various claims under Illinois law: trespass to personal property (Count I); consumer fraud (Count II); unjust enrichment (Count III); negligence (Count IV); and computer tampering (Count V). Plaintiff seeks injunctive relief and compensatory damages.

Defendants removed the class action to federal district court pursuant to 28 U.S.C. § 1332(d)(2) and the Class Action Fairness Act of 2005 ("CAFA"), 28 U.S.C. § 1453. Defendants have filed [a motion to, among other things,] stay litigation in favor of arbitration pursuant to § 3 of the Federal Arbitration Act ("FAA"), 9 U.S.C. § 3.

FACTS

Plaintiff alleges that DirectRevenue deceptively downloaded Spyware, distributed by BI, on thousands of computers. Spyware allows DirectRevenue and companies that employ its services to track a computer user's web browsing behavior in order to deliver targeted advertisements to that computer. For example, if a computer with Spyware views music-related Internet sites, Spyware sends a signal of the computer user's activity back to DirectRevenue, which then targets the computer with advertisements from music-related companies that have paid for access to the computer via Spyware. DirectRevenue claims access to 12,000,000 computers in the United States, and has attracted national media attention and criticism for its alleged misconduct in gaining and maintaining such access. According to plaintiff, aQuantive and AccuQuote, or someone on their behalf, used Spyware to send advertisements to the computers.

DirectRevenue "secretly installs" Spyware by bundling it with other legitimate software that is available "free" on the Internet, such as games. When the computer user downloads and installs a game, he or she simultaneously, but unwittingly, downloads Spyware. "The computer users do not consent, let alone have knowledge," that Spyware is being installed on their computers because DirectRevenue has "deceptively caused" Spyware to download without the users' consent or knowledge. DirectRevenue has an agreement governing Spyware called the "BetterInternet End User License Agreement" ("EULA") that purports to inform a consumer that Spyware will be installed, computer use will be monitored, and the computer will receive targeted advertisements.

According to plaintiff, DirectRevenue installs Spyware in at least three different ways to avoid showing the EULA to computer users. First, for computers with Microsoft settings set to "low," Spyware automatically installs when a user downloads a free software program. These users are "never even shown the [EULA], told of its existence, or advised of the need for any sort of licensing." Second, computer users who have Microsoft Windows' Service Pack 2 (a security feature) installed on their computers receive a pop-up dialog box as the Spyware is being downloaded. The message in the dialogue box is an "unintelligible" incomplete sentence, refers only to " 'the software,' rather than a bona fide program name," and asks the user to click "Install" or "Don't Install." There is no disclosure that the software being downloaded includes Spyware. There is a link to the EULA, but users are not asked to click on the link, advised of the availability of the EULA, or asked to agree to the EULA. Third, Internet users without Microsoft Windows Service Pack 2 are asked to agree to a "Consumer Policy Agreement," but not to the EULA, and there is no such policy available on DirectRevenue's website or elsewhere for computer users to review.

According to plaintiff, Spyware is designed to be difficult to remove from a computer once it is installed. DirectRevenue engages "in a uniformly deceptive course of conduct" to prevent users from removing Spyware after it is installed, including changing its name to prevent disgruntled computer users from complaining and altering the Spyware file names so that anti-Spyware programs and computer technicians cannot locate and remove it. DirectRevenue uses misleading aliases in an effort to deceive consumers including: BestOffers, BetterInternet, Ceres, LocalNRD, MSView, MultiMPP, MXTarget, OfferOptimizer, and Twaintec. The EULA, if users ever see it, directs users who want to remove Spyware from their computers to a website address, http://mypctuneup.com/contacts.php. However, at the time of the complaint, the link did not connect to a web page, and no such site could be found. If a user attempts to use the "add or remove programs" feature to remove the legitimate software to which Spyware was bundled, Spyware "unbundles" and remains on the computer.

Through Spyware, advertisers and advertising agents, including aQuantive and AccuQuote, have access to millions of computers for their targeted advertising. These advertisers, or companies they have hired to advertise on their behalf, bombard users' computers with ads that constantly "pop up" over whatever web page a user is viewing. The pop-up advertisements are sent in a manner that breaches the security of affected computers by bypassing commonly-used software designed to block pop-ups. Once an advertisement is sent, it generally remains on the computer screen until the computer user actually closes the advertisement. Even after closing the advertisement, however, it is sent over and over again, and users receive many advertisements repeatedly. According to plaintiff, "Newsweek reported that Direct Revenue may have as many as 1.5 billion advertising impressions (i.e., pop-ups) per month."

Plaintiff alleges that Spyware wreaks havoc on a computer and its user. Spyware destroys other software programs, and Spyware and the unsolicited advertisements that clog the screen cause computers to slow down, deplete Internet bandwidth and the computer's memory, and use pixels and screen-space on monitors. Productivity is decreased because hours are wasted attempting to remove Spyware from computers, closing recurring and frequent advertisements, and waiting for slowed machines. Users are forced to keep their slowed computers running longer, which uses more electricity, decreases the useful life of an computer, and forces the user to incur increased Internet access charges. It costs approximately $30 per year to purchase software to effectively remove Spyware and unwanted advertisements, and to guard against future infections.

DISCUSSION

. . .

II. DirectRevenue and AccuQuote's motion to stay litigation in favor of arbitration

DirectRevenue and AccuQuote argue that the instant litigation must be stayed pursuant to § 3 of the FAA, 9 U.S.C. § 3, and the EULA, which contains an arbitration clause ("Arbitration Clause"). The Arbitration Clause requires the parties to submit "any and all disputes, controversies and claims relating in any way to [BI's targeted advertising software], this Agreement or the breach thereof (including the arbitration of any claim or dispute and the enforceability of this paragraph)" to arbitration before the American Arbitration Association in New York, New York. Plaintiff does not challenge defendants' assumption that the Arbitration Clause would apply to the instant dispute, but argues that he never saw or agreed to the EULA prior to the installation of Spyware on his computer, and therefore is not bound by its terms.

The FAA mandates enforcement of valid, written arbitration agreements. 9 U.S.C. § 2; Tinder v. Pinkerton Security, 305 F.3d 728, 733 (7th Cir. 2002). To give effect to the federal policy, § 3 of the FAA provides for stays of litigation when an issue presented in a case is referable to arbitration. 9 U.S.C. § 3; *Tinder*, 305 F.3d at 733. "Because arbitration is a matter of contract, a party cannot be required to submit to arbitration if it has not agreed to do so." AT & T Techs., Inc. v. Communications Workers of America, 475 U.S. 643, 648, 106 S.Ct. 1415, 89 L.Ed.2d 648 (1986). The Seventh Circuit has held that agreements to arbitrate are evaluated under the same standards as any other contract. *Tinder*, 305 F.3d at 733. A district court must promptly compel arbitration once it is satisfied that the parties agreed to arbitrate, but if the district court determines that the making of the arbitration agreement is seriously disputed, "the court shall processed summarily to the trial thereof." 9 U.S.C. § 2. . . .

In *Tinder*, an employment discrimination suit, the Seventh Circuit held that the district court had correctly compelled the plaintiff to arbitrate because she failed to raise a triable issue of fact. Id. The plaintiff did not contradict the defendants' affidavits that she was "definitely" provided with a brochure containing her employer's arbitration provision. Id. at 735–36. In the instant case, by contrast, defendants make no such assertions regarding plaintiff in particular. Rather, they submit affidavit testimony that every time Spyware is installed from DirectRevenue's website, the computer user is presented with the opportunity through a hyperlink to read the EULA prior to downloading the software. According to the affidavit of Christopher Dowhan ("Dowhan"), vice-president of distribution for DR, users downloading DirectRevenue's software cannot proceed until "they have that opportunity and either take advantage of it or opt to skip it." Even if uncontroverted and sufficient to establish that users were "definitely" provided with the opportunity to view the EULA on DirectRevenue's website, Dowhan's affidavit testimony is defeated by plaintiff's clarification in his affidavits that he downloaded software bundled with Spyware from a third-party distributor and never visited DirectRevenue's website. Plaintiff has thus raised a triable issue of fact whether he agreed to the EULA, or was even provided with notice of its existence.

DirectRevenue and AccuQuote also argue that each advertisement that plaintiff alleges he received as a result of Spyware "would have contained a link with yet another opportunity to view the EULA." According to DirectRevenue and AccuQuote, clicking on a small button with question mark in the corner of the pop-up advertisements leads to additional information about Spyware, another opportunity to read the EULA, and instructions on how to uninstall Spyware. The question box does not indicate that it links to information regarding the source of the advertisements or to any kind of user agreement, however. Moreover, by the time plaintiff began receiving the advertisements Spyware had already been installed, and the computer damage had begun.

ProCD, Inc. v. Zeidenberg, 86 F.3d 1447, 1450–53 (7th Cir. 1996), cited by DirectRevenue in support of its argument, is thus inapposite. In ProCD, the Seventh Circuit held that a license agreement was enforceable because the plaintiff was given notice of the existence of a license agreement before purchasing a product, although the terms of the agreement were sealed inside the package, and purchasers had the opportunity to return the product if the terms were unacceptable. Here, by contrast, plaintiff claims that he was not given notice of the EULA's existence prior to installation, Spyware begins consuming computer resources when it is installed, and uninstalling Spyware is significantly more confusing and vexing process than returning a product.

Because the court finds that plaintiff has raised a triable issue of fact whether he agreed to the EULA, the court need not address the parties' other arguments about the validity and the enforceability of the Arbitration Clause, or whether it inures to the benefit of third parties. Accordingly, DirectRevenue and AccuQuote's motion to stay the instant case is denied.

* * *

Questions

1. When two or more parties have a legal dispute, the default method of resolving that dispute is civil litigation. Parties may opt out of litigation by agreeing, either before or after a dispute has arisen, to use arbitration or another form of dispute resolution such as mediation. What does the court in *Sotelo* say about how to determine whether or not a party has consented to use arbitration?

2. Did the plaintiff in *Bragg* consent to arbitration?

B. WHAT IS ARBITRATION?

Arbitration is a proceeding, governed by contract, in which a dispute is resolved by an impartial adjudicator, chosen by the parties, whose decision the parties have agreed to accept as final and binding. It differs from negotiation and mediation in that the arbitrator imposes a resolution rather than a settlement which has been agreed to by the parties. It differs from litigation because it is informal: arbitration occurs in a conference room rather than a courtroom, the rules of procedure and evidence are loosely applied, and both discovery and motion practice are limited.

The Federal Arbitration Act does not define "arbitration", and courts are currently grappling with whether certain "non-binding" dispute resolution systems qualify as "arbitration" within the meaning of the FAA. The issue is important because if a dispute resolution agreement constitutes "arbitration" under the FAA, there are several consequences, including:

- A party seeking resolution of a dispute pursuant to the dispute resolution agreement can file a simple motion to compel a recalcitrant party to resolve the claim pursuant to the agreed upon procedures. On the other hand, if there is no arbitration clause, the party must file a regular lawsuit, seeking damages or specific performance.

This, of course, defeats the dispute resolution agreement's purpose, which presumably was to avoid litigation.

- There is a judicial presumption favoring enforcement of the dispute resolution agreement. The courts interpret the FAA as creating a strong presumption in favor of arbitration.
- There is a ready mechanism to have a court "confirm" or "vacate" an award. The FAA expressly permits the winner in arbitration to confirm and enforce the award, and the loser to try, usually unsuccessfully, to vacate it.

Courts can find that a contract contains an arbitration clause even if the word "arbitration" never appears. Conversely, simply terming a procedure "arbitration" does not necessarily mean that the courts will treat it as such. The following are some of the approaches courts have taken in trying to define "arbitration":

AMF Inc. v. Brunswick Corp., 621 F.Supp. 456, 460–61 (S.D.N.Y. 1985), is routinely cited and relied upon by courts when analyzing whether a non-binding resolution system constitutes "arbitration" under the FAA. AMF and Brunswick were competitors. They each manufactured the machines used in bowling alleys to reset the pins once a bowler has knocked them down. Each claimed that the other was falsely advertising the superiority of its own machines. To settle this dispute, the parties agreed that future advertising disputes would be submitted to an advisory third party, the National Advertising Division ("NAD") of the Council of Better Business Bureaus. The NAD would issue an opinion that would "not be binding upon the parties, but . . . advisory only."

A subsequent dispute arose, and Brunswick refused to submit the new claim to the NAD. AMF sued to compel. At issue was whether the court had authority under the FAA to order Brunswick's compliance. The court held that the non-binding mechanism at issue in that case constituted "arbitration" because (a) it required the submission of an issue to a "third-party" who would decide the matter, even if not conclusively, and (b) when "[v]iewed in light of [the parties'] reasonable commercial expectations," the non-binding decision would effectively "settle[]" at least part of their dispute.

Harrison v. Nissan Motor Corp. in U.S.A., 111 F.3d 343, 349–52 (3d Cir. 1997), like *AMF*, recognized that "arbitration" under the FAA in some circumstances could encompass "non-binding" dispute resolution. In defining "arbitration," *Harrison* borrowed from *AMF* and held that "arbitration" at minimum requires a "third-party" decision-maker. *Harrison*, however, also set forth an additional requirement for "arbitration" not discussed in *AMF*:

> Although it defies easy definition, the essence of arbitration, we think, is that, when the parties agree to submit their disputes to it, they have agreed to arbitrate these disputes *through to completion*, i.e. to an award made by a third-party arbitrator. *Arbitration does not occur until the process is completed and the arbitrator makes a decision.*

> Hence, if one party seeks an order compelling arbitration and it is granted, the parties must then arbitrate their dispute to an arbitrators' decision, and cannot seek recourse to the courts before that time.

Id. at 351 (emphasis added). Using this definition of arbitration, the court concluded that the dispute resolution mechanism at issue did not qualify as arbitration within the meaning of the FAA. Even though using the resolution mechanism was a precondition to litigation, the mechanism permitted an aggrieved party to withdraw from the process and file a lawsuit if a decision was not rendered in forty days. Thus, an aggrieved party would not have to "pursue the procedure to completion in all cases" because it could, in some instances, seek "recourse to the courts" before that time. According to *Harrison*, a party cannot back out of arbitration prior to a decision, even if the decision is non-binding. If a procedure permits a party to do so, then the dispute resolution mechanism is not "arbitration" under the FAA.

Wolsey, Ltd. v. Foodmaker, Inc., 144 F.3d 1205, 1209 (9th Cir. 1998), attempted to reconcile *AMF* with *Harrison*. The Ninth Circuit in *Wosley* concluded that the non-binding arbitration procedure at issue in AMF constituted arbitration within the meaning of the FAA because:

> [the agreement] clearly provides for the submission of claims to "a third party." *AMF* Inc., 621 F.Supp. at 460. Moreover, unlike [in *Harrison*], the ... [a]greement does not explicitly permit one of the parties to "seek recourse to the courts" after submitting claims for non-binding arbitration but before the "process is completed and the arbitrator makes a decision." *Harrison*, 111 F.3d at 350.

In *Brennan v. King*, 139 F.3d 258, 265 (1st Cir. 1998), the court likewise focused on the non-binding nature of the arbitration procedure, but also focused on the narrow scope of the matters to be arbitrated. A faculty member sued a university to challenge his denial of tenure. The faculty member's contract with the university contained two arbitration clauses. The first governed only non-tenure matters, such as teaching responsibilities. This arbitration clause was broad, and arbitration was final and binding. The arbitration clause that covered matters related to tenure, however, was much narrower in scope, and was not binding on the parties:

> The grievance procedure with respect to tenure disputes is wholly separate and evinces no broad arbitral authority to resolve such disputes. The handbook does allow for a proceeding within the tenure consideration process labeled "binding arbitration." But it is readily apparent that such arbitration as the handbook contemplates could not have resolved Brennan's dispute with the university. To be sure, the handbook recites that an arbitral decision "shall be final and binding on the parties to the dispute and the University." But the *scope* of what is subject to arbitration is limited to "procedural issues." Although it is not at all clear what is embraced under the rubric of "procedural issues," it is abundantly clear that among those things that the arbitrator is "without power to" do is to "grant or deny tenure." Evidently the arbitrator is confined to addressing non-sub-

stantive issues that may—but also may not—have some impact on the tenure decision ultimately made by the university's trustees.

Furthermore, to the extent that the arbitrator can be said to have authority to "bind" the parties, including the university, with respect to "procedural issues," the narrowness of that authority is plain to see. In what would be, for the university, the worst-case scenario—one in which the arbitrator "is convinced that the Provost's decision [to transmit to the president a negative tenure recommendation notwithstanding the Appeals Committee's positive recommendation] is not reasonably supported by the record," all the arbitrator is empowered to do is require the "Provost to transmit, to the President, the Standing Appeals Committee's positive recommendation in lieu of the Provost's own." And both the president and the board of trustees remain entirely free to disregard the favorable Appeals Committee recommendation forwarded by the provost pursuant to the arbitrator's directive. Consequently, the president will still receive nothing more than a recommendation, not a conclusive determination. Thus the most that a tenure candidate can achieve through arbitration is the substitution of the Appeals Committee's positive recommendation for the provost's negative recommendation.

Nor does the contract manifest an intent that arbitration be the exclusive means for addressing a dispute over tenure. The handbook speaks only of the candidate having a "right" to request arbitration. It is true that there is authority for the proposition that in some circumstances courts have the power to enforce agreements that *require* arbitration even when such arbitration is nonbinding. *See AMF, Inc. v. Brunswick Corp.,* 621 F.Supp. 456, 461 (S.D.N.Y.1985) (Weinstein, J.) (holding an agreement requiring nonbinding arbitration enforceable under the FAA when there is a "reasonable ... expectation [that] the dispute will be settled" by the procedure). In this case, however, the parties have made resort to arbitration the *prerogative,* but not the *obligation,* of the tenure candidate.[7]

The court therefore held that the university could not invoke the FAA to compel the faculty member to arbitrate his denial-of-tenure claim.

In *Fit Tech, Inc. v. Bally Total Fitness Holding Corp.*, 374 F.3d 1, 7 (1st Cir. 2004), the First Circuit took a completely different approach than *Harrison* and *Wosley*. In *Fit Tech*, a provision in the parties' asset purchase agreement required that certain financial disputes be referred to "Accountants" for "final determination within forty-five (45) days, which determina-

7. Even if applicable here, the *AMF* approach would not compel a different outcome. Because the contract at issue here imposes strict constraints on the scope of the arbitrator's authority and severely limits the effect of the arbitral decision, there is little ground for a "reasonable ... expectation" that the procedure will resolve the dispute. *Accord Harrison v. Nissan Motor Corp.,* 111 F.3d 343, 350 (3d Cir.1997) (applying the logic of *AMF* to determine that a nonbinding dispute resolution provision contained in a warranty—and labeled by the warranty's drafter as "arbitration"—"does not constitute arbitration within the meaning of the FAA").

tion shall be final and binding on all of the parties hereto." The *Fit Tech* court analyzed whether this "accounting remedy" was arbitration by considering how closely it resembled "classic arbitration":

> This brings us to Bally's second hurdle, namely, to the question whether the accountant remedy is arbitration at all. If it is not arbitration, then remedies under the Federal Arbitration Act, including an interlocutory appeal, would be unavailable. The Act itself does not define "arbitration", see Harrison v. Nissan Motor Corp. in U.S.A., 111 F.3d 343, 350 (3d Cir. 1997). Whether the accountant remedy is "arbitration" under the federal statute is a characterization issue, which in our view is governed by federal law.
>
> That a uniform federal definition is required is obvious to us. True, the substance of the purchase agreement—who promised to do what—is governed by state law (here, the parties agree, by Illinois law), but whether what has been agreed to amounts to "arbitration" under the Federal Arbitration Act depends on what Congress meant by the term in the federal statute. Assuredly Congress intended a "national" definition for a national policy. . . .
>
> Whether the accounting remedy is "arbitration" under the federal statute is the more interesting question. The answer does not depend on the nomenclature used in the agreement, see AMF Inc. v. Brunswick Corp., 621 F.Supp. 456, 460 (E.D.N.Y. 1985); rather, the question is how closely the specified procedure resembles classic arbitration and whether treating the procedure as arbitration serves the intuited purposes of Congress. For example, other circuits (defensibly, in our view) have declined to treat an agreement for non-binding arbitration as "arbitration" within the meaning of the Act. See *Dluhos v. Strasberg*, 321 F.3d 365, 371 (3d Cir. 2003); Harrison, 111 F.3d at 349–52. *But see Wolsey, Ltd. v. Foodmaker, Inc.*, 144 F.3d 1205, 1208–09 (9th Cir. 1998).
>
> By contrast, in our case, the purchase agreement makes the [accounting] remedy "final" (whether any more final than ordinary arbitration is doubtful but need not be decided now), and other common incidents of arbitration of a contractual dispute are present: an independent adjudicator, substantive standards (the contractual terms of the payout), and an opportunity for each side to present its case. *See General Motors Corp. v. Pamela Equities Corp.*, 146 F.3d 242, 246 (5th Cir. 1998); *Harrison*, 111 F.3d at 350; *AMF Inc.*, 621 F.Supp. at 460. To us, this is arbitration in everything but name.

Finally, in *Advanced Bodycare Solutions, LLC v. Thione Int'l, Inc.*, 524 F.3d 1235 (11th Cir. 2008), the Eleventh Circuit rejected the view (taken by some lower courts) that a court can compel a party to "mediate" under the FAA. The Eleventh Circuit, using the test from *Fit Tech*, held that mediation does not constitute "arbitration" under the FAA because, among other things, it does not produce "an award," which is a necessary component of "classic arbitration."

Questions

1. Look again at the definition of arbitration at the beginning of this subsection. Assume for a minute that it is consistent with "classic arbitration". If the procedures of a purported arbitration agreement are significantly skewed in favor of one party (as in *Bragg*), does the other party have an argument that the "agreement" is not "arbitration" and therefore is not enforceable under the FAA?

2. As Thomas Stipanowich points out, the

> "classic" model of arbitration is but one—albeit highly important—alternative among a growing number of process templates for resolving domestic and international disputes. These include mediation and many forms of third-party evaluation or nonbinding adjudication, multi-step processes or integrated conflict management programs, and hybrids such as "med-arb" and "arb-med." Some are consensual approaches; others are mandated as part of a government regulatory scheme.

Thomas J. Stipanowich, *The Arbitration Penumbra: Arbitration Law and the Rapidly Changing Landscape of Dispute Resolution*, 8 Nev. L.J. 427 (2007). How useful is the *Fit Tech* court's definition of arbitration now that arbitration is no longer one-size-fits-all?

3. "Interest arbitration" involves parties who are unsuccessfully attempting to negotiate a contract. The parties select an interest arbitrator to determine the contractual language of provisions to which they are unable to agree. Interest arbitration is common in public-sector labor negotiations where, for example, police officers and firefighters are prohibited by law from striking. The Employee Free Choice Act, pending in Congress when this book went to press, would require "interest arbitration" in private-sector collective bargaining negotiations if, after a union is formed, the parties have bargained for 120 days without agreeing on a contract. For a discussion of how the interest-arbitration provision of the EFCA might work in private-sector labor negotiations, see Andrew Lee Younkins, *Comment, Judicial Review Standards for Interest Arbitration Awards Under the Employee Free Choice Act*, 43 U.S.F. L. Rev. 447 (2008).

C. WHAT DOES ARBITRATION LOOK LIKE?

Arbitration proceedings can take an almost infinite variety of forms, ranging from procedures that are highly informal and ad hoc to procedures that are as structured and formal as a court of law. Under some procedures, arbitration consists of the parties sitting around a table and taking turns telling their side of the dispute to a neutral who listens and asks questions. Alternatively, some arbitrations follow formal rules of evidence and procedure, and include motion practice, stenographic records of hearings, and post-hearing briefs. Most arbitrations fall between these two extremes. But it is axiomatic that arbitration takes whatever form the parties desire—arbitration is a creature of the parties and the parties are free to shape the scope of arbitration and the procedures to be used however they please.[1] It is not uncommon for arbitration agreements to specify particular procedures and evidentiary rules to apply to the arbitration hearing.

Just as the procedures for arbitration vary, there are many methods of designating an arbitrator. Sometimes disputants designate an arbitrator on an ad hoc basis, after a dispute has arisen. Sometimes parties in an ongoing relationship designate a standing arbitrator, or umpire, to resolve all disputes that may arise between them.

Arbitration is used frequently in commercial disputes, where trade associations or industry-specific groups have devised industry-specific procedures for the resolution of disputes between members of the trade. These procedures often call upon respected senior members of the trade, like village elders, to hear disputes and bring their knowledge of fairness and local custom to bear in their deliberations.[2]

Arbitration also is frequently used in collective bargaining settings. It is customary for collective bargaining agreements to establish formal grievance procedures, which enable an orderly method for a union and management to consult and negotiate over issues of contractual interpretation or allegations that one side has breached its contractual obligations. If agreement is not reached by the early stages of the grievance procedure, collective bargaining agreements typically specify that arbitration before an outside neutral arbitrator will be the final stage.[3]

There are several professional associations that parties can use to obtain qualified arbitrators. The best known is the American Arbitration Association ("AAA"), an organization founded in the 1920s at the time of the enactment of the Federal Arbitration Act. The AAA has become a large national organization with headquarters in New York and several regional offices. It maintains lists of arbitrators by specialty in specific subject areas, as well as general lists in the areas of commercial disputes, international disputes, mass tort disputes, energy disputes, labor-management disputes, individual employment disputes, and construction disputes. The AAA has also devised a set of standard arbitral rules and procedures for each of these subject areas. When parties contact the AAA in search of an arbitrator, the AAA provides the parties with a list of arbitrators in the relevant subject area from which the parties can choose. The parties pay the AAA an administrative fee for its services and pay the arbitrator at an agreed-upon hourly or per diem rate.

Once an arbitrator is selected, the parties usually agree upon a written submission to the arbitrator. The submission states in concise and general terms the questions to be decided. The arbitrator's task is defined and

1. See Ariana R. Levinson, *Lawyering Skills, Principles and Methods Offer Insight as to Best Practices for Arbitration*, 60 Baylor L. Rev. 1, 18–23 (2008).

2. See, Soia Mentschikoff, *Commercial Arbitration*, 61 Colum. L. Rev. 846 (1961).

3. See Harry Shulman, *Reason, Contract, and Law in Labor Relations*, 68 Harv. L. Rev. 999 (1955).

circumscribed by the submission. For example, a typical submission in a commercial dispute might say:

> Did Company X materially breach its agreement with Company Y by shipping its product three days after the date specified for performance, and if so, what shall the remedy be?

After a hearing is held, the arbitrator issues an award. Courts treat the award as a final and binding disposition of the issues submitted to the arbitrator. The award may or may not be accompanied by a written opinion. The question of whether and under what circumstances arbitrators should write opinions is hotly debated for reasons that are addressed in Chapter 4.1.B. Whether or not an arbitral award is accompanied by an opinion, judicial review of arbitral awards is extremely limited. While some judicial review of arbitral awards is possible, and indeed necessary to ensure that the arbitrator has not violated the parties' agreement to arbitrate, courts are supposed to avoid reviewing the merits of the dispute. Thus, from the perspective of disputants, arbitration is a quasi-judicial means of resolving disputes.

2. Historical Background

A. Common Law

Prior to 1920, common law courts in the United States would not specifically enforce arbitration agreements. This meant, in practice, that if one party to an arbitration agreement refused to arbitrate, the other party was powerless to compel arbitration. The party seeking arbitration could obtain neither an order compelling arbitration nor a stay of litigation if the contract-breaker sued. In most states, the party seeking arbitration could go to a court for damages for breach of the promise to arbitrate, but courts would award a nominal amount—at most the cost of preparing for the arbitration that never occurred.[4] Federal courts and most states followed the common law rule.

The doctrine that denied specific performance to a promise to arbitrate was called the revocability doctrine, and was based on an agency analogy. The arbitrator was deemed to be the agent of both sides, so that agreements to arbitrate were revocable by either party until the arbitral award was issued. Once an award was issued, the legal status of the arbitration changed. At common law, arbitral awards were binding, and in many jurisdictions, they could be converted into a judgment of the court.

There were two different justifications offered for the revocability doctrine. The first was the notion that the parties were not competent, by private contract, to "oust the court of jurisdiction." This formulation originated in England, but it quickly took hold in both federal and state

4. Harry Baum & Leon Pressman, The Enforcement of Commercial Arbitration Agreements in the Federal Courts, 8 N.Y.U. L. Rev. 238, 241–42 (1930).

courts in the United States.[5] For example, the Supreme Court said in 1874 in *Insurance Co. v. Morse*, "[a]greements in advance to oust the courts of the jurisdiction conferred by law are illegal and void."[6] It was sometimes said that parties could neither create nor diminish the jurisdiction of the courts by contract.[7]

The other rationale for the 19th century revocability doctrine was set out by Justice Story in 1845, in the case of *Tobey v. County of Bristol,* 23 Fed.Cas. 1313 (1845). In the following excerpt, Justice Story explained that although a court of equity has no objections to arbitration tribunals, a court will not compel parties to participate in arbitration because the court cannot ensure that the process will be fair and equitable. The limited-powers-of-equity rationale for the revocability doctrine has received less attention than the ouster rationale.

* * *

Tobey v. County of Bristol

23 Fed.Cas. 1313 (C.C.D.Mass.1845).

■ STORY, CIRCUIT JUSTICE.

... Courts of equity do not refuse to interfere to compel a party specifically to perform an agreement to refer to arbitration, because they wish to discourage arbitrations, as against public policy. On the contrary, they have and can have no just objection to these domestic forums, and will enforce, and promptly interfere to enforce their awards when fairly and lawfully made, without hesitation or question. But when they are asked to proceed farther and to compel the parties to appoint arbitrators whose award shall be final, they necessarily pause to consider, whether such tribunals possess adequate means of giving redress, and whether they have a right to compel a reluctant party to submit to such a tribunal, and to close against him the doors of the common courts of justice, provided by the government to protect rights and to redress wrongs. One of the established principles of courts of equity is, not to entertain a bill for the specific performance of any agreement, where it is doubtful whether it may not thereby become the instrument of injustice, or to deprive parties of rights which they are otherwise fairly entitled to have protected. The specific performance of an agreement is, by no means, a matter of right which a party has authority to demand from a court of equity. So far from this, it is a matter of sound discretion in the court, to be granted or withheld, according to its own view of the merits and circumstances of the particular case, and never amounts to a peremptory duty. Now we all know, that

5. See Julius Cohen, Commercial Arbitration, 84–102 (1918) (tracing the history of the "oust the jurisdiction" doctrine in England and America).

6. Home Insurance Co. v. Morse, 87 U.S. (20 Wall.) 445 (1874).

7. The "ouster" rationale is discussed and criticized by Judge Frank in the *Kulukundis Shipping v. Amtorg Trading* case, which appears below.

arbitrators, at the common law, possess no authority whatsoever, even to administer an oath, or to compel the attendance of witnesses. They cannot compel the production of documents, and papers and books of account, or insist upon a discovery of facts from the parties under oath. They are not ordinarily well enough acquainted with the principles of law or equity, to administer either effectually, in complicated cases; and hence it has often been said, that the judgment of arbitrators is but rusticum judicium. Ought then a court of equity to compel a resort to such a tribunal, by which, however honest and intelligent, it can in no case be clear that the real legal or equitable rights of the parties can be fully ascertained or perfectly protected?

. . . And this leads me to remark in the second place, that it is an established principle of courts of equity never to enforce the specific performance of any agreement, where it would be a vain and imperfect act, or where a specific performance is from the very nature and character of the agreement, impracticable or inequitable, to be enforced. 2 Story, Eq. Jur. § 959a. Thus, for example, courts of equity will not decree the specific performance of an agreement for a partnership in business, where it is to be merely doing the pleasure of both parties, because it may be forthwith dissolved by either party. See Story, Partn. §§ 189, 190, and Colly. Partn. (2n Ed.) bk. 2, pp. 132, 133, c. 2, § 2; 1 Story, Eq. Jur. § 666, and the cases there cited; Crawshay v. Maule, 1 Swanst. 515, the reporter's note. So, upon the like ground, courts of equity will not decree the specific performance of a contract by an author to write dramatic performances for a particular theatre, although it will restrain him from writing for another theatre, if he has contracted not to do so (2 Story, Eq. Jur. § 959a; Morris v. Colman, 18 Ves. 437; Clarke v. Price, 3 Wils. Ch. 157; Baldwin v. Society for Diffusion of Useful Knowledge, 9 Sim. 393); nor will they compel the specific performance of a contract by an actor to act a specified number of nights at a particular theatre (Kemble v. Kean, 6 Sim. 333); nor will they compel the specific performance of a contract to furnish maps to be engraved and published by the other party (Baldwin v. Society for Diffusion of Useful Knowledge, 9 Sim. 393). In all these cases the reason is the same, the utter inadequacy of the means of the court to enforce the due performance of such a contract. The same principle would apply to the case of a specific contract by a master to paint an historical picture, or a contract by a sculptor to carve a statute or a group, historical or otherwise. From their very nature, all such contracts must depend for their due execution, upon the skill, and will, and honor of the contracting party. Now this very reasoning applies with equal force to the case at bar. How can a court of equity compel the respective parties to name arbitrators; and a fortiori, how can it compel the parties mutually to select arbitrators, since each must, in such a case, agree to all the arbitrators? If one party refuses to name an arbitrator, how is the court to compel him to name one? If an arbitrator is named by one party, how is the court to ascertain, if the other party objects to him, whether he is right or wrong in his objection? If one party names an arbitrator, who will not act, how can the court compel him to select another? If one party names an arbitrator not agreed to by the other, how is the court to find out what are his reasons for refusing? If one party names an arbitrator whom the other deems incompetent, how is the court to decide upon the question of his competency? Take the present case, where the arbitrators are to be mutually selected, when and within that time are they to be appointed? How many shall they be—two, three, four, five, seventeen, or even twenty? The resolve is silent as to the number. Can the court fix the number, if the parties do not agree upon it? That would be doing what has never yet been done. If either party should refuse to name any arbitrator, or to agree upon any named by the other side, has the court authority, of itself, to appoint arbitrators, or to substitute a master for them? That would be, as Sir John Leach said in Agar v. Macklen, 2 Sim. & S. 418, 423, to bind the parties contrary to their agreement; and in Milnes v. Gery, 14 Ves. 400, 408, Sir William Grant held such an appointment to be clearly beyond the authority of the court. In Wilks v. Davis, 3 Mer. 507, 509, Lord Eldon referring to the cases of Cooth v. Jackson, 6 Ves. 34; Milnes v. Gery, 14 Ves. 400, 408; and Blundell v. Brettargh, 17 Ves. 232,—said: "It has been determined in the cases referred to, that if one party agrees to sell and another to purchase, at a price to be settled by arbitrators named by the parties, if no award has been made, the court cannot decree respecting it." In Cooth v. Jackson, 6 Ves. 34, Lord Eldon said: "I am not aware of a case even at law, nor that a court of equity has ever entertained this jurisdiction, that where a reference has been made to arbitration and the judgment of the arbitrators is not given in the time and manner according to the agreement, the court have substituted themselves for the arbitrators and made the award. I am not aware that it has been done even in a case where the substantial thing to be done is agreed between the parties, but the time and manner in which it is to be done, is that which they have put upon others to execute." The same learned judge, in Blundell v. Brettargh, 17 Ves. 232, 242, affirmed the same statement, substituting only the word "prescribe" for "execute." So that we abundantly see, that the very impracticability of compelling the parties to name arbitrators, or upon their default, for the court to appoint them, constitutes, and must forever constitute, a complete bar to any attempt on the part of a court of equity to compel the specific performance of any agreement to refer to arbitration. It is essentially, in its very nature and character, an agreement which must rest in the good faith and honor of the parties, and like an agreement to paint a picture, or to carve a statute, or to write a book, or to invent patterns for prints, must be left to the conscience of the parties, or to such remedy in damages for the breach thereof, as the law has provided....

* * *

Questions

1. The normal remedy for breach of contract is damages. When one side alleges a breach of a promise to arbitrate, why might that party seek specific performance instead? Could damages ever serve as an adequate remedy for breach of a promise to arbitrate?

2. How does Judge Story's approach differ from the "ouster rationale" for refusing to grant specific performance to a promise to arbitrate?

3. Although common law courts would not issue a specific decree to compel parties to arbitrate, if parties nonetheless chose to arbitrate a dispute and an award was issued, common law courts would enforce the arbitral award at the behest of one of the parties. See Michael H. LeRoy, Crowning the New King: The Statutory Arbitrator and the Demise of Judicial Review, 2009 J. Disp. Resol. 1 (2009). Is this treatment of arbitration consistent with Judge Story's approach in *Tobey?* Is it consistent with the "ouster rationale" for refusing to compel parties to arbitrate in the first place?

* * *

B. THE NEW YORK ARBITRATION ACT OF 1920

Modern arbitration law has its origins in the New York Arbitration Act of 1920. In the early years of the twentieth century, the commercial bar of New York mounted a concerted challenge to the revocability doctrine. Commercial trade groups used arbitration extensively, and wanted the legal system to reflect and support their arbitration practices. The role of the business community in the development and legal authorization of arbitration is described by Jerold S. Auerbach in the following passage from his book, JUSTICE WITHOUT LAW.

Jerold S. Auerbach, JUSTICE WITHOUT LAW*

> [C]ommercial arbitration ... was nourished by the convergence of business organization and government regulation during the early years of the twentieth century. After a turbulent era of competitive disorder following the Civil War, business consolidation made self-regulation possible. By the 1920s there was a high level of industrial self-government. Indeed, business interests were equated with the national interest; the ideal society was seen as a benevolent business commonwealth (although, to be sure, uncommon wealth was reserved for businessmen). As business power expanded, however, government regulatory power (with considerable lag) also expanded in an effort to contain it. But the stronger the regulatory state, the stronger the desire for spheres of voluntary activity beyond its control. The growth of the regulatory state unsettled advocates of commercial autonomy, who turned to arbitration as a shield against government intrusion. Arbitration fit neatly into their vision of industrial planning; it permitted businessmen to solve their own problems 'in their own way—

* Jerold S. Auerbach, Justice Without Law (Oxford Press 1983). Reprinted with permission.

without resort to the clumsy and heavy hand of Government.' Commercial arbitration revived as the indigenous demand of powerful economic groups who formed their own consensual communities of profit.

Before World War I, commercial arbitration was confined to trade associations whose members engaged in the continuous sale or trade of a special product, commodity, or security. (Arbitration in the New York Stock Exchange, the Chicago Board of Trade, and the fur and silk industries dated back to the nineteenth century.) In such tightly organized associations the value of an enduring commercial relationship far exceeded the value of a particular commodity. Without the internal resolution of disputes through arbitration, litigation would inevitably promote 'hard feeling and ultimate disruption' of the bonds that sustained commercial relationships. As long as disputes were settled within the association, members were assured that their shared customs, however idiosyncratic, would be respected. Trade custom, which facilitated amicable relations between buyer and seller, offered far more security than the mysterious, and threatening, procedures of the law.

Commercial arbitration was revived at the instigation of Charles L. Bernheimer, president of a cotton-goods concern, who was frustrated by the costs, delays, and uncertainties of commercial litigation. Bernheimer touted the virtues of arbitration, which resolved disputes 'in a rough and ready "Squire Justice" fashion wherein ordinary common sense, knowledge of human nature, a clean cut sense of commercial equity, patience and forbearance produce the results desired' by businessmen. More powerful than 'the force of law,' reported his Chamber of Commerce arbitration committee, was 'the collective conscience of a group.' Other businessmen were also discovering the advantages of commercial arbitration. In Illinois, where arbitration by the Chicago Board of Trade helped to rationalize the commodities market, various commodities exchanges used its arbitration processes to maintain common standards and tight discipline among members. 'Why waste time, energy and money in court trials?' read a letter of inquiry to 'Mr. Business Man' in Illinois. Arbitration 'does not result in enmity between the parties, as does the ordinary law suit.' Instead, it offered expertise, business efficiency, and just results.

Preliminary support for the principle of arbitration came from an unexpected source: the legal profession. As the administration of justice deteriorated in urban America, lawyers were thrown on the defensive. They conceded (at least in the privacy of their own company), that there was 'a widespread feeling throughout the country that our bench and bar are not meeting the demands of the present age, that there has been manifest a growing distrust of our courts and a growing disrespect for our laws.' At the annual meeting of the Missouri Bar Association in 1914 Percy Werner, a St. Louis attorney, proposed a 'simple, dignified, honest, conciliatory, and democratic' procedure for the resolution of private disputes. Ordinary citizens were entitled to a procedure 'free from technicality and mystery, "which cut" to the marrow of a controversy in a simple, speedy, direct manner.' As government regulation increased, Werner observed, courts were inundated with an unprecedented volume of public-law issues, ranging from labor-management conflict to public utilities regulation to social legislation for working women and children. To reduce judicial congestion  the ordinary private disputes of individuals should be diverted to voluntary tribunals for arbitration by a lawyer, chosen by the disputants' attorneys. Not only would these tribunals serve the public; they would benefit bench and bar. Public respect for the judiciary would increase as over-crowded dockets diminished. Since only attorneys with 'character and learning' would serve as arbitrators, 'suspicion and reproach' of the bar would recede.

The New York Chamber of Commerce expressed interest in Werner's proposal, noting the opportunity for 'cooperative usefulness between commercial organizations and the legal profession.' The New York State Bar Association established a new committee to consider a range of alternatives that its members proposed for preventing unnecessary litigation: conciliation courts; Mormon-style mediation; arbitration; and specialized merchants' tribunals. Arbitration captured the committee's interest, but lawyers and businessmen wanted different results from it. Lawyers, defensive about criticism, were eager to improve their public image, without losing clients, while retaining control over dispute resolution. Businessmen, apprehensive about outside intrusion, wanted expeditious, inexpensive justice which comported with commercial practice, free of external legal constraints.

* * *

In 1915, Judge Charles Hough of the Southern District of New York wrote in *United States Asphalt Refining Co. v. Trinidad Lake Petroleum Co.*, 222 Fed. 1006 (S.D.N.Y. 1915), that there was no basis for the revocability doctrine other than *stare decisis*. Using this decision as its cue, the New York Chamber of Commerce decided to launch a full-scale attack on the doctrine. It participated as *amicus curiae* in another pending case regarding enforcement of arbitration agreements, and it commissioned Mr. Julius Henry Cohen, a respected member of the New York commercial bar and the Chair of the New York Bar Association's Committee on Arbitration, to represent the Chamber. Cohen's brief was then expanded into a book-length treatise on the errors of the revocability doctrine and the pressing need for reform in the law of arbitration.[1]

Cohen's book was followed by an avalanche of writings from the commercial law community urging courts and legislatures to change the law of arbitration. In 1919, the New York Chamber of Commerce joined

1. Charles Bernheimer, Introduction, in Julius Henry Cohen, Commercial Arbitration and the Law, xi; Cohen, id. at pp. xiii–xiv.

with the New York Bar Association to draft a statute for the New York legislature changing the common law rule. The statute, drafted by Julius Cohen, was patterned on the English arbitration law of 1898, which had dealt the final blow to the revocability doctrine there. There was, however, one significant difference between the New York and British statutes. The proposed New York law did not contain a provision for de novo court review of questions of law, whereas the British law did. There was also some dispute within the American legal community over whether arbitration agreements should be irrevocable for existing disputes or for future disputes.[2] Those who wanted to ensure that *all* agreements to arbitrate—those pertaining to future disputes as well as to existing disputes—were legally enforceable and irrevocable prevailed. In 1920, Cohen's bill passed the New York legislature and became the New York Arbitration Act.

The New York Arbitration Act of 1920 made written agreements to arbitrate existing or future disputes "valid, enforceable, and irrevocable, save upon such grounds as exist at law or in equity for the revocation of any contract." Ch. 275, General Laws of New York of 1920, Section 2. It further provided in Section 3 that a party aggrieved by the failure of another to submit a dispute to arbitration could petition the state supreme court (i.e., the New York trial court) "for an order directing that such arbitration proceed in the manner provided for in such contract or submission." Section 4 contained a procedure by which the court could appoint an arbitrator if a party resisting arbitration failed to cooperate in the selection of one, or if no method was specifically provided in the parties' contract. And the New York statute provided in Section 5 that once any suit or proceeding was brought on a matter referable to arbitration under the statute, the court "shall stay the trial of the action until such arbitration has been had in accordance with the terms of the agreement."

The New York Arbitration Act also amended the New York Civil Practice Act in several respects to provide for arbitration. One important provision was the addition of Section 1457 of the Civil Practice Act, which specified four grounds upon which courts could vacate an arbitration award. These are:

1. Where the award was procured by corruption, fraud or other undue means.

2. Where there was evident partiality or corruption in the arbitrators, or either of them.

3. Where the arbitrators were guilty of misconduct in refusing to postpone the hearing upon sufficient cause shown, or in refusing to hear evidence pertinent and material to the controversy; or of any other misbehavior by which the rights of any party have been prejudiced.

2. See Alfred Heuston, Settlement of Disputes by Arbitration, 1 WASH. L. REV. 243, 244, n. 8 (1925).

4. Where the arbitrators exceeded their powers, or so imperfectly executed them, that a mutual, final and definite award upon the subject-matter submitted was not made.

This language of the New York Arbitration Act was adopted, almost verbatim, in the Federal Arbitration Act five years later.

* * *

Questions

1. Compare the provisions of the New York Arbitration Act of 1920 with the provisions of the Federal Arbitration Act, as it appears in Appendix A. Are there any significant differences?

2. How might arbitration of a dispute between two members of a trade association differ from arbitration between two strangers, or between a member and a nonmember of a trade association? Are the reasons why courts should enforce agreements to arbitrate stronger or weaker when a dispute is between strangers who do not share such common membership?

3. In what ways is arbitration ideally suited to resolving commercial disputes? Is it an equally ideal way to resolve the myriad other disputes for which it is used today, such as employment, civil rights, and consumer disputes?

* * *

C. THE FEDERAL ARBITRATION ACT OF 1925

In the early 1920's, several states followed the lead of New York and enacted arbitration statutes to remove the common law doctrine of revocability and provide for legal enforcement of executory promises to arbitrate. At the same time, the American Bar Association began to work on a federal arbitration law, patterned on the New York statute. The A.B.A. prepared drafts for an United States Arbitration Act (USAA) in 1921, 1922, and 1923. Congress held hearings on the proposed USAA bill in January 1924, after which the bill moved quickly through the House and Senate Committees. In 1925, Congress unanimously passed a statute patterned on the New York Arbitration law.[1] The United States Arbitration Law, later renamed the Federal Arbitration Act (FAA), was signed by President Coolidge on February 12, 1925.

The Federal Arbitration Act says that arbitration agreements contained in contracts involving maritime transactions or interstate commerce are "valid, irrevocable, and enforceable, save upon such grounds as exist at law or in equity for the revocation of any contract," 9 U.S.C. § 2. It also empowers federal courts to grant a stay of litigation for any issue referable to arbitration under a valid arbitration agreement, 9 U.S.C. § 3, and to

1. For a detailed history of the enactment of the USAA, see Ian R. Macneil, American Arbitration Law, pp. 83–101 (Oxford University Press, 1992).

grant a motion to compel arbitration when one party refuses to abide by its arbitration agreement, 9 U.S.C. § 4. The text of the FAA appears in Appendix A.

One month after the new federal arbitration law went into effect, Julius Cohen, who played a significant role in drafting the federal arbitration law, together with Kenneth Dayton, set forth their views of the goals and effects of the new enactment in an article entitled "The New Federal Arbitration Law," 12 Va. L. Rev. 265 (1926):

> Before we analyze the machinery furnished by this statute to accomplish its purposes, we must understand the end for which systems of arbitration are devised. The evils which arbitration is intended to correct are three in number: (1) The long delay usually incident to a proceeding at law, in equity or in admiralty, especially in recent years in centers of commercial activity, where there has arisen great congestion of the court calendars. This delay arises not only from congestion of the calendars, which necessitates each case awaiting its turn for consideration, but also frequently from preliminary motions and other steps taken by litigants, appeals there from, which delay consideration of the merits, and appeals from decisions upon the merits which commonly follow the decision of any case of real importance. (2) The expense of litigation. (3) The failure, through litigation, to reach a decision regarded as just when measured by the standards of the business world. This failure may result either because the courts necessarily apply general rules which do not always fit a specific case, or because, in the ordinary jury trial, the parties do not have the benefit of the judgment of persons familiar with the peculiarities of the given controversy.
>
> Making an agreement to arbitrate is not always sufficient, however. If both parties are strictly honorable and if there is no misunderstanding between them as to the scope and effect of the agreement which they have made, they will carry out the contract to arbitrate and perform the award entered upon it, and there is no necessity for a statute. Unfortunately, this situation does not commonly exist. The party refusing to proceed may believe in good faith that for one reason or another his agreement to arbitrate does not bind him (*i.e.*, he may assert that he made no such agreement or that it was not intended to cover the particular controversy). Even without this, after a dispute has arisen, one party or the other ordinarily has a certain technical advantage which may be impaired if he submits the controversy to arbitration rather than to the courts. It may be in the application of a settled rule of law. It may be in some procedural peculiarity, or it may be merely in the delay of which he is assured by the congestion of the courts before he has to meet his obligation. The result is that this party is usually loath to surrender his supposed advantage. His unwillingness is not necessarily due to dishonesty or bad faith. Unfortunately, business has become so used to the doctrine of revocability of arbitration agreements that these clauses are not regarded in the same

light as other contractual obligations, and the party who refuses to perform his agreement frequently does not realize that he is violating his word. He has no conscious intention of defaulting upon his agreement, but the rule of law has blinded him to the fact that this is an agreement. While our American courts have usually declared a friendly attitude toward arbitration, they have felt themselves bound by the long standing decisions holding that arbitration agreements were revocable at will and would not be enforced by the courts. The result has been that any party who wished to avoid an agreement which he had made to arbitrate had only to declare his refusal to proceed and the courts would not order specific performance of the contract while the alternative of a damage suit was inadequate.

Furthermore, after the completion of an arbitration proceeding and the rendition of an award, the remedy open to the successful party if his opponent refused to perform the award was not in all respects satisfactory. To be sure, the award was usually considered a determination of the merits of the controversy, and the successful party had only to plead and prove the award to recover judgment upon it. Even this remedy, however, left room for an extended law suit because of the collateral issues of fraud and misconduct and other impropriety in the proceeding which might be introduced and which meant that the delay in finally recovering judgment was substantially as great as though action had been brought upon the original dispute. The one advantage lay in the fact that proof became simpler.

To meet the situation where, through dishonesty or mistake or otherwise, one party to an arbitration agreement refuses to perform it, statutes such as those adopted by Congress and in New York and New Jersey are advocated and have met favor.

The adoption of the statute does not mean that parties who have agreed to arbitrate and, after the controversy arises, are still willing to arbitrate and abide by the results must come into court or submit to any legal interference whatever. The arbitration proceeds as though the statute were non-existent. There is no interference by the courts.

Where one party refuses to carry out the agreement, however, the other party now has a remedy formerly denied him. This remedy is not, as has been suggested, equally cumbersome with the existing actions at law, nor is there any prospect that it will ever become so.

It has been suggested that the proposed law depends entirely for its validity upon the exercise of the interstate-commerce and admiralty powers of Congress. This is not the fact. It rests upon the constitutional provision by which Congress is authorized to establish and control inferior Federal courts. So far as congressional acts relate to the procedure in such courts, they are clearly within the congressional power. This principle is so evident and so firmly established that it cannot be seriously disputed. The statute as drawn establishes a procedure in the Federal courts for the enforcement of certain arbitration agreements. It is no infringement upon the right of each State to decide for itself what contracts shall or shall not exist under its laws. To be sure, whether or not a contract exists is a question of the substantive law of the jurisdiction wherein the contract was made. But whether or not an arbitration agreement is to be enforced is a question of the law of procedure and is determined by the law of the jurisdiction wherein the remedy is sought. That the enforcement of arbitration contracts is within the law of procedure as distinguished from substantive law is well settled by the decisions of our courts. The rule must be changed for the jurisdiction in which the agreement is sought to be enforced, and a change in the jurisdiction in which it was made is of no effect. Every one of the States in the Union might declare such agreement to be valid and enforceable, and still in the Federal courts it would remain void and unenforceable without this statute....

Arbitration under the Federal and similar statutes is simply a new procedural remedy, particularly adapted to the settlement of commercial disputes. It clearly is not outside the law because it is provided for by statute. No more is it outside the established legal system, because under these statutes the proceeding from beginning to end may be brought under the supervision of the courts if either party deems it necessary. No one is required to make an agreement to arbitrate. Such action by a party is entirely voluntary. When the agreement to arbitrate is made, it is not left outside the law. Proceedings under the new arbitration law are as much a part of our legal system as any other special proceeding or form of remedy. It is merely a new method for enforcing a contract freely made by the parties thereto.

* * *

Questions

1. Cohen and Dayton mention three evils that the Federal Arbitration Act was intended to correct when it was enacted in the 1920s. Do these criticisms of the judicial system apply equally today?

2. Cohen and Dayton state that the enforcement of arbitration clauses under the Federal Arbitration Act is an aspect of procedural law. Can you argue that this is an aspect of substantive law?

3. Note that Cohen and Dayton emphasize that the FAA does not rest on Congress' Commerce Power or its Admiralty Powers, but rather on Congress' power under Article III to establish and regulate the procedures in the federal courts. Why do you think they take this position? What would be the consequences if the FAA rested on the Commerce power instead?

* * *

The *Kulukundis Shipping* case, which appears below, is an early attempt by a federal court to interpret and apply the then-new federal arbitration statute. In reading the opinion, consider whether Justice Frank's views are in tension with Justice Story's in the *Tobey* case.

Kulukundis Shipping Co., S/A v. Amtorg Trading Corporation

126 F.2d 978 (2d Cir. 1942).

■ FRANK, CIRCUIT JUDGE.

The libel alleged that appellant (respondent) had, through its authorized representatives, agreed to a charter party with appellee (libellant). Appellant's answer in effect denied that anyone authorized to act for it had so agreed. After a trial, the district court made the following

Findings of Fact

1. Libellant, Kulukundis Shipping Co. S/A, employed Blidberg Rothchild Co. Inc. as a broker and the respondent, Amtorg Trading Corporation employed Potter & Gordon, Inc. as its broker in the negotiations for the chartering of the ship 'Mount Helmos' for a trip to Japan. On March 15, 1940, Rothchild, of the firm of Blidberg Rothchild Co. Inc., and Gordon, acting on behalf of Potter & Gordon, Inc., agreed upon a charter and closed by Gordon executing and delivering to Rothchild a fixture slip which is the usual trade practice, indicating the conclusion of charter negotiations in the trade of ship brokerage. All the material items of the bargain are set forth in the fixture slip excepting demurrage, dispatch, and the date of the commencement of the charter term which all had been agreed on but were omitted by an oversight. A number of the terms, including the War Risks Clause of 1937, were fixed by the incorporation of a reference to an earlier charter of the steamer 'Norbryn.' Gordon acted with authority.

2. Thereafter, respondent refused to sign the charter but instead repudiated it.

Conclusions of Law

1. Respondent has breached a valid contract and is liable in damages to the libellant.

Pursuant to the foregoing, the court entered an order that appellee recover from appellant the damages sustained, and referred to a named commissioner the ascertainment of the damages, to be reported to the court....

The appellant, in its answer originally filed, pleaded that no contract had been made. No steps of any importance having meanwhile occurred in the suit, some nine months later and two months before the trial, it sought to amend its answer by including, as a separate defense, the fact that the alleged charter party upon which appellee was suing contained an arbitration clause, that appellee had not at any time asked appellant to proceed to arbitration, and that therefore the suit had been prematurely brought. This motion to amend was denied. If the amendment should have been allowed, the additional defense can now be urged.

The arbitration clause reads as follows: "24. Demurrage or despatch is to be settled at loading and discharging ports separately, except as per

Clause 9. Owners and Charterers agree, in case of any dispute or claim, to settle same by arbitration in New York. Also, in case of a dispute of any nature whatsoever, same is to be settled by arbitration in New York. In both cases arbitrators are to be commercial men."

[The court then quoted Sections 2, 3 & 4 of the Federal Arbitration Act.]

Appellant admits—as it must—that the district court had jurisdiction to determine whether the parties had made an agreement to arbitrate. Appellant contends, however, that, once the court determined in this suit that there was such an arbitration agreement, the court lost all power over the suit beyond that of staying further proceedings until there had been an arbitration as agreed to; in that arbitration, argues appellant, the arbitrators will have jurisdiction to determine all issues except the existence of the arbitration clause. This jurisdiction, it is urged, is broad enough to permit an independent determination, by the arbitrator, that the contract itself is not valid or binding. Appellee asserts that the defendant had repudiated the charter-party, and that, therefore, the arbitration clause must be wholly disregarded.

In considering these contentions in the light of the precedents, it is necessary to take into account the history of the judicial attitude towards arbitration: The English courts, while giving full effect to agreements to submit controversies to arbitration after they had ripened into arbitrators' awards, would—over a long period beginning at the end of the 17th century—do little or nothing to prevent or make irksome the breach of such agreements when they were still executory.[5] Prior to 1687, such a breach could be made costly: a penal bond given to abide the result of an arbitration had a real bite, since a breach of the bond's condition led to a judgment for the amount of the penalty. It was so held in 1609 in Vynoir's Case, 8 Coke Rep. 81b. To be sure, Coke there, in a dictum, citing precedents, dilated on the inherent revocability of the authority given to an arbitrator; such a revocation was not too important, however, if it resulted in a stiff judgment on a penal bond. But the Statute of Fines and Penalties (8 & 9 Wm.III c. 11, § 8), enacted in 1687, provided that, in an action on any bond given for performance of agreements, while judgment would be entered for the penalty, execution should issue only for the damages actually sustained. Coke's dictum as to revocability, uttered seventy-eight years earlier, now took on a new significance, as it was now held that for breach of an undertaking to arbitrate the damages were only nominal. Recognizing the effect of the impact of this statute on executory arbitration agreements, Parliament, eleven years later, enacted a statute, 9 Wm.III c. 15 (1698), designed to remedy the situation by providing that, if an

5. The early English history of enforcement of executory arbitration agreements is not too clear. Arbitration was used by the medieval guilds and in early maritime transactions. Some persons trace an influence back to Roman law, doubtless itself affected by Greek law; others discern the influence of ecclesiastical law. See Sayre, Development of Commercial Arbitration Law, 37 Yale L.J. (1927) 595, 597. [additional citations omitted.]

agreement to arbitrate so provided, it could be made a "rule of court" (i.e., a court order), in which event it became irrevocable, and one who revoked it would be subject to punishment for contempt of court; but the submission was revocable until such a rule of court had been obtained. This statute, limited in scope, was narrowly construed and was of little help. The ordinary executory arbitration agreement thus lost all real efficacy since it was not specifically enforceable in equity, and was held not to constitute the basis of a plea in bar in, or a stay of, a suit on the original cause of action. In admiralty, the rulings were much the same.

It has been well said that "the legal mind must assign some reason in order to decide anything with spiritual quiet."[8B] And so, by way of rationalization, it became fashionable in the middle of the 18th century to say that such agreements were against public policy because they "oust the jurisdiction" of the courts. But that was a quaint explanation, inasmuch as an award, under an arbitration agreement, enforced both at law and in equity, was no less an ouster; and the same was true of releases and covenants not to sue, which were given full effect. Moreover, the agreement to arbitrate was not illegal, since suit could be maintained for its breach. Here was a clear instance of what Holmes called a "right" to break a contract and to substitute payment of damages for non-performance;[10] as, in this type of case, the damages were only nominal, that "right" was indeed meaningful.

An effort has been made to justify this judicial hostility to the executory arbitration agreement on the ground that arbitrations, if unsupervised by the courts, are undesirable, and that legislation was needed to make possible such supervision. But if that was the reason for unfriendliness to such executory agreements, then the courts should also have refused to aid arbitrations when they ripened into awards. And what the English courts, especially the equity courts, did in other contexts, shows that, if they had the will, they could have devised means of protecting parties to arbitrations. Instead, they restrictively interpreted successive statutes intended to give effect to executory arbitrations.... Perhaps the true explanation is the hypnotic power of the phrase, "oust the jurisdiction."[17] Give a bad dogma a good name and its bite may become as bad as its bark.

In 1855, in Scott v. Avery, 5 H.C.L. 811, the tide seemed to have turned. There it was held that if a policy made an award of damages by arbitrators a condition precedent to a suit on the policy, a failure to submit to arbitration would preclude such a suit, even if the policy left to the arbitrators the consideration of all the elements of liability. But, despite later legislation, the hostility of the English courts to executory arbitrations

8B. Hough, J., in United States Asphalt R. Co. v. Trinidad Lake P. Co., D.C. 1915, 222 F. 1006, 1008. He discusses and shows the "worthlessness" of the several "causes advanced for refusing to compel men to abide by their arbitration contracts."

10. Holmes, The Path of The Law, 10 Harv.L.Rev. (1897) 457.

17. Words sometimes have such potency. For an excellent 18th century American essay on "semantics" along these lines, see Mr. Justice Wilson's opinion in Chisholm v. Georgia, 1793, 2 Dall. 419, 454ff, 1 L.Ed. 440; Cf. United States v. Forness, 2 Cir., January 20, 1942, 125 F.2d 928, 934, and note 9.

resumed somewhat after Scott v. Avery, and seems never to have been entirely dissipated.

That English attitude was largely taken over in the 19th century by most courts in this country. Indeed, in general, they would not go as far as Scott v. Avery, supra, and continued to use the "ouster of jurisdiction" concept: An executory agreement to arbitrate would not be given specific performance or furnish the basis of a stay of proceedings on the original cause of action.... In the case of broader executory agreements, no more than nominal damages would be given for a breach.

Generally speaking, then, the courts of this country were unfriendly to executory arbitration agreements. The lower federal courts, feeling bound to comply with the precedents, nevertheless became critical of this judicial hostility. There were intimations in the Supreme Court that perhaps the old view might be abandoned, but in the cases hinting at that newer attitude the issue was not raised. Effective state arbitration statutes were enacted beginning with the New York Statute of 1920.

The United States Arbitration Act of 1925 was sustained as constitutional, in its application to cases arising in admiralty. Marine Transit Corp. v. Dreyfus, 1932, 284 U.S. 263, 52 S.Ct. 166, 76 L.Ed. 282. The purpose of that Act was deliberately to alter the judicial atmosphere previously existing. The report of the House Committee stated, in part: "Arbitration agreements are purely matters of contract, and the effect of the bill is simply to make the contracting party live up to his agreement. He can no longer refuse to perform his contract when it becomes disadvantageous to him. An arbitration agreement is placed upon the same footing as other contracts, where it belongs.... The need for the law arises from an anachronism of our American law. Some centuries ago, because of the jealousy of the English courts for their own jurisdiction, they refused to enforce specific agreements to arbitrate upon the ground that the courts were thereby ousted from their jurisdiction. This jealousy survived for so long a period that the principle became firmly embedded in the English common law and was adopted with it by the American courts. The courts have felt that the precedent was too strongly fixed to be overturned without legislative enactment, although they have frequently criticized the rule and recognized its illogical nature and the injustice which results from it. The bill declares simply that such agreements for arbitration shall be enforced, and provides a procedure in the Federal courts for their enforcement.... It is particularly appropriate that the action should be taken at this time when there is so much agitation against the costliness and delays of litigation. These matters can be largely eliminated by agreements for arbitration, if arbitration agreements are made valid and enforceable."

In the light of the clear intention of Congress, it is our obligation to shake off the old judicial hostility to arbitration. Accordingly, in a case like this, involving the federal Act, we should not follow English or other decisions which have narrowly construed the terms of arbitration agreements or arbitration statutes. With this new orientation, we approach the problems here presented. They are twofold: (a) Does the arbitration provision here have the sweeping effect ascribed to it by appellant? (b) Is it, as appellee contends, wholly without efficacy because appellant asserted that there never was an agreement for a charter party? We shall consider these questions in turn:

To the appellant's sweeping contention there are several answers:

(a) Appellant, as we saw, concedes that, in such a case as this, before sending any issue to arbitrators, the court must determine whether an arbitration provision exists. As the arbitration clause here is an integral part of the charter party, the court, in determining that the parties agreed to that clause, must necessarily first have found that the charter party exists. If the court here, having so found, were now to direct the arbitrators to consider that same issue, they would be traversing ground already covered in the court trial. There would thus result precisely that needless expenditure of time and money (the "costliness and delays of litigation") which Congress sought to avoid in enacting the Arbitration Act. In the light of that fact, a reasonable interpretation of the Act compels a repudiation of appellant's sweeping contention.

(b) If the issue of the existence of the charter party were left to the arbitrators and they found that it was never made, they would, unavoidably (unless they were insane), be obliged to conclude that the arbitration agreement had never been made. Such a conclusion would (1) negate the court's prior contrary decision on a subject which, admittedly, the Act commits to the court, and (2) would destroy the arbitrators' authority to decide anything and thus make their decision a nullity. Cf. Phillips, The Paradox in Arbitration Law, 46 Harv.L.Rev. (1933) 1258, 1270–1272; Phillips, A Lawyer's Approach to Commercial Arbitration, 41 Yale L.J. (1934) 31; 6 Williston, Contracts (Rev.ed. 1938), Section 1920 (pp. 5369–5379).

(c) The Arbitration Act does not cover an arbitration agreement sufficiently broad to include a controversy as to the existence of the very contract which embodies the arbitration agreement. Section 2 of the Act describes only three types of agreement covered by the Act: One type is "an agreement . . . to submit to arbitration an existing controversy arising out of . . . a contract, transaction,' etc.; thus the parties here, after a dispute had arisen as to the existence of the charter party, might have made an agreement to submit to arbitration that 'existing' controversy. But that is not this case. Section 2 also includes a 'provision in . . . a contract evidencing a transaction . . . to settle by arbitration a controversy thereafter arising out of such contract or transaction. . . .' Plainly such a provision does not include a provision in a contract to arbitrate the issue whether the minds of the parties ever met so as to bring about the very contract of which that arbitration clause is a part; a controversy 'arising out of a transaction evidenced by a contract,' for if no contract existed then there was no such transaction evidenced by a contract and, therefore, no controversy arising out of that transaction. The third type of arbitration agreement described in Section 2 of the Act is a provision in a contract to settle by arbitration 'a controversy thereafter arising out of . . . the refusal to perform the whole or any part thereof.' This is familiar language; it refers to a controversy, which parties to a contract may easily contemplate, arising when a party to the contract, without denying that he made it, refuses performance; it does not mean a controversy arising out of the denial by one of the parties that he ever made any contract whatsoever.

It is clear then that, even assuming, arguendo, that a contract would be drawn containing an arbitration clause sufficiently broad to include a controversy as to whether the minds of the parties had ever met concerning the making of the very contract which embodies the arbitration clause, such a clause would not be within the Arbitration Act. Accordingly, it perhaps would not be immunized from the prestatutory rules inimical to arbitration, i.e., would not serve as the basis of a stay of the suit on the contract, leaving the parties to the arbitration called for by their agreement. Were the arbitration clause here sufficiently broad to call for arbitration of the dispute as to the existence of the charter party, it would, therefore, perhaps be arguable that it was entirely outside of the Act and, accordingly, irrelevant in the case before us; we need not consider that question, as we hold that the breadth of the arbitration clause is not so great and it is within the terms of Section 2 of the Act.

We conclude that it would be improper to submit to the arbitrators the issue of the making of the charter party.

But it does not follow that appellant was not entitled to a stay of the suit, under Section 3, until arbitration has been had as to the amount of the damages. Here it is important to differentiate between Sections 3 and 4 of the Act. Under Section 4, the proceeding—as the Supreme Court observed in Marine Transit Corp. v. Dreyfus, 284 U.S. 263, 278, 52 S.Ct. 166, 76 L.Ed. 516—is one for specific performance: One of the parties seeks "an order directing that ... arbitration proceed in the manner provided for" in the arbitration clause or agreement. It may well be that in a proceeding under Section 4, there are open many of the usual defenses available in a suit for specific performance.[30] It would seem that a court, when exercising equity powers, should do so on the basis of a fully informed judgment as to all the circumstances. We recognize that some authorities have held to the contrary under similarly worded state arbitration statutes, interpreting them to require the courts automatically to decree specific performance without regard to the usual equitable considerations. It is difficult for us to believe that Congress intended us so to construe Section 4, although we do not here decide that question.[32] However that may be,

30. Note the statement in the Congressional Committee's report: "An arbitration agreement is placed upon the same footing as other contracts, where it belongs." But no other contracts will be ordered to be specifically enforced where the customary equitable factors are absent. Other portions of that report, previously quoted, state that the purpose of the Act was to get rid of the effects of the earlier judicial hostility to arbitration contracts. To interpret the Act as precluding equitable considerations when a court is asked to order specific performance is to do far more than that.

32. Those sponsors of arbitration who insist that the valuable traditional powers of the equity courts are choked off under provisions like Section 4 are doing arbitration no real service. For where their position has the same equitable considerations should surely not be applicable when a defendant asks a stay pursuant to Section 3. For he is not then seeking specific performance (i.e., an order requiring that the parties proceed to arbitration) but merely a stay order of a kind long familiar in common law, equity and admiralty actions. His position is that when the court (to quote Section 3) is "satisfied that the issue involved in such suit . . . is referable to arbitration," the court must "stay the trial of the action until such arbitration has been had in accordance with the terms of the agreement." There is a well recognized distinction between such a stay and specific performance: The first merely arrests further action by the court itself in the suit until something outside the suit has occurred; but the court does not order that it shall be done. The second, through the exercise of discretionary equity powers, affirmatively orders that someone do (or refrain from doing) some act outside the suit.

. . . In the case at bar, so far as the arbitration was concerned, it was the first duty of the court, under Section 3, to determine whether there was an agreement to arbitrate and whether any of the issues raised in the suit were within the reach of that agreement. The appellant contested the existence of the charter party which contained that agreement, but also alternatively pleaded that, if it existed, then there should be a stay pending arbitration of the appropriate issues. We see no reason why a respondent should be precluded from thus pleading in the alternative.

. . . As Williston remarks: "A person who repudiates a contract wrongfully cannot sue upon it himself, but if he is sued upon it, he can be held liable only according to the terms of the contract. If, therefore, an arbitration clause amounts to a condition precedent to the defendant's promise to pay any insurance money, and such conditions are lawful, the defendant can be held liable only if that condition is performed, prevented or waived."

Arbitration under the charter party here was a condition precedent. At common law, or in admiralty, failure of a plaintiff to perform an ordinary condition precedent (unless excused) is the basis of a plea in bar. . . .

The arbitration clause here was clearly broad enough to cover the issue of damages; "a clause of general arbitration does not cease to be within the statute when the dispute narrows down to damages alone."[36] It has been suggested that the arbitration clause calls for arbitrators who are "commercial men," that they are not appropriate persons to compute damages in this case where appellant has not merely breached but denied the existence of the charter party, and that, therefore, it must follow that the parties did not contemplate arbitration of such damages. But that argument is untenable, since it rests upon an unsound assumption, i.e., that

been accepted, litigation—which the arbitration statutes are designed to reduce—is augmented. The more enthusiastic of those sponsors have thought of arbitration as a universal panacea. We doubt whether it will cure corns or bring general beatitude. Few panaceas work as well as advertised. Almost always those who propose one think solely of the disadvantages of an older method which they criticize, forget its advantages, and disregard evils which may attend the reform.

36. Shanferoke Coal & Supply Corp. v. Westchester S. Corp., 70 F.2d 297, 299 (2d Cir. 1934).

damages are to be differently computed in those two kinds of situations. In truth, it is precisely this sort of case where arbitration of damages by "commercial men" may be peculiarly useful, as they are likely to be more familiar than the average lawyer who serves as special master with the relevant background of international shipping in the state of world affairs as of the period covered by the charter party.

There remains to be considered the language of Section 3 of the Act that, "on application," such a stay shall be granted "providing the applicant for the stay is not in default in proceeding with such arbitration." We take that proviso to refer to a party who, when requested, has refused to go to arbitration or who has refused to proceed with the hearing before the arbitrators once it has commenced. The appellant was never asked by appellee to proceed with the arbitration; indeed, it is the appellee who has objected to it. . . .

Accordingly, we conclude that the defendant here was not in default within the meaning of the proviso in Section 3. It follows that the district court should have stayed the suit, pending arbitration to determine the damages. . . .

The order of the district court is reversed and the cause is remanded with directions to proceed in accordance with the foregoing opinion.

* * *

Questions

1. Compare the court's discussion of an arbitrator's ability to decide the validity of its enabling contractual clause in *Kulukundis* to a court's ability to determine its own jurisdiction. How do they differ? How are they similar? Should they be identical?

2. When parties to a dispute disagree about whether a valid contract was formed, can a court decide the issue of contract formation without deciding the merits of the case? Consider the following hypothetical:

> Osborne discusses renting her recreational vehicle to Katsiff for one month, at a particular rate. Many details are discussed, including price, liability, and the fact that Katsiff wants the car on Monday, August 1 at 10:00 to begin a family vacation. Katsiff takes notes, but nothing is signed. After their discussions, Katsiff believes they have a deal. He shows up at Osborne's house on Monday to get the vehicle, but Osborne refuses to deliver it. Katsiff rents a comparable vehicle at a higher price and then sues Osborne for breach of promise to rent the vehicle. Osborne defends on the grounds that no valid contract was formed.

If the court finds there was a contract formed, has it also decided that Osborne is in breach? If it finds that no contract was formed, can it nonetheless find Osborne liable? Is this hypothetical distinguishable from the *Kulukundis Shipping* case?

3. In the above hypothetical, suppose that the discussions between the parties included the issue of arbitration. Assume that the parties agreed that should they have disagreements about the performance of the rental arrangement, they would submit the dispute to arbitration according to the AAA commercial arbitration rules. In such case, if a court decides that there was a valid contract, is the arbitration clause necessarily also valid? If so, can the arbitrator decide that no valid contract was made?

4. Judge Frank's description of the history of judicial responses to arbitration concentrates on the interjurisdictional rivalry between courts and private tribunals. He offers a thorough critique of the "ouster of jurisdiction" rationale for the courts' restrictive approach. He only mentions Justice Story's opinion in the *Tobey* case in a footnote, even though Justice Story was one of nineteenth century America's preeminent jurists. How well does Judge Frank respond to the due process and equity arguments that Justice Story raised in the *Tobey* opinion?

* * *

3. STATE VERSUS FEDERAL JURISDICTION

Federal courts have subject-matter jurisdiction over two types of cases: cases that arise under federal law ("federal question" cases) and cases "between citizens of different states" (diversity cases). Absent diversity, it often is difficult to determine whether a dispute over arbitration belongs in federal court or state court. This problem arises because the Federal Arbitration Act, though a federal statute, has been interpreted by the Supreme Court as not conferring subject-matter jurisdiction. This means that a party seeking to enforce an arbitration agreement pursuant to the FAA can only get into federal court if the party can show an independent basis for federal jurisdiction. Otherwise, the enforceability of the arbitration agreement will be decided in a state court (though, as described in the next section of this chapter, the state court will apply the FAA).

Vaden v. Discover Bank

__ U.S. __, 129 S.Ct. 1262 (2009).

■ JUSTICE GINSBURG delivered the opinion of the Court.

Section 4 of the Federal Arbitration Act, 9 U.S.C. § 4, authorizes a United States district court to entertain a petition to compel arbitration if the court would have jurisdiction, "save for [the arbitration] agreement," over "a suit arising out of the controversy between the parties." We consider in this opinion two questions concerning a district court's subject-matter jurisdiction over a § 4 petition: Should a district court, if asked to compel arbitration pursuant to § 4, "look through" the petition and grant the requested relief if the court would have federal-question jurisdiction over the underlying controversy? And if the answer to that question is yes, may a district court exercise jurisdiction over a § 4 petition when the petitioner's complaint rests on state law but an actual or potential counterclaim rests on federal law?

The litigation giving rise to these questions began when Discover Bank's servicing affiliate filed a complaint in Maryland state court. Presenting a claim arising solely under state law, Discover [sued in state court] to recover past-due charges from one of its credit cardholders, Betty Vaden. Vaden answered and counterclaimed, alleging that Discover's finance charges, interest, and late fees violated state [usery] law. Invoking an arbitration clause in its cardholder agreement with Vaden, Discover then filed a § 4 petition in the United States District Court for the District of Maryland to compel arbitration of Vaden's counterclaims. The District Court had subject-matter jurisdiction over its petition, Discover maintained, because Vaden's state-law counterclaims were completely preempted by federal banking law. The District Court agreed and ordered arbitration. Reasoning that a federal court has jurisdiction over a § 4 petition if the parties' underlying dispute presents a federal question, the Fourth Circuit eventually affirmed.

We agree with the Fourth Circuit in part. A federal court may "look through" a § 4 petition and order arbitration if, "save for [the arbitration] agreement," the court would have jurisdiction over "the [substantive] controversy between the parties." We hold, however, that the Court of Appeals misidentified the dimensions of "the controversy between the parties." Focusing on only a slice of the parties' entire controversy, the court seized on Vaden's counterclaims, held them completely preempted, and on that basis affirmed the District Court's order compelling arbitration. Lost from sight was the triggering plea—Discover's claim for the balance due on Vaden's account. Given that entirely state-based plea and the established rule that federal-court jurisdiction cannot be invoked on the basis of a defense or counterclaim, the whole "controversy between the parties" does not qualify for federal-court adjudication. Accordingly, we reverse the Court of Appeals' judgment. . . .

II

In 1925, Congress enacted the FAA "[t]o overcome judicial resistance to arbitration," *Buckeye Check Cashing, Inc. v. Cardegna,* 546 U.S. 440, 443, 126 S.Ct. 1204, 163 L.Ed.2d 1038 (2006), and to declare " 'a national policy favoring arbitration' of claims that parties contract to settle in that manner," *Preston v. Ferrer,* 552 U.S. ___, ___, 128 S.Ct. 978, 983, 169 L.Ed.2d 917 (2008) (quoting *Southland Corp. v. Keating,* 465 U.S. 1, 10, 104 S.Ct. 852, 79 L.Ed.2d 1 (1984)). To that end, § 2 provides that arbitration agreements in contracts "involving commerce" are "valid, irrevocable, and enforceable." 9 U.S.C. § 2. Section 4—the section at issue here—provides for United States district court enforcement of arbitration agreements. Petitions to compel arbitration, § 4 states, may be brought before "any United States district court which, save for such agreement, would have jurisdiction under title 28 . . . of the subject matter of a suit arising out of the controversy between the parties."

The "body of federal substantive law" generated by elaboration of FAA § 2 is equally binding on state and federal courts. *Southland,* 465 U.S., at 12, 104 S.Ct. 852 (quoting *Moses H. Cone Memorial Hospital v. Mercury Constr. Corp.,* 460 U.S. 1, 25, n. 32, 103 S.Ct. 927, 74 L.Ed.2d 765 (1983)); accord *Allied–Bruce Terminix Cos. v. Dobson,* 513 U.S. 265, 271–272, 115 S.Ct. 834, 130 L.Ed.2d 753 (1995). "As for jurisdiction over controversies touching arbitration," however, the Act is "something of an anomaly" in the realm of federal legislation: It "bestow[s] no federal jurisdiction but rather requir[es] [for access to a federal forum] an independent jurisdictional basis" over the parties' dispute. *Hall Street Associates, L.L.C. v. Mattel, Inc.,* 552 U.S. ___, ___, 128 S.Ct. 1396, 1402, 170 L.Ed.2d 254 (2008) (quoting *Moses H. Cone,* 460 U.S., at 25, n. 32, 103 S.Ct. 927). Given the substantive supremacy of the FAA, but the Act's nonjurisdictional cast, state courts have a prominent role to play as enforcers of agreements to arbitrate. See *Southland,* 465 U.S., at 15, 104 S.Ct. 852; *Moses H. Cone,* 460 U.S., at 25, and n. 32, 103 S.Ct. 927.

The independent jurisdictional basis Discover relies upon in this case is 28 U.S.C. § 1331, which vests in federal district courts jurisdiction over "all civil actions arising under the Constitution, laws, or treaties of the United States." Under the longstanding well-pleaded complaint rule, however, a suit "arises under" federal law "only when the plaintiff's statement of his own cause of action shows that it is based upon [federal law]." *Louisville & Nashville R. Co. v. Mottley,* 211 U.S. 149, 152, 29 S.Ct. 42, 53 L.Ed. 126 (1908). Federal jurisdiction cannot be predicated on an actual or anticipated defense: "It is not enough that the plaintiff alleges some anticipated defense to his cause of action and asserts that the defense is invalidated by some provision of [federal law]." *Ibid.* Nor can federal jurisdiction rest upon an actual or anticipated counterclaim. We so ruled, emphatically, in *Holmes Group,* 535 U.S. 826, 122 S.Ct. 1889, 153 L.Ed.2d 13. . . .

A *complaint* purporting to rest on state law, we have recognized, can be recharacterized as one "arising under" federal law if the law governing the complaint is exclusively federal. See *Beneficial Nat. Bank v. Anderson,* 539 U.S. 1, 8, 123 S.Ct. 2058, 156 L.Ed.2d 1 (2003). Under this so-called "complete preemption doctrine," a plaintiff's "state cause of action [may be recast] as a federal claim for relief, making [its] removal [by the defendant] proper on the basis of federal question jurisdiction." 14B Wright & Miller § 3722.1, p. 511. A state-law-based *counterclaim,* however, even if similarly susceptible to recharacterization, would remain nonremovable. Under our precedent construing § 1331, as just explained, counterclaims, even if they rely exclusively on federal substantive law, do not qualify a case for federal-court cognizance.

III

Attending to the language of the FAA and the above-described jurisdictional tenets, we approve the "look through" approach to this extent: A federal court may "look through" a § 4 petition to determine whether it is predicated on an action that "arises under" federal law; in keeping with the well-pleaded complaint rule as amplified in *Holmes Group,* however, a federal court may not entertain a § 4 petition based on the contents, actual or hypothetical, of a counterclaim.

A

The text of § 4 drives our conclusion that a federal court should determine its jurisdiction by "looking through" a § 4 petition to the parties' underlying substantive controversy. We reiterate § 4's relevant instruction: When one party seeks arbitration pursuant to a written agreement and the other resists, the proponent of arbitration may petition for an order compelling arbitration in

> any United States district court which, save for [the arbitration] agreement, would have jurisdiction under title 28, in a civil action or in admiralty of the subject matter of a suit arising out of the controversy between the parties.

9 U.S.C. § 4. The phrase "save for [the arbitration] agreement" indicates that the district court should assume the absence of the arbitration agreement and determine whether it "would have jurisdiction under title 28" without it. See 396 F.3d, at 369, 372 (case below). Jurisdiction over what? The text of § 4 refers us to "the controversy between the parties." That phrase, the Fourth Circuit said, and we agree, is most straightforwardly read to mean the "substantive conflict between the parties." *Id.,* at 370. See also *Moses H. Cone,* 460 U.S., at 25, n. 32, 103 S.Ct. 927 (noting in dicta that, to entertain a § 4 petition, a federal court must have jurisdiction over the "underlying dispute").

The majority of Courts of Appeals to address the question, we acknowledge, have rejected the "look through" approach entirely, as Vaden asks us to do here. The relevant "controversy between the parties," Vaden insists, is simply and only the parties' discrete dispute over the arbitrability of their claims. She relies, quite reasonably, on the fact that a § 4 petition to compel arbitration seeks no adjudication on the merits of the underlying controversy. Indeed, its very purpose is to have an arbitrator, rather than a court, resolve the merits. A § 4 petition, Vaden observes, is essentially a plea for specific performance of an agreement to arbitrate, and it thus presents principally contractual questions: Did the parties validly agree to arbitrate? What issues does their agreement encompass? Has one party dishonored the agreement?

Vaden's argument, though reasonable, is difficult to square with the statutory language. Section 4 directs courts to determine whether they would have jurisdiction "save for [the arbitration] agreement." How, then, can a dispute over the existence or applicability of an arbitration agreement be the controversy that counts?

The "save for" clause, courts espousing the view embraced by Vaden respond, means only that the "antiquated and arcane" ouster notion no longer holds sway. *Drexel Burnham Lambert, Inc. v. Valenzuela Bock,* 696 F.Supp. 957, 961 (S.D.N.Y.1988). Adherents to this "ouster" explanation of § 4's language recall that courts traditionally viewed arbitration clauses as unworthy attempts to "oust" them of jurisdiction; accordingly, to guard against encroachment on their domain, they refused to order specific enforcement of agreements to arbitrate. See H.R.Rep. No. 96, 68th Cong., 1st Sess., 1–2 (1924) (discussed in *Dean Witter Reynolds Inc. v. Byrd,* 470 U.S. 213, 219–220, and n. 6, 105 S.Ct. 1238, 84 L.Ed.2d 158 (1985)). The "save for" clause, as comprehended by proponents of the "ouster" explanation, was designed to ensure that courts would no longer consider themselves ousted of jurisdiction and would therefore specifically enforce arbitration agreements. See, *e.g., Westmoreland,* 100 F.3d, at 267–268, and n. 6 (adopting the "ouster" interpretation advanced in *Drexel Burnham Lambert,* 696 F.Supp., at 961–963); *Strong,* 485 F.3d, at 631 (Marcus, J., specially concurring) (reading § 4's "save for" clause "as instructing the court to 'set aside' not the arbitration agreement ..., but merely the previous judicial hostility to arbitration agreements").

We are not persuaded that the "ouster" explanation of § 4's "save for" clause carries the day. To the extent that the ancient "ouster" doctrine continued to impede specific enforcement of arbitration agreements, § 2 of the FAA, the Act's "centerpiece provision," *Mitsubishi Motors Corp. v. Soler Chrysler–Plymouth, Inc.,* 473 U.S. 614, 625, 105 S.Ct. 3346, 87 L.Ed.2d 444 (1985), directly attended to the problem. Covered agreements to arbitrate, § 2 declares, are "valid, irrevocable, and enforceable, save upon such grounds as exist at law or in equity for the revocation of any contract." Having commanded that an arbitration agreement is enforceable just as any other contract, Congress had no cause to repeat the point. See 1 I. MacNeil, R. Speidel, & T. Stipanowich, Federal Arbitration Law § 9.2.3.3, p. 9:18 (1995) (hereinafter MacNeil) ("Th[e] effort to connect the 'save for' language to the ancient problem of 'ouster of jurisdiction' is imaginative, but utterly unfounded and historically inaccurate." (footnote omitted)). . . .

B

Having determined that a district court should "look through" a § 4 petition, we now consider whether the court "would have [federal-question] jurisdiction" over "a suit arising out of the controversy" between Discover and Vaden. 9 U.S.C. § 4. As explained above, § 4 of the FAA does not enlarge federal-court jurisdiction; rather, it confines federal courts to the jurisdiction they would have "save for [the arbitration] agreement." Mindful of that limitation, we read § 4 to convey that a party seeking to compel arbitration may gain a federal court's assistance only if, "save for" the agreement, the entire, actual "controversy between the parties," as they have framed it, could be litigated in federal court. We conclude that the parties' actual controversy, here precipitated by Discover's state-court suit for the balance due on Vaden's account, is not amenable to federal-court adjudication. Consequently, the § 4 petition Discover filed in the United States District Court for the District of Maryland must be dismissed.

As the Fourth Circuit initially stated, the "controversy between the parties" arose from the "alleged debt" Vaden owed to Discover. 396 F.3d, at 370. Discover's complaint in Maryland state court plainly did not "arise under" federal law, nor did it qualify under any other head of federal-court jurisdiction.

In holding that Discover properly invoked federal-court jurisdiction, the Fourth Circuit looked beyond Discover's complaint and homed in on Vaden's state-law-based defense and counterclaims. Those responsive pleadings, Discover alleged, and the Fourth Circuit determined, were completely preempted by the FDIA. The Fourth Circuit, however, misapprehended our decision in *Holmes Group.* Under the well-pleaded complaint rule, a completely preempted counterclaim remains a counterclaim and thus does not provide a key capable of opening a federal court's door. See also *Taylor v. Anderson,* 234 U.S. 74, 75–76, 34 S.Ct. 724, 58 L.Ed. 1218 (1914) ("[W]hether a case is one arising under [federal law] . . . must be determined from what necessarily appears in the plaintiff's statement of his own claim . . ., unaided by anything alleged in anticipation o[r] avoidance of defenses which it is thought the defendant may interpose.").

Neither Discover nor The Chief Justice, concurring in part and dissenting in part (hereinafter dissent), defends the Fourth Circuit's reasoning. Instead, the dissent insists that a federal court "would have" jurisdiction over "the controversy Discover seeks to arbitrate"—namely, "whether 'Discover Bank charged illegal finance charges, interest and late fees.' " The dissent hypothesizes two federal suits that might arise from this purported controversy: "an action by Vaden asserting that the charges violate the FDIA, or one by Discover seeking a declaratory judgment that they do not."

There is a fundamental flaw in the dissent's analysis: In lieu of focusing on the whole controversy as framed by the parties, the dissent hypothesizes discrete controversies of its own design. As the parties' state-court filings reflect, the originating controversy here concerns Vaden's alleged debt to Discover. Vaden's responsive counterclaims challenging the legality of Discover's charges are a discrete aspect of the whole controversy Discover and Vaden brought to state court. Whether one might imagine a federal-question suit involving the parties' disagreement over Discover's charges is beside the point. The relevant question is whether the whole controversy between the parties—not just a piece broken off from that controversy—is one over which the federal courts would have jurisdiction.

The dissent would have us treat a § 4 petitioner's statement of the issues to be arbitrated as the relevant controversy even when that statement does not convey the full flavor of the parties' entire dispute. Artful dodges by a § 4 petitioner should not divert us from recognizing the actual dimensions of that controversy. The text of § 4 instructs federal courts to determine whether they would have jurisdiction over "a suit arising out of *the* controversy between the parties"; it does not give § 4 petitioners license to recharacterize an existing controversy, or manufacture a new controversy, in an effort to obtain a federal court's aid in compelling arbitration.

Moreover, our reading of § 4 fully accords with the statute's subjunctive construction ("would have jurisdiction") and its reference to "*a* suit." Section 4, we recognize, enables a party to seek an order compelling arbitration even when the parties' controversy is not the subject of pending litigation. Whether or not the controversy between the parties is embodied in an existing suit, the relevant question remains the same: Would a federal court have jurisdiction over an action arising out of that full-bodied controversy? . . .

True, the outcome in this case may well have been different had Vaden initiated an FDIA claim about the legality of Discover's charges. Because that controversy likely would have been amenable to adjudication in a federal forum, Discover could have asked a federal court to send the parties to arbitration. But that is not what occurred here. Vaden did not invoke the FDIA. Indeed, she framed her counterclaims under state law and clearly preferred the Maryland forum. The dissent's hypothesizing about the case that might have been brought does not provide a basis for federal-court jurisdiction. . . .

In sum, § 4 of the FAA instructs district courts asked to compel arbitration to inquire whether the court would have jurisdiction, "save for [the arbitration] agreement," over "a suit arising out of the controversy between the parties." We read that prescription in light of the well-pleaded complaint rule and the corollary rule that federal jurisdiction cannot be invoked on the basis of a defense or counterclaim. Parties may not circumvent those rules by asking a federal court to order arbitration of the portion of a controversy that implicates federal law when the court would not have federal-question jurisdiction over the controversy as a whole. It does not suffice to show that a federal question lurks somewhere inside the parties' controversy, or that a defense or counterclaim would arise under federal law. Because the controversy between Discover and Vaden, properly perceived, is not one qualifying for federal-court adjudication, § 4 of the FAA does not empower a federal court to order arbitration of that controversy, in whole or in part.

Discover, we note, is not left without recourse. Under the FAA, state courts as well as federal courts are obliged to honor and enforce agreements to arbitrate. *Southland,* 465 U.S., at 12, 104 S.Ct. 852; *Moses H. Cone,* 460 U.S., at 25, 26, n. 34, 103 S.Ct. 927. Discover may therefore petition a Maryland court for aid in enforcing the arbitration clause of its contracts with Maryland cardholders. . . .

For the reasons stated, the District Court lacked jurisdiction to entertain Discover's § 4 petition to compel arbitration. The judgment of the Court of Appeals affirming the District Court's order is therefore reversed, and the case is remanded for further proceedings consistent with this opinion.

It is so ordered.

■ CHIEF JUSTICE ROBERTS, with whom JUSTICE STEVENS, JUSTICE BREYER, and JUSTICE ALITO join, concurring in part and dissenting in part.

I agree with the Court that a federal court asked to compel arbitration pursuant to § 4 of the Federal Arbitration Act should "look through" the dispute over arbitrability in determining whether it has jurisdiction to grant the requested relief. But look through to what? The statute provides a clear and sensible answer: The court may consider the § 4 petition if the court "would have" jurisdiction over "the subject matter of a suit arising out of the controversy between the parties." 9 U.S.C. § 4.

The § 4 petition in this case explains that the controversy Discover seeks to arbitrate is whether "Discover Bank charged illegal finance charges, interest and late fees." App. 30. Discover contends in its petition that the resolution of this dispute is controlled by federal law—specifically § 27(a) of the Federal Deposit Insurance Act (FDIA), 12 U.S.C. § 1831d(a) (setting forth the interest rates a state-chartered, federally insured bank may charge "notwithstanding any State constitution or statute which is hereby preempted"). Vaden agrees that the legality of Discover's charges and fees is governed by the FDIA. A federal court therefore "would have jurisdiction ... of the subject matter of a suit arising out of the controversy" Discover seeks to arbitrate. That suit could be an action by Vaden asserting that the charges violate the FDIA, or one by Discover seeking a declaratory judgment that they do not.

The majority is diverted off this straightforward path by the fortuity that a complaint happens to have been filed in this case. Instead of looking to the controversy the § 4 petitioner seeks to arbitrate, the majority focuses on the controversy underlying that complaint, and asks whether "the *whole* controversy," as reflected in "the parties' state-court filings," arises under federal law. Because that litigation was commenced as a state-law debt-collection claim, the majority concludes there is no § 4 jurisdiction.

This approach is contrary to the language of § 4, and sharply restricts the ability of federal courts to enforce agreements to arbitrate. The "controversy" to which § 4 refers is the dispute alleged to be subject to arbitration. The § 4 petitioner must set forth the nature of that dispute-the one he seeks to arbitrate—in the § 4 petition seeking an order to compel arbitration. Section 4 requires that the petitioner be "aggrieved" by the other party's "failure, neglect, or refusal ... to arbitrate under a written agreement for arbitration"; that language guides the district court to the specific controversy the other party is unwilling to arbitrate.

That is clear from the FAA's repeated and consistent use of the term "controversy" to mean the specific dispute asserted to be subject to arbitration, not to some broader, "full flavor[ed]" or "full-bodied" notion of the disagreement between the parties. In § 2, for example, the "controversy" is the one "to [be] settle[d] by arbitration" and the one "to [be] submit[ted] to arbitration." 9 U.S.C. § 2. In § 10(a)(3), it is a ground for vacating an arbitration award that the arbitrator refused to hear evidence "pertinent and material to the controversy"-obviously the "controversy" subject to arbitration, or the arbitrator's refusal to consider the evidence would hardly be objectionable. In § 11(c), an award may be modified if "imperfect in matter of form not affecting the merits of the controversy"—again, necessarily the controversy submitted to arbitration, and therefore the subject of the award.

There is no reason to suppose "controversy" meant the controversy subject to arbitration everywhere else in the FAA, but something quite different in § 4. The issue is whether there is jurisdiction to compel arbitration to resolve a controversy; why would the pertinent controversy for assessing jurisdiction be anything other than the same one asserted to be subject to arbitration?

The majority looks instead to the controversy the state-court litigation seeks to resolve. This produces the odd result of defining "controversy" more broadly than the § 4 petition itself. Discover's petition does not seek to arbitrate its state-law debt-collection claims, but rather Vaden's allegation that the fees Discover has been charging her (and other members of her proposed class) violate the FDIA. See App. 30. The majority does not appear to question that there would be federal jurisdiction over a suit arising out of the subject matter of that dispute. The majority finds no jurisdiction here, however, because "a federal court could not entertain Discover's state-law debt-collection claim." There is no jurisdiction to compel arbitration of a plainly federal controversy-the FDIA dispute—because there is no jurisdiction to compel arbitration of the debt-collection dispute. But why Discover should have to demonstrate federal jurisdiction over a state-court claim it does not seek to arbitrate is a mystery. Cf. *Moses H. Cone Memorial Hospital v. Mercury Constr. Corp.,* 460 U.S. 1, 19–21, 103 S.Ct. 927, 74 L.Ed.2d 765 (1983) (affirming federal-court jurisdiction over a § 4 petition seeking to arbitrate only one of two disputes pending in state-court litigation); *Dean Witter Reynolds, Inc. v. Byrd,* 470 U.S. 213, 218–221, 105 S.Ct. 1238, 84 L.Ed.2d 158 (1985) (when litigation involves multiple claims, only some of which are covered by an arbitration agreement, district court must compel arbitration of the covered claims if so requested).

The majority's approach will allow federal jurisdiction to compel arbitration of *entirely* state-law claims. Under that approach the "controversy" is not the one the § 4 petitioner seeks to arbitrate, but a broader one encompassing the "whole controversy" between the parties. If that broader dispute involves both federal and state-law claims, and the "originating" dispute is federal, *ibid.,* a party could seek arbitration of just the state-law claims. The "controversy" under the majority's view would qualify as federal, giving rise to § 4 jurisdiction to compel arbitration of a purely state-law claim.

Take this case as an example. If Vaden had filed her FDIA claim first, and Discover had responded with a state-law debt-collection counterclaim, that suit is one that "could be litigated in federal court." As a result, the majority's approach would seem to permit Vaden to file a § 4 petition to compel arbitration of the entirely state-law-based debt-collection dispute, because that dispute would be part and parcel of the "full flavor[ed]," "originating" FDIA controversy. Defining the controversy as the dispute the § 4 petitioner seeks to arbitrate eliminates this problem by ensuring that the *actual dispute* subject to arbitration is federal.

The majority's conclusion that this controversy "is not one qualifying for federal-court adjudication" stems from its mistaken focus on the existing litigation. Rather than ask whether a court "would have" jurisdiction over the "subject matter" of "a" suit arising out of the "controversy," the majority asks only whether the court *does* have jurisdiction over the subject matter of a *particular* complaint. But § 4 does not speak of actual jurisdiction over pending suits; it speaks subjunctively of prospective jurisdiction over "the subject matter of a suit arising out of the controversy between the parties." 9 U.S.C. § 4. The fact that Vaden has chosen to package the FDIA controversy in counterclaims in pending state-court litigation in no way means that a district court "would [not] have" jurisdiction over the "subject matter" of "a suit" arising out of the FDIA controversy. A big part of arbitration is avoiding the procedural niceties of formal litigation; it would be odd to have the authority of a court to compel arbitration hinge on just such niceties in a pending case. . . .

Discover and Vaden have agreed to arbitrate any dispute arising out of Vaden's account with Discover. Vaden's allegations against Discover have given rise to such a dispute. Discover seeks to arbitrate that controversy, but Vaden refuses to do so. Resolution of the controversy is governed by federal law, specifically the FDIA. There is no dispute about that. In the absence of the arbitration agreement, a federal court "would have jurisdiction . . . of the subject matter of a suit arising out of the controversy between the parties," 9 U.S.C. § 4, whether the suit were brought by Vaden or Discover. The District Court therefore may exercise jurisdiction over this petition under § 4 of the Federal Arbitration Act.

* * *

Questions

1. In *Vaden*, the Court was unanimous on an issue that previously had divided the circuit courts. However, the Court split 5–4 on a subsidiary issue. Who gets the best of this argument?

2. After reading *Vaden*, can you articulate a clear rule governing when a nondiverse case to compel arbitration can be brought in federal court?

* * *

4. STATE VERSUS FEDERAL LAW

The Federal Arbitration Act declared arbitration agreements to be "valid, enforceable and irrevocable." It also called upon federal courts to enforce arbitration agreements by staying litigation in any suit referable to arbitration (Section 3), and by granting motions to compel recalcitrant parties to arbitrate disputes that they had agreed to submit to arbitration. (Section 4). The Act, while expressly applicable to federal courts, left open many questions about the role of state law. For example, in a diversity case, is the issue of arbitration substantive or procedural for purposes of deciding whether or not to apply state substantive law under *Erie Railroad Co. v. Tompkins*? Do the provisions of the Act apply only to federal law issues in federal courts, or do they also apply to state law issues brought in federal courts pursuant to the courts' ancillary jurisdiction? Does the Act preempt conflicting state law for cases involving commerce and maritime transactions? If so, does it apply in state courts? Assuming there is preemption, does Section 3, which provides that suits brought in a *federal court* upon any issue referable to arbitration shall be stayed pending such arbitration, apply in state courts? Does the exception in Section 2, which denies enforceability for arbitration agreements "upon such grounds as exist at law or in equity for the enforcement of any contract," call upon federal courts to apply state common law defenses to arbitration agreements?

The Supreme Court has addressed these and related issues over a forty-year period. The way these issues have been resolved has had significant ramifications for the role of arbitration in our civil litigation system. However, as the following cases demonstrate, the relationship between state and federal arbitration law is far from settled. There remain significant open questions and there are still vigorous dissenting views represented on the Court.

Bernhardt v. Polygraphic Company of America, Inc.

350 U.S. 198 (1956).

■ MR. JUSTICE DOUGLAS delivered the opinion of the Court.

This suit, removed from a Vermont court to the District Court on grounds of diversity of citizenship, was brought for damages for the discharge of petitioner under an employment contract. At the time the contract was made petitioner was a resident of New York. Respondent is a New York corporation. The contract was made in New York. Petitioner later became a resident of Vermont, where he was to perform his duties under the contract, and asserts his rights there.

The contract contains a provision that in case of any dispute the parties will submit the matter to arbitration under New York law by the American Arbitration Association, whose determination "shall be final and absolute." After the case had been removed to the District Court, respondent moved for a stay of the proceedings so that the controversy could go to arbitration in New York. The motion alleged that the law of New York governs the question whether the arbitration provision of the contract is binding.

The District Court ruled that under Erie R. Co. v. Tompkins, 304 U.S. 64, 58 S.Ct. 817, 82 L.Ed. 1188, the arbitration provision of the contract was governed by Vermont law and that the law of Vermont makes revocable an agreement to arbitrate at any time before an award is actually made. The District Court therefore denied the stay, 122 F.Supp. 733. The Court of Appeals reversed, 2 Cir., 218 F.2d 948. The case is here on a petition for certiorari which we granted, 349 U.S. 943, 75 S.Ct. 873, because of the doubtful application by the Court of Appeals of Erie R. Co. v. Tompkins, supra.

A question under the United States Arbitration Act ... lies at the threshold of the case. Section 2 of that Act makes "valid, irrevocable, and enforceable" provisions for arbitration in certain classes of contracts; and § 3 provides for a stay of actions in the federal courts of issues referable to arbitration under those contracts. Section 2 makes "valid, irrevocable, and enforceable" only two types of contracts: those relating to a maritime transaction and those involving commerce. No maritime transaction is involved here. Nor does this contract evidence "a transaction involving commerce" within the meaning of § 2 of the Act. There is no showing that petitioner while performing his duties under the employment contract was working "in" commerce, was producing goods for commerce, or was engaging in activity that affected commerce, within the meaning of our decisions.[3]

The Court of Appeals went on to hold that in any event § 3 of the Act stands on its own footing. It concluded that while § 2 makes enforceable arbitration agreements in maritime transactions and in transactions involving commerce, § 3 covers all arbitration agreements even though they do not involve maritime transactions or transactions in commerce. We disagree with that reading of the Act. Sections 1, 2, and 3 are integral parts of a whole. To be sure, § 3 does not repeat the words "maritime transaction" or "transaction involving commerce", used in §§ 1 and 2. But §§ 1 and 2 define the field in which Congress was legislating. Since § 3 is a part of the regulatory scheme, we can only assume that the "agreement in writing" for arbitration referred to in § 3 is the kind of agreement which §§ 1 and 2 have brought under federal regulation. There is no intimation or suggestion in the Committee Reports that §§ 1 and 2 cover a narrower field than § 3. On the contrary, S.Rep. No. 536, 68th Cong., 1st Sess., p. 2, states that § 1 defines the contracts to which "the bill will be applicable." And H.R. Rep. No. 96, 68th Cong., 1st Sess., p. 1, states that one foundation of the new regulating measure is "the Federal control over interstate commerce and over admiralty." If respondent's contention is correct, a constitutional question might be presented. Erie R. Co. v. Tompkins indicated that

3. Section 1 defines "commerce" as: "... commerce among the several States or with foreign nations, or in any Territory of the United States or in the District of Columbia, or between any such Territory and another, or between any such Territory and any State or foreign nation, or between the District of Columbia and any State or Territory or foreign nation, but nothing herein contained shall apply to contracts of employment of seamen, railroad employees, or any other class of workers engaged in foreign or interstate commerce." Since no transaction involving commerce appears to be involved here, we do not reach the further question whether in any event petitioner would be included in "any other class of workers" within the exceptions of § 1 of the Act.

Congress does not have the constitutional authority to make the law that is applicable to controversies in diversity of citizenship cases. Shanferoke Coal & Supply Corp. of Delaware v. Westchester Service Corp., 293 U.S. 449, 55 S.Ct. 313, 79 L.Ed. 583, applied the Federal Act in a diversity case. But that decision antedated Erie R. Co. v. Tompkins; and the Court did not consider the larger question presented here—that is, whether arbitration touched on substantive rights, which Erie R. Co. v. Tompkins held were governed by local law, or was a mere form of procedure within the power of the federal courts or Congress to prescribe. Our view, as will be developed, is that § 3, so read, would invade the local law field. We therefore read § 3 narrowly to avoid that issue. Federal Trade Commission v. American Tobacco Co., 264 U.S. 298, 307, 44 S.Ct. 336, 337, 68 L.Ed. 696. We conclude that the stay provided in § 3 reaches only those contracts covered by §§ 1 and 2.

The question remains whether, apart from the Federal Act, a provision of a contract providing for arbitration is enforceable in a diversity case.

The Court of Appeals, in disagreeing with the District Court as to the effect of an arbitration agreement under Erie R. Co. v. Tompkins, followed its earlier decision of Murray Oil Products Co. v. Mitsui & Co., 2 Cir., 146 F.2d 381, 383, which held that, "Arbitration is merely a form of trial, to be adopted in the action itself, in place of the trial at common law: it is like a reference to a master, or an 'advisory trial' under Federal Rules of Civil Procedure. . . ."

We disagree with that conclusion. We deal were with a right to recover that owes its existence to one of the States, not to the United States. The federal court enforces the state-created right by rules of procedure which it has acquired from the Federal Government and which therefore are not identical with those of the state courts. Yet, in spite of that difference in procedure, the federal court enforcing a state-created right in a diversity case is, as we said in Guaranty Trust Co. of New York v. York, 326 U.S. 99, 108, 65 S.Ct. 1464, 1469, 89 L.Ed. 2079, in substance "only another court of the State." The federal court therefore may not "substantially affect the enforcement of the right as given by the State." Id., 326 U.S. 109, 65 S.Ct. 1470. If the federal court allows arbitration where the state court would disallow it, the outcome of litigation might depend on the court-house where suit is brought. For the remedy by arbitration, whatever its merits or shortcomings, substantially affects the cause of action created by the State. The nature of the tribunal where suits are tried is an important part of the parcel of rights behind a cause of action. The change from a court of law to an arbitration panel may make a radical difference in ultimate result. Arbitration carries no right to trial by jury that is guaranteed both by the Seventh Amendment and by Ch. 1, Art. 12th, of the Vermont Constitution. Arbitrators do not have the benefit of judicial instruction on the law; they need not give their reasons for their results; the record of their proceedings is not as complete as it is in a court trial; and judicial review of an award is more limited than judicial review of a trial—all as discussed in Wilko v. Swan, 346 U.S. 427, 435–438, 74 S.Ct. 182, 186, 188,

98 L.Ed. 168.[4] We said in the York case that "The nub of the policy that underlies Erie R. Co. v. Tompkins is that for the same transaction the accident of a suit by a non-resident litigant in a federal court instead of in a State court a block away, should not lead to a substantially different result." 326 U.S. at 109, 65 S.Ct. 1470. There would in our judgment be a resultant discrimination if the parties suing on a Vermont cause of action in the federal court were remitted to arbitration, while those suing in the Vermont court could not be.

The District Court found that if the parties were in a Vermont court, the agreement to submit to arbitration would not be binding and could be revoked at any time before an award was made. He gave as his authority Mead's Adm'x v. Owen, 83 Vt. 132, 135, 74 A. 1058, and Sartwell v. Sowles, 72 Vt. 270, 277, 48 A. 11, decided by the Supreme Court of Vermont. In the Owen case the court, in speaking of an agreement to arbitrate, held that "... either party may revoke the submission at any time before the publication of an award." 83 Vt. at page 135, 74 A. at page 1059. That case was decided in 1910. But it was agreed on oral argument that there is no later authority from the Vermont courts, that no fracture in the rules announced in those cases has appeared in subsequent rulings or dicta, and that no legislative movement is under way in Vermont to change the result of those cases. Since the federal judge making those findings is from the Vermont bar, we give special weight to his statement of what the Vermont law is.... We agree with him that if arbitration could not be compelled in the Vermont courts, it should not be compelled in the Federal District Court. Were the question in doubt or deserving further canvass, we would of course remand the case to the Court of Appeals to pass on this question of Vermont law. But, as we have indicated, there appears to be no confusion in the Vermont decisions, no developing line of authorities that casts a shadow over the established ones, no dicta, doubts or ambiguities in the opinions of Vermont judges on the question, no legislative development that promises to undermine the judicial rule. We see no reason, therefore, to remand the case to the Court of Appeals to pass on this question of local law.

Respondent argues that since the contract was made in New York and the parties contracted for arbitration under New York law, New York arbitration law should be applied to the enforcement of the contract. A question of conflict of laws is tendered, a question that is also governed by Vermont law. See Klaxon Co. v. Stentor Electric Mfg. Co., 313 U.S. 487, 61

4. Whether the arbitrators misconstrued a contract is not open to judicial review. The Hartbridge, 2 Cir., 62 F.2d 72. Questions of fault or neglect are solely for the arbitrators' consideration. James Richardson & Sons v. W. E. Hedger Transportation Corp., 2 Cir., 98 F.2d 55. Arbitrators are not bound by the rules of evidence.... They may draw on their personal knowledge in making an award. American Almond Products Co. v. Consolidated Pecan Sales Co., 2 Cir., 144 F.2d 448.... Absent agreement of the parties, a written transcript of the proceedings is unnecessary. A. O. Andersen Trading Co. v. Brimberg. Swearing of witnesses may not be required. Application of Shapiro, supra. And the arbitrators need not disclose the facts or reasons behind their award. Shirley Silk Co. v. American Silk Mills, Inc., 257 App.Div. 375, 377, 13 N.Y.S.2d 309, 311.

S.Ct. 1020, 85 L.Ed. 1477. It is not clear to some of us that the District Court ruled on that question. We mention it explicitly so that it will be open for consideration on remand of the cause to the District Court.

The judgment of the Court of Appeals is reversed and the cause is remanded to the District Court for proceedings in conformity with this opinion.

Reversed and remanded.

■ MR. JUSTICE FRANKFURTER, concurring.

It is my view that the judgment of the Court of Appeals should be reversed and the case remanded to that court and not to the District Court.

This action was brought in the Bennington County Court of the State of Vermont by petitioner, a citizen of Vermont, against respondent, a corporation of the State of New York. Respondent removed the case to the United States District Court for the District of Vermont. The subject matter of the litigation is a contract made between the parties in New York, and the sole basis of the jurisdiction of the District Court is diversity of citizenship. Not only was the contract made in New York, but the parties agreed to the following provision in it: "Fourteenth: The parties hereto do hereby stipulate and agree that it is their intention and covenant that this agreement and performance hereunder and all suits and special proceedings hereunder be construed in accordance with and under and pursuant to the laws of the State of New York and that in any action special proceeding or other proceeding that may be brought arising out of, in connection with or by reason of this agreement, the laws of the State of New York shall be applicable and shall govern to the exclusion of the law of any other forum, without regard to the jurisdiction in which any action or special proceeding may be instituted." Respondent invoked another provision of the contract whereby disputes under the agreement were to be submitted to arbitration subject to the regulations of the American Arbitration Association and the pertinent provisions of the New York Arbitration Act, Civil Practice Act, § 1468 et seq. It did so by a motion to stay the proceeding in the District Court pending arbitration.

The District Court denied the stay because, on its reading of the Vermont cases, Vermont law, while recognizing the binding force of such an agreement by way of a suit for damages, does not allow specific performance or a stay pending arbitration. It rested on a decision rendered by the Supreme Court of Vermont in a bill for an accounting evidently between two Vermonters and relating wholly to a Vermont transaction, i.e., a controversy about personal property on a Vermont farm. Mead's Adm'x v. Owen, 83 Vt. 132, 74 A. 1058. This case was decided in 1910 and, in turn, relied on Aspinwall v. Tousey, 2 Tyler, Vt., 328, decided in 1803, authorizing revocation of a submission to arbitration at any time before the publication of an award.

The Court of Appeals found it unnecessary to consider what the Vermont law was today, for it held that the arbitration provision did not concern a matter of "substantive" law, for which, in this diversity case,

Vermont law would be controlling on the United States District Court sitting in Vermont. It held that the arbitration provision fell within the law of "procedure" governing an action in the federal court, whatever the source of the jurisdiction. So holding, the Court of Appeals found § 3 of the United States Arbitration Act, 9 U.S.C. § 3, 9 U.S.C.A. § 3, applicable and, accordingly, directed the District Court to heed that Act and allow the matter to go to arbitration. 2 Cir., 218 F.2d 948.

This Court explained in Guaranty Trust Co. of New York v. York, 326 U.S. 99, 65 S.Ct. 1464, 89 L.Ed. 2079, why the categories of "substance" and "procedure" are, in relation to the application of the doctrine of Erie R. Co. v. Tompkins, 304 U.S. 64, 58 S.Ct. 817, 82 L.Ed. 1188, less than self-defining. They are delusive. The intrinsic content of what is thought to be conveyed by those terms in the particular context of a particular litigation becomes the essential inquiry. This mode of approaching the problem has had several applications since the York decision. I agree with the Court's opinion that the differences between arbitral and judicial determination of a controversy under a contract sufficiently go to the merits of the outcome, and not merely because of the contingencies of different individuals passing on the same question, to make the matter one of "substance" in the sense relevant for Erie R. Co. v. Tompkins. In view of the ground that was taken in that case for its decision, it would raise a serious question of constitutional law whether Congress could subject to arbitration litigation in the federal courts which is there solely because it is "between Citizens of different States", U.S.Const. Art. III, § 2, in disregard of the law of the State in which a federal court is sitting. Since the United States Arbitration Act of 1925 does not obviously apply to diversity cases, in the light of its terms and the relevant interpretive materials, avoidance of the constitutional question is for me sufficiently compelling to lead to a construction of the Act as not applicable to diversity cases....

Vermont law regarding such an arbitration agreement as the one before us, therefore, becomes decisive of the litigation. But what is Vermont law? One of the difficulties, of course, resulting from Erie R. Co. v. Tompkins, is that it is not always easy and sometimes difficult to ascertain what the governing state law is. The essence of the doctrine of that case is that the difficulties of ascertaining state law are fraught with less mischief than disregard of the basic nature of diversity jurisdiction, namely, the enforcement of state-created rights and state policies going to the heart of those rights. If Judge Gibson's statement of what is the contemporary Vermont law relevant to the arbitration provision now before him were determinative, that would be that. But the defendant is entitled to have the view of the Court of Appeals on Vermont law and cannot, under the Act of Congress, be foreclosed by the District Court's interpretation.

As long as there is diversity jurisdiction, "estimates" are necessarily often all that federal courts can make in ascertaining what the state court would rule to be its law.... This Court ought not to by-pass the Court of Appeals on an issue which, if the Court of Appeals had made a different estimate from the District Court's, of contemporaneous Vermont law regarding such a contract as the one before us, this Court, one can confidently say, would not have set its view of Vermont law against that of the Court of Appeals. For the mere fact that Vermont in 1910 restated its old law against denying equitable relief for breach of a promise to arbitrate a contract made under such Vermont law, is hardly a conclusive ground for attributing to the Vermont Supreme Court application of this equitable doctrine in 1956 to a contract made in New York with explicit agreement by the parties that the law of New York which allows such a stay as was here sought, New York Civil Practice Act, § 1451, should govern.... Law does change with times and circumstances, and not merely through legislative reforms. It is also to be noted that law is not restricted to what is found in Law Reports, or otherwise written. See Nashville, C. & St. L.R. Co. v. Browning, 310 U.S. 362, 369, 60 S.Ct. 968, 84 L.Ed. 1254. The Supreme Court of Vermont last spoke on this matter in 1910. The doctrine that it referred to was not a peculiar indigenous Vermont rule. The attitude reflected by that decision nearly half a century ago was the current traditional judicial hostility against ousting courts, as the phrase ran, of their jurisdiction.... To be sure, a vigorous legislative movement got under way in the 1920's expressive of a broadened outlook of view on this subject. But courts do not always wait for legislation to find a judicial doctrine outmoded....

Surely in the light of all that has happened since 1910 in the general field of the law of arbitration, it is not for us to assume that the Court of Appeals, if it had that question for consideration, could not have found that the law of Vermont today does not require disregard of a provision of a contract made in New York, with a purposeful desire to have the law of New York govern, to accomplish a result that today may be deemed to be a general doctrine of the law. Of course, if the Court of Appeals, versed in the general jurisprudence of Vermont and having among its members a Vermont lawyer, should find that the Vermont court would, despite the New York incidents of the contract, apply Vermont law and that it is the habit of the Vermont court to adhere to its precedents and to leave changes to the legislature, it would not be for the federal court to gainsay that policy. I am not suggesting what the Court of Appeals' answer to these questions would be, still less what it should be. I do maintain that the defendant does have the right to have the judgment of the Court of Appeals on that question and that it is not for us to deny him that right.

I would remand the case to the Court of Appeals for its determination of Vermont law on matters which the basis of its decision heretofore rendered it needless to consider.

■ [MR. JUSTICE HARLAN's separate concurrence and MR. JUSTICE BURTON's dissenting opinion have been omitted.]

* * *

Questions

1. According to Justice Douglas, what is the constitutional basis of the FAA? Can his view be squared with that of Julius Cohen, who drafted the statute, as described in the Cohen and Dayton article above? What is the constitutional problem with the Respondent's position, to which Justice Douglas alludes?

2. If Justice Douglas had decided that the FAA is procedural rather than substantive, what would have been the outcome of this case?

3. Once the Court decided that the FAA is substantive for purposes of *Erie*, do the provisions of the Act apply in diversity cases?

* * *

Southland Corporation v. Keating

465 U.S. 1 (1984).

■ CHIEF JUSTICE BURGER delivered the opinion of the Court.

We noted probable jurisdiction to consider (a) whether the California Franchise Investment Law, which invalidates certain arbitration agreements covered by the Federal Arbitration Act, violates the Supremacy Clause and (b) whether arbitration under the Federal Act is impaired when a class action structure is imposed on the process by the state courts.

I

Appellant The Southland Corporation is the owner and franchisor of 7–Eleven convenience stores. Southland's standard franchise agreement provides each franchisee with a license to use certain registered trademarks, a lease or sublease of a convenience store owned or leased by Southland, inventory financing, and assistance in advertising and merchandising. The franchisees operate the stores, supply bookkeeping data, and pay Southland a fixed percentage of gross profits. The franchise agreement also contains the following provision requiring arbitration:

> Any controversy or claim arising out of or relating to this Agreement or the breach thereof shall be settled by arbitration in accordance with the Rules of the American Arbitration Association . . . and judgment upon any award rendered by the arbitrator may be entered in any court having jurisdiction thereof.

Appellees are 7–Eleven franchisees. Between September 1975 and January 1977, several appellees filed individual actions against Southland in California Superior Court alleging, among other things, fraud, oral misrepresentation, breach of contract, breach of fiduciary duty, and violation of the disclosure requirements of the California Franchise Investment Law, Cal.Corp.Code § 31000 et seq. (West 1977). Southland's answer, in all but one of the individual actions, included the affirmative defense of failure to arbitrate.

In May 1977, appellee Keating filed a class action against Southland on behalf of a class that assertedly includes approximately 800 California franchisees. Keating's principal claims were substantially the same as those asserted by the other franchisees. After the various actions were consolidated, Southland petitioned to compel arbitration of the claims in all cases, and appellees moved for class certification.

The Superior Court granted Southland's motion to compel arbitration of all claims except those claims based on the Franchise Investment Law. The court did not pass on appellees' request for class certification. Southland appealed from the order insofar as it excluded from arbitration the claims based on the California statute. Appellees filed a petition for a writ of mandamus or prohibition in the California Court of Appeal arguing that the arbitration should proceed as a class action.

The California Court of Appeal reversed the trial court's refusal to compel arbitration of appellees' claims under the Franchise Investment Law. 109 Cal.App.3d 784, 167 Cal.Rptr. 481 (1980). That court interpreted the arbitration clause to require arbitration of all claims asserted under the Franchise Investment Law, and construed the Franchise Investment Law not to invalidate such agreements to arbitrate. Alternatively, the court concluded that if the Franchise Investment Law rendered arbitration agreements involving commerce unenforceable, it would conflict with § 2 of the Federal Arbitration Act, 9 U.S.C. § 2 (1976), and therefore be invalid under the Supremacy Clause. 167 Cal.Rptr. at 493–494. The Court of Appeal also determined that there was no "insurmountable obstacle" to conducting an arbitration on a class-wide basis, and issued a writ of mandate directing the trial court to conduct class certification proceedings. Id., at 492.

The California Supreme Court, by a vote of 4–2, reversed the ruling that claims asserted under the Franchise Investment Law are arbitrable. 31 Cal.3d 584, 183 Cal.Rptr. 360, 645 P.2d 1192 (1982). The California Supreme Court interpreted the Franchise Investment Law to require judicial consideration of claims brought under that statute and concluded that the California statute did not contravene the federal Act. Id., at 604, 183 Cal.Rptr., at 371–372, 645 P.2d, at 1203–1204. The court also remanded the case to the trial court for consideration of appellees' request for class-wide arbitration.

We postponed consideration of the question of jurisdiction pending argument on the merits. 103 S.Ct. 721, 74 L.Ed.2d 948 (1983). We reverse in part and dismiss in part....

III

The California Franchise Investment Law provides:

> Any condition, stipulation or provision purporting to bind any person acquiring any franchise to waive compliance with any provision of this law or any rule or order hereunder is void. Cal.Corp.Code § 31512 (West 1977).

The California Supreme Court interpreted this statute to require judicial consideration of claims brought under the State statute and accordingly refused to enforce the parties' contract to arbitrate such claims. So interpreted the California Franchise Investment Law directly conflicts with § 2 of the Federal Arbitration Act and violates the Supremacy Clause.

In enacting § 2 of the federal Act, Congress declared a national policy favoring arbitration and withdrew the power of the states to require a judicial forum for the resolution of claims which the contracting parties agreed to resolve by arbitration. The Federal Arbitration Act provides:

> A written provision in any maritime transaction or a contract evidencing a transaction involving commerce to settle by arbitration a controversy thereafter arising out of such contract or transaction, or the refusal to perform the whole or any part thereof, or an agreement in writing to submit to arbitration an existing controversy arising out of such a contract, transaction, or refusal, shall be valid, irrevocable, and enforceable, save upon such grounds as exist at law or in equity for the revocation of any contract.

9 U.S.C. § 2 (1976). Congress has thus mandated the enforcement of arbitration agreements.

We discern only two limitations on the enforceability of arbitration provisions governed by the Federal Arbitration Act: they must be part of a written maritime contract or a contract "evidencing a transaction involving commerce" and such clauses may be revoked upon "grounds as exist at law or in equity for the revocation of any contract." We see nothing in the Act indicating that the broad principle of enforceability is subject to any additional limitations under State law.

The Federal Arbitration Act rests on the authority of Congress to enact substantive rules under the Commerce Clause. In Prima Paint Corp. v. Flood & Conklin Manufacturing Corp., 388 U.S. 395, 87 S.Ct. 1801, 18 L.Ed.2d 1270 (1967), the Court examined the legislative history of the Act and concluded that the statute "is based upon . . . the incontestable federal foundations of 'control over interstate commerce and over admiralty.' " Id., at 405, 87 S.Ct., at 1806 (quoting H.R.Rep. No. 96, 68th Cong., 1st Sess. 1 (1924)). The contract in Prima Paint, as here, contained an arbitration clause. One party in that case alleged that the other had committed fraud in the inducement of the contract, although not of arbitration clause in particular, and sought to have the claim of fraud adjudicated in federal court. The Court held that, notwithstanding a contrary state rule, consideration of a claim of fraud in the inducement of a contract "is for the arbitrators and not for the courts," id., at 400, 87 S.Ct., at 1804. The Court relied for this holding on Congress' broad power to fashion substantive rules under the Commerce Clause.

At least since 1824 Congress' authority under the Commerce Clause has been held plenary. Gibbons v. Ogden, 22 U.S. 1, 196, 9 Wheat. 1, 196, 6 L.Ed. 23 (1824). In the words of Chief Justice Marshall, the authority of Congress is "the power to regulate; that is, to prescribe the rule by which commerce is to be governed." Ibid. The statements of the Court in Prima Paint that the Arbitration Act was an exercise of the Commerce Clause power clearly implied that the substantive rules of the Act were to apply in state as well as federal courts. As Justice Black observed in his dissent, when Congress exercises its authority to enact substantive federal law under the Commerce Clause, it normally creates rules that are enforceable in state as well as federal courts. Prima Paint, 388 U.S., at 420, 87 S.Ct., at 1814 (Black, J., dissenting). . . .

Congressional Intent →

Although the legislative history is not without ambiguities, there are strong indications that Congress had in mind something more than making arbitration agreements enforceable only in the federal courts. The House Report plainly suggests the more comprehensive objectives:

> The purpose of this bill is to make valid and enforceable agreements for arbitration contained in *contracts involving interstate commerce* or within the jurisdiction or admiralty, or which may be the subject of litigation in the Federal courts. H.R.Rep. No. 96, 68th Cong., 1st Sess. 1 (1924) (emphasis added.)

This broader purpose can also be inferred from the reality that Congress would be less likely to address a problem whose impact was confined to federal courts than a problem of large significance in the field of commerce. The Arbitration Act sought to "overcome the rule of equity, that equity will not specifically enforce any arbitration agreement." Hearing on S. 4214 Before a Subcomm. of the Senate Comm. on the Judiciary, 67th Cong., 4th Sess. 6 (1923) ("Senate Hearing") (remarks of Sen. Walsh). The House Report accompanying the bill stated:

> [t]he need for the law arises from . . . the jealousy of the English courts for their own jurisdiction. . . . This jealousy survived for so lon[g] a period that the principle became firmly embedded in the English common law and was adopted with it by the American courts. The courts have felt that the precedent was too strongly fixed to be overturned without legislative enactment. . . . H.R.Rep. No. 96, supra, 1–2 (1924).

Surely this makes clear that the House Report contemplated a broad reach of the Act, unencumbered by state law constraints. As was stated in Metro Industrial Painting Corp. v. Terminal Construction Corp., 287 F.2d 382, 387 (C.A.2 1961) (Lumbard, Chief Judge, concurring), "the purpose of the act was to assure those who desired arbitration and whose contracts related to interstate commerce that their expectations would not be undermined by federal judges, or . . . by state courts or legislatures." Congress also showed its awareness of the widespread unwillingness of state courts to enforce arbitration agreements, e.g., Senate Hearing, supra, at 8, and that such courts were bound by state laws inadequately providing for

> technical arbitration by which, if you agree to arbitrate under the method provided by the statute, you have an arbitration by statute[;] but [the statutes] ha[d] nothing to do with validating the contract to arbitrate. Ibid.

The problems Congress faced were therefore twofold: the old common law hostility toward arbitration, and the failure of state arbitration statutes to mandate enforcement of arbitration agreements. To confine the scope of the Act to arbitrations sought to be enforced in federal courts would frustrate what we believe Congress intended to be a broad enactment appropriate in scope to meet the large problems Congress was addressing.

Justice O'Connor argues that Congress viewed the Arbitration Act "as a procedural statute, applicable only in federal courts." Post, at 865. If it is correct that Congress sought only to create a procedural remedy in the federal courts, there can be no explanation for the express limitation in the Arbitration Act to contracts "involving commerce." 9 U.S.C. § 2. For example, when Congress has authorized this Court to prescribe the rules of procedure in the federal Courts of Appeals, District Courts, and bankruptcy courts, it has not limited the power of the Court to prescribe rules applicable only to causes of action involving commerce. See, e.g., 28 U.S.C. §§ 2072, 2075, 2076 (1976). We would expect that if Congress, in enacting the Arbitration Act, was creating what it thought to be a procedural rule applicable only in federal courts, it would not so limit the Act to transactions involving commerce. On the other hand, Congress would need to call on the Commerce Clause if it intended the Act to apply in state courts. Yet at the same time, its reach would be limited to transactions involving interstate commerce. We therefore view the "involving commerce" requirement in § 2, not as an inexplicable limitation on the power of the federal courts, but as a necessary qualification on a statute intended to apply in state and federal courts.

Under the interpretation of the Arbitration Act urged by Justice O'Connor, claims brought under the California Franchise Investment Law are not arbitrable when they are raised in state court. Yet it is clear beyond question that if this suit had been brought as a diversity action in a federal district court, the arbitration clause would have been enforceable.[7] Prima Paint, supra. The interpretation given to the Arbitration Act by the California Supreme Court would therefore encourage and reward forum shopping. We are unwilling to attribute to Congress the intent, in drawing on the comprehensive powers of the Commerce Clause, to create a right to enforce an arbitration contract and yet make the right dependent for its enforcement on the particular forum in which it is asserted. And since the overwhelming proportion of all civil litigation in this country is in the state courts, we cannot believe Congress intended to limit the Arbitration Act to disputes subject only to federal court jurisdiction.[9] Such an interpretation

7. Appellees contend that the arbitration clause, which provides for the arbitration of "any controversy or claim arising out of or relating to this Agreement or the breach hereof," does not cover their claims under the California Franchise Investment Law. We find the language quoted above broad enough to cover such claims. Cf. Prima Paint, supra, 388 U.S., at 403–404, 406, 87 S.Ct., at 1805–1806, 1807 (finding nearly identical language to cover a claim that a contract was induced by fraud).

9. While the Federal Arbitration Act creates federal substantive law requiring the parties to honor arbitration agreements, it does not create any independent federal-question jurisdiction under 28 U.S.C. § 1331 (1976) or otherwise. Moses H. Cone, 103 S.Ct., at 942 n. 32. This seems implicit in the provisions in § 3 for a stay by a "court in which such suit is pending" and in § 4 that enforcement may be ordered by "any United States district court which, save for such agreement, would have jurisdiction under Ti-

would frustrate Congressional intent to place "[a]n arbitration agreement ... upon the same footing as other contracts, where it belongs." H.R.Rep. No. 96, supra, 1.

In creating a substantive rule applicable in state as well as federal courts,[10] Congress intended to foreclose state legislative attempts to undercut the enforceability of arbitration agreements. We hold that § 31512 of the California Franchise Investment Law violates the Supremacy Clause....

It is so ordered.

■ JUSTICE STEVENS, concurring in part and dissenting in part.

The Court holds that an arbitration clause that is enforceable in an action in a federal court is equally enforceable if the action is brought in a state court. I agree with that conclusion. Although Justice O'Connor's review of the legislative history of the Federal Arbitration Act demonstrates that the 1925 Congress that enacted the statute viewed the statute as essentially procedural in nature, I am persuaded that the intervening developments in the law compel the conclusion that the Court has reached. I am nevertheless troubled by one aspect of the case that seems to trouble none of my colleagues.

For me it is not "clear beyond question that if this suit had been brought as a diversity action in a Federal District Court, the arbitration clause would have been enforceable." Ante, at 860. The general rule prescribed by § 2 of the Federal Arbitration Act is that arbitration clauses in contracts involving interstate transactions are enforceable as a matter of federal law. That general rule, however, is subject to an exception based on "such grounds as exist at law or in equity for the revocation of any contract." I believe that exception leaves room for the implementation of certain substantive state policies that would be undermined by enforcing certain categories of arbitration clauses.

The exercise of State authority in a field traditionally occupied by State law will not be deemed preempted by a federal statute unless that was the clear and manifest purpose of Congress. Ray v. Atlantic Richfield Co., 435 U.S. 151, 157, 98 S.Ct. 988, 994, 55 L.Ed.2d 179 (1978); see generally, Hamilton, The Federalist, No. 32, 300 (Van Doren Ed.1945). Moreover, even where a federal statute does displace State authority, it "rarely occupies a legal field completely, totally excluding all participation by the

tle 28, in a civil action or in admiralty of the subject matter of a suit arising out of the controversy between the parties." Ibid.; Prima Paint, supra, 388 U.S., at 420 and n. 24, 87 S.Ct., at 1814 (Black, J., dissenting); Krauss Bros. Lumber Co. v. Louis Bossert & Sons, Inc., 62 F.2d 1004, 1006 (C.A.2 1933) (L. Hand, J.)

10. The contention is made that the Court's interpretation of § 2 of the Act renders §§ 3 and 4 "largely superfluous." Post, at 869, n. 20. This misreads our holding and the Act. In holding that the Arbitration Act preempts a state law that withdraws the power to enforce arbitration agreements, we do not hold that §§ 3 and 4 of the Arbitration Act apply to proceedings in state courts. Section 4, for example, provides that the Federal Rules of Civil Procedure apply in proceedings to compel arbitration. The Federal Rules do not apply in such state court proceedings.

legal systems of the states.... Federal legislation, on the whole, has been conceived and drafted on an ad hoc basis to accomplish limited objectives. It builds upon legal relationships established by the states, altering or supplanting them only so far as necessary for the special purpose." P. Bator, P. Mishkin, D. Shapiro, & H. Wechsler, Hart and Wechsler's The Federal Courts and the Federal System 470–471 (2d ed. 1973).

The limited objective of the Federal Arbitration Act was to abrogate the general common law rule against specific enforcement of arbitration agreements, S.Rep. No. 536, 68th Cong., 1st Sess., 2–3 (1924), and a state statute which merely codified the general common law rule—either directly by employing the prior doctrine of revocability or indirectly by declaring all such agreements void—would be preempted by the Act. However, beyond this conclusion, which seems compelled by the language of § 2 and case law concerning the Act, it is by no means clear that Congress intended entirely to displace State authority in this field. Indeed, while it is an understatement to say that "the legislative history of the ... Act ... reveals little awareness on the part of Congress that state law might be affected," it must surely be true that given the lack of a "clear mandate from Congress as to the extent to which state statutes and decisions are to be superseded, we must be cautious in construing the act lest we excessively encroach on the powers which Congressional policy, if not the Constitution, would reserve to the states." Metro Industrial Painting Corp. v. Terminal Construction Co., 287 F.2d 382, 386 (C.A.2 1961) (Lumbard, C.J., concurring).

The textual basis in the Act for avoiding such encroachment is the provision of § 2 which provides that arbitration agreements are subject to revocation on such grounds as exist at law or in equity for the revocation of any contract. The Act, however, does not define what grounds for revocation may be permissible, and hence it would appear that the judiciary must fashion the limitations as a matter of federal common law. Cf. Textile Workers v. Lincoln Mills, 353 U.S. 448, 77 S.Ct. 912, 1 L.Ed.2d 972 (1957). In doing so, we must first recognize that as the " 'saving clause' in § 2 indicates, the purpose of Congress in 1925 was to make arbitration agreements as enforceable as other contracts, but not more so." Prima Paint Corp. v. Flood & Conklin Mfg. Co., 388 U.S. 395, 404 n. 12, 87 S.Ct. 1801, 1806 n. 12, 18 L.Ed.2d 1270 (1967); see also, H.R.Rep. No. 96, 68th Cong., 1st Sess. 1 (1924). The existence of a federal statute enunciating a substantive federal policy does not necessarily require the inexorable application of a uniform federal rule of decision notwithstanding the differing conditions which may exist in the several States and regardless of the decisions of the States to exert police powers as they deem best for the welfare of their citizens.... Indeed, the lower courts generally look to State law regarding questions of formation of the arbitration agreement under § 2, see, e.g., Comprehensive Merchandising Cat., Inc. v. Madison Sales Corp., 521 F.2d 1210 (C.A.7 1975), which is entirely appropriate so long as the state rule does not conflict with the policy of § 2.

A contract which is deemed void is surely revocable at law or in equity, and the California legislature has declared all conditions purporting to waive compliance with the protections of the Franchise Disclosure Act, including but not limited to arbitration provisions, void as a matter of public policy. Given the importance to the State of franchise relationships, the relative disparity in the bargaining positions between the franchisor and the franchisee, and the remedial purposes of the California Act, I believe this declaration of State policy is entitled to respect. . . .

We should not refuse to exercise independent judgment concerning the conditions under which an arbitration agreement, generally enforceable under the Act, can be held invalid as contrary to public policy simply because the source of the substantive law to which the arbitration agreement attaches is a State rather than the Federal Government. I find no evidence that Congress intended such a double standard to apply, and I would not lightly impute such an intent to the 1925 Congress which enacted the Arbitration Act.

A state policy excluding wage claims from arbitration, cf. Merrill Lynch, Pierce, Fenner & Smith v. Ware, 414 U.S. 117, 94 S.Ct. 383, 38 L.Ed.2d 348 (1973), or a state policy of providing special protection for franchisees, such as that expressed in California's Franchise Investment Law, can be recognized without impairing the basic purposes of the federal statute. Like the majority of the California Supreme Court, I am not persuaded that Congress intended the pre-emptive effect of this statute to be "so unyielding as to require enforcement of an agreement to arbitrate a dispute over the application of a regulatory statute which a state legislature, in conformity with analogous federal policy, has decided should be left to judicial enforcement." App. to Juris. Statement 18a.

Thus, although I agree with most of the Court's reasoning and specifically with its jurisdictional holdings, I respectfully dissent from its conclusion concerning the enforceability of the arbitration agreement. On that issue, I would affirm the judgment of the California Supreme Court.

■ JUSTICE O'CONNOR with whom JUSTICE REHNQUIST joins, dissenting.

Section 2 of the Federal Arbitration Act (FAA), 9 U.S.C. § 2, provides that a written arbitration agreement "shall be valid, irrevocable, and enforceable, save upon such grounds as exist at law or in equity for the revocation of any contract." § 2 does not, on its face, identify which judicial forums are bound by its requirements or what procedures govern its enforcement. The FAA deals with these matters in §§ 3 and 4. § 3 provides:

> If any suit or proceeding be brought in any of the courts of the United States upon any issue referable to arbitration . . . the court . . . shall on application of one of the parties stay the trial of the action until such arbitration has been had in accordance with the terms of the agreement. . . .

§ 4 specifies that a party aggrieved by another's refusal to arbitrate

> "may petition any United States district court which, save for such agreement, would have jurisdiction under Title 28, in a civil action or in admiralty of the subject matter . . . for an order directing that such

arbitration proceed in the manner provided for in such agreement...."

Today, the Court takes the facial silence of § 2 as a license to declare that state as well as federal courts must apply § 2. In addition, though this is not spelled out in the opinion, the Court holds that in enforcing this newly-discovered federal right state courts must follow procedures specified in § 3. The Court's decision is impelled by an understandable desire to encourage the use of arbitration, but it utterly fails to recognize the clear congressional intent underlying the FAA. Congress intended to require federal, not state, courts to respect arbitration agreements.

I

The FAA (originally the "United States Arbitration Act") was enacted in 1925. As demonstrated below, infra, at 865–868, Congress thought it was exercising its power to dictate either procedure or "general federal law" in federal courts. The issue presented here is the result of three subsequent decisions of this Court.

In 1938 this Court decided Erie Railroad Co. v. Tompkins, 304 U.S. 64, 58 S.Ct. 817, 82 L.Ed. 1188. Erie denied the federal government the power to create substantive law solely by virtue of the Article III power to control federal court jurisdiction. Eighteen years later the Court decided Bernhardt v. Polygraphic Co., 350 U.S. 198, 76 S.Ct. 273, 100 L.Ed. 199 (1956). *Bernhardt* held that the duty to arbitrate a contract dispute is outcome-determinative—i.e. "substantive"—and therefore a matter normally governed by state law in federal diversity cases.

Bernhardt gave rise to concern that the FAA could thereafter constitutionally be applied only in federal court cases arising under federal law, not in diversity cases. In Prima Paint v. Flood & Conklin, 388 U.S. 395, 404–405, 87 S.Ct. 1801, 1806–1807, 18 L.Ed.2d 1270 (1967), we addressed that concern, and held that the FAA may constitutionally be applied to proceedings in a federal diversity court. The FAA covers only contracts involving interstate commerce or maritime affairs, and Congress "plainly has the power to legislate" in that area. 388 U.S., at 405, 87 S.Ct., at 1807.

Nevertheless, the *Prima Paint* decision "carefully avoided any explicit endorsement of the view that the Arbitration Act embodied substantive policies that were to be applied to all contracts within its scope, whether sued on in state or federal courts." P. Bator, P. Mishkin, D. Shapiro, & H. Wechsler, Hart and Wechsler's The Federal Courts and the Federal System 731–732 (2d ed. 1973). Today's case is the first in which this Court has had occasion to determine whether the FAA applies to state court proceedings. One statement on the subject did appear in Moses H. Cone Memorial Hospital v. Mercury Construction Corp., 103 S.Ct. 927, 74 L.Ed.2d 765 (1983), but that case involved a federal, not a state, court proceeding; its dictum concerning the law applicable in state courts was wholly unnecessary to its holding.

II

The majority opinion decides three issues. First, it holds that § 2 creates federal substantive rights that must be enforced by the state courts. Second, though the issue is not raised in this case, the Court states, ante, at 861, n. 9, that § 2 substantive rights may not be the basis for invoking federal court jurisdiction under 28 U.S.C. § 1331. Third, the Court reads § 2 to require state courts to enforce § 2 rights using procedures that mimic those specified for federal courts by FAA §§ 3 and 4. The first of these conclusions is unquestionably wrong as a matter of statutory construction; the second appears to be an attempt to limit the damage done by the first; the third is unnecessary and unwise.

A

One rarely finds a legislative history as unambiguous as the FAA's. That history establishes conclusively that the 1925 Congress viewed the FAA as a procedural statute, applicable only in federal courts, derived, Congress believed, largely from the federal power to control the jurisdiction of the federal courts....

B

The structure of the FAA itself runs directly contrary to the reading the Court today gives to § 2. § 3 and § 4 are the implementing provisions of the Act, and they expressly apply only to federal courts. § 4 refers to the "United States district court[s]," and provides that it can be invoked only in a court that has jurisdiction under Title 28 of the United States Code. As originally enacted, § 3 referred, in the same terms as § 4, to "courts [or court] of the United States." There has since been a minor amendment in § 4's phrasing, but no substantive change in either section's limitation to federal courts.

None of this Court's prior decisions has authoritatively construed the Act otherwise. It bears repeating that both Prima Paint and Moses H. Cone involved federal court litigation. The applicability of the FAA to state court proceedings was simply not before the Court in either case. Justice Black would surely be surprised to find either the majority opinion or his dissent in Prima Paint cited by the Court today, as both are, ante, at 858, 859. His dissent took pains to point out:

> "The Court here does not hold ... that the body of federal substantive law created by federal judges under the Arbitration Act is required to be applied by state courts. A holding to that effect—which the Court seems to leave up in the air—would flout the intention of the framers of the Act." 388 U.S., at 424, 87 S.Ct., at 1816 (Black, J., dissenting) (footnotes omitted).

Nothing in the Prima Paint majority opinion contradicts this statement.

The Prima Paint majority gave full but precise effect to the original congressional intent—it recognized that notwithstanding the intervention of Erie the FAA's restrictive focus on maritime and interstate contracts permits its application in federal diversity courts. Today's decision, in contrast, glosses over both the careful crafting of Prima Paint and the historical reasons that made Prima Paint necessary, and gives the FAA a reach far broader than Congress intended.

III

Section 2, like the rest of the FAA, should have no application whatsoever in state courts. Assuming, to the contrary, that § 2 does create a federal right that the state courts must enforce, state courts should nonetheless be allowed, at least in the first instance, to fashion their own procedures for enforcing the right. Unfortunately, the Court seems to direct that the arbitration clause at issue here must be specifically enforced; apparently no other means of enforcement is permissible.

It is settled that a state court must honor federally created rights and that it may not unreasonably undermine them by invoking contrary local procedure. "[T]he assertion of Federal rights, when plainly and reasonably made, is not to be defeated under the name of local practice." Brown v. Western R., 338 U.S. 294, 299, 70 S.Ct. 105, 108, 94 L.Ed. 100 (1949). But absent specific direction from Congress the state courts have always been permitted to apply their own reasonable procedures when enforcing federal rights. Before we undertake to read a set of complex and mandatory procedures into § 2's brief and general language, we should at a minimum allow state courts and legislatures a chance to develop their own methods for enforcing the new federal rights. Some might choose to award compensatory or punitive damages for the violation of an arbitration agreement; some might award litigation costs to the party who remained willing to arbitrate; some might affirm the "validity and enforceability" of arbitration agreements in other ways. Any of these approaches could vindicate § 2 rights in a manner fully consonant with the language and background of that provision.

In summary, even were I to accept the majority's reading of § 2, I would disagree with the Court's disposition of this case. After articulating the nature and scope of the federal right it discerns in § 2, the Court should remand to the state court, which has acted, heretofore, under a misapprehension of federal law. The state court should determine, at least in the first instance, what procedures it will follow to vindicate the newly articulated federal rights. Compare Missouri ex rel. Southern R. v. Mayfield, 340 U.S. 1, 5, 71 S.Ct. 1, 3, 95 L.Ed. 3 (1950).

IV

The Court, ante, at 860–861, rejects the idea of requiring the FAA to be applied only in federal courts partly out of concern with the problem of forum shopping. The concern is unfounded. Because the FAA makes the federal courts equally accessible to both parties to a dispute, no forum shopping would be possible even if we gave the FAA a construction faithful to the congressional intent. In controversies involving incomplete diversity of citizenship there is simply no access to federal court and therefore no possibility of forum shopping. In controversies with complete diversity of citizenship the FAA grants federal court access equally to both parties; no party can gain any advantage by forum shopping. Even when the party resisting arbitration initiates an action in state court, the opposing party can invoke FAA § 4 and promptly secure a federal court order to compel arbitration. See, e.g., Moses H. Cone, supra.

Ironically, the FAA was passed specifically to rectify forum shopping problems created by this Court's decision in Swift v. Tyson, 41 U.S. 1, 16 Pet. 1, 10 L.Ed. 865 (1842). By 1925 several major commercial states had passed state arbitration laws, but the federal courts refused to enforce those laws in diversity cases. The drafters of the FAA might have anticipated Bernhardt by legislation and required federal diversity courts to adopt the arbitration law of the state in which they sat. But they deliberately chose a different approach. As was pointed out at congressional hearings, an additional goal of the Act was to make arbitration agreements enforceable even in federal courts located in states that had no arbitration law. The drafters' plan for maintaining reasonable harmony between state and federal practices was not to bludgeon states into compliance, but rather to adopt a uniform federal law, patterned after New York's path-breaking state statute, and simultaneously to press for passage of coordinated state legislation. The key language of the Uniform Act for Commercial Arbitration was, accordingly, identical to that in § 2 of the FAA.

In summary, forum shopping concerns in connection with the FAA are a distraction that do not withstand scrutiny. The Court ignores the drafters' carefully devised plan for dealing with those problems.

V

Today's decision adds yet another chapter to the FAA's already colorful history. In 1842 this Court's ruling in Swift v. Tyson, 41 U.S. 1, 16 Pet. 1, 10 L.Ed. 865 (1842), set up a major obstacle to the enforcement of state arbitration laws in federal diversity courts. In 1925 Congress sought to rectify the problem by enacting the FAA; the intent was to create uniform law binding only in the federal courts. In Erie (1938), and then in Bernhardt (1956), this Court significantly curtailed federal power. In 1967 our decision in Prima Paint upheld the application of the FAA in a federal court proceeding as a valid exercise of Congress' Commerce Clause and Admiralty powers. Today the Court discovers a federal right in FAA § 2 that the state courts must enforce. Apparently confident that state courts are not competent to devise their own procedures for protecting the newly discovered federal right, the Court summarily prescribes a specific procedure, found nowhere in § 2 or its common law origins, that the state courts are to follow.

Today's decision is unfaithful to congressional intent, unnecessary, and, in light of the FAA's antecedents and the intervening contraction of federal power, inexplicable. Although arbitration is a worthy alternative to litigation, today's exercise in judicial revisionism goes too far. I respectfully dissent.

* * *

Questions

1. Can the Supreme Court's opinion in *Southland* be reconciled with that in *Bernhardt?*

2. In 1924, when Congress was considering the bill that became the Federal Arbitration Act, the Committee Report on the bill stated:

> The purpose of this bill is to make valid and enforcible [sic] agreements for arbitration contained in contracts involving interstate commerce or within the jurisdiction of [sic] admiralty, or which may be the subject of litigation in the Federal courts. . . .
>
> Whether an agreement for arbitration shall be enforced or not is a question of procedure to be determined by the law court in which the proceeding is brought and not one of substantive law to be determined by the law of the forum in which the contract is made.

Report from the Committee on the Judiciary, H. Rep. No. 96, 68th Congress, 1st Sess. (January 24, 1924).

Was the majority opinion in *Southland* faithful to this legislative history?

3. Recall that in *Bernhardt v. Polygraphic Co.*, the Supreme Court held that for *Erie* purposes, the enforceability of an agreement to arbitrate was a matter of substantive law, and thus to be governed by state law in diversity cases. Later, in *Prima Paint v. Flood & Conklin*, 388 U.S. 395 (1967), the Court ruled that the FAA was based upon Congress' power to regulate interstate commerce, thus making it applicable in state courts as well as in federal courts by virtue of the Supremacy Clause. As a result, however, the Court created a jurisdictional anomaly: arbitration is substantive for *Erie* purposes (*Bernhardt*), but the Commerce Clause basis for the Act makes it substantive *federal* law and thus applicable in state courts and in federal courts in diversity cases. How can this anomaly be justified?

4. In *Southland*, and in *Moses H. Cone Memorial Hospital v. Mercury Construction Corp.*, 460 U.S. 1 (1983) discussed therein (and again in Chapter 2.2.A), the Supreme Court stated that the FAA does not create federal question jurisdiction. Can the FAA be substantive and yet not give rise to a federal question? Why does the Court hold that the FAA does not create federal question jurisdiction? Is this another jurisdictional anomaly?

* * *

Note on Perry v. Thomas

In *Perry v. Thomas*, 482 U.S. 483 (1987), the Supreme Court addressed the question of whether the FAA preempts restrictions on arbitration enacted by state legislatures. Thomas, an employee of the securities firm Kidder, Peabody, & Co., had a dispute over commissions he alleged he had earned on the sale of securities. When Thomas initially applied for employment with the firm, he had signed a Uniform Application for Securities Industry Registration, which provided for arbitration of all disputes between himself and the firm. Thomas sued for his commissions in state court, and the defendants sought to stay proceedings and compel arbitration. The California Labor Code provided that actions for the collection of wages could be maintained "without regard to the existence of any private agreement to arbitrate." Cal. Lab. Code § 229 (West 1971).

The California Superior Court and Court of Appeal held that the claim was not subject to arbitration. It based its decision on the Supreme Court's decision in Merrill Lynch, Pierce, Fenner & Smith v. Ware, 414 U.S. 117 (1973), where the Court rejected a Supremacy Clause challenge to Section 229 of the California Labor Code in a case that arose under the 1934 Securities Exchange Act. Having concluded that *Merrill Lynch v. Ware* was dispositive, the California Superior Court also did not address Thomas's alternative argument that the arbitration agreement in his case constituted an unconscionable, unenforceable contract of adhesion because "(a) the selection of arbitrators is made by the New York Stock Exchange and is presumptively biased in favor of management; and (b) the denial of meaningful discovery is unduly oppressive and frustrates an employee's claim for relief."

Justice Marshall, writing for the majority of the Supreme Court, reversed. He found that the California Labor Code provision was preempted by the FAA and ordered the litigation stayed and the case sent to arbitration in accordance with the FAA. The Court distinguished *Ware* on the grounds that the specific federal substantive law that was claimed to preempt state law in that case emanated from the 1934 Exchange Act, an Act which the Court interpreted to contain no policy favoring arbitration and no necessity for uniformity in "an exchange's housekeeping affairs."

"By contrast," wrote Justice Marshall,

> the present appeal addresses the pre-emptive effect of the Federal Arbitration Act, a statute that embodies Congress' intent to provide for the enforcement of arbitration agreements within the full reach of the Commerce Clause. Its general applicability reflects that [t]he preeminent concern of Congress in passing the Act was to enforce private agreements into which parties had entered.... Byrd, 470 U.S., at 221, 105 S.Ct., at 1242. We have accordingly held that these agreements must be 'rigorously enforce[d].' Ibid. ... This clear federal policy places § 2 of the Act in unmistakable conflict with California's § 229 requirement that litigants be provided a judicial forum for resolving wage disputes. Therefore, under the Supremacy Clause, the state statute must give way.

The majority also declined to address Thomas's claim that the arbitration agreement in this case constituted an unconscionable, unenforceable contract of adhesion. However, in footnote 9, Marshall added:

> We note, however, the choice-of-law issue that arises when defenses such as Thomas' so-called "standing" and unconscionability arguments are asserted. In instances such as these, the text of § 2 provides the touchstone for choosing between state-law principles and the principles of federal common law envisioned by the passage of that statute: An agreement to arbitrate is valid, irrevocable, and enforceable, as a matter of federal law, see Moses H. Cone Memorial Hospital v. Mercury Construction Corp., 460 U.S. 1, 24, 103 S.Ct. 927, 941, 74 L.Ed.2d 765 (1983), "save upon such grounds as exist at law or in equity for the revocation of any contract." 9 U.S.C. § 2. Thus state law, whether of legislative or judicial origin, is applicable if that law arose to govern issues concerning the validity, revocability, and enforceability of contracts generally. A state-law principle that takes its meaning precisely from the fact that a contract to arbitrate is at issue does not comport with this requirement of § 2. See Prima Paint, supra, 388 U.S., at 404, 87 S.Ct., at 1806; Southland Corp. v. Keating, 465 U.S., at 16–17, n. 11, 104 S.Ct., at 861, n. 11. A court may not, then, in assessing the rights of litigants to enforce an arbitration agreement, construe that agreement in a manner different from that in which it otherwise construes nonarbitration agreements under state law. Nor may a court rely on the uniqueness of an agreement to arbitrate as a basis for a state-law holding that enforcement would be unconscionable, for this would enable the court to effect what we hold today the state legislature cannot.

Justice O'Connor, dissenting, argued,

> Even if I were not to adhere to my position that the Act is inapplicable to state court proceedings, however, I would still dissent. We have held that Congress can limit or preclude a waiver of a judicial forum, and that Congress' intent to do so will be deduced from a statute's text or legislative history, or "from an inherent conflict between arbitration and the statute's underlying purposes." Shearson/American Express Inc. v. McMahon, 482 U.S. 220, 227, 107 S.Ct. 2332, 96 L.Ed.2d 185, 55 USLW 4757 (1987). As Justice Stevens has observed, the Court has not explained why state legislatures should not also be able to limit or preclude waiver of a judicial forum.
>
> [T]he California Legislature intended to preclude waiver of a judicial forum; it is clear, moreover, that this intent reflects an important state policy. Section 229 of the California Labor Code specifically provides that actions for the collection of wages may be maintained in the state courts" without regard to the existence of any private agreement to arbitrate." Cal.Lab.Code Ann. § 229 (West 1971). The California Legislature thereby intended "to protect the worker from the exploitative employer who would demand that a prospective employee sign away in advance his right to resort to the judicial system for redress of an employment grievance," and § 229 has "manifested itself as an important state policy through interpretation by the

California courts.'' Merrill Lynch, Pierce, Fenner & Smith v. Ware, 414 U.S. 117, 131, 132–133, 94 S.Ct. 383, 391, 392, 38 L.Ed.2d 348 (1973).

In my view, therefore, even if the Act applies to state court proceedings, California's policy choice to preclude waivers of a judicial forum for wage claims is entitled to respect.

Justice Stevens, also dissenting, stated that he shared Justice O'Connor's opinion that "the States' power to except certain categories of disputes from arbitration should be preserved unless Congress decides otherwise."

* * *

Questions

1. How does *Perry* differ from *Southland?* What issues are presented in *Perry* that were not already decided in *Southland*? Is *Perry* a harder or easier case than *Southland* for finding the state law claims preempted?

2. What does footnote 9 in *Perry* say about the role of state law doctrines under the FAA? According to the Court, which state law doctrines survive the very broad preemptive reach of the FAA?

3. What if a state statute, instead of requiring *judicial* resolution of a claim, requires an initial, nonbinding *administrative* resolution of the claim? This issue was raised in Preston v. Ferrer, ___ U.S. ___, 128 S.Ct. 978 (2008). In that case, a television judge, "Judge Alex" [E. Ferrer], signed an agreement containing an arbitration clause with Artist Manager Arnold Preston. When Judge Alex failed to make the stipulated payments, Preston filed for arbitration. Judge Alex challenged the legality of the entire agreement under the California Talent Agencies Act on the ground that Preston was not properly licensed under the state Talent Agency Act. This Act, among other things, provides that disputes under it must be referred to the California Labor Commissioner. California courts ruled that the legality of the Alex–Ferrer agreement should be decided by the Labor Commissioner. The Supreme Court reversed, holding that "when parties agree to arbitrate all questions arising under a contract, state laws lodging primary jurisdiction in another forum, whether judicial or administrative, are superseded by the FAA."

* * *

Volt Information Sciences, Inc. v. Board of Trustee of Stanford University

489 U.S. 468 (1989).

■ CHIEF JUSTICE REHNQUIST delivered the opinion of the Court.

Unlike its federal counterpart, the California Arbitration Act, Cal. Civ. Proc. Code Ann. § 1280 et seq. (West 1982), contains a provision allowing a court to stay arbitration pending resolution of related litigation. We hold application of the California statute is not pre-empted by the Federal Arbitration Act (FAA or Act), 9 U.S.C. § 1 et seq., in a case where the parties have agreed that their arbitration agreement will be governed by the law of California.

Appellant Volt Information Sciences, Inc. (Volt), and appellee Board of Trustees of Leland Stanford Junior University (Stanford) entered into a construction contract under which Volt was to install a system of electrical conduits on the Stanford campus. The contract contained an agreement to arbitrate all disputes between the parties "arising out of or relating to this contract or the breach thereof." The contract also contained a choice-of-law clause providing that "[t]he Contract shall be governed by the law of the place where the Project is located." App. 37. During the course of the project, a dispute developed regarding compensation for extra work, and Volt made a formal demand for arbitration. Stanford responded by filing an action against Volt in California Superior Court, alleging fraud and breach of contract; in the same action, Stanford also sought indemnity from two other companies involved in the construction project, with whom it did not have arbitration agreements. Volt petitioned the Superior Court to compel arbitration of the dispute.[2] Stanford in turn moved to stay arbitration pursuant to Cal.Civ.Proc.Code Ann. § 1281.2(c) (West 1982), which permits a court to stay arbitration pending resolution of related litigation between a party to the arbitration agreement and third parties not bound by it, where "there is a possibility of conflicting rulings on a common issue of law or fact."[3] The Superior Court denied Volt's motion to compel arbitration and stayed the arbitration proceedings pending the outcome of the litigation on the authority of § 1281.2(c). App. 59–60.

The California Court of Appeal affirmed. The court acknowledged that the parties' contract involved interstate commerce, that the FAA governs contracts in interstate commerce, and that the FAA contains no provision permitting a court to stay arbitration pending resolution of related litigation involving third parties not bound by the arbitration agreement. App. 64–65. However, the court held that by specifying that their contract would be governed by " 'the law of the place where the project is located,' " the parties had incorporated the California rules of arbitration, including § 1281.2(c), into their arbitration agreement. Id., at 65. Finally, the court

2. Volt also asked the court to stay the Superior Court litigation until the arbitration was completed, presumably pursuant to § 3 of the FAA, 9 U.S.C. § 3, and the parallel provision of the California Arbitration Act, Cal.Civ.Proc.Code Ann. § 1281.2(c)(3) (West 1982). App. 45–46.

3. Section 1281.2(c) provides, in pertinent part, that when a court determines that "[a] party to the arbitration agreement is also a party to a pending court action or special proceeding with a third party, arising out of the same transaction or series of related transactions and there is a possibility of conflicting rulings on a common issue of law or fact[,] . . . the court (1) may refuse to enforce the arbitration agreement and may order intervention or joinder of all parties in a single action or special proceeding; (2) may order intervention or joinder as to all or only certain issues; (3) may order arbitration among the parties who have agreed to arbitration and stay the pending court action or special proceeding pending the outcome of the arbitration proceeding; or (4) may stay arbitration pending the outcome of the court action or special proceeding."

rejected Volt's contention that, even if the parties had agreed to arbitrate under the California rules, application of § 1281.2(c) here was nonetheless pre-empted by the FAA because the contract involved interstate commerce. Id., at 68–80.

The court reasoned that the purpose of the FAA was " 'not [to] mandate the arbitration of all claims, but merely the enforcement ... of privately negotiated arbitration agreements.' " Id., at 70 (quoting Dean Witter Reynolds Inc. v. Byrd, 470 U.S. 213, 219, 105 S.Ct. 1238, 1242, 84 L.Ed.2d 158 (1985)). While the FAA therefore pre-empts application of state laws which render arbitration agreements unenforceable, "[i]t does not follow, however, that the federal law has preclusive effect in a case where the parties have chosen in their [arbitration] agreement to abide by state rules." App. 71. To the contrary, because "[t]he thrust of the federal law is that arbitration is strictly a matter of contract," ibid., the parties to an arbitration agreement should be "at liberty to choose the terms under which they will arbitrate." Id., at 72. Where, as here, the parties have chosen in their agreement to abide by the state rules of arbitration, application of the FAA to prevent enforcement of those rules would actually be "inimical to the policies underlying state and federal arbitration law," id., at 73, because it would "force the parties to arbitrate in a manner contrary to their agreement." Id., at 65. The California Supreme Court denied Volt's petition for discretionary review. Id., at 87. We postponed consideration of our jurisdiction to the hearing on the merits ... We now hold that we have appellate jurisdiction and affirm.

Appellant devotes the bulk of its argument to convincing us that the Court of Appeal erred in interpreting the choice-of-law clause to mean that the parties had incorporated the California rules of arbitration into their arbitration agreement.... Appellant acknowledges, as it must, that the interpretation of private contracts is ordinarily a question of state law, which this Court does not sit to review ... But appellant nonetheless maintains that we should set aside the Court of Appeal's interpretation of this particular contractual provision for two principal reasons.

Appellant first suggests that the Court of Appeal's construction of the choice-of-law clause was in effect a finding that appellant had "waived" its "federally guaranteed right to compel arbitration of the parties' dispute," a waiver whose validity must be judged by reference to federal rather than state law ... This argument fundamentally misconceives the nature of the rights created by the FAA. The Act was designed "to overrule the judiciary's longstanding refusal to enforce agreements to arbitrate," Byrd, supra, 470 U.S., at 219–220, 105 S.Ct., at 1241–1242, and place such agreements " 'upon the same footing as other contracts,' " Scherk v. Alberto–Culver Co., 417 U.S. 506, 511 ... Section 2 of the Act therefore declares that a written agreement to arbitrate in any contract involving interstate commerce or a maritime transaction "shall be valid, irrevocable, and enforceable, save upon such grounds as exist at law or in equity for the revocation of any contract," 9 U.S.C. § 2, and § 4 allows a party to such an arbitration agreement to "petition any United States district court ... for an order directing that such arbitration proceed in the manner provided for in such agreement."

But § 4 of the FAA does not confer a right to compel arbitration of any dispute at any time; it confers only the right to obtain an order directing that "arbitration proceed in the manner provided for in [the parties'] agreement." 9 U.S.C. § 4 (emphasis added). Here the Court of Appeal found that, by incorporating the California rules of arbitration into their agreement, the parties had agreed that arbitration would not proceed in situations which fell within the scope of Calif.Code Civ.Proc.Ann. § 1281.2(c) (West 1982). This was not a finding that appellant had "waived" an FAA-guaranteed right to compel arbitration of this dispute, but a finding that it had no such right in the first place, because the parties' agreement did not require arbitration to proceed in this situation. Accordingly, appellant's contention that the contract interpretation issue presented here involves the "waiver" of a federal right is without merit.

Second, appellant argues that we should set aside the Court of Appeal's construction of the choice-of-law clause because it violates the settled federal rule that questions of arbitrability in contracts subject to the FAA must be resolved with a healthy regard for the federal policy favoring arbitration. Brief for Appellant 49–52; id., at 92–96, citing Moses H. Cone Memorial Hospital v. Mercury Construction Corp., 460 U.S. 1, 24–25, 103 S.Ct. 927, 941–942, 74 L.Ed.2d 765 (1983) (§ 2 of the FAA "create[s] a body of federal substantive law of arbitrability, applicable to any arbitration agreement within the coverage of the Act," which requires that "questions of arbitrability ... be addressed with a healthy regard for the federal policy favoring arbitration," and that "any doubts concerning the scope of arbitrable issues ... be resolved in favor of arbitration"); Mitsubishi Motors Corp. v. Soler Chrysler–Plymouth, Inc., 473 U.S. 614, 626, 105 S.Ct. 3346, 3353, 87 L.Ed.2d 444 (1985) (in construing an arbitration agreement within the coverage of the FAA, "as with any other contract, the parties' intentions control, but those intentions are generously construed as to issues of arbitrability"). These cases of course establish that, in applying general state-law principles of contract interpretation to the interpretation of an arbitration agreement within the scope of the Act, ... due regard must be given to the federal policy favoring arbitration, and ambiguities as to the scope of the arbitration clause itself resolved in favor of arbitration.

But we do not think the Court of Appeal offended the Moses H. Cone principle by interpreting the choice-of-law provision to mean that the parties intended the California rules of arbitration, including the § 1281.2(c) stay provision, to apply to their arbitration agreement. There is no federal policy favoring arbitration under a certain set of procedural rules; the federal policy is simply to ensure the enforceability, according to their terms, of private agreements to arbitrate. Interpreting a choice-of-law clause to make applicable state rules governing the conduct of arbitration—rules which are manifestly designed to encourage resort to the arbitral process—simply does not offend the rule of liberal construction set forth in Moses H. Cone, nor does it offend any other policy embodied in the FAA.[5]

The question remains whether, assuming the choice-of-law clause meant what the Court of Appeal found it to mean, application of Cal.Civ. Proc.Code Ann. § 1281.2(c) is nonetheless pre-empted by the FAA to the extent it is used to stay arbitration under this contract involving interstate commerce. It is undisputed that this contract falls within the coverage of the FAA, since it involves interstate commerce, and that the FAA contains no provision authorizing a stay of arbitration in this situation. Appellee contends, however, that §§ 3 and 4 of the FAA, which are the specific sections claimed to conflict with the California statute at issue here, are not applicable in this state-court proceeding and thus cannot pre-empt application of the California statute. See Brief for Appellee 43–50. While the argument is not without some merit,[6] we need not resolve it to decide this case, for we conclude that even if §§ 3 and 4 of the FAA are fully applicable in state-court proceedings, they do not prevent application of Cal.Civ.Proc. Code Ann. § 1281.2(c) to stay arbitration where, as here, the parties have agreed to arbitrate in accordance with California law.

The FAA contains no express pre-emptive provision, nor does it reflect a congressional intent to occupy the entire field of arbitration. See Bernhardt v. Polygraphic Co., 350 U.S. 198, 76 S.Ct. 273, 100 L.Ed. 199 (1956) (upholding application of state arbitration law to arbitration provision in contract not covered by the FAA). But even when Congress has not completely displaced state regulation in an area, state law may nonetheless be pre-empted to the extent that it actually conflicts with federal law—that is, to the extent that it "stands as an obstacle to the accomplishment and execution of the full purposes and objectives of Congress." Hines v. Davidowitz, 312 U.S. 52, 67, 61 S.Ct. 399, 404, 85 L.Ed. 581 (1941). The question before us, therefore, is whether application of Cal.Civ.Proc.Code Ann. § 1281.2(c) to stay arbitration under this contract in interstate commerce, in accordance with the terms of the arbitration agreement itself,

5. Unlike the dissent, see post at 1259–1260, we think the California arbitration rules which the parties have incorporated into their contract generally foster the federal policy favoring arbitration. As indicated, the FAA itself contains no provision designed to deal with the special practical problems that arise in multiparty contractual disputes when some or all of the contracts at issue include agreements to arbitrate. California has taken the lead in fashioning a legislative response to this problem, by giving courts authority to consolidate or stay arbitration proceedings in these situations in order to minimize the potential for contradictory judgments. See Calif.Civ.Proc.Code Ann. § 1281.2(c).

6. While we have held that the FAA's "substantive" provisions—§§ 1 and 2—are applicable in state as well as federal court, see Southland Corp. v. Keating, 465 U.S. 1, 12, 104 S.Ct. 852, 859, 79 L.Ed.2d 1 (1984), we have never held that §§ 3 and 4, which by their terms appear to apply only to proceedings in federal court, see 9 U.S.C. § 3 (referring to proceedings "brought in any of the courts of the United States"); § 4 (referring to "any United States district court"), are nonetheless applicable in state court. See Southland Corp. v. Keating, supra, at 16, n. 10, 104 S.Ct., at 861 n. 10 (expressly reserving the question whether "§§ 3 and 4 of the Arbitration Act apply to proceedings in state courts"); see also id., at 29, 104 S.Ct., at 867 (O'Connor, J., dissenting) (§§ 3 and 4 of the FAA apply only in federal court).

would undermine the goals and policies of the FAA. We conclude that it would not.

... In recognition of Congress' principal purpose of ensuring that private arbitration agreements are enforced according to their terms, we have held that the FAA pre-empts state laws which "require a judicial forum for the resolution of claims which the contracting parties agreed to resolve by arbitration." Southland Corp. v. Keating, 465 U.S. 1, 10 ... But it does not follow that the FAA prevents the enforcement of agreements to arbitrate under different rules than those set forth in the Act itself. Indeed, such a result would be quite inimical to the FAA's primary purpose of ensuring that private agreements to arbitrate are enforced according to their terms. Arbitration under the Act is a matter of consent, not coercion, and parties are generally free to structure their arbitration agreements as they see fit. Just as they may limit by contract the issues which they will arbitrate, see Mitsubishi, supra, 473 U.S., at 628, 105 S.Ct., at 3353, so too may they specify by contract the rules under which that arbitration will be conducted. Where, as here, the parties have agreed to abide by state rules of arbitration, enforcing those rules according to the terms of the agreement is fully consistent with the goals of the FAA, even if the result is that arbitration is stayed where the Act would otherwise permit it to go forward. By permitting the courts to "rigorously enforce" such agreements according to their terms ... we give effect to the contractual rights and expectations of the parties, without doing violence to the policies behind by the FAA.

The judgment of the Court of Appeals is

Affirmed.

■ JUSTICE O'CONNOR took no part in the consideration or decision of this case.

■ JUSTICE BRENNAN, with whom JUSTICE MARSHALL joins, dissenting.

The litigants in this case were parties to a construction contract which contained a clause obligating them to arbitrate disputes and making that obligation specifically enforceable. The contract also incorporated provisions of a standard form contract prepared by the American Institute of Architects and endorsed by the Associated General Contractors of America; among these general provisions was § 7.1.1: "The Contract shall be governed by the law of the place where the Project is located." When a dispute arose between the parties, Volt invoked the arbitration clause, while Stanford attempted to avoid it (apparently because the dispute also involved two other contractors with whom Stanford had no arbitration agreements).

The Federal Arbitration Act (FAA), 9 U.S.C. § 1 et seq., requires courts to enforce arbitration agreements in contracts involving interstate commerce. See ante, at 1253. The California courts nonetheless rejected Volt's petition to compel arbitration in reliance on a provision of state law that, in the circumstances presented, permitted a court to stay arbitration pending the conclusion of related litigation. Volt, not surprisingly, suggested that the Supremacy Clause compelled a different result. The California Court of Appeal found, however, that the parties had agreed that their contract would be governed solely by the law of the State of California, to the exclusion of federal law. In reaching this conclusion the court relied on no extrinsic evidence of the parties' intent, but solely on the language of the form contract that the " 'law of the place where the project is located' " would govern. App. 66–67.

This Court now declines to review that holding, which denies effect to an important federal statute, apparently because it finds no question of federal law involved. I can accept neither the state court's unusual interpretation of the parties' contract, nor this Court's unwillingness to review it. I would reverse the judgment of the California Court of Appeal.[4]

I

Contrary to the Court's view, the state court's construction of the choice-of-law clause is reviewable for two independent reasons.

A

The Court's decision not to review the state court's interpretation of the choice-of-law clause appears to be based on the principle that "the interpretation of private contracts is ordinarily a question of state law, which this Court does not sit to review." . . . I have no quarrel with the general proposition that the interpretation of contracts is a matter of state law. By ending its analysis at that level of generality, however, the Court overlooks well-established precedent to the effect that, in order to guard against arbitrary denials of federal claims, a state court's construction of a contract in such a way as to preclude enforcement of a federal right is not immune from review in this Court as to its "adequacy."

While in this case the federal right at issue is a statutory, not a constitutional, one, the principle under which we review the antecedent question of state law is the same. Where "the existence or the application of a federal right turns on a logically antecedent finding on a matter of state law, it is essential to the Court's performance of its function that it exercise an ancillary jurisdiction to consider the state question. Federal rights could otherwise be nullified by the manipulation of state law." Wechsler, The Appellate Jurisdiction of the Supreme Court: Reflections on the Law and the Logistics of Direct Review, 34 Wash. & Lee L.Rev. 1043, 1052 (1977) . . .

No less than in the cited cases, the right of the instant parties to have their arbitration agreement enforced pursuant to the FAA could readily be circumvented by a state-court construction of their contract as having intended to exclude the applicability of federal law. It is therefore essential

4. I do not disagree with the Court's holding, ante, at 1254–1255, that the FAA does not pre-empt state arbitration rules, even as applied to contracts involving interstate commerce, when the parties have agreed to arbitrate by those rules to the exclusion of federal arbitration law. I would not reach that question, however, because I conclude that the parties have made no such agreement.

that, while according due deference to the decision of the state court, we independently determine whether we "clearly would have judged the issue differently if [we] were the state's highest court." Wechsler, supra, at 1052.

B

Arbitration is, of course, "a matter of contract and a party cannot be required to submit to arbitration any dispute which he has not agreed so to submit." Steelworkers v. Warrior & Gulf Co., 363 U.S. 574, 582, 80 S.Ct. 1347, 1353, 4 L.Ed.2d 1409 (1960). I agree with the Court that "the FAA does not require parties to arbitrate when they have not agreed to do so." Ante, at 1254. Since the FAA merely requires enforcement of what the parties have agreed to, moreover, they are free if they wish to write an agreement to arbitrate outside the coverage of the FAA. Such an agreement would permit a state rule, otherwise pre-empted by the FAA, to govern their arbitration. The substantive question in this case is whether or not they have done so. And that question, we have made clear in the past, is a matter of federal law....

While appearing to recognize that the state court's interpretation of the contract does raise a question of federal law, the Court nonetheless refuses to determine whether the state court misconstrued that agreement. There is no warrant for failing to do so. The FAA requires that a court determining a question of arbitrability not stop with the application of state-law rules for construing the parties' intentions, but that it also take account of the command of federal law that "those intentions [be] generously construed as to issues of arbitrability." Mitsubishi Motors, supra, 473 U.S., at 626, 105 S.Ct., at 3354. Thus, the decision below is based on both state and federal law, which are thoroughly intertwined. In such circumstances the state-court judgment cannot be said to rest on an "adequate and independent state ground" so as to bar review by this Court. See Enterprise Irrigation Dist. v. Farmers Mutual Canal Co., 243 U.S. 157, 164, 37 S.Ct. 318, 320, 61 L.Ed. 644 (1917) ("But where the non-federal ground is so interwoven with the other as not to be an independent matter ... our jurisdiction is plain") ...

II

Construed with deference to the opinion of the California Court of Appeal, yet "with a healthy regard for the federal policy favoring arbitration," Moses H. Cone, 460 U.S., at 24, 103 S.Ct., at 941, it is clear that the choice-of-law clause cannot bear the interpretation the California court assigned to it.

Construction of a contractual provision is, of course, a matter of discerning the parties' intent. It is important to recall, in the first place, that in this case there is no extrinsic evidence of their intent. We must therefore rely on the contract itself. But the provision of the contract at issue here was not one that these parties drafted themselves. Rather, they incorporated portions of a standard form contract commonly used in the construction industry. That makes it most unlikely that their intent was in any way at variance with the purposes for which choice-of-law clauses are commonly written and the manner in which they are generally interpreted....

Choice-of-law clauses simply have never been used for the purpose of dealing with the relationship between state and federal law. There is no basis whatever for believing that the parties in this case intended their choice-of-law clause to do so.

III

Most commercial contracts written in this country contain choice-of-law clauses, similar to the one in the Stanford–Volt contract, specifying which State's law is to govern the interpretation of the contract. See Scoles & Hay, Conflict of Laws, at 632–633 ("Party autonomy means that the parties are free to select the law governing their contract, subject to certain limitations. They will usually do so by means of an express choice-of-law clause in their written contract"). Were every state court to construe such clauses as an expression of the parties' intent to exclude the application of federal law, as has the California Court of Appeal in this case, the result would be to render the Federal Arbitration Act a virtual nullity as to presently existing contracts. I cannot believe that the parties to contracts intend such consequences to flow from their insertion of a standard choice-of-law clause. Even less can I agree that we are powerless to review decisions of state courts that effectively nullify a vital piece of federal legislation. I respectfully dissent.

* * *

Questions

1. After *Volt*, will a choice of law clause in a contract always supplant the application of the FAA? Under what circumstances will it so operate?

2. Would the results in *Southland* or *Perry* have been different if those cases had involved a choice of law clause similar to that involved in *Volt*?

3. How can *Perry* be distinguished from *Volt*?

4. Is the holding of *Volt* limited to state law procedural rules regulating arbitration, or does it also apply to state law substantive rules that bear on arbitration? That is, in *Southland*, could the parties have retained the benefits of the California Franchise Investment Act by enumerating its provisions in their contract? Could they have done so by incorporating the CFIA by reference?

5. Is *Volt* in tension with the federal policy of the FAA to favor arbitration as a means of resolving disputes?

* * *

Allied–Bruce Terminix Companies, Inc., and Tern International Company v. Dobson

513 U.S. 265 (1995).

■ JUSTICE BREYER delivered the opinion of the Court.

This case concerns the reach of § 2 of the Federal Arbitration Ac That section makes enforceable a written arbitration provision in "a contract *evidencing* a transaction *involving* commerce." 9 U.S.C. § 2 (emphasis added). Should we read this phrase broadly, extending the Act's reach to the limits of Congress' Commerce Clause power? Or, do the two underscored words—"involving" and "evidencing"—significantly restrict the Act's application? We conclude that the broader reading of the Act is the correct one; and we reverse a State Supreme Court judgment to the contrary.

I

In August 1987 Steven Gwin, a respondent, who owned a house in Birmingham, Alabama, bought a lifetime "Termite Protection Plan" (Plan) from the local office of Allied–Bruce Terminix Companies, a franchise of Terminix International Company. In the Plan, Allied–Bruce promised "to protect" Gwin's house "against the attack of subterranean termites," to reinspect periodically, to provide any "further treatment found necessary," and to repair, up to $100,000, damage caused by new termite infestations. App. 69. Terminix International "guarantee[d] the fulfillment of the terms" of the Plan. Ibid. The Plan's contract document provided in writing that "*any controversy or claim* ... arising out of or relating to the interpretation, performance or breach of any provision of this agreement *shall be settled exclusively by arbitration*." Id., at 70 (emphasis added).

In the Spring of 1991 Mr. and Mrs. Gwin, wishing to sell their house to Mr. and Mrs. Dobson, had Allied–Bruce reinspect the house. They obtained a clean bill of health. But, no sooner had they sold the house and transferred the Termite Protection Plan to Mr. and Mrs. Dobson than the Dobsons found the house swarming with termites. Allied–Bruce attempted to treat and repair the house, but the Dobsons found Allied–Bruce's efforts inadequate. They therefore sued the Gwins, and (along with the Gwins, who cross-claimed) also sued Allied–Bruce and Terminix in Alabama state court. Allied–Bruce and Terminix, pointing to the Plan's arbitration clause and 2 of the Federal Arbitration Act, immediately asked the court for a stay, to allow arbitration to proceed. The court denied the stay. Allied–Bruce and Terminix appealed.

The Supreme Court of Alabama upheld the denial of the stay on the basis of a state statute, Ala.Code § 8–1–41(3) (1993), making written, predispute arbitration agreements invalid and "unenforceable." 628 So.2d 354, 355 (Ala. 1993). To reach this conclusion, the court had to find that the Federal Arbitration Act, which pre-empts conflicting state law, did not apply to the termite contract. It made just that finding. The court considered the federal Act inapplicable because the connection between the termite contract and interstate commerce was too slight. In the court's view, the Act applies to a contract only if " 'at the time [the parties entered into the contract] and accepted the arbitration clause, they *contemplated* substantial interstate activity.' " Ibid. (emphasis in original) (quoting Metro Industrial Painting Corp. v. Terminal Constr. Co., 287 F.2d 382, 387 (CA2) (Lumbard, C.J., concurring), cert. denied, 368 U.S. 817, 82 S.Ct. 31, 7 L.Ed.2d 24 (1961)). Despite some interstate activities (e.g., Allied–Bruce, like Terminix, is a multistate firm and shipped treatment and repair material from out of state), the court found that the parties "contemplated" a transaction that was primarily local and not "substantially" interstate.

Several state courts and federal district courts, like the Supreme Court of Alabama, have interpreted the Act's language as requiring the parties to a contract to have "contemplated" an interstate commerce connection. See, e.g., Burke County Public Schools Bd. of Ed. v. Shaver Partnership, 303 N.C. 408, 417–420, 279 S.E.2d 816, 822–823 (1981); R.J. Palmer Constr. Co. v. Wichita Band Instrument Co., 7 Kan.App.2d 363, 367, 642 P.2d 127, 130 (1982); Lacheney v. Profitkey Int'l, Inc., 818 F.Supp. 922, 924 (E.D.Va. 1993). Several federal appellate courts, however, have interpreted the same language differently, as reaching to the limits of Congress' Commerce Clause power. See, e.g., Foster v. Turley, 808 F.2d 38, 40 (C.A.10 1986); Robert Lawrence Co. v. Devonshire Fabrics, Inc., 271 F.2d 402, 406–407 (C.A.2 1959), cert. dism'd, 364 U.S. 801, 81 S.Ct. 27, 5 L.Ed.2d 37 (1960); cf. Snyder v. Smith, 736 F.2d 409, 417–418 (CA7), cert. denied, 469 U.S. 1037, 105 S.Ct. 513, 83 L.Ed.2d 403 (1984). We granted certiorari to resolve this conflict, 510 U.S. 1190, 114 S.Ct. 1292, 127 L.Ed.2d 646 (1994); and, as we said, we conclude that the broader reading of the statute is the right one . . .

[R]espondents, supported by 20 state attorneys general, now ask us to overrule Southland and thereby to permit Alabama to apply its anti-arbitration statute in this case irrespective of the proper interpretation of § 2. The Southland Court, however, recognized that the pre-emption issue was a difficult one, and it considered the basic arguments that respondents and amici now raise (even though those issues were not thoroughly briefed at the time). Nothing significant has changed in the 10 years subsequent to Southland; no later cases have eroded Southland's authority; and, no unforeseen practical problems have arisen. Moreover, in the interim, private parties have likely written contracts relying upon Southland as authority. Further, Congress, both before and after Southland, has enacted legislation extending, not retracting, the scope of arbitration. See, e.g., 9 U.S.C. § 15 (eliminating the Act of State doctrine as a bar to arbitration); 9 U.S.C. §§ 201–208 (international arbitration). For these reasons, we find it inappropriate to reconsider what is by now well-established law.

We therefore proceed to the basic interpretive questions aware that we are interpreting an Act that seeks broadly to overcome judicial hostility to arbitration agreements and that applies in both federal and state courts. We must decide in this case whether that Act used language about interstate commerce that nonetheless limits the Act's application, thereby carving out an important statutory niche in which a State remains free to apply its anti-arbitration law or policy. We conclude that it does not.

III

The Federal Arbitration Act, § 2, provides that a "written provision in any maritime transaction or a *contract evidencing a transaction involving commerce* to settle by arbitration a controversy thereafter arising out of such contract or transaction ... shall be valid, irrevocable, and enforceable, save upon such grounds as exist at law or in equity for the revocation of any contract." 9 U.S.C. § 2 (emphasis added).

The initial interpretive question focuses upon the words "involving commerce." These words are broader than the often-found words of art "in commerce." They therefore cover more than " 'only persons or activities within the flow of interstate commerce.' " United States v. American Building Maintenance Industries, 422 U.S. 271, 276, 95 S.Ct. 2150, 2154, 45 L.Ed.2d 177 (1975), quoting Gulf Oil Corp. v. Copp Paving Co., 419 U.S. 186, 195, 95 S.Ct. 392, 398, 42 L.Ed.2d 378 (1974) (defining "in commerce" as related to the "flow" and defining the "flow" to include "the generation of goods and services for interstate markets and their transport and distribution to the consumer"); see also FTC v. Bunte Brothers, Inc., 312 U.S. 349, 351, 61 S.Ct. 580, 582, 85 L.Ed. 881 (1941). But, how far beyond the flow of commerce does the word "involving" reach? Is "involving" the functional equivalent of the word "affecting"? That phrase—"affecting commerce"—normally signals a congressional intent to exercise its Commerce Clause powers to the full. See Russell v. United States, 471 U.S. 858, 859, 105 S.Ct. 2455, 2456, 85 L.Ed.2d 829 (1985). We cannot look to other statutes for guidance for the parties tell us that this is the only federal statute that uses the word "involving" to describe an interstate commerce relation.

After examining the statute's language, background, and structure, we conclude that the word "involving" is broad and is indeed the functional equivalent of "affecting." For one thing, such an interpretation, linguistically speaking, is permissible. The dictionary finds instances in which "involve" and "affect" sometimes can mean about the same thing. V Oxford English Dictionary 466 (1st ed. 1933) (providing examples dating back to the mid-nineteenth century, where "involve" means to "include or affect in ... operation"). For another, the Act's legislative history, to the extent that it is informative, indicates an expansive congressional intent. See, e.g., H.R.Rep. No. 96, 68th Cong., 1st Sess., 1 (1924) (the Act's "control over interstate commerce reaches not only the actual physical interstate shipment of goods but also contracts relating to interstate commerce"); 65 Cong.Rec. 1931 (1924) (the Act "affects contracts relating to interstate subjects and contracts in admiralty") (remarks of Rep. Graham); Joint Hearings on S. 1005 and H.R. 646 before the Subcommittees of the Committees on the Judiciary, 68th Cong., 1st Sess., 7 (1924) (hereinafter Joint Hearings) (testimony of Charles L. Bernheimer, chairman of the

Committee on Arbitration of the Chamber of Commerce of the State of New York, agreeing that the proposed bill "relates to contracts arising in interstate commerce"); id., at 16 (testimony of Julius H. Cohen, drafter for the American Bar Association of much of the proposed bill's language, that the Act reflects part of a strategy to rid the law of an "anachronism" by "get[ting] a Federal law to cover interstate and foreign commerce and admiralty"); see also 9 U.S.C. § 1 (defining the word "commerce" in the language of the Commerce Clause itself).

Further, this Court has previously described the Act's reach expansively as coinciding with that of the Commerce Clause. See, e.g., Perry v. Thomas, 482 U.S. 483, 490, 107 S.Ct. 2520, 2525–26, 96 L.Ed.2d 426 (1987) (the Act "embodies Congress' intent to provide for the enforcement of arbitration agreements within the full reach of the Commerce Clause"); Southland Corp. v. Keating, 465 U.S., at 14–15, 104 S.Ct., at 860 (the " 'involving commerce' " requirement is a constitutionally "necessary qualification" on the Act's reach, marking its permissible outer limit); see also Prima Paint Corp. v. Flood & Conklin Mfg. Co., 388 U.S., at 407, 87 S.Ct., at 1807–08 (Harlan, J., concurring) (endorsing Robert Lawrence Co. v. Devonshire Fabrics, Inc., 271 F.2d 402, 407 (C.A.2 1959) (Congress, in enacting the FAA, "took pains to utilize as much of its power as it could . . .")).

Finally, a broad interpretation of this language is consistent with the Act's basic purpose, to put arbitration provisions on "the same footing" as a contract's other terms. Scherk v. Alberto–Culver Co., 417 U.S., at 511, 94 S.Ct., at 2453. Conversely, a narrower interpretation is not consistent with the Act's purpose, for (unless unreasonably narrowed to the flow of commerce) such an interpretation would create a new, unfamiliar, test lying somewhere in a no-man's land between "in commerce" and "affecting commerce," thereby unnecessarily complicating the law and breeding litigation from a statute that seeks to avoid it.

We recognize arguments to the contrary: The pre-New Deal Congress that passed the Act in 1925 might well have thought the Commerce Clause did not stretch as far as has turned out to be so. But, it is not unusual for this Court in similar circumstances to ask whether the scope of a statute should expand along with the expansion of the Commerce Clause power itself, and to answer the question affirmatively—as, for the reasons set forth above, we do here. See, e.g., McLain v. Real Estate Bd. of New Orleans, Inc., 444 U.S. 232, 241, 100 S.Ct. 502, 508–509, 62 L.Ed.2d 441 (1980); Hospital Building Co. v. Trustees of Rex Hospital, 425 U.S. 738, 743, n. 2, 96 S.Ct. 1848, 1852, n. 2, 48 L.Ed.2d 338 (1976) . . .

The Gwins and Dobsons, with far better reason, point to a different case, Bernhardt v. Polygraphic Co. of America, 350 U.S. 198, 76 S.Ct. 273, 100 L.Ed. 199 (1956). In that case, Bernhardt, a New York resident, had entered into an employment contract (containing an arbitration clause) in New York with Polygraphic, a New York corporation. But, Bernhardt "was to perform" that contract after he "later became a resident of Vermont." Id., at 199, 76 S.Ct., at 274. This Court was faced with the question whether, in light of Erie, a federal court should apply the Federal Arbitration Act in a diversity case when faced with state law hostile to arbitration. Id., at 200, 76 S.Ct., at 274–75. The Court did not reach that question, however, for it decided that the contract itself did not "involv[e]" interstate commerce and therefore fell outside the Act. Id., at 200–202, 76 S.Ct., at 274–276. Since Congress, constitutionally speaking, could have applied the Act to Bernhardt's contract, say the parties, how then can we say that the Act's word "involving" reaches as far as the Commerce Clause itself?

The best response to this argument is to point to the way in which the Court reasoned in Bernhardt, and to what the Court said. It said that the *reason* the Act did not apply to Bernhardt's contract was that there was "*no showing that petitioner* while performing his duties under the employment contract was working 'in' commerce, was producing goods for commerce, or *was engaging in activity that affected commerce*, within the meaning of our decisions." Bernhardt, supra, at 200–201, 76 S.Ct., at 274–275 (emphasis added) (footnote omitted).

Thus, the Court interpreted the words "involving commerce" as broadly as the words "affecting commerce"; and, as we have said, these latter words normally mean a full exercise of constitutional power. At the same time, the Court's opinion does not discuss the implications of the "interstate" facts to which the respondents now point. For these reasons, Bernhardt does not require us to narrow the scope of the word "involving." And, we conclude that the word "involving," like "affecting," signals an intent to exercise Congress' commerce power to the full.

IV

Section 2 applies where there is "a contract *evidencing a transaction* involving commerce." 9 U.S.C. § 2 (emphasis added). The second interpretive question focuses on the underscored words. Does "evidencing a transaction" mean only that the transaction (that the contract "evidences") must turn out, in fact, to have involved interstate commerce? Or, does it mean more?

Many years ago, Second Circuit Chief Judge Lumbard said that the phrase meant considerably more. He wrote: "The significant question ... is not whether, in carrying out the terms of the contract, the parties did cross state lines, but whether, *at the time they entered into it* and accepted the arbitration clause, they *contemplated* substantial interstate activity. Cogent evidence regarding their state of mind at the time would be the terms of the contract, and if it, on its face, evidences interstate traffic ..., the contract should come within § 2. In addition, evidence as to how the parties expected the contract to be performed and how it was performed is relevant to whether substantial interstate activity was contemplated." Metro Industrial Painting Corp. v. Terminal Constr. Co., 287 F.2d 382, 387 (C.A.2 1961) (Lumbard, C.J., concurring) (second emphasis added).

The Supreme Court of Alabama, and several other courts, have followed this view, known as the "contemplation of the parties" test. See supra, at 837.

We find the interpretive choice difficult, but for several reasons we conclude that the first interpretation ("commerce in fact") is more faithful to the statute than the second ("contemplation of the parties"). First, the "contemplation of the parties" interpretation, when viewed in terms of the statute's basic purpose, seems anomalous. That interpretation invites litigation about what was, or was not, "contemplated." Why would Congress intend a test that risks the very kind of costs and delay through litigation (about the circumstances of contract formation) that Congress wrote the Act to help the parties avoid? See Moses H. Cone Memorial Hospital v. Mercury Constr. Corp., 460 U.S. 1, 29, 103 S.Ct. 927, 944, 74 L.Ed.2d 765 (1983) (the Act "calls for a summary and speedy disposition of motions or petitions to enforce arbitration clauses").

Moreover, that interpretation too often would turn the validity of an arbitration clause on what, from the perspective of the statute's basic purpose, seems happenstance, namely whether the parties happened to think to insert a reference to interstate commerce in the document or happened to mention it in an initial conversation. After all, parties to a sales contract with an arbitration clause might naturally think about the goods sold, or about arbitration, but why should they naturally think about an interstate commerce connection?

Further, that interpretation fits awkwardly with the rest of § 2. That section, for example, permits parties to agree to submit to arbitration "an existing controversy arising out of" a contract made earlier. Why would Congress want to risk non-enforceability of this later arbitration agreement (even if fully connected with interstate commerce) simply because the parties did not properly "contemplate" (or write about) the interstate aspects of the earlier contract? The first interpretation, requiring only that the "transaction" in fact involve interstate commerce, avoids this anomaly, as it avoids the other anomalous effects growing out of the "contemplation of the parties" test.

Second, the statute's language permits the "commerce in fact" interpretation. That interpretation, we concede, leaves little work for the word "evidencing" (in the phrase "a contract evidencing a transaction") to perform, for every contract evidences some transaction. But, perhaps Congress did not want that word to perform much work. The Act's history, to the extent informative, indicates that the Act's supporters saw the Act as part of an effort to make arbitration agreements universally enforceable. They wanted to "get a Federal law" that would "cover" areas where the Constitution authorized Congress to legislate, namely "interstate and foreign commerce and admiralty." Joint Hearings, at 16 (testimony of Julius H. Cohen). They urged Congress to model the Act after a New York statute that made enforceable a written arbitration provision "in a written contract," Act of Apr. 19, 1920, ch. 275, § 2, 1920 N.Y.Laws 803, 804. Hearing on S. 4213 and S. 4214 before the Subcommittee of the Senate Committee on the Judiciary, 67th Cong., 4th Sess., 2 (1923) (testimony of Charles L. Bernheimer). Early drafts made enforceable a written arbitration provision "in any contract or maritime transaction or transaction involving commerce." S. 4214, 67th Cong., 4th Sess. § 2 (1922) (emphasis added); S. 1005, 68th Cong., 1st Sess. (1923); H.R. 646, 68th Cong., 1st Sess. (1924). Members of Congress, looking at that phrase, might have thought the words "any contract" standing alone went beyond Congress' constitutional authority. And, if so, they might have simply connected those words with the later words "transaction involving commerce," thereby creating the phrase that became law. Nothing in the Act's history suggests any other, more limiting, task for the language.

Third, the basic practical argument underlying the "contemplation of the parties" test was, in Judge Lumbard's words, the need to "be cautious in construing the act lest we excessively encroach on the powers which Congressional policy, if not the Constitution, would reserve to the states." Metro Industrial Painting Corp., supra, at 386 (Lumbard, C.J., concurring). The practical force of this argument has diminished in light of this Court's later holdings that the Act does displace state law to the contrary. See Southland Corp. v. Keating, 465 U.S., at 10–16, 104 S.Ct., at 858–861; Perry v. Thomas, 482 U.S., at 489–492, 107 S.Ct., at 2525–2527.

Finally, we note that an amicus curiae argues for an "objective" ("reasonable person" oriented) version of the "contemplation of the parties" test on the ground that such an interpretation would better protect consumers asked to sign form contracts by businesses. We agree that Congress, when enacting this law, had the needs of consumers, as well as others, in mind. See S.Rep. No. 536, 68th Cong., 1st Sess., 3 (1924) (the Act, by avoiding "the delay and expense of litigation," will appeal "to big business and little business alike, ... corporate interests [and] ... individuals"). Indeed, arbitration's advantages often would seem helpful to individuals, say, complaining about a product, who need a less expensive alternative to litigation. See, e.g., H.R.Rep. No. 97–542, p. 13 (1982) ("The advantages of arbitration are many: it is usually cheaper and faster than litigation; it can have simpler procedural and evidentiary rules; it normally minimizes hostility and is less disruptive of ongoing and future business dealings among the parties; it is often more flexible in regard to scheduling of times and places of hearings and discovery devices ..."). And, according to the American Arbitration Association (also an amicus here), more than one-third of its claims involve amounts below $10,000, while another third involve claims of $10,000 to $50,000 (with an average processing time of less than six months). App. to Brief for American Arbitration Association as Amicus Curiae 26–27.

We are uncertain, however, just how the "objective" version of the "contemplation" test would help consumers. Sometimes, of course, it would permit, say, a consumer with potentially large damage claims, to disavow a contract's arbitration provision and proceed in court. But, if so, it would equally permit, say, local business entities to disavow a contract's arbitration provisions, thereby leaving the typical consumer who has only a small damage claim (who seeks, say, the value of only a defective refrigerator or television set) without any remedy but a court remedy, the costs and delays of which could eat up the value of an eventual small recovery.

In any event, § 2 gives States a method for protecting consumers against unfair pressure to agree to a contract with an unwanted arbitration provision. States may regulate contracts, including arbitration clauses, under general contract law principles and they may invalidate an arbitration clause "upon such grounds as exist at law or in equity for the revocation of *any* contract." 9 U.S.C. § 2 (emphasis added). What States may not do is decide that a contract is fair enough to enforce all its basic terms (price, service, credit), but not fair enough to enforce its arbitration clause. The Act makes any such state policy unlawful, for that kind of policy would place arbitration clauses on an unequal "footing," directly contrary to the Act's language and Congress' intent. See Volt Information Sciences, Inc., 489 U.S., at 474, 109 S.Ct., at 1253.

For these reasons, we accept the "commerce in fact" interpretation, reading the Act's language as insisting that the "transaction" in fact "involve" interstate commerce, even if the parties did not contemplate an interstate commerce connection.

V

The parties do not contest that the transaction in this case, in fact, involved interstate commerce. In addition to the multistate nature of Terminix and Allied–Bruce, the termite-treating and house-repairing material used by Allied–Bruce in its (allegedly inadequate) efforts to carry out the terms of the Plan, came from outside Alabama.

Consequently, the judgment of the Supreme Court of Alabama is reversed and the case is remanded for further proceedings consistent with this opinion.

It is so ordered.

■ JUSTICE O'CONNOR, concurring.

I agree with the Court's construction of § 2 of the Federal Arbitration Act. As applied in federal courts, the Court's interpretation comports fully with my understanding of congressional intent. A more restrictive definition of "evidencing" and "involving" would doubtless foster pre-arbitration litigation that would frustrate the very purpose of the statute. As applied in state courts, however, the effect of a broad formulation of § 2 is more troublesome. The reading of § 2 adopted today will displace many state statutes carefully calibrated to protect consumers, see, e.g., Mont.Code Ann. § 27–5–114(2)(b) (1993) (refusing to enforce arbitration clauses in consumer contracts where the consideration is $5,000 or less), and state procedural requirements aimed at ensuring knowing and voluntary consent, see, e.g., S.C.Code Ann. § 15–48–10(a) (Supp.1993) (requiring that notice of arbitration provision be prominently placed on first page of contract). I have long adhered to the view, discussed below, that Congress designed the Federal Arbitration Act to apply only in federal courts. But if we are to apply the Act in state courts, it makes little sense to read § 2 differently in that context. In the end, my agreement with the Court's construction of § 2 rests largely on the wisdom of maintaining a uniform standard.

I continue to believe that Congress never intended the Federal Arbitration Act to apply in state courts, and that this Court has strayed far afield in giving the Act so broad a compass....

Were we writing on a clean slate, I would adhere to that view and affirm the Alabama court's decision. But, as the Court points out, more than 10 years have passed since Southland, several subsequent cases have built upon its reasoning, and parties have undoubtedly made contracts in reliance on the Court's interpretation of the Act in the interim. After reflection, I am persuaded by considerations of stare decisis, which we have said "have special force in the area of statutory interpretation," Patterson v. McLean Credit Union, 491 U.S. 164, 172–173, 109 S.Ct. 2363, 2370–2371, 105 L.Ed.2d 132 (1989), to acquiesce in today's judgment. Though wrong, Southland has not proved unworkable, and, as always, "Congress remains free to alter what we have done." Ibid.

Today's decision caps this Court's effort to expand the Federal Arbitration Act. Although each decision has built logically upon the decisions preceding it, the initial building block in Southland laid a faulty foundation. I acquiesce in today's judgment because there is no "special justification" to overrule Southland. Arizona v. Rumsey, 467 U.S. 203, 212, 104 S.Ct. 2305, 2310–11, 81 L.Ed.2d 164 (1984). It remains now for Congress to correct this interpretation if it wishes to preserve state autonomy in state courts.

■ JUSTICE THOMAS, with whom JUSTICE SCALIA joins, dissenting.

I disagree with the majority at the threshold of this case, and so I do not reach the question that it decides. In my view, the Federal Arbitration Act (FAA) does not apply in state courts. I respectfully dissent.

I

In Southland Corp. v. Keating, 465 U.S. 1, 104 S.Ct. 852, 79 L.Ed.2d 1 (1984), this Court concluded that § 2 of the FAA "appl[ies] in state as well as federal courts," id., at 12, 104 S.Ct., at 859, and "withdr[aws] the power of the states to require a judicial forum for the resolution of claims which the contracting parties agreed to resolve by arbitration," id., at 10, 104 S.Ct., at 858. In my view, both aspects of Southland are wrong.

A

Section 2 of the FAA declares that an arbitration clause contained in "a contract evidencing a transaction involving commerce" shall be "valid, irrevocable, and enforceable, save upon such grounds as exist at law or in equity for the revocation of any contract." 9 U.S.C. § 2 ... On its face, and considered out of context, § 2 draws no apparent distinction between federal courts and state courts. But not until 1959—nearly 35 years after Congress enacted the FAA—did any court suggest that § 2 applied in state courts, ... and this Court waited until 1984 to conclude, over a strong dissent by Justice O'Connor, that § 2 extends to the States. See Southland, supra, 465 U.S., at 10–16, 104 S.Ct., at 858–861.

The explanation for this delay is simple: the statute that Congress enacted actually applies only in federal courts. At the time of the FAA's passage in 1925, laws governing the enforceability of arbitration agreements were generally thought to deal purely with matters of procedure rather than substance, because they were directed solely to the mechanisms for resolving the underlying disputes. As then-Judge Cardozo explained: "Arbitration is a form of procedure whereby differences may be settled. It is not a definition of the rights and wrongs out of which differences grow." Berkovitz v. Arbib & Houlberg, Inc., 230 N.Y. 261, 270, 130 N.E. 288, 290 (1921) (holding the New York arbitration statute of 1920, from which the FAA was copied, to be purely procedural). It would have been extraordinary for Congress to attempt to prescribe procedural rules for state courts. See, e.g., Ex parte Gounis, 304 Mo. 428, 437, 263 S.W. 988, 990 (1924) (describing the rule that Congress cannot "regulate or control [state courts'] modes of procedure" as one of the "general principles which have come to be accepted as settled constitutional law")....

It is easy to understand why lawyers in 1925 classified arbitration statutes as procedural. An arbitration agreement is a species of forum-selection clause: without laying down any rules of decision, it identifies the adjudicator of disputes. A strong argument can be made that such forum-selection clauses concern procedure rather than substance. Cf. Fed.Rules Civ.Proc. 73 (district court, with consent of the parties, may refer case to magistrate for resolution), 53 (district court may refer issues to special master). And if a contractual provision deals purely with matters of judicial procedure, one might well conclude that questions about whether and how it will be enforced also relate to procedure ...

The distinction between "substance" and "procedure" acquired new meaning after Erie Railroad Co. v. Tompkins, 304 U.S. 64, 58 S.Ct. 817, 82 L.Ed. 1188 (1938). Thus, in 1956 we held that for Erie purposes, the question whether a court should stay litigation brought in breach of an arbitration agreement is one of "substantive" law. Bernhardt v. Polygraphic Co. of America, Inc., 350 U.S. 198, 203–204, 76 S.Ct. 273, 276–277, 100 L.Ed. 199. But this later development could not change the original meaning of the statute that Congress enacted in 1925. Although Bernhardt classified portions of the FAA as "substantive" rather than "procedural," it does not mean that they were so understood in 1925 or that Congress extended the FAA's reach beyond the federal courts....

II

Rather than attempting to defend Southland on its merits, petitioners rely chiefly on the doctrine of stare decisis in urging us to adhere to our mistaken interpretation of the FAA. See Reply Brief for Petitioners 3–6. In my view, that doctrine is insufficient to save Southland.

The majority (ante, at 838) and Justice O'Connor (ante, at 844) properly focus on whether overruling Southland would frustrate the legitimate expectations of people who have drafted and executed contracts in the belief that even state courts will strictly enforce arbitration clauses. I do not doubt that innumerable contracts containing arbitration clauses have been written since 1984, or that arbitrable disputes might yet arise out of a large proportion of these contracts. Some of these contracts might well have been written differently in the absence of Southland. Still, I see no reason to think that the costs of overruling Southland are unacceptably high. Certainly no reliance interests are involved in cases like the present one, where the applicability of the FAA was not within the contemplation of the parties at the time of contracting. In many other cases, moreover, the parties will simply comply with their arbitration agreement, either on the theory that they should live up to their promises or on the theory that arbitration is the cheapest and best way of resolving their dispute. In a fair number of the remaining cases, the party seeking to enforce an arbitration agreement will be able to get into federal court, where the FAA will apply. And even if access to federal court is impossible (because § 2 creates no independent basis for federal-question jurisdiction), many cases will arise in States whose own law largely parallels the FAA. Only Alabama, Mississippi, and Nebraska still hold all executory arbitration agreements to be unenforceable, though some other States refuse to enforce particular classes of such agreements. See Strickland, The Federal Arbitration Act's Interstate Commerce Requirement: What's Left for State Arbitration Law?, 21 Hofstra L.Rev. 385, 401–403, and n. 93 (1992)....

Because I believe that the FAA ... is wholly inapplicable in [state] courts, I would affirm the Alabama Supreme Court's judgment.

[Justice SCALIA wrote a separate dissenting opinion in which he argued that "Adhering to Southland entails a permanent, unauthorized eviction of state-court power to adjudicate a potentially large class of disputes." He also stated that he "stand[s] ready to join four other Justices in overruling [Southland], since Southland will not become more correct over time, * * * the course of future lawmaking seems unlikely to be affected by its existence, and the accumulated private reliance will not likely increase beyond the level it has already achieved (few contracts not terminable at will have more than a 5–year term)".]

* * *

Note on the FAA's Reach Under the Commerce Clause

Ruling on the breadth of the FAA, the Court in *Perry* determined that Congress intended that the statute be enforceable to "the full reach of the Commerce Clause." The Court reiterated and amplified this holding in *Allied–Bruce Terminix*, but in that same term the Court also decided a case with far-reaching implications for the scope of the Commerce Power.

In *United States v. Lopez*, 514 U.S. 549 (1995), the Supreme Court, for the first time in almost sixty years and the ninth time in its history, struck down a federal statute for exceeding the scope of Congress' authority under the Commerce Clause. The Respondent, Alfonso Lopez, was convicted under the Gun–Free School Zones Act of 1990, which made the carrying of a gun within 1,000 feet of a school a federal offense. Lopez was convicted in district court, and the conviction was reversed by the Fifth Circuit. A five-justice majority invalidated the statute. The majority reaffirmed Congress' power to regulate under the clause in "three broad areas": (1) "the use of the channels of interstate commerce"; (2) "the instrumentalities of interstate commerce, or persons or things in interstate commerce, even though the threat [against which legislation is directed] may come only from intrastate activities"; and (3) "those activities having a substantial relation to interstate commerce." The *Lopez* case involved the third (and historically broadest) basis of the Commerce power. The Court reasoned that Congress can only regulate activities that "substantially affect interstate commerce" under the *NLRB v. Jones & Laughlin Steel Co.* line of cases if the activities so regulated are "commercial" in nature. Finding that "the possession of a gun in a local school zone is in no sense an economic activity," the Court, speaking through Chief Justice Rehnquist, concluded that the federal sovereign had no authority to criminalize the activity. In doing so, the Court rejected the government's proffered syllogism: the presence of weapons in or around schools interferes with the educational mission of schools; education is central to the national economy; therefore, the presence of guns in the vicinity of the nation's schools has predictably dire consequences for national productivity and thereby affects commerce.

The majority conceded that its distinction between commercial and noncommercial activity "may in some cases result in legal uncertainty." In an apparent effort to provide some guidance for future cases, the Court staked out certain areas of activity in which the states "have historically been sovereign," and which are thus by implication off limits to federal regulation: "family law . . . (including marriage, divorce, and child custody), [and] criminal law enforcement or education."

Justices Kennedy and Thomas concurred separately. Justice Kennedy emphasized the need for the regulated activity to have a "commercial character" and for the legislation itself to "have an evident commercial nexus" to withstand Commerce Clause scrutiny. Justice Breyer wrote the principal dissent, in which Justices Ginsburg, Souter and Stevens joined.

Lopez seemed to restrict the reach of the FAA under the Commerce Clause. Not so, said the Court in *Citizens Bank v. Alafabco, Inc.*, 539 U.S. 52 (2003). *Alafabco* involved a commercial loan contract containing an arbitration clause. Some courts, including the Alabama Supreme Court in this case, had taken the cramped view that to come within the purview of the FAA and Congress' Commerce Power, the underlying transaction, by itself, had to have a substantial effect on interstate commerce. In *Alafabco*, the Supreme Court rejected this view and held that the FAA is satisfied when either:

(1) The transaction at issue has *some* nexus to interstate commerce (e.g., in *Alafabco,* the borrower used the commercial loan money to conduct its business in multiple states, and the commercial loan

money was secured by the borrower inventory which came from different states), or

(2) The transaction at issue is economic in nature, and, when similar types of transactions are aggregated together, Congress could regulate the "general practice" of which the transaction is a part (e.g., in *Alafabco*, the Supreme Court did not doubt that Congress could regulate "commercial lending".) Only the general practice must "bear on interstate commerce in a substantial way."

In *Alafabco*, the Supreme Court held that "*Lopez* did not restrict the reach of the FAA."

* * *

Questions

1. The language of the FAA does not merely require a transaction "involving commerce"—a term which Justice Breyer equates with "affecting commerce" in *Allied–Bruce Terminix*—it also requires that there be a contract "evidencing" a transaction involving commerce. Was the Dobsons' contract to exterminate pests in their home clearly a "contract evidencing a transaction involving interstate commerce"?

2. Can a court determine whether a contract involves interstate commerce without examining the facts of the case? If a court examines the facts, is it displacing the role of the arbitrator?

3. The FAA was enacted in 1925, before the expansion of Congress' Commerce Power in the 1930s. Leaving aside the issue of whether the statutory grant should expand with the expanding interpretations of the Commerce Power, does the fact that the statute was passed before it was evident that the Commerce Power would be interpreted expansively suggest that the basis for the statute might have been Article III rather than the Commerce Power, as the dissenters in *Allied–Bruce* suggest?

4. How should *Alafabco* be reconciled with *Lopez*?

* * *

5. ENFORCEABILITY OF AGREEMENTS TO ARBITRATE

It is frequently stated that arbitration is a creature of contract. This axiom means that arbitration cannot be imposed on parties without their consent and that the form of arbitration to be used is determined by the parties' agreement. Similarly, the issues subject to arbitration are determined by the agreement between the parties. Traditionally, parties in contractual relations have used arbitration to resolve disputes that arise during the course of their contractual relationship about issues of contract interpretation, performance, and breach. The contractual core of arbitration means that arbitrators are expected to base their awards on the terms of the parties' agreement.[1]

Contracting parties often include broadly worded arbitration clauses in their agreements. A typical clause is one whereby the parties promise to arbitrate "all disputes that arise out of or in relation" to a specified transaction. In such cases, courts are called upon to decide how broadly to interpret the arbitration clause. For example, should a broad boilerplate arbitration clause be deemed to refer only to disputes over contractual interpretation and performance, or should it be deemed to refer also to disputes that arise outside of the parties' contractual obligations? For example, should a boilerplate clause obligate parties to arbitrate tort law claims that arise incidentally to their contractual dealings? Should such a clause compel arbitration of disputes over public law claims—claims that one side or the other has violated a statute? Or, to put it differently, should parties be able to use private contracting to take public law claims out of the courts and place them in an arbitral forum instead? To what extent should courts permit parties to select the forum for resolving their disputes when the disputes implicate issues of statutory or common law rights?

The Supreme Court has grappled with these questions in relation to the Federal Arbitration Act for fifty years. Initially the Court interpreted the FAA to compel arbitration of parties' contractual disputes, but not to compel arbitration of ancillary statutory or tort law claims. But in a series of cases in the 1980s, the Court reversed its previous position and found a large number of public law claims to be amenable to arbitration. These cases define the scope of arbitration today.

* * *

Wilko v. Swan

346 U.S. 427 (1953).

■ MR. JUSTICE REED delivered the opinion of the Court.

This action by petitioner, a customer, against respondents, partners in a securities brokerage firm, was brought in the United States District Court for the Southern District of New York, to recover damages under § 12(2) of the Securities Act of 1933. The complaint alleged that on or about January 17, 1951, through the instrumentalities of interstate commerce, petitioner was induced by Hayden, Stone and Company to purchase 1,600 shares of the common stock of Air Associates, Incorporated, by false representations that pursuant to a merger contract with the Borg Warner

1. In the past, arbitrators in some settings such as trade associations and craft guilds have used customs and norms of the trade as well as express contractual terms to inform their decisions. In these settings, the parties arguably understood that the arbitrator's role was not merely to interpret the parties' agreement, but it was also to impose on the parties the norms of the community within which the parties were mutually engaged. See, e.g., Katherine Van Wezel Stone, Rustic Justice: Community and Coercíon Under the Federal Arbitration Act, 77 U. N.Car. L. Rev. 931 (1999).

Corporation, Air Associates' stock would be valued at $6.00 per share over the then current market price, and that financial interests were buying up the stock for the speculative profit. It was alleged that he was not told that Haven B. Page (also named as a defendant but not involved in this review), a director of, and counsel for, Air Associates was then selling his own Air Associates' stock, including some or all that petitioner purchased. Two weeks after the purchase, petitioner disposed of the stock at a loss. Claiming that the loss was due to the firm's misrepresentations and omission of information concerning Mr. Page, he sought damages.

Without answering the complaint, the respondent moved to stay the trial of the action pursuant to § 3 of the United States Arbitration Act until an arbitration in accordance with the terms of identical margin agreements was had. An affidavit accompanied the motion stating that the parties' relationship was controlled by the terms of the agreements and that while the firm was willing to arbitrate petitioner had failed to seek or proceed with any arbitration of the controversy.

Finding that the margin agreements provide that arbitration should be the method of settling all future controversies, the District Court held that the agreement to arbitrate deprived petitioner of the advantageous court remedy afforded by the Securities Act, and denied the stay. A divided Court of Appeals concluded that the Act did not prohibit the agreement to refer future controversies to arbitration, and reversed.

The question is whether an agreement to arbitrate a future controversy is a "condition, stipulation, or provision binding any person acquiring any security to waive compliance with any provision" of the Securities Act which § 14[6] declares "void." We granted certiorari, 345 U.S. 969, 73 S.Ct. 1112, to review this important and novel federal question affecting both the Securities Act and the United States Arbitration Act . . .

In response to a Presidential message urging that there be added to the ancient rule of caveat emptor the further doctrine of "let the seller also beware," Congress passed the Securities Act of 1933. Designed to protect investors, the Act requires issuers, underwriters, and dealers to make full and fair disclosure of the character of securities sold in interstate and foreign commerce and to prevent fraud in their sale. To effectuate this policy, § 12(2) created a special right to recover for misrepresentation which differs substantially from the common-law action in that the seller is made to assume the burden of proving lack of scienter. The Act's special right is enforceable in any court of competent jurisdiction—federal or state—and removal from a state court is prohibited. If suit be brought in a federal court, the purchaser has a wide choice of venue, the privilege of nation-wide service of process and the jurisdictional $3,000 requirement of diversity cases is inapplicable.

6. 48 Stat. 84, 15 U.S.C. s 77n, 15 U.S.C.A. § 77n. Section 14 provides: "Any condition, stipulation, or provision binding any person acquiring any security to waive compliance with any provision of this subchapter or of the rules and regulations of the Commission shall be void."

The United States Arbitration Act establishes by statute the desirability of arbitration as an alternative to the complications of litigation. The reports of both Houses on that Act stress the need for avoiding the delay and expense of litigation, and practice under its terms raises hope for its usefulness both in controversies based on statutes or on standards otherwise created. This hospitable attitude of legislatures and courts toward arbitration, however, does not solve our question as to the validity of petitioner's stipulation by the margin agreements, set out below, to submit to arbitration controversies that might arise from the transactions.[15]

Petitioner argues that § 14, note 6, supra, shows that the purpose of Congress was to assure that sellers could not maneuver buyers into a position that might weaken their ability to recover under the Securities Act. He contends that arbitration lacks the certainty of a suit at law under the Act to enforce his rights. He reasons that the arbitration paragraph of the margin agreement is a stipulation that waives "compliance with" the provision of the Securities Act, set out in the margin, conferring jurisdiction of suits and special powers.

Respondent asserts that arbitration is merely a form of trial to be used in lieu of a trial at law, and therefore no conflict exists between the Securities Act and the United States Arbitration Act either in their language or in the congressional purposes in their enactment. Each may function within its own scope, the former to protect investors and the latter to simplify recovery for actionable violations of law by issuers or dealers in securities.

Respondent is in agreement with the Court of Appeals that the margin agreement arbitration paragraph, note 15, supra, does not relieve the seller from either liability or burden of proof, note 1, supra, imposed by the Securities Act. We agree that in so far as the award in arbitration may be affected by legal requirements, statutes or common law, rather than by considerations of fairness, the provisions of the Securities Act control. This is true even though this proposed agreement has no requirement that the arbitrators follow the law. This agreement of the parties as to the effect of the Securities Act includes also acceptance of the invalidity of the paragraph of the margin agreement that relieves the respondent sellers of liability for all "representation or advice by you or your employees or agents regarding the purchase or sale by me of any property. . . ."

The words of § 14, note 6, supra, void any "stipulation" waiving compliance with any "provision" of the Securities Act. This arrangement to arbitrate is a "stipulation," and we think the right to select the judicial forum is the kind of "provision" that cannot be waived under § 14 of the

15. "Any controversy arising between us under this contract shall be determined by arbitration pursuant to the Arbitration Law of the State of New York, and under the rules of either the Arbitration Committee of the Chamber of Commerce of the State of New York, or of the American Arbitration Association, or of the Arbitration Committee of the New York Stock Exchange or such other Exchange as may have jurisdiction over the matter in dispute, as I may elect. Any arbitration hereunder shall be before at least three arbitrators."

Securities Act. That conclusion is reached for the reasons set out above in the statement of petitioner's contention on this review. While a buyer and seller of securities, under some circumstances, may deal at arm's length on equal terms, it is clear that the Securities Act was drafted with an eye to the disadvantages under which buyers labor. Issuers of and dealers in securities have better opportunities to investigate and appraise the prospective earnings and business plans affecting securities than buyers. It is therefore reasonable for Congress to put buyers of securities covered by that Act on a different basis from other purchasers.

When the security buyer, prior to any violation of the Securities Act, waives his right to sue in courts, he gives up more than would a participant in other business transactions. The security buyer has a wider choice of courts and venue. He thus surrenders one of the advantages the Act gives him and surrenders it at a time when he is less able to judge the weight of the handicap the Securities Act places upon his adversary.

Even though the provisions of the Securities Act, advantageous to the buyer, apply, their effectiveness in application is lessened in arbitration as compared to judicial proceedings. Determination of the quality of a commodity or the amount of money due under a contract is not the type of issue here involved. This case requires subjective findings on the purpose and knowledge of an alleged violator of the Act. They must be not only determined but applied by the arbitrators without judicial instruction on the law. As their award may be made without explanation of their reasons and without a complete record of their proceedings, the arbitrators' conception of the legal meaning of such statutory requirements as "burden of proof," "reasonable care" or "material fact," see, note 1, supra, cannot be examined. Power to vacate an award is limited. While it may be true, as the Court of Appeals thought, that a failure of the arbitrators to decide in accordance with the provisions of the Securities Act would "constitute grounds for vacating the award pursuant to section 10 of the Federal Arbitration Act," that failure would need to be made clearly to appear. In unrestricted submission, such as the present margin agreements envisage, the interpretations of the law by the arbitrators in contrast to manifest disregard are not subject, in the federal courts, to judicial review for error in interpretation. The United States Arbitration Act contains no provision for judicial determination of legal issues such as is found in the English law. As the protective provisions of the Securities Act require the exercise of judicial direction to fairly assure their effectiveness, it seems to us that Congress must have intended § 4, note 6, supra, to apply to waiver of judicial trial and review. . . .

Two policies, not easily reconcilable, are involved in this case. Congress has afforded participants in transactions subject to its legislative power an opportunity generally to secure prompt, economical and adequate solution of controversies through arbitration if the parties are willing to accept less certainty of legally correct adjustment. On the other hand, it has enacted the Securities Act to protect the rights of investors and has forbidden a waiver of any of those rights. Recognizing the advantages that prior agreements for arbitration may provide for the solution of commercial controversies, we decide that the intention of Congress concerning the sale of securities is better carried out by holding invalid such an agreement for arbitration of issues arising under the Act.

Reversed.

■ MR. JUSTICE JACKSON, concurring.

I agree with the Court's opinion insofar as it construes the Securities Act to prohibit waiver of a judicial remedy in favor of arbitration by agreement made before any controversy arose. I think thereafter the parties could agree upon arbitration. However, I find it unnecessary in this case, where there has not been and could not be any arbitration, to decide that the Arbitration Act precludes any judicial remedy for the arbitrators' error of interpretation of a relevant statute.

■ MR. JUSTICE FRANKFURTER, whom MR. JUSTICE MINTON joins, dissenting.

If arbitration inherently precluded full protection of the rights § 12(2) of the Securities Act affords to a purchaser of securities, or if there were no effective means of ensuring judicial review of the legal basis of the arbitration, then, of course, an agreement to settle the controversy by arbitration would be barred by § 14, the anti-waiver provision, of that Act.

There is nothing in the record before us, nor in the facts of which we can take judicial notice, to indicate that the arbitral system as practiced in the City of New York, and as enforceable under the supervisory authority of the District Court for the Southern District of New York, would not afford the plaintiff the rights to which he is entitled.

The impelling considerations that led to the enactment of the Federal Arbitration Act are the advantages of providing a speedier, more economical and more effective enforcement of rights by way of arbitration than can be had by the tortuous course of litigation, especially in the City of New York. These advantages should not be assumed to be denied in controversies like that before us arising under the Securities Act, in the absence of any showing that settlement by arbitration would jeopardize the rights of the plaintiff.

Arbitrators may not disregard the law. Specifically they are, as Chief Judge Swan pointed out, "bound to decide in accordance with the provisions of section 12(2)." On this we are all agreed. It is suggested, however, that there is no effective way of assuring obedience by the arbitrators to the governing law. But since their failure to observe this law "would ... constitute grounds for vacating the award pursuant to section 10 of the Federal Arbitration Act," 201 F.2d 439, 445, appropriate means for judicial scrutiny must be implied, in the form of some record or opinion, however informal, whereby such compliance will appear, or want of it will upset the award.

We have not before us a case in which the record shows that the plaintiff in opening an account had no choice but to accept the arbitration stipulation, thereby making the stipulation an unconscionable and unenforceable provision in a business transaction. The Securities and Exchange Commission, as amicus curiae, does not contend that the stipulation which the Court of Appeals respected, under the appropriate safeguards defined by it, was a coercive practice by financial houses against customers incapable of self-protection. It is one thing to make out a case of overreaching as between parties bargaining not at arm's length. It is quite a different thing to find in the anti-waiver provision of the Securities Act a general limitation on the Federal Arbitration Act.

On the state of the record before us, I would affirm the decision of the Court of Appeals.

* * *

Questions

1. According to Justice Reed, what particular features of the Securities Act of 1933 suggest a Congressional intent to override the FAA? Could these features be interpreted in any other way?

2. Justice Frankfurter suggests that courts have the authority to overturn arbitration decisions that do not follow the law. Does the majority agree? Is Frankfurter basing this claim on the FAA? If not, then on what authority does he rely?

3. Justice Frankfurter's dissent suggests that arbitrators have an obligation to explain their awards with written opinions, yet the American Arbitration Association takes the opposite position in its Commercial Arbitration Rules. The AAA advises arbitrators in commercial cases not to write opinions unless both parties request them to do so. What are the pros and cons of Frankfurter's position? Why might the AAA take the position it does?

* * *

Dean Witter Reynolds, Inc. v. Byrd

470 U.S. 213 (1985).

■ JUSTICE MARSHALL delivered the opinion of the Court.

The question presented is whether, when a complaint raises both federal securities claims and pendent state claims, a Federal District Court may deny a motion to compel arbitration of the state-law claims despite the parties' agreement to arbitrate their disputes. We granted certiorari to resolve a conflict among the Federal Courts of Appeals on this question. 467 U.S. 1240, 104 S.Ct. 3509, 82 L.Ed.2d 818 (1984).

I

In 1981, A. Lamar Byrd sold his dental practice and invested $160,000 in securities through Dean Witter Reynolds Inc., a securities broker-dealer. The value of the account declined by more than $100,000 between September 1981 and March 1982. Byrd filed a complaint against Dean Witter in the United States District Court for the Southern District of California, alleging a violation of §§ 10(b), 15(c), and 20 of the Securities Exchange Act of 1934, 15 U.S.C. §§ 78j(b), 78o(c), and 78t, and of various state-law provisions. Federal jurisdiction over the state-law claims was based on diversity of citizenship and the principle of pendent jurisdiction. In the complaint, Byrd alleged that an agent of Dean Witter had traded in his account without his prior consent, that the number of transactions executed on behalf of the account was excessive, that misrepresentations were made by an agent of Dean Witter as to the status of the account, and that the agent acted with Dean Witter's knowledge, participation, and ratification.

When Byrd invested his funds with Dean Witter in 1981, he signed a Customer's Agreement providing that "[a]ny controversy between you and the undersigned arising out of or relating to this contract or the breach thereof, shall be settled by arbitration." App. to Pet. for Cert. 11. Dean Witter accordingly filed a motion for an order severing the pendent state claims, compelling their arbitration, and staying arbitration of those claims pending resolution of the federal-court action. App. 12. It argued that the Federal Arbitration Act (Arbitration Act or Act), 9 U.S.C. §§ 1–14, which provides that arbitration agreements "shall be valid, irrevocable, and enforceable, save upon such grounds as exist at law or in equity for the revocation of any contract," § 2, required that the District Court compel arbitration of the state-law claims. The Act authorizes parties to an arbitration agreement to petition a federal district court for an order compelling arbitration under *Wilko*, of any issue referable to arbitration under the agreement. §§ 3, 4. Because Dean Witter assumed that the federal securities claim was not subject to the arbitration provision of the contract and could be resolved only in the federal forum, it did not seek to compel arbitration of that claim. The District Court denied in its entirety the motion to sever and compel arbitration of the pendent state claims, and on an interlocutory appeal the Court of Appeals for the Ninth Circuit affirmed. 726 F.2d 552 (1984).

II

Confronted with the issue we address—whether to compel arbitration of pendent state-law claims when the federal court will in any event assert jurisdiction over a federal-law claim—the Federal Courts of Appeals have adopted two different approaches. Along with the Ninth Circuit in this case, the Fifth and Eleventh Circuits have relied on the "doctrine of intertwining." When arbitrable and nonarbitrable claims arise out of the same transaction, and are sufficiently intertwined factually and legally, the district court, under this view, may in its discretion deny arbitration as to the arbitrable claims and try all the claims together in federal court. These courts acknowledge the strong federal policy in favor of enforcing arbitration agreements but offer two reasons why the district courts nevertheless should decline to compel arbitration in this situation. First, they assert that such a result is necessary to preserve what they consider to be the court's exclusive jurisdiction over the federal securities claim; otherwise, they suggest, arbitration of an "intertwined" state claim might precede the federal proceeding and the fact finding done by the arbitrator might thereby bind the federal court through collateral estoppel. The second reason they cite is efficiency; by declining to compel arbitration, the court avoids bifurcated proceedings and perhaps redundant efforts to litigate the same factual questions twice.

In contrast, the Sixth, Seventh, and Eighth Circuits have held that the Arbitration Act divests the district courts of any discretion regarding arbitration in cases containing both arbitrable and nonarbitrable claims, and instead requires that the courts compel arbitration of arbitrable claims, when asked to do so. These courts conclude that the Act, both through its plain meaning and the strong federal policy it reflects, requires courts to enforce the bargain of the parties to arbitrate, and "not substitute [its] own views of economy and efficiency" for those of Congress. Dickinson v. Heinold Securities, Inc., 661 F.2d 638, 646 (C.A.7 1981).

We agree with these latter courts that the Arbitration Act requires district courts to compel arbitration of pendent arbitrable claims when one of the parties files a motion to compel, even where the result would be the possibly inefficient maintenance of separate proceedings in different forums. Accordingly, we reverse the decision not to compel arbitration.

III

The Arbitration Act provides that written agreements to arbitrate controversies arising out of an existing contract "shall be valid, irrevocable, and enforceable, save upon such grounds as exist at law or in equity for the revocation of any contract." 9 U.S.C. § 2. By its terms, the Act leaves no place for the exercise of discretion by a district court, but instead mandates that district courts shall direct the parties to proceed to arbitration on issues as to which an arbitration agreement has been signed. §§ 3, 4. Thus, insofar as the language of the Act guides our disposition of this case, we would conclude that agreements to arbitrate must be enforced, absent a ground for revocation of the contractual agreement.

It is suggested, however, that the Act does not expressly address whether the same mandate—to enforce arbitration agreements—holds true where, as here, such a course would result in bifurcated proceedings if the arbitration agreement is enforced. Because the Act's drafters did not explicitly consider the prospect of bifurcated proceedings, we are told, the clear language of the Act might be misleading. Thus, courts that have adopted the view of the Ninth Circuit in this case have argued that the Act's goal of speedy and efficient decision making is thwarted by bifurcated proceedings, and that, given the absence of clear direction on this point, the intent of Congress in passing the Act controls and compels a refusal to compel arbitration. They point out, in addition, that in the past the Court on occasion has identified a contrary federal interest sufficiently compelling to outweigh the mandate of the Arbitration Act, see n. 1, supra, and they conclude that the interest in speedy resolution of claims should do so in this case. See, e.g., Miley v. Oppenheimer & Co., 637 F.2d 318, 336 (5th Cir. 1981); Cunningham v. Dean Witter Reynolds, Inc., 550 F.Supp. 578, 585 (E.D.Cal. 1982).

We turn, then, to consider whether the legislative history of the Act provides guidance on this issue. The congressional history does not expressly direct resolution of the scenario we address. We conclude, however, on consideration of Congress' intent in passing the statute, that a court must compel arbitration of otherwise arbitrable claims, when a motion to compel arbitration is made.

The legislative history of the Act establishes that the purpose behind its passage was to ensure judicial enforcement of privately made agreements to arbitrate. We therefore reject the suggestion that the overriding goal of the Arbitration Act was to promote the expeditious resolution of claims. The Act, after all, does not mandate the arbitration of all claims, but merely the enforcement—upon the motion of one of the parties—of privately negotiated arbitration agreements. The House Report accompanying the Act makes clear that its purpose was to place an arbitration agreement "upon the same footing as other contracts, where it belongs," H.R.Rep. No. 96, 68th Cong., 1st Sess., 1 (1924), and to overrule the judiciary's longstanding refusal to enforce agreements to arbitrate. This is not to say that Congress was blind to the potential benefit of the legislation for expedited resolution of disputes. Far from it, the House Report expressly observed:

> It is practically appropriate that the action should be taken at this time when there is so much agitation against the costliness and delays of litigation. These matters can be largely eliminated by agreements for arbitration, if arbitration agreements are made valid and enforceable. Id., at 2.

Nonetheless, passage of the Act was motivated, first and foremost, by a congressional desire to enforce agreements into which parties had entered, and we must not overlook this principal objective when construing the statute, or allow the fortuitous impact of the Act on efficient dispute resolution to overshadow the underlying motivation . . .

We therefore are not persuaded by the argument that the conflict between two goals of the Arbitration Act—enforcement of private agreements and encouragement of efficient and speedy dispute resolution—must be resolved in favor of the latter in order to realize the intent of the drafters. The preeminent concern of Congress in passing the Act was to enforce private agreements into which parties had entered, and that concern requires that we rigorously enforce agreements to arbitrate, even if the result is "piecemeal" litigation, at least absent a countervailing policy manifested in another federal statute. See n. 1, supra. By compelling arbitration of state-law claims, a district court successfully protects the contractual rights of the parties and their rights under the Arbitration Act.

IV

It is also suggested, however, and some Courts of Appeals have held, that district courts should decide arbitrable pendent claims when a nonarbitrable federal claim is before them, because otherwise the findings in the arbitration proceeding might have collateral-estoppel effect in a subsequent federal proceeding. This preclusive effect is believed to pose a threat to the federal interest in resolution of securities claims, and to warrant a refusal to compel arbitration. Other courts have held that the claims should be separately resolved, but that this preclusive effect warrants a stay of arbitration proceedings pending resolution of the federal securities claim. In this case, Dean Witter also asked the District Court to stay the arbitration proceedings pending resolution of the federal claim, and we suspect it did so in response to such holdings.

We believe that the preclusive effect of arbitration proceedings is significantly less well settled than the lower court opinions might suggest, and that the consequences of this misconception has been the formulation of unnecessarily contorted procedures. We conclude that neither a stay of proceedings, nor joined proceedings, is necessary to protect the federal interest in the federal-court proceeding, and that the formulation of collateral-estoppel rules affords adequate protection to that interest.

Initially, it is far from certain that arbitration proceedings will have any preclusive effect on the litigation of nonarbitrable federal claims. Just last Term, we held that neither the full-faith-and-credit provision of 28 U.S.C. § 1738, nor a judicially fashioned rule of preclusion, permits a federal court to accord res judicata or collateral-estoppel effect to an unappealed arbitration award in a case brought under 42 U.S.C. § 1983. McDonald v. West Branch, 466 U.S. 284, 104 S.Ct. 1799, 80 L.Ed.2d 302 (1984). The full-faith-and-credit statute requires that federal courts give the same preclusive effect to a State's judicial proceedings as would the courts of the State rendering the judgment, and since arbitration is not a judicial proceeding, we held that the statute does not apply to arbitration awards. Id., at 287–288, 104 S.Ct., at 1801–1802. The same analysis inevitably would apply to any unappealed state arbitration proceedings. We also declined, in *McDonald*, to fashion a federal common-law rule of preclusion, in part on the ground that arbitration cannot provide an adequate substitute for a judicial proceeding in protecting the federal statutory and constitutional rights that § 1983 is designed to safeguard. We therefore recognized that arbitration proceedings will not necessarily have a preclusive effect on subsequent federal-court proceedings.

Significantly, *McDonald* also establishes that courts may directly and effectively protect federal interests by determining the preclusive effect to be given to an arbitration proceeding. Since preclusion doctrine comfortably plays this role, it follows that neither a stay of the arbitration proceedings, nor a refusal to compel arbitration of state claims, is required in order to assure that a precedent arbitration does not impede a subsequent federal-court action. The Courts of Appeals that have assumed collateral-estoppel effect must be given to arbitration proceedings have therefore sought to accomplish indirectly that which they erroneously assumed they could not do directly.

The question of what preclusive effect, if any, the arbitration proceedings might have is not yet before us, however, and we do not decide it. The collateral-estoppel effect of an arbitration proceeding is at issue only after arbitration is completed, of course, and we therefore have no need to consider now whether the analysis in *McDonald* encompasses this case. Suffice it to say that in framing preclusion rules in this context, courts shall take into account the federal interests warranting protection. As a result, there is no reason to require that district courts decline to compel arbitration, or manipulate the ordering of the resulting bifurcated proceedings, simply to avoid an infringement of federal interests.

Finding unpersuasive the arguments advanced in support of the ruling below, we hold that the District Court erred in refusing to grant the motion of Dean Witter to compel arbitration of the pendent state claims. Accordingly, we reverse the decision of the Court of Appeals insofar as it upheld the District Court's denial of the motion to compel arbitration, and we remand for further proceedings consistent with this opinion.

It is so ordered.

■ JUSTICE WHITE, concurring.

I join the Court's opinion. I write separately only to add a few words regarding two issues that it leaves undeveloped.

The premise of the controversy before us is that respondent's claims under the Securities Exchange Act of 1934 are not arbitrable, notwithstanding the contrary agreement of the parties. The Court's opinion rightly concludes that the question whether that is so is not before us. Ante, at 1240, n. 1. Nonetheless, I note that this is a matter of substantial doubt. In Wilko v. Swan, 346 U.S. 427, 74 S.Ct. 182, 98 L.Ed. 168 (1953), the Court held arbitration agreements unenforceable with regard to claims under § 12(2) the 1933 Act . . .

Wilko's reasoning cannot be mechanically transplanted to the 1934 Act. While § 29 of that Act, 15 U.S.C. § 78cc(a), is equivalent to § 14 of the 1933 Act, counterparts of the other two provisions are imperfect or absent altogether. Jurisdiction under the 1934 Act is narrower, being restricted to the federal courts. 15 U.S.C. § 78aa. More important, the cause of action under § 10(b) and Rule 10b–5, involved here, is implied rather than express.... The phrase "waive compliance with any *provision of this chapter*," 15 U.S.C. § 78cc(a) (emphasis added), is thus literally inapplicable. Moreover, *Wilko's* solicitude for the federal cause of action—the "special right" established by Congress, 346 U.S., at 431, 74 S.Ct., at 184—is not necessarily appropriate where the cause of action is judicially implied and not so different from the common-law action.

. . . The Court's opinion makes clear that a district court should not stay arbitration, or refuse to compel it at all, for fear of its preclusive effect. And I can perceive few, if any, other possible reasons for staying the arbitration pending the outcome of the lawsuit. Belated enforcement of the arbitration clause, though a less substantial interference than a refusal to enforce it at all, nonetheless significantly disappoints the expectations of the parties and frustrates the clear purpose of their agreement. In addition, once it is decided that the two proceedings are to go forward independently, the concern for speedy resolution suggests that neither should be delayed. While the impossibility of the lawyers being in two places at once may require some accommodation in scheduling, it seems to me that the heavy presumption should be that the arbitration and the lawsuit will each proceed in its normal course. And while the matter remains to be determined by the District Court, I see nothing in the record before us to indicate that arbitration in the present case should be stayed.

* * *

Questions

1. To what extent do the majority and concurring opinions in *Byrd* modify the holding of *Wilko*?

2. What does the Court in *Byrd* say about the effect of an arbitral ruling on a federal court's subsequent determination of a federal claim? Is it possible that an arbitral award, while not technically preclusive, could have a *de facto* preclusive effect? Is the Court's analogy to its treatment of full-faith-and-credit preclusion persuasive? What are the relevant differences?

3. Does the Court suggest that federal courts should decide on a case-by-case basis what collateral-estoppel effect to give an arbitral award? If so, what factors should a court use to make that determination? Can a court make that determination without considering the merits of the arbitrated claim? Does this amount to de facto judicial review of the merits of an arbitration award?

4. The Court in *Byrd* states that there is a tension between two goals of the FAA—to provide expeditious resolution of disputes and to enforce private agreements to arbitrate. It concludes that when these goals are in tension, the latter should take precedence. On what basis is it making this choice? What are the consequences of this interpretation for the FAA?

* * *

Scherk v. Alberto–Culver Company

417 U.S. 506 (1974).

■ MR. JUSTICE STEWART delivered the opinion of the Court.

Alberto–Culver Co., the respondent, is an American company incorporated in Delaware with its principal office in Illinois. It manufactures and distributes toiletries and hair products in this country and abroad. During the 1960s Alberto–Culver decided to expand its overseas operations, and as part of this program it approached the petitioner Fritz Scherk, a German citizen residing at the time of trial in Switzerland. Scherk was the owner of three interrelated business entities, organized under the laws of Germany and Liechtenstein, that were engaged in the manufacture of toiletries and the licensing of trademarks for such toiletries. An initial contact with Scherk was made by a representative of Alberto–Culver in Germany in June 1967, and negotiations followed at further meetings in both Europe and the United States during 1967 and 1968. In February 1969 a contract was signed in Vienna, Austria, which provided for the transfer of the ownership of Scherk's enterprises to Alberto–Culver, along with all rights held by these enterprises to trademarks in cosmetic goods. The contract contained a number of express warranties whereby Scherk guaranteed the sole and unencumbered ownership of these trademarks. In addition, the contract contained an arbitration clause providing that "any controversy or claim (that) shall arise out of this agreement or the breach thereof" would be referred to arbitration before the International Chamber of Commerce in Paris, France, and that "(t)he laws of the State of Illinois, U.S.A. shall apply to and govern this agreement, its interpretation and performance."[1]

The closing of the transaction took place in Geneva, Switzerland, in June 1969. Nearly one year later Alberto–Culver allegedly discovered that the trademark rights purchased under the contract were subject to substantial encumbrances that threatened to give others superior rights to the trademarks and to restrict or preclude Alberto–Culver's use of them. Alberto–Culver thereupon tendered back to Scherk the property that had been transferred to it and offered to rescind the contract. Upon Scherk's refusal, Alberto–Culver commenced this action for damages and other relief in a Federal District Court in Illinois, contending that Scherk's fraudulent representations concerning the status of the trademark rights constituted violations of § 10(b) of the Securities Exchange Act of 1934, . . . and Rule 10b–5 promulgated thereunder . . .

In response, Scherk filed a motion to dismiss the action for want of personal and subject-matter jurisdiction as well as on the basis of forum non conveniens, or, alternatively, to stay the action pending arbitration in Paris pursuant to the agreement of the parties. Alberto–Culver, in turn, opposed this motion and sought a preliminary injunction restraining the prosecution of arbitration proceedings. On December 2, 1971, the District Court denied Scherk's motion to dismiss, and, on January 14, 1972, it granted a preliminary order enjoining Scherk from proceeding with arbitration. In taking these actions the court relied entirely on this Court's

1. The arbitration clause relating to the transfer of one of Scherk's business entities, similar to the clauses covering the other two, reads in its entirety as follows:

> The parties agree that if any controversy or claim shall arise out of this agreement or the breach thereof and either party shall request that the matter shall be settled by arbitration, the matter shall be settled exclusively by arbitration in accordance with the rules then obtaining of the International Chamber of Commerce, Paris, France.... All arbitration proceedings shall be held in Paris, France, and each party agrees to comply in all respects with any award made in any such proceeding and to the entry of a judgment in any jurisdiction upon any award rendered in such proceeding. The laws of the State of Illinois, U.S.A. shall apply to and govern this agreement, its interpretation and performance.

decision in Wilko v. Swan, 346 U.S. 427, 74 S.Ct. 182, 98 L.Ed. 168, which held that an agreement to arbitrate could not preclude a buyer of a security from seeking a judicial remedy under the Securities Act of 1933, in view of the language of § 14 of that Act, barring "(a)ny condition, stipulation, or provision binding any person acquiring any security to waive compliance with any provision of this subchapter" ... The Court of Appeals for the Seventh Circuit, with one judge dissenting, affirmed, upon what it considered the controlling authority of the Wilko decision. 484 F.2d 611. Because of the importance of the question presented we granted Scherk's petition for a writ of certiorari. 414 U.S. 1156, 94 S.Ct. 913, 39 L.Ed.2d 108.

I

The United States Arbitration Act, now 9 U.S.C. § 1 et seq., reversing centuries of judicial hostility to arbitration agreements, was designed to allow parties to avoid "the costliness and delays of litigation," and to place arbitration agreements "upon the same footing as other contracts".... Accordingly the Act provides that an arbitration agreement such as is here involved "shall be valid, irrevocable, and enforceable, save upon such grounds as exist at law or in equity for the revocation of any contract." 9 U.S.C. § 2. The Act also provides in § 3 for a stay of proceedings in a case where a court is satisfied that the issue before it is arbitrable under the agreement, and § 4 of the Act directs a federal court to order parties to proceed to arbitration if there has been a "failure, neglect, or refusal" of any party to honor an agreement to arbitrate.

In Wilko v. Swan, supra, this Court acknowledged that the Act reflects a legislative recognition of the "desirability of arbitration as an alternative to the complications of litigation," 346 U.S., at 431, 74 S.Ct., at 185, but nonetheless declined to apply the Act's provisions ...[6] Thus, Wilko's advance agreement to arbitrate any disputes subsequently arising out of his contract to purchase the securities was unenforceable under the terms of § 14 of the Securities Act of 1933.

Alberto–Culver, relying on this precedent, contends that the District Court and Court of Appeals were correct in holding that its agreement to arbitrate disputes arising under the contract with Scherk is similarly unenforceable in view of its contentions that Scherk's conduct constituted violations of the Securities Exchange Act of 1934 and rules promulgated

6. The arbitration agreement involved in *Wilko* was contained in a standard form margin contract. But see the dissenting opinion of Mr. Justice Frankfurter, 346 U.S. 427, 439, 440, 74 S.Ct. 182, 189, concluding that the record did not show that "the plaintiff (Wilko) in opening an account had no choice but to accept the arbitration stipulation...." The petitioner here would limit the decision in *Wilko* to situations where the parties exhibit a disparity of bargaining power, and contends that, since the negotiations leading to the present contract took place over a number of years and involved the participation on both sides of knowledgeable and sophisticated business and legal experts, the *Wilko* decision should not apply. See also the dissenting opinion of Judge Stevens of the Court of Appeals in this case, 484 F.2d 611, 615. Because of our disposition of this case on other grounds, we need not consider this contention.

thereunder. For the reasons that follow, we reject this contention and hold that the provisions of the Arbitration Act cannot be ignored in this case.

At the outset, a colorable argument could be made that even the semantic reasoning of the *Wilko* opinion does not control the case before us. Wilko concerned a suit brought under § 12(2) of the Securities Act of 1933, which provides a defrauded purchaser with the "special right" of a private remedy for civil liability, 346 U.S., at 431, 74 S.Ct., at 184. There is no statutory counterpart of § 12(2) in the Securities Exchange Act of 1934, and neither § 10(b) of that Act nor Rule 10b–5 speaks of a private remedy to redress violations of the kind alleged here. While federal case law has established that § 10(b) and Rule 10b–5 create an implied private cause of action, see 6 L. Loss, Securities Regulation 3869–3873 (1969) and cases cited therein; ... the Act itself does not establish the "special right" that the Court in *Wilko* found significant ...

Accepting the premise, however, that the operative portions of the language of the 1933 Act relied upon in *Wilko* are contained in the Securities Exchange Act of 1934, the respondent's reliance on Wilko in this case ignores the significant and, we find, crucial differences between the agreement involved in Wilko and the one signed by the parties here. Alberto–Culver's contract to purchase the business entities belonging to Scherk was a truly international agreement. Alberto–Culver is an American corporation with its principal place of business and the vast bulk of its activity in this country, while Scherk is a citizen of Germany whose companies were organized under the laws of Germany and Liechtenstein. The negotiations leading to the signing of the contract in Austria and to the closing in Switzerland took place in the United States, England, and Germany, and involved consultations with legal and trademark experts from each of those countries and from Liechtenstein. Finally, and most significantly, the subject matter of the contract concerned the sale of business enterprises organized under the laws of and primarily situated in European countries, whose activities were largely, if not entirely, directed to European markets.

Such a contract involves considerations and policies significantly different from those found controlling in *Wilko*. In *Wilko*, quite apart from the arbitration provision, there was no question but that the laws of the United States generally, and the federal securities laws in particular, would govern disputes arising out of the stock-purchase agreement. The parties, the negotiations, and the subject matter of the contract were all situated in this country, and no credible claim could have been entertained that any international conflict-of-laws problems would arise. In this case, by contrast, in the absence of the arbitration provision considerable uncertainty existed at the time of the agreement, and still exists, concerning the law applicable to the resolution of disputes arising out of the contract.

Such uncertainty will almost inevitably exist with respect to any contract touching two or more countries, each with its own substantive laws and conflict-of-laws rules. A contractual provision specifying in advance the forum in which disputes shall be litigated and the law to be applied is, therefore, an almost indispensable precondition to achievement of the orderliness and predictability essential to any international business transaction. Furthermore, such a provision obviates the danger that a dispute under the agreement might be submitted to a forum hostile to the interests of one of the parties or unfamiliar with the problem area involved.

A parochial refusal by the courts of one country to enforce an international arbitration agreement would not only frustrate these purposes, but would invite unseemly and mutually destructive jockeying by the parties to secure tactical litigation advantages. In the present case, for example, it is not inconceivable that if Scherk had anticipated that Alberto–Culver would be able in this country to enjoin resort to arbitration he might have sought an order in France or some other country enjoining Alberto–Culver from proceeding with its litigation in the United States. Whatever recognition the courts of this country might ultimately have granted to the order of the foreign court, the dicey atmosphere of such a legal no-man's-land would surely damage the fabric of international commerce and trade, and imperil the willingness and ability of businessmen to enter into international commercial agreements.[11]

The exception to the clear provisions of the Arbitration Act carved out by *Wilko* is simply inapposite to a case such as the one before us. In *Wilko* the Court reasoned that "(w)hen the security buyer, prior to any violation of the Securities Act, waives his right to sue in courts, he gives up more than would a participant in other business transactions. The security buyer has a wider choice of courts and venue. He thus surrenders one of the advantages the Act gives him...." 346 U.S., at 435, 74 S.Ct., at 187. In the context of an international contract, however, these advantages become chimerical since, as indicated above, an opposing party may by speedy resort to a foreign court block or hinder access to the American court of the purchaser's choice.

Two Terms ago in The Bremen v. Zapata Off–Shore Co., 407 U.S. 1, 92 S.Ct. 1907, 32 L.Ed.2d 513, we rejected the doctrine that a forum-selection clause of a contract, although voluntarily adopted by the parties, will not be respected in a suit brought in the United States "unless the selected state

11. The dissenting opinion argues that our conclusion that *Wilko* is inapplicable to the situation presented in this case will vitiate the force of that decision because parties to transactions with many more direct contacts with this country than in the present case will nonetheless be able to invoke the "talisman" of having an "international contract." Post, at 2461. Concededly, situations may arise where the contacts with foreign countries are so insignificant or attenuated that the holding in *Wilko* would meaningfully apply. Judicial response to such situations can and should await future litigation in concrete cases. This case, however, provides no basis for a judgment that only United States laws and United States courts should determine this controversy in the face of a solemn agreement between the parties that such controversies be resolved elsewhere. The only contact between the United States and the transaction involved here is the fact that Alberto–Culver is an American corporation and the occurrence of some—but by no means the greater part—of the pre-contract negotiations in this country. To determine that "American standards of fairness," post, at 2461, must nonetheless govern the controversy demeans the standards of justice elsewhere in the world, and unnecessarily exalts the primacy of United States law over the laws of other countries.

would provide a more convenient forum than the state in which suit is brought." Id., at 7, 92 S.Ct., at 1912. Rather, we concluded that a "forum clause should control absent a strong showing that it should be set aside." Id., at 15, 92 S.Ct., at 1916. We noted that "much uncertainty and possibly great inconvenience to both parties could arise if a suit could be maintained in any jurisdiction in which an accident might occur or if jurisdiction were left to any place (where personal or in rem jurisdiction might be established). The elimination of all such uncertainties by agreeing in advance on a forum acceptable to both parties is an indispensable element in international trade, commerce, and contracting." Id., at 13 . . .

An agreement to arbitrate before a specified tribunal is, in effect, a specialized kind of forum-selection clause that posits not only the situs of suit but also the procedure to be used in resolving the dispute. The invalidation of such an agreement in the case before us would not only allow the respondent to repudiate its solemn promise but would, as well, reflect a "parochial concept that all disputes must be resolved under our laws and in our courts . . . We cannot have trade and commerce in world markets and international waters exclusively on our terms, governed by our laws, and resolved in our courts." Id., at 9, 92 S.Ct., at 1912.

For all these reasons we hold that the agreement of the parties in this case to arbitrate any dispute arising out of their international commercial transaction is to be respected and enforced by the federal courts in accord with the explicit provisions of the Arbitration Act.

Accordingly, the judgment of the Court of Appeals is reversed and the case is remanded to that court with directions to remand to the District Court for further proceedings consistent with this opinion.

■ MR. JUSTICE DOUGLAS, with whom MR. JUSTICE BRENNAN, MR. JUSTICE WHITE, and MR. JUSTICE MARSHALL concur, dissenting.

. . . The basic dispute between the parties concerned allegations that the trademarks which were basic assets in the transaction were encumbered and that their purchase was induced through serious instances of fraudulent representations and omissions by Scherk and his agents within the jurisdiction of the United States. If a question of trademarks were the only one involved, the principle of The Bremen v. Zapata Off–Shore Co., 407 U.S. 1, 92 S.Ct. 1907, 32 L.Ed.2d 513, would be controlling.

We have here, however, questions under the Securities Exchange Act of 1934 . . .

. . . It could perhaps be argued that *Wilko* does not govern because it involved a little customer pitted against a big brokerage house, while we deal here with sophisticated buyers and sellers: Scherk, a powerful German operator, and Alberto–Culver, an American business surrounded and protected by lawyers and experts. But that would miss the point of the problem. The Act does not speak in terms of "sophisticated" as opposed to "unsophisticated" people dealing in securities. The rules when the giants play are the same as when the pygmies enter the market.

If there are victims here, they are not Alberto–Culver the corporation, but the thousands of investors who are the security holders in Alberto–Culver. If there is fraud and the promissory notes are excessive, the impact is on the equity in Alberto–Culver....

There has been much support for arbitration of disputes; and it may be the superior way of settling some disagreements. If A and B were quarreling over a trade-mark and there was an arbitration clause in the contract, the policy of Congress in implementing the United Nations Convention on the Recognition and Enforcement of Foreign Arbitral Awards, as it did in 9 U.S.C. § 201 et seq., would prevail. But the Act does not substitute an arbiter for the settlement of disputes under the 1933 and 1934 Acts. Art. II(3) of the Convention says:

> The court of a Contracting State, when seized of an action in a matter in respect of which the parties have made an agreement within the meaning of this article, shall, at the request of one of the parties, refer the parties to arbitration, unless it finds that the said agreement is null and void, inoperative or incapable of being performed....

But § 29(a) of the 1934 Act makes agreements to arbitrate liabilities under § 10 of the Act "void" and "inoperative." Congress has specified a precise way whereby big and small investors will be protected and the rules under which the Alberto–Culvers of this Nation shall operate. They or their lawyers cannot waive those statutory conditions, for our corporate giants are not principalities of power but guardians of a host of wards unable to care for themselves. It is these wards that the 1934 Act tries to protect ... It is peculiarly appropriate that we adhere to *Wilko*—more so even than when *Wilko* was decided. Huge foreign investments are being made in our companies. It is important that American standards of fairness in security dealings govern the destinies of American investors until Congress changes these standards.

... The Court appears to attach some significance to the fact that the specific provisions of the 1933 Act involved in *Wilko* are not duplicated in the 1934 Act, which is involved in this case. While Alberto–Culver would not have the right to sue in either a state or federal forum as did the plaintiff in *Wilko*, 346 U.S., at 431, 74 S.Ct., at 184, the Court deprives it of its right to have its Rule 10b–5 claim heard in a federal court. We spoke at length in *Wilko* of this problem, elucidating the undesirable effects of remitting a securities plaintiff to an arbitral, rather than a judicial, forum. Here, as in *Wilko*, the allegations of fraudulent misrepresentation will involve "subjective findings on the purpose and knowledge" of the defendant, questions ill-determined by arbitrators without judicial instruction on the law. See id., at 435, 74 S.Ct., at 187. An arbitral award can be made without explication of reasons and without development of a record, so that the arbitrator's conception of our statutory requirement may be absolutely incorrect yet functionally unreviewable, even when the arbitrator seeks to apply our law. We recognized in *Wilko* that there is no judicial review corresponding to review of court decisions. Id., at 436–437, 74 S.Ct., at 187–188. The extensive pretrial discovery provided by the Federal Rules of Civil

Procedure for actions in district court would not be available. And the wide choice of venue provided by the 1934 Act, 15 U.S.C. § 78aa, would be forfeited. See Wilko v. Swan, supra, at 431, 435, 74 S.Ct. at 186. The loss of the proper judicial forum carries with it the loss of substantial rights.

When a defendant, as alleged here, has, through proscribed acts within our territory, brought itself within the ken of federal securities regulation, a fact not disputed here, those laws—including the controlling principles of *Wilko*—apply whether the defendant is foreign or American, and whether or not there are transnational elements in the dealings. Those laws are rendered a chimera when foreign corporations or funds—unlike domestic defendants—can nullify them by virtue of arbitration clauses which send defrauded American investors to the uncertainty of arbitration on foreign soil, or, if those investors cannot afford to arbitrate their claims in a far-off forum, to no remedy at all.

Moreover, the international aura which the Court gives this case is ominous. We now have many multinational corporations in vast operations around the world—Europe, Latin America, the Middle East, and Asia. The investments of many American investors turn on dealings by these companies. Up to this day, it has been assumed by reason of *Wilko* that they were all protected by our various federal securities Acts. If these guarantees are to be removed, it should take a legislative enactment. I would enforce our laws as they stand, unless Congress makes an exception.

* * *

Questions

1. How does the *Scherk* Court interpret the Court's previous holding in *Wilko*? How does the dissent's interpretation differ from the majority's? Which is the better reading of the text?

2. What are the special concerns the majority gives for upholding arbitration awards in international agreements? Does it suggest that the holding of *Scherk* is limited to the international context? Or, is the reasoning in *Scherk* applicable in a purely domestic context? Does the dissent agree that international arbitration poses unique concerns that are not present in domestic arbitrations?

3. According to the majority, what will protect investors against an international commercial arbitrator misconstruing or misapplying U.S. securities laws? How does the majority address the concerns about the procedural inadequacy of arbitration that are raised by the dissent?

4. Is it accurate for the dissent to claim that the result of this case will be the evisceration of federal securities law when international parties are involved?

5. Note the majority's analogizing an arbitration clause to a forum selection clause. This is a significant departure from prior cases., and the analogy becomes a critical underpinning of later cases. Is this analogy persuasive? What are the relevant differences between the two types of clauses?

* * *

Mitsubishi Motors Corporation v. Soler Chrysler–Plymouth, Inc.

473 U.S. 614 (1985).

■ JUSTICE BLACKMUN delivered the opinion of the Court.

The principal question presented by these cases is the arbitrability, pursuant to the Federal Arbitration Act, 9 U.S.C. § 1 et seq., and the Convention on the Recognition and Enforcement of Foreign Arbitral Awards (Convention), [1970] 21 U.S.T. 2517, T.I.A.S. No. 6997, of claims arising under the Sherman Act, 15 U.S.C. § 1 et seq., and encompassed within a valid arbitration clause in an agreement embodying an international commercial transaction.

I

Petitioner-cross-respondent Mitsubishi Motors Corporation (Mitsubishi) is a Japanese corporation which manufactures automobiles and has its principal place of business in Tokyo, Japan. Mitsubishi is the product of a joint venture between, on the one hand, Chrysler International, S.A. (CISA), a Swiss corporation registered in Geneva and wholly owned by Chrysler Corporation, and, on the other, Mitsubishi Heavy Industries, Inc., a Japanese corporation. The aim of the joint venture was the distribution through Chrysler dealers outside the continental United States of vehicles manufactured by Mitsubishi and bearing Chrysler and Mitsubishi trademarks. Respondent-cross-petitioner Soler Chrysler–Plymouth, Inc. (Soler), is a Puerto Rico corporation with its principal place of business in Pueblo Viejo, Guaynabo, Puerto Rico.

On October 31, 1979, Soler entered into a Distributor Agreement with CISA which provided for the sale by Soler of Mitsubishi-manufactured vehicles within a designated area, including metropolitan San Juan ... On the same date, CISA, Soler, and Mitsubishi entered into a Sales Procedure Agreement (Sales Agreement) which, referring to the Distributor Agreement, provided for the direct sale of Mitsubishi products to Soler and governed the terms and conditions of such sales ... Paragraph VI of the Sales Agreement, labeled "Arbitration of Certain Matters," provides:

> All disputes, controversies or differences which may arise between [Mitsubishi] and [Soler] out of or in relation to Articles I–B through V of this Agreement or for the breach thereof, shall be finally settled by arbitration in Japan in accordance with the rules and regulations of the Japan Commercial Arbitration Association....

Initially, Soler did a brisk business in Mitsubishi-manufactured vehicles. As a result of its strong performance, its minimum sales volume, specified by Mitsubishi and CISA, and agreed to by Soler, for the 1981 model year was substantially increased ... In early 1981, however, the new-car market slackened. Soler ran into serious difficulties in meeting the expected sales volume, and by the spring of 1981 it felt itself compelled to request that Mitsubishi delay or cancel shipment of several orders.... About the same time, Soler attempted to arrange for the transshipment of a quantity of its vehicles for sale in the continental United States and Latin America. Mitsubishi and CISA, however, refused permission for any such diversion, citing a variety of reasons,[1] and no vehicles were transshipped. Attempts to work out these difficulties failed. Mitsubishi eventually withheld shipment of 966 vehicles, apparently representing orders placed for May, June, and July 1981 production, responsibility for which Soler disclaimed in February 1982 ...

The following month, Mitsubishi brought an action against Soler in the United States District Court for the District of Puerto Rico under the Federal Arbitration Act and the Convention.[2] Mitsubishi sought an order, pursuant to 9 U.S.C. §§ 4 and 201, to compel arbitration in accord with 57 VI of the Sales Agreement ... Shortly after filing the complaint, Mitsubishi filed a request for arbitration before the Japan Commercial Arbitration Association ...

Soler denied the allegations and counterclaimed against both Mitsubishi and CISA. It alleged numerous breaches by Mitsubishi of the Sales Agreement, raised a pair of defamation claims, and asserted causes of action under the Sherman Act, 15 U.S.C. § 1 et seq.; the federal Automobile Dealers' Day in Court Act, 70 Stat. 1125, 15 U.S.C. § 1221 et seq.; the Puerto Rico competition statute, P.R.Laws Ann., Tit. 10, § 257 et seq. (1976); and the Puerto Rico Dealers' Contracts Act, P.R.Laws Ann., Tit. 10, § 278 et seq. (1978 and Supp.1983). In the counterclaim premised on the Sherman Act, Soler alleged that Mitsubishi and CISA had conspired to divide markets in restraint of trade. To effectuate the plan, according to Soler, Mitsubishi had refused to permit Soler to resell to buyers in North, Central, or South America vehicles it had obligated itself to purchase from

1. The reasons advanced included concerns that such diversion would interfere with the Japanese trade policy of voluntarily limiting imports to the United States, App. 143, 177–178; that the Soler-ordered vehicles would be unsuitable for use in certain proposed destinations because of their manufacture, with use in Puerto Rico in mind, without heaters and defoggers, id., at 182; that the vehicles would be unsuitable for use in Latin America because of the unavailability there of the unleaded, high-octane fuel they required, id., at 177, 181–182; that adequate warranty service could not be ensured, id., at 176, 182; and that diversion to the mainland would violate contractual obligations between CISA and Mitsubishi, id., at 144, 183.

2. The complaint alleged that Soler had failed to pay for 966 ordered vehicles; that it had failed to pay contractual "distress unit penalties," intended to reimburse Mitsubishi for storage costs and interest charges incurred because of Soler's failure to take shipment of ordered vehicles; that Soler's failure to fulfill warranty obligations threatened Mitsubishi's reputation and goodwill; that Soler had failed to obtain required financing; and that the Distributor and Sales Agreements had expired by their terms or, alternatively, that Soler had surrendered its rights under the Sales Agreement. Id., at 11–14.

Mitsubishi; had refused to ship ordered vehicles or the parts, such as heaters and defoggers, that would be necessary to permit Soler to make its vehicles suitable for resale outside Puerto Rico; and had coercively attempted to replace Soler and its other Puerto Rico distributors with a wholly owned subsidiary which would serve as the exclusive Mitsubishi distributor in Puerto Rico . . .

After a hearing, the District Court ordered Mitsubishi and Soler to arbitrate each of the issues raised in the complaint and in all the counterclaims save two and a portion of a third. With regard to the federal antitrust issues, it recognized that the Courts of Appeals, following American Safety Equipment Corp. v. J.P. Maguire & Co., 391 F.2d 821 (2d Cir. 1968), uniformly had held that the rights conferred by the antitrust laws were " 'of a character inappropriate for enforcement by arbitration.' " . . . The District Court held, however, that the international character of the Mitsubishi–Soler undertaking required enforcement of the agreement to arbitrate even as to the antitrust claims. It relied on Scherk v. Alberto–Culver Co., 417 U.S. 506, 515–520, 94 S.Ct. 2449, 2455–2458, 41 L.Ed.2d 270 (1974), in which this Court ordered arbitration, pursuant to a provision embodied in an international agreement, of a claim arising under the Securities Exchange Act of 1934 notwithstanding its assumption, arguendo, that *Wilko*, supra, which held nonarbitrable claims arising under the Securities Act of 1933, also would bar arbitration of a 1934 Act claim arising in a domestic context.

The United States Court of Appeals for the First Circuit affirmed in part and reversed in part. 723 F.2d 155 (1983). It first rejected Soler's argument that Puerto Rico law precluded enforcement of an agreement obligating a local dealer to arbitrate controversies outside Puerto Rico. It also rejected Soler's suggestion that it could not have intended to arbitrate statutory claims not mentioned in the arbitration agreement. Assessing arbitrability "on an allegation-by-allegation basis," id., at 159, the court then read the arbitration clause to encompass virtually all the claims arising under the various statutes, including all those arising under the Sherman Act.

Finally, after endorsing the doctrine of American Safety, precluding arbitration of antitrust claims, the Court of Appeals concluded that neither this Court's decision in Scherk nor the Convention required abandonment of that doctrine in the face of an international transaction. 723 F.2d, at 164–168. Accordingly, it reversed the judgment of the District Court insofar as it had ordered submission of "Soler's antitrust claims" to arbitration. Affirming the remainder of the judgment, the court directed the District Court to consider in the first instance how the parallel judicial and arbitral proceedings should go forward.

We granted certiorari primarily to consider whether an American court should enforce an agreement to resolve antitrust claims by arbitration when that agreement arises from an international transaction. . . .

II

At the outset, we address the contention raised in Soler's cross-petition that the arbitration clause at issue may not be read to encompass the statutory counterclaims stated in its answer to the complaint. In making this argument, Soler does not question the Court of Appeals' application of ¶ VI of the Sales Agreement to the disputes involved here as a matter of standard contract interpretation. Instead, it argues that as a matter of law a court may not construe an arbitration agreement to encompass claims arising out of statutes designed to protect a class to which the party resisting arbitration belongs "unless [that party] has expressly agreed" to arbitrate those claims, see Pet. for Cert. in No. 83–1733, pp. 8, I, by which Soler presumably means that the arbitration clause must specifically mention the statute giving rise to the claims that a party to the clause seeks to arbitrate. See 723 F.2d, at 159. Soler reasons that, because it falls within the class for whose benefit the federal and local antitrust laws and dealers' Acts were passed, but the arbitration clause at issue does not mention these statutes or statutes in general, the clause cannot be read to contemplate arbitration of these statutory claims.

We do not agree, for we find no warrant in the Arbitration Act for implying in every contract within its ken a presumption against arbitration of statutory claims. The Act's centerpiece provision makes a written agreement to arbitrate "in any maritime transaction or a contract evidencing a transaction involving commerce ... valid, irrevocable, and enforceable, save upon such grounds as exist at law or in equity for the revocation of any contract." 9 U.S.C. § 2. The "liberal federal policy favoring arbitration agreements," Moses H. Cone Memorial Hospital v. Mercury Construction Corp., 460 U.S. 1, 24, 103 S.Ct. 927, 941, 74 L.Ed.2d 765 (1983), manifested by this provision and the Act as a whole, is at bottom a policy guaranteeing the enforcement of private contractual arrangements: the Act simply "creates a body of federal substantive law establishing and regulating the duty to honor an agreement to arbitrate." Id., at 25, n. 32, 103 S.Ct., at 942, n. 32. As this Court recently observed, "[t]he preeminent concern of Congress in passing the Act was to enforce private agreements into which parties had entered," a concern which "requires that we rigorously enforce agreements to arbitrate." Dean Witter Reynolds Inc. v. Byrd, 470 U.S. 213, 221 ...

Accordingly, the first task of a court asked to compel arbitration of a dispute is to determine whether the parties agreed to arbitrate that dispute. The court is to make this determination by applying the "federal substantive law of arbitrability, applicable to any arbitration agreement within the coverage of the Act." Moses H. Cone Memorial Hospital, 460 U.S., at 24, 103 S.Ct., at 941 ... And that body of law counsels

> that questions of arbitrability must be addressed with a healthy regard for the federal policy favoring arbitration ... The Arbitration Act establishes that, as a matter of federal law, any doubts concerning the scope of arbitrable issues should be resolved in favor of arbitration, whether the problem at hand is the construction of the contract

> language itself or an allegation of waiver, delay, or a like defense to arbitrability. Moses H. Cone Memorial Hospital, 460 U.S., at 24–25, 103 S.Ct., at 941–942.

See, e.g., Steelworkers v. Warrior & Gulf Navigation Co., 363 U.S. 574, 582–583, 80 S.Ct. 1347, 1352–1353, 4 L.Ed.2d 1409 (1960). Thus, as with any other contract, the parties' intentions control, but those intentions are generously construed as to issues of arbitrability.

There is no reason to depart from these guidelines where a party bound by an arbitration agreement raises claims founded on statutory rights. Some time ago this Court expressed "hope for [the Act's] usefulness both in controversies based on statutes or on standards otherwise created," Wilko v. Swan, 346 U.S. 427, 432, . . . (1953) (footnote omitted); . . ., and we are well past the time when judicial suspicion of the desirability of arbitration and of the competence of arbitral tribunals inhibited the development of arbitration as an alternative means of dispute resolution. Just last Term in *Southland Corp.*, supra, where we held that § 2 of the Act declared a national policy applicable equally in state as well as federal courts, we construed an arbitration clause to encompass the disputes at issue without pausing at the source in a state statute of the rights asserted by the parties resisting arbitration. 465 U.S., at 15, and n. 7, 104 S.Ct., at 860, and n. 7. Of course, courts should remain attuned to well-supported claims that the agreement to arbitrate resulted from the sort of fraud or overwhelming economic power that would provide grounds "for the revocation of any contract." 9 U.S.C. § 2; . . . But, absent such compelling considerations, the Act itself provides no basis for disfavoring agreements to arbitrate statutory claims by skewing the otherwise hospitable inquiry into arbitrability.

That is not to say that all controversies implicating statutory rights are suitable for arbitration. There is no reason to distort the process of contract interpretation, however, in order to ferret out the inappropriate. Just as it is the congressional policy manifested in the Federal Arbitration Act that requires courts liberally to construe the scope of arbitration agreements covered by that Act, it is the congressional intention expressed in some other statute on which the courts must rely to identify any category of claims as to which agreements to arbitrate will be held unenforceable. See Wilko v. Swan, 346 U.S., at 434–435, 74 S.Ct., at 186–187; *Southland Corp.*, 465 U.S., at 16, n. 11, 104 S.Ct., at 861, n.11; Dean Witter Reynolds Inc., 470 U.S., at 224–225, 105 S.Ct., at 1244–1245 (concurring opinion). For that reason, Soler's concern for statutorily protected classes provides no reason to color the lens through which the arbitration clause is read. By agreeing to arbitrate a statutory claim, a party does not forgo the substantive rights afforded by the statute; it only submits to their resolution in an arbitral, rather than a judicial, forum. It trades the procedures and opportunity for review of the courtroom for the simplicity, informality, and expedition of arbitration. We must assume that if Congress intended the substantive protection afforded by a given statute to include protection against waiver of the right to a judicial forum, that intention will be deducible from text or legislative history. See Wilko v. Swan, supra. Having made the bargain to arbitrate, the party should be held to it unless Congress itself has evinced an intention to preclude a waiver of judicial remedies for the statutory rights at issue. Nothing, in the meantime, prevents a party from excluding statutory claims from the scope of an agreement to arbitrate. See Prima Paint Corp., 388 U.S., at 406, 87 S.Ct., at 1807.

In sum, the Court of Appeals correctly conducted a two-step inquiry, first determining whether the parties' agreement to arbitrate reached the statutory issues, and then, upon finding it did, considering whether legal constraints external to the parties' agreement foreclosed the arbitration of those claims. We endorse its rejection of Soler's proposed rule of arbitration-clause construction.

III

We now turn to consider whether Soler's antitrust claims are nonarbitrable even though it has agreed to arbitrate them. In holding that they are not, the Court of Appeals followed the decision of the Second Circuit in American Safety Equipment Corp. v. J.P. Maguire & Co., 391 F.2d 821 (1968). Notwithstanding the absence of any explicit support for such an exception in either the Sherman Act or the Federal Arbitration Act, the Second Circuit there reasoned that "the pervasive public interest in enforcement of the antitrust laws, and the nature of the claims that arise in such cases, combine to make ... antitrust claims ... inappropriate for arbitration." Id., at 827–828. We find it unnecessary to assess the legitimacy of the *American Safety* doctrine as applied to agreements to arbitrate arising from domestic transactions. As in Scherk v. Alberto–Culver Co., 417 U.S. 506, 94 S.Ct. 2449, 41 L.Ed.2d 270 (1974), we conclude that concerns of international comity, respect for the capacities of foreign and transnational tribunals, and sensitivity to the need of the international commercial system for predictability in the resolution of disputes require that we enforce the parties' agreement, even assuming that a contrary result would be forthcoming in a domestic context.

Even before *Scherk*, this Court had recognized the utility of forum-selection clauses in international transactions.... Recognizing that "agreeing in advance on a forum acceptable to both parties is an indispensable element in international trade, commerce, and contracting," id., at 13–14, 92 S.Ct., at 1914–1916 the decision in *The Bremen* clearly eschewed a provincial solicitude for the jurisdiction of domestic forums....

The Bremen and *Scherk* establish a strong presumption in favor of enforcement of freely negotiated contractual choice-of-forum provisions. Here, as in *Scherk*, that presumption is reinforced by the emphatic federal policy in favor of arbitral dispute resolution. And at least since this Nation's accession in 1970 to the Convention, see [1970] 21 U.S.T. 2517, T.I.A.S. 6997, and the implementation of the Convention in the same year by amendment of the Federal Arbitration Act, that federal policy applies with special force in the field of international commerce. Thus, we must weigh the concerns of American Safety against a strong belief in the efficacy of arbitral procedures for the resolution of international commercial disputes and an equal commitment to the enforcement of freely negotiated choice-of-forum clauses.

At the outset, we confess to some skepticism of certain aspects of the *American Safety* doctrine. As distilled by the First Circuit, 723 F.2d, at 162, the doctrine comprises four ingredients. First, private parties play a pivotal role in aiding governmental enforcement of the antitrust laws by means of the private action for treble damages. Second, "the strong possibility that contracts which generate antitrust disputes may be contracts of adhesion militates against automatic forum determination by contract." Third, antitrust issues, prone to complication, require sophisticated legal and economic analysis, and thus are "ill-adapted to strengths of the arbitral process, i.e., expedition, minimal requirements of written rationale, simplicity, resort to basic concepts of common sense and simple equity." Finally, just as "issues of war and peace are too important to be vested in the generals, ... decisions as to antitrust regulation of business are too important to be lodged in arbitrators chosen from the business community—particularly those from a foreign community that has had no experience with or exposure to our law and values." See American Safety, 391 F.2d, at 826–827.

Initially, we find the second concern unjustified. The mere appearance of an antitrust dispute does not alone warrant invalidation of the selected forum on the undemonstrated assumption that the arbitration clause is tainted. A party resisting arbitration of course may attack directly the validity of the agreement to arbitrate. See Prima Paint Corp. v. Flood & Conklin Mfg. Co., 388 U.S. 395, 87 S.Ct. 1801, 18 L.Ed.2d 1270 (1967). Moreover, the party may attempt to make a showing that would warrant setting aside the forum-selection clause—that the agreement was "[a]ffected by fraud, undue influence, or overweening bargaining power"; that "enforcement would be unreasonable and unjust"; or that proceedings "in the contractual forum will be so gravely difficult and inconvenient that [the resisting party] will for all practical purposes be deprived of his day in court." The Bremen, 407 U.S., at 12, 15, 18, 92 S.Ct., at 1914, 1916, 1917. But absent such a showing—and none was attempted here—there is no basis for assuming the forum inadequate or its selection unfair.

Next, potential complexity should not suffice to ward off arbitration. We might well have some doubt that even the courts following *American Safety* subscribe fully to the view that antitrust matters are inherently insusceptible to resolution by arbitration, as these same courts have agreed that an undertaking to arbitrate antitrust claims entered into after the dispute arises is acceptable.... And the vertical restraints which most frequently give birth to antitrust claims covered by an arbitration agreement will not often occasion the monstrous proceedings that have given antitrust litigation an image of intractability. In any event, adaptability and access to expertise are hallmarks of arbitration. The anticipated subject matter of the dispute may be taken into account when the arbitrators are appointed, and arbitral rules typically provide for the participation of experts either employed by the parties or appointed by the tribunal. Moreover, it is often a judgment that streamlined proceedings and expeditious results will best serve their needs that causes parties to agree to arbitrate their disputes; it is typically a desire to keep the effort and expense required to resolve a dispute within manageable bounds that prompts them mutually to forgo access to judicial remedies. In sum, the factor of potential complexity alone does not persuade us that an arbitral tribunal could not properly handle an antitrust matter.

For similar reasons, we also reject the proposition that an arbitration panel will pose too great a danger of innate hostility to the constraints on business conduct that antitrust law imposes. International arbitrators frequently are drawn from the legal as well as the business community; where the dispute has an important legal component, the parties and the arbitral body with whose assistance they have agreed to settle their dispute can be expected to select arbitrators accordingly. We decline to indulge the presumption that the parties and arbitral body conducting a proceeding will be unable or unwilling to retain competent, conscientious, and impartial arbitrators.

We are left, then, with the core of the *American Safety* doctrine—the fundamental importance to American democratic capitalism of the regime of the antitrust laws ... Without doubt, the private cause of action plays a central role in enforcing this regime ... The treble-damages provision wielded by the private litigant is a chief tool in the antitrust enforcement scheme, posing a crucial deterrent to potential violators ...

The importance of the private damages remedy, however, does not compel the conclusion that it may not be sought outside an American court. Notwithstanding its important incidental policing function, the treble-damages cause of action conferred on private parties by § 4 of the Clayton Act, 15 U.S.C. § 15, and pursued by Soler here by way of its third counterclaim, seeks primarily to enable an injured competitor to gain compensation for that injury ...

There is no reason to assume at the outset of the dispute that international arbitration will not provide an adequate mechanism. To be sure, the international arbitral tribunal owes no prior allegiance to the legal norms of particular states; hence, it has no direct obligation to vindicate their statutory dictates. The tribunal, however, is bound to effectuate the intentions of the parties. Where the parties have agreed that the arbitral body is to decide a defined set of claims which includes, as in these cases, those arising from the application of American antitrust law, the tribunal therefore should be bound to decide that dispute in accord with the national law giving rise to the claim ... And so long as the prospective litigant effectively may vindicate its statutory cause of action in the arbitral forum, the statute will continue to serve both its remedial and deterrent function.

Having permitted the arbitration to go forward, the national courts of the United States will have the opportunity at the award-enforcement stage to ensure that the legitimate interest in the enforcement of the antitrust laws has been addressed. The Convention reserves to each signatory country the right to refuse enforcement of an award where the "recognition or enforcement of the award would be contrary to the public policy of that country." ... While the efficacy of the arbitral process requires that substantive review at the award-enforcement stage remain minimal, it would not require intrusive inquiry to ascertain that the tribunal took cognizance of the antitrust claims and actually decided them.

As international trade has expanded in recent decades, so too has the use of international arbitration to resolve disputes arising in the course of that trade. The controversies that international arbitral institutions are called upon to resolve have increased in diversity as well as in complexity. Yet the potential of these tribunals for efficient disposition of legal disagreements arising from commercial relations has not yet been tested. If they are to take a central place in the international legal order, national courts will need to "shake off the old judicial hostility to arbitration," Kulukundis Shipping Co. v. Amtorg Trading Corp., 126 F.2d 978, 985 (2d Cir. 1942), and also their customary and understandable unwillingness to cede jurisdiction of a claim arising under domestic law to a foreign or transnational tribunal. To this extent, at least, it will be necessary for national courts to subordinate domestic notions of arbitrability to the international policy favoring commercial arbitration. See *Scherk*, supra.

Accordingly, we "require this representative of the American business community to honor its bargain," Alberto–Culver Co. v. Scherk, 484 F.2d 611, 620 (7th Cir. 1973) (Stevens, J., dissenting), by holding this agreement to arbitrate "enforce[able] ... in accord with the explicit provisions of the Arbitration Act." *Scherk*, 417 U.S., at 520, 94 S.Ct., at 2457

The judgment of the Court of Appeals is affirmed in part and reversed in part, and the cases are remanded for further proceedings consistent with this opinion.

It is so ordered.

■ JUSTICE POWELL took no part in the decision of these cases.

■ JUSTICE STEVENS, with whom JUSTICE BRENNAN joins, and with whom JUSTICE MARSHALL joins except as to Part II, dissenting.

... This Court agrees with the Court of Appeals' interpretation of the scope of the arbitration clause, but disagrees with its conclusion that the clause is unenforceable insofar as it purports to cover an antitrust claim against a Japanese company. This Court's holding rests almost exclusively on the federal policy favoring arbitration of commercial disputes and vague notions of international comity arising from the fact that the automobiles involved here were manufactured in Japan. Because I am convinced that the Court of Appeals' construction of the arbitration clause is erroneous, and because I strongly disagree with this Court's interpretation of the relevant federal statutes, I respectfully dissent. In my opinion, (1) a fair construction of the language in the arbitration clause in the parties' contract does not encompass a claim that auto manufacturers entered into a conspiracy in violation of the antitrust laws; (2) an arbitration clause should not normally be construed to cover a statutory remedy that it does not expressly identify; (3) Congress did not intend § 2 of the Federal Arbitration Act to apply to antitrust claims; and (4) Congress did not intend the Convention on the Recognition and Enforcement of Foreign Arbitral Awards to apply to disputes that are not covered by the Federal Arbitration Act.

I

On October 31, 1979, respondent, Soler Chrysler–Plymouth, Inc. (Soler), entered into a "distributor agreement" to govern the sale of Plymouth passenger cars to be manufactured by petitioner, Mitsubishi Motors Corporation of Tokyo, Japan (Mitsubishi). Mitsubishi, however, was not a party to that agreement. Rather the "purchase rights" were granted to Soler by a wholly owned subsidiary of Chrysler Corporation that is referred to as "Chrysler" in the agreement. The distributor agreement does not contain an arbitration clause. Nor does the record contain any other agreement providing for the arbitration of disputes between Soler and Chrysler.

Paragraph 26 of the distributor agreement authorizes Chrysler to have Soler's orders filled by any company affiliated with Chrysler, that company thereby becoming the "supplier" of the products covered by the agreement with Chrysler. Relying on paragraph 26 of their distributor agreement, Soler, Chrysler, and Mitsubishi entered into a separate Sales Procedure Agreement designating Mitsubishi as the supplier of the products covered by the distributor agreement. The arbitration clause the Court construes today is found in that agreement. As a matter of ordinary contract interpretation, there are at least two reasons why that clause does not apply to Soler's antitrust claim against Chrysler and Mitsubishi.

First, the clause only applies to two-party disputes between Soler and Mitsubishi. The antitrust violation alleged in Soler's counterclaim is a three-party dispute. Soler has joined both Chrysler and its associated company, Mitsubishi, as counter defendants....

Second, the clause only applies to disputes "which may arise between MMC and BUYER out of or in relation to Articles I–B through V of this Agreement or for the breach thereof...." Id., at 52. [Neither apply here.]

The federal policy favoring arbitration cannot sustain the weight that the Court assigns to it. A clause requiring arbitration of all claims "relating to" a contract surely could not encompass a claim that the arbitration clause was itself part of a contract in restraint of trade ... Nor in my judgment should it be read to encompass a claim that relies, not on a failure to perform the contract, but on an independent violation of federal law. The matters asserted by way of defense do not control the character, or the source, of the claim that Soler has asserted. Accordingly, simply as a matter of ordinary contract interpretation, I would hold that Soler's antitrust claim is not arbitrable.

II

Section 2 of the Federal Arbitration Act describes three kinds of arbitrable agreements. Two—those including maritime transactions and those covering the submission of an existing dispute to arbitration—are not involved in this case. The language of § 2 relating to the Soler–Mitsubishi arbitration clause reads as follows:

> A written provision in ... a contract evidencing a transaction involving commerce to settle by arbitration a controversy thereafter arising out of such contract ... or the refusal to perform the whole or any part thereof, ... shall be valid, irrevocable, and enforceable, save upon such grounds as exist at law or in equity for the revocation of any contract.

The plain language of this statute encompasses Soler's claims that arise out of its contract with Mitsubishi, but does not encompass a claim arising under federal law, or indeed one that arises under its distributor agreement with Chrysler. Nothing in the text of the 1925 Act, nor its legislative history, suggests that Congress intended to authorize the arbitration of any statutory claims.

Until today all of our cases enforcing agreements to arbitrate under the Arbitration Act have involved contract claims. In one, the party claiming a breach of contractual warranties also claimed that the breach amounted to fraud actionable under § 10(b) of the Securities Exchange Act of 1934. Scherk v. Alberto–Culver Co., 417 U.S. 506, 94 S.Ct. 2449, 41 L.Ed.2d 270 (1974). But this is the first time the Court has considered the question whether a standard arbitration clause referring to claims arising out of or relating to a contract should be construed to cover statutory claims that have only an indirect relationship to the contract. In my opinion, neither the Congress that enacted the Arbitration Act in 1925, nor the many parties who have agreed to such standard clauses, could have anticipated the Court's answer to that question.

On several occasions we have drawn a distinction between statutory rights and contractual rights and refused to hold that an arbitration barred the assertion of a statutory right. Thus, in Alexander v. Gardner–Denver Co., 415 U.S. 36, 94 S.Ct. 1011, 39 L.Ed.2d 147 (1974), we held that the arbitration of a claim of employment discrimination would not bar an employee's statutory right to damages under Title VII of the Civil Rights Act of 1964, 42 U.S.C. §§ 2000e–2000e–17, notwithstanding the strong federal policy favoring the arbitration of labor disputes. In that case the Court explained at some length why it would be unreasonable to assume that Congress intended to give arbitrators the final authority to implement the federal statutory policy:

> Arbitral procedures, while well suited to the resolution of contractual disputes, make arbitration a comparatively inappropriate forum for the final resolution of rights created by Title VII. This conclusion rests first on the special role of the arbitrator, whose task is to effectuate the intent of the parties rather than the requirements of enacted legislation.... But other facts may still render arbitral processes compara-

> tively inferior to judicial processes in the protection of Title VII rights. Among these is the fact that the specialized competence of arbitrators pertains primarily to the law of the shop, not the law of the land. United Steelworkers of America v. Warrior & Gulf Navigation Co., 363 U.S. 574, 581–583, [80 S.Ct. 1347, 1352–1353, 4 L.Ed.2d 1409] (1960). Parties usually choose an arbitrator because they trust his knowledge and judgment concerning the demands and norms of industrial relations. On the other hand, the resolution of statutory or constitutional issues is a primary responsibility of courts, and judicial construction has proved especially necessary with respect to Title VII, whose broad language frequently can be given meaning only by reference to public law concepts.

415 U.S., at 56–57, 94 S.Ct., at 1023–1024 (footnote omitted).

In addition, the Court noted that the informal procedures which make arbitration so desirable in the context of contractual disputes are inadequate to develop a record for appellate review of statutory questions. Such review is essential on matters of statutory interpretation in order to assure consistent application of important public rights.

In Barrentine v. Arkansas–Best Freight System, Inc., 450 U.S. 728, 101 S.Ct. 1437, 67 L.Ed.2d 641 (1981), we reached a similar conclusion with respect to the arbitrability of an employee's claim based on the Fair Labor Standards Act, 29 U.S.C. §§ 201–219. We again noted that an arbitrator, unlike a federal judge, has no institutional obligation to enforce federal legislative policy . . .

The Court's opinions in *Alexander*, *Barrentine*, *McDonald*, and *Wilko* all explain why it makes good sense to draw a distinction between statutory claims and contract claims. In view of the Court's repeated recognition of the distinction between federal statutory rights and contractual rights, together with the undisputed historical fact that arbitration has functioned almost entirely in either the area of labor disputes or in "ordinary disputes between merchants as to questions of fact," see n. 11, supra, it is reasonable to assume that most lawyers and executives would not expect the language in the standard arbitration clause to cover federal statutory claims. Thus, in my opinion, both a fair respect for the importance of the interests that Congress has identified as worthy of federal statutory protection, and a fair appraisal of the most likely understanding of the parties who sign agreements containing standard arbitration clauses, support a presumption that such clauses do not apply to federal statutory claims.

III

The Court has repeatedly held that a decision by Congress to create a special statutory remedy renders a private agreement to arbitrate a federal statutory claim unenforceable . . . The reasons that motivated those decisions apply with special force to the federal policy that is protected by the antitrust laws . . .

The Sherman and Clayton Acts reflect Congress' appraisal of the value of economic freedom; they guarantee the vitality of the entrepreneurial spirit. Questions arising under these Acts are among the most important in public law.

The unique public interest in the enforcement of the antitrust laws is repeatedly reflected in the special remedial scheme enacted by Congress. Since its enactment in 1890, the Sherman Act has provided for public enforcement through criminal as well as civil sanctions. The pre-eminent federal interest in effective enforcement once justified a provision for special three-judge district courts to hear antitrust claims on an expedited basis, as well as for direct appeal to this Court bypassing the courts of appeals. See, e.g., United States v. National Assn. of Securities Dealers, Inc., 422 U.S. 694, 95 S.Ct. 2427, 45 L.Ed.2d 486 (1975)....

This Court would be well advised to endorse the collective wisdom of the distinguished judges of the Courts of Appeals who have unanimously concluded that the statutory remedies fashioned by Congress for the enforcement of the antitrust laws render an agreement to arbitrate antitrust disputes unenforceable. Arbitration awards are only reviewable for manifest disregard of the law, 9 U.S.C. §§ 10, 207, and the rudimentary procedures which make arbitration so desirable in the context of a private dispute often mean that the record is so inadequate that the arbitrator's decision is virtually unreviewable.[31] Despotic decision making of this kind is fine for parties who are willing to agree in advance to settle for a best approximation of the correct result in order to resolve quickly and inexpensively any contractual dispute that may arise in an ongoing commercial relationship. Such informality, however, is simply unacceptable when every error may have devastating consequences for important businesses in our national economy and may undermine their ability to compete in world markets. Instead of "muffling a grievance in the cloakroom of arbitration," the public interest in free competitive markets would be better served by having the issues resolved "in the light of impartial public court adjudication." See Merrill Lynch, Pierce, Fenner & Smith, Inc. v. Ware, 414 U.S. 117.

IV

The Court assumes for the purposes of its decision that the antitrust issues would not be arbitrable if this were a purely domestic dispute, ante, at 3355, but holds that the international character of the controversy makes it arbitrable. The holding rests on vague concerns for the international implications of its decision and a misguided application of Scherk v. Alberto–Culver, Co., 417 U.S. 506, 94 S.Ct. 2449, 41 L.Ed.2d 270 (1974).

31. The arbitration procedure in this case does not provide any right to evidentiary discovery or a written decision, and requires that all proceedings be closed to the public. App. 220–221. Moreover, Japanese arbitrators do not have the power of compulsory process to secure witnesses and documents, nor do witnesses who are available testify under oath. Id., at 218–219. Cf. 9 U.S.C. § 7 (arbitrators may summon witnesses to attend proceedings and seek enforcement in a district court).

International Obligations of the United States

... As the Court acknowledges, the only treaty relevant here is the Convention on the Recognition and Enforcement of Foreign Arbitral Awards. [1970] 21 U.S.T. 2517, T.I.A.S. No. 6997.... Article III provides that each "Contracting State shall recognize arbitral awards as binding and enforce them." However, if an arbitration award is "contrary to the public policy of [a] country" called upon to enforce it, or if it concerns a subject matter which is "not capable of settlement by arbitration under the law of that country," the Convention does not require that it be enforced. Arts. V(2)(a) and (b). Thus, reading Articles II and V together, the Convention provides that agreements to arbitrate disputes which are nonarbitrable under domestic law need not be honored, nor awards rendered under them enforced ...

International Comity

It is clear then that the international obligations of the United States permit us to honor Congress' commitment to the exclusive resolution of antitrust disputes in the federal courts. The Court today refuses to do so, offering only vague concerns for comity among nations. The courts of other nations, on the other hand, have applied the exception provided in the Convention, and refused to enforce agreements to arbitrate specific subject matters of concern to them.

It may be that the subject-matter exception to the Convention ought to be reserved—as a matter of domestic law—for matters of the greatest public interest which involve concerns that are shared by other nations. The Sherman Act's commitment to free competitive markets is among our most important civil policies. Supra, at 3366–3370. This commitment, shared by other nations which are signatory to the Convention, is hardly the sort of parochial concern that we should decline to enforce in the interest of international comity ...

V

The Court's repeated incantation of the high ideals of "international arbitration" creates the impression that this case involves the fate of an institution designed to implement a formula for world peace. But just as it is improper to subordinate the public interest in enforcement of antitrust policy to the private interest in resolving commercial disputes, so is it equally unwise to allow a vision of world unity to distort the importance of the selection of the proper forum for resolving this dispute. Like any other mechanism for resolving controversies, international arbitration will only succeed if it is realistically limited to tasks it is capable of performing well—the prompt and inexpensive resolution of essentially contractual disputes between commercial partners. As for matters involving the political passions and the fundamental interests of nations, even the multilateral convention adopted under the auspices of the United Nations recognizes that private international arbitration is incapable of achieving satisfactory results.

In my opinion, the elected representatives of the American people would not have us dispatch an American citizen to a foreign land in search of an uncertain remedy for the violation of a public right that is protected by the Sherman Act. This is especially so when there has been no genuine bargaining over the terms of the submission, and the arbitration remedy provided has not even the most elementary guarantees of fair process. Consideration of a fully developed record by a jury, instructed in the law by a federal judge, and subject to appellate review, is a surer guide to the competitive character of a commercial practice than the practically unreviewable judgment of a private arbitrator.

Unlike the Congress that enacted the Sherman Act in 1890, the Court today does not seem to appreciate the value of economic freedom. I respectfully dissent.

* * *

Questions

1. Do you agree with the *Mitsubishi* Court that an arbitration clause should be treated the same as a choice of forum clause in the international context? Are there differences between the types of clauses that the Court is ignoring that might argue for a different outcome in this case?

2. What features of the Sherman Antitrust Act led some lower courts to hold that Sherman Act claims are inappropriate for arbitration? How does the Supreme Court majority in *Mitsubishi* respond to these objections? What other federal statutes might be amenable to arbitration? What types of statutes would not be amenable?

3. How important to the majority's reasoning is the availability of judicial review for arbitration awards that construe the Sherman Act?

4. Does the Court's opinion leave the *American Safety* doctrine intact for wholly domestic disputes involving arbitration of antitrust claims?

* * *

Note on International Arbitration

Arbitration is a particularly important way to resolve international disputes. Parties to an international dispute often distrust the judicial system of other countries, and no party wants to adjudicate a dispute on the other party's home field. Arbitration provides a neutral forum. As one commentator has noted:

> [I]nternational commercial arbitration eliminates many of the drawbacks associated with hometown litigation. For example, while parties from developing states might complain about the supposedly Western orientation of major arbitration institutions, one probably cannot accuse them of the strong parochial biases often embedded in national judicial systems.... In addition, the increasing harmonization of inter-

> national arbitration rules and laws means that all parties can reap the benefits of familiar procedures specifically designed for international commercial disputes. Furthermore, those instruments generally allow parties to employ their regular counsel without regard to bar membership at the place of arbitration. Finally, the opportunity to appoint an arbitrator, and the New York Convention's widespread ratification help to ensure that tribunal members will have relevant expertise, that they will collectively appreciate the business and legal cultures of the disputing parties, and that their awards can be enforced in summary proceedings under uniform standards from "Albania to Zimbabwe." Thus, because it combines neutrality with high levels of convenience for both parties, and because it promotes finality through worldwide guarantees of enforcement, arbitration has eclipsed judicial settlement as the predominant means of adjudicating international commercial disputes.

Charles H. Brower II, The Functions and Limits of Arbitration and Judicial Settlement Under Private and Public International Law, 18 Duke J. Comp. & Int'l L. 259, 263–64 (2008).

The enforceability of international arbitration agreements raises many of the same issues as the enforceability of domestic arbitration agreements. International agreements, however, are governed not only by national law, but also by treaties. The most significant is the Convention on the Recognition and Enforcement of Foreign Arbitral Awards (the "New York Convention"), which requires signatory nations to honor and enforce arbitration agreements falling within the scope of the Convention. Another significant treaty is the Inter–American Convention on International Commercial Arbitration (the "Panama Convention"). The United States has implemented its obligations under both treaties in Chapters 2 and 3 of the FAA, respectively.

Though arbitration dominates the resolution of international *commercial* disputes, it is not firmly embedded as a dispute resolution method for international *public* disputes. For discussions of why this might be so, see Mark L. Movsesian, International Commercial Arbitration and International Courts, 18 Duke J. Comp. & Int'l L. 423 (2008), and Thomas E. Carbonneau, *Commercial Peace and Political Competition in the Crosshairs of International Arbitration*, 18 Duke J. Comp. & Int'l L. 311 (2008).

* * *

Shearson/American Express, Inc. v. McMahon

482 U.S. 220 (1987).

■ JUSTICE O'CONNOR delivered the opinion of the Court.

This case presents two questions regarding the enforceability of predispute arbitration agreements between brokerage firms and their customers. The first is whether a claim brought under § 10(b) of the Securities Exchange Act of 1934 (Exchange Act), 48 Stat. 891, 15 U.S.C. § 78j(b), must be sent to arbitration in accordance with the terms of an arbitration agreement. The second is whether a claim brought under the Racketeer Influenced and Corrupt Organizations Act (RICO), 18 U.S.C. § 1961 et seq., must be arbitrated in accordance with the terms of such an agreement.

I

Between 1980 and 1982, respondents Eugene and Julia McMahon, individually and as trustees for various pension and profit-sharing plans, were customers of petitioner Shearson/American Express Inc. (Shearson), a brokerage firm registered with the Securities and Exchange Commission (SEC or Commission). Two customer agreements signed by Julia McMahon provided for arbitration of any controversy relating to the accounts the McMahons maintained with Shearson. The arbitration provision provided in relevant part as follows:

> Unless unenforceable due to federal or state law, any controversy arising out of or relating to my accounts, to transactions with you for me or to this agreement or the breach thereof, shall be settled by arbitration in accordance with the rules, then in effect, of the National Association of Securities Dealers, Inc. or the Boards of Directors of the New York Stock Exchange, Inc. and/or the American Stock Exchange, Inc. as I may elect. 618 F.Supp. 384, 385 (1985).

In October 1984, the McMahons filed an amended complaint against Shearson and petitioner Mary Ann McNulty, the registered representative who handled their accounts, in the United States District Court for the Southern District of New York. The complaint alleged that McNulty, with Shearson's knowledge, had violated § 10(b) of the Exchange Act and Rule 10b–5, 17 CFR § 240.10b–5 (1986), by engaging in fraudulent, excessive trading on respondents' accounts and by making false statements and omitting material facts from the advice given to respondents. The complaint also alleged a RICO claim, 18 U.S.C. § 1962(c), and state law claims for fraud and breach of fiduciary duties.

Relying on the customer agreements, petitioners moved to compel arbitration of the McMahons' claims pursuant to § 3 of the Federal Arbitration Act, 9 U.S.C. § 3. The District Court granted the motion in part. 618 F.Supp. 384 (1985). The court first rejected the McMahons' contention that the arbitration agreements were unenforceable as contracts of adhesion. It then found that the McMahons' § 10(b) claims were arbitrable under the terms of the agreement, concluding that such a result followed from this Court's decision in Dean Witter Reynolds Inc. v. Byrd, 470 U.S. 213, 105 S.Ct. 1238, 84 L.Ed.2d 158 (1985), and the "strong national policy favoring the enforcement of arbitration agreements." 618 F.Supp., at 388. The District Court also held that the McMahons' state law claims were arbitrable under Dean Witter Reynolds Inc. v. Byrd, supra. It concluded, however, that the McMahons' RICO claim was not arbitrable "because of the important federal policies inherent in the enforcement of RICO by the federal courts." 618 F.Supp., at 387.

The Court of Appeals affirmed the District Court on the state law and RICO claims, but it reversed on the Exchange Act claims. 788 F.2d 94 (2d Cir. 1986). With respect to the RICO claim, the Court of Appeals concluded that "public policy" considerations made it "inappropriat[e]" to apply the provisions of the Arbitration Act to RICO suits. Id., at 98. The court reasoned that RICO claims are "not merely a private matter." Ibid. Because a RICO plaintiff may be likened to a "private attorney general" protecting the public interest, ibid., the Court of Appeals concluded that such claims should be adjudicated only in a judicial forum. It distinguished this Court's reasoning in Mitsubishi Motors Corp. v. Soler Chrysler–Plymouth, Inc., 473 U.S. 614, 105 S.Ct. 3346, 87 L.Ed.2d 444 (1985), concerning the arbitrability of antitrust claims, on the ground that it involved international business transactions and did not affect the law "as applied to agreements to arbitrate arising from domestic transactions." 788 F.2d, at 98.

With respect to respondents' Exchange Act claims, the Court of Appeals noted that under Wilko v. Swan, 346 U.S. 427, 74 S.Ct. 182, 98 L.Ed. 168 (1953), claims arising under § 12(2) of the Securities Act of 1933 (Securities Act), 48 Stat. 84, 15 U.S.C. § 77l(2), are not subject to compulsory arbitration. The Court of Appeals observed that it previously had extended the *Wilko* rule to claims arising under § 10(b) of the Exchange Act and Rule 10b–5 . . . The court acknowledged that Scherk v. Alberto–Culver Co., 417 U.S. 506, 94 S.Ct. 2449, 41 L.Ed.2d 270 (1974), and Dean Witter Reynolds Inc. v. Byrd, supra, had "cast some doubt on the applicability of *Wilko* to claims under § 10(b)." 788 F.2d, at 97. The Court of Appeals nevertheless concluded that it was bound by the "clear judicial precedent in this Circuit," and held that *Wilko* must be applied to Exchange Act claims. 788 F.2d, at 98.

We granted certiorari, 479 U.S. 812, 107 S.Ct. 60, 93 L.Ed.2d 20 (1986), to resolve the conflict among the Courts of Appeals regarding the arbitrability of § 10(b) and RICO claims.

II

The Federal Arbitration Act, 9 U.S.C. § 1 et seq., provides the starting point for answering the questions raised in this case. The Act was intended to "revers[e] centuries of judicial hostility to arbitration agreements," Scherk v. Alberto–Culver Co., supra, 417 U.S., at 510, 94 S.Ct., at 2453, by "plac[ing] arbitration agreements 'upon the same footing as other contracts.' " 417 U.S., at 511, 94 S.Ct., at 2453, quoting H.R.Rep. No. 96, 68th Cong., 1st Sess., 1, 2 (1924). The Arbitration Act accomplishes this purpose by providing that arbitration agreements "shall be valid, irrevocable, and enforceable, save upon such grounds as exist at law or in equity for the revocation of any contract." 9 U.S.C. § 2. The Act also provides that a court must stay its proceedings if it is satisfied that an issue before it is arbitrable under the agreement, § 3; and it authorizes a federal district court to issue an order compelling arbitration if there has been a "failure, neglect, or refusal" to comply with the arbitration agreement, § 4.

The Arbitration Act thus establishes a "federal policy favoring arbitration," Moses H. Cone Memorial Hospital v. Mercury Construction Corp., 460 U.S. 1, 24, 103 S.Ct. 927, 941, 74 L.Ed.2d 765 (1983), requiring that "we rigorously enforce agreements to arbitrate." Dean Witter Reynolds Inc. v. Byrd, supra, 470 U.S., at 221, 105 S.Ct., at 1242. This duty to enforce arbitration agreements is not diminished when a party bound by an agreement raises a claim founded on statutory rights. As we observed in Mitsubishi Motors Corp. v. Soler Chrysler–Plymouth, Inc., "we are well past the time when judicial suspicion of the desirability of arbitration and of the competence of arbitral tribunals" should inhibit enforcement of the Act " 'in controversies based on statutes.' " 473 U.S., at 626–627, 105 S.Ct., at 3354, quoting Wilko v. Swan, supra, 346 U.S., at 432, 74 S.Ct., at 185. Absent a well-founded claim that an arbitration agreement resulted from the sort of fraud or excessive economic power that "would provide grounds 'for the revocation of any contract,' " 473 U.S., at 627, 105 S.Ct., at 3354, the Arbitration Act "provides no basis for disfavoring agreements to arbitrate statutory claims by skewing the otherwise hospitable inquiry into arbitrability." Ibid.

The Arbitration Act, standing alone, therefore mandates enforcement of agreements to arbitrate statutory claims. Like any statutory directive, the Arbitration Act's mandate may be overridden by a contrary congressional command. The burden is on the party opposing arbitration, however, to show that Congress intended to preclude a waiver of judicial remedies for the statutory rights at issue. See id., at 628, 105 S.Ct., at 3354. If Congress did intend to limit or prohibit waiver of a judicial forum for a particular claim, such an intent "will be deducible from [the statute's] text or legislative history," ibid., or from an inherent conflict between arbitration and the statute's underlying purposes . . .

To defeat application of the Arbitration Act in this case, therefore, the McMahons must demonstrate that Congress intended to make an exception to the Arbitration Act for claims arising under RICO and the Exchange Act, an intention discernible from the text, history, or purposes of the statute. We examine the McMahons' arguments regarding the Exchange Act and RICO in turn.

III

When Congress enacted the Exchange Act in 1934, it did not specifically address the question of the arbitrability of § 10(b) claims. The McMahons contend, however, that congressional intent to require a judicial forum for the resolution of § 10(b) claims can be deduced from § 29(a) of the Exchange Act, 15 U.S.C. § 78cc(a), which declares void "[a]ny condition, stipulation, or provision binding any person to waive compliance with any provision of [the Act]."

First, we reject the McMahons' argument that § 29(a) forbids waiver of § 27 of the Exchange Act, 15 U.S.C. § 78aa. Section 27 provides in relevant part:

> The district courts of the United States ... shall have exclusive jurisdiction of violations of this title or the rules and regulations thereunder, and of all suits in equity and actions at law brought to enforce any liability or duty created by this title or the rules and regulations thereunder.

The McMahons contend that an agreement to waive this jurisdictional provision is unenforceable because § 29(a) voids the waiver of "any provision" of the Exchange Act. The language of § 29(a), however, does not reach so far. What the antiwaiver provision of § 29(a) forbids is enforcement of agreements to waive "compliance" with the provisions of the statute. But § 27 itself does not impose any duty with which persons trading in securities must "comply." By its terms, § 29(a) only prohibits waiver of the substantive obligations imposed by the Exchange Act. Because § 27 does not impose any statutory duties, its waiver does not constitute a waiver of "compliance with any provision" of the Exchange Act under § 29(a).

We do not read Wilko v. Swan, 346 U.S. 427, 74 S.Ct., 182, 98 L.Ed. 168 (1953), as compelling a different result. In Wilko, the Court held that a predispute agreement could not be enforced to compel arbitration of a claim arising under § 12(2) of the Securities Act, 15 U.S.C. § 77l(2). The basis for the ruling was § 14 of the Securities Act, which, like § 29(a) of the Exchange Act, declares void any stipulation "to waive compliance with any provision" of the statute. At the beginning of its analysis, the *Wilko* Court stated that the Securities Act's jurisdictional provision was "the kind of 'provision' that cannot be waived under § 14 of the Securities Act." 346 U.S., at 435, 74 S.Ct., at 186. This statement, however, can only be understood in the context of the Court's ensuing discussion explaining why arbitration was inadequate as a means of enforcing "the provisions of the Securities Act, advantageous to the buyer." Ibid. The conclusion in *Wilko* was expressly based on the Court's belief that a judicial forum was needed to protect the substantive rights created by the Securities Act: "As the protective provisions of the Securities Act require the exercise of judicial direction to fairly assure their effectiveness, it seems to us that Congress must have intended § 14 ... to apply to waiver of judicial trial and review." Id., at 437, 74 S.Ct., at 188. *Wilko* must be understood, therefore, as holding that the plaintiff's waiver of the "right to select the judicial forum," id., at 435, 74 S.Ct., at 186, was unenforceable only because arbitration was judged inadequate to enforce the statutory rights created by § 12(2).

Indeed, any different reading of Wilko would be inconsistent with this Court's decision in Scherk v. Alberto–Culver Co., 417 U.S. 506, 94 S.Ct. 2449, 41 L.Ed.2d 270 (1974). In *Scherk*, the Court upheld enforcement of a predispute agreement to arbitrate Exchange Act claims by parties to an international contract ... The decision in *Scherk* thus turned on the Court's judgment that under the circumstances of that case, arbitration was an adequate substitute for adjudication as a means of enforcing the parties' statutory rights. *Scherk* supports our understanding that *Wilko* must be read as barring waiver of a judicial forum only where arbitration is inadequate to protect the substantive rights at issue. At the same time, it confirms that where arbitration does provide an adequate means of enforcing the provisions of the Exchange Act, § 29(a) does not void a predispute waiver of § 27—*Scherk* upheld enforcement of just such a waiver.

The second argument offered by the McMahons is that the arbitration agreement effects an impermissible waiver of the substantive protections of the Exchange Act. Ordinarily, "[b]y agreeing to arbitrate a statutory claim, a party does not forgo the substantive rights afforded by the statute; it only submits to their resolution in an arbitral, rather than a judicial, forum." Mitsubishi Motors Corp. v. Soler Chrysler–Plymouth, Inc., 473 U.S., at 628, 105 S.Ct., at 3354. The McMahons argue, however, that § 29(a) compels a different conclusion. Initially, they contend that predispute agreements are void under § 29(a) because they tend to result from broker overreaching. They reason, as do some commentators, that Wilko is premised on the belief "that arbitration clauses in securities sales agreements generally are not freely negotiated." See, e.g., Sterk, Enforceability of Agreements to Arbitrate: An Examination of the Public Policy Defense, 2 Cardozo L.Rev. 481, 519 (1981). According to this view, *Wilko* barred enforcement of predispute agreements because of this frequent inequality of bargaining power, reasoning that Congress intended for § 14 generally to ensure that sellers did not "maneuver buyers into a position that might weaken their ability to recover under the Securities Act." 346 U.S., at 432, 74 S.Ct., at 185. The McMahons urge that we should interpret § 29(a) in the same fashion.

We decline to give *Wilko* a reading so far at odds with the plain language of § 14, or to adopt such an unlikely interpretation of § 29(a). The concern that § 29(a) is directed against is evident from the statute's plain language: it is a concern with whether an agreement "waive[s] compliance with [a] provision" of the Exchange Act. The voluntariness of the agreement is irrelevant to this inquiry: if a stipulation waives compliance with a statutory duty, it is void under § 29(a), whether voluntary or not. Thus, a customer cannot negotiate a reduction in commissions in exchange for a waiver of compliance with the requirements of the Exchange Act, even if the customer knowingly and voluntarily agreed to the bargain. Section 29(a) is concerned, not with whether brokers "maneuver[ed customers] into" an agreement, but with whether the agreement "weaken[s] their ability to recover under the [Exchange] Act." 346 U.S., at 432, 74 S.Ct., at 185. The former is grounds for revoking the contract under ordinary principles of contract law; the latter is grounds for voiding the agreement under § 29(a).

The other reason advanced by the McMahons for finding a waiver of their § 10(b) rights is that arbitration does "weaken their ability to recover under the [Exchange] Act." Ibid. That is the heart of the Court's decision in *Wilko*, and respondents urge that we should follow its reasoning. *Wilko* listed several grounds why, in the Court's view, the "effectiveness [of the Act's provisions] in application is lessened in arbitration." 346 U.S., at 435,

74 S.Ct., at 185. First, the *Wilko* Court believed that arbitration proceedings were not suited to cases requiring "subjective findings on the purpose and knowledge of an alleged violator." Id., at 435–436, 74 S.Ct., at 186–187. *Wilko* also was concerned that arbitrators must make legal determinations "without judicial instruction on the law," and that an arbitration award "may be made without explanation of [the arbitrator's] reasons and without a complete record of their proceedings." Id., at 436, 74 S.Ct., at 187. Finally, *Wilko* noted that the "[p]ower to vacate an award is limited," and that "interpretations of the law by the arbitrators in contrast to manifest disregard are not subject, in the federal courts, to judicial review for error in interpretation." Id., at 436–437, 74 S.Ct., at 187–188. *Wilko* concluded that in view of these drawbacks to arbitration, § 12(2) claims "require[d] the exercise of judicial direction to fairly assure their effectiveness." Id., at 437, 74 S.Ct., at 187.

As Justice Frankfurter noted in his dissent in *Wilko*, the Court's opinion did not rest on any evidence, either "in the record ... [or] in the facts of which [it could] take judicial notice," that "the arbitral system ... would not afford the plaintiff the rights to which he is entitled." Id., at 439, 74 S.Ct., at 189. Instead, the reasons given in *Wilko* reflect a general suspicion of the desirability of arbitration and the competence of arbitral tribunals—most apply with no greater force to the arbitration of securities disputes than to the arbitration of legal disputes generally. It is difficult to reconcile *Wilko*'s mistrust of the arbitral process with this Court's subsequent decisions involving the Arbitration Act ...

The suitability of arbitration as a means of enforcing Exchange Act rights is evident from our decision in *Scherk*. Although the holding in that case was limited to international agreements, the competence of arbitral tribunals to resolve § 10(b) claims is the same in both settings. Courts likewise have routinely enforced agreements to arbitrate § 10(b) claims where both parties are members of a securities exchange or the National Association of Securities Dealers (NASD), suggesting that arbitral tribunals are fully capable of handling such matters ... And courts uniformly have concluded that *Wilko* does not apply to the submission to arbitration of existing disputes, see, e.g., Gardner v. Shearson, Hammill & Co., 433 F.2d 367 (5th Cir. 1970); Moran v. Paine, Webber, Jackson & Curtis, 389 F.2d 242 (3d Cir. 1968), even though the inherent suitability of arbitration as a means of resolving § 10(b) claims remains unchanged. Cf. Mitsubishi, 473 U.S., at 633, 105 S.Ct., at 3357.

Thus, the mistrust of arbitration that formed the basis for the Wilko opinion in 1953 is difficult to square with the assessment of arbitration that has prevailed since that time. This is especially so in light of the intervening changes in the regulatory structure of the securities laws. Even if Wilko's assumptions regarding arbitration were valid at the time Wilko was decided, most certainly they do not hold true today for arbitration procedures subject to the SEC's oversight authority....

In 1953, when Wilko was decided, the Commission had only limited authority over the rules governing self-regulatory organizations (SROs)—

the national securities exchanges and registered securities associations—and this authority appears not to have included any authority at all over their arbitration rules. See Brief for Securities and Exchange Commission as Amicus Curiae 14–15. Since the 1975 amendments to § 19 of the Exchange Act, however, the Commission has had expansive power to ensure the adequacy of the arbitration procedures employed by the SROs. No proposed rule change may take effect unless the SEC finds that the proposed rule is consistent with the requirements of the Exchange Act, 15 U.S.C. § 78s(b)(2); and the Commission has the power, on its own initiative, to "abrogate, add to, and delete from" any SRO rule if it finds such changes necessary or appropriate to further the objectives of the Act, 15 U.S.C. § 78s(c). In short, the Commission has broad authority to oversee and to regulate the rules adopted by the SROs relating to customer disputes, including the power to mandate the adoption of any rules it deems necessary to ensure that arbitration procedures adequately protect statutory rights.

In the exercise of its regulatory authority, the SEC has specifically approved the arbitration procedures of the New York Stock Exchange, the American Stock Exchange, and the NASD, the organizations mentioned in the arbitration agreement at issue in this case. We conclude that where, as in this case, the prescribed procedures are subject to the Commission's § 19 authority, an arbitration agreement does not effect a waiver of the protections of the Act. While stare decisis concerns may counsel against upsetting Wilko's contrary conclusion under the Securities Act, we refuse to extend Wilko's reasoning to the Exchange Act in light of these intervening regulatory developments. The McMahons' agreement to submit to arbitration therefore is not tantamount to an impermissible waiver of the McMahons' rights under § 10(b), and the agreement is not void on that basis under § 29(a).

The final argument offered by the McMahons is that even if § 29(a) as enacted does not void predispute arbitration agreements, Congress subsequently has indicated that it desires § 29(a) to be so interpreted. According to the McMahons, Congress expressed this intent when it failed to make more extensive changes to § 28(b), 15 U.S.C. § 78bb(b), in the 1975 amendments to the Exchange Act.... But the amended version of § 28(b), like the original, mentions neither customers nor arbitration. It is directed at an entirely different problem: enhancing the self-regulatory function of the SROs under the Exchange Act.

The McMahons nonetheless argue that we should find it significant that Congress did not take this opportunity to address the general question of the arbitrability of Exchange Act claims. Their argument is based entirely on a sentence from the Conference Report, which they contend amounts to a ratification of *Wilko*'s extension to Exchange Act claims. The Conference Report states:

> The Senate bill amended section 28 of the Securities Exchange Act of 1934 with respect to arbitration proceedings between self-regulatory organizations and their participants, members, or persons dealing with

> members or participants. The House amendment contained no comparable provision. The House receded to the Senate. It was the clear understanding of the conferees that this amendment did not change existing law, as articulated in Wilko v. Swan, 346 U.S. 427 [74 S.Ct. 182, 98 L.Ed. 168] (1953), concerning the effect of arbitration proceedings provisions in agreements entered into by persons dealing with members and participants of self-regulatory organizations....

The McMahons contend that the conferees would not have acknowledged *Wilko* in a revision of the Exchange Act unless they were aware of lower court decisions extending *Wilko* to § 10(b) claims and intended to approve them. We find this argument fraught with difficulties. We cannot see how Congress could extend *Wilko* to the Exchange Act without enacting into law any provision remotely addressing that subject. See Train v. City of New York, 420 U.S. 35, 45, 95 S.Ct. 839, 845, 43 L.Ed.2d 1 (1975). And even if it could, there is little reason to interpret the Report as the McMahons suggest. At the outset, the committee may well have mentioned Wilko for a reason entirely different from the one postulated by the McMahons—lower courts had applied § 28(b) to the Securities Act, see, e.g., Axelrod & Co. v. Kordich, Victor & Neufeld, supra, at 843, and the committee may simply have wished to make clear that the amendment to § 28(b) was not otherwise intended to affect Wilko's construction of the Securities Act. Moreover, even if the committee were referring to the arbitrability of § 10(b) claims, the quoted sentence does not disclose what committee members thought "existing law" provided. The conference members might have had in mind the two Court of Appeals decisions extending *Wilko* to the Exchange Act, as the McMahons contend. See Greater Continental Corp. v. Schechter, 422 F.2d 1100 (C.A.2 1970); Moran v. Paine, Webber, Jackson & Curtis, 389 F.2d 242 (C.A.3 1968). It is equally likely, however, that the committee had in mind this Court's decision the year before expressing doubts as to whether *Wilko* should be extended to § 10(b) claims. See Scherk v. Alberto–Culver Co., 417 U.S., at 513, 94 S.Ct., at 2454 ("[A] colorable argument could be made that even the semantic reasoning of the *Wilko* opinion does not control [a case based on § 10(b)]"). Finally, even assuming the conferees had an understanding of existing law that all agreed upon, they specifically disclaimed any intent to change it. Hence, the *Wilko* issue was left to the courts: it was unaffected by the amendment to § 28(b). This statement of congressional inaction simply does not support the proposition that the 1975 Congress intended to engraft onto unamended § 29(a) a meaning different from that of the enacting Congress.

We conclude, therefore, that Congress did not intend for § 29(a) to bar enforcement of all predispute arbitration agreements. In this case, where the SEC has sufficient statutory authority to ensure that arbitration is adequate to vindicate Exchange Act rights, enforcement does not effect a waiver of "compliance with any provision" of the Exchange Act under § 29(a). Accordingly, we hold the McMahons' agreements to arbitrate Exchange Act claims "enforce[able] ... in accord with the explicit provisions of the Arbitration Act." Scherk v. Alberto–Culver Co., supra, at 520, 94 S.Ct., at 2457.

IV

Unlike the Exchange Act, there is nothing in the text of the RICO statute that even arguably evinces congressional intent to exclude civil RICO claims from the dictates of the Arbitration Act. This silence in the text is matched by silence in the statute's legislative history. The private treble-damages provision codified as 18 U.S.C. § 1964(c) was added to the House version of the bill after the bill had been passed by the Senate, and it received only abbreviated discussion in either House. See Sedima, S.P.R.L. v. Imrex Co., 473 U.S. 479, 486–488, 105 S.Ct. 3275, 3280–3281, 87 L.Ed.2d 346 (1985). There is no hint in these legislative debates that Congress intended for RICO treble-damages claims to be excluded from the ambit of the Arbitration Act. See Genesco, Inc. v. T. Kakiuchi & Co., Ltd., 815 F.2d 840, 850–851 (2d Cir. 1987); Mayaja, Inc. v. Bodkin, 803 F.2d 157, 164 (C.A.5 1986).

Because RICO's text and legislative history fail to reveal any intent to override the provisions of the Arbitration Act, the McMahons must argue that there is an irreconcilable conflict between arbitration and RICO's underlying purposes. Our decision in Mitsubishi Motors Corp. v. Soler Chrysler–Plymouth, Inc., 473 U.S. 614, 105 S.Ct. 3346, 87 L.Ed.2d 444 (1985), however, already has addressed many of the grounds given by the McMahons to support this claim . . .

Not only does Mitsubishi support the arbitrability of RICO claims, but there is even more reason to suppose that arbitration will adequately serve the purposes of RICO than that it will adequately protect private enforcement of the antitrust laws. Antitrust violations generally have a widespread impact on national markets as a whole, and the antitrust treble-damages provision gives private parties an incentive to bring civil suits that serve to advance the national interest in a competitive economy. See Lindsay, "Public" Rights and Private Forums: Predispute Arbitration Agreements and Securities Litigation, 20 Loyola (LA) L.Rev. 643, 691–692 (1987). RICO's drafters likewise sought to provide vigorous incentives for plaintiffs to pursue RICO claims that would advance society's fight against organized crime. See Sedima, S.P.R.L. v. Imrex Co., supra, at 498, 105 S.Ct., at 3286. But in fact RICO actions are seldom asserted "against the archetypal, intimidating mobster." Id., at 499, 105 S.Ct., at 3286; see also id., at 506, 105 S.Ct., at 3295 (MARSHALL, J., dissenting) ("[O]nly 9% of all civil RICO cases have involved allegations of criminal activity normally associated with professional criminals"). The special incentives necessary to encourage civil enforcement actions against organized crime do not support non-arbitrability of run-of-the-mill civil RICO claims brought against legitimate enterprises. The private attorney general role for the typical RICO plaintiff is simply less plausible than it is for the typical antitrust plaintiff, and does not support a finding that there is an irreconcilable conflict between arbitration and enforcement of the RICO statute.

In sum, we find no basis for concluding that Congress intended to prevent enforcement of agreements to arbitrate RICO claims. The McMahons may effectively vindicate their RICO claim in an arbitral forum, and therefore there is no inherent conflict between arbitration and the purposes underlying § 1964(c). Moreover, nothing in RICO's text or legislative history otherwise demonstrates congressional intent to make an exception to the Arbitration Act for RICO claims. Accordingly, the McMahons, "having made the bargain to arbitrate," will be held to their bargain. Their RICO claim is arbitrable under the terms of the Arbitration Act.

V

Accordingly, the judgment of the Court of Appeals for the Second Circuit is reversed, and the case is remanded for further proceedings consistent with this opinion.

It is so ordered.

■ JUSTICE BLACKMUN, with whom JUSTICE BRENNAN and JUSTICE MARSHALL join, concurring in part and dissenting in part.

I concur in the Court's decision to enforce the arbitration agreement with respect to respondents' RICO claims and thus join Parts I, II, and IV of the Court's opinion. I disagree, however, with the Court's conclusion that respondents' § 10(b) claims also are subject to arbitration.

Both the Securities Act of 1933 and the Securities Exchange Act of 1934 were enacted to protect investors from predatory behavior of securities industry personnel. In Wilko v. Swan, 346 U.S. 427, 74 S.Ct. 182, 98 L.Ed. 168 (1953), the Court recognized this basic purpose when it declined to enforce a predispute agreement to compel arbitration of claims under the Securities Act. Following that decision, lower courts extended Wilko's reasoning to claims brought under § 10(b) of the Exchange Act, and Congress approved of this extension. In today's decision, however, the Court effectively overrules *Wilko* by accepting the Securities and Exchange Commission's newly adopted position that arbitration procedures in the securities industry and the Commission's oversight of the self-regulatory organizations (SROs) have improved greatly since *Wilko* was decided. The Court thus approves the abandonment of the judiciary's role in the resolution of claims under the Exchange Act and leaves such claims to the arbitral forum of the securities industry at a time when the industry's abuses towards investors are more apparent than ever.

I

At the outset, it is useful to review the manner by which the issue decided today has been kept alive inappropriately by this Court. As the majority explains, *Wilko* was limited to the holding "that a predispute agreement could not be enforced to compel arbitration of a claim arising under § 12(2) of the Securities Act." Ante, at 2338. Relying, however, on the reasoning of *Wilko* and the similarity between the pertinent provisions of the Securities Act and those of the Exchange Act, lower courts extended the *Wilko* holding to claims under the Exchange Act and refused to enforce predispute agreements to arbitrate them as well . . .

If, however, there could have been any doubts about the extension of *Wilko's* holding to § 10(b) claims, they were undermined by Congress in its 1975 amendments to the Exchange Act. The Court questions the significance of these amendments, which, as it notes, concerned, among other things, provisions dealing with dispute resolution and disciplinary action by an SRO towards its own members. See ante, at 2342–2343. These amendments, however, are regarded as "the 'most substantial and significant revision of this country's Federal securities laws since the passage of the Securities Exchange Act in 1934.' " . . . More importantly, in enacting these amendments, Congress specifically was considering exceptions to § 29(a), 15 U.S.C. § 78cc, the nonwaiver provision of the Exchange Act, a provision primarily designed with the protection of investors in mind. The statement from the legislative history, cited by the Court, ante, at 2343, on its face indicates that Congress did not want the amendments to overrule *Wilko*. . . .

II

There are essentially two problems with the Court's conclusion that predispute agreements to arbitrate § 10(b) claims may be enforced. First, the Court gives *Wilko* an overly narrow reading so that it can fit into the syllogism offered by the Commission and accepted by the Court, namely, (1) *Wilko* was really a case concerning whether arbitration was adequate for the enforcement of the substantive provisions of the securities laws; (2) all of the *Wilko* Court's doubts as to arbitration's adequacy are outdated; (3) thus *Wilko* is no longer good law . . . Second, the Court accepts uncritically petitioners' and the Commission's argument that the problems with arbitration, highlighted by the *Wilko* Court, either no longer exist or are not now viewed as problems by the Court. This acceptance primarily is based upon the Court's belief in the Commission's representations that its oversight of the SROs ensures the adequacy of arbitration.

A

I agree with the Court's observation that, in order to establish an exception to the Arbitration Act, 9 U.S.C. § 1 et seq., for a class of statutory claims, there must be "an intention discernible from the text, history, or purposes of the statute." Ante, at 2338. Where the Court first goes wrong, however, is in its failure to acknowledge that the Exchange Act, like the Securities Act, constitutes such an exception. This failure is made possible only by the unduly narrow reading of *Wilko* that ignores the Court's determination there that the Securities Act was an exception to the Arbitration Act. The Court's reading is particularly startling because it is in direct contradiction to the interpretation of *Wilko* given by the Court in Mitsubishi Motors Corp. v. Soler Chrysler–Plymouth, Inc., 473 U.S. 614, 105 S.Ct. 3346, 87 L.Ed.2d 444 (1985), a decision on which the Court relies for its strong statement of a federal policy in favor of arbitration. But we observed in *Mitsubishi*:

> Just as it is the congressional policy manifested in the Federal Arbitration Act that requires courts liberally to construe the scope of arbitration agreements covered by that Act, it is the congressional intention expressed in some other statute on which the courts must rely to identify any category of claims as to which agreements to arbitrate will be held unenforceable. See Wilko v. Swan, 346 U.S., at 434–435 [74 S.Ct., at 186–187] ... We must assume that if Congress intended the substantive protection afforded by a given statute to include protection against waiver of the right to a judicial forum, that intention will be deducible from text or legislative history. See Wilko v. Swan, supra. Id., at 627–628, 105 S.Ct., at 3354.

Such language clearly suggests that, in Mitsubishi, we viewed Wilko as holding that the text and legislative history of the Securities Act—not general problems with arbitration—established that the Securities Act constituted an exception to the Arbitration Act. In a surprising display of logic, the Court uses *Mitsubishi* as support for the virtues of arbitration and thus as a means for undermining *Wilko's* holding, but fails to take into account the most pertinent language in *Mitsubishi*....

Accordingly, the Court seriously errs when it states that the result in Wilko turned only on the perceived inadequacy of arbitration for the enforcement of § 12(2) claims. It is true that the Wilko Court discussed the inadequacies of this process, 346 U.S., at 435–437, 74 S.Ct., at 186–188, and that this discussion constituted one ground for the Court's decision. The discussion, however, occurred after the Court had concluded that the language, legislative history, and purposes of the Securities Act mandated an exception to the Arbitration Act for these securities claims....

In light of a proper reading of *Wilko*, the pertinent question then becomes whether the language, legislative history, and purposes of the Exchange Act call for an exception to the Arbitration Act for § 10(b) claims. The Exchange Act waiver provision is virtually identical to that of the Securities Act. More importantly, the same concern with investor protection that motivated the Securities Act is evident in the Exchange Act, although the latter, in contrast to the former, is aimed at trading in the secondary securities market ... We have recognized that both Acts were designed with this common purpose in mind ... Indeed, the application of both Acts to the same conduct, ... suggests that they have the same basic goal. And we have approved a cumulative construction of remedies under the securities Acts to promote the maximum possible protection of investors ...

In sum, the same reasons that led the Court to find an exception to the Arbitration Act for § 12(2) claims exist for § 10(b) claims as well. It is clear that *Wilko*, when properly read, governs the instant case and mandates that a predispute arbitration agreement should not be enforced as to § 10(b) claims.

B

Even if I were to accept the Court's narrow reading of *Wilko*, as a case dealing only with the inadequacies of arbitration in 1953, I do not think that this case should be resolved differently today so long as the policy of investor protection is given proper consideration in the analysis. Despite improvements in the process of arbitration and changes in the judicial attitude towards it, several aspects of arbitration that were seen by the *Wilko* court to be inimical to the policy of investor protection still remain. Moreover, I have serious reservations about the Commission's contention that its oversight of the SROs' arbitration procedures will ensure that the process is adequate to protect an investor's rights under the securities Acts.

As the Court observes, ante, at 2339–2340, in *Wilko* the Court was disturbed by several characteristics of arbitration that made such a process inadequate to safeguard the special position in which the Securities Act had placed the investor. The Court concluded that judicial review of the arbitrators' application of the securities laws would be difficult because arbitrators were required neither to give the reasons for their decisions nor to make a complete record of their proceedings. See 346 U.S., at 436, 74 S.Ct., at 187. The Court also observed that the grounds for vacating an arbitration award were limited. The Court noted that, under the Arbitration Act, there were only four grounds for vacation of an award: fraud in procuring the award, partiality on the part of arbitrators, gross misconduct by arbitrators, and the failure of arbitrators to render a final decision. Id., at 436, n. 22, 74 S.Ct., at 187, n. 22, quoting 9 U.S.C. § 10 (1952 Ed., Supp. V). The arbitrators' interpretation of the law would be subject to judicial review only under the "manifest disregard" standard. 346 U.S., at 436, 74 S.Ct., at 187....

Furthermore, there remains the danger that, at worst, compelling an investor to arbitrate securities claims puts him in a forum controlled by the securities industry. This result directly contradicts the goal of both securities Acts to free the investor from the control of the market professional. The Uniform Code provides some safeguards[19] but despite them, and indeed because of the background of the arbitrators, the investor has the impression, frequently justified, that his claims are being judged by a forum composed of individuals sympathetic to the securities industry and not drawn from the public. It is generally recognized that the codes do not define who falls into the category "not from the securities industry." ... Accordingly, it is often possible for the "public" arbitrators to be attorneys or consultants whose clients have been exchange members or SROs. See Panel of Arbitrators 1987–1988, CCH American Stock Exchange Guide 158–160 (1987) (71 out of 116 "public" arbitrators are lawyers). The uniform opposition of investors to compelled arbitration and the over-

19. The Uniform Code mandates that a majority of an arbitration panel, usually composed of between three to five arbitrators, be drawn from outside the industry. Fifth SICA Report § 8(a), p. 31. Each arbitrator, moreover, is directed to disclose "any circumstances which might preclude such arbitrator from rendering an objective and impartial determination." § 11, p. 32. In addition, the parties are informed of the business associations of the arbitrators, § 9, and each party has the right to one peremptory challenge and to unlimited challenges for cause, § 10, p. 32. The arbitrators are usually individuals familiar with the federal securities laws. See Brener v. Becker Paribas Inc., 628 F.Supp. 442, 448 (S.D.N.Y. 1985).

whelming support of the securities industry for the process suggest that there must be some truth to the investors' belief that the securities industry has an advantage in a forum under its own control. . . .

More surprising than the Court's acceptance of the present adequacy of arbitration for the resolution of securities claims is its confidence in the Commission's oversight of the arbitration procedures of the SROs to ensure this adequacy. Such confidence amounts to a wholesale acceptance of the Commission's present position that this oversight undermines the force of Wilko and that arbitration therefore should be compelled because the Commission has supervisory authority over the SROs' arbitration procedures. The Court, however, fails to acknowledge that, until it filed an amicus brief in this case, the Commission consistently took the position that § 10(b) claims, like those under § 12(2), should not be sent to arbitration, that predispute arbitration agreements, where the investor was not advised of his right to a judicial forum, were misleading, and that the very regulatory oversight upon which the Commission now relies could not alone make securities-industry arbitration adequate. It is most questionable, then, whether the Commission's recently adopted position is entitled to the deference that the Court accords it. . . .

In the meantime, the Court leaves lower courts with some authority, albeit limited, to protect investors before Congress acts. Courts should take seriously their duty to review the results of arbitration to the extent possible under the Arbitration Act. As we explained in Mitsubishi Motors Corp. v. Soler Chrysler–Plymouth, Inc., "courts should remain attuned to well-supported claims that the agreement to arbitrate resulted from the sort of fraud or overwhelming economic power that would provide grounds 'for the revocation of any contract.' " 473 U.S., at 627, 105 S.Ct., at 3354, quoting 9 U.S.C. § 2. Indeed, in light of today's decision compelling the enforcement of predispute arbitration agreements, it is likely that investors will be inclined, more than ever, to bring complaints to federal courts that arbitrators were partial or acted in "manifest disregard" of the securities laws. See Brown, Shell, & Tyson at 36. It is thus ironic that the Court's decision, no doubt animated by its desire to rid the federal courts of these suits, actually may increase litigation about arbitration.

I therefore respectfully dissent in part.

■ JUSTICE STEVENS, concurring in part and dissenting in part.

Gaps in the law must, of course, be filled by judicial construction. But after a statute has been construed, either by this Court or by a consistent course of decision by other federal judges and agencies, it acquires a meaning that should be as clear as if the judicial gloss had been drafted by the Congress itself. This position reflects both respect for Congress' role, see Boys Markets, Inc. v. Retail Clerks, 398 U.S. 235, 257–258, 90 S.Ct. 1583, 1595–1596, 26 L.Ed.2d 199 (1970) (Black, J., dissenting), and the compelling need to preserve the courts' limited resources, see B. Cardozo, The Nature of the Judicial Process 149 (1921).

During the 32 years immediately following this Court's decision in Wilko v. Swan, 346 U.S. 427, 74 S.Ct. 182, 98 L.Ed. 168 (1953), each of the eight Circuits that addressed the issue concluded that the holding of *Wilko* was fully applicable to claims arising under the Securities Exchange Act of 1934. See ante, at 2349, n. 6 (opinion of Blackmun, J.). This longstanding interpretation creates a strong presumption, in my view, that any mistake that the courts may have made in interpreting the statute is best remedied by the Legislative, not the Judicial, Branch. The history set forth in Part I of Justice Blackmun's opinion adds special force to that presumption in this case.

For this reason, I respectfully dissent from the portion of the Court's judgment that holds *Wilko* inapplicable to the 1934 Act. Like Justice Blackmun, however, I join Parts I, II, and IV of the Court's opinion.

* * *

Questions

1. Do the provisions of the Securities and Exchange Act of 1934 differ sufficiently from those of the Securities Act of 1933 to warrant the conclusion that the latter but not the former statute was intended to override the FAA?

2. Is it disingenuous of the Court to argue that nothing in the text or history of the Exchange Act or RICO evinces Congressional intent to preclude arbitration? The Exchange Act, of course, was enacted at a time when arbitration was being used almost exclusively to resolve commercial disputes, and RICO was enacted when *Wilko* was undisputedly good law. Why in either case would it even have occurred to Congress that claims brought under those statutes might be arbitrable?

3. How convincing is Justice O'Connor's interpretation of the 1975 amendments to the Securities Acts? Is there another view of those amendments that might argue for a different result in this case?

4. Compare the interpretation of *Wilko* by the majority and the dissent in *Shearson/American Express v. McMahon*. How do the two opinions differ as to what was held in that previous case?

5. Is there tension between Justice O'Connor's opinion in this case and her dissent in *Southland*? Can these two opinions be reconciled?

6. What are the differing views of the majority and dissent about the virtues and shortcomings of the arbitration process?

* * *

Rodriguez de Quijas v. Shearson/American Express, Inc.

490 U.S. 477 (1989).

■ JUSTICE KENNEDY delivered the opinion of the Court.

The question here is whether a predispute agreement to arbitrate claims under the Securities Act of 1933 is unenforceable, requiring resolution of the claims only in a judicial forum.

I

Petitioners are individuals who invested about $400,000 in securities. They signed a standard customer agreement with the broker, which included a clause stating that the parties agreed to settle any controversies "relating to [the] accounts" through binding arbitration that complies with specified procedures. The agreement to arbitrate these controversies is unqualified, unless it is found to be unenforceable under federal or state law. Customer's Agreement ¶ 13. The investments turned sour, and petitioners eventually sued respondent and its broker-agent in charge of the accounts, alleging that their money was lost in unauthorized and fraudulent transactions. In their complaint they pleaded various violations of federal and state law, including claims under § 12(2) of the Securities Act of 1933, 15 U.S.C. § 77l (2), and claims under three sections of the Securities Exchange Act of 1934.

The District Court ordered all the claims to be submitted to arbitration except for those raised under § 12(2) of the Securities Act. It held that the latter claims must proceed in the court action under our clear holding on the point in Wilko v. Swan, 346 U.S. 427, 74 S.Ct. 182, 98 L.Ed. 168 (1953). The District Court reaffirmed its ruling upon reconsideration and also entered a default judgment against the broker, who is no longer in the case. The Court of Appeals reversed, concluding that the arbitration agreement is enforceable because this Court's subsequent decisions have reduced Wilko to "obsolescence." Rodriguez de Quijas v. Shearson/Lehman Bros., Inc., 845 F.2d 1296, 1299 (C.A.5 1988). We granted certiorari, 488 U.S. 954, 109 S.Ct. 389, 102 L.Ed.2d 379 (1988).

II

The *Wilko* case, decided in 1953, required the Court to determine whether an agreement to arbitrate future controversies constitutes a binding stipulation "to waive compliance with any provision" of the Securities Act, which is nullified by § 14 of the Act. 15 U.S.C. § 77n. The Court considered the language, purposes, and legislative history of the Securities Act and concluded that the agreement to arbitrate was void under § 14. But the decision was a difficult one in view of the competing legislative policy embodied in the Arbitration Act, which the Court described as "not easily reconcilable," and which strongly favors the enforcement of agreements to arbitrate as a means of securing "prompt, economical and adequate solution of controversies." 346 U.S., at 438, 74 S.Ct., at 188.

It has been recognized that *Wilko* was not obviously correct, for "the language prohibiting waiver of 'compliance with any provision of this title' could easily have been read to relate to substantive provisions of the Act without including the remedy provisions." Alberto–Culver Co. v. Scherk,

484 F.2d 611, 618, n. 7 (C.A.7 1973) (Stevens, J., dissenting), rev'd, 417 U.S. 506, 94 S.Ct. 2449, 41 L.Ed.2d 270 (1974)....

The Court's characterization of the arbitration process in *Wilko* is pervaded by what Judge Jerome Frank called "the old judicial hostility to arbitration." Kulukundis Shipping Co. v. Amtorg Trading Corp., 126 F.2d 978, 985 (2d Cir. 1942). That view has been steadily eroded over the years, beginning in the lower courts. See Scherk, supra, at 616 (Stevens, J., dissenting) (citing cases) ... To the extent that Wilko rested on suspicion of arbitration as a method of weakening the protections afforded in the substantive law to would-be complainants, it has fallen far out of step with our current strong endorsement of the federal statutes favoring this method of resolving disputes.

Once the outmoded presumption of disfavoring arbitration proceedings is set to one side, it becomes clear that the right to select the judicial forum and the wider choice of courts are not such essential features of the Securities Act that § 14 is properly construed to bar any waiver of these provisions. Nor are they so critical that they cannot be waived under the rationale that the Securities Act was intended to place buyers of securities on an equal footing with sellers. *Wilko* identified two different kinds of provisions in the Securities Act that would advance this objective. Some are substantive, such as the provision placing on the seller the burden of proving lack of scienter when a buyer alleges fraud. See 346 U.S., at 431, 74 S.Ct., at 184, citing 15 U.S.C. § 77l (2). Others are procedural. The specific procedural improvements highlighted in Wilko are the statute's broad venue provisions in the federal courts; the existence of nationwide service of process in the federal courts; the extinction of the amount-in-controversy requirement that had applied to fraud suits when they were brought in federal courts under diversity jurisdiction rather than as a federal cause of action; and the grant of concurrent jurisdiction in the state and federal courts without possibility of removal. See 346 U.S., at 431, 74 S.Ct., at 184, citing 15 U.S.C. § 77v(a).

There is no sound basis for construing the prohibition in § 14 on waiving "compliance with any provision" of the Securities Act to apply to these procedural provisions. Although the first three measures do facilitate suits by buyers of securities, the grant of concurrent jurisdiction constitutes explicit authorization for complainants to waive those protections by filing suit in state court without possibility of removal to federal court. These measures, moreover, are present in other federal statutes which have not been interpreted to prohibit enforcement of predispute agreements to arbitrate. See Shearson/American Express Inc. v. McMahon, supra (construing the Securities Exchange Act of 1934; see 15 U.S.C. § 78aa); ibid. (construing the RICO statutes; see 18 U.S.C. § 1965); Mitsubishi Motors Corp. v. Soler Chrysler–Plymouth, Inc., supra (construing the antitrust laws; see 15 U.S.C. 15).

Indeed, in *McMahon* the Court declined to read § 29(a) of the Securities Exchange Act of 1934, the language of which is in every respect the same as that in § 14 of the 1933 Act, compare 15 U.S.C. § 77v(a) with

§ 78aa, to prohibit enforcement of predispute agreements to arbitrate. The only conceivable distinction in this regard between the Securities Act and the Securities Exchange Act is that the former statute allows concurrent federal-state jurisdiction over causes of action and the latter statute provides for exclusive federal jurisdiction. But even if this distinction were thought to make any difference at all, it would suggest that arbitration agreements, which are "in effect, a specialized kind of forum-selection clause," Scherk v. Alberto–Culver Co., 417 U.S. 506, 519, 94 S.Ct. 2449, 2457, 41 L.Ed.2d 270 (1974), should not be prohibited under the Securities Act, since they, like the provision for concurrent jurisdiction, serve to advance the objective of allowing buyers of securities a broader right to select the forum for resolving disputes, whether it be judicial or otherwise . . .

Finally, in *McMahon* we stressed the strong language of the Arbitration Act, which declares as a matter of federal law that arbitration agreements "shall be valid, irrevocable, and enforceable, save upon such grounds as exist at law or in equity for the revocation of any contract." 9 U.S.C. § 2. Under that statute, the party opposing arbitration carries the burden of showing that Congress intended in a separate statute to preclude a waiver of judicial remedies, or that such a waiver of judicial remedies inherently conflicts with the underlying purposes of that other statute. 482 U.S., at 226–227, 107 S.Ct., at 2337–2338. But as Justice Frankfurter said in dissent in *Wilko*, so it is true in this case: "There is nothing in the record before us, nor in the facts of which we can take judicial notice, to indicate that the arbitral system ... would not afford the plaintiff the rights to which he is entitled." 346 U.S., at 439, 74 S.Ct., at 189. Petitioners have not carried their burden of showing that arbitration agreements are not enforceable under the Securities Act.

The language quoted above from § 2 of the Arbitration Act also allows the courts to give relief where the party opposing arbitration presents "well-supported claims that the agreement to arbitrate resulted from the sort of fraud or overwhelming economic power that would provide grounds 'for the revocation of any contract.' " *Mitsubishi*, 473 U.S., at 627, 105 S.Ct., at 3354. This avenue of relief is in harmony with the Securities Act's concern to protect buyers of securities by removing "the disadvantages under which buyers labor" in their dealings with sellers. *Wilko*, supra, 346 U.S., at 435, 74 S.Ct., at 187. Although petitioners suggest that the agreement to arbitrate here was adhesive in nature, the record contains no factual showing sufficient to support that suggestion.

III

We do not suggest that the Court of Appeals on its own authority should have taken the step of renouncing *Wilko*. If a precedent of this Court has direct application in a case, yet appears to rest on reasons rejected in some other line of decisions, the Court of Appeals should follow the case which directly controls, leaving to this Court the prerogative of overruling its own decisions. We now conclude that *Wilko* was incorrectly decided and is inconsistent with the prevailing uniform construction of other federal statutes governing arbitration agreements in the setting of business transactions. Although we are normally and properly reluctant to overturn our decisions construing statutes, we have done so to achieve a uniform interpretation of similar statutory language, Commissioner v. Estate of Church, 335 U.S. 632, 649–650, 69 S.Ct. 322, 330–331, 93 L.Ed. 288 (1949), and to correct a seriously erroneous interpretation of statutory language that would undermine congressional policy as expressed in other legislation, see, e.g., Boys Markets, Inc. v. Retail Clerks, 398 U.S. 235, 240–241, 90 S.Ct. 1583, 1586–1587, 26 L.Ed.2d 199 (1970) (overruling Sinclair Refining Co. v. Atkinson, 370 U.S. 195, 82 S.Ct. 1328, 8 L.Ed.2d 440 (1962)). Both purposes would be served here by overruling the *Wilko* decision.

It also would be undesirable for the decisions in *Wilko* and *McMahon* to continue to exist side by side. Their inconsistency is at odds with the principle that the 1933 and 1934 Acts should be construed harmoniously because they "constitute interrelated components of the federal regulatory scheme governing transactions in securities." Ernst & Ernst v. Hochfelder, 425 U.S. 185, 206, 96 S.Ct. 1375, 1387, 47 L.Ed.2d 668 (1976). In this case, for example, petitioners' claims under the 1934 Act were subjected to arbitration, while their claim under the 1933 Act was not permitted to go to arbitration, but was required to proceed in court. That result makes little sense for similar claims, based on similar facts, which are supposed to arise within a single federal regulatory scheme. In addition, the inconsistency between *Wilko* and *McMahon* undermines the essential rationale for a harmonious construction of the two statutes, which is to discourage litigants from manipulating their allegations merely to cast their claims under one of the securities laws rather than another. For all of these reasons, therefore, we overrule the decision in *Wilko*.

. . . The judgment of the Court of Appeals is Affirmed.

■ JUSTICE STEVENS, with whom JUSTICE BRENNAN, JUSTICE MARSHALL, and JUSTICE BLACKMUN join, dissenting.

The Court of Appeals refused to follow Wilko v. Swan, 346 U.S. 427, 74 S.Ct. 182, 98 L.Ed. 168 (1953), a controlling precedent of this Court. As the majority correctly acknowledges, ante, at 1921, the Court of Appeals therefore engaged in an indefensible brand of judicial activism. We, of course, are not subject to the same restraint when asked to upset one of our own precedents. But when our earlier opinion gives a statutory provision concrete meaning, which Congress elects not to amend during the ensuing 3½ decades, our duty to respect Congress' work product is strikingly similar to the duty of other federal courts to respect our work product.

In the final analysis, a Justice's vote in a case like this depends more on his or her views about the respective lawmaking responsibilities of Congress and this Court than on conflicting policy interests. Judges who have confidence in their own ability to fashion public policy are less hesitant to change the law than those of us who are inclined to give wide latitude to the views of the voters' representatives on nonconstitutional matters.... As I pointed out years ago, Alberto–Culver Co. v. Scherk, 484 F.2d 611, 615–620 (C.A.7 1973) (dissenting opinion), rev'd, 417 U.S. 506, 94 S.Ct. 2449, 41 L.Ed.2d 270 (1974), there are valid policy and textual arguments on both sides regarding the interrelation of federal securities and arbitration Acts. See ante, at 1919–1921. None of these arguments, however, carries sufficient weight to tip the balance between judicial and legislative authority and overturn an interpretation of an Act of Congress that has been settled for many years.

I respectfully dissent.

* * *

Questions

1. Was the result in *Rodriguez* inevitable in light of the reasoning in *Scherk, Mitsubishi*, and *McMahon?*

2. Is the Court's statement that *Wilko*'s reasoning "has fallen far out of step with our current strong endorsement" of arbitration based on anything other than its own opinions in post-*Wilko* cases? If that is the only basis for the statement, is the Court's reasoning anything more than bootstrapping?

3. Does the Court accept a distinction between a waiver of the substantive provisions of a statute and a waiver of a remedy, as was mentioned in dicta in *Scherk*? Is this distinction a useful means to determine whether claims arising under the Securities Act are amenable to arbitration? Does this distinction help determine whether other statutory claims are amenable to arbitration? Is there some other basis for deciding which statutory claims are amenable to arbitration and which are not?

* * *

Gilmer v. Interstate/Johnson Lane Corp.

500 U.S. 20 (1991).

■ JUSTICE WHITE delivered the opinion of the Court.

The question presented in this case is whether a claim under the Age Discrimination in Employment Act of 1967 (ADEA), 81 Stat. 602, as amended, 29 U.S.C. § 621 et seq., can be subjected to compulsory arbitration pursuant to an arbitration agreement in a securities registration application. The Court of Appeals held that it could, 895 F.2d 195 (C.A.4 1990), and we affirm.

I

Respondent Interstate/Johnson Lane Corporation (Interstate) hired petitioner Robert Gilmer as a Manager of Financial Services in May 1981. As required by his employment, Gilmer registered as a securities representative with several stock exchanges, including the New York Stock Exchange (NYSE). See App. 15–18. His registration application, entitled "Uniform Application for Securities Industry Registration or Transfer," provided, among other things, that Gilmer "agree[d] to arbitrate any dispute, claim or controversy" arising between him and Interstate "that is required to be arbitrated under the rules, constitutions or by-laws of the organizations with which I register." Id., at 18. Of relevance to this case, NYSE Rule 347 provides for arbitration of "[a]ny controversy between a registered representative and any member or member organization arising out of the employment or termination of employment of such registered representative." App. to Brief for Respondent 1.

Interstate terminated Gilmer's employment in 1987, at which time Gilmer was 62 years of age. After first filing an age discrimination charge with the Equal Employment Opportunity Commission (EEOC), Gilmer subsequently brought suit in the United States District Court for the Western District of North Carolina, alleging that Interstate had discharged him because of his age, in violation of the ADEA. In response to Gilmer's complaint, Interstate filed in the District Court a motion to compel arbitration of the ADEA claim. In its motion, Interstate relied upon the arbitration agreement in Gilmer's registration application, as well as the Federal Arbitration Act (FAA), 9 U.S.C. § 1 et seq. The District Court denied Interstate's motion, based on this Court's decision in Alexander v. Gardner–Denver Co., 415 U.S. 36, 94 S.Ct. 1011, 39 L.Ed.2d 147 (1974), and because it concluded that "Congress intended to protect ADEA claimants from the waiver of a judicial forum." App. 87. The United States Court of Appeals for the Fourth Circuit reversed, finding "nothing in the text, legislative history, or underlying purposes of the ADEA indicating a congressional intent to preclude enforcement of arbitration agreements." 895 F.2d, at 197. We granted certiorari, 498 U.S. 809, 111 S.Ct. 41, 112 L.Ed.2d 18 (1990), to resolve a conflict among the Courts of Appeals regarding the arbitrability of ADEA claims.

II

The FAA was originally enacted in 1925, 43 Stat. 883, and then reenacted and codified in 1947 as Title 9 of the United States Code. Its purpose was to reverse the longstanding judicial hostility to arbitration agreements that had existed at English common law and had been adopted by American courts, and to place arbitration agreements upon the same footing as other contracts. Dean Witter Reynolds Inc. v. Byrd, 470 U.S. 213, 219–220, and n. 6 (1985); Scherk v. Alberto–Culver Co., 417 U.S. 506, 510, n. 4 (1974). Its primary substantive provision states that "[a] written provision in any maritime transaction or a contract evidencing a transaction involving commerce to settle by arbitration a controversy thereafter arising out of such contract or transaction ... shall be valid, irrevocable, and enforceable, save upon such grounds as exist at law or in equity for the revocation of any contract." 9 U.S.C. § 2. The FAA also provides for stays of proceedings in federal district courts when an issue in the proceeding is referable to arbitration, § 3, and for orders compelling arbitration when one party has failed, neglected, or refused to comply with an arbitration agreement, § 4. These provisions manifest a "liberal federal policy favoring arbitration agreements." Moses H. Cone Memorial Hospital v. Mercury Construction Corp., 460 U.S. 1, 24, 103 S.Ct. 927, 941, 74 L.Ed.2d 765 (1983).[2]

It is by now clear that statutory claims may be the subject of an arbitration agreement, enforceable pursuant to the FAA. Indeed, in recent years we have held enforceable arbitration agreements relating to claims arising under the Sherman Act, 15 U.S.C. §§ 1–7; 10(b) of the Securities Exchange Act of 1934, 15 U.S.C. § 78j(b); the civil provisions of the Racketeer Influenced and Corrupt Organizations Act (RICO), 18 U.S.C. § 1961 et seq.; and § 12(2) of the Securities Act of 1933, 15 U.S.C. § 77l(2). See Mitsubishi Motors Corp. v. Soler Chrysler–Plymouth, Inc., 473 U.S. 614, 105 S.Ct. 3346, 87 L.Ed.2d 444 (1985); Shearson/American Express Inc. v. McMahon, 482 U.S. 220, 107 S.Ct. 2332, 96 L.Ed.2d 185 (1987); Rodriguez de Quijas v. Shearson/American Express, Inc., 490 U.S. 477, 109 S.Ct. 1917, 104 L.Ed.2d 526 (1989). In these cases we recognized that "[b]y agreeing to arbitrate a statutory claim, a party does not forgo the substantive rights afforded by the statute; it only submits to their resolution in an arbitral, rather than a judicial, forum." *Mitsubishi*, 473 U.S., at 628, 105 S.Ct., at 3354.

Although all statutory claims may not be appropriate for arbitration, "[h]aving made the bargain to arbitrate, the party should be held to it unless Congress itself has evinced an intention to preclude a waiver of judicial remedies for the statutory rights at issue." Ibid. In this regard, we note that the burden is on Gilmer to show that Congress intended to preclude a waiver of a judicial forum for ADEA claims. See *McMahon*, 482 U.S., at 227, 107 S.Ct., at 2337. If such an intention exists, it will be

2. Section 1 of the FAA provides that "nothing herein contained shall apply to contracts of employment of seamen, railroad employees, or any other class of workers engaged in foreign or interstate commerce." 9 U.S.C. § 1. Several amici curiae in support of Gilmer argue that section excludes from the coverage of the FAA all "contracts of employment." Gilmer, however, did not raise the issue in the courts below, it was not addressed there, and it was not among the questions presented in the petition for certiorari. In any event, it would be inappropriate to address the scope of the § 1 exclusion because the arbitration clause being enforced here is not contained in a contract of employment. The FAA requires that the arbitration clause being enforced be in writing. See 9 U.S.C. §§ 2, 3. The record before us does not show, and the parties do not contend, that Gilmer's employment agreement with Interstate contained a written arbitration clause. Rather, the arbitration clause at issue is in Gilmer's securities registration application, which is a contract with the securities exchanges, not with Interstate. The lower courts addressing the issue uniformly have concluded that the exclusionary clause of § 1 of the FAA is inapplicable to arbitration clauses contained in such registration applications.... We implicitly assumed as much in Perry v. Thomas, 482 U.S. 483, 107 S.Ct. 2520, 96 L.Ed.2d 426 (1987), where we held that the FAA required a former employee of a securities firm to arbitrate his statutory wage claim against his former employer, pursuant to an arbitration clause in his registration application. Unlike the dissent, see post, at 1659–1660, we choose to follow the plain language of the FAA and the weight of authority, and we therefore hold that § 1's exclusionary clause does not apply to Gilmer's arbitration agreement. Consequently, we leave for another day the issue raised by amici curiae.

discoverable in the text of the ADEA, its legislative history, or an "inherent conflict" between arbitration and the ADEA's underlying purposes. See ibid. Throughout such an inquiry, it should be kept in mind that "questions of arbitrability must be addressed with a healthy regard for the federal policy favoring arbitration." *Moses H. Cone*, supra, 460 U.S., at 24, 103 S.Ct., at 941.

III

Gilmer concedes that nothing in the text of the ADEA or its legislative history explicitly precludes arbitration. He argues, however, that compulsory arbitration of ADEA claims pursuant to arbitration agreements would be inconsistent with the statutory framework and purposes of the ADEA. Like the Court of Appeals, we disagree.

A

Congress enacted the ADEA in 1967 "to promote employment of older persons based on their ability rather than age; to prohibit arbitrary age discrimination in employment; [and] to help employers and workers find ways of meeting problems arising from the impact of age on employment." 29 U.S.C. § 621(b). To achieve those goals, the ADEA, among other things, makes it unlawful for an employer "to fail or refuse to hire or to discharge any individual or otherwise discriminate against any individual with respect to his compensation, terms, conditions, or privileges of employment, because of such individual's age." § 623(a)(1). This proscription is enforced both by private suits and by the EEOC. . . .

As Gilmer contends, the ADEA is designed not only to address individual grievances, but also to further important social policies. See, e.g., EEOC v. Wyoming, 460 U.S. 226, 231, 103 S.Ct. 1054, 1057–1058, 75 L.Ed.2d 18 (1983). We do not perceive any inherent inconsistency between those policies, however, and enforcing agreements to arbitrate age discrimination claims. It is true that arbitration focuses on specific disputes between the parties involved. The same can be said, however, of judicial resolution of claims. Both of these dispute resolution mechanisms nevertheless also can further broader social purposes. The Sherman Act, the Securities Exchange Act of 1934, RICO, and the Securities Act of 1933 all are designed to advance important public policies, but, as noted above, claims under those statutes are appropriate for arbitration. "[S]o long as the prospective litigant effectively may vindicate [his or her] statutory cause of action in the arbitral forum, the statute will continue to serve both its remedial and deterrent function." *Mitsubishi*, supra, 473 U.S., at 637, 105 S.Ct., at 3359.

We also are unpersuaded by the argument that arbitration will undermine the role of the EEOC in enforcing the ADEA. An individual ADEA claimant subject to an arbitration agreement will still be free to file a charge with the EEOC, even though the claimant is not able to institute a private judicial action. Indeed, Gilmer filed a charge with the EEOC in this case. In any event, the EEOC's role in combating age discrimination is not dependent on the filing of a charge; the agency may receive information concerning alleged violations of the ADEA "from any source," and it has independent authority to investigate age discrimination. See 29 CFR § 1626.4, 1626.13 (1990). Moreover, nothing in the ADEA indicates that Congress intended that the EEOC be involved in all employment disputes. Such disputes can be settled, for example, without any EEOC involvement ...[6] Finally, the mere involvement of an administrative agency in the enforcement of a statute is not sufficient to preclude arbitration. For example, the Securities Exchange Commission is heavily involved in the enforcement of the Securities Exchange Act of 1934 and the Securities Act of 1933, but we have held that claims under both of those statutes may be subject to compulsory arbitration. See Shearson/American Express Inc. v. McMahon, 482 U.S. 220, 107 S.Ct. 2332, 96 L.Ed.2d 185 (1987); Rodriguez de Quijas v. Shearson/American Express, Inc., 490 U.S. 477, 109 S.Ct. 1917, 104 L.Ed.2d 526 (1989).

Gilmer also argues that compulsory arbitration is improper because it deprives claimants of the judicial forum provided for by the ADEA. Congress, however, did not explicitly preclude arbitration or other nonjudicial resolution of claims, even in its recent amendments to the ADEA. "[I]f Congress intended the substantive protection afforded [by the ADEA] to include protection against waiver of the right to a judicial forum, that intention will be deducible from text or legislative history." Mitsubishi, 473 U.S., at 628, 105 S.Ct., at 3354. Moreover, Gilmer's argument ignores the ADEA's flexible approach to resolution of claims. The EEOC, for example, is directed to pursue "informal methods of conciliation, conference, and persuasion," 29 U.S.C. § 626(b), which suggests that out-of-court dispute resolution, such as arbitration, is consistent with the statutory scheme established by Congress. In addition, arbitration is consistent with Congress' grant of concurrent jurisdiction over ADEA claims to state and federal courts, see 29 U.S.C. § 626(c)(1) (allowing suits to be brought "in any court of competent jurisdiction"), because arbitration agreements, "like the provision for concurrent jurisdiction, serve to advance the objective of allowing [claimants] a broader right to select the forum for resolving disputes, whether it be judicial or otherwise." *Rodriguez de Quijas*, supra, at 483, 109 S.Ct., at 1921.

B

In arguing that arbitration is inconsistent with the ADEA, Gilmer also raises a host of challenges to the adequacy of arbitration procedures. Initially, we note that in our recent arbitration cases we have already rejected most of these arguments as insufficient to preclude arbitration of statutory claims. Such generalized attacks on arbitration "res[t] on suspicion of arbitration as a method of weakening the protections afforded in the substantive law to would-be complainants," and as such, they are "far out

6. In the recently enacted Older Workers Benefits Protection Act, Pub.L. 101–433, 104 Stat. 978, Congress amended the ADEA to provide that "[a]n individual may not waive any right or claim under this Act unless the waiver is knowing and voluntary." See § 201. Congress also specified certain conditions that must be met in order for a waiver to be knowing and voluntary. Ibid.

of step with our current strong endorsement of the federal statutes favoring this method of resolving disputes." *Rodriguez de Quijas*, supra, at 481, 109 S.Ct., at 1920. Consequently, we address these arguments only briefly.

Gilmer first speculates that arbitration panels will be biased. However, "[w]e decline to indulge the presumption that the parties and arbitral body conducting a proceeding will be unable or unwilling to retain competent, conscientious and impartial arbitrators." *Mitsubishi*, supra, 473 U.S., at 634, 105 S.Ct., at 3357–3358. In any event, we note that the NYSE arbitration rules, which are applicable to the dispute in this case, provide protections against biased panels. The rules require, for example, that the parties be informed of the employment histories of the arbitrators, and that they be allowed to make further inquiries into the arbitrators' backgrounds. See 2 CCH New York Stock Exchange Guide ¶ 2608, p. 4314 (Rule 608) (1991) (hereinafter 2 N.Y.S.E. Guide). In addition, each party is allowed one peremptory challenge and unlimited challenges for cause. Id., ¶ 2609, at 4315 (Rule 609). Moreover, the arbitrators are required to disclose "any circumstances which might preclude [them] from rendering an objective and impartial determination." Id., ¶ 2610, at 4315 (Rule 610). The FAA also protects against bias, by providing that courts may overturn arbitration decisions "[w]here there was evident partiality or corruption in the arbitrators." 9 U.S.C. § 10(b). There has been no showing in this case that those provisions are inadequate to guard against potential bias.

Gilmer also complains that the discovery allowed in arbitration is more limited than in the federal courts, which he contends will make it difficult to prove discrimination. It is unlikely, however, that age discrimination claims require more extensive discovery than other claims that we have found to be arbitrable, such as RICO and antitrust claims. Moreover, there has been no showing in this case that the NYSE discovery provisions, which allow for document production, information requests, depositions, and subpoenas, see 2 N.Y.S.E. Guide ¶ 2619, pp. 4318–4320 (Rule 619); Securities and Exchange Commission Order Approving Proposed Rule Changes by New York Stock Exchange, Inc., Nat. Assn. of Securities Dealers, Inc., and the American Stock Exchange, Inc., Relating to the Arbitration Process and the Use of Predispute Arbitration Clauses, 54 Fed.Reg. 21144, 21149–21151 (1989), will prove insufficient to allow ADEA claimants such as Gilmer a fair opportunity to present their claims. Although those procedures might not be as extensive as in the federal courts, by agreeing to arbitrate, a party "trades the procedures and opportunity for review of the courtroom for the simplicity, informality, and expedition of arbitration." *Mitsubishi*, supra, at 628, 105 S.Ct., at 3354. Indeed, an important counterweight to the reduced discovery in NYSE arbitration is that arbitrators are not bound by the rules of evidence. See 2 N.Y.S.E. Guide ¶ 2620, p. 4320 (Rule 620).

A further alleged deficiency of arbitration is that arbitrators often will not issue written opinions, resulting, Gilmer contends, in a lack of public knowledge of employers' discriminatory policies, an inability to obtain effective appellate review, and a stifling of the development of the law. The

NYSE rules, however, do require that all arbitration awards be in writing, and that the awards contain the names of the parties, a summary of the issues in controversy, and a description of the award issued. See id., ¶¶ 2627(a), (e), at 4321 (Rules 627(a), (e)). In addition, the award decisions are made available to the public. See id., ¶ 2627(f), at 4322 (Rule 627(f)). Furthermore, judicial decisions addressing ADEA claims will continue to be issued because it is unlikely that all or even most ADEA claimants will be subject to arbitration agreements. Finally, Gilmer's concerns apply equally to settlements of ADEA claims, which, as noted above, are clearly allowed.[4]

It is also argued that arbitration procedures cannot adequately further the purposes of the ADEA because they do not provide for broad equitable relief and class actions. As the court below noted, however, arbitrators do have the power to fashion equitable relief. 895 F.2d, at 199–200. Indeed, the NYSE rules applicable here do not restrict the types of relief an arbitrator may award, but merely refer to "damages and/or other relief." 2 N.Y.S.E. Guide ¶ 2627(e), p. 4321 (Rule 627(e)). The NYSE rules also provide for collective proceedings. Id., ¶ 2612(d), at 4317 (Rule 612(d)). But "even if the arbitration could not go forward as a class action or class relief could not be granted by the arbitrator, the fact that the [ADEA] provides for the possibility of bringing a collective action does not mean that individual attempts at conciliation were intended to be barred." Nicholson v. CPC Int'l Inc., 877 F.2d 221, 241 (C.A.3 1989) (Becker, J., dissenting). Finally, it should be remembered that arbitration agreements will not preclude the EEOC from bringing actions seeking class-wide and equitable relief.

C

An additional reason advanced by Gilmer for refusing to enforce arbitration agreements relating to ADEA claims is his contention that there often will be unequal bargaining power between employers and employees. Mere inequality in bargaining power, however, is not a sufficient reason to hold that arbitration agreements are never enforceable in the employment context. Relationships between securities dealers and investors, for example, may involve unequal bargaining power, but we nevertheless held in *Rodriguez de Quijas* and *McMahon* that agreements to arbitrate in that context are enforceable. See 490 U.S., at 484, 109 S.Ct., at 1921–1922; 482 U.S., at 230, 107 S.Ct., at 2339–2340. As discussed above, the FAA's purpose was to place arbitration agreements on the same footing as other contracts. Thus, arbitration agreements are enforceable "save upon such grounds as exist at law or in equity for the revocation of any contract." 9 U.S.C. § 2. "Of course, courts should remain attuned to well-supported claims that the agreement to arbitrate resulted from the sort of fraud or overwhelming economic power that would provide grounds 'for the

4. Gilmer also contends that judicial review of arbitration decisions is too limited. We have stated, however, that "although judicial scrutiny of arbitration awards necessarily is limited, such review is sufficient to ensure that arbitrators comply with the requirements of the statute" at issue. Shearson/American Express Inc. v. McMahon, 482 U.S. 220, 232, 107 S.Ct. 2332, 2340, 96 L.Ed.2d 185 (1987).

revocation of any contract.' " *Mitsubishi*, 473 U.S., at 627, 105 S.Ct., at 3354. There is no indication in this case, however, that Gilmer, an experienced businessman, was coerced or defrauded into agreeing to the arbitration clause in his registration application. As with the claimed procedural inadequacies discussed above, this claim of unequal bargaining power is best left for resolution in specific cases.

IV

In addition to the arguments discussed above, Gilmer vigorously asserts that our decision in Alexander v. Gardner–Denver Co., 415 U.S. 36, 94 S.Ct. 1011, 39 L.Ed.2d 147 (1974), and its progeny—Barrentine v. Arkansas–Best Freight System, Inc., 450 U.S. 728, 101 S.Ct. 1437, 67 L.Ed.2d 641 (1981), and McDonald v. West Branch, 466 U.S. 284, 104 S.Ct. 1799, 80 L.Ed.2d 302 (1984)—preclude arbitration of employment discrimination claims. Gilmer's reliance on these cases, however, is misplaced.

In *Gardner–Denver*, the issue was whether a discharged employee whose grievance had been arbitrated pursuant to an arbitration clause in a collective-bargaining agreement was precluded from subsequently bringing a Title VII action based upon the conduct that was the subject of the grievance. In holding that the employee was not foreclosed from bringing the Title VII claim, we stressed that an employee's contractual rights under a collective-bargaining agreement are distinct from the employee's statutory Title VII rights:

> In submitting his grievance to arbitration, an employee seeks to vindicate his contractual right under a collective-bargaining agreement. By contrast, in filing a lawsuit under Title VII, an employee asserts independent statutory rights accorded by Congress. The distinctly separate nature of these contractual and statutory rights is not vitiated merely because both were violated as a result of the same factual occurrence. 415 U.S., at 49–50, 94 S.Ct., at 1020.

We also noted that a labor arbitrator has authority only to resolve questions of contractual rights. Id., at 53–54, 94 S.Ct., at 1022–1023. The arbitrator's "task is to effectuate the intent of the parties" and he or she does not have the "general authority to invoke public laws that conflict with the bargain between the parties." Id., at 53, 94 S.Ct., at 1022. By contrast, "in instituting an action under Title VII, the employee is not seeking review of the arbitrator's decision. Rather, he is asserting a statutory right independent of the arbitration process." Id., at 54, 94 S.Ct., at 1022. We further expressed concern that in collective-bargaining arbitration "the interests of the individual employee may be subordinated to the collective interests of all employees in the bargaining unit." Id., at 58, n. 19, 94 S.Ct., at 1024, n. 19. . . .

There are several important distinctions between the *Gardner–Denver* line of cases and the case before us. First, those cases did not involve the issue of the enforceability of an agreement to arbitrate statutory claims. Rather, they involved the quite different issue whether arbitration of contract-based claims precluded subsequent judicial resolution of statutory claims. Since the employees there had not agreed to arbitrate their statutory claims, and the labor arbitrators were not authorized to resolve such claims, the arbitration in those cases understandably was held not to preclude subsequent statutory actions. Second, because the arbitration in those cases occurred in the context of a collective-bargaining agreement, the claimants there were represented by their unions in the arbitration proceedings. An important concern therefore was the tension between collective representation and individual statutory rights, a concern not applicable to the present case. Finally, those cases were not decided under the FAA, which, as discussed above, reflects a "liberal federal policy favoring arbitration agreements." *Mitsubishi*, 473 U.S., at 625, 105 S.Ct., at 3353. Therefore, those cases provide no basis for refusing to enforce Gilmer's agreement to arbitrate his ADEA claim.

V

We conclude that Gilmer has not met his burden of showing that Congress, in enacting the ADEA, intended to preclude arbitration of claims under that Act. Accordingly, the judgment of the Court of Appeals is

Affirmed.

■ JUSTICE STEVENS, with whom JUSTICE MARSHALL joins, dissenting.

Section 1 of the Federal Arbitration Act (FAA) states:

> [N]othing herein contained shall apply to contracts of employment of seamen, railroad employees, or any other class of workers engaged in foreign or interstate commerce. 9 U.S.C. § 1.

The Court today, in holding that the FAA compels enforcement of arbitration clauses even when claims of age discrimination are at issue, skirts the antecedent question whether the coverage of the Act even extends to arbitration clauses contained in employment contracts, regardless of the subject matter of the claim at issue. In my opinion, arbitration clauses contained in employment agreements are specifically exempt from coverage of the FAA, and for that reason respondent Interstate/Johnson Lane Corporation cannot, pursuant to the FAA, compel petitioner to submit his claims arising under the Age Discrimination in Employment Act of 1967 (ADEA), 29 U.S.C. § 621 et seq., to binding arbitration....

II

The Court, declining to reach the issue for the reason that petitioner never raised it below, nevertheless concludes that "it would be inappropriate to address the scope of the § 1 exclusion because the arbitration clause being enforced here is not contained in a contract of employment ... Rather, the arbitration clause at issue is in Gilmer's securities registration application, which is a contract with the securities exchanges, not with Interstate." Ante, at 1651–1652, n. 2. In my opinion the Court too narrowly construes the scope of the exclusion contained in § 1 of the FAA.

There is little dispute that the primary concern animating the FAA was the perceived need by the business community to overturn the common-law rule that denied specific enforcement of agreements to arbitrate in contracts between business entities. The Act was drafted by a committee of the American Bar Association (ABA), acting upon instructions from the ABA to consider and report upon "the further extension of the principle of commercial arbitration." Report of the Forty-third Annual Meeting of the ABA, 45 A.B.A.Rep. 75 (1920). At the Senate Judiciary Subcommittee hearings on the proposed bill, the chairman of the ABA committee responsible for drafting the bill assured the Senators that the bill "is not intended [to] be an act referring to labor disputes, at all. It is purely an act to give the merchants the right or the privilege of sitting down and agreeing with each other as to what their damages are, if they want to do it. Now that is all there is in this." Hearing on S. 4213 and S. 4214 before a Subcommittee of the Senate Committee on the Judiciary, 67th Cong., 4th Sess., 9 (1923). At the same hearing, Senator Walsh stated:

> The trouble about the matter is that a great many of these contracts that are entered into are really not [voluntary] things at all. Take an insurance policy; there is a blank in it. You can take that or you can leave it. The agent has no power at all to decide it. Either you can make that contract or you can not make any contract. It is the same with a good many contracts of employment. A man says, 'These are our terms. All right, take it or leave it.' Well, there is nothing for the man to do except to sign it; and then he surrenders his right to have his case tried by the court, and has to have it tried before a tribunal in which he has no confidence at all. Ibid.

Given that the FAA specifically was intended to exclude arbitration agreements between employees and employers, I see no reason to limit this exclusion from coverage to arbitration clauses contained in agreements entitled "Contract of Employment." In this case, the parties conceded at oral argument that Gilmer had no "contract of employment" as such with respondent. Gilmer was, however, required as a condition of his employment to become a registered representative of several stock exchanges, including the New York Stock Exchange (NYSE). Just because his agreement to arbitrate any "dispute, claim or controversy" with his employer that arose out of the employment relationship was contained in his application for registration before the NYSE rather than in a specific contract of employment with his employer, I do not think that Gilmer can be compelled pursuant to the FAA to arbitrate his employment-related dispute. Rather, in my opinion the exclusion in § 1 should be interpreted to cover any agreements by the employee to arbitrate disputes with the employer arising out of the employment relationship, particularly where such agreements to arbitrate are conditions of employment....

III

Not only would I find that the FAA does not apply to employment-related disputes between employers and employees in general, but also I would hold that compulsory arbitration conflicts with the congressional purpose animating the ADEA, in particular. As this Court previously has noted, authorizing the courts to issue broad injunctive relief is the cornerstone to eliminating discrimination in society. Albemarle Paper Co. v. Moody, 422 U.S. 405, 415, 95 S.Ct. 2362, 2370, 45 L.Ed.2d 280 (1975). The ADEA, like Title VII of the Civil Rights Act of 1964, authorizes courts to award broad, class-based injunctive relief to achieve the purposes of the Act. 29 U.S.C. § 626(b). Because commercial arbitration is typically limited to a specific dispute between the particular parties and because the available remedies in arbitral forums generally do not provide for class-wide injunctive relief, see Shell, ERISA and Other Federal Employment Statutes: When is Commercial Arbitration an "Adequate Substitute" for the Courts?, 68 Texas L.Rev. 509, 568 (1990), I would conclude that an essential purpose of the ADEA is frustrated by compulsory arbitration of employment discrimination claims.... The Court's holding today clearly eviscerates the important role played by an independent judiciary in eradicating employment discrimination.

IV

When the FAA was passed in 1925, I doubt that any legislator who voted for it expected it to apply to statutory claims, to form contracts between parties of unequal bargaining power, or to the arbitration of disputes arising out of the employment relationship. In recent years, however, the Court "has effectively rewritten the statute", and abandoned its earlier view that statutory claims were not appropriate subjects for arbitration. See Mitsubishi Motors v. Soler Chrysler–Plymouth, Inc., 473 U.S. 614, 646–651, 105 S.Ct. 3346, 3363–3367, 87 L.Ed.2d 444 (1985) (Stevens, J., dissenting). Although I remain persuaded that it erred in doing so, the Court has also put to one side any concern about the inequality of bargaining power between an entire industry, on the one hand, and an individual customer or employee, on the other. See ante, at 1655–1656. Until today, however, the Court has not read § 2 of the FAA as broadly encompassing disputes arising out of the employment relationship. I believe this additional extension of the FAA is erroneous. Accordingly, I respectfully dissent.

* * *

Questions

1. What does the *Gilmer* opinion have to say about how a court should determine which statutory claims are amenable to arbitration? How does the Court address the plaintiff's argument that the Age Discrimination Act embodies important policies that should be determined by a public tribunal?

2. Why might an employee prefer to litigate rather than arbitrate an age discrimination claim?

3. Does the Court's opinion in *Gilmer* mean that employees of brokerage firms who have Title VII claims must submit those claims to arbitration? Empirical studies have found that, arbitrators are overwhelmingly white males over the age of 60. How might that fact affect a female employee's confidence in the fairness of arbitration if she had a sexual harassment complaint? Should this be relevant to the court's analysis of whether the claim was amenable to arbitration? Is it relevant that federal judges fit the same demographic profile as arbitrators?

4. Are there special concerns about the use of arbitration in employment disputes that should lead the Court to scrutinize the process of forming an arbitration agreement? To impose stricter scrutiny on the bargaining process that led the parties to conclude an arbitration agreement? Should a court also scrutinize the arbitration procedures when employment claims are asserted?

5. Does the *Gilmer* court impose a set of minimal due process norms on arbitration? If so, what are they? Should an award that results from an arbitration proceeding that does not contain the *Gilmer* procedures be vacated by a court?

6. Might the Court's enthusiastic endorsement of compulsory arbitration be motivated in part by a self-interested desire to reduce the number of employment cases in already overloaded federal dockets? See Rebecca Hanner White, Arbitration and the Administrative State, 38 Wake Forest Law Review 1283, 1296 (2003) (courts, by enforcing predispute arbitration agreements, can achieve more manageable caseloads and avoid becoming "super-personnel departments."). If so, is this an appropriate justification for a judicial doctrine?

7. The National Academy of Arbitrators (NAA) is the primary professional association of labor arbitrators. It has issued a Statement on Individual Contracts of Employment which provides: "At the hearing, the arbitrator should seek a comfortable balance between the traditional informality and efficiency of arbitration and court-like diligence in respecting and safeguarding the substantive statutory rights of the parties." Is this realistic?

* * *

6. ARBITRATION UNDER THE LABOR MANAGEMENT RELATIONS ACT—AN ALTERNATIVE STATUTORY FRAMEWORK

Arbitration has been a prominent feature of American collective bargaining agreements since World War II. At present, approximately 95 percent of collective bargaining agreements contain grievance procedures that utilize arbitration as the last step. Thus arbitration has become the primary method for interpreting and enforcing collective bargaining agreements in the United States.

Labor arbitration pursuant to a collective bargaining agreement is governed by a federal labor statute—Section 301(a) of the Labor Management Relations Act. Ironically, Section 301, which was enacted in 1947, does not mention arbitration at all. Rather, it creates jurisdiction in federal courts to enforce collective bargaining agreements. It was enacted to enable employers to enforce promises not to strike that were contained in collective bargaining agreements. Section 301(a) says:

> Suits for violation of contacts between an employer and a labor organization representing employees in an industry affecting commerce as defined in this Act, or between any such labor organizations, may be brought in any district court of the United States having jurisdiction of the parties, without respect to the amount in controversy or without regard to the citizenship of the parties. 29 U.S.C. § 185(a).

Despite its brevity, Section 301 has generated considerable judicial and scholarly attention. Its bare words have served as a foundation upon which an entire legal structure for regulating collective bargaining has been built. Through a process of inventive judicial construction which began with the Supreme Court decision in *Textile Workers v. Lincoln Mills,* 353 U.S. 448 (1957), Section 301 has generated a common law of labor relations centered on judicial support for labor arbitration.

Section 301 and the federal common law of labor arbitration defined the role of arbitration within the American collective bargaining system. In a series of cases interpreting Section 301, the Supreme Court delineated a delicate relationship between the judicial system and private labor arbitration. These doctrines have had a major influence on the law of arbitration in other areas as well. Indeed, many of the expansive interpretations of the Federal Arbitration Act in the 1980s are based upon labor precedents from Section 301 cases in the 1950s and 1960s. Thus it is instructive to study the evolution of the legal doctrines under Section 301 both to understand the role of law in labor arbitration and to understand the evolving law of arbitration in the nonlabor areas that are governed by the Federal Arbitration Act.

Textile Workers Union of America v. Lincoln Mills of Alabama

353 U.S. 448 (1957).

■ MR. JUSTICE DOUGLAS delivered the opinion of the Court.

Petitioner-union entered into a collective bargaining agreement in 1953 with respondent-employer, the agreement to run one year and from year to year thereafter, unless terminated on specified notices. The agreement provided that there would be no strikes or work stoppages and that grievances would be handled pursuant to a specified procedure. The last step in the grievance procedure—a step that could be taken by either party—was arbitration.

This controversy involves several grievances that concern work loads and work assignments. The grievances were processed through the various steps in the grievance procedure and were finally denied by the employer. The union requested arbitration, and the employer refused. Thereupon the union brought this suit in the District Court to compel arbitration.

The District Court concluded that it had jurisdiction and ordered the employer to comply with the grievance arbitration provisions of the collective bargaining agreement. The Court of Appeals reversed by a divided vote. 230 F.2d 81. It held that, although the District Court had jurisdiction to entertain the suit, the court had no authority founded either in federal or state law to grant the relief. The case is here on a petition for a writ of certiorari which we granted because of the importance of the problem and the contrariety of views in the courts. 352 U.S. 821, 77 S.Ct. 54, 1 L.Ed.2d 46.

The starting point of our inquiry is § 301 of the Labor Management Relations Act of 1947, 61 Stat. 156, 29 U.S.C. § 185, 29 U.S.C.A. § 185, which provides:

> (a) Suits for violation of contracts between an employer and a labor organization representing employees in an industry affecting commerce as defined in this chapter, or between any such labor organizations, may be brought in any district court of the United States having jurisdiction of the parties, without respect to the amount in controversy or without regard to the citizenship of the parties.
>
> (b) Any labor organization which represents employees in an industry affecting commerce as defined in this chapter and any employer whose activities affect commerce as defined in this chapter shall be bound by the acts of its agents. Any such labor organization may sue or be sued as an entity and in behalf of the employees whom it represents in the courts of the United States. Any money judgment against a labor organization in a district court of the United States shall be enforceable only against the organization as an entity and against its assets, and shall not be enforceable against any individual member or his assets.

There has been considerable litigation involving § 301 and courts have construed it differently. There is one view that § 301(a) merely gives federal district courts jurisdiction in controversies that involve labor organizations in industries affecting commerce, without regard to diversity of citizenship or the amount in controversy. Under that view § 301(a) would not be the source of substantive law; it would neither supply federal law to resolve these controversies nor turn the federal judges to state law for answers to the questions. Other courts—the overwhelming number of them—hold that § 301(a) is more than jurisdictional—that it authorizes federal courts to fashion a body of federal law for the enforcement of these collective bargaining agreements and includes within that federal law specific performance of promises to arbitrate grievances under collective bargaining agreements. Perhaps the leading decision representing that point of view is the one rendered by Judge Wyzanski in Textile Workers Union of America (C.I.O.) v. American Thread Co., D.C., 113 F.Supp. 137. That is our construction of § 301(a), which means that the agreement to arbitrate grievance disputes, contained in this collective bargaining agreement, should be specifically enforced.

From the face of the Act it is apparent that § 301(a) and § 301(b) supplement one another. Section 301(b) makes it possible for a labor organization, representing employees in an industry affecting commerce, to sue and be sued as an entity in the federal courts. Section 301(b) in other words provides the procedural remedy lacking at common law. Section 301(a) certainly does something more than that. Plainly, it supplies the basis upon which the federal district courts may take jurisdiction and apply the procedural rule of § 301(b). The question is whether § 301(a) is more than jurisdictional.

The legislative history of § 301 is somewhat cloudy and confusing. But there are a few shafts of light that illuminate our problem.

The bills, as they passed the House and the Senate, contained provisions which would have made the failure to abide by an agreement to arbitrate an unfair labor practice. S.Rep. No. 105, 80th Cong., 1st Sess., pp. 20–21, 23; H.R.Rep. No. 245, 80th Cong., 1st Sess., p. 21. This feature of the law was dropped in Conference. As the Conference Report stated, "Once parties have made a collective bargaining contract, the enforcement of that contract should be left to the usual processes of the law and not to the National Labor Relations Board." H.R.Conf.Rep. No. 510, 80th Cong., 1st Sess., p. 42.

Both the Senate and the House took pains to provide for "the usual processes of the law" by provisions which were the substantial equivalent of § 301(a) in its present form. Both the Senate Report and the House Report indicate a primary concern that unions as well as employees should be bound to collective bargaining contracts. But there was also a broader concern—a concern with a procedure for making such agreements enforceable in the courts by either party. At one point the Senate Report, supra, p. 15, states, "We feel that the aggrieved party should also have a right of action in the Federal courts. Such a policy is completely in accord with the purpose of the Wagner Act which the Supreme Court declared was 'to compel employers to bargain collectively with their employees to the end that an employment contract, binding on both parties, should be made. . . .' "

Congress was also interested in promoting collective bargaining that ended with agreements not to strike. The Senate Report, supra, p. 16 states:

> If unions can break agreements with relative impunity, then such agreements do not tend to stabilize industrial relations. The execution of an agreement does not by itself promote industrial peace. The chief advantage which an employer can reasonably expect from a collective labor agreement is assurance of uninterrupted operation during the term of the agreement. Without some effective method of assuring freedom from economic warfare for the term of the agreement, there is little reason why an employer would desire to sign such a contract.
>
> Consequently, to encourage the making of agreements and to promote industrial peace through faithful performance by the parties, collective

> agreements affecting interstate commerce should be enforceable in the Federal courts. Our amendment would provide for suits by unions as legal entities and against unions as legal entities in the Federal courts in disputes affecting commerce.

Thus collective bargaining contracts were made "equally binding and enforceable on both parties." Id., p. 15. As stated in the House Report, supra, p. 6, the new provision "makes labor organizations equally responsible with employers for contract violations and provides for suit by either against the other in the United States district courts." ...

Plainly the agreement to arbitrate grievance disputes is the quid pro quo for an agreement not to strike. Viewed in this light, the legislation does more than confer jurisdiction in the federal courts over labor organizations. It expresses a federal policy that federal courts should enforce these agreements on behalf of or against labor organizations and that industrial peace can be best obtained only in that way....

It seems, therefore, clear to us that Congress adopted a policy which placed sanctions behind agreements to arbitrate grievance disputes, by implication rejecting the common-law rule, discussed in Red Cross Line v. Atlantic Fruit Co., 264 U.S. 109, 44 S.Ct. 274, 68 L.Ed. 582, against enforcement of executory agreements to arbitrate. We would undercut the Act and defeat its policy if we read § 301 narrowly as only conferring jurisdiction over labor organizations.

The question then is, what is the substantive law to be applied in suits under § 301(a)? We conclude that the substantive law to apply in suits under § 301(a) is federal law, which the courts must fashion from the policy of our national labor laws. See Mendelsohn, Enforceability of Arbitration Agreements Under Taft–Hartley Section 301, 66 Yale L.J. 167. The Labor Management Relations Act expressly furnishes some substantive law. It points out what the parties may or may not do in certain situations. Other problems will lie in the penumbra of express statutory mandates. dates. Some will lack express statutory sanction but will be solved by looking at the policy of the legislation and fashioning a remedy that will effectuate that policy. The range of judicial inventiveness will be determined by the nature of the problem ... Federal interpretation of the federal law will govern, not state law ... But state law, if compatible with the purpose of § 301, may be resorted to in order to find the rule that will best effectuate the federal policy.... Any state law applied, however, will be absorbed as federal law and will not be an independent source of private rights.

It is not uncommon for federal courts to fashion federal law where federal rights are concerned. See Clearfield Trust Co. v. United States, 318 U.S. 363, 366–367 ... Congress has indicated by § 301(a) the purpose to follow that course here. There is no constitutional difficulty. Article III, § 2, extends the judicial power to cases "arising under ... the Laws of the United States ..." The power of Congress to regulate these labor-management controversies under the Commerce Clause is plain. Houston East & West Texas R. Co. v. United States, 234 U.S. 342, 34 S.Ct. 833, 58 L.Ed.

1341; National Labor Relations Board v. Jones & Laughlin Corp., 301 U.S. 1, 57 S.Ct. 615, 81 L.Ed. 893. A case or controversy arising under s 301(a) is, therefore, one within the purview of judicial power as defined in Article III . . .

The judgment of the Court of Appeals is reversed and the cause is remanded to that court for proceedings in conformity with this opinion.

Reversed.

■ MR. JUSTICE BLACK took no part in the consideration or decision of this case.

■ MR. JUSTICE FRANKFURTER (dissenting).

The Court has avoided the difficult problems raised by § 301 of the Taft–Hartley Act, . . . by attributing to the section an occult content. This plainly procedural section is transmuted into a mandate to the federal courts to fashion a whole body of substantive federal law appropriate for the complicated and touchy problems raised by collective bargaining. I have set forth in my opinion in Association of Westinghouse Salaried Employees v. Westinghouse Electric Corp. the detailed reasons why I believe that § 301 cannot be so construed, even if constitutional questions cannot be avoided. 348 U.S. 437. But the Court has a "clear" and contrary conclusion emerge from the "somewhat," to say the least, "cloudy and confusing legislative history." This is more than can be fairly asked even from the alchemy of construction. Since the Court relies on a few isolated statements in the legislative history which do not support its conclusion, however favorably read, I have deemed in necessary to set forth in an appendix the entire relevant legislative history of the Taft–Hartley Act and its predecessor, the Case Bill. This legislative history reinforces the natural meaning of the statute as an exclusively procedural provision, affording, that is, an accessible federal forum for suits on agreements between labor organizations and employers, but not enacting federal law for such suits . . .

Even on the Court's attribution to § 301 of a direction to the federal courts to fashion, out of bits and pieces elsewhere to be gathered, a federal common law of labor contracts, it still does not follow that Congress has enacted that an agreement to arbitrate industrial differences be specifically enforceable in the federal courts. On the contrary, the body of relevant federal law precludes such enforcement of arbitration clauses in collective-bargaining agreements.

Prior to 1925, the doctrine that executory agreements to arbitrate any kind of dispute would not be specifically enforced still held sway in the federal courts . . . Legislation was deemed necessary to assure such power to the federal courts. In 1925, Congress passed the United States Arbitration Act, . . . making executory agreements to arbitrate specifically enforceable in the federal courts, but explicitly excluding "contracts of employment" of workers engaged in interstate commerce from its scope. Naturally enough, I find rejection, though not explicit, of the availability of the Federal Arbitration Act to enforce arbitration clauses in collective-bargaining agreements in the silent treatment given that Act by the Court's opinion. If an Act that authorizes the federal courts to enforce arbitration provisions in contracts generally, but specifically denies authority to decree that remedy for "contracts of employment," were available, the Court would hardly spin such power out of the empty darkness of § 301. I would make this rejection explicit, recognizing that when Congress passed legislation to enable arbitration agreements to be enforced by the federal courts, it saw fit to exclude this remedy with respect to labor contracts ...

Even though the Court glaringly ignores the Arbitration Act, it does at least recognize the common-law rule against enforcement of executory agreements to arbitrate. It nevertheless enforces the arbitration clause in the collective-bargaining agreements in these cases. It does so because it finds that Congress "by implication" rejected the common-law rule. I would add that the Court, in thus deriving power from the unrevealing words of the Taft–Hartley Act, has also found that Congress "by implication" repealed its own statutory exemption of collective-bargaining agreements in the Arbitration Act, an exemption made as we have seen for well-defined reasons of policy.

... [T]he rule that is departed from "by implication" had not only been "judicially formulated" but had purposefully been congressionally formulated in the Arbitration Act of 1925. And it is being departed from on the tenuous basis of the legislative history of § 301, for which the utmost that can be claimed is that insofar as there was any expectation at all, it was only that conventional remedies, including equitable remedies, would be available. But of course, as we have seen, "equitable remedies" in the federal courts had traditionally excluded specific performance of arbitration clauses, except as explicitly provided by the 1925 Act. Thus, even assuming that § 301 contains directions for some federal substantive law of labor contracts, I see no justification for translating the vague expectation concerning the remedies to be applied into an overruling of previous federal common law and, more particularly, into the repeal of the previous congressional exemption of collective-bargaining agreements from the class of agreements in which arbitration clauses were to be enforced.

The second ground of my dissent from the Court's action is more fundamental. Since I do not agree with the Court's conclusion that federal substantive law is to govern in actions under § 301, I am forced to consider the serious constitutional question that was adumbrated in the Westinghouse case, 348 U.S. at 449–452, the constitutionality of a grant of jurisdiction to federal courts over contracts that came into being entirely by virtue of state substantive law, a jurisdiction not based on diversity of citizenship, yet one in which a federal court would, as in diversity cases, act in effect merely as another court of the State in which it sits. The scope of allowable federal judicial power that this grant must satisfy is constitutionally described as "Cases, in Law and Equity, arising under this Constitution, the Laws of the United States, and Treaties made, or which shall be made, under their Authority." Art. III, § 2 ...

Almost without exception, decisions under the general statutory grants have tested jurisdiction in terms of the presence, as an integral part of plaintiff's cause of action, of an issue calling for interpretation or application of federal law ... Although it has sometimes been suggested that the "cause of action" must derive from federal law, ... it has been found sufficient that some aspect of federal law is essential to plaintiff's success ... The litigation-provoking problem has been the degree to which federal law must be in the forefront of the case and not collateral, peripheral or remote.

To be sure, the full scope of a substantive regulation is frequently in dispute and must await authoritative determination by courts. Congress declares its purpose imperfectly or partially, and compatible judicial construction completes it. But in this case we start with a provision that is wholly jurisdictional and as such bristles with constitutional problems under Article III. To avoid them, interpolation of substantive regulation has been proposed. From what materials are we to draw a determination that § 301 is something other than what it declares itself? Is the Court justified in creating all the difficult problems of choice within a sphere of delicate policy without any direction from Congress and merely for the sake of giving effect to a provision that seems to deal with a different subject? ...

Assuming, however, that we would be justified in pouring substantive content into a merely procedural vehicle, what elements of federal law could reasonably be put into the provisions of § 301? The suggestion that the section permits the federal courts to work out, without more, a federal code governing collective-bargaining contracts must, for reasons that have already been stated, be rejected. Likewise the suggestion that § 301 may be viewed as a congressional authorization to the federal courts to work out a concept of the nature of the collective-bargaining contract, leaving detailed questions of interpretation to state law ...

Nor will Congress' objective be furthered by an attempt to limit the grant of a federal forum to certain types of actions between unions and employers. It would be difficult to find any basis for, or principles of, selection, either in the terms of § 301 or in considerations relevant to promotion of stability in labor relations. It is true that a fair reading of § 301 in the context of its enactment shows that the suit that Congress primarily contemplated was the suit against a union for strike in violation of contract. From this it might be possible to imply a federal right to bring an action for damages based on such an event. In the interest of mutuality, so close to the heart of Congress, we might in turn find a federal right in the union to sue for a lockout in violation of contract. But neither federal right would be involved in the present cases. Moreover, it bears repetition that Congress chose not to make this the basis of federal law, i.e., it chose not to make such conduct an unfair labor practice ...

In the wise distribution of governmental powers, this Court cannot do what a President sometimes does in returning a bill to Congress. We cannot return this provision to Congress and respectfully request that body to face the responsibility placed upon it by the Constitution to define the jurisdiction of the lower courts with some particularity and not to leave these courts at large. Confronted as I am, I regretfully have no choice. For all the reasons elaborated in this dissent, even reading into § 301 the limited federal rights consistent with the purposes of that section, I am impelled to the view that it is unconstitutional in cases such as the present ones where it provides the sole basis for exercise of jurisdiction by the federal courts.

[The concurring opinion of Mr. Justice Burton, with which Mr. Justice Harlan joins, has been omitted.]

* * *

Questions

1. Why was this case brought under Section 301 of the Labor Management Relations Act rather than under the FAA?

2. Why does Justice Douglas emphasize that Section 301 is not merely procedural? What constitutional problem would be posed if it were merely procedural?

3. Justice Douglas ultimately concludes that Section 301 is substantive. What is the substance that he finds in the provision? From what source does he derive it? How does he use the substance he attributes to the statute to decide the narrow question in the case? What is the specific issue in the case?

4. What does Justice Douglas mean by his statement that no-strike clauses and arbitration promises stand in a *quid pro quo* relationship to each other? Is this an empirical claim that the clauses are in fact negotiated and found together in collective bargaining agreements? If so, does he give any evidence for that? What kind of evidence might be relevant to support such a claim? Alternatively, is Douglas's assertion of a *quid pro quo* relationship between arbitration and a no-strike promise a logical claim, i.e., a claim that if there is one clause in a collective bargaining agreement, the other must also be present? Does the opinion provide any reasoning to support such a logical linkage? Or does Douglas mean there is some relationship between the two clauses other than an empirical or logical link? If so, what does he mean by his statement that there is a *quid pro quo* relationship between arbitration and a no-strike promise?

5. What is Justice Frankfurter's view about the constitutionality of Section 301?

6. When he was Professor Frankfurter, a law professor at Harvard Law School, Justice Frankfurter drafted the Norris–LaGuardia Act. That statute withdraws the power of a federal court to issue an injunction in a labor dispute except under narrowly defined circumstances not present in the *Lincoln Mills* case. Is Frankfurter's dissent here based solely on his view that the Norris LaGuardia Act prohibits an injunctive decree in a labor dispute, or does he have another ground for his objection? What is Justice

Frankfurter's view on the power of courts to grant specific performance to promises to arbitrate?

7. What evidence is there that Congress intended, when it enacted Section 301, to create a federal common law of collective bargaining agreements? Doesn't the simple language of Section 301(a) suggest otherwise? The decision in *Lincoln Mills* has been criticized as an extreme and illegitimate instance of judicial law-making. Is judicial law-making justified in this case? Is it ever justified?

* * *

Note on Local 174, Teamsters v. Lucas Flour Company

In *Local 174, Teamsters, Chauffeurs, Warehousemen & Helpers of America v. Lucas Flour Company*, 369 U.S. 95 (1962), the company and union had a collective bargaining agreement that called for arbitration of "any difference as to the true interpretation of this agreement." It further provided that "during such arbitration, there shall be no suspension of work." The contract also stated that "The Employer reserves the right to discharge any man in his employ if his work is not satisfactory."

In May 1958, the company fired an employee for unsatisfactory work after the employee damaged a fork-lift truck. The union called a strike to protest the discharge, and the strike lasted eight days. After the strike ended, the union submitted the issue of the employee's dismissal to arbitration. Five months later, the arbitration board ruled in favor of the employer. In the meantime, the employer brought an action against the union in state court seeking damages caused by the strike. The state court applied state law and awarded damages to the employer. Although the union had not violated any express term of the no-strike clause, the state court stated, "the strike was a violation of the collective bargaining contract, because it was an attempt to coerce the employer to forego his contractual right to discharge an employee for unsatisfactory work." The Supreme Court granted certiorari on two issues: Should the state court apply state or federal law, and was the union in violation of its collective bargaining agreement?

The Court first held that the state court erred in applying state law to a Section 301 case. It said:

> The dimensions of § 301 require the conclusion that substantive principles of federal labor law must be paramount in the area covered by the statute. Comprehensiveness is inherent in the process by which the law is to be formulated under the mandate of Lincoln Mills, requiring issues raised in suits of a kind covered by § 301 to be decided according to the precepts of federal labor policy.
>
> More important, the subject matter of § 301(a) 'is peculiarly one that calls for uniform law.' The possibility that individual contract terms might have different meanings under state and federal law would inevitably exert a disruptive influence upon both the negotiation and

> administration of collective agreements. Because neither party could be certain of the rights which it had obtained or conceded, the process of negotiating an agreement would be made immeasurably more difficult by the necessity of trying to formulate contract provisions in such a way as to contain the same meaning under two or more systems of law which might someday be invoked in enforcing the contract. Once the collective bargain was made, the possibility of conflicting substantive interpretation under competing legal systems would tend to stimulate and prolong disputes as to its interpretation. Indeed, the existence of possibly conflicting legal concepts might substantially impede the parties' willingness to agree to contract terms providing for final arbitral or judicial resolution of disputes.
>
> The importance of the area which would be affected by separate systems of substantive law makes the need for a single body of federal law particularly compelling. The ordering and adjusting of competing interests through a process of free and voluntary collective bargaining is the keystone of the federal scheme to promote industrial peace. State law which frustrates the effort of Congress to stimulate the smooth functioning of that process thus strikes at the very core of federal labor policy. With due regard to the many factors which bear upon competing state and federal interests in this area ... we cannot but conclude that in enacting § 301 Congress intended doctrines of federal labor law uniformly to prevail over inconsistent local rules.

Having determined that federal law applied, the Court applied the evolving federal law of Section 301 to decide the ultimate issue in the case—whether the union violated the agreement. The union argued that there was no violation of the collective bargaining agreement because there was not a no-strike clause in the contract explicitly covering the subject of the dispute over which the strike was called. The Court disagreed:

> The collective bargaining contract expressly imposed upon both parties the duty of submitting the dispute in question to final and binding arbitration. In a consistent course of decisions the Courts of Appeals of at least five Federal Circuits have held that a strike to settle a dispute which a collective bargaining agreement provides shall be settled exclusively and finally by compulsory arbitration constitutes a violation of the agreement.... We approve that doctrine. To hold otherwise would obviously do violence to accepted principles of traditional contract law. Even more in point, a contrary view would be completely at odds with the basic policy of national labor legislation to promote the arbitral process as a substitute for economic warfare ...
>
> What has been said is not to suggest that a no-strike agreement is to be implied beyond the area which it has been agreed will be exclusively covered by compulsory terminal arbitration. Nor is it to suggest that there may not arise problems in specific cases as to whether compulsory and binding arbitration has been agreed upon, and, if so, as to what disputes have been made arbitrable. But no such problems are present in this case. The grievance over which the union struck was, as it

> concedes, one which it had expressly agreed to settle by submission to final and binding arbitration proceedings. The strike which it called was a violation of that contractual obligation.

Justice Black, in a strongly worded dissent, accused the majority of rewriting the contract between the parties. As he said:

> The Court now finds—out of clear air, so far as I can see—that the union, without saying so in the agreement, not only agreed to arbitrate such differences, but also promised that there would be no strike while arbitration of a dispute was pending under this provision. And on the basis of its 'discovery' of this additional unwritten promise by the union, the Court upholds a judgment awarding the company substantial damages for a strike in breach of contract . . .

Justice Black also questioned what principles of "traditional contract law" the Court referred to when it so disregarded the parties express contractual language:

> I had supposed, however—though evidently the Court thinks otherwise—that the job of courts enforcing contracts was to give legal effect to what the contracting parties actually agree to do, not to what courts think they ought to do. In any case, I have been unable to find any accepted principle of contract law—traditional or otherwise—that permits courts to change completely the nature of a contract by adding new promises that the parties themselves refused to make in order that the new court-made contract might better fit into whatever social, economic, or legal policies the courts believe to be so important that they should have been taken out of the realm of voluntary contract by the legislative body and furthered by compulsory legislation.

* * *

Questions

1. How does the relationship between state and federal law in the *Lucas Flour* case compare to the relationship set out in *Volt v. Board of Trustees?*

2. Justice Black accuses the majority of departing from ordinary notions of contractual consent by implying a no-strike clause where none exists. What doctrines of "traditional contract law" was the majority referring to? Is Justice Black correct—has the court rewritten the agreement between the parties, or has it merely interpreted the agreement?

3. Can parties counteract the impact of *Lucas Flour* by expressly stating, in their collective agreement, that even though there is an arbitration provision, there is no obligation of the union to refrain from striking in certain specified situations, such as in disputes concerning imminent threat to safety? After *Lucas Flour*, will courts enforce those private agreements? If so, does *Lucas Flour* really signify a court disregarding the parties' intent, or is it a default term that applies when the parties are silent as to their intent?

4. After *Lucas Flour*, courts can imply a no-strike clause in a collective agreement that has an applicable arbitration clause. However, courts do not imply an arbitration clause where there is an applicable no-strike clause. Why this difference in treatment? Is this a departure from the notion that the two clauses are mirror images of each other as the *quid pro quo* language of *Lincoln Mills* would suggest?

* * *

United Steelworkers of America v. American Manufacturing Co.

363 U.S. 564 (1960).

■ Opinion of the Court by MR. JUSTICE DOUGLAS, announced by MR. JUSTICE BRENNAN.

This suit was brought by petitioner union in the District Court to compel arbitration of a "grievance" that petitioner, acting for one Sparks, a union member, had filed with the respondent, Sparks' employer. The employer defended on the ground (1) that Sparks is estopped from making his claim because he had a few days previously settled a workmen's compensation claim against the company on the basis that he was permanently partially disabled, (2) that Sparks is not physically able to do the work, and (3) that this type of dispute is not arbitrable under the collective bargaining agreement in question.

The agreement provided that during its term there would be "no strike," unless the employer refused to abide by a decision of the arbitrator. The agreement sets out a detailed grievance procedure with a provision for arbitration (regarded as the standard form) of all disputes between the parties "as to the meaning, interpretation and application of the provisions of this agreement."

The agreement reserves to the management power to suspend or discharge any employee "for cause." It also contains a provision that the employer will employ and promote employees on the principle of seniority "where ability and efficiency are equal." Sparks left his work due to an injury and while off work brought an action for compensation benefits. The case was settled, Sparks' physician expressing the opinion that the injury had made him 25% "permanently partially disabled." That was on September 9. Two weeks later the union filed a grievance which charged that Sparks was entitled to return to his job by virtue of the seniority provision of the collective bargaining agreement. Respondent refused to arbitrate and this action was brought. The District Court held that Sparks, having accepted the settlement on the basis of permanent partial disability, was estopped to claim any seniority or employment rights and granted the motion for summary judgment. The Court of Appeals affirmed, 264 F.2d 624, for different reasons. After reviewing the evidence it held that the grievance is "a frivolous, patently baseless one, not subject to arbitration under the collective bargaining agreement." Id., at page 628. The case is here on a writ of certiorari, 361 U.S. 881.

Section 203(d) of the Labor Management Relations Act, 1947, 61 Stat. 154, 29 U.S.C. § 173(d), 29 U.S.C.A. § 173(d), states, "Final adjustment by a method agreed upon by the parties is hereby declared to be the desirable method for settlement of grievance disputes arising over the application or interpretation of an existing collective-bargaining agreement...." That policy can be effectuated only if the means chosen by the parties for settlement of their differences under a collective bargaining agreement is given full play.

A state decision that held to the contrary announced a principle that could only have a crippling effect on grievance arbitration. The case was International Ass'n of Machinists v. Cutler–Hammer, Inc., 271 App.Div. 917, 67 N.Y.S.2d 317, affirmed 297 N.Y., 519, 74 N.E.2d 464. It held that "If the meaning of the provision of the contract sought to be arbitrated is beyond dispute, there cannot be anything to arbitrate and the contract cannot be said to provide for arbitration." 271 App.Div. at page 918, 67 N.Y.S.2d at page 318. The lower courts in the instant case had a like preoccupation with ordinary contract law. The collective agreement requires arbitration of claims that courts might be unwilling to entertain. In the context of the plant or industry the grievance may assume proportions of which judges are ignorant. Yet, the agreement is to submit all grievances to arbitration, not merely those that a court may deem to be meritorious. There is no exception in the "no strike" clause and none therefore should be read into the grievance clause, since one is the quid pro quo for the other. The question is not whether in the mind of the court there is equity in the claim. Arbitration is a stabilizing influence only as it serves as a vehicle for handling any and all disputes that arise under the agreement.

The collective agreement calls for the submission of grievances in the categories which it describes, irrespective of whether a court may deem them to be meritorious. In our role of developing a meaningful body of law to govern the interpretation and enforcement of collective bargaining agreements, we think special heed should be given to the context in which collective bargaining agreements are negotiated and the purpose which they are intended to serve. See Lewis v. Benedict Coal Corp., 361 U.S. 459, 468, 80 S.Ct. 489, 495, 4 L.Ed.2d 442. The function of the court is very limited when the parties have agreed to submit all questions of contract interpretation to the arbitrator. It is confined to ascertaining whether the party seeking arbitration is making a claim which on its face is governed by the contract. Whether the moving party is right or wrong is a question of contract interpretation for the arbitrator. In these circumstances the moving party should not be deprived of the arbitrator's judgment, when it was his judgment and all that it connotes that was bargained for.

The courts, therefore, have no business weighing the merits of the grievance, considering whether there is equity in a particular claim, or determining whether there is particular language in the written instrument which will support the claim. The agreement is to submit all grievances to arbitration, not merely those which the court will deem meritorious. The processing of even frivolous claims may have therapeutic values of which those who are not a part of the plant environment may be quite unaware.

The union claimed in this case that the company had violated a specific provision of the contract. The company took the position that it had not violated that clause. There was, therefore, a dispute between the parties as to "the meaning, interpretation and application" of the collective bargaining agreement. Arbitration should have been ordered. When the judiciary undertakes to determine the merits of a grievance under the guise of interpreting the grievance procedure of collective bargaining agreements, it usurps a function which under that regime is entrusted to the arbitration tribunal.

Reversed.

■ MR. JUSTICE FRANKFURTER concurs in the result.

■ MR. JUSTICE WHITTAKER, believing that the District Court lacked jurisdiction to determine the merits of the claim which the parties had validly agreed to submit to the exclusive jurisdiction of a Board of Arbitrators (Textile Workers v. Lincoln Mills, 353 U.S. 448), concurs in the result of this opinion.

* * *

Questions

1. Does the Court in *American Manufacturing* decide that an employer must arbitrate any grievance a union wants to arbitrate, no matter how frivolous? Suppose an employee filed a grievance claiming that she is entitled to overtime pay for a certain day, and it turns out, on investigation, that the employee did not work at all on that day because she was away on vacation. Should the employer be forced to arbitrate her claim? Are there costs in requiring an employer to arbitrate all frivolous cases? What is the countervailing benefit, if any?

2. What are the reasons Justice Douglas advances for holding that all cases, even frivolous ones, must be arbitrated? Could he have interpreted the parties agreement in this case to mean that they agree to arbitrate all *reasonable* grievances? Would the latter approach change the role of arbitration in the collective bargaining system?

3. According to Justice Douglas, what is the role of a court when presented with a petition to compel arbitration? Is it to simply rubber stamp the petition as "granted"? Or must the court engage in some sort of review?

4. Why does the Court impliedly limit arbitration to claims that on their face are covered by an arbitration clause? Why not hold that all disputes must be arbitrated?

5. Can courts rule on the issue of arbitrability without considering the merits of a dispute? Even with the light once-over look that Douglas calls for, are courts required to make some initial foray into the merits of the dispute? Could the court have formulated a test for arbitrability that avoids this result?

* * *

United Steelworkers of America v. Warrior and Gulf Navigation Co.

363 U.S. 574 (1960).

■ Opinion of the Court by MR. JUSTICE DOUGLAS, announced by MR. JUSTICE BRENNAN.

Respondent transports steel and steel products by barge and maintains a terminal at Chickasaw, Alabama, where it performs maintenance and repair work on its barges. The employees at that terminal constitute a bargaining unit covered by a collective bargaining agreement negotiated by petitioner union. Respondent between 1956 and 1958 laid off some employees, reducing the bargaining unit from 42 to 23 men. This reduction was due in part to respondent contracting maintenance work, previously done by its employees, to other companies. The latter used respondent's supervisors to lay out the work and hired some of the laid-off employees of respondent (at reduced wages). Some were in fact assigned to work on respondent's barges. A number of employees signed a grievance which petitioner presented to respondent, the grievance reading:

> We are hereby protesting the Company's actions, of arbitrarily and unreasonably contracting out work to other concerns, that could and previously has been performed by Company employees.
>
> This practice becomes unreasonable, unjust and discriminatory in lieu (sic) of the fact that at present there are a number of employees that have been laid off for about 1 and 1/2 years or more for allegedly lack of work.
>
> Confronted with these facts we charge that the Company is in violation of the contract by inducing a partial lock-out, of a number of the employees who would otherwise be working were it not for this unfair practice.

The collective agreement had both a "no strike" and a "no lockout" provision. It also had a grievance procedure which provided in relevant part as follows:

> Issues which conflict with any Federal statute in its application as established by Court procedure or matters which are strictly a function of management shall not be subject to arbitration under this section.
>
> Should differences arise between the Company and the Union or its members employed by the Company as to the meaning and application of the provisions of this Agreement, or should any local trouble of any kind arise, there shall be no suspension of work on account of such differences but an earnest effort shall be made to settle such differ-

ences immediately [through a first-step procedure ending with arbitration.]

Settlement of this grievance was not had and respondent refused arbitration. This suit was then commenced by the union to compel it.

The District Court granted respondent's motion to dismiss the complaint [and the Court of Appeals affirmed].

We held in Textile Workers v. Lincoln Mills, 353 U.S. 448, that a grievance arbitration provision in a collective agreement could be enforced by reason of § 301(a) of the Labor Management Relations Act and that the policy to be applied in enforcing this type of arbitration was that reflected in our national labor laws ... The present federal policy is to promote industrial stabilization through the collective bargaining agreement ... A major factor in achieving industrial peace is the inclusion of a provision for arbitration of grievances in the collective bargaining agreement.[4]

Thus the run of arbitration cases, illustrated by Wilko v. Swan, 346 U.S. 427, becomes irrelevant to our problem. There the choice is between the adjudication of cases or controversies in courts with established procedures or even special statutory safeguards on the one hand and the settlement of them in the more informal arbitration tribunal on the other. In the commercial case, arbitration is the substitute for litigation. Here arbitration is the substitute for industrial strife. Since arbitration of labor disputes has quite different functions from arbitration under an ordinary commercial agreement, the hostility evinced by courts toward arbitration of commercial agreements has no place here. For arbitration of labor disputes under collective bargaining agreements is part and parcel of the collective bargaining process itself.

The collective bargaining agreement states the rights and duties of the parties. It is more than a contract; it is a generalized code to govern a myriad of cases which the draftsmen cannot wholly anticipate ... The collective agreement covers the whole employment relationship. It calls into being a new common law—the common law of a particular industry or of a particular plant. As one observer has put it:[6]

> ... (I)t is not unqualifiedly true that a collective-bargaining agreement is simply a document by which the union and employees have imposed upon management limited, express restrictions of its otherwise absolute right to manage the enterprise, so that an employee's claim must fail unless he can point to a specific contract provision upon which the claim is founded. There are too many people, too many problems, too many unforeseeable contingencies to make the words of the contract the exclusive source of rights and duties. One cannot reduce all the

4. Complete effectuation of the federal policy is achieved when the agreement contains both an arbitration provision for all unresolved grievances and an absolute prohibition of strikes, the arbitration agreement being the "quid pro quo" for the agreement not to strike. Textile Workers v. Lincoln Mills, 353 U.S. 448, 455, 77 S.Ct. 912, 917.

6. Cox, Reflections Upon Labor Arbitration, 72 Harv. L. Rev. 1482, 1498–1499 (1959).

rules governing a community like an industrial plant to fifteen or even fifty pages. Within the sphere of collective bargaining, the institutional characteristics and the governmental nature of the collective-bargaining process demand a common law of the shop which implements and furnishes the context of the agreement. We must assume that intelligent negotiators acknowledged so plain a need unless they stated a contrary rule in plain words.

A collective bargaining agreement is an effort to erect a system of industrial self-government. When most parties enter into contractual relationship they do so voluntarily, in the sense that there is no real compulsion to deal with one another, as opposed to dealing with other parties. This is not true of the labor agreement. The choice is generally not between entering or refusing to enter into a relationship, for that in all probability pre-exists the negotiations. Rather it is between having that relationship governed by an agreed-upon rule of law or leaving each and every matter subject to a temporary resolution dependent solely upon the relative strength, at any given moment, of the contending forces. The mature labor agreement may attempt to regulate all aspects of the complicated relationship, from the most crucial to the most minute over an extended period of time. Because of the compulsion to reach agreement and the breadth of the matters covered, as well as the need for a fairly concise and readable instrument, the product of negotiations (the written document) is, in the words of the late Dean Shulman, "a compilation of diverse provisions: some provide objective criteria almost automatically applicable; some provide more or less specific standards which require reason and judgment in their application; and some do little more than leave problems to future consideration with an expression of hope and good faith." Shulman, supra, at 1005. Gaps may be left to be filled in by reference to the practices of the particular industry and of the various shops covered by the agreement. Many of the specific practices which underlie the agreement may be unknown, except in hazy form, even to the negotiators. Courts and arbitration in the context of most commercial contracts are resorted to because there has been a breakdown in the working relationship of the parties; such resort is the unwanted exception. But the grievance machinery under a collective bargaining agreement is at the very heart of the system of industrial self-government. Arbitration is the means of solving the unforeseeable by molding a system of private law for all the problems which may arise and to provide for their solution in a way which will generally accord with the variant needs and desires of the parties. The processing of disputes through the grievance machinery is actually a vehicle by which meaning and content are given to the collective bargaining agreement.

Apart from matters that the parties specifically exclude, all of the questions on which the parties disagree must therefore come within the scope of the grievance and arbitration provisions of the collective agreement. The grievance procedure is, in other words, a part of the continuous collective bargaining process. It, rather than a strike, is the terminal point of a disagreement.

The labor arbitrator performs functions which are not normal to the courts; the considerations which help him fashion judgments may indeed by foreign to the competence of courts.

> A proper conception of the arbitrator's function is basic. He is not a public tribunal imposed upon the parties by superior authority which the parties are obliged to accept. He has no general charter to administer justice for a community which transcends the parties. He is rather part of a system of self-government created by and confined to the parties.... Shulman, supra, at 1016.

The labor arbitrator's source of law is not confined to the express provisions of the contract, as the industrial common law—the practices of the industry and the shop—is equally a part of the collective bargaining agreement although not expressed in it. The labor arbitrator is usually chosen because of the parties' confidence in his knowledge of the common law of the shop and their trust in his personal judgment to bring to bear considerations which are not expressed in the contract as criteria for judgment. The parties expect that his judgment of a particular grievance will reflect not only what the contract says but, insofar as the collective bargaining agreement permits, such factors as the effect upon productivity of a particular result, its consequence to the morale of the shop, his judgment whether tensions will be heightened or diminished. For the parties' objective in using the arbitration process is primarily to further their common goal of uninterrupted production under the agreement, to make the agreement serve their specialized needs. The ablest judge cannot be expected to bring the same experience and competence to bear upon the determination of a grievance, because he cannot be similarly informed.

The Congress, however, has by § 301 of the Labor Management Relations Act, assigned the courts the duty of determining whether the reluctant party has breached his promise to arbitrate. For arbitration is a matter of contract and a party cannot be required to submit to arbitration any dispute which he has not agreed so to submit. Yet, to be consistent with congressional policy in favor of settlement of disputes by the parties through the machinery of arbitration, the judicial inquiry under § 301 must be strictly confined to the question whether the reluctant party did agree to arbitrate the grievance or did agree to give the arbitrator power to make the award he made. An order to arbitrate the particular grievance should not be denied unless it may be said with positive assurance that the arbitration clause is not susceptible of an interpretation that covers the asserted dispute. Doubts should be resolved in favor of coverage.

We do not agree with the lower courts that contracting-out grievances were necessarily excepted from the grievance procedure of this agreement. To be sure, the agreement provides that "matters which are strictly a function of management shall not be subject to arbitration." But it goes on to say that if "differences" arise or if "any local trouble of any kind" arises, the grievance procedure shall be applicable.

Collective bargaining agreements regulate or restrict the exercise of management functions; they do not oust management from the performance of them. Management hires and fires, pays and promotes, supervises and plans. All these are part of its function, and absent a collective bargaining agreement, it may be exercised freely except as limited by public law and by the willingness of employees to work under the particular, unilaterally imposed conditions. A collective bargaining agreement may treat only with certain specific practices, leaving the rest to management but subject to the possibility of work stoppages. When, however, an absolute no-strike clause is included in the agreement, then in a very real sense everything that management does is subject to the agreement, for either management is prohibited or limited in the action it takes, or if not, it is protected from interference by strikes. This comprehensive reach of the collective bargaining agreement does not mean, however, that the language, "strictly a function of management," has no meaning.

"Strictly a function of management" might be thought to refer to any practice of management in which, under particular circumstances prescribed by the agreement, it is permitted to indulge. But if courts, in order to determine arbitrability, were allowed to determine what is permitted and what is not, the arbitration clause would be swallowed up by the exception. Every grievance in a sense involves a claim that management has violated some provision of the agreement.

Accordingly, "strictly a function of management" must be interpreted as referring only to that over which the contract gives management complete control and unfettered discretion. Respondent claims that the contracting out of work falls within this category. Contracting out work is the basis of many grievances; and that type of claim is grist in the mills of the arbitrators. A specific collective bargaining agreement may exclude contracting out from the grievance procedure. Or a written collateral agreement may make clear that contracting out was not a matter for arbitration. In such a case a grievance based solely on contracting out would not be arbitrable. Here, however, there is no such provision. Nor is there any showing that the parties designed the phrase "strictly a function of management" to encompass any and all forms of contracting out. In the absence of any express provision excluding a particular grievance from arbitration, we think only the most forceful evidence of a purpose to exclude the claim from arbitration can prevail, particularly where, as here, the exclusion clause is vague and the arbitration clause quite broad. Since any attempt by a court to infer such a purpose necessarily comprehends the merits, the court should view with suspicion an attempt to persuade it to become entangled in the construction of the substantive provisions of a labor agreement, even through the back door of interpreting the arbitration clause, when the alternative is to utilize the services of an arbitrator.

The grievance alleged that the contracting out was a violation of the collective bargaining agreement. There was, therefore, a dispute "as to the meaning and application of the provisions of this Agreement" which the parties had agreed would be determined by arbitration.

The judiciary sits in these cases to bring into operation an arbitral process which substitutes a regime of peaceful settlement for the older regime of industrial conflict. Whether contracting out in the present case violated the agreement is the question. It is a question for the arbiter, not for the courts.

Reversed.

■ MR. JUSTICE FRANKFURTER concurs in the result.

■ MR. JUSTICE BLACK took no part in consideration or decision of this case.

■ MR. JUSTICE WHITTAKER, dissenting.

Until today, I have understood it to be the unquestioned law, as this Court has consistently held, that arbitrators are private judges chosen by the parties to decide particular matters specifically submitted; that the contract under which matters are submitted to arbitrators is at once the source and limit of their authority and power; and that their power to decide issues with finality, thus ousting the normal functions of the courts, must rest upon a clear, definitive agreement of the parties, as such powers can never be implied. United States v. Moorman, 338 U.S. 457, 462 ... I believe that the Court today departs from the established principles announced in these decisions....

The Court ... holds that the arbitrator's source of law is "not confined to the express provisions of the contract," that arbitration should be ordered "unless it may be said with positive assurance that the arbitration clause is not susceptible of an interpretation that covers the asserted dispute," that "(d)oubts (of arbitrability) should be resolved in favor of coverage," and that when, as here, "an absolute no-strike clause is included in the agreement, then ... everything that management does is subject to (arbitration)." I understand the Court thus to hold that the arbitrators are not confined to the express provisions of the contract, that arbitration is to be ordered unless it may be said with positive assurance that arbitration of a particular dispute is excluded by the contract, that doubts of arbitrability are to be resolved in favor of arbitration, and that when, as here, the contract contains a no-strike clause, everything that management does is subject to arbitration.

This is an entirely new and strange doctrine to me. I suggest, with deference, that it departs from both the contract of the parties and the controlling decisions of this Court. I find nothing in the contract that purports to confer upon arbitrators any such general breadth of private judicial power. The Court cites no legislative or judicial authority that creates for or gives to arbitrators such broad general powers. And I respectfully submit that today's decision cannot be squared with the statement of Judge, later Mr. Justice, Cardozo in Marchant that "No one is under a duty to resort to these conventional tribunals, however helpful their processes, *except to the extent that he has signified his willingness*. Our own favor or disfavor of the cause of arbitration is not to count as a factor in the appraisal of the thought of others." (emphasis added), 252 N.Y., at page 299, 169 N.E., at page 391 ...

With respect, I submit that there is nothing in the contract here to indicate that the employer "signified (its) willingness" (Marchant, supra,

252 N.Y. at page 299, 169 N.E. at page 391) to submit to arbitrators whether it must cease contracting out work. Certainly no such intention is "made manifest by plain language" (Moorman, supra, 338 U.S. at page 462, 70 S.Ct. at page 291), as the law "requires," because such consent "is not to be implied." Hensey, supra, 205 U.S. at page 309, 27 S.Ct. at page 539. To the contrary, the parties by their conduct over many years interpreted the contracting out of major repair work to be "strictly a function of management," and if, as the concurring opinion suggests, the words of the contract can "be understood only by reference to the background which gave rise to their inclusion," then the interpretation given by the parties over 19 years to the phrase "matters which are strictly a function of management" should logically have some significance here....

* * *

Questions

1. Consider the following hypothetical:

> A collective bargaining agreement contains a provision stating that disputes over safety issues are subject to arbitration but disputes over job assignments are not. The agreement also states that in the event of a safety dispute, an employee is entitled to refuse to perform unsafe work if an expedited grievance is filed. One day an employee named Fletcher is given an assignment that she claims is dangerous. She refuses to perform and instead files a grievance seeking to arbitrate. The employer claims that it is not arbitrable because it is a job assignment dispute, and disciplines Fletcher for refusing the assignment. The union grieves the discipline action and the employer refuses to arbitrate. The union brings suit to compel arbitration.

How should the court rule?

2. Suppose the employer, in the previous hypothetical, has evidence that shows that Fletcher fabricated her safety concerns in order to obtain arbitration of the job assignment. Would that alter the outcome under the *Warrior and Gulf* court's analysis? What would Justice Whittaker say about the relevance and admissibility of the employer's evidence? What would the majority say?

3. It is often said that the decision in *Warrior and Gulf* creates a presumption of arbitrability for cases arising under Section 301 of the Labor Management Relations Act. In what sense is it a presumption? Is it a conclusive presumption? How can a party challenging arbitrability overcome the presumption? What reasons does the Court give for creating such a presumption?

4. On what basis does the Court in *Warrior & Gulf* distinguish *Wilko v. Swan*? Are you persuaded?

5. The Supreme Court says in *Warrior & Gulf* that "[a] collective bargaining agreement is an effort to erect a system of industrial self-government."

What does the Court mean? What, according to the Court, are the components of this self-government? What is the "law," and how is it created? What is the role of the federal and state governments? What is the role of the arbitrator? Are there any drawbacks to this paradigm for how labor relations should be ordered?

6. How do Section 301 and the FAA fit together? Should case law under one be applicable to issues arising under the other? Consider the following case.

* * *

14 Penn Plaza LLC v. Pyett

___ U.S. ___, 129 S.Ct. 1456 (2009).

■ JUSTICE THOMAS delivered the opinion of the Court.

The question presented by this case is whether a provision in a collective-bargaining agreement that clearly and unmistakably requires union members to arbitrate claims arising under the Age Discrimination in Employment Act of 1967 (ADEA), 81 Stat. 602, as amended, 29 U.S.C. § 621 *et seq.*, is enforceable. The United States Court of Appeals for the Second Circuit held that this Court's decision in *Alexander v. Gardner–Denver Co.,* 415 U.S. 36, 94 S.Ct. 1011, 39 L.Ed.2d 147 (1974), forbids enforcement of such arbitration provisions. We disagree and reverse the judgment of the Court of Appeals.

I

Respondents are members of the Service Employees International Union, Local 32–J (Union).... Since the 1930s, the Union has engaged in industry-wide collective bargaining with the Realty Advisory Board on Labor Relations, Inc. (RAB), a multiemployer bargaining association for the New York City real-estate industry. The agreement between the Union and the RAB is embodied in their Collective Bargaining Agreement for Contractors and Building Owners (CBA). The CBA requires union members to submit all claims of employment discrimination to binding arbitration under the CBA's grievance and dispute resolution procedures:

> § 30 NO DISCRIMINATION. There shall be no discrimination against any present or future employee by reason of race, creed, color, age, disability, national origin, sex, union membership, or any other characteristic protected by law, including, but not limited to, claims made pursuant to Title VII of the Civil Rights Act, the Americans with Disabilities Act, the Age Discrimination in Employment Act, the New York State Human Rights Law, the New York City Human Rights Code, ... or any other similar laws, rules, or regulations. All such claims shall be subject to the grievance and arbitration procedures (Articles V and VI) as the sole and exclusive remedy for violations. Arbitrators shall apply appropriate law in rendering decisions based upon claims of discrimination. App. to Pet. for Cert. 48a.

Petitioner 14 Penn Plaza LLC is a member of the RAB. It owns and operates the New York City office building where, prior to August 2003, respondents worked as night lobby watchmen and in other similar capacities. Respondents were directly employed by petitioner Temco Service Industries, Inc. (Temco), a maintenance service and cleaning contractor. In August 2003, with the Union's consent, 14 Penn Plaza [outsourced the watchmen positions and reassigned Respondents to jobs as night porters and light duty cleaners]. Respondents contend that these reassignments [violated seniority and overtime rules and discriminated against them on the basis of race. The Union brought a grievance and requested arbitration under the CBA].

After the initial arbitration hearing, the Union withdrew the first set of respondents' grievances—the age-discrimination claims—from arbitration. Because it had consented to the contract for new security personnel at 14 Penn Plaza, the Union believed that it could not legitimately object to respondents' reassignments as discriminatory. But the Union continued to arbitrate the seniority and overtime claims, and, after several hearings, the claims were denied.

. . . [R]espondents filed a complaint with the Equal Employment Opportunity Commission (EEOC) [which subsequently issued a right-to-sue letter.] Respondents thereafter filed suit against petitioners in the United States District Court for the Southern District of New York, alleging that their reassignment violated the ADEA and state and local laws prohibiting age discrimination. Petitioners filed a motion to compel arbitration of respondents' claims pursuant to § 3 and § 4 of the Federal Arbitration Act (FAA), 9 U.S.C. §§ 3, 4. The District Court denied the motion because under Second Circuit precedent, "even a clear and unmistakable union-negotiated waiver of a right to litigate certain federal and state statutory claims in a judicial forum is unenforceable." App. to Pet. for Cert. 21a. Respondents immediately appealed the ruling under § 16 of the FAA . . .

The Court of Appeals affirmed. 498 F.3d 88. According to the Court of Appeals, it could not compel arbitration of the dispute because *Gardner–Denver,* which "remains good law," held "that a collective bargaining agreement could not waive covered workers' rights to a judicial forum for causes of action created by Congress." 498 F.3d, at 92, 91, n. 3 (citing *Gardner–Denver,* 415 U.S., at 49–51, 94 S.Ct. 1011). . . . As a result, an individual employee would be free to choose compulsory arbitration under [*Gilmer v. Interstate/Johnson Lane Corp.,* 500 U.S. 20, 111 S.Ct. 1647, 114 L.Ed.2d 26 (1991)], but a labor union could not collectively bargain for arbitration on behalf of its members. We granted certiorari, 552 U.S. ___, 128 S.Ct. 1223, 170 L.Ed.2d 57 (2008), to address the issue left unresolved in *Wright,* which continues to divide the Courts of Appeals, and now reverse.

II

A

The NLRA governs federal labor-relations law. As permitted by that statute, respondents designated the Union as their "exclusive representativ[e] ... for the purposes of collective bargaining in respect to rates of pay, wages, hours of employment, or other conditions of employment." 29 U.S.C. § 159(a). As the employees' exclusive bargaining representative, the Union "enjoys broad authority ... in the negotiation and administration of [the] collective bargaining contract." *Communications Workers v. Beck,* 487 U.S. 735, 739, 108 S.Ct. 2641, 101 L.Ed.2d 634 (1988) (internal quotation marks omitted). But this broad authority "is accompanied by a responsibility of equal scope, the responsibility and duty of fair representation." *Humphrey v. Moore,* 375 U.S. 335, 342, 84 S.Ct. 363, 11 L.Ed.2d 370 (1964). The employer has a corresponding duty under the NLRA to bargain in good faith "with the representatives of his employees" on wages, hours, and conditions of employment. 29 U.S.C. § 158(a)(5); see also § 158(d).

In this instance, the Union and the RAB, negotiating on behalf of 14 Penn Plaza, collectively bargained in good faith and agreed that employment-related discrimination claims, including claims brought under the ADEA, would be resolved in arbitration. This freely negotiated term between the Union and the RAB easily qualifies as a "conditio[n] of employment" that is subject to mandatory bargaining under § 159(a)....

As a result, the CBA's arbitration provision must be honored unless the ADEA itself removes this particular class of grievances from the NLRA's broad sweep. See *Mitsubishi Motors Corp. v. Soler Chrysler-Plymouth, Inc.,* 473 U.S. 614, 628, 105 S.Ct. 3346, 87 L.Ed.2d 444 (1985). It does not. This Court has squarely held that the ADEA does not preclude arbitration of claims brought under the statute. See *Gilmer,* 500 U.S., at 26–33, 111 S.Ct. 1647....

The *Gilmer* Court's interpretation of the ADEA fully applies in the collective-bargaining context. Nothing in the law suggests a distinction between the status of arbitration agreements signed by an individual employee and those agreed to by a union representative. This Court has required only that an agreement to arbitrate statutory antidiscrimination claims be "explicitly stated" in the collective-bargaining agreement. [*Wright v. Universal Maritime Service Corp.,* 525 U.S. 70, 80, 119 S.Ct. 391, 142 L.Ed.2d 361 (1998)]. The CBA under review here meets that obligation....

Examination of the two federal statutes at issue in this case, therefore, yields a straightforward answer to the question presented: The NLRA provided the Union and the RAB with statutory authority to collectively bargain for arbitration of workplace discrimination claims, and Congress did not terminate that authority with respect to federal age-discrimination claims in the ADEA. Accordingly, there is no legal basis for the Court to strike down the arbitration clause in this CBA, which was freely negotiated by the Union and the RAB, and which clearly and unmistakably requires respondents to arbitrate the age-discrimination claims at issue in this appeal. Congress has chosen to allow arbitration of ADEA claims. The Judiciary must respect that choice.

B

The CBA's arbitration provision is also fully enforceable under the *Gardner–Denver* line of cases. Respondents interpret *Gardner–Denver* and its progeny to hold that "a union cannot waive an employee's right to a judicial forum under the federal antidiscrimination statutes" because "allowing the union to waive this right would substitute the union's interests for the employee's antidiscrimination rights." Brief for Respondents 12. The "combination of union control over the process and inherent conflict of interest with respect to discrimination claims," they argue, "provided the foundation for the Court's holding [in *Gardner–Denver*] that arbitration under a collective-bargaining agreement could not preclude an individual employee's right to bring a lawsuit in court to vindicate a statutory discrimination claim." *Id.,* at 15. We disagree.

1

The holding of *Gardner–Denver* is not as broad as respondents suggest. [In that case, t]he District Court issued a decision, affirmed by the Court of Appeals, which granted summary judgment to the employer because it concluded that "the claim of racial discrimination had been submitted to the arbitrator and resolved adversely to [the employee]." *Id.,* at 43, 94 S.Ct. 1011. In the District Court's view, "having voluntarily elected to pursue his grievance to final arbitration under the nondiscrimination clause of the collective-bargaining agreement," the employee was "bound by the arbitral decision" and precluded from suing his employer on any other grounds, such as a statutory claim under Title VII. *Ibid.*

This Court reversed the judgment on the narrow ground that the arbitration was not preclusive because the collective-bargaining agreement did not cover statutory claims. As a result, the lower courts erred in relying on the "doctrine of election of remedies" to bar the employee's Title VII claim. *Id.,* at 49, 94 S.Ct. 1011. "That doctrine, which refers to situations where an individual pursues remedies that are legally or factually inconsistent" with each other, did not apply to the employee's dual pursuit of arbitration and a Title VII discrimination claim in district court. The employee's collective-bargaining agreement did not mandate arbitration of statutory antidiscrimination claims. *Id.,* at 49–50, 94 S.Ct. 1011.... Because the collective-bargaining agreement gave the arbitrator "authority to resolve only questions of contractual rights," his decision could not prevent the employee from bringing the Title VII claim in federal court "regardless of whether certain contractual rights are similar to, or duplicative of, the substantive rights secured by Title VII." *Id.,* at 53–54, 94 S.Ct. 1011; see also *id.,* at 50, 94 S.Ct. 1011....

The Court's decisions following *Gardner–Denver* have not broadened its holding to make it applicable to the facts of this case....

[The Court discussed *Barrentine v. Arkansas–Best Freight System, Inc.,* 450 U.S. 728, 101 S.Ct. 1437, 67 L.Ed.2d 641 (1981) and *McDonald v. West Branch,* 466 U.S. 284, 104 S.Ct. 1799, 80 L.Ed.2d 302 (1984).] The facts underlying *Gardner–Denver, Barrentine,* and *McDonald* reveal the narrow scope of the legal rule arising from that trilogy of decisions. Summarizing those opinions in *Gilmer,* this Court made clear that the *Gardner–Denver* line of cases "did not involve the issue of the enforceability of an agreement to arbitrate statutory claims." 500 U.S., at 35, 111 S.Ct. 1647. Those decisions instead "involved the quite different issue whether arbitration of contract-based claims precluded subsequent judicial resolution of statutory claims. Since the employees there had not agreed to arbitrate their statutory claims, and the labor arbitrators were not authorized to resolve such claims, the arbitration in those cases understandably was held not to preclude subsequent statutory actions." *Ibid.;* see also *Wright,* 525 U.S., at 76, 119 S.Ct. 391; *Livadas v. Bradshaw,* 512 U.S. 107, 127, n. 21, 114 S.Ct. 2068, 129 L.Ed.2d 93 (1994). *Gardner–Denver* and its progeny thus do not control the outcome where, as is the case here, the collective-bargaining agreement's arbitration provision expressly covers both statutory and contractual discrimination claims.[8]

2

We recognize that apart from their narrow holdings, the *Gardner–Denver* line of cases included broad dicta that was highly critical of the use of arbitration for the vindication of statutory antidiscrimination rights. That skepticism, however, rested on a misconceived view of arbitration that this Court has since abandoned.

First, the Court in *Gardner–Denver* erroneously assumed that an agreement to submit statutory discrimination claims to arbitration was tantamount to a waiver of those rights.... The Court was correct in concluding that federal antidiscrimination rights may not be prospectively waived, ... but it confused an agreement to arbitrate those statutory claims with a prospective waiver of the substantive right. The decision to resolve ADEA claims by way of arbitration instead of litigation does not waive the statutory right to be free from workplace age discrimination; it waives only the right to seek relief from a court in the first instance. See *Gilmer, supra,* at 26, 111 S.Ct. 1647 ("'[B]y agreeing to arbitrate a statutory claim, a party does not forgo the substantive rights afforded by the statute; it only submits to their resolution in an arbitral, rather than a judicial, forum'" (quoting *Mitsubishi Motors Corp.,* 473 U.S., at 628, 105 S.Ct. 3346))....

Second, *Gardner–Denver* mistakenly suggested that certain features of arbitration made it a forum "well suited to the resolution of contractual disputes," but "a comparatively inappropriate forum for the final resolution of rights created by Title VII." 415 U.S., at 56, 94 S.Ct. 1011. According to the Court, the "factfinding process in arbitration" is "not

8. Because today's decision does not contradict the holding of *Gardner–Denver,* we need not resolve the *stare decisis* concerns raised by the dissenting opinions. See *post,* at 1478, 1481 (opinion of Souter, J.); *post,* at 1477–1478 (opinion of Stevens, J.). But given the development of this Court's arbitration jurisprudence in the intervening years, see *infra,* at 1469–1471 *Gardner–Denver* would appear to be a strong candidate for overruling if the dissent's broad view of its holding, see *post,* at 1479–1480 (opinion of Souter, J.), were correct....

equivalent to judicial factfinding" and the "informality of arbitral procedure ... makes arbitration a less appropriate forum for final resolution of Title VII issues than the federal courts." *Id.*, at 57, 58, 94 S.Ct. 1011. The Court also questioned the competence of arbitrators to decide federal statutory claims....

These misconceptions have been corrected. For example, the Court has "recognized that arbitral tribunals are readily capable of handling the factual and legal complexities of antitrust claims, notwithstanding the absence of judicial instruction and supervision" and that "there is no reason to assume at the outset that arbitrators will not follow the law." *McMahon, supra,* at 232, 107 S.Ct. 2332; *Mitsubishi Motors Corp.,* 473 U.S., at 634, 105 S.Ct. 3346 ("We decline to indulge the presumption that the parties and arbitral body conducting a proceeding will be unable or unwilling to retain competent, conscientious, and impartial arbitrators"). An arbitrator's capacity to resolve complex questions of fact and law extends with equal force to discrimination claims brought under the ADEA.... At bottom, objections centered on the nature of arbitration do not offer a credible basis for discrediting the choice of that forum to resolve statutory antidiscrimination claims.[10]

Third, the Court in *Gardner–Denver* raised in a footnote a "further concern" regarding "the union's exclusive control over the manner and extent to which an individual grievance is presented." 415 U.S., at 58, n. 19, 94 S.Ct. 1011. The Court suggested that in arbitration, as in the collective-bargaining process, a union may subordinate the interests of an individual employee to the collective interests of all employees in the bargaining unit. *Ibid.;* see also *McDonald, supra,* at 291, 104 S.Ct. 1799 ("The union's interests and those of the individual employee are not always identical or even compatible. As a result, the union may present the employee's grievance less vigorously, or make different strategic choices, than would the employee") ...

We cannot rely on this judicial policy concern as a source of authority for introducing a qualification into the ADEA that is not found in its text.... Congress is fully equipped "to identify any category of claims as to which agreements to arbitrate will be held unenforceable." *Mitsubishi Motors Corp., supra,* at 627, 105 S.Ct. 3346. Until Congress amends the ADEA to meet the conflict-of-interest concern identified in the *Gardner–Denver* dicta, and seized on by respondents here, there is "no reason to color the lens through which the arbitration clause is read" simply because of an alleged conflict of interest between a union and its members....

The conflict-of-interest argument also proves too much. Labor unions certainly balance the economic interests of some employees against the

10. Moreover, an arbitrator's decision as to whether a unionized employee has been discriminated against on the basis of age in violation of the ADEA remains subject to judicial review under the FAA. 9 U.S.C. § 10(a). "[A]lthough judicial scrutiny of arbitration awards necessarily is limited, such review is sufficient to ensure that arbitrators comply with the requirements of the statute." *Shearson/American Express Inc. v. McMahon,* 482 U.S. 220, 232, 107 S.Ct. 2332, 96 L.Ed.2d 185 (1987).

needs of the larger work force as they negotiate collective-bargain agreements and implement them on a daily basis. But this attribute of organized labor does not justify singling out an arbitration provision for disfavored treatment.... It was Congress' verdict that the benefits of organized labor outweigh the sacrifice of individual liberty that this system necessarily demands. Respondents' argument that they were deprived of the right to pursue their ADEA claims in federal court by a labor union with a conflict of interest is therefore unsustainable; it amounts to a collateral attack on the NLRA.

In any event, Congress has accounted for this conflict of interest in several ways. [For example], the NLRA has been interpreted to impose a "duty of fair representation" on labor unions, which a union breaches "when its conduct toward a member of the bargaining unit is arbitrary, discriminatory, or in bad faith." *Marquez v. Screen Actors,* 525 U.S. 33, 44, 119 S.Ct. 292, 142 L.Ed.2d 242 (1998).... In addition, a union is subject to liability under the ADEA if the union itself discriminates against its members on the basis of age. See 29 U.S.C. § 623(d) ... Union members may also file age-discrimination claims with the EEOC and the National Labor Relations Board, which may then seek judicial intervention under this Court's precedent. See *EEOC v. Waffle House, Inc.,* 534 U.S. 279, 295–296, 122 S.Ct. 754, 151 L.Ed.2d 755 (2002). In sum, Congress has provided remedies for the situation where a labor union is less than vigorous in defense of its members' claims of discrimination under the ADEA.

III

... Respondents also argue that the CBA operates as a substantive waiver of their ADEA rights because it not only precludes a federal lawsuit, but also allows the Union to block arbitration of these claims. Brief for Respondents 28–30. Petitioners contest this characterization of the CBA, see Reply Brief for Petitioners 23–27, and offer record evidence suggesting that the Union has allowed respondents to continue with the arbitration even though the Union has declined to participate, see App. to Pet. for Cert. 42a. But not only does this question require resolution of contested factual allegations, it was not fully briefed to this or any court and is not fairly encompassed within the question presented, see this Court's Rule 14.1(a). Thus, although a substantive waiver of federally protected civil rights will not be upheld, see *Mitsubishi Motors Corp.*, 473 U.S., at 637, and n. 19, 105 S.Ct. 3346; *Gilmer,* 500 U.S., at 29, 111 S.Ct. 1647, we are not positioned to resolve in the first instance whether the CBA allows the Union to prevent respondents from "effectively vindicating" their "federal statutory rights in the arbitral forum," *Green Tree Financial Corp.–Ala. v. Randolph,* 531 U.S. 79, 90, 121 S.Ct. 513, 148 L.Ed.2d 373 (2000). Resolution of this question at this juncture would be particularly inappropriate in light of our hesitation to invalidate arbitration agreements on the basis of speculation. See *id.*, at 91, 121 S.Ct. 513.

IV

We hold that a collective-bargaining agreement that clearly and unmistakably requires union members to arbitrate ADEA claims is enforceable as a matter of federal law. The judgment of the Court of Appeals is reversed, and the case is remanded for further proceedings consistent with this opinion.

It is so ordered.

■ JUSTICE STEVENS, dissenting.

Justice Souter's dissenting opinion, which I join in full, explains why our decision in *Alexander v. Gardner–Denver Co.,* 415 U.S. 36, 94 S.Ct. 1011, 39 L.Ed.2d 147 (1974), answers the question presented in this case. My concern regarding the Court's subversion of precedent to the policy favoring arbitration prompts these additional remarks. . . .

Today the majority's preference for arbitration again leads it to disregard our precedent. Although it purports to ascertain the relationship between the Age Discrimination in Employment Act of 1967 (ADEA), the National Labor Relations Act, and the Federal Arbitration Act, the Court ignores our earlier determination of the relevant provisions' meaning. The Court concludes that "[i]t was Congress' verdict that the benefits of organized labor outweigh the sacrifice of individual liberty" that the system of organized labor "necessarily demands," even when the sacrifice demanded is a judicial forum for asserting an individual statutory right. *Ante* But in *Gardner–Denver* we determined that "Congress' verdict" was otherwise when we held that Title VII does not permit a CBA to waive an employee's right to a federal judicial forum. Because the purposes and relevant provisions of Title VII and the ADEA are not meaningfully distinguishable, it is only by reexamining the statutory questions resolved in *Gardner–Denver* through the lens of the policy favoring arbitration that the majority now reaches a different result. . . .

As was true in *Rodriguez de Quijas,* there are competing arguments in this case regarding the interaction of the relevant statutory provisions. But the Court in *Gardner–Denver* considered these arguments, including "the federal policy favoring arbitration of labor disputes," 415 U.S., at 59, 94 S.Ct. 1011, and held that Congress did not intend to permit the result petitioners seek. In the absence of an intervening amendment to the relevant statutory language, we are bound by that decision. It is for Congress, rather than this Court, to reassess the policy arguments favoring arbitration and revise the relevant provisions to reflect its views.

■ JUSTICE SOUTER, with whom JUSTICE STEVENS, JUSTICE GINSBURG, and JUSTICE BREYER join, dissenting.

The issue here is whether employees subject to a collective-bargaining agreement (CBA) providing for conclusive arbitration of all grievances, including claimed breaches of the Age Discrimination in Employment Act of 1967 (ADEA), 29 U.S.C. § 621 *et seq.,* lose their statutory right to bring an ADEA claim in court, § 626(c). Under the 35–year–old holding in *Alexander v. Gardner–Denver Co.,* 415 U.S. 36, 94 S.Ct. 1011, 39 L.Ed.2d 147 (1974), they do not, and I would adhere to *stare decisis* and so hold today.

I

Like Title VII of the Civil Rights Act of 1964, 42 U.S.C. § 2000e *et seq.*, the ADEA is aimed at " 'the elimination of discrimination in the workplace,' " *McKennon v. Nashville Banner Publishing Co.*, 513 U.S. 352, 358, 115 S.Ct. 879, 130 L.Ed.2d 852 (1995) (quoting *Oscar Mayer & Co. v. Evans*, 441 U.S. 750, 756, 99 S.Ct. 2066, 60 L.Ed.2d 609 (1979)), and, again like Title VII, the ADEA "contains a vital element. . . : It grants an injured employee a right of action to obtain the authorized relief," 513 U.S., at 358, 115 S.Ct. 879. "Any person aggrieved" under the Act "may bring a civil action in any court of competent jurisdiction for legal or equitable relief," 29 U.S.C. § 626(c), thereby "not only redress[ing] his own injury but also vindicat[ing] the important congressional policy against discriminatory employment practices," *Gardner–Denver, supra,* at 45, 94 S.Ct. 1011.

Gardner–Denver considered the effect of a CBA's arbitration clause on an employee's right to sue under Title VII. One of the employer's arguments was that the CBA entered into by the union had waived individual employees' statutory cause of action subject to a judicial remedy for discrimination in violation of Title VII. Although Title VII, like the ADEA, "does not speak expressly to the relationship between federal courts and the grievance-arbitration machinery of collective-bargaining agreements," 415 U.S., at 47, 94 S.Ct. 1011, we unanimously held that "the rights conferred" by Title VII (with no exception for the right to a judicial forum) cannot be waived as "part of the collective bargaining process," *id.*, at 51, 94 S.Ct. 1011. We stressed the contrast between two categories of rights in labor and employment law. There were "statutory rights related to collective activity," which "are conferred on employees collectively to foster the processes of bargaining [, which] properly may be exercised or relinquished by the union as collective-bargaining agent to obtain economic benefits for union members." *Ibid.* But "Title VII . . . stands on plainly different [categorical] ground; it concerns not majoritarian processes, but an individual's right to equal employment opportunities." *Ibid.* Thus, as the Court previously realized, *Gardner–Denver* imposed a "seemingly absolute prohibition of union waiver of employees' federal forum rights." *Wright v. Universal Maritime Service Corp.*, 525 U.S. 70, 80, 119 S.Ct. 391, 142 L.Ed.2d 361 (1998).

We supported the judgment with several other lines of complementary reasoning. First, we explained that antidiscrimination statutes "have long evinced a general intent to accord parallel or overlapping remedies against discrimination," and Title VII's statutory scheme carried "no suggestion . . . that a prior arbitral decision either forecloses an individual's right to sue or divests federal courts of jurisdiction." *Gardner–Denver,* 415 U.S., at 47, 94 S.Ct. 1011. We accordingly concluded that "an individual does not forfeit his private cause of action if he first pursues his grievance to final arbitration under the nondiscrimination clause of a collective-bargaining agreement." *Id.*, at 49, 94 S.Ct. 1011.

Second, we rejected the District Court's view that simply participating in the arbitration amounted to electing the arbitration remedy and waiving the plaintiff's right to sue. We said that the arbitration agreement at issue covered only a contractual right under the CBA to be free from discrimination, not the "independent statutory rights accorded by Congress" in Title VII. *Id.,* at 49–50, 94 S.Ct. 1011. Third, we rebuffed the employer's argument that federal courts should defer to arbitral rulings. We declined to make the "assumption that arbitral processes are commensurate with judicial processes," *id.,* at 56, 94 S.Ct. 1011, and described arbitration as "a less appropriate forum for final resolution of Title VII issues than the federal courts," *id.,* at 58, 94 S.Ct. 1011.

Finally, we took note that "[i]n arbitration, as in the collective bargaining process, the interests of the individual employee may be subordinated to the collective interests of all employees in the bargaining unit," *ibid.,* n. 19, a result we deemed unacceptable when it came to Title VII claims. In sum, *Gardner–Denver* held that an individual's statutory right of freedom from discrimination and access to court for enforcement were beyond a union's power to waive.

Our analysis of Title VII in *Gardner–Denver* is just as pertinent to the ADEA in this case. . . .

II

The majority evades the precedent of *Gardner–Denver* as long as it can simply by ignoring it. The Court never mentions the case before concluding that the ADEA and the National Labor Relations Act, 29 U.S.C. § 151 *et seq.,* "yiel[d] a straightforward answer to the question presented," *ante,* that is, that unions can bargain away individual rights to a federal forum for antidiscrimination claims. If this were a case of first impression, it would at least be possible to consider that conclusion, but the issue is settled and the time is too late by 35 years to make the bald assertion that "[n]othing in the law suggests a distinction between the status of arbitration agreements signed by an individual employee and those agreed to by a union representative." *Ante,* at 1465. In fact, we recently and unanimously said that the principle that "federal forum rights cannot be waived in union-negotiated CBAs even if they can be waived in individually executed contracts ... assuredly finds support in" our case law, *Wright,* 525 U.S., at 77, 119 S.Ct. 391, and every Court of Appeals save [the Fourth Circuit] has read our decisions as holding to this position ...

Equally at odds with existing law is the majority's statement that "[t]he decision to fashion a CBA to require arbitration of employment-discrimination claims is no different from the many other decisions made by parties in designing grievance machinery." *Ante.* That is simply impossible to square with our conclusion in *Gardner–Denver* that "Title VII ... stands on plainly different ground" from "statutory rights related to collective activity": "it concerns not majoritarian processes, but an individual's right to equal employment opportunities." 415 U.S., at 51, 94 S.Ct. 1011 ...

When the majority does speak to *Gardner–Denver,* it misreads the case in claiming that it turned solely "on the narrow ground that the arbitration was not preclusive because the collective-bargaining agreement did not cover statutory claims." *Ante.* That, however, was merely one of several reasons given in support of the decision, see *Gardner–Denver,* 415 U.S., at 47–59, 94 S.Ct. 1011, and we raised it to explain why the District Court made a mistake in thinking that the employee lost his Title VII rights by electing to pursue the contractual arbitration remedy, see *id.,* at 49–50, 94 S.Ct. 1011. One need only read *Gardner–Denver* itself to know that it was not at all so narrowly reasoned . . . Indeed, if the Court can read *Gardner–Denver* as resting on nothing more than a contractual failure to reach as far as statutory claims, it must think the Court has been wreaking havoc on the truth for years, since (as noted) we have unanimously described the case as raising a "seemingly absolute prohibition of union waiver of employees' federal forum rights." *Wright, supra,* at 80, 119 S.Ct. 391. Human ingenuity is not equal to the task of reconciling statements like this with the majority's representation that *Gardner–Denver* held only that "the arbitration was not preclusive because the collective-bargaining agreement did not cover statutory claims." *Ante.*

Nor, finally, does the majority have any better chance of being rid of another of *Gardner–Denver*'s statements supporting its rule of decision, set out and repeated in previous quotations: "in arbitration, as in the collective-bargaining process, a union may subordinate the interests of an individual employee to the collective interests of all employees in the bargaining unit," *ante,* (citing 415 U.S., at 58, n. 19, 94 S.Ct. 1011), an unacceptable result when it comes to "an individual's right to equal employment opportunities," *id.,* at 51, 94 S.Ct. 1011. The majority tries to diminish this reasoning, and the previously stated holding it supported, by making the remarkable rejoinder that "[w]e cannot rely on this judicial policy concern as a source of authority for introducing a qualification into the ADEA that is not found in its text." *Ante.* It is enough to recall that respondents are not seeking to "introduc[e] a qualification into" the law; they are justifiably relying on statutory-interpretation precedent decades old, never overruled, and serially reaffirmed over the years. See, *e.g., McDonald v. West Branch,* 466 U.S. 284, 291, 104 S.Ct. 1799, 80 L.Ed.2d 302 (1984); *Barrentine, supra,* at 742, 101 S.Ct. 1437. With that precedent on the books, it makes no sense for the majority to claim that "judicial policy concern[s]" about unions sacrificing individual antidiscrimination rights should be left to Congress.[4]

For that matter, Congress has unsurprisingly understood *Gardner–Denver* the way we have repeatedly explained it and has operated on the assumption that a CBA cannot waive employees' rights to a judicial forum to enforce antidiscrimination statutes. See, *e.g.,* H.R.Rep. No. 102–40, pt. 1, p. 97 (1991) (stating that, "consistent with the Supreme Court's interpreta-

4. The majority says it would be "particularly inappropriate" to consider *Gardner–Denver*'s conflict-of-interest rationale because "Congress has made available" another "avenue" to protect workers against union discrimination, namely, a duty of fair representation claim. *Ante,* at 1472–1473. This answer misunderstands the law, for unions may decline for a variety of reasons to pursue potentially meritorious discrimination claims without succumbing to a member's suit for failure of fair representation.

tion of Title VII in [*Gardner–Denver*]," "any agreement to submit disputed issues to arbitration . . . in the context of a collective bargaining agreement . . . does not preclude the affected person from seeking relief under the enforcement provisions of Title VII"). . . .

III

On one level, the majority opinion may have little effect, for it explicitly reserves the question whether a CBA's waiver of a judicial forum is enforceable when the union controls access to and presentation of employees' claims in arbitration, *ante,* which "is usually the case," *McDonald, supra,* at 291, 104 S.Ct. 1799. But as a treatment of precedent in statutory interpretation, the majority's opinion cannot be reconciled with the *Gardner–Denver* Court's own view of its holding, repeated over the years and generally understood, and I respectfully dissent.

* * *

Questions

1. Note that although the arbitration clause at issue in this case was in a collective bargaining agreement, the motion to compel arbitration was brought pursuant to the FAA. Does *Penn Plaza* represent a conflation of the two sources of law?

2. The arbitration clause at issue in this case is unusual—employers seldom demand at the bargaining table a clause subjecting all discrimination claims to grievance arbitration, and unions even less often agree to such a clause. Is the existence of the broad waiver clause in Section 30 essential to the holding of *Penn Plaza,* or might courts reach the same outcome in cases involving more general arbitration clauses? If the broad waiver clause is essential to the *Penn Plaza,* the practical effect of the case likely will be very limited.

3. What, if anything, is left of *Gardner–Denver* after *Penn Plaza*? Is it limited to labor cases where there is no express grant of authority to the arbitrator to decide the statutory questions? If so, then what are we to make of arbitration decisions in which the arbitrator applies a statute because the parties have at least implicitly incorporated it in the collective bargaining agreement? Consider the following cases decided shortly after *Penn Plaza* was released.

In *Mathews v. Denver Newspaper Agency*, LLP, 2009 WL 1231776 (D. Colo. 2009), the arbitration clause at issue gave the arbitrator the authority to decide statutory discrimination claims, but also provided that employees were not required to arbitrate these claims and could pursue them in court. Rather than doing so, however, an employee pursued his discrimination claim through collective-bargaining arbitration. Instead of relying on the union to represent him, the employee hired his own counsel to prepare and present his case in the grievance arbitration hearing. At the hearing, the employee apparently presented evidence and argument that the employer had violated federal law by discriminating against him. After losing in arbitration, the employee took his claim to court. The court dismissed, holding that by electing to take his statutory discrimination claim to grievance arbitration and then vigorously pursuing it there, the employee had waived his right to pursue the same claim in litigation. The court also held that the arbitrated resolution of the claim precluded subsequent litigation on res judicata grounds.

Contrast *Mathews* with *Kravar v. Triangle Services, Inc.*, 2009 WL 1392595 (S.D.N.Y. 2009) in which the arbitration clause at issue was identical to the one in *Penn Plaza*—it provided that all discrimination claims were subject to grievance arbitration. The employee filed a grievance and told the union that she wanted to arbitrate it, but the union declined to take the case to arbitration. The employee then sued in court. The employer moved to dismiss, citing *Penn Plaza*. The court denied the motion, holding that the union's refusal to take the case to arbitration was an impermissible waiver of the employee's substantive antidiscrimination rights. The court held, therefore, that the employee was entitled to pursue her claim in court.

If courts go the *Kravar* route, then *Gardner–Denver* survives *Penn Plaza* and Part III of *Penn Plaza* becomes the exception swallowing the "rule." But what if courts go the *Mathews* route? In many ways, *Mathews* is factually similar to *Gardner–Denver*. As in *Mathews*, the *Gardner–Denver* plaintiff had gone to arbitration, had an opportunity to present his discrimination claim, and lost. The Supreme Court cited the arbitrator's possible lack of authority as one reason for allowing Alexander to sue, but that didn't seem to be a critical basis for the holding. The *Mathews* court applied the same election/preclusion arguments the *Gardner–Denver* Court had declined to apply.

4. What are the benefits and drawbacks of using labor arbitration to resolve statutory claims? Consider this question from the perspective of the company, the union, and the individual members of the union.

5. Note the majority's footnote 10. Does this portend expansive judicial review of labor arbitration awards? Of arbitration awards involving statutory claims such as employment discrimination? Of only labor arbitration awards involving statutory claims? Or is it just window dressing?

6. Does the Court in *Penn Plaza* hold that judicial review of arbitrated discrimination cases will be governed by the FAA standard of review rather than that the *Steelworkers Trilogy*?

7. The apparent conflation in *Penn Plaza* of labor and employment arbitration raises but does not answer a host of other issues. For example: (a) Is the cost of pursuing a complex employment claim appropriately shared by all employees paying dues? (b) What is the applicable time period for bringing a discrimination claim—the few days typically listed in the contract for bringing grievances or the longer statute of limitations for discrimination claims under statutes? (c) May a collective bargaining agreement restrict the remedies available when statutory rights are arbitrated?

May it restrict the ability to bring class claims? (d) How should the parties handle choice-of-law issues that may arise under state antidiscrimination laws when a collective bargaining agreement covers employees in more than one state? (e) Does *Penn Plaza* give employers a new argument to make in union organizing campaigns—if you choose a union, you can lose your ability to bring any claims under employment statutes?

CHAPTER TWO

DEFENSES TO ARBITRATION

1. INTRODUCTION

The decision to arbitrate rather than litigate a dispute can have enormous strategic and tactical consequences for the parties. The decision can arise at two points in time: when a contract is drafted, or during the course of performance after a dispute has arisen. Even if parties have inserted an arbitration clause into their initial agreement, it is common for one side to attempt to resist arbitration when a dispute arises.

When the prospect of arbitration arises in the context of an actual dispute, parties often bring different considerations to bear on the issue than they did at the contract-drafting stage. Whether it is in a party's interest to arbitrate rather than litigate depends on many factors, such as the nature of the dispute, the nature of the arbitral tribunal, the types of procedures used in the procedure, the method of selecting the arbitrators, and the types of remedies sought. Many of these factors were not present when the contract was drafted. In addition, by the time there is a dispute requiring resolution, the parties usually perceive themselves as being in an adversarial rather than cooperative relationship with each other, i.e., a relationship in which one party's gain will be the other party's loss. The zero-sum framework applies not only to the anticipated outcome of the dispute, but also to the issue of whether or not to use arbitration. That is, when one side wants to arbitrate a dispute, the other side usually does not. The party seeking to use arbitration does so because it believes it will obtain a strategic or practical advantage in the arbitral forum. But in the looking-glass logic of litigation, where one party sees its interest lie, the other party sees what is in its interest to avoid. Thus, parties who might have agreed to arbitration clauses at the time of contract-drafting often find themselves seeking to avoid arbitration at the time of disputing.

Sometimes, a party's resistance to arbitration is well founded. A party may fear that the particular makeup of the arbitral panel or the method of selection will yield an arbitrator who will be unsympathetic to its position. Or, the party may want to raise certain legal claims or defenses that it believes an arbitrator will not adequately understand or weigh in the determination. Or, the party resisting arbitration may want the discovery tools or remedy powers available only in a court. Thus, there are many reasons why a party might seek to avoid arbitration.

This chapter explores the circumstances under which a party can avoid an arbitration clause under the Federal Arbitration Act. Section 2 of the Act states that:

> A written provision in any maritime transaction or a contract evidencing a transaction involving commerce to settle by arbitration a controversy arising thereafter arising out of such contract or transaction, or the refusal to perform the whole or any part thereof, or an agreement in writing to submit to arbitration an existing controversy arising out of such a contract, transaction, or refusal, shall be valid, irrevocable and enforceable, *save upon such grounds as exist at law or in equity for the revocation of any contract.* (Emphasis added).

According to this provision, a party can resist arbitration if it can effectively assert a defense that would constitute grounds at law or in equity for the revocation of any contract. As we saw in Chapter 1, a court will look to state law to govern such a defense.[1] However, we also saw that to succeed, a state law defense to arbitration must be a matter of general state law, not state law specific to arbitration.[2]

Defenses to arbitration are raised in two contexts. First, if one party to a dispute brings an action in court on its claim, the opponent can move for a stay of the judicial proceedings under Section 3 of the FAA on the ground that the dispute is subject to arbitration. Section 3 states:

> If any suit or proceeding be brought in any of the courts of the United States upon any issue referable to arbitration under an agreement in writing for such arbitration, the court in which the suit is pending, upon being satisfied that the issue involved in such suit or proceeding is referable to arbitration under such an agreement, *shall on application of one of the parties stay the trial of the action until such arbitration has been had in accordance with the terms of the agreement* . . . (Emphasis added).

If there is a written arbitration clause that comes under the FAA, the plaintiff that originally brought the action in court has the burden of showing why the arbitration clause should not be enforced.

Alternately, a party seeking arbitration can bring a petition under Section 4 of the FAA for a motion to compel its opponent to arbitrate. Section 4 provides that:

> A party aggrieved by the alleged failure, neglect, or refusal of another to arbitrate under a written agreement for arbitration may petition any United States district court . . . for an order directing that such arbitration proceed in the manner provided for in such agreement. . . . The court shall hear the parties, and upon being satisfied that the making of the agreement for arbitration or the failure to comply therewith is not in issue, *the court shall make an order directing the parties to proceed to arbitration* in accordance with the terms of the agreement. (Emphasis added).

In such case, the party resisting arbitration must assert a valid defense.

1. See, e.g., *Volt v. Board of Trustees*, Chapter 1.4.

2. See *Perry v. Thomas*, Chapter 1.4.

Whether a defense to arbitration is raised by a plaintiff in response to a defendant's motion under § 3 to stay litigation, or by a defendant in response to a plaintiff's § 4 petition to compel arbitration, the principles that a court will apply are the same. The following cases demonstrate how courts treat the most common defenses to arbitration.

2. ARBITRABILITY

A. WHAT CLAIMS ARE ARBITRABLE?

Country Mutual Insurance Company v. Kosmos

116 Ill.App.3d 914, 452 N.E.2d 547 (1983).

■ ROMITI, PRESIDING JUSTICE:

The sole issue in this case is whether an insurer can be forced to arbitrate an uninsured motorist claim even where it is clear as a matter of law from the pleadings that there is no coverage. We hold there is no duty to arbitrate under such circumstances and reverse the trial court which ordered arbitration.

Plaintiff Country Mutual Insurance Company filed this action to obtain a declaration that there was no insurance coverage and no duty to arbitrate. In its complaint the insurer alleged that the insured, after suffering an accident, made a claim and demanded arbitration. When interviewed the insured stated that the accident occurred when as a result of swerving to avoid another motor vehicle his car left the roadway and collided with a light pole. The insurer thereupon denied coverage since there was no contact with another motor vehicle.

The insured has never denied that there was no contact, either in the trial court or on appeal.

As required by statute, the automobile liability policy issued by Country Mutual to defendant provided uninsured motorist coverage including accidents caused by hit and run vehicles. (Ill.Rev.Stat.1979, ch. 73, par. 755a.) It is well established in Illinois that a provision, statutory or otherwise, limiting coverage to accidents caused by hit and run vehicles affords coverage only where the hit and run vehicle makes contact with the insured or his vehicle. Finch v. Central National Insurance Group of Omaha (1974), 59 Ill.2d 123.

The insurance policy does provide for arbitration but only where the parties disagree over whether the insured is "legally entitled to recover damages from the owner or operator of an uninsured motor vehicle" or the amount of such damages. Under this provision only questions of negligence and damages can be submitted to the arbitrator. (Flood v. Country Mutual Insurance Co. (1968), 41 Ill.2d 91, 242 N.E.2d 149.) Questions of law or fact concerning coverage cannot, under this clause, be submitted to arbitration.

(Flood; Liberty Mutual Fire Insurance Co. v. Loring (1968), 91 Ill.App.2d 372, 235 N.E.2d 418.) Thus the question whether there was contact is not arbitrable under this clause but is decided by the trial court in a declaratory judgment action. (Loring.) "[I]f no contact; no hit-and-run automobile. If no uninsured motorist; no right to arbitration ..." Cruger v. Allstate Insurance Co. (Fla.App.1964), 162 So.2d 690, 693.

The insured contends that this limitation on the right to arbitration is invalid in light of the 1978 amendment to the statute providing in part:

> No such policy shall be renewed or delivered or issued for delivery in this State after July 1, 1978 unless it is provided therein that any dispute with respect to such coverage shall be submitted for arbitration to the American Arbitration Association or for determination in the following manner: Upon the insured requesting arbitration, each party to the dispute shall select an arbitrator and the two arbitrators so named shall select a third arbitrator. If such arbitrators are not selected within 45 days from such request, either party may request that such arbitration be submitted to the American Arbitration Association. (Ill.Rev.Stat.1979, ch. 73, par. 755a.)

If, in fact, the policy provision is in conflict with the statute then of course the statute is controlling. If not, then the parties are bound by the policy provisions.

The language "disputes with respect to such coverage" is ambiguous. It is not clear whether it refers to issues of the existence of coverage or merely disputes arising under the policy provision where coverage is established. Accordingly, it would be appropriate to look at the construction of the legislature when enacting the bill ... But the legislative debates, as cited by the insurer (80th Illinois General Assembly, Third Reading of Senate Bill 1041, May 23, 1977, pp. 46–47), indicate that the statute was enacted solely to curb delays in arbitration and not to extend the scope of arbitration.

However we need not resolve that question because in this case no bona fide dispute has been raised by the pleadings. As already noted, the insurer alleged that there was no contact and the insured has not alleged that there was contact. Yet absent an allegation of physical contact with the unidentified driver, the insured's claim is insufficient and must be dismissed. (Finch v. Central National Insurance Group of Omaha (1974), 59 Ill.2d 123, 319 N.E.2d 468.) To allow an arbitrator to rule for an insured despite the clearly established absence of coverage would be to give the arbitrator unconstitutional powers to decide questions solely of law, and to overrule the Illinois Supreme Court, something even this court cannot do.

Accordingly, the judgment of the trial court is reversed and judgment entered for the plaintiff.

■ JOHNSON and JIGANTI, JJ., concur.

* * *

Questions

1. Why do you think the insurance company in this case seeks to avoid arbitration where the facts seem to favor its position so clearly?

2. The court finds that there is "clearly established absence of coverage." Is this so clear? Is the question "solely a matter of law" as the court suggests? Is the court using its power to determine questions of law or fact concerning the scope of coverage to pre-screen the insured's claim?

3. Should there be a general requirement for pleadings in arbitration to set out the factual basis for a legal claim? If not, how would arbitrability be determined under the standard of the Illinois Court of Appeals?

4. How is the court interpreting the 1978 amendment to the state statute? Can there be arbitration "with respect to such coverage" without an arbitrator considering the scope of coverage? What, in the court's view, is left for an arbitrator to decide concerning coverage? Why does the court believe it should not permit an arbitrator to decide the scope of coverage?

5. Note that the court says it would be unconstitutional to submit questions of law to the arbitrator. *Country Mutual Insurance* was decided in 1983, the same year as *Southland* and two years before *Mitsubishi Motors,* which were studied in the last chapter. Do you think the court would take the same position today?

* * *

Bowmer v. Bowmer

50 N.Y.2d 288, 406 N.E.2d 760 (1980).

■ FUCHSBERG, JUDGE.

Confronting in this case the increasingly common use of arbitration in the context of a dispute between former spouses, we hold that a separation agreement's broadly worded arbitration clause, which additionally draws attention to matters specifically made arbitrable elsewhere in the agreement, does not confer authority upon the arbitrator to pass on the husband's claim that changed circumstances warranted a downward modification of the agreement's support provisions.

After nearly 17 years of marriage, in April of 1972 John and Dorothy Bowmer entered into a lengthy and detailed separation agreement which, as later incorporated but not merged in a judgment of divorce, provided for the husband's payment of alimony and support for their three minor children pursuant to a carefully arranged formula. Its arbitration clause, numbered paragraph 17, reads in pertinent part: "Any claim, dispute or misunderstanding arising out of or in connection with this Agreement, or any breach hereof, or any default in payment by the Husband, or any matter herein made the subject matter of arbitration, shall be arbitrated".

As the clause suggests, at various points the agreement delineated certain matters that were expressly made arbitrable, including adjustments in the support formula (upon the stated contingencies that the tax laws were amended to make support payments taxable to the husband and that the Government's cost of living index was discontinued or its method of publication altered) and in the extent of the husband's obligation to underwrite college costs should the parties disagree over the husband's ability to meet them.

The present dispute had its genesis in July, 1977, when Bowmer informed his former wife that, because of changed circumstances, as of February, 1978 he would reduce his support payments by almost $1,000 per month and make no further tuition payments.[1] She refused to accede to this plan or to his alternative informal request that they submit the question to arbitration. Thereafter, when he nevertheless unilaterally undertook to make these downward adjustments, Ms. Bowmer invoked the arbitration clause to compel him to pay the arrearages. Her former husband then commenced this proceeding to stay the arbitration she had commenced and to compel arbitration on the issues of whether he was entitled to downward modification of his monetary obligations consistent with the steps he had taken. Contemporaneously, Bowmer filed his own demand for arbitration on these and a third issue.[2] She, in turn, cross-moved to stay the arbitration he had initiated, contending that, except for the question of his deferment of the children's educational expenses, the issues he raised were nonarbitrable.[3] In due course, Special Term consolidated both arbitration proceedings, denied her motion and directed that arbitration proceed on the issues Bowmer had raised.

But, on Ms. Bowmer's appeal from so much of the order that directed arbitration on the issue of reduction in the level of support payments, the Appellate Division modified, holding that issue to be nonarbitrable (67 A.D.2d 8, 10, 414 N.Y.S.2d 340). On the former husband's appeal to us, therefore, the sole question is whether the arbitrator may properly consider the claim for downward modification on the support obligations. For the reasons which follow, we conclude he may not and, therefore, we now affirm the order from which this appeal arises.

Arbitration clauses are by now familiar provisos in separation agreements. Indeed, aside from expressing the parties' preference for a means of dispute resolution more informal, more expedient and possibly less costly than litigation (Matter of Siegel (Lewis), 40 N.Y.2d 687, 689, 389 N.Y.S.2d

1. Petitioner asserted that it was no longer economically feasible for him to meet the support obligations in the agreement because his second wife was no longer employed and because, with all three children in college, the additional payments for educational expenses had grown to $12,000 per year.

2. In his demand, Bowmer also sought to direct the sale of the marital abode, reading the agreement as permitting his former spouse to reside there only while the children, then attending college away from home, lived there on a full-time basis. Although Ms. Bowmer unsuccessfully contested the arbitrability of this issue below, it was not appealed to the Appellate Division.

3. The separation agreement specifically provided: "If the Husband is of the opinion that he cannot afford to pay for the (college) education of a particular Child, and if the Wife does not agree with his alleged inability to do so, she shall have the right to have the matter arbitrated, pursuant to Article '17' of this Agreement".

800, 358 N.E.2d 484), an arbitration provision may well have been intended to furnish insulation from the potential for notoriety and other stresses that so often accompanies the airing of marital disputes in court (see Matter of Lasek v. Lasek, 13 A.D.2d 242, 244, 215 N.Y.S.2d 983). Moreover, resort to the arbitral forum may afford the spouses an opportunity to have their grievances heard by someone who they think may be especially well qualified in matrimonial matters.

But as with such provisions in the commercial context generally, the rule is clear that unless the agreement to arbitrate expressly and unequivocally encompasses the subject matter of the particular dispute, a party cannot be compelled to forego the right to seek judicial relief and instead submit to arbitration ... Examining the clause in paragraph 17 with this precept in mind, we first observe the standard, broadly framed directive to submit to arbitration "Any claim, dispute or misunderstanding arising out of or in connection with" the agreement ... However, there is more. As indicated earlier, the clause goes on to state that elsewhere in the agreement particular matters, apparently of special import to the spouses, are expressly made arbitrable. Paragraph 17 therefore seems to be something of a hybrid, containing wording ordinarily present in both broad and limited arbitration clauses; hence, we should not reflexively attribute to the parties an intention to have every possible dispute go to arbitration....

For, though the parties might well have thought that the particularized matters were subsumed under the general arbitration language—in which case they could be understood as merely intending to emphasize the arbitrability of certain disputes—the inclusion perhaps more reasonably suggests that the spouses viewed the general language somewhat qualifiedly. This accords with the rule of construction that, in such cases, the specific provisions tend to restrict the general (see 4 Williston, Contracts (3d ed.), § 624, pp. 822–825). Thus, rather than place reliance on a single boilerplate proviso, the parties were careful to direct explicitly that arbitration be the remedy for several critical and foreseeable conflicts on the extent of the husband's support obligation.

Further evidence that the arbitration clause was not intended to encompass the dispute here comes from the fact that the support provisions themselves were particularly detailed and drawn flexibly to anticipate changes in the spouses' circumstances. Exemplifying this is the agreement's design for a sliding scale of support payments equivalent to 50% of the husband's gross income, but in no event less than $14,000 or more than $30,000, less an amount equivalent to one half of the wife's gross income over $9,000. "Gross income" was itself meticulously defined and made to reflect, at least in part, the financial condition of the parties: for instance, depending on whether Bowmer's gross income was below or above $50,000 he was either to include or exclude from that figure payments from his employer's profit-sharing plan. On top of all this, of course, the cost of living index guaranteed a broader kind of responsiveness to economic variations.

The sense of these provisions, taken together, is to indicate that the parties gave their attention to the possibility of changed circumstances and tried to address the problem by injecting elasticity into the support formula itself. Given this and the fact that the husband's obligation to pay for the costs of his children's college education was expressly made modifiable under changed circumstances and specifically made the subject of arbitration, it is significant that neither the modification nor arbitrability of the more fundamental support obligation is addressed by any term of the 37–page separation agreement.

The omission becomes especially important in light of the inability of courts to effect any change in an adequate level of support fixed by a valid and unimpeached separation agreement unless it has been merged in a judgment of divorce . . . Of course, had they so intended, the parties could have agreed that the support provisions be modifiable by judicial proceedings under appropriate circumstances . . . But they did not. And, although the power to alter the support provisions in a separation agreement may likewise be conferred upon an arbitrator . . ., the cases so holding have involved contracts explicitly authorizing such relief (see Braverman v. Braverman, 9 Misc.2d 661, 168 N.Y.S.2d 348, supra; Storch v. Storch, 38 A.D.2d 904, 329 N.Y.S.2d 474). Against this background the frame of reference of the drafters of this detailed and comprehensive document appellant's claim that a downward modification of support "arises out of or in connection with" the terms of the agreement is hardly persuasive.

More fundamentally, what appellant seeks, in essence, is to have the arbitrator rewrite the terms of the agreement because he now views them as onerous. This cannot be considered merely a claim arising from the contract. Instead, it requires the making of a new contract, not by the parties, but by the arbitrator. Obviously, the parties never agreed to such a procedure for it would mean that, once the agreement made provision for arbitration, the arbitrator would be completely unfettered by the terms of the contract in resolving disputes. Nor is our refusal to place the power to change the support provisions within the scope of the arbitration clause to be considered an impermissible attempt to precensor the type of relief available to the arbitrator. While, as a general rule, once a controversy is properly before the arbitrator he has wide discretion in his choice of remedies . . ., the power to formulate flexible solutions cannot be used as a bootstrap for an unpredictable expansion of the parameters of arbitral authority (cf. Garrity v. Lyle Stuart, Inc., 40 N.Y.2d 354).

Appellant insists that our decision in Matter of SCM Corp. (Fisher Park Lane Co.), 40 N.Y.2d 788, sanctions such an arbitral rewriting. However, the rationale of that case was considerably more limited. There, though holding that a landlord's counterclaim for reformation was time-barred, we took the occasion to state that the arbitrator, acting pursuant to a broad arbitration clause, could permissibly reform the terms of a lease on the landlord's assertion that the instrument failed to conform to the parties' original intent (40 N.Y.2d, supra, at pp. 792–794). Reformation of a contract to express what the parties in fact agreed upon has been held to be a claim which arises out of the contract, in contradistinction to modification of contract terms to reflect changed circumstances, a claim of a fundamentally different nature, which finds no basis at all in the agreement. Pointedly, appellant nowhere suggests that by reason of accident, mistake or fraud the agreement failed to express the real intentions of the contracting parties; he seeks instead to create a wholly new contract. . . . Accordingly, the order of the Appellate Division should be affirmed.

■ GABRIELLI, JUDGE (dissenting).

I am impelled to dissent, for I cannot concur in the misapplication of previously well-settled principles of law to this rather simple case. The dispositive issue presented by this appeal is whether a separation agreement requiring arbitration of "(a)ny claim, dispute or misunderstanding arising out of or in connection with" the agreement authorizes arbitration of the husband's claim that his support obligations under the agreement should be modified because of a change in circumstances. Also implicated, because of the analysis employed by the majority of this court, is whether an arbitrator's power to grant certain requested relief may be challenged by an application to stay arbitration.

. . . It is beyond dispute that the parties to a separation agreement may agree to arbitrate disputes concerning the support provisions of that agreement (see Hirsch v. Hirsch, 37 N.Y.2d 312, 372 N.Y.S.2d 71, 333 N.E.2d 371). Hence, the only issue in this case is whether in fact the Bowmers have so agreed. As is noted above, the agreement provides for arbitration of "(a)ny claim, dispute or misunderstanding arising out of or in connection with" the separation agreement, it is difficult to conceive of a broader declaration of arbitrability. Appellant's claim, whether it be viewed as an attempt to modify the agreement or, more accurately, as a claim that the agreement itself impliedly contemplated modification of the support obligation by an arbitrator, certainly must fall within the purview of that wide-sweeping language. Hence, it appears evident that the instant dispute is arbitrable.

The majority, however, now concludes that this seemingly broad language does not truly mean what it says, but is instead limited in some inarticulable manner and to some uncertain extent. Unfortunately, there exists no support for such an interpretation in the language of the agreement. As noted above, the arbitration clause explicitly provides for arbitration of "(a)ny claim, dispute or misunderstanding arising out of or in connection with this Agreement, or any breach hereof, or any default in payment by the Husband, or any matter herein made the subject matter of arbitration." The majority suggests that the provision for the arbitration of "any claim, dispute or misunderstanding arising out of or in connection with" the agreement has no real application or meaning, and that the only controversies actually made arbitrable by the agreement are those involving "any breach hereof, or any default in payment by the Husband, or any matter herein made the subject matter of arbitration." To so hold is to simply read the opening words of the arbitration provision out of existence entirely, and that is something which a court may not do under the guise of contract interpretation. Had the parties desired to provide for arbitration of only those disputes mentioned in the latter phrases of the arbitration clause, there would have been no reason to include the broad opening words. However, that language was made an integral part of the agreement and should be given effect by the courts.

This judicial evisceration of an extremely broad arbitration provision portends a return to that outmoded and heavy-handed judicial scrutiny of arbitration agreements which I had thought this court had abandoned by its decision in Matter of Weinrott (Carp), 32 N.Y.2d 190, 344 N.Y.S.2d 848, 298 N.E.2d 42. Today's decision resurrects, in new guise, the so-called "specifically enumerated" approach to arbitration clauses which we explicitly rejected in Weinrott. The effect of this decision is to render meaningless the otherwise broad provisions of any arbitration agreement in which the parties, possibly from an excess of caution, have taken the care to specify those particular types of disputes which they feared might not be covered by the general language of the arbitration agreement. I cannot concur in such an approach. It serves no valid purpose where, as here, the intent of the parties is plainly to submit to arbitration all disputes "arising out of or in connection with" the separation agreement. Rather, it will merely encourage those who wish to delay final resolution of a dispute to turn to the courts in the hope of preventing the submission to arbitration of matters clearly intended to be determined in that forum.

No more persuasive is the majority's suggestion that the instant dispute is not arbitrable because appellant is attempting to have the arbitrator "rewrite" the agreement and not merely interpret it. Initially, I note that there exists no reason why two persons may not enter into an agreement authorizing an arbitrator to modify the terms of that agreement upon the application of one of the parties. Any objections to the concept of an arbitrator "rewriting" a contract for the parties stems not from some evil inherent in the idea itself, but rather from the more general doctrine that, at least in the area of consensual arbitration, a party may be bound by the decision of an arbitrator only to the extent that he has agreed to be bound. Normally, the parties to an agreement will not wish to confer upon an arbitrator the power to modify their agreement, and it is for that reason that the arbitrator will lack the power to "rewrite" the agreement. Such objections, however, pertain not to the arbitrability of a dispute, but rather to the power of the arbitrator to provide certain relief, and as such may only be raised by application to vacate an award, not by application to stay arbitration (compare CPLR 7503, with 7511; see Board of Educ. v. Barni, 49 N.Y.2d 311, 425 N.Y.S.2d 554, 401 N.E.2d 912).

That the instant application to stay involves no more than a premature contention that the arbitrator will exceed his power is shown by the fact that regardless of the outcome of this appeal, arbitration will proceed on the question of appellant's obligations under the contract. The only effect of this proceeding can be to limit the range of remedies which the arbitrator may employ in an attempt to resolve the dispute between the Bowmers. The expenditure of so much time and effort merely to inform an arbitrator in advance of arbitration that he may not grant certain requested relief is hardly consistent with the function of arbitration as an inexpensive and swift alternative forum. Moreover, it serves to take from the arbitrator the power to determine, at least in the first instance, the range of remedies authorized by the agreement, and creates yet another preliminary inquiry to be made by the courts before ordering arbitration.

Accordingly, I vote to reverse the order of the Appellate Division and reinstate the order of Supreme Court.

■ JASEN, JONES, WACHTLER and MEYER, JJ., concur with FUCHSBERG, J.

■ GABRIELLI, J., dissents and votes to reverse in a separate opinion in which COOKE, C. J., concurs.

* * *

Questions

1. How does the majority reach its conclusion on the issue of arbitrability? Is the disagreement between the majority and the dissent a disagreement about how to interpret the contractual provision or a difference in attitude about arbitration?

2. What would be wrong with permitting an arbitrator to rewrite an agreement in light of changed circumstances? In some situations, of which family law is a prime example, courts have the power to revise contracts in light of changed circumstances. If that were the case under New York's matrimonial law, should an arbitrator also have that power? Is there a difference between permitting a court to revise a contract and permitting an arbitrator to do so?

3. Consider the following hypothetical:

> A landowner, who owns a large apartment complex of 1,000 units, gets into a dispute with a tenant. The lease, which is a standard lease that he uses for all his units, states:
>
>> Landlord will maintain premises and make reasonable repairs. If damage requiring repair is the result of Tenant's intentional act or negligence, Landlord has the right to bill Tenant for the cost of repairs, and if said bill is not paid promptly, Landlord may treat the repair bill as rent for purposes of remedies.
>
> The lease also states:
>
>> Tenant will keep apartment in reasonable repair, and refrain from any activity that will cause undue damage or undue wear and tear.
>>
>> All obligations concerning condition of the apartment are subject to arbitration.
>
> Also under the lease, the tenant has the usual obligation to pay rent every month, and the obligations of tenant to pay rent are subject to state law, which gives landlord a right to evict after 10 days notice.

> A dispute arises when the tenant's upstairs neighbor leaves his bathtub running and it overflows, dripping water through tenant's kitchen ceiling. The water gets into the tenant's light fixtures, causing the lights to short out. The tenant tries to get the landlord to repair the damage, but the landlord does not do so. After two weeks in which the tenant has no lights in her kitchen, she withholds rent, and sends the landlord a letter explaining that she will pay rent when her ceiling and kitchen light is repaired. The landlord sends her a notice that continued nonpayment of rent for 10 days will give him right to evict. After 10 days, he moves to evict in state court. The tenant makes a motion to stay the proceeding and compel arbitration. The state has an arbitration law identical to FAA.

How would you argue this case for the tenant? Would the approach of the majority or the dissent in *Bowmer* be more useful to cite in favor or your position? How should a court decide the issue?

* * *

Moses H. Cone Memorial Hospital v. Mercury Construction Corp.

460 U.S. 1 (1983).

■ JUSTICE BRENNAN delivered the opinion of the Court.

This case, commenced as a petition for an order to compel arbitration under § 4 of the United States Arbitration Act of 1925 (Arbitration Act or Act), 9 U.S.C. § 4, presents the question whether, in light of the policies of the Act and of our decisions in Colorado River Water Conservation District v. United States, 424 U.S. 800 (1976), and Will v. Calvert Fire Insurance Co., 437 U.S. 655 (1978), the District Court for the Middle District of North Carolina properly stayed this diversity action pending resolution of a concurrent state-court suit. The Court of Appeals for the Fourth Circuit reversed the stay. We granted certiorari. We affirm.

I

Petitioner Moses H. Cone Memorial Hospital ("Hospital") is located in Greensboro, North Carolina. Respondent Mercury Construction Corp. ("Mercury"), a construction contractor, has its principal place of business in Alabama. In July 1975, Mercury and the Hospital entered into a contract for the construction of additions to the Hospital building. The contract, drafted by representatives of the Hospital, included provisions for resolving disputes arising out of the contract or its breach. All disputes involving interpretation of the contract or performance of the construction work were to be referred in the first instance to J.N. Pease Associates ("Architect"), an independent architectural firm hired by the Hospital to design and oversee the construction project. With certain stated exceptions, any dispute decided by the Architect (or not decided by it within a stated time) could be submitted by either party to binding arbitration under a broad arbitration clause in the contract:

> All claims, disputes and other matters in question arising out of, or relating to, this Contract or the breach thereof, . . . shall be decided by arbitration in accordance with the Construction Industry Arbitration Rules of the American Arbitration Association then obtaining unless the parties mutually agree otherwise. This agreement to arbitrate shall be specifically enforceable under the prevailing arbitration law. The award rendered by the arbitrators shall be final, and judgment may be entered upon it in accordance with applicable law in any court having jurisdiction thereof. App. 29–30.

The contract also specified the time limits for arbitration demands.

Construction on the project began in July 1975. Performance was to be completed by October 1979. In fact, construction was substantially completed in February 1979, and final inspections were made that June.

At a meeting in October 1977 (during construction), attended by representatives of Mercury, the Hospital, and the Architect, Mercury agreed, at the Architect's request, to withhold its claims for delay and impact costs (i.e., claims for extended overhead or increase in construction costs due to delay or inaction by the Hospital) until the work was substantially completed. On this record, the Hospital does not contest the existence of this agreement, although it asserts that the Architect lacked authority to agree to a delay in presentation of claims or to entertain claims after the contract work was completed.

In January 1980, Mercury submitted to the Architect its claims for delay and impact costs. Mercury and the Architect discussed the claims over several months, substantially reducing the amount of the claims. According to the Hospital, it first learned of the existence of Mercury's claims in April 1980; its lawyers assumed active participation in the claim procedure in May. The parties differ in their characterizations of the events of the next few months—whether there were "ongoing negotiations," or merely an "investigation" by the Hospital. In any event, it appears from the record that lawyers for the Hospital requested additional information concerning Mercury's claims. As a result, on August 12, 1980, Mercury gave a detailed presentation of its claims at a meeting attended by Mercury's representatives and lawyers, the Hospital's representatives and lawyers, and representatives of the Architect. Mercury agreed to send copies of its files to an expert hired by the Hospital, and the parties agreed to meet again on October 13.

On October 6, Mercury's counsel telephoned the Hospital's counsel to confirm that the scheduled meeting would go forward. The Hospital's counsel said he would call back the next day. When he did, he informed Mercury's counsel that the Hospital would pay nothing on Mercury's claim. He also said that the Hospital intended to file a declaratory judgment action in North Carolina state court.

True to its word, the Hospital filed an action on the morning of October 8 in the Superior Court of Guilford County, North Carolina, naming Mercury and the Architect as defendants. The complaint alleged that Mercury's claim was without factual or legal basis and that it was barred by the statute of limitations. It alleged that Mercury had lost any right to arbitration under the contract due to waiver, laches, estoppel, and failure to make a timely demand for arbitration. The complaint also alleged various delinquencies on the part of the Architect. As relief, the Hospital sought a declaration that there was no right to arbitration; a stay of arbitration; a declaration that the Hospital bore no liability to Mercury; and a declaration that if the Hospital should be found liable in any respect to Mercury, it would be entitled to indemnity from the Architect. The complaint was served on Mercury on October 9. On that same day, Mercury's counsel mailed a demand for arbitration.

On October 15, without notice to Mercury, the Hospital obtained an ex parte injunction from the state court forbidding Mercury to take any steps directed toward arbitration. Mercury objected, and the stay was dissolved on October 27. As soon as the stay was lifted, Mercury filed the present action in the District Court, seeking an order compelling arbitration under § 4 of the Arbitration Act, 9 U.S.C. § 4.[4] Jurisdiction was based on diversity of citizenship. On the Hospital's motion, the District Court stayed Mercury's federal-court suit pending resolution of the state-court suit because the two suits involved the identical issue of the arbitrability of Mercury's claims . . .

Mercury sought review of the District Court's stay by both a notice of appeal and a petition for mandamus. A panel of the Court of Appeals for the Fourth Circuit heard argument in the case, but before the panel issued any decision, the Court informed the parties that it would consider the case en banc. After reargument, the en banc Court held that it had appellate jurisdiction over the case under 28 U.S.C. § 1291. It reversed the District Court's stay order and remanded the case to the District Court with instructions for entry of an order to arbitrate.

[The District Court's stay] was plainly erroneous in view of Congress's clear intent, in the Arbitration Act, to move the parties to an arbitrable dispute out of court and into arbitration as quickly and easily as possible. The Act provides two parallel devices for enforcing an arbitration agreement: a stay of litigation in any case raising a dispute referable to arbitration, 9 U.S.C. § 3, and an affirmative order to engage in arbitration, § 4. Both of these sections call for an expeditious and summary hearing, with only restricted inquiry into factual issues. Assuming that the state court would have granted prompt relief to Mercury under the Act, there still would have been an inevitable delay as a result of the District Court's

4. Simultaneously, Mercury filed a petition for removal of the Hospital's state-court action. The District Court remanded the removed case on the ground that, because the Hospital and the Architect are both North Carolina corporations, there was no complete diversity. The propriety of the removal or remand is not before this Court.

stay. The stay thus frustrated the statutory policy of rapid and unobstructed enforcement of arbitration agreements.

... [T]he basic issue presented in Mercury's federal suit was the arbitrability of the dispute between Mercury and the Hospital. Federal law in the terms of the Arbitration Act governs that issue in either state or federal court. Section 2 is the primary substantive provision of the Act, declaring that a written agreement to arbitrate "in any maritime transaction or a contract evidencing a transaction involving commerce ... shall be valid, irrevocable, and enforceable, save upon such grounds as exist at law or in equity for the revocation of any contract." 9 U.S.C. § 2. Section 2 is a congressional declaration of a liberal federal policy favoring arbitration agreements, notwithstanding any state substantive or procedural policies to the contrary. The effect of the section is to create a body of federal substantive law of arbitrability, applicable to any arbitration agreement within the coverage of the Act. In Prima Paint Corp. v. Flood & Conklin Mfg. Corp., 388 U.S. 395, 87 S.Ct. 1801, 18 L.Ed.2d 1270 (1967), for example, the parties had signed a contract containing an arbitration clause, but one party alleged that there had been fraud in the inducement of the entire contract (although the alleged fraud did not go to the arbitration clause in particular). The issue before us was whether the issue of fraud in the inducement was itself an arbitrable controversy. We held that the language and policies of the Act required the conclusion that the fraud issue was arbitrable. Id., at 402–404, 87 S.Ct., at 1805–06. Although our holding in Prima Paint extended only to the specific issue presented, the courts of appeals have since consistently concluded that questions of arbitrability must be addressed with a healthy regard for the federal policy favoring arbitration. We agree. The Arbitration Act establishes that, as a matter of federal law, any doubts concerning the scope of arbitrable issues should be resolved in favor of arbitration, whether the problem at hand is the construction of the contract language itself or an allegation of waiver, delay, or a like defense to arbitrability.

To be sure, the source-of-law factor has less significance here than in Calvert, since the federal courts' jurisdiction to enforce the Arbitration Act is concurrent with that of the state courts.[32] But we emphasize that our task in cases such as this is not to find some substantial reason for the

32. See n. 34, infra. The Arbitration Act is something of an anomaly in the field of federal-court jurisdiction. It creates a body of federal substantive law establishing and regulating the duty to honor an agreement to arbitrate, yet it does not create any independent federal-question jurisdiction under 28 U.S.C. § 1331 (1976 ed., Supp. IV) or otherwise. Section 4 provides for an order compelling arbitration only when the federal district court would have jurisdiction over a suit on the underlying dispute; hence, there must be diversity of citizenship or some other independent basis for federal jurisdiction before the order can issue. E.g., Commercial Metals Co. v. Balfour, Guthrie, & Co., 577 F.2d 264, 268–269 (C.A.5 1978), and cases cited. Section 3 likewise limits the federal courts to the extent that a federal court cannot stay a suit pending before it unless there is such a suit in existence. Nevertheless, although enforcement of the Act is left in large part to the state courts, it nevertheless represents federal policy to be vindicated by the federal courts where otherwise appropriate. We need not address whether a federal court might stay a state-court suit pending arbitration under 28 U.S.C. § 2283.

exercise of federal jurisdiction by the district court; rather, the task is to ascertain whether there exist "exceptional" circumstances, the "clearest of justifications," that can suffice under Colorado River to justify the surrender of that jurisdiction. Although in some rare circumstances the presence of state-law issues may weigh in favor of that surrender, the presence of federal-law issues must always be a major consideration weighing against surrender.

Finally, in this case an important reason against allowing a stay is the probable inadequacy of the state-court proceeding to protect Mercury's rights. We are not to be understood to impeach the competence or procedures of the North Carolina courts. Moreover, state courts, as much as federal courts, are obliged to grant stays of litigation under § 3 of the Arbitration Act.[34] It is less clear, however, whether the same is true of an order to compel arbitration under § 4 of the Act.[35] We need not resolve that question here; it suffices to say that there was, at a minimum, substantial room for doubt that Mercury could obtain from the state court an order compelling the Hospital to arbitrate.[36] In many cases, no doubt, a § 3 stay is quite adequate to protect the right to arbitration. But in a case such as this, where the party opposing arbitration is the one from whom payment or performance is sought, a stay of litigation alone is not enough. It leaves the recalcitrant party free to sit and do nothing—neither to litigate nor to arbitrate. If the state court stayed litigation pending arbitration but declined to compel the Hospital to arbitrate, Mercury would have no sure way to proceed with its claims except to return to federal court to obtain a § 4

34. Although § 3 refers ambiguously to a suit "in any of the courts of the United States," the state courts have almost unanimously recognized that the stay provision of § 3 applies to suits in state as well as federal courts, requiring them to issue the same speedy relief when a dispute is referable to arbitration. (The North Carolina Supreme Court has so held, although not until after the District Court ordered this stay. Burke County Public Schools Board of Education v. Shaver Partnership, 303 N.C. 408, 279 S.E.2d 816 (1981).) This is necessary to carry out Congress's intent to mandate enforcement of all covered arbitration agreements; Congress can hardly have meant that an agreement to arbitrate can be enforced against a party who attempts to litigate an arbitrable dispute in federal court, but not against one who sues on the same dispute in state court. See also Prima Paint, 388 U.S., at 404, 87 S.Ct., at 1806.

35. Section 4, unlike § 3, speaks only of a petition to "any United States district court." Nonetheless, at least one state court has held that § 4 does require state courts to issue § 4 orders to arbitrate where the section's conditions are met. Main v. Merrill Lynch, Pierce, Fenner & Smith Inc., 67 Cal. App.3d 19, 24–25, 136 Cal.Rptr. 378, 380–381 (1977).

36. As a historical matter, there was considerable doubt at the time of the District Court's stay that the North Carolina court would have granted even a § 3 stay of litigation. The then-controlling precedent in North Carolina was to the effect that a contract such as that between Mercury and the Hospital was not subject to the Arbitration Act at all, on the reasoning that a construction project is not "commerce" within the meaning of §§ 1 and 2 of the Act. Burke County Public Schools Board of Education v. Shaver Partnership, 46 N.C.App. 573, 265 S.E.2d 481 (1980); Bryant–Durham Electric Co. v. Durham County Hospital Corp., 42 N.C.App. 351, 256 S.E.2d 529 (1979). The North Carolina Supreme Court has, however, since repudiated those decisions. Burke County Public Schools Board of Education v. Shaver Partnership, 303 N.C. 408, 279 S.E.2d 816 (1981).

order—a pointless and wasteful burden on the supposedly summary and speedy procedures prescribed by the Arbitration Act.

[I]n addition to reversing the District Court's stay, the Court of Appeals decided that the underlying contractual dispute between Mercury and the Hospital is arbitrable under the Arbitration Act and the terms of the parties' arbitration agreement. It reversed the District Court's judgment and remanded the case "with instructions to proceed in conformity herewith." 656 F.2d, at 946. In effect, the Court of Appeals directed the District Court to enter a § 4 order to arbitrate.

In this Court, the Hospital does not contest the substantive correctness of the Court of Appeals's holding on arbitrability. It does raise several objections to the procedures the Court of Appeals used in considering and deciding this case. In particular, it points out that the only issue formally appealed to the Court of Appeals was the propriety of the District Court's stay order. Ordinarily, we would not expect the Court of Appeals to pass on issues not decided in the District Court. In the present case, however, we are not disposed to disturb the Court's discretion in its handling of the case in view of the special interests at stake and the apparent lack of any prejudice to the parties. 28 U.S.C. § 2106 gives a court of appeals some latitude in entering an order to achieve justice in the circumstances. The Arbitration Act calls for a summary and speedy disposition of motions or petitions to enforce arbitration clauses. The Court of Appeals had in the record full briefs and evidentiary submissions from both parties on the merits of arbitrability, and held that there were no disputed issues of fact requiring a jury trial before a § 4 order could issue. Under these circumstances, the Court acted within its authority in deciding the legal issues presented in order to facilitate the prompt arbitration that Congress envisaged.

Affirmed.

■ JUSTICE REHNQUIST, with whom THE CHIEF JUSTICE and JUSTICE O'CONNOR join, dissent.

* * *

Questions

1. What is the issue of arbitrability in this case? In what way does it differ from the issue of arbitrability in *Bowmer*?

2. How does the Court decide the question of arbitrability in *Moses H. Cone*? Is the standard for arbitrability the court applied in *Moses H. Cone* different from that applied in *Bowmer*? How can we account for the difference?

3. One commentator has written that although a presumption of arbitrability is justifiable in the labor relations context due to the role of arbitration in preserving labor peace, such a presumption cannot be justified in interpreting of the Federal Arbitration Act. In the latter context,

"The Supreme Court has no clear expression of congressional policy upon which to base its own program of promoting commercial arbitration." Jonathan R. Nelson, *Judge–Made Law and the Presumption of Arbitrability*, 58 Brooklyn L. Rev. 279, 328 (1992). Do you agree? Suppose Congress declared that arbitration is a valuable device for resolving disputes because it conserves on scarce judicial resources and provides an efficient and speedy method of resolving most disputes. Would this statement then support the presumption of arbitrability in the FAA context? Could one infer such a statement from Congress' silence in the face of the many Supreme Court decisions in the past decade that have expanded the role of arbitration in commercial and other settings under the FAA?

4. In cases arising under Section 301 of the Labor Management Relations Act, the Supreme Court has determined that issues of procedural arbitrability are to be treated differently than questions of substantively arbitrability for purposes of whether a court or arbitrator is to decide them. See *John Wiley & Sons v. Livingston*, 376 U.S. 543 (1964). From what we have seen to date, does the Court make the same distinction in the FAA cases? Should it make such a distinction?

5. Alan Scott Rau has argued that the term "arbitrability" adds nothing "to our understanding of the problems of arbitration practice" and should be "renounce[d]" with "all the other detritus of our case law." Alan Scott Rau, *Everything You Really Need to Know About "Separability" in Seventeen Simple Propositions*, 14 Am. Rev. Int'l Arb. 1, 120 (2003). Do you agree? In considering the usefulness of the term, the following typology might be helpful.

"Arbitrability" can mean at least six different things:

- Statutory arbitrability: whether arbitration is permitted or forbidden by statute.
- Contract-scope arbitrability: whether a dispute is contractually encompassed within an agreement to arbitrate.
- Contract-enforcement arbitrability: whether the parties have entered into an enforceable agreement to arbitrate.
- Procedural arbitrability: whether contractual prerequisites to arbitration (e.g., time limits and notice requirements) have been fulfilled.
- Decisional arbitrability$_1$: whether the above issues should be decided by a court or by an arbitrator.
- Decisional arbitrability$_2$: whether the issue immediately above should be decided by a court or by an arbitrator.

See Richard A. Bales, *Contract Formation Issues in Employment Arbitration*, 44 Brandeis L.J. 415, 426–27 (2006).

Might it be more helpful to distinguish arbitrability—i.e., whether a dispute falls within a particular arbitration clause—from "amenability"—i.e., whether a particular dispute is a type that can be arbitrated? If so, arbitrability refers to the scope of the parties' own contractual language in relation to the dispute, whereas amenability refers to statutory or other impediments imposed externally to the contract.

6. The last two bullet points above are about *who decides* whether a given dispute is arbitrable. This is critically important at a practical level. On the one hand, an arbitrator has an obvious self-interest in ruling in favor of arbitrability, so one might expect courts to make these decisions. On the other hand, as William Park has pointed out, permitting courts to make the decisions allows a party opposing arbitration to derail arbitration and send the dispute to court merely by asserting an arbitrability issue. William Park, *Determining an Arbitrator's Jurisdiction: Timing and Finality in American Law*, 8 Nevada L.J. 135, 138 (2007). Would this be inconsistent with the parties' agreement to arbitrate their disputes?

* * *

B. Who Decides What Claims Are Arbitrable?

First Options of Chicago, Inc. v. Kaplan

514 U.S. 938 (1995).

■ Justice Breyer delivered the opinion of the Court.

In this case we consider ... how a district court should review an arbitrator's decision that the parties agreed to arbitrate a dispute ...

I

The case concerns several related disputes between, on one side, First Options of Chicago, Inc., a firm that clears stock trades on the Philadelphia Stock Exchange, and, on the other side, three parties: Manuel Kaplan; his wife, Carol Kaplan; and his wholly owned investment company, MK Investments, Inc. (MKI), whose trading account First Options cleared. The disputes center around a "workout" agreement, embodied in four separate documents, which governs the "working out" of debts to First Options that MKI and the Kaplans incurred as a result of the October 1987 stock market crash. In 1989, after entering into the agreement, MKI lost an additional $1.5 million. First Options then took control of, and liquidated, certain MKI assets; demanded immediate payment of the entire MKI debt; and insisted that the Kaplans personally pay any deficiency. When its demands went unsatisfied, First Options sought arbitration by a panel of the Philadelphia Stock Exchange.

MKI, having signed the only workout document (out of four) that contained an arbitration clause, accepted arbitration. The Kaplans, however, who had not personally signed that document, denied that their disagreement with First Options was arbitrable and filed written objections to that effect with the arbitration panel. The arbitrators decided that they had the power to rule on the merits of the parties' dispute, and did so in favor of First Options. The Kaplans then asked the Federal District Court to vacate the arbitration award, see 9 U.S.C. § 10 (1988 Ed., Supp. V), and

First Options requested its confirmation, see § 9. The court confirmed the award. Nonetheless, on appeal the Court of Appeals for the Third Circuit agreed with the Kaplans that their dispute was not arbitrable; and it reversed the District Court's confirmation of the award against them.

We granted certiorari to consider two questions regarding the standards that the Court of Appeals used to review the determination that the Kaplans' dispute with First Options was arbitrable. First, the Court of Appeals said that courts "should independently decide whether an arbitration panel has jurisdiction over the merits of any particular dispute." 19 F.3d, at 1509 (emphasis added). First Options asked us to decide whether this is so (i.e., whether courts, in "reviewing the arbitrators' decision on arbitrability," should "apply a de novo standard of review or the more deferential standard applied to arbitrators' decisions on the merits") when the objecting party "submitted the issue to the arbitrators for decision." Pet. for Cert. I. Second, the Court of Appeals stated that it would review a district court's denial of a motion to vacate a commercial arbitration award (and the correlative grant of a motion to confirm it) "de novo." 19 F.3d, at 1509. First Options argues that the Court of Appeals instead should have applied an "abuse of discretion" standard. See Robbins v. Day, 954 F.2d 679, 681–682 (11th Cir. 1992).

II

The first question—the standard of review applied to an arbitrator's decision about arbitrability—is a narrow one. To understand just how narrow, consider three types of disagreement present in this case. First, the Kaplans and First Options disagree about whether the Kaplans are personally liable for MKI's debt to First Options. That disagreement makes up the merits of the dispute. Second, they disagree about whether they agreed to arbitrate the merits. That disagreement is about the arbitrability of the dispute. Third, they disagree about who should have the primary power to decide the second matter. Does that power belong primarily to the arbitrators (because the court reviews their arbitrability decision deferentially) or to the court (because the court makes up its mind about arbitrability independently)? We consider here only this third question.

Although the question is a narrow one, it has a certain practical importance. That is because a party who has not agreed to arbitrate will normally have a right to a court's decision about the merits of its dispute (say, as here, its obligation under a contract). But, where the party has agreed to arbitrate, he or she, in effect, has relinquished much of that right's practical value. The party still can ask a court to review the arbitrator's decision, but the court will set that decision aside only in very unusual circumstances. See, e.g., 9 U.S.C. § 10 (award procured by corruption, fraud, or undue means; arbitrator exceeded his powers); Wilko v. Swan, 346 U.S. 427, 436–437, 74 S.Ct. 182, 187–188, 98 L.Ed. 168 (1953) (parties bound by arbitrator's decision not in "manifest disregard" of the law), overruled on other grounds, Rodriguez de Quijas v. Shearson/American Express, Inc., 490 U.S. 477 (1989). Hence, who—court or arbitrator—

has the primary authority to decide whether a party has agreed to arbitrate can make a critical difference to a party resisting arbitration.

We believe the answer to the "who" question (i.e., the standard-of-review question) is fairly simple. Just as the arbitrability of the merits of a dispute depends upon whether the parties agreed to arbitrate that dispute, see, e.g., Mastrobuono v. Shearson Lehman Hutton, Inc., 514 U.S. 52, 58, 115 S.Ct. 1212, 1216, 131 L.Ed.2d 76 (1995); Mitsubishi Motors Corp. v. Soler Chrysler–Plymouth, Inc., 473 U.S. 614, 626 (1985), so the question "who has the primary power to decide arbitrability" turns upon what the parties agreed about that matter. Did the parties agree to submit the arbitrability question itself to arbitration? If so, then the court's standard for reviewing the arbitrator's decision about that matter should not differ from the standard courts apply when they review any other matter that parties have agreed to arbitrate. See AT & T Technologies, Inc. v. Communications Workers, 475 U.S. 643, 649, 106 S.Ct. 1415, 1418, 89 L.Ed.2d 648 (1986) (parties may agree to arbitrate arbitrability); Steelworkers v. Warrior & Gulf Navigation Co., 363 U.S. 574, 583, n. 7, 80 S.Ct. 1347, 1353, n. 7, 4 L.Ed.2d 1409 (1960) (same). That is to say, the court should give considerable leeway to the arbitrator, setting aside his or her decision only in certain narrow circumstances. See, e.g., 9 U.S.C. § 10. If, on the other hand, the parties did not agree to submit the arbitrability question itself to arbitration, then the court should decide that question just as it would decide any other question that the parties did not submit to arbitration, namely independently. These two answers flow inexorably from the fact that arbitration is simply a matter of contract between the parties; it is a way to resolve those disputes—but only those disputes—that the parties have agreed to submit to arbitration. See, e.g., AT & T Technologies, supra, at 649, 106 S.Ct., at 1418; Mastrobuono, supra, at 58–60, and n. 9, 115 S.Ct., at 1216–1217, and n. 9 . . . (Additional citations omitted.)

We agree with First Options, therefore, that a court must defer to an arbitrator's arbitrability decision when the parties submitted that matter to arbitration. Nevertheless, that conclusion does not help First Options win this case. That is because a fair and complete answer to the standard-of-review question requires a word about how a court should decide whether the parties have agreed to submit the arbitrability issue to arbitration. And, that word makes clear that the Kaplans did not agree to arbitrate arbitrability here.

When deciding whether the parties agreed to arbitrate a certain matter (including arbitrability), courts generally (though with a qualification we discuss below) should apply ordinary state-law principles that govern the formation of contracts. See, e.g., Mastrobuono, supra, at 62–64, and n. 9, 115 S.Ct., at 1219, and n. 9. . . . The relevant state law here, for example, would require the court to see whether the parties objectively revealed an intent to submit the arbitrability issue to arbitration. See, e.g., Estate of Jesmer v. Rohlev, 241 Ill.App.3d 798, 803, 182 Ill.Dec. 282, 286, 609 N.E.2d 816, 820 (1993) (law of the State whose law governs the workout agreement); . . . See generally Mitsubishi Motors, supra, at 626, 105 S.Ct., at 3353.

This Court, however, has (as we just said) added an important qualification, applicable when courts decide whether a party has agreed that arbitrators should decide arbitrability: Courts should not assume that the parties agreed to arbitrate arbitrability unless there is "clea[r] and unmistakabl[e]" evidence that they did so. AT & T Technologies, supra, at 649, 106 S.Ct., at 1418–1419; see Warrior & Gulf, supra, at 583, n. 7, 80 S.Ct., at 1353, n. 7. In this manner the law treats silence or ambiguity about the question "who (primarily) should decide arbitrability" differently from the way it treats silence or ambiguity about the question "whether a particular merits-related dispute is arbitrable because it is within the scope of a valid arbitration agreement"—for in respect to this latter question the law reverses the presumption. See Mitsubishi Motors, supra, at 626, 105 S.Ct., at 3353 ("[A]ny doubts concerning the scope of arbitrable issues should be resolved in favor of arbitration") (quoting Moses H. Cone Memorial Hospital v. Mercury Constr. Corp., 460 U.S. 1, 24–25, 103 S.Ct. 927, 941, 74 L.Ed.2d 765 (1983)); Warrior & Gulf, supra, at 582–583, 80 S.Ct., at 1352–1353.

But, this difference in treatment is understandable. The latter question arises when the parties have a contract that provides for arbitration of some issues. In such circumstances, the parties likely gave at least some thought to the scope of arbitration. And, given the law's permissive policies in respect to arbitration, see, e.g., Mitsubishi Motors, supra, at 626, 105 S.Ct., at 3353, one can understand why the law would insist upon clarity before concluding that the parties did not want to arbitrate a related matter. See Domke § 2.02, p. 156 (issues will be deemed arbitrable unless "it is clear that the arbitration clause has not included" them). On the other hand, the former question—the "who (primarily) should decide arbitrability" question—is rather arcane. A party often might not focus upon that question or upon the significance of having arbitrators decide the scope of their own powers. Cf. Cox, Reflections Upon Labor Arbitration, 72 Harv.L.Rev. 1482, 1508–1509 (1959), cited in Warrior & Gulf, 363 U.S., at 583, n. 7, 80 S.Ct., at 1353, n. 7. And, given the principle that a party can be forced to arbitrate only those issues it specifically has agreed to submit to arbitration, one can understand why courts might hesitate to interpret silence or ambiguity on the "who should decide arbitrability" point as giving the arbitrators that power, for doing so might too often force unwilling parties to arbitrate a matter they reasonably would have thought a judge, not an arbitrator, would decide. Ibid. See generally Dean Witter Reynolds Inc. v. Byrd, 470 U.S. 213, 219–220, 105 S.Ct. 1238, 1241–1242, 84 L.Ed.2d 158 (1985) (Arbitration Act's basic purpose is to "ensure judicial enforcement of privately made agreements to arbitrate").

On the record before us, First Options cannot show that the Kaplans clearly agreed to have the arbitrators decide (i.e., to arbitrate) the question of arbitrability. First Options relies on the Kaplans' filing with the arbitrators a written memorandum objecting to the arbitrators' jurisdiction. But merely arguing the arbitrability issue to an arbitrator does not indicate a clear willingness to arbitrate that issue, i.e., a willingness to be effectively bound by the arbitrator's decision on that point. To the contrary, insofar as the Kaplans were forcefully objecting to the arbitrators deciding their dispute with First Options, one naturally would think that they did not want the arbitrators to have binding authority over them. This conclusion draws added support from (1) an obvious explanation for the Kaplans' presence before the arbitrators (i.e., that MKI, Mr. Kaplan's wholly owned firm, was arbitrating workout agreement matters); and (2) Third Circuit law that suggested that the Kaplans might argue arbitrability to the arbitrators without losing their right to independent court review, Teamsters v. Western Pennsylvania Motor Carriers Assn., 574 F.2d 783, 786–788 (1978); see 19 F.3d, at 1512, n. 13.

First Options makes several counter arguments: (1) that the Kaplans had other ways to get an independent court decision on the question of arbitrability without arguing the issue to the arbitrators (e.g., by trying to enjoin the arbitration, or by refusing to participate in the arbitration and then defending against a court petition First Options would have brought to compel arbitration, see 9 U.S.C. § 4); (2) that permitting parties to argue arbitrability to an arbitrator without being bound by the result would cause delay and waste in the resolution of disputes; and (3) that the Arbitration Act therefore requires a presumption that the Kaplans agreed to be bound by the arbitrators' decision, not the contrary. The first of these points, however, while true, simply does not say anything about whether the Kaplans intended to be bound by the arbitrators' decision. The second point, too, is inconclusive, for factual circumstances vary too greatly to permit a confident conclusion about whether allowing the arbitrator to make an initial (but independently reviewable) arbitrability determination would, in general, slow down the dispute resolution process. And, the third point is legally erroneous, for there is no strong arbitration-related policy favoring First Options in respect to its particular argument here. After all, the basic objective in this area is not to resolve disputes in the quickest manner possible, no matter what the parties' wishes, Dean Witter Reynolds, supra, at 219–220, 105 S.Ct., at 1241–1242, but to ensure that commercial arbitration agreements, like other contracts, " 'are enforced according to their terms,' " Mastrobuono, 514 U.S., at 54, 115 S.Ct., at 1214 (quoting Volt Information Sciences, 489 U.S., at 479, 109 S.Ct., at 1256), and according to the intentions of the parties, Mitsubishi Motors, 473 U.S., at 626, 105 S.Ct., at 3353. See Allied–Bruce, 513 U.S., at 268–69, 115 S.Ct., at 837. That policy favors the Kaplans, not First Options.

We conclude that, because the Kaplans did not clearly agree to submit the question of arbitrability to arbitration, the Court of Appeals was correct in finding that the arbitrability of the Kaplan/First Options dispute was subject to independent review by the courts. . . .

The judgment of the Court of Appeals is affirmed.

* * *

Questions

1. If parties can consent to have an arbitrator determine the issue of arbitrability, and if, as *Moses H. Cone* concludes, there is a presumption of arbitrability for issues of contract construction, then why doesn't the Court order the parties to arbitrate the issue of arbitrability in *First Options*? Is *First Options* consistent with *Moses H. Cone*? Or does *First Options* represent a retreat from the expansive conception of arbitrability enunciated in *Moses H. Cone*?

2. Why doesn't the Court apply the presumption of arbitrability in *First Options*? Why does it require "clear and unmistakable evidence" of such an intent on the issue of who is to decide arbitrability, but not on other issues concerning arbitrability? Does the Court make a serious encroachment on the presumption of arbitrability by doing so? Is the Court distinguishing arbitrability determinations on the basis of its own view as to which issues the parties are likely to have considered and which ones they are not likely to have considered in the contract formation process? What is the basis for the Court's conclusion that the parties were not likely to have considered the issue of who is to decide arbitrability? Are there other types of issues that parties are unlikely to consider at the time of contract formation? Should those likewise be excluded from the presumption of arbitrability?

3. Is there a conflict between a liberal federal policy favoring arbitration and the Court's commitment to treating arbitration agreements like ordinary contracts? Can the result in *First Options* be explained on the basis of the court's desire to enforce the will of the parties, or is it an instance of the court enforcing a federal policy favoring arbitration?

4. In decisions of arbitrability, what are the respective institutional advantages of arbitrators and district courts? How should this affect the standard of review by district courts of arbitral decisions on arbitrability? Should it affect the standard of review on the merits of a dispute?

* * *

Green Tree Fin. Corp. v. Bazzle

539 U.S. 444 (2003).

■ JUSTICE BREYER announced the judgment of the Court and delivered an opinion, in which JUSTICE SCALIA, JUSTICE SOUTER, and JUSTICE GINSBURG join.

This case concerns contracts between a commercial lender and its customers, each of which [sic] contains a clause providing for arbitration of all contract-related disputes. The Supreme Court of South Carolina held (1) that the arbitration clauses are silent as to whether arbitration might take the form of class arbitration, and (2) that, in that circumstance, South Carolina law interprets the contracts as permitting class arbitration. 351 S.C. 244, 569 S.E.2d 349 (2002). We granted certiorari to determine whether this holding is consistent with the Federal Arbitration Act, 9 U.S.C. § 1 *et seq.*

We are faced at the outset with a problem concerning the contracts' silence. Are the contracts in fact silent, or do they forbid class arbitration as petitioner Green Tree Financial Corp. contends? Given the South Carolina Supreme Court's holding, it is important to resolve that question. But we cannot do so, not simply because it is a matter of state law, but also because it is a matter for the arbitrator to decide. Because the record suggests that the parties have not yet received an arbitrator's decision on that question of contract interpretation, we vacate the judgment of the South Carolina Supreme Court and remand the case so that this question may be resolved in arbitration.

I

In 1995, respondents Lynn and Burt Bazzle secured a home improvement loan from petitioner Green Tree. The Bazzles and Green Tree entered into a contract, governed by South Carolina law, which included the following arbitration clause:

> ARBITRATION—All disputes, claims, or controversies arising from or relating to this contract or the relationships which result from this contract ... *shall be resolved by binding arbitration by one arbitrator selected by us with consent of you.* This arbitration contract is made pursuant to a transaction in interstate commerce, and shall be governed by the Federal Arbitration Act at 9 U.S.C. section 1.... THE PARTIES VOLUNTARILY AND KNOWINGLY WAIVE ANY RIGHT THEY HAVE TO A JURY TRIAL, EITHER PURSUANT TO ARBITRATION UNDER THIS CLAUSE OR PURSUANT TO A COURT ACTION BY U.S. (AS PROVIDED HEREIN).... The parties agree and understand that the arbitrator shall have all powers provided by the law and the contract. These powers shall include all legal and equitable remedies, including, but not limited to, money damages, declaratory relief, and injunctive relief. App. 34 (emphasis added, capitalization in original).

Respondents Daniel Lackey and George and Florine Buggs entered into loan contracts and security agreements for the purchase of mobile homes with Green Tree. These agreements contained arbitration clauses that were, in all relevant respects, identical to the Bazzles' arbitration clause. (Their contracts substitute the word "you" with the word "Buyer[s]" in the italicized phrase.) 351 S.C., at 264, n. 18, 569 S.E.2d, at 359, n. 18 (emphasis deleted).

At the time of the loan transactions, Green Tree apparently failed to provide these customers with a legally required form that would have told them that they had a right to name their own lawyers and insurance agents and would have provided space for them to write in those names. See S.C.Code Ann. § 37–10–102 (West 2002). The two sets of customers before us now as respondents each filed separate actions in South Carolina state courts, complaining that this failure violated South Carolina law and seeking damages.

In April 1997, the Bazzles asked the court to certify their claims as a class action. Green Tree sought to stay the court proceedings and compel arbitration. On January 5, 1998, the court both (1) certified a class action and (2) entered an order compelling arbitration. App. 7. Green Tree then selected an arbitrator with the Bazzles' consent. And the arbitrator, administering the proceeding as a class arbitration, eventually awarded the class $10,935,000 in statutory damages, along with attorney's fees. The trial court confirmed the award, App. to Pet. for Cert. 27a–35a, and Green Tree appealed to the South Carolina Court of Appeals claiming, among other things, that class arbitration was legally impermissible.

Lackey and the Buggses had earlier begun a similar court proceeding in which they, too, sought class certification. Green Tree moved to compel arbitration. The trial court initially denied the motion, finding the arbitration agreement unenforceable, but Green Tree pursued an interlocutory appeal and the State Court of Appeals reversed. *Lackey v. Green Tree Financial Corp.,* 330 S.C. 388, 498 S.E.2d 898 (1998). The parties then chose an arbitrator, indeed the same arbitrator who was subsequently selected to arbitrate the Bazzles' dispute.

In December 1998, the arbitrator certified a class in arbitration. App. 18. The arbitrator proceeded to hear the matter, ultimately ruled in favor of the class, and awarded the class $9,200,000 in statutory damages in addition to attorney's fees. The trial court confirmed the award. App. to Pet. for Cert. 36a–54a. Green Tree appealed to the South Carolina Court of Appeals claiming, among other things, that class arbitration was legally impermissible.

The South Carolina Supreme Court withdrew both cases from the Court of Appeals, assumed jurisdiction, and consolidated the proceedings. 351 S.C., at 249, 569 S.E.2d, at 351. That court then held that the contracts were silent in respect to class arbitration, that they consequently authorized class arbitration, and that arbitration had properly taken that form. We granted certiorari to consider whether that holding is consistent with the Federal Arbitration Act.

II

The South Carolina Supreme Court's determination that the contracts are silent in respect to class arbitration raises a preliminary question. Green Tree argued there, as it argues here, that the contracts are not silent—that they forbid class arbitration. And we must deal with that argument at the outset, for if it is right, then the South Carolina court's holding is flawed on its own terms; that court neither said nor implied that it would have authorized class arbitration had the parties' arbitration agreement forbidden it.

Whether Green Tree is right about the contracts themselves presents a disputed issue of contract interpretation. THE CHIEF JUSTICE believes that Green Tree is right; indeed, that Green Tree is so clearly right that we should ignore the fact that state law, not federal law, normally governs such matters, see *post,* at 2408 (Stevens, J., concurring in judgment and dissenting in part), and reverse the South Carolina Supreme Court outright, see *post,* at 2410–2411 (Rehnquist, C.J., dissenting). The Chief Justice points out that the contracts say that disputes "shall be resolved ... by one arbitrator selected by us [Green Tree] with consent of you [Green Tree's customer]." App. to Pet. for Cert. 110a. See *post,* at 2410. And it finds that class arbitration is clearly inconsistent with this requirement. After all, class arbitration involves an arbitration, not simply between Green Tree and a *named customer,* but also between Green Tree and *other* (represented) customers, all taking place before the arbitrator chosen to arbitrate the initial, *named customer's* dispute.

We do not believe, however, that the contracts' language is as clear as THE CHIEF JUSTICE believes. The class arbitrator *was* "selected by" Green Tree "with consent of" Green Tree's customers, the named plaintiffs. And insofar as the other class members agreed to proceed in class arbitration, they consented as well.

Of course, Green Tree did *not* independently select *this* arbitrator to arbitrate its disputes with the *other* class members. But whether the contracts contain this additional requirement is a question that the literal terms of the contracts do not decide. The contracts simply say (I) "selected by us [Green Tree]." And that is literally what occurred. The contracts do not say (II) "selected by us [Green Tree] to arbitrate this dispute and no other (even identical) dispute with another customer." The question whether (I) in fact implicitly means (II) is the question at issue: Do the contracts forbid class arbitration? Given the broad authority the contracts elsewhere bestow upon the arbitrator, see, *e.g.,* App. to Pet. for Cert. 110a (the contracts grant to the arbitrator "all powers," including certain equitable powers "provided by the law and the contract"), the answer to this question is not completely obvious.

At the same time, we cannot automatically accept the South Carolina Supreme Court's resolution of this contract-interpretation question. Under the terms of the parties' contracts, the question—whether the agreement forbids class arbitration—is for the arbitrator to decide. The parties agreed to submit to the arbitrator *"[a]ll* disputes, claims, or controversies arising from or relating to this contract or the relationships which result from this contract." *Ibid.* (emphasis added). And the dispute about what the arbitration contract in each case means (*i.e.,* whether it forbids the use of class arbitration procedures) is a dispute "relating to this contract" and the resulting "relationships." Hence the parties seem to have agreed that an arbitrator, not a judge, would answer the relevant question. See *First Options of Chicago, Inc. v. Kaplan,* 514 U.S. 938, 943, 115 S.Ct. 1920, 131 L.Ed.2d 985 (1995) (arbitration is a "matter of contract"). And if there is doubt about that matter-about the " 'scope of arbitrable issues' "-we should resolve that doubt " 'in favor of arbitration.' " *Mitsubishi Motors Corp. v. Soler Chrysler–Plymouth, Inc.,* 473 U.S. 614, 626, 105 S.Ct. 3346, 87 L.Ed.2d 444 (1985).

In certain limited circumstances, courts assume that the parties intended courts, not arbitrators, to decide a particular arbitration-related matter (in the absence of "clea[r] and unmistakabl[e]" evidence to the contrary). *AT & T Technologies, Inc. v. Communications Workers,* 475 U.S. 643, 649, 106 S.Ct. 1415, 89 L.Ed.2d 648 (1986). These limited instances typically involve matters of a kind that "contracting parties would likely have expected a court" to decide. *Howsam v. Dean Witter Reynolds, Inc.,* 537 U.S. 79, 83, 123 S.Ct. 588, 154 L.Ed.2d 491 (2002). They include certain gateway matters, such as whether the parties have a valid arbitration agreement at all or whether a concededly binding arbitration clause applies to a certain type of controversy. See generally *Howsam, supra.* See also *John Wiley & Sons, Inc. v. Livingston,* 376 U.S. 543, 546–547, 84 S.Ct. 909, 11 L.Ed.2d 898 (1964) (whether an arbitration agreement survives a corporate merger); *AT & T, supra,* at 651–652, 106 S.Ct. 1415 (whether a labor-management layoff controversy falls within the scope of an arbitration clause).

The question here—whether the contracts forbid class arbitration—does not fall into this narrow exception. It concerns neither the validity of the arbitration clause nor its applicability to the underlying dispute between the parties. Unlike *First Options,* the question is not whether the parties wanted a judge or an arbitrator to decide *whether they agreed to arbitrate a matter.* 514 U.S., at 942–945, 115 S.Ct. 1920. Rather the relevant question here is what *kind of arbitration proceeding* the parties agreed to. That question does not concern a state statute or judicial procedures, cf. *Volt Information Sciences, Inc. v. Board of Trustees of Leland Stanford Junior Univ.,* 489 U.S. 468, 474–476, 109 S.Ct. 1248, 103 L.Ed.2d 488 (1989). It concerns contract interpretation and arbitration procedures. Arbitrators are well situated to answer that question. Given these considerations, along with the arbitration contracts' sweeping language concerning the scope of the questions committed to arbitration, this matter of contract interpretation should be for the arbitrator, not the courts, to decide. Cf. *Howsam, supra,* at 83, 123 S.Ct. 588 (finding for roughly similar reasons that the arbitrator should determine a certain procedural "gateway matter").

III

With respect to this underlying question—whether the arbitration contracts forbid class arbitration—the parties have not yet obtained the arbitration decision that their contracts foresee. As far as concerns the *Bazzle* plaintiffs, the South Carolina Supreme Court wrote that the "trial court" issued "an order granting class certification" and the arbitrator subsequently "administered" class arbitration proceedings "without further involvement of the trial court." 351 S.C., at 250–251, 569 S.E.2d, at 352. Green Tree adds that "the class arbitration was imposed on the parties and the arbitrator by the South Carolina trial court." Brief for Petitioner 30. Respondents now deny that this was so, Brief for Respondents 13, but we can find no convincing record support for that denial.

As far as concerns the *Lackey* plaintiffs, what happened in arbitration is less clear. On the one hand, the *Lackey* arbitrator (the same individual who later arbitrated the *Bazzle* dispute) wrote: "*I* determined that a class action should proceed in arbitration based upon *my* careful review of the broadly drafted arbitration clause prepared by Green Tree." App. to Pet. for Cert. 84a (emphasis added). And respondents suggested at oral argument that the arbitrator's decision was independently made. Tr. of Oral Arg. 39.

On the other hand, the *Lackey* arbitrator decided this question after the South Carolina trial court had determined that the identical contract in the *Bazzle* case authorized class arbitration procedures. And there is no question that the arbitrator was aware of the *Bazzle* decision, since the *Lackey* plaintiffs had argued to the arbitrator that it should impose class arbitration procedures in part because the state trial court in *Bazzle* had done so. Record on Appeal 516–518. In the court proceedings below (where Green Tree took the opposite position), the *Lackey* plaintiffs maintained that "to the extent" the arbitrator decided that the contracts permitted class procedures (in the *Lackey* case or the *Bazzle* case), "it was a reaffirmation and/or adoption of [the *Bazzle* c]ourt's prior determination." Record on Appeal 1708, n. 2. See also App. 31–32, n. 2.

On balance, there is at least a strong likelihood in *Lackey* as well as in *Bazzle* that the arbitrator's decision reflected a court's interpretation of the contracts rather than an arbitrator's interpretation. That being so, we remand the case so that the arbitrator may decide the question of contract interpretation—thereby enforcing the parties' arbitration agreements according to their terms. 9 U.S.C. § 2; *Volt, supra,* at 478–479, 109 S.Ct. 1248.

The judgment of the South Carolina Supreme Court is vacated, and the case is remanded for further proceedings.

So ordered.

■ JUSTICE STEVENS, concurring in the judgment and dissenting in part.

The parties agreed that South Carolina law would govern their arbitration agreement. The Supreme Court of South Carolina has held as a matter of state law that class-action arbitrations are permissible if not prohibited by the applicable arbitration agreement, and that the agreement between these parties is silent on the issue. 351 S.C. 244, 262–266, 569 S.E.2d 349, 359–360 (2002). There is nothing in the Federal Arbitration Act that precludes either of these determinations by the Supreme Court of South Carolina. See *Volt Information Sciences, Inc. v. Board of Trustees of Leland Stanford Junior Univ.,* 489 U.S. 468, 475–476, 109 S.Ct. 1248, 103 L.Ed.2d 488 (1989).

Arguably the interpretation of the parties' agreement should have been made in the first instance by the arbitrator, rather than the court. See *Howsam v. Dean Witter Reynolds, Inc.,* 537 U.S. 79, 123 S.Ct. 588, 154 L.Ed.2d 491 (2002). Because the decision to conduct a class-action arbitration was correct as a matter of law, and because petitioner has merely challenged the merits of that decision without claiming that it was made by the wrong decisionmaker, there is no need to remand the case to correct that possible error.

Accordingly, I would simply affirm the judgment of the Supreme Court of South Carolina. Were I to adhere to my preferred disposition of the case, however, there would be no controlling judgment of the Court. In order to avoid that outcome, and because Justice Breyer's opinion expresses a view of the case close to my own, I concur in the judgment. See *Screws v. United States,* 325 U.S. 91, 134, 65 S.Ct. 1031, 89 L.Ed. 1495 (1945) (Rutledge, J., concurring in result).

■ CHIEF JUSTICE REHNQUIST, with whom JUSTICE O'CONNOR and JUSTICE KENNEDY join, dissenting.

The parties entered into contracts with an arbitration clause that is governed by the Federal Arbitration Act (FAA), 9 U.S.C. § 1 *et seq.* The Supreme Court of South Carolina held that arbitration under the contracts could proceed as a class action even though the contracts do not by their terms permit class-action arbitration. The plurality now vacates that judgment and remands the case for the arbitrator to make this determination. I would reverse because this determination is one for the courts, not for the arbitrator, and the holding of the Supreme Court of South Carolina contravenes the terms of the contracts and is therefore pre-empted by the FAA.

The agreement to arbitrate involved here, like many such agreements, is terse. Its operative language is contained in one sentence:

> All disputes, claims, or controversies arising from or relating to this contract or the relationships which result from this contract . . . shall be resolved by binding arbitration by one arbitrator selected by us with consent of you. App. 34.

The decision of the arbitrator on matters agreed to be submitted to him is given considerable deference by the courts. See *Major League Baseball Players Assn. v. Garvey,* 532 U.S. 504, 509–510, 121 S.Ct. 1724, 149 L.Ed.2d 740 (2001) *(per curiam).* The Supreme Court of South Carolina relied on this principle in deciding that the arbitrator in this case did not abuse his discretion in allowing a class action. 351 S.C. 244, 266–268, 569 S.E.2d 349, 361–362 (2002). But the decision of *what* to submit to the arbitrator is a matter of contractual agreement by the parties, and the interpretation of that contract is for the court, not for the arbitrator. As we stated in *First Options of Chicago, Inc. v. Kaplan,* 514 U.S. 938, 945, 115 S.Ct. 1920, 131 L.Ed.2d 985 (1995):

> [G]iven the principle that a party can be forced to arbitrate only those issues it specifically has agreed to submit to arbitration, one can understand why courts might hesitate to interpret silence or ambiguity on the 'who should decide arbitrability' point as giving the arbitrators that power, for doing so might too often force unwilling parties to arbitrate a matter they reasonably would have thought a judge, not an arbitrator, would decide.

Just as fundamental to the agreement of the parties as *what* is submitted to the arbitrator is to *whom* it is submitted. Those are the two provisions in the sentence quoted above, and it is difficult to say that one is more important than the other. I have no hesitation in saying that the choice of arbitrator is as important a component of the agreement to arbitrate as is the choice of what is to be submitted to him.

Thus, this case is controlled by *First Options,* and not by our more recent decision in *Howsam v. Dean Witter Reynolds, Inc.,* 537 U.S. 79, 123 S.Ct. 588, 154 L.Ed.2d 491 (2002). There, the agreement provided that any dispute "shall be determined by arbitration before any self-regulatory organization or exchange of which Dean Witter is a member." *Id.,* at 81, 123 S.Ct. 588 (internal quotation marks omitted). Howsam chose the National Association of Securities Dealers (NASD), and agreed to that organization's "Uniform Submission Agreement" which provided that the arbitration would be governed by NASD's "Code of Arbitration Procedure." *Id.,* at 82, 123 S.Ct. 588. That code, in turn, contained a limitation. This Court held that it was for the arbitrator to interpret that limitation provision:

> "[P]rocedural" questions which grow out of the dispute and bear on its final disposition" are presumptively *not* for the judge, but for an arbitrator, to decide. *John Wiley [& Sons, Inc. v. Livingston,* 376 U.S. 543, 557, 84 S.Ct. 909, 11 L.Ed.2d 898 (1964)] (holding that an arbitrator should decide whether the first two steps of a grievance procedure were completed, where these steps are prerequisites to arbitration). So, too, the presumption is that the arbitrator should decide "allegation[s] of waiver, delay, or a like defense to arbitrability." *Id.,* at 84, 84 S.Ct. 909.

I think that the parties' agreement as to how the arbitrator should be selected is much more akin to the agreement as to what shall be arbitrated, a question for the courts under *First Options,* than it is to "allegations of waiver, delay, or like defenses to arbitrability," which are questions for the arbitrator under *Howsam.* . . .

Under the FAA, "parties are generally free to structure their arbitration agreements as they see fit." *Volt, supra,* at 479, 109 S.Ct. 1248. Here, the parties saw fit to agree that any disputes arising out of the contracts "shall be resolved by binding arbitration by one arbitrator selected by us with consent of you." App. 34. Each contract expressly defines "us" as petitioner, and "you" as the respondent or respondents named in that specific contract. *Id.,* at 33 (" 'We' and 'us' means the Seller *above,* its successors and assigns;" " 'You' and 'your' means each Buyer *above* and guarantor, jointly and severally" (emphasis added)). Each contract also specifies that it governs all "disputes . . . arising from . . . *this* contract or the relationships which result from *this* contract." *Id.,* at 34 (emphasis added). These provisions, which the plurality simply ignores, see *ante,* at 2406, make quite clear that petitioner must select, and each buyer must agree to, a particular arbitrator for disputes between petitioner and that specific buyer.

While the observation of the Supreme Court of South Carolina that the agreement of the parties was silent as to the availability of class-wide arbitration is literally true, the imposition of class-wide arbitration contravenes the just-quoted provision about the selection of an arbitrator. To be sure, the arbitrator that administered the proceedings was "selected by [petitioner] with consent of" the Bazzles, Lackey, and the Buggses. App. 34–36. But petitioner had the contractual right to choose an arbitrator for each dispute with the other 3,734 individual class members, and this right was denied when the same arbitrator was foisted upon petitioner to resolve those claims as well. Petitioner may well have chosen different arbitrators for some or all of these other disputes; indeed, it would have been reasonable for petitioner to do so, in order to avoid concentrating all of the risk of substantial damages awards in the hands of a single arbitrator. As petitioner correctly concedes, Brief for Petitioner 32, 42, the FAA does not prohibit parties from choosing to proceed on a classwide basis. Here, however, the parties simply did not so choose.

"Arbitration under the Act is a matter of consent, not coercion." *Volt, supra,* at 479, 109 S.Ct. 1248. Here, the Supreme Court of South Carolina imposed a regime that was contrary to the express agreement of the parties as to how the arbitrator would be chosen. It did not enforce the "agreemen[t] to arbitrate . . . according to [its] terms." *Mastrobuono, supra,* at 54, 115 S.Ct. 1212 (internal quotation marks omitted). I would therefore reverse the judgment of the Supreme Court of South Carolina.

■ JUSTICE THOMAS, dissenting.

I continue to believe that the Federal Arbitration Act (FAA), 9 U.S.C. § 1 *et seq.,* does not apply to proceedings in state courts. . . . For that reason, the FAA cannot be a ground for pre-empting a state court's interpretation of a private arbitration agreement. Accordingly, I would leave undisturbed the judgment of the Supreme Court of South Carolina.

* * *

Questions

1. Did the plurality adequately distinguish *First Options* on the issue of *who decides* arbitrability issues?

2. Given the absence of a majority opinion and Justice Stevens's waffling concurrence, how much precedential value does *Green Tree* have? What do you think of the Seventh Circuit's assessment?:

> Taking [the opinions of Justices Breyer and Stevens] together, we cannot identify a single rationale endorsed by a majority of the Court. Justice Breyer reasoned that 1) consolidation is a procedural question for the arbitrator; 2) the Supreme Court should not reach the question whether the parties' agreements forbid class arbitration; and 3) remand is required so that the arbitrators can address whether the agreements forbid class arbitration. Justice Stevens, in contrast, reasoned that 1) the South Carolina Supreme Court correctly held as a

> matter of state law that the parties' agreements do not forbid class arbitration; and 2) remand was not required, because the parties did not argue that the arbitrator, rather than the court, should have decided the appropriateness of class arbitration. The Justices' rationales do not overlap.

Employers Ins. Co. of Wausau v. Century Indem. Co., 443 F.3d 573, 581 (7th Cir. 2006); cf. Pedcor Management Co., Inc. Welfare Benefit Plan v. Nations Personnel of Texas, Inc., 343 F.3d 355 (5th Cir. 2003) (finding that the narrowest ground for decision in *Green Tree* is that the validity of class arbitration is to be decided by the arbitrator, absent evidence that the parties intended the court to resolve the issue).

3. Consumer arbitration usually occurs in one of two contexts. In the first, a company uses arbitration as a shield against complaints brought by consumers. An example is Green Tree's attempt to use its arbitration clause (with the class action prohibition) to make it difficult or impossible for the Bazzles to bring their claim. In the second, a company uses arbitration as a sword in a debt-collection case: arbitration is an expedited path to judgment against a consumer who owes the company money. See, e.g., MBNA Am. Bank, N.A. v. Nelson, 841 N.Y.S.2d 826 (N.Y. Civ. Ct. 2007). Should the law distinguish between these two types of cases? See Note, Mandatory Arbitration Clauses: Proposals for Reform of Consumer–Defendant Arbitration, 122 Harv. L. Rev. 1170 (2009).

4. What is the appropriate role of an ethical attorney in advising her or his client about drafting an arbitration clause for consumer contracts? If a credit card company instructs its attorney to draft an arbitration clause for the company's consumer contracts, should the attorney draft a clause that strongly favors the company by, for example, prohibiting class actions and imposing a high filing fee? What should the attorney do if specifically instructed to do so by the company? For consumer and employment cases that follow throughout this book, consider where the ethical line should be drawn between vigorous client representation and commitment to justice. See Amy J. Schmitz, Ethical Considerations in Drafting and Enforcing Consumer Arbitration Clauses, 49 S. Tex. L. Rev. 841 (2008).

5. Does this case resolve the issues of how courts should construe contractual silence about whether to allow arbitral class actions and whether courts should enforce class action waivers? We revisit these issues in Chapter 3.

* * *

PacifiCare Health Sys. v. Book

538 U.S. 401 (2003).

■ JUSTICE SCALIA delivered the opinion of the Court.

In this case, we are asked to decide whether respondents can be compelled to arbitrate claims arising under the Racketeer Influenced and

Corrupt Organizations Act (RICO), 18 U.S.C. § 1961 *et seq.*, notwithstanding the fact that the parties' arbitration agreements may be construed to limit the arbitrator's authority to award damages under that statute.

I

Respondents are members of a group of physicians who filed suit against managed-health-care organizations including petitioners PacifiCare Health Systems, Inc., and PacifiCare Operations, Inc. (collectively, PacifiCare), and UnitedHealthcare, Inc., and UnitedHealth Group Inc. (collectively, United). These physicians alleged that the defendants unlawfully failed to reimburse them for health-care services that they had provided to patients covered by defendants' health plans. They brought causes of action under RICO, the Employee Retirement Income Security Act of 1974 (ERISA), and federal and state prompt-pay statutes, as well as claims for breach of contract, unjust enrichment, and *in quantum meruit. In re Managed Care Litigation,* 132 F.Supp.2d 989, 992 (S.D. Fla. 2000).

Of particular concern here, PacifiCare and United moved the District Court to compel arbitration, arguing that provisions in their contracts with respondents required arbitration of these disputes, including those arising under RICO. *Ibid.* Respondents opposed the motion on the ground that, because the arbitration provisions prohibit an award of punitive damages, see App. 107, 147, 168, 212, respondents could not obtain "meaningful relief" in arbitration for their claims under the RICO statute, which authorizes treble damages, 18 U.S.C. § 1964(c). See *Paladino v. Avnet Computer Technologies, Inc.,* 134 F.3d 1054, 1062 (11th Cir. 1998) (holding that where a remedial limitation in an arbitration agreement prevents a plaintiff from obtaining "meaningful relief" for a statutory claim, the agreement to arbitrate is unenforceable with respect to that claim).

The District Court denied petitioners' request to compel arbitration of the RICO claims. 132 F.Supp.2d, at 1007. The court concluded that given the remedial limitations in the relevant contracts, it was, indeed, "faced with a potential *Paladino* situation . . . , where the plaintiff may not be able to obtain meaningful relief for allegations of statutory violations in an arbitration forum." *Id.,* at 1005. Accordingly, it found the arbitration agreements unenforceable with respect to respondents' RICO claims. *Id.,* at 1007. The Eleventh Circuit affirmed "for the reasons set forth in [the District Court's] comprehensive opinion," *In re Humana Inc. Managed Care Litigation,* 285 F.3d 971, 973 (2002), and we granted certiorari, 537 U.S. 946, 123 S.Ct. 409, 154 L.Ed.2d 289 (2002).

II

Petitioners argue that whether the remedial limitations render their arbitration agreements unenforceable is not a question of "arbitrability," and hence should have been decided by an arbitrator, rather than a court, in the first instance. They also claim that even if this question is one of arbitrability, and is therefore properly within the purview of the courts at this time, the remedial limitations at issue do not require invalidation of their arbitration agreements. Either way, petitioners contend, the lower courts should have compelled arbitration. We conclude that it would be premature for us to address these questions at this time.

Our decision in *Vimar Seguros y Reaseguros, S.A. v. M/V Sky Reefer,* 515 U.S. 528, 115 S.Ct. 2322, 132 L.Ed.2d 462 (1995), supplies the analytic framework for assessing the ripeness of this dispute. In *Vimar,* we dealt with a bill of lading concerning a shipment of goods from Morocco to Massachusetts. Upon receipt of the goods, the purchaser discovered that they had been damaged, and, along with its insurer (Vimar), filed suit against the shipper. The shipper sought to compel arbitration, relying on choice-of-law and arbitration clauses in the bill of lading under which disputes arising out of the parties' agreement were to be governed by Japanese law and resolved through arbitration before the Tokyo Maritime Arbitration Commission. Vimar countered by arguing that the arbitration clause violated the Carriage of Goods by Sea Act (COGSA), 46 U.S.C.App. § 1300 *et seq.,* and hence was unenforceable. 515 U.S., at 531–532, 115 S.Ct. 2322. In particular, Vimar claimed that "there is no guarantee foreign arbitrators will apply COGSA"; that the foreign arbitrator was likely to apply rules of Japanese law under which respondents' liability might be less than what it would be under COGSA; and that this would violate "[t]he central guarantee of [COGSA] § 3(8) . . . that the terms of a bill of lading may not relieve the carrier of obligations or diminish the legal duties specified by the Act." *Id.,* at 539, 115 S.Ct. 2322.

Notwithstanding Vimar's insistence that the arbitration agreement violated federal policy as embodied in COGSA, we declined to reach the issue and held that the arbitration clause was, at least initially, enforceable. "At this interlocutory stage," we explained, "it is not established what law the arbitrators will apply to petitioner's claims or that petitioner will receive diminished protection as a result. The arbitrators may conclude that COGSA applies of its own force or that Japanese law does not apply so that, under another clause of the bill of lading, COGSA controls." *Id.,* at 540, 115 S.Ct. 2322. We further emphasized that "mere speculation that the foreign arbitrators *might* apply Japanese law which, depending on the proper construction of COGSA, *might* reduce respondents' legal obligations, does not in and of itself lessen liability under COGSA § 3(8)," nor did it provide an adequate basis upon which to declare the relevant arbitration agreement unenforceable. *Id.,* at 541, 115 S.Ct. 2322 (emphases added). We found that "[w]hatever the merits of petitioner's comparative reading of COGSA and its Japanese counterpart, its claim is premature." *Id.,* at 540, 115 S.Ct. 2322.

The case at bar arrives in a similar posture. Two of the four arbitration agreements at issue provide that "punitive damages shall not be awarded [in arbitration]," App. 107, 147; one provides that "[t]he arbitrators . . . shall have no authority to award any punitive or exemplary damages," *id.,* at 212; and one provides that "[t]he arbitrators . . . shall have no authority to award extra contractual damages of any kind, including punitive or exemplary damages . . .," *id.,* at 168. Respondents insist, and the District

Court agreed, 132 F.Supp.2d, at 1000–1001, 1005, that these provisions preclude an arbitrator from awarding treble damages under RICO. We think that neither our precedents nor the ambiguous terms of the contracts make this clear.

Our cases have placed different statutory treble-damages provisions on different points along the spectrum between purely compensatory and strictly punitive awards. Thus, in *Vermont Agency of Natural Resources v. United States ex rel. Stevens,* 529 U.S. 765, 784, 120 S.Ct. 1858, 146 L.Ed.2d 836 (2000), we characterized the treble-damages provision of the False Claims Act, 31 U.S.C. §§ 3729–3733, as "essentially punitive in nature." In *Brunswick Corp. v. Pueblo Bowl–O–Mat, Inc.,* 429 U.S. 477, 485, 97 S.Ct. 690, 50 L.Ed.2d 701 (1977), on the other hand, we explained that the treble-damages provision of § 4 of the Clayton Act, 15 U.S.C. § 15, "is in essence a remedial provision." Likewise in *American Soc. of Mechanical Engineers, Inc. v. Hydrolevel Corp.,* 456 U.S. 556, 575, 102 S.Ct. 1935, 72 L.Ed.2d 330 (1982), we noted that "the antitrust private action [which allows for treble damages] was created primarily as *a remedy* for the victims of antitrust violations." (Emphasis added.) And earlier this Term, in *Cook County v. United States ex rel. Chandler, ante,* 538 U.S. 119, 130, 123 S.Ct. 1239, we stated that "it is important to realize that treble damages have a compensatory side, serving remedial purposes in addition to punitive objectives." Indeed, we have repeatedly acknowledged that the treble-damages provision contained in RICO itself is remedial in nature. In *Agency Holding Corp. v. Malley–Duff & Associates, Inc.,* 483 U.S. 143, 151, 107 S.Ct. 2759, 97 L.Ed.2d 121 (1987), we stated that "[b]oth RICO and the Clayton Act are designed *to remedy* economic injury by providing for the recovery of treble damages, costs, and attorney's fees." (Emphasis added.) And in *Shearson/American Express Inc. v. McMahon,* 482 U.S. 220, 241, 107 S.Ct. 2332, 96 L.Ed.2d 185 (1987) we took note of the "remedial function" of RICO's treble-damages provision.

In light of our case law's treatment of statutory treble damages, and given the uncertainty surrounding the parties' intent with respect to the contractual term "punitive," the application of the disputed language to respondents' RICO claims is, to say the least, in doubt. And *Vimar* instructs that we should not, on the basis of "mere speculation" that an arbitrator might interpret these ambiguous agreements in a manner that casts their enforceability into doubt, take upon ourselves the authority to decide the antecedent question of how the ambiguity is to be resolved.[2] 515

2. If the contractual ambiguity could itself be characterized as raising a "gateway" question of arbitrability, then it would be appropriate for a court to answer it in the first instance. But we noted just this Term that "the phrase 'question of arbitrability' has a ... limited scope." *Howsam v. Dean Witter Reynolds, Inc.,* 537 U.S. 79, 83, 123 S.Ct. 588, 154 L.Ed.2d 491 (2002). Indeed, we have "found the phrase [question of arbitrability] applicable in the kind of narrow circumstance where contracting parties would likely have expected a court to have decided the gateway matter, where they are not likely to have thought that they had agreed that an arbitrator would do so, and, consequently, where reference of the gateway dispute to the court avoids the risk of forcing parties to arbitrate a matter that they may well not have agreed to arbitrate." *Id.,* at 83–84. Giv-

U.S., at 541, 115 S.Ct. 2322. In short, since we do not know how the arbitrator will construe the remedial limitations, the questions whether they render the parties' agreements unenforceable and whether it is for courts or arbitrators to decide enforceability in the first instance are unusually abstract. As in *Vimar,* the proper course is to compel arbitration. The judgment of the Court of Appeals is reversed, and the case is remanded for further proceedings consistent with this opinion.

It is so ordered.

* * *

Questions

1. What are the advantages of waiting until the arbitrator has ruled on the issue of whether the arbitration agreement precludes an award of treble damages versus getting a rule from the Court now? Is there a tension between the competing policies of preventing unwarranted attacks on arbitral authority and avoiding unwarranted arbitrations? See William W. Park, *Determining an Arbitrator's Jurisdiction: Timing and Finality in American Law*, 8 Nev. L.J. 135 (2007).

2. Can you draft an arbitration clause that clearly states the intent of the parties with respect to the issues raised in the preceding three cases? The preceding six cases? Must such a clause be complex, or can it be as simple as "the arbitrator has jurisdiction to decide all issues"?

3. In *Moses H. Cone*, the Court stated that the FAA "establishes that, as a matter of federal law, any doubts concerning the scope of arbitrable issues should be resolved in favor of arbitration, whether the problem at hand is the construction of the contract language itself or an allegation of *waiver*, delay, or like defense to arbitrability." (Emphasis added.) Should a court, or an arbitrator, entertain a claim that a party has waived its right to arbitrate by engaging in certain conduct (e.g., by conducting extensive discovery and engaging in motion practice and then later requesting the court to compel arbitration in accordance with the parties pre-dispute arbitration agreement)? The First Circuit has ruled that "waiver by conduct, at least where due to litigation-related activity, is presumptively an issue for the court." See Marie v. Allied Home Mortg. Corp., 402 F.3d 1 (1st Cir. 2005). Do you agree?

4. Should a court enforce an arbitral award in which an arbitrator applied a contractual limitation on remedies in a case involving a statute that did not impose such remedial limitations? Does this deprive the winning party of a substantive right? We will return to this question in Chapter 4.2.C.

* * *

en our presumption in favor of arbitration, *Moses H. Cone Memorial Hospital v. Mercury Constr. Corp.,* 460 U.S. 1, 24–25, 103 S.Ct. 927, 74 L.Ed.2d 765 (1983), we think the preliminary question whether the remedial limitations at issue here prohibit an award of RICO treble damages is not a question of arbitrability.

3. MUTUAL ASSENT

When a court is presented with a petition to stay litigation under Section 3 or a petition to compel arbitration under Section 4 of the Federal Arbitration Act, the Court must engage in a two-step inquiry. First, it must determine whether there is a valid agreement to arbitrate between the parties, and then it must determine whether the dispute comes within the arbitration clause. See *Pennzoil Exploration & Production Co. v. Ramco Energy Ltd.*, 139 F.3d 1061 (5th Cir. 1998). The first step requires the court to consider the validity of the agreement on the basis of state contract law principles. In applying state law to determine whether a valid agreement to arbitrate exists, a court considers such contract formation issues as mutual assent, consideration, and the Statute of Frauds. The second step requires the court to construe the scope of the arbitration clause to determine whether it applies to the particular dispute. In doing so, the court must interpret the arbitration clause in light of the FAA's presumption of arbitrability. Thus, litigation under Section 3 or 4 of the FAA involves a complex blend of state and federal law.

In the last section we observed the operation of the second step of the inquiry. We saw how the presumption of arbitrability inserts a powerful pro-arbitration tilt into the interpretation of arbitration agreements. In this section, we examine how state courts treat one frequently raised issue of contract formation—lack of mutual assent. In following sections, we will explore how the contract defenses of fraud, illegality, duress, and unconscionability bear on the enforcement of arbitration agreements.

* * *

A. KNOWING CONSENT

Specht v. Netscape Communications Corp.

306 F.3d 17 (2d Cir. 2002).

■ SOTOMAYOR, CIRCUIT JUDGE.

This is an appeal from a judgment of the Southern District of New York denying a motion by defendants-appellants Netscape Communications Corporation and its corporate parent, America Online, Inc. (collectively, "defendants" or "Netscape"), to compel arbitration and to stay court proceedings. In order to resolve the central question of arbitrability presented here, we must address issues of contract formation in cyberspace. Principally, we are asked to determine whether plaintiffs-appellees ("plaintiffs"), by acting upon defendants' invitation to download free software made available on defendants' webpage, agreed to be bound by the software's license terms (which included the arbitration clause at issue), even though plaintiffs could not have learned of the existence of those terms unless, prior to executing the download, they had scrolled down the webpage to a screen located below the download button. We agree with the district court that a reasonably prudent Internet user in circumstances such as these would not have known or learned of the existence of the license terms before responding to defendants' invitation to download the free software, and that defendants therefore did not provide reasonable notice of the license terms. In consequence, plaintiffs' bare act of downloading the software did not unambiguously manifest assent to the arbitration provision contained in the license terms. . . .

We therefore affirm the district court's denial of defendants' motion to compel arbitration and to stay court proceedings.

BACKGROUND

I. Facts

In three related putative class actions, plaintiffs alleged that, unknown to them, their use of SmartDownload transmitted to defendants private information about plaintiffs' downloading of files from the Internet, thereby effecting an electronic surveillance of their online activities in violation of two federal statutes, the Electronic Communications Privacy Act, 18 U.S.C. §§ 2510 *et seq.*, and the Computer Fraud and Abuse Act, 18 U.S.C. § 1030.

Specifically, plaintiffs alleged that when they first used Netscape's Communicator—a software program that permits Internet browsing—the program created and stored on each of their computer hard drives a small text file known as a "cookie" that functioned "as a kind of electronic identification tag for future communications" between their computers and Netscape. Plaintiffs further alleged that when they installed SmartDownload—a separate software "plug-in" that served to enhance Communicator's browsing capabilities—SmartDownload created and stored on their computer hard drives another string of characters, known as a "Key," which similarly functioned as an identification tag in future communications with Netscape. According to the complaints in this case, each time a computer user employed Communicator to download a file from the Internet, SmartDownload "assume[d] from Communicator the task of downloading" the file and transmitted to Netscape the address of the file being downloaded together with the cookie created by Communicator and the Key created by SmartDownload. These processes, plaintiffs claim, constituted unlawful "eavesdropping" on users of Netscape's software products as well as on Internet websites from which users employing SmartDownload downloaded files.

In the time period relevant to this litigation, Netscape offered on its website various software programs, including Communicator and SmartDownload, which visitors to the site were invited to obtain free of charge. It is undisputed that five of the six named plaintiffs—Michael Fagan, John Gibson, Mark Gruber, Sean Kelly, and Sherry Weindorf—downloaded Communicator from the Netscape website. These plaintiffs acknowledge that when they proceeded to initiate installation of Communicator, they were automatically shown a scrollable text of that program's license agreement and were not permitted to complete the installation until they had clicked on a "Yes" button to indicate that they accepted all the license terms.[4] If a user attempted to install Communicator without clicking "Yes," the installation would be aborted. All five named user plaintiffs [plaintiffs suing for harm they allegedly incurred as computer users] expressly agreed to Communicator's license terms by clicking "Yes." The Communicator license agreement that these plaintiffs saw made no mention of SmartDownload or other plug-in programs, and stated that "[t]hese terms apply to Netscape Communicator and Netscape Navigator" and that "all disputes relating to this Agreement (excepting any dispute relating to intellectual property rights)" are subject to "binding arbitration in Santa Clara County, California."

Although Communicator could be obtained independently of SmartDownload, all the named user plaintiffs, except Fagan, downloaded and installed Communicator in connection with downloading SmartDownload. Each of these plaintiffs allegedly arrived at a Netscape webpage captioned "SmartDownload Communicator" that urged them to "Download With Confidence Using SmartDownload!" At or near the bottom of the screen facing plaintiffs was the prompt "Start Download" and a tinted button labeled "Download." By clicking on the button, plaintiffs initiated the download of SmartDownload. Once that process was complete, SmartDownload, as its first plug-in task, permitted plaintiffs to proceed with downloading and installing Communicator, an operation that was accompanied by the clickwrap display of Communicator's license terms described above.

The signal difference between downloading Communicator and downloading SmartDownload was that no clickwrap presentation accompanied the latter operation. Instead, once plaintiffs Gibson, Gruber, Kelly, and Weindorf had clicked on the "Download" button located at or near the bottom of their screen, and the downloading of SmartDownload was complete, these plaintiffs encountered no further information about the plug-in program or the existence of license terms governing its use. The sole reference to SmartDownload's license terms on the "SmartDownload Com-

4. This kind of online software license agreement has come to be known as "clickwrap" (by analogy to "shrinkwrap," used in the licensing of tangible forms of software sold in packages) because it "presents the user with a message on his or her computer screen, requiring that the user manifest his or her assent to the terms of the license agreement by clicking on an icon. The product cannot be obtained or used unless and until the icon is clicked." *Specht,* 150 F.Supp.2d at 593–94 (footnote omitted). Just as breaking the shrinkwrap seal and using the enclosed computer program after encountering notice of the existence of governing license terms has been deemed by some courts to constitute assent to those terms in the context of tangible software, *see, e.g., ProCD, Inc. v. Zeidenberg,* 86 F.3d 1447, 1451 (7th Cir.1996), so clicking on a webpage's clickwrap button after receiving notice of the existence of license terms has been held by some courts to manifest an Internet user's assent to terms governing the use of downloadable intangible software, *see, e.g., Hotmail Corp. v. Van$Money Pie Inc.,* 47 U.S.P.Q.2d 1020, 1025 (N.D.Cal.1998).

municator'' webpage was located in text that would have become visible to plaintiffs only if they had scrolled down to the next screen.

Had plaintiffs scrolled down instead of acting on defendants' invitation to click on the ''Download'' button, they would have encountered the following invitation: ''Please review and agree to the terms of the *Netscape SmartDownload software license agreement* before downloading and using the software.'' Plaintiffs Gibson, Gruber, Kelly, and Weindorf averred in their affidavits that they never saw this reference to the SmartDownload license agreement when they clicked on the ''Download'' button. They also testified during depositions that they saw no reference to license terms when they clicked to download SmartDownload, although under questioning by defendants' counsel, some plaintiffs added that they could not ''remember'' or be ''sure'' whether the screen shots of the SmartDownload page attached to their affidavits reflected precisely what they had seen on their computer screens when they downloaded SmartDownload.

In sum, plaintiffs Gibson, Gruber, Kelly, and Weindorf allege that the process of obtaining SmartDownload contrasted sharply with that of obtaining Communicator. Having selected SmartDownload, they were required neither to express unambiguous assent to that program's license agreement nor even to view the license terms or become aware of their existence before proceeding with the invited download of the free plug-in program. Moreover, once these plaintiffs had initiated the download, the existence of SmartDownload's license terms was not mentioned while the software was running or at any later point in plaintiffs' experience of the product.

Even for a user who, unlike plaintiffs, did happen to scroll down past the download button, SmartDownload's license terms would not have been immediately displayed in the manner of Communicator's clickwrapped terms. Instead, if such a user had seen the notice of SmartDownload's terms and then clicked on the underlined invitation to review and agree to the terms, a hypertext link would have taken the user to a separate webpage entitled ''License & Support Agreements.'' The first paragraph on this page read, in pertinent part:

> The use of each Netscape software product is governed by a license agreement. You must read and agree to the license agreement terms BEFORE acquiring a product. Please click on the appropriate link below to review the current license agreement for the product of interest to you before acquisition. For products available for download, you must read and agree to the license agreement terms BEFORE you install the software. If you do not agree to the license terms, do not download, install or use the software.

Below this paragraph appeared a list of license agreements, the first of which was ''*License Agreement for Netscape Navigator and Netscape Communicator Product Family* (Netscape Navigator, Netscape Communicator and Netscape SmartDownload).'' If the user clicked on that link, he or she would be taken to yet another webpage that contained the full text of a license agreement that was identical in every respect to the Communicator license agreement except that it stated that its "terms apply to Netscape Communicator, Netscape Navigator, and Netscape SmartDownload." The license agreement granted the user a nonexclusive license to use and reproduce the software, subject to certain terms:

> BY CLICKING THE ACCEPTANCE BUTTON OR INSTALLING OR USING NETSCAPE COMMUNICATOR, NETSCAPE NAVIGATOR, OR NETSCAPE SMARTDOWNLOAD SOFTWARE (THE "PRODUCT"), THE INDIVIDUAL OR ENTITY LICENSING THE PRODUCT ("LICENSEE") IS CONSENTING TO BE BOUND BY AND IS BECOMING A PARTY TO THIS AGREEMENT. IF LICENSEE DOES NOT AGREE TO ALL OF THE TERMS OF THIS AGREEMENT, THE BUTTON INDICATING NON-ACCEPTANCE MUST BE SELECTED, AND LICENSEE MUST NOT INSTALL OR USE THE SOFTWARE.

Among the license terms was a provision requiring virtually all disputes relating to the agreement to be submitted to arbitration:

> Unless otherwise agreed in writing, all disputes relating to this Agreement (excepting any dispute relating to intellectual property rights) shall be subject to final and binding arbitration in Santa Clara County, California, under the auspices of JAMS/EndDispute, with the losing party paying all costs of arbitration....

II. Proceedings Below

In the district court, defendants moved to compel arbitration and to stay court proceedings pursuant to the Federal Arbitration Act ("FAA"), 9 U.S.C. § 4, arguing that the disputes reflected in the complaints, like any other dispute relating to the SmartDownload license agreement, are subject to the arbitration clause contained in that agreement. Finding that Netscape's webpage, unlike typical examples of clickwrap, neither adequately alerted users to the existence of SmartDownload's license terms nor required users unambiguously to manifest assent to those terms as a condition of downloading the product, the court held that the user plaintiffs had not entered into the SmartDownload license agreement. *Specht,* 150 F.Supp.2d at 595–96. [Defendants appealed.] . . .

DISCUSSION

I. Standard of Review and Applicable Law

. . . The FAA provides that a "written provision in any . . . contract evidencing a transaction involving commerce to settle by arbitration a controversy thereafter arising out of such contract or transaction . . . shall be valid, irrevocable, and enforceable, save upon such grounds as exist at law or in equity for the revocation of any contract." 9 U.S.C. § 2. It is well settled that a court may not compel arbitration until it has resolved "the question of the very existence" of the contract embodying the arbitration clause. *Interocean Shipping Co. v. Nat'l Shipping & Trading Corp.,* 462 F.2d 673, 676 (2d Cir.1972). "[A]rbitration is a matter of contract and a party cannot be required to submit to arbitration any dispute which he has not agreed so to submit." *AT & T Techs., Inc. v. Communications Workers of Am.,* 475 U.S. 643, 648, 106 S.Ct. 1415, 89 L.Ed.2d 648 (1986) (quotation marks omitted). Unless the parties clearly provide otherwise, "the question of arbitrability—whether a[n] .... agreement creates a duty for the parties to arbitrate the particular grievance-is undeniably an issue for judicial determination." *Id.* at 649, 106 S.Ct. 1415.

The district court properly concluded that in deciding whether parties agreed to arbitrate a certain matter, a court should generally apply state-law principles to the issue of contract formation. *Mehler v. Terminix Int'l Co.,* 205 F.3d 44, 48 (2d Cir. 2000); see also *Perry v. Thomas,* 482 U.S. 483, 492 n. 9, 107 S.Ct. 2520, 96 L.Ed.2d 426 (1987) ("[S]tate law, whether of legislative or judicial origin, is applicable [to the determination of whether the parties agreed to arbitrate] *if* that law arose to govern issues concerning the validity, revocability, and enforceability of contracts generally."). Therefore, state law governs the question of whether the parties in the present case entered into an agreement to arbitrate disputes relating to the SmartDownload license agreement. The district court further held that California law governs the question of contract formation here; the parties do not appeal that determination....

III. Whether the User Plaintiffs Had Reasonable Notice of and Manifested Assent to the SmartDownload License Agreement

... [A] transaction, in order to be a contract, requires a manifestation of agreement between the parties. See *Windsor Mills, Inc. v. Collins & Aikman Corp.,* 25 Cal.App.3d 987, 991, 101 Cal.Rptr. 347, 350 (1972) ("[C]onsent to, or acceptance of, the arbitration provision [is] necessary to create an agreement to arbitrate."); *see also* Cal. Com.Code § 2204(1) ("A contract for sale of goods may be made in any manner sufficient to show agreement, including conduct by both parties which recognizes the existence of such a contract"). Mutual manifestation of assent, whether by written or spoken word or by conduct, is the touchstone of contract. *Binder v. Aetna Life Ins. Co.,* 75 Cal.App.4th 832, 848, 89 Cal.Rptr.2d 540, 551 (1999); *cf.* Restatement (Second) of Contracts § 19(2) (1981) ("The conduct of a party is not effective as a manifestation of his assent unless he intends to engage in the conduct and knows or has reason to know that the other party may infer from his conduct that he assents"). Although an onlooker observing the disputed transactions in this case would have seen each of the user plaintiffs click on the SmartDownload "Download" button, see *Cedars Sinai Med. Ctr. v. Mid–West Nat'l Life Ins. Co.,* 118 F.Supp.2d 1002, 1008 (C.D.Cal.2000) ("In California, a party's intent to contract is judged objectively, by the party's outward manifestation of consent"), a consumer's clicking on a download button does not communicate assent to contractual terms if the offer did not make clear to the consumer that clicking on the download button would signify assent to those terms, see *Windsor Mills,* 25 Cal.App.3d at 992, 101 Cal.Rptr. at 351 ("[W]hen the offeree does not know that a proposal has been made to him this objective standard does not apply"). California's common law is clear that "an offeree, regardless of apparent manifestation of his consent, is not bound by inconspicuous contractual provisions of which he is unaware, contained in a document whose contractual nature is not obvious." Id.; see also *Marin Storage & Trucking, Inc. v. Benco Contracting & Eng'g, Inc.,* 89 Cal. App.4th 1042, 1049, 107 Cal.Rptr.2d 645, 651 (2001) (same).

Arbitration agreements are no exception to the requirement of manifestation of assent. "This principle of knowing consent applies with particular force to provisions for arbitration." *Windsor Mills,* 101 Cal.Rptr. at 351. Clarity and conspicuousness of arbitration terms are important in securing informed assent.... Thus, California contract law measures assent by an objective standard that takes into account both what the offeree said, wrote, or did and the transactional context in which the offeree verbalized or acted.

A. The Reasonably Prudent Offeree of Downloadable Software

Defendants argue that plaintiffs must be held to a standard of reasonable prudence and that, because notice of the existence of SmartDownload license terms was on the next scrollable screen, plaintiffs were on "inquiry notice" of those terms. We disagree with the proposition that a reasonably prudent offeree in plaintiffs' position would necessarily have known or learned of the existence of the SmartDownload license agreement prior to acting, so that plaintiffs may be held to have assented to that agreement with constructive notice of its terms.... It is true that "[a] party cannot avoid the terms of a contract on the ground that he or she failed to read it before signing." *Marin Storage & Trucking,* 89 Cal.App.4th at 1049, 107 Cal.Rptr.2d at 651. But courts are quick to add: "An exception to this general rule exists when the writing does not appear to be a contract and the terms are not called to the attention of the recipient. In such a case, no contract is formed with respect to the undisclosed term." *Id.; cf. Cory v. Golden State Bank,* 95 Cal.App.3d 360, 364, 157 Cal.Rptr. 538, 541 (1979) ("[T]he provision in question is effectively hidden from the view of money order purchasers until after the transactions are completed.... Under these circumstances, it must be concluded that the Bank's money order purchasers are not chargeable with either actual or constructive notice of the service charge provision, and therefore cannot be deemed to have consented to the provision as part of their transaction with the Bank").

Most of the cases cited by defendants in support of their inquiry-notice argument are drawn from the world of paper contracting. *See, e.g., Taussig v. Bode & Haslett,* 134 Cal. 260, 66 P. 259 (1901) (where party had opportunity to read leakage disclaimer printed on warehouse receipt, he had duty to do so); *In re First Capital Life Ins. Co.,* 34 Cal.App.4th 1283, 1288, 40 Cal.Rptr.2d 816, 820 (1995) (purchase of insurance policy after opportunity to read and understand policy terms creates binding agreement) ... [string citations omitted].

As the foregoing cases suggest, receipt of a physical document containing contract terms or notice thereof is frequently deemed, in the world of paper transactions, a sufficient circumstance to place the offeree on inquiry notice of those terms. "Every person who has actual notice of circumstances sufficient to put a prudent man upon inquiry as to a particular fact, has constructive notice of the fact itself in all cases in which, by prosecuting such inquiry, he might have learned such fact." Cal. Civ.Code § 19. These principles apply equally to the emergent world of online product delivery, pop-up screens, hyperlinked pages, clickwrap licensing, scrollable documents, and urgent admonitions to "Download Now!". What plaintiffs saw when they were being invited by defendants to download this fast, free plug-in called SmartDownload was a screen containing praise for the product and, at the very bottom of the screen, a "Download" button. Defendants argue that under the principles set forth in the cases cited above, a "fair and prudent person using ordinary care" would have been on inquiry notice of SmartDownload's license terms. *Shacket,* 651 F.Supp. at 690.

We are not persuaded that a reasonably prudent offeree in these circumstances would have known of the existence of license terms. Plaintiffs were responding to an offer that did not carry an immediately visible notice of the existence of license terms or require unambiguous manifestation of assent to those terms. Thus, plaintiffs' "apparent manifestation of ... consent" was to terms "contained in a document whose contractual nature [was] not obvious." *Windsor Mills,* 25 Cal.App.3d at 992, 101 Cal.Rptr. at 351. Moreover, the fact that, given the position of the scroll bar on their computer screens, plaintiffs may have been aware that an unexplored portion of the Netscape webpage remained below the download button does not mean that they reasonably should have concluded that this portion contained a notice of license terms. In their deposition testimony, plaintiffs variously stated that they used the scroll bar "[o]nly if there is something that I feel I need to see that is on-that is off the page," or that the elevated position of the scroll bar suggested the presence of "mere[ ] formalities, standard lower banner links" or "that the page is bigger than what I can see." Plaintiffs testified, and defendants did not refute, that plaintiffs were in fact unaware that defendants intended to attach license terms to the use of SmartDownload.

We conclude that in circumstances such as these, where consumers are urged to download free software at the immediate click of a button, a reference to the existence of license terms on a submerged screen is not sufficient to place consumers on inquiry or constructive notice of those terms. The SmartDownload webpage screen was "printed in such a manner that it tended to conceal the fact that it was an express acceptance of [Netscape's] rules and regulations." *Larrus,* 266 P.2d at 147. Internet users may have, as defendants put it, "as much time as they need[ ]" to scroll through multiple screens on a webpage, but there is no reason to assume that viewers will scroll down to subsequent screens simply because screens are there. When products are "free" and users are invited to download them in the absence of reasonably conspicuous notice that they are about to bind themselves to contract terms, the transactional circumstances cannot be fully analogized to those in the paper world of arm's-length bargaining. In the next two sections, we discuss case law and other legal authorities that have addressed the circumstances of computer sales, software licensing, and online transacting. Those authorities tend strongly to support our conclusion that plaintiffs did not manifest assent to SmartDownload's license terms.

B. Shrinkwrap Licensing and Related Practices

Defendants cite certain well-known cases involving shrinkwrap licensing and related commercial practices in support of their contention that plaintiffs became bound by the SmartDownload license terms by virtue of inquiry notice. For example, in *Hill v. Gateway 2000, Inc.,* 105 F.3d 1147 (7th Cir.1997), the Seventh Circuit held that where a purchaser had ordered a computer over the telephone, received the order in a shipped box containing the computer along with printed contract terms, and did not return the computer within the thirty days required by the terms, the purchaser was bound by the contract. *Id.* at 1148–49. In *ProCD, Inc. v. Zeidenberg,* the same court held that where an individual purchased software in a box containing license terms which were displayed on the computer screen every time the user executed the software program, the user had sufficient opportunity to review the terms and to return the software, and so was contractually bound after retaining the product. *ProCD,* 86 F.3d at 1452 ... [string citations omitted].

These cases do not help defendants. To the extent that [it holds] that the purchaser of a computer or tangible software is contractually bound after failing to object to printed license terms provided with the product, *Hill* do[es] not differ markedly from the cases involving traditional paper contracting discussed in the previous section. Insofar as the purchaser in *ProCD* was confronted with conspicuous, mandatory license terms every time he ran the software on his computer, that case actually undermines defendants' contention that downloading in the absence of conspicuous terms is an act that binds plaintiffs to those terms....

C. Online Transactions

Cases in which courts have found contracts arising from Internet use do not assist defendants, because in those circumstances there was much clearer notice than in the present case that a user's act would manifest assent to contract terms. *See, e.g., Hotmail Corp. v. Van$Money Pie Inc.,* 47 U.S.P.Q.2d 1020, 1025 (N.D.Cal.1998) (granting preliminary injunction based in part on breach of "Terms of Service" agreement, to which defendants had assented); *America Online, Inc. v. Booker,* 781 So.2d 423, 425 (Fla.Dist.Ct.App. 2001) (upholding forum selection clause in "freely negotiated agreement" contained in online terms of service); *Caspi v. Microsoft Network, L.L.C.,* 323 N.J.Super. 118, 732 A.2d 528, 530, 532–33 (N.J.Super.Ct.App.Div.1999) (upholding forum selection clause where subscribers to online software were required to review license terms in scrollable window and to click "I Agree" or "I Don't Agree"); *Barnett v. Network Solutions, Inc.,* 38 S.W.3d 200, 203–04 (Tex.App. 2001) (upholding forum selection clause in online contract for registering Internet domain names that required users to scroll through terms before accepting or rejecting them); . . .

After reviewing the California common law and other relevant legal authority, we conclude that under the circumstances here, plaintiffs' downloading of SmartDownload did not constitute acceptance of defendants' license terms. Reasonably conspicuous notice of the existence of contract terms and unambiguous manifestation of assent to those terms by consumers are essential if electronic bargaining is to have integrity and credibility. We hold that a reasonably prudent offeree in plaintiffs' position would not have known or learned, prior to acting on the invitation to download, of the reference to SmartDownload's license terms hidden below the "Download" button on the next screen. We affirm the district court's conclusion that the user plaintiffs, including Fagan, are not bound by the arbitration clause contained in those terms.

CONCLUSION

For the foregoing reasons, we affirm the district court's denial of defendants' motion to compel arbitration and to stay court proceedings.

* * *

Questions

1. How does the court in *Specht v. Netscape* distinguish the decisions in *ProCD v. Zeidenberg* and *Hill v. Gateway 2000?* Why is there sufficient manifestation of assent in those cases but not in *Specht*? After this case, how would you advise Netscape to redesign its SmartDownload software to make the arbitration clause enforceable? Would it be sufficient if there were a web page that noted the existence of a license, gave an optional website where the terms could be found, and required the user to click on "I assent" to continue, all without displaying to the user the terms of the license? If so, is *Specht* really a requirement to ensure knowing consent, or is it merely a meaningless formality?

2. How does the court distinguish the cases holding that a party failing to read a contract's terms is nonetheless bound to the contract's provisions? Isn't the objection to the kind of "browse-wrap" used here that the viewers failed to click on, and read, the terms of the contract that were available to them? If that is the objection, how does it differ from a buyer who fails to read the fine print on the back of a form and later complains that the terms were onerous? Do you find the distinction convincing?

3. Does the court in this case suggest that in all cases involving contract enforcement, a court should engage in a detailed factual examination of the conditions under which a contract is formed to determine whether there was knowing and voluntary assent? Should it hold a hearing to determine assent? Is a hearing required in all cases, or only in cases in which there is an arbitration clause? If the latter, wouldn't such a ruling be preempted by the FAA pursuant to the command of *Perry v. Thomas* that state law rules that are specific to arbitration are preempted?

4. Similarly, note that the *Specht* court, quoting another case, stated that "the principle of knowing consent applies with particular force to provisions for arbitration. *Windsor Mills,* 101 Cal.Rptr. at 351." Is the court suggesting that it should impose a more stringent scrutiny of contractual consent when arbitration clauses are involved? If so, is this ruling preempted?

5. If there is an arbitration clause in the contract, should issues of contract formation be left for the arbitrator to decide? If not, why not?

6. In *Specht*, the plaintiffs alleged that the defendant had violated federal statutes designed to protect consumers against computer fraud and electronic invasions of privacy. Could the plaintiffs successfully argue that even if they had consented to the arbitration clause, these claims should not fall within the promise to arbitrate? Would it help if they could show, for example, that Congress intended in these statutes to give individuals a right to sue in a federal court? Could they argue that the very concerns about fraud and surreptitious electronic manipulation that led to the enactment of the statutes were at work in the arbitration clause here?

7. Consent issues often arise when arbitration clauses are buried in fine print, a prolix form agreement, or a mountain of documents. See, e.g., Gaylord Dep't Stores of Alabama, Inc. v. Stephens, 404 So.2d 586, 588 (Ala. 1981) (jury trial waiver provision "buried in paragraph thirty-four in a contract containing forty-six paragraphs"); Kinkel v. Cingular Wireless, LLC, 828 N.E.2d 812 (Ill. App. 2005) (extremely small typeface); Shaffer v. ACS Government Services, Inc., 321 F.Supp.2d 682 (D.Md. 2004) (refusing to enforce arbitration clause contained on page 56 of a 71–page employee guidebook); but see Nagrampa v. Mailcoups Inc., 401 F.3d 1024, 1029 (9th Cir. 2005) (enforcing arbitration clause found on the twenty-fifth page of a thirty-page franchise agreement). In the employment context, courts sometimes find lack of consent when the employer pressures an employee to sign an arbitration agreement without reading it. See, e.g., Brennan v. Bally Total Fitness, 198 F.Supp.2d 377, 383 (S.D.N.Y. 2002) (refusing to enforce arbitration agreement where employer gave employee no more than fifteen minutes to review a sixteen-page single-spaced agreement). Should there be a uniform standard of consent that is applied to consumer, employment, commercial, and other contexts in which arbitration clauses are used?

8. Can consent issues also arise in *post-dispute* arbitration agreements? Consider *Metters v. Ralphs Grocery Co.*, 74 Cal.Rptr.3d 210 (Cal.App.2008). An employee of Ralphs Grocery was told to sign a company "form" if he wanted to pursue informal means of resolving an actual dispute he was having. The employee signed the form; however, the form, which contained an arbitration clause, did not appear to be a contract and the form did not clearly inform the employee that he was agreeing to arbitrate. Thus, the court held that the employee was not bound by the arbitration clause:

> Ralphs relies on the general rule that "ordinarily one who signs an instrument which on its face is a contract is deemed to assent to all its terms. A party cannot avoid the terms of a contract on the ground that he or she failed to read it before signing. [Citations.]" (Marin Storage & Trucking, Inc. v. Benco Contracting & Engineering, Inc. (2001) 89 Cal.App.4th 1042, 1049 [107 Cal.Rptr.2d 645].) This is so even where the contracting party relied on misrepresentations by the other party that it was not necessary to read the contract before signing. "[O]ne party's unreasonable reliance on the other's misrepresentations, resulting in a failure to read a written agreement before signing it, is an insufficient basis, under the doctrine of fraud in the execution, for permitting that party to avoid an arbitration agreement contained in the contract." (Rosenthal v. Great Western Financial Securities Corp. (1996) 14 Cal.4th 394, 423 [58 Cal.Rptr.2d 875, 926 P.2d 1061].)
>
> But if the one who signs the instrument is unaware of the contractual provisions, he cannot be said to have agreed to them. Thus, "[a]n exception to [the] general rule exists when the writing does not appear to be a contract and the terms are not called to the attention of the recipient. In such a case, no contract is formed with respect to the undisclosed term. [Citations omitted.]

9. As the *Specht* court notes, the FAA applies only to "written" arbitration agreements. Can an argument be made that cyber agreements are not "written", and therefore are not governed by the FAA? See Stephen E. Friedman, *Protecting Consumers from Arbitration Provisions in Cyberspace, the Federal Arbitration Act and E–Sign Act Notwithstanding*, 57 Cath. U. L. Rev. 377 (2008).

* * *

B. UNSIGNED ARBITRATION AGREEMENTS

Daisy Manufacturing Co., Inc. v. NCR Corporation

29 F.3d 389 (8th Cir. 1994).

■ FRIEDMAN, SENIOR CIRCUIT JUDGE.

I

A. In 1976, the appellant NCR Corporation (NCR) entered into an agreement with Daisy Division Victor Comptometer Corporation governing the "terms and conditions" under which the customer would obtain "equipment, programs, and systems and maintenance services" from NCR. The contract, called a "Universal Agreement," was a detailed printed document that, according to NCR, it "typically signs . . . at the onset of a commercial relationship with its customers." The "Universal Agreement" included the following arbitration provision:

> Disputes—Any controversy or claim, including any claim of misrepresentation, arising out of or related to this Agreement and/or any

Arbit. clause

contract hereafter entered into between NCR and Customer, or the breach thereof, or the furnishing of any equipment or service by NCR to Customer, shall be settled by arbitration.

. . . On November 15, 1983, Daisy Manufacturing Company, Inc., was created and "purchased certain of the assets of the Daisy Division" of Kidde Recreation Products, Inc., which in turn had acquired the Daisy Division from Victor Comptometer Corp. Frank Tarr, who had signed the Universal Agreement Amendment as Vice–President Finance and Administration of Daisy Manufacturing Co., assumed the same position in the new entity.

Daisy Manufacturing Company, Inc., continued the same line of business as Daisy Manufacturing Co., at the same address and with some of the same senior management.

Both before and after October 15, 1983, Daisy placed a number of orders with NCR for computers and computer-related equipment. Both NCR and Daisy used the names "Daisy Manufacturing Co." and "Daisy Manufacturing Co., Inc." interchangeably.

The record contains no evidence that after November 15, 1983, (1) Daisy told NCR (a) that a new entity had supplanted Daisy Manufacturing Co. or (b) that the Daisy Manufacturing Co. with which NCR continued to deal was not the same company with which it had previously dealt for a number of years, or (2) that when NCR continued to show Daisy Manufacturing Co., as the customer, Daisy attempted to correct the alleged improper designation. . . .

B. In October 1991, Daisy ordered from NCR the computer system that gave rise to this litigation. Mr. James Moody, as Executive Vice–President and Chief Financial Officer, signed the purchase order for "Daisy Manufacturing Co." The purchase order included the following statement:

> [ ] Except as indicated below, furnishing of equipment, programs and/or services specified herein shall be pursuant to the terms of the Universal Agreement entered into by NCR and Customer.
>
> [ ] Terms and conditions on reverse side apply.

On the reverse side, the purchase order form set forth various terms, including the following arbitration clause:

> DISPUTES—Any controversy or claim, including any claim of misrepresentation, rising out of or related to this Agreement or the breach thereof, or the furnishing of any equipment or service by NCR to Customer, shall be settled by arbitration.

Daisy did not check either box.

Daisy's complaint states that "[i]mmediately upon the delivery" of the computer software "Daisy began experiencing numerous problems which have greatly compromised the performance and operation of their business."

C. In April 1993, Daisy Manufacturing Co., Inc., filed the present district court diversity action against NCR ... The complaint accused NCR of breach of contract (the October 1991 purchase order), fraud, and violation of the Racketeer Influenced and Corrupt Organizations Act [RICO], 18 U.S.C. § 1961 et seq. (1988).

NCR moved, pursuant to Sections 3 and 4 of the Federal Arbitration Act, 9 U.S.C. (1988) and the Arkansas Uniform Arbitration Act, Ark.Code Ann. §§ 16–108–201 (1987), to compel arbitration and to stay the judicial proceedings. In a 10–page letter opinion, the district court denied the motion because it "cannot say that Daisy is contractually bound to arbitrate the disputes that are the subject of this action." The court held that

> ... The mere fact that Daisy as a newly formed corporation continued a business relationship that had previously existed between NCR and the Daisy Division of a separate corporation is insufficient to subject Daisy to the agreement.... Daisy was incorporated in 1983 and thus became a separate and distinct legal entity. The fact that it may have had the same or some of the same officers, directors, or shareholders, or continued business at the same physical location is insufficient to allow the court to disregard the corporate existence.

The court apparently concluded that Daisy's failure to check either box on the purchase order prevented the application of the arbitration provision on the reverse side of that order....

II

... The district court held that Daisy Manufacturing Co., Inc. was not bound by the arbitration provisions in the amended Universal Agreement because those documents had been signed not by that entity but by its predecessors, Daisy Division Victor Comptometer Corporation and Daisy Manufacturing Co. The court stated that "[t]he mere fact that Daisy as a newly formed corporation continued a business relationship that had previously existed between NCR and the Daisy Division of a separate corporation is insufficient to subject Daisy to the agreement ... The fact that it may have had the same or some of the same officers, directors, or shareholders, or continued business at the same physical location is insufficient to allow the court to disregard the corporate existence."

The issues, however, were not whether the new corporate entity "continued a business relationship that had previously existed" between its predecessors and NCR or whether the court should "disregard the corporate existence" of Daisy Manufacturing Co., Inc. The issues were (A) whether the course of dealing between the parties after Daisy Manufacturing Co., Inc. was formed in 1983, in which both treated the latter as the same customer as its predecessor Daisy Manufacturing Co., bound Daisy Manufacturing Co., Inc. to the arbitration provision of the amended Universal Agreement that the predecessor had signed, and (B) whether Daisy Manufacturing Co., Inc. was not bound by the arbitration provision in the Universal Agreement or the purchase order agreement because it had not checked either box on the purchase order to indicate which terms and conditions it wanted to govern the computer system purchase order. We hold that the district court erred in both of the grounds upon which it concluded that Daisy Manufacturing Co., Inc. was not bound by the arbitration provision of the Universal Agreement or the purchase order . . .

[The court found that although Daisy Manufacturing was formed as a separate entity in 1983, it continued to deal with NCR as Daisy Division had done previously. The court reasoned that because Daisy Manufacturing did not notify NCR that it was a new entity, by its conduct it ratified and accepted the amended Universal Agreement that its predecessor had signed and, therefore, was bound by it.]

B. The next question is whether Daisy's failure to check either box on the purchase order avoided Daisy's obligation under the Universal Agreement (and the purchase order itself) to arbitrate its dispute with NCR. The failure to check did not have that effect.

The two boxes gave Daisy the opportunity to decide whether the terms governing the computer system sale would be those in the "Universal Agreement entered into by NCR and customer" or those on the reverse side of the purchase order. The purchase order thus reflected the parties' understanding that the customer had entered into, and was bound by, the Universal Agreement. The arbitration clause of the Universal Agreement covered any dispute "arising out of or related to . . . any contract hereafter entered into between NCR and Customer . . .," which included the 1991 purchase order.

The box-checking provisions thus gave Daisy the opportunity to have the terms on the reverse side of the purchase order rather than those in the Universal Agreement govern the particular transaction. That provision, however, cannot fairly be interpreted as giving Daisy a third choice: avoiding the application of either the Universal Agreement or the purchase order by not checking either box. The effect of Daisy's failure to check either box was to confirm the applicability of the Universal Agreement to the particular purchase contract between NCR and its customer, as the Universal Agreement contemplated.

Daisy relies on the earlier decision of the Seventh Circuit in *Matterhorn Inc. v. NCR Corporation,* 763 F.2d 866 (1985). That case involved a similar situation, and the district court, on being requested to stay Matterhorn's suit for breach of contract and to order arbitration, submitted to the jury the question whether the purchase order on which Matterhorn had not checked either box incorporated the arbitration clause of the Universal Agreement. The jury answered that question "no" and the court refused to order arbitration. The court of appeals affirmed, on the ground it could not say that the jury verdict was "irrational." *Id.* at 875. Daisy points to the following statement in the opinion:

> The purchase order can therefore be interpreted, if barely, as giving the buyer two options that are not exclusive and a residual option—to be governed by the general law, with dispute resolution by courts rather than arbitrators.

Id. at 874.

This passing dictum is insufficient to refute our reasoning above. More in point is the following statement in *Matterhorn:*

> The question of arbitrability ought to turn not on what the method of supersession is called, but on whether the court can infer from the whole course of dealings between the parties that they intended the arbitration clause in their initial contract to govern disputes arising out of the alleged attempt to supersede that contract.

Id. at 873.

Here, as we have shown, "the whole course of dealings between the parties" indicates that they understood and intended that the Universal Agreement signed by Daisy Manufacturing Co., Inc.'s predecessors, which included the arbitration provision, would "govern disputes" arising out of or relating to the purchase of the computer system by Daisy from NCR.

If, when it signed the purchase order, Daisy did not want to be bound by the arbitration provisions of either that order or the Universal Agreement, it could have explicitly so stated on the purchase order by writing something like "no arbitration of any dispute arising out of this purchase order." That would have alerted NCR to Daisy's position and given NCR the opportunity, if it did not want to do business on that basis, to decline to sell the computer system to Daisy. Daisy's mere failure to check one of the boxes on the purchase order, however, did not vitiate its continued obligation to arbitrate the dispute under the Universal Agreement . . .

The order of the district court is reversed, and the case is remanded with instructions to order arbitration and stay the judicial proceedings pending such arbitration.

* * *

Questions

1. Did Daisy Manufacturing objectively manifest consent to the arbitration clause? Was its refusal to check either box on the form a manifestation of its non-agreement to an arbitration clause? How could Daisy Manufacturing have indicated its non-agreement more clearly?

2. Who has the burden of proof on the issue of contract formation: the party refusing to agree to arbitration, or the party asserting the existence of mutual assent to arbitrate?

3. In this case, did the court conclude that a prior course of dealings between the parties overrides a manifestation of non-consent? How else could you understand the court's opinion?

* * *

Note on Unsigned Arbitration Agreements Sent By Email

Unsigned agreements often occur when one party sends "notice" of an arbitration agreement to another party via email. For example, in Campbell v. General Dynamics Gov't Sys. Corp., 407 F.3d 546 (1st Cir. 2005),

General Dynamics sent employees an e-mail message containing intranet links to its new Dispute Resolution Policy (DRP). The DRP itself stated that an employee's continued employment would constitute acceptance of the DRP, which included mandatory arbitration. The text of the e-mail message, however, said little of arbitration and nothing of discrimination claims; nor did it state that employees would be bound by arbitration if they continued to work for the employer. An employee denied having read the e-mail or learning of the arbitration clause until after he had been fired. General Dynamics responded with a tracking log demonstrating that the employee had opened the e-mail, but General Dynamics could not show that the employee had clicked on the link. The United States District Court for the District of Massachusetts held that General Dynamics' notice was insufficient:

> General Dynamics did nothing but send the email.... Plainly, even email technology enables the company to do better. The company did not, for example, require an employee to signify by return email that he had read the email, or more importantly, that he had read the attachments and understood their implications.... The practice of reflexively opening (so as to remove the unread tag) and deleting a mass email without reading it, or even being aware of it, is not uncommon.... [R]eceiving an email in a virtual mailbox is not the same as receiving a letter in a real mailbox.

Campbell v. General Dynamics Gov't Sys. Corp., 321 F.Supp.2d 142, 145, 148–49 (D. Mass. 2004).

On appeal, the First Circuit rejected the district court's skepticism toward e-mail as a method of communicating notice of an arbitration agreement. 407 F.3d 546 (2005). Nonetheless, the First Circuit affirmed the district court's finding that the notice provided in this case was insufficient to create a binding arbitration agreement. The court noted that General Dynamics had implemented all previous personnel matters via signed documents; in this context, the failure to require some sort of affirmative response (such as signing an acknowledgment or clicking a box on a computer screen) was insufficient to alert employees that they were entering into a contract. Moreover, the e-mail was worded so vaguely that "a reasonable employee could read the e-mail announcement and conclude that the [arbitration] Policy presented an optional alternative to litigation rather than a mandatory replacement for it." Thus, the court held that the e-mail failed to put employees "on inquiry notice of the unilateral contract offer contained in the linked materials."

* * *

C. ARBITRATION ARISING FROM A COURSE OF DEALINGS

Woodcrest Fabrics, Inc. v. B & R Textile Corporation

95 A.D.2d 656, 464 N.Y.S.2d 359 (App.Div.1st Dept. 1983).

■ SANDLER, J.P.

The petitioner-respondent Woodcrest Fabrics Inc. (Woodcrest) is a New York corporation, with offices in New York City, primarily engaged in converting textile fabrics purchased in the greige from various sources. The respondent-appellant B & R Textile Corp. (B & R) is a New York corporation, also with offices in New York City, primarily engaged in the conversion of textile fabrics. On seven occasions during 1981 B & R, acting through B.J. Stein Ltd. (Stein), textile brokers, sold Woodcrest various quantities of 100% textured polyester tissue faille. The procedure followed in these transactions was that Stein, acting on behalf of B & R, offered to sell the fabrics to Woodcrest, which accepted the offers and ordered the fabrics. For each transaction Stein sent sales notes to both the buyer and the seller confirming the sale. The sales notes set forth the terms of the transaction and provided for the settlement of any controversy arising under the contract by arbitration in accordance with the rules then obtaining of the General Arbitration Council of the Textile Industry. These notes included above the arbitration clause a notice in prominent print to the effect that duplicate copies of the note have been simultaneously sent to the buyer and seller, and that "the acknowledgment of sale by either party shall bind both parties to all of the terms and conditions set forth herein unless written notice of objection to its contents shall be made within 10 days after receipt of the sale note." The sales notes further included the statement that Stein was acting solely as broker . . .

The controversy with which we are concerned developed as a result of Woodcrest's refusal to pay for goods received pursuant to the transactions reflected in sales notes dated December 1 and December 23, 1981 on the claim that the goods were substandard and defective. By a demand for arbitration dated March 11, 1982, B & R sought to initiate arbitration proceedings against petitioner with regard to the failure to pay for these two shipments. Claiming that arbitration had never been discussed or agreed to with either the broker or B & R, and that the arbitration clauses on the sales notes were unauthorized and not binding, Woodcrest moved by order to show cause for an order staying the arbitration proceedings on the ground that there were no valid agreements to arbitrate. In opposition to the petition B & R submitted affidavits by an employee of Stein familiar with the transactions, B & R's President, and two independent brokers. Each affidavit attested that it is normal practice and usage for textile brokers in New York City to confirm transactions with the sending of a sales note to both the buyer and seller, and that it is standard in the textile industry in New York City for such notes to embody an arbitration provision. Indeed, the affidavits by the two independent brokers assert that all such sales notes contain an arbitration provision. No reply affidavits were submitted by Woodcrest. Notwithstanding Woodcrest's failure to put in issue the prevailing practice in the textile industry in New York City, or to disclaim its knowledge at any pertinent time of that practice, or its awareness of the arbitration clause on the face of the sales notes, Special Term stayed arbitration. The court concluded that there had been a failure to establish an agreement by Woodcrest to arbitrate . . .

We disagree and would accordingly reverse the order staying arbitration for two separate reasons. First, under long established principles, retention without objection for a reasonable period of time of broker's sales notes in which "the broker professes to act for both parties" constitutes a ratification of the broker's authority to enter into the purported transaction, and where the sales notes include an arbitration provision, constitutes a ratification of the broker's authority to include such a provision. [Citations omitted.] Second, applying what we believe to be the principle set forth in *Schubtex, Inc. v. Allen Snyder, Inc., supra,* the undisputed evidence of industry practice and custom, together with all the other circumstances presented, make this a proper case for "a determination that a written provision for arbitration has, in fact, been incorporated into the oral agreement of the parties in consequence of either trade usage or a prior course of dealings ..." (49 N.Y.2d at p. 6, 424 N.Y.S.2d 133, 399 N.E.2d 1154).

[On the first ground, the court found that each party had ratified the broker's authority. On the second ground, the court stated the following:]

An agreement to arbitrate, supplementing the express terms of a contract for the sale of goods, may be implied in a proper case from a course of past conduct or the custom and practice in the industry. An arbitration provision in a memorandum thereafter received by a party to the transaction would not ... constitute a material alteration of the terms of the contract. A party who receives such a memorandum without communicating its objection within a reasonable period of time would be bound by the arbitration provision, that provision having been (p. 6, 424 N.Y.S.2d 133, 399 N.E.2d 1154) "incorporated in the oral agreement of the parties in consequence of either trade usage or a prior course of dealings...." See UCC § 2–207. The undisputed facts in the record make this a compelling case for applying this principle.

The evidence is uncontested that it is the practice in the textile industry in New York City for broker negotiated transactions to be followed by sales notes to both parties setting forth the terms of the transaction and including arbitration provisions. Two of the affidavits by independent textile brokers assert that "all" such sales notes include arbitration provisions. Woodcrest is a New York corporation engaged in the textile business, and with an office in New York City. It did not deny that the practice in the industry was as described in the affidavits submitted on behalf of B & R, nor did it disclaim any knowledge of that practice. Nor did Woodcrest claim that it had not read the prominently printed arbitration provision on the face of the sales notes. Although not by itself sufficient to justify an inference of an agreement to arbitrate, the circumstance that there had been five previous transactions between the parties embodied in sales notes including an arbitration provision that had been retained without objection by Woodcrest provides additional support here for the inference of an agreement to arbitrate.

... Woodcrest entered into a number of textile transactions with B & R, knowing that B & R understood, and had a right to understand, that any dispute with regard to these transactions would be resolved by arbitration, and chose not to communicate its disagreement with that understanding, if it in fact had disagreed, until a dispute occurred. For the reasons set forth above we are persuaded that the sales notes received by Woodcrest with regard to each transaction, in the absence of any communication of objection to the arbitration provision within a reasonable time, constituted enforceable written agreements to arbitrate.

■ MILONAS, J. (Dissenting).

... The law is clear that an arbitration provision printed on a written confirmation of an order constitutes a material alteration of that proposed purchase order. Therefore, absent evidence of an express intention by the parties to resort to arbitration, they will not be found to have obligated themselves thereto. [Citations omitted.] In the instant matter, appellant asserts that the intent of the parties to employ arbitration is reflected by the previous dealings between them, as well as the custom and usage in the industry. However, the subject of arbitration was never discussed between appellant's broker and Woodcrest. Respondent did not sign or return its sales notes, nor is there any proof that it had actual knowledge of the arbitration clause. The fact that it may be the practice of textile brokers to use sales notes which include an arbitration provision is hardly sufficient indication of a common industry-wide custom or usage such as would bind the buyer to arbitration, thereby foreclosing its right to legal redress in the courts ... In *Schubtex, Inc. v. Allen Snyder, Inc., supra,* 49 N.Y.2d at 6, 424 N.Y.S.2d 133, 399 N.E.2d 1154, the Court of Appeals stated that:

> Although evidence of a prior course of dealing is relevant in determining whether the parties have agreed to submit their dispute to arbitration and a determination that their oral agreement included a provision for arbitration could in a proper case be implied from a course of past conduct or the custom and practice in the industry, such a determination must be supported by evidence which affirmatively establishes that the parties expressly agreed to arbitrate their disputes. As the concurring members of the court concede, "evidence of a trade usage or of a prior course of dealings may normally be utilized to supplement the express terms of a contract for the sale of goods" ... We would note also that this doctrine has been held to be applicable to arbitration agreements ...

... There is nothing in the record of this case to demonstrate that Woodcrest ever contracted itself to arbitrate its disputes with appellant. Respondent simply agreed to purchase certain material from B & R Textile and received a standard broker's sales note containing a provision for arbitration from the broker originally retained by the seller. Additional transactions ensued in the same manner. It cannot be inferred that Woodcrest obligated itself to arbitration because it did not cancel the order after arrival of the sales note or because it failed expressly to disavow the arbitration clause. Accordingly, Special Term appropriately granted the application to stay arbitration.

* * *

Questions

1. In *Woodcrest*, does the majority or the dissent present the more convincing argument?

2. The majority states that this is a "compelling case" for application of the principles of § 2–207 of the UCC. To what principle or provision of § 2–207 is the court referring? Section 2–207 provides:

> (1) A definite and seasonable expression of acceptance or a written confirmation, which is sent within a reasonable time operates as an acceptance even though it states terms additional to or different from those offered or agreed upon, unless acceptance is expressly made conditional on assent to the additional or different terms.
>
> (2) The additional terms are to be construed as proposals for additions to the contract. Between merchants such terms become part of the contract unless:
>
> > (a) they offer expressly limits acceptance to the terms of the offer;
> >
> > (b) they materially alter it; or
> >
> > (c) notification of objection to them has already been given or is given within a reasonable time after notice of them is received.
>
> (3) Conduct by both parties which recognizes the existence of a contract is sufficient to establish a contract for sale although the writings of the parties do not otherwise establish a contract. In such case the terms of the particular contract consist of those terms on which the writings of the parties agree, together with any supplementary terms incorporated under any other provision of this Act.

3. Is there a tension between the principle that a litigant should not be forced to arbitrate absent evidence of an express intent to do so, and the proposition, endorsed and applied by the majority in *Woodcrest Fabrics,* that a provision for arbitration can be implied from trade usage or a prior course of dealings?

* * *

Note on § 2–207 of the UCC and Arbitration

Arbitration clauses often are found in the forms that merchants use to signify their transactions. Thus, for example, an arbitration clause will sometimes appear on the back of a buyer's purchase order or the back of a seller's confirmation form. When an arbitration clause is present in only one of the forms, parties often disagree as to whether their disputes must be arbitrated or litigated. Such a "battle of the forms" problem requires the application of UCC § 2–207. Under § 2–207, once it is established that the parties are "merchants" for purposes of the UCC, and that the forms did not expressly condition acceptance upon assent to the additional terms on the form, then a court must determine whether the contract includes an arbitration clause or not. This inquiry turns on whether an arbitration clause is a "material" alteration for purposes of § 2–207(2). If the additional term *is not* a material alteration, then § 2–207 provides that the term becomes part of the contract unless a timely objection is made. If the term *is* a material alteration, then it is not part of the contract unless the recipient manifested an assent to its inclusion.[1]

Courts have taken two approaches to the issue of the materiality of an additional arbitration clause. The New York courts have taken the position that an arbitration clause is per se material, so that it does not become part of the contract between the parties absent specific agreement to do so.[2] Other courts have adopted what is termed the "modern approach," pursuant to which the additional terms are examined to determine whether they cause undue surprise or hardship to the parties. Under this approach, a court must decide the materiality *vel non* of an arbitration term on the basis of evidence that shows whether or not the objecting party had reason to know that the arbitration clause was in the contract.[3] As one court stated, "[i]n Illinois, the *sole* test for the determination of the materiality of an alteration is whether the addition constitutes unreasonable surprise to one of the parties." *Schulze and Burch Biscuit Co. v. Tree Top, Inc.,* 831 F.2d 709, 714 (7th Cir. 1987) (emphasis supplied). In determining whether the objecting party is subjected to unreasonable surprise, courts will examine the prior course of dealings between the parties and trade usages in the industry to determine whether the parties should have expected that arbitration would be used to resolve their disputes. Thus, for example, in *Schulze and Burch Bisquit Co.,* supra, the court found that the arbitration clause was not a material addition and hence was included in the contract, where the two parties had contracted for the same goods on nine previous occasions, each time using forms with an arbitration clause.

In contrast, in the court in *PCS Nitrogen Fertilizer, L.P. v. Christy Refractories, L.L.C.,* 225 F.3d 974 (8th Cir. 2000) analyzed the parties' forms and concluded that there was no contract formed from the various conflicting written documents. However, the court found that the parties concluded a contract by their conduct under § 2–207(3). The court also concluded that the contract did not include the arbitration clause because there was not a sufficient course of dealing between the parties to integrate the arbitration provision into the parties' contract. While there had been many customer forms exchanged between the parties, all but one involved the very transaction in dispute. Thus, the objecting party only received one customer acknowledgement form containing an arbitration provision prior

1. See *Willow Valley Manor v. Trouvailles, Inc.,* 977 F.Supp. 700, 704–05 (E.D.Pa. 1997).

2. See *Bayway Refining Co. v. Oxygenated Marketing & Trading A.G.,* 215 F.3d 219 (2d Cir. 2000); *Coastal Industries, Inc. v. Automatic Steam Products Corp.,* 654 F.2d 375, 379 (5th Cir. 1981) (applying New York law to question of materiality for purposes of § 2–207); *Marlene Indus. v. Carnac Textiles, Inc.,* 380 N.E.2d 239 (N.Y.1978).

3. See *Willow Valley Manor,* supra, 977 F.Supp. at 705; *Bergquist Company v. Sunroc Corp.,* 777 F.Supp. 1236 (E.D.Pa. 1991).

to the instant dispute. "This in and of itself hardly establishes a prior course of dealing . . ." Id. at 982.

* * *

D. Arbitration Clauses Incorporated By Reference

When arbitration provisions are inserted into a contract by reference, the non-drafting party may not know what the arbitration provisions say, or even that there is an arbitration provision. For example, when parties conclude a contract that states that "this contract shall be governed by the rules of the XYZ Trade Association" and one party to the contract is not a member of the named association, the reference may or may not put the non-member party on notice that there is an arbitration provision that bears on the contract. Thus arbitration clauses that are incorporated by reference pose special problems for ascertaining mutual assent.

In the past, many courts were reluctant to enforce arbitration clauses that were incorporated by reference on the grounds that they lacked the requisite mutual assent. Some courts gave careful scrutiny to arbitration clauses that were inserted by reference because they believed that a contractual provision as important as an arbitration clause—which is in effect a waiver of a right to sue—should be express to be enforceable. See, e.g. *Riverdale Fabrics Corp. v. Tillinghast–Stiles Co.*, 118 N.E.2d 104, 106 (N.Y. 1954). As the New York Court of Appeals stated, "Parties are not to be led into arbitration unwittingly through subtlety." Id. at 106. But in the late 1980s, courts abandoned their policing approach and began to enforce arbitration clauses that were incorporated by reference even when the contract was silent on the existence of the arbitration clause. The following case illustrates the new approach.

Hodge Brothers, Inc. v. DeLong Co., Inc.

942 F.Supp. 412 (W.D.Wis. 1996).

■ Crabb, District Judge.

This is a civil action in which plaintiffs seek declaratory relief, rescission and money damages for violation of the Commodity Exchange Act, 7 U.S.C. §§ 1–25, and the Racketeer Influenced and Corrupt Organizations Act, 18 U.S.C. §§ 1961–1968, and for common law fraud, breach of contract, breach of fiduciary duties and other wrongs . . . Defendants have counterclaimed, seeking declaratory and injunctive relief and money damages. Defendants allege violations of the Warehouse Keepers and Grain Dealers Security Act, Wis.Stat. §§ 127.01–.18, breach of contract and fraudulent misrepresentation, among other things. The case turns on the interpretation and validity of various contracts entered into between the parties for the sale of grain and soybeans. It is presently before the court on defendants' motion to stay all proceedings in this court and compel arbitration pursuant to §§ 3 and 4 of the Federal Arbitration Act, 9 U.S.C. §§ 1–16. Defendants contend that this action is subject to arbitration under the Federal Arbitration Act because the parties incorporated by reference into each of their grain purchase contracts a mandatory arbitration provision that encompasses the present dispute. Plaintiffs resist arbitration, contending the incorporated arbitration provisions apply only to members of the National Grain and Feed Association and not to nonmembers such as plaintiffs . . .

For the sole purpose of deciding this motion, I have found as fact the following relevant allegations from the complaint, the counterclaim and the attachments to the parties' briefs.

FACTS

Plaintiffs have a grain and soybean farming operation located in Janesville, Wisconsin. Defendant The DeLong Co. is a grain dealer located in Clinton, Wisconsin. Defendants William DeLong and David DeLong are citizens of Wisconsin and "principals, officers and directors" of defendant DeLong Co.

In late 1995, plaintiffs and defendant DeLong Co. entered into several "Grain Purchase" contracts. Each contract contained a provision stating that the contract "is made in accordance with the Trade Rules of the National Grain & Feed Association governing transactions in grain except as modified herein and both parties agree to be bound thereby." The trade rules to which the provision refers are contained in a booklet entitled, "Trade Rules and Arbitration Rules." The booklet begins with a "General Explanation of NGFA Trade Rules and Arbitration System," which specifies both that the "Grain Trade Rules . . . govern all disputes of a financial, mercantile, or commercial nature involving grain" and that the "Trade Rules are the basis for the NGFA's Arbitration System." The "Preamble" to the trade rules states that the rules:

> shall govern all disputes of a financial, mercantile, or commercial character connected with grain . . . arising between Active members of the National Grain and Feed Association, and shall be the basis of arbitration on such controversies, unless otherwise and specifically agreed to.

Rule 42 of the trade rules reads, in part, as follows:

> Arbitration: (a) Where differences between members of this Association cannot be amicably adjusted, said differences shall, at the request of either party, be submitted to the NGFA Arbitration Committee. (b) The decision of an Arbitration Committee of this Association shall be final except as provided in Section 9 of the Arbitration Rules.

The arbitration rules follow the trade rules in the booklet. Section one of the arbitration rules falls under the heading, "The Arbitration System Description and Purpose," and provides that the arbitration system is made up of three-person "National Arbitration Committees." Section three of the arbitration rules falls under the heading "Jurisdiction" and provides:

> (a) A National Arbitration Committee may properly consider a case involving a dispute between or among any of the following:

(1) active members . . . of the National Association. . . .

(2) Members . . . and nonmembers, by consent of both parties or by court order. In the absence of a court order a case between a member and a nonmember may not be properly considered by the National Arbitration Committee without the consent of both parties. If the contract in dispute between a member and nonmember provides for arbitration by the National Association or under its Arbitration Rules, the parties to the contract shall be deemed to have consented to arbitration under these Arbitration Rules.

The "National Arbitration Committee" is defined in section four of the arbitration rules.

OPINION

. . . The question raised in this case is whether the arbitration provisions incorporated by reference into the hedge-to-arrive grain purchase contracts require a stay of proceedings pursuant to section 3 of the arbitration act . . .

A determination of defendants' motion to stay proceedings and compel arbitration depends on the resolution of two related questions: 1) whether the parties entered into a valid and enforceable agreement to arbitrate; and if so, 2) whether the claims arising out of the present dispute fall within the scope of the claims they agreed to arbitrate. [citation omitted] As to the first question, plaintiffs contend that when they signed the contracts they did not believe they were agreeing to the arbitration provision incorporated in the contracts because they do not belong to the National Grain and Feed Association. Alternatively, they argue that even if they should have understood they were agreeing to application of the provision, the provision is illegal and unenforceable either because the contracts as a whole are illegal or because the arbitration agreement fails to meet the requirements of 17 C.F.R. pt. 180. . . .

A. *Agreement to Arbitrate: Did the parties enter into a valid and enforceable agreement?*

"An agreement to arbitrate is treated like any other contract." *Kresock v. Bankers Trust Co.,* 21 F.3d 176, 178 (7th Cir.1994) (citing 9 U.S.C. § 2). Therefore, it is necessary to decide as a matter of contract law whether plaintiffs agreed to arbitrate the claims involved in this dispute. [Citation omitted.]

Although plaintiffs do not dispute that a contract may incorporate by reference an arbitration clause from another document, *see, e.g., R.J. O'Brien & Assoc.,* 64 F.3d at 260 ("A contract . . . need not contain an explicit arbitration clause if it validly incorporates by reference an arbitration clause in another document.") (citing cases), they contend that they did not agree to be bound by the arbitration provision in Trade Rule 42(a) because that rule applies by its own terms only to "members" of the association. Defendants do not dispute plaintiffs' assertion that they are not members, but contend that membership is irrelevant because the parties agreed to use the trade rules as the governing standard for their agreements. Defendants are correct. Parties are free to stipulate to any procedures they choose for the procedures governing the arbitration of their disputes, "short of authorizing trial by battle or ordeal or, more doubtfully, by a panel of three monkeys." *Baravati v. Josephthal, Lyon & Ross, Inc.,* 28 F.3d 704, 709 (7th Cir. 1994).

If I were to accept plaintiffs' argument that their non-membership serves to exempt them from the arbitration clause, I would have to conclude that plaintiffs did not agree to be bound by any of the trade rules. Such a conclusion would be in direct contravention of the plain and unambiguous language in each hedge-to-arrive contract that the contract was being made "in accordance with the Trade Rules of the . . . Association . . . and both parties agree to be bound thereby." [citations omitted].

A similar "membership" argument was rejected by the Court of Appeals for the Seventh Circuit in *Paper Express, Ltd.,* 972 F.2d 753. A purchaser (the plaintiff) and a vendor had incorporated into their contract the following clause: "Warranty: 6 months according to the rules of VDMA and ZVEI." *Id.* at 754. The rules of the VDMA, a German machine manufacturer association, contained a rule regarding warranties and a forum selection clause that the purchaser did not wish to honor. The court held that when the parties agreed in the warranty section of their contract to apply the "rules of VDMA and ZVEI," they agreed to incorporate all of the VDMA rules, not just the warranty rule. *Id.* at 755. The court rejected plaintiff's argument that the rules did not apply because it was not a "qualified businessman" under the VDMA. Not only was the plaintiff wrong about his status under the rules, it could not escape their application. "Even if the VDMA rules do not apply *by their own force* to the transaction at issue here, the parties could still choose to incorporate them into their contract." *Id.* at 757 (emphasis in original).

Even though Rule 42 does not apply to the transactions between plaintiffs and defendant DeLong Co. by its own force, the parties "agree[d] to be bound" by the trade rules; no exception was made for Rule 42. Plaintiffs' non-membership in the National Grain and Feed Association is irrelevant to the application of Rule 42 or any other trade rule incorporated by reference into their contracts with defendants. *See Wilson Fertilizer & Grain, Inc. v. ADM Milling Co.,* 654 N.E.2d 848 (Ind.App.1995) (seller of grain who was not member of National Grain and Feed Association agreed to arbitrate under Trade Rule 42 where buyer's confirmation order provided that "This Contract is also subject to the Trade Rules of the National Grain and Feed Association currently in effect").

Plaintiffs argue that even if they agreed that their underlying contracts were governed by the trade rules, they did not agree to subject their disputes to the National Grain and Feed Association's Arbitration Rules. In plaintiffs' views, these arbitration rules are separate rules not referenced in the parties' hedge-to-arrive contracts. Plaintiffs are mistaken. The trade rules make clear reference to the arbitration rules as the proper method for carrying out the compulsory arbitration required under Trade Rule 42.

Plaintiffs cite Arbitration Rule 3(a)(2) in support of their argument that there are distinctions between the two sets of rules, but in fact, this rule supports defendants' argument that the parties did not have to incorporate the arbitration rules expressly into the hedge-to-arrive contracts. Arbitration Rule 3(a)(2) provides that "[i]f the contract in dispute between a member and nonmember provides for arbitration by the National Association ... the parties to the contract shall be deemed to have consented to arbitration under these Arbitration Rules." By agreeing to be bound by Trade Rule 42, the parties agreed to arbitrate before the national committee.

... I conclude that defendants are entitled to an order 1) compelling arbitration of this dispute under 9 U.S.C. § 4; and 2) staying this proceeding pending arbitration under 9 U.S.C. § 3.

* * *

Questions

1. Why do you think courts have abandoned their previous approach of requiring evidence of knowing consent when an arbitration clause is inserted by reference?

2. Under what circumstances should a party be deemed to have assented to terms that do not appear on the face of a contract? Should the answer depend upon whether the non-drafting party had reason to know what was in the referenced material? Or, do all parties have a duty to read contractual terms, even contractual terms that are not presented to them? Should it depend upon whether they have an ability to obtain the contractual terms should they so request?

3. Is there a difference between a reference to an incorporated document that mentions arbitration and a reference that is silent about the existence of an arbitration term? Should a non-drafting party be deemed to have assented to an arbitration clause in the former situation, but not in the latter? If so, does this place a limit on the duty to read? Is this the position taken by the court in *Hodge Brothers v. DeLong?*

4. The court cites Richard Posner in *Baravati* for the proposition that parties are free to stipulate to any arbitral procedures they choose, "short of authorizing trial by battle or ordeal or, more doubtfully, by a panel of three monkeys." Is this literally true? What if the parties are arbitrating a statutory claim?

5. In a dispute between a pay phone owner (the plaintiff) and MCI (the defendant), the evidence showed that the parties had a contract that stated that "service is provided in accordance with MCI's Tariff with the FCC." The contract made no reference to arbitration. Some time after the contract was made, MCI amended its Tariff on file with the Federal Communications Commission (FCC) to provide for binding arbitration of all disputes. The plaintiff was unaware of the tariff amendment and had never consented to arbitrate disputes with MCI. When a service-related dispute arose with MCI, should the plaintiff be required to submit to arbitration? See *Pay Phone Concepts, Inc. v. MCI Telecommunications Corp.*, 904 F.Supp. 1202 (D.Kan. 1995).

6. Cases subsequent to *Hodge Brothers* have cast doubt on the notion that words of party coverage such as "member" can be ignored in construing an arbitration clause incorporated by reference. For example, in *Blanchard Valley Farmers Coop., Inc. v. Carl Niese & Sons Farms, Inc.*, 758 N.E.2d 1238 (Ohio App.2001), the Ohio Court of Appeals squarely disagreed with *Hodge Brothers* and held that a non-member cannot be compelled to arbitrate a claim under the NGFA:

> Here, it is undisputed that the agreements made no reference to the Arbitration Rules. Rather, each of the agreements merely stated, "this purchase is made subject to the trade rules of the National Grain and Feed Association." This language is clearly sufficient to incorporate the NGFA Trade Rules into the agreements. However, no provision of the Trade Rules requires that disputes between members and non-members be arbitrated, and Niese Farms did not become a "member" of the NGFA merely by entering into an agreement that was governed in part by its Trade Rules.
>
> Therefore, we cannot say that Niese Farms consented to arbitration when it entered into the agreements with BVFC. But see Hodge Bros., Inc. v. The DeLong Co., Inc., 942 F.Supp. 412, 416 (W.D. Wis. 1996) (holding that parties consented to NGFA arbitration), criticized in Nicholas P. Iavarone, Arbitration, Expediency, and the Demise of Justice in District Courts: Another Side of the Hedge-to-Arrive Controversy (1998), 3 Drake J. Agric. L. 319, 359–62.

Similarly, in *World Rentals & Sales, LLC v. Volvo Constr. Equip. Rents, Inc.*, 517 F.3d 1240 (11th Cir. 2008), the Eleventh Circuit faithfully adhered to the party-limiting language of an arbitration clause that was incorporated, by reference, into the parties' agreement. There, the parties' Loan Documents incorporated, by reference, all agreements "referred" to in the Loan Documents. The Loan Documents referred to "Franchise Agreements," and these Franchise Agreements contained arbitration clauses. The court first held that these arbitration clauses were validly incorporated into the Loan Documents even though the arbitration clauses were not explicitly referred to in the incorporation language. The court held, however, that the particular party who was unwilling to arbitrate, "Volvo Finance," could not be compelled to arbitrate because it was not a party (a "Franchisor" or "Franchisee") that was covered by the arbitration clauses:

> Those provisions [in the Franchise Agreements] cover "[a]ll disputes, claims, controversies or causes of action arising between Franchisee and Franchisor."
>
> The Franchise Agreements define the term "Franchisor" this way: Franchisee [i.e., World Rentals] further acknowledges that: (i) the term "Franchisor" as used in this Agreement shall refer only to Volvo Construction Equipment Rents, Inc. and not Franchisor's parents or

affiliates; (ii) Franchisor is not authorized to contract for or on behalf of its parent or any of its affiliates; and (iii) this Agreement shall not be deemed to bind or otherwise restrict Franchisor's parent or any of its affiliates.

It could not be clearer that the term "Franchisor" refers "only" to Volvo Rents and not to any of Volvo Rents' "affiliates," such as Volvo Finance. Thus, the applicable arbitration clause unambiguously limits its reach only to disputes between the World Parties and Volvo Rents; plainly and expressly it excludes any disputes between the World Parties and Volvo Finance....

More recently, the Second Circuit has explained the general point ...: "[A]n arbitration agreement restricted to the immediate parties does not bind a non-party, notwithstanding words of incorporation or reference in a separate contract by which that non-party is bound." Progressive Cas. Ins. Co. v. C.A. Reaseguradora Nacional de Venezuela, 991 F.2d 42, 47 (2d Cir. 1993) (internal quotation marks omitted). (Emphasis added.)

In short, *World Rentals* conflicts with *Hodge Brothers* in that *Hodge Brothers* ignored the language in the arbitration provision that restricted its coverage to "members," whereas *World Rentals* dictates that party-limiting language (such as "Franchisor") must be given effect.

Which is the better approach?

* * *

4. Fraud, Illegality, and the Separability Doctrine

A. Fraud in the Inducement

Ericksen v. 100 Oak Street

35 Cal.3d 312, 673 P.2d 251 (1983).

■ GRODIN, JUSTICE.

The question presented here is whether a party to an agreement which includes an arbitration clause may bypass the arbitral process, and invoke the jurisdiction of the courts, by asserting that the agreement itself was the product of fraud. We conclude, in accord with the United States Supreme Court and the overwhelming majority of state courts which have considered the question, that the arbitration commitment is severable from the underlying agreement and that where, as in this case, the arbitration clause may reasonably be construed to encompass the fraud claim, the entire dispute should be resolved through arbitration.

Facts and Procedural History

The underlying dispute concerns a lease executed by plaintiff and respondent Ericksen, Arbuthnot, McCarthy, Kearney and Walsh, Inc., an Oakland law firm, hereinafter referred to as Ericksen, and 100 Oak Street, a California limited partnership which owns a three-story office building in Oakland. The lease, dated August 15, 1979, was for a five-year term and provided that Ericksen would occupy the first floor of the 100 Oak Street building, starting November 15, 1979.

Shortly after it occupied the premises, Ericksen began complaining that the air conditioning in the building was defective. Halfway through the lease term, Ericksen vacated the premises, moving to another office during Memorial Day weekend, 1982.

Notwithstanding a lease clause in which it agreed to arbitrate "[i]n the event of any dispute between the parties hereto with respect to the provisions of this Lease exclusive of those provisions relating to payment of rent," Ericksen filed suit on June 30, 1982. The complaint sought damages and declaratory relief and alleged a breach of the implied covenant of quiet enjoyment; breach of the implied warranty of habitability; frustration of purpose; simple breach of contract; constructive eviction; and fraud. Ericksen claimed it was entitled to rescind the agreement, and sought general and punitive damages.

Within a few days after it was served with the complaint, 100 Oak Street filed a petition to compel arbitration of the dispute (Code Civ.Proc., § 1281.2), and to stay the civil proceedings. Ericksen filed a response in which it admitted that it and 100 Oak Street had "entered into a written agreement requiring that the controversy alleged in the petition to be submitted to arbitration," but asserted that "[g]rounds exist for revocation of the agreement to arbitrate the alleged controversy in that [Ericksen] was falsely and fraudulently induced to enter into the lease agreement." On the basis of this general and unverified allegation,[1] the trial court denied 100 Oak Street's petition, and this appeal followed.

Discussion

Code of Civil Procedure section 1281.2 provides, in relevant part: "On the petition of a party to an arbitration agreement alleging the existence of a written agreement to arbitrate a controversy and that a party thereto refuses to arbitrate such controversy, the court shall order the petitioner and the respondent to arbitrate the controversy if it determines that an

1. Ericksen's complaint, also unverified, alleged in part that before and after the signing of the lease defendants "falsely and fraudulently, and with intent to deceive and defraud the plaintiff, represented to plaintiff that the leased premises were in a tenantable condition," and that those representations were false, and known to be false, because "in truth the air conditioning was inadequate, making the leased premises untenantable." At oral argument before this court, Ericksen's attorney confirmed that this was the fraud referred to in its response to the petition to compel arbitration. Ericksen's complaint also asserted that there had been a mutual rescission of the agreement, but this was not a stated ground for opposing arbitration in the trial court.

agreement to arbitrate the controversy exists, unless it determines that: . . . [¶] (b) Grounds exist for the revocation of the agreement."

The language of the statute on its face would not appear to countenance the trial court's view that the mere general assertion of fraud in an unverified response is sufficient basis for the denial of a petition to compel arbitration. Rather, the statute calls for a "determination" by the court as to the existence of the requisite agreement, and manifestly no such determination has been made.

There exists a more fundamental question, however, and that is whether the California Arbitration Act contemplates that a court, confronted with an agreement containing an arbitration clause and a petition to compel arbitration, will preliminarily entertain and decide a party's claim that the underlying agreement (as distinguished from the agreement to arbitrate) was produced by fraud. The question is one of first impression in this state.... We therefore turn to decisions of the federal courts and the courts of our sister states for guidance.

I. The Federal Rule

In Robert Lawrence Company v. Devonshire Fabrics, Inc. (2d Cir. 1959) 271 F.2d 402, cert. dism. (1960) 364 U.S. 801, 81 S.Ct. 27, 5 L.Ed.2d 37, plaintiff sought damages for allegedly fraudulent misrepresentations made by defendant in inducing it to pay for a quantity of woolen fabric, which, plaintiff claimed, was not of "first quality" as the agreement provided. Defendant moved to stay the suit pending arbitration pursuant to a provision of the sales agreement calling for arbitration of "[a]ny complaint, controversy or question which may arise with respect to this contract that cannot be settled by the parties thereto." The trial court denied the stay on the ground that the existence of a valid contract was a question which must first be determined by the court.

The court of appeals, in what proved to be a seminal decision on this issue, reversed. Calling the trial court's approach an "oversimplification of the problem," the court held that the federal arbitration statute "envisages a distinction between the entire contract between the parties on the one hand and the arbitration clause of the contract on the other." (271 F.2d at p. 409.) Such a construction was compelled, the court reasoned, not only by the language of the statute but also by other pertinent considerations as well. "Historically arbitration clauses were treated as separable parts of the contract, although such treatment generally meant the agreement was being deprived of its efficacy. [Citations.] And since the passage of the [federal] Arbitration Act, the courts have similarly held that the illegality of part of the contract does not operate to nullify an agreement to arbitrate. [Citations.] Nor does the alleged breach or repudiation of the contract preclude the right to arbitrate. [Citations.] [¶] Finally, any doubts as to the construction of the Act ought to be resolved in line with its liberal policy of promoting arbitration both to accord with the original intention of the parties and to help ease the current congestion of court calendars. Such policy has been consistently reiterated by the federal courts and we think it deserves to be heartily endorsed.'' (271 F.2d at p. 410.)

Referring to the case before it, the court observed that ''[t]he issue of fraud seems inextricably enmeshed in the other factual issues of the case. Indeed, the difference between fraud in the inducement and mere failure of performance by delivery of defective merchandise depends upon little more than legal verbiage and the formulation of legal conclusions. Once it is settled that arbitration agreements are 'valid, irrevocable, and enforceable' we know of no principle of law that stands as an obstacle to a determination by the parties to the effect that arbitration should not be denied or postponed upon the mere cry of fraud in the inducement, as this would permit the frustration of the very purposes sought to be achieved by the agreement to arbitrate, i.e. a speedy and relatively inexpensive trial before commercial specialists.'' (Id., at p. 410, emphasis added.) It would be different, the court suggested, if there were a claim, supported by a showing of substance, that the arbitration clause was itself induced by fraud, but ''[i]t is not enough that there is substance to the charge that the contract to deliver merchandise of a certain quality was induced by fraud.'' (Id., at p. 411.) Since the contract language was broad enough to include a claim of fraud in the inducement of the contract itself, that was a question for the arbitrator to determine.

Other cases

In Prima Paint v. Flood & Conklin (1967) 388 U.S. 395, 87 S.Ct. 1801, 18 L.Ed.2d 1270 the United States Supreme Court confronted the Devonshire issue in the context of a consulting agreement in which Flood & Conklin agreed to perform certain services for and not to compete with Prima Paint. The agreement contained an arbitration clause providing that '' '[a]ny controversy or claim arising out of or relating to this Agreement ... shall be settled by arbitration in the City of New York ...' '' (388 U.S. at p. 398, 87 S.Ct. at p. 1803). Flood & Conklin, contending that Prima had failed to make a payment under the contract, sent Prima a notice requesting arbitration. Prima responded with an action in federal district court to rescind the entire consulting agreement on the ground of fraud. The fraud allegedly consisted of Flood & Conklin's misrepresentation at the time the contract was made, that it was solvent and able to perform the agreement, when in fact it was completely insolvent. Flood & Conklin moved to stay Prima's lawsuit pending arbitration of the fraud issue. The lower courts, relying on the Second Circuit's decision in Devonshire, held that the action should be stayed to permit arbitration of the issue.

The Supreme Court noted it was the view of the Second Circuit in Devonshire and other cases that ''except where the parties otherwise intend, arbitration clauses ... are 'separable' from the contracts in which they are embedded, and that where no claim is made that fraud was directed to the arbitration clause itself, a broad arbitration clause will be held to encompass arbitration of the claim that the contract itself was induced by fraud. [Fn. omitted.]'' (388 U.S. at p. 402, 87 S.Ct. at p. 1805, emphasis in original.) And, the high court adopted the Devonshire rule as a proper interpretation of the federal statute, binding upon federal courts in suits involving agreements subject to that statute—i.e., maritime contracts and those evidencing transactions in "commerce." (388 U.S. at pp. 403–404, 87 S.Ct. at pp. 1805–1806.) "In so concluding," the court stated, "we not only honor the plain meaning of the statute but also the unmistakably clear congressional purpose that the arbitration procedure, when selected by the parties to a contract, be speedy and not subject to delay and obstruction in the courts." (Id., at p. 404, 87 S.Ct. at 1806.)

The United States Supreme Court in Moses H. Cone Memorial Hosp. v. Mercury Const., supra, 460 U.S. 1, 103 S.Ct. 927, 74 L.Ed.2d 765 has recently reconfirmed Prima Paint, stating its holding in broad terms, and approving an even broader, derivative, proposition which had been accepted by the courts of appeals: "that questions of arbitrability must be addressed with a healthy regard for the federal policy favoring arbitration.... The Arbitration Act establishes that, as a matter of federal law, any doubts concerning the scope of arbitrable issues should be resolved in favor of arbitration, whether the problem at hand is the construction of the contract language itself or an allegation of waiver, delay, or a like defense to arbitrability." (103 S.Ct. at pp. 941–942.)

II. The Rule in Other States

The high courts of our sister states with cognate arbitration acts have followed the rule in Prima Paint with near unanimity. The only exceptions appear to be Louisiana ... and Minnesota ...

The treatment of this issue in New York, where courts have had the longest and most extensive exposure to arbitration law, is particularly instructive. In 1957, prior to Prima Paint, the New York Court of Appeals interpreted that state's arbitration law to mean that fraud in the inducement of a contract was an issue for the court, and not for the arbitrators. (Wrap–Vertiser Corporation v. Plotnick (1957) 3 N.Y.2d 17, 163 N.Y.S.2d 639, 143 N.E.2d 366.) After Prima Paint the court reversed itself and adopted the federal rule on the basis of legal and policy arguments which it found "compelling." (Weinrott v. Carp (1973) 32 N.Y.2d 190, 344 N.Y.S.2d 848, 856, 298 N.E.2d 42, 47.) The theoretical underpinning of its prior rule had been the concept that an arbitration agreement was not separable from the principal contract, so that if the substantive provisions of the contract were to fall, the entire contract including an arbitration clause would fall with it. (Id., 344 N.Y.S.2d at p. 854, 298 N.E.2d at p. 46.) But the court observed, "[j]udicial intervention, based upon a nonseparability contract theory in arbitration matters prolongs litigation, and defeats, as this case conclusively demonstrates, two of arbitration's primary virtues, speed and finality [citations]." (Id., 344 N.Y.S.2d at p. 855 ...) Such conduct "has the effect of frustrating both the initial intent of the parties as well as legislative policy." (Ibid.)

An "additional and desirable result" of its decision, the New York court noted, was to bring that state's law in accord with federal law as declared in Prima Paint, thus avoiding the awkwardness of applying different rules depending upon whether the case involved a contract subject to the federal statute. "[I]t is a rather technical distinction to apply one law or another depending on whether interstate commerce is involved. If we were to adhere to our former approach, we would be making the existence of interstate commerce (or the lack of it) determinative with respect to the application of the arbitration provision. Clearly no party makes a decision on the scope of arbitration based on whether the contract in question involves interstate commerce." (344 N.Y.S.2d at p. 857, fn. 2, 298 N.E.2d at p. 48, fn. 2.)

III. Evaluation

Contrary to plaintiff's contention, the majority rule, as reflected in cases like Prima Paint, Devonshire, and Weinrott, is compatible with California's arbitration statute. The difference between Code of Civil Procedure section 1281.2, which calls for arbitration unless grounds exist for revocation of the agreement, and the federal statute, which mandates arbitration "save upon such grounds as exist at law or in equity for the revocation of any contract" is inconsequential, and does not require or point to a different rule. Likewise, the New York statute, calling for arbitration when "there is no substantial question whether a valid agreement was made or complied with" (N.Y.Civ.Prac.Law, § 7503, subd. (a) (1980 McKinney)), is harmonious. As in the case of these statutes, the term "agreement" may properly be construed to refer to the agreement to arbitrate, as distinguished from the overall contract in which that agreement is contained. (Weinrott v. Carp, supra, 344 N.Y.S.2d at p. 855, 298 N.E.2d at p. 47.)

In addition, the majority rule is in accord with this state's strong public policy in favor of arbitration as a speedy and relatively inexpensive means of dispute resolution ... This is particularly true in cases such as this, where parties of presumptively equal bargaining power have entered into an agreement containing a commitment to arbitrate by a procedure of unchallenged fairness, and one of the parties seeks to avoid arbitration by asserting that the other party fraudulently induced the agreement because he never intended to perform. (See fn. 1, ante.) The difference between a breach of contract and such fraudulent inducement turns upon determination of a party's state of mind at the time the contract was entered into, and we ought not close our eyes to the practical consequences of a rule which would allow a party to avoid an arbitration commitment by relying upon that distinction.

California courts have observed in other contexts the dangers inherent in committing preliminary issues to the courts. "If participants in the arbitral process begin to assert all possible legal or procedural defenses in court proceedings before the arbitration itself can go forward, 'the arbitral wheels would very soon grind to a halt.'" ... And, we have recently warned against "procedural gamesmanship" aimed at undermining the advantages of arbitration. (Christensen v. Dewor Developments, supra, 33 Cal.3d 778, 784, 191 Cal.Rptr. 8, 661 P.2d 1088.) A statutory interpretation which would yield such results is not to be preferred.

We conclude that this court should adopt the majority rule. The scope of arbitration is, of course, a matter of agreement between the parties, and if they choose to limit that scope so as to exclude questions of fraud in the inducement of the contract that choice must be respected. In this state, as under federal law ... doubts concerning the scope of arbitrable issues are to be resolved in favor of arbitration ... Therefore, in the absence of indication of contrary intent, and where the arbitration clause is reasonably susceptible of such an interpretation, claims of fraud in the inducement of the contract (as distinguished from claims of fraud directed to the arbitration clause itself) will be deemed subject to arbitration.

We proceed to apply these principles to the instant case, where the parties agreed to arbitrate "any dispute between the parties hereto with respect to the provisions of this Lease exclusive of those provisions relating to payment of rent." Although this language is not as broad as that considered in Prima Paint other cases have found allegations of fraud covered by quite similar arbitration clauses. (See, e.g., J.P. Stevens & Co., Inc. v. Harrell International, Inc. (Fla.App.1974) 299 So.2d 69, cert. dism. (Fla. 1975) 313 So.2d 707.) Moreover, as in Devonshire, the issue of fraud which is asserted here "seems inextricably enmeshed in the other factual issues of the case." (271 F.2d at p. 410; see also Comprehensive Merch. Cat., Inc. v. Madison Sales Corp. (7th Cir.1975) 521 F.2d 1210, 1214.) Indeed, the claim of substantive breach—that the air conditioning did not perform properly—is totally embraced within the claim of fraud—that the lessor knew, at the time of the lease, that the air conditioning would not perform. Thus, if the trial court were to proceed to determine the fraud claim it would almost certainly have to decide the claim of substantive breach as well, and the original expectations of the parties—that such questions would be determined through arbitration—would be totally defeated. However the fraud claim were determined, there would be virtually nothing left for the arbitrator to decide. We conclude that the arbitration clause is broad enough to include this claim of fraud in the inducement.

Accordingly, the judgment is reversed and the superior court is directed to vacate its order denying 100 Oak Street's petition to compel arbitration and to enter an order granting the petition.

■ RICHARDSON, KAUS, BROUSSARD and REYNOSO, JJ., concur.

■ MOSK, JUSTICE, dissenting.

The majority establish a rule that earns a high rank in the cart-before-the-horse category. Instead of first requiring determination of whether the entire agreement was induced by fraud and then, if it was not, proceeding to arbitrate the issue of compliance with its terms, my colleagues order arbitration first and then sometime in the vague future the underlying validity of the very agreement which provided, among other matters, for the arbitration, is to be ascertained. This is resupination: logic and procedure turned upside down.

Code of Civil Procedure section 1281.2 provides that the court shall order arbitration "unless it determines that: ... [¶](b) Grounds exist for the revocation of the agreement." It seems obvious that the "it" refers to the court, and that the Legislature intended the court, not the arbitrator, to determine if grounds exist for revocation of the agreement.

The majority rather curiously admit that the statute calls for determination by the court whether a valid agreement exists, and then they announce that "manifestly no such determination has been made." Obviously. Nor will it be made if the matter must proceed to arbitration before a court can ascertain whether the agreement was induced by fraud.

Another paragraph in Code of Civil Procedure section 1281.2 makes clear the legislative intent in a situation comparable to that before us. The statute declares: "If *the court determines* that there are other issues between the petitioner and the respondent which are not subject to arbitration and which are the subject of *a pending action* or special proceeding *between the petitioner and the respondent* and that a determination of such issues *may make the arbitration unnecessary*, the court may delay its order to arbitrate until the determination of such other issues or until such earlier time as the court specifies" (italics added).

Here again, the Legislature refers to "the court determines," not the arbitrator. It seems to cover our case: if the court finds there was fraud in the inducement of the underlying contract "a determination of such issues may make the arbitration unnecessary"; therefore the court may delay any order for arbitration until the fraud issue is heard and decided. As Justice Black said in another context, the language raises no doubts about its meaning "except to someone anxious to find doubts." (Prima Paint v. Flood & Conklin (1967) 388 U.S. 395, 412, 87 S.Ct. 1801, 1810, 18 L.Ed.2d 1270 (dis. opn.)).

Pursuant to that section, the Court of Appeal in Gustafson v. State Farm Mut. Auto. Ins. Co. (1973) 31 Cal.App.3d 361, 107 Cal.Rptr. 243, held that the trial court should have determined the issue of waiver before ordering arbitration—that it was a matter for the court, not the arbitrator.

I cannot quarrel with federal decisions relied on by the majority, since they are based on provisions of the federal arbitration act, which in turn is bottomed on admiralty and the commerce clause of the Federal Constitution. I must concede, however, that I find the decisions unpersuasive, for the federal act specifically exempts from arbitration all contracts that are invalid "upon such grounds as exist at law or in equity for the revocation of any contract." (9 U.S.C. § 2.) This would certainly seem to embrace fraud in the inducement, as alleged in the instant case.

That was the view expressed in the irrefutable dissent by Justices Black, Douglas and Stewart in Prima Paint v. Flood & Conklin, supra, 388 U.S. 395, 412–413, 87 S.Ct. 1801, 1810, 18 L.Ed.2d 1270: "Let us look briefly at the language of the Arbitration Act itself as Congress passed it. Section 2, the key provision of the Act, provides that '[a] written provision in . . . a contract . . . involving commerce to settle by arbitration a controversy thereafter arising out of such contract . . . shall be valid, irrevocable, and enforceable, save upon such grounds as exist at law or in equity for the revocation of any contract.' Section 3 provides that '[i]f any suit . . . be brought . . . upon any issue referable to arbitration under an agreement in writing for such arbitration, the court . . . upon being satisfied that the issue involved in such suit . . . is referable to arbitration under such an agreement, shall . . . stay the trial of the action until such arbitration has been had. . . .' The language of these sections could not, I think, raise doubts about their meaning except to someone anxious to find doubts. They simply mean this: an arbitration agreement is to be enforced by a federal court unless the court, not the arbitrator, finds grounds 'at law or in equity for the revocation of any contract.' Fraud, of course, is one of the most common grounds for revoking a contract. If the contract was procured by fraud, then, unless the defrauded party elects to affirm it, there is absolutely no contract, nothing to be arbitrated. Sections 2 and 3 of the Act assume the existence of a valid contract. They merely provide for enforcement where such a valid contract exists. These provisions were plainly designed to protect a person against whom arbitration is sought to be enforced from having to submit his legal issues as to validity of the contract to the arbitrator. The legislative history of the Act makes this clear." (Fn. omitted.)

Justice Fortas' prevailing opinion in *Prima Paint* observes that the First Circuit in *Lummus Company v. Commonwealth Oil Refining Co.* (1960) 280 F.2d 915, held that if the arbitration clause is regarded by a state as an inseparable part of the contract, a claim of fraud in the inducement must be decided by the court. The high court did not disapprove Lummus; it merely went on to distinguish federal court proceedings, based as they were in Prima Paint on a maritime contract.

. . . While there are a number of other state courts that support the conclusion of the majority here, I am persuaded by the Louisiana court. In George Engine Co., Inc. v. Southern Shipbldg. Corp. (La.1977) 350 So.2d 881, 884–885, the court held that the issue of misrepresentation in the inducement of a contract is not to be submitted to arbitration even though the contract contains an arbitration clause. The court observed that under the Louisiana arbitration act an arbitration agreement was to be judicially enforced unless a court, not an arbitrator, found grounds at law or in equity for revocation of the contract. It reasoned that courts historically have had jurisdiction over legal issues presented by a petition to rescind a contract because of error in its inducement. Fraud in the inducement therefore was to be decided by the courts. The function of arbitrators, the court declared, is to resolve factual controversies arising out of valid contracts. It added that the courts are much better equipped than arbitrators to determine the legal question of misrepresentation or of fraud in the inducement of a contract.

It is one of the essential elements of a contract that the parties enter into it knowingly and consensually, not through fraud, duress, menace, undue influence or mistake. If consent to entering into a contract is obtained by any of the foregoing elements, a court may declare the entire contract to be unenforceable—the entire contract, without exception for any single provision. I can see no reason for selecting one provision of a potentially unenforceable contract, the arbitration clause, and stamping it with our imprimatur.

I would affirm the judgment.

■ BIRD, C.J., concurs.

* * *

Note on Prima Paint v. Flood & Conklin

Before 1967, most courts held that if a party raised a contractual defense grounded in state law that would render the entire contract unenforceable or void, a court rather than an arbitrator must rule on the defense.[1] They reasoned that if the contract is invalid, then so too is any promise to arbitrate contained in the contract.[2] But in *Prima Paint v. Flood & Conklin*, 388 U.S. 395 (1967), discussed in *Ericksen v. 100 Oak Street*, supra, the Supreme Court rejected this approach, and instead ruled that allegations of fraud in the inducement did not defeat a duty to arbitrate under the contract.

In *Prima Paint*, the plaintiff and Flood & Conklin Mfg. (F & C) entered into two contracts pursuant to which Prima Paint purchased F & C's paint business, F & C provided Prima Paint with current customer lists, and F & C promised not to compete for existing customers or within existing sales areas. F & C also promised to provide consulting services in connection with its manufacturing operations, sales, and services for six years. The contract had a broad arbitration clause, covering "any controversy or claim arising out of or relating to this Agreement." One week after the contract was signed, F & C filed for bankruptcy under Chapter XI of the Bankruptcy Act. Prima Paint, which had promised to provide F & C a percentage of receipts from the former F & C customers, ceased making payments.

F & C sought to arbitrate the payment dispute, and Prima Paint sued in District Court seeking recission of the consulting agreement on the basis of alleged fraudulent inducement. Jurisdiction was based on diversity of citizenship. Prima Paint also moved to enjoin the pending arbitration and F & C responded with a motion to stay litigation pending arbitration pursuant to Section 3 of the FAA. F & C contended that the issue of fraud in the inducement was an issue for the arbitrator to decide, not an issue to be decided by the court.

The District Court granted F & C's motion and stayed the litigation. It relied on an earlier Second Circuit case, *Robert Lawrence Co. v. Devonshire Fabrics, Inc.*, 271 F.2d 402 (2d Cir. 1959), which held that an allegation of

1. See Linda R. Hirshman, *The Second Arbitration Trilogy: The Federalization of Arbitration Law*, 71 Va. L. Rev. 1305, 1330 (1985).

2. See, e.g., American Airlines v. Louisville and Jefferson County Air Board, 269 F.2d 811, 816–17 (6th Cir. 1959); Kulukundis Shipping v. Amtorg Trading Corp., 126 F.2d 978 (2d Cir. 1942). But see, Robert Lawrence Co. v. Devonshire Fabrics, Inc., 271 F.2d 402 (2d Cir. 1959) (adopting and explaining separability doctrine).

fraud in the inducement of a contract generally—as opposed to an allegation of fraud in the inducement of an arbitration clause itself—was a matter for an arbitrator, not a court, to decide. The Court of Appeals affirmed, and the Supreme Court accepted review.

The Supreme Court affirmed the lower courts. Justice Fortas, writing for the majority, endorsed the view of the Second Circuit that "*except where the parties otherwise intend*—arbitration clauses as a matter of federal law are 'separable' from the contracts in which they are embedded, and that where no claim is made that fraud was directed to the arbitration clause itself, a broad arbitration clause will be held to encompass arbitration of the claim that the contract itself was induced by fraud." 388 U.S. at 402 (emphasis in original). Fortas found support for the "separability doctrine" in Section 4 of the FAA, which states that courts must compel parties to arbitrate a dispute "once it is satisfied that 'the making of the agreement for arbitration or the failure to comply [with the arbitration agreement] is not in issue.' " 388 U.S. at 403. He reasoned that Section 4, and Section 3 by analogy, means that "if the claim is fraud in the inducement of the arbitration clause itself—an issue which goes to the 'making' of the agreement to arbitrate—the federal court may proceed to adjudicate it. But the statutory language does not permit the federal court to consider claims of fraud in the inducement of the contract generally." Id. at 403–04.

Justice Black, along with Justices Douglas and Stewart, dissented. He argued that:

> The Court here holds that the United States Arbitration Act, 9 U.S.C. §§ 1–14, as a matter of federal substantive law, compels a party to a contract containing a written arbitration provision to carry out his "arbitration agreement" even though a court might, after a fair trial, hold the entire contract—including the arbitration agreement—void because of fraud in the inducement. The Court holds, what is to me fantastic, that the legal issue of a contract's voidness because of fraud is to be decided by persons designated to arbitrate factual controversies arising out of a valid contract between the parties. And the arbitrators who the Court holds are to adjudicate the legal validity of the contract need not even be lawyers, and in all probability will be nonlawyers, wholly unqualified to decide legal issues, and even if qualified to apply the law, not bound to do so. I am by no means sure that thus forcing a person to forgo his opportunity to try his legal issues in the courts where, unlike the situation in arbitration, he may have a jury trial and right to appeal, is not a denial of due process of law. I am satisfied, however that Congress did not impose any such procedures in the Arbitration Act.
>
> . . . The plain purpose of the Act as written by Congress was this and no more: Congress wanted federal courts to enforce contracts to arbitrate and plainly said so in the Act. But Congress also plainly said that whether a contract containing an arbitration clause can be rescinded on the ground of fraud is to be decided by the courts and not by the arbitrators. Prima here challenged in the courts the validity of

its alleged contract with F & C as a whole, not in fragments. If there has never been any valid contract, then there is not now and never has been anything to arbitrate. If Prima's allegations are true, the sum total of what the Court does here is to force Prima to arbitrate a contract which is void and unenforceable before arbitrators who are given the power to make final legal determinations of their own jurisdiction, not even subject to effective review by the highest court in the land. That is not what Congress said Prima must do. It seems to be what the Court thinks would promote the policy of arbitration. I am completely unable to agree to this new version of the Arbitration Act.

Questions

1. What reasons does the *Ericksen* court give for the separability doctrine? How convincing is the argument for the doctrine? How convincing are the dissents in *Ericksen* and *Prima Paint*?

2. In *Ericksen,* is the court correct that it could not have decided the issue of fraud in the inducement without deciding the issue of breach of the agreement?

3. In *Prima Paint*, what reason does Justice Fortas give for the separability doctrine? Is it based on statutory construction or on the presumption of arbitrability? Or, is it based on the unstated proposition that the parties consented by implication to have disputes about a contract's validity determined by an arbitrator? If so, can parties introduce evidence of nonconsent? What kind of evidence would be sufficient to rebut the existence of implied consent?

4. What do the *Ericksen* court and the Supreme Court in *Prima Paint* mean when they state that the separability doctrine does not require an arbitrator to determine an allegation of fraud directed at the arbitration clause itself? What might such fraud consist of?

5. Is the separability doctrine consistent with the holding of *First Options*? Is it consistent with ordinary contract law?

The doctrine has been roundly criticized on many grounds. See Richard C. Reuben, *First Options, Consent to Arbitration, and the Demise of Separability: Restoring Access to Justice for Contracts with Arbitration Provisions,* 56 SMU L. Rev. 819, 838 (2003); Pierre H. Bergeron, *At the Crossroads of Federalism and Arbitration: The Application of Prima Paint to Purportedly Void Contracts*, 93 Ky. L.J. 423, 427, 458–60 (2005). One criticism is that the doctrine is incorrect as a matter of statutory interpretation: the Court's *Prima Paint* interpretation of the FAA § 4 is inconsistent with § 2's assurance that arbitration clauses should not be enforced unless they are valid under state contract law.

A second criticism is that the separability doctrine perverts contract law by implying consent to arbitration from an agreement to which at least one of the parties claims it never consented. See Stephen J. Ware, *Arbitration Law's Separability Doctrine After Buckeye Check Cashing, Inc. v.*

Cardegna, 8 Nev. L.J. 107 (2007). An example is AmSouth Bank v. Bowens, 351 F.Supp.2d 571, 573–75 (S.D. Miss. 2005). Bank customers alleged that a bank employee had forged their signatures and thereby had stolen money out of their accounts. The allegedly forged "signature cards" used by the employee to access the customers' accounts referred to a customer agreement containing an arbitration clause. When the customers sued the bank in state court, the bank sued in federal court to compel arbitration pursuant to the arbitration clause on the signature cards. The customers filed affidavits denying they had ever agreed to arbitrate anything—they had never received copies of the customer agreement and their names had been forged on the signature cards. Nonetheless, the court sent the case to arbitration because the "forgery allegation regards the customer agreement as a whole and not just the arbitration clause of the customer agreement."

A third criticism is that the separability doctrine is just another instrumental method by which federal courts may send cases to arbitration. Professor Jean Sternlight, for example, has pointed out that it is exceptionally improbable that issues of fraud or assent tainting the arbitration agreement would not also affect the container contract generally: a party intending to defraud another is unlikely to focus on the arbitration provision, and instead is far more likely to focus on "something big like the price or quality of the goods or services at issue." Because nearly all contract-formation issues will affect the container contract and not just the arbitration agreement, nearly all cases will be arbitrable. See Jean R. Sternlight, Rethinking the Constitutionality of the Supreme Court's Preference for Binding Arbitration: A Fresh Assessment of Jury Trial, Separation of Powers, and Due Process Concerns, 72 Tul. L. Rev. 1, 24 n.87 (1997).

* * *

Chastain v. Robinson–Humphrey Company, Inc.

957 F.2d 851 (11th Cir. 1992).

[In a securities dispute, the plaintiff, Brenda Chastain, claimed that she never signed or agreed to an arbitration agreement and that her signature on such an agreement was a forgery. The securities firm admitted that Chastain never signed the requisite documents, but sought arbitration, claiming that under the separability doctrine or *Prima Paint,* the arbitrator should determine whether the dispute was subject to arbitration. The court refused to compel arbitration of the issue of arbitrability.]

Under normal circumstances, an arbitration provision within a contract admittedly signed by the contractual parties is sufficient to require the district court to send any controversies to arbitration. [Citation omitted.] Under such circumstances, the parties have at least presumptively agreed to arbitrate any disputes, including those disputes about the validity of the contract *in general.* See *Prima Paint,* 388 U.S. at 403–04, 87 S.Ct. at 1806. Because the making of the arbitration agreement *itself* is rarely in issue when the parties have signed a contract containing an arbitration provision, the district court usually must compel arbitration immediately after one of the contractual parties so requests. *Id.*

The calculus changes when it is undisputed that the party seeking to avoid arbitration has not signed any contract requiring arbitration. In such a case, that party is challenging the very existence of *any* agreement, *including the existence of an agreement to arbitrate.* Under these circumstances, there is no presumptively valid general contract which would trigger the district court's duty to compel arbitration pursuant to the Act. If a party has not signed an agreement containing arbitration language, such a party may not have agreed to submit grievances to arbitration at all. Therefore, before sending any such grievances to arbitration, *the district court itself* must first decide whether or not the non-signing party can nonetheless be bound by the contractual language ... In cases of this type, the proper rule has been stated by our predecessor court:

> To make a genuine issue entitling the [party seeking to avoid arbitration] to a trial by jury [on the arbitrability question], an unequivocal denial that the agreement had been made [is] needed, and some evidence should [be] produced to substantiate the denial.

... *Prima Paint* has never been extended to require arbitrators to adjudicate a party's contention, supported by substantial evidence, that a contract *never existed at all.* See *Three Valleys Mun. Water Dist. v. E.F. Hutton & Co.,* 925 F.2d 1136, 1140 (9th Cir. 1991). Here, Robinson–Humphrey is arguing that Chastain must arbitrate because of a purported contract which *indisputably* lacks the formalities necessary to signal Chastain's *ex ante* assent to the agreement as a whole. Clearly, the trigger of the court's power to compel arbitration in cases like *Prima Paint, Coleman,* and *Haydu*—the existence of a presumptively valid arbitration agreement contained within a contract signed by the parties—is entirely absent in this case.... Therefore, *Prima Paint* does not govern our decision ...

A party cannot place the making of the arbitration agreement in issue simply by opining that no agreement exists. Rather, that party must substantiate the denial of the contract with enough evidence to make the denial colorable. [Citation omitted.] Here, Robinson–Humphrey's concession that it did not obtain Chastain's signature or a power of attorney adequately substantiates Chastain's denial of entering into a contract. If such admissions were insufficient to entitle Chastain to a trial on the issue of her duty to arbitrate, we would invite a far more realistic fear: Party A could forge Party B's name to a contract and compel Party B to arbitrate the question of the genuineness of its signature. Similarly, any citizen of Los Angeles could sign a contract on behalf of the city and Los Angeles would be required to submit to an arbitrator the question whether it was bound to the contract, even if its charter prevented it from engaging in *any* arbitration.

... [T]he two issues pressed by the company—whether a party has authority to bind another to an arbitration agreement and whether a party can ratify an arbitration agreement by her conduct—should ordinarily be decided in the trial court *before* final resolution of a motion to compel arbitration. [Citations omitted.] The district court may find merit in Robinson–Humphrey's arguments and subsequently order Chastain to submit her securities allegations to arbitration. Until that time, however, the district court has no authority to compel the arbitration of Chastain's complaints.

* * *

Questions

1. Why does the court in *Chastain* refuse to apply the separability doctrine? Is there a basis to distinguish between fraud in the inducement and fraud in the execution for purposes of the application of the separability doctrine? What about the *Amsouth Bank* case, discussed in the note immediately preceding *Chastain*? Are the two cases inconstant or distinguishable?

Is there a basis to distinguish between a contract that is void and one that is voidable for purposes of the doctrine? A *voidable* contract is a contract which one of the parties has the power to void on the ground that the contract was induced by fraud, duress, or mistake. A *void* contract is not a contract at all because one of its essential elements, such as mutual assent or consideration, is missing. Some courts considering arbitration clauses within void contracts have distinguished *Prima Paint* and held that the separability doctrine does not apply when the validity of the entire contract is challenged. See, e.g., Sandvik AB v. Advent Int'l Corp., 220 F.3d 99, 107 (3d Cir. 2000). Other courts, however, have held that the separability doctrine applies to both void and voidable contracts. See, e.g., Bess v. Check Express, 294 F.3d 1298 (11th Cir. 2002). For more on this topic, see the Supreme Court's decision in Buckeye Check Cashing, Inc. v. Cardegna, infra chapter 2.4.B.

2. Does *Chastain* suggest that all allegations that a contract is void *ab initio* should be determined by a court? See *Bess, supra*; Burden v. Check into Cash of Kentucky, LLC, 267 F.3d 483 (6th Cir. 2001). If not, then how can we determine which challenges to contract formation are subject to the separability doctrine and which are not?

3. For purposes of the separability doctrine, is a contract that is void *ab initio* the same as one that never came into existence in the first place? Judge Esterbrook, in Sphere Drake Insurance Limited v. All American Insurance Co., 256 F.3d 587 (7th Cir. 2001), attempted to explain why a claim that no contract was ever formed is different from other types of challenges to contract formation for purposes of the separability doctrine. In that case, an insurance company, All American, sought to hold a reinsurer, Sphere Drake, liable for certain losses, and the reinsurance company denied that it had agreed to provide such reinsurance. Rather, it claimed that EUI, the broker who wrote the reinsurance policies on Sphere Drake's behalf, did so without actual or apparent authority to do so. Because the reinsurance contract had an arbitration provision, All American sought to arbitrate the question of Sphere Drake's responsibility under the contract. Sphere Drake maintains that "even if EIU plastered the papers with arbitration clauses that can't kick Sphere Drake out of court on the question whether EIU was its agent. To arbitrate the agency issue, Sphere Drake insists, would be circular, for arbitration is proper if and only if EIU indeed could bind Sphere Drake." 256 F.3d at 588–89. Judge Esterbrook agreed, and explained:

> *Prima Paint* holds that, unless the arbitration clause excludes such disputes, an arbitrator resolves a claim of fraud in the inducement. This means, All American believes, that all disputes about contract *formation* go to arbitrators; only disputes about the scope of arbitration clauses (as in *AT & T Technologies*) are resolved in advance by courts. That is, we suppose, a possible reading of *Prima Paint*, which sits uneasily alongside *AT & T Technologies* and *First Options*. But it is not a plausible reading, for it would disregard the principle that arbitration is contractual. Unless the parties agree otherwise, they are entitled to have courts resolve their disputes. The parties in *Prima Paint* did agree otherwise and promised to have the arbitrator resolve "[a]ny controversy or claim arising out of *or relating to* this Agreement" (emphasis added), the broadest possible clause. Whether one party defrauded another during the negotiations for the agreement "related to" that agreement. There was no doubt that the arbitration agreement (and the contract of which it was a part) had been signed; both sides knew what they were getting. A claim of fraud in the inducement—which boils down to "we wouldn't have signed this contract had we known the full truth about our trading partner"—supposes that the unhappy party did agree, but now wishes it hadn't. If a claim of "we wish we hadn't agreed" could be litigated, even when the arbitration clause is so broad, this would move a good portion of contract disputes back to court and defeat this part of the agreement at the outset, for it is easy to cry fraud. *Prima Paint* thought it important that no one argued that the arbitration clause was itself the result of fraud; that enabled an arbitrator to resolve defenses to enforcement of the contract without calling into question the arbitrator's own authority to act.
>
> Fraud in the inducement does not negate the fact that the parties actually reached an agreement. That's what was critical in *Prima Paint*. But whether there was *any* agreement is a distinct question. *Chastain* sensibly holds a claim of forgery must be resolved by a court. A person whose signature was forged has never agreed to anything. Likewise with a person whose name was written on a contract by a faithless agent who lacked authority to make that commitment. This is not a defense to enforcement, as in *Prima Paint*; it is a situation in which no contract came into being; and as arbitration depends on a valid contract an argument that the contract does not exist can't logically be resolved by the arbitrator (unless the parties agree to arbitrate this issue after the dispute arises). It was possible to arbitrate in *Prima Paint* without circularity; in forgery and agency cases, by

> contrast, the arbitrator's authority to resolve the dispute would depend on one particular answer to that very dispute. Only a court can break that circle.

Id. at 590–91.

* * *

B. ILLEGALITY AND THE LIMITS OF SEPARABILITY

The separability doctrine of *Prima Paint* is not limited to the defense of fraud in the inducement, but often is applied also to contractual defenses such as mistake, impossibility, duress, unconscionability, and illegality. The separability doctrine is a severe restriction on the types of contractual defenses that can be raised as a bar to arbitration. The following cases illustrate some of the problems that arise when a court applies the separability doctrine to the defense of illegality.

Party Yards, Inc. v. Templeton

751 So.2d 121 (Fla.App. 2000).

■ W. SHARP, J.

Party Yards, Inc., Pete Dorney and Andrew Baron (hereinafter "Party Yards") appeal an order granting Templeton's motion to stay litigation and denying their motion to stay arbitration. They contend it was error for the trial court *not to first* determine whether the contract was illegal under the usury statutes. We agree and reverse.

Party Yard designs, creates, produces and markets beverage containers with logos or other advertisement-type information printed on them. During the fall of 1996, they entered into a contract with Miller Brewing Company to produce beverage containers. Miller wanted prompt production and shipment of the products for the 1997 Super Bowl. Party Yards sought to borrow in excess of $200,000 for production costs and expenses in connection with this contract. They initially obtained a $100,000 loan, but sought a second lender—Templeton—for the remainder of the funds needed.

Templeton offered to lend Party Yards $160,000, and this offer was ultimately accepted. The contract, which contained three subparts, was executed on December 18, 1996. The subparts include a promissory note, a security agreement, and a representation agreement (collectively referred to as the contract).[1] The $160,000 was lent in three installments, and Party Yards repaid the principal in April of 1997. In addition to any interest provided for in the note (18% if the note was not paid by its due date, March 18, 1997), Templeton received, *inter alia,* "commissions" on the *gross* revenue of *all* of Party Yards products (not just the products sold or

1. It is apparent that these three "agreements" are in reality one contract, and we treat them as such in this appeal.

marketed by him), plus a percentage of the gross invoice price. Party Yards was required to continue to pay these sums for twenty years after Templeton's death to his heirs. Templeton was not required to render any services or perform any acts on Party Yards' behalf in order to receive these "commissions."

Because Templeton's sole obligation under the contract was the $160,000 loan, the interest and additional "commissions," may well render the contract usurious. In Florida, contracts for payment of interest exceeding eighteen percent per annum are usurious. § 687.02(1).[2] An unlawful rate of interest exists when a person reserves, charges, or takes, directly or indirectly, a rate of interest exceeding that amount:

> [B]y way of commission for advances, discounts, or exchange, or by *any contract, contrivance, or device whatever whereby the debtor is required or obligated to pay a sum of money greater than the actual principal sum received, together with interest at the rate of the equivalent of 18 percent per annum simple interest.* (Emphasis added.)

§ 687.03(1), Fla. Stat.

In usury cases, courts look to substance over form because the purpose of the statute is to protect the needy borrower by penalizing the unconscionable lender. *Jersey Palm–Gross v. Paper,* 639 So.2d 664 (Fla. 4th DCA 1994), *approved,* 658 So.2d 531 (Fla. 1995); *Bermil Corp. v. Sawyer,* 353 So.2d 579 (Fla. 3d DCA 1977). To establish that a transaction is usurious, the party must show: (1) an express or implied loan; (2) a repayment requirement; (3) an agreement to pay interest in excess of the legal rate; and (4) a corrupt intent to take more than the legal rate for the use of the money loaned. *Antonelli v. Neumann,* 537 So.2d 1027, 1028 (Fla. 3d DCA 1988). Corrupt intent is established if the evidence indicates that the lender knowingly charged or received excessive interest, considering all of the surrounding circumstances. *Antonelli* at 1029.

The contract in this case contained an arbitration provision. When the motions were heard below, the court determined that the Federal Arbitration Act (the FAA), Title 9 U.S.C. § 2, which governs the enforcement of arbitration provisions, was applicable. The court also concluded it must order arbitration, based on *Prima Paint Corp. v. Flood & Conklin Mfg. Co.,* 388 U.S. 395, 87 S.Ct. 1801, 18 L.Ed.2d 1270 (1967). But see *First Options of Chicago, Inc. v. Kaplan,* 514 U.S. 938, 944, 115 S.Ct. 1920, 131 L.Ed.2d 985 (1995).

The issue here, one of first impression, is whether a contract that violates state law and is criminal in nature, can be referred to arbitration. We find that the trial court's reliance on *Prima Paint* was misplaced because that case is inapplicable under the facts presented here. In this

2. Interest exceeding 25% is criminal usury. § 687.071(2) and (3). Charging interest between 25% and 40% constitutes a misdemeanor. § 687.071(2). A third degree felony occurs when a loan shark or shylock charges interest exceeding 45%. § 687.071(3). Section 687.146 provides that *any* contract which violates the chapter is a felony of the third degree.

case, the language in the arbitration provision of the contract is not broad enough to encompass a usury violation. The arbitration provision contained in this contract provides that:

> [*A*]*ny controversy arising under this Agreement* shall be submitted to arbitration, with three (3) Arbitrators presiding, before the American Arbitration Association in New York, New York, in accordance with its rules, and judgment confirming the Arbitrator's award may be entered in any court of competent jurisdiction. (Emphasis added.)

As a matter of law, a usury violation does not arise under an agreement. Rather it arises under state statutory law. A claim that a contract is illegal and, as in this case, criminal in nature, is not a matter which can be determined by an arbitrator. An arbitrator cannot order a party to perform an illegal act. See *Hill v. Norfolk & W.Ry. Co.,* 814 F.2d 1192, 1195 (7th Cir. 1987). Further, the FAA puts arbitration clauses on an equal footing with other clauses in a contract. See *Paladino v. Avnet Computer Technologies, Inc.,* 134 F.3d 1054, 1060 (11th Cir. 1998) (Florida law), citing *Allied–Bruce Terminix Cos., Inc. v. Dobson,* 513 U.S. 265, 275, 115 S.Ct. 834, 130 L.Ed.2d 753 (1995). It does not put such clauses above state law or other contractual provisions.

A court's failure to first determine whether the contract violates Florida's usury laws could breathe life into a contract that not only violates state law, but also is criminal in nature, by use of an arbitration provision. This would lead to an absurd result. Legal authorities from the earliest time have unanimously held that no court will lend its assistance in any way towards carrying out the terms of an illegal contract. *McMullen v. Hoffman,* 174 U.S. 639, 19 S.Ct. 839, 43 L.Ed. 1117 (1899). Illegal promises will not be enforced in cases controlled by federal law. *Kaiser Steel Corp. v. Mullins,* 455 U.S. 72, 102 S.Ct. 851, 70 L.Ed.2d 833 (1982).

A party who alleges and offers colorable evidence that a contract is illegal cannot be compelled to arbitrate the threshold issue of the *existence* of the agreement to arbitrate; only a court can make that determination. [Citations omitted] Where the facts alleged by the plaintiff are sufficient to put the making of a lawful agreement at issue, the trial court must determine the validity of the agreement before compelling a party to submit to arbitration. *Chastain v. Robinson–Humphrey Co., Inc.,* 957 F.2d 851, 854, 855 (11th Cir. 1992).

In this case, Party Yards submitted sufficient evidence below to warrant the court's resolution of whether the contract was illegal based upon violation of Florida's usury statutes. We therefore REVERSE and REMAND to the trial court for such determination.

* * *

Questions

1. Why didn't the court apply the separability doctrine in *Party Yards?* Is the result of *Party Yards* consistent with *Prima Paint*? Is it consistent with *Ericksen*?

2. Are usury laws special for purposes of the separability doctrine? Or does *Party Yards* mean that all allegations of illegality under state law must be determined by a court rather than by an arbitrator?

3. Does the result in *Party Yards* depend upon the fact that in Florida, violation of the state usury statute is a criminal violation? Would the result be different if it were a civil violation? Would it be different if the state statute provided that usurious contracts were void?

4. Does *Party Yards* suggest that the presumption of arbitrability not apply to the question of who decides the determination of an allegation that a party violated state law? Or, does the presumption of arbitrability spring back once a court has determined the issue of the contract's legality *vel non*? Is this a minor exception to the otherwise broad presumption, or a retreat from broad presumption?

* * *

Buckeye Check Cashing, Inc. v. Cardegna

546 U.S. 440 (2006).

■ JUSTICE SCALIA delivered the opinion of the Court.

We decide whether a court or an arbitrator should consider the claim that a contract containing an arbitration provision is void for illegality.

I

Respondents John Cardegna and Donna Reuter entered into various deferred-payment transactions with petitioner Buckeye Check Cashing (Buckeye), in which they received cash in exchange for a personal check in the amount of the cash plus a finance charge. For each separate transaction they signed a "Deferred Deposit and Disclosure Agreement" (Agreement), which included the following arbitration provisions:

> 1. *Arbitration Disclosure* By signing this Agreement, you agree that i[f] a dispute of any kind arises out of this Agreement or your application therefore or any instrument relating thereto, th[e]n either you or we or third-parties involved can choose to have that dispute resolved by binding arbitration as set forth in Paragraph 2 below....
>
> 2. *Arbitration Provisions* Any claim, dispute, or controversy ... arising from or relating to this Agreement ... or the validity, enforceability, or scope of this Arbitration Provision or the entire Agreement (collectively 'Claim'), shall be resolved, upon the election of you or us or said third-parties, by binding arbitration.... This arbitration Agreement is made pursuant to a transaction involving interstate commerce, and shall be governed by the Federal Arbitration Act ('FAA'), 9 U.S.C. Sections 1–16. The arbitrator shall apply applicable substantive law constraint [sic] with the FAA and applicable statu[t]es of limitations and shall honor claims of privilege recognized by law ...

Respondents brought this putative class action in Florida state court, alleging that Buckeye charged usurious interest rates and that the Agreement violated various Florida lending and consumer-protection laws, rendering it criminal on its face. Buckeye moved to compel arbitration. The trial court denied the motion, holding that a court rather than an arbitrator should resolve a claim that a contract is illegal and void *ab initio*. The District Court of Appeal of Florida for the Fourth District reversed, holding that because respondents did not challenge the arbitration provision itself, but instead claimed that the entire contract was void, the agreement to arbitrate was enforceable, and the question of the contract's legality should go to the arbitrator.

Respondents appealed, and the Florida Supreme Court reversed, reasoning that to enforce an agreement to arbitrate in a contract challenged as unlawful " 'could breathe life into a contract that not only violates state law, but also is criminal in nature . . .' " 894 So.2d 860, 862 (2005) (quoting *Party Yards, Inc. v. Templeton,* 751 So.2d 121, 123 (Fla.App. 2000)). We granted certiorari. 545 U.S. 1127, 125 S.Ct. 2937, 162 L.Ed.2d 864 (2005).

II

A

To overcome judicial resistance to arbitration, Congress enacted the Federal Arbitration Act (FAA), 9 U.S.C. §§ 1–16. Section 2 embodies the national policy favoring arbitration and places arbitration agreements on equal footing with all other contracts ... Challenges to the validity of arbitration agreements "upon such grounds as exist at law or in equity for the revocation of any contract" can be divided into two types. One type challenges specifically the validity of the agreement to arbitrate. See, *e.g., Southland Corp. v. Keating,* 465 U.S. 1, 4–5, 104 S.Ct. 852, 79 L.Ed.2d 1 (1984) (challenging the agreement to arbitrate as void under California law insofar as it purported to cover claims brought under the state Franchise Investment Law). The other challenges the contract as a whole, either on a ground that directly affects the entire agreement (*e.g.,* the agreement was fraudulently induced), or on the ground that the illegality of one of the contract's provisions renders the whole contract invalid.[1] Respondents' claim is of this second type. The crux of the complaint is that the contract as a whole (including its arbitration provision) is rendered invalid by the usurious finance charge.

1. The issue of the contract's validity is different from the issue whether any agreement between the alleged obligor and obligee was ever concluded. Our opinion today addresses only the former, and does not speak to the issue decided in the cases cited by respondents (and by the Florida Supreme Court), which hold that it is for courts to decide whether the alleged obligor ever signed the contract, *Chastain v. Robinson–Humphrey Co.,* 957 F.2d 851 (11th Cir. 1992), whether the signor lacked authority to commit the alleged principal, *Sandvik AB v. Advent Int'l Corp.,* 220 F.3d 99 (3d Cir. 2000); *Sphere Drake Ins. Ltd. v. All American Ins. Co.,* 256 F.3d 587 (7th Cir. 2001), and whether the signor lacked the mental capacity to assent, *Spahr v. Secco,* 330 F.3d 1266 (10th Cir. 2003).

In *Prima Paint Corp. v. Flood & Conklin Mfg. Co.,* 388 U.S. 395, 87 S.Ct. 1801, 18 L.Ed.2d 1270 (1967), we addressed the question of who—court or arbitrator—decides these two types of challenges. The issue in the case was "whether a claim of fraud in the inducement of the entire contract is to be resolved by the federal court, or whether the matter is to be referred to the arbitrators." *Id.*, at 402, 87 S.Ct. 1801. Guided by § 4 of the FAA, we held that "if the claim is fraud in the inducement of the arbitration clause itself—an issue which goes to the making of the agreement to arbitrate—the federal court may proceed to adjudicate it. But the statutory language does not permit the federal court to consider claims of fraud in the inducement of the contract generally." *Id.*, at 403–404, 87 S.Ct. 1801 (internal quotation marks and footnote omitted). We rejected the view that the question of "severability" was one of state law, so that if state law held the arbitration provision not to be severable a challenge to the contract as a whole would be decided by the court. See *id.*, at 400, 402–403, 87 S.Ct. 1801.

Subsequently, in *Southland Corp.*, we held that the FAA "create[d] a body of federal substantive law," which was "applicable in state and federal courts." 465 U.S., at 12, 104 S.Ct. 852 (internal quotation marks omitted). We rejected the view that state law could bar enforcement of § 2, even in the context of state-law claims brought in state court. See *id.*, at 10–14, 104 S.Ct. 852; see also *Allied–Bruce Terminix Cos. v. Dobson,* 513 U.S. 265, 270–273, 115 S.Ct. 834, 130 L.Ed.2d 753 (1995).

B

Prima Paint and *Southland* answer the question presented here by establishing three propositions. First, as a matter of substantive federal arbitration law, an arbitration provision is severable from the remainder of the contract. Second, unless the challenge is to the arbitration clause itself, the issue of the contract's validity is considered by the arbitrator in the first instance. Third, this arbitration law applies in state as well as federal courts. The parties have not requested, and we do not undertake, reconsideration of those holdings. Applying them to this case, we conclude that because respondents challenge the Agreement, but not specifically its arbitration provisions, those provisions are enforceable apart from the remainder of the contract. The challenge should therefore be considered by an arbitrator, not a court.

In declining to apply *Prima Paint's* rule of severability, the Florida Supreme Court relied on the distinction between void and voidable contracts. "Florida public policy and contract law," it concluded, permit "no severable, or salvageable, parts of a contract found illegal and void under Florida law." 894 So.2d, at 864. *Prima Paint* makes this conclusion irrelevant. That case rejected application of state severability rules to the arbitration agreement *without discussing* whether the challenge at issue would have rendered the contract void or voidable. See 388 U.S., at 400–404, 87 S.Ct. 1801. Indeed, the opinion expressly disclaimed any need to decide what state-law remedy was available, *id.,* at 400, n. 3, 87 S.Ct. 1801, (though Justice Black's dissent *asserted* that state law rendered the contract void, *id.,* at 407, 87 S.Ct. 1801). Likewise in *Southland,* which arose in state court, we did not ask whether the several challenges made there—fraud, misrepresentation, breach of contract, breach of fiduciary duty, and violation of the California Franchise Investment Law—would render the contract void or voidable. We simply rejected the proposition that the enforceability of the arbitration agreement turned on the state legislature's judgment concerning the forum for enforcement of the state-law cause of action. See 465 U.S., at 10, 104 S.Ct. 852. So also here, we cannot accept the Florida Supreme Court's conclusion that enforceability of the arbitration agreement should turn on "Florida public policy and contract law," 894 So.2d, at 864.

C

Respondents assert that *Prima Paint*'s rule of severability does not apply in state court. They argue that *Prima Paint* interpreted only §§ 3 and 4—two of the FAA's procedural provisions, which appear to apply by their terms only in federal court—but not § 2, the only provision that we have applied in state court. This does not accurately describe *Prima Paint.* Although § 4, in particular, had much to do with *Prima Paint*'s understanding of the rule of severability, see 388 U.S., at 403–404, 87 S.Ct. 1801, this rule ultimately arises out of § 2, the FAA's substantive command that arbitration agreements be treated like all other contracts. The rule of severability establishes how this equal-footing guarantee for "a written [arbitration] provision" is to be implemented. Respondents' reading of *Prima Paint* as establishing nothing more than a federal-court rule of procedure also runs contrary to *Southland*'s understanding of that case. One of the bases for *Southland's* application of § 2 in state court was precisely *Prima Paint*'s "reli[ance] for [its] holding on Congress' broad power to fashion substantive rules under the Commerce Clause." 465 U.S., at 11, 104 S.Ct. 852; see also *Prima Paint, supra,* at 407, 87 S.Ct. 1801 (Black, J., dissenting) ("[t]he Court here holds that the [FAA], as a matter of *federal substantive law* ..." (emphasis added)). *Southland* itself refused to "believe Congress intended to limit the Arbitration Act to disputes subject only to *federal*-court jurisdiction." 465 U.S., at 15, 104 S.Ct. 852.

Respondents point to the language of § 2, which renders "valid, irrevocable, and enforceable" "a written provision in" or "an agreement in writing to submit to arbitration an existing controversy arising out of" a "contract." Since, respondents argue, the only arbitration agreements to which § 2 applies are those involving a "contract," and since an agreement void *ab initio* under state law is not a "contract," there is no "written provision" in or "controversy arising out of" a "contract," to which § 2 can apply. This argument echoes Justice Black's dissent in *Prima Paint:* "Sections 2 and 3 of the Act assume the existence of a valid contract. They merely provide for enforcement where such a valid contract exists." 388 U.S., at 412–413, 87 S.Ct. 1801. We do not read "contract" so narrowly. The word appears four times in § 2. Its last appearance is in the final clause, which allows a challenge to an arbitration provision "upon such grounds as exist at law or in equity for the revocation of any *contract*." (Emphasis added.) There can be no doubt that "contract" as used this last time must include contracts that later prove to be void. Otherwise, the grounds for revocation would be limited to those that rendered a contract voidable—which would mean (implausibly) that an arbitration agreement could be challenged as voidable but not as void. Because the sentence's final use of "contract" so obviously includes putative contracts, we will not read the same word earlier in the same sentence to have a more narrow meaning. We note that neither *Prima Paint* nor *Southland* lends support to respondents' reading; as we have discussed, neither case turned on whether the challenge at issue would render the contract voidable or void.

It is true, as respondents assert, that the *Prima Paint* rule permits a court to enforce an arbitration agreement in a contract that the arbitrator later finds to be void. But it is equally true that respondents' approach permits a court to deny effect to an arbitration provision in a contract that the court later finds to be perfectly enforceable. *Prima Paint* resolved this conundrum—and resolved it in favor of the separate enforceability of arbitration provisions. We reaffirm today that, regardless of whether the challenge is brought in federal or state court, a challenge to the validity of the contract as a whole, and not specifically to the arbitration clause, must go to the arbitrator.

The judgment of the Florida Supreme Court is reversed, and the case is remanded for further proceedings not inconsistent with this opinion.

It is so ordered.

■ JUSTICE ALITO took no part in the consideration or decision of this case.

■ JUSTICE THOMAS, dissenting.

I remain of the view that the Federal Arbitration Act (FAA), 9 U.S.C. § 1 *et seq.*, does not apply to proceedings in state courts.... Thus, in state-court proceedings, the FAA cannot be the basis for displacing a state law that prohibits enforcement of an arbitration clause contained in a contract that is unenforceable under state law. Accordingly, I would leave undisturbed the judgment of the Florida Supreme Court.

* * *

Questions

1. What, if anything, is left of *Chastain* and *Party Yards* after *Buckeye*?

After the U.S. Supreme Court's decision in *Buckeye*, the Florida Supreme Court officially "approved" of the decision rendered by the Florida Court of Appeals. Thus, the Court of Appeals's decision is now law in Florida. See Cardegna v. Buckeye Check Cashing, Inc., 930 So.2d 610, 611 (Fla. 2006) (recognizing that "the United States Supreme Court has reversed this Court's decision, and, in effect approved the holding of the Fourth District ... [C]onsistent with and pursuant to the United States

Supreme Court's decision, we withdraw our previous opinion and now approve the decision of the Fourth District").

2. Is there a difference between a challenge to the content of a contract and a challenge to its existence? Does the concept of voidness mean that a valid contract never actually came into existence?

3. Which approach to allegations of illegality is more consistent with the value of freedom of contract, that of *Party Yards* or that of *Buckeye*?

4. Is there a policy justification for the separability doctrine? What is it?

5. Recall *Preston v. Ferrer*, ___ U.S. ___, 128 S.Ct. 978 (2008), discussed in Chapter 1.4, in which a California statute required that certain talent agency disputes be first sent to the California Labor Commissioner who would render a nonbinding decision on the matter. Afterwards, the losing party could compel arbitration if the parties had an arbitration agreement encompassing the dispute. The Supreme Court held that the FAA preempted the California statute's initial lodging of an arbitrable dispute with the state Labor Commissioner. Did the Court treat *Preston* as a *Buckeye*-type of case by couching the analysis in terms of whether, in the first instance, the dispute between the parties is one for the arbitrator or for the court to decide? Can the cases be distinguished?

* * *

5. Adhesion Contracts, Duress and Unconscionability

Graham v. Scissor–Tail, Inc.

623 P.2d 165 (Cal. 1981).

■ The Court:

These are two consolidated appeals. Plaintiff Graham appeals from a judgment confirming the award of an arbitrator . . . Defendant Scissor–Tail, Inc., appeals from a special order after judgment taxing costs relating to attorney's fees . . . We will reverse the judgment confirming the award, directing the trial court to vacate its order compelling arbitration (see fn. 1, ante) and conduct further proceedings. We will dismiss the appeal from the special order after judgment as moot, 103 Cal.App.3d 115, 162 Cal.Rptr. 798.

I

Plaintiff Bill Graham is an experienced promoter and producer of musical concerts. Defendant C. Russell Bridges, also known as Leon Russell (Russell), is a successful performer and recording artist and the leader of a musical group; he is also a member of the American Federation of Musicians (A.F. of M.). Defendant Scissor–Tail, Inc. (Scissor–Tail) is a California corporation, wholly owned by Russell, which serves as the vehicle by which the services of Russell and his group are marketed. Defendant David Forest

Agency, Ltd. (Forest) was, at the time here relevant, acting in the ca[illegible] of booking agent for Scissor–Tail.

Early in 1973, Scissor–Tail and Russell decided to formulate [illegible] structure a personal appearance tour for the latter and his group. For[illegible] was engaged to assist in this project, and at the suggestion of Den[illegible] Cordell, Russell's personal manager and an officer of Scissor–Tail, contac[illegible]ed plaintiff Graham, who had previously promoted a number of Russe[illegible] concerts, to request that he provide his services for four of the twelve concerts on the projected tour. A series of four contracts was prepared covering, respectively, concerts at Ontario, Oakland, Long Island, and Philadelphia. Graham signed all four contracts; Scissor–Tail (per Dennis Cordell), for reasons to appear, signed only those relating to the Ontario and Oakland concerts, which were to occur on July 29 and August 5, 1973.

The four contracts in question were all prepared on an identical form known in the industry as an A.F. of M. Form B Contract; in this case each bore the heading of the Forest agency. Aside from matters such as date and time, they differed from one another in only two areas i. e., the contents of the blanks designated "hours of employment" and "wage agreed upon." The former dealt with matters such as hours of performance and the provision of a guest artist to appear on the program prior to the Russell group. The latter provided that payment was to be "applicable A.F. of M. scale" or a specified percentage (85 percent in the case of Ontario, Oakland, and Philadelphia; 90 percent in the case of Long Island) "of the gross receipts after bonafide, receipted, sanctioned expenses and taxes, whichever is greater." Also here indicated in each case was the capacity of the concert site, the price of tickets, and the potential gross.

The contracts designated Graham as the "purchaser of music" or "employer," the seven members of the group as "musicians." They did not speak explicitly to the question of who was to bear any eventual net losses. The contract forms also provided: "9. In accordance with the Constitution, By-laws, Rules and Regulations of the Federation, the parties will submit every claim, dispute, controversy or difference involving the musical services arising out of or connected with this contract and the engagement covered thereby for determination by the International Executive Board of the Federation or a similar board of an appropriate local thereof and such determination shall be conclusive, final and binding upon the parties."

As indicated above, all four contracts were signed by plaintiff Graham, his signature appearing below his typed name on a blank designated "signature of employer." Only those contracts relating to the Ontario and Oakland concerts bore a corresponding signature; on those contracts, below the typed name "Scissor–Tail, Inc. by C. Russell Bridges aka Leon Russell" and on a blank designated "signature of leader," is the signature of Dennis Cordell, who as above indicated was Russell's personal manager and an officer of Scissor–Tail.

On the second page of each contract is a list of the seven musicians involved (including Russell), together with an indication of the A.F. of M. local of each.

The Ontario concert took place as scheduled and had gross receipts of $173,000 (out of a potential gross reflected in the contract of "$450,000 plus"), with expenses of $236,000, resulting in a net loss of some $63,000. The Oakland concert also took place, resulting in a net profit of some $98,000. Following this second concert a dispute arose among the parties over who was to bear the loss sustained in the Ontario concert and whether that loss could be offset against the profits of the Oakland concert, Scissor–Tail and Forest taking the position that under the contract Graham was to bear all losses from any concert without offset, Graham urging that under standard industry practice and custom relating to 8 5/15 and 9 0/10 contracts such losses should accrue without offset to Scissor–Tail, et al. This dispute remaining unresolved, Scissor–Tail declined to execute the contracts for the Long Island and Philadelphia concerts; apparently these concerts took place as scheduled, but some party other than Graham performed the promotional services.

In October 1973, Graham filed an action for breach of contract, declaratory relief, and rescission against all defendants. Scissor–Tail responded with a petition to compel arbitration. After once ordering arbitration, the trial court in 1974 granted reconsideration in order to permit discovery "limited to the issues of whether an agreement to arbitrate was entered into and whether grounds exist to rescind such agreement. . . ." Following such discovery, and in light of resulting depositions lodged with it, the court in March of 1976 finally granted the petition and ordered arbitration. Along with its order, and at Graham's request, the court filed formal findings of fact and conclusions of law.

By letter dated April 12, 1976, the A.F. of M. was advised of the court's order. By late June, however, no hearing date had been set and counsel for Scissor–Tail wrote to the union requesting that a date be set and suggesting certain dates convenient to him. Rather than comply with this request, however, the union, through its International Executive Board, on July 6 issued its decision awarding the full amount of Scissor–Tail's claim against Graham, or some $53,000. Counsel for Graham, protesting against this procedure, was informed by the A.F. of M. that it conformed with normal practice, which contemplated the entry of award without hearing. Thereupon counsel for Graham enlisted the assistance of Scissor–Tail's counsel in the matter and, upon securing the latter's consent, was successful in reopening the matter and having it set for hearing.

In the meantime, on August 10, 1976, Graham had been placed on the union's "defaulter's list" [sic] apparently a list of persons with whom union members may not do business. . . .

On October 29, 1976, a hearing was held at the union's western (Hollywood) office before a "referee" appointed by the union president. The referee was a former executive officer and a long-time member of the union; he had acted as a hearing officer in many previous union matters. All parties (excluding Russell himself) and counsel were present. Graham sought to have the proceedings transcribed by a court reporter brought by him; the request was denied and the reporter excused. The hearing thereupon proceeded. Graham produced considerable evidence consisting of his own testimony, the testimony of another promoter, the stipulated testimony of a third promoter, and three sworn statements by others engaged in the popular music concert field to the effect that under common and widely held custom and practice in the industry, the promoter under a 9 0/10 or 8 5/15 contract was understood to bear no risk of loss because his share of the profits under such contracts was considerably smaller than under the "normal" contract, under which the promoter takes a larger percentage of the profits but is understood to bear the risk of loss; no contrary evidence was offered by Scissor–Tail. The referee also heard evidence regarding the propriety of certain expenses claimed by Graham and questioned by Scissor–Tail.

On November 5, 1976, in his report to the union's International Executive Board, the referee recommended that Graham be ordered to pay to Scissor–Tail the amount of its original claim (some $53,000; see fn. 6, ante). The balance of the claim consisting of the items added by Scissor–Tail's September 10 request was denied, the referee noting that the union had issued no directions to him regarding it.

On February 22, 1977, the union's International Executive Board made its award in conformity with the recommendation of the referee.

Scissor–Tail thereupon filed a petition in the superior court to confirm the award; Graham filed a petition to vacate it. (See Code Civ.Proc., § 1285.) The court granted the former petition and denied the latter; judgment was entered accordingly. (Code Civ.Proc., § 1287.4.) . . .

Graham appeals from the judgment confirming the arbitrator's award. Scissor–Tail appeals from the order taxing costs.

II

We first turn our attention to the validity of the order compelling arbitration. Plaintiff, as we have indicated, is entitled to challenge this order on the instant appeal.

Plaintiff's basic contention in this respect is that the order compelling arbitration was in error because the underlying agreement at least insofar as it required arbitration of disputes before the A.F. of M. was an unenforceable contract of adhesion. Two separate questions are thus presented, each of which requires separate consideration: (1) Is this a contract of adhesion? (2) If so, is it unenforceable?

A.

The term "contract of adhesion," now long a part of our legal vocabulary, has been variously defined in the cases and other legal literature. The serviceable general definition first suggested by Justice Tobriner in 1961, however, has well stood the test of time and will bear little improvement: "The term signifies a standardized contract, which, imposed and drafted by the party of superior bargaining strength, relegates to the subscribing party only the opportunity to adhere to the contract or reject it." (Neal v. State Farm Ins. Cos. (1961) 188 Cal.App.2d 690, 694, 10 Cal.Rptr. 781.)

Such contracts are, of course, a familiar part of the modern legal landscape, in which the classical model of "free" contracting by parties of equal or near-equal bargaining strength is often found to be unresponsive to the realities brought about by increasing concentrations of economic and other power. They are an inevitable fact of life for all citizens businessman and consumer alike. While not lacking in social advantages, they bear within them the clear danger of oppression and overreaching. It is in the context of this tension between social advantage in the light of modern conditions on the one hand, and the danger of oppression on the other that courts and legislatures have sometimes acted to prevent perceived abuses.

We believe that the contract here in question, in light of all of the circumstances presented, may be fairly described as adhesive. Although defendant and its supporting amicus curiae are strenuous in their insistence that Graham's prominence and success in the promotion of popular music concerts afforded him considerable bargaining strength in the subject negotiations, the record before us fairly establishes that he, for all his asserted stature in the industry, was here reduced to the humble role of "adherent." It appears that all concert artists and groups of any significance or prominence are members of the A.F. of M.; that pursuant to express provision of the A.F. of M.'s constitution and bylaws members are not permitted to sign any form of contract other than that issued by the union; that the A.F. of M. Form B. Contract in use at the time here relevant included the arbitration provisions here in question; and that Scissor–Tail insisted upon the use of 8 5/15 and 9 0/10 contractual arrangements. In these circumstances it must be concluded that Graham, whatever his asserted prominence in the industry, was required by the realities of his business as a concert promoter to sign A.F. of M. form contracts with any concert artist with whom he wished to do business and that in the case before us he, wishing to promote the Russell concerts, was presented with the nonnegotiable option of accepting such contracts on an 8 5/15 or 9 0/10 basis or not at all.

It is argued, however, that other provisions of the contract e. g., those relating to the length, time, and date of the concert and the selection of a special guest artist to appear on the program preceding the Russell group were subject to negotiation and that this consideration operated to mitigate or remove all adhesive characteristics from the contract. We do not agree.... The terms here asserted to be subject to negotiation, assuming that they were in fact so, were of relatively minor significance in comparison to those imposed by Scissor–Tail, which included not only the provision concerning the manner and rate of compensation but that dictating a union forum for the resolution of any disputes. In these circumstances we cannot conclude that the presence of other assertedly negotiable terms acted to remove the taint of adhesion.

B.

To describe a contract as adhesive in character is not to indicate its legal effect. It is, rather, "the beginning and not the end of the analysis insofar as enforceability of its terms is concerned." (Wheeler v. St. Joseph Hospital, supra, 63 Cal.App.3d 345, 357, 133 Cal.Rptr. 775.) Thus, a contract of adhesion is fully enforceable according to its terms ... unless certain other factors are present which, under established legal rules legislative or judicial operate to render it otherwise.

Generally speaking, there are two judicially imposed limitations on the enforcement of adhesion contracts or provisions thereof. The first is that such a contract or provision which does not fall within the reasonable expectations of the weaker or "adhering" party will not be enforced against him ... The second a principle of equity applicable to all contracts generally is that a contract or provision, even if consistent with the reasonable expectations of the parties, will be denied enforcement if, considered in its context, it is unduly oppressive or "unconscionable." ... We proceed to examine whether the instant contract, and especially that provision thereof requiring the arbitration of disputes before the A.F. of M., should have been denied enforcement under either of these two principles.

We cannot conclude on the record before us that the contractual provision requiring arbitration of disputes before the A.F. of M. was in any way contrary to the reasonable expectations of plaintiff Graham. By his own declarations and testimony, he had been a party to literally thousands of A.F. of M. contracts containing a similar provision; indeed it appears that during the 3 years preceding the instant contracts he had promoted 15 or more concerts with Scissor–Tail, on each occasion signing a contract containing arbitration provisions similar to those here in question. It also appears that he had been involved in prior proceedings before the A.F. of M. regarding disputes with other musical groups arising under prior contracts. Finally, the discussions taking place following the Oakland concert, together with his telegram indicating that he himself would file charges with the A.F. of M. if the matter were not settled to his satisfaction, all strongly suggest an abiding awareness on his part that all disputes arising under the contracts were to be resolved by arbitration before the A.F. of M. For all of these reasons it must be concluded that the provisions requiring such arbitration were wholly consistent with Graham's reasonable expectations upon entering into the contract.

We are thus brought to the question whether the contract provision requiring the arbitration of disputes before the A.F. of M. because it designates an arbitrator who, by reason of its status and identity, is presumptively biased in favor of one party is for that reason to be deemed unconscionable and unenforceable. Graham, although couching his arguments in other terminology, essentially maintains that it is the thrust of his position being that to allow the A.F. of M. to sit in judgment of a dispute arising between one of its members and a contracting nonmember is so inimical to fundamental notions of fairness as to require nonenforcement. We proceed to a consideration of this contention.

We are met at the outset of our inquiry with certain provisions of the California Arbitration Act which, it would seem, contemplate complete contractual autonomy in the choice of an arbitrator. Section 1281.6 of the Code of Civil Procedure provides that "(I)f the arbitration agreement provides a method of appointing an arbitrator, such method shall be followed." Section 1282 of the same code states that "(u)nless the arbitration agreement otherwise provides," arbitration shall be by a neutral arbitrator either alone or in combination with other neutral and/or nonneutral arbitrators. Subsection (d) of the same section provides: "If there is no neutral arbitrator, the powers and duties of a neutral arbitrator may be exercised by a majority of the arbitrators."

In Federico v. Frick (1970) 3 Cal.App.3d 872, 84 Cal.Rptr. 74, a case factually similar to that here before us, it was held that these provisions "expressly permit[ ] the parties to an arbitration to agree to the conduct of arbitration proceedings by a nonneutral arbitrator.... [A]rbitration being a creature of statute, the statute controls." (3 Cal.App.3d at p. 876, fn. omitted.) This result followed, the court concluded, even though "(e)lementary fairness may seem to demand that arbitration proceedings be under the control of a neutral and impartial arbitrator, ..."(Id.) The court noted by way of footnote that "many government contracts customarily provide that all disputes arising under them shall be arbitrated by a specified official of the governmental entity which is one of the contracting parties." ...

There are, of course, a host of cases from other jurisdictions which bear upon the problem. We here note only one, which we consider of particular interest. In the Arbitration Between Cross & Brown Company and Nelson (1957) 4 A.D.2d 501, 167 N.Y.S.2d 573, the court considered the validity of a contractual provision in an employment contract which provided that any dispute under the contract was to be arbitrated before the employer, whose decision was to be final. The court, in essence, found the provision unconscionable; enforcement was denied. "A well-recognized principle of 'natural justice,'" the court stated, "is that a man may not be a judge in his own cause. Irrespective of any proof of actual bias or prejudice, the law presumes that a party to a dispute cannot have that disinterestedness and impartiality necessary to act in a judicial or quasi-judicial capacity regarding that controversy. This absolute disqualification to act rests upon sound public policy. Any other rule would be repugnant to a proper sense of justice." (Id., at p. 575.) The court went on, however, to explain the limits of its holding in the following terms: "As a general rule, since arbitration is a contractual method of settling disputes, whom the parties choose to act as an arbitrator is a matter of their own judgment. An interest in the dispute or a relationship with a party, if known to the parties to the agreement when the arbitrator is chosen, will not disqualify the arbitrator from acting. In Lipschutz v. Gutwirth, 304 N.Y. 58, 61–62, 106 N.E.2d 8, 10, the Court said: 'The spirit of the arbitration law being the fuller effectuation of contractual rights, the method for selecting arbitrators and the composition of the arbitral tribunal have been left to the contract of the parties.' ... By our decision herein we do not intend to limit the power of contracting parties to designate arbitrators who, with the knowledge of the parties, may have an interest in the dispute or who sustain some relationship to a party which would otherwise disqualify the arbitrator from serving. What we do hold is that no party to a contract, or someone so identified with the party as to be in fact, even though not in name, the party, can be designated as an arbitrator to decide disputes under it. Apart from outraging public policy, such an agreement is illusory; for while in form it provides for arbitration, in substance it yields the power to an adverse party to decide disputes under the contract." (Id., at p. 576.)

We believe that what was said in the Cross & Brown case, viewed against the provisions of our arbitration act, provides an instructive framework for the consideration of cases such as that now confronting us. The Arbitration Act, as we read it, expressly recognizes the right of contractual parties to provide for the resolution of contractual disputes by arbitral machinery of their own design and composition ... In so doing we do not believe and the Arbitration Act does not require that the parties are or should be strictly precluded from designating as arbitrator a person or entity who, by reason of relationship to a party or some similar factor, can be expected to adopt something other than a "neutral" stance in determining disputes. At the same time we must note that when as here the contract designating such an arbitrator is the product of circumstances suggestive of adhesion, the possibility of overreaching by the dominant party looms large; contracts concluded in such circumstances, then, must be scrutinized with particular care to insure that the party of lesser bargaining power, in agreeing thereto, is not left in a position depriving him of any realistic and fair opportunity to prevail in a dispute under its terms.

As the United States Supreme Court has said in a related context, "Congress has put its blessing on private dispute settlement arrangements ..., but it was anticipated, we are sure, that the contractual machinery would operate within some minimum levels of integrity." (Hines v. Anchor Motor Freight (1976) 424 U.S. 554, 571, 96 S.Ct. 1048, 1059, 47 L.Ed.2d 231.) By the same token it appears that the Legislature has determined that the parties shall have considerable leeway in structuring the dispute settlement arrangements by which they are bound; while recognizing that the leeway may permit the establishment of arrangements which vary to some extent from the dead-center of "neutrality," we at the same time must insist and most especially in circumstances smacking of adhesion that certain "minimum levels of integrity" be achieved if the arrangement in question is to pass judicial muster.

It is for the courts of course to determine largely on a case by case basis what these "minimum levels of integrity" shall be. In doing so it must not be lost sight of that the "contractual machinery" of the parties is intended by them to serve as a substitute for although of course not a duplicate of formal judicial proceedings. What is contemplated, then, is a tribunal i.e., an entity or body which "hears and decides" disputes. (See Webster's New Internat. Dict. (2d ed. 1941) p. 2707.) As the Cross & Brown case indicates, an entity or body which by its nature is incapable of "deciding" on the basis of what it has "heard" as, in that case, one of the principal parties to the contract does not qualify. "Unless we close our eyes to realities," the court there said, "the agreement here becomes, not a contract to arbitrate, but an engagement to capitulate." (167 N.Y.S.2d at p. 576.) The same result would follow, the court there suggests, when one "so identified with the party as to be in fact, even though not in name, the party" is designated. (Id.) In such cases as this, the agreement to arbitrate is essentially illusory. Here, clearly, "minimum levels of integrity" are not achieved, and the "agreement to arbitrate" should be denied enforcement on grounds of unconscionability.

There is we think a second basis, related to that just discussed, for denying enforcement on such grounds. The fact that an entity or body designated by contract to act as arbitrator of contractual disputes is one capable of acting as a tribunal i.e., in the sense of hearing a dispute and deciding fairly and rationally on the basis of what it has heard is of little consequence if it proceeds under rules which deny a party the fair opportunity to present his side of the dispute. Thus, if a party resisting arbitration can show that the rules under which arbitration is to proceed will operate to deprive him of what we in other contexts have termed the common law right of fair procedure, the agreement to arbitrate should not be enforced. In this respect it is well to reiterate, adapting it to the present context, what we said in the seminal case on this subject. "The common law requirement of a fair procedure does not compel formal proceedings with all the embellishments of a court trial (citation), nor adherence to a single mode of process. It may be satisfied by any one of a variety of procedures which afford a fair opportunity for (a disputant) to present his position. As such, this court should not attempt to fix a rigid procedure that must invariably be observed." (Pinsker v. Pacific Coast Society of Orthodontists (1974) 12 Cal.3d 541, 555, 116 Cal.Rptr. 245.) When it can be demonstrated, however, that the clear effect of the established procedure of the arbitrator will be to deny the resisting party a fair opportunity to present his position, the court should refuse to compel arbitration.[23]

We thus return to the narrow question here before us: Is the contract we here consider, insofar as it requires the arbitration of all disputes arising thereunder before the A.F. of M., to be deemed unconscionable and unenforceable?

The answer to this question, we have concluded, must clearly be yes. Although our review of the record has disclosed nothing which would indicate that A.F. of M. procedures operate to deny any party a fair opportunity to present his position prior to decision, we are of the view that

23. Enforcement of an agreement to arbitrate should be denied on this ground, we think, only in the clearest of cases, i.e., when the applicable procedures essentially preclude the possibility of a fair hearing. In all other cases the matter should be permitted to proceed to arbitration. If, in the course of arbitration proceedings, the resisting party is actually denied a fair opportunity to present his position, ample means for relief are available through a subsequent petition to vacate the award. . .

the "minimum levels of integrity" which are requisite to a contractual arrangement for the nonjudicial resolution of disputes are not achieved by an arrangement which designates the union of one of the parties as the arbitrator of disputes arising out of employment especially when, as here, the arrangement is the product of circumstances indicative of adhesion.

As we have indicated above, drawing from the teaching of the Cross & Brown case, a contract which purports to designate one of the parties as the arbitrator of all disputes arising thereunder is to this extent illusory the reason being that the party so designated will have an interest in the outcome which, in the view of the law, will render fair and reasoned decision, based on the evidence presented, a virtual impossibility. Because, as we have explained, arbitration (as a contractually structured substitute for formal judicial proceedings) contemplates just such a decision, a contractual party may not act in the capacity of arbitrator and a contractual provision which designates him to serve in that capacity is to be denied enforcement on grounds of unconscionability. We have also indicated that the same result would follow, and for the same reasons, when the designated arbitrator is not the party himself but one whose interests are so allied with those of the party that, for all practical purposes, he is subject to the same disabilities which prevent the party himself from serving. Again, a contractual provision designating such an entity as arbitrator must be denied enforcement on the ground that it would be unconscionable to permit that entity to so serve.

A labor union is an association or combination of workers organized for the purpose of securing through united action the most favorable conditions as regards wages or rates of pay, hours, and conditions of employment for its members; the primary function of such an organization is that of bargaining with employers on behalf of its membership in order to achieve these objectives ... By its very nature, therefore, a labor union addresses disputes concerning compensation arrangements between its members and third parties with interests identical to those of the affected members; to suppose that it would do otherwise is to suppose that it would act in a manner inconsistent with its reason for being.

In the view of these considerations we think it must be concluded that a contractual provision designating the union of one of the parties to the contract as the arbitrator of all disputes arising thereunder including those concerning the compensation due under the contract does not achieve the "minimum levels of integrity" which we must demand of a contractually structured substitute for judicial proceedings. Such a provision, being inimical to the concept of arbitration as we understand it, would be denied enforcement in any circumstances; clearly it cannot stand in a case which, like that before us, requires the careful and searching scrutiny appropriate to a contract with manifestly adhesive characteristics. The trial court's order compelling arbitration in the instant case was therefore in error and must be reversed.

III

[The Court rejected the Defendant's argument that the agreement was arbitrable under § 301 of the LMRA.]

IV

We have held that the provision of the instant contract requiring arbitration of disputes arising thereunder before the A.F. of M. is unconscionable and unenforceable, and that the order compelling arbitration pursuant to it was in error. In light of the strong public policy of this state in favor of resolving disputes by arbitration, however, we do not believe that the parties herein should for this reason be precluded from availing themselves of nonjudicial means of settling their differences. The parties have indeed agreed to arbitrate, but in so doing they have named as sole and exclusive arbitrator an entity which we cannot permit to serve in that broad capacity. In these circumstances we do not believe that the parties should now be precluded from attempting to agree on an arbitrator who is not subject to the disabilities we have discussed. We therefore conclude that upon remand the trial court should afford the parties a reasonable opportunity to agree on a suitable arbitrator and, failing such agreement, the court should on petition of either party appoint the arbitrator. (See and cf. Code Civ.Proc., § 1281.6.) In the absence of an agreement or petition to appoint, the court should proceed to a judicial determination of the controversy.

The judgment is reversed and the cause remanded to the trial court with directions to vacate its order compelling arbitration and undertake further proceedings in conformity with the views expressed in this opinion....

* * *

Questions

1. Under the *Graham* Court's reasoning, if Graham were to obtain a membership in the American Federation of Musicians, would the arbitration agreement still be unconscionable?

2. Can parties decide on any arbitration process they choose? Recall Richard Posner, cited in *Hodge Brothers* and Note 4 after the case, stating that parties are free to stipulate to any arbitral procedures they choose, "short of authorizing trial by battle or ordeal or, more doubtfully, by a panel of three monkeys."

Suppose, for example, two parties agree to an arbitration procedure in which the brother-in-law of one of them will decide who wins and who loses in any dispute that might arise. Should this be enforceable? Can parties decide to toss a coin in the event of a dispute? Can they decide that one of the parties will decide all disputes? Is Posner's position fully consistent with the contractualist nature of arbitration? Or, does the *Graham v. Scissor–Tail* court suggest that there is some essential minimum due process built into the concept of "arbitration" itself? If so, what kinds of minimal procedures are required? What kinds of procedures would so violate that essential meaning of the term "arbitration" as to no longer come under the FAA?

* * *

Armendariz v. Foundation Health Psychcare Services, Inc.

6 P.3d 669 (Cal. 2000).

■ MOSK, J.

In this case, we consider a number of issues related to the validity of a mandatory employment arbitration agreement, i.e., an agreement by an employee to arbitrate wrongful termination or employment discrimination claims rather than filing suit in court, which an employer imposes on a prospective or current employee as a condition of employment. The employees in this case claim that employees may not be compelled to arbitrate antidiscrimination claims brought under the California Fair Employment and Housing Act (FEHA) (Gov. Code, § 12900 et seq.) We conclude that such claims are in fact arbitrable *if* the arbitration permits an employee to vindicate his or her statutory rights. As explained, in order for such vindication to occur, the arbitration must meet certain minimum requirements, including neutrality of the arbitrator, the provision of adequate discovery, a written decision that will permit a limited form of judicial review, and limitations on the costs of arbitration.

The employees further claim that several provisions of the arbitration agreement are unconscionable, both because they fail to meet these minimum requirements and because the arbitration agreement is not bilateral. We conclude that the agreement possesses a damages limitation that is contrary to public policy, and that it is unconscionably unilateral.

Finally, the employees contend that the presence of these unconscionable provisions renders the entire arbitration agreement unenforceable. The employer argues that even if some of the provisions are unconscionable or contrary to public policy, the proper remedy is to strike or restrict those clauses pursuant to Civil Code section 1670.5, and to enforce the rest of the arbitration agreement. The trial court chose the employees' preferred solution of refusing to enforce the arbitration agreement, but the Court of Appeal sided with the employer and enforced the agreement minus the one provision it found unconscionable. We conclude, for reasons explained below, that the arbitration agreement is unenforceable and that therefore the Court of Appeal's judgment must be reversed.

I. Statement of Facts and Procedural Issues

Marybeth Armendariz and Dolores Olague–Rodgers (hereafter the employees) filed a complaint for wrongful termination against their former employer, Foundation Health Psychcare Services, Inc. (hereafter the employer).... In July and August of 1995, the employer hired the employees in the "Provider Relations Group" and they were later given supervisory positions with annual salaries of $38,000. On June 20, 1996, they were informed that their positions were being eliminated and that they were being terminated. During their year of employment, they claim that their supervisors and coworkers engaged in sexually based harassment and discrimination. The employees alleged that they were "terminated . . . because of their perceived and/or actual sexual orientation (heterosexual)."

Both employees had filled out and signed employment application forms, which included an arbitration clause pertaining to any future claim of wrongful termination. Later, they executed a separate employment arbitration agreement, containing the same arbitration clause. The clause states in full: "I agree as a condition of my employment, that in the event my employment is terminated, and I contend that such termination was wrongful or otherwise in violation of the conditions of employment or was in violation of any express or implied condition, term or covenant of employment, whether founded in fact or in law, including but not limited to the covenant of good faith and fair dealing, or otherwise in violation of any of my rights, I and Employer agree to submit any such matter to binding arbitration pursuant to the provisions of title 9 of Part III of the California Code of Civil Procedure, commencing at section 1280 et seq. or any successor or replacement statutes. I and Employer further expressly agree that in any such arbitration, my exclusive remedies for violation of the terms, conditions or covenants of employment shall be limited to a sum equal to the wages I would have earned from the date of any discharge until the date of the arbitration award. I understand that I shall not be entitled to any other remedy, at law or in equity, including but not limited to reinstatement and/or injunctive relief."

The employees' complaint against the employer alleges a cause of action for violation of the FEHA and three additional causes of action for wrongful termination based on tort and contract theories of recovery. The complaint sought general damages, punitive damages, injunctive relief, and the recovery of attorney fees and costs of suit.

The employer countered by filing a motion for an order to compel arbitration pursuant to Code of Civil Procedure section 1281.2. . . . [T]he trial court denied the motion on the ground that the arbitration provision in question was an unconscionable contract. The . . . Court of Appeal reversed. . . . We granted review.

II. Discussion

[The Court held that employment discrimination claims are arbitrable, an issue open at the time that since has been resolved in favor of arbitrability. The Court next held that the FAA covered employment contracts, another issue open at the time that since has been resolved in favor of coverage.]

C. *Arbitration of FEHA Claims*

The United States Supreme Court's dictum that a party, in agreeing to arbitrate a statutory claim, "does not forgo the substantive rights afforded by the statute [but] only submits to their resolution in an arbitral ... forum" (*Mitsubishi Motors, supra*, 473 U.S. at p. 628) is as much prescriptive as it is descriptive. That is, it sets a standard by which arbitration agreements and practices are to be measured, and disallows forms of arbitration that in fact compel claimants to forfeit certain substantive statutory rights....

1. *Limitation of Remedies*

The principle that an arbitration agreement may not limit statutorily imposed remedies such as punitive damages and attorney fees appears to be undisputed.... [I]n *Graham Oil v. ARCO Products Co.* (9th Cir. 1994) 43 F.3d 1244 (*Graham Oil*), the court refused to enforce an arbitration agreement between a petroleum franchiser and franchisee that did not allow for the punitive damages and attorney fees remedies available under the Petroleum Marketing Practices Act, because both of these remedies are "important to the effectuation of the PMPA's policies." (*Gaham Oil, supra*, 43 F.3d at p. 1248.)

As stated, the arbitration agreement in this case [limits damages to back pay]. The employees claim that the agreement compels them to arbitrate statutory claims without affording the full range of statutory remedies, including punitive damages and attorney fees to a prevailing plaintiff, available under the FEHA.... We conclude this damages limitation is contrary to public policy and unlawful.

2. *Adequate Discovery*

The employees argue that employers typically have in their possession many of the documents relevant for bringing an employment discrimination case, as well as having in their employ many of the relevant witnesses. The denial of adequate discovery in arbitration proceedings leads to the de facto frustration of the employee's statutory rights....

We agree that adequate discovery is indispensable for the vindication of FEHA claims. The employer does not dispute the point, but contends that the arbitration agreement at issue in this case does provide for adequate discovery by incorporating by reference all the rules set forth in the [California Arbitration Act. We find these discovery rules sufficient to vindicate the employees' FEHA rights.]

3. *Judicial Review*

The employees argue that lack of judicial review of arbitration awards makes the vindication of FEHA rights in arbitration illusory.... [However,] the employees' claim that they are unable to vindicate their FEHA rights because of inadequate judicial review of an arbitration award is premature.

4. *Employee Not to Pay Unreasonable Costs and Arbitration Fees*

The employees point to the fact that the agreement is governed by Code of Civil Procedure section 1284.2, which provides that "each party to the arbitration shall pay his pro rata share of the expenses and fees of the neutral arbitrator, together with other expenses of the arbitration incurred or approved by the neutral arbitrator . . ." They argue that requiring them to share the often substantial costs of arbitrators and arbitration effectively prevents them from vindicating their FEHA rights. . . .

[W]e conclude that when an employer imposes mandatory arbitration as a condition of employment, the arbitration agreement or arbitration process cannot generally require the employee to bear any *type* of expense that the employee would not be required to bear if he or she were free to bring the action in court. This rule will ensure that employees bringing FEHA claims will not be deterred by costs greater than the usual costs incurred during litigation, costs that are essentially imposed on an employee by the employer. . . .

We therefore hold that a mandatory employment arbitration agreement that contains within its scope the arbitration of FEHA claims impliedly obliges the employer to pay all types of costs that are unique to arbitration. Accordingly, we interpret the arbitration agreement in the present case as providing, consistent with the above, that the employer must bear the arbitration forum costs. The absence of specific provisions on arbitration costs would therefore not be grounds for denying the enforcement of an arbitration agreement.

D. *Unconscionability of the Arbitration Agreement*

1. *General Principles of Unconscionability*

In the previous part of this opinion, we focused on the minimum requirements for the arbitration of unwaivable statutory claims. In this part, we will consider objections to arbitration that apply more generally to any type of arbitration imposed on the employee by the employer as a condition of employment, regardless of the type of claim being arbitrated. These objections fall under the rubric of unconscionability.

We explained the judicially created doctrine of unconscionability in *Scissor–Tail*, *supra*, 28 Cal.3d 807. . . . Because unconscionability is a reason for refusing to enforce contracts generally, it is also a valid reason for refusing to enforce an arbitration agreement under Code of Civil Procedure section 1281, which, as noted, provides that arbitration agreements are "valid, enforceable and irrevocable, save upon such grounds as exist for the revocation of any contract." The United States Supreme Court, in interpreting the same language found in section 2 of the FAA (9 U.S.C. § 2), recognized that "generally applicable contract defenses, such as fraud, duress, or *unconscionability*, may be applied to invalidate arbitration agreements. . . ." (*Doctor's Associates, Inc. v. Casarotto*, *supra*, 517 U.S. 681, 687 [116 S.Ct. 1652, 1656], italics added.)

As explained in *A & M Produce Co.*, *supra*, 135 Cal.App.3d 473, "unconscionability has both a 'procedural' and a 'substantive' element," the former focusing on " 'oppression' " or " 'surprise' " due to unequal bargaining power, the latter on " 'overly harsh' " or " 'one-sided' " results.

(*Id.* at pp. 486–487.) "The prevailing view is that [procedural and substantive unconscionability] must *both* be present in order for a court to exercise its discretion to refuse to enforce a contract or clause under the doctrine of unconscionability." (*Stirlen v. Supercuts, Inc.*, 51 Cal.App.4th at p. 1533). But they need not be present in the same degree. "Essentially a sliding scale is invoked which disregards the regularity of the procedural process of the contract formation, that creates the terms, in proportion to the greater harshness or unreasonableness of the substantive terms themselves." (15 Williston on Contracts (3d ed. 1972) § 1763A, pp. 226–227; see also *A & M Produce Co., supra*, 135 Cal.App.3d at p. 487.) In other words, the more substantively oppressive the contract term, the less evidence of procedural unconscionability is required to come to the conclusion that the term is unenforceable, and vice versa.

2. *Unconscionability and Mandatory Employment Arbitration*

Applying the above principles to this case, we first determine whether the arbitration agreement is adhesive. There is little dispute that it is. It was imposed on employees as a condition of employment and there was no opportunity to negotiate.

Moreover, in the case of preemployment arbitration contracts, the economic pressure exerted by employers on all but the most sought-after employees may be particularly acute, for the arbitration agreement stands between the employee and necessary employment, and few employees are in a position to refuse a job because of an arbitration requirement. While arbitration may have its advantages in terms of greater expedition, informality, and lower cost, it also has, from the employee's point of view, potential disadvantages: waiver of a right to a jury trial, limited discovery, and limited judicial review. . . .

Arbitration is favored in this state as a voluntary means of resolving disputes, and this voluntariness has been its bedrock justification. . . . Given the lack of choice and the potential disadvantages that even a fair arbitration system can harbor for employees, we must be particularly attuned to claims that employers with superior bargaining power have imposed one-sided, substantively unconscionable terms as part of an arbitration agreement. . . . With this in mind, we turn to the employees' specific unconscionability claims.

Aside from FEHA issues discussed in the previous part of this opinion, the employees contend that the agreement is substantively unconscionable because it requires only employees to arbitrate their wrongful termination claims against the employer, but does not require the employer to arbitrate claims it may have against the employees. In asserting that this lack of mutuality is unconscionable, they rely primarily on the opinion of the Court of Appeal in *Stirlen, supra*, 51 Cal.App.4th 1519. The employee in that case was hired as a vice-president and chief financial officer; his employment contract provided for arbitration " 'in the event there is any dispute arising out of [the employee's] employment with the Company,' " including "the termination of that employment." (*Stirlen, supra*, 51 Cal.

App.4th at p. 1528.) The agreement specifically excluded certain types of disputes from the scope of arbitration, including those relating to the protection of the employer's intellectual and other property and the enforcement of a postemployment covenant not to compete, which were to be litigated in state or federal court.... The *Stirlen* court concluded that the agreement was one of adhesion [and that it] was substantively unconscionable.

We conclude that a "modicum of bilaterality" [is required] in an arbitration agreement. Given the disadvantages that may exist for plaintiffs arbitrating disputes, it is unfairly one-sided for an employer with superior bargaining power to impose arbitration on the employee as plaintiff but not to accept such limitations when it seeks to prosecute a claim against the employee, without at least some reasonable justification for such one-sidedness based on "business realities." ... If the arbitration system established by the employer is indeed fair, then the employer as well as the employee should be willing to submit claims to arbitration. Without reasonable justification for this lack of mutuality, arbitration appears less as a forum for neutral dispute resolution and more as a means of maximizing employer advantage. Arbitration was not intended for this purpose.

The employer cites a number of cases that have held that a lack of mutuality in an arbitration agreement does not render the contract illusory as long as the employer agrees to be bound by the arbitration of employment disputes. (*Michalski v. Circuit City Stores, Inc.* (7th Cir. 1999) 177 F.3d 634; *Johnson v. Circuit City Stores* (4th Cir. 1998) 148 F.3d 373, 378.) We agree that such lack of mutuality does not render the contract illusory, i.e., lacking in mutual consideration. We conclude, rather, that in the context of an arbitration agreement imposed by the employer on the employee, such a one-sided term is unconscionable. Although parties are free to contract for asymmetrical remedies and arbitration clauses of varying scope, ... the doctrine of unconscionability limits the extent to which a stronger party may, through a contract of adhesion, impose the arbitration forum on the weaker party without accepting that forum for itself....

We agree with the *Stirlen* court that the ordinary principles of unconscionability may manifest themselves in forms peculiar to the arbitration context. One such form is an agreement requiring arbitration only for the claims of the weaker party but a choice of forums for the claims of the stronger party. The application of this principle to arbitration does not disfavor arbitration. It is no disparagement of arbitration to acknowledge that it has, as noted, both advantages and disadvantages. The perceived advantages of the judicial forum for plaintiffs include the availability of discovery and the fact that courts and juries are viewed as more likely to adhere to the law and less likely than arbitrators to "split the difference" between the two sides, thereby lowering damages awards for plaintiffs.... An employer may accordingly consider a court to be a forum superior to arbitration when it comes to vindicating its own contractual and statutory rights, or may consider it advantageous to have a choice of arbitration or litigation when determining how best to pursue a claim against an employee. It does not disfavor arbitration to hold that an employer may not impose a system of arbitration on an employee that seeks to maximize the advantages and minimize the disadvantages of arbitration for itself at the employee's expense. On the contrary, a unilateral arbitration agreement imposed by the employer without reasonable justification reflects the very mistrust of arbitration that has been repudiated by the United States Supreme Court in *Doctors' Associates, Inc. v. Casarotto*, *supra*, 517 U.S. 681, and other cases. We emphasize that if an employer does have reasonable justification for the arrangement—i.e., a justification grounded in something other than the employer's desire to maximize its advantage based on the perceived superiority of the judicial forum—such an agreement would not be unconscionable. Without such justification, we must assume that it is.

Applying these principles to the present case, we note the arbitration agreement was limited in scope to employee claims regarding wrongful termination. Although it did not expressly authorize litigation of the employer's claims against the employee, ... such was the clear implication of the agreement....

This is not to say that an arbitration clause must mandate the arbitration of all claims between employer and employee in order to avoid invalidation on grounds of unconscionability. Indeed, as the employer points out, the present arbitration agreement does not require arbitration of all conceivable claims that an employee might have against an employer, only wrongful termination claims. But an arbitration agreement imposed in an adhesive context lacks basic fairness and mutuality if it requires one contracting party, but not the other, to arbitrate all claims arising out of the same transaction or occurrence or series of transactions or occurrences. The arbitration agreement in this case lacks mutuality in this sense because it requires the arbitration of employee—but not employer—claims arising out of a wrongful termination. An employee terminated for stealing trade secrets, for example, must arbitrate his or her wrongful termination claim under the agreement while the employer has no corresponding obligation to arbitrate its trade secrets claim against the employee.

The unconscionable one-sidedness of the arbitration agreement is compounded in this case by the fact that it does not permit the full recovery of damages for employees, while placing no such restriction on the employer. Even if the limitation on FEHA damages is severed as contrary to public policy, the arbitration clause in the present case still does not permit full recovery of ordinary contract [or tort] damages....

E. *Severability of Unconscionable Provisions*

... Two reasons for severing or restricting illegal terms rather than voiding the entire contract appear implicit in case law. The first is to prevent parties from gaining undeserved benefit or suffering undeserved detriment as a result of voiding the entire agreement—particularly when there has been full or partial performance of the contract.... Second, more generally, the doctrine of severance attempts to conserve a contractual relationship if to do so would not be condoning an illegal scheme.

In this case, two factors weigh against severance of the unlawful provisions. First, the arbitration agreement contains more than one unlawful provision; it has both an unlawful damages provision and an unconscionably unilateral arbitration clause. Such multiple defects indicate a systematic effort to impose arbitration on an employee not simply as an alternative to litigation, but as an inferior forum that works to the employer's advantage.

Second, in the case of the agreement's lack of mutuality, such permeation is indicated by the fact that there is no single provision a court can strike or restrict in order to remove the unconscionable taint from the agreement. Rather, the court would have to, in effect, reform the contract, not through severance or restriction, but by augmenting it with additional terms.

III. Disposition

The judgment of the Court of Appeal upholding the employer's petition to compel arbitration is reversed, and the cause is remanded to the Court of Appeal with directions to affirm the judgment of the trial court.

* * *

Questions

1. Note the Court's two distinct sources of authority for striking arbitral provisions that it considered offensive: (1) that these provisions eviscerated substantive statutory rights, and (2) unconscionability. How would the first argument work if the employees' claims had been based only on contract or tort?

2. The employees in this case were low-level supervisors. What if, instead, this same arbitration agreement had been challenged by a CEO, and the company were able to show lots of give-and-take in the negotiation of the employment contract of which the arbitration agreement was a part, including give-and-take over provisions of the arbitration clause? Would such a contract be adhesive? If not, would or could it be unconscionable? Should the law distinguish negotiated contracts from "cram-down" contracts? How?

3. The *Armendariz* court states that "ordinary principles of unconscionability may manifest themselves in forms peculiar to the arbitration context." *Perry v. Thomas* and progeny state that the FAA preempts state laws that restrict enforcement of arbitration agreements but not other contracts. How should courts deal with contract provisions that are specific to arbitration clauses? Clearly, a court may not invalidate an arbitration clause simply because the court believes in the superiority of a judicial forum, but what about provisions "that go beyond the choice of arbitration itself," and instead specify, for example, how that arbitration is to occur?

See David S. Schwartz, *The Federal Arbitration Act and the Power of Congress Over State Courts*, 83 Or. L. Rev. 541, 568 (2004). For example, may a state court strike in its entirety an employment arbitration clause that gives the employer unilateral authority to select the pool of potential arbitrators, or that restricts an arbitrator's authority to award punitive damages? The unconscionability doctrine is a "general" contract doctrine applicable to all contracts, but applied in this way it may be said to single out arbitration clauses. See Christopher R. Drahozal, *Federal Arbitration Act Preemption*, 79 Ind. L.J. 393, 411 (2004).

4. The *Armendariz* court finds that two terms are unconscionable: limitations on remedies and lack of mutuality. The latter is a relatively mild rationale for finding unconscionability—compare, for example, some of the lopsided arbitration terms discussed below in Chapter 3. *Armendariz* holds only that lack of mutuality is unconscionable absent justification. Employers argue that preserving judicial remedies for employers but not employees is justified because the few employer causes of action against employees (such as attempts to protect trade secrets) cannot be cured by damages, and therefore require immediate judicial intervention in the form of restraining orders and injunctions, whereas typical employee claims (such as wrongful discharge) can be cured by damages. Are you persuaded?

5. The *Armendariz* court found that lack of mutuality could support a finding of unconscionability. Other courts have found, as *Armendariz* alluded, that lack of mutuality causes a failure of consideration. See, e.g., Gibson v. Neighborhood Health Clinics, Inc., 121 F.3d 1126, 1131 (7th Cir. 1997). Still other courts have held that mutuality is not required so long as the employer has provided the employee with some other type of consideration. For example, in Circuit City Stores, Inc. v. Najd, 294 F.3d 1104, 1108 (9th Cir. 2002), the Ninth Circuit held that an employer's "promise to be bound by the arbitration process itself" is adequate consideration to support the employee's promise to arbitrate his claims; it was irrelevant that the employer did not promise to arbitrate its own claims against the employee. Most courts fall somewhere between these extremes, requiring that the employer agree to arbitrate at least some claims against the employee or give the employee at least something of value in exchange for the employee's arbitration agreement. There is a split of authority over whether at-will employment can constitute adequate consideration for an arbitration agreement. See Richard A. Bales, *Contract Formation Issues in Employment Arbitration*, 44 Brandeis L.J. 415, 455–58 (2006).

6. Do you agree that the *Armendariz* court's discussion of lack of mutuality is not premised on a disparagement of arbitration?

7. When a court finds that one or more terms in an arbitration agreement are unconscionable, should the court sever the offending terms(s) or refuse to enforce the entire arbitration agreement? What are the advantages and disadvantages of each approach?

8. Both *Graham v. Scissor*–Tail and *Armendariz* are California decisions. They should not necessarily be taken as representative of the other 49 states on the issue of unconscionability. Many other states, for example, impose a much higher standard for both substantive and procedural unconscionability. Is the California approach to unconscionability anti-arbitration?

* * *

Broemmer v. Abortion Services of Phoenix, Ltd.

840 P.2d 1013 (Ariz. 1992).

■ MOELLER, VICE CHIEF JUSTICE.

Melinda Kay Broemmer (plaintiff) asks this court to review a court of appeals opinion that held that an "Agreement to Arbitrate" which she signed prior to undergoing a clinical abortion is an enforceable, albeit an adhesive, contract. Broemmer v. Otto, 169 Ariz. 543, 821 P.2d 204 (1991). The opinion affirmed the trial court's grant of summary judgment in favor of Abortion Services of Phoenix and Dr. Otto (defendants). Because we hold the agreement to arbitrate is unenforceable as against plaintiff, we reverse the trial court and vacate in part the court of appeals opinion. We have jurisdiction pursuant to Ariz. Const. art. 6, § 5(3) and A.R.S. § 12–120.24.

FACTS AND PROCEDURAL HISTORY

In December 1986, plaintiff, an Iowa resident, was 21 years old, unmarried, and 16 or 17 weeks pregnant. She was a high school graduate earning less than $100.00 a week and had no medical benefits. The father-to-be insisted that plaintiff have an abortion, but her parents advised against it. Plaintiff's uncontested affidavit describes the time as one of considerable confusion and emotional and physical turmoil for her.

Plaintiff's mother contacted Abortion Services of Phoenix and made an appointment for her daughter for December 29, 1986. During their visit to the clinic that day, plaintiff and her mother expected, but did not receive, information and counseling on alternatives to abortion and the nature of the operation. When plaintiff and her mother arrived at the clinic, plaintiff was escorted into an adjoining room and asked to complete three forms, one of which is the agreement to arbitrate at issue in this case. The agreement to arbitrate included language that "any dispute aris[ing] between the Parties as a result of the fees and/or services" would be settled by binding arbitration and that "any arbitrators appointed by the AAA [American Arbitration Association] shall be licensed medical doctors who specialize in obstetrics/gynecology." The two other documents plaintiff completed at the same time were a 2–page consent-to-operate form and a questionnaire asking for a detailed medical history. Plaintiff completed all three forms in less than 5 minutes and returned them to the front desk. Clinic staff made no attempt to explain the agreement to plaintiff before or after she signed, and did not provide plaintiff with copies of the forms. After plaintiff returned the forms to the front desk, she was taken into an examination room where pre-operation procedures were performed. She was then instructed to return at 7:00 a.m. the next morning for the termination procedure. Plaintiff returned the following day and Doctor Otto performed the abortion. As a result of the procedure, plaintiff suffered a punctured uterus that required medical treatment.

Plaintiff filed a malpractice complaint in June 1988, approximately 1 ½ years after the medical procedure. By the time litigation commenced, plaintiff could recall completing and signing the medical history and consent-to-operate forms, but could not recall signing the agreement to arbitrate. Defendants moved to dismiss, contending that the trial court lacked subject matter jurisdiction because arbitration was required. In opposition, plaintiff submitted affidavits that remain uncontroverted. The trial court considered the affidavits, apparently treated the motion to dismiss as one for summary judgment, and granted summary judgment to the defendants. Plaintiff's motion to vacate, quash or set aside the order, or to stay the claim pending arbitration, was denied.

On appeal, the court of appeals held that although the contract was one of adhesion, it was nevertheless enforceable because it did not fall outside plaintiff's reasonable expectations and was not unconscionable ... We granted plaintiff's petition for review.

We will resolve the one issue which is dispositive: Under the undisputed facts in this case, is the agreement to arbitrate enforceable against plaintiff? We hold that it is not.

DISCUSSION

I. The Contract is One of Adhesion

When the facts are undisputed, this court is not bound by the trial court's conclusions and may make its own analysis of the facts or legal instruments on which the case turns. Tovrea Land & Cattle Co. v. Linsenmeyer, 100 Ariz. 107, 114, 412 P.2d 47, 51 (1966). A.R.S. § 12–1501 authorizes written agreements to arbitrate and provides that they are "valid, enforceable and irrevocable, save upon such grounds as exist at law or in equity for the revocation of any contract." Thus, the enforceability of the agreement to arbitrate is determined by principles of general contract law. The court of appeals concluded, and we agree, that, under those principles, the contract in this case was one of adhesion.

An adhesion contract is typically a standardized form "offered to consumers of goods and services on essentially a 'take it or leave it' basis without affording the consumer a realistic opportunity to bargain and under such conditions that the consumer cannot obtain the desired product or services except by acquiescing in the form contract." Wheeler v. St. Joseph Hosp., 63 Cal.App.3d 345, 356, 133 Cal.Rptr. 775, 783 (1976) (citations omitted); see also Burkons v. Ticor Title Ins. Co. of Cal., 165 Ariz. 299, 311, 798 P.2d 1308, 1320 (App. 1989), rev'd on other grounds, 168 Ariz. 345, 813 P.2d 710 (1991) (essence of adhesion contract is that it is offered to consumers on essentially a "take it or leave it" basis). The Wheeler court further stated that "[t]he distinctive feature of a contract of adhesion is that the weaker party has no realistic choice as to its terms."

63 Cal.App.3d at 356, 133 Cal.Rptr. at 783 (citations omitted). Likewise, in Contractual Problems in the Enforcement of Agreements to Arbitrate Medical Malpractice, 58 Va.L.Rev. 947, 988 (1972), Professor Stanley Henderson recognized "the essence of an adhesion contract is that bargaining position and leverage enable one party 'to select and control risks assumed under the contract.'" (quoting Friedrich Kessler, Contracts of Adhesion–Some Thoughts About Freedom of Contract, 43 Colum.L.Rev. 629 (1943)).

The printed form agreement signed by plaintiff in this case possesses all the characteristics of a contract of adhesion. The form is a standardized contract offered to plaintiff on a "take it or leave it" basis. In addition to removing from the courts any potential dispute concerning fees or services, the drafter inserted additional terms potentially advantageous to itself requiring that any arbitrator appointed by the American Arbitration Association be a licensed medical doctor specializing in obstetrics/gynecology. The contract was not negotiated but was, instead, prepared by defendant and presented to plaintiff as a condition of treatment. Staff at the clinic neither explained its terms to plaintiff nor indicated that she was free to refuse to sign the form; they merely represented to plaintiff that she had to complete the three forms. The conditions under which the clinic offered plaintiff the services were on a "take it or leave it" basis, and the terms of service were not negotiable. Applying general contract law to the undisputed facts, the court of appeals correctly held that the contract was one of adhesion.

II. Reasonable Expectations

Our conclusion that the contract was one of adhesion is not, of itself, determinative of its enforceability. "[A] contract of adhesion is fully enforceable according to its terms [citations omitted] unless certain other factors are present which, under established legal rules—legislative or judicial—operate to render it otherwise." Graham v. Scissor–Tail, Inc., 28 Cal.3d 807, (1981) (footnotes omitted). To determine whether this contract of adhesion is enforceable, we look to two factors: the reasonable expectations of the adhering party and whether the contract is unconscionable . . .

Plaintiff argues that the trial court should have adopted, and we should now adopt, the analysis provided in Obstetrics & Gynecologists v. Pepper, 101 Nev. 105, 693 P.2d 1259 (1985), because it is virtually indistinguishable from the present case. In Pepper, the patient was required to sign an agreement before receiving treatment which waived her right to jury trial [sic] and submitted all disputes to arbitration. The clinic did not explain the contents of the agreement to the patient. The clinic's practice was to have staff instruct patients to complete two medical history forms and the agreement to arbitrate and to inform patients that any questions would be answered. If the patient refused to sign the agreement, the clinic refused treatment.

The plaintiff in Pepper signed the agreement, but did not recall doing so, nor did she recall having the agreement explained to her. The plaintiff later brought suit for injuries suffered due to improperly prescribed oral contraceptives. The trial court made no findings of fact or conclusions of law, but the Nevada Supreme Court, upon review of the record before it, held the agreement unenforceable because plaintiff did not give a knowing consent to the agreement to arbitrate.

The facts in the instant case present an even stronger argument in favor of holding the agreement unenforceable than do the facts in Pepper. In both cases, plaintiffs stated that they did not recall signing the agreement to arbitrate or having it explained to them. Unlike the clinic in Pepper, the clinic in this case did not show that it was the procedure of clinic staff to offer to explain the agreement to patients. The clinic did not explain the purpose of the form to plaintiff and did not show whether plaintiff was required to sign the form or forfeit treatment. In Pepper, the fact that both parties were waiving their right to a jury trial was explicit, which is not so in the present case.

Clearly, the issues of knowing consent and reasonable expectations are closely related and intertwined. In Darner Motor Sales, Inc. v. Universal Underwriters Ins. Co., 140 Ariz. 383, 682 P.2d 388 (1984), this court used the Restatement (Second) of Contracts § 211 (Standardized Agreements), as a guide to analyzing, among other things, contracts that contain non-negotiated terms. The comment to subsection (3), quoted with approval in Darner, states in part:

> Although customers typically adhere to standardized agreements and are bound by them without even appearing to know the standard terms in detail, they are not bound to unknown terms which are beyond the range of reasonable expectation.

See 140 Ariz. at 391, 682 P.2d at 396.

The Restatement focuses our attention on whether it was beyond plaintiff's reasonable expectations to expect to arbitrate her medical malpractice claims, which includes waiving her right to a jury trial, as part of the filling out of the three forms under the facts and circumstances of this case. Clearly, there was no conspicuous or explicit waiver of the fundamental right to a jury trial or any evidence that such rights were knowingly, voluntarily and intelligently waived. The only evidence presented compels a finding that waiver of such fundamental rights was beyond the reasonable expectations of plaintiff. Moreover, as Professor Henderson writes, "[i]n attempting to effectuate reasonable expectations consistent with a standardized medical contract, a court will find less reason to regard the bargaining process as suspect if there are no terms unreasonably favorable to the stronger party." Henderson, supra, at 995. In this case failure to explain to plaintiff that the agreement required all potential disputes, including malpractice disputes, to be heard only by an arbitrator who was a licensed obstetrician/gynecologist requires us to view the "bargaining" process with suspicion. It would be unreasonable to enforce such a critical term against plaintiff when it is not a negotiated term and defendant failed to explain it to her or call her attention to it.

Personal Facts

Plaintiff was under a great deal of emotional stress, had only a high school education, was not experienced in commercial matters, and is still not sure "what arbitration is." Given the circumstances under which the agreement was signed and the nature of the terms included therein, our reading of Pepper, Darner, the Restatement and the affidavits in this case compel us to conclude that the contract fell outside plaintiff's reasonable expectations and is, therefore, unenforceable. Because of this holding, it is unnecessary for us to determine whether the contract is also unconscionable.

III. A Comment on The Dissent

In view of the concern expressed by the dissent, we restate our firm conviction that arbitration and other methods of alternative dispute resolution play important and desirable roles in our system of dispute resolution. We encourage their use. When agreements to arbitrate are freely and fairly entered, they will be welcomed and enforced. They will not, however, be exempted from the usual rules of contract law, as A.R.S. § 12–1501 itself makes clear . . .

The dissent is concerned that our decision today sends a "mixed message." It is, however, our intent to send a clear message. That message is: Contracts of adhesion will not be enforced unless they are conscionable and within the reasonable expectations of the parties. This is a well-established principle of contract law; today we merely apply it to the undisputed facts of the case before us.

DISPOSITION

Those portions of the opinion of the court of appeals inconsistent with this opinion are vacated. The judgment of the trial court is reversed and this case is remanded for further proceedings consistent with this opinion. Because plaintiff has successfully overcome defendant's claimed contractual defense, the trial court may entertain an application for fees incurred at the trial court and appellate level. Wagenseller v. Scottsdale Memorial Hosp., 147 Ariz. 370, 391–95, 710 P.2d 1025, 1046–50 (1985).

■ FELDMAN, C.J., and CORCORAN and ZLAKET, JJ., concur.

■ MARTONE, JUSTICE, dissenting.

The court's conclusion that the agreement to arbitrate was outside the plaintiff's reasonable expectations is without basis in law or fact. I fear today's decision reflects a preference for litigation over alternative dispute resolution that I had thought was behind us. I would affirm the court of appeals.

We begin with the undisputed facts that the court ignores. Appendix "A" to this dissent is the agreement to arbitrate. At the top it states in bold capital letters "PLEASE READ THIS CONTRACT CAREFULLY AS IT EFFECTS [sic] YOUR LEGAL RIGHTS." Directly under that in all capital letters are the words "AGREEMENT TO ARBITRATE." The recitals indicate that "the Parties deem it to be in their respective best interest to settle any such dispute as expeditiously and economically as possible." The parties agreed that disputes over services provided would be settled by arbitration in accordance with the rules of the American Arbitration Association. They further agreed that the arbitrators appointed by the American Arbitration Association would be licensed medical doctors who specialize in obstetrics/gynecology. Plaintiff, an adult, signed the document....

The court seizes upon the doctrine of reasonable expectations to revoke this contract. But there is nothing in this record that would warrant a finding that an agreement to arbitrate a malpractice claim was not within the reasonable expectations of the parties. On this record, the exact opposite is likely to be true. For all we know, both sides in this case might wish to avoid litigation like the plague and seek the more harmonious waters of alternative dispute resolution. Nor is there anything in this record that would suggest that arbitration is bad. Where is the harm? In the end, today's decision reflects a preference in favor of litigation that is not shared by the courts of other states and the courts of the United States.

In Doyle v. Giuliucci, 62 Cal.2d 606, 43 Cal.Rptr. 697, 699, 401 P.2d 1, 3 (1965), Chief Justice Roger J. Traynor of the California Supreme Court said, in connection with a medical malpractice claim, that "[t]he arbitration provision in such contracts is a reasonable restriction, for it does no more than specify a forum for the settlement of disputes." And, in Madden v. Kaiser Foundation Hospitals, 17 Cal.3d 699, 131 Cal.Rptr. 882, 890, 552 P.2d 1178, 1186 (1976), the California Supreme Court outlined "the benefits of the arbitral forum":

> [t]he speed and economy of arbitration, in contrast to the expense and delay of jury trial, could prove helpful to all parties; the simplified procedures and relaxed rules of evidence in arbitration may aid an injured plaintiff in presenting his case. Plaintiffs with less serious injuries, who cannot afford the high litigation expenses of court or jury trial, disproportionate to the amount of their claim, will benefit especially from the simplicity and economy of arbitration; that procedure could facilitate the adjudication of minor malpractice claims which cannot economically be resolved in a judicial forum....

Against this background, how does this court reach its conclusion that arbitration is beyond the reasonable expectations of the parties? Its reliance on Obstetrics and Gynecologists v. Pepper, 101 Nev. 105, 693 P.2d 1259 (1985), Darner Motor Sales, Inc. v. Universal Underwriters Insurance Co., 140 Ariz. 383, 682 P.2d 388 (1984), and the Restatement (Second) of Contracts § 211 (1979), is misplaced.

Pepper is a brief per curiam opinion of the Nevada Supreme Court which merely affirmed the finding of a trial court. The trial court held a hearing to determine whether there was an enforceable arbitration contract. However, the trial court did not make findings of facts and conclusions of law. That court simply denied a motion to stay pending arbitration. The Nevada Supreme Court said "[t]he district court could certainly have found that the arbitration agreement was an adhesion contract." 693 P.2d at 1260. It then said "[s]ince appellant's counsel failed to pursue the entry of findings of facts and conclusions of law, we are bound to presume that the district court found that respondent did not give a knowing consent to the arbitration agreement prepared by appellant clinic." Id., 693 P.2d at 1261. If Pepper stands for anything, it stands for the proposition that "knowing consent" is a factual question, and that an appellate court will affirm a factual finding if there is any evidence to support it. The basis for the court's decision was "knowing consent" under Nevada law, not reasonable expectations under ours.

Nor are Darner and the Restatement support for this court's conclusion. Darner held that an adhesive contract term that is "contrary to the negotiated agreement made by the parties," 140 Ariz. at 387, 682 P.2d at 392, will not be enforced because it collides with expectations that "have been induced by the making of a promise." 140 Ariz. at 390, 682 P.2d at 395 (quoting 1 Corbin, Contracts § 1 at 2 (1963)). The defendant here did not promise the plaintiff that malpractice claims could be litigated. Thus, the agreement to arbitrate is not contrary to any negotiated deal.

Gordinier v. Aetna Casualty & Surety Co., 154 Ariz. 266, 742 P.2d 277 (1987), of course, extended Darner to the entire scope of the Restatement (Second) of Contracts § 211 (1979). But even that section does not support today's decision. Under Restatement (Second) of Contracts § 211(3), standardized agreements are enforceable except where a party has reason to believe that the other party would not manifest assent if he knew that the writing contained a particular term. Comment f to § 211 tells us:

> Such a belief or assumption may be shown by the prior negotiations or inferred from the circumstances. Reason to believe may be inferred from the fact that the term is bizarre or oppressive, from the fact that it eviscerates the non-standard terms explicitly agreed to, or from the fact that it eliminates the dominant purpose of the transaction. The inference is reinforced if the adhering party never had an opportunity to read the term, or if it is illegible or otherwise hidden from view.

Plainly, there are no facts in this case to support any of these factors. There were no prior negotiations that were contrary to arbitration. An agreement to arbitrate is hardly bizarre or oppressive. It is a preferred method of alternative dispute resolution that our legislature has expressly acknowledged in A.R.S. § 12–1501. Arbitration does not eviscerate any agreed terms. Nor does it eliminate the dominant purpose of the transaction. The plaintiff here had an opportunity to read the document, the document was legible and was hardly hidden from plaintiff's view. This arbitration agreement was in bold capital letters. Thus, the reasonable expectations standard of the Restatement (Second) of Contracts § 211 does not support this court's conclusion....

Today's decision sends a mixed message. In light of all of these developments, how can it be that an agreement to arbitrate "fell outside plaintiff's reasonable expectations?" The court's answer, Part III, ante, at 152, 840 P.2d at 1017, merely confuses the concept of a contract of adhesion with the doctrine of reasonable expectations. The court says it will enforce arbitration agreements "freely and fairly entered," ante, at 153, 840 P.2d at 1018, and that "the document involved is a contract of adhesion." Id. But the court's own framework of analysis acknowledges that its "conclusion that the contract was one of adhesion is not, of itself, determinative of its enforceability." Ante, at 151, 840 P.2d at 1016. It acknowledges that once it is determined that an adhesive contract exists, one looks to (1) reasonable expectations and (2) conscionability. Id. No one doubts that this was a contract of adhesion. And the court holds that because "the contract fell outside plaintiff's reasonable expectations" it is unenforceable, and therefore it is not necessary "to determine whether the contract is also unconscionable." Ante, at 152, 840 P.2d at 1017. Thus the court does not reach conscionability.

The only basis for the court's decision is "reasonable expectations," but words such as "freely and fairly entered," or "contract of adhesion" are irrelevant to that inquiry. If it is not "free" it is a contract of adhesion. If it is "unfair" it is unconscionable. Nowhere does the court's "Comment on The Dissent" provide the basis for its legal conclusion that this adhesive agreement to arbitrate fell outside of plaintiff's reasonable expectations. In the end we are left to conclude that people reasonably expect litigation over alternative dispute resolution. For all these reasons, I dissent.

* * *

Questions

1. Was the arbitration agreement in this case unconscionable? Given that the plaintiff was a literate adult, was the court's decision really based on the lack of consent, or was it based on the court's view of the oppressiveness of the terms?

2. How would the case come out if instead of an arbitration clause, the contract had specified a very short statute of limitations? How would it have been decided if it specified a low cap on damages?

3. In evaluating an arbitration clause in a contract of adhesion, how should the reasonable expectations of the parties be determined? Is an arbitration clause truly beyond the *reasonable* expectations of the parties? Would the case come out differently in a locality where medical forms frequently contained arbitration provisions?

4. The dissent argues that arbitration "does not eviscerate any agreed terms" of the contract. Do you agree? In what respect might it be argued that an arbitration clause does just that? Would one know *ex ante*, or is it necessary to await the result of an arbitration to know whether agreed terms were eviscerated or not?

* * *

Note on Consent in Consumer Arbitration[1]

Consumers who are given form contracts by a large manufacturer that contain arbitration provisions hidden in a sea of standardized terms often resist arbitration on the ground that they did not truly assent. The problem arises most acutely when one of the parties is a member of an industry or trade association that advocates a standard arbitration procedure for its members to use. Such entities frequently give their customers contracts that state the contract incorporates the rules of a given trade association without mentioning that an arbitration procedure is one component of the rules. When a dispute subsequently arises, the consumer claims that she had no knowledge of the arbitration term, and thus did not consent to be bound.

It is a well known principle of contract law that parties are responsible for the contracts they sign, even if they have not read them.[2] This "duty to read" means, *inter alia*, that courts hold parties to terms the parties have incorporated by reference into their contracts, even if the party seeking to avoid the incorporated term had no knowledge of these terms at the time the contract was made.[3] However, a competing principle of contract law says that a party is not bound by a contractual term of which he was unaware and which he had no reason to suspect was in the agreement. "A person is not bound by the terms of a written agreement if he had no knowledge of its terms because the manner in which they are embodied in the instrument would not lead a reasonable person to suspect that the terms are part of the contract."[4] This principle is embodied in § 211 of the RESTATEMENT OF CONTRACTS (2d), which states:

> (1) Except as stated in Subsection (3), where a party to an agreement signs or otherwise manifests assent to a writing . . ., he adopts the writing as an integrated agreement with respect to the terms included in the writing. . . .
>
> (3) Where the other party has reason to believe that the party manifesting such assent would not do so if he knew that the writing contained a particular term, the term is not part of the agreement.

One application of the no-enforcement-of-unexpected-terms principle is that courts scrutinize contracts and invalidate terms if the terms are oppressive and not within a party's reasonable expectation, i.e., not within the range of terms the offeree could reasonably expect to find in the contract. The same principle applies to terms contained in standard form

1. See Katherine Van Wezel Stone, *Rustic Justice: Community and Coercion Under the Federal Arbitration Act*, 77 N. Car. L. Rev. 931 (1999).

2. See, John D. Calamari, *Duty to Read–A Changing Concept*, 43 Fordham L. Rev. 341, 341 (1974).

3. E. Allen Farnsworth, CONTRACTS 2d Edition, 195 & 295 (1982); John D. Calamari and Joseph M. Perillo, CONTRACTS, 3rd Edition, 410 (1987).

4. *Drans v. Providence College*, 383 A.2d 1033, 1037–38 (R.I.1978).

contracts but which are either buried in a sea of fine print or otherwise not conspicuous to the signing party.[5]

Because courts exercise a policing role when confronted with one-sided incorporated terms in contracts generally, one might also expect courts to police arbitration agreements that are incorporated by reference for unfairness, oppression, or surprise. Until the late 1980s, this was the case. Courts were reluctant to uphold arbitration clauses when the arbitration provision was contained in a document that parties incorporated by reference into their contracts but did not mention expressly.[6] For example, the New York courts adopted a principle that "an agreement to arbitrate must be clear and direct, and must not depend upon implication, inveiglement or subtlety" to be enforceable.[7] The New York Court of Appeals stated in 1954, "[P]arties are not to be led into arbitration unwittingly through subtlety."[8]

Until the 1980s, courts were particularly skeptical of arbitration clauses in contracts in which the drafter was a member of the trade association and the party seeking to avoid arbitration was not. The New York Court of Appeals noted that such contracts appear to have been drafted with a deliberate intent to avoid the mention of arbitration, leaving "unwary traders" to learn of the arbitration provision only when a dispute arises.[9] It said: "The form of words favored by these trade associations appears to have been designed to avoid any resistance that might arise if arbitration were brought to the attention of the contracting parties as the exclusive remedy in case of disputes." Id. at 292.

In the late 1980s, state courts abandoned their policing approach to arbitration clauses incorporated by reference. Instead, they began to enforce arbitration clauses which were incorporated by reference even when the contract was silent on the existence of the arbitration clause. In part, the change was the result of the Supreme Court's opinion in 1987 in Perry v. Thomas, 482 U.S. 483 (1987), discussed in Chapter 5 above. In *Perry*, the Court held that under the FAA the existence of a valid agreement to arbitrate must be determined by reference to state law, but any state law or legal doctrine which is specific to arbitration is preempted by the FAA. Thus, only state laws governing the enforceability of contracts generally can be used as a defense to arbitration under the FAA. Id. at 492 & n. 9. *Perry*'s admonition that courts may not rely on arbitration-specific doctrines to invalidate arbitration agreements led courts to hold that state law doctrines that required strict scrutiny of arbitration clauses that were

5. See, Williams v. Walker–Thomas Furniture Co., 350 F.2d 445 (D.C.Cir. 1965); Henningsen v. Bloomfield Motors, Inc., 161 A.2d 69 (N.J.1960).

6. See e.g., Medical Development Corp. v. Industrial Molding, 479 F.2d 345 (10th Cir. 1973); C. Itoh & Co. v. Jordan Int'l, 552 F.2d 1228 (7th Cir. 1977); Amoco Oil v. M.T. Mary Ellen, 529 F.Supp. 227 (S.D.N.Y. 1981). See generally, Robert Whitman, Incorporation by Reference in Commercial Contracts, 21 Md. L. Rev. 1, 16–17 (1961).

7. Matter of Doughboy Industries, 233 N.Y.S.2d 488, 493 (App.Div.1962) (J. Breitel).

8. Riverdale Fabrics v. Tillinghast–Stiles Co., 118 N.E.2d 104 (N.Y.1954).

9. Riverdale Fabrics v. Tillinghast–Stiles, 306 N.Y. at 292.

incorporated by reference were no longer valid.[10] Similarly, state contract law doctrines that required there be an explicit and unequivocal waiver of a right to sue before finding that parties had agreed to binding arbitration were held to be preempted.[11] The result was that whereas general contract law provides latitude for courts to protect consumers in their dealings with large organized interests by relieving them of oppressive and unexpected contractual terms, many courts interpreted *Perry* to deny courts that same latitude when they were dealing with arbitration clauses.

Recently in the employment context, some courts have begun to lean in the other direction, holding that a form contract drafted by an employer that incorporates an arbitration process without giving an employee fair notice that arbitration is included will not be enforceable. For example, in Rosenberg v. Merrill Lynch, Pierce, Fenner & Smith, 170 F.3d 1 (1st Cir. 1999), the First Circuit held that a standard form an employee was required to sign to register with the New York Stock Exchange that required her to arbitrate "any dispute, claim or controversy that may arise that is required to be arbitrated under the rules, constitutions or by-laws of the [New York Stock Exchange]" did not require her to arbitrate her employment discrimination claims against her brokerage firm employer. The court reasoned that the form arbitration agreement:

> did not by itself define the range of claims subject to arbitration, even though Merrill Lynch expressly represented that she would be advised of the rules. But those rules were not given to Rosenberg or described to her. The question then becomes which party should bear the risk of her ignorance. Given Congress' concern that agreements to arbitrate employment discrimination claims should be enforced only where 'appropriate' . . . Merrill Lynch should, we believe, bear that risk.

It remains to be seen whether courts will similarly shift the burden of uncertainty to manufacturers in situations where consumers find they lose their rights to sue because of arbitration provisions buried in fine print or hidden in incorporated terms.

The following case addresses some of these issues.

* * *

Aguillard v. Auction Mgmt. Corp.

908 So.2d 1 (La. 2005).

■ KNOLL, JUSTICE.

This civil case addresses the legal question of whether the court of appeal erred in declaring a contract, including its arbitration agreement,

10. See e.g., Progressive Casualty Insurance Co. v. C.A. Reaseguradora Nacional De Venezuela, 991 F.2d 42, 46 (2d Cir. 1993); Cook Chocolate Co. v. Salomon, Inc., 684 F.Supp. 1177, 1182 (S.D.N.Y. 1988).

11. Progressive Casualty Insurance Co. v. C.A. Reaseguradora Nacional De Venezuela, 991 F.2d at 45–46.

adhesionary. The district court denied the defendants' motion to stay proceedings pending arbitration. The court of appeal affirmed the district court's ruling. We granted this writ particularly to address the validity of the arbitration agreement and to resolve a split among the circuits regarding the enforceability of arbitration agreements contained within consumer standard form contracts under a "contract of adhesion" analysis, a *res nova* issue before this court. *Dave F. Aguillard v. Auction Management Corp.,* 04–2804 c/w 04–2857 (La.3/11/05), 896 So.2d 47. For the following reasons we reverse, finding the lower courts erred in failing to stay the proceedings pending arbitration and adopt a liberal policy favoring arbitrability.

FACTS AND PROCEDURAL HISTORY

On March 25, 2003, defendant, Gilmore Auction & Realty Company ("Gilmore Realty"), a duly licensed Louisiana auctioneer, conducted a public auction of certain real estate property located in Sulphur, Louisiana. Gilmore Realty, along with Auction Management Corporation ("Auction Management"), the closing coordinator, acted as agents for the owner of the property defendant Bank of New York. . . .

Prior to the auction, Auction Management and Gilmore Realty disseminated a sales brochure to prospective bidders, which pictured and described each of the auctioned properties and the rules that governed the auction. Plaintiff, Dave F. Aguillard, obtained a brochure prior to the event.

On the day of the auction, plaintiff, along with approximately seventeen other individuals, attended [an] onsite auction ... Prior to bidding and receiving his bidder number, plaintiff was required to sign and deliver before the commencement of the auction the document entitled "Auction Terms & Conditions," which contained the arbitration clause in dispute. By signing the document, plaintiff "acknowledge[d] that he or she ha[d] read and underst[ood] these *AUCTION TERMS & CONDITIONS* and agree[d] to be bound thereby." ...

At the auction, plaintiff submitted the highest bid on the residential dwelling and was thereupon required to sign a document entitled "Auction Real Estate Sales Agreement" and to submit his check to Auction Management and Gilmore Realty in the amount of $4,290, which represented ten percent of the sales price on the property, in accordance with the Auction Terms & Conditions.

The seller, Bank of New York, subsequently rejected plaintiff's bid of $42,900, and refused to close the sale of the property, refusing as well to execute the Auction Real Estate Sales Agreement. Bank of New York argued the auction was not an "absolute auction" and any offer to purchase was subject to the seller's confirmation. On or around April 17, 2003, the seller submitted a counter-offer of $53,000. Plaintiff rejected this offer.

Subsequently, plaintiff filed suit to enforce the Auction Real Estate Sales Agreement against Bank of New York and its servicer New South Federal Savings Bank ("New South"), Auction Management, and Gilmore

Auction ("defendants"). In response, the defendants filed a joint motion to stay proceedings pending arbitration . . . , contending the arbitration clause contained in the Auction Terms & Conditions document governs this dispute. The district court denied the motion.

[Defendants appealed.] The court of appeal affirmed the district court's ruling, finding the entire contract between the parties, including the arbitration clause, was adhesionary and lacked mutuality. *Dave F. Aguillard v. Auction Management Corp.,* 04–393, p. 8 (La.App. 3 Cir. 10/13/04), 884 So.2d 1257, 1261. Relying on its previous decisions in *Sutton's Steel & Supply, Inc. v. Bellsouth Mobility, Inc.,* 00–511 (La.App. 3 Cir. 12/13/00), 776 So.2d 589, *writ denied,* 01–0152 (La.3/16/01), 787 So.2d 316, and *Simpson v. Grimes,* 02–0869 (La.App. 3 Cir. 5/21/03), 849 So.2d 740, *writ denied,* 03–2497 (La.12/19/03), 861 So.2d 567, the Third Circuit concluded plaintiff was not in a position to bargain regarding the terms of the agreement with the defendants and was required to sign the document prior to receiving a bid number and participating in the auction. The defendants were clearly in a superior bargaining position. The court noted (1) the document was printed in extremely small type and "the arbitration clause was not distinguished in any way"; (2) the defendants reserved to themselves methods of dispute resolution other than arbitration, which were not available to the auction customer, e.g., the seller had the option to retain the earnest money deposit as liquidated damages and re-offer and resell the property in situations of buyer default; and (3) provisions in the documents provided the defendants the unilateral power to change any or all parts of the contract, including the arbitration clause, simply by verbal announcement at the auction block. . . .

We granted this writ to address whether the court of appeal erred in declaring the arbitration clause adhesionary and to resolve a split among the circuits regarding the enforceability of arbitration agreements in consumer standard form contracts under a "contract of adhesion" analysis, a *res nova* issue before this Court. . . .

Contracts of Adhesion

Broadly defined, a contract of adhesion is a standard contract, usually in printed form, prepared by a party of superior bargaining power for adherence or rejection of the weaker party. Often in small print, these contracts sometimes raise a question as to whether or not the weaker party actually consented to the terms. . . .

. . . [A]lthough a contract of adhesion is a contract executed in a standard form in the vast majority of instances, not every contract in standard form may be regarded as a contract of adhesion.Therefore, we are not willing to declare all standard form contracts adhesionary; rather, we find standard form serves merely as a possible indicator of adhesion.

Consent is called into question by the standard form, small print, and most especially the disadvantageous position of the accepting party, which is further emphasized by the potentially unequal bargaining positions of the parties. An unequal bargaining position is evident when the contract unduly burdens one party in comparison to the burdens imposed upon the drafting party and the advantages allowed to that party. Once consent is called into question, the party seeking to invalidate the contract as adhesionary must then demonstrate the non-drafting party either did not consent to the terms in dispute or his consent was vitiated by error, which in turn, renders the contract or provision unenforceable.

In summation, a contract is one of adhesion when either its form, print, or unequal terms call into question the consent of the non-drafting party and it is demonstrated that the contract is unenforceable, due to lack of consent or error, which vitiates consent. Accordingly, even if a contract is standard in form and printed in small font, if it does not call into question the non-drafting party's consent and if it is not demonstrated that the non-drafting party did not consent or his consent is vitiated by error, the contract is not a contract of adhesion. . . .

Analysis of Auction Terms & Conditions

In light of the strong presumption in both federal and state law of arbitrability, we find the Third Circuit erred as a matter of law in declaring the arbitration clause adhesionary for several reasons. First, although the arbitration agreement is in relatively small print, neither the print nor the font size of the arbitration agreement differs in any way from the other clauses in the standard form contract. Moreover, the print is not unreasonably small. We further note that the contract at issue was only a two-page document and that each paragraph was separated from the preceding and following paragraphs by what appears to be double spacing. Additionally, the arbitration provision at issue was contained in a single sentence paragraph within the section of the document labeled in capital letters ANNOUNCEMENTS.

Secondly, the court of appeal erroneously found the arbitration agreement unenforceable because it was not distinguished in any way. The United States Supreme Court in *Doctor's Associates, Inc. v. Casarotto,* 517 U.S. 681, 687, 116 S.Ct. 1652, 134 L.Ed.2d 902 (1996), specifically found that the FAA presumption of arbitrability preempted a state statute requiring special notice requirements applicable only to arbitration agreements before an arbitration clause could be enforced. In this case, the arbitration provision, although not distinguished, was not concealed in any way, but rather was contained in a single sentence paragraph separated from the preceding and following paragraphs by double spacing.

Thirdly, we disagree with the appellate court's conclusion that the contract lacked mutuality as to the arbitration agreement, and we find the arbitration clause severely limits both the defendants' and the plaintiff's right to litigate. Nowhere in the document do the defendants reserve to themselves the right to litigate any issue arising from the contract, and further, the reservation of rights contained within the DEFAULT provisions to which the appellate court took such exception, can only be invoked when the purchaser fails to comply with the Auction Terms & Conditions.

According to the arbitration agreement, a finding of default must be determined through arbitration.

Moreover, it does not appear that there was such a difference in bargaining positions between the parties so as to justify the application of the principle of contract of adhesion to the arbitration clause. As the dissenting judge noted, the underlying transaction, a real estate auction, does not indicate that it was such a necessary transaction to establish the plaintiff was compelled to enter it. As noted above, each party was strictly limited to arbitration for dispute resolution, and if the plaintiff did not agree with the terms of arbitration or the terms in general, he could have either attempted to negotiate the terms of the contract or refused to participate in the auction.

We find the court of appeal erred in declaring the whole contract governing the terms and conditions of the auction adhesionary and lacking in mutuality.

It is well settled that a party who signs a written instrument is presumed to know its contents and cannot avoid its obligations by contending that he did not read it, that he did not understand it, or that the other party failed to explain it to him. *See, e.g., Tweedel v. Brasseaux,* 433 So.2d 133, 137 (La.1983) (stating: "The presumption is that parties are aware of the contents of writings to which they have affixed their signatures . . . The burden of proof is upon them to establish with reasonable certainty that they have been deceived." "If a party can read, it behooves him to examine an instrument before signing it; and if he cannot read, it behooves him to have the instrument read to him and listen attentatively whilst this is being done."). The plaintiff in this case signed the contract "acknowledg[ing] that he . . . read and [understood the] *AUCTION TERMS & CONDITIONS* and agree[d] to be bound thereby."

The parties were free to contract to the terms which provided the defendants with the right to make announcements from the Auction Block that would take precedence over all previously printed materials or any other oral statements made or that the Auction Agreement for the Purchase and Sale of Real Estate represented the final contracted terms or even that the Auctioneer would resolve any dispute over matters at the auction and could remove a listed property from the auction at any time with the seller's direction. Moreover, there was no evidence that the plaintiff was not in an equal bargaining position as the defendants because the plaintiff could have avoided arbitration and the contractual provisions as a whole by simply not signing the agreement.

After careful review of the terms of the arbitration clause, we find nothing sufficient to establish the defendants were in such a superior bargaining position as to render the plaintiff a far weaker party or the contract adhesionary, nor do we find anything in the document itself that would call into question the validity of plaintiff's consent to the terms of the agreement as indicated by his signature. The doctrine of contract of adhesion is inapplicable in this case. We now address the defendants' motion for stay pending arbitration. . . .

DECREE

For the foregoing reasons, the judgments of the lower courts that found the contract, including the arbitration clause, adhesionary and lacking in mutuality are reversed, and this matter is stayed pending arbitration.

REVERSED; STAY PENDING ARBITRATION GRANTED.

* * *

Questions

1. Arbitration clauses in consumer transactions are becoming ubiquitous. For example, cell phone contracts often contain arbitration clauses buried in the fine print. Cell-contract arbitration clauses almost always contain provisions forbidding class actions. Because damages in individual claims tend to be low in these types of cases (the underlying dispute usually involves a claim that the cell phone company overcharged consumers a few dollars per billing cycle), enforcing the class-action waiver effectively would make it impossible for consumers to bring valid claims. Under these circumstances, many courts have held that the class-action waivers are unconscionable. Do you think these arbitration clauses should be enforced? Why or why not?

2. Suppose a consumer or employee challenges an arbitration clause embedded in a larger contract on the ground that the clause is unconscionable. As part of the argument as to why the arbitration clause is unconscionable, the complainant claims that the larger contract itself was adhesive, i.e., presented on a "take it or leave it basis," and the consumer/employee had no opportunity to negotiate the larger contract. However, the complainant does not challenge the validity of the larger contract or otherwise seek to invalidate the larger contract—he only attacks the arbitration clause. Nor does the complainant claim that the arbitration clause itself was adhesive, just the larger contract. In this context, can a court, after *Buckeye*, entertain an argument that an arbitration clause in a larger contract is unconscionable in part because the larger contract itself was adhesive?

The Ninth Circuit (over a vigorous dissent) has held that a *court* can entertain this type of argument. Nagrampa v. MailCoups, Inc., 469 F.3d 1257 (9th Cir. 2006) (en banc). *Nagrampa* distinguished *Buckeye* on the ground that *Buckeye* deals with situations in which a party is claiming that the *entire* larger contract is void or voidable, and thus, by extension, the arbitration clause is invalid too. By contrast, in *Nagrampa* the party was not actually attacking the validity of the entire contract, only the arbitration clause itself. That is, the party was not actually seeking the invalidation of the larger contract. Even though the adhesive nature of the larger contract could, in theory, support a defense to the enforcement of the larger contract, this theoretical consideration was not controlling. What *was* controlling is whether the party is actually, in fact, seeking the invalidation of the larger contract.

The opposite post-*Buckeye* view is captured in *Toledano v. O'Connor*, 501 F.Supp.2d 127 (D.D.C. 2007), which refused to entertain an argument that the arbitration clause was procedurally unconscionable because the plaintiff "did not participate in the crafting of the language of the [larger] agreement" in which the arbitration clause was embedded. *Id.* at 146. In a footnote, the court criticized *Nagrampa* while noting other pre-*Buckeye* opinions that conflicted with *Nagrampa*:

> The Ninth Circuit has observed, however, that "[a]n argument that the arbitration agreement itself is procedurally unconscionable may be informed, as required by California state substantive law, by a determination of whether it is contained within a larger contract of adhesion." *Nagrampa*, 469 F.3d at 1276. The correctness of this statement is doubtful in light of the Supreme Court's decision in *Buckeye Check Cashing*. *See Nagrampa*, 469 F.3d at 1298–1300 (O'Scannlain, J., dissenting) (arguing that *Buckeye Check Cashing* precludes [a] district court from considering whether [the larger] contract is adhesive as part of [an] unconscionability analysis); see also, e.g., *Jenkins v. First Am. Cash Advance of Ga.*, LLC, 400 F.3d 868, 877 (11th Cir. 2005) ("[T]he FAA does not permit a federal court to consider claims alleging the contract as a whole was adhesive."); *Madol v. Dan Nelson Auto. Group*, 372 F.3d 997, 1000 (8th Cir. 2004) ("The law required that the plaintiffs' claims be referred to arbitration because their arguments of unconscionability 'cannot fairly be limited to the making of the arbitration clause.'" (citation omitted)). *Id.* at 146 n. 5 (brackets added).

A final approach is found in *Bruni v. Didion*, 160 Cal.App.4th 1272 (2008). The court in *Bruni* noted that a footnote in *Buckeye* limited the scope of the holding. That footnote states:

> The issue of the contract's validity is different from the issue whether any agreement between the alleged obligor and obligee was ever concluded. Our opinion today addresses only the former, and does not speak to the issue decided in the cases cited by respondents (and by the Florida Supreme Court), which hold that it is for courts to decide whether the alleged obligor ever signed the contract, Chastain v. Robinson–Humphrey Co., 957 F.2d 851 (CA11 1992), whether the signor lacked authority to commit the alleged principal, Sandvik AB v. Advent Int'l Corp., 220 F.3d 99 (CA3 2000); Sphere Drake Ins. Ltd. v. All American Ins. Co., 256 F.3d 587 (CA7 2001), and whether the signor lacked the mental capacity to assent, Spahr v. Secco, 330 F.3d 1266 (CA10 2003).

Accordingly, relying on this limitation, *Bruni* concluded that a court "still must consider one type of challenge to the overall contract: a claim that the party resisting arbitration never actually agreed to be bound" to the overall contract. *Id.* at 1284. In *Bruni*, much like *Nagrampa*, the arbitration clause appeared in a larger contract of adhesion. The *Bruni* court first held that the adhesive nature of the larger contract called into question whether the plaintiffs ever "agreed to be bound" to the larger contract—i.e., the "imposition" of the contract upon them vitiated their consent. Thus, because the adhesive nature of the larger contract called into question whether they ever "agreed to be bound" to it terms, the court could properly consider the adhesive nature of the larger contract as one factor that cut against enforcement of the arbitration clause. The *Bruni* court then considered other attacks that were specifically directed at the arbitration clause itself. Ultimately, the court found that these arbitration-specific attacks were valid and, when *combined* with the adhesive nature of the larger contract, rendered the arbitration agreement unconscionable.

* * *

6. State Consumer Protection Law

Casarotto v. Lombardi and Doctor's Associates, Inc.

886 P.2d 931 (Mont.1994).

Plaintiffs Paul and Pamela Casarotto filed this suit in the District Court for the Eighth Judicial District in Cascade County to recover damages which they claim were caused by the defendants' breach of contract and tortious conduct. Defendants Nick Lombardi and Doctor's Associates, Inc. (DAI), moved the District Court for an order dismissing plaintiffs' complaint, or in the alternative, staying further judicial proceedings pending arbitration of plaintiffs' claims pursuant to a provision in DAI's franchise agreement with plaintiffs which required that disputes "arising out of or relating to" that contract be settled by arbitration. The District Court granted defendants' motion, and ordered that further judicial proceedings be stayed until arbitration proceedings were completed in accordance with the terms of the parties' agreement. Plaintiffs appeal from that order. We reverse the order of the District Court.

The issues raised on appeal are:

1. Based on conflict of law principles, is the franchise agreement entered into between the Casarottos and DAI governed by Connecticut law or Montana law?

2. If the contract is governed by Montana law, is the notice requirement in § 27–5–114(4), MCA, of Montana's Uniform Arbitration Act, preempted by the Federal Arbitration Act found at 9 U.S.C. §§ 1–15 (1988)?

FACTUAL BACKGROUND

On October 29, 1992, Paul and Pamela Casarotto filed an amended complaint naming Doctor's Associates, Inc., and Nick Lombardi as defendants. For purposes of our review of the District Court's order, we presume the facts alleged in the complaint to be true.

DAI is a Connecticut corporation which owns Subway Sandwich Shop franchises, and Lombardi is their development agent in Montana. The Casarottos entered into a franchise agreement with DAI which allowed them to open a Subway Sandwich Shop in Great Falls, Montana. However, they were told by Lombardi that their first choice for a location in Great Falls was unavailable.

According to their complaint, the Casarottos agreed to open a shop at a less desirable location, based on a verbal agreement with Lombardi that when their preferred location became available, they would have the exclusive right to open a store at that location. Contrary to that agreement, the preferred location was subsequently awarded by Lombardi and DAI to another franchisee. As a result, the Casarottos' business suffered irreparably, and they lost their business, along with the collateral which secured their SBA loan.

This action is based on the Casarottos' allegation that Lombardi and DAI breached their agreement with the Casarottos, defrauded them, breached the covenant of good faith and fair dealing, and engaged in other tortious conduct, all of which directly caused the Casarottos loss of business and the resulting damage.

DAI's franchise agreement with the Casarottos was executed on April 25, 1988. There was no indication on the first page of the contract that it was subject to arbitration. However, paragraph 10(c) of the contract, found on page 9, included the following provision:

> Any controversy or claim arising out of or relating to this contract or the breach thereof shall be settled by Arbitration in accordance with the Commercial Arbitration Rules of the American Arbitration Association at a hearing to be held in Bridgeport, Connecticut and judgment upon an award rendered by the Arbitrator(s) may be entered in any court having jurisdiction thereof. The commencement of arbitration proceedings by an aggrieved party to settle disputes arising out of or relating to this contract is a condition precedent to the commencement of legal action by either party. The cost of such a proceeding will be born equally by the parties.

On January 29, 1993, DAI moved the District Court to dismiss the Casarottos' complaint, or at least stay further judicial proceedings, pending arbitration pursuant to paragraph 10(c) of the franchise agreement. DAI alleged that the franchise agreement affected interstate commerce, and therefore, was subject to the Federal Arbitration Act found at 9 U.S.C. §§ 1–15 (1988). They sought a stay of proceedings pursuant to § 3 of that Act . . .

DAI claimed that Montana law could not be raised as a bar to enforcement of the arbitration provision for two reasons: First, the contract specifically called for the application of Connecticut law; and second, Montana law was preempted by the Federal Arbitration Act.

The Casarottos opposed DAI's motion on the grounds that Montana law applied, in spite of the choice of law provision in the contract, and that based on § 27–5–114(4), MCA, the contract's arbitration provision was unenforceable because DAI had not provided notice on the first page of the agreement that the contract was subject to arbitration.

On June 2, 1993, the District Court issued its order granting DAI's motion to stay further judicial proceedings pursuant to 9 U.S.C. § 3 . . .

ISSUE 1

Based on conflict of law principles, is the franchise agreement entered into between the Casarottos and DAI governed by Connecticut law or Montana law?

Paragraph 12 of the franchise agreement entered into between the parties provides as follows: "This agreement shall be governed by and construed in accordance with the laws of the State of Connecticut and contains the entire understanding of the parties." DAI contends that, therefore, Connecticut law governs our interpretation of the contract and that since Connecticut law is identical to the Federal Arbitration Act see Conn.Gen.Stat. § 52–409 (1993), conspicuous notice that the contract was subject to arbitration was not required and we need not concern ourselves with the issue of whether Montana law is preempted.

The Casarottos respond that the issue of whether to apply Connecticut or Montana law involves a conflict of law issue and that the answer can be found in our prior decisions. We agree . . .

In this case, there is a choice of law provision in the parties' contract. The question is whether it was an "effective" choice. We recently held in Youngblood v. American States Ins. Co. (1993), 262 Mont. 391, 394, 866 P.2d 203, 205, that this State's public policy will ultimately determine whether choice of law provisions in contracts are "effective." In that case, we stated:

> [T]he choice of law provision will be enforced unless enforcement of the contract provision requiring application of Oregon law as regards subrogation of medical payments violates Montana's public policy or is against good morals.

Youngblood, 866 P.2d at 205.

Based on our conclusion in that case that subrogation of medical payment benefits was contrary to our public policy, we held that:

> [T]he choice of law provision in the insurance contract would result in medical payment subrogation under Oregon law. Because such subrogation violates Montana's public policy, that term of the insurance contract at issue here is not enforceable.

Youngblood, 866 P.2d at 208.

Restatement (Second) of Conflict of Laws § 187(2) (1971) is consistent with our decision in Youngblood, and expands upon the factors to be considered under the circumstances in this case. It provides that:

(2) The law of the state chosen by the parties to govern their contractual rights and duties will be applied, even if the particular issue is one which the parties could not have resolved by an explicit provision in their agreement directed to that issue, unless either

(a) the chosen state has no substantial relationship to the parties or the transaction and there is no other reasonable basis for the parties' choice, or

(b) application of the law of the chosen state would be contrary to a fundamental policy of a state which has a materially greater interest than the chosen state in the determination of the particular issue and which, under the rule of § 188, would be the state of the applicable law in the absence of an effective choice of law by the parties.

Adopting § 187, then, as our guide, we first look to § 188 to determine whether Montana law would be applicable absent an "effective" choice of law by the parties.

According to the affidavit of Paul Casarotto filed in opposition to DAI's motion to dismiss, he executed the contract in neither Connecticut nor Montana. It was executed while he was traveling in New York. However, it appears from that same affidavit, and from the allegations in the complaint, that original negotiations were conducted by him in Great Falls, the contract was to be performed in Great Falls, the subject matter of the contract (the Subway Sandwich Shop) was located in Great Falls, and that he and Pamela Casarotto resided in Great Falls at the time that the contract was executed. The only connection to Connecticut was that DAI was incorporated in that state and apparently had its home office in that state at the time of the parties' agreement. We conclude that based upon the application of the criteria set forth in § 188, and our prior decision in Emerson, Montana has a materially greater interest than Connecticut in the contract issue that is presented, and that absent an "effective" choice of law by the parties, Montana law would apply.

Our remaining inquiry, then, is whether application of Connecticut law would be contrary to a fundamental policy of this State by eliminating the requirement that notice be provided when a contract is subject to arbitration.

In Trammel v. Brotherhood of Locomotive Firemen and Enginemen (1953), 126 Mont. 400, 409, 253 P.2d 329, 334, we held that the public policy of a state is established by its express legislative enactments. Here, the legislative history for §27–5–114(4), MCA, makes clear that the legislative committee members considering adoption of the Uniform Arbitration Act had two primary concerns. First, they did not want Montanans to waive their constitutional right of access to Montana's courts unknowingly, and second, they were concerned about Montanans being compelled to arbitrate disputes at distant locations beyond the borders of our State.

The facts in this case, and our recent decision in another case, justify those concerns.

Regardless of the amount in controversy between these parties, the arbitration clause in the Subway Sandwich Shop Franchise Agreement requires that the Casarottos travel thousands of miles to Connecticut to have their dispute arbitrated. Furthermore, it requires that they share equally in the expense of arbitration, regardless of the merits of their claim. Presumably, that expense could be substantial, since under the Commercial Arbitration Rules of the American Arbitration Association (1992), those expenses would, at a minimum, include: the arbitrator's fees and travel expenses, the cost of witnesses chosen by the arbitrator, the American Arbitration Association's administrative charges, and a filing fee of up to $4000, depending on the amount in controversy. For a proceeding involving multiple arbitrators, the administrative fee alone, for which the Casarottos would be responsible, is $150 a day. In addition, since the contract called for the application of Connecticut law, the Casarottos would be required to retain the services of a Connecticut attorney.

In spite of the expense set forth above, the procedural safeguards which have been established in Montana to assure the reliability of the outcome in dispute resolutions are absent in an arbitration proceeding. The extent of pretrial discovery is within the sole discretion of the arbitrator and the rules of evidence are not applicable. The arbitrator does not have to follow any law, and there does not have to be a factual basis for the arbitrator's decision. See May v. First National Pawn Brokers, Ltd. (Mont. 1994), 269 Mont. 19, 887 P.2d 185.

Based upon the determination by the Legislature of this State that the citizens of this State are at least entitled to notice before entering into an agreement which will limit their future resolution of disputes to a procedure as potentially inconvenient, expensive, and devoid of procedural safeguards as the one provided for by the rules of the American Arbitration Association, and the terms of this contract, we conclude that the notice requirement of § 27–5–114, MCA, does establish a fundamental public policy in Montana, and that the application of Connecticut law would be contrary to that policy. Therefore, we conclude that the law of Montana governs the franchise agreement entered into between the Casarottos and Doctor's Associates, Inc.

ISSUE 2

If the contract is governed by Montana law, is the notice requirement in § 27–5–114(4), MCA, of Montana's Uniform Arbitration Act, preempted by the Federal Arbitration Act found at 9 U.S.C. §§ 1–15 (1988)?

DAI contends that even if Montana law is applicable, § 27–5–114(4), MCA, is preempted by the Federal Arbitration Act because it would void an otherwise enforceable arbitration agreement. In support of its argument, DAI relies on U.S. Supreme Court decisions in Perry v. Thomas (1987), 482 U.S. 483, 107 S.Ct. 2520, 96 L.Ed.2d 426, Southland Corp. v. Keating (1984), 465 U.S. 1, 104 S.Ct. 852, 79 L.Ed.2d 1, and Moses H. Cone Memorial Hospital v. Mercury Construction Corp. (1983), 460 U.S. 1, 103 S.Ct. 927, 74 L.Ed.2d 765. These cases have been referred to as "[a] trilogy of United States Supreme Court cases" which "developed the federal policy favoring arbitration and the principle that the FAA is substantive law enacted pursuant to Congress's commerce powers that preempts contrary state provisions." David P. Pierce, The Federal Arbitration Act: Conflicting Interpretations of its Scope 61 Cinn.L.Rev. 623, 630 (1992). From this trilogy, Southland and Perry appear to be closest on point and warrant some discussion.

Southland Corporation was the owner and franchisor of 7–Eleven Convenience Stores. Its standard franchise agreements, like DAI's included an arbitration provision. Southland was sued in California by several of its franchisees, based on claims which included violations of the disclosure requirements of the California Franchise Investment Law, Cal.Corp.Code § 31000, et seq. (West 1977). The California Supreme Court held that the Franchise Investment Law required judicial consideration of claims brought under that statute, and therefore, held that arbitration could not be compelled. The U.S. Supreme Court disagreed, and held that:

> In creating a substantive rule applicable in state as well federal courts, Congress intended to foreclose state legislative attempts to undercut the enforceability of arbitration agreements. We hold that § 31512 of the California Franchise Investment Law violates the Supremacy Clause.

Southland, 465 U.S. at 16, 104 S.Ct. at 861 (footnotes omitted).

In Perry, the Supreme Court was called upon to reconcile 9 U.S.C. § 2 which mandates enforcement of arbitration agreements, with § 229 of the California Labor Code, "which provides that actions for the collection of wages may be maintained 'without regard to the existence of any private agreement to arbitrate.'" Perry, 482 U.S. at 484, 107 S.Ct. at 2523 (quoting Cal.Lab.Code § 229 (West 1971)). In that case, Kenneth Thomas sued his former employer for commissions he claimed were due for the sale of securities. His employer sought to stay the proceedings pursuant to §§ 2 and 4 of the Federal Arbitration Act, based on the arbitration provision found in Thomas's application for employment. Perry, 482 U.S. at 484–85, 107 S.Ct. at 2522–23. In an opinion affirmed by the California Court of Appeals and the California Supreme Court, the California Superior Court denied the motion to compel arbitration. On appeal, the U.S. Supreme Court held that § 2 of the FAA reflected a strong national policy favoring arbitration agreements, notwithstanding "state substantive or procedural policies to the contrary." Perry, 482 U.S. at 489, 107 S.Ct. at 2525. Citing its decision in Southland, the Court held that:

> Congress intended to foreclose state legislative attempts to undercut the enforceability of arbitration agreements" Id. [465 U.S.] at 16 [104 S.Ct. at 858] (footnote omitted). Section 2, therefore, embodies a clear federal policy of requiring arbitration unless the agreement to arbitrate is not part of a contract evidencing interstate commerce or is revocable "upon such grounds as exist at law or in equity for the revocation of any contract." 9 U.S.C. § 2. "We see nothing in the Act indicating that the broad principle of enforceability is subject to any additional limita-

> tions under state law." Keating, supra, 465 U.S. at 11 [104 S.Ct. at 858].

Perry, 482 U.S. at 489–90, 107 S.Ct. at 2525.

As additional authority, DAI cites to our own previous decisions which have enforced arbitration agreements in Montana based on Southland and Perry. See Downey v. Christensen (1992), 251 Mont. 386, 825 P.2d 557; Vukasin v. D.A. Davidson & Co. (1990), 241 Mont. 126, 785 P.2d 713; William Gibson, Jr., Inc. v. James Graff Communications (1989), 239 Mont. 335, 780 P.2d 1131; Larsen v. Opie (1989), 237 Mont. 108, 771 P.2d 977; Passage v. Prudential–Bache Securities, Inc. (1986), 223 Mont. 60, 727 P.2d 1298.

The Casarottos, however, contend that Southland and Perry must be considered in light of the Supreme Court's more recent decision in Volt Information Sciences, Inc. v. Board of Trustees of Leland Stanford Junior University (1989), 489 U.S. 468, 109 S.Ct. 1248, 103 L.Ed.2d 488, and that our prior arbitration decisions did not deal with the enforceability of arbitration agreements which violated Montana's statutory law. We agree.

In Volt, the parties entered into a construction contract which contained an agreement to arbitrate all disputes between the parties relating to the contract. The contract also provided that it would be governed by the law in the state where the project was located. Volt, 489 U.S. at 470, 109 S.Ct. at 1251.

As a result of a contract dispute between the parties, Stanford filed an action in California Superior Court naming Volt and two other companies involved in the construction project. Volt petitioned the Superior Court to compel arbitration of the dispute. However, the California Arbitration Act found at Cal.Civ.Proc.Code § 1280, et seq. (West 1982), contained a provision allowing the court to stay arbitration pending resolution of related litigation. On that basis, the Superior Court denied Volt's motion to compel arbitration, and instead, stayed arbitration proceedings pending outcome of the litigation. The California Court of Appeals affirmed that decision, and the California Supreme Court denied Volt's petition for discretionary review. The U.S. Supreme Court granted review and affirmed the decision of the California courts. Volt, 489 U.S. at 471–73, 109 S.Ct. at 1251–52.

On appeal, the Supreme Court considered Volt's argument that California's arbitration laws were preempted by the Federal Arbitration Act. In its analysis of the preemption issue, the Supreme Court stated that:

> The FAA contains no express pre-emptive provision, nor does it reflect a congressional intent to occupy the entire field of arbitration. But even when Congress has not completely displaced state regulation in an area, state law may nonetheless be pre-empted to the extent that it actually conflicts with federal law—that is, to the extent that it "stands as an obstacle to the accomplishment and execution of the full purposes and objectives of Congress." Hines v. Davidowitz, 312 U.S. 52, 67 [61 S.Ct. 399, 404, 85 L.Ed. 581] (1941). The question before us, therefore, is whether application of Cal.Civ.Proc.Code Ann. § 1281.2(c)

> to stay arbitration under this contract in interstate commerce, in accordance with the terms of the arbitration agreement itself, would undermine the goals and policies of the FAA. We conclude that it would not.

Volt, 489 U.S. at 477–78, 109 S.Ct. at 1255 (citation omitted; emphasis added).

The Supreme Court explained that the purpose of the Federal Arbitration Act was to enforce lawful agreements entered into by the parties, and not to impose arbitration on the parties involuntarily. It noted that in this case the parties' agreement was to be bound by the arbitration rules from California. Therefore, it held that:

> Where, as here, the parties have agreed to abide by state rules of arbitration, enforcing those rules according to the terms of the agreement is fully consistent with the goals of the FAA, even if the result is that arbitration is stayed where the Act would otherwise permit it to go forward. By permitting the courts to "rigorously enforce" such agreements according to their terms, see [Dean Witter Reynolds, Inc. v.] Byrd, [470 U.S. 213] at 221 [105 S.Ct. 1238, 1242, 84 L.Ed.2d 158 (1985)], we give effect to the contractual rights and expectations of the parties, without doing violence to the policies behind the FAA.

Volt, 489 U.S. at 479, 109 S.Ct. at 1256.

While the Court in Volt applied state laws that had been chosen by the parties in their contract, and this case involves state law which is applied pursuant to conflict of law principles, it has been observed that:

> The real significance of the Volt decision is not in the Court's holding, but rather in what the Court failed to hold. For example, the Court found no preemption of the California arbitration law by the FAA. Instead, the Court merely stated that Congress did not intend that the FAA occupy the entire field of arbitration law. Thus, enforcing the California law was merely a procedural issue and did not frustrate the policy behind the FAA of enforcing the agreement.

David P. Pierce, The Federal Arbitration Act: Conflicting Interpretations of its Scope 61 Cinn.L.Rev. 623, 635 (1992) (footnotes omitted).

Based upon the Supreme Court's decision in Volt, we conclude that the nature of our inquiry is whether Montana's notice requirement found at § 27–5–114(4), MCA, would "undermine the goals and policies of the FAA." We conclude that it does not ...

Our conclusion that Montana's notice requirement does not undermine the policies of the FAA is based on the Supreme Court's conclusion that it was never Congress's intent when it enacted the FAA to preempt the entire field of arbitration, and its further conclusion that the FAA does not require parties to arbitrate when they have not agreed to do so. That Court held that the purpose of the FAA is simply to enforce arbitration agreements into which parties had entered, and acknowledged that the interpretation of contracts is ordinarily a question of state law. Volt, 489 U.S. at 474, 109 S.Ct. at 1253.

Presumably, therefore, the Supreme Court would not find it a threat to the policies of the Federal Arbitration Act for a state to require that before arbitration agreements are enforceable, they be entered knowingly. To hold otherwise would be to infer that arbitration is so onerous as a means of dispute resolution that it can only be foisted upon the uninformed. That would be inconsistent with the conclusion that the parties to the contract are free to decide how their disputes should be resolved.

Montana's notice requirement does not preclude parties from knowingly entering into arbitration agreements, nor do our courts decline to enforce arbitration agreements which are entered into knowingly.

Therefore, we conclude that Montana's notice statute found at § 27–5–114(4), MCA, would not undermine the goals and policies of the FAA, and is not preempted by 9 U.S.C. § 2 (1988).

Because the agreement of the parties in this case did not comply with Montana's statutory notice requirement, it is not subject to arbitration, according to the law of Montana. The District Court's order dated June 2, 1993, is, therefore, reversed, and this case is remanded to the District Court for further proceedings consistent with this opinion.

■ HARRISON, HUNT and NELSON, JJ., concur.

■ TRIEWEILER, JUSTICE, specially concurring.

The majority opinion sets forth principles of law agreeable to the majority of this Court in language appropriate for judicial precedent. I offer this special concurring opinion as my personal observation regarding many of the federal decisions which have been cited to us as authority.

To those federal judges who consider forced arbitration as the panacea for their "heavy case loads" and who consider the reluctance of state courts to buy into the arbitration program as a sign of intellectual inadequacy, I would like to explain a few things.

In Montana, we are reasonably civilized and have a sophisticated system of justice which has evolved over time and which we continue to develop for the primary purpose of assuring fairness to those people who are subject to its authority.

Over the previous 100 years of our history as a state, our courts have developed rules of evidence for the purpose of assuring that disputes are resolved on the most reliable bases possible.

Based on the presumption that all men and women are fallible and make mistakes, we have developed standards for appellate review which protect litigants from human error or the potential arbitrariness of any one individual.

We believe in the rule of law so that people can plan their commercial and personal affairs. If our trial courts decline to follow those laws, our citizens are assured that this Court will enforce them.

We have rules for venue, and jurisdictional requirements based on the assumption that it is unfair to force people to travel long distances from their homes at great expense and inconvenience to prosecute or defend against lawsuits.

We believe that our courts should be accessible to all, regardless of their economic status, or their social importance, and therefore, provide courts at public expense and guarantee access to everyone.

We have developed liberal rules of discovery (patterned after the federal courts) based on the assumption that the open and candid exchange of information is the surest way to resolve claims on their merits and avoid unnecessary trials.

We have contract laws and tort laws. We have laws to protect our citizens from bad faith, fraud, unfair business practices, and oppression by the many large national corporations who control many aspects of their lives but with whom they have no bargaining power.

While our system of justice and our rules are imperfect, they have as their ultimate purpose one overriding principle. They are intended, and continue to evolve, for the purpose of providing fairness to people, regardless of their wealth or political influence.

What I would like the people in the federal judiciary, especially at the appellate level, to understand is that due to their misinterpretation of congressional intent when it enacted the Federal Arbitration Act, and due to their naive assumption that arbitration provisions and choice of law provisions are knowingly bargained for, all of these procedural safeguards and substantive laws are easily avoided by any party with enough leverage to stick a choice of law and an arbitration provision in its pre-printed contract and require the party with inferior bargaining power to sign it.

The procedures we have established, and the laws we have enacted, are either inapplicable or unenforceable in the process we refer to as arbitration.

I am particularly offended by the attitude of federal judges, typified by the remarks of Judge Selya in the First Circuit, which were articulated in Securities Industry Ass'n v. Connolly (1st Cir. 1989), 883 F.2d 1114, cert. denied (1990), 495 U.S. 956, 110 S.Ct. 2559, 109 L.Ed.2d 742.

Judge Selya considered "[i]ncreased resort to the courts" as the cause for "tumefaction of already-swollen court calendars." He refers to arbitration as "a contractual device that relieves some of the organic pressure by operating as a shunt, allowing parties to resolve disputes outside of the legal system." Connolly, 883 F.2d at 1116. He states that "[t]he hope has long been that the Act could serve as a therapy for the ailment of the crowded docket." Connolly, 883 F.2d at 1116. He then bemoans that fact that, "[a]s might be expected, there is a rub: the patient, and others in interest, often resist the treatment." Connolly, 883 F.2d at 1116.

Judge Selya refers to the preference in the various state jurisdictions to resolve disputes according to traditional notions of fairness, and then suggests that "[t]he FAA was enacted to overcome this 'anachronism'." Connolly, 883 F.2d at 1119 (citation omitted). He considers it the role of federal courts to be "on guard for artifices in which the ancient suspicion of arbitration might reappear." Connolly, 883 F.2d at 1119.

This type of arrogance not only reflects an intellectual detachment from reality, but a self-serving disregard for the purposes for which courts exist.

With all due respect, Judge Selya's opinion illustrates an all too frequent preoccupation on the part of federal judges with their own case load and a total lack of consideration for the rights of individuals. Nowhere in Judge Selya's lengthy opinion is there any consideration for the total lack of procedural safeguards inherent in the arbitration process. Nowhere in his opinion does he consider the financial hardship that contracts, like the one in this case, impose on people who simply cannot afford to enforce their rights by the process that has been forced upon them. Nowhere does Judge Selya acknowledge that the "patient" (presumably courts like this one) who resists the "treatment" (presumably the imposition of arbitration in lieu of justice) has a case load typically three times as great as Justice Selya's case load.

The notion by federal judges, like Judge Selya, that people like the Casarottos have knowingly and voluntarily bargained and agreed to resolve their contractual disputes or tort claims by arbitration, is naive at best, and self-serving and cynical at worst. To me, the idea of a contract or agreement suggests mutuality. There is no mutuality in a franchise agreement, a securities brokerage agreement, or in any other of the agreements which typically impose arbitration as the means for resolving disputes. National franchisors, like the defendant in this case, and brokerage firms, who have been the defendants in many other arbitration cases, present form contracts to franchisees and consumers in which choice of law provisions and arbitration provisions are not negotiable, and the consequences of which are not explained. The provision is either accepted, or the business or investment opportunity is denied. Yet these provisions, which are not only approved of, but encouraged by people like Judge Selya, do, in effect, subvert our system of justice as we have come to know it. If any foreign government tried to do the same, we would surely consider it a serious act of aggression.

Furthermore, if the Federal Arbitration Act is to be interpreted as broadly as some of the decisions from our federal courts would suggest, then it presents a serious issue regarding separation of powers. What these interpretations do, in effect, is permit a few major corporations to draft contracts regarding their relationship with others that immunizes them from accountability under the laws of the states where they do business, and by the courts in those states. With a legislative act, the Congress, according to some federal decisions, has written state and federal courts out of business as far as these corporations are concerned. They are not subject to California's labor laws or franchise laws, they are not subject to our contract laws or tort laws. They are, in effect, above the law.

These insidious erosions of state authority and the judicial process threaten to undermine the rule of law as we know it.

Nothing in our jurisprudence appears more intellectually detached from reality and arrogant than the lament of federal judges who see this system of imposed arbitration as "therapy for their crowded dockets." These decisions have perverted the purpose of the FAA from one to accomplish judicial neutrality, to one of open hostility to any legislative effort to assure that unsophisticated parties to contracts of adhesion at least understand the rights they are giving up.

It seems to me that judges who have let their concern for their own crowded docket overcome their concern for the rights they are entrusted with should step aside and let someone else assume their burdens. The last I checked, there were plenty of capable people willing to do so.

■ WEBER, JUSTICE, dissents as follows.

I respect the majority opinion in its expression of the deeply held conviction that arbitration of the type expressed in the contract in this case should not be enforced in Montana and thereby deprive the parties of access to the court system. . . .

The majority opinion analyzes the United States Supreme Court's decision in Volt and from that concludes that the nature of the inquiry is whether Montana's notice requirement under (§ 27–5–11494), MCA, would undermine the goals and policy of the FAA and further concludes it does not. I disagree with that analysis of Volt.

. . . It is essential to keep in mind that the key holding of Volt as expressed by the United State Supreme Court was that the agreement to arbitrate should be enforced according to its terms—and that allowed application of the California law which provided for the stay in proceedings where other parties besides the arbitration parties were involved in the case. That conclusion does not assist the majority opinion. The rationale of the Volt decision in the present case would require enforcement of the contract as agreed upon by the parties—which would require application of the American Arbitration Association rules as well as the laws of the State of Connecticut. I conclude that the contract here should be enforced to require application of the American Arbitration Association Rules and the laws of the State of Connecticut under Volt. . . .

■ TURNAGE, C.J., concurs in the foregoing dissent. The dissenting opinion of JUSTICE GRAY is omitted.

* * *

Questions

1. In the foregoing case, suppose the Montana and Connecticut common law differ with respect to the standard for establishing liability on the basis of promissory estoppel, or the relevant statute of limitations. Which state's law would apply? Why might the choice of law analysis be different for an arbitration clause? Do all laws of a state reflect the state's public policies? If so, for a contract entered into or performed in Montana, would a choice of law of a state other than Montana ever be effective?

2. If the court's decision means that Montana arbitration law is somehow more reflective of public policies than other state laws, is the state applying an arbitration-specific doctrine in contravention to the rule of *Perry v. Thomas,* that only state law defenses of a general type can be raised to defeat arbitration?

3. Does the Supreme Court's decision in *Volt* mean that the nature of the inquiry into the validity of the Montana notice requirement must be based on whether the requirement would "undermine the goals and policies of the FAA"? Under that standard, how should this case come out?

4. This case was remanded by the Supreme Court in light of Allied–Bruce Terminix v. Dobson, 513 U.S. 265 (1995). See 515 U.S. 1129 (1995). What in the *Allied–Bruce Terminix* case might be relevant for the Montana Supreme Court on remand?

* * *

On remand, the Montana court adhered to its earlier opinion. Subsequently, the case again was appealed to the Supreme Court. The Court accepted the case and rendered the following opinion.

Doctor's Associates, Inc. v. Casarotto

517 U.S. 681 (1996).

■ JUSTICE GINSBURG delivered the opinion of the Court.

This case concerns a standard form franchise agreement for the operation of a Subway sandwich shop in Montana. When a dispute arose between parties to the agreement, franchisee Paul Casarotto sued franchisor Doctor's Associates, Inc. (DAI) and DAI's Montana development agent, Nick Lombardi, in a Montana state court. DAI and Lombardi sought to stop the litigation pending arbitration pursuant to the arbitration clause set out on page nine of the franchise agreement.

The Federal Arbitration Act (FAA or Act) declares written provisions for arbitration "valid, irrevocable, and enforceable, save upon such grounds as exist at law or in equity for the revocation of any contract." 9 U.S.C. § 2. Montana law, however, declares an arbitration clause unenforceable unless "[n]otice that [the] contract is subject to arbitration" is "typed in underlined capital letters on the first page of the contract." Mont.Code Ann. § 27–5–114(4) (1995). The question here presented is whether Montana's law is compatible with the federal Act. We hold that Montana's first-page notice requirement, which governs not "any contract," but specifically and solely contracts "subject to arbitration," conflicts with the FAA and is therefore displaced by the federal measure.

I

Petitioner DAI is the national franchisor of Subway sandwich shops. In April 1988, DAI entered a franchise agreement with respondent Paul Casarotto, which permitted Casarotto to open a Subway shop in Great Falls, Montana. The franchise agreement stated, on page nine and in ordinary type: "Any controversy or claim arising out of or relating to this contract or the breach thereof shall be settled by Arbitration...." App. 75.

In October 1992, Casarotto sued DAI and its agent, Nick Lombardi, in Montana state court, alleging state-law contract and tort claims relating to the franchise agreement. DAI demanded arbitration of those claims, and successfully moved in the Montana trial court to stay the lawsuit pending arbitration. Id., at 10–11.

The Montana Supreme Court reversed. Casarotto v. Lombardi, 268 Mont. 369, 886 P.2d 931 (1994). That court left undisturbed the trial court's findings that the franchise agreement fell within the scope of the FAA and covered the claims Casarotto stated against DAI and Lombardi. The Montana Supreme Court held, however, that Mont.Code Ann. § 27–5–114(4) rendered the agreement's arbitration clause unenforceable. The Montana statute provides:

> Notice that a contract is subject to arbitration ... shall be typed in underlined capital letters on the first page of the contract; and unless such notice is displayed thereon, the contract may not be subject to arbitration.

Notice of the arbitration clause in the franchise agreement did not appear on the first page of the contract. Nor was anything relating to the clause typed in underlined capital letters. Because the State's statutory notice requirement had not been met, the Montana Supreme Court declared the parties' dispute "not subject to arbitration." 268 Mont., at 382, 886 P.2d, at 939.

DAI and Lombardi unsuccessfully argued before the Montana Supreme Court that § 27–5–114(4) was preempted by § 2 of the FAA. DAI and Lombardi dominantly relied on our decisions in Southland Corp. v. Keating, 465 U.S. 1, 104 S.Ct. 852, 79 L.Ed.2d 1 (1984), and Perry v. Thomas, 482 U.S. 483, 107 S.Ct. 2520, 96 L.Ed.2d 426 (1987). In Southland, we held that § 2 of the FAA applies in state as well as federal courts, see 465 U.S., at 12, 104 S.Ct., at 859, and "withdr[aws] the power of the states to require a judicial forum for the resolution of claims which the contracting parties agreed to resolve by arbitration," id., at 10, 104 S.Ct., at 858. We noted in the path-marking Southland decision that the FAA established a "broad principle of enforceability," id., at 11, 104 S.Ct., at 858, and that § 2 of the federal Act provided for revocation of arbitration agreements only upon "grounds as exist at law or in equity for the revocation of any contract." In Perry, we reiterated: "[S]tate law, whether of legislative or judicial origin, is applicable if that law arose to govern issues concerning the validity, revocability, and enforceability of contracts generally. A state-law principle that takes its meaning precisely from the fact that a contract to arbitrate is at issue does not comport with [the text of § 2]." 482 U.S., at 492, n. 9, 107 S.Ct., at 2527, n. 9.

The Montana Supreme Court, however, read our decision in Volt Information Sciences, Inc. v. Board of Trustees of Leland Stanford Junior Univ., 489 U.S. 468, 109 S.Ct. 1248, 103 L.Ed.2d 488 (1989), as limiting the preemptive force of § 2 and correspondingly qualifying Southland and Perry. 268 Mont., at 378–381, 886 P.2d, at 937–939. As the Montana Supreme Court comprehended Volt, the proper inquiry here should focus not on the bare words of § 2, but on this question: Would the application of Montana's notice requirement, contained in § 27–5–114(4), "undermine the goals and policies of the FAA." 268 Mont., at 381, 886 P.2d, at 938 (internal quotation marks omitted). Section 27–5–114(4), in the Montana court's judgment, did not undermine the goals and policies of the FAA, for the notice requirement did not preclude arbitration agreements altogether; it simply prescribed "that before arbitration agreements are enforceable, they be entered knowingly." Id., at 381, 886 P.2d, at 939.

DAI and Lombardi petitioned for certiorari. Last Term, we granted their petition, vacated the judgment of the Montana Supreme Court, and remanded for further consideration in light of Allied–Bruce Terminix Cos. v. Dobson, 513 U.S. 265, 115 S.Ct. 834, 130 L.Ed.2d 753 (1995). See 515 U.S. 1129, 115 S.Ct. 2552, 132 L.Ed.2d 807 (1995). In Allied–Bruce, we restated what our decisions in Southland and Perry had established:

> States may regulate contracts, including arbitration clauses, under general contract law principles and they may invalidate an arbitration clause 'upon such grounds as exist at law or in equity for the revocation of any contract.' 9 U.S.C. § 2. What States may not do is decide that a contract is fair enough to enforce all its basic terms (price, service, credit), but not fair enough to enforce its arbitration clause. The Act makes any such state policy unlawful, for that kind of policy would place arbitration clauses on an unequal 'footing,' directly contrary to the Act's language and Congress's intent. 513 U.S. at 281, 115 S.Ct. at 843.

On remand, without inviting or permitting further briefing or oral argument, the Montana Supreme Court adhered to its original ruling. The court stated: "After careful review, we can find nothing in the [Allied–Bruce] decision which relates to the issues presented to this Court in this case." Casarotto v. Lombardi, 274 Mont. 3, 7, 901 P.2d 596, 598 (1995). Elaborating, the Montana court said it found "no suggestion in [Allied–Bruce] that the principles from Volt on which we relied [to uphold § 27–5–114(4)] have been modified in any way." Id., at 8, 901 P.2d, at 598–599. We again granted certiorari, 516 U.S. 1036, 116 S.Ct. 690, 133 L.Ed.2d 594 (1996), and now reverse.

II

Section 2 of the FAA provides that written arbitration agreements "shall be valid, irrevocable, and enforceable, save upon such grounds as exist at law or in equity for the revocation of any contract." 9 U.S.C. § 2.

Repeating our observation in Perry, the text of § 2 declares that state law may be applied "if that law arose to govern issues concerning the validity, revocability, and enforceability of contracts generally." 482 U.S., at 492, n. 9, 107 S.Ct., at 2527, n. 9. Thus, generally applicable contract defenses, such as fraud, duress or unconscionability, may be applied to invalidate arbitration agreements without contravening § 2. See Allied–Bruce, 513 U.S., at 281, 115 S.Ct., at 843; Rodriguez de Quijas v. Shearson/American Express, Inc., 490 U.S. 477, 483–484, 109 S.Ct. 1917, 1921–1922, 104 L.Ed.2d 526 (1989); Shearson/American Express Inc. v. McMahon, 482 U.S. 220, 226, 107 S.Ct. 2332, 2337, 96 L.Ed.2d 185 (1987).

Courts may not, however, invalidate arbitration agreements under state laws applicable only to arbitration provisions. See Allied–Bruce, 513 U.S., at 281, 115 S.Ct., at 842–843; Perry, 482 U.S., at 492, n. 9, 107 S.Ct., at 2527, n. 9. By enacting § 2, we have several times said, Congress precluded States from singling out arbitration provisions for suspect status, requiring instead that such provisions be placed "upon the same footing as other contracts." Scherk v. Alberto–Culver Co., 417 U.S. 506, 511, 94 S.Ct. 2449, 2453, 41 L.Ed.2d 270 (1974) (internal quotation marks omitted). Montana's § 27–5–114(4) directly conflicts with § 2 of the FAA because the State's law conditions the enforceability of arbitration agreements on compliance with a special notice requirement not applicable to contracts generally. The FAA thus displaces the Montana statute with respect to arbitration agreements covered by the Act. See 2 I. Macneil, R. Speidel, T. Stipanowich, & G. Shell, Federal Arbitration Law § 19.1.1, pp. 19:4–19:5 (1995) (under Southland and Perry, "state legislation requiring greater information or choice in the making of agreements to arbitrate than in other contracts is preempted").[3]

The Montana Supreme Court misread our Volt decision and therefore reached a conclusion in this case at odds with our rulings. Volt involved an arbitration agreement that incorporated state procedural rules, one of which, on the facts of that case, called for arbitration to be stayed pending the resolution of a related judicial proceeding. The state rule examined in

3. At oral argument, counsel for Casarotto urged a broader view, under which § 27–5–114(4) might be regarded as harmless surplus. See Tr. of Oral Arg. 29–32. Montana could have invalidated the arbitration clause in the franchise agreement under general, informed consent principles, counsel suggested. She asked us to regard § 27–5–114(4) as but one illustration of a cross-the-board rule: unexpected provisions in adhesion contracts must be conspicuous. See also Brief for Respondents 21–24. But the Montana Supreme Court announced no such sweeping rule. The court did not assert as a basis for its decision a generally applicable principle of "reasonable expectations" governing any standard form contract term. Cf. Transamerica Ins. Co. v. Royle, 202 Mont. 173, 180, 656 P.2d 820, 824 (1983) (invalidating provision in auto insurance policy that did not "honor the reasonable expectations" of the insured). Montana's decision trains on and upholds a particular statute, one setting out a precise, arbitration-specific limitation. We review that disposition, and no other. It bears reiteration, however, that a court may not "rely on the uniqueness of an agreement to arbitrate as a basis for a state-law holding that enforcement would be unconscionable, for this would enable the court to effect what . . . the state legislature cannot." Perry v. Thomas, 482 U.S. 483, 492, n. 9, 107 S.Ct. 2520, 2527, n. 9, 96 L.Ed.2d 426 (1987).

Volt determined only the efficient order of proceedings; it did not affect the enforceability of the arbitration agreement itself. We held that applying the state rule would not "undermine the goals and policies of the FAA," 489 U.S., at 478, 109 S.Ct., at 1255, because the very purpose of the Act was to "ensur[e] that private agreements to arbitrate are enforced according to their terms," id., at 479, 109 S.Ct., at 1256.

Applying § 27–5–114(4) here, in contrast, would not enforce the arbitration clause in the contract between DAI and Casarotto; instead, Montana's first-page notice requirement would invalidate the clause. The "goals and policies" of the FAA, this Court's precedent indicates, are antithetical to threshold limitations placed specifically and solely on arbitration provisions. Section 2 "mandate[s] the enforcement of arbitration agreements," Southland, 465 U.S., at 10, 104 S.Ct., at 858, "save upon such grounds as exist at law or in equity for the revocation of any contract," 9 U.S.C. § 2. Section 27–5–114(4) of Montana's law places arbitration agreements in a class apart from "any contract," and singularly limits their validity. The State's prescription is thus inconsonant with, and is therefore preempted by, the federal law.

For the reasons stated, the judgment of the Supreme Court of Montana is reversed, and the case is remanded for further proceedings not inconsistent with this opinion.

It is so ordered.

■ JUSTICE THOMAS, dissenting.

For the reasons given in my dissent last term in Allied–Bruce Terminix Cos. v. Dobson, 513 U.S. 265 (1995), I remain of the view that § 2 of the Federal Arbitration Act, 9 U.S.C. § 2, does not apply to proceedings in state courts. Accordingly, I respectfully dissent.

* * *

Questions

1. How does the majority reinterpret *Volt?* Is this the only reading of *Volt* that is possible?

2. Does footnote 3 raise the possibility of challenges to arbitration clauses based on unconscionability or lack of consent? How must such challenges be framed in order to succeed?

3. Are decisions like *Casarotto*, *Southland*, and *Green Tree v. Bazzle* consistent with the Supreme Court's deference in recent decades to principles of federalism? What, exactly, is left of state arbitration law after these decisions? Do you think the Congress that passed the FAA in the 1920s intended it to be interpreted as broadly as the Court does today? See Edward Brunet, *The Minimal Role of Federalism and State Law in Arbitration*, 8 Nev. L.J. 326 (2007); Maureen A. Weston, *Preserving the Federal*

Arbitration Act by Reining in Judicial Expansion and Mandatory Use, 8 Nev. L.J. 385 (2007).

* * *

7. ALLOCATING THE COSTS OF ARBITRATION

Unlike a judicial proceeding, the parties to an arbitration must pay not only filing fees, but also fees for the arbitrator's time spent in a hearing and deciding a case. In addition, there can be travel costs for the arbitrator, the parties, and witnesses if the hearing is in a distant location. Some arbitration providers also pass along to the parties the costs of renting hearing rooms and other administrative expenses. Thus arbitration can be very expensive. For example, the American Arbitration Association (AAA) charges the party requesting arbitration a filing fee that can be as high as $5,000 just to initiate a case. In addition, many arbitrators charge $1,000–1,500 for each day of an arbitral hearing and each day spent reaching their decision. When parties arbitrate claims that would otherwise be heard in a judicial forum, they must bear these costs themselves.

There are very few studies comparing the cost of arbitration to the cost of litigation, so it is difficult to generalize about the cost advantages or disadvantages of each method. One study, conducted by the *Public Citizen* and published in May 2002, found:

- The cost to a plaintiff of initiating an arbitration is almost always higher than the cost of instituting a lawsuit. Our comparison of court fees to the fees charged by the three primary arbitration provider organizations demonstrates that *forum costs*—the costs charged by the tribunal that will decide the dispute—can be up to five thousand percent higher in arbitration than in court litigation. These costs have a deterrent effect, often preventing a claimant from even filing a case.

- Arbitration costs will probably always be higher than court costs in any event, because the expenses of a private legal system are so substantial. The same support personnel that expedite cases at a courthouse, such as file clerks and court administrators, are also necessary to manage arbitration cases. But because arbitration provider organizations handle fewer cases over larger geographic areas, the economy of scale in a court clerk's office cannot be achieved, increasing the administrative cost per case. Thus, while it costs the Clerk of the Circuit Court of Cook County an average of $44.20 to administer a case, AAA's administrative cost per case averages $340.63, about 700 percent more.

- Arbitration saddles claimants with a plethora of extra fees that they would not be charged if they went to court. For example, the National Arbitration Forum charges $75 to issue a subpoena. A lawsuit litigant can obtain a subpoena form for free from the court, oftentimes downloading it off the Internet. NAF also charges fees for discovery requests

> ($150) and continuances ($100), occurrences so ubiquitous in litigation that they must be viewed as inevitable. The American Arbitration Association (AAA) charges extra fees for use of a hearing room ...

The *Public Citizen* report hypothesized that the high costs of arbitration were the result of a lack of competition among arbitration providers and a lack of incentives to control costs on behalf of parties drafting arbitration agreements. It wrote:

> Arbitration costs are high under a pre-dispute arbitration clause because there is no price competition among providers. Companies that want to use arbitration costs as a barrier, to prevent consumers and others from asserting their legal rights, have no incentive to arrange low-cost arbitration services. Instead, it is to their advantage to seek out the highest-cost arbitration providers. While experience has shown that many lawyers are willing to serve as arbitrators for nominal fees, the market provides no mechanism to match volunteer arbitrators to cases in which they are needed the most.

Public Citizen, *Report on Costs of Arbitration*, May 1, 2002, available at http://www.citizen.org/publications/release.cfm?ID=7173&secID=1052&catID=126.

In addition to the costs charged by the arbitration provider, parties to an arbitration often have to pay large costs for travel to the hearing. If parties do not designate a location for the hearing, then under the rules of the AAA, the arbitrator has the power to designate the location. As one commentator notes,

> When the employment contract does not designate a location, the AAA's procedure for selecting a location does not present any special problems when the employer and employee are located in the same city or state, since presumably, both parties will request arbitration to take place near the employment setting. However, difficulties arise when an employee works for a national employer, headquartered in another state. Customarily, the employer will outline in the employment contract that arbitration is to take place in the state where the national headquarters are located. Such a provision can impose a severe hardship on the employee, who may have to travel long distances for resolution of a dispute. Adding yet another burden, the AAA directs that the arbitrator's travel expenses are to shared equally by the parties, unless the employment contract provides differently or the arbitrator directs otherwise, making an employee responsible for even greater expenses if the arbitrator is also from another state ...
>
> Travel expenses also effect the production of witnesses. For instance, the AAA provides that any travel expenses for witnesses are to be borne equally by both parties, unless otherwise agreed by the parties or otherwise awarded by the arbitrator. When a party requires the production of witnesses, having them travel across several states is usually not feasible. This is especially true for the employee's witnesses, because employees would choose, in many instances, to forego

> the calling of some witnesses in lieu of fronting expensive travel costs and awaiting apportionment of travel expenses at the end of arbitration. The employer, on the other hand, usually has more than sufficient funds to advance the costs of travel and has easier access to witnesses as most will be the company's employees. Consequently, unless otherwise agreed, if an employer calls numerous witnesses, the employee will be assessed for one-half of the opposing party's presentation of witnesses.

Melissa G. Lamm, *Who Pays Arbitration Fees?: The Unanswered Question in Circuit City Stores, Inc. v. Adams,* 24 Campbell L. Rev. 93 (2001).

Some arbitration agreements explicitly allocate the respective financial burdens. For example, many arbitration agreements state that the costs of the arbitration are shared equally between the parties. Alternatively, some impose the arbitration costs on the losing party. And some arbitration systems expressly limit the financial liability of the weaker party. For example, the employment arbitration system at the Halliburton Corporation (formerly Brown & Root) specifies that an employee must pay a processing fee of $50.00 and the company will pay the rest of the costs of arbitration.[1] Most arbitration agreements are either silent about the allocation of costs or leave the cost allocation question to the discretion of the arbitrator.

When an individual is required to arbitrate a statutory claim against a large corporation, the high cost of arbitration itself works an injustice. If the arbitration system requires the individual to pay a substantial share of the cost, the individual may not have the financial resources even to have her case heard. If the system permits the arbitrator to allocate costs at the end of the case, the individual may not want to take the risk of not only losing but being saddled with a sizeable liability for the arbitrator's fees.

Courts have addressed the question of whether it is unconscionable for an arbitration system to require an individual to bear the costs of having her claims heard. The following cases illustrate the issues that have arisen and the approaches that courts are taking.

* * *

Green Tree Financial Corp. v. Randolph

531 U.S. 79 (2000).

■ CHIEF JUSTICE REHNQUIST delivered the opinion of the Court.

... Respondent Larketta Randolph purchased a mobile home from Better Cents Home Builders, Inc., in Opelika, Alabama. She financed this purchase through petitioners Green Tree Financial Corporation and its wholly owned subsidiary, Green Tree Financial Corp.-Alabama. Petitioners'

1. For a detailed description of the Brown & Root arbitration system, see Richard A. Bales, *Compulsory Arbitration: The Grand Experiment in Employment* 108–09 (1997).

Manufactured Home Retail Installment Contract and Security Agreement required that Randolph buy Vendor's Single Interest insurance, which protects the vendor or lienholder against the costs of repossession in the event of default. The agreement also provided that all disputes arising from, or relating to, the contract, whether arising under case law or statutory law, would be resolved by binding arbitration.

Randolph later sued petitioners, alleging that they violated the Truth in Lending Act (TILA), 15 U.S.C. § 1601 *et seq.*, by failing to disclose as a finance charge the Vendor's Single Interest insurance requirement. She later amended her complaint to add a claim that petitioners violated the Equal Credit Opportunity Act, 15 U.S.C. §§ 1691–1691f, by requiring her to arbitrate her statutory causes of action. She brought this action on behalf of a similarly situated class. In lieu of an answer, petitioners filed a motion to compel arbitration, to stay the action, or, in the alternative, to dismiss. The District Court granted petitioners' motion to compel arbitration, denied the motion to stay, and dismissed Randolph's claims with prejudice. The District Court also denied her request to certify a class. 991 F.Supp. 1410 (M.D.Ala. 1997). She requested reconsideration, asserting that she lacked the resources to arbitrate, and as a result, would have to forgo her claims against petitioners. See Plaintiff's Motion for Reconsideration, Record Doc. No. 53, p. 9. The District Court denied reconsideration. 991 F.Supp., at 1425–1426. Randolph appealed.

[The Court of Appeals for the Eleventh Circuit first found the district court ruling appealable.] The court then determined that the arbitration agreement failed to provide the minimum guarantees that respondent could vindicate her statutory rights under the TILA. Critical to this determination was the court's observation that the arbitration agreement was silent with respect to payment of filing fees, arbitrators' costs, and other arbitration expenses. On that basis, the court held that the agreement to arbitrate posed a risk that respondent's ability to vindicate her statutory rights would be undone by "steep" arbitration costs, and therefore was unenforceable. We granted certiorari, 529 U.S. 1052, 120 S.Ct. 1552, 146 L.Ed.2d 458 (2000), and we now affirm the Court of Appeals with respect to the first conclusion, and reverse it with respect to the second . . .

III

We now turn to the question whether Randolph's agreement to arbitrate is unenforceable because it says nothing about the costs of arbitration, and thus fails to provide her protection from potentially substantial costs of pursuing her federal statutory claims in the arbitral forum. Section 2 of the FAA provides that "[a] written provision in any maritime transaction or a contract evidencing a transaction involving commerce to settle by arbitration a controversy thereafter arising out of such contract . . . shall be valid, irrevocable, and enforceable, save upon such grounds as exist at law or in equity for the revocation of any contract." 9 U.S.C. § 2. In considering whether respondent's agreement to arbitrate is unenforceable, we are mindful of the FAA's purpose "to reverse the longstanding judicial hostility to arbitration agreements . . . and to place arbitration agreements upon the same footing as other contracts." *Gilmer v. Interstate/Johnson Lane Corp.,* 500 U.S. 20, 24, 111 S.Ct. 1647, 114 L.Ed.2d 26 (1991).

In light of that purpose, we have recognized that federal statutory claims can be appropriately resolved through arbitration, and we have enforced agreements to arbitrate that involve such claims. [Citations omitted.] We have likewise rejected generalized attacks on arbitration that rest on "suspicion of arbitration as a method of weakening the protections afforded in the substantive law to would-be complainants." *Rodriguez de Quijas,* 109 S.Ct. 1917. These cases demonstrate that even claims arising under a statute designed to further important social policies may be arbitrated because " 'so long as the prospective litigant effectively may vindicate [his or her] statutory cause of action in the arbitral forum,' " the statute serves its functions. See *Gilmer, supra,* at 28, 111 S.Ct. 1647 (quoting *Mitsubishi,* 105 S.Ct. 3346).

In determining whether statutory claims may be arbitrated, we first ask whether the parties agreed to submit their claims to arbitration, and then ask whether Congress has evinced an intention to preclude a waiver of judicial remedies for the statutory rights at issue. See *Gilmer, supra,* at 26, 111 S.Ct. 1647; *Mitsubishi,* 105 S.Ct. 3346. In this case, it is undisputed that the parties agreed to arbitrate all claims relating to their contract, including claims involving statutory rights. Nor does Randolph contend that the TILA evinces an intention to preclude a waiver of judicial remedies. She contends instead that the arbitration agreement's silence with respect to costs and fees creates a "risk" that she will be required to bear prohibitive arbitration costs if she pursues her claims in an arbitral forum, and thereby forces her to forgo any claims she may have against petitioners. Therefore, she argues, she is unable to vindicate her statutory rights in arbitration. See Brief for Respondent 29–30.

It may well be that the existence of large arbitration costs could preclude a litigant such as Randolph from effectively vindicating her federal statutory rights in the arbitral forum. But the record does not show that Randolph will bear such costs if she goes to arbitration. Indeed, it contains hardly any information on the matter.[5] As the Court of Appeals recognized,

5. In Randolph's motion for reconsideration in the District Court, she asserted that "[a]rbitration costs are high" and that she did not have the resources to arbitrate. But she failed to support this assertion. She first acknowledged that petitioners had not designated a particular arbitration association or arbitrator to resolve their dispute. Her subsequent discussion of costs relied entirely on unfounded assumptions. She stated that "[f]or the purposes of this discussion, we will assume filing with the [American Arbitration Association], the filing fee is $500 for claims under $10,000 and this does not include the cost of the arbitrator or administrative fees." . . . She then noted: "[The American Arbitration Association] further cites $700 per day as the average arbitrator's fee." . . . Randolph plainly failed to make any factual showing that the American Arbitration Association would conduct the arbitration, or that, if it did, she would be charged the filing fee or arbitrator's fee that she identified. These unsupported statements provide no basis on which to ascertain the actual costs and fees to which she would be subject in arbitration. In this Court, Randolph's brief lists fees incurred in cases involving other arbitrations as reflected in opinions of other Courts of

"we lack ... information about how claimants fare under Green Tree's arbitration clause." 178 F.3d, at 1158. The record reveals only the arbitration agreement's silence on the subject, and that fact alone is plainly insufficient to render it unenforceable. The "risk" that Randolph will be saddled with prohibitive costs is too speculative to justify the invalidation of an arbitration agreement.

To invalidate the agreement on that basis would undermine the "liberal federal policy favoring arbitration agreements." *Moses H. Cone Memorial Hospital,* 460 U.S., at 24, 103 S.Ct. 927. It would also conflict with our prior holdings that the party resisting arbitration bears the burden of proving that the claims at issue are unsuitable for arbitration. See *Gilmer, supra,* at 26, 111 S.Ct. 1647; *McMahon, supra,* at 227, 107 S.Ct. 2332. We have held that the party seeking to avoid arbitration bears the burden of establishing that Congress intended to preclude arbitration of the statutory claims at issue. See *Gilmer, supra; McMahon, supra.* Similarly, we believe that where, as here, a party seeks to invalidate an arbitration agreement on the ground that arbitration would be prohibitively expensive, that party bears the burden of showing the likelihood of incurring such costs. Randolph did not meet that burden. How detailed the showing of prohibitive expense must be before the party seeking arbitration must come forward with contrary evidence is a matter we need not discuss; for in this case neither during discovery nor when the case was presented on the merits was there any timely showing at all on the point. The Court of Appeals therefore erred in deciding that the arbitration agreement's silence with respect to costs and fees rendered it unenforceable.

The judgment of the Court of Appeals is affirmed in part and reversed in part.

It is so ordered.

■ JUSTICE GINSBURG, with whom JUSTICE STEVENS and JUSTICE SOUTER join, and with whom JUSTICE BREYER joins as to Parts I and III, concurring in part and dissenting in part. . . .

II

The Court today deals with a "who pays" question, specifically, who pays for the arbitral forum. The Court holds that Larketta Randolph bears the burden of demonstrating that the arbitral forum is financially inaccessible to her. Essentially, the Court requires a party, situated as Randolph is, either to submit to arbitration without knowing who will pay for the forum or to demonstrate up front that the costs, if imposed on her, will be prohibitive. *Ante,* at 522–523. As I see it, the case in its current posture is not ripe for such a disposition.

The Court recognizes that "the existence of large arbitration costs could preclude a litigant such as Randolph from effectively vindicating her

Appeals, while petitioners' counsel states that arbitration fees are frequently waived by petitioners. None of this information affords a sufficient basis for concluding that Randolph would in fact have incurred substantial costs in the event her claim went to arbitration.

federal statutory rights in the arbitral forum." *Ante,* at 522. But, the Court next determines, "the party resisting arbitration bears the burden of proving that the claims at issue are unsuitable for arbitration" and "Randolph did not meet that burden." *Ante,* at 522. In so ruling, the Court blends two discrete inquiries: First, is the arbitral forum *adequate* to adjudicate the claims at issue; second, is that forum *accessible* to the party resisting arbitration.

Our past decisions deal with the first question, the *adequacy* of the arbitral forum to adjudicate various statutory claims. See, *e.g., Gilmer v. Interstate/Johnson Lane Corp.,* 500 U.S. 20 (1991) (Age Discrimination in Employment Act claims are amenable to arbitration); *Shearson/American Express Inc. v. McMahon,* 482 U.S. 220 (1987) (Claims under Racketeer Influenced and Corrupt Organizations Act and Securities Exchange Act are amenable to arbitration). These decisions hold that the party resisting arbitration bears the burden of establishing the inadequacy of the arbitral forum for adjudication of claims of a particular genre. See *Gilmer,* 500 U.S., at 26; *McMahon,* 482 U.S., at 227. It does not follow like the night the day, however, that the party resisting arbitration should also bear the burden of showing that the arbitral forum would be financially inaccessible to her.

The arbitration agreement at issue is contained in a form contract drawn by a commercial party and presented to an individual consumer on a take-it-or-leave-it basis. The case on which the Court dominantly relies, *Gilmer,* also involved a nonnegotiated arbitration clause. But the "who pays" question presented in this case did not arise in *Gilmer.* Under the rules that governed in *Gilmer*—those of the New York Stock Exchange—it was the standard practice for securities industry parties, arbitrating employment disputes, to pay all of the arbitrators' fees. See *Cole v. Burns Int'l Security Servs.,* 105 F.3d 1465, 1483 (C.A.D.C. 1997). Regarding that practice, the Court of Appeals for the District of Columbia Circuit recently commented:

> [I]n *Gilmer,* the Supreme Court endorsed a system of arbitration in which employees are not required to pay for the arbitrator assigned to hear their statutory claims. There is no reason to think that the Court would have approved arbitration in the absence of this arrangement. Indeed, we are unaware of any situation in American jurisprudence in which a beneficiary of a federal statute has been required to pay for the services of the judge assigned to hear her or his case. *Id.,* at 1484.

III

The form contract in this case provides no indication of the rules under which arbitration will proceed or the costs a consumer is likely to incur in arbitration. Green Tree, drafter of the contract, could have filled the void by specifying, for instance, that arbitration would be governed by the rules of the American Arbitration Association (AAA). Under the AAA's Consumer Arbitration Rules, consumers in small-claims arbitration incur no filing fee and pay only $125 of the total fees charged by the arbitrator. All other fees and costs are to be paid by the business party. Brief for American

Arbitration Association as *Amicus Curiae* 15–16. Other national arbitration organizations have developed similar models for fair cost and fee allocation.[2] It may be that in this case, as in *Gilmer,* there is a standard practice on arbitrators' fees and expenses, one that fills the blank space in the arbitration agreement. Counsel for Green Tree offered a hint in that direction. See Tr. of Oral Arg. 26 ("Green Tree does pay [arbitration] costs in a lot of instances . . .") But there is no reliable indication in this record that Randolph's claim will be arbitrated under any consumer-protective fee arrangement.

As a repeat player in the arbitration required by its form contract, Green Tree has superior information about the cost to consumers of pursuing arbitration. [Citations omitted.] In these circumstances, it is hardly clear that Randolph should bear the burden of demonstrating up front the arbitral forum's inaccessibility, or that she should be required to submit to arbitration without knowing how much it will cost her.

As I see it, the Court has reached out prematurely to resolve the matter in the lender's favor . . . [I]f the arbitral forum were in this case financially accessible to Randolph, there would be no occasion to reach the decision today rendered by the Court. Before writing a term into the form contract, as the District of Columbia Circuit did,[3] see *Cole,* 105 F.3d, at 1485, or leaving cost allocation initially to each arbitrator, as the Court does, I would remand for clarification of Green Tree's practice . . .

* * *

Phillips v. Associates Home Equity Services, Inc.

179 F.Supp.2d 840 (N.D.Ill. 2001).

■ KENNELLY, DISTRICT JUDGE.

Plaintiff Juan Phillips filed a class action complaint alleging violations of the Truth in Lending Act, 15 U.S.C. § 1601 *et seq.,* in connection with defendants' handling of residential mortgage transactions. This case is before the Court on defendants' motion to compel arbitration and stay these proceedings based on an arbitration agreement executed by Phillips and defendant Associates Home Equity, and defendants' motion to dismiss all class claims pursuant to Fed.R.Civ.P. 23(d)(4) and 12(b)(6). For the reasons outlined below, defendants' motion to compel arbitration is denied, and ruling on defendants' motion to dismiss is deferred.

FACTUAL BACKGROUND

In May 2000, Phillips obtained a residential mortgage loan in the amount of $72,900 from defendant Associates Home Equity to finance

2. They include National Arbitration Forum provisions that limit small-claims consumer costs to between $49 and $175 and a National Consumer Disputes Advisory Committee protocol recommending that consumer costs be limited to a reasonable amount. . . .

3. The court interpreted a form contract to arbitrate employment disputes, silent as to costs, to require the employer "to pay all of the arbitrator's fees necessary for a full and fair resolution of [the discharged employee's] statutory claims." 105 F.3d, at 1485.

home improvements and pay off her existing consumer debts. Associates Home Equity offers financial products and services such as home equity loans, personal loans, automobile loans, and retail sales financing to consumers, and it specializes in providing credit to the "subprime" market, which consists of persons who are considered to be poor credit risks. Phillips' loan was initially arranged by a mortgage broker, Ficus Financial, which is not named in the complaint. As part of her loan transaction, Phillips received and/or signed a standard form mortgage broker agreement, a loan agreement, a rate reduction rider, a trust deed, a TILA disclosure statement, a HUD–1 settlement statement, and a notice of her right to cancel.

On May 23, 2000, in connection with the loan transaction, Phillips and Associates Home Equity also entered into a written arbitration agreement. Among other things, the agreement contains a section entitled "DISPUTES COVERED" that provides that the parties agree to arbitrate "all claims and disputes between you [Phillips] and us [Associates Home Equity]," including "without limitation, all claims and disputes arising out of, in connection with, or relating to" the May 2000 loan. *See* Arbitration Agreement, Plaintiff's Objection to Arbitration, Exhibit D. The agreement further provides that arbitration will be conducted through the American Arbitration Association ("AAA"), pursuant to its then-current "Commercial Arbitration Rules."

In addition, the agreement includes a provision governing the costs associated with arbitration:

> COSTS OF ARBITRATION: If you start arbitration, you agree to pay the initial filing fee and required deposit required by the American Arbitration Association. If we start arbitration, we will pay the filing fee and required deposit. If you believe you are financially unable to pay such fees, you may ask the American Arbitration Association to defer or reduce such fees, pursuant to the Commercial Arbitration Rules. If the American Arbitration Association does not defer or reduce such fees so that you are able to afford them, we will, upon your written request, pay the fees, subject to any later allocation of the fees and expenses between you and us by the arbitrator. There may be other costs during the arbitration, such as attorney's fees, expenses of travel to the arbitration, and the costs of the arbitration hearings. The Commercial Arbitration Rules determine who will pay those fees.

Arbitration Agreement, p. 2, Plaintiff's Objection to Arbitration, Exhibit D.

On March 19, 2001, Phillips wrote a letter to Associates Home Equity purporting to rescind her loan agreement pursuant to TILA. One day later, Phillips filed this suit seeking declaratory rulings and damages based on Defendants' alleged TILA violations.

ANALYSIS

"It is beyond peradventure that the Federal Arbitration Act embodies a strong federal policy in favor of arbitration." *Sweet Dreams Unlimited,*

Inc. v. Dial–A–Mattress International, Ltd., 1 F.3d 639, 641 (7th Cir.1993) (citing *Moses H. Cone Memorial Hospital v. Mercury Construction,* 460 U.S. 1, 103 S.Ct. 927, 74 L.Ed.2d 765 (1983)). The party opposing arbitration bears the burden of proving that the claims at issue are not subject to arbitration. *Green Tree Financial Corp. v. Randolph,* 531 U.S. 79, 91–92 (2000). Phillips makes five arguments in opposition to arbitration: (1) she rescinded the entire May 2000 loan transaction (which included the arbitration agreement), and therefore the arbitration agreement cannot now be enforced; (2) the arbitration agreement is an unenforceable waiver of her substantive rights under TILA because it does not guarantee her an award of attorneys' fees and litigation expenses if she is successful in arbitration; (3) the arbitral forum is prohibitively expensive; (4) the American Arbitration Association is biased in favor of the defendants; and (5) the arbitration agreement was the result of fraud in the inducement. Only Phillips' argument regarding the expense of the arbitral forum is sufficient to defeat defendants' motion to compel, and on this basis we deny the motion.

[The court rejected Phillips' arguments concerning rescission, waiver, bias, and fraud.]

We finally address Phillips' argument that the costs associated with pursuing her claims in the arbitral forum are prohibitively high. As the Supreme Court recognized in *Green Tree,* "[i]t may well be that the existence of large arbitration costs could preclude a litigant ... from effectively vindicating her federal statutory rights in the arbitral forum." *Green Tree,* 531 U.S. at 90, 121 S.Ct. 513. The Court further determined that where "a party seeks to invalidate an arbitration agreement on the ground that arbitration would be prohibitively expensive, that party bears the burden of showing the likelihood of incurring such costs." *Id.* at 92, 121 S.Ct. 513. At that point, the onus is on the party seeking arbitration to provide contrary evidence. *Id.* In *Green Tree,* the record contained no evidence regarding the costs associated with arbitration, and the Court thus refused to invalidate the arbitration agreement based on an entirely speculative "risk" that the plaintiff would be "saddled with prohibitive costs." *Id.* at 91, 121 S.Ct. 513.

In contrast to the plaintiff in *Green Tree,* Phillips has come forward with evidence that the costs associated with arbitration would effectively preclude her from pursuing her TILA claims. Specifically, Phillips offers evidence from the AAA that she will be forced to pay upwards of $4,000 simply to file her claim. Plaintiff's Opposition to Arbitration, p. 14 and Exhibit E. It is true that the arbitration agreement provides that defendants agreed in the parties' contract to front this amount, but the agreement makes this subject to later allocation by the arbitrator. Furthermore, the initial filing fee is far from the only cost involved in the arbitration. The AAA's Commercial Rules provide that the arbitrator's fees (which range from $750 to $5,000 per day, with an average of $1800 per day in the Chicago area), travel expenses, rental of a hearing room, and other costs are borne equally by the parties, absent some agreement between the parties—an agreement that is lacking in this case—or a different division made at the discretion of the arbitrator. In further support of her argument, Phillips provides an affidavit stating that she "cannot afford to pay" the filing fees and other costs, and that she is in "severe financial straits." Plaintiff's Opposition to Arbitration, Exhibit F, ¶ 9, 10. We see no reason to doubt Phillips' assertion regarding her financial viability, particularly in light of Phillips' inclusion in the "subprime" market targeted by Associates Home Equity. Thus even if we disregard the filing fee, the cost of pursuing arbitration appears to be prohibitive for Phillips, and it is likely to be at least twelve times what it currently costs to file a case in federal court.

In response, defendants do not dispute that Phillips cannot afford the costs associated with arbitration. Instead, defendants argue that the AAA's Commercial Rules contain certain safeguards to protect Phillips against incurring exorbitant costs. These arguments are unavailing. First, defendants argue that Phillips is protected from the expenses of the arbitration because the parties can agree that the costs will be borne by one party. That argument is beside the point here, as defendants have not offered to bear the costs (aside from their agreement to front the filing fee). Second, defendants note that the arbitrator at his or her discretion can assess all expenses to one party at the conclusion of the case. Defendants' Reply in Support of Arbitration, p. 8. But that is nothing more than an argument that there exists *some possibility* that Phillips ultimately may not have to bear a prohibitively expensive portion of the arbitration costs. This is not enough to defeat Phillips' evidence that she would have to expend thousands of dollars that she does not have in order to pursue her claim, with no solid way of getting the money back. Finally, defendants' assertions that AAA arbitrators "customarily" serve without compensation for the first day of service in smaller cases does not appear to apply here, as Phillips is seeking rescission of a loan agreement involving over $70,000, and the AAA rules cited by defendants apply to claims involving less than $10,000. *See* Defendants' Memorandum in Support of Arbitration, p. 7, n. 5.

Defendants further argue that Phillips' cost showing amounts only to "pure speculation," and that Phillips' "generalized assertions" of possible costs should not defeat arbitration. Defendants' Reply in Support of Arbitration, p. 8. We disagree. Phillips has made a reasonable, good faith effort to estimate her arbitration costs with assistance from the AAA, and without actually going through arbitration and receiving a final bill, we see no way for her to provide a more precise showing of her costs than she has done here. We are satisfied that Phillips has met her burden under *Green Tree* of showing that the expense of arbitration would be prohibitive in this case, and we find that defendants have failed to adequately contest that showing. *See Green Tree,* 531 U.S. at 92, 121 S.Ct. 513; *See also Giordano v. Pep Boys—Manny, Moe & Jack, Inc.,* No. 99–1281, 2001 WL 484360 (E.D.Pa. March 29, 2001) (finding that arbitration costs in the thousands of dollars would deter plaintiff's vindication of his claims; thus the cost-sharing provisions of the arbitration agreement were unenforceable). We caution, however, that the cost showing made by Phillips does not create some bright-line rule for future litigants. Instead, the inquiry must be determined on a case-by-case basis.

In sum, Phillips has carried her burden of proving that the costs associated with arbitration would effectively preclude her from vindicating her federal statutory rights. Accordingly, we deny defendants' motion to compel. In the event, however, that defendants were to agree to bear the costs associated with the arbitration, the Court would be willing entertain a motion to reconsider its ruling on that basis.

* * *

Questions

1. According to the *Green Tree* majority, what must a plaintiff show to successfully challenge an arbitration system that imposes significant costs on the party seeking to vindicate substantive rights? Must a plaintiff show that she will definitely incur substantial costs, or merely that she is likely to incur substantial costs? How much certainty need there be for the plaintiff to succeed? Does the court in *Phillips v. Associates Home Equity* impose a somewhat different test?

2. How will a court determine whether an arbitration system imposes such burdensome costs on a party as to prevent the party from vindicating her substantive rights in the arbitral forum? What factors will a court use to make this determination: the estimated costs of the arbitration? the value of the claim? the income of the plaintiff? the overall wealth of both parties? Should a court hold a hearing to determine whether the arbitration is excessively burdensome?

3. What does the Supreme Court in *Green Tree* mean when it states that there are circumstances in which steep arbitration costs could abrogate a party's "substantive rights"? Is the right to have one's legal claim heard and decided by an impartial tribunal a "substantive right"? If it is, then why is it an abrogation of a "substantive right" to impose a financial cost on a party seeking to vindicate a statutory right?

4. Under *Green Tree,* if an arbitration agreement is silent about fee allocation, is a court ever permitted to mandate that one of the parties bear all the costs of arbitration?

* * *

Cole v. Burns International Security Services

105 F.3d 1465 (D.C.Cir. 1997).

■ HARRY T. EDWARDS, CHIEF JUDGE:

... In this case, the appellant, Clinton Cole, seeks to overturn an order of the District Court dismissing his complaint under Title VII of the Civil Rights Act of 1964, as amended, and compelling arbitration of his disputes with Burns International Security Services ("Burns" or "Burns Security"). Although Cole seemingly raised a viable action under Title VII, the District

Court held that his statutory claims of employment discrimination should be dismissed pursuant to the Federal Arbitration Act ("FAA" or "Act") . . .

BACKGROUND

Clinton Cole used to work as a security guard at Union Station in Washington, D.C. for a company called LaSalle and Partners ("LaSalle"). In 1991, Burns Security took over LaSalle's contract to provide security at Union Station and required all LaSalle employees to sign a "Pre–Dispute Resolution Agreement" in order to obtain employment with Burns. The Pre–Dispute Resolution Agreement ("agreement" or "contract") [contained a predispute arbitration agreement] . . . On August 5, 1991, Cole signed the agreement and began working for Burns.

In October 1993, Burns Security fired Cole. After filing charges with the Equal Employment Opportunity Commission, Cole filed the instant complaint in the United States District Court for the District of Columbia, alleging racial discrimination, harassment based on race, retaliation for his writing a letter of complaint regarding sexual harassment of a subordinate employee by another supervisor at Burns, and intentional infliction of emotional distress. Burns moved to compel arbitration of the dispute and to dismiss Cole's complaint pursuant to the terms of the contract.

The District Court found that the arbitration agreement clearly covered Cole's claims. The court also rejected Cole's suggestions (1) that the Pre–Dispute Resolution Agreement was excluded from coverage under the Federal Arbitration Act under 9 U.S.C. § 1, and (2) that the agreement was an unenforceable and unconscionable contract of adhesion. As a result, the trial court granted Burns Security's motion to compel arbitration and dismissed Cole's complaint.

DISCUSSION

[The court first held that the exemption in Section 1 of the Federal Arbitration Act does not exclude all contracts of employment that affect commerce, but rather that section 1 of the FAA exempts only the employment contracts of workers actually engaged in the movement of goods in interstate commerce.]

We turn now to the heart of the problem in this case, i.e., the enforceability of conditions of employment requiring individual employees to use arbitration in place of judicial fora for the resolution of statutory claims . . .

[After noting that the parties agreed to arbitrate under the AAA rules for the conduct of the arbitration, the court went on to state:]

The provisions of the AAA Rules immediately relevant to our analysis are as follows: . . .

(4) Rule 35: A filing fee of $500 must be advanced by the initiating party, subject to final apportionment by the arbitrator in the award, and an administrative fee of $150 per hearing day must be paid by each

party, but the AAA "may, in the event of extreme hardship on any party, defer or reduce the administrative fees;"

(5) Rule 36: The expenses of the arbitration, including required travel and other expenses of the arbitrator, AAA representatives, and witnesses, will be shared equally by the parties, unless the parties agree otherwise or the arbitrator directs otherwise in the award;

(6) Rule 37: The parties are to agree with the arbitrator on appropriate compensation for the arbitrator's work, but if the parties cannot agree with the arbitrator on a rate of compensation, the arbitrator's fee will be set by AAA. Payment of the arbitrator's fee is made through AAA, not directly between the parties and the arbitrator.

The parties stipulated that arbitrators' fees are commonly $500 to $1,000 or more per day.[8] Significantly, however, the AAA Rules do not prescribe any particular allocation of responsibility for the payment of the arbitrators' fees.

Nothing in these rules indicates how an arbitrator's compensation is to be allocated. Instead, it is quite clear that AAA hedged on this question in the National Rules for the Resolution of Employment Disputes (effective June 1, 1996) (probably because the issue was seen to be so controversial). In contrast, in the AAA Labor Arbitration Rules, at 16 (as amended and effective January 1, 1996), it is clearly provided that, "[u]nless mutually agreed otherwise, the arbitrator's compensation shall be borne equally by the parties, in accordance with the fee structure disclosed in the arbitrator's biographical profile submitted to the parties." There is no such provision in the National Rules for the Resolution of Employment Disputes. It is therefore unclear in the instant case whether an arbitrator's fees (as distinguished from "administrative fees") are to be paid by the employee alone, the employer alone, or by the parties together. For the reasons that follow, we hold that an arbitrator's compensation and expenses must be paid by the employer alone.

3. The Obligation to Pay Arbitrators' Fees

Although we find that the disputed arbitration agreement is legally valid, there is one point that requires amplification. The arbitration agreement in this case presents an issue not raised by the agreement in *Gilmer:* can an employer condition employment on acceptance of an arbitration agreement that requires the employee to submit his or her statutory claims to arbitration and then requires the employee to pay all or part of the

Issue

8. AAA cites $700 per day as the average arbitrator's fee. Kenneth May, Labor Lawyers at ABA Session Debate Role of American Arbitration Association, Daily Lab. Rep. (BNA) No. 31, at A–12 (Feb. 15, 1996). JAMS/Endispute arbitrators charge an average of $400 per hour. See Alleyne, 13 Hofstra Lab. L.J. at 410 n.189. However, fees of $500 or $600 per hour are not uncommon. [citations] CPR Institute for Dispute Resolution estimates arbitrators' fees of $250–$350 per hour and 15–40 hours of arbitrator time in a typical employment case, for total arbitrators' fees of $3,750 to $14,000 in an "average" case. See CPR Inst. for Dispute Resolution, Employment ADR: A Dispute Resolution Program for Corporate Employers I–13 (1995).

arbitrators' fees? This was not an issue in Gilmer (and other like cases), because, under NYSE Rules and NASD Rules, it is standard practice in the securities industry for employers to pay all of the arbitrators' fees. See Daily Lab. Rep. (BNA) No. 93 at A–3 (May 14, 1996). Employees may be required to pay a filing fee, expenses, or an administrative fee, but these expenses are routinely waived in the event of financial hardship.

Thus, in *Gilmer,* the Supreme Court endorsed a system of arbitration in which employees are not required to pay for the arbitrator assigned to hear their statutory claims. There is no reason to think that the Court would have approved arbitration in the absence of this arrangement. Indeed, we are unaware of any situation in American jurisprudence in which a beneficiary of a federal statute has been required to pay for the services of the judge assigned to hear her or his case. Under *Gilmer,* arbitration is supposed to be a reasonable substitute for a judicial forum. Therefore, it would undermine Congress's intent to prevent employees who are seeking to vindicate statutory rights from gaining access to a judicial forum and then require them to pay for the services of an arbitrator when they would never be required to pay for a judge in court.

There is no doubt that parties appearing in federal court may be required to assume the cost of filing fees and other administrative expenses, so any reasonable costs of this sort that accompany arbitration are not problematic.[12] However, if an employee like Cole is required to pay arbitrators' fees ranging from $500 to $1,000 per day or more, in addition to administrative and attorney's fees, is it likely that he will be able to pursue his statutory claims? We think not. See David W. Ewing, JUSTICE ON THE JOB: RESOLVING GRIEVANCES IN THE NONUNION WORKPLACE (Harvard Business School Press 1989) at 291 (quoting corporate director of industrial relations at Northrop explaining why Northrop pays arbitrators' fees: "[W]e bear the cost of the arbitration for the very practical reason that most of the employees who seek arbitration of their grievances simply couldn't afford it if we did not"). There is no indication in AAA's rules that an arbitrator's fees may be reduced or waived in cases of financial hardship. These fees would be prohibitively expensive for an employee like Cole, especially after being fired from his job, and it is unacceptable to require Cole to pay arbitrators' fees, because such fees are unlike anything that he would have to pay to pursue his statutory claims in court.

Arbitration will occur in this case only because it has been mandated by the employer as a condition of employment. Absent this requirement, the employee would be free to pursue his claims in court without having to pay for the services of a judge. In such a circumstance—where arbitration

12. Even if an employee is not required to pay any portion of an arbitrator's fee, arbitration in a program such as the one administered by AAA is hardly inexpensive. Under the AAA plan, Cole could be required to pay a filing file of $500.00 (as compared with the $120.00 filing fee that he paid to pursue his claim in District Court), administrative fees of $150.00 per day, room rental fees, and court reporter fees (and, of course, attorneys' fees, if he employs an attorney).

has been imposed by the employer and occurs only at the option of the employer—arbitrators' fees should be borne solely by the employer.

Some commentators have suggested that it would be a perversion of the arbitration process to have the arbitrator paid by only one party to the dispute. We fail to appreciate the basis for this concern. If an arbitrator is likely to "lean" in favor of an employer—something we have no reason to suspect—it would be because the employer is a source of future arbitration business, and not because the employer alone pays the arbitrator. It is doubtful that arbitrators care about who pays them, so long as they are paid for their services.

Furthermore, there are several protections against the possibility of arbitrators systematically favoring employers because employers are the source of future business. For one thing, it is unlikely that such corruption would escape the scrutiny of plaintiffs' lawyers or appointing agencies like AAA. Corrupt arbitrators will not survive long in the business. In addition, wise employers and their representatives should see no benefit in currying the favor of corrupt arbitrators, because this will simply invite increased judicial review of arbitral judgments.

In sum, we hold that Cole could not be required to agree to arbitrate his public law claims as a condition of employment if the arbitration agreement required him to pay all or part of the arbitrator's fees and expenses. In light of this holding, we find that the arbitration agreement in this case is valid and enforceable. We do so because we interpret the agreement as requiring Burns Security to pay all of the arbitrator's fees necessary for a full and fair resolution of Cole's statutory claims . . .

So ordered.

■ KAREN LECRAFT HENDERSON, CIRCUIT JUDGE, concurring in part and dissenting in part:

By conditioning arbitration on the employer's assumption of arbitrator costs, the majority engages in pure judicial fee shifting which finds no support in the FAA, Gilmer or the parties' agreement, not one of which addresses arbitration fee allocation. Yet, relying on this very silence, the majority now declares that the employer must bear the costs, regardless of the outcome or the merits of the parties' positions, because of the majority's own speculation on what the arbitration costs will be and who will be required to pay them—factual matters never presented to the district court or even argued by the parties on appeal. The issues of costs and their allocation were first posed by the panel sua sponte during oral argument . . . I would at a minimum remand to afford [the district] court the opportunity to develop an evidentiary record and to make findings of fact regarding the likely costs and their allocation . . .

Morrison v. Circuit City Stores

317 F.3d 646 (6th Cir. 2003), en banc.

■ MOORE, J.

Lillian Pebbles Morrison submitted an application for a managerial position at a Circuit City store in Cincinnati, Ohio. As part of the application process, Morrison was required to sign a document entitled "Dispute Resolution Agreement." This document contained an arbitration clause that required resolution of all disputes or controversies arising out of employment with Circuit City in an arbitral forum....

Pursuant to Rule 13 of the Dispute Resolution Agreement, Circuit City is required to advance all costs for the arbitration, but each party is required to pay one-half of the costs of arbitration following the issuance of an arbitration award, unless the arbitrator decides to use her discretionary power to require the losing party to pay all arbitration costs. Such costs include "the daily or hourly fees and expenses (including travel) of the Arbitrator who decides the case, filing or administrative fees charged by the Arbitration Service, the cost of a reporter [to] transcribe[ ] the proceeding, and expenses of renting a room in which the arbitration is held," as well as incidental costs such as "photocopying or the costs of producing witnesses or proof." Rule 13 further provides that all arbitration costs must be paid within ninety calendar days of the issuance of the arbitration award. In addition, that rule provides that, if an employee is able to pay her share of the arbitration costs within this ninety day period, her costs (not including attorney fees) are then limited to the greater of either five hundred dollars or three percent of her most recent annual compensation. An employee who is not able to arrange to pay this amount within ninety days of the award's issuance, however, must pay her entire share of the costs. Circuit City also reserves the right to deduct up to five percent of the employee's compensation per pay period to satisfy any outstanding obligation....

Morrison began her employment at Circuit City on or about December 1, 1995. Two years later, on December 12, 1997, she was terminated. Morrison alleges that her termination was the result of race and sex discrimination. She filed this lawsuit on December 11, 1998 ...

Morrison argue[s] on appeal that the cost-splitting provisions in the arbitration agreements have the effect of denying her an effective forum for the vindication of [her] statutory rights. The Supreme Court has made clear that statutory rights, such as those created by Title VII, may be subject to mandatory arbitration only if the arbitral forum permits the effective vindication of those rights. If, then, the splitting or sharing of the costs of the arbitral forum under a particular arbitration agreement effectively prevents the vindication of a plaintiff's statutory rights, those rights cannot be subject to mandatory arbitration under that agreement. [E]mployers should not be permitted to draft arbitration agreements that deter a substantial number of potential litigants from seeking any forum for the vindication of their rights. To allow this would fatally undermine the federal anti-discrimination statutes, as it would enable employers to evade the requirements of federal law altogether.

Although the Tenth, Eleventh, and D.C. Circuits have suggested that such cost-splitting provisions *per se* deny litigants an effective forum for the vindication of their statutory rights, most courts, including this one, that have addressed this question have held that this issue must be decided on a case-by-case basis. In *Green Tree Financial Corp.–Alabama v. Randolph,* 531 U.S. 79, 121 S.Ct. 513, 148 L.Ed.2d 373 (2000), the Supreme Court adopted a case-by-case approach to determining whether a cost-splitting provision in an arbitration agreement denies potential litigants the opportunity to vindicate their statutory rights.

We believe that the following propositions of law can be derived from *Green Tree*. First, in some cases, the potential of incurring large arbitration costs and fees will deter potential litigants from seeking to vindicate their rights in the arbitral forum. Under *Gilmer,* the arbitral forum must provide litigants with an effective substitute for the judicial forum; if the fees and costs of the arbitral forum deter potential litigants, then that forum is clearly not an effective, or even adequate, substitute for the judicial forum. Second, where that prospect deters potential litigants, the arbitration agreement, or, at minimum, the cost-splitting provision contained within it, is unenforceable under *Gilmer*. Third, the burden of demonstrating that incurring such costs is likely under a given set of circumstances rests, at least initially, with the party opposing arbitration.

However, *Green Tree* does not provide us with a standard for "[h]ow detailed the showing of prohibitive expenses must be" to support the conclusion that the provision, at minimum, is unenforceable. In that case, of course, the plaintiff had relied solely on the arbitration agreement's silence on the allocation of arbitration costs, and thus the risk of incurring such prohibitive costs was highly speculative, indeed. In the case[ ] before us, however, the arbitration agreement[ ] explicitly provide[s] for cost-splitting. Thus, we must determine the appropriate standard for determining whether a cost-splitting provision contained in an arbitration agreement is invalid.

The Fourth Circuit has posited such a standard. Under *Bradford v. Rockwell Semiconductor Systems, Inc.,* 238 F.3d 549, 556 (4th Cir. 2001), the inquiry can be broken into three parts: (1) the potential litigant's ability to pay arbitration costs and fees; (2) the difference between the expected cost of arbitration to the litigant and the expected cost of a judicial forum; and (3) whether that difference "is so substantial as to deter the bringing of claims" in the arbitral forum. With respect to (1) and (2), *Bradford* emphasized that "an appropriate case-by-case inquiry must focus upon a claimant's expected or actual arbitration costs and his ability to pay those costs, measured against a baseline of the claimant's expected costs for litigation and his ability to pay those costs." *Id.* n. 5. In keeping with *Green Tree*, the party opposing arbitration—*i.e.*, the plaintiff—bears the burden of demonstrating these elements. *See Bradford,* 238 F.3d. at 557.

The *Bradford* test and similar approaches, however, suffer from at least two infirmities. First, requiring the plaintiff to come forward with concrete estimates of anticipated or expected arbitration costs asks too much at this initial stage in the proceedings. Before an arbitrator has been selected, for example, a plaintiff can only estimate the hourly rate that the arbitrator will charge. Under the *Bradford* case-by-case approach, such average figures may appear "too speculative" to support a finding that the costs are prohibitively expensive, even though the plaintiff has no other evidence of costs. Moreover, where arbitration agreements provide for the shifting of fees and costs by the arbitrator on the basis of the arbitrator's decision on the merits, potential litigants (and reviewing courts) may not be able to gauge the likelihood of success or cost-shifting, especially prior to discovery.

Second, the *Bradford* case-by-case approach is inadequate to protect the deterrent functions of the federal anti-discrimination statutes at issue. The issue is not only whether an individual claimant would be precluded from effectively vindicating his or her rights in an arbitral forum by the risk of incurring substantial costs, but also whether other similarly situated individuals would be deterred by those risks as well. A cost-splitting provision should be held unenforceable whenever it would have the "chilling effect" of deterring a substantial number of potential litigants from seeking to vindicate their statutory rights.

A number of courts have suggested that judicial review of arbitration awards will adequately safeguard the remedial and deterrent functions of federal anti-discrimination statutes. *Post hoc* judicial review of arbitration awards as a means of guaranteeing the adequacy of the arbitral forum for protecting federal statutory rights has a kind of superficial attractiveness.... Requiring plaintiffs to arbitrate their claims and then argue, either to the arbitrator or to the reviewing court, that the costs were prohibitive avoids the problem identified in *Green Tree,* namely the "speculative" or "conjectural" nature of the costs of arbitration....

This attractiveness is, however, only superficial; there are at least two problems with this approach. First, judicial review of arbitration awards is very narrow. Second, ... [a]fter the plaintiff has arbitrated her claims, reviewing courts will not likely determine that this risk deterred the plaintiff; after all, the plaintiff has already arbitrated her claims. Deterrence occurs early in the process. If we do not know who will prevail on the ultimate cost-splitting question until the end, we know who has lost from the beginning: those whom the cost-splitting provision deterred from initiating their claims at all.

In sum, the *post hoc* judicial review approach places plaintiffs in a kind of "Catch–22." They cannot claim, in advance of arbitration, that the risk of incurring arbitration costs would deter them from arbitrating their claims because they do not know what the costs will be, but if they arbitrate and actually incur costs, they cannot then argue that the costs deterred them because they have already arbitrated their claims. Just as Yossarian could not escape flying combat missions by claiming that he was crazy because anyone wanting to be released from combat must be sane, under this approach potential litigants cannot escape arbitration by claiming that the costs are prohibitive until after arbitration, at which point the costs were not prohibitive, because the litigants actually arbitrated their disputes.

For these reasons, we reject the judicial-review approach ... [W]e adopt a case-by-case approach to this issue that we believe is more protective of statutory rights than that adopted by the Fourth Circuit in *Bradford.*

We hold that potential litigants must be given an opportunity, prior to arbitration on the merits, to demonstrate that the potential costs of arbitration are great enough to deter them and similarly situated individuals from seeking to vindicate their federal statutory rights in the arbitral forum. Our approach differs from the case-by-case approach advocated in *Bradford* by looking to the possible "chilling effect" of the cost-splitting provision on similarly situated potential litigants, as opposed to its effect merely on the actual plaintiff in any given case. This difference in approach is premised on *Gilmer,* which held that "[s]o long as the prospective litigant effectively may vindicate [his or her] statutory cause of action in the arbitral forum, the statute will continue to serve both its remedial and deterrent function." 500 U.S. at 28, 111 S.Ct. 1647 (quotation omitted). As *Gilmer* makes clear, federal anti-discrimination statutes play both a remedial and deterrent role. Although the former role is largely a matter of the rights of particular aggrieved individuals, the latter is a question of "broader social purposes." *Id.* The deterrent function of the laws in question is, in part, that employers who engage in discriminatory practices are aware that they may incur liability in more than one case. If, however, a cost-splitting provision would deter a substantial number of potential litigants, then that provision undermines the deterrent effect of the anti-discrimination statutes. Thus, in order to protect the statutory rights at issue, the reviewing court must look to more than just the interests and conduct of a particular plaintiff. [I]f the reviewing court finds that the cost-splitting provision would deter a substantial number of similarly situated potential litigants, it should refuse to enforce the cost-splitting provision in order to serve the underlying functions of the federal statute. In conducting this analysis, the reviewing court should define the class of such similarly situated potential litigants by job description and socioeconomic background. It should take the actual plaintiff's income and resources as representative of this larger class's ability to shoulder the costs of arbitration....

In analyzing this issue, reviewing courts should consider the costs of litigation as the alternative to arbitration, as in *Bradford,* but they must weigh the potential costs of litigation in a realistic manner. In many, if not most, cases, employees (and former employees) bringing discrimination claims will be represented by attorneys on a contingency-fee basis. Thus, many litigants will face minimal costs in the judicial forum, as the attorney will cover most of the fees of litigation and advance the expenses incurred in discovery....

This analysis will yield different results in different cases. It will find, in many cases, that high-level managerial employees and others with substantial means can afford the costs of arbitration, thus making cost-splitting provisions in such cases enforceable. In the case of other employees, however, this standard will render cost-splitting provisions unenforceable in many, if not most, cases.

On appeal, Circuit City argues that Morrison could have avoided having to pay half of the cost of the arbitration, under the terms of Rule 13, if she could have arranged to pay the greater of $500 or three percent of her annual salary (in this case, three percent of $54,060, or $1,622) within ninety days of the arbitrator's award. Circuit City argues that, given this provision, we must reach the conclusion that Morrison did not face prohibitive costs in the present case because, at most, she would have been required to pay $1,622 for the arbitral forum.

In the abstract, this sum may not appear prohibitive, but it must be considered from the vantage point of the potential litigant in a case such as this. Recently terminated, the potential litigant must continue to pay for housing, utilities, transportation, food, and the other necessities of life in contemporary society despite losing her primary, and most likely only, source of income. Unless she is exceedingly fortunate, the potential litigant will experience at least a brief period of unemployment. Turning to the arbitration agreement with her employer, the potential litigant finds that, as the default rule, she will be obligated to pay half the costs of any arbitration which she initiates.

Minimal research will reveal that the potential costs of arbitrating the dispute easily reach thousands, if not tens of thousands, of dollars, far exceeding the costs that a plaintiff would incur in court. Courts charge plaintiffs initial filing fees, but they do not charge extra for in-person hearings, discovery requests, routine motions, or written decisions, costs that are all common in the world of private arbitrators. Based on one recent study using costs and estimates provided by three major arbitration providers themselves, a plaintiff forced to arbitrate a typical $60,000 employment discrimination claim will incur costs, depending on which company is chosen to provide the arbitration, that range from three to nearly *fifty* times the basic costs of litigating in a judicial, rather than arbitral, forum. . . . Based on these considerations, along with the evidence that Morrison presented regarding her previous salary, we conclude that the default cost-splitting rule in the Circuit City arbitration agreement would deter a substantial percentage of potential litigants from bringing their claims in the arbitral forum. . . .

Based on this reasoning, we hold that Morrison has satisfied her burden in the present case in demonstrating that the cost-splitting arrangement in the Circuit City arbitration agreement would deter a substantial number of similarly situated persons from attempting to vindicate their statutory rights in the arbitral forum, and thus that the cost-splitting provision in the agreement was unenforceable with respect to her claims.

* * *

Questions

1. Is it possible to distinguish *Cole v. Burns* from *Green Tree?* Does the fact that *Cole* was an employment case suggest that there were special considerations not present in *Green Tree?* If so, what might those factors be? Should employment cases be treated differently from other cases in regard to the allocation of the costs of arbitration?

2. In both *Green Tree* and *Cole,* the parties' arbitration agreement was silent as to allocation of the costs of arbitration. After these cases, what would you advise a client who is seeking to include an arbitration agreement in a contract to specify concerning allocation of arbitration fees? Would your advice depend upon the nature of the transaction? Would it depend upon your view of the relative economic resources of the parties?

3. Prior to *Cole*, the prevailing view of legal commentators seemed to be that sharing the cost of the arbitrator was an essential term of an enforceable employment arbitration agreement, on the theory that arbitrators might be perceived as biased if they were paid solely by employers. See, e.g., Shalu Tandon Buckley, *Practical Concerns Regarding the Arbitration of Statutory Employment Claims*, 11 Ohio State Journal on Dispute Resolution 149, 179–80 (1996); Reginald Alleyne, *Arbitrators' Fees: The Dagger in the Heart of Mandatory Arbitration for Statutory Discrimination Claims*, 6 University of Pennsylvania Journal of Labor & Employment Law 1 (2003). After *Cole* but before *Green Tree*, the judicial pendulum seemed to shift; many courts concluded that employee access to the dispute resolution forum is a more important concern, and that arbitration agreements that require employees to pay a significant part of the arbitrator's fees were unenforceable. See, e.g., Shankle v. B–G Maintenance Management of Colorado, Inc., 163 F.3d 1230 (10th Cir. 1999) (refusing to enforce arbitration agreement that required employee to pay for one-half of the arbitration fees).

Since *Green Tree*, the pendulum seems to have shifted again, with most courts evaluating fee-splitting provisions on a case-by-case basis and requiring employees to prove that they cannot afford the costs of arbitration. See, e.g., Faber v. Menard, Inc., 367 F.3d 1048, 1053–54 (8th Cir. 2004); EEOC v. Rappaport, Hertz, Cherson & Rosenthal, P.C., 448 F.Supp.2d 458, 462–63 (E.D.N.Y. 2006) (listing cases). In *Blair v. Scott Specialty Gases*, 283 F.3d 595, 608 (3d Cir. 2002), the Third Circuit held that an employee's affidavit demonstrating that she had negative income and negative assets did not relieve the district court of making a factual determination of her ability to afford the probable arbitration fees, but in Spinetti v. Service Corporation International, 324 F.3d 212 (3d Cir. 2003), the Third Circuit affirmed the district court's determination of inability to pay. Cf. Cooper v. MRM Investment Co., 199 F.Supp.2d 771 (M.D. Tenn. 2002) (finding that plaintiff could not afford arbitral fees where her income for the previous year was only $7253.74). Compare Roberson v. Clear Channel Broadcasting, Inc., 144 F.Supp.2d 1371 (S.D. Fla. 2001) (even where employee demonstrates inability to afford arbitral fees, employer may still obtain order compelling arbitration by agreeing to pay those fees) with *Cooper*, 199 F.Supp.2d 771 (employer's agreement to pay fees does not entitle employer to order compelling arbitration if the fee provision might deter other employees from pursuing their claims).

Even the D.C. Circuit seems to be backing away from the categorical approach it adopted in *Cole*. See Brown v. Wheat First Securities, Inc., 257 F.3d 821 (D.C. Cir. 2001) (holding that *Cole* does not apply to state common law retaliatory discharge claims); LaPrade v. Kidder, Peabody & Co., 246 F.3d 702 (D.C. Cir. 2001) (enforcing an award which taxed $8,376 in fees against successful plaintiff).

In light of these developments, does *Cole* survive *Green Tree*? Is there any aspect of *Cole* that is still good law?

4. Is the Sixth Circuit's determination in *Morrison* that courts should consider the effect of a fee-shifting provision on other employees consistent with *Green Tree*? Does *Green Tree* limit a court's consideration to the particular employee who has challenged the fee-shifting provision?

5. A recent empirical study comparing the cost of arbitration to litigation found that:

> First, the upfront costs of arbitration will in many cases be higher than, and at best be the same as, the upfront costs in litigation. Whether arbitration is less costly than litigation thus depends on how attorneys' fees and other costs compare, and the evidence here is inconclusive. Second, for employees and consumers with small and mid-sized claims, the availability of low-cost arbitration makes arbitration an accessible forum, and possibly a more accessible forum than litigation. But for consumers with large claims, and for employees not able to use low-cost arbitration, the evidence is less clear.

Christopher R. Drahozal, *Arbitration Costs and Forum Accessibility: Empirical Evidence*, 41 U. Mich. J.L. Reform 813 (2008). How does this empirical finding affect the reasoning in *Green Tree*? If a party could show that in a particular arbitration, the costs would be less than litigation, would that fact alone satisfy *Green Tree*'s criteria for shifting the cost to an employee?

6. Class action arbitrations can raise significant cost issues. For example, in Gonzalez v. Menard, Inc., 534 F.Supp.2d 815 (N.D. Ill. 2008), employees Irene Gonzalez and Kenneth Stanley attempted to bring a class action alleging employment discrimination on the basis of race. The predispute arbitration agreement that the employer Menard had drafted and required the employees to sign specified that claims would be arbitrated by the American Arbitration Association. AAA rules would have imposed a $3250 filing fee and a supplemental filing fee of $14,000. The court stated:

> [T]his Court sought a possible path to accommodate Menard's desire for arbitration by asking its counsel whether his client would be prepared to treat the [fee of $350 for filing an individual discrimination claim] as extending to the class claims here, with Menard committing itself to pick up the balance of the AAA tab. That inquiry was met with a flat-out refusal, with Menard's counsel offering the response that a division of those very large class action expenses among the members of a certified class would not be onerous for any individual member of the class, including Gonzalez and Stanley as class representatives. But the short answer to that "generous" response is that AAA costs are

> incurred up front, so that Menard's proposed "solution" would force Gonzalez and Stanley to gamble on being successful in obtaining class certification, a highly unfair risk to impose on persons of such modest means (and a risk that does not exist in any federal class action lawsuit where the class-based claim is non-frivolous).
>
> Thus Menard's response equates to an in terrorem effort to discourage this or any other proposed class action, an effort that runs counter to the basic principles that are implicit in Fed.R.Civ.P. 23....
>
> In sum, Menard's motion for referral to AAA arbitration must be and is denied. Gonzalez and Stanley have satisfied the test of demonstrating "prohibitively expensive" arbitration within the teaching of Green Tree. Because Employee Agreement ¶ 6's arbitration requirement is invalid and unenforceable in the circumstances of this case, the action will go forward in this District Court.

Does this case remove all class action claims from arbitration, at least under the AAA cost structure? Class action arbitrations will be discussed in more detail in Chapter 3.7.

8. An empirical study of AAA employment arbitration found that AAA employment arbitrators exercised their discretion to reallocate arbitrator's fees to the employer in 70.25% of the cases, hearing fees in 71.3% of the cases, and some or all of the filing fees in 85.12% of the cases. Even when employees lost on the merits, the arbitrator nonetheless shifted some or all of the employee's share of these fees to the employer in approximately 65% of the cases. Elizabeth Hill, *Due Process at Low Cost: An Empirical Study of Employment Arbitration Under the Auspices of the American Arbitration Association*, 18 Ohio State Journal on Dispute Resolution 777, 812 (2003). Is this finding significant for employers seeking to uphold arbitration decisions that purport to impose costs on employees?

8. EMPLOYMENT CONTRACTS

The following case addresses an aspect of *Gilmer v. Interstate/Johnson Lane Corp.,* 500 U.S. 20 (1991), *supra,* that was not addressed earlier. Recall that in the *Gilmer* case, an employee of a brokerage house sued his employer alleging a violation of the Age Discrimination in Employment Act. In finding the dispute to be amenable to arbitration, the Court refused to address the argument, raised by *amicus curiae* on appeal, that arbitration of the plaintiff's claim could not be compelled under the Federal Arbitration Act because it fell within the "contracts of employment" exclusion in Section 1 of the Act. The FAA states, in Section 1 that:

> nothing herein shall apply to contracts of employment of seamen, railroad employees, or any other class of workers engaged in foreign or interstate commerce.

9 U.S.C. 1. The *Gilmer* majority refused to consider the argument on the ground that it had not been raised at the trial court. 500 U.S. at 21 & n. 2.

Furthermore, the Supreme Court said that the arbitration agreement at issue was not between the plaintiff and his employer but rather was with a third party, the National Association of Security Dealers, so the exclusion did not apply.

After *Gilmer*, lower federal courts grappled with the question of how to interpret the "contracts of employment" exclusion contained in the FAA. By 2001, every Court of Appeals except the Ninth Circuit had decided that the Section 1 exclusion applied only to workers who were directly involved in transporting goods across state lines. See, e.g. *McWilliams v. Logicon, Inc.*, 143 F.3d 573 (10th Cir. 1998); *Asplundh Tree Expert Co. v. Bates*, 71 F.3d 592 (6th Cir. 1995); *Tenney Engineering, Inc. v. United Electrical Workers, Local 437*, 207 F.2d 450 (3d Cir. 1953). Following *Tenney,* the other circuits held that under the principle of *ejusdem generis,* the exclusion in Section 1 applied only to employees who were similar to the expressly mentioned seamen and railroad employees—*i.e.,* only those who moved goods across state lines.

The Ninth Circuit disagreed. In *Craft v. Campbell Soup,* 177 F.3d 1083 (9th Cir. 1998), the Ninth Circuit held that the FAA does not apply to any employment contracts. The Ninth Circuit reasoned on the basis of the language and history of the provision that:

> Congress' Commerce Clause power at the time of the FAA's enactment was limited to employees who actually transported people or goods in interstate commerce.
>
> Under these circumstances, when Congress drafted § 2, that section could only apply to those employees. Section 1, however, exempts those very same employees from the scope of the FAA. Thus, when Congress drafted the FAA in 1925, the Act did not apply to any labor or employment contracts. See Arce v. Cotton Club of Greenville, Inc., 883 F.Supp. 117, 123 (N.D. Miss.1995) . . .

The Supreme Court resolved the split between the circuits in *Circuit City Stores v. Adams.*

* * *

A. The Contracts of Employment Exclusion From the FAA

Circuit City Stores, Inc. v. Adams

532 U.S. 105 (2001).

■ JUSTICE KENNEDY delivered the opinion of the Court.

I

[Saint Clair Adams applied for a job at Circuit City Stores, Inc., which until its bankruptcy in early 2009 was a national retailer of consumer electronics. Adams signed an employment application containing an arbitration clause. Two years after she was hired, Adams filed an employment discrimination lawsuit against Circuit City in state court, asserting state law discrimination and tort claims. Circuit City sued in federal court under the FAA to enjoin the state-court action and to compel arbitration. The district court entered the requested order, and Adams appealed. The Ninth Circuit reversed, holding that the arbitration agreement between Adams and Circuit City was contained in a "contract of employment," and so was not subject to the FAA. Circuit City appealed, noting that the Ninth Circuit's conclusion that all employment contracts are excluded from the FAA conflicted with every other Court of Appeals to have addressed the question.]

II

A

[This case involves] the exemption from coverage under § 1. The exemption clause provides the Act shall not apply "to contracts of employment of seamen, railroad employees, or any other class of workers engaged in foreign or interstate commerce." 9 U.S.C. § 1. Most Courts of Appeals conclude the exclusion provision is limited to transportation workers, defined, for instance, as those workers "actually engaged in the movement of goods in interstate commerce." *Cole, supra,* at 1471. [T]he Court of Appeals for the Ninth Circuit takes a different view and interprets the § 1 exception to exclude all contracts of employment from the reach of the FAA . . .

B

. . . Respondent, endorsing the reasoning of the Court of Appeals for the Ninth Circuit that the provision excludes all employment contracts, relies on the asserted breadth of the words "contracts of employment of . . . any other class of workers engaged in . . . commerce." Referring to our construction of § 2's coverage provision in *Allied–Bruce*—concluding that the words "involving commerce" evidence the congressional intent to regulate to the full extent of its commerce power—respondent contends § 1's interpretation should have a like reach, thus exempting all employment contracts. The two provisions, it is argued, are coterminous; under this view the "involving commerce" provision brings within the FAA's scope all contracts within the Congress' commerce power, and the "engaged in . . . commerce" language in § 1 in turn exempts from the FAA all employment contracts falling within that authority.

This reading of § 1, however, runs into an immediate and, in our view, insurmountable textual obstacle. Unlike the "involving commerce" language in § 2, the words "any other class of workers engaged in . . . commerce" constitute a residual phrase, following, in the same sentence, explicit reference to "seamen" and "railroad employees." Construing the residual phrase to exclude all employment contracts fails to give independent effect to the statute's enumeration of the specific categories of workers which precedes it; there would be no need for Congress to use the phrases "seamen" and "railroad employees" if those same classes of workers were subsumed within the meaning of the "engaged in . . . commerce" residual clause. The wording of § 1 calls for the application of the maxim *ejusdem generis,* the statutory canon that "[w]here general words follow specific words in a statutory enumeration, the general words are construed to embrace only objects similar in nature to those objects enumerated by the preceding specific words." 2A N. Singer, Sutherland on Statutes and Statutory Construction § 47.17 (1991) . . . Under this rule of construction the residual clause should be read to give effect to the terms "seamen" and "railroad employees," and should itself be controlled and defined by reference to the enumerated categories of workers which are recited just before it; the interpretation of the clause pressed by respondent fails to produce these results.

Canons of construction need not be conclusive and are often countered, of course, by some maxim pointing in a different direction. The application of the rule *ejusdem generis* in this case, however, is in full accord with other sound considerations bearing upon the proper interpretation of the clause. For even if the term "engaged in commerce" stood alone in § 1, we would not construe the provision to exclude all contracts of employment from the FAA. Congress uses different modifiers to the word "commerce" in the design and enactment of its statutes. The phrase "affecting commerce" indicates Congress' intent to regulate to the outer limits of its authority under the Commerce Clause. See, *e.g., Allied–Bruce,* 513 U.S., at 277, 115 S.Ct. 834. The "involving commerce" phrase, the operative words for the reach of the basic coverage provision in § 2, was at issue in *Allied–Bruce.* That particular phrase had not been interpreted before by this Court. Considering the usual meaning of the word "involving," and the pro-arbitration purposes of the FAA, *Allied–Bruce* held the "word 'involving,' like 'affecting,' signals an intent to exercise Congress' commerce power to the full." *Ibid.* Unlike those phrases, however, the general words "in commerce" and the specific phrase "engaged in commerce" are understood to have a more limited reach. In *Allied–Bruce* itself the Court said the words "in commerce" are "often-found words of art" that we have not read as expressing congressional intent to regulate to the outer limits of authority under the Commerce Clause. *Id.,* at 273 . . . [Citations omitted.]

It is argued that we should assess the meaning of the phrase "engaged in commerce" in a different manner here, because the FAA was enacted when congressional authority to regulate under the commerce power was to a large extent confined by our decisions . . . When the FAA was enacted in 1925, respondent reasons, the phrase "engaged in commerce" was not a term of art indicating a limited assertion of congressional jurisdiction; to the contrary, it is said, the formulation came close to expressing the outer limits of Congress' power as then understood . . . [Citations omitted.] Were this mode of interpretation to prevail, we would take into account the scope of the Commerce Clause, as then elaborated by the Court, at the date of the FAA's enactment in order to interpret what the statute means now.

A variable standard for interpreting common, jurisdictional phrases would contradict our earlier cases and bring instability to statutory interpretation ...

In sum, the text of the FAA forecloses the construction of § 1 followed by the Court of Appeals in the case under review, a construction which would exclude all employment contracts from the FAA.... Section 1 exempts from the FAA only contracts of employment of transportation workers.

C

As the conclusion we reach today is directed by the text of § 1, we need not assess the legislative history of the exclusion provision. [citation] We do note, however, that the legislative record on the § 1 exemption is quite sparse. Respondent points to no language in either committee report addressing the meaning of the provision, nor to any mention of the § 1 exclusion during debate on the FAA on the floor of the House or Senate. Instead, respondent places greatest reliance upon testimony before a Senate subcommittee hearing suggesting that the exception may have been added in response to the objections of the president of the International Seamen's Union of America. See Hearing on S. 4213 and S. 4214 before a Subcommittee of the Senate Committee on the Judiciary, 67th Cong., 4th Sess., 9 (1923). Legislative history is problematic even when the attempt is to draw inferences from the intent of duly appointed committees of the Congress. It becomes far more so when we consult sources still more steps removed from the full Congress and speculate upon the significance of the fact that a certain interest group sponsored or opposed particular legislation. Cf. *Kelly v. Robinson,* 479 U.S. 36, 51, n. 13, 107 S.Ct. 353, 93 L.Ed.2d 216 (1986) ("[N]one of those statements was made by a Member of Congress, nor were they included in the official Senate and House Reports. We decline to accord any significance to these statements"). We ought not attribute to Congress an official purpose based on the motives of a particular group that lobbied for or against a certain proposal—even assuming the precise intent of the group can be determined, a point doubtful both as a general rule and in the instant case. It is for the Congress, not the courts, to consult political forces and then decide how best to resolve conflicts in the course of writing the objective embodiments of law we know as statutes....

For the foregoing reasons, the judgment of the Court of Appeals for the Ninth Circuit is reversed, and the case is remanded for further proceedings consistent with this opinion.

■ JUSTICE STEVENS, with whom JUSTICE GINSBURG and JUSTICE BREYER join, and with whom JUSTICE SOUTER joins as to Parts II and III, dissenting....

I

... The history of the Act, which is extensive and well-documented, makes clear that the FAA was a response to the refusal of courts to enforce commercial arbitration agreements, which were commonly used in the maritime context. The original bill was drafted by the Committee on Commerce, Trade, and Commercial Law of the American Bar Association (ABA) upon consideration of "the further extension of the principle of *commercial* arbitration." Report of the Forty-third Annual Meeting of the ABA, 45 A.B.A. Rep. 75 (1920) (emphasis added). As drafted, the bill was understood by Members of Congress to "simply provid[e] for one thing, and that is to give an opportunity to enforce an agreement in *commercial* contracts and *admiralty* contracts." 65 Cong. Rec.1931 (1924) (remarks of Rep. Graham) (emphasis added). It is no surprise, then, that when the legislation was first introduced in 1922, it did not mention employment contracts, but did contain a rather precise definition of the term "maritime transactions" that underscored the commercial character of the proposed bill. Indeed, neither the history of the drafting of the original bill by the ABA, nor the records of the deliberations in Congress during the years preceding the ultimate enactment of the Act in 1925, contains any evidence that the proponents of the legislation intended it to apply to agreements affecting employment.

Nevertheless, the original bill was opposed by representatives of organized labor, most notably the president of the International Seamen's Union of America,[13] because of their concern that the legislation might authorize federal judicial enforcement of arbitration clauses in employment contracts and collective-bargaining agreements. In response to those objections, the chairman of the ABA committee that drafted the legislation emphasized at a Senate Judiciary Subcommittee hearing that "[i]t is not intended that this shall be an act referring to labor disputes at all," but he also observed that "if your honorable committee should feel that there is any danger of that, they should add to the bill the following language, 'but nothing herein contained shall apply to seamen or any class of workers in interstate and foreign commerce.' " Hearing 9. Similarly, another supporter of the bill, then Secretary of Commerce Herbert Hoover, suggested that "[i]f objection appears to the inclusion of workers' contracts in the law's scheme, it might be well amended by stating 'but nothing herein contained shall apply to contracts of employment of seamen, railroad employees, or any other class of workers engaged in interstate or foreign commerce.' " *Id.*, at 14. The legislation was reintroduced in the next session of Congress with Secretary Hoover's exclusionary language added to § 1, and the amendment eliminated organized labor's opposition to the proposed law.[14]

13. He stated: "[T]his bill provides for reintroduction of forced or involuntary labor, if the freeman through his necessities shall be induced to sign. Will such contracts be signed? Esau agreed, because he was hungry. It was the desire to live that caused slavery to begin and continue. With the growing hunger in modern society, there will be but few that will be able to resist. The personal hunger of the *seaman,* and the hunger of the wife and children of the *railroad man* will surely tempt them to sign, and so with *sundry other workers in 'Interstate and Foreign Commerce.'* " Proceedings of the 26th Annual Convention of the International Seamen's Union of America 203–204 (1923) (emphasis added).

14. Indeed, in a post-enactment comment on the amendment, the Executive Council of the American Federation of Labor reported:

> Protests from the American Federation of Labor and the International Seamen's

That amendment is what the Court construes today. History amply supports the proposition that it was an uncontroversial provision that merely confirmed the fact that no one interested in the enactment of the FAA ever intended or expected that § 2 would apply to employment contracts....

II.

A quarter century after the FAA was passed, many Courts of Appeals were presented with the question whether collective-bargaining agreements were "contracts of employment" for purposes of § 1's exclusion. The courts split over that question ... In *Textile Workers v. Lincoln Mills of Ala.*, 353 U.S. 448, 77 S.Ct. 923, 1 L.Ed.2d 972 (1957), [this] Court ... held that § 301 [ ] provided the authority to compel arbitration. The fact that the Court relied on § 301 of the LMRA, a statutory provision that does not mention arbitration, rather than the FAA, a statute that expressly authorizes the enforcement of arbitration agreements, strongly implies that the Court had concluded that the FAA simply did not apply because § 1 exempts labor contracts.

III.

Times have changed. Judges in the 19th century disfavored private arbitration. The 1925 Act was intended to overcome that attitude, but a number of this Court's cases decided in the last several decades have pushed the pendulum far beyond a neutral attitude and endorsed a policy that strongly favors private arbitration....

It is not necessarily wrong for the Court to put its own imprint on a statute. But when its refusal to look beyond the raw statutory text enables it to disregard countervailing considerations that were expressed by Members of the enacting Congress and that remain valid today, the Court misuses its authority. As the history of the legislation indicates, the potential disparity in bargaining power between individual employees and large employers was the source of organized labor's opposition to the Act, which it feared would require courts to enforce unfair employment contracts.... When the Court simply ignores the interest of the unrepresented employee, it skews its interpretation with it own policy preferences....

I respectfully dissent.

■ JUSTICE SOUTER, with whom JUSTICE STEVENS, JUSTICE GINSBURG, and JUSTICE BREYER join, dissenting....

[T]he majority today finds great significance in the fact that the generally phrased exemption for the employment contracts of workers "engaged in commerce" does not stand alone, but occurs at the end of a

Union brought an amendment which provides that "nothing herein contained shall apply to contracts of employment of seamen, railroad employees or any other class of workers engaged in foreign or interstate commerce." This exempted labor from the provisions of the law, although its sponsors denied there was any intention to include labor disputes. Proceedings of the 45th Annual Convention of the American Federation of Labor 52 (1925).

sequence of more specific exemptions: for "contracts of employment of seamen, railroad employees, or any other class of workers engaged in foreign or interstate commerce." ... Like many interpretive canons, however, *ejusdem generis* is a fallback, and if there are good reasons not to apply it, it is put aside. There are good reasons here. As Adams argued, it is imputing something very odd to the working of the congressional brain to say that Congress took care to bar application of the Act to the class of employment contracts it most obviously had authority to legislate about in 1925, contracts of workers employed by carriers and handlers of commerce, while covering only employees "engaged" in less obvious ways, over whose coverage litigation might be anticipated with uncertain results ...

* * *

Questions

1. How convincing is the majority's argument about *ejusdem generis*? Does the principle of construction require that the contracts of employment exclusion be interpreted narrowly, or is there a competing principle of construction that might argue for a broad interpretation?

2. As Justice Souter points out in his dissent, Congress believed in 1925 that it only had the power to regulate employment relations of seamen and railroad workers, due to its limited view of the scope of the commerce power. Since then its view has changed dramatically. Today, Congress and the courts view Congressional power under the Commerce Clause as permitting Congress to regulate widely in private sector employment. See, *NLRB v. Jones & Laughlin Steel Corp.*, 301 U.S. 1 (1937). How might this change in the power of Congress to regulate private employment affect your view of congressional intent?

3. What weight does the majority give to Congressional intent? Does it treat Congressional intent as wholly irrelevant, or does it state that it is impossible to discern Congressional intent in this case? If it were unequivocally established that in 1925 Congress intended to exclude all workers from the FAA, would the Court in *Circuit City* have reached a different result? How could such intent be established?

4. Are you convinced by the Court's distinction of the phrases "involving commerce" and "engaged in ... commerce"? Is there anything "plain" about the meanings the Court attributes to these phrases? For insightful historical discussions of the FAA exclusion, see Matthew W. Finkin, "*Workers' Contracts" Under the United States Arbitration Act: An Essay in Historical Clarification*, 17 Berkeley Journal of Employment & Labor Law 282 (1996); Matthew W. Finkin, *Employment Contracts Under the FAA—Reconsidered*, 48 Labor Law Journal 329 (1997).

5. Recall that in the 1956 case of *Bernhardt v. Polygraphic Co. of Am., supra* Chapter 1.4, the Supreme Court rejected the view that the FAA contained two different definitions of interstate commerce, one for Section

2 and a different one for Section 3. Is *Circuit City* consistent with this ruling?

* * *

Note on Circuit City Case on Remand

After the Supreme Court decision in *Circuit City*, the case was remanded to the Ninth Circuit. On remand, the Ninth Circuit found that the arbitration agreement involved in the case was unconscionable and hence unenforceable. The finding of unconscionability rested on three grounds. First, the court noted that Circuit City's Dispute Resolution Agreement (DRA) obligated the employee to arbitrate all employment-related legal disputes but did not require Circuit City to arbitrate its claims against employees. "Circuit City has offered no justification for this asymmetry, nor is there any indication that 'business realities' warrant the one-sided obligation." Second, the court noted that the DRA limited the relief available so that a prevailing employee could not recover the full amount that would otherwise be recoverable under the applicable employment statute. Third, the court found that the Circuit City DRA required employees to pay half the arbitrator's fees. "This fee allocation scheme alone would render an arbitration agreement unenforceable." In addition, the court mentioned that the DRA imposed a short statute of limitation that would operate to deprive a party of the benefit of the "continuing violation" doctrine available under the fair employment law at issue. See Circuit City v. Adams, 279 F.3d 889 (9th Cir. 2002).

* * *

B. Contract Formation Issues in Employment Arbitration

The use of arbitration in the employment context poses interpretive and practical problems that go beyond the problem of interpreting the Section 1 exclusion in the FAA. The *Gilmer* case opened the door for employers to require their nonunion employees to use arbitration in a wide range of settings, and it has significantly impacted employment discrimination and unjust dismissal litigation. Often these employment arbitration systems, designed by an employer and presented to an employee as a precondition of hire, contain serious due process deficiencies that make it difficult for employees to prevail. For example, some shift the burden of proof, shorten the limitations periods, or eliminate the possibility for discovery. In addition, some impose strict limitations on remedies or require employees to pay high fees to have their cases heard. Employees have challenged nonunion arbitration systems on many grounds, including lack of consent, unconscionability, and inadequate due process.[1] The cases that follow illustrate some of the issues that have been raised.

* * *

1. See Katherine Van Wezel Stone, *Mandatory Arbitration of Individual Employment Rights: The Yellow Dog Contract of the 1990s*, 73 Denver L. Rev. 1017 (1996).

Melena v. Anheuser–Busch, Inc.[2]

847 N.E.2d 99 (Ill. 2006).

■ JUSTICE FREEMAN delivered the judgment of the court, with opinion:

This case arises from a complaint filed by plaintiff, Joann Melena, alleging that her employer, defendant Anheuser–Busch, Inc., terminated her employment in retaliation for her filing of a workers' compensation claim with the Illinois Industrial Commission. The circuit court of Jefferson County denied Anheuser–Busch's motion to dismiss and compel arbitration or, in the alternative, to stay the proceedings and compel arbitration. The appellate court affirmed the circuit court's order and remanded the matter for further proceedings. 352 Ill.App.3d 699, 287 Ill.Dec. 859, 816 N.E.2d 826. We granted leave to appeal and now reverse the judgment of the appellate court.

BACKGROUND

Plaintiff joined Anheuser–Busch as a nonunion employee at its distribution center in Mt. Vernon, Illinois, on February 22, 1999. In February 2000, Anheuser–Busch mailed to all of its Mt. Vernon employees, including plaintiff, a letter which announced the impending implementation of a "Dispute Resolution Program." Attached to the letter were materials describing the new program, including a "Dispute Resolution Program Guide," "Dispute Resolution Program Highlights," and the "Dispute Resolution Program Policy Statement."

The various materials explained the new program. For example, the policy statement set forth:

> This procedure is an agreement to arbitrate pursuant to the Federal Arbitration Act, 9 U.S.C.A. Sections 1–14, or if that Act is held to be inapplicable for any reason, the arbitration law in the state in which the arbitration hearing is held.

The concept of binding arbitration was described in the following manner:

> At the binding arbitration level, disputes that cannot be resolved through Level 1 . . . or Level 2 . . . are presented to a neutral third-party arbitrator for a final and binding decision. The arbitrator essentially substitutes for a judge and jury who might decide the case in a court setting. At the arbitration hearing, the arbitrator makes a decision after both sides have presented their positions. If the arbitrator decides in favor of the employee, the arbitrator can award the same remedies that would have been available in court for the type of claim that was brought.

2. For a detailed discussion of Anheuser–Busch's dispute resolution system, see Richard A. Bales & Jason N.W. Plowman, *Compulsory Arbitration as Part of a Broader Employment Dispute Resolution Process: The Anheuser–Busch Example*, 26 Hofstra Labor & Employment L.J. 1 (2008).

The policy statement further explained that "by continuing or accepting an offer of employment" with Anheuser–Busch, all employees to whom the policy was applicable "agree as a condition of employment to submit all covered claims to the dispute resolution program." The statement defined "covered claims" as "employment-related claims against the company and individual managers acting within the scope of their employment, regarding termination and/or alleged unlawful or illegal conduct on the part of the company ..." Moreover, the policy made clear that the new procedure did not operate "to change the employment-at-will relationship between the company and its employees."

In addition to the written materials included in the letter, Anheuser–Busch arranged for a brief presentation of the new program to be delivered to Mt. Vernon employees on February 23, 2000, which was to be followed by a question-and-answer session. Anheuser–Busch also placed posters explaining the program throughout its Mt. Vernon facility. The new program became effective on April 1, 2000.

In April 2001, Anheuser–Busch distributed "The Promotional Products Group [PPG] Distribution Center Handbook" to Mt. Vernon employees. This handbook included a description of the dispute resolution program and referenced the written program materials noted above. On April 27, 2001, plaintiff signed the following "Employee Acknowledgment and Understanding":

> I acknowledge that I have received the PPG Mt. Vernon employee handbook. I understand that the information in the handbook represents guidelines only and that the company reserves the right to modify this handbook or amend or terminate any policies, procedures, or employee benefit programs at any time, whether or not described in this handbook. I understand that I am responsible for reading the handbook, familiarizing myself with its contents and adhering to all company policies and procedures, whether set forth in this handbook or elsewhere.
>
> I further understand and acknowledge that this handbook is not a contract of employment or guarantee of employment for any specific duration, express or implied, between me and PPG Mt. Vernon.

On September 11, 2002, plaintiff suffered a work-related injury for which she filed a claim for workers' compensation with the Illinois Industrial Commission. While plaintiff was receiving temporary total disability benefits, Anheuser–Busch terminated her employment on March 14, 2003.

Plaintiff filed a complaint in the circuit court of Jefferson County on May 8, 2003. In the complaint, she alleged that Anheuser–Busch discharged her in retaliation for exercising her rights under the Illinois Workers' Compensation Act. Anheuser–Busch moved to dismiss the complaint and compel arbitration or, in the alternative, to stay the proceedings and compel arbitration. The circuit court denied the motion without comment.

On appeal, the appellate court affirmed the circuit court's order. The appellate court held that, in order to be enforceable, an agreement to arbitrate claims like the one at issue must be entered into knowingly and voluntarily. After considering the facts of this case, the appellate court concluded that a remand was not necessary because "even if the plaintiff entered into the agreement knowingly, she did not do so voluntarily." 352 Ill.App.3d at 707, 287 Ill.Dec. 859, 816 N.E.2d 826. Noting that it had "serious reservations" about whether an agreement to arbitrate, offered as a condition of employment, "is ever voluntary," the court deemed "illusory" whatever choice plaintiff was said to have had in this matter. 352 Ill.App.3d at 707–08, 287 Ill.Dec. 859, 816 N.E.2d 826. The court remanded the cause to the circuit court for further proceedings on the underlying cause for retaliatory discharge.

ANALYSIS

The issue presented in this case is whether the mandatory arbitration provisions of the "Dispute Resolution Program" instituted by Anheuser–Busch constitute an enforceable contract binding on plaintiff. Anheuser–Busch assigns error to the appellate court's holding that the arbitration agreement, to be enforceable, must be entered into knowingly and voluntarily. Rather, Anheuser–Busch contends that, like any other contract, an arbitration agreement is enforceable, based on fundamental principles of contract law. Plaintiff, urging affirmance of the appellate court, contends that the arbitration agreement was not enforceable because she did not enter into the contract knowingly and voluntarily. . . .

Section 2 of the FAA compels judicial enforcement of arbitration agreements "in any . . . contract evidencing a transaction involving commerce." 9 U.S.C. § 2 (1994). The United States Supreme Court has held that employment contracts are subject to the terms of the FAA except for those employment contracts which deal with transportation workers. *Circuit City Stores, Inc. v. Adams,* 532 U.S. 105, 121 S.Ct. 1302, 149 L.Ed.2d 234 (2001). Section 2 further provides that such a written provision

> shall be valid, irrevocable, and enforceable, *save upon such grounds as exist at law or in equity for the revocation of any contract.* (Emphasis added.) 9 U.S.C. § 2 (1994).

. . . The parties disagree over whether the *choice* of litigating a claim for retaliatory discharge, based on statutory rights under the Illinois Workers' Compensation Act (820 ILCS 305/1 *et seq.* (West 2000)), in state court is an important right which may only be relinquished through a knowing and voluntary waiver. In this context, the parties, as well as the appellate court, have likened the claim at issue here, *i.e.,* retaliatory discharge based on statutory rights under the Workers' Compensation Act, to federal statutory claims such as those advanced under Title VII of the Civil Rights Act. In *Alexander v. Gardner–Denver Co.,* 415 U.S. 36, 94 S.Ct. 1011, 39 L.Ed.2d 147 (1974), the United States Supreme Court indicated that an employee could not *forfeit* substantive rights under Title VII without a voluntary and knowing waiver. In other words, before an employee gives up a substantive right predicated upon federal statutory law, it must be clear that the employee understands and freely makes the decision to do so. See *Pierce v. Atchison, Topeka & Santa Fe Ry. Co.,* 65 F.3d 562, 571 (7th Cir. 1995). However, as the Seventh Circuit Court of Appeals has noted, "[l]ess clear is whether the right to have one's federal claims determined judicially rather than in an arbitration proceeding qualifies to this added protection." *Gibson v. Neighborhood Health Clinics,* 121 F.3d 1126, 1129 (7th Cir. 1997).

The United States Supreme Court has not directly addressed this issue. Rather, since the decision in *Alexander,* the Court's views on arbitration have evolved and become more favorable. For example, the Court has repeatedly "rejected generalized attacks on arbitration that rest on 'suspicion of arbitration as a method of weakening the protections afforded in the substantive law.' " *Green Tree Financial Corp.–Ala. v. Randolph,* 531 U.S. 79, 89–90, 121 S.Ct. 513, 521, 148 L.Ed.2d 373, 383 (2000), quoting *Rodriguez de Quijas v. Shearson/American Express, Inc.,* 490 U.S. 477, 481, 109 S.Ct. 1917, 1920, 104 L.Ed.2d 526, 535–36 (1989). The Court has emphasized that "federal statutory claims may be the subject of arbitration agreements ... enforceable pursuant to the FAA because the agreement only determines the choice of forum." *Equal Employment Opportunity Comm'n v. Waffle House, Inc.,* 534 U.S. 279, 295 n. 10, 122 S.Ct. 754, 765 n. 10, 151 L.Ed.2d 755, 770 n. 10 (2002). According to the Court, "[b]y agreeing to arbitrate a statutory claim, a party does not forgo the substantive rights afforded by the statute; it only submits their resolution in an arbitral, rather than a judicial, forum." *Mitsubishi Motors Corp. v. Soler Chrysler–Plymouth, Inc.,* 473 U.S. 614, 628, 105 S.Ct. 3346, 3354, 87 L.Ed.2d 444, 456 (1985).

The Supreme Court has held, however, that statutory rights may be subject to mandatory arbitration only if the arbitral forum permits the effective vindication of those rights:

> It is by now clear that statutory claims may be the subject of an arbitration agreement, enforceable pursuant to the FAA. Indeed, in recent years we have held enforceable arbitration agreements relating to claims arising under the Sherman Act [citation], § 10(b) of the Securities Exchange Act of 1934 [citation], the civil provisions of the Racketeer Influenced and Corrupt Organizations Act (RICO) [citation], and § 12(2) of the Securities Act of 1933 [citation]. See *Mitsubishi Motors Corp. v. Soler Chrysler–Plymouth, Inc.,* 473 U.S. 614 [105 S.Ct. 3346, 87 L.Ed.2d 444] (1985); *Shearson/American Express Inc. v. McMahon,* 482 U.S. 220 [107 S.Ct. 2332, 96 L.Ed.2d 185] (1987); *Rodriguez de Quijas v. Shearson/American Express, Inc.,* 490 U.S. 477 [109 S.Ct. 1917, 104 L.Ed.2d 526] (1989). In these cases we recognized that "[b]y agreeing to arbitrate a statutory claim, a party does not forgo the substantive rights afforded by the statute; it only submits to their resolution in an arbitral, rather than a judicial, forum." *Gilmer,* 500 U.S. at 26, 111 S.Ct. at 1652, 114 L.Ed.2d at 37, quoting *Mitsubishi,* 473 U.S. at 628, 105 S.Ct. at 3354, 87 L.Ed.2d at 456....

Although the Supreme Court has not spoken on the need for a knowing and voluntary standard in this context, several federal circuit courts of appeal have weighed in on the matter. As noted by the appellate court in this case, a split exists amongst the various circuits regarding the knowing and voluntary standard. 352 Ill.App.3d at 705, 287 Ill.Dec. 859, 816 N.E.2d 826. The appellate court found persuasive the reasoning espoused by the Ninth Circuit Court of Appeals in *Prudential Insurance Co. of America v. Lai,* 42 F.3d 1299 (9th Cir. 1994). There, the Ninth Circuit reversed a district court order compelling arbitration on a sexual discrimination claim because the employees had not knowingly entered into the agreement to arbitrate employment disputes. The employees, when applying for the positions of sales representatives with the employer, were required to sign forms containing agreements to arbitrate any dispute, claim or controversy required to be arbitrated under the rules of any organization with which the employees registered. They subsequently registered with the National Association of Securities Dealers, which required that disputes arising in connection with the business of its members be arbitrated. The employees contended that when they signed the forms, arbitration was never mentioned and they were never given a copy of the NASD Manual, which contained the actual terms of the arbitration agreement. *Lai,* 42 F.3d at 1301.

In considering the enforceability of the arbitration agreement, the court of appeals framed the issue thusly: "The issue before us, however, is not whether employees may ever agree to arbitrate statutory employment claims; they can. The issue here is whether these particular employees entered into such a binding arbitration agreement, thereby waiving statutory court remedies otherwise available." *Lai,* 42 F.3d at 1303. The court recognized that certain causes of action are entitled to a heightened level of protection pursuant to various federal statutes, such as the Age Discrimination Employment Act, the Civil Rights Act or the Americans with Disabilities Act. It noted that, " 'Legislative enactments in this area have long evinced a general intent to accord parallel or overlapping remedies against discrimination. In the Civil Rights Act of 1964, Congress indicated that they considered the policy against discrimination to be of the "highest priority." ... Moreover, the legislative history of Title VII manifests a congressional intent to allow an individual to pursue independently his rights under both Title VII and other applicable state and federal statutes.' " *Lai,* 42 F.3d at 1304, quoting *Alexander v. Gardner–Denver Co.,* 415 U.S. 36, 47–48, 94 S.Ct. 1011, 1019, 39 L.Ed.2d 147, 158 (1974). The court held that the employees were not bound by any valid agreement to arbitrate the disputes because they did not *knowingly* enter into a contract to forgo their statutory remedies in favor of arbitration.

The court further cited specific provisions of legislative history to support its adoption of the "knowing and voluntary" standard. H.R.Rep. No. 102–40(I), at 97 (1991), *reprinted in* 1991 U.S.C.C.A.N. 549, 635. Speaking of proposed section 118, Senator Dole explicitly declared that the arbitration provision encourages arbitration only "where the parties knowingly and voluntarily elect to use these methods." 137 Cong. Rec. S15472, S15478 (daily ed. October 30, 1991) (statement of Senator Dole). The knowing and voluntary standard enunciated in *Lai* has been adopted by other courts, as well. See, *e.g., Rosenberg v. Merrill Lynch, Pierce, Fenner & Smith, Inc.,* 170 F.3d 1 (1st Cir. 1999).

As the appellate court noted, however, the Ninth Circuit's approach to this issue has not "garnered universal support." 352 Ill.App.3d at 705, 287 Ill.Dec. 859, 816 N.E.2d 826. A countervailing point of view to the knowing and voluntary standard is one which holds that the determination of the enforceability of a mandatory arbitration agreement between employer and employee turns upon fundamental principles of contract law. Under this approach,

> The nondrafting party ... consents to arbitration by signing the form or by manifesting assent in another way, such as by performance of the contract. That the consumer did not read or understand the arbitration clause does not prevent the consumer from consenting to it. Nor does the consumer's ignorance that an arbitration clause is included on the form. These are statements of ordinary, plain-vanilla contract law. S. Ware, *Arbitration Clauses, Jury–Waiver Clauses, and other Contractual Waivers of Constitutional Rights,* 67 Law & Contemp. Probs. 167, 171 (Winter/Spring 2004).

Several federal circuit courts of appeal have endorsed this approach, as exemplified by the decision of the United States Court of Appeals for the Third Circuit in *Seus v. John Nuveen & Co.,* 146 F.3d 175 (3d Cir. 1998).

In *Seus,* the court of appeals affirmed the district court's order granting the employer's motion to compel arbitration in a suit by an employee alleging multiple claims of discrimination under Title VII of the Civil Rights Act of 1964 and the Age in Discrimination in Employment Act of 1967. The employee joined Nuveen brokerage firm in 1982. Nuveen is required to register all employees who deal in securities with the National Association of Securities Dealers. In order to comply with this requirement, employees must sign a U–4 form in which the employee agrees to arbitrate any dispute which is required "to be arbitrated under the Rules." Although the employee in *Seus* executed this form, she contended that Congress, "in legislation subsequent to the FAA, has carved out an exception to its provisions for pre-dispute agreements to arbitrate claims under the ADEA." *Seus,* 146 F.3d at 179. The court, rejected this argument by citing *Gilmer v. Interstate/Johnson Lane Corp.,* 500 U.S. 20, 111 S.Ct. 1647, 114 L.Ed.2d 26 (1991), stating:

> The Supreme Court began its analysis by making it clear that exceptions to the FAA's rule requiring enforcement of agreements to arbitrate are not to be recognized lightly. Because of the strong federal policy favoring arbitration, any exception must be founded on clear indicia of congressional intent. *Seus,* 146 F.3d at 179.

Rejecting the "knowing and voluntary" standard, the court went on to hold:

> By "knowing" and "voluntary", Seus means more than with an understanding that a binding agreement is being entered and without fraud or duress. Determining whether an agreement to arbitrate is

> "knowing" and "voluntary", in her view, requires an inquiry into such matters as the specificity of the language of the agreement, the plaintiff's education and experience, plaintiff's opportunity for deliberation and negotiation, and whether plaintiff was encouraged to consult counsel. She does not contend that this heightened "knowing" and "voluntary" standard is a generally applicable principle of contract law.... Nothing short of a showing of fraud, duress, mistake or some other ground recognized by the law applicable to contracts generally would have excused the district court from enforcing Seus's agreement. *Seus,* 146 F.3d at 183–84.

Similarly, the Eleventh, Fifth, Eighth and District of Columbia Circuit Courts of Appeal have rejected the knowing and voluntary standard. [Citations omitted.]

After careful consideration, we agree with those federal circuit courts of appeal which base their analysis upon principles of fundamental contract law because we believe that approach is more faithful to the FAA. The Seventh Circuit Court of Appeals has recently questioned the "continued validity" of the Ninth Circuit's knowing and voluntary waiver standard in the wake of recent United States Supreme Court decisions, noting "it is clear that arbitration agreements in the employment context, like arbitration agreements in other contexts, are to be evaluated according to the same standards as any other contract." *Penn v. Ryan's Family Steak Houses, Inc.,* 269 F.3d 753, 758 (7th Cir.2001). The Seventh Circuit also has recognized that

> [w]hile the Supreme Court has stressed in recent years that federal policy under the FAA favors the enforcement of valid arbitration agreements [citations], the Court has been equally adamant that a party can be forced into arbitration only if she has in fact entered into a valid, enforceable contract waiving her right to a judicial forum. *AT & T Technologies, Inc. v. Communications Workers of America,* 475 U.S. 643, 106 S.Ct. 1415, 89 L.Ed.2d 648 (1986) ("[A]rbitration is a matter of contract and a party cannot be required to submit to arbitration any dispute which he has not agreed so to submit.") Whether the parties have agreed to arbitrate is determined under ordinary state law contract principles. *Penn,* 269 F.3d at 758–59.

In our view, the FAA's plain language makes clear that arbitration agreements are enforceable except for state-law grounds for ordinary contract revocation. 9 U.S.C. § 2 (1994).... Similarly, the failure to apply general contract doctrines to arbitration agreements which require waiver of fundamental, statutory rights would raise arbitration agreements to an elevated status not contemplated by the FAA or Congress. "As the 'saving clause' in § 2 indicates, the purpose of Congress in 1925 was to make arbitration agreements as enforceable as other contracts, but not more so." *Prima Paint Corp. v. Flood & Conklin Mfg. Co.,* 388 U.S. 395, 404 n. 12, 87 S.Ct. 1801, 1806 n. 12, 18 L.Ed.2d 1270, 1277 n. 12 (1967). We agree with the Eleventh Circuit Court of Appeals in that, by "knowing" and "voluntary," plaintiff means "much more than a general understanding that a binding agreement or contract is being entered into." *Caley,* 428 F.3d at 1370 n. 12. Such an approach is contrary to the usual maxim of contract law that a party to an agreement is charged with knowledge of and assent to the agreement signed. *Black v. Wabash, St. Louis & Pacific Ry. Co.,* 111 Ill. 351, 358, 1884 WL 9967 (1884); *Hintz v. Lazarus,* 58 Ill.App.3d 64, 66, 15 Ill.Dec. 546, 373 N.E.2d 1018 (1978). For these reasons, we view the heightened "knowing and voluntary" standard as being inconsistent with the FAA.

Notwithstanding the above, plaintiff, citing *People v. Braggs,* 209 Ill.2d 492, 284 Ill.Dec. 682, 810 N.E.2d 472 (2003), argues that before a constitutional right may be waived, it must be clear the waiver was entered into voluntarily and knowingly. In light of this, she argues, the arbitration agreement is ineffective to waive her seventh amendment and statutory trial rights, such as the right to access to the courts and the right to a jury trial. Similar arguments have been rejected by several federal circuit courts of appeal. In discussing this same issue, the Eleventh Circuit recently stated:

> [A]s the Fifth Circuit has noted, "[t]he *Seventh Amendment* does not confer the right to a trial, but only the right to have a jury hear the case *once it is determined that the litigation should proceed before a court.* If the claims are properly before an arbitral forum pursuant to an arbitration agreement, the jury trial right vanishes." *American Heritage Life Ins. Co. v. Orr,* 294 F.3d 702, 711 (5th Cir. 2002) (emphasis added); *see also Sydnor v. Conseco Fin. Serv. Corp.,* 252 F.3d 302, 307 (4th Cir. 2001) ("[t]he right to a jury trial attaches in the context of judicial proceedings *after it is determined that litigation should proceed before a court.* Thus, the loss of the right to a jury trial is a necessary and fairly obvious consequence of an agreement to arbitrate." (quotation marks and citation omitted) (emphasis added))
>
> . . .

We find this reasoning persuasive and so hold.

Having concluded that the regular principles of contract law apply in this case, we must now apply our state contract law in analyzing the contract question. In other words, we must now decide whether the parties' agreement to arbitrate amounted to an enforceable contract under Illinois law. We hold that it did.

In Illinois, an offer, an acceptance and consideration are the basic ingredients of a contract. *Steinberg v. Chicago Medical School,* 69 Ill.2d 320, 329, 13 Ill.Dec. 699, 371 N.E.2d 634 (1977). We believe that Anheuser–Busch's introduction of the Dispute Resolution Program, its mailing of materials related to the program to its employees, constitutes Anheuser–Busch's "offer." By continuing her employment with Anheuser–Busch, plaintiff both accepted the offer and provided the necessary consideration. See *Duldulao v. Saint Mary of Nazareth Hospital Center,* 115 Ill.2d 482, 490, 106 Ill.Dec. 8, 505 N.E.2d 314 (1987). As Anheuser–Busch correctly notes, under Illinois law, continued employment is sufficient consideration for the enforcement of employment agreements.... [Citations omitted.]

Plaintiff continued working for Anheuser–Busch for three years after the initial implementation of the Dispute Resolution Program in 2000 and for just shy of two years after signing the acknowledgment form in 2001. Under these facts, the agreement to arbitrate covered claims arising from the employment relationship is enforceable.

In so holding, we necessarily reject the appellate court's implication that plaintiff's acceptance of the dispute resolution provisions in this case was illusory by virtue of the fact that Anheuser–Busch gave her little choice in the matter. 352 Ill.App.3d at 707–08, 287 Ill.Dec. 859, 816 N.E.2d 826. In other words, because the agreement was offered on a "take it or leave it" basis, the contract is unenforceable. The appellate court's implication here contravenes federal, as well as Illinois, decisional law. The United States Supreme Court in *Gilmer* stated that inequality in bargaining power "is not a sufficient reason to hold that arbitration agreements are never enforceable in the employment context." *Gilmer,* 500 U.S. at 33, 111 S.Ct. at 1655, 114 L.Ed.2d at 41. . . .

CONCLUSION

For the foregoing reasons, we find that the "Dispute Resolution Program" is an enforceable agreement between plaintiff and Anheuser–Busch. As such, we find that the circuit court erred in denying defendant's motion to dismiss and compel arbitration. We reverse the judgment of the appellate court and the order of the circuit court and remand the cause to the circuit court for further proceedings consonant with this opinion.

Judgments reversed; cause remanded.

■ JUSTICE KILBRIDE, dissenting:

I respectfully dissent from the majority's opinion in this matter [because, among other things,] employer-mandated arbitration provisions are effectively contracts of adhesion and raise serious issues concerning employees' actual knowledge and voluntariness when being bound by them. . . .

IV

I am troubled by an employer's unilateral imposition of a mandatory binding arbitration provision requiring employees to forfeit their constitutional rights to judicial process far in advance of any actual dispute. This places employees such as the plaintiff here in the fundamentally unfair position of being required to seek remedies exclusively in a forum mandated by employment agreements that can no longer logically bind them because they are no longer "covered employees." Furthermore, while there may be certain types of disputes that a given employee may be willing to submit to arbitration, there are undoubtedly other types that the same employee would choose to seek vindication of the employee's rights in a traditional judicial forum. By being economically coerced into signing a take-it-or-leave-it employer-mandated arbitration agreement just to maintain employment, the employee is often unwittingly stripped of the future ability to treat issues on a case-by-case basis. Moreover, as noted earlier in this dissent, nearly all employees lack sufficient knowledge of the differences in the procedural protections afforded to them in the two forums to make truly informed and voluntary decisions to enter into mandatory binding arbitration provisions. Common sense and experience dictate that, without that knowledge, employees accept the provisions solely in order to keep their current jobs.

Indeed, the true voluntariness of such an anticipatory employment agreement has been the subject of much criticism. See, *e.g.*, D. Schwartz, *Enforcing Small Print to Protect Big Business: Employee and Consumer Rights Claims in an Age of Compelled Arbitration,* 1997 Wis. L.Rev. 33, 76, 114–19 (1997) (noting that the drafters and proponents of the Federal Arbitration Act did not intend it to apply to contracts of adhesion such as employment contracts, that there is often a disparity of bargaining power and information between employers and employees pertaining to these agreements, and reviewing the critical differences between the use of settlements and prospective waivers such as predispute arbitration agreements); M. Eisenberg, *The Limits of Cognition and the Limits of Contract,* 47 Stan. L.Rev. 211, 251–52 (1995) (concluding that employees may be exploited by arbitration provisions due to their "limited cognition" of the long-term impact of their agreement to mandatory binding arbitration over disputes that have not yet even arisen); Comment, C. Reilly, *Achieving Knowing and Voluntary Consent in Pre–Dispute Mandatory Arbitration Agreements at the Contracting Stage of Employment,* 90 Cal. L. Rev. 1203, 1225–26, 1234–35 (2002) (citing empirical studies showing that the majority of employees of all types are ignorant of their legal employment rights, the available legal processes, the procedural and remedial implications of agreeing to arbitration of future disputes, their substantive protections as employees, and that the economic pressures at work in these contracts of adhesion make truly knowing and voluntary consent unlikely).

I find these matters particularly troublesome in the context of the plaintiff's claims in this case. The plaintiff alleged she was discharged from her employment in retaliation for the exercise of her statutory rights under the Illinois workers' compensation statute. Without a doubt, retaliatory discharge is contrary to the public policy of this state. *Gonzalez v. Prestress Engineering Corp.,* 115 Ill.2d 1, 9, 104 Ill.Dec. 751, 503 N.E.2d 308 (1986); *Kelsay v. Motorola, Inc.,* 74 Ill.2d 172, 187, 23 Ill.Dec. 559, 384 N.E.2d 353 (1978).

This court has long recognized the vital importance of the public policy protecting employees who assert their rights under the Workers' Compensation Act. *Gonzalez,* 115 Ill.2d at 9, 104 Ill.Dec. 751, 503 N.E.2d 308. In addition, the legislature's intent to protect employees' rights through third-party oversight is apparent from its statutory requirement of state approval prior to the settlement of certain types of workers' compensation claims. 820 ILCS 305/10.1 (West 2002). Here, the DRP deprives employees of the Act's third-party oversight protections by barring any state oversight. A refusal to recognize the serious question involving the voluntariness and the actual knowledge of employees about the ramifications of signing predispute arbitration clauses seriously undermines these intentions.

V

In sum, the majority's analysis ... ignores the real-world factors militating against an employee's truly voluntary and knowing agreement to a mandatory binding arbitration provision imposed by an employer in a contract of adhesion. When viewed in light of this court's previous concerted efforts to uphold the strong public policy protecting employees who file Workers' Compensation Act claims, this analysis is particularly disconcerting. For these reasons, I respectfully dissent.

* * *

Questions

1. What might satisfy the *Lai* court's requirement that an arbitration agreement be entered into knowingly and voluntarily? Is the "knowing" requirement the same as the "voluntary" requirement, or could we imagine cases in which an agreement was entered into knowingly but not voluntarily, or vice versa? On the problematic nature of consent in the employment setting, see Stephen J. Ware, *Employment Arbitration and Voluntary Consent*, 25 Hofstra L. Rev. 83 (1996); Jeffrey W. Stempel, *Reconsidering the Employment Contract Exclusion in Section 1 of the Federal Arbitration Act*, 1991 J. Dispute Resolution 259 (1991); Jean Sternlight, *Rethinking the Constitutionality of the Supreme Court's Preference for Binding Arbitration*, 72 Tulane L. Rev. 1 (1997).

2. Do you agree with the majority's analysis of the jury-trial-waiver issue? Is it circular? Do you think it is true that from the perspective of most employees and consumers, "the loss of the right to a jury trial is a necessary and fairly obvious consequence of an agreement to arbitrate"? For a thorough discussion of jury-trial waivers, see the point-counterpoint arguments of Jean Sternlight and Steve Ware: Jean R. Sternlight, *The Rise and Spread of Mandatory Arbitration as a Substitute for the Jury Trial*, 38 U.S.F. L. Rev. 17 (2003); Jean R. Sternlight, *Mandatory Binding Arbitration and the Demise of the Seventh Amendment Right to a Jury Trial*, 16 Ohio St. J. Disp. Resol. 669 (2001); Stephen J. Ware, *Contractual Arbitration, Mandatory Arbitration, and State Constitutional Jury–Trial Rights*, 38 U.S.F. L. Rev. 39 (2003); Stephen J. Ware, *Arbitration Clauses, Jury–Waiver Clauses and Other Contractual Waivers of Constitutional Rights*, 67 Law & Contemp. Probs. 167 (2004).

3. Katherine Stone has argued that there should be heightened judicial scrutiny of arbitral awards in cases in which employers coerce employees into signing a take-it-or-leave-it employer-mandated arbitration agreements, see Katherine Van Wezel Stone, *Rustic Justice: Community and Coercion Under the Federal Arbitration Act*, 77 N.C. L. Rev. 931 (1999); Katherine Van Wezel Stone, *Mandatory Arbitration of Individual Employ-*

ment Rights: The Yellow Dog Contract of the 1990s, 73 Denv. U. L. Rev. 1017 (1996). Do you agree?

* * *

Seawright v. American Gen. Fin. Inc.

507 F.3d 967 (6th Cir. 2007).

■ BOGGS, CHIEF JUDGE.

Lisa Seawright worked for American General Financial Services ("AGF") from November 1978 until April 2005. AGF terminated Seawright's employment in April 2005. In response, Seawright filed suit in the United States District Court for the Western District of Tennessee, alleging that AGF discharged her in violation of Tennessee antidiscrimination law and the Family and Medical Leave Act, 29 U.S.C. § 2601 *et seq.* AGF moved to compel arbitration, proffering an arbitration agreement to which Seawright had previously agreed. Seawright denies that she agreed to arbitrate. At issue is whether an agreement exists between AGF and Seawright, and if so, whether the agreement is enforceable. The district court found that no enforceable agreement existed. We hold that Seawright's knowing continuation of employment after the effective date of the arbitration program constituted acceptance of a valid and enforceable contract to arbitrate. We therefore reverse the district court's denial of AGF's motion to compel arbitration.

I

In April 1999, AGF began notifying its employees that it would be implementing an Employee Dispute Resolution ("EDR") Program. It introduced the EDR Program through a series of announcements and informational meetings. The company first informed employees about the EDR Program on April 6, 1999 in a "Home Office Bulletin," a publication circulated to all company offices, including the office where Seawright was a branch manager. Around the same time, AGF also mailed letters to its employees informing them that the EDR Program would become effective June 1, 1999. Included with the letter was an informational brochure, which stated:

> The AGF Employee Dispute Resolution Program is the sole means of resolving employment-related disputes between you and the company or you and another employee, including disputes for legally protected rights such as freedom from discrimination, retaliation, or harassment, unless otherwise prohibited by law. . . .
>
> Seeking, accepting, or continuing employment with AGF means that you agree to resolve employment related claims against the company or another employee through this process instead of through the court system. . . .

AGF then held group informational meetings explaining the program. A pamphlet distributed to the employees during the informational meeting repeated the information above. Seawright signed an attendance sheet acknowledging that she had attended an informational session and received a copy of the AGF Employment Dispute Resolution Pamphlet. The EDR Program went into effect on June 1, 1999. Seawright remained an AGF employee.

Two years after the program went into effect, in June 2001, AGF mailed its employees a letter that reminded them that the EDR Program was still in effect and explained how to locate additional information on the program on the company's intranet website. The letter also included a brochure summarizing the EDR Program. The brochure was similar to the other two brochures that had been distributed by mail and at the informational meetings. It also included the same three paragraphs regarding the binding nature of the arbitration agreement and reiterating that, "[s]eeking, accepting, or continuing employment with AGF means that you agree to resolve employment related claims against the company or another employee through this process instead of through the court system."

Seawright continued her employment with AGF until AGF terminated her on April 26, 2005. She filed suit against AGF shortly thereafter and AGF responded with a motion to compel arbitration. In Seawright's answer to the motion to compel arbitration, she acknowledged the above facts but argued that (1) she did not assent to the EDR Program and that there was no bargained-for exchange; (2) she did not enter into a written agreement as required by the Federal Arbitration Act, ("FAA"), 9 U.S.C. § 1 *et seq.*; and (3) in the alternative, the arbitration agreement is void because it is a contract of adhesion or unconscionable. The district court agreed with Seawright's first argument, holding that "merely receiving information and acknowledging the EDR program is not tantamount to assent. There was no bargained for exchange, and [Seawright] had no ability to affect the terms of the company's policy." *Seawright v. Amer. Gen. Fin. Serv.*, No. 06–2339 DV, 4 (W.D. Tenn. Dec 22, 2006) (order denying motion to compel arbitration and stay proceedings). It thus denied the order to compel arbitration on the basis that there was no valid and enforceable agreement. *Ibid.* AGF now appeals. . . .

III

. . . Because arbitration agreements are fundamentally contracts, we review the enforceability of an arbitration agreement according to the applicable state law of contract formation. *First Options of Chicago, Inc. v. Kaplan,* 514 U.S. 938, 943–44, 115 S.Ct. 1920, 131 L.Ed.2d 985 (1995). Any arguments based on the applicability of the FAA to the agreement at issue are, of course, evaluated in accordance with federal case law. Seawright makes four arguments based on state contract law and a fifth argument based on the FAA. Seawright's state contract law arguments are: (1) there was no valid arbitration agreement because she did not actually assent to the EDR Program; (2) there was no valid arbitration agreement because there was no consideration; (3) even if there had been assent and consideration, the arbitration agreement is unenforceable because it is illusory; and (4) alternatively, the arbitration agreement is unenforceable because it is an unconscionable contract of adhesion. Seawright's argument under the FAA is that she did not enter into a *written* agreement as required by the Federal Arbitration Act. We begin by addressing Seawright's arguments based on state contract law.

A. Assent

The issue at hand is whether Seawright's continued employment with AGF constituted assent. "Tennessee law recognizes the validity of unilateral contracts, in which acceptance is indicated by action under the contract." *Fisher v. GE Med. Sys.,* 276 F.Supp.2d 891, 895 (M.D.Tenn. 2003). The written materials accompanying the arbitration agreement clearly stated that continued employment after the effective date of the EDR Program would constitute the employee's acceptance of the agreement to arbitrate. Thus, under Tennessee law, Seawright expressed a valid assent when she continued to work for AGF.

The district court acknowledged that "[g]enerally, continued employment constitutes acceptance of an employer's arbitration policy." *Seawright,* No. 06–2339 DV at 3. Nevertheless, . . . the district court concluded that "merely receiving information and acknowledging the EDR program is not tantamount to assent." This misstates the issue. The question is not whether the mere receipt of an offer constitutes acceptance but whether an action—continuing one's employment—can constitute acceptance. Under Tennessee law, continued employment can constitute acceptance. *Fisher,* 276 F.Supp.2d at 895 ("By continuing to work at GE, the plaintiffs accepted the terms of [the arbitration agreement], a binding contract.") . . .

Noticeably absent from Seawright's brief is a discussion of the "knowing and voluntary waiver" requirement established by this circuit in *Morrison v. Circuit City Stores, Inc.,* 317 F.3d 646 (6th Cir. 2003) (en banc). In *Morrison,* the court applied "ordinary contract principles in determining whether" a binding arbitration agreement that included a waiver of a right to sue in court was valid. *Id.* at 668 (citing *Adams v. Philip Morris, Inc.,* 67 F.3d 580, 583 (6th Cir.1995)). In determining whether an employee "knowingly and voluntarily" waived the right, the court considers: "(1) plaintiff's experience, background, and education; (2) the amount of time the plaintiff had to consider whether to sign the waiver, including whether the employee had an opportunity to consult with a lawyer; (3) the clarity of the waiver; (4) consideration for the waiver; as well as (5) the totality of the circumstances." *Id.* at 668. In *Morrison,* the court found that the plaintiff knowingly and voluntarily waived her right to sue based on the fact that she was "a highly educated managerial employee who was capable of understanding the terms of the agreement" and that the "waiver of the right to file suit in federal court was plain." Seawright is similarly situated: She is an educated, managerial employee, who was capable of understanding the EDR Program's provisions. Also, like Morrison, Seawright had ample time (in Seawright's case, two months) between AGF's announcement of the EDR Program and the Program's commencement during which she could have consulted with an attorney or decided she did not wish to waive her rights. Finally, the EDR Program clearly stated that employees, by agreeing to the EDR Program, would be waiving their rights to sue in federal court.

Though Morrison signaled her assent to the arbitration agreement through a signature and Seawright signaled her assent through action, nowhere in *Morrison* does the court hold that the waiver must be express and in writing. Indeed, such a requirement would likely be inconsistent with federal case law interpreting the FAA itself. As we elaborate below, arbitration agreements under the FAA need only be written, not necessarily signed. If this court were to equate "knowing and voluntary" with "express and written" then we would effectively require that all arbitration agreements be signed to be enforceable. This would be in conflict with both the plain reading of the statute and with past precedent interpreting the statute. Accordingly, we find that, although Seawright did not sign a waiver, her acceptance of the EDR Program-which stated that parties to the agreement waived their right to sue in court-was knowing and voluntary.

B. Consideration

Addressing the issue of consideration, the district court stated that the agreement lacked "bargained for exchange." The district court seemed to base this conclusion on the fact that Seawright "had no ability to affect the terms of the company's policy." That fact, however, is irrelevant to whether there is a bargained-for exchange. Under Tennessee contract law, "[m]utuality of promises is 'ample' consideration for a contract. A mutual promise 'in itself would constitute a sufficient consideration.'" *Pyburn v. Bill Heard Chevrolet,* 63 S.W.3d 351 (Tenn.Ct.App. 2001) (quoting *Rodgers v. Southern Newspapers, Inc.,* 214 Tenn. 335 379 S.W.2d 797, 800 (1964)); *see also Buraczynski v. Eyring,* 919 S.W.2d 314, 321 n. 6 (Tenn. 1996). In the agreement at issue, the arbitration process was binding on both employer and employee, regardless of who requested arbitration. Thus, employer and employee were equally obligated to arbitrate those disputes falling within the coverage of the plan. This is enough to ensure mutuality of obligation and thus constitute consideration.

C. Illusory Contracts

Though Seawright's brief does not explicitly argue this point, her statement that "in contrast to the employee's inability to challenge the EDR program, the Companies maintained the right to change or terminate the program at any time" (Appellee's Br. 6–7) might be construed as an argument that the agreement was illusory and therefore void. Tennessee law requires that a contract not be illusory, that is, that it impose genuine obligations on both parties. *Parks v. Morris,* 914 S.W.2d 545, 550 (Tenn.Ct. App. 1995) ("If one or both parties to a contract have the right to cancel or terminate the agreement, then the contract lacks mutuality and is unenforceable") (internal quotation omitted). In *Floss v. Ryan's Family Steak Houses, Inc.*, 211 F.3d 306 (6th Cir. 2000) the court found the arbitration agreement to be "fatally indefinite" because the employer "reserved the right to alter the applicable rules and procedures without any obligation to notify, much less receive consent from" the employees. *Id.* at 315–16. The arbitration agreement in this case is distinguishable. While the defendant companies reserved the right to terminate the EDR at any time, they also agreed to be bound by the terms of the agreement for 90 days after giving reasonable notice of the termination and as to all known disputes arising before the date termination. J.A. 341. Thus, the companies were bound by the terms for at least 90 days after the agreement came into effect. This reciprocal obligation to arbitrate at least those claims arising in the 90–day period after the effective date of the agreement satisfies the mutuality requirement.

D. Contracts of Adhesion and Unconscionability

1

Seawright argues that the arbitration agreement is "unenforceable and/or void because it is a contract of adhesion entered into with unequal bargaining power and because it is substantively unconscionable." (Appellee's Br. 22). The Supreme Court has made it clear that "[m]ere inequality in bargaining power, however, is not a sufficient reason to hold that arbitration agreements are never enforceable in the employment context." *Gilmer v. Interstate/Johnson Lane Corp.*, 500 U.S. 20, 32, 111 S.Ct. 1647, 114 L.Ed.2d 26 (1991). The Court went on to write, "Of course, courts should remain attuned to well-supported claims that the agreement to arbitrate resulted from the sort of fraud or overwhelming economic power that would provide grounds for the revocation of any contract." *Id.* at 33, 111 S.Ct. 1647 (citing *Mitsubishi Motors Corp. v. Soler Chrysler–Plymouth, Inc.*, 473 U.S. 614, 627, 105 S.Ct. 3346, 87 L.Ed.2d 444 (1985)). Thus, to determine whether a contract is unenforceable we must follow Tennessee law governing the enforceability of contracts of adhesion.

The Supreme Court of Tennessee has defined an adhesion contract as being "a standardized form offered on what amounts to a 'take it or leave it' basis, without affording the weaker party a realistic opportunity to bargain, and under conditions whereby the weaker party can only obtain the desired product or service by submitting to the form of the contract." *Buraczynski v. Eyring*, 919 S.W.2d 314, 320 (Tenn. 1996) . . . However, a contract is not adhesive merely because it is a standardized form offered on a take-it-or-leave-it basis. The last element of adhesion, "the absence of a meaningful choice for the party occupying the weaker bargaining position," must also be present. *Cooper v. MRM Inv. Co.*, 367 F.3d 493 (6th Cir. 2004). While the agreement at issue here may fulfill the first three conditions, Seawright has not demonstrated the final element. Applying Tennessee state law, the Sixth Circuit in *Cooper* held that an employer's mandatory arbitration agreement was not a contract of adhesion based on the failure of a similar condition:

> To find *this* contract adhesive, however, there must be evidence that [the employee] would be unable to find suitable employment if she refused to sign [the employer's] agreement. She presented no such evidence. For instance, she did not allege that she looked for comparable jobs but was unable to find one. Generalizations about employer practices in the modern economy cannot substitute for such evidence. *See Andersons, Inc. v. Horton Farms,* 166 F.3d 308, 324 (6th Cir. 1998) (no procedural unconscionability where grain seller "failed to present evidence that it searched for other alternatives and that there were none").
>
> *Cooper,* 367 F.3d at 502.

. . . Seawright has presented no evidence that she would be unable to find suitable employment if she had refused to be a party to the arbitration agreement. Thus, we hold that the agreement is not a contract of adhesion.

2

Even if Seawright could show that the arbitration agreement was adhesive, she would also have to demonstrate that it was unconscionable. *Cooper,* 367 F.3d at 503. In Tennessee, adhesion contracts are unenforceable only when the terms are "beyond the reasonable expectations of an ordinary person, or oppressive or unconscionable." *Buraczynski,* 919 S.W.2d at 320; *see also Pyburn,* 63 S.W.3d at 359 (Tenn. App. 2001). A contract is unconscionable when the "inequality of the bargain is so manifest as to shock the judgment of a person of common sense, and where the terms are so oppressive that no reasonable person would make them on the one hand, and no honest and fair person would accept them on the other." *Haun v. King,* 690 S.W.2d 869, 872 (Tenn. Ct. App. 1984). Courts will not enforce adhesion contracts which are "oppressive to the weaker party or which serve to limit the obligations and liability of the stronger party." *Buraczynski,* 919 S.W.2d at 320 (Tenn. 1996). The Tennessee Supreme Court recognizes both substantive and procedural elements of unconscionability. *Taylor v. Butler,* 142 S.W.3d 277, 285 (Tenn. 2004) ("The determination that a contract or term is or is not unconscionable is made in the light of its setting, purpose and effect. Relevant factors include weaknesses in the contracting process like those involved in more specific rules as to contractual capacity, fraud, and other invalidating causes. . . .") (citing Restatement (Second) of Contract § 208, cmt. a (1981)).

Seawright does not argue, and this court could not hold, that the arbitration agreement was *substantively* unconscionable. The underlying arbitration agreement is equitable in that it binds both employer and employee to arbitration and does not "limit the obligations and liability of the stronger party"—the employer. This distinguishes the EDR Program from the arbitration agreements that Tennessee courts have held unconscionable. *See, e.g., Taylor v. Butler,* 142 S.W.3d 277 (Tenn. 2004) ("City Auto has a judicial forum for practically all claims that it could have against Taylor. . . . At the same time, Taylor is required to arbitrate any claim that she might have against City Auto.").

Seawright's only argument that the contract was procedurally unconscionable is her contention that there was unequal bargaining power. The finding that "an employee had less bargaining power *is* relevant to the procedural-unconscionability analysis." *Cooper,* 367 F.3d at 504. Seawright did not present evidence of any "factors bearing on the relative bargaining position of the contracting parties, including their age, education, intelligence, business acumen and experience, and relative bargaining power." *Ibid.* (citing *Morrison,* 317 F.3d at 666). Moreover, given Seawright's education and position as a branch office manager who had worked for the company for two and a half decades, it is unlikely that she could marshal such evidence. This distinguishes Seawright from a low-level employee who may be "required to sign an arbitration agreement precisely at the time that he or she is most willing to sign anything just to get a job." *Cooper,* 367 F.3d at 504 (citing *Cooper v. MRM Inv. Co.,* 199 F.Supp.2d 771, 780 & n. 8 (M.D. Tenn. 2002)).

For the forgoing reasons we find that Seawright entered into a valid and enforceable agreement to arbitrate.

E. The Federal Arbitration Act

In addition to Seawright's four arguments that the agreement is unenforceable under Tennessee state contract law, she asserts a fifth argument that a federal court cannot compel arbitration pursuant to the FAA because the arbitration agreement at issue was not written as required by the FAA. The FAA provides:

> A written provision in any maritime transaction or a contract evidencing a transaction involving commerce ... shall be valid, irrevocable, and enforceable, save upon such grounds as exist at law or in equity for the revocation of any contract.

9 U.S.C. § 2 (2006). Seawright analogizes the FAA to the Statute of Frauds; however, unlike contracts that fall under the Statute of Frauds, arbitration agreements under the FAA need to be written, but not necessarily *signed. Fisher,* 276 F.Supp.2d at 895. The agreement at issue here was written. A pamphlet entitled "American General Finance Company's Employee Dispute Resolution Program," was distributed via United States mail to employees. That pamphlet describes the arbitration procedures, makes it clear that the agreement is one for binding arbitration in lieu of a trial, and asserts that "[s]eeking, accepting, or continuing employment with AGF means that you agree to resolve employment related claims against the company or another employee through this process instead of through the court system." J.A. 291. Thus, the arbitration agreement, including the provision that continued employment would constitute acceptance, was written. This is in line with the conclusions of other circuits....

IV

... The employer at issue here did not try to hide its mandatory arbitration policy or try to trick its employees into agreeing to the policy. Nor did the employer choose an arbitration forum that would discourage employees from submitting disputes or favor the employer in the resolution of those disputes. In the absence of evidence that assent to the arbitration agreement was procured though unfair means or that the agreement itself was substantively unfair, courts should enforce mandatory arbitration agreements on the same basis as any other agreement that employers require as a condition of employment. Seawright has failed to demonstrate any state grounds upon which the agreement might be void or unenforceable and has failed to demonstrate the agreement did not comply with the "written" requirement of the FAA. We therefore REVERSE the district court's decision denying the order to compel arbitration and REMAND to the district court for further proceedings consistent with this opinion.

■ BOYCE F. MARTIN, JR., CIRCUIT JUDGE, dissenting.

The Court's ruling today goes too far in subordinating the constitutional rights of employees to the convenience of employers. The "agreement" between Seawright and AGF-which was not signed, contained a unilateral working-as-acceptance provision, and constituted a total waiver of the right to access a court-goes past the acceptable limit of what employers can force upon their employees without the employees' consent.

First and foremost, Seawright's signature appears nowhere on any arbitration agreement. Thus we have no proof that she manifested assent to the contract. Although Tennessee law does permit unilateral contracts, no Tennessee court has decided whether continuing employment is effective as a waiver of constitutional rights. A unilateral contract is one where an offeror "reasonably expects to induce action of a definite and substantial character" from the offeree. *See Curtiss Candy Co. v. Silberman,* 45 F.2d 451, 453 (6th Cir. 1930). Implicit in this understanding is that the offeree is aware of the significance of the act performed. Without a signal that she understands that a contract is being made, how is one to know if she has truly accepted?[1]

The majority cites Seawright's failure to express her lack of assent as evidence that she assented (distinguishing her from the plaintiff in *Lee,* who told her boss she did not agree to the program). *See Lee v. Red Lobster Inns of Am., Inc.,* 92 Fed.Appx. 158, 162 (6th Cir. 2004). As we held in that case, however, it is too onerous to require employees to object to new agreements imposed upon them: "a contract such as this places the burden on the employee to repeatedly object to a company's unilaterally adopted arbitration policy or risk being found to have agreed to it. This is not how contracts are formed." *Id.* "The mere receipt of an unsolicited offer does not impair the offeree's freedom of action or inaction or impose on him any duty to speak." *Id.* (citing Restatement (Second) of Contracts § 69, cmt. a (1981)). After today, however, an employee apparently must expressly reject the agreement in order not to be bound by it.

1. Homer Simpson talking to God: "Here's the deal: you freeze everything as it is, and I won't ask for anything more. If that is OK, please give me absolutely no sign. [no response] OK, deal. In gratitude, I present you this offering of cookies and milk. If you want me to eat them for you, please give me no sign. [no response] Thy will be done." *The Simpsons: And Maggie Makes Three* (Fox television broadcast, Jan. 22, 1995).

... Here, Seawright's only signature was on an "Information Session Sign–In Sheet," in which "I acknowledge that I have *attended* the information session and *received* a copy of the AGF Employee Dispute Resolution pamphlet." Joint App'x 319 (emphasis added). The script for the information session says that the sign-in sheet "confirms that you attended the information session," not that the employees read or understood the policy's binding nature. *Id.* at 315. Without a signature on a document that proves Seawright was at least aware of the nature of the agreement, it is impossible to say she knowingly waived her rights....

Because Seawright never performed any action that signaled that she knowingly and voluntarily entered into the agreement (and waived her rights), it is unreasonable to hold her to the agreement's terms. Thus I respectfully DISSENT from the majority's opinion.

* * *

Questions

1. Did Seawright accept AGF's arbitration agreement? On this issue, note especially the dissent's footnote 1.

2. In Hardin v. First Cash Financial Services, Inc., 465 F.3d 470 (10th Cir. 2006), an employer distributed an employment arbitration agreement to employees and announced that employees who continued to work would be deemed to have accepted its terms.

> Shortly after receiving these materials, [employee Shellee] Hardin discussed the DRP with her supervisor and unequivocally refused to consent to the DRP. Hardin stated that, although she would not quit, her continued employment was not intended to serve as her assent. Her supervisor responded that despite her statements to the contrary her continued employment with First Cash would manifest her acceptance. There was no further communication between Hardin and First Cash, and Hardin never signed the Agreement.

The Tenth Circuit held that Hardin had accepted the arbitration agreement. The court reasoned the employer had made an initial offer to Hardin of continued employment based on her assent to the dispute resolution program, and that she then made a counteroffer to continue working under unchanged employment terms. The employer rejected the counteroffer and repeated its initial offer, after which Hardin, by continuing to work, "assented to [the employer]'s offer to modify the terms of her at-will employment."

Do you agree? Is there any way Hardin could have dodged arbitration other than by quitting her job?

3. A law firm shareholder sues her firm for sex discrimination. The firm seeks to compel arbitration, citing to an arbitration agreement in the firm's corporate bylaws. The employee claims she was never aware of nor received a copy of the arbitration provision. The firm points out that her compensation and benefits are governed by the bylaws, and that as a member of various committees she was supposed to be familiar with the bylaws. Should the employee be bound by the arbitration agreement?

No, held the Third Circuit in Kirleis v. Dickie, McCamey & Chilcote, P.C., 560 F.3d 156 (3d Cir. 2009). Under Pennsylvania law, the court said, "explicit agreement is essential to the formation of an enforceable arbitration contract." If Pennsylvania law does not require such "explicit agreement" for the formation of other contracts, would the law be preempted? What if Pennsylvania law says that standard-form contracts signed by consumers are enforceable even if consumers have not read all the terms?

4. In an at-will employment relationship, must there be independent consideration given by an employer to support an arbitration agreement presented to a current employee? Ordinarily, an employer may modify the terms of at-will employment (such as the rate of pay or scheduled work hours) at any time, so long as the employer notifies the employee. In some contexts, however, courts have found that the promises underlying at-will employment are insufficient consideration to support a major change in the employment relationship. A traditional example is the non-compete agreement. Some courts have held that continued at-will employment cannot serve as consideration for a non-compete agreement because the at-will employer's right to fire the employee at any time nullifies the employer's "promise" of continued employment. See, e.g., Labriola v. Pollard Group, Inc., 100 P.3d 791, 794–95 (Wash. 2004). Some courts apply the same analysis to arbitration agreements. An example is Vedachalam v. Tata America Intern. Corp., 477 F.Supp.2d 1080 (N.D. Cal. 2007), in which the court held that consideration was lacking when a purported arbitration agreement applied only to employee claims against the employer but not vice versa.

5. Is there a lack of consideration where an employer expressly reserves the right to unilaterally modify or terminate the arbitration agreement? This issue arises when an employer inserts an arbitration clause into an employment handbook that contains a unilateral modification clause. In *Douglass v. Pflueger Haw., Inc.*, 135 P.3d 129 (Haw. 2006), the court held that such a contract was illusory and therefore unenforceable, at least where the employer puts *no* restrictions on its ability to amend or terminate arbitration provisions. By contrast, in *Hardin* (discussed in note 2 above), the court held that an arbitration agreement containing a unilateral modification clause is enforceable if there are some restrictions on the employer's ability to amend or terminate. In *Hardin*, the employer had to give advance notice of any change to its arbitration clause, could not make any changes to the arbitration clause with respect to any potential claim or dispute of which it had actual notice, and could not terminate the arbitration clause with respect to any claim arising prior to the date of termination. For more on this issue, see Michael L. DeMichele & Richard A. Bales, *Unilateral–Modification Provisions in Employment Arbitration Agreements*, 24 Hofstra Labor & Employment L.J. 63 (2006).

6. Does the contract law doctrine of unconscionability provide a satisfactorily predictable guide for employers who want to draft arbitration agreements? Note how the Tennessee law of adhesion and unconscionability as discussed in *Seawright* differs from California law as discussed in *Armendariz* (supra Chapter 2.5).

* * *

C. Unconscionability in Employment Arbitration Agreements

Armendariz v. Foundation Health Psychcare Services, Inc., 6 P.3d 669 (Cal. 2000), discussed above in Chapter 2.5, contains a detailed discussion of unconscionability in employment arbitration agreements, so we will not present another principal case here.

Some employment arbitration agreements are negotiated. Examples include employment contracts for high-level executives, and post-dispute arbitration agreements. Other employment arbitration agreements are drafted by employers who are legitimately looking for a way to resolve employment disputes that is better than litigation. Some employers, however, have used their bargaining power over at-will employees and applicants to put their thumb on the arbitral scales by designing arbitration systems that seem clearly designed to make it impossible for employees to pursue even legitimate claims.

The Supreme Court's FAA preemption doctrine, presumption of arbitrability, and strong federal policy favoring arbitration have made it difficult, however, to challenge all but the most egregiously lopsided employment arbitration agreements on federal grounds. Many courts, therefore, have looked to other sources of law to void lopsided employment arbitration agreements.

Recall that the FAA makes arbitration agreements enforceable save for grounds that would make *any* contract unenforceable. Routine judicial enforcement of most standard-form contracts therefore makes it difficult to use a "knowing and voluntary" standard, or even notice and consent standards, to void most arbitration agreements. Unconscionability seems to be the vehicle of choice at the moment for voiding lopsided agreements. It only works, however, in jurisdictions (such as California—see *Armendariz*) that have robust unconscionability/adhesion doctrines that apply to contracts generally. In states with weaker doctrines (such as Tennessee, as discussed in *Seawright* above), the doctrine cannot be widely applied to arbitration agreements.

The paradigmatic case dealing with a lopsided employment arbitration agreement is *Hooters of America, Inc. v. Phillips*, 173 F.3d 933 (4th Cir. 1999). In this case, the court took a second approach to voiding a lopsided employment arbitration agreement—it found that the lopsided arbitration terms breached an implied contract that arbitration would be fair. Other courts, such as the D.C. Circuit's *Cole* decision (discussed in Chapter 2.7 on allocating the costs of arbitration) have taken a third approach to voiding lopsided arbitration agreements: they have found that the lopsided arbitration terms make it impossible to vindicate substantive statutory rights such as the right to be free from employment discrimination. Recall that the Supreme Court has stated, in *Mitsubishi* and *Gilmer* among other cases, that arbitration is merely a substitute forum and not a waiver of substantive rights.

Hooters, though technically not an unconscionability case, is nonetheless instructive here because it illustrates so many of the ways that an employer can make an employment arbitration agreement lopsided. In that case, an employee quit her job and threatened to bring a Title VII claim over allegations of sexual harassment. Two years earlier, the company had instituted an alternative dispute resolution program, pursuant to which the company had conditioned eligibility for raises and promotions on employees signing an "agreement to arbitrate employment-related disputes." The agreement provided that the "employee and the company agree to resolve any claims pursuant to the company's rules and procedures for alternative resolution of employment-related disputes, as promulgated by the company from time to time." Phillips had twice signed the agreement, but neither she nor any other employee was given a copy of Hooter's arbitration rules and procedures. Two years later, when she raised her harassment allegations, the employer sued to compel arbitration of her claim under the FAA. Phillips counterclaimed for violations of Title VII and for declaration that employer's arbitration agreements were unenforceable. The District Court denied the employer's motions to compel arbitration and the employer appealed. The Fourth Circuit held that the employer materially breached the agreement to arbitrate by promulgating egregiously unfair arbitration rules. The court stated:

> Hooters argues that Phillips gave her assent to a bilateral agreement to arbitrate. That contract provided for the resolution by arbitration of all employment-related disputes, including claims arising under Title VII. Hooters claims the agreement to arbitrate is valid because Phillips twice signed it voluntarily. Thus, it argues the courts are bound to enforce it and compel arbitration.
>
> We disagree. The judicial inquiry, while highly circumscribed, is not focused solely on an examination for contractual formation defects such as lack of mutual assent and want of consideration ... Courts also can investigate the existence of "such grounds as exist at law or in equity for the revocation of any contract." 9 U.S.C. § 2. However, the grounds for revocation must relate specifically to the arbitration clause and not just to the contract as a whole. Prima Paint Corp. v. Flood & Conklin Mfg. Co., 388 U.S. 395, 402–04, 87 S.Ct. 1801, 18 L.Ed.2d 1270 (1967) ... In this case, the challenge goes to the validity of the arbitration agreement itself. Hooters materially breached the arbitration agreement by promulgating rules so egregiously unfair as to constitute a complete default of its contractual obligation to draft arbitration rules and to do so in good faith.

Hooters and Phillips agreed to settle any disputes between them not in a judicial forum, but in another neutral forum—arbitration. Their agreement provided that Hooters was responsible for setting up such a forum by promulgating arbitration rules and procedures. To this end, Hooters instituted a set of rules in July 1996.

The Hooters rules when taken as a whole, however, are so one-sided that their only possible purpose is to undermine the neutrality of the proceeding. The rules require the employee to provide the company notice of her claim at the outset, including "the nature of the Claim" and "the specific act(s) or omissions(s) which are the basis of the Claim." Rule 6–2(1), (2). Hooters, on the other hand, is not required to file any responsive pleadings or to notice its defenses. Additionally, at the time of filing this notice, the employee must provide the company with a list of all fact witnesses with a brief summary of the facts known to each. Rule 6–2(5). The company, however, is not required to reciprocate.

The Hooters rules also provide a mechanism for selecting a panel of three arbitrators that is crafted to ensure a biased decisionmaker. Rule 8. The employee and Hooters each select an arbitrator, and the two arbitrators in turn select a third. Good enough, except that the employee's arbitrator and the third arbitrator must be selected from a list of arbitrators created exclusively by Hooters. This gives Hooters control over the entire panel and places no limits whatsoever on whom Hooters can put on the list. Under the rules, Hooters is free to devise lists of partial arbitrators who have existing relationships, financial or familial, with Hooters and its management. In fact, the rules do not even prohibit Hooters from placing its managers themselves on the list. Further, nothing in the rules restricts Hooters from punishing arbitrators who rule against the company by removing them from the list. Given the unrestricted control that one party (Hooters) has over the panel, the selection of an impartial decision maker would be a surprising result.

Nor is fairness to be found once the proceedings are begun. Although Hooters may expand the scope of arbitration to any matter, "whether related or not to the Employee's Claim," the employee cannot raise "any matter not included in the Notice of Claim." Rules 4–2, 8–9. Similarly, Hooters is permitted to move for summary dismissal of employee claims before a hearing is held whereas the employee is not permitted to seek summary judgment. Rule 14–4. Hooters, but not the employee, may record the arbitration hearing "by audio or videotaping or by verbatim transcription." Rule 18–1. The rules also grant Hooters the right to bring suit in court to vacate or modify an arbitral award when it can show, by a preponderance of the evidence, that the panel exceeded its authority. Rule 21–4. No such right is granted to the employee.

In addition, the rules provide that upon 30 days notice Hooters, but not the employee, may cancel the agreement to arbitrate. Rule 23–

1. Moreover, Hooters reserves the right to modify the rules, "in whole or in part," whenever it wishes and "without notice" to the employee. Rule 24–1. Nothing in the rules even prohibits Hooters from changing the rules in the middle of an arbitration proceeding . . .

We hold that the promulgation of so many biased rules—especially the scheme whereby one party to the proceeding so controls the arbitral panel—breaches the contract entered into by the parties. The parties agreed to submit their claims to arbitration—a system whereby disputes are fairly resolved by an impartial third party. Hooters by contract took on the obligation of establishing such a system. By creating a sham system unworthy even of the name of arbitration, Hooters completely failed in performing its contractual duty . . .

By promulgating this system of warped rules, Hooters so skewed the process in its favor that Phillips has been denied arbitration in any meaningful sense of the word. To uphold the promulgation of this aberrational scheme under the heading of arbitration would undermine, not advance, the federal policy favoring alternative dispute resolution. This we refuse to do.

* * *

Questions

1. Would a nonunion arbitration agreement that required employees to bring all disputes to arbitration and to prove any allegation of discrimination beyond a reasonable doubt be unconscionable? Does any change in the standard of proof that imposes additional burdens on the complaining party render an arbitration agreement unconscionable?

2. Would it be unconscionable for an employer to require an employee to agree, as a condition of hire, to waive all her rights to bring a discrimination complaint against the employer at any time in the future? Alexander v. Gardner–Denver, 423 U.S. 1058 (1976), says that this would violate Title VII. Then why doesn't it violate Title VII for an employer to require an employee to sign a predispute arbitration agreement and thereby waive her right to sue for enforcement of her Title VII rights?

3. Suppose an employer requires an employee, at the time of hire, to agree to arbitrate any dispute that might arise, including complaints of discrimination, before an arbitrator designated by the employer's vice president for human relations. Would this agreement be enforceable? Would/should it matter (1) Whether there is knowing and voluntary consent to the arbitrator-selection clause? (2) Whether the employee was the company vice president, and there was copious give-and-take in the negotiation of many of the terms of her employment contract, including both salary and the arbitration clause?

4. Is it unjust for the Supreme Court to apply a strict contractualist construction of the FAA to contexts such as consumer and employee arbitration?

* * *

D. THIRD-PARTY ARBITRATION PROVIDERS

Some employers have contracted for third-party providers to establish and operate arbitration systems for their employees' disputes. At first glance, such systems appear to obviate some concerns of employer bias in the operation of an arbitral system or in the selection of the decisionmaker. However, third-party arbitration systems give rise to some additional concerns, as the following case explores.

Walker v. Ryan's Family Steak Houses, Inc.

400 F.3d 370 (6th Cir. 2005).

■ CLAY, CIRCUIT JUDGE.

Defendant Ryan's Family Steak Houses, Inc. appeals the October 2, 2003 order of the district court, denying its motion to dismiss and petition to compel arbitration, pursuant to the Federal Arbitration Act, 9 U.S.C. §§ 3 and 4, of Plaintiff Erric Walker's, Steve Ricketts', and Vickie Atchley's claims for violations of the Fair Labor Standards Act of 1938 ("FLSA"), 29 U.S.C. §§ 201–219. For the reasons that follow, we AFFIRM.

I.

On November 12, 2002, Plaintiffs Erric Walker, Steve Ricketts, and Vickie Atchley filed a self-styled "collective action" complaint for violations of the FLSA against Defendant Ryan's Family Steak Houses, Inc. ("Ryan's") in the United States District Court for the Middle District of Tennessee. Ryan's is a Delaware corporation, with its principal place of business in South Carolina, and owns and operates a chain of over 300 restaurants in 22 states. Plaintiffs, former employees at various Ryan's locations in Tennessee, allege that Ryan's failed to pay them the minimum wage and/or one-and-one-half their regular rate of pay for all hours worked in excess of each 40 hour work week, in violation of the FLSA. After Plaintiffs filed suit, 18 additional unnamed plaintiffs filed their consent to become party plaintiffs in the lawsuit. Ryan's moved to dismiss Plaintiffs' complaint and petitioned for an order compelling Plaintiffs to arbitrate their claims pursuant to the Federal Arbitration Act ("FAA"), 9 U.S.C. §§ 3 and 4. Ryan's argued that Plaintiffs federal court claims were foreclosed by the arbitration agreements that each had executed at the outset of their employment. [The district court denied Ryan's motion, and Ryan's appealed.] . . .

Since 1996 or 1997, any individual who applies for employment with Ryan's has been presented with a 12–page application packet. The second page of the packet notifies the applicant that he or she is required to complete and sign the "Job Application Agreement to Arbitration of Employment–Related Disputes" (hereafter "Arbitration Agreement") in order to be considered for a position. Failure to sign and accept the Arbitration Agreement and its related rules and procedures purportedly terminates the job application process. . . .

Unlike the typical pre-employment arbitration agreement which involves a contract between the applicant and his or her potential employer, Ryan's Arbitration Agreement is not between the applicant and Ryan's. Rather, it is between the applicant and Employment Dispute Services, Inc. ("EDSI"). EDSI is a South Carolina corporation whose sole business is the marketing and administration of the Employment Dispute Resolution Program. The program is a third-party arbitration system which was established in 1992 to provide employers and employees outside of the securities industry with a purportedly fair and expeditious means of resolving employment-related disputes. EDSI has contracts with a total of seven companies, including Ryan's.

The Arbitration Agreement that Plaintiffs executed explains that Ryan's (referred to therein as the "Company") had entered into a separate agreement with EDSI "to arbitrate and resolve any and all employment-related disputes between the Company's employees (and job applicants) and the Company." Although Plaintiffs were not provided with a copy of Ryan's separate agreement with EDSI, that agreement obligates EDSI to, *inter alia,* "administer and provide access to the EDSI alternative dispute resolution procedures and forum for all Company job applicants, employees, and the Company itself, as provided in the EDSI Rules and Procedures"; train managers and supervisors about the alternative dispute resolution program; and train managers and employees selected to serve as potential "adjudicators" in the program. Also, for an additional fee, EDSI will conduct "an employee relations audit (personnel polices and procedures, handbooks and other personnel forms), management training, and employee attitude surveys with recommended management responses." Ryan's agreement with EDSI is renewable from year to year, but Ryan's may cancel the contract with ten days' written notice.

By executing the Arbitration Agreement with EDSI, Plaintiffs agreed to (a) bring any employment disputes that he or she may have against Ryan's and that would otherwise be decided in a state or federal court only in EDSI's arbitral forum and (b) be bound by a final decision of the EDSI arbitration panel. The purported consideration for Plaintiffs' promise to arbitrate is EDSI's agreement "to provide an arbitration forum, Rules and Procedures, and a hearing and decision based on any claim or dispute [that the applicant] may file or defend[.]" According to the agreement, Ryan's is a third party beneficiary of the agreement between Plaintiffs and EDSI, and Plaintiffs are third party beneficiaries of Ryan's agreement with EDSI. The agreement continues for the period of Plaintiffs' employment with Ryan's, unless mutually terminated in writing by Plaintiffs and EDSI.

The 2000 version of EDSI's Employment Dispute Resolution Rules and Procedures—the most recent version of the rules—provides that the substantive rights and remedies in EDSI's arbitration forum are the same as are available in a federal or state court. The rules govern all legal disputes, claims, or causes of action that arise out of the employment or possible employment of all parties signatory to an employment dispute resolution agreement with EDSI. The rules govern both the claims of a "claimant" (i.e., an applicant or employee) and any claims that a signatory defendant might bring against a claimant who has signed the Arbitration Agreement.

The rules further provide that a panel of three "adjudicators" resolves arbitration claims and are chosen from three separate selection pools: (1) supervisors or managers of an employer signatory to an agreement with EDSI; (2) employees who are non-exempt from the wage and hour protections of the Fair Labor Standards Act; and (3) attorneys, retired judges, or other competent legal professional persons not associated with either party. No individual who has been employed by an employer involved in the dispute can serve as an adjudicator.

EDSI provides the parties with a list of three potential adjudicators in each of the three selection pools. The parties have access to a schedule of the adjudicators' fees and their employment history for at least the previous five years, along with related biographical information. Potential adjudicators also are required to disclose any information which may preclude them from making an objective and impartial decision.

Once EDSI selects the pools of potential adjudicators, the claimant and the defendant alternately strike names from each of the three selection pools until one name from each pool remains. Any potential adjudicator may be struck for cause. As a matter of EDSI practice, if an adjudicator is removed from the pool for cause, EDSI provides another potential adjudicator.

Once arbitration proceedings commence, any party may serve a request for production of documents, and counsel for the parties have subpoena power. The rules also permit each party to schedule a deposition of one individual. A party may file a request for additional depositions, "but such requests are not encouraged and shall be granted in extraordinary fact situations and for good cause shown." . . .

III.

[T]he district court held that the [arbitration] agreements are unenforceable because they do not allow Plaintiffs to effectively vindicate their rights under the FLSA. We agree for the reasons discussed below.

Even if there is no contract-based defense to the enforceability of an arbitration agreement, a court cannot enforce the agreement as to a claim if the specific arbitral forum provided under the agreement does not "allow for the effective vindication of that claim." *Floss* [v. Ryan's Family Steak Houses, Inc., 211 F.3d 306, 313 (6th Cir. 2000)]. Generally, a party cannot avoid the arbitration process simply by alleging that the arbitration panel will be biased, because the FAA "protects against bias, by providing that courts may overturn arbitration decisions '[w]here there was evident partiality or corruption in the arbitrators.' " *Gilmer,* 500 U.S. at 30, 111 S.Ct. 1647 (quoting 9 U.S.C. § 10(b)) . . . However, the general rule prohibiting pre-arbitration challenges to an allegedly biased arbitration panel does not extend to an allegation that the arbitrator-selection process itself is fundamentally unfair. *McMullen* [v. Meijer, Inc., 355 F.3d 485, 494 n.7 (6th Cir.

2004) (per curiam)]. In such a case, "the arbitral forum is not an effective substitute for a judicial forum," and, therefore, the party need not arbitrate first and then allege bias through post-arbitration judicial review. *Id.*

The Arbitration Agreements and related rules and procedures at issue in this case demonstrate that EDSI's arbitral forum is not neutral and, therefore, the agreements are unenforceable. As previously described, under EDSI's rules, three "adjudicators" are selected from three separate selection pools to preside over the arbitration hearing. The first of these pools consists of supervisors and managers from another EDSI signatory company; the second consists of employees from another signatory; and the third contains attorneys, retired judges, and other "competent legal professional persons not associated with either party." Although dictum, language in *Floss* signaled this Court's extreme disapproval of this arbitrator selection mechanism:

> We have serious reservations as to whether the arbitral forum provided under the current version of the EDSI Rules and Procedures is suitable for the resolution of statutory claims. Specifically, the neutrality of the forum is far from clear in light of the uncertain relationship between Ryan's and EDSI. [Plaintiffs] Floss and Daniels suggest that EDSI is biased in favor of Ryan's and other employers because it has a financial interest in maintaining its arbitration service contracts with employers. Though the record does not clearly reflect whether EDSI, in contrast to the American Arbitration Association, operates on a for-profit basis, the potential for bias exists. In light of EDSI's role in determining the pool of potential arbitrators, any such bias would render the arbitral forum fundamentally unfair. *See Cole v. Burns Int'l Security Services,* 105 F.3d 1465, 1482 (D.C.Cir.1997) ("At a minimum, statutory rights include both a substantive protection and access to a neutral forum in which to enforce those protections.").

[*Floss*, 211 F.3d] at 314; *see also McMullen, supra,* 355 F.3d at 493–94 (following dictum in *Floss* to strike down arbitration scheme in which employer had exclusive control over selection of arbitrator pool).

The record in this case removes any of the uncertainties surrounding the relationship between Ryan's and EDSI that the Court noted in *Floss.* EDSI is clearly a for-profit business, and Ryan's annual fee accounted for over 42% of EDSI's gross income in 2002. Given the symbiotic relationship between Ryan's and EDSI, Ryan's effectively determines the three pools of arbitrators, thereby rendering the arbitral forum fundamentally unfair to claimants who are applicants or employees. *See Geiger* [v. Ryan's Family Steak Houses, Inc., 134 F.Supp.2d 985, 995 (S.D.Ind. 2001)] (holding that there is a strong potential for bias in the selection of the arbitration panel because EDSI receives payment from its agreements with various employers to provide a forum for resolving employment disputes, but no comparable payment is made by or received from an employee for agreeing to submit to the forum; further holding that EDSI's full authority to select both the Rules for arbitration as well as the pools of potential arbitrators, combined with EDSI's potential bias in favor of employers like Ryan's, rendered it "unlikely that applicants/employees will participate in an unbiased forum"); *McMullen,* 355 F.3d at 493–94 (holding that the employer's exclusive control over the pool of potential arbitrators prevented the plaintiff from effectively vindicating her Title VII rights: "[T]he arbitrator-selection procedure used by Meijer allows it to create the type of symbiotic relationship with its arbitrators that we feared would promulgate bias in *Floss.*"); *Hooters of Am., Inc. v. Phillips,* 173 F.3d 933, 938–39 (4th Cir. 1999) (affirming denial of motion to compel because the arbitration rules provided a mechanism for selecting a panel of three arbitrators that was crafted to ensure a biased decisionmaker; the employer created the list of potential arbitrators).

The bias against employees and applicants is significantly enhanced by the lack of any criteria governing employees of signatory companies who are eligible to serve as adjudicators. There are no minimum educational requirements, potential arbitrators do not need to have any relevant experience as an adjudicator, and there is no explicit requirement that they be unbiased. Similarly, the rules do not require that the legal professionals who comprise the third pool possess either substantive or procedural knowledge of dispute resolution or of the employment law issues involved in the arbitration. The names of potential arbitrators for the legal professional pool purportedly are provided to EDSI by an unaffiliated company, Resolute Systems, Inc.; however, there is no information in the record regarding how Resolute Systems selects potential adjudicators for EDSI's program.

The bias is exacerbated by the lack of a protocol governing EDSI's selection of potential adjudicators from the three pools. The individuals in the supervisor and employee pools are neither randomly selected nor chosen by a disinterested person for their skills. Instead, all members of these two pools are chosen by the small number of employers who, like Ryan's, have signed alternative dispute resolution agreements with EDSI: Golden Corral Steak Houses, K & W Cafeterias, Papa John's Pizza, Sticky Fingers Restaurants, The Cliffs at Glass, Inc., and Wieland Investments, Inc. In addition, the rules do not prevent a supervisor of a signatory company from sitting on an adjudication panel with a non-supervisory employee from the same company, including someone whom the supervisor directly supervises. Further, EDSI has no policy in place that prohibits a signatory company from discussing the arbitration process or specific claims with its employee adjudicators or from attempting to improperly influence its employee adjudicators.

Finally, the limited discovery that the EDSI forum provides could significantly prejudice employees or applicants. The rules allow "just one deposition as of right and additional depositions only at the discretion of the (arguably biased) panel, with the express policy that depositions 'are not encouraged and shall be granted in extraordinary fact situations only for good cause shown.' " *Geiger,* 134 F.Supp.2d at 996 (quoting EDSI Rules, Art. XII, § 6; reproduced at J.A. 315.). We agree with the district court's conclusion in *Geiger* that "the limited discovery, controlled by a potentially biased arbitration panel, . . . creates the unfairness to claimants." *Id.* We acknowledge that the opportunity to undertake extensive discovery is not necessarily appropriate in an arbitral forum, the purpose of which is to reduce the costs of dispute resolution. Indeed, when parties enter arbitration agreements at arms-length they typically should expect that the extent of discovery will be more circumscribed than in a judicial setting. But parties to a valid arbitration agreement also expect that neutral arbitrators will preside over their disputes regarding both the resolution on the merits and the critical steps, including discovery, that precede the arbitration award. A structural bias in the make-up of the arbitration panel, which would stymie a party's attempt to marshal the evidence to prove or defend a claim, can be just as prejudicial as arbitral bias in the final decision on the merits. Such is the case here, providing an additional basis to conclude that EDSI's and Ryan's arbitration scheme does not allow for the effective vindication of Plaintiffs' FLSA claims.

IV.

For all the foregoing reasons, we AFFIRM the district court's holdings that state law contract defenses preclude enforcement of Plaintiffs' arbitration agreements and that Plaintiffs' arbitration agreements are unenforceable under the FAA because they do not allow for effective vindication of their FLSA claims.

* * *

Questions

1. How would you advise an employer who wanted to use a third-party arbitrator provider to hear and decide disputes concerning its employees? How should the arbitration system be designed to avoid a finding that it is unconscionable? How should the system be presented to employees to avoid a finding of lack of consent or lack of consideration?

2. Is there an inherent risk of bias when one party is a repeat player in arbitration and the other party (e.g., a consumer or employee) is not? A repeat-player effect might result in two systemic employer advantages. The first is that the employer is more familiar with the pool of potential arbitrators and therefore is in a better position than an employee to select an arbitrator favorable to its side. The second is that an arbitrator interested in generating future business will be predisposed to favor the employer. See Lisa B. Bingham, *On Repeat Players, Adhesive Contracts, and the Use of Statistics in Judicial Review of Employment Arbitration Awards*, 29 McGeorge Law Review 223 (1998); Lisa B. Bingham, *Employment Arbitration: The Repeat Player Effect*, 1 Employee Rights and Employment Policy Journal 189 (1997). But see Lisa B. Bingham & Shimon Sarraf, *Employment Arbitration Before and After the Due Process Protocol for Mediation and Arbitration Disputes Arising Out of Employment: Preliminary Evidence That Self–Regulation Makes A Difference*, in Alternative Dispute Resolution in the Employment Arena: Proceedings of New York

University's 53d Annual Conference on Labor (Samuel Estreicher ed. 2001) (finding no statistically significant evidence that employers confronting the same arbitrator in a second case have a higher probability of success); see also Jeffrey W. Stempel, *Keeping Arbitrations from Becoming Kangaroo Courts*, 8 Nev. L.J. 251 (2007) (suggesting that arbitrators be licensed by the states).

* * *

E. Effects of Employment Arbitration Agreements on Third Parties

EEOC v. Waffle House, 534 U.S. 279 (2002), involved an employee who was fired from his job as a Waffle House grill operator after he suffered seizure at work. The employee, who had signed a predispute arbitration agreement, did not pursue arbitration, but instead filed a charge of discrimination with the Equal Employment Opportunity Commission (EEOC).[3] The EEOC subsequently filed a complaint in federal district court against Waffle House for unlawful disability discrimination against the employee. Waffle House moved to stay the suit and compel arbitration. The district court denied the motion. The court of appeals reversed, ordering arbitration, but limiting the EEOC's potential remedies to injunctive relief.

The issue before the Court was whether an arbitration agreement between an employer and the employee barred the EEOC from pursuing victim-specific judicial relief, such as backpay, reinstatement, and damages, in an enforcement action. The Court, in a 6–3 decision authored by Justice Stevens, reversed the court of appeals, and held that the EEOC was free to seek victim-specific relief. The Court reasoned that Title VII, which created the EEOC, "makes the EEOC the master of its own case," and that the statute gave the agency—not the courts—the authority "to determine whether public resources should be committed to the recovery of victim-specific relief."

Justice Thomas, writing for the dissent, focused on § 706(g)(1)of Title VII. This section provides that, after a finding of liability, "the court may enjoin the respondent from engaging in such unlawful employment practice, and order *such affirmative action as may be appropriate,* which may include, but is not limited to, reinstatement or hiring of employees, with or without back pay ... *or any other equitable relief as the court deems appropriate*" (emphasis added). Justice Thomas reasoned that it was not "appropriate" to allow the EEOC to do on behalf of an employee that

3. The EEOC is the administrative agency created by Congress to administer Title VII, the Age Discrimination in Employment Act, and the Americans with Disabilities Act. The agency has only procedural rulemaking authority under Title VII, but has both substantive and procedural rulemaking authority under the other two statutes. See 29 U.S.C. § 628 (ADEA). The EEOC does not have statutory authority to interpret the Federal Arbitration Act; nor does it have adjudicatory authority under any of the antidiscrimination statutes. The EEOC has consistently opposed the enforcement of predispute arbitration agreements, but has been roundly ignored by the courts on this issue.

which the employee is precluded from doing for himself—i.e., to seek victim-specific relief in court on behalf of an employee who had agreed to arbitrate, rather than litigate, his claims.

* * *

Questions

1. Does the holding in *Waffle House* mean that parties to an arbitration agreement can never bind third parties who were not signatories? Or is the *Waffle House* holding limited to the impact of a private arbitration agreement on a government enforcement agency?

2. Suppose an employer has a contract with a health maintenance organization to provide health coverage for its employees, and that agreement contains a provision requiring arbitration of all disputes that arise between the employer and the HMO pertaining to the contract. An employee has a dispute with the HMO concerning an allegation of malpractice. Can the HMO require the employee to arbitrate as a third party beneficiary of the employer-HMO agreement? See Spear, Leeds & Kellogg v. Central Life Assurance Co., 85 F.3d 21 (2d Cir. 1996).

3. The Court left open the issue of whether the EEOC may pursue a claim that an employee already has brought to arbitration. How should lower courts resolve this issue? What if an employee signs a waiver or release instead of an arbitration agreement? See Senich v. American–Republican, Inc., 215 F.R.D. 40, 44–45 (D.Conn. 2003) (permitting EEOC to seek victim-specific relief for employees who had signed a waiver and release as a condition of receiving benefits under an employer severance program).

4. Justices Souter, Stevens, Ginsburg, and Breyer dissented in *Circuit City Stores, Inc. v. Adams, supra.* However, each of these Justices joined the majority in *Waffle House*, and cited *Circuit City* for the proposition that the FAA applies to employment contracts. Can *Waffle House*, then, be seen as strengthening the institution of employment arbitration?

* * *

9. Arbitration Involving Nonparties

There are a number of circumstances under which someone who was not a party to an arbitration clause seeks to enforce an arbitration clause against one who was a party to the clause. For example, a construction subcontractor in a payment dispute with a general contractor might want to utilize an arbitration provision in the general contractor's contract with the owner. Or, a successor or assignee of a party might seek to utilize an arbitration agreement. Further, there are circumstances in which a party to an arbitration clause might seek to compel a non-party to arbitrate. For example, a party to an agreement containing an arbitration clause might seek to force a non-party to arbitrate a matter that arises out of and/or is related to a transaction that is subject to an arbitration agreement. In these situations, a court must decide whether the arbitration agreement binds one who was not a party to it.

Under the general law of contract, third party beneficiaries, assignees, and certain other third parties can have rights and/or obligations under a contract that they did not participate in making. A non-party's actions can create an estoppel or a waiver that can also bind them to arbitrate a dispute. In the arbitration context, imposing a duty to arbitrate on a non-party presents novel issues of balancing the strong federal policy favoring arbitration against the equally strong policy of grounding arbitration in consent so as to avoid implied waivers of a judicial forum. The cases that follow explore these issues.

* * *

A. ASSIGNING THE OBLIGATION TO ARBITRATE

Kaufman v. William Iselin & Co.

74 N.Y.S.2d 23 (N.Y.App.Div. 1947).

■ SHIENTAG, JUSTICE.

J. B. Kaufman Co., petitioner (hereinafter called "Kaufman"), brought this proceeding to compel appellant factor, William Iselin & Co., Inc. (hereinafter called "Iselin"), to arbitrate an alleged dispute arising out of the purchase by Kaufman of certain goods from Crest–Tex Mills, Inc. (hereinafter called "Crest–Tex"). Iselin was not a party to the contract of sale of the goods made between Kaufman and Crest–Tex. The claim against Iselin is based upon the proposition that when a seller's factor receives an assignment of invoices of accounts and of the merchandise covered thereby, that transfer carries with it as matter of law an assignment pro tanto of the contract to which the invoices relate and the assignee becomes bound by the terms of the seller's agreement with the buyer.

In the instant proceeding the buyer claims that after the merchandise was received and after the invoices had been paid to the factor, certain defects were discovered and it was found that the goods delivered were not in accordance with the specifications originally agreed upon. Notice of the defect was given to the seller Crest–Tex, to its selling agent, and to the seller's factor, Iselin. The invoices were paid by the buyer to Iselin, the seller's factor, in accordance with the billing requirements, and prior to the discovery that the merchandise was defective.

Under the agreement between the buyer and seller, it was provided that 'Any controversy arising under or in relation to this contract shall be settled by arbitration.'

The terms under which Iselin received the assignment of the invoices are as follows:

> This bill is assigned to and payable only to our factors William Iselin & Co., Inc., 357 Fourth Avenue, New York 10, N. Y., to whom notice must be given of any merchandise returns or claims for shortage, nondelivery or for other grounds.
>
> In consideration of $1.00 and other valuable consideration receipt of which is hereby acknowledged, we hereby sell, assign and transfer to William Iselin & Co., Inc., in confirmation of their title thereto, all our right, title and interest in and to the above stated accounts, invoices numbered ___ to ___ inclusive and in and to the merchandise therein described, and we hereby fully guarantee the validity and correctness of said accounts and due acceptance of said merchandise by the purchasers named without objection or claim.
>
> This assignment is made pursuant to the written agreement.

On petitioner's motion, the court at Special Term directed arbitration of the controversy between buyer and seller and factor. The only appellant is the factor, Iselin, who contends that as assignee of certain specific invoices, which were paid before the proceeding began, it is not subject to any claim for defective goods. The factor argues that it had no interest in the contract other than a security interest to cover advances made to the seller of the goods, that as an assignee with merely a security title it had no duty to perform in relation to delivery of goods of any special quality, and, finally, it claims that the mere assignment of a security title does not bind the assignee to any of the terms of the contract including the provision for arbitration.

The only question to be decided at this time is whether the petition supports a claim, at least prima facie, that Iselin is bound in any respect by the arbitration clause in the contract between the buyer and seller.

The question whether an assignee assumes the duties as well as the rights under an assigned contract was considered at length by the Court of Appeals in Langel v. Betz, 250 N.Y. 159, 163, 164 N.E. 890, 891. There, the court took up the American Law Institute's Restatement of the Law of Contracts, Section 164(2), which reads as follows:

> (2) Acceptance by the assignee of such an assignment is interpreted, in the absence of circumstances showing a contrary intention, as both an assent to become an assignee of the assignor's rights and as a promise to the assignor to assume the performance of the assignor's duties.

In referring to this provision of the Restatement the Court of Appeals said:

> This promise to the assignor would then be available to the other party to the contract. Lawrence v. Fox, 20 N.Y. 268; I Williston on Contracts, § 412. The proposed change is a complete reversal of our present rule of interpretation as to the probable intention of the parties. It is, perhaps, more in harmony with modern ideas of contractual relations than is 'the archaic view of a contract as creating a strictly personal obligation between the creditor and debtor' (Pollock

on Contracts [9th Ed.] 232), which prohibited the assignee from suing at law in his own name and which denied a remedy to third party beneficiaries. The fountains out of which these resolutions issue have been broken up if not destroyed (Seaver v. Ransom, 224 N.Y. 233, 237, 120 N.E. 639 [640], 2 A.L.R. 1187), but the law remains that no promise of the assignee to assume the assignor's duties is to be inferred from the acceptance of an assignment of a bilateral contract, in the absence of circumstances surrounding the assignment itself which indicate a contrary intention.

The court finally took the position that one must consider the dealings between the parties to discover whether the assignee entered into such agreements that it might be said to have assumed the duty of performance of the contract.

Obviously, the mere assignment of an invoice and of the merchandise covered thereby for purposes of securing a loan made by a commercial banker is not a situation in which it may be said that it was the intention of the parties that the factor should assume performance of the basic contract. Since that is all that is here present, we find that there is no showing of the assumption of contract duties by the appellant, Iselin.

We limit our decision to holding that on the present record no case is made out to justify a finding that the factor, under the conditions herein presented, has assumed the duty to arbitrate. This is not a situation where the assignee has taken any affirmative action under the contract to enforce its terms; in such event it is proper to hold that having taken steps to adopt the terms of the contract he had assumed the obligations as well as the rights thereunder. (Citations omitted.) Here, no affirmative action having been taken by the assignee, the factor, the situation may be said to be analogous to that present in Langel v. Betz, 250 N.Y. 159, 164 N.E. 890, supra.

The order, in so far as it directs William Iselin & Co., Inc., to proceed to arbitration, should be reversed with $20 costs and disbursements to the appellant against the petitioners-respondents and the motion to that extent denied.

All concur.

* * *

Questions

1. Note that the court distinguished the facts of *Kaufman* from "a situation where the assignee has taken any affirmative action under the contract to enforce its terms." Suppose that the appellant, Iselin wanted to enforce the arbitration clause against Kaufman on a claim for nonpayment. Could Iselin, as an assignee of the agreement, affirmatively enforce the arbitration clause?

2. Under the *Kaufman* court's reasoning, is there any circumstance in which an assignee would assume a contractual duty to arbitrate? What might those circumstances be? Are there circumstances in which a third party beneficiary can be forced to arbitrate a claim based on a contract between two contracting parties? Would the same reasoning apply?

3. Does the court apply the same reasoning to the assignability of an obligation to arbitrate as it would to the assignability of contractual obligations generally?

4. Does a parent who signs a contract on behalf of her minor child bind her child (a non-signatory) to an arbitration clause in that contract? Yes, said the New Jersey Supreme Court, in *Hojnowski v. Vans Skate Park*, 901 A.2d 381 (N.J. 2006). A mother had signed a release form on behalf of her 12–year old son so that her son could enter, and skateboard in, a private skate park owned by Vans. Her son was injured and sued Vans; Vans moved to compel arbitration. The court held that a parent can bind her minor child to an agreement to arbitrate future tort claims. The court reasoned that is consistent with the strong policy in favor of arbitration and that binding the child does not operate as a "waiver" of any substantive rights—it merely alters the forum in which the child's rights must be asserted.

5. In labor arbitration, the union generally controls whether a given case goes to arbitration, subject to the union's duty to fairly represent individual employees. If a union does not want to take a grievance to arbitration, can the union assign the grievance to the grievant? See Mitchell H. Rubinstein, *Assignment of Labor Arbitration*, 81 St. John's L. Rev. 41 (2007) (arguing that unions should be permitted to do so). Would employers be happy with this arrangement?

This issue may take on increased importance in the wake of the Supreme Court's ruling in 14 Penn Plaza v. Pyett, ___ U.S. ___, 129 S.Ct. 1456 (2009) (see Chapter 1.6), holding that unions may agree to arbitrate the statutory claims of individual employees.

* * *

Note on Assigning the Obligation to Arbitrate

In *Gruntal & Co. v. Steinberg*, 854 F.Supp. 324 (D.N.J. 1994), Gruntal, a securities broker, acquired the assets of Philips, another broker pursuant to an Asset Purchase Agreement. The Purchase Agreement purported to include customer accounts. Subsequently, one of Philips' customers, Steinberg, sought to arbitrate a claim regarding the account under the arbitration procedures of the NASD. Gruntal sought a declaratory judgment that it did not have an obligation to arbitrate Philips' customers complaints for transactions that predated Gruntal's accession to the accounts. The District Court held that while there was an arbitration provision in the contract between Philips, the original broker, and his customers, the agreement did not bind the successor broker to arbitrate. The court explained:

The Steinbergs do not argue that they and Gruntal are signatories to a contract to arbitrate. Ronald Steinberg, in fact, testified at trial that he never signed an agreement of any sort with Gruntal. Instead, the Steinbergs rely on two alternative bases for Gruntal's asserted obligation to arbitrate in the Arbitration Proceedings: (1) the transfer of the Steinberg Accounts, and the arbitration clauses in the accompanying Philips Contracts, to Gruntal as a result of the Asset Purchase Agreement and (2) Gruntal's membership in the NASD.

Significant doubt exists as to whether the Steinberg Accounts and the attendant Philips Contracts were ever transferred to Gruntal pursuant to the transfer provision in the Asset Purchase Agreement . . . It is not necessary, however, to conclusively decide this issue here. Even if the Steinberg Accounts and Philips Contracts were transferred to Gruntal, such a transfer cannot, by itself, create an obligation to arbitrate on Gruntal's part.

Under New York law, made applicable by [the Asset Purchase Agreement], the assignee of rights under a bilateral contract is not bound to perform the assignor's duties unless he expressly assumes to do so. Lachmar v. Trunkline LNG Co., 753 F.2d 8, 9–10 (2d Cir.1985) . . . Included among the duties to which this rule has reference is the duty to arbitrate. Lachmar, 753 F.2d at 10; Matter of Kaufman, 272 A.D. 578, 581–82, 74 N.Y.S.2d 23 (App.Div. 1st Dept.1947) . . .

In the instant case, the record establishes conclusively that Gruntal never expressly assumed Philips' duty to arbitrate in the Arbitration Proceedings. As indicated, the Arbitration Proceedings involve transactions and events which took place on or before 15 February 1988, over two months prior to the Closing Date [of the Purchase Agreement]. Also as indicated, Gruntal, by the Asset Purchase Agreement, expressly renounced any obligations of Philips, to arbitrate or otherwise, "arising as a result of or in connection with the business or activities of [Philips] at the [Fort Lee] Office prior to the Closing Date." Asset Purchase Agreement, 2. Silverman, the Gruntal officer who negotiated the Asset Purchase Agreement with Philips, testified at Trial that Gruntal had no intention of assuming any responsibilities of Philips which arose prior to the Closing Date.

* * *

Questions

1. Why doesn't the court order Gruntal to arbitrate, among other things, the issue of which obligations it assumed under its agreement with Philips? Has the court in *Gruntal* ignored the presumption of arbitrability?

2. By invoking the law of assignment under New York law, has the court in *Gruntal* disregarded the rule of *Perry v. Thomas* that arbitration-specific state law doctrines should not be used to defeat arbitration? Can this opinion be understood as consistent with prevailing arbitration law under the FAA?

* * *

B. EQUITABLE ESTOPPEL

J. A. Construction Management Corporation v. Insurance Company of North America

659 F.2d 836 (7th Cir. 1981).

■ CUDAHY, CIRCUIT JUDGE.

J. A. Construction Management Corporation ("J.A.") appeals from the district court's denial of its motion to compel arbitration. We vacate and remand for further proceedings consistent with this opinion.

I.

On February 15, 1975, James Associates Architects and Engineers, Inc. ("James Associates") entered into an agreement with the Greater Clark County School Building Corporation ("Clark") to provide the architectural and construction management services necessary for the construction of the Charlestown and Jeffersonville Middle Schools in Clark County, Indiana. James Associates was authorized under this agreement to assign project managers at both sites to oversee and coordinate all construction operations. Pursuant to this authority, James Associates executed a contract with J. A., under which J. A. was to perform the construction management services relating to the middle school projects.

On November 30, 1976, Hughes Masonry Company, Inc. ("Hughes") entered into an agreement with Clark to provide masonry services for construction of the two schools. Pursuant to the terms of this contract, J. A. was designated as construction manager for both projects. The contract also incorporated by reference the American Institute of Architects' "General Conditions," which, together with other contract documents, outlined the responsibilities of Clark, James Associates, J. A. and Hughes. Section 7.10.1 of the "General Conditions" provided that all disputes "arising out of, or relating to, this contract or the breach thereof . . . shall be decided by arbitration."[1]

Several disputes arose soon after Hughes began its work on the school building projects in late summer of 1977, and, on March 18, 1978, Clark terminated its contract with Hughes. Clark's action was based on Hughes' alleged breach of its contractual obligations. Clark hired another contractor, allegedly at a substantial increase in cost, to complete the masonry work for the building projects. Therefore, in an effort to recover its alleged

1. The contracts between Clark and James Associates and James Associates and J. A. contained similar arbitration clauses.

increase in costs from Hughes, Clark filed, on April 17, 1978, pursuant to Section 7.10.1 of the "General Conditions," a demand for arbitration of its dispute with Hughes with the American Arbitration Association.

Hughes subsequently filed separate actions against Clark in the United States District Court for the Southern District of Indiana and against J. A. in the Superior Court of Marion County, Indiana. In the district court, after Clark sought to compel arbitration, Hughes moved to enjoin any arbitration proceedings. On September 18, 1979, Hughes amended its complaint in federal court to add J. A. and the American Arbitration Association as defendants. Thirteen days later, on October 1, 1979, before J. A. had answered the amended complaint, the district court entered an order enjoining all defendants, including J. A., from proceeding to arbitration.

On May 28, 1980, after filing an answer which raised arbitration as an affirmative defense, J. A. filed a motion to compel arbitration of all contract disputes between itself, Hughes and Clark. The district court denied J. A.'s motion in an order dated December 12, 1980, and J. A. filed a timely appeal from that decision.

II.

... Hughes now argues, however, that it cannot be required to arbitrate because J.A. is not entitled to invoke the arbitration provision of the Hughes–Clark agreement since it is not a party to that agreement.

Whatever the merit of this argument, we believe Hughes is equitably estopped from asserting it in this case, because the very basis of Hughes' claim against J.A. is that J.A. breached the duties and responsibilities assigned and ascribed to J.A. by the agreement between Clark and Hughes.

Hughes has characterized its claims against J.A. as sounding in tort, i. e., intentional and negligent interference with contract. In substance, however, Hughes is attempting to hold J.A. to the terms of the Hughes–Clark agreement. Hughes' complaint is thus fundamentally grounded in J.A.'s alleged breach of the obligations assigned to it in the Hughes–Clark agreement.[4] Therefore, we believe it would be manifestly inequitable to permit Hughes to both claim that J.A. is liable to Hughes for its failure to perform the contractual duties described in the Hughes–Clark agreement and at the same time deny that J.A. is a party to that agreement in order to avoid arbitration of claims clearly within the ambit of the arbitration clause. "In short, (plaintiff) cannot have it both ways. (It) cannot rely on

4. ... [I]n response to Clark's motion for a stay, Hughes argued, inter alia, that J.A.'s acts "amounted to an abandonment of the contract both by Clark and J.A." Similarly, an affidavit of Hughes' president submitted in support of Hughes' March 12, 1979, brief states in part that "(f)rom the very inception of the agreement, Clark, in conjunction with its construction manager, committed acts that breached the covenants, representations and warranties set out in the construction agreement" and that "Clark and the construction manager, by committing the acts (which are listed in subparagraphs A through E and J of paragraph 30 of Hughes' complaint, see note 6, infra) as well as other acts, specifically and intentionally abandoned the agreement from its very inception ..." Hughes cannot now be heard to say for purposes of avoiding arbitration that its claims against J.A. are not fundamentally grounded in the contract.

the contract when it works to its advantage, and repudiate it when it works to (its) disadvantage.'' Tepper Realty Co. v. Mosaic Tile Co., 259 F.Supp. 688, 692 (S.D.N.Y. 1966). [Citation omitted.]

Although only Hughes and Clark are signatories to the Hughes–Clark agreement, that agreement identifies James Associates as the architect and J.A. as the construction manager for the school projects. Section 2.3.1 of the agreement provides that the ''Architect and Construction Manager will be the Owner's representatives during construction (and) will have authority to act on behalf of the Owner, to the extent provided in the Contract Documents....'' Subsequent provisions of the agreement set forth various duties that James Associates and J.A. are to perform on behalf of the owner ...

Presumably, James Associates and J.A. are not contractually liable for breach of obligations set forth in the Hughes–Clark agreement since they are not parties to that agreement. Rather, James Associates was obligated to perform the duties of construction management by virtue of its contract with Clark, which imposed those duties upon James Associates in consideration of 7.5% of the total construction cost. The construction management duties were in turn imposed on J.A. by virtue of the James Associates–J.A. contract (under which J.A. was to receive 3% of the total construction costs).

But Hughes seeks in this action to hold J.A. responsible for its failure to perform (or its improper performance of) the obligations set forth in the Hughes–Clark agreement. In Count I of its amended complaint, for example, Hughes alleges that ''Clark and/or its construction manager'' breached and were in default of the Hughes–Clark agreement. And, in Count III, Hughes alleges that J.A., ''instead of carrying out its duties and responsibilities contained in the agreement,'' interfered with the contractual relationship between Clark and Hughes. Although Count III sounds in tort, the acts that Hughes alleges as constituting interference with the agreement in fact consist essentially of J.A.'s alleged failure to properly perform various duties ascribed to J.A. by the Hughes–Clark agreement. Similarly, in its ''Specific Contentions'' filed at the request of the district court on August 29, 1980, Hughes alleged, as the basis for its claims against J.A., that J.A., as Clark's ''agent,'' failed to carry out various duties and responsibilities specified in the Hughes–Clark agreement and therefore ''intentionally interfered'' with that agreement.

The district court's order is therefore vacated and remanded for further proceedings in accordance with this opinion.

* * *

Questions

1. If, as the court states, J.A. is not contractually liable for breach of the Hughes–Clark agreement, why can J.A. get the benefit of the arbitration provision in that same agreement?

2. Would the outcome be the same if it were Hughes trying to force J.A. to arbitrate a claim brought by J.A. related to the construction project? Is there any difference between permitting a non-signatory to arbitrate and requiring a non-signatory to arbitrate?

* * *

Note on Estoppel in Arbitration Claims Against Third Parties

Equitable estoppel is raised to compel a nonparty to arbitrate when it would be unfair not to. Generally, courts use it to prevent parties from enjoying the benefits of a contract but not its burdens. The Second Circuit explained the application of equitable estoppel, as well as other theories of third party obligations to arbitrate, in Thomson–CSF S.A. v. American Arbitration Association, 64 F.3d 773 (2d Cir. 1995). The court was presented with an effort by a signatory to an agreement containing an arbitration clause to force a non-signatory to arbitrate. Plaintiff Thomson–CSF's (Thomson's) subsidiary, Rediffusion Simulation Limited (Rediffusion) entered into an agreement with E & S Computer Corporation (E & S) to purchase certain computer-generated image equipment. The agreement called for arbitration of all disputes between the "parties" to the Agreement. When a dispute arose concerning the performance of the agreement, E & S filed a demand for arbitration against both Rediffusion and the parent, Thomson. Thomson brought an action in federal district court to enjoin the arbitration, and E & S cross-motioned to compel arbitration. The district court ruled that both Rediffusion and Thomson were bound by the arbitration clause. On appeal, the Second Circuit reversed in relation to Thomson. It wrote:

> This Court has recognized a number of theories under which nonsignatories may be bound to the arbitration agreements of others. Those theories arise out of common law principles of contract and agency law. Accordingly, we have recognized five theories for binding nonsignatories to arbitration agreements: 1) incorporation by reference; 2) assumption; 3) agency; 4) veil-piercing/alter ego; and 5) estoppel. The district court properly rejected each of these traditional theories as sufficient justification for binding Thomson to the arbitration agreement of its subsidiary.
>
> A. *Incorporation by Reference*
>
> A nonsignatory may compel arbitration against a party to an arbitration agreement when that party has entered into a separate contractual relationship with the nonsignatory which incorporates the existing arbitration clause. *See Import Export Steel Corp. v. Mississippi Valley Barge Line Co.,* 351 F.2d 503, 505–506 (2d Cir. 1965) (separate agreement with nonsignatory expressly "assum[ing] all the obligations and privileges of [signatory party] under the ... subcharter" constitutes grounds for enforcement of arbitration clause by nonsignatory); *Matter of Arbitration Between Keystone Shipping Co. and Texport Oil*

Co., 782 F.Supp. 28, 31 (S.D.N.Y. 1992); *Continental U.K. Ltd. v. Anagel Confidence Compania Naviera, S.A.,* 658 F.Supp. 809, 813 (S.D.N.Y. 1987) (if a "party's arbitration clause is expressly incorporated into a bill of lading, nonsignatories ... who are linked to that bill through general principles of contract law or agency law may be bound").

B. *Assumption*

In the absence of a signature, a party may be bound by an arbitration clause if its subsequent conduct indicates that it is assuming the obligation to arbitrate. *See Gvozdenovic v. United Air Lines, Inc.,* 933 F.2d 1100, 1105 (2d Cir.) (flight attendants manifested a clear intention to arbitrate by sending a representative to act on their behalf in arbitration process), *cert. denied,* 502 U.S. 910, 112 S.Ct. 305, 116 L.Ed.2d 248 (1991); *Keystone Shipping,* 782 F.Supp. at 31; *In re Transrol Navegacao S.A.,* 782 F.Supp. 848, 851 (S.D.N.Y. 1991).

C. *Agency*

Traditional principles of agency law may bind a nonsignatory to an arbitration agreement. *See Interbras Cayman Co. v. Orient Victory Shipping Co., S.A.,* 663 F.2d 4, 6–7 (2d Cir. 1981); *A/S Custodia,* 503 F.2d at 320; *Fisser,* 282 F.2d at 233–38; *Keystone Shipping,* 782 F.Supp. at 31–32.

D. *Veil Piercing/Alter Ego*

In some instances, the corporate relationship between a parent and its subsidiary are sufficiently close as to justify piercing the corporate veil and holding one corporation legally accountable for the actions of the other. As a general matter, however, a corporate relationship alone is not sufficient to bind a nonsignatory to an arbitration agreement. *See Keystone Shipping,* 782 F.Supp. at 30–31. Nonetheless, the courts will pierce the corporate veil "in two broad situations: to prevent fraud or other wrong, or where a parent dominates and controls a subsidiary." *Carte Blanche (Singapore) Pte., Ltd. v. Diners Club Int'l, Inc.,* 2 F.3d 24, 26 (2d Cir. 1993); *see also Wm. Passalacqua Builders, Inc. v. Resnick Developers S., Inc.,* 933 F.2d 131, 138–39 (2d Cir. 1991) ("Liability ... may be predicated either upon a showing of fraud or upon complete control by the dominating corporation that leads to a wrong against third parties.").

E. *Estoppel*

This Court has also bound nonsignatories to arbitration agreements under an estoppel theory. In *Deloitte Noraudit A/S v. Deloitte Haskins & Sells, U.S.,* 9 F.3d 1060, 1064 (2d Cir.1993), a foreign accounting firm received a settlement agreement concerning the use of the trade name "Deloitte" in association with accounting practices. Under the agreement—containing an arbitration clause—local affiliates of the international accounting association Deloitte Haskins & Sells International were entitled to use the trade name "Deloitte" in exchange for compliance with the dictates of the agreement. A Norwegian accounting firm received the agreement, made no objection to the terms of the agreement, and proceeded to utilize the trade name. This Court held that by knowingly exploiting the agreement, the accounting firm was estopped from avoiding arbitration despite having never signed the agreement. *See* 9 F.3d at 1064 . . .

Several courts of appeal have recognized an alternative estoppel theory requiring arbitration between a signatory and nonsignatory. *See Sunkist Soft Drinks, Inc. v. Sunkist Growers, Inc.,* 10 F.3d 753, 757–58 (11th Cir.1993), *cert. denied,* 513 U.S. 869, 115 S.Ct. 190, 130 L.Ed.2d 123 (1994); *J.J. Ryan & Sons, Inc. v. Rhone Poulenc Textile, S.A.,* 863 F.2d 315, 320–21 (4th Cir.1988) . . . In these cases, a signatory was bound to arbitrate with a nonsignatory at the nonsignatory's insistence because of "the close relationship between the entities involved, as well as the relationship of the alleged wrongs to the nonsignatory's obligations and duties in the contract . . . and [the fact that] the claims were 'intimately founded in and intertwined with the underlying contract obligations.' " *Sunkist,* 10 F.3d at 757 (quoting *McBro Planning,* 741 F.2d at 344).

As these cases indicate, the circuits have been willing to estop a *signatory* from avoiding arbitration with a nonsignatory when the issues the nonsignatory is seeking to resolve in arbitration are intertwined with the agreement that the estopped party has signed . . . [H]owever, "[t]he situation here is inverse: E & S, as signatory, seeks to compel Thomson, a non-signatory." While E & S suggests that this is a non-distinction, the nature of arbitration makes it important. Arbitration is strictly a matter of contract; if the parties have not agreed to arbitrate, the courts have no authority to mandate that they do so. *See United Steelworkers,* 363 U.S. at 582, 80 S.Ct. at 1352–53. In the line of cases discussed above, the courts held that the parties were estopped from avoiding arbitration because they had entered into written arbitration agreements, albeit with the affiliates of those parties asserting the arbitration and not the parties themselves. Thomson, however, cannot be estopped from denying the existence of an arbitration clause to which it is a signatory because no such clause exists.

* * *

C. THIRD PARTY BENEFICIARIES

Parker v. Center for Creative Leadership

15 P.3d 297 (Colo.App. 2000).

■ JUDGE DAILEY.

Defendant, Center for Creative Leadership (CCL), appeals the order of the trial court denying its request to require plaintiff, Daniel J. Parker, to submit to arbitration. We reverse and remand with directions.

CCL and plaintiff's employer, U.S. West Marketing Resources Group, Inc., entered into a Service Agreement. Plaintiff suffered injuries while attending a corporate leadership workshop sponsored by employer and conducted by CCL. Plaintiff filed suit against CCL, asserting claims for negligence, breach of contract, negligent misrepresentation, and intentional misrepresentation.

. . . CCL sought to enforce the arbitration clause contained in the Service Agreement. Section 20.6 of the Service Agreement, entitled "Dispute Resolution," reads, in pertinent part:

> 20.6.1 *Any claim,* controversy or dispute, whether sounding in contract, statute, tort, fraud, misrepresentation or other legal theory, *between the parties to this Agreement or between one of the parties to this Agreement and the employees . . . of the other party,* shall be resolved by arbitration as prescribed in this section. The Federal Arbitration Act, 9 U.S.C. § 1–15, not state law, shall govern the arbitrability of all claims (emphasis added).

The trial court denied the motion, finding that, because plaintiff did not sign the Service Agreement, the arbitration clause did not apply to him.

I.

CCL contends on appeal that plaintiff is bound by the arbitration clause as an alleged third-party beneficiary of the Service Agreement. We agree.

The question of arbitrability is one for the court to decide. *Jefferson County School District No. R–1 v. Shorey,* 826 P.2d 830 (Colo. 1992).

The right to compel arbitration of a dispute is derived from contract. Thus, one who is not a party to the contract generally cannot compel, or be compelled to participate in, arbitration. *Eychner v. Van Vleet,* 870 P.2d 486 (Colo.App. 1993). However, a nonparty, such as a third-party beneficiary, may fall within the scope of an arbitration agreement if the parties to the contract so intend. *Everett v. Dickinson & Co.,* 929 P.2d 10 (Colo.App. 1996); *Eychner v. Van Vleet, supra.*

In the present case, although the information in the record is limited, it appears that the Service Agreement was entered into so that CCL could provide leadership training services for the benefit of employer and its employees. In return, CCL and employer agreed to arbitrate any disputes arising between them and/or their employees.

In his complaint, plaintiff brought claims for relief based upon CCL's alleged responsibilities under the Service Agreement. Consequently, plaintiff may not, while seeking to enforce CCL's duties and obligations under the agreement, at the same time argue that the provisions of that contract do not apply to him. *See Lee v. Grandcor Medical Systems, Inc.,* 702 F.Supp. 252 (D.Colo. 1988) (third-party beneficiary must accept contract's burdens along with its benefits); *Georgia Power Co. v. Partin,* 727 So.2d 2 (Ala. 1998) (same).

Here, the contract between employer and CCL expressly provided that all claims, regardless of theory, between the parties or an employee of one of the parties must be submitted to arbitration. The employer and CCL thus demonstrated their intent to create enforceable rights in or duties to third parties, including plaintiff. Thus, based on the language of the Service Agreement, as well as the surrounding circumstances, we determine that all of plaintiff's claims are subject to the arbitration clause . . .

The order of the trial court denying CCL's request for arbitration is reversed and the cause is remanded for further proceedings consistent with the views expressed in this opinion.

■ JUDGE NEY and JUDGE KAPELKE concur.

* * *

Questions

1. Is it relevant to the outcome in *Parker v. Center for Creative Leadership* that the contract between the plaintiff's employer and the Center called for arbitration of "any claim . . . between one of the parties to this Agreement and the employees of the other party"? Can parties to a contract require nonsignatories to arbitrate claims simply by inserting their names, or as in this case, designating them by category in the text of an agreement? If not, what role, if any, does the contractual language play in the court's decision?

2. Different states have different standards for finding a third party beneficiary relationship. For example, Delaware requires that (1) the contracting parties must have intended to confer rights on the third party; (2) the benefit must have been intended as a gift or as satisfaction of a pre-existing obligation; and (3) the intent to benefit must be a material part of the parties' purpose in entering the contract. See E.I. DuPont de Nemours v. Rhone Poulenc Fiber and Resin, 269 F.3d 187 (3d Cir. 2001). In contrast, in Alabama, a third party has rights under a contract if the contracting parties intended to confer rights upon the third party. Wilson v. Waverlee Homes, 954 F.Supp. 1530 (M.D.Ala. 1997) (overruled other grounds). Yet other states require that the contract name the third party. What standard is the court applying in the *Parker* case?

3. The court states that the plaintiff cannot seek to enforce CCL's duties under the agreement but attempt to avoid arbitration under the agreement. The plaintiff, however, was suing for injuries sustained at the defendant's workshop, and several of his causes of action sounded in tort. Does the court suggest that if the plaintiff's case were a simple personal injury lawsuit, then the arbitration clause would not bind the plaintiff?

4. In *Ex parte Dickinson,* 711 So.2d 984 (Ala. 1998) a husband and wife signed a Retail Installment Contract for the purchase of an automobile. Only the husband signed a further document, a Retail Buyer's Order, that contained an arbitration clause. Subsequently, the husband and wife sued the automobile dealer for fraud, breach of contract, conversion and wrongful repossession. The court held that the husband was required to arbitrate his claim, but the wife was not because she was not a signatory to the arbitration clause and had not agreed to arbitrate. Could the wife be considered a third party beneficiary of the Retail Buyer's Order? If so, can this case be distinguished from *Parke*?

5. In *Parker,* the plaintiff was required to submit to an arbitration procedure to which he did not expressly agree. Would the outcome be the same if the plaintiff were attempting to force the defendant to use the arbitration system negotiated between the defendant and the plaintiff's employer? See Grigson v. Creative Artists Agency*, L.L.C.,* 210 F.3d 524 (5th Cir. 2000).

6. Should state contract law of the forum state determine the standard for finding a third party beneficiary for purposes of the Federal Arbitration Act? Or, is there a federal rule of third party beneficiary status that is imported into the FAA through the operation of preemption and the liberal federal policy supporting arbitration? Does the presumption of arbitrability require state courts to grant third party beneficiary status whenever there is a colorable claim that a nonsignatory should come under an arbitration clause? If so, what happens to the bedrock principle that arbitration is grounded in consent of the parties?

* * *

Jackson v. Iris.com

524 F.Supp.2d 742 (E.D. Va. 2007).

■ ROBERT G. DOUMAR, DISTRICT JUDGE.

On May 15, 2007, Iris.com ("Defendant" or "Iris") filed a Demand for Arbitration with the American Arbitration Association ("AAA") against Curtis James Jackson III, p/k/a/ 50 Cent, ("Plaintiff" or "Jackson"). On August 30, 2007, Jackson filed a Complaint to Stay the Arbitration and for Declaratory Judgment. On October 11, 2007, Jackson filed a Motion for a Preliminary Injunction to Stay Arbitration. The arbitration is scheduled for January 21–23, 2008. On December 5, 2007, this Court notified the parties of its intent to consider entering summary judgment *sua sponte* for the Defendant and advised the Plaintiff to submit any additional evidence. For the reasons set forth herein, the Court hereby DECLARES that the claims against the Plaintiff are subject to arbitration, GRANTS summary judgment *sua sponte* for the Defendant, and DISMISSES the case without prejudice to any claims presented in arbitration.

DISCUSSION

I. FACTUAL AND PROCEDURAL BACKGROUND

The essential facts of this case are not in dispute and are contained in affidavits and exhibits accompanying the parties' various filings. Iris was responsible for producing the "Night of Music" concert series, an event scheduled to take place on July 15, 2006, in Libreville, Gabon, Africa. On February 22, 2006, Iris entered into two separate contracts with G*Town

Entertainment, Inc. ("G*Town") whereby G*Town agreed to "furnish the services of" performers Jackson and Melissa Arnette Elliot, p/k/a Missy Elliot ("Elliot") at the July 15, 2006, concert. Iris paid a total of $550,000 to G*Town in exchange for the performances: $350,000 pursuant to the contract for Jackson ("G*Town Contract") and $200,000 pursuant to the contract for Elliot. The G*Town Contract contains an arbitration provision . . .

The G*Town Contract also contains a liquidated damages provision which states that the $350,000 "payment shall be deemed a non-refundable deposit if [Iris] breeches the terms of the agreement or if [Jackson] breeches the terms of this agreement [Iris] will be refunded his/her deposit minus an [sic] (five percent) 5% commission." Pursuant to the contracts, G*Town paid $450,000 to American Talent Agency ("ATA"), a booking agent for Jackson and Elliot, in two installments: $45,000 on May 24, 2006, and $405,000 on June 8, 2006. G*Town allegedly retained the remaining $100,000 as a commission. ATA then paid $150,000 to Jackson on June 28, 2006, and $75,000 to Elliot on June 30, 2006. Plaintiff has allegedly been unable to locate the remaining $225,000 paid to ATA.

While the above essential facts are fairly straightforward, the facts regarding the breakdown in negotiations between the parties are somewhat more complex. As a threshold matter, the parties do not dispute that ATA was Jackson's booking agent. Violator Management ("Violator"), Jackson's manager, admits that it "engaged" ATA to negotiate for Jackson's performance in Africa. In addition, negotiations between Iris and Jackson over Jackson's performance in Africa appear to have proceeded in two distinct stages. The first stage involved Iris indirectly negotiating with ATA using G*Town as an intermediary, whereas the second stage involved Iris directly negotiating with ATA.

At the first stage, Iris entered into the contract with G*Town containing the arbitration provision at issue, and G*Town proceeded to negotiate with ATA for Jackson's performance. G*Town's negotiations with ATA are memorialized in several documents . . .

The negotiations between G*Town and ATA apparently broke down, and Jackson failed to perform on July 15, 2006. Iris argues that Jackson breached the G*Town Contract by failing to perform. G*Town argues that Iris breached the G*Town Contract by failing to provide agreed-upon travel arrangements. Jackson argues that he was never a party to the G*Town Contract. However, as discussed further below, it is unnecessary for the Court to entangle itself in this factual dispute because the only issue presently before the Court is whether Jackson is subject to the G*Town Contract's arbitration provision.

At the second stage, Sedlmayr & Associates, PC ("Sedlmayr"), counsel for Jackson, negotiated for Jackson's performance directly with Arent Fox, PLLC ("Arent Fox"), counsel for Iris. In fact, ATA and Sedlmayr allegedly took over negotiations with Iris prior to the original July 15, 2006, performance date. When negotiations broke down regarding the July 15, 2006, performance date, Sedlmayr and Arent Fox began negotiations for an alternative performance date of August 12, 2006. *Id.* These negotiations are similarly memorialized in several documents . . .

The Draft Contract between Iris and Jackson does not contain an arbitration provision. Rather, it requires all disputes to be litigated in state or federal courts in New York City. The Draft Contract also provides for liquidated damages in the event of default:

> 3. *COMPENSATION*
>
> PURCHASER [Iris] agrees to pay FURNISHER [Jackson] Three Hundred Thousand and 00/100 U.S. Dollars ($300,000.00) for the show (the "Compensation") free of all foreign taxes (such as box office, admission, license, franchise, property or other similar taxes) and without deductions of any kind, provided, however, that *FURNISHER acknowledges that purchaser has previously paid and shall receive a credit of $150,000 against the Compensation, leaving a sum of One Hundred Fifty Thousand and 00/100 U.S. Dollars ($150,000.00) to be paid.*
>
> Deposits are to be paid to ATA o/b/o FURNISHER as follows (it being agreed by FURNISHER that all payments be made to FURNISHER hereunder shall be made to ATA and that payments made to ATA shall be deemed payments made to FURNISHER for all purposes of this Agreement).
>
> 16. *REMEDIES*
>
> In the event that PURCHASER fails to fulfill in any material respect of any of PURCHASER'S obligations hereunder, on or before the dates and terms specified above or otherwise defaults in performing its obligations under this Agreement, in such event FURNISHER shall be entitled to collect/retain the Compensation as liquidated damages, whereupon this Agreement shall be terminated.

(Pl.'s Mem. Ex. 1D ¶¶ 3, 16.) (emphasis added). Similarly, a July 18, 2006, email from Violator to Arent Fox stated:

> Fee as agreed upon and as follows: 50% of fee already paid shall serve as nonrefundable forfeited deposit. The remaining 50% of initial payment to serve as front end for new date with $150K balance on [Jackson] and $75K balance on [Elliot] due and payable immediately.

(Def.'s Opp. Ex. 7.) From these two documents, it is clear that the Draft Contract contemplated putting a portion of the $450,000 that Iris already paid to ATA pursuant to the G*Town Contract toward the alternative August 12, 2006, concert date. However, the parties do not allege that this Draft Contract, or any other contract besides the G*Town Contract, was ever actually executed by the parties. Nevertheless, Jackson argues, without citing any authority, that the above provisions of the Draft Contract entitled him to retain the $150,000 paid by Iris as a "kill fee" to compensate him for his preparation once the deal fell through. (Pl.'s Mem. 6–7.)

On May 15, 2007, once the deal fell through, Iris filed a Demand for Arbitration with the AAA against Jackson, G*Town, and Elliot pursuant to the arbitration provision in the G*Town Contract. On August 30, 2007, Jackson filed a Complaint to Stay Arbitration and for Declaratory Judgment in the Circuit Court of Arlington County, Virginia. On September 24, 2007, Iris removed the Complaint to this Court. On October 10, 2007, Iris filed an Answer to Jackson's Complaint. On October 11, 2007, Jackson filed a Motion for Preliminary Injunction to Stay Arbitration. On October 25, 2007, Iris filed a Response in Opposition to Plaintiff's Motion to Stay Arbitration. On October 31, 2007, Jackson filed a Reply in Support of his Motion to Stay Arbitration. On November 9, 2007, this Court issued an Order directing the Plaintiff to account for the $550,000 Iris paid to G*Town. On November 30, 2007, Jackson filed a Response to the Court's Order. On December 5, 2007, this Court issued an Order notifying the Plaintiff of its intent to consider entering summary judgment *sua sponte* and directing the Plaintiff to submit any additional evidence within eleven (11) days. On December 17, 2007, Jackson filed a Response to the Court's Order. Arbitration is scheduled for January 21–23, 2008. . . .

III. ANALYSIS

In his December 17, 2007, Submission in Response to this Court's December 5, 2007, Order, Jackson alleges that there are essentially two material factual disputes that preclude this Court's entry of summary judgment at this time: (1) whether G*Town was an agent or apparent agent of Jackson, and (2) whether the G*Town Contract or the Draft Contract controls the dispute between the parties for purposes of this proceeding. However, for the reasons set forth below, the Court hereby FINDS that there is no genuine issue of material fact with respect to which contract controls the narrow dispute between the parties over whether Iris' claims against Jackson are subject to arbitration.

Furthermore, Jackson is correct in noting that the central factual dispute between the parties appears to be G*Town's agency status. Therefore, as a threshold matter, viewing the facts in the light most favorable to Jackson, the Court will assume, without deciding, that G*Town is neither Jackson's agent nor Jackson's apparent agent for purposes of this opinion. However, whether G*Town is Jackson's agent is immaterial, and Iris is nevertheless entitled to summary judgment as a matter of law pursuant to Fed.R.Civ.P. 56(c). Under the doctrine of equitable estoppel as applied by the Fourth Circuit, a party (or his agent) need not actually sign a contract in order to be bound by the contract's arbitration clause so long as the party retains a "direct benefit" of the contract. *Schwabedissen,* 206 F.3d at 418 (internal quotations and citations omitted). As the Defendant correctly notes, "[t]he obligation and entitlement to arbitrate does not attach only to one who has personally signed the written arbitration provision. Rather, well-established common law principles dictate that in an appropriate case a nonsignatory can enforce, or be bound by, an arbitration provision within a contract executed by other parties." *Washington Square Sec., Inc. v.*

Aune, 385 F.3d 432, 435 (4th Cir. 2004) (internal quotations and citations omitted).

It is an axiomatic rule of contract law that a party may not "rely on the contract when it works to its advantage, and repudiate it when it works to its disadvantage." *Hughes Masonry Co. v. Greater Clark County Sch. Bldg. Corp.,* 659 F.2d 836, 839 (7th Cir. 1981) (internal quotations and citations omitted). Generally, the doctrine of "[e]quitable estoppel precludes a party from asserting rights he otherwise would have had against another when his own conduct renders assertion of those rights contrary to equity." *Schwabedissen,* 206 F.3d at 417–18 (internal quotations and citations omitted). Under the federal substantive law of arbitrability incorporated into the FAA, the Fourth Circuit has explicitly applied the common-law doctrine of equitable estoppel to the arbitration context:

> In the arbitration context, the doctrine recognizes that a party may be estopped from asserting that the lack of his signature on a written contract precludes enforcement of the contract's arbitration clause when he has consistently maintained that other provisions of the same contract should be enforced to benefit him. *To allow a [party] to claim the benefit of the contract and simultaneously avoid its burdens would both disregard equity and contravene the purpose underlying the enactment of the [FAA].*

Id. at 418 (internal quotations and citations omitted) (emphasis added). In the specific situation where, as in this case, a signatory seeks to enforce an arbitration agreement against a non-signatory, the doctrine estops the non-signatory from claiming that he is not bound to the arbitration agreement when he receives a "direct benefit" from a contract containing an arbitration clause. *Id.* (internal quotations and citations omitted); *see also Am. Bankers Ins. Group, v. Long,* 453 F.3d 623, 628 (4th Cir.2006); *R.J. Griffin,* 384 F.3d at 162; *Am. Bureau of Shipping v. Tencara Shipyard S.P.A.,* 170 F.3d 349, 353 (2d Cir.1999) (holding that non-signatory was estopped from denying applicability of arbitration clause where nonsignatory received "direct benefits" from contract including lowered insurance rates and the ability to sail under the French flag).

For example, in *Schwabedissen,* International Paper bought an industrial saw from Wood Systems, a distributor. 206 F.3d at 414. The saw was manufactured by Schwabedissen pursuant to a contract between Wood Systems and Schwabedissen containing an arbitration clause. *Id.* International Paper was not a signatory to the contract. *Id.* The industrial saw was defective, and International Paper sued Schwabedissen for breach of the terms and warranties of the contract. *Id.* The Fourth Circuit found that International Paper was equitably estopped from denying the applicability of the arbitration clause to its claims against Schwabedissen because International Paper could not both accept the contract's benefits (the warranty provisions) and, at the same time, reject the contract's burdens (the arbitration provisions). *Id.* at 416–19.

In this case, just like International Paper in *Schwabedissen,* Jackson seeks to have his cake and eat it too. Iris paid G*Town $550,000 pursuant to the G*Town Contract. No other sums were paid by Iris. G*Town then paid $450,000 to ATA, Jackson's undisputed agent. ATA then paid $150,000 to Jackson and $75,000 to Elliot. Jackson concedes that he retained the $150,000 payment. The $150,000 ultimately retained by Jackson was a "direct benefit" of the G*Town Contract executed by Iris and G*town. Pursuant to the test outlined by the Fourth Circuit, Jackson is therefore equitably estopped from denying the applicability of the arbitration clause, even though, allegedly, neither he nor his agents signed the G*Town Contract. *Schwabedissen,* 206 F.3d at 418. Iris' $150,000 payment to Jackson, albeit indirect, was intended to be partial consideration for his performance in Africa pursuant to the G*Town Contract. It would be inequitable to permit Jackson to retain the direct benefits of the G*Town Contract (the $150,000 paid by Iris) while, at the same time, permitting him to deny the contract's burdens (the arbitration provision).

Furthermore, Jackson did not retain the $150,000 as a mere "third-party beneficiary" of the G*Town Contract. Rather, the only possible justification for Jackson's retention of the $150,000 is that he is entitled to damages for Iris' alleged breach of the G*Town Contract pursuant to the contract's liquidated damages provision. Jackson's claim to the $150,000 is therefore certainly a "direct," rather than indirect, benefit of the G*Town Contract. Just like International Paper in *Schwabedissen,* Jackson cannot simply choose to enforce favorable provisions of the G*Town Contract (the liquidated damages provision) and, at the same time, avoid the unfavorable provisions (the arbitration provision). Although Jackson may, in fact, be entitled to retain the $150,000 as a "kill fee" or otherwise pursuant to the liquidated damages provision of the G*Town Contract, the merits of his claim to the $150,000 are of no consequence to this proceeding and shall be decided by an arbitrator. All that matters for purposes of the proceeding before this Court is that Jackson implicitly asserts a claim to $150,000 based on a provision of the G*Town Contract that "directly benefits" him, and that he is therefore subject to the contract's arbitration provision as well.

Jackson nevertheless argues that, once the deal fell through, he was entitled to retain the $150,000 Iris paid him as a "kill fee" pursuant *not* to the G*Town Contract but, rather, pursuant to a *subsequent* contract between Iris and Jackson ("Draft Contract") that did *not* contain an arbitration provision. (Pl.'s Mem. 6–7.) Indeed, Jackson correctly identifies the only factual dispute between the parties relevant to this Court's equitable estoppel inquiry: whether Iris paid the $150,000 pursuant to the G*Town Contract or the Draft Contract. Unfortunately for Jackson, *the Draft Contract was never executed by the parties,* and therefore cannot serve as the basis for Jackson's claim to the $150,000. In essence, Jackson argues that he may retain the funds paid by Iris pursuant to terms of a contract that were never agreed upon. Despite the many opportunities the Court has given Jackson to provide support for this argument, he cites no precedent for such an extraordinary proposition, and this Court is aware of none. In addition, even if the Draft Contract was executed, pursuant to its terms, Jackson would be entitled to liquidated damages (his supposed "kill fee") only if Iris "defaults in performing its obligations under [the Draft Contract]." (Pl.'s Mem. Ex. 1D ¶¶ 3, 16.) This Court is unable to fathom how Iris can breach the terms of a contract that was never executed.

Furthermore, the facts and circumstances surrounding the payment of $150,000 to Jackson clearly indicate that the funds were intended as payment pursuant to the G*Town Contract and not pursuant to the Draft Contract. First, it is undisputed that the funds ultimately received by Jackson and ATA, Jackson's agent, passed through G*Town. However, because Jackson vehemently denies that G*Town was involved in any way with subsequent negotiations over the Draft Contract, the funds must have been originally paid pursuant to the G*Town Contract. Second, the timing of the various transactions establishes that the money changed hands pursuant to the original G*Town Contract. G*Town and Iris entered into the G*Town Contract on February 22, 2006. G*Town paid ATA on May 24, 2006, and June 8, 2006. ATA paid Jackson $150,000 on June 28, 2006. The original concert date was July 15, 2006. It was not until July 18, 2006, that Violator even suggested the "do over of the Gabon date" that was contemplated in the Draft Contracts. (Def.'s Opp. Ex. 7.) In fact, the Draft Contracts specifying an August 12, 2006, concert date were dated July 24, 2006–a full month after Jackson was paid. This Court cannot fathom how Iris could have paid Jackson an "advance" on June 28, 2006, pursuant to the Draft Contract, when the circumstances necessitating that Draft Contract (Jackson's failure to perform in Africa) did not arise until July 15, 2006.

Nevertheless, various documents indicate that the parties did *contemplate* entering into an agreement by which the money Iris already paid pursuant to the G*Town Contract would be put toward the alternative August 12, 2006, concert date. For example, the Draft Contract states: "[Jackson] acknowledges that [Iris] has previously paid and shall receive a credit of $150,000 against the Compensation, leaving a sum of One Hundred Fifty Thousand and 00/100 U.S. Dollars ($150,000.00) to be paid." Similarly, a July 18, 2006, email from Violator to Arent Fox states: "50% of fee already paid shall serve as non-refundable forfeited deposit. The remaining 50% of initial payment to serve as front end for new date." (Def.'s Opp. Ex. 7.) However, this agreement was *never consummated.* Iris and Jackson never agreed to alter the original purpose of the $150,000 Iris initially paid because they never agreed on the terms of the subsequent Draft Contract. Therefore, this Court hereby FINDS that the $150,000 was paid pursuant to the original G*Town Contract, the only contract that actually was executed between the parties at the time Iris paid, and Jackson received, the funds. . . .

CONCLUSION

Viewing the facts in the light most favorable to the Plaintiff, the Court hereby FINDS that the Defendant has established that there is no genuine issue as to any material fact and that the Defendant is therefore entitled to judgment as a matter of law pursuant to Fed.R.Civ.P. 56(c). Furthermore, the Court hereby FINDS that the Plaintiff has failed to show that there is a genuine issue as to any material fact that would preclude this Court's entry of summary judgment for the Defendant holding that Iris' claims against Jackson are subject to arbitration.

Therefore, for the foregoing reasons, the Court hereby DECLARES that the claims against the Plaintiff are subject to arbitration, GRANTS summary judgment *sua sponte* for the Defendant, and DISMISSES the case without prejudice to any claims presented in arbitration.

CHAPTER THREE

ARBITRAL DUE PROCESS

1. INTRODUCTION

Arbitration is a term that applies to an almost infinite variety of procedures. There is no one standard, or even dominant, off-the-rack arbitration procedure. This is because arbitration procedure, like an initial promise to arbitrate, is a matter of private contract.[1] Sometimes contracting parties create detailed arbitration procedures in their initial agreement to arbitrate. At other times, parties may contractually incorporate a pre-existing arbitration procedure, such as the Commercial Procedures of the American Arbitration Association (see Appendix C), or the procedures of a trade association to which the contracting parties belong. However, if an arbitration agreement is silent on the procedures to be followed, then courts generally assume that the parties have delegated to the arbitrator the task of determining procedures.

Courts have grappled with the problem of determining how far a party's and/or arbitrator's control over procedure in arbitration should go, and the extent to which courts should police such proceedings for minimum due process concerns. Questions arise such as: Which elements of due process can the parties waive? Does the arbitrator have ultimate control over the proceeding, or will a proceeding that does not rise to some minimal level of due process result in a court vacating the arbitration award? If there is some due process minima that courts will impose on arbitration proceedings, of what is it comprised? Should courts require arbitration to provide a "full and fair hearing"? What are the elements of such a hearing?

Courts cannot be expected to import the entire Federal Rules of Civil Procedure into arbitration, or arbitration would lose its distinctive advantages of providing flexibility, informality, and speed. Arbitration procedures typically are less formal and contain fewer procedural protections than a full-blown trial. But how relaxed can arbitration procedures be and still accord with fundamental notions of due process? Due process concerns are particularly salient now that courts are asked to defer to arbitration for the resolution of not only contractual but also statutory disputes. Are there minimal due process norms that courts must impose to justify such delegation of authority?

Section 10 of the Federal Arbitration Act sets out four grounds on which a court may vacate an arbitral award:

1. For a variation on this theme, see Henry S. Noyes, *If You (Re)–Build It, They Will Come: Contracts to Remake the Rules of Litigation in Arbitration's Image*, 30 Harv. J. L. & Pub. Pol'y 579 (2007) (arguing that disputing parties should, by contract, make litigation rules more like arbitration).

(a) Where the award was procured by corruption, fraud, or undue means.

(b) Where there was evident partiality or corruption in the arbitrators.

(c) Where the arbitrators were guilty of misconduct in refusing to postpone the hearing, upon sufficient cause shown, or in refusing to hear evidence pertinent and material to the controversy, or in any other misbehavior by which the rights of any party have been prejudiced.

(d) Where the arbitrators exceeded their powers, or so imperfectly executed them that a mutual, final, and definite award upon the subject matter was not made.

Of the statutory grounds for vacating arbitral awards, (a), (b) and (c), are directed toward the arbitral process rather than the merits of a final arbitral award. (d) seems to address both procedural and substantive concerns. In the cases that follow, we see how courts have interpreted the four statutory grounds for vacating awards. In addition, some courts hold that the statutory grounds do not exhaust the grounds for setting aside awards, and have found an additional ground for vacating an award when the process is found to be "fundamentally unfair." Some courts have added additional factors to their scrutiny of the merits, saying for example that they should vacate awards that do not "draw their essence" from the parties' agreement or are "fundamentally irrational."

The scope of fundamental fairness, minimal due process, and judicial review in arbitration, both within the statutory framework and as judge-made common law, are explored in the materials that follow.

2. Notice, Ex Parte Hearings, and Default

Gingiss International, Inc. v. Bormet

58 F.3d 328 (7th Cir. 1995).

■ BAUER, CIRCUIT JUDGE.

Gingiss International, Inc. ("Gingiss") and H–K Formalwear Corporation ("H–K Formalwear") entered into a franchise agreement on December 18, 1984, under which H–K Formalwear was granted the right to operate a Gingiss Formalwear Center store in Industry, California. The franchise agreement contained an arbitration clause which provided that all disputes between the parties relating to the agreement would be subject to arbitration in Chicago under the Federal Arbitration Act ("FAA"), 9 U.S.C. §§ 1–16, and the Rules of the American Arbitration Association ("AAA"), unless Gingiss elected to pursue certain claims in a judicial forum. The franchise agreement also contained a California choice-of-law provision. Norman E. Bormet and Phyllis M. Bormet were officers of H–K Formalwear, and each owned one-third of the shares of the corporation. The store was managed by Mrs. Bormet's son, Howard Parks, who was also the president of H–K Formalwear and owned one-third of its shares.

Gingiss entered into a Shareholder's and Officer's Agreement with the Bormets and Parks contemporaneously with the franchise agreement. The Shareholder's and Officer's Agreement provided that the Bormets and Parks agreed to be bound by all obligations of H–K Formalwear under the franchise agreement as if each was the franchisee. The Bormets and Parks also agreed to be bound by all obligations of H–K Formalwear under a related sublease of the California store.

In December 1993, following the expiration of the franchise agreement, Gingiss initiated arbitration proceedings against H–K Formalwear, the Bormets, and Parks. Gingiss sought damages for several breaches of the franchise agreement and the sublease, including the failure to pay royalties and advertising fund contributions. Gingiss also sought damages for trademark infringement and unfair competition under the Lanham Act, 15 U.S.C. §§ 1051–1128, and its attorney's fees incurred in prosecuting an earlier unlawful detainer action against H–K Formalwear in California state court.

Gingiss' attorney sent a copy of Gingiss' arbitration demand by regular mail to the Bormets at a post office box in Old Fort, North Carolina. This was the same address to which Gingiss had previously sent correspondence to the Bormets, and the Bormets had regularly replied. The AAA sent a letter by regular mail to the same address on December 30, 1993, notifying the Bormets of the arbitration proceeding. The AAA sent three additional letters concerning the arbitration proceeding by regular mail to the Bormets at this address in January 1994. Neither Gingiss' arbitration demand nor any of the AAA's letters was ever returned as undelivered.

An arbitration hearing was held on March 30, 1994, at the AAA's offices in Chicago. The Bormets and Parks did not appear at the hearing. Gingiss, nonetheless, presented evidence in support of its claims pursuant to the AAA's Commercial Arbitration Rule 30. On April 14, 1994, the arbitrator awarded Gingiss $60,629.25 against H–K Formalwear, the Bormets, and Parks jointly and severally. This award remains unsatisfied. The arbitrator awarded Gingiss an additional $57,142.44 against H–K Formalwear and Parks.

Gingiss then filed this application in the district court to confirm the arbitration award rendered against the Bormets. 9 U.S.C. § 9. Jurisdiction was premised upon diversity of citizenship. The Bormets petitioned to vacate the award on several grounds. 9 U.S.C. § 10(a). The district court granted Gingiss' motion for summary judgment and confirmed the award.

. . . The Bormets contend that the arbitration award should be vacated because they did not receive proper notice of the arbitration proceedings. We have repeatedly held that 9 U.S.C. § 10(a) provides the exclusive grounds for setting aside an arbitration award under the FAA. E.g., Baravati v. Josephthal, Lyon & Ross, Inc., 28 F.3d 704, 706 (7th Cir. 1994); Eljer, 14 F.3d at 1256; Moseley, Hallgarten, Estabrook & Weeden, Inc. v.

Ellis, 849 F.2d 264, 267 (7th Cir. 1988) (collecting cases). Inadequate notice is not one of these grounds, and the Bormets' claim therefore fails.

To the extent that the Bormets are asserting that the arbitrator committed misconduct by failing to notify them of the arbitration, 9 U.S.C. § 10(a)(3), their argument is without merit. Under the AAA's Commercial Arbitration Rule 40, notice "may be served on a party by mail addressed to the party or its representative at the last known address." Gingiss sent a copy of its arbitration demand by regular mail to the Bormets at their last known address, a post office box in Old Fort, North Carolina, and the AAA sent four letters by regular mail to the Bormets at this address. None of these notices was ever returned as undelivered. The Bormets nevertheless claim that they did not receive any of these notices.

The Bormets had no right under the franchise agreement to receive actual notice of the arbitration. Rule 40 does not require that notice be served by certified or registered mail. Although the Bormets point out that both Illinois and California state law require notice by registered mail or personal service, 710 ILCS 5/5(a); Cal. Code Civ.Proc. § 1282.2(a)(1), these laws are inapplicable. The parties expressly agreed in the arbitration clause that the AAA's Rules would govern in the arbitration proceeding. See Volt Info. Sciences, Inc. v. Board of Trustees of Leland Stanford Junior Univ., 489 U.S. 468, 479, 109 S.Ct. 1248, 1256, 103 L.Ed.2d 488 (1989) (the parties may specify by contract the rules under which arbitration will be conducted). The Bormets' reliance on section eighteen of the franchise agreement, which provided that "[a]ll written notices permitted or required to be delivered by the provisions of this Agreement" shall be delivered by hand or by registered or certified mail, is also misplaced. "[A] document should be read to give effect to all its provisions and to render them consistent with each other." Mastrobuono v. Shearson Lehman Hutton, Inc., 514 U.S. 52, 115 S.Ct. 1212, 1219, 131 L.Ed.2d 76 (1995). Section eighteen, by its terms, applied only to notices which were required to be sent under the franchise agreement, such as default or termination notices. The arbitration clause, which is contained in section sixteen of the agreement, governed the notice procedures in the arbitration.

AFFIRMED.

* * *

Amalgamated Cotton Garment & Allied Industries Fund v. J.B.C. Company of Madera, Inc.

608 F.Supp. 158 (W.D.Pa. 1984).

■ Mansmann, District Judge.

Plaintiff Amalgamated Cotton Garment & Allied Industries Fund (the "Fund") brought this action to recover contributions allegedly due the Fund on behalf of the employees of Campo Slacks, Inc. ("Campo Slacks") and J & E Sportswear, Inc. ("J & E Sportswear"). The Fund seeks to recover these contributions from Defendants J.B.C. Company of Madera, Inc. ("J.B.C."), Joseph Campolong, Betty Campolong and David Campolong, all of whom are allegedly jointly and severally liable for said contributions. The case was tried before this Court nonjury. We hereby make the following findings of fact and conclusions of law pursuant to Fed.R.Civ.P. 52(a):

FINDINGS OF FACT

The Fund is an "employee benefit plan" within the meaning of § 3(3) of the Employee Retirement Security Act of 1974, as amended ("ERISA"), 29 U.S.C. § 1002(3). [Plaintiffs allege that the Defendants were contractually obligated, pursuant to several collective bargaining agreements, to contribute to the fund. Plaintiffs allege that Defendants contributed approximately $70,000 less than they were supposed to.] . . .

In the meantime, the Fund, pursuant to the collective bargaining agreements, initiated several arbitration proceedings against Joseph Campolong and J.B.C., as "alter egos" of Campo Slacks and J & E Sportswear, to recover delinquent contributions. The arbitrator found that due notice was given to the parties for each proceeding yet neither Mr. Campolong nor J.B.C. entered an appearance at any of the arbitration hearings.[3]

The arbitrator issued four arbitration awards in which he found Joseph Campolong and J.B.C. jointly and severally liable for the delinquent contributions. Specifically, the arbitrator found as a factual matter that Joseph Campolong, J.B.C., Campo Slacks and J & E Sportswear constitute a single joint enterprise.[4]

Joseph Campolong and J.B.C. did not move to vacate or to modify any of the arbitration awards until filing a counterclaim to this action more than a year after the fourth arbitration decision.

Joseph Campolong and J.B.C. have failed and refused to pay the amount of the delinquency.

The Fund brought the present action to confirm the arbitration awards . . . Defendants have counterclaimed to vacate the arbitration awards. In addition, at trial, the three individual Defendants orally moved for dismissal of the case against them. . . .

[W]e cannot enforce an arbitration award where the evidence does not establish that the parties did in fact receive proper notice and the opportunity to be present at the arbitration proceeding. In this regard, it is axiomatic that all parties to an arbitration hearing must be given an opportunity to be heard, which implies the right to receive notice of the hearing. See Ryan–Walsh Stevedoring Co. v. General Longshore Workers

3. The evidence at trial showed that for each arbitration proceeding, a notice of intention to arbitrate was sent by certified mail to Joseph Campolong and J.B.C. In every instance, the certified mail was marked "unclaimed" and returned to the Fund.

4. The evidence showed that upon the issuance of each arbitration award, the Fund mailed a copy of the award to Joseph Campolong and J.B.C. by certified mail. Each arbitration award, as with the notices of intention to arbitrate, was returned unclaimed.

Union, Local No. 3000, 509 F.Supp. 463, 467 (E.D.La. 1981); Wright–Bernet, Inc. v. Amalgamated Local Union No. 41, 501 F.Supp. 72, 74 (S.D.Ohio 1980). . . .

In Local 149, Boot and Shoe Workers Union v. Faith Shoe Co. [201 F.Supp. 234 (M.D.Pa. 1962)], the court, in an action to enforce an arbitration award, examined the question of whether an ex parte arbitration award was void and unenforceable. The court essentially held that an ex parte award was enforceable if the other side received notice of the time and place of the hearing but did not request an adjournment or otherwise object. Since the court was considering the matter on a Fed.R.Civ.P. 12(b) Motion to Dismiss, the court took the allegations of the Complaint as stating the facts. The Complaint alleged that formal notice of the hearing had been given to Defendant and Defendant's counsel. The Complaint further alleged that on the day of the hearing, Defendant's counsel was notified again of the arbitration hearing. Upon being informed by Defendant's counsel that Defendant would not appear or be represented at the hearing, the other party advised that the hearing would proceed without representation by the Defendant. The court therefore concluded that the absent party had waived its right to be present and heard.

In the instant case, we cannot conclude that Joseph Campolong and J.B.C. waived their right to be present and heard at the arbitration hearings since the evidence at trial did not establish that Mr. Campolong and J.B.C. received notice of the arbitration proceedings. In this regard, there is no evidence that personal service was made ~~or~~ that the Fund telephonically contacted Defendants or their counsel regarding the arbitration proceedings. Moreover, the certified notices sent to Mr. Campolong and J.B.C. were never claimed and were therefore returned to the Fund.[16]

Since the evidence does not show that the absent parties received notice of the arbitration hearings, we cannot find that they waived their right to be present. Therefore, we cannot enforce the ex parte arbitration awards as requested by the Fund . . .

* * *

Questions

Contrast *Gingiss* with Choice Hotels Int'l, Inc. v. SM Prop. Mgmt., LLC, 519 F.3d 200 (4th Cir. 2008). As in *Gingiss*, the arbitration clause was embedded in a larger franchise agreement. The arbitration clause incorporated AAA rules, but the franchise agreement contained a separate notice provision that read:

> All notices required or permitted under this Agreement must be in writing, must be personally delivered or mailed by registered or certi-

16. We note in this regard that the certified notices were not marked "refused" as they could have been if Defendants had received them but refused to accept them. Rather, they were marked "unclaimed."

> fied mail, return receipt requested, or by a nationally recognized courier service . . . to you at the Designated Representative's address.

When a dispute arose, one party provided notice that complied with the AAA rules but not with the more-stringent notice provision in the franchise agreement. The dispute was arbitrated with only one party attending. The Fourth Circuit held that the notice provision in the franchise agreement controlled, and vacated the arbitral award. The court squarely disagreed with *Gingiss*:

> In support of its position that the district court committed reversible error by vacating the Arbitration Award, Franchisor relies heavily upon the Seventh Circuit's decision in Gingiss Int'l, Inc. v. Bormet, 58 F.3d 328 (7th Cir. 1995). The facts of *Gingiss* are, in certain respects, analogous to those of the present appeal . . .
>
> The Seventh Circuit's reading of the franchise agreement at issue in *Gingiss* and Franchisor's reading of the Franchise Agreement at issue in the present appeal disregard the plain and unambiguous language of those agreements. With respect to the case at hand, Section 15 unambiguously provides that "*All notices required or permitted under this Agreement* must be in writing, must be personally delivered or mailed by registered or certified mail, return receipt requested, or by a nationally recognized courier service to . . . [Franchisees] at the Designated Representative's address." (J.A. 15) (emphasis added). All means all. While the Arbitration Clause sets forth the crux of the arbitration terms of the Franchise Agreement, including that any arbitration would be governed by the Commercial Arbitration Rules of the AAA, the Arbitration Clause does not contain language otherwise trumping the all encompassing notice-to-the-properly-designated-representative language of Section 15. The logic of the district court's vacature of the Arbitration Award is even more apparent when one considers that AAA Commercial Rule R–1 provides that the Commercial Rules of AAA apply whenever the parties provide for arbitration by the AAA, but that the "parties, by written agreement, may vary the procedures set forth in these rules."

How does the reasoning in *Choice Hotels International* differ from that in *Amalgamated Cotton Garment & Allied Industries Fund*?

1. Is there a right to notice of arbitral proceedings? Or is notice a purely contractual matter?

2. If an arbitration agreement is silent on the question of notice, should a court imply a notice requirement? What should the implied notice requirement be? Should it require actual notice, or should constructive notice by mail or by publication be sufficient?

3. If an arbitration agreement permits arbitration hearings to be scheduled with no notice given to one of the contracting parties, and if an arbitration is then held to which that party was not notified, is there any basis for a court to vacate the award?

4. Do the standards for due process in arbitration vary depending upon whether the FAA, state arbitration statutes, or Section 301 of the LMRA govern the proceedings?

* * *

Waterspring, S.A. v. Trans Marketing Houston Inc.

717 F.Supp. 181 (S.D.N.Y. 1989).

■ LEISURE, DISTRICT JUDGE:

Waterspring, S.A. ("Waterspring," "Owner," or "petitioner"), brought this petition, as Owner of the M.T. OCEANIA GLORY, for an order pursuant to Section 4 of Title 9, United States Code, compelling respondent, Trans Marketing Houston, Inc. ("TMHI," "Charterer," or "Owner"), as Charterer to proceed to arbitration before a panel comprised of Stephen H. Busch ("Busch"), Manfred W. Arnold ("Arnold") and Hammond L. Cederholm ("Cederholm"), in accordance with the terms and conditions of a certain contract of charter party allegedly entered into between petitioner and respondent. TMHI has cross-moved to vacate the partial final arbitration award dated December 5, 1988.

FACTUAL BACKGROUND

A charter party agreement for the M/V COUNTESS, owned by Astor Marine S.A. and operated by Adriatic Tankers Shipping Company ("Adriatic"), was fixed on July 6, 1988 (the "Charter"). The fixture telex confirming the agreement incorporated the terms of a standard form charter party commonly know as the Asbatankvoy form. The fixture telex also provided for arbitration in New York. The COUNTESS became delayed and the Charter was amended to change the vessel to the OCEANIA GLORY, owned by Waterspring, and operated by Adriatic. The amendment was confirmed by telex. Affidavit of Glen T. Oxton, Esq., sworn to on February 15, 1989 ("Oxton Affidavit"), Exhibit 37.

The OCEANIA GLORY carried cargoes for TMHI from Houston to Santo Tomas, Guatemala and Guayaquil, Ecuador, pursuant to the Charter. Discharging in Guayaquil was completed on September 8, 1988. On September 20, 1988, the Owner submitted an invoice for demurrage in the amount of $58,122. Oxton Affidavit, Exhibit 3. Subsequently, Charterer paid $88,754.84 to Owner and withheld payment of the balance of $194,367 due to the alleged wrongful presentation of cargo documents by Owner. Oxton Affidavit, Exhibit 4.

As noted, the Charter is under the Asbatankvoy form, which provides for arbitration. Owner demanded arbitration, requested an immediate partial final award for freight and demurrage and appointed its arbitrator by a letter to Charterer sent by facsimile and mail on October 12, 1988. Oxton Affidavit, Exhibit 6. On October 25, 1988, Charterer requested time to discuss the merits of the dispute with its broker. Affidavit of Richard M. Ziccardi, Esq., sworn to on March 3, 1989 ("Ziccardi Affidavit"), Exhibit 5.

On November 2, 1988, Owner, asserting that Charterer failed to appoint its arbitrator within 20 days as provided in Clause 24 of the Charter, appointed Manfred Arnold on Charterer's behalf. Oxton Affidavit, Exhibit 9. On November 10, 1988 Cederholm and Arnold appointed Busch as the third arbitrator and set the first hearing date for November 23, 1988. Oxton Affidavit, Exhibit 10.

On or about November 10, 1988, TMHI was advised by petitioner's counsel that an arbitration hearing had been scheduled for November 23, 1988 in New York City. Ziccardi Affidavit, Exhibit 9. TMHI retained counsel, who wrote to the arbitration panel on November 16, 1988, to request an adjournment. Ziccardi Affidavit, Exhibit 12. This counsel requested an extension of time from the panel on the grounds that the scheduled arbitration hearing was for the Wednesday before Thanksgiving making travel arrangements impossible and that retained counsel was previously scheduled to be in California on that day. This request was initially refused by the arbitration panel in New York, which then tied further consideration of such request to a demand for full security of the petitioner's claim. On November 22, 1988, Charterer attempted to appoint its arbitrator, Richard E. Repetto.

On December 5, 1988, the arbitration panel granted Waterspring a partial final arbitration award of $100,000. TMHI paid $100,000 to Waterspring. TMHI contends that this payment was based upon its own good faith determination that such amount was due and owing. Allegedly, the decision to pay this amount was made in advance of any knowledge on the part of TMHI of the contents of the partial final award dated December 5, 1988. Reply Memorandum of Law in Support of Counter–Motion to Vacate Partial Final Award at 4. Owner asserts it is still owed freight and demurrage aggregating $94,367.10 plus interest, costs and attorneys' fees.

DISCUSSION

MOTION TO COMPEL ARBITRATION

Petitioner presently seeks an order pursuant to Section 4 of Title 9, United States Code, compelling respondent, TMHI to proceed to arbitration before a panel comprised of Stephen H. Busch, Manfred W. Arnold and Hammond L. Cederholm, in accordance with the terms and conditions of the Charter allegedly entered into between petitioner and respondent. Respondent opposes the motion on various grounds.

Section 4 of the Federal Arbitration Act, 9 U.S.C. § 4 provides, inter alia:

> A party aggrieved by the alleged failure, neglect, or refusal of another to arbitrate under a written agreement for arbitration may petition any United States district court ... for an order directing that such arbitration proceed in the manner provided for in such agreement ...

Clause 24 of the charter party at issue, provides in pertinent part as follows:

> Either party hereto may call for such arbitration by service upon any officer of the other, wherever he may be found, of a written notice specifying the name and address of the arbitrator chosen by the first moving party and a brief description of the disputes or differences which such party desires to put to arbitration. If the other party shall not, by notice served upon an officer of the first moving party within twenty days of the service of such notice, appoint its arbitrator to arbitrate the dispute or differences specified, then the first moving party shall have the right without further notice to appoint a second arbitrator, who shall be a disinterested person with precisely the same force and effect as if said second arbitrator has been appointed by the other party. In the event that the two arbitrators fail to appoint a third arbitrator within twenty days of the appointment of the second arbitrator, either arbitrator may apply to a Judge of any court of maritime jurisdiction in the city above-mentioned for the appointment of a third arbitrator, and the appointment of such arbitrator by such Judge on such application shall have precisely the same force and effect as if such arbitrator had been appointed by the two arbitrators. . . .

Oxton Affidavit, Exhibit 1.

TMHI urges that before seeking relief from this Court under the Arbitration Act, petitioner must exhaust its remedies under the arbitration agreement by proceeding with the arbitration to a conclusion, even though TMHI does not participate. Charterer contends that Waterspring is not a party aggrieved by a failure, neglect or refusal to arbitrate within the meaning of § 4 of the Act as it can proceed with an ex parte arbitration.

Petitioner, on the other hand, contends that before arbitration can continue, the Court must determine whether or not Waterspring is a party to the arbitration agreement, and whether the panel is properly constituted. It points out that, if it continues to go through with the arbitration, it may prove to be a nullity, and urges that this makes it an aggrieved party entitled to relief under the Act.

Section 4 of the Arbitration Act permits "a party aggrieved by the alleged failure, neglect, or refusal of another to arbitrate" under a written arbitration agreement to petition the court to compel arbitration. The basic question here is whether or not the petitioner is a party who is aggrieved by a failure to arbitrate. Unless it is, it cannot maintain this proceeding.

The arbitration agreement at issue has a self-executing mechanism. It provides that, in the event the opposing party fails to appoint its arbitrator within 20 days, the moving party may then appoint a disinterested person as the second arbitrator. The two arbitrators are then to select a third arbitrator. Thus, in the event of failure of the opposing party to appoint an arbitrator the agreement entered into by the parties provides its own remedies. If this arbitration clause is properly invoked, a duly constituted panel is formed regardless of respondent's actions and without the need to resort to Federal Court intervention. Indeed, the very purpose of such a self-executing mechanism in an arbitration clause is to avoid the time and expense of Federal Court motion practice. The case at bar is before this

Court because petitioner voluntarily suspended the ex parte arbitration in order to seek an order from this Court which, in essence, would represent a retroactive approval of petitioner's actions thus far, as well as sanction future acts by the arbitrators. Such a declaratory judgment is not provided for in Title 9 of the United States Code. A/S Ganger Rolf v. Zeeland Transportation Ltd., 191 F.Supp. 359, 362–63 (S.D.N.Y. 1961).

It is true that the issue of whether or not Waterspring was in fact a party to this charter and bound by the arbitration clause is not one for the arbitrators and must be passed upon by the court at some time. See, e.g., Kulukundis Shipping Co. S/A v. Amtorg Trading Corp., 126 F.2d 978 (2d Cir. 1942); A/S Ganger Rolf, supra. But it does not necessarily follow that this issue must be determined prior to the conclusion of the arbitration proceeding. An ex parte arbitration under the terms of an arbitration clause like the one in the case at bar is valid and an award made thereunder is enforceable against a party bound by the clause. See, e.g., Corallo v. Merrick Central Carburetor, 733 F.2d 248 (2d Cir. 1984); Standard Magnesium Corp. v. Fuchs, 251 F.2d 455 (10th Cir. 1957); A/S Ganger Rolf, supra.

Such an ex parte arbitration involves risks both to the moving party and to the party which did not appoint its own arbitrator. If the assertion of the petitioner that the panel is properly constituted and that they are parties to the agreement is unfounded petitioner may find that the arbitration was in fact a useless gesture and it was put to unnecessary expense. But it is hardly in a position to complain if its unfounded assertion leads to that result.

On the other hand, if petitioner's assertions turn out to be well-founded and the panel is properly constituted, TMHI is in the position, by its own default, of being precluded from contesting the merits. It may not complain that it has not been heard on the merits before the arbitrators since it waived the right to do so, granted to it by the arbitration agreement by which it bound itself.

The Court notes that the object of the Arbitration Act contemplates only the enforcement of the arbitration agreement made by the parties themselves in the manner they themselves provide. "Having designed their own remedy for recalcitrance [petitioner] cannot, over respondent's objection, ignore that remedy and pursue another." A/S Ganger, supra, 191 F.Supp. at 362.

What petitioner[ ] really want[s] here is a judgment declaring [the parties bound by the arbitration clause] in advance of arbitration as insurance against the possibility that [it] may be mistaken in [its] assertion that it is so bound. It does not seem to me that Sections 4, 5 and 6 of the Act contemplate such a declaratory judgment or authorize the Court to render it. These sections are designed only to insure that the parties proceed in the manner provided by the arbitration agreement which they themselves fashioned. Id. at 362–63.

Since the contract permitted petitioner to proceed with the arbitration without respondent's cooperation, petitioner is not a "party aggrieved" and 9 U.S.C. § 4 does not apply. A/S Ganger Rolf, supra, 191 F.Supp. 362–363; Cf. Aaacon Auto Transport, Inc. v. Barnes, 603 F.Supp. 1347, 1349 (S.D.N.Y. 1985) (party cannot compel arbitration where other side had demanded arbitration in another forum); Koreska v. Perry–Sherwood Corp., 253 F.Supp. 830, 832 (S.D.N.Y. 1965) (court cannot compel arbitration anywhere when parties have already submitted to arbitration in accordance with terms of contract), aff'd, 360 F.2d 212 (2d Cir. 1966) (mem.).

Accordingly, petitioner's motion to compel the continuation of the arbitration before the present panel is denied . . .

* * *

Questions

1. In *Totem Marine Tug & Barge, Inc. v. North American Towing, Inc.*, 607 F.2d 649 (5th Cir. 1979), an arbitration panel awarded the prevailing party an item of damages that had not been specifically requested. To determine the amount to award for the unrequested item, the arbitrators telephoned the counsel for the prevailing party after the hearing had been closed, and asked that a figure be supplied. The other side was neither notified of the call nor given an opportunity to contest the figure. The court found that this ex parte communication violated the Commercial Arbitration Rules of the American Arbitration Association, which require that "(a)ll evidence shall be taken in the presence of all the parties, except where any of the parties is absent, in default, or has waived his right to be present." The court further found that by receiving the ex parte communication, the arbitrators had engaged in prejudicial arbitral misconduct under Section 10(c) of the FAA. It vacated the award without prejudice so that it could be resubmitted to a new arbitration panel. Can this case be distinguished from *Waterspring v. Trans Marketing Houston Inc.*?

2. Is it ever appropriate for an arbitration to proceed *ex parte* if there is no specific self-executing mechanism in the agreement? Who should make such determination? At what stage in the proceeding?

* * *

3. Right to an Evidentiary Hearing

Federal Deposit Insurance Corporation v. Air Florida System, Inc.

822 F.2d 833 (9th Cir. 1987).

■ Fletcher, Circuit Judge.

The FDIC appeals a judgment refusing to rescind its contract with Air Florida and enforcing an arbitration award in Air Florida's favor. We reverse in part, vacate in part, and remand.

BACKGROUND

In its capacity as receiver of the United States National Bank, the FDIC became a major creditor of the Westgate–California Corporation ("Westgate"). As such, the FDIC was entitled to a large block of Westgate stock once Westgate's reorganization in bankruptcy was completed. In 1980, the FDIC sold its Westgate interests to Air Florida for $15.4 million. As part of the agreement, Air Florida promised to make a general public offer for outstanding Westgate common shares at no less than the price it paid the FDIC. If Air Florida acquired more than 80% of Westgate's common stock, and if it paid more per share to tender-offerees than the FDIC received, the FDIC was entitled to additional compensation to afford it the same price per share paid the tender-offerees.

Air Florida purchased the Westgate stock in order to acquire Air California, a Westgate controlled corporation. After Air Florida purchased the FDIC's interest in Westgate, however, Westgate's bankruptcy trustees arranged, and the district court approved, the sale of Air California to a third party for $61.5 million. The sale caused a substantial increase in the trading price of outstanding shares of Westgate common stock. Air Florida had paid approximately $18 per share for the stock, but after Air California's sale, Westgate shares traded between $21 and $26.50 per share.

In February 1982, Air Florida informed the FDIC that it had decided not to make a tender offer. On April 1, 1982, Westgate's directors announced that Westgate would be liquidated with shareholders receiving $28.25 per share of common stock.[1] On April 30, the FDIC brought suit against Air Florida seeking rescission and restitution because Air Florida had failed to make the tender offer. In defense, Air Florida denied that it had a contractual duty to make an offer at a price exceeding the price paid to the FDIC and argued that the rise in Westgate's market price excused its tender offer obligation. The FDIC asserted that Air Florida was required to make an offer reasonably calculated to acquire the shares, no matter what the market price.

Air Florida counterclaimed for $2 million it alleged was owing under a separate provision in the contract that required adjustment of the purchase price of the stock upon sale of a cannery owned by Westgate. After a bench trial, the district court adopted Air Florida's interpretation of the contract, holding that Air Florida had not breached its agreement with FDIC. FDIC v. Air Florida Sys., Inc., No. 85–0525–N(H) (S.D.Cal. Jan. 6, 1983) (Findings of Fact and Conclusions of Law). Having rejected the FDIC's rescission claim, the district court held that the contract, including the cannery adjustment provision, remained in effect. The amount of the adjustment

1. The liquidating dividend was paid on May 3, 1982. Air Florida realized a gain of more than $10 per share over the price paid to the FDIC, a $3.86 million profit on its Westgate common shares.

was left open until "determined by the parties, the parties' designated accountants or an independent accountant pursuant to the arbitration procedures set forth in ... the [purchase] Agreement." Id. at 9.

When neither the parties nor their accountants could reach an agreement on the cannery adjustment, the contractual arbitration process was invoked. Following the arbitration, which resulted in a $1,486,000 adjustment in favor of Air Florida, the FDIC moved to vacate the award because of the arbitrator's failure to hold an oral hearing. The district court held that "the arbitrator's election to resolve the question ... based on written submissions alone, did not deny the FDIC a fundamentally fair hearing." FDIC v. Air Florida, No. 82–0525–N(I) (C.D.Cal. July 10 1984) (unpublished order). The court granted Air Florida's cross-motion to enter the arbitration award as part of the judgment and allowed prejudgment interest on the award....

Right to an Oral Hearing

FDIC asserts that the arbitrator's refusal to hold an oral hearing on the issue of contractual intent violated its rights and rendered the arbitration unenforceable. The arbitrator, who was an accountant, did meet with the FDIC and Air Florida accountants, but he then refused the FDIC's request to hold a further evidentiary hearing. Rather, he requested the parties to submit in written form the materials they wished to have considered. In support of its interpretation of the cannery adjustment provision, FDIC submitted the affidavit of the attorney who negotiated the Agreement for the FDIC. The FDIC concedes that it could have submitted additional written documentation had it chosen to do so.

There is no disagreement that the federal Arbitration Act, 9 U.S.C. §§ 1–14 governs this dispute. Where the Act applies, it "provides the exclusive grounds for challenging an arbitration award within its purview." Lafarge Conseils et Etudes, S.A. v. Kaiser Cement & Gypsum Corp., 791 F.2d 1334, 1338 (9th Cir. 1986). Section 10 of the Act sets forth the circumstances under which a district court may vacate an arbitration award. 9 U.S.C. § 10. The FDIC relies on section 10(c) to support its claim of procedural deficiency. Section 10(c) permits vacation of an award

> [w]here the arbitrators were guilty of misconduct in refusing to postpone the hearing, upon sufficient cause shown, or in refusing to hear evidence pertinent and material to the controversy; or of any other misbehavior by which the rights of any party have been prejudiced.

9 U.S.C. § 10(c).

While section 10(c) assumes that the parties to an arbitration will be afforded a hearing, neither in this section nor anywhere else in the Act are hearing procedures, much less oral hearing procedures, explicitly provided for. Certainly the parties may agree upon appropriate procedures by contract, but, where they do not, procedural matters "become part of the bundle of issues committed to decisions by the arbitrator." Sheet Metal Workers Int'l Ass'n, Local 420 v. Kinney Air Conditioning Co., 756 F.2d 742, 744 (9th Cir. 1985). An arbitration award should not be vacated on procedural grounds unless the procedure employed was a "sham, substantially inadequate or substantially unavailable." Harris v. Chemical Leaman Tank Lines, 437 F.2d 167, 171 (5th Cir.1971), quoted in Dogherra v.

Safeway Stores, Inc., 679 F.2d 1293, 1296 (9th Cir.), cert. denied, 459 U.S. 990, 103 S.Ct. 346, 74 L.Ed.2d 386 (1982). So long as the hearing provided is "full and fair," a procedural attack must fail. Coast Trading Co. v. Pacific Molasses Co., 681 F.2d 1195, 1198 (9th Cir. 1982). Applying section 10(c), a hearing is full and fair unless the arbitrator (1) despite a showing of cause, refuses a postponement; (2) refuses to hear pertinent and material evidence; or (3) engages in misbehavior that prejudices the rights of a party. 9 U.S.C. § 10(c). The FDIC did not request a postponement and there is no allegation that the arbitrator refused to consider evidence the FDIC submitted. Finally, the failure to hold an oral hearing cannot be deemed misbehavior that prejudiced the FDIC's rights because the FDIC has not shown that its evidence was not amenable to presentation in written form. Admittedly, a "paper hearing" often will be an inadequate means to determine the facts upon which an arbitration decision must rely. In this case, however, the nature of the decision to be made leads us to conclude that the "paper hearing" was adequate.[9] As the district court noted:

> [W]hat the parties bargained for was not a quasi-judicial proceeding conducted by lawyers, but [rather] the professional opinion of an independent accountant on an accounting issue—the value of a business. Accountants derive their calculations not from evidentiary hearings, but from working papers and discussions with other accountants. Thus, it was predictable that the instant arbitrator would base his decision on this information. Nothing in the parties' contractual sequential valuation process manifests an intent to require an oral evidentiary hearing. Had the parties intended the arbitration to resolve primarily legal issues through evidentiary hearings, they surely would have agreed to use a lawyer, not an accountant, as the arbitrator, or declared arbitration rules as governing. Instead the parties instructed an accountant to resolve the dispute ..., leaving the procedure to the arbitrator's sound discretion.

FDIC v. Air Florida, No. 82–0525–N(I) at 8–9 (July 10, 1984) (unpublished order).

* * *

Casualty Indemnity Exchange v. Yother

439 So.2d 77 (Ala. 1983).

■ SHORES, JUSTICE.

This case grew out of the following facts:

In May 1982, Jack Yother, d/b/a Mickey Motors, purchased an automobile policy of insurance from Casualty Indemnity Exchange (CIE), covering

9. The FDIC argues also that it had a due process right to an oral hearing. The arbitration involved here was private, not state, action; it was conducted pursuant to contract by a private arbitrator. Although Congress, in the exercise of its commerce power, has provided for some governmental regulation of private arbitration agreements, we do not find in private arbitration proceedings the state action requisite for a constitutional due process claim.

Yother's 1979 International Harvester tractor-truck. During the pre-dawn hours of August 1, 1982, while this policy was in full force and effect, the tractor was stolen from the insured's place of business. The tractor was never recovered. It is undisputed that there was a loss, and that it was covered by the aforesaid policy.

Yother submitted proof of loss for the stolen tractor to his insurance agent, claiming a loss of $40,000, the policy limit. In response, he received the following letter:

> Dear Mr. Yother:
>
> This is to inform you that Casualty Indemnity Exchange has rejected your Proof of Loss which you submitted to them on September 17, 1982.
>
> The reason for the rejection is that they are not in agreement with actual cash value you have placed on the 1979 International Tractor. They consider the tractor to have a value no greater than $35,000.00.
>
> Since a dispute has arisen you are entitled to call upon that provision of your policy which provides for arbitration.
>
> Please follow the procedure outlined in the provision and direct your correspondence to the writer.
>
> Yours truly,
>
> Robert C. Carroll, Adjuster

The provision of the insurance policy referred to in Carroll's letter states:

> 2. Appraisal. If the insured and the company fail to agree as to the amount of loss, each shall, on the written demand of either, made within sixty days after receipt of proof of loss by the company, select a competent and disinterested appraiser, and the appraisal shall be made at a reasonable time and place. The appraisers shall first select a competent and disinterested umpire, and failing for fifteen days to agree upon such umpire, then, on the request of the insured or the company, such umpire shall be selected by a judge of a court of record in the county and state in which such appraisal is pending. The appraisers shall then appraise the loss, stating separately the actual cash value at the time of loss and the amount of loss, and failing to agree shall submit their differences to the umpire. An award in writing of any two shall determine the amount of loss. The insured and the company shall each pay his or its chosen appraiser and shall bear equally the other expenses of the appraisal and umpire.

The insured notified CIE by letter that he had elected to invoke the arbitration clause to settle the dispute over the actual cash value of his tractor. The insured and CIE subsequently executed a "Memorandum of Appraisal," in which the insured appointed Elmer Mann as his appraiser, and CIE named Buddy O'Neal as its appraiser.

Mann, a local International Harvester truck and tractor dealer, had sold the insured 1979 International Harvester tractor-truck. Mann was familiar with both the features and condition of the tractor at the time it was stolen. O'Neal, owner of a truck lot, had never seen the tractor and had no personal knowledge of its condition. After a telephone conversation and a personal meeting, the two men failed to agree on the value of the tractor.

Pursuant to the policy provision, Mann and O'Neal selected and appointed Leon Lucas, an employee of International Harvester Company, as umpire. Prior to submitting the matter to Lucas, however, Mann and O'Neal executed an instrument divided into the following sections: "(1) Declaration of Appraisers"; (2) "Selection of Umpire"; (3) "Qualification of Umpire"; and (4) "Award." The first three sections relate to acknowledgment by the appraisers and the umpire of their respective duties. The fourth section, entitled "Award," states that the undersigned appraisers and umpire "have appraised and determined and do hereby award as the actual value" of the stolen property, and provides a space for the amount of the award to be inserted. Although the two appraisers were still not in agreement as to the value to be awarded, both signed the form in blank and forwarded it to Lucas. Lucas, without consulting either appraiser or the insured, entered a figure of $36,500 and signed the form, dated December 16, 1982. The insured received notice of the award on January 10, 1983.

The insured appealed from the Award of Arbitration, as provided by § 6–6–15, Code 1975, and asked the circuit court to set it aside. He alleged that the award was void because it was not made in substantial compliance with applicable provisions of the Alabama Code, and because the insured was not given notice of the hearing and was not allowed to present any evidence of the value of the tractor. The award was entered as a judgment in the records of the Circuit Court of Marshall County, pursuant to § 6–6–15, Code.

Following a hearing, the trial court set aside the award, stating in part:

> (a) That the procedure contemplated in Code Sections 6–6–1 through 6–6–16 was not substantially followed in that no notice of any kind was given to the plaintiff, Jack Yother, and he had no opportunity to present any evidence to any of the arbitrators or appraisers except to the arbitrator or appraiser designated by him.
>
> (b) That said statutory scheme referred to in said Code Sections was not otherwise substantially followed....
>
> (d) That the parties hereto did not agree for the dispute between them to be resolved pursuant to said Code Sections.

CIE appeals, and we affirm.

CIE argues that the procedure employed in determining the actual cash value of Yother's tractor was an appraisal, *not* an arbitration. As such, CIE contends that the trial court, by relying on § 6–6–1, et seq., to vacate the award, erred because those Code provisions do not apply to an "appraisal award" made pursuant to an insurance contract. We agree that an appraisal is distinguishable from arbitration and is not subject to the various procedural requirements imposed upon the arbitration process. But whether the procedures required are those of an arbitration or of an appraisal must be determined from the intent of the disputants or from the character of the questions and issues to be answered, or both. 5 Am.Jur.2d *Arbitration and Award*, § 3 (1962).

CIE claims that Yother knowingly entered into an appraisal agreement to resolve the dispute over the actual cash value of his tractor, and that neither party intended for that determination to be subjected to the various procedural requirements under the arbitration article of the Code; in support of that agreement, CIE points out that neither the policy provision nor the "Memorandum of Appraisal," signed by the insured, uses the word "arbitration." However, we note that the letter from CIE's adjuster, rejecting the insured's original loss claim, advises him that he is entitled to "call upon that provision of [his] policy which provides for arbitration." And the insured responded that he desired to exercise his right "as per policy agreements of arbitration."

Arbitration and appraisal are generally distinguished in the following manner:

> A distinction is often drawn between an arbitration and a mere appraisal or valuation, or proceeding in the nature of an appraisal, the fundamental difference between the two proceedings being held to lie in the procedure to be followed and the effect of the findings. In other words, the point is made that appraisers, unlike arbitrators, act without hearing or judicial inquiry upon their own knowledge or information acquired independent of the evidence of witnesses; and that the appraisal ordinarily settles only a subsidiary or incidental matter rather than the main controversy as does an arbitration award.

6 C.J.S. *Arbitration*, § 3 (1975).

> An agreement for arbitration ordinarily encompasses the disposition of the entire controversy between the parties upon which award a judgment may be entered, whereas an agreement for appraisal extends merely to the resolution of the specific issues of actual cash value and the amount of loss, all other issues being reserved for determination in a plenary action before the court. Furthermore, appraisers are generally expected to act on their own skill and knowledge; they may reach individual conclusions and are required to meet only for the purpose of ironing out differences in the conclusions reached; and they are not obliged to give the rival claimants any formal notice or to hear evidence, but may proceed by ex parte investigation so long as the parties are given opportunity to make statements and explanations with regard to matters in issue.

5 Am.Jur.2d *Arbitration and Award*, § 3 (1962).

Conceding, as CIE argues, that the two proceedings are different, we hold that the trial court did not err in setting aside the award in this case, whether it is labeled arbitration or appraisal.

First, because the insured was given no notice of the hearing, he was denied the opportunity to offer testimony or other evidence of the condition and value of his tractor at the time of loss. He testified that he requested, on two separate occasions, that he be permitted to appear before the hearing. The insured stated that he made one request to Mann, his appraiser, and another request to his insurance agent, Gerald Martin. He further testified that Martin told him that his request would be forwarded to CIE. This evidence was not challenged. The fact that neither the policy provision nor the agreement expressly provides for notice to the parties is not determinative.

> It has been held that even though neither the insurance policy nor the arbitration or appraisal agreement provides for it, notice to the parties of a hearing before the appraisers or arbitrators appointed to determine the amount of a loss under the policy is nevertheless necessary when one of the parties manifests a desire to be heard.

Annot., 25 A.L.R.3d 711 (1969).

Secondly, a hearing was never conducted. It is undisputed that the two appraisers signed a blank award form without having agreed upon a value for the tractor-truck, and that Lucas, the umpire, entered the amount of the award without having consulted the appraisers or having received evidence from the insured as to the tractor's condition. Thus, the policy provision was not complied with. It requires concurrences of two of the three, i.e., the two appraisers and the umpire, and it is not controverted that Lucas alone made the award without notice to the insured, without a hearing, and without any evidence. Mann's testimony in this regard was undisputed:

> Q. Did you sign each of these documents on the same day?
>
> A. The two of us, yes.
>
> Q. And Mr. O'Neal signed on the same day?
>
> A. Yes.
>
> Q. Now, the bottom document says in part: We hereby certify that we have truly and conscientiously performed, et cetera, and do hereby award as the actual cash value of the property on the 16th day of December, 1982, the amount of the loss thereto by . . . blank . . . on that day . . . the following sum, to-wit: actual cash value $36,500. Was that figure, $36,500, in this document when you signed it?
>
> A. No.
>
> Q. Was it in this document when Mr. O'Neal signed it?
>
> A. No.
>
> Q. Did you agree that $36,500 was the actual cash value of Mr. Yother's truck?
>
> A. No.
>
> Q. Why did you sign the bottom document?
>
> A. Well, the idea I had and that Mr. O'Neal had on arbitration, we thought that if he and I couldn't agree . . . if we picked a third party, we were bound by his appraisal.

Q. And you all couldn't agree?

A. No.

In Dufresne v. Marine Ins. Co., 157 Minn. 390, 196 N.W. 560, 562 (1923), a case involving facts similar to those of the present case, the Supreme Court of Minnesota stated:

> [S]ince the universal idea of a proper determination of a controverted matter between man and man rests upon a fair hearing of both sides, it would seem to follow that an arbitration without such hearing should not be upheld, unless it satisfactorily is made to appear either that a hearing was not contemplated or else that it was waived. The court expressly found that plaintiff did not waive notice of the hearing, and that he expected and intended to be present and give evidence, but was prevented from attending and presenting his evidence because of lack of notice and knowledge of the meeting of the appraisers. The finding is sustained, we think. The claim cannot be successfully maintained that this is a case where no hearing was contemplated either because of the character of the subject to be appraised or because of the expert qualifications of the appraisers selected. Two of the appraisers had never seen the automobile. It could not be produced. They could therefore act only upon information obtained from others. And naturally, in such a case, the owner who has sustained the loss should have an opportunity to adduce evidence as to the value and qualities of the article.

It is fundamental that one is entitled to notice and an opportunity to be heard where property rights are affected. The insured asserted that right, and it was denied. CIE argues only that the policy provision is silent with respect to notice and, because it is, that the insured was entitled to none. We cannot agree, where the evidence is undisputed that he demanded notice and an opportunity to produce evidence. The foregoing statement by the Minnesota court is applicable under the facts of this case, whether it is considered a hearing held by "appraisers" or an arbitration hearing.

The judgment of the trial court is affirmed.

AFFIRMED.

■ TORBERT, C.J., and MADDOX, JONES and BEATTY, JJ., concur.

* * *

Questions

1. Do parties have a right to be present at their own arbitration proceedings? Does a "full and fair" hearing require an oral evidentiary hearing at all? If not, what does it require?

2. Common notions of due process would require that parties have a right to receive notice, to be present, and to give evidence in support of their claims. However, not all arbitration procedures grant parties such rights. Some expressly deny some of these due process elements in the arbitration agreements. Some permit arbitrators to fashion procedures, even procedures that might fall short of an ideal due process norm. Is the right to be present a right which parties can waive by agreement prior to a dispute arising? Is it a right a party can waive in the course of resolving an existing dispute? Or, is it a right which cannot be waived at all?

3. What is the difference between an appraisal and an arbitration? In *Casualty Indemnity*, did the court ultimately decide whether the contract called for an arbitration or an appraisal proceeding? Does it give any guidance as to how a court can determine whether parties intended to devise an appraisal procedure or an arbitration proceeding? What indicia of intent could a court use? Can it rely on the language the parties use to describe their procedure? Note that Mann's testimony in *Casualty Indemnity* uses the term "arbitration" and "appraisal" interchangeably in the same sentence. If the language of the principals is not dispositive, what other evidence could a court use to determine intent?

4. Can a court determine whether the parties' agreement called for an appraisal or an arbitration by looking at the type of procedure to which the parties impliedly agreed? Or, should the court make a determination on the basis of the procedural consequences that follow from the particular label they select? Is the latter approach circular?

5. The court in *Casualty Indemnity* says that the distinctive feature of an appraisal proceeding that justifies the lack of an evidentiary hearing is that it relies on the expertise of the decisionmaker. But one of the primary reasons that parties chose arbitration, and an important rationale for judicial delegation to arbitration, is the expertise of the decisionmakers. If both arbitration and an appraisal proceeding are chosen for the decisionmaker's expertise, then why is a hearing required in the former but not the latter?

6. Should parties in arbitration be permitted to file in arbitration dispositive motions such as motions to dismiss or motions for summary judgment? Under what circumstances, if any, should an arbitrator grant such motions? Should the arbitrator use the same legal standard that a court would? Why or why not?

The securities industry's self-regulator, the Financial Industry Regulatory Authority (FINRA), has made it much more difficult for securities firms to obtain summary dismissals in disputes brought by investors. FINRA reported receiving complaints that securities firms were filing dispositive motions routinely and repetitively, causing increased costs for retail-investor claimants. Under the new rule, effective February 23, 2009, dispositive motions may be granted only in three narrow circumstances: (a) the parties have settled their dispute in writing; (b) there is a "factual impossibility" involved, such as a claim involving auction-rate securities against a firm that doesn't sell any; or (c) a party doesn't file a claim within six years of the events at issue. Arbitrators also must conduct hearings on motions to dismiss.

Should the FINRA rule apply to other types of arbitration, such as employment and consumer arbitration? Consider these contrasting views, both from Workplace Prof Blog (post by Richard Bales and comment by Dennis Nolan, Feb. 3, 2009, http://lawprofessors.typepad.com/laborprof_blog/2009/02/motions-to-dism.html):

[Post] The rationale given by FINRA for the rule in securities arbitration applies equally to employment arbitration. One of the advantages employees get from arbitration is access to a dispute resolution forum when the value of their claim is not sufficient to attract an attorney on a contingent fee basis. Dispositive motions make it far more difficult to take a case pro se, and therefore significantly diminish the access advantage of arbitration. For this reason, I think this new securities arbitration rule should apply equally to employment arbitration.

[Comment] [D]ispositive motions [are] useful in [some] employment cases. I agree they should be rare, should only be used when the normal requirements are met, and that arbitrators should resolve all doubts in favor of the non-moving party.

That said, a motion to dismiss should be granted when, as a matter of law, the employee fails to state a legal claim or does not meet the statutory or common law requirements. A motion for summary judgment should be granted when a party's evidence is obviously insufficient to prove the charge. And so on. To deny a motion in those circumstances merely delays a decision and increases transaction costs, with no benefit to the employee.

7. Should courts enforce onerous forum selection clauses in arbitration agreements when there is a significant difference in bargaining power between the parties? Contrast, e.g., Domingo v. Ameriquest Mortgage Co., 70 F. App'x 919, 920 (9th Cir. 2003) (refusing to enforce arbitration agreement that, among other things, required an employee in Hawaii to arbitrate a claim in California); Carter v. Countrywide Credit Indus., Inc., 362 F.3d 294, 299–300 (5th Cir. 2004) (enforcing arbitration agreement containing forum selection clause because employees all lived near the designated forum); Dominguez v. Finish Line, Inc., 439 F.Supp.2d 688 (W.D. Tex. 2006) (severing from an arbitration agreement a clause that would have required employee in Austin, Texas to arbitrate in Indianapolis); Ciago v. Ameriquest Mortgage Co., 295 F.Supp.2d 324, 330 (S.D.N.Y. 2003) (holding that the validity and meaning of specific provisions within an arbitration agreement, including a forum selection clause that would require a New York employee to arbitrate in California, is a matter for the arbitrator to decide).

* * *

4. RIGHT TO COUNSEL

Mikel v. Scharf

444 N.Y.S.2d 690 (N.Y.App.Div. 1981).

MEMORANDUM BY THE COURT

In a proceeding to confirm an arbitration award made by a religious tribunal, in which proceeding respondents cross-petitioned to vacate the award, petitioner appeals from a judgment of the Supreme Court, Kings County, dated October 16, 1980, 105 Misc.2d 548, 432 N.Y.S.2d 602, that denied the petition, granted the cross petition and vacated the award.

Judgment affirmed, with costs.

CPLR 7506 (subd. [c]) provides, as here relevant, that the parties at an arbitration hearing are "entitled to be heard, to present evidence and to cross-examine witnesses." Furthermore, "[a] party has the right to be represented by an attorney ... [and t]his right may not be waived" (CPLR 7506, subd. [d]).

Proper procedure was not followed by the religious tribunal which rendered the subject award and that failure is fatal to confirmation of the award (see CPLR 7511, subd. [b], par. 1, cl. [iv]). The tribunal only permitted respondents' attorney to address it after considerable pleading on the part of respondent Asher Scharf and, even then, the attorney was not permitted to introduce evidence or to cross-examine witnesses, despite his attempts to do so. Furthermore, when respondents were notified of a second meeting of the tribunal, they were expressly told not to bring their attorney. The tribunal could not preclude that representation nor deny respondents the right to present evidence and the right to cross-examine (see CPLR 7506). This failure to observe statutory procedure was prejudicial to the respondents. Accordingly, the award was properly vacated.

We have examined petitioner's remaining contentions and find them to be without merit.

* * *

Outdoor Services, Inc. v. Pabagold, Inc.

230 Cal.Rptr. 73 (Cal.App. 1986).

■ BARRY-DEAL, ASSOCIATE JUSTICE.

BACKGROUND

In March 1981, Pabagold entered into a written contract with Mediasmith, by which Mediasmith agreed to plan and place an advertising campaign for Pabagold's product, Hawaiian Gold Pabatan suntan lotion. The contract authorized Mediasmith to enter into contracts with third parties in order to effectuate the advertising program and to make timely payments to those third parties for goods and services for Pabagold's account. Pabagold was to be fully responsible to Mediasmith for all authorized expenditures. Pabagold agreed to pay Mediasmith's fee for services, including agreed-upon special services and out-of-pocket expenses. The contract contained a provision for the recovery of attorney's fees and costs incurred in enforcing the agreement, as well as a clause that any dispute arising under the contract would be settled by arbitration.

In April 1981, Mediasmith entered into an oral contract with Outdoor Services, by which Outdoor Services agreed to purchase outdoor advertising space for Pabagold's account in exchange for a 5 percent commission on the gross billings for the advertising placements. As required by the contract, Mediasmith provided Pabagold with a written media estimate for the outdoor advertising, which was signed and authorized by Pabagold's vice president, Frank T. Fitzsimmons, Jr. Outdoor Services was not mentioned on the estimate.

Outdoor Services purchased from billboard advertisers $187,244.60 worth of posting and maintenance of outdoor advertising displays and earned $8,545.42 in commissions. Upon Outdoor Services' demand upon Mediasmith for payment, Mediasmith requested payment from Pabagold. Pabagold failed to pay Mediasmith, which in turn did not pay Outdoor Services. Certain outdoor advertising companies began claiming independent liability on the part of Outdoor Services.

Mediasmith filed a complaint for breach of contract against Pabagold in San Francisco Superior Court in July 1981 and on three occasions unsuccessfully sought a writ of attachment against Pabagold. Thereafter, in November 1981, Gannett, one of the outdoor billboard companies with whom Outdoor Services had placed advertising pursuant to its contract with Mediasmith, filed a complaint against Outdoor Services.

On November 20, 1981, Outdoor Services filed a demand against Pabagold with the American Arbitration Association for arbitration as a third party beneficiary of the Pabagold–Mediasmith contract. Mediasmith, on December 14, 1981, filed a cross-demand with the American Arbitration Association for arbitration against Pabagold. On January 5, 1982, Outdoor Services filed an answer and a cross-complaint against Mediasmith and Pabagold in the Gannett action.

The American Arbitration Association granted jurisdiction over the arbitration between Mediasmith and Pabagold based on the arbitration clause contained in their contract, but required Outdoor Services to get either the consent of the parties to the arbitration or a court order as to the ability of Outdoor Services to participate in the arbitration. Pabagold refused its consent, but on March 22, 1982, Outdoor Services' petition to compel arbitration was granted by the San Francisco Superior Court.

On May 26, 1982, counsel for Pabagold failed to appear at a duly noticed prehearing conference at which the parties were to have set a hearing date for the arbitration. On the following day, Pabagold's counsel requested a continuance, and the arbitration was continued to September 1982. Pabagold's counsel again failed to appear at a duly noticed prearbitration conference on August 27, 1982.

On September 1, 1982, officers of Pabagold informed Outdoor Services that Pabagold would represent itself at the arbitration hearing. No mention was made that Pabagold was seeking new counsel. On September 6, Pabagold requested and obtained from all counsel a stipulation to continue the arbitration one day to September 8. However, on September 8, Pabagold appeared and requested a 60–day continuance in order to obtain counsel. The arbitrator denied the request, stating that Pabagold's conduct did not entitle it to a continuance.

On September 16, after the hearing had commenced, the arbitrator granted a continuance until October 25 because Stuart G. Sall, one of Pabagold's officers who was representing Pabagold at the arbitration, was experiencing health problems. The arbitrator rendered his decision in favor of Outdoor Services on November 11. On January 21, 1983, an order confirming arbitration award and a judgment were entered. This appeal followed.

DISCUSSION

. . . [The court held that Outdoor Services was entitled to enforce the arbitration clause as a third-party beneficiary and that Outdoor Services did not waive the right to arbitrate.]

Denial of Continuance

Pabagold lastly contends that the judgment should be vacated because the arbitrator refused to continue the hearing so that Pabagold could seek new counsel. The contention lacks merit.

A party to an arbitration has the right to be represented by counsel at any arbitration proceeding. (Code Civ.Proc., § 1282.4.) The court shall vacate an arbitration award if the rights of a party were substantially prejudiced by the refusal of the arbitrators to postpone the hearing upon sufficient cause being shown therefor. (Code Civ.Proc., § 1286.2, subd. (e).)

Pabagold argues that because its counsel announced his refusal to proceed on the eve of the arbitration proceeding, Pabagold should have been granted a continuance to secure new counsel.

Contrary to appellant's assertion, there is no due process right to be represented by counsel at arbitration. (Horn v. Gurewitz (1968) 261 Cal. App.2d 255, 262, 67 Cal.Rptr. 791.) Additionally, Pabagold has failed to show sufficient cause for postponing the hearing. As early as January 26, 1982, Pabagold's counsel failed to appear at duly noticed depositions. Counsel also did not attend the prearbitration conference on May 26, 1982. However, on May 27, 1982, Pabagold's counsel requested a continuance of the arbitration scheduled for June 7, 1982. The arbitration was continued to September 7, 1982. Counsel again failed to appear at the August 27, 1982, prearbitration conference.

On September 1, 1982, Pabagold informed Outdoor Services that it would represent itself at the hearing. On September 6, 1982, Pabagold requested and obtained a stipulation by all parties to continue the arbitration for one day to September 8. On September 8, Pabagold appeared and requested a 60–day continuance to obtain new counsel. The arbitrator denied the request.

Any problems that Pabagold had with its counsel predate by several months the September arbitration. Pabagold had ample time to obtain other representation. Therefore, the arbitrator properly denied the request for a continuance.

Pabagold's lack of diligence distinguishes this case from Vann v. Shilleh (1975) 54 Cal.App.3d 192, 126 Cal.Rptr. 401. In that case, the appellant's counsel withdrew on the eve of trial because his client rejected a negotiated settlement. (Id., at p. 197) This court held that the trial court abused its discretion in denying the appellant's motion for continuance to retain an attorney because counsel had improperly abandoned his client without advance warning. (Id., at pp. 196–197.)

Here, Pabagold was well aware that its counsel had not been diligent. Pabagold had ample time to substitute counsel, but failed to do so. Under the circumstances, no continuance was justified . . .

* * *

Questions

1. Is there a due process right to be represented by an attorney at an arbitration? Would it violate due process if parties agreed upon an arbitration procedure in which neither one could use an attorney? What if an attorney could be present but was not permitted to speak to the arbitration panel or to question witnesses?

2. Would it violate due process if an arbitrator declared that no attorney shall be present in a hearing she is conducting?

3. Some arbitration agreements contain a clause similar to the following: "X has the right to be represented by an attorney at all times. However, if X elects not to bring a lawyer to the arbitration hearing, Y also will agree not to bring a lawyer to the hearing." Might such a clause be misleading, particularly in employment and consumer arbitration?

Orley Ashenfelter and David Bloom collected empirical evidence concerning the use and nonuse of attorneys in several different types of disputes. They found that the outcome of disputes is roughly the same if either both parties or neither party is represented by an attorney. Where only one party is represented by an attorney, however, that party's likelihood of prevailing increases substantially. The authors concluded that where the method of dispute resolution allows the parties a realistic option of representing themselves, the decision to retain lawyers presents a prisoner's dilemma: although it would be in both parties' best interest to represent themselves, both nonetheless will rationally hire lawyers to avoid the "sucker's payoff" a party receives when only one's opponent hires a lawyer. Orley Ashenfelter and David Bloom, *Lawyers as Agent of the Devil in a Prisoner's Dilemma Game*, 11–19 (National Bureau of Economic Research Working Paper No. 4447 (Sept. 1993)).

On the other hand, Richard Ross, former Senior Associate General Counsel for Anheuser–Busch, has argued that it is in an employer's best interest to encourage and even pay for an employee's retention of an attorney in an arbitral proceeding. He explains:

> If the employee does not have a lawyer, the selection of an arbitrator is a little more difficult just because the employee is not familiar with the process. It can also be helpful in settling some disputes if the employee has someone to lean on for advice and counsel. An attorney can help the employee assess his or her claim realistically, and give the employee some assurance that any settlement is fair and reasonable.

Richard Ross, Interview by Peter Phillips, in CPR Institute for Dispute Resolution, How Companies Manage Employment Disputes: A Compendium of Leading Corporate Employment Programs 54 (2002).

4. As the *Mikel* case exemplifies, religious tribunals often adjudicate cases in the same manner as conventional arbitrations. Are these adjudications judicially enforceable (and thereby reducible to binding legal judgments) under the FAA and parallel state arbitration laws? The answer usually is yes, but there is tension between the requirement of minimal due process (which includes some level of judicial review) and the "religious question doctrine" which prohibits civil courts from reviewing religious questions. For more on this topic, see Michael C. Grossman, Note, *Is this Arbitration?: Religious Tribunals, Judicial Review, and Due Process*, 107 Columbia L. Rev. 169 (2007).

* * *

5. Discovery

a. DISCOVERY PENDING ARBITRATION

Mississippi Power Company v. Peabody Coal Company

69 F.R.D. 558 (S.D.Miss. 1976).

■ COLEMAN, CIRCUIT JUDGE.

I. Background

Mississippi Power Company (MPC), plaintiff, has filed a civil action against Peabody Coal Company (Peabody) and Commercial Transport Corporation (Commercial), seeking $346,318,012.00 in damages for the alleged breach of a coal supply contract. Also sought were (1) a declaratory judgment that Peabody's force majeure excuse for nonperformance of the contract is not valid; (2) a judgment requiring Peabody to specifically perform said coal supply contract; and (3) an injunction, pendente lite, requiring Peabody to continue to supply the full tonnage of coal called for in the coal supply contract. Against Commercial MPC sought only a declaration that MPC was relieved from tendering for transport the minimum tonnage required by its barge contract with Commercial. MPC also sought discovery in the form of interrogatories and requests for production of documents.

The coal supply contract had an arbitration clause. Pursuant to the Federal Arbitration Act, Peabody moved for a stay pending arbitration. Peabody also filed a motion to postpone discovery, except as related to issues raised by its motion to stay while the court was considering the motion to stay.

After briefing and oral argument, District Judge Harold Cox filed a memorandum opinion on July 23, 1975. This was followed by an "Order for Arbitration" entered August 6, 1975. The opinion and order found: (1) that the contract between MPC and Peabody was one involving and affecting interstate commerce; (2) that it contained an agreement to arbitrate any unresolved controversy between the parties or claims of one party against the other under the rules of the American Arbitration Association. The Court therefore ordered the parties to proceed with such arbitration, but retained full jurisdiction of the case to make available to the parties all discovery processes provided by the Federal Rules of Civil Procedure. In this respect the order provided:

> This Court expressly retains full jurisdiction of this case and in the meantime, will make available to the parties all discovery processes provided by the Civil Rules of Federal Procedure to the extent that it may be necessary to the presentation and decision of any disputed facts in the case as may be helpful under Civil Rule 81(a)(c) [sic, 81(a)(3)] of the Federal Rules of Civil Procedure. In the meantime, this proceeding shall be stayed in this Court without prejudice or advantage to either party. The plaintiff may continue all discovery processes and have the processes of this Court available to enforce answers thereto within the time contemplated by such rules. The defendant (Peabody Coal Company) shall answer any interrogatories presently outstanding within 15 days. Further discovery processes shall be commenced and concluded within ninety days after this date.

Peabody appealed only that portion of the order which provided discovery under the Federal Rules of Civil Procedure. October 6, 1975, Peabody's appeal was dismissed because it was not taken from a final appealable order.

Subsequently, Judge Cox recused himself. Sitting by designation as a District Judge for the Southern District of Mississippi, the author of this opinion took over the case.

Discovery proceeded, but Peabody objected to certain of Miss. Power Company's interrogatories and requests for production of documents. Peabody refused certain MPC requests for production of particular documents on the ground that they were not relevant to the issues presented for arbitration and were overly broad and all-inclusive. MPC filed a motion to compel discovery. An extended hearing was held in chambers on November 21, 1975 in Ackerman, Mississippi. This Court, sua sponte, questioned

Miss. Power Company's right to discovery and requested that the issue be briefed.

II. Issues

. . . When a Court stays a suit in order that arbitration may be had, does it have any further authority or jurisdiction to order that discovery may proceed, either as to the merits of the suit or in aid of arbitration? . . .

The first sentence of Section 30 of the Commercial Arbitration Rules of the American Arbitration Association provides:

> The parties may offer such evidence as they desire *and shall produce* (emphasis added) such additional evidence as the arbitrator may deem necessary to an understanding and determination of the dispute.

Title 9 of the United States Code, Section 7, authorizes arbitrators to summon witnesses, books, records, documents, and papers deemed material as evidence in the case. United States district courts may compel compliance with the summons.

It is thus readily apparent that under the contract which the parties made, under Rule 30, and under the applicable federal statute the arbitrator can compel the production (discovery) of every book, record, document and paper deemed material to the appropriate resolution of the controversy between Mississippi Power and Peabody.

With reference to discovery, however, Judge Cox's order left the parties standing with one foot in the district court and the other in the arbitrator's office. If arbitration is to proceed, and the law looks with disfavor on delays, two discovery proceedings could be in progress simultaneously, one under the direction of the Court and the other under the control of the arbitrator.

Considerable discovery has been accomplished in compliance with Judge Cox's order, but Peabody objects on numerous grounds to additional extensive discovery proposed by the plaintiff. Plaintiff has countered with a motion to compel discovery. This motion is the issue now before this Court.

Upon a thorough exploration of the applicable law the Court concludes that the motion to compel discovery should be denied and that the arbitration process should be set in motion without further delay.

The Law as to Discovery Pending Arbitration

So far as I have been able to discover, the Court of Appeals for the Fifth Circuit has had only one occasion to consider this question. This is to be found in the per curiam opinion in Local 66, International Ass'n of Heat and Frost Insulators and Asbestos Workers v. Leona Lee Corp., 5 Cir. 1970, 434 F.2d 192. This case appears to approve discovery *on the merits* prior to arbitration. It categorically stated, 434 F.2d at 194:

> Also, the District Court did not err when it specifically made available to the parties federal discovery procedures "to the extent necessary for the presentation of matters submitted for Trade Board and Arbitration determination." Such order is consistent with the District Court's

retention of jurisdiction and effectuates the policy favoring arbitration. (footnote omitted).

This sweeping declaration appears to come down emphatically in support of the proposition that in a case ordered to arbitration discovery may proceed simultaneously in the courts and before the arbitrator. This District Court is, of course, obligated to follow the outstanding, unreversed precedents of the Fifth Circuit. The difficulty here, however, is that the *Leona Lee* per curiam never mentions, and does not discuss, outstanding judicial precedent; it does not explicate the reasoning upon which the declaration was grounded. It makes no effort to demonstrate how simultaneous discovery in arbitration cases "is consistent with the District Court's retention of jurisdiction and effectuates the policy of favoring arbitration". It is against the overwhelming weight of authority. I feel, therefore, that the decision in *Leona Lee* must have been grounded on some factor not made clear in the opinion and is not a controlling precedent.

The great weight of authority is clearly to the effect that discovery on the subject matter of a dispute to be arbitrated will be denied. See 7 Moore's Fed.Practice § 81.05[7] at 81–82 . . .

One of the earliest cases to declare that discovery was inappropriate after a stay action was Commercial Solvents Corp. v. Louisiana Liquid Fertilizer Co., S.D.N.Y.1957, 20 F.R.D. 359. There one party had served notice on the other party to arbitrate a dispute in accordance with the terms of their contract. An ex parte order allowing the taking of depositions was obtained and it was from this order that an appeal was taken. The Court found no authority to compel discovery in aid of arbitration, noting:

> By voluntarily becoming a party to a contract in which arbitration was the agreed mode for settling disputes thereunder respondent chose to avail itself of procedures peculiar to the arbitral process rather than those used in judicial determinations. "A main object of a voluntary submission to arbitration is the avoidance of formal and technical preparation of a case for the usual procedure of a judicial trial." 1 Wigmore, Evidence § 4(e) (3d ed. 1940). Arbitration may well have advantages but where the converse results a party having chosen to arbitrate cannot then vacillate and successfully urge a preference for a unique combination of litigation and arbitration.
>
> 20 F.R.D. at 361.

Numerous other district court cases have declared for various reasons that discovery as to the merits of a suit that has been stayed for arbitration is improper and should not be allowed. See Econo–Car Internat'l, Inc. v. Antilles Car Rentals, Inc., D.V.I.1973, 61 F.R.D. 8, 10, rev'd on other grounds, 3 Cir. 1974, 499 F.2d 1391 . . .

Some district courts have said that discovery may be ordered in "exceptional circumstances". See Ferro Union Corp. v. SS Ionic Coast, S.D.Tex.1967, 43 F.R.D. 11 (exceptional circumstances found where ship crew was about to leave the country and might never return to U.S. waters) . . .

From the above discussion it is apparent that the vast majority of courts that have considered the matter have concluded that allowing discovery on the merits of a case prior to arbitration is inconsistent with the aims of arbitration. The Harvard Law Review aptly stated this conclusion in one of its surveys on discovery, as follows:[1]

> As to arbitration, discovery is generally not available as an incident of the arbitration proceeding itself. Discovery is expensive and time-consuming, and is thus inconsistent with the desires of parties who refer their disputes to arbitrators rather than to formal judicial tribunals. Moreover, discovery by a collateral application in a court, although authorized in some states, is allowed with reluctance, as it tends to reduce the arbitrator's control of the proceeding. When an arbitration issue is before a court—as in a motion to stay an action allegedly referable to arbitration—discovery has usually been denied unless the stay is refused; again it is thought that the expense of discovery should not be forced on a party who has agreed to submit a controversy to a less costly method of adjudication.

See also 4 Moore's Fed.Practice § 26.54 (2nd ed. 1975) (depositions are properly taken only for the purpose of preparing for trial in a pending action in the district court and not to aid in the disposition of a collateral proceeding such as arbitration).

The Decision

Within the parameters of this case, the merits of this controversy, including its evidentiary aspects, should be left to the arbitrator.

In reaching this conclusion I need not hold that discovery pending arbitration is never to be allowed, nor am I required to hold, as pontificated in Leona Lee, supra, that it is always to be permitted.

Instead, the parties should be held to their agreement and to the availability of Rule 30 of the Rules of the American Arbitration Association. Backed up by the federal statute, this rule allows the arbitrator, in his discretion, to permit any discovery necessary to the performance of his function. There should be no necessity for double-barreled discovery, proceeding simultaneously under the supervision of the Court, on one hand, and under the supervision of the arbitrator, on the other, a situation fraught with the likelihood of conflicts, duplications, hindrances and delays, all basically in conflict with the arbitration process, as demonstrated by the many cases hereinabove cited. This course avoids anything inimical to the obligation to arbitrate, yet it will not deprive the plaintiff of the benefits of discovery, which can be had, if needed, at the hands of the arbitrator and under his direction.

V. Conclusion

Under the facts, circumstances, and governing law of this case I hold that I am not bound by Judge Cox's original order which allowed discovery

1. 74 Harv.L.Rev. 940, 943 (1961).

to proceed on the merits of this controversy pending arbitration or while arbitration is in progress. It need not be said, but I say it nevertheless, that this indicates no disrespect whatever for the prior views of Judge Cox or for his position as a Judge of the same court in which I am now sitting ...

Finding that by Section 23 the parties have contracted to submit all unresolved controversies or claims by one party against the other to arbitration, *including adjustment for gross inequities* (Section 18 of the contract), the Court directs that arbitration shall proceed without further delay.

* * *

Recognition Equipment, Inc. v. NCR Corporation

532 F.Supp. 271 (N.D.Tex. 1981).

■ ROBERT W. PORTER, DISTRICT JUDGE.

Currently pending before the Court is the motion of Defendant NRC Corporation to stay all further proceedings in this action pursuant to section 3 of the Federal Arbitration Act, 9 U.S.C. § 3. Defendant's motion presents the Court with two distinct issues for consideration: first, whether the commercial contract entered into among the respective parties to this action provides for reference of the pertinent issues in dispute to arbitration; and second, assuming a stay is granted, whether or not the Court should allow discovery under the Federal Rules of Civil Procedure, pending arbitration. Jurisdiction over this action is predicated upon 28 U.S.C. § 1332, there being complete diversity of citizenship among the parties.

Recognition Equipment, Inc., Plaintiff herein, brings this action to recover monies it asserts are due and owing from the Defendant as a consequence of a sale of certain mechanical goods and related parts. Plaintiff alleges that it provided the Defendant with said goods and related parts but received payment from the Defendant which was erroneously based upon the wrong price list. The action was originally brought in state court, but there being complete diversity among the parties, the Defendant petitioned for removal to federal court. The agreement in question has ... the following arbitration clause:

> 11. Arbitration. Any controversy or claim arising out of or relating to this Agreement or the breach thereof, shall be settled by arbitration in accordance with the Rules of the American Arbitration Association and judgment upon the award rendered by the Arbitrator(s) may be entered in any Court having jurisdiction thereof.

[Regarding the first issue before the court, the court found that the parties had agreed to arbitrate Plaintiff's claim against Defendant] ..., and that consequently, Defendant's motion to stay pursuant to section 3 of the Federal Arbitration Act should be granted.

The second issue before the Court is more troublesome. Plaintiff maintains that, assuming the Court grants Defendant's motion to stay, the parties are entitled to go forward with discovery under the Federal Rules of Civil Procedure. In support of its contention Plaintiff notes that section 3 of the Federal Arbitration Act provides only for a stay of "the trial of the action," and also cites Int'l Assoc. of Heat and Frost Insulators and Asbestos Workers v. Leona Lee Corp., 434 F.2d 192 (5th Cir. 1970) (per curiam). In Leona Lee the Fifth Circuit, in an action brought under section 301 of the Labor Management Relations Act, 29 U.S.C. § 185, affirmed an order of the lower court staying trial of the action and permitting discovery pursuant to the Federal Rules to the extent necessary for the presentation of the dispute to an arbitral forum. In so doing, the court stated that such a procedure was consistent with the lower court's retention of jurisdiction and that it effectuated the policy favoring arbitration. A later opinion by Circuit Judge Coleman, sitting by designation as a Judge of the United States District Court for the Southern District of Mississippi, however, undercuts the broad and sweeping language in Leona Lee. In Mississippi Power Company v. Peabody Coal Co., 69 F.R.D. 558 (S.D.Miss. 1976), Judge Coleman, in a case similar to the one at bar, concluded that discovery under the Federal Rules of Civil Procedure during a section 3 stay was improper, at least on the facts of that specific case. Judge Coleman noted numerous problems with allowing parties the opportunity to engage in discovery under the Federal Rules during a section 3 stay. First and foremost is that the Federal Arbitration Act provides for discovery by the arbitrator in section 7 of the Act, 9 U.S.C. § 7, and thus additional discovery under the Federal Rules would create "dual discovery." Second, he noted that the majority of the courts which have faced the issue have decided against allowing discovery to proceed under the rules. Third, those courts which have allowed discovery to proceed pending arbitration have noted "exceptional circumstances" in the facts before them to justify the decision. Finally, Judge Coleman also noted that the purpose of arbitration is to avoid the attendant delay and expense of litigation....

Subsequent to the Mississippi Power case, the Fifth Circuit has recognized the issue raised by Judge Coleman concerning "dual discovery" preceding arbitration. Yeargin Construction Co. v. Parsons & Whittemore Alabama Machinery and Services Corp., 609 F.2d 829, 831 (5th Cir. 1980). In addition, the United States Supreme Court has cited the Mississippi Power case with approval for the proposition that "when the purpose of a discovery request is to gather information for use in proceedings other than the pending suit, discovery is properly denied." Oppenheimer Fund, Inc. v. Sanders, 437 U.S. 340, 352 n. 17, 98 S.Ct. 2380, 2390 n. 17, 57 L.Ed.2d 253 (1978) (dictum).

The Court is persuaded that Judge Coleman's opinion in Mississippi Power accurately reflects the law with respect to discovery under the Federal Rules pending arbitration under the Federal Arbitration Act. Perhaps the greatest distinction between the Mississippi Power case, and Leona Lee, is that the latter case was brought under section 301 of the LMRA, 29 U.S.C. § 185. There is nothing in the opinion to indicate that the arbitral forum which would hear the claim in Leona Lee had any discovery powers. Thus, "dual discovery" may not have been an issue there and this aspect of the case could be the "factor not made clear" of which Judge Coleman spoke. Therefore, the Court is of the opinion that Leona Lee is not binding precedent for the instant case. In addition, for the reasons set forth so persuasively in Mississippi Power, the Court is of the opinion that, on the facts of this case, discovery under the Federal Rules should not proceed pending arbitration. Time and again courts have concluded that the purposes of arbitration under the Federal Arbitration Act are to facilitate and expedite the resolution of disputes, ease court congestion, and provide disputants with a less costly alternative to litigation . . .

The Court in Mississippi Power did not hold that discovery pending arbitration is never to be permitted and acknowledged other decisions in which it was held that such discovery may be granted under "exceptional circumstances." 69 F.R.D. at 566–67, citing Ferro Union Corp. v. SS Ionic Coast, 43 F.R.D. 11 (S.D. Tex.1967). In the immediate action Plaintiff has failed to demonstrate any "exceptional circumstances" which would justify pre-arbitration discovery. Some courts have stated that the granting of discovery during a stay lies within the Court's discretion. Bigge Crane and Rigging Co. v. Docutel Corp., 371 F.Supp. 240 (E.D.N.Y. 1973). The Court is of the opinion that the better exercise of discretion in the instant case is to deny Plaintiff's request for pre-arbitration discovery.[4] Accordingly,

It is ORDERED that Defendant's motion for a stay or proceedings in this action pending arbitration of the dispute raised by the original complaint is GRANTED: the parties are directed to submit the matter to arbitration in a manner consistent with paragraph 28.11 of the contract in issue and the Court retains jurisdiction over the matter to enforce sections 4 and 7 of the Federal Arbitration Act;

It is further ORDERED that the Plaintiff's request for discovery pursuant to the Federal Rules of Civil Procedure pending arbitration is DENIED.

* * *

Questions

1. What is the problem of dual discovery that the court mentions in *Recognition Equipment*? Could the problem be overcome without denying parties access to the discovery provisions of the Federal Rules of Civil Procedure?

2. Under what circumstances might a court order discovery pending arbitration? What authority or policy rationale might justify such judicial action? How much weight should a court or arbitrator give to an argument that discovery will delay resolution of a dispute and undermine the ratio-

4. A further reason for denying discovery pending arbitration lies in the potential for interference with the arbitral function. By retaining jurisdiction over this action and allowing pre-arbitration discovery the Court would be duty bound to administer the discovery process. In so doing, there is a likelihood that its administration of the discovery issues could pre-shape the issues before the arbitrator.

nale that led the parties to select arbitration in the first place? See Note, *Arbitration and Award–Discovery–Court May Permit Discovery on the Merits When It Will Not Delay Arbitration*, 44 U. Cinn. L. Rev. 151 (1975).

3. If a court were to hear discovery requests in matters in which arbitration was pending, presumably the court would have to determine which discovery requests were reasonable and relevant. How can a court determine issues of reasonableness and relevance without some attention to the merits of the underlying dispute? Must an arbitrator who hears discovery requests also make a pre-determination as to reasonableness and relevancy? Is such a determination subject to judicial review?

4. Some arbitration procedures provide for limited discovery. See, e.g., C. Edward Fletcher III, *Privatizing Securities Disputes through the Enforcement of Arbitration Agreements*, 71 Minn. L. Rev. 393 (1987) (describing discovery provisions of securities industry arbitrations). Should a court presume that an arbitration procedure that does not expressly provide for discovery intends to preclude parties from engaging in discovery?

* * *

b. DISCOVERY OF NON–PARTIES

Meadows Indemnity Company, Limited v. Nutmeg Insurance Co.

157 F.R.D. 42 (M.D.Tenn. 1994).

■ SANDIDGE, UNITED STATES MAGISTRATE JUDGE.

I. BACKGROUND

The referred matter comes to the Court on the Court's general docket as a small scene from a larger litigation picture which includes a currently pending arbitration action as well as lawsuits in New York and California. The underlying theme behind these proceedings involves events related to the operation of a casualty insurance/reinsurance pool....

In 1989, Meadows Indemnity Company, Ltd. ("Meadows") filed a lawsuit in the Eastern District of New York against several insurance companies and other related companies. Willis Corroon is the successor in interest to one defendant in the lawsuit, the Corroon & Black Corporation, and wholly owns another defendant, Baccala & Shoop Insurance Services ("BSIS"). Meadows complains that beginning in the late 1970's and continuing into the 1980's, BSIS established and managed an insurance/reinsurance pool ("the pool") and acted as an agent with respect to the pool for several policy issuing insurance companies. Meadows alleges, among other things, that BSIS and the companies, individually and in conspiracy, gained excessive commissions and fees from the pool and fraudulently concealed information from reinsurers participating in the pool regarding premium inadequacy, severity of expected loss, amount of commissions and fees diverted from premiums, etc.

The District Court in New York ordered arbitration of Meadows' claims against the defendant insurance companies and stayed the claims against BSIS and Willis Corroon until completion of the arbitration proceedings. Shortly thereafter, several of the defendant insurance companies filed suit against Meadows in California. The California lawsuit is also stayed pending the arbitration results.

The arbitration currently underway involves Meadows' claims against the several insurance companies, one of which is the Hartford Group. As part of the arbitration, Meadows petitioned the arbitration panel to subpoena certain documents and records of BSIS because of its role as agent for Hartford and as manager of the pool. Hartford objected to the petition and the panel heard both written and oral arguments from both sides as to Meadows' request. On February 22, 1993, the arbitration panel issued the subpoena to BSIS, in the care of Willis Corroon, requiring the production of documents according to a schedule of documents attached to the subpoena. The schedule sets out 53 categories or types of documents which are to be produced pursuant to the subpoena, and states that production of the documents is to take place at Willis Corroon's Nashville, Tennessee office or at another location as agreed to by the parties. It appears from the parties' briefs that the documents covered by the subpoena are in fact located in a California warehouse. See Docket Entry No. 13.

At oral argument the Court was informed by the parties that the District Court in New York had recently issued an order, on June 14, 1993, which vacated the stay of proceedings in the New York lawsuit to the extent that Meadows is allowed to proceed with pretrial discovery against BSIS.

II. ANALYSIS

The only issue before the Court is whether Willis Corroon, which is not a party to the arbitration proceedings, must comply with an order from the arbitration panel requiring it to produce numerous documents, not for the panel's review at a hearing, but for inspection and copying by Meadows prior to a hearing before the panel.

Section 7 of the Federal Arbitration Act, 9 U.S.C. §§ 1–307, provides in relevant part:

> The arbitrators ... may summon in writing any person to attend before them or any of them as a witness and in a proper case to bring with him or them any book, record, document, or paper which may be deemed material as evidence in the case ...

Willis Corroon's main argument for the protective order is that the arbitration panel has acted beyond their [sic] statutory authority by ordering production of documents unrelated to an order to appear before the arbitration panel, and by ordering production of the documents for review not by the arbitration panel but by a party to the arbitration. Willis Corroon's arguments are unpersuasive and I find that the arbitration panel's action of issuing the subpoena is within its authority under the Federal Arbitration Act.

Initially, I note that the arbitration panel has already determined that the documents to be provided are relevant to the arbitration proceedings. Given this Court's minimal contact with the issues involved in the litigation surrounding the pool, and the arbitration panel's expertise in this matter, there is no reason to second guess the panel's determination as to relevance.

There is little dispute the arbitration panel, pursuant to its authority under Section 7, could require a witness in the name of Willis Corroon to appear before the panel and bring all of the documents at issue to a hearing. Considering the sheer number of documents addressed by the subpoena, however, this scenario seems quite fantastic and practically unreasonable. With this in mind, the arbitration panel issued the disputed subpoena as a method of dealing with complex and voluminous discovery matters in an orderly and efficient manner. See Docket Entry No. 9. Mindful that one of the ultimate goals of the arbitration panel is to make a full and fair determination of the issues involved, and the underlying policies behind arbitration include the resolution of issues in an efficient and less costly manner, the panel's decision to issue the subpoena seems entirely reasonable.

Contrary to the arguments of Willis Corroon, I find that Section 7 authorizes the action taken by the arbitration panel. Stanton v. Paine Webber Jackson & Curtis, 685 F.Supp. 1241 (S.D.Fla. 1988). The power of the panel to compel production of documents from third-parties for the purposes of a hearing implicitly authorizes the lesser power to compel such documents for arbitration purposes prior to a hearing. Willis Corroon's argument requires adoption of an unnecessarily constrictive and unreasonable reading of Section 7 which would limit the ability of the arbitration panel to deal effectively with a large and complex case such as the one at hand, and generally hamper the use of arbitration as a forum for dispute resolution.

With respect to Willis Corroon's arguments about the burdensome nature of the subpoena, nothing has been presented which indicates that producing the documents will in fact be unduly burdensome. While Willis Corroon and BSIS are not parties to the arbitration, they are intricately related to the parties involved in the arbitration and are not mere third-parties who have been pulled into this matter arbitrarily. The documents appear to be at a central location to which Meadows has agreed to travel. The burden of sifting through the documents and copying those needed is on Meadows. At this stage there is simply no merit to Willis Corroon's arguments about an undue burden on them. If one should arise during the course of the document production, Willis Corroon may seek protection through the appropriate district court.

It appears that whether through the arbitration proceedings or the lawsuit in New York, the documents possessed by Willis Corroon relating to the pool are going to be produced for Meadows' review. As I find that the arbitration panel acted within its authority, I see no reason to grant the protective order sought by Willis Corroon and further delay the arbitration proceedings.

The arbitration panel's subpoena is valid under the Federal Arbitration Act. The requested documents should be produced at a time and location agreed on by the parties and should be made available for inspection by Meadows. Meadows shall be responsible, at its own costs, of arranging for the copying of any documents desired. An order denying the motion for a protective order will be entered.

* * *

Integrity Insurance Co. v. American Centennial Insurance Co.

885 F.Supp. 69 (S.D.N.Y. 1995).

■ SCHEINDLIN, DISTRICT JUDGE.

Thomas Lennon and Eugene McGee petition this Court to quash subpoenas duces tecum issued by an arbitrator pursuant to a dispute between Integrity Insurance Company, in liquidation ("Integrity"), and American Centennial Insurance Company ("ACIC"). The subpoenas were issued by the arbitrator at the request of ACIC, and direct the petitioners to appear for pre-hearing depositions and to produce documents.

BACKGROUND

The dispute between Integrity and ACIC arises from a number of reinsurance agreements. See Affidavit of Brendan M. Kennedy ("Kennedy Aff."), Attorney for Integrity, at § 2. The Liquidator instituted arbitration proceedings against ACIC pursuant to those agreements. Id. Separate and apart from the arbitration proceeding, the Liquidator has filed an action in New Jersey on behalf of Integrity's policyholders, creditors, reinsurers and others, against former officers and directors of Integrity, including petitioner McGee ("D & O action"). See Affidavit of Eugene Wollan, Attorney for ACIC, in Support of Petition ("Wollan Aff.") at § 8. McGee is a former Vice President of Integrity and Lennon is McGee's attorney in the D & O action. Petition ("Pet.") at §§ 3–4. Lennon also represents Leonard Stern, a former President of Integrity and a defendant in the D & O action. Wollan Aff. at § 8. Discovery in the D & O action has been stayed pending the outcome of settlement negotiations. Pet. at § 7.

Neither petitioner is a party to the arbitration proceeding. The subpoenas require them to appear for a deposition and to produce all relevant documents relating to the reinsurance agreements at issue between ACIC and Integrity. The subpoenas further require production of documents relating to the D & O action. Wollan Aff. at § 8. Additionally, ACIC seeks to depose Lennon in order to learn the whereabouts of Stern, so that Stern can be served with a deposition subpoena. Lennon has refused to voluntarily disclose Stern's address, claiming that it is privileged. Wollan Aff. at § 9; Brief in Support of Petition at 9.

Petitioners request that this Court quash these subpoenas, on the grounds that an arbitrator has no authority to compel a non-party to appear at a deposition prior to an arbitration hearing....

DISCUSSION

A. Depositions of Nonparties

The issue of whether an arbitrator has the authority to compel a nonparty to appear at a pre-hearing deposition appears to be a case of first impression within this district. This Court recognizes that federal policy strongly favors arbitration as an alternative dispute resolution process, see Moses H. Cone Memorial Hosp. v. Mercury Constr. Corp., 460 U.S. 1, 24, 103 S.Ct. 927, 941, 74 L.Ed.2d 765 (1983), and that courts should interpret the Federal Arbitration Act ("FAA"), 9 U.S.C. §§ 1 et seq., so "as to further, rather than impede, arbitration." Bigge Crane and Rigging Co. v. Docutel Corp., 371 F.Supp. 240, 246 (E.D.N.Y. 1973).

Arbitration is, however, a creation of contract, bargained for and voluntarily agreed to by the parties. The petitioners, who are not parties to the arbitration agreement, never bargained for or voluntarily agreed to participate in an arbitration. After weighing the policy favoring arbitration against the rights and privileges of nonparties, this Court concludes that an arbitrator does not have the authority to compel nonparty witnesses to appear for pre-arbitration depositions.

To determine the extent of an arbitrator's authority, one must begin with the source of that authority. An arbitrator's power *over the parties* derives from both the arbitration agreement and the FAA. Arbitrators can exert no more control over parties than that which the parties, through their agreements, granted to the arbitrators. The four reinsurance agreements contain different arbitration clauses. Agreements 1080 and 4013 state "[t]he arbitrators ... are relieved of all judicial formalities and may abstain from following the strict rules of law." Agreements 1021 and 978 state: "[t]he arbitrators will not be obliged to follow judicial formalities or the rules of evidence except to the extent required by the state law of the site of arbitration.... Except as provided above, arbitration will be based upon the procedures of the American Arbitration Association [('AAA')]." The rules of the AAA state that "[a]n arbitrator or other person authorized by law to subpoena witnesses or documents may do so upon the request of any party." American Arbitration Association, *Commercial Arbitration Rules*, Rule 31 (1993). Thus, there is nothing within the reinsurance agreements that explicitly limits the power of an arbitrator to order discovery. See Chiarella v. Viscount Indus. Co. Ltd., No. 92 Civ. 9310, 1993 WL 497967 (S.D.N.Y. Dec.1, 1993).

Because the parties to a contract cannot bind nonparties, they certainly cannot grant such authority to an arbitrator. Thus, an arbitrator's power *over nonparties* derives solely from the FAA. The contested subpoenas were issued by the arbitrator pursuant to section 7 of the FAA.

> The arbitrators ... may summon in writing any person to attend before them or any of them as a witness and in a proper case to bring with him or them any book, record, document, or paper which may be deemed material as evidence in the case.... [I]f any person or persons so summoned to testify shall refuse or neglect to obey said summons, upon petition the United States district court for the district in which such arbitrators, or a majority of them, are sitting may compel the attendance of such person or persons before said arbitrator or arbitrators, or punish said person or persons for contempt in the same manner provided by law for securing the attendance of witnesses or their punishment for neglect or refusal to attend in the courts of the United States.

9 U.S.C. § 7.

Implicit within the power to compel compliance with an arbitrator's summons must be the power to quash that summons if it was improperly issued. Oceanic Transport Corp. v. Alcoa S.S. Co., 129 F.Supp. 160 (S.D.N.Y. 1954) (rejecting petition to sanction nonparty for failure to comply and vacating subpoena because evidence sought was not material). The court may also consider a petition to quash; there is no requirement that a petition to compel be made first. See Commercial Metals Co. v. International Union Marine Corp., 318 F.Supp. 1334 (S.D.N.Y. 1970) (denying motion to quash subpoena duces tecum issued by arbitrator because evidence sought by arbitrator—documents from a party—was relevant to inquiry).

Though the language of the statute speaks only to the arbitrators power to summon a witness to "attend before them," i.e. at the hearing, the courts have permitted arbitrators to order prehearing discovery of parties. See, e.g., In re Technostroyexport, 853 F.Supp. 695, 697 (S.D.N.Y. 1994) (pre-hearing discovery *between parties* is "a matter governed by the applicable arbitration rules (as distinct from court rules) and by what the arbitrator decides."); Chiarella v. Viscount Indus. Co. Ltd., No. 92 Civ. 9310, 1993 WL 497967 (S.D.N.Y. Dec.1, 1993) (arbitrators did not exceed authority by ordering *the parties* "to mutually exchange all documents and witness lists (i.e. full discovery)"). Two cases from other districts address discovery from nonparties and appear to be the most closely analogous to the instant case.

In Stanton v. Paine Webber Jackson & Curtis, Inc., 685 F.Supp. 1241 (S.D.Fla. 1988) the arbitrator, at the request of the defendants, had issued subpoenas to nonparties, requiring prehearing production of documents. The plaintiff objected, contending that issuance of the subpoenas was improper, and constituted impermissible pre-hearing discovery. The court held that:

> [the] plaintiffs ... are asking the court to impose judicial control over the arbitration proceedings. Such action by the court would vitiate the

> purposes of the Federal Arbitration Act: 'to facilitate and expedite the resolution of disputes, ease court congestion, and provide disputants with a less costly alternative to litigation.' Recognition Equip., Inc. v. NCR Corp., 532 F.Supp. 271, 275 (N.D. Tex.1981).
>
> Furthermore, the court finds that under the Arbitration Act, the arbitrators may order and conduct such discovery as they find necessary. See Corcoran v. Shearson/American Express, Inc., 596 F.Supp. 1113, 1117 (N.D.Ga. 1984); Mississippi Power Co. v. Peabody Coal Co., 69 F.R.D. 558 (S.D.Miss. 1976).... Plaintiff's contention that § 7 of the Arbitration Act only permits the arbitrators to compel witnesses at the hearing, and prohibits pre-hearing appearances, is unfounded.

Stanton, 685 F.Supp. at 1242–43. Stanton differs from the instant case in two significant ways. First, the objections to the subpoenas in Stanton were made by one of the parties to the arbitration, not by the subpoenaed nonparty. Second, the subpoenas in Stanton were for the production of documents, and did not require pre-hearing depositions.

When contracting parties stipulate that disputes will be arbitrated, they agree to submit to arbitration procedures rather than court procedures.... At issue here, however, is an objection by *nonparties*. Petitioners are not parties to the reinsurance agreements nor did they agree to arbitration; there is no "bargained for" advantage to the nonparty. Thus, references to cases concerning pre-hearing discovery disputes *between parties* are not persuasive.

The only reported case that explicitly addresses the plight of a nonparty who objects to arbitrator-ordered discovery is Meadows Indem. Co., Ltd. v. Nutmeg Ins. Co., 157 F.R.D. 42 (M.D.Tenn. 1994). There, an arbitration panel ordered a nonparty to produce documents, for inspection by a party, prior to the arbitration hearing. Upon the nonparty's motion for a protective order, the court ruled that the arbitrators' subpoena was valid under the FAA.... The court further noted that because the documents requested would ultimately have to be produced at the hearing, if not prior to it, no added burden was placed on the nonparty. Id.

It is the burden placed on the nonparty that distinguishes Meadows from the instant case. Documents are only produced once, whether it is at the arbitration or prior to it. Common sense encourages the production of documents prior to the hearing so that the parties can familiarize themselves with the content of the documents. Depositions, however, are quite different. The nonparty may be required to appear twice—once for deposition and again at the hearing. That a nonparty might suffer this burden in a litigation is irrelevant; arbitration is not litigation, and the nonparty never consented to be a part of it. Furthermore, as the deposition is not held before the arbitrator, there is nothing to protect the nonparty from harassing or abusive discovery. The nonparty would, of necessity, turn to the court, obligating the court to become enmeshed in the merits of the matter being arbitrated. This would leave "the parties with one foot in court and the other in arbitration." Mississippi Power Co. v. Peabody Coal Co., 69 F.R.D. 558, 564 (S.D.Miss. 1976). Though the Mississippi Power court was addressing "dual discovery"—discovery proceeding simultaneously under the direction of the court and the arbitrators—the considerations of "minimizing the time, expense, and formality of arbitration; preventing duplicative efforts by the federal courts and the arbitrators; and avoiding interference with the arbitrators," Thompson v. Zavin, 607 F.Supp. 780, 782–83 (N.D.Cal. 1984), is equally applicable here.

Thus, an arbitrator may not compel attendance of a nonparty at a pre-hearing deposition. The subpoenas issued by the arbitrators are modified accordingly . . .

* * *

Questions

1. In *COMSAT Corporation v. National Science Foundation*, 190 F.3d 269, 275 (4th Cir. 1999), the Fourth Circuit agreed with the *Integrity* court that depositions of nonparties were not permitted, but it presented a different rationale. The court emphasized Section 7 of the FAA, which provides that "[a]rbitrators . . . may summon in writing any person to appear before them . . . as a witness . . . and to bring with him or them any book, record, document, or paper which may be deemed material." According to the Fourth Circuit, the words "before them" meant before the arbitrator at the hearing, and not during any pre-hearing discovery. Coupling this language with the absence of any expressly stated authority to compel pre-hearing discovery on non-parties, the Fourth Circuit limited the arbitrator's power over non-parties to the actual hearing. See also Hay Group, Inc. v. E.B.S. Acquisition Corp., 360 F.3d 404 (3d Cir. 2004). Cf. Security Life Ins. Co. of Am. v. Duncanson & Holt, Inc. (In re Sec. Life Ins. Co. of Am.), 228 F.3d 865, 870–71 (8th Cir. 2000) ("We thus hold that implicit in an arbitration panel's power to subpoena relevant documents for production at a hearing is the power to order the production of relevant documents for review by a party prior to the hearing," and further stating that it did not matter whether the subpoenaed person was technically a "party" so long as the person was not "a mere bystander pulled into this matter arbitrarily.")

What are the implications of the *COMSAT* rationale for other forms of pre-hearing discovery? Which is the better rationale for limiting nonparty depositions?

2. Should the same considerations govern discovery directed to non-parties as those pertaining to parties? What would a non-party have to do to quash an arbitral discovery subpoena? Is a court more likely to quash an arbitral subpoena issued to a non-party than to a party? Which decision-maker has more authority to order discovery of non-parties—courts under the Federal Rules or arbitrators under the FAA? For more on this topic, see Anne B. O'Hagen, Comment, *Balancing Burdens: Clarifying the Discovery Standard in Arbitration Proceedings*, 117 Yale L.J. 1559 (2008); Jason F.

Darnall & Richard Bales, *Arbitral Discovery of Non–Parties*, 2001 J. Dispute Resol. 321.

3. Does the same policy rationale that supports broad discovery power by judges in a federal court support broad discovery power for arbitrators?

* * *

c. ARBITRATOR AUTHORITY OVER PRE–HEARING PROCEDURES

Golub v. Spivey

520 A.2d 394 (Md.App. 1987).

■ KARWACKI, JUDGE.

FACTS

On July 25, 1979, Mrs. Spivey (Ms. Nagle at that time) was sent by her personal physician to Dr. Golub, a radiologist, for an intravenous pyelogram, a procedure permitting study of a patient's kidney function. Although the pyelogram administered by Dr. Golub revealed inflammation and dysfunction of the left kidney, Dr. Golub erroneously reported a negative finding, i.e., a normal pyelogram. In reliance on Dr. Golub's inaccurate report, Mrs. Spivey's treating physicians failed to provide the immediate care required by her condition. The condition went untreated until the spring of 1980 when Mrs. Spivey visited a urologist. The urologist conducted tests which disclosed that Mrs. Spivey had suffered permanent damage to her left kidney due to an untreated infection.

Mrs. Spivey filed a claim with the Director of the HCAO in August 1980. In addition to Dr. Golub, other health care providers named as defendants in the statement of claim were Richard Berkowitz, M.D., and George N. Karkar, M.D. An arbitration panel consisting of an attorney, a health care provider, and a lay person was appointed pursuant to [Maryland statute] § 3–2A–04(c) to (e).*

On September 9, 1983, three days before the scheduled start of the arbitration hearing, Mrs. Spivey filed a motion in limine seeking to preclude Dr. Golub from presenting expert testimony at the hearing. Previously, on February 17, 1983, the panel chairman had issued an order requiring all counsel in the case to provide the names of experts to each other by July 15, 1983. The other two defendant health care providers each provided the names of two experts by that date, but Dr. Golub did not identify any experts. The panel granted Mrs. Spivey's motion in limine over Dr. Golub's objection that he intended to call the experts named by the other defendant health care providers. The panel also denied Dr. Golub's request for a continuance.

* Eds. Note: The Maryland statute at issue in *Golub* is almost identical to Section 10(a)(3) of the FAA.

A hearing was conducted before the arbitration panel on September 15 and 16, 1983. At the beginning of the hearing, Mrs. Spivey voluntarily dismissed Dr. Berkowitz and Dr. Karkar as defendants. Dr. Golub admitted liability at the hearing, and at its conclusion on September 16, the arbitration panel rendered an award against Dr. Golub in the amount of $150,000. [Dr. Golub sued to vacate the award, arguing that the arbitrator had erred by excluding his expert.] . . .

In his motion to vacate, Dr. Golub relied on § 3–224(b)(4), which states:

> The court shall vacate an award if: . . .
>
> (4) The arbitrators refused to postpone the hearing upon sufficient cause being shown for the postponement, refused to hear evidence material to the controversy, or otherwise so conducted the hearing, contrary to the provisions of § 3–213, as to prejudice substantially the rights of a party.

Dr. Golub contends that the arbitration panel, in granting Mrs. Spivey's motion in limine precluding Dr. Golub from presenting expert testimony at the arbitration hearing, "refused to hear evidence material to the controversy." Furthermore, Dr. Golub posits that the surprise caused by the granting of the motion in limine just prior to the scheduled start of the hearing constituted "sufficient cause" for granting his requested postponement. We think the court was correct in denying Dr. Golub's Motion to Vacate Award. Dr. Golub's argument overlooks the arbitration panel's basis for granting Mrs. Spivey's motion in limine. A deadline for naming experts had been established by the panel chairman in a scheduling order issued on February 17, 1983. That deadline was July 15, 1983. Dr. Golub not only failed to name any experts by that date, but he did not provide any names until the motion in limine was filed on September 9, 1983, at which point he sought to claim as his own the experts identified by the other two defendants.

The panel chairman in a health claims arbitration proceeding has the authority to decide all prehearing procedures including issues relating to discovery. § 3–2A–05(c). We believe exclusion of expert testimony on Dr. Golub's behalf was an appropriate sanction for Dr. Golub's failure to comply with the discovery deadline in the panel chairman's scheduling order. Therefore, the Circuit Court did not err in denying Dr. Golub's Motion to Vacate Award . . .

JUDGMENT AFFIRMED; COSTS TO BE PAID BY THE APPELLANT.

* * *

Questions

1. Are the arbitrators and court in *Golub* importing judicial procedures into the arbitral setting? Is this appropriate?

2. The court in *Golub* states that the arbitrators have authority over all pre-hearing procedures. Are there limits on the arbitrator's authority over the conduct of pre-hearing procedures? Should there be? Should there be limits to the arbitrator's authority over hearing procedures?

* * *

d. CONTRACTUAL RESTRICTIONS ON DISCOVERY

Continental Airlines, Inc. v. Mason

87 F.3d 1318 (9th Cir. 1996).

■ MEMORANDUM OPINION.

Alecia B. Mason ... appeals the district court's Order compelling arbitration of her claims against Continental Airlines of employment discrimination, wrongful termination, and infliction of emotional distress.... Mason['s] claim that the ... arbitration procedure [contained in the company's employee handbook] was unconscionable because it did not provide for discovery or legal counsel is meritless. In order to be unconscionable, a contract clause must "shock the conscience." ... There is nothing that shocks the conscience about an arbitration procedure that does not provide for discovery or legal representation....

* * *

Wilks v. Pep Boys

241 F.Supp.2d 860 (M.D. Tenn. 2003).

■ TRAUGHER, DISTRICT JUDGE.

[A group of employees sued their employer for alleged violations of the Fair Labor Standards Act. The employer moved to dismiss and compel arbitration. Each of the employees had signed an arbitration agreement. However, because the employer had modified its arbitration agreement on several occasions, each plaintiff had signed a different version of the arbitration agreement. Apparently, some of the arbitration agreements provided that arbitration would be conducted under rules promulgated by the American Arbitration Association (AAA), and other agreements provided that arbitration would be conducted under rules promulgated by the Judicial Arbitration and Mediation Services/Endispute (JAMS).]

The Agreement provides for the following discovery:

> Each party shall have the right to take the deposition of one individual and any expert witness designated by another party. Each party also shall have the right to propound requests for production of documents to any party.... Additional discovery may be had only where the Arbitrator selected so orders, upon a showing of substantial need.

The plaintiffs contend that, in the context of this collective FLSA case, that provision is "lopsided" and, therefore, unconscionable. The plaintiffs maintain that the defendant will only need to depose each plaintiff (its one deposition), but that the plaintiffs will need to depose numerous managers and other supervisory personnel in order to prove their claims. . . .

[T]he rules of AAA and JAMS provide relief for the plaintiffs from this discovery provision. Rule 7 of AAA's National Rules provides that: "The arbitrator shall have the authority to order such discovery ... as the arbitrator considers necessary to a full and fair exploration of the issues in dispute, consistent with the expedited nature of arbitration." This standard, more liberal than the "substantial need" standard in the Agreement, would determine the scope of discovery because Rule 1 of the National Rules provides that if an "adverse material inconsistency exists between the arbitration agreement and these rules, the arbitrator shall apply these rules."

Likewise, JAMS procedure forecloses lopsided discovery in favor of the employer. Standard No. 4 of the Minimum Standards provides for the "exchange of core information prior to the arbitration," and the Comment to that Standard provides that, in addition to one deposition for each side, "[o]ther discovery should be available at the arbitrator's discretion." Rule 2 of the JAMS Rules & Procedures mandates that these Minimum Standards prevail over any inconsistent agreement between the parties. . . .

The various versions of the Agreement, as it must be administered by AAA and JAMS, is [sic] valid and enforceable. Therefore, as to the plaintiffs and prospective plaintiffs who have executed the Mutual Agreement to Arbitrate Claims in versions that do not differ in material respects from the versions before the court, this litigation will be dismissed, and those plaintiffs will be compelled to arbitrate their FLSA claims.

* * *

Walker v. Ryan's Family Steak Houses, Inc.

289 F.Supp.2d 916 (M.D. Tenn. 2003), aff'd, 400 F.3d 370 (6th Cir. 2005).

■ TRAUGHER, DISTRICT JUDGE.

[A group of employees sued their employer for alleged violations of the Fair Labor Standards Act. The employer moved to dismiss and compel arbitration.]

Since 1993, Ryan's has had in place an agreement with Employment Dispute Services, Inc. ("EDSI") under which EDSI [a for-profit arbitration provider] agrees to provide an arbitral forum for all Ryan's job applicants, employees, and the company itself, in exchange for annual payment from Ryan's. In turn, Ryan's requires all job applicants, prior to being considered for employment, to sign a document ... under which applicants agree to submit any and all employment-related disputes to EDSI's arbitration process and forego their right to have claims heard in a judicial forum. If an applicant refuses to sign the Agreement, she will not be considered for employment with Ryan's. Ryan's is named in the Agreement as a third party beneficiary.

Although limited discovery provisions are common in arbitration as a means of streamlining the process, the limited discovery available in the EDSI forum burdens the employee-claimant far more heavily than the employer, suggesting structural bias in favor of the employer. Both parties may request production of documents and are required to exchange witness lists and documents to be offered into evidence prior to arbitration. (Docket No. 82, Ex. 1, 2000 Rules at 4–6.) However, parties are able to schedule only one deposition as of right, and additional depositions are strongly disfavored, even under the current Rules: "Either party may file a request with the adjudication panel for additional depositions, but such requests are not encouraged and shall be granted *in extraordinary fact situations only and for good cause shown.*" *Id.* at 6 (emphasis added). Employment claims often require an employee to conduct many depositions (e.g., co-workers, supervisors, etc.) to make out her case, while employers are often able to defend such claims with only one deposition—that of the employee. Thus, employees usually have a need for more discovery than employers, and stringent limitations on depositions such as those promulgated by EDSI more heavily burden the employee than the employer. Additionally, this court has previously noted that the rules of the American Arbitration Association and the Judicial Arbitration and Mediation Services/Endispute are relatively liberal in affording additional discovery "where necessary to a full and fair exploration of the issues in dispute." *See Wilks v. Pep Boys,* 241 F.Supp.2d 860, 865 (M.D. Tenn.2003). This liberal attitude towards discovery stands in stark contrast to EDSI's strict requirement that additional discovery should issue only in "extraordinary fact situations" and "for good cause shown." . . .

Although this court recognizes the liberal federal policy favoring arbitration, it finds that the circumstances of this case preclude submitting these claims to the EDSI arbitral forum. For the reasons stated herein, the defendant's motion to dismiss and petition to compel arbitration and stay proceedings will be denied.

* * *

Ostroff v. Alterra Healthcare Corp.

433 F.Supp.2d 538 (E.D.Pa. 2006).

[A daughter sued on behalf of her mother, who had been injured while residing in a nursing home.]

While plaintiff in this case is allowed "permissible discovery per the Pennsylvania Rules of Civil Procedure," she is only allowed to depose defendant's expert witnesses. This restriction means that plaintiff cannot depose any of defendant's employees or any of the other residents of [the nursing home]. Under the facts of this case, the only individuals who know exactly how Restine was injured are employees of [the nursing home], and possibly other residents of the facility. Without depositions, plaintiff will be limited to obtaining statements from other [the nursing home] residents on a voluntary basis. With respect to defendant's employees, Pennsylvania Rule of Professional Conduct 4.2 prohibits plaintiff's lawyer from communicating with any employee who might establish the liability of the defendant.... If plaintiff cannot depose other residents of [the nursing home] or defendant's employees, she will be forced to proceed to arbitration with only limited information as to how the accident in question occurred.... Plaintiff's limited information will put her at a distinct disadvantage in arbitration ...

* * *

Williams v. Katten, Muchin & Zavis

1996 WL 717447 (N.D. Ill.).

■ MAROVICH, DISTRICT JUDGE.

[Plaintiff Elaine Williams moved to vacate an arbitration award in her favor and to reinstate her employment discrimination claims in federal court. The arbitration award did not give Williams any front pay damages or compensatory damages for her alleged medical expenses and emotional harm. One of Williams' arguments supporting vacatur was that KMZ had refused to produce three of four of her proposed deponents. The arbitrator, after holding a pre-hearing discovery conference, had denied Williams' deposition requests.]

The AAA Rules, incorporated into the [arbitration] agreement, authorize an arbitrator to subpoena a witness and documents either independently or upon the request of a party, and empower the arbitrator to determine the appropriate scope of discovery.... While it may be true that Williams was not permitted to engage in discovery to the extent she had hoped, it is also true that "by agreeing to arbitrate, a party trades the procedures and opportunity for review of the courtroom for the simplicity, informality, and expedition of arbitration." *Gilmer*, 500 U.S. at 26 (citation omitted)....

Williams ... claims that the arbitrator's discovery rulings in KMZ's favor prevented her from presenting facts critical to her claim and thereby denied her a fundamentally fair hearing. The Court is permitted to vacate an arbitrator's award where the arbitrators "refuse[d] to hear evidence pertinent and material to the controversy." 9 U.S.C. § 10(a)(3). However, the informal nature of arbitration proceedings effectuates the national policy favoring arbitration, and such proceedings require "expeditious and summary hearing, with only restricted inquiry into factual issues."

At the discovery hearing, the [a]rbitrator Simon ruled on the relevance of each discovery request, and explained, for example, why it would be inappropriate for Williams to depose the three individuals she had requested ... [The arbitrator's] discovery rulings were not arbitrary and capricious as Williams would like this Court to believe; rather, the arbitrator offered the parties the opportunity to present to the panel "the most relevant evidence in support of [their] respective sides." Williams has failed to demonstrate that the arbitrator's discovery rulings in this case constitute the kind of fundamental error necessary to find that Williams was deprived of a fair hearing.

* * *

Questions

1. Though courts are not entirely consistent, the trend seems to be that courts in employment and consumer cases will enforce arbitration agreements that give the arbitrator discretion to permit or limit discovery, but refuse to enforce agreements that impose absolute limitations on discovery or that forbid discovery altogether. See Martin H. Malin, *Privatizing Justice–But By How Much? Questions Gilmer Did Not Answer*, 16 Ohio State Journal on Dispute Resolution 589 (2001) (arguing that discovery in employment arbitration should be left to the discretion of the arbitrator to determine on a case-by-case basis). What about where the arbitrator has discretion, but exercises it to forbid the consumer/employee from conducting any discovery? Should it matter whether restrictions on discovery come from the contract or from the arbitrator?

2. Is there an appropriate way to balance the parties' need for discovery against the desire for a quick and inexpensive resolution of the dispute?

3. How do these cases fit with the cases in the preceding section about discovery of nonparties? Are the nursing home residents in *Ostroff*, and the supervisors and other decisionmakers in the employment cases, nonparties?

4. Note that the first four discovery cases excerpted above are before the court on the defendant's motion to compel arbitration. The last case is before the court on the employee's motion to vacate an arbitration award. Should the procedural posture of the case affect the court's analysis of the discovery issue?

* * *

6. Evidence

Totem Marine Tug & Barge, Inc. v. North American Towing, Inc.

607 F.2d 649 (5th Cir. 1979).

■ Reavley, Circuit Judge:

North American Towing, Inc. (North American) applied for confirmation of an arbitration award against Totem Marine Tug and Barge, Inc. (Totem), which sought to vacate or modify the award. The arbitrators' decision held that Totem had breached the charter agreement between the parties and awarded North American damages of $74,568.08. The district court confirmed the award. 429 F.Supp. 452 (E.D.La. 1977). Because of irregularities in the conduct of the arbitration hearing which materially prejudiced Totem, we reverse.

FACTS

On June 19, 1975, Totem and North American entered a six month time charter agreement for the M/V KIRT CHOUEST owned by North American. The vessel was to be delivered to Totem at Galliano, Louisiana, and to be returned there or to any other mutually agreed port at the expiration of the charter term. Totem was to use the vessel to tow a loaded barge from Houston through the Panama Canal and into the Pacific, to Los Angeles and then Seattle, and finally to Anchorage, Alaska. On October 19, 1975, Totem terminated the charter allegedly because of excessive repairs and delays caused by the vessel. North American requested arbitration. Totem responded by seeking a clarification of North American's claim. North American provided an itemized statement of the claim, the first and largest item being the "Specific contract amount for returning vessel $45,000.00" (R. at 29). Totem counterclaimed alleging that the vessel was unfit for the purposes of the charter and that the vessel had been redelivered at a mutually agreed port: Anchorage.

Although North American never requested damages for charter hire, the contract amount for use of the vessel between October 19 (the date of Totem's alleged breach) and December 19 (the end of the charter term), the arbitration panel awarded it nonetheless. The panel stated: "North American erroneously asked only for its return expense (plus some miscellaneous accounting items) in damages. The proper measure of North American's damages was the balance of charter hire due under the charter less the earnings of the vessel during that period." (R. at 118). Totem contends that by this action the arbitrators exceeded their powers and awarded on a matter not submitted to them, thereby impairing the award under the provisions of 9 U.S.C.A. § 10(d) and § 11(b) (1970).

The panel then computed North American's damages as the charter hire due under the contract from October 19 to December 19, less the earnings of the KIRT CHOUEST during the same time period, plus some miscellaneous expenses. It is undisputed that after the close of the arbitration proceedings, during deliberations, the arbitrators realized that each had a different figure in his notes on the earnings of the KIRT CHOUEST from October to December. The arbitrator appointed by North American then telephoned North American's counsel who supplied the figure which the arbitrators used to complete their computations. Totem was neither notified of this telephone conversation nor given any opportunity to respond to the figure provided by North American. Totem contends that this ex parte communication constituted prejudicial misconduct by the arbitrators in violation of 9 U.S.C.A. § 10(c).

UNLAWFUL EXTENSION OF SUBJECT MATTER

Totem contends that the issue of charter hire was never placed in issue in the arbitration proceeding and that an award on that basis denied it due process. North American acknowledges that it never specifically requested damages for charter hire but claims that the matter was naturally intertwined in the general scope of the breach of contract claim.

An arbitration proceeding is much less formal than a trial in court. "In handling evidence an arbitrator need not follow all the niceties observed by the federal courts. He need only grant the parties a fundamentally fair hearing." Bell Aerospace Co. Div. of Textron, Inc. v. Local 516, UAW, 500 F.2d 921, 923 (2d Cir. 1974). All parties in an arbitration proceeding are entitled to notice and an opportunity to be heard. Citizens Bldg. of West Palm Beach, Inc. v. Western Union Tel. Co., 120 F.2d 982, 984 (5th Cir. 1941); Seldner Corp. v. W. R. Grace & Co., 22 F.Supp. 388, 391–93 (D.Md. 1938). Although arbitrators enjoy a broad grant of authority to fashion remedies (Commercial Arbitration Rules of the American Arbitration Association § 42), arbitrators are restricted to those issues submitted ...

Arbitration is contractual and arbitrators derive their authority from the scope of the contractual agreement. United Steelworkers of America v. Enterprise Wheel and Car Corp., 363 U.S. 593, 597, 80 S.Ct. 1358, 4 L.Ed.2d 1424 (1960); Gulf and South America Steamship Co., Inc. v. National Maritime Union of America, 360 F.2d 63, 65 (5th Cir. 1966). The award of an arbitration panel may be vacated where the arbitrators exceed their powers. 9 U.S.C.A. § 10(d) (1970) ...

The arbitration panel exceeded its powers by awarding damages for charter hire to North American. Not only did North American fail to list charter hire in its itemized statement of damages submitted to Totem, but in its brief submitted to the arbitration panel, North American conceded that charter hire was not an issue in the arbitration. Totem prepared and argued a case in which return expenses, and not charter hire, was the main issue. North American originally claimed damages totalling $74,713.63, later amended to a total of $87,047.82, the first and largest item claimed being $45,000.00 for return of the vessel. With the exception of the $45,000 claim for returning the vessel, and a few other very minor exceptions totalling less than $1,000, the arbitration panel fully upheld North American's claim. In place of the $45,000 North American requested for return of the vessel, the arbitrators awarded charter hire totalling $117,440.00, bringing the total damages due North American to $157,887.63, before Totem's offsets and counterclaims. It is anomalous for the arbitration panel to award an unrequested item of damages three times larger than any item claimed by North American and then to hear the panel action supported with an argument that the awarded item was naturally intertwined within the scope of the arbitration.

In its letter of February 4, 1976, responding to Totem's request for a clarification of the matters to be submitted to arbitration, North American set forth the nature of the dispute and the amount involved by itemizing its damages. Although return expenses were specifically listed, damages for charter hire were not. By awarding charter hire, the arbitrators ignored the arbitral dispute submitted by the parties and dispensed their "own brand of industrial justice." United Steelworkers of America v. Enterprise Wheel and Car Corp., supra, 363 U.S. at 597, 80 S.Ct. 1358.

EX PARTE COMMUNICATION

After the arbitrators decided to base North American's damages on charter hire instead of the expenses of returning the vessel, it became necessary to determine the earnings of the KIRT CHOUEST between October and December as an offset. Because charter hire had never been placed in issue and the vessel's earnings had arisen only as related to the issue of whether the vessel had been returned to North American at Anchorage, each of the arbitrators had a different figure in his notes and none were confident that he had the correct figure. Consequently, although the hearings had been closed several days earlier, and despite the fact that the office of Totem's counsel was in the same building in which the arbitrators were deliberating, a long distance call was placed to North American's counsel to ascertain the earnings of the KIRT CHOUEST. The figure supplied by North American's counsel was adopted by the panel although it matched none of their figures. Totem was never notified of the call or given any opportunity to contest the figure supplied.

In clause twenty-four of the charter agreement, Totem and North American incorporated the Commercial Arbitration Rules of the American Arbitration Association for the resolution of any dispute between them. Section thirty of the Arbitration Rules states that "(a)ll evidence shall be taken in the presence of all the parties, except where any of the parties is absent in default or has waived his right to be present." Evidence was received from North American's counsel out of Totem's presence when the telephone call was made and the figure given by North American was adopted by the arbitrators as the basis for their computations. Totem neither defaulted nor waived its rights, but instead, timely filed a motion to vacate in district court. The arbitration rules provide specific procedures for the receipt of evidence[7] and the close of hearings,[8] procedures violated by the ex parte communication with North American.

7. Section 31 provides as follows:

Section 31. EVIDENCE BY AFFIDAVIT AND FILING OF DOCUMENTS

The Arbitrator shall receive and consider the evidence of witnesses by affidavit, but shall give it only such weight as he deems it entitled to after consideration of any objections made to its admission. All documents not filed with the Arbitrator at the hearing, but arranged for at the hearing or subsequently by agreement of the parties, shall be filed with the AAA for transmission to the Arbitrator. All parties shall be afforded opportunity to examine such documents.

8. Section 34 provides as follows:

Section 34. CLOSING OF HEARINGS

The Arbitrator shall specifically inquire of all parties whether they have any further proofs to offer or witnesses to be heard. Upon receiving negative replies, the Arbitrator shall declare the hearings closed and a minute thereof shall be recorded. If briefs are to be filed, the hearings shall be declared closed as of the final date set by the Arbitrator for the receipt of briefs. If documents are to be filed as provided for in Section 31 and the date set for their receipt is later than that set for the receipt of briefs, the later date shall be the date of closing the hearing. The time limit within which the Arbitrator is required to make his award shall commence to run, in the absence of other agreements by the parties, upon the closing of the hearings.

After the arbitration panel improperly extended the scope of arbitration to include charter hire, the extent of Totem's liability hinged on the determination of the earnings of the KIRT CHOUEST between October and December. The ex parte receipt of evidence bearing on this matter constituted misbehavior by the arbitrators prejudicial to Totem's rights in violation of 9 U.S.C.A. § 10(c); E. g., Chevron Transport Corp. v. Astro Vencedor Compania Naviera, S. A., 300 F.Supp. 179 (S.D.N.Y. 1969) (the failure of maritime arbitrators to make the ship's logs in the hand of one party fully and timely available to the other party was considered sufficient grounds for vacating the award where the party could show that he was thereby prejudiced); Katz v. Uvegi, 18 Misc.2d 576, 187 N.Y.S.2d 511 (Sup.Ct. 1959), aff'd, 11 A.D.2d 773, 205 N.Y.S.2d 972 (App.Div. 1960): "Arbitrators cannot conduct ex parte hearings or receive evidence except in the presence of each other and of the parties, unless otherwise stipulated." 18 Misc.2d at 583, 187 N.Y.S.2d at 518.

We vacate the award without prejudice to the resubmission of the dispute between the parties before a new arbitration panel in accordance with the terms of the contract.

* * *

Questions

1. In *Totem Marine Tug & Barge*, suppose the rules governing the arbitration were silent about whether the parties should be present for all evidence. How would the case have been decided in that event?

2. How can a court know if the evidence heard *ex parte* was prejudicial? Can it interrogate the arbitrator to find out?

* * *

Smaligo v. Fireman's Fund Insurance Company

247 A.2d 577 (Pa. 1968).

■ JONES, JUSTICE.

Michael and Mary Smaligo, as personal representatives of their daughter's estate, instituted arbitration proceedings to recover for the daughter's death caused by a hit-and-run driver on March 27, 1967, at a time said daughter, aged 37, was on a home week-end visit from Mayview State Hospital where she had been a patient since 1962. Arbitration proceeded under the "Uninsured Motorist Clause" of Smaligos' policy of insurance with Fireman's Fund Insurance Company, which resulted in an award to Smaligos of only $243.00 (a figure which represented one-third of the cost of the family memorial monument).

Smaligos moved to vacate the award on the ground of certain irregularities in the arbitration proceedings, to-wit: (1) that the arbitrator proceeded to make an award even though informed by Smaligos' counsel of their acceptance of a settlement offer made prior to the arbitration proceedings, which offer Smaligos claimed was still outstanding; and (2) that the arbitrator denied a request of Smaligos' counsel for a recess to obtain the testimony of Dr. Parsons, decedent's attending physician, as to decedent's future work expectancy, the arbitrator holding such testimony not to be necessary. Smaligos argued that these irregularities resulted in an unjust, inequitable and unconscionable award for the death of a 37–year old woman who had been gainfully employed prior to her commitment to Mayview State Hospital in 1962. After a hearing on Smaligos' motion the court below issued an order vacating the award and remanding the case for hearing *de novo* before another arbitrator to be selected from the American Arbitration Association Panel.

The insurance company has appealed from said order, contending that, since the proceedings were admittedly under the common law, the court was bound by the arbitrator's action. In making this argument, the insurance company relies on our holding in Harwitz v. Selas Corporation of America, 406 Pa. 539, 178 A.2d 617 (1962), as follows: "If the appeal is from a common law award, Appellant, to succeed, must show by clear, precise and indubitable evidence that he was denied a hearing, or that there was fraud, misconduct, corruption or some other irregularity of this nature on the part of the arbitrator which caused him to render an unjust, inequitable and unconscionable award, the arbitrator being the final judge of both law and fact, his award not being subject to disturbance for a mistake of either."

A review of the record reveals the following facts: Elizabeth Smaligo, the decedent—a high school graduate who had also attended night classes at Duquesne University—had been gainfully employed as a secretary by Westinghouse Electric Corporation from 1949 until October, 1962, when she was admitted to Western Psychiatric Hospital and there diagnosed as schizophrenic. Later she was committed to Mayview State Hospital and, at the time of her death, was still so committed though permitted to visit her home on weekends and holidays. During such a home a weekend stay she was struck by a hit-and-run driver on March 27, 1967. Smaligos then made claim against their insurance company under the terms of the Uninsured Motorist Provisions of an automobile liability policy that had been issued to them by that company wherein the company had agreed to pay "all sums which the insured or his legal representative shall be legally entitled to recover as damages." The company refused to pay the $9,750.00 asked by Smaligos in settlement and on July 27, 1967 the company notified Smaligos' counsel by letter as follows: "We concede that there is a settlement value to the case but that it is not worth $9,750. as demanded by you. In an effort to avoid further expenses and time to both, I will now make an offer to conclude this claim on an amicable basis and for the sum of $7,500. which you may convey to your clients. If the offer of $7,500. is not acceptable, I would then suggest that your arbitration papers be prepared as we have no intention of increasing this offer, feeling that it is fair and just to all parties concerned.''

On August 30, 1967, Smaligos' counsel made a demand for arbitration to the American Arbitration Association and on October 11, 1967 Thomas J. Reinstadtler, Jr., Esquire, was appointed as arbitrator. A hearing was held on December 18, 1967 which, as before stated, resulted in the arbitrator awarding only $243, being one-third of the cost of a family memorial monument. The arbitrator determined that the funeral bill of $1,016.30 was payable under the Medical Payment Clause of the policy and thus not recoverable under the Uninsured Motorist Clause.

It must be conceded that there was no evidence in the record that decedent would ever again be gainfully employed. However, Smaligos' counsel testified at the hearing on the motion to vacate that he had asked the arbitrator for a continuance in order to secure the expert testimony of Dr. Parsons on the question of decedent's future earning ability and capacity and that the arbitrator stated that such testimony was not necessary. Dr. Parsons was decedent's attending physician. The arbitrator, on the other hand, testified that no formal motion for continuance was made and that he could not remember ''specifically what Mr. Maurizi asked or what my response was,'' although he did not deny that he had said Dr. Parsons' testimony was unnecessary. In fact, counsel who had represented defendant company during the arbitration proceedings testified that the arbitrator did state that the doctor's testimony was unnecessary.

Whether or not a formal motion for continuance was made is not as governing as the arbitrator seeks to make it. The important fact that stands clear is that Smaligos' counsel did proffer medical testimony which was relevant and of great import in the determination of loss of future earnings of the decedent and that the arbitrator determined such testimony was not necessary. It may be true that Smaligos' counsel should have come prepared with the medical testimony at the time of the hearing and that perhaps the necessity of such testimony came to him as an ''afterthought'' (as stated by the arbitrator), but such observations cannot militate from the all-important fact that counsel did at the time of the hearing make an offer to present the medical testimony and the arbitrator viewed such testimony as ''unnecessary''.

This was not a mere mistake of law or of fact binding upon all parties and the court. The arbitrator's failure to regard Dr. Parsons' testimony of any import resulted in Smaligos being denied a full and fair hearing. That an award is not binding where there has been a denial of a hearing has been clearly stated by this Court on several occasions. In Newspaper Guild of Greater Philadelphia v. Philadelphia Daily News, Inc., 401 Pa. 337, 346, 164 A.2d 215, 220 (1960), we stated: ''The defenses available to the News in a proceeding to enforce a common law award are extremely limited. Such an award of arbitrators is conclusive and binding and cannot be attacked unless it can be shown by clear, precise and indubitable evidence that the parties were denied a hearing, or that there was fraud, misconduct, corruption or some other irregularity of this nature on the part of the arbitrators which caused them to render an unjust, inequitable and unconscionable award." We repeated this holding in Harwitz v. Selas Corporation of America, 406 Pa. 539, 542, 178 A.2d 617, 619 (1962), the very case relied upon by defendant as hereinbefore quoted and again here quoted as follows: "If the appeal is from a common law award, Appellant, to succeed, must show by clear, precise and indubitable evidence that he was denied a hearing, or that there was fraud, misconduct, corruption or some other irregularity of this nature on the part of the arbitrator which caused him to render an unjust, inequitable and unconscionable award, the arbitrator being the final judge of both law and fact, his award not being subject to disturbance for a mistake of either. Newspaper Guild of Greater Philadelphia v. Philadelphia Daily News, Inc., 401 Pa. 337, 164 A.2d 215 (1960)"...

Though the arbitrator's conduct in this case may not have constituted fraud, misconduct, corruption or some other irregularity "of this nature", yet it was conduct which amounted to a denial of a full and fair hearing of Smaligos' cause of action. It is our opinion, therefore, that the court below properly vacated the award and remanded it for arbitration before another arbitrator....

Order affirmed.

■ MUSMANNO, COHEN and ROBERTS, JJ., did not participate in this decision.

* * *

Questions

1. The court in *Smaligo* decided that the disputed evidence was relevant and therefore should have been admitted by the arbitrator. How can a court determine the relevance of the evidence in an arbitration proceeding? To what degree does this require the court to consider the merits of the case?

2. What does the *Smaligo* decision indicate about the minimal due process protections required to constitute a "full and fair" hearing?

* * *

Note on Robbins v. Day

In *Robbins v. Day*, 954 F.2d 679 (11th Cir. 1992),[1] the plaintiffs initiated arbitration proceedings against the defendant stockbrokers based on a claim of excessive trading constituting churning of the plaintiffs' accounts. At arbitration, the defendant-stockbrokers asserted the Fifth Amendment's provision against self-incrimination and refused to testify because they were under indictment for securities fraud arising from the same set of facts. The stockbrokers also sought to continue the hearing until after the securities fraud trial was completed. The plaintiffs opposed

1. The Supreme Court overruled Robbins v. Day on grounds unrelated to the issue for which it is cited here. See First Options of Chicago, Inc. v. Kaplan, 514 U.S. 938 (1995).

the continuance, which was refused on the ground that the stockbrokers' testimony was unimportant to the proceedings. The stockbrokers prevailed in the arbitration. Subsequently, in seeking to have the award vacated, the plaintiffs argued that the arbitrators should have compelled the stockbrokers to testify. The Eleventh Circuit refused to vacate, noting that "[a] federal court may vacate an arbitrator's award ... only if the arbitrator's refusal to hear pertinent and material evidence prejudices the rights of the parties and denies them a fair hearing. Further, an arbitration award must not be set aside for the arbitrator's refusal to hear evidence that is cumulative or irrelevant."

In reaching its decision to refuse to vacate the award, the court emphasized the systemic virtues of arbitration:

> In applying the statutory grounds for the granting of a motion to vacate an award, we always bear in mind that the basic policy of conducting arbitration is to offer a means of deciding disputes expeditiously and at lower costs. Thus the Federal Arbitration Act allows arbitration to proceed with only a summary hearing and with restricted inquiry into factual issues. The arbitrator is not bound to hear all the evidence tendered by the parties; he need only give each party the opportunity to present its arguments and evidence.... We will not undermine the expediency of arbitration to determine the materiality or pertinence of excluded evidence that the moving party agreed was unimportant.

How might a court determine whether excluded evidence is "cumulative or irrelevant" or "central and decisive"? Suppose an arbitration award was not accompanied by an opinion, but merely stated which party prevailed and the amount of monetary damages. How should a reviewing court evaluate the relevance of excluded evidence in that case?

* * *

Bonar v. Dean Witter Reynolds, Inc.

835 F.2d 1378 (11th Cir. 1988).

■ KRAVITCH, CIRCUIT JUDGE:

Arbitrators of a dispute between the Bonars and Dean Witter Reynolds awarded punitive as well as compensatory damages to the Bonars. Dean Witter claims that the district court abused its discretion in refusing to vacate the award of punitive damages because (1) it was obtained through fraud; (2) the arbitrators lacked authority to award punitive damages; (3) the appellees contractually waived any right they may have had to punitive damages; and (4) the punitive damages award was so irrational as to be an abuse of the arbitrators' discretion. Concluding that the district court abused its discretion in not vacating the award on the ground of fraud, we reverse and remand for a new hearing on the issue of punitive damages.

I

[In July, 1982, appellees James and Beverly Bonar opened a securities trading account at Dean Witter's Orlando, Florida office, with an initial deposit of $16,436.77. Their account executive, Ed Leavenworth, stole funds from their account so that, by November, 1983, it was depleted. Leavenworth stole funds from another account in 1984, and deposited those stolen funds into appellees account. In September, 1984, Leavenworth left the employ of Dean Witter and went to another investment firm. Appellees closed their Dean Witter account and moved it to Leavenworth's new firm. When they closed their Dean Witter Account, it had a market value of $11,489.90. In January, 1985, Dean Witter discovered Leavenworth's embezzlement and notified all his former customers, including appellees. In addition, Dean Witter turned over the results of its investigation to the State Attorney for Orange County, Florida, and assisted in the criminal prosecution and ultimate incarceration of Leavenworth.]

On August 9, 1985, the appellees filed a complaint and demand for arbitration with the American Arbitration Association alleging violations of various state and federal laws, breach of fiduciary duty, negligence, and gross negligence in the handling of their account. The complaint, seeking compensatory and punitive damages, named as defendants Dean Witter, John McNally, Jr., the branch manager of the Orlando office, and Leavenworth. Leavenworth was never served with process and thus never became a party to the arbitration proceedings.

A three member arbitration panel heard the appellees' case on May 8–9, 1986. At the hearing, Dean Witter and McNally admitted liability for compensatory damages.[2] Because of this admission, the central factual issue for the arbitrators to decide was whether the conduct of Dean Witter and McNally justified the imposition of punitive damages. At the hearing, in addition to the testimony from lay witnesses, the appellees presented the testimony of two expert witnesses to support their claim for punitive damages. The second expert, Thomas E. Nix, testified that he was president and owner of an investment advisory firm, that he graduated from the University of Alabama in 1980 with a bachelor's degree in finance and that in 1981 he attended Columbia University and received a bachelor's degree in accounting. Nix further testified that after his graduation from Columbia he worked for St. Paul in New York as the money manager of a $30 million portfolio and that in the summer of 1985 he received an honorary doctorate in finance from the Technical University of Vienna.

During voir dire, Nix admitted that he was not, and never had been, a licensed securities broker or branch manager of a securities brokerage house. Based on this, Dean Witter requested that Nix not be allowed to testify on the ground that he was "not qualified as an expert to render testimony on the trading in any account." After the panel rejected this

2. McNally and Dean Witter admitted liability for compensatory damages in the amount of $5,886.77. This figure represents the appellees' original deposit of $16,436.77, less the $11,489.90 value of the stock transferred to appellees when they closed their account, plus interest of 12%.

request, Nix testified that, in his opinion, the trading in the appellees' account was excessive, and that Dean Witter and McNally had not properly supervised the appellees' account. On June 5, 1986, the arbitrators assessed compensatory damages against both Dean Witter and McNally, and punitive damages of $150,000 against Dean Witter alone. Following the award, Dean Witter applied to the arbitration panel for a reduction in, or the elimination of, the award of punitive damages. The arbitrators denied that application on July 15, 1986.

On July 30, 1986, Dean Witter moved to vacate or modify the arbitration award pursuant to the Federal Arbitration Act, 9 U.S.C. §§ 10 and 11, (the "Arbitration Act") on the grounds that the arbitrators lacked authority to award punitive damages, that the appellees contractually waived any right to punitive damages, and that the punitive damage award was based upon a manifest disregard of the evidence and was so irrational as to be an abuse of the arbitrators' discretion. Before the district court decided this motion, Dean Witter discovered that the credentials asserted by Nix as a basis for his testimony as an expert witness were completely false. Nix was an engineering student at the University of Alabama and never graduated from that institution. Furthermore, he never attended Columbia University or worked for St. Paul.

Accordingly, on November 20, 1986, Dean Witter filed an amended motion to vacate or modify the arbitration award adding as grounds that the award should be vacated under 9 U.S.C. § 10(a) because it was procured through fraud ... Shortly thereafter, the appellees filed motions to confirm the arbitration award, ... and to strike as untimely Dean Witter's amended motion to vacate. In the motion to strike, the appellees admitted that Nix had committed perjury at the arbitration hearing.

By orders dated December 9, 1986, the district court granted appellees' motion to confirm the arbitration award, denied Dean Witter's amended motion to vacate or modify the award, and denied all other motions of both parties. The district court took the above actions by stamping GRANTED or DENIED on the face of the parties' motions. As a result, there is no written order explaining the basis for these decisions. The district court entered a final judgment based on the arbitration award against Dean Witter and McNally on April 2, 1987 and this appeal followed.

II

* * *

B.

... [W]e must now decide whether the district court, in denying the motion, abused its discretion under the Arbitration Act. Section 10 of the Arbitration Act specifies the grounds for vacating an arbitration award and provides as follows:

> (a) In either of the following cases the United States court in and for the district wherein the award was made may make an order vacating the award upon the application of any party to the arbitration award—
>
> (1) Where the award was procured by corruption, fraud, or undue means.

In reviewing cases under § 10(a), courts have relied upon a three part test to determine whether an arbitration award should be vacated for fraud.[7] First, the movant must establish the fraud by clear and convincing evidence.... Second, the fraud must not have been discoverable upon the exercise of due diligence prior to or during the arbitration. Third, the person seeking to vacate the award must demonstrate that the fraud materially related to an issue in the arbitration. This last element does not require the movant to establish that the result of the proceedings would have been different had the fraud not occurred. [Citations omitted.]

Mindful that we are reviewing the district court's refusal to vacate under the narrow "abuse of discretion" standard, we nevertheless hold that under the above test, Nix's perjury requires vacation of the punitive damages portion of the arbitration award. First, along with its amended motion to vacate the award, Dean Witter submitted to the district court clear and convincing evidence of Nix's perjury. Letters from the relevant university officials revealed that, contrary to his testimony, Nix had never graduated from the University of Alabama and had never attended Columbia University. Furthermore, an affidavit from the Human Resources Officer at St. Paul Fire and Marine Insurance Company confirmed that Nix had never worked for either St. Paul or its banking subsidiary. Second, Dean Witter has shown that it could not have discovered Nix's perjury before or during the arbitration hearing. Because the rules of the American Arbitration Association do not provide for a pre-hearing exchange of witness lists, Dean Witter did not know who would testify as appellees' expert witnesses until the time of the hearing. Without a pre-hearing opportunity to thoroughly investigate Nix's credentials, Dean Witter could not have known the extent to which he lied about them at the hearing.

Dean Witter has also demonstrated that Nix's perjury materially related to an issue in the arbitration, thus satisfying its burden under the third prong of the test. As Dean Witter stressed in its brief, because the appellants admitted liability for compensatory damages, the only factual issue before the arbitrators was whether the appellants' conduct was negligent enough to justify the imposition of punitive damages. In support of the appellees' claim for punitive damages, Nix testified at considerable length about how, in his opinion, Dean Witter had mishandled the appellees' account. For example, Nix testified that compared to the average turnover in a portfolio with objectives similar to the appellees' objectives, the turnover rate he calculated for the appellees' account was "extremely

7. There is no doubt that perjury constitutes fraud within the meaning of the Arbitration Act....

high." In addition, when asked whether he thought the appellees' account had been excessively traded, Nix responded: "Briefly I would have to say that it was not so [sic only] excessive but gross and abusive." Appellees' counsel ended his direct examination by asking Nix for his expert opinion as to whether there had been a disregard for the best interests of the customer. Nix responded:

> Yes, I do. Mr. Leavenworth and Dean Witter were the fiduciaries for the Bonars' account, in my opinion. They had control, they ran the show. Ed Leavenworth may have been the first mate on the ship, but John McNally was the captain. John McNally may have delegated the responsibility of reviewing the checks, reviewing transactions, the daily blotter, whatever, but ultimately it comes back down to him.
>
> With regard to that you can't dismiss the responsibility involved here. The ultimate responsibility comes back down to the office manager. There was disregard for the customer. They embezzled from them. They embezzled from other people to put money into their account, they churned it. They even went so far as to run an excessive margin balance for three months.
>
> And from all appearances here and from the testimony it would seem that while Mr. McNally did show concern and couldn't understand why it went for ninety days or more, the evidence from my perspective during that time frame is that Dean Witter didn't care. You wouldn't let a margin balance run for ninety days if you did care.

If Nix had not committed perjury by falsifying his credentials, it is extremely doubtful that he would have been permitted to testify as an expert, and the arbitrators would have heard none of the above testimony. The arbitrators' written award, although brief, reflects the influence of Nix's testimony. Nix was the only expert, and in fact the only witness, who unequivocally pinpointed Dean Witter as the party who "didn't care," and who testified that McNally was less culpable for showing some concern over the state of the appellees' account. The arbitrators' award of punitive damages against Dean Witter, but not against McNally, unquestionably reflects the influence of this testimony. Thus, by establishing the foundation that allowed the panel to hear influential expert testimony on the central issue of negligent supervision, the fraud materially related to an issue in the arbitration.[12]

12. The appellees argue that Nix's testimony was merely cumulative and therefore could not have prejudiced Dean Witter's case. To support this argument, the appellees point out that Paul Landauer, the expert who testified before Nix, also opined that the appellees' account had been excessively traded and negligently supervised. This, however, does not mean that the arbitrators ignored Nix's testimony on the same subject. In fact, given that only two experts testified on the crucial issue of negligent supervision, Nix's testimony was invaluable to the appellees in that it corroborated the testimony of their only other expert witness. Perhaps if Nix's testimony had followed a number of other experts who had all testified that the account had been negligently supervised, we would agree that his testimony was merely cumulative. On these facts, however, the appellees' characterization of Nix's testimony as merely "cumu-

... Accordingly, Dean Witter is entitled to a new hearing on the issue of punitive damages before a different panel of arbitrators.[14]

III.

[The court also considered and rejected Dean Witter's arguments that the arbitrators exceeded their powers by awarding punitive damages, and that appellees had waived their right to punitive damages by agreeing to the customer agreement in this case.]

* * *

Questions

1. To what extent does the test for vacating an award due to perjury require a court to examine the conduct of the hearing or the merits of the underlying dispute? In *Bonar*, the court quotes testimony from the hearing to establish that Nix's perjury was "materially related to an issue in the arbitration." Could the movant have established grounds to vacate if there had been no record of such testimony? Without a transcript, how can a party meet the test for vacating an award due to perjury? Can the movant subpoena the arbitrator to testify to the materiality of the false testimony? Is there any other means by which a court could make such a determination?

2. One of the grounds for vacating the award is that Dean Witter could not have discovered the perjury before or during the hearing due to the absence of pre-hearing exchange of witness lists under the American Arbitration Association rules. To what degree should the court remedy deficiencies in the procedural rules the parties themselves have selected? Would it be preferable to require as a general rule that arbitration rules

lative" unfairly minimizes its importance in these proceedings.

The appellees also argue that Nix's testimony on negligent supervision "merely reflects the obvious, and the conclusion—unsatisfactory supervision—is something counsel on these facts could argue even in the absence of expert testimony." They argue that testimony from Dean Witter employees, revealing that Dean Witter did not follow its own internal guidelines for safeguarding investors, was enough to support the arbitrators' award of punitive damages. However, what appellees *could* have done is irrelevant; what matters is that they *did* offer Nix's extensive "expert" testimony to buttress testimony of lay witnesses and now must live with the consequences of that decision.

14. The appellees argue that if this court reverses the judgment and vacates the arbitration award, the matter should be remanded to the original panel of arbitrators, who should then state the weight given to Nix's testimony, and whether they would have made the same award in the absence of that testimony. Although we are authorized to remand to the original panel, see 9 U.S.C. § 10(e), we are not required to do so, see Electronics Corp. of America v. International Union of Electrical, Radio & Machine Workers, Local 272, 492 F.2d 1255, 1257 (1st Cir. 1974). In a case such as this, where the perjury of an expert witness has so tainted the proceedings, we agree with Dean Witter that it would be difficult for the arbitrators now to determine the importance or weight given to Nix's testimony.

meet certain procedural standards to obviate the necessity of *post hoc* judicial intervention?

* * *

7. CLASS ACTIONS

The FAA does not say anything about class or collective actions. Historically, most federal courts have held that, where an arbitration agreement is silent regarding class actions or other collective procedures, plaintiffs may bring in arbitration only their individualized claims.[1] Today, however, courts are split on this issue, and also on the related issue of whether to enforce arbitration agreements that expressly waive a party's right to bring a class action.

Much of the current confusion emanates from the 2003 U.S. Supreme Court decision of Green Tree Financial Corp. v. Bazzle, 539 U.S. 444 (2003), which you may recall from Chapter 2.2.B. For a nice summary of the splintered decision in *Bazzle*, see Imre S. Szalai, *Aggregate Dispute Resolution: Class and Labor Arbitration*, 13 Harv. Negot. L. Rev. 399 (2008). In *Bazzle*, a state court, construing an arbitration agreement that arguably was silent regarding class arbitration, ordered class arbitration. The issue before the Supreme Court was whether the state court's decision was consistent with the FAA. A four-Justice plurality focused on a threshold question of whether the underlying arbitration agreement was in fact silent regarding class arbitration or whether it forbade arbitration, and held that this determination must be made by an arbitrator and not a court. The plurality therefore vacated the state court judgment and returned the case to the arbitrator for a determination of whether the arbitration agreement permitted or forbade class arbitration. Justice Stevens wrote a separate opinion stating his belief that the FAA permits a state court to determine that an arbitration agreement is silent regarding class arbitration and to find that class arbitration is permissible on that basis. However, Justice Stevens concurred in the judgment only because he recognized that if he stuck to his guns, there would be no controlling judgment. A group of dissenting Justices argued that a court, not an arbitrator, should decide the threshold question of whether an arbitration agreement permits class actions; and that in this case, the contract did not permit class arbitration. Justice Thomas dissented on the basis that the FAA does not apply in state court.

The impact of *Bazzle* on class action waivers is unclear. Perhaps the plurality decision, by not holding outright that class arbitration is inconsistent with the FAA, implicitly reversed the then commonly held assumption that the FAA disfavors class arbitration. This would augur favorably for the

1. *See* Jay W. Waks & William Poorten, *Employment Class Arbitration: An Oxymoron? Or a Matter of Contract?*, 24 Alternatives to the High Cost of Litig. 145 (Oct. 2006).

future of class arbitration. On the other hand, perhaps the plurality decision, by not holding outright that the purported class action waiver was invalid, implicitly endorsed the use of class action waivers. This would augur unfavorably for the future of class arbitration. Recall that the Seventh Circuit has found that *Bazzle* should be given no weight at all on this issue: "[t]aking these two opinions [of the plurality and Justice Stevens] together, we cannot identify a single rationale endorsed by a majority of the Court." Employers Ins. Co. of Wausau v. Century Indem. Co., 443 F.3d 573, 580 (7th Cir. 2006).

* * *

Johnson v. West Suburban Bank

225 F.3d 366 (3d Cir. 2000).

■ BECKER, CHIEF JUDGE.

[The plaintiff Terry Johnson applied for and received a short-term loan for $250 from West Suburban Bank. The loan agreement imposed a finance charge of $88 for the two-week loan, amounting to an annual percentage rate of 917%. The loan agreement also contained a broad arbitration clause. Johnson sued on behalf of a putative class in the District Court for the District of Delaware, alleging that the Bank and Tele–Cash, Inc., the bank's agent for the loan transaction, violated both the Truth in Lending Act (TILA) and the Electronic Fund Transfer Act (EFTA) by failing to properly disclose the high rate of interest, and by requiring loan applicants to open accounts from which they were required to irrevocably preauthorize electronic fund transfers to pay the loan.

The defendant Bank moved to dismiss the action on the ground that it was subject to arbitration under the agreement. The plaintiff countered that the arbitration clause was not enforceable because Congress consciously inserted language into the TILA statute with the intent of encouraging district court judges to certify class actions. He further argued that in the legislative history of amendments to the TILA, Congress communicated that class action remedies play a central role in the TILA and EFTA enforcement schemes. Rather than simply provide restitution, Johnson asserted, such litigation is meant to serve public policy goals through plaintiffs who act as private attorneys general, and that the class action device is necessary to ensure meaningful deterrence to creditors who might violate the acts.

The District Court agreed with the plaintiff, and denied defendant's motion to dismiss the action. The Court of Appeals for the Third Circuit reversed.]

... Whether a court can compel arbitration of TILA claims when the parties' loan agreement contains an arbitration clause but the plaintiff seeks to bring claims on behalf of multiple claimants is a question of first impression for this court ... The burden of establishing that Congress meant to preclude arbitration for a statutory claim rests with the party who seeks to avoid arbitration. *See Gilmer,* 500 U.S. at 26, 111 S.Ct. 1647. Such intention may be found in the text, legislative history, or in an "inherent conflict" between arbitration and the statute's underlying purposes. *Id.* (citing *Shearson/American Express, Inc. v. McMahon*, 482 U.S. 220, 227, 107 S.Ct. 2332, 96 L.Ed.2d 185 (1987)).

[The court examined the text and legislative history of the TILA, and found nothing to suggest that Congress, in enacting the TILA, meant to preclude a waiver of a right to bring claims as a class action. The court then considered whether there was an "inherent conflict" between arbitration and the statute.]

. . . Because nothing in the legislative history or the statutory text of the TILA clearly expresses congressional intent to preclude the ability of parties to engage in arbitration, Johnson must demonstrate that arbitration irreconcilably conflicts with the purposes of the TILA. While Johnson may be correct in arguing that Congress contemplated class actions as a part of the TILA enforcement scheme, and even that class actions were self-consciously promoted by Congress in amending the statute, he falls short of demonstrating irreconcilable conflict between arbitration and the TILA.

1. TILA's public policy goals

Johnson focuses on the ability of a class action award to act as a penalty against lenders who violate the TILA. This focus is logical. The prospect of a class action award will doubtless deter TILA violations more effectively than the prospect that debtors will pursue individual actions, either in court or in arbitration, because the damages available to individuals are generally limited. *See* 15 U.S.C. § 1640. In this manner, argues Johnson, class actions are central to TILA's purposes, because the statute's civil damages provisions are not remedial, but rather, given the frequent absence of actual damages, are designed to *deter* unfair credit practices. Phrased another way, the TILA, in Johnson's submission, is meant to encourage private attorneys general, and the statute as a whole is intended for public purposes rather than private grievances. While these arguments carry force, they are ultimately unpersuasive, for they do not translate into a conclusion that class actions are necessary to provide deterrence or fulfill any of the other goals of the Act.

a. The effects of arbitration on private litigation

First, even if plaintiffs who sign valid arbitration agreements lack the procedural right to proceed as part of a class, they retain the full range of rights created by the TILA. These rights remain available in individual arbitration proceedings. The Supreme Court has made clear that when arbitration will preserve a plaintiff's substantive rights, compelling arbitration in accordance with an arbitration clause will not impede a statute's deterrent function. '[S]o long as the prospective litigant effectively may vindicate [his or her] statutory cause of action in the arbitral forum, the statute will continue to serve both its remedial and deterrent function.'

Mitsubishi Motors Corp. v. Soler Chrysler–Plymouth, Inc., 473 U.S. 614, 637, 105 S.Ct. 3346, 87 L.Ed.2d 444 (1985). Johnson does not argue that the arbitral forum selected in his agreement is somehow inadequate to vindicate any of his rights under the TILA or that arbitrators would be unable to afford him any relief that he could individually obtain in a court proceeding, including injunctive relief or attorney's fees. *Cf. Randolph v. Green Tree Fin. Corp.*, 178 F.3d 1149, 1158 (11th Cir. 1999), *cert. granted*, 529 U.S. 1052, 120 S.Ct. 1552, 146 L.Ed.2d 458 (2000) (reversing order compelling arbitration in a TILA case because the clause at issue 'raises serious concerns with respect to filing fees, arbitrators' costs and other arbitration expenses that may curtail or bar a plaintiff's access to the arbitral forum'); *Baron v. Best Buy Co., Inc.*, 75 F.Supp.2d 1368, 1370 (S.D.Fla. 1999) (appeal pending) (refusing to compel arbitration in a TILA case when the arbitration agreement required parties to bear own expense for attorneys' costs in contravention of TILA provisions that provide for recovery of attorneys' fees).

Under the prevailing jurisprudence, when the right made available by a statute is capable of vindication in the arbitral forum, the public policy goals of that statute do not justify refusing to arbitrate. The notion that there is a meaningful distinction between vindicating a statute's social purposes and adjudicating private grievances for purposes of determining whether a statute precludes compelling arbitration under a valid arbitration clause was rejected by the Supreme Court in *Gilmer v. Interstate/Johnson Lane Corp.*, 500 U.S. 20, 111 S.Ct. 1647, 114 L.Ed.2d 26 (1991). That case concerned whether claims under the Age Discrimination in Employment Act (ADEA) must be available in a judicial forum. The Court concluded otherwise, despite arguments based on the ADEA's important social policy goals. 'As Gilmer contends, the ADEA is designed not only to address individual grievances, but also to further important social policies. We do not perceive any inherent inconsistency between those policies, however, and enforcing agreements to arbitrate age discrimination claims.' *Id.* at 27, 500 U.S. 20, 111 S.Ct. 1647 (citation omitted). Class actions could be similarly effective in promoting the ADEA's social policies, and, as discussed below, that statute lends itself more easily to being construed as creating a substantive right to a class action. *Gilmer* therefore appears to foreclose much of Johnson's argument.

We also note that while arbitrating claims that might have been pursued as part of class actions potentially reduces the number of plaintiffs seeking to enforce the TILA against creditors, arbitration does not eliminate plaintiff incentives to assert rights under the Act. The sums available in recovery to individual plaintiffs are not automatically increased by use of the class forum. Indeed, individual plaintiff recoveries available in a class action may be lower than those possible in individual suits because the recovery available under TILA's statutory cap on class recoveries is spread over the entire class. Nor will arbitration necessarily choke off the supply of lawyers willing to pursue claims on behalf of debtors. Attorneys' fees are recoverable under the TILA, *see* 15 U.S.C. § 1640(a)(3), and would therefore appear to be recoverable in arbitration, as arbitrators possess the power to fashion the same relief as courts. In sum, though pursuing individual claims in arbitration may well be less attractive than pursuing a class action in the courts, we do not agree that compelling arbitration of the claim of a prospective class action plaintiff irreconcilably conflicts with TILA's goal of encouraging private actions to deter violations of the Act. Whatever the benefits of class actions, the FAA "*requires* piecemeal resolution when necessary to give effect to an arbitration agreement." *Moses H. Cone Mem'l Hosp. v. Mercury Constr. Co.*, 460 U.S. 1, 20, 103 S.Ct. 927, 74 L.Ed.2d 765 (1983) (emphasis in the original)....

In sum, Johnson's arguments that the TILA precludes arbitration are unpersuasive. "[I]f Congress intended the substantive protection afforded by a given statute to include protection against waiver of the right to a judicial forum, that intention will be deducible from text or legislative history." Mitsubishi Motors Corp. v. Soler Chrysler–Plymouth, Inc., 473 U.S. 614, 628, 105 S.Ct. 3346, 87 L.Ed.2d 444 (1985). No such intent is deducible here....

The order of the District Court denying the motion to stay proceedings and compel arbitration will be reversed and the case remanded for further proceedings consistent with this opinion.

* * *

Kristian v. Comcast Corp.

446 F.3d 25 (1st Cir. 2006).

■ LIPEZ, CIRCUIT JUDGE.

* * *

I.

Plaintiffs ... are Boston area subscribers of cable services obtained from Defendant–Appellant Comcast Corporation ("Comcast").... [Their complaints] allege that the prices that they have been paying for cable services are inflated as a result of anticompetitive practices on the part of Comcast and AT & T Broadband, Comcast's predecessor-in-interest.

The complaints allege that Comcast has been consolidating its hold on markets and territories through agreements to swap or exchange cable television assets ("swapping agreements").[1] The complaints specifically reference two swapping agreements, one in 1999 and another in 2001. Plaintiffs Kristian and Masterman allege that Comcast engages in conduct that excludes, prevents, or interferes with competition, including Comcast's refusal to provide programming access to competitors either before or after

1. Swapping agreements allegedly violate antitrust laws because, by using them, cable providers can divide and allocate markets so that a cable subscriber can only obtain cable service from a single provider in his or her location. Simply put, through swapping agreements, companies trade territory, eliminating competition in a given geographical area.

Comcast merged with AT & T Broadband in 2002. Plaintiffs seek certification of class actions comprised of individuals who subscribed to Comcast cable services in the Boston area at anytime from December 1999 to the present.

When Plaintiffs first subscribed for cable services, none of their service agreements contained an arbitration provision. In 2001, Comcast began including an arbitration provision in the terms and conditions governing the relationship between Comcast and its subscribers. These terms and conditions are contained, in part, in notices that inform subscribers at the time of cable installation—and at least annually thereafter—of the terms and conditions governing their subscriptions ("Policies & Practices"). Comcast included the Policies & Practices with each Boston area subscriber's invoice as a billing stuffer during the November 2001 billing cycle.

The version of the Policies & Practices mailed in November/December 2002 contained an arbitration agreement that, at first blush, substantially differed from the one in the 2001 Policies & Practices. The arbitration agreement contained in the November/December 2003 Policies & Practices remained unchanged from 2002. Comcast seeks to compel arbitration pursuant to the language of the arbitration agreements contained in the 2002/2003 Policies & Practices; the 2002/2003 arbitration agreements are the focus of this appeal.

II.

[One group of plaintiffs sued in state court; the other group in federal court. Comcast removed the state-court action to federal court and filed motions to compel arbitration in both cases. Plaintiffs opposed arbitration, arguing, among other things,] that the arbitration agreements prevented them from vindicating their causes of action under federal antitrust law, and that they violated public policy and were unconscionable under state law.... Comcast filed an interlocutory appeal contesting the district court's denial of its motions to compel arbitration. Both cases are currently stayed, pending resolution of this appeal. As the district court's order refusing to compel arbitration applied to both ... complaints, the two cases have been consolidated for purposes of this appeal....

V.

* * *

G. Class arbitration

i. The question of arbitrability

The ... arbitration agreements clearly prohibit any type of class or consolidated action:

> THERE SHALL BE NO RIGHT OR AUTHORITY FOR ANY CLAIMS TO BE ARBITRATED ON A CLASS ACTION OR CONSOLIDATED BASIS OR ON BASES INVOLVING CLAIMS BROUGHT IN A PURPORTED REPRESENTATIVE CAPACITY ON BEHALF OF THE

GENERAL PUBLIC (SUCH AS A PRIVATE ATTORNEY GENERAL), OTHER SUBSCRIBERS, OR OTHER PERSONS SIMILARLY SITUATED UNLESS YOUR STATE'S LAWS PROVIDE OTHERWISE.

Comcast cites *Bazzle* for the proposition that class actions are a procedural issue left properly for an arbitrator to decide. However, ... Comcast misreads the decision.

... [T]he Court in *Bazzle* was "faced at the outset with a problem concerning the contracts' silence. Are the contracts in fact silent, or do they forbid class arbitration ...?" *Bazzle,* 539 U.S. at 447, 123 S.Ct. 2402. Since the literal terms of the agreement did not resolve the class arbitration question, the Court concluded that "the question-whether the agreement forbids class arbitration-is for the arbitrator to decide." *Bazzle,* 539 U.S. at 451, 123 S.Ct. 2402. However, we do not confront that situation here. Unlike the arbitration agreement in *Bazzle,* the ... arbitration agreements unmistakably forbid the use of class procedures in arbitration.... *Bazzle* does not apply here because of the clarity of the prohibition against class arbitration.

We recognize that the arbitration agreements' class mechanism prohibition is *not* in direct conflict with the relevant antitrust statutes, state and federal, which do not mention class actions or the like. However, the arbitration agreements' language ostensibly conflicts with the Federal Rules of Civil Procedure, which provide for class actions. *See* Fed.R.Civ.P. 23. We say ostensibly because the Policies & Practices explicitly forbids only class *arbitration,* and not class actions. However, because the Policies & Practices creates a mandatory arbitration regime, a ban on class arbitration effectively forecloses the use of any class-based mechanism.

The bar has substantial implications for the enforceability of the arbitration agreements. We have said that the legitimacy of the arbitral forum rests on "the presumption that arbitration provides a fair and adequate mechanism for enforcing statutory rights." *Rosenberg,* 170 F.3d at 14. The Supreme Court has stated this same premise. In *Mitsubishi,* the Court held that "[s]o long as the prospective litigant effectively may vindicate its statutory cause of action in the arbitral forum, the [federal substantive] statute will continue to serve both its remedial and deterrent function." 473 U.S. at 637, 105 S.Ct. 3346. The bar on class arbitration threatens the premise that arbitration can be "a fair and adequate mechanism for enforcing statutory rights." *Rosenberg,* 170 F.3d at 14.

In *Amchem Prods., Inc. v. Windsor,* 521 U.S. 591, 117 S.Ct. 2231, 138 L.Ed.2d 689 (1997), the Supreme Court stated that "[t]he policy at the very core of the class action mechanism is to overcome the problem that small recoveries do not provide the incentive for any individual to bring a solo action prosecuting his or her rights," *id.* at 617, 117 S.Ct. 2231 (quoting *Mace v. Van Ru Credit Corp.,* 109 F.3d 338, 344 (7th Cir. 1997)). In *Carnegie v. Household Int'l, Inc.,* 376 F.3d 656, 661 (7th Cir. 2004), the Seventh Circuit stated the proposition even more bluntly: "It would hardly be an improvement to have in lieu of this single class action 17,000,000 suits each seeking damages of $15.00 to $30.00.... The *realistic* alternative to a class action is not 17,000,000 individual suits, but zero individual suits, as only a lunatic or a fanatic sues for $30.00." While Comcast is correct when it categorizes the class action (and class arbitration) as a procedure for redressing claims-and not a substantive or statutory right in and of itself—we cannot ignore the substantive implications of this procedural mechanism.

Here, the putative class would consist of Comcast's Boston area subscribers. According to the factual information contained in the unopposed expert declarations Plaintiffs submitted to the district court below, each putative class member's estimated recovery—assuming the damage award was trebled pursuant to the applicable antitrust statute—would range from a few hundred dollars to perhaps a few thousand dollars. By contrast, the expert fees alone are estimated to be in the hundreds of thousands of dollars; and attorney's fees could reach into the millions of dollars. To say that each potential class member is unlikely to have or make available the up-front costs needed to prosecute this costly antitrust suit is a large understatement. The class mechanism ban—"particularly its implicit ban on spreading across multiple plaintiffs the costs of experts, depositions, neutrals' fees, and other disbursements"—forces the putative class member "to assume financial burdens so prohibitive as to deter the bringing of claims.... And these costs ... will exceed the value of the recovery she is seeking." Myriam Gilles, *Opting Out of Liability: The Forthcoming, Near-Total Demise of the Modern Class Action,* 104 Mich. L. Rev. 373, 407 (2005).

In *Randolph,* the plaintiff asserted that:

> the arbitration agreement's silence with respect to costs and fees creates a "risk" that she will be required to bear prohibitive arbitration costs if she pursues her claims in an arbitral forum, and thereby forces her to forgo any claims she may have against petitioners. Therefore, she argues, she is unable to vindicate her statutory rights in arbitration.

531 U.S. at 90, 121 S.Ct. 513. In response, the Supreme Court acknowledged that "the existence of large arbitration costs could preclude a litigant such as Randolph from effectively vindicating her federal statutory rights in the arbitral forum." *Id.* Here, there is no doubt about these large arbitration costs.

Although neither the Supreme Court nor the First Circuit has decided a case that presents the exact issue we face here, other courts of appeals have. These courts concluded that there was a question of arbitrability presented by the bar on class arbitration. *See, e.g., Jenkins v. First Am. Cash Advance of Georgia,* 400 F.3d 868 (11th Cir. 2005)[18] *Livingston v.*

18. In *Jenkins,* the Eleventh Circuit decided a similar case using an unconscionability rationale. However, the court relied on another of its decisions, which used a "vindication of statutory rights" rationale. The *Jenkins* court equated the two rationales. *See Jenkins,* 400 F.3d at 877–78; *see also Randolph v. Green Tree Fin. Corp.-Alabama,* 244 F.3d 814, 819 (11th Cir. 2001) (hereinafter *Randolph II*).

Associates Fin., Inc., 339 F.3d 553 (7th Cir.2003). We see no reason not to do the same here. The class arbitration bar is unmistakable. Because the denial of class arbitration in the pursuit of antitrust claims has the potential to prevent Plaintiffs from vindicating their statutory rights, Plaintiffs present a question of arbitrability with respect to the . . . arbitration agreements' class arbitration prohibition.

ii. The merits

a. Relevant federal law

On the merits, the decisions of other courts of appeal appear to weigh against Plaintiffs, although not overwhelmingly so. Four of our sister circuits—the Third, Fourth, Seventh, and Eleventh—enforce consumer arbitration clauses barring the use of class mechanisms (class action and/or class arbitration). *See Johnson v. West Suburban Bank,* 225 F.3d 366, 374 (3d Cir. 2000) ("Because there is no irreconcilable conflict between arbitration and the goals of the TILA [Truth in Lending Act], we similarly hold that claims arising under the EFTA [Electronic Fund Transfer Act] may also be subject to arbitration notwithstanding the desire of a plaintiff who previously consented to arbitration to bring his or her claims as part of a class."); *Snowden v. CheckPoint Check Cashing,* 290 F.3d 631, 638 (4th Cir. 2002) ("We also reject [the plaintiff's] argument that the Arbitration Agreement is unenforceable as unconscionable because without the class action vehicle, she will be unable to maintain her legal representation given the small amount of her individual damages."); *Livingston,* 339 F.3d at 559 ("[H]aving found the Arbitration Agreement enforceable we must give full force to its terms. . . . The Arbitration Agreement at issue here explicitly precludes . . . class claims or pursuing 'class action arbitration' "); *Randolph II,* 244 F.3d at 819 ("[W]e hold that a contractual provision to arbitrate TILA claims is enforceable even if it precludes a plaintiff from utilizing class action procedures in vindicating statutory rights under TILA.").

These four decisions have two important commonalities. First, attorney's fees and costs were either recoverable by the plaintiffs who contested the arbitral forum on the basis of the class arbitration ban, or the fees and costs issue was moot. For example, in *Johnson,* the court stated "[n]or will arbitration necessarily choke off the supply of lawyers willing to pursue claims on behalf of debtors. Attorneys' fees are recoverable under the TILA." *Johnson,* 225 F.3d at 374. In *Livingston,* the defendant agreed to pay all costs associated with arbitration. *Livingston,* 339 F.3d at 557. Here, too, because of the general savings clause in the Policies & Practices, we have ruled that attorney's fees and costs must be available in the arbitral forum.

Second, in all four decisions, the plaintiffs raised claims against banks or other financial lenders primarily under the TILA. This is not the case here, where we are dealing with federal and state antitrust claims. That is a potentially important distinction. Therefore, we must examine the rationale for these decisions more closely. For this purpose, we will discuss the

Third Circuit's *Johnson* decision. Each of the other circuits relies on *Johnson. See Snowden,* 290 F.3d at 638–39 (citing *Johnson,* 225 F.3d at 374); *Livingston,* 339 F.3d at 559 (citing *Johnson,* 225 F.3d at 369); *Randolph II,* 244 F.3d at 818 ("Our thinking in this respect is consistent with the Third Circuit's decision that '[arbitration] clauses are effective even though they may render class actions to pursue statutory claims under the TILA . . . unavailable.' ") (quoting *Johnson,* 225 F.3d at 369). In supporting the bar on class arbitration, *Johnson* also contains the most extensive analysis for that position. *See generally Johnson,* 225 F.3d at 370–77.

b. The *Johnson* decision

The *Johnson* decision begins its analysis of the validity of a class mechanism bar with the Supreme Court's decision in *Gilmer.* In *Gilmer,* the plaintiff brought an age discrimination claim, and then contested arbitration of that claim because, *inter alia,* the arbitral forum did not offer all of the procedures a judicial forum would, such as full discovery and class actions. *See Gilmer,* 500 U.S. at 29–33, 111 S.Ct. 1647. *Gilmer's* holding—that an ADEA plaintiff can be compelled to arbitrate his ADEA claim—is based on the proposition from *Mitsubishi* that "so long as the prospective litigant effectively may vindicate [his or her] statutory cause of action in the arbitral forum, the statute will continue to serve both its remedial and deterrent function." *Gilmer,* 500 U.S. at 28, 111 S.Ct. 1647 (quoting *Mitsubishi,* 473 U.S. at 637, 105 S.Ct. 3346) (internal quotation marks omitted).

Johnson extends *Gilmer* to the TILA context and enforces a class action bar in arbitration, based on three assertions. First, class actions do not necessarily give plaintiffs better incentives to bring private enforcement actions:

> [t]he sums available in recovery to individual plaintiffs are not automatically increased by use of the class forum. Indeed, individual plaintiff recoveries available in a class action may be lower than those possible in individual suits because the recovery available under TILA's statutory cap on class recoveries is spread over the entire class.

Johnson, 225 F.3d at 374.

Second, plaintiffs will still be able to find representation without the class action mechanism because of the availability of attorney's fees and costs:

> Nor will arbitration necessarily choke off the supply of lawyers willing to pursue claims on behalf of debtors. Attorneys' fees are recoverable under the TILA, *see* 15 U.S.C. § 1640(a)(3), and would therefore appear to be recoverable in arbitration, as arbitrators possess the power to fashion the same relief as courts.

Johnson, 225 F.3d at 374–75 (internal citations omitted). According to the *Johnson* court, "though pursuing individual claims in arbitration may well be less attractive than pursuing a class action in the courts, we do not agree that compelling arbitration of the claim of a prospective class action plaintiff irreconcilably conflicts with TILA's goal of encouraging private actions to deter violations of the Act." *Id.*

Third, *Johnson* asserts that even if TILA plaintiffs are discouraged from bringing private enforcement actions, administrative enforcement exists to fill the void. "Our conclusion that there is no irreconcilable conflict between the TILA's social policy goals and arbitration of claims that could have been heard as part of a class action is bolstered by the statute's administrative enforcement provisions. These provisions offer meaningful deterrents to violators of the TILA if private enforcement actions should fail to fulfill that role." *Id.* at 375.

In our view, these rationales drawn from the TILA context do not support the validity of a bar to class arbitration of Plaintiffs' antitrust claims.

c. The inapplicability of *Johnson* to the antitrust context

As an initial matter, prosecuting a typical TILA claim is vastly different from prosecuting an antitrust claim because of the sheer complexity of the latter. For example, in *Snowden,* the plaintiff engaged in "deferred deposit" transactions, where "a customer tenders a check to the store that is cashed for a service fee with the understanding that the check will not be negotiated until some later, agreed upon time." 290 F.3d at 633. The plaintiff alleged in her complaint that: (1) the "deferred deposit transactions with [the defendant] were loans; and (2) that the service fee charged by [the defendant] for such transactions constituted interest." *Id.* at 635. As a result, the plaintiff asserted that the defendant had violated, *inter alia,* the TILA.

In a cases such as *Snowden,* there is a specific transaction at issue. Whether there is a TILA violation usually hinges on whether the facts about that transaction do or do not establish a violation of the TILA. This is not a particularly difficult analysis. As one commentator has summarized, in TILA cases, "one must be cognizant of the type of credit being extended as well as the terms of the credit contract to determine which disclosures, in addition to the APR and finance charge, are required under TILA and any other applicable Federal and state laws." Matthew A. Edwards, *Empirical and Behavioral Critiques of Mandatory Disclosure: Socioeconomics and the Quest for Truth in Lending,* 14 Cornell J.L. & Pub. Pol'y 199, 216 (2005). By contrast, whether a company's action constitutes an antitrust violation is usually a complicated question of fact. The law that then applies to those facts is equally complex. This complexity of prosecuting an antitrust claim is confirmed by the unopposed experts' affidavits provided by Plaintiffs, which describe the great expense and labor required by such a case. . . .

The complexity of an antitrust case generally, and the complexity and cost required to prosecute a case against Comcast specifically, undermine the *Johnson* court's rationales for supporting a bar to class arbitration. *Johnson* first asserts that a class action does not necessarily provide greater incentives for private enforcement actions in the TILA context. Yet, Plaintiffs have provided uncontested and unopposed expert affidavits demonstrating that without some form of class mechanism—be it class action or class arbitration—a consumer antitrust plaintiff will not sue at all....

Johnson's second assertion—that the availability of attorney's fees provides the necessary incentive for private enforcement actions—similarly finds little to no purchase in the antitrust context. A plaintiff's attorney in the consumer antitrust context would be required to invest a large initial outlay in time and money, including "opportunity costs"—estimated in the hundreds of thousands of dollars—for only a portion of an individual plaintiff's recovery, which at most is a few thousand dollars. Then, factoring in the uncertainty of success, the appeal for an attorney to take on an individual plaintiff's antitrust claim shrinks even further. As two commentators have noted:

> [t]he court decisions striking class action prohibitions have all emphasized that many small-dollar claims are simply not feasible if brought individually. In essence, these cases recognize ... that by increasing plaintiffs' transaction costs, defendants can induce them to accept lower settlements or even drop their claims altogether. Citing the Supreme Court's oft-stated justification for supporting class actions, courts invalidating class action prohibitions explain that it is often not rational for individual consumers or attorneys to bring small claims, whether through litigation or arbitration.

Jean B. Sternlight & Elizabeth J. Jensen, *Using Arbitration to Eliminate Consumer Class Actions: Efficient Business Practice or Unconscionable Abuse?,* 67–SPG Law & Contemp. Probs. 75, 85–86 (2004)....

If, as a practical matter, there will be no incentive for private enforcement of antitrust claims by consumers, the *Johnson* court's third assertion—that any decrease in private enforcement actions will be redressed by administrative enforcement—becomes even more suspect. When Congress enacts a statute that provides for both private and administrative enforcement actions, Congress envisions a role for both types of enforcement. Otherwise, Congress would not have provided for both. Weakening one of those enforcement mechanisms seems inconsistent with the Congressional scheme. Eliminating one of them entirely is surely incompatible with Congress's choice.

In summary, we find *Johnson's* rationale for allowing arbitration to move forward in the TILA context despite a bar on the use of class mechanisms unpersuasive when applied to Plaintiffs' antitrust claims. Because of the presence of the bar on class mechanisms in arbitration, Plaintiffs cannot be compelled to arbitrate their antitrust claims, both state and federal, if that bar remains in place.

d. The position of other courts

There is support for this conclusion in the holdings of other courts. Although these courts—be they state courts or federal courts applying state law—have generally refused to compel arbitration on state unconscionability grounds, these decisions contain reasoning that mirrors our own.[22] These decisions emphasize that a class mechanism bar can impermissibly frustrate the prosecution of claims in *any* forum, arbitral or judicial. As the California Supreme Court has observed, "class actions and arbitrations are, particularly in the consumer context, often inextricably linked to the vindication of substantive rights." *Discover Bank v. Superior Court,* 36 Cal.4th 148, 161, 30 Cal.Rptr.3d 76, 113 P.3d 1100 (Cal. 2005)....

VI.

... We [have] determined that Plaintiffs' challenges to the Policies & Practices's ... class arbitration bar [does] pose questions of arbitrability. On the merits, we concluded that th[is] provision[ ], if applied in the arbitral forum, would prevent the vindication of statutory rights. However, we then applied the savings clauses of the arbitration agreements to sever th[is] provision[ ] from the arbitration agreements as applied to Plaintiffs' antitrust claims. With these provisions removed, arbitration of the antitrust claims can proceed....

For the reasons stated, the district court's holding that the arbitration clause in the ... Policies & Practices, in its entirety, does not apply to Plaintiffs' antitrust claims is *reversed.* We *remand* for further proceedings not inconsistent with this opinion. The parties shall bear their own costs.

* * *

Discover Bank v. Superior Court

113 P.3d 1100 (Cal.2005).

■ MORENO, J.

This case concerns the validity of a provision in an arbitration agreement between Discover Bank and a credit cardholder forbidding classwide arbitration. The credit cardholder, a California resident, alleges that Discover Bank had a practice of representing to cardholders that late payment fees would not be assessed if payment was received by a certain date, whereas in actuality they were assessed if payment was received after 1:00 p.m. on that date, thereby leading to damages that were small as to individual consumers but large in the aggregate. Plaintiff filed a complaint

22. We realize that a state unconscionability analysis, based on the particulars of state contract law, may include considerations not present in the vindication of statutory rights analysis applied here, which is not dependent on state law. However, the unconscionability analysis always includes an element that is the essence of the vindication of statutory rights analysis—the frustration of the right to pursue claims granted by statute. For example, in *Faber v. Menard, Inc.,* 367 F.3d 1048 (8th Cir. 2004), the Eighth Circuit held that "[a] fee-splitting arrangement may be unconscionable if information specific to the circumstances indicates that fees are cost-prohibitive and preclude the vindication of statutory rights in an arbitral forum" while citing *Randolph,* 531 U.S. at 90, 121 S.Ct. 513, a vindication of statutory rights case. *Faber,* 367 F.3d at 1053; *see also, supra* n. 18; *Jenkins,* 400 F.3d at 877–78.

claiming damages for this alleged deceptive practice, and Discover Bank successfully moved to compel arbitration pursuant to its arbitration agreement with plaintiff.

Plaintiff now seeks to pursue a classwide arbitration, which is well accepted under California law. (See *Keating v. Superior Court* (1982) 31 Cal.3d 584, 613–614, 183 Cal.Rptr. 360, 645 P.2d 1192 (*Keating*), overruled on other grounds in *Southland Corp. v. Keating* (1984) 465 U.S. 1, 104 S.Ct. 852, 79 L.Ed.2d 1 (*Southland*).) But plaintiff's arbitration agreement with Discover Bank has a clause forbidding classwide arbitration.[†] ... The trial court ruled that the class arbitration waiver was unconscionable and enforced the arbitration agreement with the proviso that plaintiff could seek classwide arbitration. The Court of Appeal, without disputing that such class arbitration waivers may be unconscionable under California law and without addressing the choice-of-law issue, nonetheless held that the Federal Arbitration Act (FAA) (9 U.S.C. § 1 et seq.) preempts the state law rule that class arbitration waivers are unconscionable.

As explained below, we conclude that, at least under some circumstances, the law in California is that class action waivers in consumer contracts of adhesion are unenforceable, whether the consumer is being asked to waive the right to class action litigation or the right to classwide arbitration. We further conclude that the Court of Appeal is incorrect that the FAA preempts California law in this respect....

II. Discussion

A. Class Action Law Suits and Class Action Arbitration

...

B. The Enforceability of Class Action Waivers

Keating judicially authorized classwide arbitration in a case in which the arbitration agreement at issue was silent on the matter. It did not answer directly the question whether a class action waiver may be unenforceable as contrary to public policy or unconscionable. * * * [P]laintiff contends that class action or arbitration waivers in consumer contracts, and in this particular contract, should be invalidated as unconscionable under California law.

To briefly recapitulate the principles of unconscionability, the doctrine has both a "procedural and a "substantive" element, the former focusing on "oppression" or "surprise" due to unequal bargaining power, the latter on "overly harsh" or "one-sided" results. [Citation.] The procedural element of an unconscionable contract generally takes the form of a contract of

† The relevant clause of the arbitration agreement provides:

... NEITHER YOU NOR WE SHALL BE ENTITLED TO JOIN OR CONSOLIDATE CLAIMS IN ARBITRATION BY OR AGAINST OTHER CARDMEMBERS WITH RESPECT TO OTHER ACCOUNTS, OR ARBITRATE ANY CLAIM AS A REPRESENTATIVE OR MEMBER OF A CLASS OR IN A PRIVATE ATTORNEY GENERAL CAPACITY.

adhesion, "which, imposed and drafted by the party of superior bargaining strength, relegates to the subscribing party only the opportunity to adhere to the contract or reject it." . . . [¶] Substantively unconscionable terms may take various forms, but may generally be described as unfairly one-sided. *Little v. Auto Stiegler, Inc.* (2003) 29 Cal.4th 1064, 1071, 130 Cal.Rptr.2d 892, 63 P.3d 979 (*Little*), cert. den. *sub nom. Auto Stiegler, Inc. v. Little* (2003) 540 U.S. 818, 124 S.Ct. 83, 157 L.Ed.2d 35.

We agree that at least some class action waivers in consumer contracts are unconscionable under California law. First, when a consumer is given an amendment to its cardholder agreement in the form of a "bill stuffer" that he would be deemed to accept if he did not close his account, an element of procedural unconscionability is present. (*Szetela, supra,* 97 Cal.App.4th at p. 1100, 118 Cal.Rptr.2d 862.) Moreover, although adhesive contracts are generally enforced (*Graham v. Scissor–Tail, Inc.* (1981) 28 Cal.3d 807, 817–818, 171 Cal.Rptr. 604, 623 P.2d 165), class action waivers found in such contracts may also be substantively unconscionable inasmuch as they may operate effectively as exculpatory contract clauses that are contrary to public policy. As stated in Civil Code section 1668: "All contracts *which have for their object, directly or indirectly, to exempt anyone from responsibility for his own fraud, or willful injury* to the person or property of another, or violation of law, whether willful or negligent, are against the policy of the law." (Italics added.)

Class action and arbitration waivers are not, in the abstract, exculpatory clauses. But . . . damages in consumer cases are often small and because " '[a] company which wrongfully exacts a dollar from each of millions of customers will reap a handsome profit' " (*Linder, supra,* 23 Cal.4th at p. 446, 97 Cal.Rptr.2d 179, 2 P.3d 27), " 'the class action is often the only effective way to halt and redress such exploitation.' " (*Ibid.*) Moreover, such class action or arbitration waivers are indisputably one-sided. "Although styled as a mutual prohibition on representative or class actions, it is difficult to envision the circumstances under which the provision might negatively impact Discover [Bank], because credit card companies typically do not sue their customers in class action lawsuits." (*Szetela, supra,* 97 Cal.App.4th at p. 1101, 118 Cal.Rptr.2d 862.) Such one-sided, exculpatory contracts in a contract of adhesion, at least to the extent they operate to insulate a party from liability that otherwise would be imposed under California law, are generally unconscionable.

We acknowledge that other courts disagree. Some courts have viewed class actions or arbitrations as a merely procedural right, the waiver of which is not unconscionable. (See, e.g., *Strand v. U.S. Bank National Association ND* (N.D. 2005) 693 N.W.2d 918, 926 (*Strand*); *Blaz v. Belfer* (5th Cir. 2004) 368 F.3d 501, 504–505; *Johnson v. West Suburban Bank* (3d Cir. 2000) 225 F.3d 366, 369; *Champ v. Siegel Trading Co., Inc.* (1995) 55 F.3d 269, 277; but see *Leonard v. Terminix Intern. Co. L.P.* (Ala. 2002) 854 So.2d 529, 538 (class action waiver together with limitation of damages clause in adhesive consumer arbitration agreement deprives plaintiffs of a "meaningful remedy" and is therefore unconscionable); *State v. Berger* (2002) 211 W.Va. 549, 567 S.E.2d 265, 278 [holding contract provision limiting class action rights unconscionable]; *Powertel v. Bexley* (Fla.Dist.Ct. App. 1999) 743 So.2d 570, 576 [same].) But as the above cited cases of this court have continually affirmed, class actions and arbitrations are, particularly in the consumer context, often inextricably linked to the vindication of substantive rights. Affixing the "procedural" label on such devices understates their importance and is not helpful in resolving the unconscionability issue.

Nor are we persuaded by the rationale stated by some courts that the potential availability of attorney fees to the prevailing party in arbitration or litigation ameliorates the problem posed by such class action waivers. (*Strand, supra,* 693 N.W.2d at p. 926; *Snowden v. Checkpoint Check Cashing* (4th Cir. 2002) 290 F.3d 631, 638.) There is no indication other than these courts' unsupported assertions that, in the case of small individual recovery, attorney fees are an adequate substitute for the class action or arbitration mechanism. Nor do we agree with the concurring and dissenting opinion that small claims litigation, government prosecution, or informal resolution are adequate substitutes.

We do not hold that all class action waivers are necessarily unconscionable. But when the waiver is found in a consumer contract of adhesion in a setting in which disputes between the contracting parties predictably involve small amounts of damages, and when it is alleged that the party with the superior bargaining power has carried out a scheme to deliberately cheat large numbers of consumers out of individually small sums of money, then, at least to the extent the obligation at issue is governed by California law, the waiver becomes in practice the exemption of the party "from responsibility for [its] own fraud, or willful injury to the person or property of another." (Civ.Code, § 1668.) Under these circumstances, such waivers are unconscionable under California law and should not be enforced.

C. FAA Preemption of California Rules Against Class Action Waivers

1. The Court of Appeal Opinion

The Court of Appeal ... [concluded] that when class action waivers are contained in arbitration agreements, California law prohibiting such waivers is preempted by section 2 of the FAA (9 U.S.C. § 2). We conclude the Court of Appeal erred....

At the outset of our discussion, we note that the FAA is silent on the matter of class actions and class action arbitration. Indeed, not only is classwide arbitration a relatively recent development, but class action litigation for damages was for the most part unknown in federal jurisdictions at the time the FAA was enacted in 1925. (Act of Feb. 12, 1925, ch. 213, 43 Stat. 883.) The Congress that enacted the FAA therefore cannot be said to have contemplated the issues before us. Accordingly, our conclusions with respect to FAA preemption must come from the United States Supreme Court's articulation of general principles regarding such preemption.

In support of its conclusion, the Court of Appeal cited *Perry v. Thomas* (1987) 482 U.S. 483, 107 S.Ct. 2520, 96 L.Ed.2d 426 (*Perry*), in which the United States Supreme Court concluded that section 2 of the FAA preempted California Labor Code section 229, which authorizes an action for the collection of wages " 'without regard to the existence of any private agreement to arbitrate.' " (*Perry, supra,* 482 U.S. at p. 484, 107 S.Ct. 2520.) As *Perry* stated, the FAA "embodies Congress' intent to provide for the enforcement of arbitration agreements within the full reach of the Commerce Clause. Its general applicability reflects that '[t]he preeminent concern of Congress in passing the Act was to enforce private agreements into which parties had entered.... This clear federal policy places § 2 of the Act in unmistakable conflict with California's § 229 requirement that litigants be provided a judicial forum for resolving wage disputes. Therefore, under the Supremacy Clause, the state statute must give way." (*Perry, supra,* 482 U.S. at pp. 490–491, 107 S.Ct. 2520.)

The Court of Appeal observed that the court in *Perry* did not address whether the contract was unconscionable, because this issue had not been addressed in the lower courts. But while noting that the issue may be considered on remand, the *Perry* court clarified the limits the FAA imposed on the unconscionability defense:

> We note ... the choice-of-law issue that arises when defenses such as [plaintiff's] so-called 'standing' and unconscionability arguments are asserted. In instances such as these, the text of § 2 provides the touchstone for choosing between state-law principles and the principles of federal common law envisioned by the passage of that statute: An agreement to arbitrate is valid, irrevocable, and enforceable, as a matter of federal law [citation], 'save upon such grounds as exist at law or in equity for the revocation of any contract.' 9 U.S.C. § 2.... Thus state law, whether of legislative or judicial origin, is applicable *if that law arose to govern issues concerning the validity, revocability, and enforceability of contracts generally.* A state-law principle that takes its meaning precisely from the fact that a contract to arbitrate is at issue does not comport with this requirement of § 2. [Citations.] A court may not, then, in assessing the rights of litigants to enforce an arbitration agreement, construe that agreement in a manner different from that in which it otherwise construes nonarbitration agreements under state law. Nor may a court rely on the uniqueness of an agreement to arbitrate as a basis for a state-law holding that enforcement would be unconscionable, for this would enable the court to effect what we hold today the state legislature cannot.

(*Perry, supra,* 482 U.S. at pp. 492–493, fn. 9, 107 S.Ct. 2520 italics omitted and added.) The Court of Appeal quoted the above language and also noted similar reasoning in the seminal case of *Southland, supra,* 465 U.S. at page 16, 104 S.Ct. 852 in which the Supreme Court held that a California statute prohibiting arbitration of certain claims under the Franchise Investment Law was preempted by the FAA.[5]

Based on the above, the Court of Appeal concluded:

> While a state may prohibit the contractual waiver of statutory consumer remedies, including the right to seek relief in a class action, such protections fall by the wayside when the waiver is contained in a validly formed arbitration agreement governed by the FAA. The antiwaiver provisions in statutes such as section 229 of the Labor Code . . . are preempted by section 2 of the FAA. Similarly, we conclude the antiwaiver language found in judicial decisions such as *America Online* and *Szetela* also has been preempted by section 2 of the FAA.

The Court of Appeal's conclusion is puzzling, because it ignores the critical distinction made by the *Perry* court between a "state-law principle that takes its meaning precisely from the fact that a contract to arbitrate is at issue," which is preempted by section 2 of the FAA, and a state law that "govern[s] issues concerning the validity, revocability, and enforceability of contracts generally," which is not. (*Perry, supra,* 482 U.S. at p. 493, fn. 9, 107 S.Ct. 2520.) "[U]nder section 2 of the FAA, a state court may refuse to enforce an arbitration agreement based on 'generally applicable contract defenses, such as fraud, duress, or unconscionability.' " (*Little, supra,* 29 Cal.4th at p. 1079, 130 Cal.Rptr.2d 892, 63 P.3d 979, quoting *Doctor's Associates, Inc. v. Casarotto* (1996) 517 U.S. 681, 687, 116 S.Ct. 1652, 134 L.Ed.2d 902.) In the present case, the principle that class action waivers are, under certain circumstances, unconscionable as unlawfully exculpatory is a principle of California law that does not specifically apply to arbitration agreements, but to contracts generally. In other words, it applies equally to class action litigation waivers in contracts without arbitration agreements as it does to class arbitration waivers in contracts with such agreements. (See *America Online, supra,* 90 Cal.App.4th at pp. 17–18, 108 Cal.Rptr.2d 699.) In that important respect it differs from the provision under consideration in *Perry,* which singled out certain arbitration agreements as unenforceable. . . .

The Court of Appeal opinion below also relied on the supposed shortcomings of arbitration to bolster its conclusion that a class action waiver is enforceable under the FAA. As the court stated: "Although California courts have recognized the consumer protection value of classwide arbitration, that is not the sole consideration. Courts should also consider the 'California rule which prevents reweighing the merits of an arbitrator's decision.' [Citation.] The FAA does not preempt this rule. [Citation.] As judicial review of the merits of an arbitrator's decision may not be had under California law, a multi-million dollar class arbitration award entered on nothing more than mere whim cannot be corrected under California law."

5. We note that although the *Southland* court overruled the portion of our *Keating* decision holding that the statute was not preempted by the FAA, it expressly declined to rule on the portion of the *Keating* decision regarding classwide arbitrations, concluding the issue had not been properly raised below. (*Southland, supra,* 465 U.S. at p. 17, 104 S.Ct. 852.)

Far from holding that the invalidation of a class action waiver discriminates against arbitration, the Court of Appeal below reasoned in effect that arbitration is an inferior forum and therefore cannot be entrusted with classwide claims. The court's conclusion regarding the unsuitability of arbitration to class actions reflects, as we stated in the context of another proposed limitation on arbitration, "the very mistrust of arbitration that has been repudiated by the United States Supreme Court." (*Armendariz, supra,* 24 Cal.4th at p. 120, 99 Cal.Rptr.2d 745, 6 P.3d 669.) Moreover, as explained below, there is nothing to indicate that class action and arbitration are inherently incompatible....

3. Green Tree Financial Corp. v. Bazzle

Discover Bank argues that *Green Tree Financial Corp. v. Bazzle* (2003) 539 U.S. 444, 123 S.Ct. 2402, 156 L.Ed.2d 414 (*Bazzle*), issued after the filing of the Court of Appeal opinion, supports the position that a state law rule against class arbitration waivers is preempted by the FAA. We disagree.... The *Bazzle* court addressed a narrow question: Green Tree disputed whether the arbitration clause was silent on classwide arbitration, arguing that the contract language in fact prohibited such arbitrations.... Even on this narrow issue, *Bazzle* produced no majority opinion.... Reading the plurality opinion together with Justice Stevens's opinion, the most that might be derived from *Bazzle* is a narrow holding: that when the question of whether a class action arbitration is available depends on whether or not the arbitration agreement is silent on the matter or expressly forbids class action arbitration, then it is up to the arbitrator, not the court, to determine whether the arbitration agreement is in fact silent.

More significant than *Bazzle's* holding, for purposes of the present case, is what it did *not* decide. The court did not address whether a state court can, consistent with the FAA, hold a class action waiver appearing in a contract of adhesion for arbitration unconscionable or contrary to public policy, as part of an arbitration-neutral law that finds all such waivers unenforceable.... Under California law, as discussed, class arbitration may be authorized, even when a contract of adhesion forbids it, because a class arbitration waiver may be unconscionable. *Bazzle* does not call into question the principle that state courts may enforce general contract rules regarding unconscionability and public policy that preclude class action waivers.... Nor did the court address the question whether that determination of unconscionability should be made by a court or an arbitrator....

We reiterate what this court said over 20 years ago in *Keating:* "Classwide arbitration, as Sir Winston Churchill said of democracy, must be evaluated, not in relation to some ideal but in relation to its alternatives." (*Keating,* 31 Cal.3d at p. 613, 183 Cal.Rptr. 360, 645 P.2d 1192.) We continue to believe that the alternatives—either not enforcing arbitration agreements and requiring class action litigation, or allowing arbitration agreements to be used as a means of completely inoculating parties against class liability—are unacceptable. Nothing in the FAA nor in *Bazzle* requires us to reconsider that assessment....

III. Disposition

The judgment of the Court of Appeal is reversed, and the cause is remanded for proceedings consistent with this opinion.

■ We concur: GEORGE, C.J., KENNARD AND WERDEGAR, JJ.

■ Concurring and Dissenting Opinion by BAXTER, J.

I concur in part and dissent in part. I agree with the majority that *federal* law does not *compel* enforcement of contractual class action waivers simply because they are contained in arbitration agreements. But I lament the majority's determination to use this case as a vehicle to resolve the issue of *California's* policy on class action waivers. [W]e need not, and should not, confront that question here.

[B]ecause the Court of Appeal upheld the instant waiver solely by finding federal preemption of any California antiwaiver policy, that court did not decide whether such a policy exists. Ordinarily, we do not address, on review, issues that were not decided by the Court of Appeal.

* * *

Questions

1. Should class actions be permitted in arbitration even if the agreement is silent on this issue? As of the date this book went to press, the Supreme Court had granted certiorari, but not decided, a case raising the issue of whether an arbitral class action is permitted when the underlying arbitration agreement says nothing about class actions. Stolt–Nielsen v. AnimalFeeds Int'l Corp., 129 S.Ct. 2793 (2009), cert. granted June 15, 2009.

2. Do the *Kristian* and *Discover Bank* courts adequately distinguish *Bazzle*? Why isn't the class-action-waiver issue one for the arbitrator to decide?

3. Do you agree with the *Kristian* court's distinction of antitrust claims from TILA claims? How do these arguments cut with regard to other types of claims, such as employment claims? Should there be a difference between statutory and nonstatutory claims? Must courts now decide, statute by statute, which claims are subject to class-action waivers and which are not? Should *all* class action waivers in consumer arbitration agreements be unenforceable?

4. Recall the discussion in Chapter 2.8.C in which we presented several different legal theories courts have used to justify reforming or refusing to enforce lopsided arbitration agreements, including: (a) the lopsided terms are inconsistent with state statutory law because the terms interfere with the enforcement of statutory rights, (b) the lopsided terms are unconscionable under state law, and (c) the lopsided terms are inconsistent with the concept of arbitration. Which of these theories, if any, are reflected in the *Kristian* and *Discover Bank* opinions?

5. Many statutes permit a court to award attorneys' fees to a prevailing party. Both *Kristian* and *Discover Bank* discuss briefly whether the availability of such fees is sufficient to attract attorneys to small-dollar cases. Why might the possibility of recovering attorneys' fees be insufficient to attract an attorney to a small-dollar case?

6. The California Supreme Court in *Discover Bank* rejects the conclusion of the Court of Appeal that class actions and arbitration are inherently incompatible. Are you persuaded? Consider the observations of Thomas Doyle and Mark Irvings, each of whom has arbitrated class action cases.[1] They point out that class arbitration can create at least two difficult ethical issues for arbitrators:

a. A judge in class-action litigation often must decide which of several competing lawyers will serve as class counsel. See Fed. R. Civ. P. 23(g)(2). An arbitrator faced with the same decision may have a conflict of interest. If the original class counsel chose the arbitrator, and/or advanced arbitration fees, this would create at least the appearance that the arbitrator is likely to favor that candidate.

b. When a class action lawsuit settles, the trial judge must ensure that absent class members receive a fair settlement—i.e., that class counsel have not colluded with the defendant to sell out the class in exchange for large attorneys' fees. See Fed. R. Civ. P. 23(e). An obvious conflict of interest occurs if this role must be played by an arbitrator because

> [that same arbitrator] has been retained by, and paid by, the parties in a lengthy arbitration. That role may be even more awkward if the arbitrator has to make a fee award to Class Counsel out of a common fund from a settlement; worse still, the arbitrator may have to decide whether that common fund should reimburse Class Counsel for arbitration expenses (including the arbitrator's own fees) that Class Counsel advanced during the course of the proceedings.[2]

One way an arbitrator might avoid these conflicts is by "certifying" these issues to a trial court for judicial resolution. But this presents problems of its own, such as: (a) Is it consistent with the parties' agreement that their dispute will be decided in arbitration? (b) What if there is no pending case—i.e., neither party has challenged the enforceability of the arbitration agreement? How would the arbitrator decide to which court s/he should certify the issues? And would the arbitrator have to file suit to get the issues before the court? File suit against whom? What would be the "case or controversy"? (c) If the underlying dispute is based on state law, would the "certification" belong in state court or federal court? (d) What if a losing suitor in a class-counsel contest, or a class-member-objector to a proposed settlement, wants discovery? (e) Is the bouncing back-and-forth

1. Thomas A. Doyle, *Practical and Ethical Issues Involving Non–Party Class Members in Class Arbitrations,* Paper presented at the American Bar Association, Section of Labor & Employment Law, Midwinter Meeting of the Committee on ADR in Labor and Employment Law (Feb. 15–18, 2009); Mark Irvings panel presentation at same.

2. Doyle, *supra*, at 10.

between arbitral and judicial forums likely to turn arbitration into a lengthy and expensive way to resolve the dispute? Cf. W. Mark C. Weidemaier, *Arbitration and the Individuation Critique*, 49 Ariz. L. Rev. 69 (2007) (arguing that classwide arbitration should be encouraged).

7. If large corporations and large employers can use arbitration agreements to preclude their customers and employees from bringing class actions, will it become increasingly difficult to secure enforcement of consumer protection or worker rights statutes?

8. Where individual enforcement in arbitration would be predictably ineffective, should there be some other mechanism to achieve compliance with such protective measures? Would it be desirable, for example, for a consumers' union or a labor union to negotiate agreements that preserve the right to proceed on a class basis? Alternatively, should Congress amend its consumer and employment statutes to provide that the right to bring a class action is nonwaivable? What other mechanisms are available to ensure enforcement of protective legislation?

9. The California Supreme Court addressed the enforceability of class arbitration waivers in the employment contract setting in *Gentry v. Superior Court*, 165 P.3d 556 (Cal.2007). The court split 4–3, and there was a vigorous dissent. The court held:

> We cannot say categorically that all class arbitration waivers in overtime cases are unenforceable. As Circuit City points out, some 40 published cases over the last 70 years in California have involved individual employees prosecuting overtime violations without the assistance of class litigation or arbitration.... Not all overtime cases will necessarily lend themselves to class actions, nor will employees invariably request such class actions. Nor in every case will class action or arbitration be demonstrably superior to individual actions.
>
> Nonetheless, when it is alleged that an employer has systematically denied proper overtime pay to a class of employees and a class action is requested notwithstanding an arbitration agreement that contains a class arbitration waiver, the trial court must consider the factors discussed above: the modest size of the potential individual recovery, the potential for retaliation against members of the class, the fact that absent members of the class may be ill informed about their rights, and other real world obstacles to the vindication of class members' rights to overtime pay through individual arbitration. If it concludes, based on these factors, that a class arbitration is likely to be a significantly more effective practical means of vindicating the rights of the affected employees than individual litigation or arbitration, and finds that the disallowance of the class action will likely lead to a less comprehensive enforcement of overtime laws for the employees alleged to be affected by the employer's violations, it must invalidate the class arbitration waiver to ensure that these employees can "vindicate [their] unwaivable rights in an arbitration forum."

* * *

8. Arbitral Bias and Misconduct

Commonwealth Coatings Corp. v. Continental Casualty Co.

393 U.S. 145 (1968).

■ Mr. Justice Black delivered the opinion of the Court.

At issue in this case is the question whether elementary requirements of impartiality taken for granted in every judicial proceeding are suspended when the parties agree to resolve a dispute through arbitration.

The petitioner, Commonwealth Coatings Corporation, a subcontractor, sued the sureties on the prime contractor's bond to recover money alleged to be due for a painting job. The contract for painting contained an agreement to arbitrate such controversies. Pursuant to this agreement petitioner appointed one arbitrator, the prime contractor appointed a second, and these two together selected the third arbitrator. This third arbitrator, the supposedly neutral member of the panel, conducted a large business in Puerto Rico, in which he served as an engineering consultant for various people in connection with building construction projects. One of his regular customers in this business was the prime contractor that petitioner sued in this case. This relationship with the prime contractor was in a sense sporadic in that the arbitrator's services were used only from time to time at irregular intervals, and there had been no dealings between them for about a year immediately preceding the arbitration. Nevertheless, the prime contractor's patronage was repeated and significant, involving fees of about $12,000 over a period of four of five years, and the relationship even went so far as to include the rendering of services on the very projects involved in this lawsuit. An arbitration was held, but the facts concerning the close business connections between the third arbitrator and the prime contractor were unknown to petitioner and were never revealed to it by this arbitrator, by the prime contractor, or by anyone else until after an award had been made. Petitioner challenged the award on this ground, among others, but the District Court refused to set aside the award. The Court of Appeals affirmed, 382 F.2d 1010 (C.A.1st Cir. 1967), and we granted certiorari, 390 U.S. 979, 88 S.Ct. 1098, 19 L.Ed.2d 1276 (1968).

In 1925 Congress enacted the United States Arbitration Act, 9 U.S.C. §§ 14–14, which sets out a comprehensive plan for arbitration of controversies coming under its terms, and both sides here assume that this Federal Act governs this case. Section 10 ... sets out the conditions upon which awards can be vacated. The two courts below held, however, that § 10 could not be construed in such a way as to justify vacating the award in this case. We disagree and reverse. Section 10 does authorize vacation of an award where it was "procured by corruption, fraud, or undue means" or "[w]here there was evident partiality ... in the arbitrators." These provisions show a desire of Congress to provide not merely for *any* arbitration but for an impartial one. It is true that petitioner does not charge before us that the third arbitrator was actually guilty of fraud or bias in deciding this case, and we have no reason, apart from the undisclosed business relationship, to suspect him of any improper motives. But neither this arbitrator nor the prime contractor gave to petitioner even an intimation of the close financial relations that had existed between them for a period of years. We have no doubt that if a litigant could show that a foreman of a jury or a judge in a court of justice had, unknown to the litigant, any such relationship, the judgment would be subject to challenge. This is shown beyond doubt by Tumey v. State of Ohio, 273 U.S. 510, 47 S.Ct. 437, 71 L.Ed. 749 (1927), where this Court held that a conviction could not stand because a small part of the judge's income consisted of court fees collected from convicted defendants. Although in Tumey it appeared the amount of the judge's compensation actually depended on whether he decided for one side or the other, that is too small a distinction to allow this manifest violation of the strict morality and fairness Congress would have expected on the part of the arbitrator and the other party in this case. Nor should it be at all relevant, as the Court of Appeals apparently thought it was here, that "[t]he payments received were a very small part of (the arbitrator's) income ..." [382 F.2d, at 1011.] For in Tumey the Court held that a decision should be set aside where there is "the slightest pecuniary interest" on the part of the judge, and specifically rejected the State's contention that the compensation involved there was "so small that it is not to be regarded as likely to influence improperly a judicial officer in the discharge of his duty ..." [273 U.S., at 524, 47 S.Ct., at 441.] Since in the case of courts this is a *constitutional* principle, we can see no basis for refusing to find the same concept in the broad statutory language that governs arbitration proceedings and provides that an award can be set aside on the basis of "evident partiality" or the use of "undue means." See also Rogers v. Schering Corp., 165 F.Supp. 295, 301 (D.C.N.J. 1958). It is true that arbitrators cannot sever all their ties with the business world, since they are not expected to get all their income from their work deciding cases, but we should, if anything, be even more scrupulous to safeguard the impartiality of arbitrators than judges, since the former have completely free rein to decide the law as well as the facts and are not subject to appellate review. We can perceive no way in which the effectiveness of the arbitration process will be hampered by the simple requirement that arbitrators disclose to the parties any dealings that might create an impression of possible bias.

While not controlling in this case, § 18 of the Rules of the American Arbitration Association, in effect at the time of this arbitration, is highly significant. It provided as follows:

> Section 18. Disclosure by Arbitrator of Disqualification—At the time of receiving his notice of appointment, the prospective Arbitrator is requested to disclose any circumstances likely to create a presumption of bias or which he believes might disqualify him as an impartial

> Arbitrator. Upon receipt of such information, the Tribunal Clerk shall immediately disclose it to the parties, who if willing to proceed under the circumstances disclosed, shall, in writing, so advise the Tribunal Clerk. If either party declines to waive the presumptive disqualification, the vacancy thus created shall be filled in accordance with the applicable provisions of this Rule.

And based on the same principle as this Arbitration Association rule is that part of the 33d Canon of Judicial Ethics which provides:

> 33. Social Relations.... [A judge] should, however, in pending or prospective litigation before him be particularly careful to avoid such action as may reasonably tend to awaken the suspicion that his social or business relations or friendships, constitute an element in influencing his judicial conduct.

This rule of arbitration and this canon of judicial ethics rest on the premise that any tribunal permitted by law to try cases and controversies not only must be unbiased but also must avoid even the appearance of bias. We cannot believe that it was the purpose of Congress to authorize litigants to submit their cases and controversies to arbitration boards that might reasonably be thought biased against one litigant and favorable to another.

Reversed.

■ MR. JUSTICE WHITE, with whom MR. JUSTICE MARSHALL joins, concurring.

While I am glad to join my Brother Black's opinion in this case, I desire to make these additional remarks. The Court does not decide today that arbitrators are to be held to the standards of judicial decorum of Article III judges, or indeed of any judges. It is often because they are men of affairs, not apart from but of the marketplace, that they are effective in their adjudicatory function. Cf. United Steelworkers of America v. Warrior & Gulf Navigation Co., 363 U.S. 574, 80 S.Ct. 1347, 4 L.Ed.2d 1409 (1960). This does not mean the judiciary must overlook outright chicanery in giving effect to their awards; that would be an abdication of our responsibility. But it does mean that arbitrators are not automatically disqualified by a business relationship with the parties before them if both parties are informed of the relationship in advance, or if they are unaware of the facts but the relationship is trivial. I see no reason automatically to disqualify the best informed and most capable potential arbitrators.

The arbitration process functions best when an amicable and trusting atmosphere is preserved and there is voluntary compliance with the decree, without need for judicial enforcement. This end is best served by establishing an atmosphere of frankness at the outset, through disclosure by the arbitrator of any financial transactions which he has had or is negotiating with either of the parties. In many cases the arbitrator might believe the business relationship to be so insubstantial that to make a point of revealing it would suggest he is indeed easily swayed, and perhaps a partisan of that party. But if the law requires the disclosure, no such imputation can arise. And it is far better that the relationship be disclosed at the outset, when the parties are free to reject the arbitrator or accept him with knowledge of the relationship and continuing faith in his objectivity, than to have the relationship come to light after the arbitration, when a suspicious or disgruntled party can seize on it as a pretext for invalidating the award. The judiciary should minimize its role in arbitration as judge of the arbitrator's impartiality. That role is best consigned to the parties, who are the architects of their own arbitration process, and are far better informed of the prevailing ethical standards and reputations within their business.

Of course, an arbitrator's business relationships may be diverse indeed, involving more or less remote commercial connections with great numbers of people. He cannot be expected to provide the parties with his complete and unexpurgated business biography. But it is enough for present purposes to hold, as the Court does, that where the arbitrator has a substantial interest in a firm which has done more than trivial business with a party, that fact must be disclosed. If arbitrators err on the side of disclosure, as they should, it will not be difficult for courts to identify those undisclosed relationships which are too insubstantial to warrant vacating an award.

■ MR. JUSTICE FORTAS, with whom MR. JUSTICE HARLAN and MR. JUSTICE STEWART join, dissenting.

I dissent and would affirm the judgment.

The facts in this case do not lend themselves to the Court's ruling. The Court sets aside the arbitration award despite the fact that the award is unanimous and no claim is made of actual partiality, unfairness, bias, or fraud.

The arbitration was held pursuant to provisions in the contracts between the parties. It is not subject to the rules of the American Arbitration Association. It is governed by the United States Arbitration Act, 9 U.S.C. §§ 1–14.

Each party appointed an arbitrator and the third arbitrator was chosen by those two. The controversy relates to the third arbitrator.

. . . The third arbitrator is a leading and respected consulting engineer who has performed services for "most of the contractors in Puerto Rico." He was well known to petitioner's counsel and they were personal friends. Petitioner's counsel candidly admitted that if he had been told about the arbitrator's prior relationship "I don't think I would have objected because I know Mr. Capacete (the arbitrator)."

Clearly, the District Judge's conclusion, affirmed by the Court of Appeals for the First Circuit, was correct, that "the arbitrators conducted fair, impartial hearings; that they reached a proper determination of the issues before them, and that plaintiff's objections represent a 'situation where the losing party to an arbitration is now clutching at straws in an attempt to avoid the results of the arbitration to which it became a party.' "

The Court nevertheless orders that the arbitration award be set aside. It uses this singularly inappropriate case to announce a per se rule that in my judgment has no basis in the applicable statute or jurisprudential principles: that, regardless of the agreement between the parties, if an arbitrator has any prior business relationship with one of the parties of which he fails to inform the other party, however innocently, the arbitration award is always subject to being set aside. This is so even where the award is unanimous; where there is no suggestion that the nondisclosure indicates partiality or bias; and where it is conceded that there was in fact no irregularity, unfairness, bias, or partiality. Until the decision today, it has not been the law that an arbitrator's failure to disclose a prior business relationship with one of the parties will compel the setting aside of an arbitration award regardless of the circumstances.

I agree that failure of an arbitrator to volunteer information about business dealings with one party will, prima facie, support a claim of partiality or bias. But where there is no suggestion that the nondisclosure was calculated, and where the complaining party disclaims any imputation of partiality, bias, or misconduct, the presumption clearly is overcome.[2]

I do not believe that it is either necessary, appropriate, or permissible to rule, as the Court does, that, regardless of the facts, innocent failure to volunteer information constitutes the "evident partiality" necessary under § 10(b) of the Arbitration Act to set aside an award. "Evident partiality" means what it says: conduct—or at least an attitude or disposition—by the arbitrator favoring one party rather than the other. This case demonstrates that to rule otherwise may be a palpable injustice, since all agree that the arbitrator was innocent of either "evident partiality" or anything approaching it.

Arbitration is essentially consensual and practical. The United States Arbitration Act is obviously designed to protect the integrity of the process with a minimum of insistence upon set formulae and rules. The Court applies to this process rules applicable to judges and not to a system characterized by dealing on faith and reputation for reliability. Such formalism is not contemplated by the Act nor is it warranted in a case where no claim is made of partiality, of unfairness, or of misconduct in any degree.

* * *

Questions

1. Is it a fundamental requirement of due process to have one's case decided by an impartial decisionmaker? Should arbitrators be held to the same standard of impartiality as judges? Why does Justice Black contend

2. At the time of the contract and the arbitration herein, § 18 of the Rules of the American Arbitration Association, which the Court quotes, was phrased merely in terms of a "request" that the arbitrator "disclose any circumstances likely to create a presumption of bias or which he believes might disqualify him as an impartial Arbitrator." In 1964, the rule was changed to provide that "the prospective neutral Arbitrator *shall* disclose any circumstances likely to create a presumption of bias or which he believes might disqualify him as an impartial Arbitrator." (Emphasis supplied.)

that an even higher standard of impartiality should apply to arbitrators than to judges? Do the other Justices agree? For a detailed comparison of the standards of impartiality of arbitrators and judges, see Steven J. Goering, *The Standard of Impartiality As Applied to Arbitrators by Federal Courts and Codes of Ethics*, 3 GEO. J. LEG. Ethics 821 (1990).

2. What are the dangers of having a biased decisionmaker? Is the presence or absence of bias an all-or-nothing proposition, or can there be degrees of bias and partiality? If so, how much bias and how far a departure from impartiality render a proceeding fundamentally unfair?

3. In *Commonwealth Coatings*, Justices White and Marshall take the position that arbitrators should not automatically be disqualified on the basis of a prior business relationship so long as the prior relationship is disclosed. Why, in their view, is disclosure a sufficient protection against the dangers of bias? Do you agree? Does disclosure and consent address all the problems of bias in a decision-maker? If a party consents on the basis of full information to an arbitration process that is loaded in favor of the other side, should the court ever set the award aside? What if the party consents because she was in desperate need of the contracted-for service? See, e.g., *Broemmer v. Abortion Services*, supra. Would it matter whether the disclosure was made at the time of contracting or after the dispute arose? What standard for demonstrating consent should be imposed?

4. What is the relationship between disclosure and bias? Should nondisclosure of a significant prior business relationship give rise to an inference of bias? Is such an inference justified? Is the opposite inference—that nondisclosure gives rise to an inference of no bias—equally plausible?

5. What is the basis for Justice Fortas' conclusion that there was no actual bias involved in this case? How can a court tell whether an arbitrator was biased? Might an arbitrator who had a prior business relationship with one party have an incentive to conceal the prior relationship in order to be retained as an arbitrator? Would such an arbitrator necessarily be biased? Would Fortas advocate that a court should hold an evidentiary hearing in order to determine whether an arbitrator was actually biased? See, e.g., Sanko Steamship Co. v. Cook Industries, 495 F.2d 1260 (2d Cir. 1973); Totem Marine Tug & Barge, Inc. v. North American Towing, 607 F.2d 649 (5th Cir. 1979). What kinds of evidence might bear on the issue? Would it be appropriate to call the arbitrator to testify? See Legion Insurance Co. v. Insurance General Agency, Inc., 822 F.2d 541 (5th Cir. 1987) (discussed in Chapter 3.9).

6. Should an arbitrator be disqualified whenever there is a possibility of bias? A probability of bias? A showing of actual bias? What factors would be relevant to establish each? Would it be sufficient, in an employment discrimination case, to show that all (90%?) arbitrators in the pool are white males over age 50?

* * *

Merit Insurance Company v. Leatherby Insurance Company

714 F.2d 673 (7th Cir.1983).

■ Before CUMMINGS, CHIEF JUDGE, POSNER, CIRCUIT JUDGE, and FAIRCHILD, SENIOR CIRCUIT JUDGE.

■ POSNER, CIRCUIT JUDGE.

This appeal from an order under Rule 60(b) of the Federal Rules of Civil Procedure setting aside an arbitration award requires us to decide whether the failure of one of the arbitrators to disclose a prior business relationship with a principal of one of the parties to the arbitration justified the district court in using its powers under Rule 60(b) and the United States Arbitration Act, 9 U.S.C. §§ 1 et seq., to set aside the award.

In 1972 Merit Insurance Company made a contract with Leatherby Insurance Company to reinsure claims under certain insurance policies that Leatherby had issued. Merit later sued Leatherby in federal district court for fraud in inducing the contract. Jurisdiction was based on diversity of citizenship. Leatherby moved the court for an order under 9 U.S.C. § 4 directing the parties to arbitrate their dispute in accordance with the arbitration clause in the contract, and in 1977 the district court entered such an order. See Merit Ins. Co. v. Leatherby Ins. Co., 581 F.2d 137, 139 (7th Cir.1978), and for collateral litigation Merit Ins. Co. v. Colao, 603 F.2d 654 (7th Cir.1979).

The arbitration was conducted under the auspices of the American Arbitration Association. Each party appointed one arbitrator and together the parties appointed from a list formulated by the AAA the third or "neutral" arbitrator, a Chicago lawyer named Jack Clifford. At the first meeting of the arbitration panel the panel agreed that the other two arbitrators would also be neutrals, rather than representatives of the parties that had appointed them.

After an arbitration that lasted three years and produced a hearing transcript of 16,000 pages, the panel on December 1, 1980, unanimously awarded Merit $10,675,000 on its claim. Merit petitioned the district court to confirm the award under 9 U.S.C. § 9. Leatherby opposed confirmation in part on the ground that the arbitrators had been biased, as indicated by certain evidentiary rulings in Merit's favor and by a comment the arbitrator appointed by Merit had made in the course of the proceedings. No charge of bias was leveled against Clifford specifically. The district judge rejected all of Leatherby's arguments and on November 19, 1981, confirmed the award. A month later he rejected Leatherby's first motion under Rule 60(b) to set it aside. Leatherby appealed to this court from both the order confirming the award and the order denying the Rule 60(b) motion. On May 12, 1982, while the appeal was pending, Leatherby filed a second Rule 60(b) motion, this one based on Leatherby's alleged discovery the previous month that Clifford had once worked under Merit's president and principal stockholder, Jerome Stern, at Cosmopolitan Insurance Company. The appeal was dismissed on Leatherby's motion, and an evidentiary hearing on its new charge of bias was held in the district court at the end of August. On November 4, 1982, in an oral opinion, the court granted Leatherby's Rule 60(b) motion and set aside the arbitration award, and Merit has appealed under 28 U.S.C. § 1291. See University Life Ins. Co. of America v. Unimarc Ltd., 699 F.2d 846, 848 (7th Cir.1983).

The hearing in the district court brought out the following facts. The chairman of the board of Cosmopolitan had hired Clifford late in 1960 to be head of the claims department. At the same time Stern had been promoted to executive vice-president of the company. As the vice-president in charge of the claims department Clifford reported to Stern. This relationship lasted till the beginning of 1963 when Stern left Cosmopolitan to enter private practice. Clifford left Cosmopolitan shortly afterward. Clifford and Stern both testified that they had had little professional contact while at Cosmopolitan and no social contacts then or since. Clifford had been promised substantial autonomy by the chairman of the board when he took over the claims department, and Stern—who had no background in claims evaluation and was preoccupied with corporate acquisitions and other matters unrelated to Clifford's responsibilities—gave Clifford a loose rein. Their principal contact came in meetings held at intervals of several months between Stern and the department heads who reported to him. They also had occasional brief discussions over specific claims; once Clifford was asked to review the claims reserves of an insurance company that Cosmopolitan was thinking of buying; and, on orders from above, Stern once required all of his subordinates, including Clifford, to take lie-detector tests. After Clifford and Stern entered private practice they spoke to each other on the phone on one or two occasions but these contacts were of no significance, and until the arbitration the two men had not met face to face since 1963. Rotheiser, a vice-president of Merit, was also employed at Cosmopolitan during Clifford's tenure, but he was the head of a separate department and according to both his testimony and Clifford's they had no dealings with one another.

The foregoing account is drawn in large part from the testimony of Clifford himself, of whom the district judge stated, "I do not find Mr. Clifford to be a credible witness." But read in context this statement principally refers not to Clifford's testimony about his time at Cosmopolitan—testimony corroborated by Stern and Rotheiser, whom the district judge did not find to be incredible and who were not contradicted by any other witness—but to Clifford's explanation of why he omitted to mention his affiliation with Cosmopolitan either when he filled out the forms that the American Arbitration Association requires from its prospective arbitrators or when he first saw Stern at the arbitration hearing. In 1975 the AAA had sent Clifford a "panel data sheet" which contained a space headed, "My prior occupational affiliations have been...." All that Clifford listed in this space (having listed private practice as his current occupation) was his job as claims manager for Firemen's Fund American Insurance Companies from 1949 to 1960. Clifford testified that he had not mentioned Cosmopolitan in part because he was not interested in doing the kind of arbitration for which his experience there would have been relevant. The judge disbelieved this because it was the same kind of work Clifford had done at Firemen's Fund. (The judge made no comment on Clifford's other, and more plausible, explanation for not mentioning his work for Cosmopolitan: it was not a useful reference. Since the company had been liquidated, getting an evaluation of Clifford's work for the company would have been difficult.) But the judge could not have believed that the purpose of the omission was to prevent Clifford from being disqualified as an arbitrator, for the Merit–Leatherby arbitration was still two years in the future when Clifford mailed back the form. The judge conjectured, rather, that Clifford had been embarrassed to broadcast his relationship with Cosmopolitan, because after he had left it the company had gone broke, which resulted, in the district judge's words, in "an explosion in the industry." But when Clifford filled out another panel data sheet at the AAA's request three years later, he again omitted any reference to his work at Cosmopolitan; and when the arbitration began and Clifford recognized Stern and realized that the president of Merit and the former executive vice-president of Cosmopolitan were one and the same, he had said nothing.

Leatherby argues that by failing at each of these junctures to disclose his former relationship with Stern, Clifford violated the ethical norms applicable to arbitrators, and that the only effective sanction for such a violation is to set aside the arbitration award. It also argues that Clifford did more than just fail to disclose his former relationship with Stern, that he tried to put Leatherby off the scent by calling Stern "Mr. Stern" rather than calling him by his first name; but there is no evidence that Clifford was doing anything other than maintaining the decorum of the arbitration proceeding.

The panel data sheet that the American Arbitration Association requires prospective arbitrators to fill out does not indicate that the information sought is for the purpose of determining whether grounds for disqualification exist, so no significance can be attached to Clifford's initial omission of his job history with Cosmopolitan. But section 18 of the AAA's Commercial Arbitration Rules requires the neutral arbitrator to "disclose to the AAA any circumstances likely to affect his impartiality, including any bias or any financial or personal interest in the result of the arbitration or any past or present relationship with the parties or their counsel." And Canon IIA of the Code of Ethics for Arbitrators in Commercial Disputes (jointly adopted by the American Arbitration Association and the American Bar Association) requires arbitrators to disclose "any existing or past financial, business, professional, family or social relationships which are likely to affect impartiality or which might reasonably create an appearance of partiality or bias." The requirement of disclosure is a continuing one, so the fact that Clifford's failure to disclose his relationship with Cosmopolitan in his first panel data sheet was innocent could not excuse his later failure to disclose the relationship when he accepted appointment as an arbitrator of the Merit–Leatherby dispute and when he recognized Stern on the first day of the arbitration hearing.

Notwithstanding the broad language of section 18, no one supposes that either the Commercial Arbitration Rules or the Code of Ethics for Arbitrators requires disclosure of every former social or financial relationship with a party or a party's principals. The Code states that its provisions relating to disclosure "are intended to be applied realistically so that the burden of detailed disclosure does not become so great that it is impractical for persons in the business world to be arbitrators, thereby depriving the parties of the services of those who might be best informed and qualified to decide particular types of cases." Quoting from Justice White's concurring opinion in Commonwealth Coatings Corp. v. Continental Casualty Co., 393 U.S. 145, 150–52, 89 S.Ct. 337, 340–41, 21 L.Ed.2d 301 (1968)—of which more anon—the Code states that although "arbitrators 'should err on the side of disclosure' . . ., it must be recognized that 'an arbitrator's business relationships may be diverse indeed, involving more or less remote commercial connections with great numbers of people' [so that] an arbitrator 'cannot be expected to provide the parties with his complete and unexpurgated business biography,' . . . [or] to disclose interests or relationships which are merely 'trivial.' "

The ethical obligations of arbitrators can be understood only by reference to the fundamental differences between adjudication by arbitrators and adjudication by judges and jurors. No one is forced to arbitrate a commercial dispute unless he has consented by contract to arbitrate. The voluntary nature of commercial arbitration is an important safeguard for the parties that is missing in the case of the courts. See Corey v. New York Stock Exchange, 691 F.2d 1205, 1210 (6th Cir.1982). Courts are coercive, not voluntary, agencies, and the American people's traditional fear of government oppression has resulted in a judicial system in which impartiality is prized above expertise. Thus, people who arbitrate do so because they prefer a tribunal knowledgeable about the subject matter of their dispute to a generalist court with its austere impartiality but limited knowledge of subject matter. "The professional competence of the arbitrator is attractive to the businessman because a commercial dispute arises out of an environment that usually possesses its own folkways, mores, and technology. Most businessmen interviewed contended that commercial disputes should be considered within the framework of such an environment. No matter how determinedly judge and lawyer work to acquire an understanding of a given business or industry, they cannot hope to approximate the practical wisdom distilled from 30 or 40 years of experience." American Management Ass'n, Resolving Business Disputes 51 (1965).

There is a tradeoff between impartiality and expertise. The expert adjudicator is more likely than a judge or juror not only to be precommitted to a particular substantive position but to know or have heard of the parties (or if the parties are organizations, their key people). "Expertise in an industry is accompanied by exposure, in ways large and small, to those engaged in it. . . ." Andros Compania Maritima, S.A. v. Marc Rich & Co., 579 F.2d 691, 701 (2d Cir.1978). The different weighting of impartiality and expertise in arbitration compared to adjudication is dramatically illustrated by the practice whereby each party appoints one of the arbitrators to be his representative rather than a genuine umpire. See Note, *The Use of Tripartite Boards in Labor, Commercial, and International Arbitration*, 68 Harv. L.Rev. 293 (1954). No one would dream of having a judicial panel composed of one part-time judge and two representatives of the parties, but that is the standard arbitration panel, the panel Leatherby chose—presumably because it preferred a more expert to a more impartial tribunal—when it wrote an arbitration clause into its reinsurance contract with Merit.

If Leatherby had wanted its dispute with Merit resolved by an Article III judge (to whom it had access under the diversity jurisdiction), it would not have inserted an arbitration clause in the contract, or having done so move for arbitration against Merit's wishes. Leatherby wanted something different from judicial dispute resolution. It wanted dispute resolution by experts in the insurance industry, who were bound to have greater knowledge of the parties, based on previous professional experience, than an Article III judge, or a jury. The parties to an arbitration choose their method of dispute resolution, and can ask no more impartiality than inheres in the method they have chosen. Cf. American Almond Products Co. v. Consolidated Pecan Sales Co., 144 F.2d 448, 451 (2d Cir.1944) (L. Hand, J.).

It is no surprise, therefore, that the standards for disqualification in the Commercial Arbitration Rules and the Code of Ethics for Arbitrators are not so stringent as those in the federal statutes on judges, see, e.g., 28 U.S.C. § 455, or in Canons 2 and 3(C) of the Code of Judicial Conduct for United States Judges and the ABA's Code of Judicial Conduct. (In fact the arbitration rules and code do not contain any standards for disqualification as such, though such standards are implicit in the disclosure requirements of the AAA's Rules and the AAA–ABA Code.) We thus do not agree with Leatherby that the test for disqualification here is whether the former relationship between Stern and Clifford was "trivial" in relation to the subject matter of the arbitration. If it were trivial Clifford would not have had to disqualify himself even if he had been a judge. See, e.g., Chitimacha Tribe of Louisiana v. Harry L. Laws Co., 690 F.2d 1157, 1166 (5th Cir.1982). . . .

Maybe it was trivial. Chitimacha held that a district judge did not have to disqualify himself from a case in which the defendant was a corporation that the judge had represented when he was in private practice, since the representation had terminated at least six years before. That was a professional relationship, like Clifford's with Stern—only a more recent one. But the test in this case is not whether the relationship was trivial; it is whether, having due regard for the different expectations regarding impartiality that parties bring to arbitration than to litigation, the relationship between Clifford and Stern was so intimate—personally, socially, professionally, or financially—as to cast serious doubt on Clifford's impartiality. Although Stern had been Clifford's supervisor for two years and was a key witness in an arbitration where the stakes to the party of which he was the president and principal shareholder were big, their relationship had ended 14 years before, Clifford had no possible financial stake in the outcome of the arbitration, and his relationship with Stern during their period together at Cosmopolitan had been distant and impersonal. The fact that they had never socialized, either while working for the same company or afterward (though both were practicing law in Chicago all this time), indicates a lack of intimacy. And when a former employee sits in judgment on a former employer there is no presumption that he will be biased in favor of the former employer; he may well be prejudiced against him. The fact that Clifford passed his lie-detector test with flying colors might have made him grateful to Stern, or might have fanned the flames of outrage at having been subjected to such an indignity, or more likely made no difference at all because it happened so long ago. Time cools emotions, whether of gratitude or resentment.

Section 18 of the Commercial Arbitration Rules makes the AAA itself the final arbiter of disqualification once the arbitrator has been appointed, subject only (so far as relevant here) to the limited judicial review allowed by section 10 of the Arbitration Act, 9 U.S.C. § 10, after an arbitration award is made and judicial confirmation of it sought. On the basis of the facts reviewed above, considered in the light of the less stringent standards applicable to disqualification of arbitrators than to disqualification of judges, we doubt that the AAA would have disqualified Clifford—or that Leatherby would have wanted it to.

But even if the failure to disclose was a material violation of the ethical standards applicable to arbitration proceedings, it does not follow that the arbitration award may be nullified judicially. Although we have great respect for the Commercial Arbitration Rules and the Code of Ethics for Arbitrators, they are not the proper starting point for an inquiry into an award's validity under section 10 of the United States Arbitration Act and Rule 60(b) of the Federal Rules of Civil Procedure. The arbitration rules and code do not have the force of law. If Leatherby is to get the arbitration award set aside it must bring itself within the statute and the federal rule. The statute specifies limited grounds for setting aside an arbitration award. The only one relevant here is, "Where there was evident partiality or corruption in the arbitrators, or either of them." 9 U.S.C. § 10(b). (Leatherby does not argue that the award can be set aside on any other ground in the statute, such as "misbehavior" of an arbitrator, in section 10(c).) This is strong language. It makes the grounds for setting aside an arbitrator's award because of bias narrower than the grounds for disqualification in the arbitration rules and code, not to mention the statutes and ethical codes pertaining to judges. Read literally, section 10(b) would require proof of actual bias ("evident partiality"). And not only the arbitrator appointed by Merit, as one might expect, but also the arbitrator appointed by Leatherby—a member of a distinguished Chicago law firm—gave a detailed affidavit denying absolutely and in detail that Clifford had ever evinced any partiality during the three years of the arbitration.

Of course actual bias might be present yet impossible to prove; Clifford might have given no indication of his vote yet have been irrevocably committed to Merit out of some obscure sense of gratitude toward, or exaggerated respect for, Stern. If circumstances are such that a man of average probity might reasonably be suspected of partiality, maybe the language of section 10(b) can be stretched to require disqualification. But the circumstances must be powerfully suggestive of bias, and are not here.

The American Arbitration Association is in competition not only with other private arbitration services but with the courts in providing—in the case of the private services, selling—an attractive form of dispute settlement. It may set its standards as high or as low as it thinks its customers want. The statute has a different purpose—to make arbitration effective by putting the coercive force of the federal courts behind arbitration decrees that affect interstate commerce or are otherwise of federal concern. See 9 U.S.C. § 1; S.Rep. No. 536, 68th Cong., 1st Sess. 3 (1924). The statute does not provide a dispute settlement mechanism; it facilitates private dispute settlement. The standards for judicial intervention are therefore narrowly drawn to assure the basic integrity of the arbitration process without meddling in it. Section 10 is full of words like corruption and misbehavior and fraud. The standards it sets are minimum ones. The ethical concerns expressed by Leatherby are remote from the draftsmen's concerns. The Senate Report, for example, refers approvingly to "arrangements for avoiding the delay and expense of litigation and referring a dispute to friends . . .," S.Rep. No. 536, supra, at 3. The fact that the AAA went beyond the statutory standards in drafting its own code of ethics does not lower the threshold for judicial intervention. If Clifford violated current ethical norms for commercial arbitrators, his was at worst a technical violation that does not justify setting aside an arbitration award on the statutory ground of evident partiality or corruption. Concern with professional reputation will provide some deterrent to such violations, especially where the arbitrator is a lawyer, as he was here.

We have discussed the issue of the award's validity as if it had to be decided on the basis of first principles—as it very largely does. Prior cases involve factual situations very different from the one here and do not yield general principles. The only Supreme Court decision, Commonwealth Coatings Corp. v. Continental Casualty Co., 393 U.S. 145, 89 S.Ct. 337, 21 L.Ed.2d 301 (1968), provides little guidance because of the inability of a majority of Justices to agree on anything but the result. Justice Black, joined by three other Justices, took a very hard line on the ethical standards of arbitrators. His opinion contains language suggesting that arbitrators are subject to the same ethical standards as judges, although this is dictum because the facts of the case required disqualification even under a narrow reading of section 10(b): the "neutral" arbitrator was a regular supplier of one of the parties to the arbitration, and had even rendered services on projects involved in the arbitration. Justice White, concurring, purported to join Justice Black's opinion but actually took a quite different tack, the sense of which is captured in the passages we quoted earlier from the Code of Ethics for Arbitrators—which treats Justice White's opinion as a surer guide to the view of a majority of the Supreme Court than Justice Black's. Justice White stated, "The Court does not decide today that arbitrators are to be held to the standards of judicial decorum of Article III judges," 393 U.S. at 150, 89 S.Ct. at 340, and since his vote was essential to a majority, what he said the Court did not decide the Court did not decide, whatever Justice Black may have hoped. Our court, in United States Wrestling Federation v. Wrestling Division of AAU, Inc., 605 F.2d 313, 319 (7th Cir.1979), treated Justice White's opinion as authoritative.

Although it is difficult to extract from the cases more than a mood, the mood is one of reluctance to set aside arbitration awards for failure of the arbitrator to disclose a relationship with a party. See, e.g., Andros Compania Maritima, S.A. v. Marc Rich & Co., supra, 579 F.2d at 700. In Andros, the arbitration award was confirmed although the neutral arbitrator, Nelson, had not disclosed that he had in the recent past sat on 19 arbitration panels with the president of one of the firms involved in the arbitration and in 12 of these panels the president had been one of the arbitrators who had selected Nelson to be the neutral. Disqualification of the neutral arbitrator was also rejected in International Produce, Inc. v. A/S Rosshavet, 638 F.2d 548, 551 (2d Cir.1981), even though, during the arbitration, he had been a witness in another case between the same law firms that were trying the arbitration matter before him. In Middlesex Mutual Ins. Co. v. Levine, 675 F.2d 1197 (11th Cir.1982) (per curiam), an arbitration award was set aside for "evident partiality," but there a company owned by the neutral arbitrator's family was entangled in a dispute with the parties to the litigation in which he personally had lost $85,000, and he also was under investigation for alleged unethical conduct involving those parties.

The suggestion in Tamari v. Bache Halsey Stuart Inc., 619 F.2d 1196 (7th Cir.1980), that "appearance of bias" is a proper standard for disqualification of arbitrators is not inconsistent with anything in our present opinion; it just means that it is unnecessary to demonstrate—what is almost impossible to demonstrate—that the arbitrator had an actual bias. The standard is an objective one, but less exacting than the one governing judges.

... Furthermore, as it is likely that if Leatherby had known about Clifford's former relationship with Stern it would not have cared, because it would not have been able to figure out any more than we can how that relationship would cut in terms of partiality toward or prejudice against Merit, we think Leatherby was required, and it failed, to support its Rule 60(b) motion with affidavits that its officers did not know of the relationship. It had to negate any inference that it had implicitly consented to have Clifford as an arbitrator knowing all it now knows but saying nothing. We note in this regard the perfunctory investigation that Leatherby made into Clifford's background when the AAA first listed him as a possible arbitrator. Leatherby argues that it would have been burdensome to investigate all 26 names on the list and that it was entitled to trust any potential arbitrator to comply with the AAA's disclosure requirements. It points out that the cost of arbitration will be increased if parties, not being able to trust the disclosure requirements, must conduct elaborate background investigations. It is true that the disclosure requirements are intended in part to avoid the costs of background investigations. But this is a $10 million case. If Leatherby had been worried about putting its fate into the hands of someone who might be linked in the distant past to the adversary's principal, it would have done more than it did to find out about Clifford. That it did so little suggests that its fear of a prejudiced panel is a tactical response to having lost the arbitration.

We do not want to encourage the losing party to every arbitration to conduct a background investigation of each of the arbitrators in an effort to uncover evidence of a former relationship with the adversary. This would only increase the cost and undermine the finality of arbitration, contrary to the purpose of the United States Arbitration Act of making arbitration a swift, inexpensive, and effective substitute for judicial dispute resolution. This lawsuit is already eight years old. To uphold the district court's vacation of the arbitration award in the absence of evidence of actual or probable partiality or corruption would open a new and, we fear, an interminable chapter in the efforts of people who have chosen arbitration and been disappointed in their choice to get the courts—to which they could have turned in the first instance for resolution of their disputes—to undo the results of their preferred method of dispute resolution.

The judgment of the district court setting aside his earlier judgment confirming the arbitration award in favor of Merit is reversed, and the case is remanded with directions to reinstate the previous judgment.

* * *

Positive Software Solutions, Inc. v. New Century Mortg. Corp.

476 F.3d 278 (5th Cir. 2007).

■ EDITH H. JONES, CHIEF JUDGE, joined by E. GRADY JOLLY, PATRICK E. HIGGINBOTHAM, W. EUGENE DAVIS, JERRY E. SMITH, RHESA H. BARKSDALE, DEMOSS, DENNIS, EDITH BROWN CLEMENT, PRADO and OWEN, CIRCUIT JUDGES:

The court reconsidered this case en banc in order to determine whether an arbitration award must be vacated for "evident partiality," 9 U.S.C. § 10(a)(2), where an arbitrator failed to disclose a prior professional association with a member of one of the law firms that engaged him. We conclude that the Federal Arbitration Act ("FAA") does not mandate the extreme remedy of vacatur for nondisclosure of a trivial past association, and we reverse the district court's contrary judgment, but it is necessary to remand for consideration of appellee's other objections to the arbitral award.

BACKGROUND

The facts are undisputed. In January 2001, New Century Mortgage Corporation ("New Century") licensed an automated software support program from Positive Software Solutions, Inc. ("Positive Software"). In December 2002, during negotiations for a renewal of that license, Positive

Software alleged that New Century copied the program in violation of the parties' agreement and applicable copyright law. Positive Software then filed this lawsuit against New Century in the Northern District of Texas alleging breach of contract, misappropriation of trade secrets, misappropriation of intellectual property, copyright infringement, fraud, and other causes of action. Positive Software sought specific performance, money damages, and injunctive relief.

In April 2003, the district court granted Positive Software's motion to preliminarily enjoin New Century from using the program and, pursuant to the parties' contract, submitted the matter to arbitration. Following American Arbitration Association ("AAA") procedures, the AAA provided the parties with a list of potential arbitrators and asked the parties to rank the candidates. After reviewing biographical information, the parties selected Peter Shurn to arbitrate the case, as he had the highest combined ranking. The AAA contacted Shurn about serving as an arbitrator, and he agreed, after stating that he had nothing to disclose regarding past relationships with either party or their counsel.

After a seven-day hearing, Shurn issued an eighty-six page written ruling, concluding that New Century did not infringe Positive Software's copyrights, did not misappropriate trade secrets, did not breach the contract, and did not defraud or conspire against Positive Software. He ordered that Positive Software take nothing on its claims and granted New Century $11,500 on its counterclaims and $1.5 million in attorney's fees.

Upon losing the arbitration, Positive Software conducted a detailed investigation of Shurn's background. It discovered that several years earlier, Shurn and his former law firm, Arnold, White, & Durkee ("Arnold White"), had represented the same party as New Century's counsel, Susman Godfrey, L.L.P., in a patent litigation between Intel Corporation and Cyrix Corporation ("the Intel litigation"). One of Susman Godfrey's attorneys in the New Century arbitration, Ophelia Camiña, had been involved in the Intel litigation.

The Intel litigation involved six different lawsuits in the early 1990s. Intel was represented by seven law firms and at least thirty-four lawyers, including Shurn and Camiña. The dispute involved none of the parties to the arbitration. Camiña participated in representing Intel in three of the lawsuits from August 1991 until July 1992, although her name remained on the pleadings in one of the cases until June 1993. In September 1992, Shurn, along with twelve other Arnold White attorneys, entered an appearance in two of the three cases on which Camiña worked. Although their names appeared together on pleadings, Shurn and Camiña never attended or participated in any meetings, telephone calls, hearings, depositions, or trials together.

Positive Software filed a motion to vacate the arbitration award, alleging that the award had been procured by fraud, Shurn had manifestly disregarded applicable laws, and, despite the lack of contact between Shurn and Camiña, Shurn had been biased, as evidenced by his failure to disclose his past connection to Camiña. In September 2004, the district court granted Positive Software's motion and vacated the award, finding that Shurn failed to disclose "a significant prior relationship with New Century's counsel," thus creating an appearance of partiality requiring vacatur. *Positive Software Solutions, Inc. v. New Century Mortgage Corp.,* 337 F.Supp.2d 862, 865 (N.D.Tex. 2004). New Century appealed, and a panel of this court affirmed the district court's vacatur on the ground that the prior relationship "might have conveyed an impression of possible partiality to a reasonable person." *Positive Software Solutions, Inc. v. New Century Mortgage Corp.,* 436 F.3d 495, 504 (5th Cir. 2006). Neither the district court nor the appellate panel found that Shurn was actually biased toward New Century. This court granted New Century's petition for rehearing en banc.

DISCUSSION

To assure that arbitration serves as an efficient and cost-effective alternative to litigation, and to hold parties to their agreements to arbitrate, the FAA narrowly restricts judicial review of arbitrators' awards. The ground of vacatur alleged here is that "there was evident partiality" in the arbitrator. The meaning of evident partiality is discernible definitionally and as construed by the Supreme Court and a number of our sister circuits.

On its face, "evident partiality" conveys a stern standard. Partiality means bias, while "evident" is defined as "clear to the vision or understanding" and is synonymous with manifest, obvious, and apparent. *Webster's Ninth New Collegiate Dictionary* 430 (1985). The statutory language, with which we always begin, seems to require upholding arbitral awards unless bias was clearly evident in the decisionmakers.

The panel decision here disagreed with the straightforward interpretation, however, and concluded that, in "a nondisclosure case in which the parties chose the arbitrator," the "arbitrator selected by the parties displays evident partiality by the very failure to disclose facts that might create a reasonable impression of the arbitrator's partiality." 436 F.3d at 502. The panel acknowledged a lack of any actual bias in this award even as it substituted a reasonable impression of partiality standard for "evident" partiality in cases of an arbitrator's nondisclosure to the parties. The panel believed this different standard to be required by the Supreme Court's decision in *Commonwealth Coatings Corp. v. Continental Cas. Co.,* 393 U.S. 145, 89 S.Ct. 337, 21 L.Ed.2d 301 (1968), which interpreted § 10(b).[2]

How *Commonwealth Coatings* guides this court is a critical issue. Reasonable minds can agree that *Commonwealth Coatings,* like many plurality-plus Supreme Court decisions, is not pellucid. Justice Black delivered the opinion of the Court and imposed "the simple requirement that arbitrators disclose to the parties any dealings that might create an impression of possible bias." *Id.* at 149, 89 S.Ct. at 339. He noted that, while arbitrators are not expected to sever all ties with the business world, courts must be scrupulous in safeguarding the impartiality of arbitrators, who are given the ability to decide both the facts and the law and whose

2. What was then § 10(b) is now contained in § 10(a)(2).

decisions are not subject to appellate review. *Id.* at 148–49, 89 S.Ct. at 339. Thus, arbitrators "not only must be unbiased but also must avoid even the appearance of bias," *Id.* at 150, 89 S.Ct. at 340, in order to maintain confidence in the arbitration system.

Justice White, the fifth vote in the case, together with Justice Marshall, purported to be "glad to join" Justice Black's opinion, but he wrote to make "additional remarks." *Id.* (White, J., concurring). Justice White emphasized that "[t]he Court does not decide today that arbitrators are to be held to the standards of judicial decorum of Article III judges, or indeed of any judges." *Id.* Indeed, Justice White wrote that arbitrators are not "automatically disqualified by a business relationship with the parties before them if . . . [the parties] are unaware of the facts but the relationship is trivial." *Id.* While supporting a policy of disclosure by arbitrators to enhance the selection process, Justice White also concluded, in a practical vein, that an arbitrator "cannot be expected to provide the parties with his complete and unexpurgated business biography." *Id.* at 151, 89 S.Ct. at 340. His opinion fully envisions upholding awards when arbitrators fail to disclose insubstantial relationships. *Id.* at 152, 89 S.Ct. at 341.

If one lays primary emphasis on Justice White's statement that he was "glad to join" the plurality, his opinion can be deemed reconcilable with that of Justice Black. Only in that event is the plurality opinion binding on lower courts.

Another compelling reading of the opinions is also possible, however. Justice Black's opinion uses an egregious set of facts as the vehicle to require broad disclosure of "any dealings that might create an impression of possible bias." *Id.* at 149, 89 S.Ct. at 339. Justice White, for his part, hews closely to the facts and finds it "enough for present purposes to hold, as the Court does, that where the arbitrator has a *substantial interest* in a firm which has done *more than trivial business* with a party, that fact must be disclosed." 393 U.S. at 151–52, 89 S.Ct. at 340–41 (emphasis added). Justice White, thus read, supports ample but not unrealistic disclosure, and he supports a cautious approach to vacatur for nondisclosure. His "joinder" is magnanimous but significantly qualified.

The latter reading is more persuasive, because it accords scope to the full White opinion, unlike the view that focuses on the introductory "glad to join" sentence. Thus, Justice White's concurrence, pivotal to the judgment, is based on a narrower ground than Justice Black's opinion, and it becomes the Court's effective ratio decidendi. *See Marks v. United States,* 430 U.S. 188, 193–94, 97 S.Ct. 990, 993–94, 51 L.Ed.2d 260 (1977).

A majority of circuit courts have concluded that Justice White's opinion did not lend majority status to the plurality opinion. [Citations to cases from the Second, Fourth, Fifth, Sixth, Seventh, Tenth, and Eleventh Circuits omitted.] While these courts' interpretations of *Commonwealth Coatings* may differ in particulars, they all agree that nondisclosure alone does not require vacatur of an arbitral award for evident partiality. An arbitrator's failure to disclose must involve a significant compromising connection to the parties. . . .

Only the Ninth Circuit has interpreted *Commonwealth Coatings,* as the panel majority did, to de-emphasize Justice White's narrowing language. *See Schmitz v. Zilveti,* 20 F.3d 1043 (9th Cir. 1994). In *Schmitz,* the court criticized case law suggesting "that an impression of bias is sufficient while an appearance [of bias] is not." *Id.* at 1047. *Commonwealth Coatings,* it held, does not merit such a "hairline distinction." *Id. Schmitz* not only interpreted *Commonwealth Coatings* to mandate a "reasonable impression of bias" standard in nondisclosure cases but went on to vacate an arbitral award where the arbitrator had not himself been aware of the potential conflict and had failed to undertake due diligence to ascertain and then disclose it to the parties.[4] Even if one ignores the extension of *Commonwealth Coatings* by *Schmitz,* the undisclosed relationship between the arbitrator's firm and Pru–Bache's parent company was more current, concrete and financially meaningful than the co-counsel relationship in the present case. *Schmitz* is an outlier that lends little support to Positive Software.

As we have concluded, the better interpretation of *Commonwealth Coatings* is that which reads Justice White's opinion holistically. The resulting standard is that in nondisclosure cases, an award may not be vacated because of a trivial or insubstantial prior relationship between the arbitrator and the parties to the proceeding. The "reasonable impression of bias" standard is thus interpreted practically rather than with utmost rigor.

According to this interpretation of *Commonwealth Coatings,* the outcome of this case is clear: Shurn's failure to disclose a trivial former business relationship does not require vacatur of the award. The essential charge of bias is that the arbitrator, Peter Shurn, worked on the same litigation as did Ophelia Camiña, counsel for one of the parties. They represented Intel in protracted patent litigation that lasted from 1990 to 1996. Camiña and Shurn each signed the same ten pleadings, but they never met or spoke to each other before the arbitration. They were two of thirty-four lawyers, and from two of seven firms, that represented Intel during the lawsuit, which ended at least seven years before the instant arbitration.

No case we have discovered in research or briefs has come close to vacating an arbitration award for nondisclosure of such a slender connection between the arbitrator and a party's counsel. In fact, courts have refused vacatur where the undisclosed connections are much stronger. *See, e.g., Montez v. Prudential Sec., Inc.,* 260 F.3d 980, 982, 984 (8th Cir. 2001) (no vacatur; as general counsel for a company, arbitrator had employed

4. In *Schmitz,* the arbitrator's law firm previously had represented Prudential Insurance Co., the parent of Pru–Bache Securities, the prevailing party in the arbitration. The representation involved at least nineteen cases over a thirty-five year period, including a case that ended less than two years before the arbitration. The arbitrator had reviewed documents naming the parent company, but did not run a conflict check for the parent or disclose any of his firm's earlier representations of the parent company prior to the arbitration.

sixty-eight attorneys, paying them $2.8 million in fees, from the law firm representing one of the parties in the arbitration); *ANR Coal,* 173 F.3d at 495–96 (no vacatur; arbitrator's law firm represented company that indirectly caused the dispute in the arbitration by buying less from the defendant, who in turn sought to buy less from the plaintiff); *Al–Harbi v. Citibank, N.A.,* 85 F.3d 680, 682 (D.C. Cir. 1996) (no vacatur where arbitrator's former law firm represented party to the arbitration on unrelated matters); *Lifecare Int'l, Inc. v. CD Med., Inc.,* 68 F.3d 429, 432–34 & n. 3 (11th Cir. 1995) (no vacatur where arbitrator had memorialized prior scheduling dispute with an attorney from the law firm representing one of the parties and mentioned it eighteen months later at the arbitration; arbitrator also failed to disclose that he became "of counsel" to a law firm the prevailing party had interviewed for the purpose of obtaining representation in the instant dispute and that had reviewed the contract involved in the case two years prior; court found this, at best, showed a "remote, uncertain, and speculative partiality"); *Health Servs. Mgmt. Corp. v. Hughes,* 975 F.2d 1253, 1255, 1264 (7th Cir. 1992) (arbitrator knew one of the parties, had worked in the same office with him twenty years ago, and saw him about once a year since; the court found this relationship "minimal" and insufficient to vacate); *Merit Ins.,* 714 F.2d at 677, 680 (no vacatur; arbitrator had worked directly under the president and principal stockholder of one of the parties for three years, ending fourteen years prior to the arbitration; the Seventh Circuit noted that "[t]ime cools emotions, whether of gratitude or resentment"); *Ormsbee Dev. Co.,* 668 F.2d at 1149–50 (no vacatur where arbitrator and law firm representing a party had clients in common; requiring vacatur under such facts would "request that potential neutral arbitrators sever all their ties with the business world" (internal quotation omitted)).

The relationship in this case pales in comparison to those in which courts have granted vacatur. *See, e.g., Commonwealth Coatings,* 393 U.S. at 146, 89 S.Ct. at 338 (business relationship between arbitrator and party was "repeated and significant"; the party to the arbitration was one of the arbitrator's "regular customers"; "the relationship even went so far as to include the rendering of services on the very projects involved in this lawsuit"); *Olson v. Merrill Lynch, Pierce, Fenner & Smith, Inc.,* 51 F.3d 157, 159 (8th Cir. 1995) (arbitrator was a high-ranking officer in a company that had a substantial ongoing business relationship with one of the parties); *Schmitz,* 20 F.3d at 1044 (arbitrator's law firm represented parent company of a party for decades, including within two years of the arbitration); *Morelite,* 748 F.2d at 81 (arbitrator's father was General President of the union involved in the arbitrated dispute).

Finally, even if Justice White's "joinder" is not read as a limitation on Justice Black's opinion in *Commonwealth Coatings,* and the controlling opinion emphatically requires arbitrators to "disclose to the parties any dealings that might create an impression of possible bias," 393 U.S. at 149, 89 S.Ct. at 339, we cannot find the standard breached in this case. The facts of *Commonwealth Coatings* are easily distinguishable. In *Commonwealth Coatings,* the arbitrator and a party had a "repeated and significant" business relationship. *Id.* at 146, 89 S.Ct. at 338. The relationship involved fees of about $12,000 paid to the arbitrator by the party, extended over a period of four or five years, ended only one year before the arbitration, and even included the rendering of services on the very projects involved in the arbitration before him. *Id.* Such a relationship bears little resemblance to the tangential, limited, and stale contacts between Shurn and Camiña. Nothing in *Commonwealth Coatings* requires vacatur for the undisclosed relationship in this case.

CONCLUSION

Awarding vacatur in situations such as this would seriously jeopardize the finality of arbitration. Just as happened here, losing parties would have an incentive to conduct intensive, after-the-fact investigations to discover the most trivial of relationships, most of which they likely would not have objected to if disclosure had been made. Expensive satellite litigation over nondisclosure of an arbitrator's "complete and unexpurgated business biography" will proliferate. Ironically, the "mere appearance" standard would make it easier for a losing party to challenge an arbitration award for nondisclosure than for actual bias.

Moreover, requiring vacatur based on a mere appearance of bias for nondisclosure would hold arbitrators to a higher ethical standard than federal Article III judges. In his concurrence, Justice White noted that the Court did not decide whether "arbitrators are to be held to the standards of judicial decorum of Article III judges, or indeed of any judges." *Id.* at 150, 89 S.Ct. at 340 (White, J., concurring). This cannot mean that arbitrators are held to a *higher* standard than Article III judges. Had this same relationship occurred between an Article III judge and the same lawyer, neither disclosure nor disqualification would have been forced or even suggested. *See Chitimacha Tribe of La. v. Harry L. Laws Co.,* 690 F.2d 1157, 1166 (5th Cir. 1982) (rejecting a finding of judicial bias where the federal judge had represented a party to the case in an unrelated matter at least six years prior). While it is true that disclosure of prior significant contacts and business dealings between a prospective arbitrator and the parties furthers informed selection, it is not true, as Justice White's opinion perceptively explains, that "the best informed and most capable potential arbitrators" should be automatically disqualified (and their awards nullified) by failure to inform the parties of trivial relationships. *Commonwealth Coatings,* 393 U.S. at 150, 89 S.Ct. at 340.

Finally, requiring vacatur on these attenuated facts would rob arbitration of one of its most attractive features apart from speed and finality—expertise. Arbitration would lose the benefit of specialized knowledge, because the best lawyers and professionals, who normally have the longest lists of potential connections to disclose, have no need to risk blemishes on their reputations from post-arbitration lawsuits attacking them as biased.

Neither the FAA nor the Supreme Court, nor predominant case law, nor sound policy countenances vacatur of FAA arbitral awards for nondisclosure by an arbitrator unless it creates a concrete, not speculative impression of bias. Arbitration may have flaws, but this is not one of them. The draconian remedy of vacatur is only warranted upon nondisclosure that involves a significant compromising relationship. This case does not come close to meeting this standard.

The judgment of the district court is REVERSED, and the case is REMANDED FOR FURTHER PROCEEDINGS.

■ REAVLEY, CIRCUIT JUDGE, dissenting, joined by WIENER, EMILIO M. GARZA, BENAVIDES and CARL E. STEWART, CIRCUIT JUDGES:

In 1968 the Supreme Court held that an arbitral award could not stand where the arbitrator had failed to disclose a past relationship that might give the impression of possible partiality. [*Commonwealth Coatings Corp. v. Continental Cas. Co.,* 393 U.S. 145, 89 S.Ct. 337, 21 L.Ed.2d 301 (1968).] The Court has never changed that holding; it is the law that rules us today. But the majority of this court disapprove of that law because they prefer to protect arbitrators and their awards when they fail to disclose prior relationships with parties or counsel. They therefore change the law for this case and, to make it appear as if their transgression does not matter, trivialize their report of the past relationship. I dissent because this court may not overrule a decision of the Supreme Court.

* * *

Questions

1. What standard for impartiality should apply under the FAA? Can there can be degrees of impartiality and bias? How much bias is grounds to set aside an arbitral award? How can parties ensure total impartiality? Can they bargain for an arbitration procedure that guarantees the parties total impartiality?

2. In *Leatherby Insurance Company,* why does Judge Posner say there is a tradeoff between impartiality and expertise? How does expertise obviate the concern about prior relationships raising a potential for bias? Is Posner relying on a view of professionalism that says experts, like professionals, can ignore self-interest and prior relationships when asked to apply professional judgment? Or is he saying that bias is not objectionable when parties have consented to it? Would he take the consent rationale so far as to uphold an arbitral award that was rendered by a relative of one of the parties, when the initial agreement provided for the relative to arbitrate all disputes that arise? Would he uphold an award by an agreement that called for a panel of three monkeys? A coin toss?

3. Is Judge Posner's rationale more persuasive than the rationale in *Positive Software*? Which gives more protection to parties against the dangers of arbitral bias?

4. Does Posner's position rest primarily on consent or on the indeterminate nature of the bias that is produced by the prior employer-employee relationship? If the latter, can't relations between siblings also be indeterminate in terms of creating either good will or ill-will? Or, parent-child relations, or even spousal relations? Should an award by an arbitrator who is a close relative of one of the parties also be upheld if there was initial consent? What if the other contracting party did not know that the arbitrator was a relation of one of the parties? Is such a scenario distinguishable from the facts of *Leatherby*?

5. Posner gives, as one reason for his refusal to set aside the award on ground of bias, the explanation that there is no a priori way to know whether the prior relationship of employer-employee created bias in favor of or in opposition to the party who is the former employer. While a judge may not know the answer to that question, presumably the former employer knows, or at least has a reasonably good guess. If the former employer believes that the former employee will be hostile, we can expect that party to speak up rather than remain silent on the issue of bias. Can't we assume, then, that if the party who is the former employer remains silent on the issue, it is because he believes that the prior relationship may be beneficial to him? Is the existence of important information that is available only to one side, be it helpful or harmful, an element of impermissible bias?

6. Positive Software investigated the background of the arbitrator only "upon losing the arbitration." Would you select an arbitrator for an eight-figure case without doing the kind of investigation that Positive Software here did only *after* arbitration? If you were representing a party about to go to arbitration, and prior to the hearing the arbitrator disclosed the type of prior relationship at issue in *Positive Software,* would you have objected?

* * *

Note on Other Sources of Disclosure Standards

Disclosure standards are imposed not only by common law and the FAA, but also by many other sources.[1] These sources include the American Bar Association Code of Ethics for Arbitrators in Commercial Disputes, the National Arbitration Forum Standards, state statutes, state codes of judicial conduct, the rules of professional responsibility for lawyers, and the Guidelines on Conflicts of Interest in International Arbitration.

In 2002, the Judicial Council of California adopted comprehensive ethics standards for contractual arbitrators in California. These standards, the most far-reaching in the country, establish minimum standards of conduct for persons appointed as neutral arbitrators under an arbitration agreement subject to the California Arbitration Act or an arbitration agreement in which the arbitration hearing is to be conducted in California. The standards include:

1. See David Allen Larson, *Conflicts of Interest and Disclosures: Are We Making a Mountain Out of a Molehill?*, 49 S. Tex. L. Rev. 879 (2008).

1. Establish the arbitrators' overarching ethical duty to act in a manner that upholds the integrity and fairness of the arbitration process and to maintain impartiality toward all participants at all times.

2. Expand arbitrators' existing statutory disclosure obligations, including the following:

   - Expand the existing duty of reasonable inquiry that applies with respect to financial interests to require arbitrators to make a reasonable effort to inform themselves about all matters that must be disclosed.

   - Expand required disclosures about the relationships of arbitrators' family members to include those of arbitrators' domestic partners.

   - Expand required disclosures about prior service as an arbitrator to include prior service as a neutral arbitrator selected by a party arbitrator in the current arbitration and service as any other type of dispute resolution neutral for a party or attorney in the current arbitration.

   - Establish specific requirements for arbitrators to disclose if they or a member of their immediate family is or, within the previous two years was, an employee, expert witness, or consultant for a party or a lawyer in the current arbitration.

   - Require that, in consumer arbitrations, arbitrators disclose information about any financial or professional relationship between any dispute resolution provider organization that is administering the arbitration and parties or attorneys in the arbitration, including information about prior cases involving those parties or attorneys in which the provider administered dispute resolution services. If any such relationship is disclosed, an arbitrator also is required to provide information about his or her relationship with that provider organization; and

   - Establish a specific requirement that arbitrators disclose membership in organizations that practice invidious discrimination on the basis of race, sex, religion, national origin, or sexual orientation.

3. Restrict an arbitrator's acceptance of subsequent employment or professional relationships (including subsequent arbitrations) involving a party or a lawyer in a prior arbitration.

4. Restrict an arbitrator's acceptance of a gift, bequest, favor, or honoraria from any person or entity whose interests are reasonably likely to come before the arbitrator in the arbitration, or that may come before the arbitrator within two years after the arbitration concludes.

What are the costs and benefits of such far-reaching disclosure standards?[2] Should the remedy for nondisclosure be to vacate the award or to sanction the arbitrator? Should it depend on the circumstances?

* * *

Morris v. Metriyakool

344 N.W.2d 736 (Mich.1984).

■ KAVANAGH, JUSTICE.

These cases concern arbitration of medical malpractice claims. The most significant issue presented is whether the malpractice arbitration act of 1975, M.C.L. § 600.5040 et seq.; M.S.A. § 27A.5040 et seq., deprives plaintiffs of constitutional rights to an impartial decision maker. We hold that it does not.

Plaintiff Diane Jackson was treated in November, 1977, at defendant Detroit Memorial Hospital by defendant Dr. William J. Bloom for a dental malady. At that time, plaintiff agreed to submit to arbitration "any claims or disputes (except for disputes over charges for services rendered) which may arise in the future out of or in connection with the health care rendered to me ... by this hospital, its employees and those of its independent staff doctors and consultants who have agreed to arbitrate." In August, 1979, plaintiff brought action for malpractice against defendants in the Wayne Circuit Court. Defendants moved for accelerated judgment, on the basis of the agreement to arbitrate. After a hearing, the court found the act constitutional and, finding no duress, mistake, or incompetency in the execution of the agreement, granted defendants' motion.

The Court of Appeals reversed, holding that M.C.L. § 600.5044(2); M.S.A. § 27A.5044(2) violates the constitutional guarantee of due process by " 'forcing the litigant to submit his or her claim to a tribunal which is composed in such a way that a high probability exists that such tribunal will be biased against the claimant without mandating the use of an arbitration form explicitly detailing the nature of the panel's makeup.' " Jackson v. Detroit Memorial Hospital, 110 Mich.App. 202, 204, 312 N.W.2d 212 (1981), quoting Morris v. Metriyakool, 107 Mich.App. 110, 134, 309 N.W.2d 910 (1981) (Bronson, J., dissenting in part and concurring in part). The court also held that the arbitration agreement is not a contract of adhesion and that, on the present facts, it is not unconscionable. Defendants applied for leave to appeal, and plaintiffs sought leave to cross-appeal, which we granted. 412 Mich. 885 (1981).

In the second case before us, plaintiff Delores M. Morris was admitted to defendant South Memorial Hospital on November 9, 1976. At the time of her admission, plaintiff executed an agreement similar to the one executed

2. See Merrick T. Rossein & Jennifer Hope, *Disclosure and Disqualification Standards for Neutral Arbitrators: How Far to Cast the Net and What is Sufficient to Vacate Award*, 81 St. John's L. Rev. 203 (2007).

by plaintiff Jackson to arbitrate any claims against defendant hospital and defendant Dr. S. Metriyakool arising out of her treatment for a hysterectomy. Subsequently, plaintiff brought suit against defendants alleging negligence in the surgical procedure, which caused her to develop peritonitis, and negligence in failing to promptly diagnose and treat the condition. Defendants each moved to submit plaintiff's claims to arbitration in accordance with the agreement. The trial court dismissed plaintiff's complaint with prejudice, but without prejudice to her right to file a claim for arbitration.

The Court of Appeals rejected plaintiff's argument that the composition of the arbitration panel was unconstitutionally biased. It also held that the act does not unconstitutionally or unconscionably deprive a patient of a meaningful opportunity to decide whether to relinquish access to a court and a jury trial. The Court further held that the agreement was not a contract of adhesion. Judge Bronson dissented from the holding of constitutionality. Morris v. Metriyakool, supra. We granted plaintiff's application for leave to appeal. 412 Mich. 884 (1981).

The malpractice arbitration act provides that a patient "may, if offered, execute an agreement to arbitrate a dispute, controversy, or issue arising out of health care or treatment by a health care provider," M.C.L. § 600.5041(1); M.S.A. § 27A.5041(1), or by a hospital, M.C.L. § 600.5042(1); M.S.A. § 27A.5042(1). A patient executing such an agreement with a health-care provider may revoke it within 60 days after execution, M.C.L. § 600.5041(3); M.S.A. § 27A.5041(3), or, in the case of a hospital, within 60 days after discharge, M.C.L. § 600.5042(3); M.S.A. § 27A.5042(3), options which must be stated in the agreement. All such agreements must provide in 12-point boldface type immediately above the space for the parties' signatures that agreement to arbitrate is not a prerequisite to the receipt of health care. M.C.L. §§ 600.5041(5), 600.5042(4); M.S.A. §§ 27A.5041(5), 27A.5042(4).

For those who have elected arbitration, the act requires a three-member panel composed of an attorney, who shall be chairperson, a physician, preferably from the respondent's medical specialty, and a person who is not a licensee of the health care profession, involved, a lawyer, or a representative of a hospital or an insurance company. M.C.L. § 600.5044(2); M.S.A. § 27A.5044(2). Where the claim is against a hospital only, a hospital administrator may be substituted for the physician. If the claim is against a health-care provider other than a physician, a licensee of the health-care profession involved shall be substituted.

Defendants Detroit Memorial Hospital and Dr. Bloom appeal from the holding that the presence of the medical member unconstitutionally created a biased panel. First, they argue that because the state does not compel arbitration, but only regulates it, state action is not involved.

A basic requirement of due process is a "fair trial in a fair tribunal". In re Murchison, 349 U.S. 133, 136, 75 S.Ct. 623, 625, 99 L.Ed. 942 (1955) . . . Essential to this notion is a fair and impartial decision maker. Crampton v. Department of State, 395 Mich. 347, 351, 235 N.W.2d 352 (1975). The Due

Process Clause, ... limits state action ... Private conduct abridging individual rights does not implicate the Due Process Clause unless to some significant extent the state, in any of its manifestations, has been found to have become involved in it, see Burton v. Wilmington Parking Authority, 365 U.S. 715, 81 S.Ct. 856, 6 L.Ed.2d 45 (1961), or to have compelled the conduct, Flagg Brothers, Inc. v. Brooks, 436 U.S. 149, 164, 98 S.Ct. 1729, 1737, 56 L.Ed.2d 185 (1978) ...

We find it unnecessary, however, to determine here whether the state has significantly involved itself in the challenged action because, even if we were to find so, we have concluded that the composition of the arbitration panel does not offend guarantees of due process.

In holding the act unconstitutional, the Court of Appeals in Jackson agreed with Judge Bronson's partial dissent in Morris that the arbitration panel presents too high a probability of actual bias to be constitutionally tolerable. In his partial dissent in Morris, Judge Bronson found the statute creating the panel unconstitutional because the medical member of the arbitration panel had such an interest in the outcome that there is too great a risk that he will not be impartial. Judge Bronson cited two affidavits submitted in Morris from malpractice insurance underwriters. They averred that any hospital administrator or physician would have a direct and substantial interest in the outcome of arbitrated cases because the cost and availability of medical malpractice insurance would be affected. Judge Bronson also said that the act in question is supported by health care professionals, which indicates that they believe they will fare better under this type of system. He also concluded that anti-plaintiff attitudes exist among large numbers of doctors. "Their 'function and frame of reference' may be expected to make them partisans of their professional colleagues." Morris, 107 Mich.App. 110, 309 N.W.2d 910 (Bronson, J., dissenting in part and concurring in part).

No showing of actual bias on the part of a particular arbitration panel is claimed, the parties having appealed from motions for accelerated judgment and no arbitration panel having been convened. That does not prevent a party from claiming that the risk of actual bias is too high to be constitutionally tolerable. "[O]ur system of law has always endeavored to prevent even the probability of unfairness." Murchison, supra, 349 U.S. 136, 75 S.Ct. 625. "In pursuit of this end, various situations have been identified in which experience teaches that the probability of actual bias on the part of the judge or decision maker is too high to be constitutionally tolerable." Withrow, supra, 421 U.S. 47, 95 S.Ct. 1464. Included in those situations is that of a decision maker who has a direct or substantial pecuniary interest in the outcome of the controversy. E.g., Gibson v. Berryhill, 411 U.S. 564, 93 S.Ct. 1689, 36 L.Ed.2d 488 (1973); see Crampton, supra, 395 Mich. 351–355, 235 N.W.2d 352.

Such a pecuniary interest is claimed here—the decision maker's interest in lower malpractice insurance premiums will influence his decision towards reducing the number and size of malpractice awards. In their affidavits, the underwriters averred that physicians and hospital administrators have a vested interest in the medical malpractice claims made against others; the claims made do affect the rate of insurance premiums and the availability of insurance. Premium rates for all doctors, they averred, are generally determined by the number of all claims, settlements, and judgments against physicians and hospitals in Michigan. The effect of an arbitration award on insurance rates is thus said to be direct and substantial.

This situation is aggravated, contends plaintiff Jackson, by the composition of the advisory committee, which selects the pool of candidates from which all members of the arbitration panel are chosen. The statute provides:

> An arbitration advisory committee is created within the bureau of insurance and shall be appointed by the commission and shall consist of 18 members. One-half of the advisory committee shall be broadly composed of licensed physicians and other health care providers, licensed hospital or institutional health care providers, malpractice insurance carriers and licensed legal practitioners. One-half shall be broadly composed of nongovernmental, nonlawyer, nonhealth care provider, and noninsurance carrier persons. The committee may appoint 1 or more specialized subcommittees with the approval of the commissioner. M.C.L. § 500.3054; M.S.A. § 24.13054.

The medical part of the committee, which includes the malpractice insurance carriers and health-care providers, has a direct interest in reducing the number and size of malpractice awards. There is a substantial possibility, plaintiff Jackson insists, that they will select candidates who are similarly inclined.

All that has been shown here with any degree of certainty is that there is a relationship between the number and size of malpractice awards on the one hand, and the cost and availability of malpractice insurance on the other. This may be taken for granted. It may also be assumed that, because physicians and hospital administrators are concerned with the cost and availability of malpractice insurance, they are members of a class which is affected by the decision in a case between other parties. See Tumey v. Ohio, 273 U.S. 510, 522, 47 S.Ct. 437, 441, 71 L.Ed. 749, 50 A.L.R. 1243 (1927). More than that must be shown, however, to make out a case which offends due process.

In Tumey, the village mayor was disqualified from sitting as a judge where he was compensated from fines imposed for violation of the state prohibition act. The Court concluded that the mayor "had a direct, personal, pecuniary interest in convicting the defendant who came before him for trial, in the twelve dollars of costs imposed in his behalf, which he would not have received if the defendant had been acquitted." Tumey, p. 523, 47 S.Ct. p. 441.

In Ward v. Monroeville, 409 U.S. 57, 93 S.Ct. 80, 34 L.Ed.2d 267 (1972), although the mayor was not directly compensated from fines imposed for traffic offenses, he held wide executive powers and was responsible for village finances. The Court disqualified the mayor from sitting as a judge because the mayor's executive responsibilities for village finances might have made him partisan to maintain the high level of contribution from the mayor's court. Revenue from fines, costs, and fees collected in the mayor's court annually contributed almost half of the total village revenues.

Also, in Gibson, supra, the Court affirmed the district court's finding that the Alabama Board of Optometry was biased and could not provide a fair and impartial hearing to optometrists charged with unprofessional conduct for working for a corporation. The board was composed solely of independent doctors not employed by corporations. The Court held that the board had a substantial pecuniary interest in the proceedings because what was sought was the revocation of the licenses of nearly half of all optometrists in the state which, if successful, would possibly redound to the personal benefit of members of the board.

In the present case, by contrast, it has not been demonstrated that the medical members of these panels have a direct pecuniary interest or that their decision may have any substantial effect on the availability of insurance or insurance premiums. We have been shown no grounds sufficient for us to conclude that these decision makers will not act with honesty and integrity. We look for a pecuniary interest which creates a probability of unfairness, a risk of actual bias which is too high to be constitutionally tolerable. It has not been shown here.

Plaintiff Jackson also argues that as a class physicians and hospital administrators possess a subliminal bias against patients who claim medical malpractice.

We interpret this as a claim made out under Crampton, supra. In Crampton, we held that the probability of actual bias was too high where a prosecutor and a police officer sat on an appeal board to review the revocation of Crampton's driver's license for refusal to submit to a chemical test upon arrest for driving under the influence of intoxicating liquor. Police officers and prosecutors are full-time law enforcement officials, we said, deeply and personally involved in the fight against law violators. "[T]hey are identified and aligned with the state as the adversary of the citizen who is charged with violation of the law. Their function and frame of reference may be expected to make them 'partisan to maintain' their own authority and that of their fellow officers." Crampton, supra, 395 Mich. 357, 235 N.W.2d 352.

We do not believe that the medical members of these panels are so identified and aligned with respondents in malpractice cases that they may be expected to favor the respondents. Physicians and other health professionals are trained in the medical arts and are oath-bound to treat the ill. Hospital administrators are trained in the proper functioning of hospitals. Neither physicians nor hospital administrators have professional interests that are adverse to patients or even malpractice claimants on a consistent, daily basis. Any identity of interest with respondents is not so strong as to create a subliminal bias for one side and against the other. . . .

[The court rejected plaintiffs' allegations of adhesion, unconscionability, and fraud.]

In Jackson, we reverse the finding of unconstitutionality and reinstate the order of the trial court submitting the matter to arbitration.

In Morris, we affirm.

■ CAVANAGH, JUSTICE (dissenting).

The central issue in these two cases is whether the Due Process Clauses of the United States Constitution, and the Michigan Constitution, which bar the state from depriving any person of life, liberty, or property without due process of law, are violated by the medical malpractice arbitration act of 1975, M.C.L. § 600.5040 et seq.; M.S.A. § 27A.5040 et seq. I am persuaded that they are because the act unconstitutionally deprives these plaintiffs of their due process rights to a fair hearing before an impartial decision maker.

Accepting in principle the analytical approach advanced by my brother Ryan, I am convinced that (1) plaintiffs have been deprived of the constitutionally cognizable right to a fair hearing before an impartial decision maker, (2) because of state action, (3) without due process of law.

I

While it is difficult to know whether to classify the right to a fair hearing before an impartial decision maker as a liberty or property right, there can be no doubt that it is a constitutionally cognizable right. Indeed, a basic tenet of due process is that decision makers must be unbiased and impartial. As the Supreme Court stated in In re Murchison, 349 U.S. 133 (1955):

> A fair trial in a fair tribunal is a basic requirement of due process. Fairness of course requires an absence of actual bias in the trial of cases. But our system of law has always endeavored to prevent even the probability of unfairness. To this end no man can be a judge in his own case and no man is permitted to try cases where he has an interest in the outcome. That interest cannot be defined with precision. Circumstances and relationships must be considered. This Court has said, however, that 'every procedure which would offer a possible temptation to the average man as a judge ... not to hold the balance nice, clear and true between the State and the accused, denies the latter due process of law.' Tumey v. Ohio, 273 U.S. 510 (1927). Such a stringent rule may sometimes bar trial by judges who have no actual bias and who would do their very best to weigh the scales of justice equally between contending parties. But to perform its high function in the best way 'justice must satisfy the appearance of justice.' Offutt v. United States, 348 U.S. 11, 14 (1954).

Thus, the potential for actual bias on the part of the decision maker may be too great in some circumstances for our system of justice to risk, despite the fact that such potential might never be realized.

One situation which presents too great a probability of actual bias is when the decision maker has a direct or substantial pecuniary interest in the outcome of the controversy. Crampton v. Department of State, 395 Mich. 347, 351, 235 N.W.2d 352 (1975). This is what the plaintiffs claim exists here, i.e., that a health care provider who must decide a medical malpractice case will be inclined to minimize the size of any award because the number and size of malpractice awards directly affect the availability and cost of medical malpractice insurance coverage.[6]

There is no dispute that the medical malpractice arbitration act was the legislative response to an alleged malpractice insurance crisis which supposedly resulted from the spiraling costs of insurance coverage for health-care providers and the reduction in actual availability of such coverage. Submission of malpractice controversies to arbitration was perceived as a way to reduce the costs of such disputes because arbitration is less complicated and quicker than litigation and usually results in a decision that is final. A reduction in the costs of bringing malpractice disputes to a resolution was to then result in a reduction in the costs of malpractice insurance coverage for health-care providers. However, since the relationship between malpractice controversies and malpractice insurance rates is so direct, it is clear that a reduction in the number and size of malpractice awards, in addition to a reduction in the costs of resolving such disputes, would be of substantial benefit to those paying for the cost of malpractice insurance coverage.

The cost of malpractice insurance premiums has a significant effect on a health-care provider's ability to practice in the medical profession. If the number and size of malpractice awards directly affect the cost of these premiums so that the premiums are more costly after an increase in the number and size of such awards, then health-care providers have a direct pecuniary interest in seeing that the number and size of malpractice awards remain small, and they have the opportunity to further this interest when they sit as decision makers in medical malpractice cases.

The fact that the direct effect of a particular malpractice award upon a single health-care provider's insurance rate may be minimal does not make the health-care provider's potential for bias on the basis of a pecuniary interest remote enough to be constitutionally permissible. Since the overall effect of malpractice claims and awards significantly affects insurance rates, the threat of a subliminal systematic bias exists in the medical profession. This results in a temptation for the medical-member decision maker to forget the requisite burden of proof and fail to hold the balance true and clear between the adverse parties.

The interests of health-care providers may vary according to the situation in which they find themselves. When a patient is sick and in need

6. The affidavits of experienced underwriters of medical malpractice insurance, which are part of this record, specifically aver that any malpractice award in favor of a plaintiff affects the availability and cost of malpractice insurance coverage and thus any health care provider would have a direct and substantial interest in the outcome of arbitrated malpractice cases.

of treatment, the health-care provider's interests are clearly not adverse to the patient. At this point the patient's welfare is undoubtedly of paramount importance to the members of the medical profession. However, in a malpractice case the focus of attention is no longer on how to make the patient well; rather, it is on whether the patient is entitled to compensation for any mistreatment received from a member of the medical profession and, if so, the amount of compensation due. Members of the medical profession are no longer in a position to use their skills to improve the patient's health. At this point they are solely in a position of choosing whether to award the patient any money for alleged wrongful medical treatment. I believe that in this situation the interests of the health-care providers in relation to those of the patient change and, in light of the effect a malpractice award may have on their pecuniary interests, the health care providers may be expected to align themselves with and favor a member of their own profession.

This is not to say that health-care providers as a group are not fair-minded. However, in the context of medical malpractice litigation, their function as arbitrators and their frame of reference may make them partisans of their professional colleagues, producing partisan results. This situation thus presents too high a risk of actual bias on the part of the medical-member decision makers to be constitutionally permissible.

In light of this potential for bias on the part of health-care providers deciding malpractice cases, I conclude that the medical malpractice arbitration act's requirement of a health-care provider in the composition of the arbitration panel violates the plaintiffs' constitutional right to a fair hearing before an impartial decision maker . . .

* * *

Questions

1. The majority says that there was no showing of actual bias in this case. What evidence does it use to reach this conclusion? Do you agree? Is the court insisting that there be actual bias, or does it suggest that potential bias would be grounds to set aside an arbitral award in some circumstances? How does the majority distinguish *Gibson v. Berryhill,* the optometrist case? What does the dissent mean by "subliminal systematic bias"? Should "subliminal systematic bias" be a ground to invalidate an arbitration award? See Martin H. Malin & Monica Biernat, *Do Cognitive Biases Infect Adjudication? A Study of Labor Arbitrators*, 11 U. Pa. J. Bus. & Emp. L. 175 (2008).

2. How central is it to the court's reasoning that the parties had a sixty-day period in which to rescind their arbitration agreement? This factor suggests that issues of consent to arbitrate are bound up with questions of due process—the more confident the court is that there is genuine consent to arbitration, the less it needs to police the process for due process shortcomings. Should protections for consent to arbitration obviate all scrutiny of due process concerns?

3. Suppose a state law provided that in all arbitrations of malpractice claims, the arbitration agreement must appear in bold print on the first page of a contract, must be in type size no smaller than 14 point, and must contain an explanation of the legal consequences of arbitration. Would such a law be enforceable after *Southland?* Would the result be different if the state law allocated the burden of proof for malpractice arbitrations, specified the composition of the arbitration panel, or mandated a 60–day rescission period? *See Doctor's Associates v. Casarotto*, supra Chapter 2.6. Should the *Casarotto* holding apply to the Michigan statutory provision requiring arbitration agreements to state, in 12–point boldface type, that the agreement to arbitrate is not a prerequisite to the receipt of health care?

* * *

9. ARBITRATOR IMMUNITY AND OBLIGATIONS TO TESTIFY

Corey v. New York Stock Exchange

691 F.2d 1205 (6th Cir. 1982).

■ KENNEDY, CIRCUIT JUDGE.

Corey appeals from the District Court's dismissal of his lawsuit against the New York Stock Exchange (NYSE) in which he claimed that the procedures followed in an arbitration proceeding sponsored by the NYSE and to which he was a party were wrongful and caused him injury. Corey sought to hold the NYSE liable for the conduct of the arbitrators and the NYSE's arbitration director, Cavell. We agree with the District Court that Corey's claims against the NYSE for the acts of the arbitrators are barred by arbitral immunity and those based on Cavell's acts constitute no more than an impermissible collateral attack on the arbitrators' award.

In 1965, Corey began to invest in the stock market under the guidance of a long-time friend, Wright, who was an account executive with Merrill Lynch, Pierce, Fenner & Smith (Merrill Lynch). Wright suffered a paralyzing stroke in 1968, but returned to work thereafter and reestablished his business relationship with Corey. In 1972 and 1973, Corey invested heavily in the stock market, allegedly because of Wright's advice. Medical concerns prompted Wright's retirement in 1973 and Corey's account was transferred to another Merrill Lynch employee. The stock in Corey's portfolio depreciated in value and he was forced to liquidate it to meet the margin requirements of his account. Corey claims to have lost approximately $175,000 as a result of the liquidation.

Corey elected to initiate arbitration proceedings against Merrill Lynch in April 1976. Article VIII of the Constitution of the NYSE, gives nonmembers the option of submitting a claim against a member brokerage corporation for arbitration, instead of pursuing remedies at law. In his statement of claim Corey alleged that his loss resulted directly from Wright's impaired judgment as a result of his stroke and from the negligence of Merrill Lynch in permitting Wright to return to work before he was capable of intelligently advising customers. The rules of the NYSE, which sponsored the arbitration, governed the selection of the five arbitrators responsible for Corey's case as well as the procedural rules to be followed. Cavell, the Assistant Arbitration Director for the NYSE, administered arbitrations between members and non-members of the NYSE. He was responsible for overseeing the preliminary arrangements for arbitrations, including the obtaining of written submissions, arranging for the appointment of arbitration panels, scheduling hearing dates, acting as a moderator on behalf of the arbitration panel and furnishing the parties with written notification of arbitration decisions. Upon selection of the arbitration panel, two hearings were held in Detroit at which Corey appeared without counsel. In March 1977, the arbitrators dismissed Corey's claim against Merrill Lynch and assessed $700 in costs against him. Cavell mailed a copy of this decision to Corey in early April 1977. Corey was not informed of his right to appeal and did not avail himself of the appeal provisions of the federal Arbitration Act. 9 U.S.C. §§ 1 et seq.

In early 1978, Corey filed suit in Ingham County Circuit Court against Merrill Lynch claiming Merrill Lynch and the NYSE conspired to deprive him of a fair hearing before the arbitrators. Neither the NYSE, Cavell nor the individual arbitrators were named as defendants. Corey challenged the composition of the arbitration panel as violative of the NYSE rules and asserted procedural irregularities that prevented him from submitting evidence, caused hearings to be postponed over his objection and allowed the arbitrators to dominate the proceedings with the purpose of defeating his claims. A motion for accelerated judgment was granted in favor of Merrill Lynch on the ground that the arbitrators' award was final and binding and that the court lacked jurisdiction over the parties and the subject matter of the suit. Corey did not appeal this decision.

In August 1978, Corey filed suit against the NYSE in Ingham County Circuit Court making allegations virtually identical to those in his suit against Merrill Lynch. He did not name Cavell or the individual arbitrators as defendants, although complaining of their acts, presumedly pursuing the NYSE on some theory of vicarious liability. Specifically, Corey alleged that the acts of Cavell during the arbitration hearings sponsored by the NYSE deprived him of a fair hearing because Cavell selected members of the arbitration panel in violation of the NYSE rules and adjourned and rescheduled hearings over Corey's objection. Although the wrongdoing is alleged to be that of Cavell, other allegations address matters unique to the arbitrators, such as their alleged refusal to allow Corey to present evidence and their prejudgment as to the merit of Corey's claims. Corey sought $1,000,000 in punitive damages for mental anguish and long-standing physical problems brought about as a result of these acts.

Following the removal of this action to federal district court, the NYSE successfully moved for summary judgment. Corey v. New York Stock Exchange, 493 F.Supp. 51 (W.D.Mich. 1980). Corey appeals this determination.

I. ARBITRAL IMMUNITY

To the extent that Corey's complaint may be construed to allege wrongdoing by the arbitrators for which the NYSE is liable, we agree with the District Court that the NYSE, acting through its arbitrators, is immune from civil liability for the acts of the arbitrators arising out of contractually agreed upon arbitration proceedings. Our decision to extend immunity to arbitrators and the boards which sponsor arbitration finds support in the case law, the policies behind the doctrines of judicial and quasi-judicial immunity and policies unique to contractually agreed upon arbitration proceedings.

The Supreme Court has long recognized that there are certain persons whose special functions require a full exemption from liability for acts committed within the scope of their duties.[4] The rationale behind the Supreme Court decisions is that the independence necessary for principled and fearless decision-making can best be preserved by protecting these persons from bias or intimidation caused by the fear of a lawsuit arising out of the exercise of official functions within their jurisdiction . . . In Butz the Court stated that immunity is not extended to individuals because of their particular location in government but because of the special nature of their responsibilities. Butz, supra, 438 U.S. at 511, 98 S.Ct. at 2913. The Court said that the relevant consideration in evaluating whether immunity should attach to the acts of persons in certain roles and with certain responsibilities was the "functional comparability" of their judgments to those of a judge. Id. 512, 98 S.Ct. at 2913; Imbler, supra, 424 U.S. at 423 n. 20, 96 S.Ct. at 991 n. 20. In each instance, safeguards were present to protect other participants and the integrity of the decision-making process. Paramount among these safeguards is the right of judicial review. Butz, supra, 438 U.S. at 512–14, 98 S.Ct. at 2913–14; Pierson v. Ray, 386 U.S. 547, 554, 87 S.Ct. 1213, 1217, 18 L.Ed.2d 288 (1967).

We believe that determinations made by the panel of arbitrators in the case on appeal are functionally comparable to those of a judge or an agency

4. The principle behind the doctrine of judicial immunity first adopted by the Supreme Court in Bradley v. Fisher, 80 U.S. 335, 20 L.Ed. 646 (1871), has been extended to state judges, Pierson v. Ray, 386 U.S. 547, 87 S.Ct. 1213, 18 L.Ed.2d 288 (1967) (judicial immunity), to federal prosecutors, Yaselli v. Goff, 275 U.S. 503, 48 S.Ct. 155, 72 L.Ed. 395 (1927), aff'g, 12 F.2d 396 (2d Cir. 1926) (quasi-judicial immunity), and state prosecutors, Imbler v. Pachtman, 424 U.S. 409, 96 S.Ct. 984, 47 L.Ed.2d 128 (1976) (quasi-judicial immunity). The principle in Bradley has also been extended to federal agency examiners, administrative law judges and agency officials performing functions analogous to prosecutors, Butz v. Economou, 438 U.S. 478, 98 S.Ct. 2894, 57 L.Ed.2d 895 (1978) (quasi-judicial immunity). To ensure unintimidated independence of action, legislators also enjoy complete immunity, Tenney v. Brandhove, 341 U.S. 367, 71 S.Ct. 783, 95 L.Ed. 1019 (1951).

hearing examiner even though this was not a statutory arbitration or one where the arbitrators were court appointed. In Burchell v. Marsh, 58 U.S. 344, 15 L.Ed. 96 (1854), the Supreme Court stated that "[a]rbitrators are judges chosen by the parties to decide the matters submitted to them...." Id. 58 U.S. at 349. The submission of the parties replaces a statute or court order as the source of the arbitrators' power with regard to subject matter and procedural rules. The arbitrators in this case were appointed by private agreement of the parties and empowered by the parties to resolve disputes between them. By agreement, the parties invoked the arbitrators' independent judgment and discretion ... By private agreement the parties have substituted the arbitrators for a judge as the decision-maker in their case. Jurisdiction by consent is recognized by reviewing and enforcing courts. See 9 U.S.C. §§ 2, 9, 10, 11 ...

Several safeguards exist to protect the participants in the decision-making process and the integrity of the arbitration proceedings. First, arbitration proceedings resemble judicial proceedings in several respects. Arbitration is adversarial. Both parties had a right to be represented by an attorney—a right Corey did not exercise. Discovery was available and hearings were held at which the arbitrators received evidence and entertained arguments. Both parties had the opportunity to present witnesses and other evidence and to cross-examine or impeach those of their adversary. After a period of deliberation, the arbitrators issued a written opinion deciding the claim. The second safeguard is the automatic right of judicial review provided by the Federal Arbitration Act, 9 U.S.C. §§ 1 et seq., applicable because of the commerce clause nexus present in transactions involving the purchase and sale of securities ... Judicial review by a district court in the jurisdiction where the award by an arbitrator is made is provided for in sections 9, 10 and 11 of the Arbitration Act. Although the scope of review differs slightly, the same protection is present in judicial review of arbitrators' decisions under the Arbitration Act as is present in the review of judicial or administrative decisions. The circumstances under which an award may be vacated include procurement of an award by fraud, corruption, undue means, partiality or corruption in the arbitrators, misconduct on the part of the arbitrators in refusing to hear pertinent evidence, arbitrators acting in excess of their powers, arbitrators committing errors of law, etc. 9 U.S.C. §§ 9, 10, 11. The district court has the power to modify or correct an award or direct a rehearing by the arbitrators. Id. §§ 9, 10. The final safeguard is the voluntary use of arbitration as a means of dispute resolution. A person such as Corey could elect to submit his claim to arbitration or pursue his remedy at law. Presumably, individuals will not avail themselves of arbitration by contractual agreement if they lack confidence in the impartiality and reliability of the arbitration process. In light of these safeguards, the risk of a wrongful act by the arbitrators is outweighed by the need for preserving the independence of their decision-making. See Butz, supra, 514, 98 S.Ct. at 2914.

A number of policy arguments support our decision. From Butz it is clear that immunity does not depend upon the source of the decision-making power but rather upon the nature of that power. Accordingly, the limits of immunity should be fixed in part by federal policy. The functional comparability of the arbitrators' decision-making process and judgments to those of judges and agency hearing examiners generates the same need for independent judgment, free from the threat of lawsuits. Immunity furthers this need. As with judicial and quasi-judicial immunity, arbitral immunity is essential to protect the decision-maker from undue influence and protect the decision-making process from reprisals by dissatisfied litigants. Federal policy, as manifested in the Arbitration Act and case law, favors final adjudication of differences by a means selected by the parties . . . Because federal policy encourages arbitration and arbitrators are essential actors in furtherance of that policy, it is appropriate that immunity be extended to arbitrators for acts within the scope of their duties and within their jurisdiction. Corbin, supra, 396–97; Hill, supra, 326. The extension of immunity to arbitrators where arbitration is pursuant to a private agreement between the parties is especially compelling because arbitration is the means selected by the parties themselves for disposing of controversies between them. By immunizing arbitrators and their decisions from collateral attacks, arbitration as the contractual choice of the parties is respected yet the arbitrators are protected. Arbitrators have no interest in the outcome of the dispute and should not be compelled to become parties to that dispute. Tamari, supra, 781. "[I]ndividuals cannot be expected to volunteer to arbitrate disputes if they can be caught up in the struggle between the litigants and saddled with the burdens of defending a lawsuit." Tamari, supra, 781. Accord, Raitport, supra, 527. An aggrieved party alleging a due process violation in the conduct of the proceedings, fraud, misconduct, a violation of public policy, lack of jurisdiction, etc., by arbitrators should pursue remedies against the "real" adversary through the appeal process. To allow a collateral attack against arbitrators and their judgments would also emasculate the appeal provisions of the federal Arbitration Act. 9 U.S.C. §§ 9, 10. For these reasons we believe that arbitral immunity is essential to the maintenance of arbitration by contractual agreement as a viable alternative to the judicial process for the settlement of controversies and must be applied in this case.

Extension of arbitral immunity to encompass boards which sponsor arbitration is a natural and necessary product of the policies underlying arbitral immunity; otherwise the immunity extended to arbitrators is illusionary. It would be of little value to the whole arbitral procedure to merely shift the liability to the sponsoring association.

II. ARBITRATION ACT AS EXCLUSIVE REMEDY

Corey's complaint may also be construed as alleging wrongdoing by Cavell for which the NYSE is liable, such as improper selection of the panel of five arbitrators so that they were biased against Corey and adjournments of Corey's hearing dates which caused him prejudice. It is implicit in Corey's complaint that these acts compromised the arbitration award thereby causing him mental anguish and physical problems. We agree with the District Court that the federal Arbitration Act provides the exclusive remedy for challenging acts that taint an arbitration award and that

Corey's attempt to sue the NYSE for the acts of Cavell is no more, in substance, than an impermissible collateral attack on the award itself.[1]

Sections 10, 11 and 12 of the Arbitration Act provide a mechanism whereby parties to an arbitration proceeding may obtain judicial review in the federal district court in the district in which the arbitration award is made. The scope of review is limited by these provisions. Section 10 provides that an award may be vacated if it was procured by fraud, corruption or undue means, where there has been evident partiality or corruption in the arbitrators, where there has been misconduct or misbehavior by which the rights of any party may have been prejudiced and where the arbitrators exceeded their powers. A rehearing by the arbitrators may be ordered in certain circumstances. Section 11 allows a district court to modify or correct an order for any miscalculation of figures or mistake in description, where the arbitrators have awarded upon a matter not submitted to them and where the award is imperfect in a matter of form not affecting the merits of the controversy. An order so compromised may be modified or corrected to effect the intent of the award and promote justice between the parties. Section 12 of the Arbitration Act requires that notice of a motion to vacate, modify or correct an award must be served on the adverse party or his attorney within three months after the award is filed or delivered. Failure to comply with this statutory precondition of timely service of notice forfeits the right to judicial review of the award. Piccolo v. Dain, Kalman & Quail, Inc., 641 F.2d 598, 600 (8th Cir. 1981). * * * Allegations of wrongdoing raised by Corey in his complaint are squarely within the scope of section 10 of the Arbitration Act. Evident partiality on the part of the arbitrators toward Merrill Lynch as a result of the manner in which they were selected is covered by section 10(b). Adjournments allegedly causing prejudice are reviewable under section 10(c). The issues raised by Corey's complaint could have been resolved by timely pursuit of a remedy under this section.

The federal Arbitration Act provides the exclusive remedy for challenging an award on the grounds raised by Corey. Section 2 of the Arbitration Act states that a contractual provision wherein the parties agree to submit a dispute to arbitration is valid, irrevocable and enforceable, except on such grounds in law or equity as exist for the revocation of the contract to arbitrate. Once an arbitrator has rendered a decision the award is binding on the parties unless they challenge the underlying contract to arbitrate pursuant to section 2 or avail themselves of the review provisions of sections 10 and 11. Corey has not alleged that there was any defect in the underlying agreement to arbitrate the dispute with Merrill Lynch, which he himself initiated, which would provide a basis for revoking that agreement. Nor has he availed himself of the review provisions of sections 10 and 11. Barring these two situations, the Arbitration Act provides no other avenue by which an arbitration award may be challenged. Two circuit courts have held that allegations within the purview of section 10 are reviewable only

1. This same argument may be made with respect to the allegations against arbitrators which we have found to be protected by arbitral immunity.

under the authority of the federal Arbitration Act. Piccolo, supra, 600 (alleged no fair and impartial hearing); Tamari v. Bache & Co., 565 F.2d 1194, 1202 (7th Cir. 1977), cert. denied, 435 U.S. 905, 98 S.Ct. 1450, 55 L.Ed.2d 495 (1978) (arbitrators biased).

To confine challenges to an award within the scope of section 10 and 11 exclusively to the review provisions of the Arbitration Act is also consistent with section 12 of that Act. The three month notice requirement in section 12 for an appeal of the award on section 10 or 11 grounds is meaningless if a party to the arbitration proceedings may bring an independent direct action asserting such claims outside of the statutory time period provided for in section 12.

Corey's claims constitute a collateral attack against the award even though Corey is presently suing a different defendant than his original adversary in the arbitration proceeding and is requesting damages for the acts of wrongdoing rather than the vacation, modification or correction of the arbitration award. Corey was not harmed by the selection of the arbitrators and the adjournments of the hearings in and of themselves; he did not and cannot raise a constitutional due process claim. Rather, he was harmed by the impact these acts had on the award. Corey's complaint has no purpose other than to challenge the very wrongs affecting the award for which review is provided under section 10 of the Arbitration Act. The mere presence of the NYSE, Cavell or the arbitrators or the prayer for damages does not change the substance of his claim. Very simply, Corey did not avail himself of the review provisions of section 10 of the Arbitration Act and may not transform what would ordinarily constitute an impermissible collateral attack into a proper independent direct action by changing defendants and altering the relief sought.

Accordingly, the judgment of the District Court is affirmed.

* * *

Morgan Phillips, Inc. v. JAMS/Endispute, L.L.C.

44 Cal.Rptr.3d 782 (Cal.App. 2 Dist. 2006).

■ WILLHITE, J.

If an arbitrator withdraws from an arbitration proceeding for no stated ethical reason following evidence and argument, and offers to continue mediation efforts but refuses to render an arbitration award, does the doctrine of arbitral immunity protect the arbitrator from suit? We hold that because such conduct defeats rather than serves the adjudicatory purpose of arbitration, arbitral immunity does not apply.

BACKGROUND

Plaintiff Morgan Phillips, Inc. appeals from the judgment dismissing its claims against defendants John B. Bates, JAMS/Endispute, L.L.C., and JAMS, Inc. The trial court entered the judgment after sustaining defendants' demurrer to Morgan Phillips' first amended complaint without leave to amend, on the ground that Morgan Phillips' claims are barred by the doctrine of arbitral immunity. We reverse.

[Because the trial court dismissed this case on the pleadings, we take the facts stated in the complaint as true.]

Morgan Phillips, a retailer of specialty bedding products, contracted with two suppliers for mattresses and box springs made according to Morgan Phillips' specifications. In October 1999, after discovering that the suppliers were not manufacturing the products as specified, Morgan Phillips sued the suppliers. The parties retained JAMS and Bates to mediate the dispute. In September 2000, Bates assisted the parties in reaching a settlement. The "stipulation for settlement" provided that "[d]isputes regarding this matter will be submitted to [Bates] for binding resolution."

In 2002, Morgan Phillips again became dissatisfied with the suppliers' products, and invoked the dispute resolution clause of the stipulation for settlement. JAMS and Bates entered a contract with Morgan Phillips that was partly written, oral, and implied by law. Under the contract, JAMS and Bates agreed to conduct a "binding arbitration" pursuant to the dispute resolution term of the settlement agreement.

On or about September 11, 2002, Bates held "a four-hour hearing" at which Morgan Phillips produced an "actual demonstration of settlement merchandise cut open to reveal that ... the bedding did not conform" to the requirements of the settlement agreement. After this evidence was presented, Bates continued the hearing to October 25, 2002, and "specifically informed the parties at that time that if the parties were unable to settle the dispute before the next scheduled arbitration session Bates would exercise his authority as arbitrator to render a binding arbitration decision. In addition, Bates specifically instructed counsel for [the suppliers] that at the next hearing counsel should be prepared to rebut the evidence proffered by Morgan Phillips and further, requested that Morgan Phillips prepare an updated damage study from its economic expert." Bates was "specifically and directly informed" that Morgan Phillips was in severe financial distress as a result of the breach, and that "there was a substantial risk that Morgan Phillips would be unable to continue in business if the dispute was not decided promptly."

When the arbitration reconvened on October 25, 2002, Morgan Phillips offered "evidence of laboratory testing" showing that the suppliers' merchandise breached the settlement agreement, and also submitted an updated damage study. Bates then gave the suppliers the opportunity to present evidence in their defense. When the suppliers finished, "all evidence had now been submitted to Bates for determination of the dispute. Bates did not request that either side present any additional evidence or to prepare any written statement of the evidence or legal argument. The arbitration hearing was now concluded and the case was now ready for Mr. Bates' arbitration decision."

Bates then "separated the parties into different rooms and [met] with each side separately in an apparent effort to settle the case without rendering an arbitration award. Over the course of next few hours, and until the lunchtime break, Bates shuttled back and forth between the parties to discuss various alternative resolutions. However, as the lunchtime break was ending, Bates suddenly announced, with no lawful justification, that he decided to withdraw as the arbitrator. Bates thereafter failed and refused to issue a binding arbitration award." . . .

JAMS advertises to the general public that it employs arbitrators who make decisions in a timely and cost-effective manner. JAMS fails to disclose, however, that its arbitrators "secretly retain the right" to abandon the arbitration "for no lawful reason" without rendering an award.

Based on these allegations, Morgan Phillips alleged two causes of action against both JAMS and Bates: the sixth, for breach contract, and the seventh, for negligent breach of the duty to provide binding arbitration services. Morgan Phillips alleged one cause of action against JAMS alone: the eighth, a representative action for unfair competition and false advertising, in violation of Business and Professions Code sections 17200 and 17500.

JAMS and Bates demurred to the first amended complaint on several grounds, including that Morgan Phillips' claims were barred by the doctrine of arbitral immunity. Adopting that reasoning, the trial court sustained the demurrer to the sixth through eighth causes of action without leave to amend.

DISCUSSION

. . . As we have noted, Morgan Phillips alleged two causes of action against both JAMS and Bates: the sixth, for breach contract, and the seventh, for negligent breach of the duty to provide binding arbitration services. The factual core of these claims is the allegation that Bates improperly withdrew from the arbitration proceeding, without cause, following evidence and argument in order to coerce a settlement, and refused to render an arbitration award. Morgan Phillips alleged one cause of action against JAMS alone: the eighth, for unfair competition and false advertising, in violation of Business and Professions Code sections 17200 and 17500. The basis of this claim is JAMS' allegedly deceptive public representations that its affiliated arbitrators will render binding arbitration decisions.

Morgan Phillips contends that arbitral immunity does not bar these claims. We agree.

[The] California common law [of] arbitral immunity . . . protects arbitrators from civil liability for conduct in their quasi-judicial capacity, including the exhibition of bias or prejudice in the rendering of their decisions. (*Stasz* [v. *Schwab* (2004) 121 Cal.App.4th 420, 434, 17 Cal. Rptr.3d 116)]. The purpose of arbitral immunity is to encourage fair and independent decision-making by immunizing arbitrators from lawsuits arising from conduct in their decision-making role. (*Thiele v. RML Realty Partners* (1993) 14 Cal.App.4th 1526, 1531, 18 Cal.Rptr.2d 416); [Additional citations omitted.] Thus, generally speaking, arbitral immunity "shields all functions which are 'integrally related to the arbitral process.' [Citations.]" (*Thiele, supra,* 14 Cal.App.4th at p. 1530, 18 Cal.Rptr.2d 416.)

California common law has recognized a narrow exception to arbitral immunity: the immunity does not apply to the arbitrator's breach of contract by failing to make any decision at all. (*Baar v. Tigerman* (1983) 140 Cal.App.3d 979, 983–985, 211 Cal.Rptr. 426 (*Baar*); see Knight et al., California Practice Guide: Alternative Dispute Resolution (The Rutter Group 2005), ¶ 5:41, p. 5–28.) The exception is supported by a common sense rationale. The failure to render an arbitration award is not integral to the arbitration process; it is, rather, a breakdown of that process. Moreover, for nonfeasance by a judge, litigants can petition for an extraordinary writ to compel action. For nonfeasance by an arbitrator who has conducted the arbitration but fails to render an award, the parties' only the remedy is a civil suit for specific performance or damages. As stated by one court, by failing to make a timely decision the arbitrator "loses his claim to immunity because he loses his resemblance to a judge. He has simply defaulted on a contractual duty to both parties." (*E.C. Ernst, Inc. v. Manhattan Const. Co. of Texas* (5th Cir. 1977) 551 F.2d 1026, 1033, mod. 559 F.2d 268.)

The scope of the exception is best explained by the decision in *Baar, supra,* which created it. In *Baar,* the plaintiffs had engaged the American Arbitration Association (AAA) and the arbitrator to conduct an arbitration proceeding. Over a four-year period, the arbitrator held 43 days of hearings and 10 days of argument. After expiration of an extended deadline, and seven months after the matter had been submitted for decision, the arbitrator still had not rendered an award. The plaintiffs filed objections to the arbitrator making an award, thereby divesting the arbitrator of jurisdiction. They then sued the arbitrator and the AAA for breach of contract, negligence, and other claims. (*Baar, supra,* 140 Cal.App.3d at pp. 981–982, 211 Cal.Rptr. 426.) On these facts, the Court of Appeal held that the arbitrator was not entitled to arbitral immunity. The court observed that "[c]ases in which courts have clothed arbitrators with immunity have involved disgruntled litigants who sought to hold an arbitrator liable for *alleged misconduct in arriving at a decision.* [Citations.] By contrast, the present case involves [the arbitrator's] *failure to make an award* without any allegation of misconduct similar to that charged in the above cases." (*Id.* at p. 983, 211 Cal.Rptr. 426, italics in original.) Further, the court noted that arbitration is primarily governed by contract, and the contract at issue set a deadline for the award: "A judge has discretion in terms of when a decision is made, but an arbitrator loses jurisdiction if a timely award is not forthcoming. [Citations.] While we must protect an arbitrator acting in a *quasi-judicial capacity,* we must also uphold the contractual obligations of an arbitrator to the parties involved." (*Id.* at p. 985, 211 Cal.Rptr. 426, italics in original.)

In the instant case, taking the relevant allegations as a whole, Morgan Phillips alleges that after completion of the evidence and argument at the arbitration proceeding, Bates conducted failed settlement talks. He then he sought to coerce an unfavorable settlement from Morgan Phillips, and avoid having to issue an award, by withdrawing as arbitrator without justification. He offered to continue mediation efforts, but he refused to issue an award. There is no indication that Bates gave any reason for his withdrawal.

Although we are mindful of the need to protect arbitrators from vexatious litigation arising from conduct in their quasi-judicial function, Morgan Phillips' allegations portray conduct foreign to that function—conduct that is the antithesis of the adjudicatory purpose of arbitration. Because arbitral immunity is designed to foster " 'principled and fearless decision-making' " (*Thiele, supra,* 14 Cal.App.4th at p. 1531, 18 Cal.Rptr.2d 416, quoting *Corey v. New York Stock Exchange* (6th Cir. 1982) 691 F.2d 1205, 1209), it cannot be used to immunize the unprincipled abandonment of the arbitration and refusal to make a decision. Accepting Morgan Phillips' allegations as true, Bates' conduct is not "sufficiently associated with the adjudicative phase of the arbitration to justify immunity." (*Thiele, supra,* 14 Cal.App.4th at p. 1530, 18 Cal.Rptr.2d 416; see *Baar, supra,* 140 Cal.App.3d at p. 985, 211 Cal.Rptr. 426.)

Relying on *Stasz, supra,* JAMS and Bates argue that arbitral immunity protects all actions taken in an arbitrator's quasi-judicial capacity, except "complete nonperformance." In *dicta, Stasz* referred to one commentator's limited interpretation of *Baar, supra,* as providing an exception to arbitral immunity only when the arbitrator " 'completely fails to do his job,' " and to another's suggestion that under *Baar* arbitrators should be immune for " '[a]nything short of complete nonperformance.' " (*Stasz, supra,* 121 Cal. App.4th at p. 437, 17 Cal.Rptr.3d 116.) Precisely what these commentators mean by "complete nonperformance" is not clear. If they mean that conducting some or all of the arbitration proceeding creates immunity for the unjustified failure to render an award, we disagree. In the instant case, Morgan Phillips alleges that Bates entered a contract to conduct a binding arbitration. Bates' alleged unjustified abandonment of the arbitration and refusal to render an award while offering to continue mediation (if true) is effectively a "complete nonperformance" of the ultimate object of the arbitration he contracted to conduct.

JAMS and Bates argue that an arbitrator's withdrawal from an arbitration proceeding before rendering an award is a quasi-judicial act entitled to immunity. We emphasize that we are at the pleading stage of the litigation, before a full evidentiary picture has been developed. Certainly, a decision to withdraw because of substantial doubt of the ability to be fair and impartial, or because of a conflict of interest, is entitled to immunity. . . . An arbitrator's decision to withdraw based on ethical standards is integral to the arbitral function; the act itself, as well as the consequent failure to render an arbitration award, is covered by arbitral immunity. Further, we do not mean to suggest that parties to an arbitration proceeding are entitled to litigate the validity of an arbitrator's stated ethical grounds for recusal in support of a later civil suit against the arbitrator or the sponsoring organization for breach of the duty to conduct a binding arbitration.

But in the instant case, we must accept as true the allegations of Morgan Phillips' first amended complaint. The allegations of the complaint do not reveal whether Bates gave any reason for his withdrawal. Morgan Phillips alleges that Bates withdrew without justification in order to coerce a settlement, while at the same time offering to continue mediation efforts and refusing to render an award. If these facts are true, and in the absence of any other showing, Bates' withdrawal (and the resultant refusal to render an award) is not immunized as a decision necessitated by ethical strictures. Rather, it is conduct inconsistent with those strictures and with his quasi judicial role as an arbitrator. It amounts to a breach of his contractual duty to conduct a binding arbitration....

Assuming the allegations of the first amended complaint to be true, we conclude that the trial court erred in ruling that the doctrine of arbitral immunity bars Morgan Phillips' claims against JAMS and Bates.

DISPOSITION

The judgment is reversed. Morgan Phillips shall recover its costs on appeal.

* * *

Questions

1. To what extent are arbitrators similar to federal prosecutors, hearing agency examiners, administrative law judges, and legislators, as the *Corey* court suggests? Do these similarities suggest that arbitrators should be granted the same level of immunity that these other officials enjoy? Are there significant differences which might point toward a different result on the issue of immunity?

2. The *Corey* court noted that there were safeguards to protect participants in arbitration even in the face of arbitrator immunity. The safeguards include assurances of certain non-waivable due process protections, a right of judicial review, the ability to vacate an award on the basis of fraud or partiality, and the fact that arbitration is voluntary in the first place. How effective are these safeguards under current interpretations of the FAA?

3. Can *Morgan Phillips* be distinguished from *Corey?* The court attempts to distinguish arbitral action that is quasi-judicial from arbitral action that is contractual in nature, but isn't the arbitrator's entire responsibility defined by the contract between the parties? Is an arbitrator's failure to abide by a contractual timetable any different, for purposes of immunity, than an arbitrator's failure to hold a fair hearing or render a fair award?

4. Is broad arbitral immunity necessary for arbitration to function effectively? Other countries have taken a wide variety of approaches to arbitral liability:

> In some countries, such as Austria, the civil code expressly provides for arbitrators' liability in certain circumstances such as the failure to meet the obligations of their appointments. In others, courts have implied limited liability through interpretation of more general provisions of their codes. German law and some Islamic countries treat arbitrator liability as a matter of contract law. Yet others treat arbitrators as having duties arising out of tort law principles. A few countries limit the arbitrator's liability to certain acts of misconduct such as wrongful withdrawal or failure to render a timely award.

Peter B. Rutledge, *Toward a Contractual Approach for Arbitral Immunity*, 39 Ga. L. Rev. 151 (2004); see also Susan D. Franck, *The Liability of International Arbitrators: A Comparative Analysis and Proposal for Qualified Immunity*, 20 N.Y.L. Sch. J. Int'l & Comp. L. 1, 7–8 (2000).

5. Maureen Wesson writes: "Individuals of nearly every profession are held accountable for complying with their contractual obligations and for exercising a reasonable degree of competency. Does it continue to make sense to exempt from the law the entire arbitration industry?" Maureen A. Weston, *Reexamining Arbitral Immunity in an Age of Mandatory and Professional Arbitration*, 88 Minn. L. Rev. 449, 459 (2004); see also Rutledge, supra.

6. How does the *Corey* court justify extending arbitral immunity to arbitral service providers? Is this a valid reason to expand immunity? Are there countervailing factors which should be considered? Should it matter whether the arbitral service provider is an industry board (NYSE), a nonprofit (AAA), or a for-profit (e.g., EDSI, discussed in Chapter 2.8.D.)?

In Pfannenstiel v. Merrill Lynch Pierce Fenner & Smith, 477 F.3d 1155 (10th Cir. 2007), an investor sued an arbitration service provider, the National Association of Securities Dealers (NASD), for having lost the exhibits and audiotapes of an arbitration hearing. The investor argued that arbitral immunity does not apply to misconduct that is separate from the provider's judicial function. The court agreed with the investor that arbitral immunity "does not protect arbitrators or their employing organizations from all claims asserted against them," stating that the key question is whether the claim at issue arises out of a "decisional act." The court concluded, however, that the investor's claim was a veiled attack on the NASD panel's decision, and for that reason gave the NASD immunity.

Similarly, in Malik v. Ruttenberg, 942 A.2d 136 (N.J. App. Div. 2008), a home remodeler arbitrated a dispute with a homeowner. During a recess in the arbitration hearing, a fight apparently broke out between the remodeler and the homeowner's attorney. The remodeler sued the arbitrator and the American Arbitration Association (AAA), arguing the arbitrator and the AAA knew of this attorney's dangerous tendencies but failed to exercise reasonable care to control them. The court agreed with the homeowner that arbitral immunity applies only to "judicial acts" performed within the arbitrator's subject matter jurisdiction, but held that controlling the hearing was a "judicial act" and was therefore entitled to immunity.

* * *

Legion Insurance Company v. Insurance General Agency, Inc.

822 F.2d 541 (5th Cir. 1987).

■ Before POLITZ, WILLIAMS, and JONES, CIRCUIT JUDGES.

■ EDITH H. JONES, CIRCUIT JUDGE:

Insurance General Agency, Inc. ("IGAI") appeals the district court's entry of judgment pursuant to 9 U.S.C. § 9 confirming an adverse arbitration award. Confronted with a motion to confirm the arbitration award by Legion and with a cross-motion to vacate or correct under 9 U.S.C. §§ 10, 11 by IGAI, the district court concluded that Legion had failed to meet its burden of proof in challenging the award. We AFFIRM.

Legion first asserts that the district court's entry of judgment on the basis of the parties' cross-motions and supporting documents, without a hearing, was inappropriate and prejudicial because it denied them fair notice and an opportunity to be heard. This argument is meritless. Title 9 U.S.C. § 6 provides that "[a]ny application to the court hereunder shall be made and heard in the manner provided by law for the making and hearing of motions...." Under this directive both parties specifically requested the court to enter an order pursuant to their respective motions. Neither party requested a hearing. Appellant cannot complain on appeal that the district court erred in granting relief specifically requested by the parties under the statutory scheme for confirming or vacating arbitration awards.

Appellant also claims that the district court's failure to take evidence, other than that submitted in the parties' motion papers, severely prejudiced its ability to present the merits of its claim. Specifically, appellant claims that the district court's decision, based solely on the motion papers and supporting exhibits, was in direct violation of the Federal Rules of Civil Procedure.[1] See Fed.R.Civ.P. 81(a)(3) (Federal Rules applicable to proceedings under Title 9 U.S.C.). We are equally unpersuaded.

Appellant cited the following bases under 9 U.S.C. §§ 10, 11 for vacating or modifying the arbitration tribunal's award: (1) The award was clearly erroneous because it exceeded the damages requested and was unsupported by the evidence; (2) The arbitrators exceeded their authority in awarding a sum which was greater than Legion's proven claim; (3) No evidence was offered supporting an award of $269,091.00, making the

1. We are called upon in this appeal to consider only whether the district court abused its discretion by deciding the motion based solely on documents submitted by the parties rather than by receiving evidence. Appellant does not now reassert its challenges to the arbitration tribunal's award.

award irrational; (4) The arbitrators failed to adhere to the agreement providing for arbitration because it is unclear whether they considered the calculations submitted by the defendant, or, alternatively, they failed to consider the calculations which constituted material evidence; (5) The award was a result of material miscalculation of figures; and (6) The award was based on a matter not submitted to the tribunal.

The district court had before it and analyzed the relevant records from the arbitration hearing, comprising 10 documents including the arbitration agreement, the demand for arbitration, calculations setting forth the specific amount of requested damages, memoranda submitted by both parties, and the premium rates and commission schedules upon which Legion based its claim. The arbitration proceeding was not transcribed. The district court determined that there was no support for assertions 1, 2, and 6; the district court also rejected challenges 3, 4, and 5 based on the documentary evidence. Technically, the documentation before the district court was not "in evidence" because its admissibility was not supported by affidavits until after the court entered judgment. Neither party disputed the authenticity of the documents, however, and the district court evidently relied upon them as if admitted by stipulation.

We recognize that some motions challenging arbitration awards may require evidentiary hearings outside the scope of the pleadings and arbitration record. Appellant cites, for example, Sanko Steamship Co. v. Cook Industries, 495 F.2d 1260, 1265 (2d Cir. 1973), in which the court of appeals reversed an order confirming an arbitration award when the question of an arbitrator's impartiality was decided on an incomplete record. There the court determined that discrepancies between the judge's opinion and the facts in the record required remand to explore fully the relationships between the arbitrator and the parties involved. See also Totem Marine Tug & Barge, Inc. v. North American Towing, 607 F.2d 649 (5th Cir. 1979) (hearing held and arbitral award vacated because of prejudicial misbehavior of arbitrators). Such matters as misconduct or bias of the arbitrators cannot be gauged on the face of the arbitral record alone.

No such case is here presented. The district court was not required by the Federal Rules to conduct a full hearing on appellant's motion. See Fed.R.Civ.P. 43(e) (providing that court may direct that motions be decided on the papers rather than after oral testimony); Fed.R.Civ.P. 78 (providing that court may decide motions on written statements of reasons in support and opposition to expedite business). See also Commerce Park at DFW Freeport v. Mardian Construction Co., 729 F.2d 334, 340–41 (5th Cir. 1984) (holding that unsupported assertions on the issue of arbitrability did not require evidentiary hearing under 9 U.S.C. § 3); Imperial Ethiopian Gov't v. Baruch–Foster Corp., 535 F.2d 334, 337 n. 10 (5th Cir. 1976) (holding that under Convention on the Recognition and Enforcement of Foreign Arbitral Awards, 9 U.S.C. §§ 201–208, which involves summary procedures, district court "was not required to resort to the formal taking of testimony or deposition procedures in order to determine" the issue before it). The error in Appellant's argument with respect to its case is exposed by the remedy it would adopt. Although it asserts no fact sought to be proved if we were to remand for evidentiary development, appellant suggests it would depose "anyone present" at the arbitration proceeding, including the arbitrators, to "recreate the evidence presented as completely as possible." Appellant's bases for vacating or modifying the arbitration award amounted, however, to evidentiary challenges and unsupported assertions that the arbitrators impermissibly calculated the award. Courts have repeatedly condemned efforts to depose members of an arbitration panel to impeach or clarify their awards. See, e.g., Andros Compania Maritima v. Marc Rich & Co., 579 F.2d 691, 702 (2d Cir. 1978). To permit time-consuming, costly discovery simply to replicate the substance of the arbitration would thwart its goal. The statutory bases for overturning an arbitral tribunal are precisely and narrowly drawn to prohibit such complete de novo review of the substance of the award, as distinguished from gross calculation errors or inadequacies in the makeup of the tribunal itself. The district court was well within its discretion to dispose of the issues before it on the record submitted by the parties.

Arbitration proceedings are summary in nature to effectuate the national policy favoring arbitration, and they require "expeditious and summary hearing, with only restricted inquiry into factual issues." Moses H. Cone Memorial Hospital v. Mercury Construction Corp., 460 U.S. 1, 22, 103 S.Ct. 927, 940, 74 L.Ed.2d 765 (1983). This case posed no factual issues that required the court, pursuant to the Arbitration Act, to delve beyond the documentary record of the arbitration and the award rendered. Discovery of the sort desired by IGAI would result in the court's reviewing the factual and legal accuracy of the award, a task this circuit has foreclosed. Local Union 59, Int'l. Brotherhood of Elec. Workers, AFL–CIO v. Green Corp., 725 F.2d 264, 268 (5th Cir.), cert. denied, 469 U.S. 833, 105 S.Ct. 124, 83 L.Ed.2d 66 (1984). The policy of expediting judicial enforcement of arbitral awards, albeit confuted here, counsels our courts to pierce the rhetoric of parties like IGAI who would embark on a costly legal path solely to challenge the factual or legal accuracy of an arbitration award.

The judgment of the district court is AFFIRMED.

* * *

Question

1. Why do courts reject efforts to depose or compel testimony of arbitrators to impeach their awards? Is it merely to avoid delay, or are there additional reasons not to compel such testimony? Why does the court state that allegations of misconduct or bias by arbitrators may justify an evidentiary hearing but allegations concerning arbitrability or gross error do not?

* * *

CHAPTER FOUR

JUDICIAL REVIEW, REMEDIES, AND FINALITY

1. STANDARD OF REVIEW OF ARBITRAL AWARDS

Under Section 10 the Federal Arbitration Act, a party can petition a court to vacate an arbitral award. The appropriate standard of review of arbitral awards is a subject of great importance and considerable controversy. A court asked to review an arbitral award to determine whether it should be enforced can take a number of approaches. If it engages in *de novo* review, then the court essentially substitutes its judgment for that of the arbitrator. If the standard of review is more deferential, then the arbitrator's decision is accorded more finality.

Many viewpoints about the proper scope of judicial review of arbitral awards have been advocated by commentators, ranging from *de novo* review on the merits to complete abstention. For example, until recently, in Great Britain arbitral awards received de novo judicial review on issues of law but great deference on issues of fact.

Deferential review promotes finality, which was important to the merchants who advocated the passage of the FAA in the 1920s to facilitate speedy resolution of their contractual issues. Consider whether a less-deferential review standard is more appropriate for statutory claims in which, presumably, it is more important to get the "right" decision than it is to get a speedy one.

The standard of judicial review of arbitral awards defines the line between public justice and private justice, and it is a line that is constantly shifting in subtle but significant ways. In the cases that follow, we see the doctrinal framework that courts have developed to define the scope of judicial review of arbitral awards. The cases also discuss the competing considerations involved and illustrate some of the more recent modifications and refinements.

* * *

A. Judicial Review Under Section 301 of the Labor Management Relations Act

United Steelworkers of America v. Enterprise Wheel and Car Corp.

363 U.S. 593 (1960).

■ Opinion of the Court by MR. JUSTICE DOUGLAS, announced by MR. JUSTICE BRENNAN.

Petitioner union and respondent during the period relevant here had a collective bargaining agreement which provided that any differences "as to the meaning and application" of the agreement should be submitted to arbitration and that the arbitrator's decision "shall be final and binding on the parties." Special provisions were included concerning the suspension and discharge of employees. The agreement stated:

> Should it be determined by the Company or by an arbitrator in accordance with the grievance procedure that the employee has been suspended unjustly or discharged in violation of the provisions of this Agreement, the Company shall reinstate the employee and pay full compensation at the employee's regular rate of pay for the time lost.

The agreement also provided:

> . . . It is understood and agreed that neither party will institute civil suits or legal proceedings against the other for alleged violation of any of the provisions of this labor contract; instead all disputes will be settled in the manner outlined in this Article III—Adjustment of Grievances.

A group of employees left their jobs in protest against the discharge of one employee. A union official advised them at once to return to work. An official of respondent at their request gave them permission and then rescinded it. The next day they were told they did not have a job any more "until this thing was settled one way or the other."

A grievance was filed; and when respondent finally refused to arbitrate, this suit was brought for specific enforcement of the arbitration provisions of the agreement. The District Court ordered arbitration. The arbitrator found that the discharge of the men was not justified, though their conduct, he said, was improper. In his view the facts warranted at most a suspension of the men for 10 days each. After their discharge and before the arbitration award the collective bargaining agreement had expired. The union, however, continued to represent the workers at the plant. The arbitrator rejected the contention that expiration of the agreement barred reinstatement of the employees. He held that the provision of the agreement above quoted imposed an unconditional obligation on the employer. He awarded reinstatement with back pay, minus pay for a 10-day suspension and such sums as these employees received from other employment.

Respondent refused to comply with the award. Petitioner moved the District Court for enforcement. The District Court directed respondent to comply. 168 F.Supp. 308. The Court of Appeals, while agreeing that the District Court had jurisdiction to enforce an arbitration award under a collective bargaining agreement, held that the failure of the award to specify the amounts to be deducted from the back pay rendered the award unenforceable. That defect, it agreed, could be remedied by requiring the parties to complete the arbitration. It went on to hold, however, that an award for back pay subsequent to the date of termination of the collective bargaining agreement could not be enforced. It also held that the requirement for reinstatement of the discharged employees was likewise unenforceable because the collective bargaining agreement had expired. 269 F.2d 327. We granted certiorari. 361 U.S. 929, 80 S.Ct. 371.

The refusal of courts to review the merits of an arbitration award is the proper approach to arbitration under collective bargaining agreements. The federal policy of settling labor disputes by arbitration would be undermined if courts had the final say on the merits of the awards. As we stated in united Steelworkers of America v. Warrior & Gulf Navigation Co., 363 U.S. 574, 80 S.Ct. 1347, the arbitrators under these collective agreements are indispensable agencies in a continuous collective bargaining process. They sit to settle disputes at the plant level—disputes that require for their solution knowledge of the custom and practices of a particular factory or of a particular industry as reflected in particular agreements.

When an arbitrator is commissioned to interpret and apply the collective bargaining agreement, he is to bring his informed judgment to bear in order to reach a fair solution of a problem. This is especially true when it comes to formulating remedies. There the need is for flexibility in meeting a wide variety of situations. The draftsmen may never have thought of what specific remedy should be awarded to meet a particular contingency. Nevertheless, an arbitrator is confined to interpretation and application of the collective bargaining agreement; he does not sit to dispense his own brand of industrial justice. He may of course look for guidance from many sources, yet his award is legitimate only so long as it draws its essence from the collective bargaining agreement. When the arbitrator's words manifest an infidelity to this obligation, courts have no choice but to refuse enforcement of the award.

The opinion of the arbitrator in this case, as it bears upon the award of back pay beyond the date of the agreement's expiration and reinstatement, is ambiguous. It may be read as based solely upon the arbitrator's view of the requirements of enacted legislation, which would mean that he exceeded the scope of the submission. Or it may be read as embodying a construction of the agreement itself, perhaps with the arbitrator looking to 'the law' for help in determining the sense of the agreement. A mere ambiguity in the opinion accompanying an award, which permits the inference that the arbitrator may have exceeded his authority, is not a reason for refusing to enforce the award. Arbitrators have no obligation to the court to give their reasons for an award. To require opinions free of ambiguity may lead arbitrators to play it safe by writing no supporting opinions. This would be undesirable for a well-reasoned opinion tends to engender confidence in the integrity of the process and aids in clarifying the underlying agreement. Moreover, we see no reason to assume that this arbitrator has abused the trust the parties confided in him and has not stayed within the areas marked out for his consideration. It is not apparent that he went beyond the submission. The Court of Appeals' opinion refusing to enforce the reinstatement and partial back pay portions of the award was not based upon any finding that the arbitrator did not premise his award on his construction of the contract. It merely disagreed with the arbitrator's construction of it.

The collective bargaining agreement could have provided that if any of the employees were wrongfully discharged, the remedy would be reinstatement and back pay up to the date they were returned to work. Respondent's major argument seems to be that by applying correct principles of law to the interpretation of the collective bargaining agreement it can be determined that the agreement did not so provide, and that therefore the arbitrator's decision was not based upon the contract. The acceptance of this view would require courts, even under the standard arbitration clause, to review the merits of every construction of the contract. This plenary review by a court of the merits would make meaningless the provisions that the arbitrator's decision is final, for in reality it would almost never be final. This underlines the fundamental error which we have alluded to in United Steelworkers of America v. American Manufacturing Co., 363 U.S. 564, 80 S.Ct. 1343. As we there emphasized, the question of interpretation of the collective bargaining agreement is a question for the arbitrator. It is the arbitrator's construction which was bargained for; and so far as the arbitrator's decision concerns construction of the contract, the courts have no business overruling him because their interpretation of the contract is different from his.

[T]he judgment of the District Court should be modified so that the amounts due the employees may be definitely determined by arbitration. In all other respects we think the judgment of the District Court should be affirmed. Accordingly, we reverse the judgment of the Court of Appeals. . . .

* * *

Questions

1. What does the *Enterprise Wheel and Car* Court say are the grounds for overturning an arbitral award in a labor arbitration under Section 301 of the Labor Management Relations Act? Justice Reed, writing in 1953 in *Wilko v. Swan*, supra Chapter 1.5, suggested that an arbitral award under the FAA could be overturned if it betrayed a "manifest disregard of the law." Are these standards of review the same? How do they differ? Which one sets a higher standard?

2. Why is the Court reluctant to review the merits of a labor arbitration award? Does the *Enterprise* test prevent courts from scrutinizing the merits of an arbitral award? Without some consideration of the merits of the dispute and some view of the meaning of the contract, how can a court determine whether the arbitrator's award drew its essence from the contract?

3. When the Court states that if there is "mere ambiguity" the award should be enforced, is it stating a presumption that arbitral awards are proper? Is this a rebuttable presumption? What would it take to overcome the presumption?

* * *

United Paperworkers International Union, AFL–CIO v. Misco, Inc.

484 U.S. 29 (1987).

■ JUSTICE WHITE delivered the opinion of the Court.

The issue for decision involves several aspects of when a federal court may refuse to enforce an arbitration award rendered under a collective-bargaining agreement.

I

Misco, Inc. (Misco, or the Company), operates a paper converting plant in Monroe, Louisiana. The Company is a party to a collective-bargaining agreement with the United Paperworkers International Union, AFL–CIO, and its union local (the Union); the agreement covers the production and maintenance employees at the plant. Under the agreement, the Company or the Union may submit to arbitration any grievance that arises from the interpretation or application of its terms, and the arbitrator's decision is final and binding upon the parties. The arbitrator's authority is limited to interpretation and application of the terms contained in the agreement itself. The agreement reserves to management the right to establish, amend, and enforce "rules and regulations regulating the discipline or discharge of employees" and the procedures for imposing discipline. Such rules were to be posted and were to be in effect "until ruled on by grievance and arbitration procedures as to fairness and necessity." For about a decade, the Company's rules had listed as causes for discharge the bringing of intoxicants, narcotics, or controlled substances on to plant property or consuming any of them there, as well as reporting for work under the influence of such substances. At the time of the events involved in this case, the Company was very concerned about the use of drugs at the plant, especially among employees on the night shift.

Isiah Cooper, who worked on the night shift for Misco, was one of the employees covered by the collective-bargaining agreement. He operated a slitter-rewinder machine, which uses sharp blades to cut rolling coils of paper. The arbitrator found that this machine is hazardous and had caused numerous injuries in recent years. Cooper had been reprimanded twice in a few months for deficient performance. On January 21, 1983, one day after the second reprimand, the police searched Cooper's house pursuant to a warrant, and a substantial amount of marijuana was found. Contemporaneously, a police officer was detailed to keep Cooper's car under observation at the Company's parking lot. At about 6:30 p.m., Cooper was seen walking in the parking lot during work hours with two other men. The three men entered Cooper's car momentarily, then walked to another car, a white Cutlass, and entered it. After the other two men later returned to the plant, Cooper was apprehended by police in the backseat of this car with marijuana smoke in the air and a lighted marijuana cigarette in the front-seat ashtray. The police also searched Cooper's car and found a plastic scales case and marijuana gleanings. Cooper was arrested and charged with marijuana possession.[3]

On January 24, Cooper told the Company that he had been arrested for possession of marijuana at his home; the Company did not learn of the marijuana cigarette in the white Cutlass until January 27. It then investigated and on February 7 discharged Cooper, asserting that in the circumstances, his presence in the Cutlass violated the rule against having drugs on the plant premises. Cooper filed a grievance protesting his discharge the same day, and the matter proceeded to arbitration. The Company was not aware until September 21, five days before the arbitration hearing was scheduled, that marijuana had been found in Cooper's car. That fact did not become known to the Union until the hearing began. At the hearing it was stipulated that the issue was whether the Company had "just cause to discharge the Grievant under Rule II.1" and, "[i]f not, what if any should be the remedy." App. to Pet. for Cert. 26a.

The arbitrator upheld the grievance and ordered the Company to reinstate Cooper with back pay and full seniority. The arbitrator based his finding that there was not just cause for the discharge on his consideration of seven criteria.[5] In particular, the arbitrator found that the Company failed to prove that the employee had possessed or used marijuana on company property: finding Cooper in the backseat of a car and a burning cigarette in the front-seat ashtray was insufficient proof that Cooper was using or possessed marijuana on company property. Id., at 49a–50a. The arbitrator refused to accept into evidence the fact that marijuana had been found in Cooper's car on company premises because the Company did not know of this fact when Cooper was discharged and therefore did not rely on it as a basis for the discharge.

3. Cooper later pleaded guilty to that charge, which was not related to his being in a car with a lighted marijuana cigarette in it. The authorities chose not to prosecute for the latter incident.

5. These considerations were the reasonableness of the employer's position, the notice given to the employee, the timing of the investigation undertaken, the fairness of the investigation, the evidence against the employee, the possibility of discrimination, and the relation of the degree of discipline to the nature of the offense and the employee's past record.

The Company filed suit in District Court, seeking to vacate the arbitration award on several grounds, one of which was that ordering reinstatement of Cooper, who had allegedly possessed marijuana on the plant premises, was contrary to public policy. The District Court agreed that the award must be set aside as contrary to public policy because it ran counter to general safety concerns that arise from the operation of dangerous machinery while under the influence of drugs, as well as to state criminal laws against drug possession. The Court of Appeals affirmed, with one judge dissenting. The court ruled that reinstatement would violate the public policy "against the operation of dangerous machinery by persons under the influence of drugs or alcohol." 768 F.2d 739, 743 (C.A.5 1985). The arbitrator had found that Cooper was apprehended on company premises in an atmosphere of marijuana smoke in another's car and that marijuana was found in his own car on the company lot. These facts established that Cooper had violated the Company's rules and gave the Company just cause to discharge him. The arbitrator did not reach this conclusion because of a "narrow focus on Cooper's procedural rights" that led him to ignore what he "knew was in fact true: that Cooper did bring marijuana onto his employer's premises." Ibid. Even if the arbitrator had not known of this fact at the time he entered his award, "it is doubtful that the award should be enforced today in light of what is now known." Ibid.

Because the Courts of Appeals are divided on the question of when courts may set aside arbitration awards as contravening public policy, we granted the Union's petition for a writ of certiorari, 479 U.S. 1029, 107 S.Ct. 871, 93 L.Ed.2d 826 (1987), and now reverse the judgment of the Court of Appeals.

II

The Union asserts that an arbitral award may not be set aside on public policy grounds unless the award orders conduct that violates the positive law, which is not the case here. But in the alternative, it submits that even if it is wrong in this regard, the Court of Appeals otherwise exceeded the limited authority that it had to review an arbitrator's award entered pursuant to a collective-bargaining agreement. Respondent, on the other hand, defends the public policy decision of the Court of Appeals but alternatively argues that the judgment below should be affirmed because of erroneous findings by the arbitrator. We deal first with the opposing alternative arguments.

A

... The reasons for insulating arbitral decisions from judicial review are grounded in the federal statutes regulating labor-management relations. These statutes reflect a decided preference for private settlement of labor disputes without the intervention of government ... The courts have jurisdiction to enforce collective-bargaining contracts; but where the contract provides grievance and arbitration procedures, those procedures must first be exhausted and courts must order resort to the private settlement mechanisms without dealing with the merits of the dispute. Because the parties have contracted to have disputes settled by an arbitrator chosen by them rather than by a judge, it is the arbitrator's view of the facts and of the meaning of the contract that they have agreed to accept. Courts thus do not sit to hear claims of factual or legal error by an arbitrator as an appellate court does in reviewing decisions of lower courts . . . As the Court has said, the arbitrator's award settling a dispute with respect to the interpretation or application of a labor agreement must draw its essence from the contract and cannot simply reflect the arbitrator's own notions of industrial justice. But as long as the arbitrator is even arguably construing or applying the contract and acting within the scope of his authority, that a court is convinced he committed serious error does not suffice to overturn his decision. Of course, decisions procured by the parties through fraud or through the arbitrator's dishonesty need not be enforced. But there is nothing of that sort involved in this case.

B

The Company's position, simply put, is that the arbitrator committed grievous error in finding that the evidence was insufficient to prove that Cooper had possessed or used marijuana on company property. But the Court of Appeals, although it took a distinctly jaundiced view of the arbitrator's decision in this regard, was not free to refuse enforcement because it considered Cooper's presence in the white Cutlass, in the circumstances, to be ample proof that Rule II.1 was violated. No dishonesty is alleged; only improvident, even silly, fact finding is claimed. This is hardly a sufficient basis for disregarding what the agent appointed by the parties determined to be the historical facts.

Nor was it open to the Court of Appeals to refuse to enforce the award because the arbitrator, in deciding whether there was just cause to discharge, refused to consider evidence unknown to the Company at the time Cooper was fired. The parties bargained for arbitration to settle disputes and were free to set the procedural rules for arbitrators to follow if they chose. Article VI of the agreement, entitled "Arbitration Procedure," did set some ground rules for the arbitration process. It forbade the arbitrator to consider hearsay evidence, for example, but evidentiary matters were otherwise left to the arbitrator. App. 19. Here the arbitrator ruled that in determining whether Cooper had violated Rule II.1, he should not consider evidence not relied on by the employer in ordering the discharge, particularly in a case like this where there was no notice to the employee or the Union prior to the hearing that the Company would attempt to rely on after-discovered evidence. This, in effect, was a construction of what the contract required when deciding discharge cases: an arbitrator was to look only at the evidence before the employer at the time of discharge. As the arbitrator noted, this approach was consistent with the practice followed by other arbitrators. And it was consistent with our observation in John Wiley & Sons, Inc. v. Livingston, 376 U.S. 543, 557 (1964), that when the subject matter of a dispute is arbitrable, "procedural" questions which grow out of the dispute and bear on its final disposition are to be left to the arbitrator . . .

C

[The Court of Appeals] ... held that the evidence of marijuana in Cooper's car required that the award be set aside because to reinstate a person who had brought drugs onto the property was contrary to the public policy "against the operation of dangerous machinery by persons under the influence of drugs or alcohol." 768 F.2d, at 743. We cannot affirm that judgment.

A court's refusal to enforce an arbitrator's award under a collective-bargaining agreement because it is contrary to public policy is a specific application of the more general doctrine, rooted in the common law, that a court may refuse to enforce contracts that violate law or public policy ... That doctrine derives from the basic notion that no court will lend its aid to one who founds a cause of action upon an immoral or illegal act, and is further justified by the observation that the public's interests in confining the scope of private agreements to which it is not a party will go unrepresented unless the judiciary takes account of those interests when it considers whether to enforce such agreements.... In the common law of contracts, this doctrine has served as the foundation for occasional exercises of judicial power to abrogate private agreements.

In W.R. Grace, we recognized that "a court may not enforce a collective-bargaining agreement that is contrary to public policy," and stated that "the question of public policy is ultimately one for resolution by the courts." 461 U.S., at 766. We cautioned, however, that a court's refusal to enforce an arbitrator's interpretation of such contracts is limited to situations where the contract as interpreted would violate "some explicit public policy" that is "well defined and dominant, and is to be ascertained 'by reference to the laws and legal precedents and not from general considerations of supposed public interests.'" Ibid. ... Two points follow from our decision in W.R. Grace. First, a court may refuse to enforce a collective-bargaining agreement when the specific terms contained in that agreement violate public policy. Second, it is apparent that our decision in that case does not otherwise sanction a broad judicial power to set aside arbitration awards as against public policy. Although we discussed the effect of that award on two broad areas of public policy, our decision turned on our examination of whether the award created any explicit conflict with other "laws and legal precedents" rather than an assessment of "general considerations of supposed public interests." 461 U.S., at 766 ...

As we see it, the formulation of public policy set out by the Court of Appeals did not comply with the statement that such a policy must be "ascertained 'by reference to the laws and legal precedents and not from general considerations of supposed public interests.'" Ibid. (quoting Muschany v. United States, supra, 324 U.S., at 66, 65 S.Ct., at 451). The Court of Appeals made no attempt to review existing laws and legal precedents in order to demonstrate that they establish a "well-defined and dominant" policy against the operation of dangerous machinery while under the influence of drugs. Although certainly such a judgment is firmly rooted in common sense, we explicitly held in W.R. Grace that a formulation of public policy based only on "general considerations of supposed public interests" is not the sort that permits a court to set aside an arbitration award that was entered in accordance with a valid collective-bargaining agreement.

Even if the Court of Appeals' formulation of public policy is to be accepted, no violation of that policy was clearly shown in this case . . . [T]he assumed connection between the marijuana gleanings found in Cooper's car and Cooper's actual use of drugs in the workplace is tenuous at best and provides an insufficient basis for holding that his reinstatement would actually violate the public policy identified by the Court of Appeals "against the operation of dangerous machinery by persons under the influence of drugs or alcohol." 768 F.2d, at 743. A refusal to enforce an award must rest on more than speculation or assumption.

In any event, it was inappropriate for the Court of Appeals itself to draw the necessary inference. To conclude from the fact that marijuana had been found in Cooper's car that Cooper had ever been or would be under the influence of marijuana while he was on the job and operating dangerous machinery is an exercise in fact finding about Cooper's use of drugs and his amenability to discipline, a task that exceeds the authority of a court asked to overturn an arbitration award. The parties did not bargain for the facts to be found by a court, but by an arbitrator chosen by them who had more opportunity to observe Cooper and to be familiar with the plant and its problems . . .

The judgment of the Court of Appeals is reversed.

[The concurring opinion of JUSTICE BLACKMUN, with whom JUSTICE BRENNAN joins, has been omitted.]

* * *

Questions

1. How does the Court apply the *Enterprise Wheel* "essence test" in this case? What consideration does it give to the company's claim that the arbitrator's fact-finding was erroneous?

2. What does the Court say about its power to overturn an award on the ground of public policy? Where does this additional standard of review come from? How is it applied in this case? Who decides issues of public policy—an arbitrator or a court? Given that there is a strong public policy against illicit drugs, embodied in the criminal laws of all states and the federal government, why does the Court refuse to vacate the award on public policy grounds?

* * *

Note on Eastern Associated Coal Corporation v. United Mine Workers of America

In *Eastern Associated Coal Corporation v. United Mine Workers of America, District 17, et al.,* 531 U.S. 57 (2000), the Supreme Court again was asked to set aside an arbitral award that reinstated an employee who tested positive for marijuana use on the job. James Smith worked for Eastern as a driver of heavy truck-like vehicles on public highways. As a truck driver, he was subject to Department of Transportation (DOT) regulations requiring random drug testing of workers engaged in "safety-sensitive" tasks. 49 CFR §§ 382.301, 382.305 (1999). Smith tested positive for marijuana use in 1996 and Eastern discharged him. After an arbitration, he was reinstated on condition that he accept a suspension and participate in a substance-abuse program. In July 1997, he again tested positive for marijuana use, and again Eastern fired him. Again an arbitrator reinstated him, while imposing a suspension and certain other conditions. Eastern sued to vacate the arbitral award. It argued that the Omnibus Employee Transportation Employee Testing Act of 1991 and the DOT's implementing regulations established a clear public policy against the operation of dangerous machinery by workers who test positive for drugs.

The District Court held that the arbitral award reinstating Smith subject to conditions did not violate public policy against drug use by workers who perform safety-sensitive functions, 66 F.Supp.2d 796 (S.D.W.Va. 1998). The Court of Appeals affirmed, 188 F.3d 501 (4th Cir. 1999). The Supreme Court affirmed. In an opinion by Justice Breyer, the Court reaffirmed its position that an arbitral award can only be overturned on grounds of public policy when the policy is " 'explicit, well defined, and dominant.' " (quoting W.R. Grace & Co. v. Rubber Workers, 461 U.S. 757 (1983)).

> ... [T]he question to be answered is not whether Smith's drug use itself violates public policy, but whether the agreement to reinstate him does so. To put the question more specifically, does a contractual agreement to reinstate Smith with specified conditions ... run contrary to an explicit, well-defined, and dominant public policy, as ascertained by reference to positive law and not from general considerations of supposed public interests?

The Court then summarized the federal laws and regulations concerning drug use and drug testing, and concluded that they reflected not only a policy against drug use by employees in safety-sensitive transportation positions, but also a policy in favor of rehabilitation of employees who use drugs:

> The award before us is not contrary to these several policies, taken together. The award does not condone Smith's conduct or ignore the risk to public safety that drug use by truck drivers may pose. Rather, the award punishes Smith by suspending him for three months, thereby depriving him of nearly $9,000 in lost wages, Record Doc. 29, App. A, p. 2; it requires him to pay the arbitration costs of both sides; it insists upon further substance-abuse treatment and testing; and it makes clear (by requiring Smith to provide a signed letter of resignation) that one more failed test means discharge.

The award violates no specific provision of any law or regulation. It is consistent with DOT rules requiring completion of substance-abuse treatment before returning to work, see 49 CFR § 382.605(c)(2)(i) (1999), for it does not preclude Eastern from assigning Smith to a non-safety-sensitive position until Smith completes the prescribed treatment program. It is consistent with the Testing Act's 1-year and 10-year driving license suspension requirements, for those requirements apply only to drivers who, unlike Smith, actually operated vehicles under the influence of drugs. See 49 U.S.C. §§ 31310(b), (c). The award is also consistent with the Act's rehabilitative concerns, for it requires substance-abuse treatment and testing before Smith can return to work.

The fact that Smith is a recidivist—that he has failed drug tests twice—is not sufficient to tip the balance in Eastern's favor.

Major League Baseball Players Association v. Garvey

532 U.S. 504 (2001).

■ PER CURIAM

The Court of Appeals for the Ninth Circuit here rejected an arbitrator's factual findings and then resolved the merits of the parties' dispute instead of remanding the case for further arbitration proceedings. Because the Court's determination conflicts with our cases limiting review of an arbitrator's award entered pursuant to an agreement between an employer and a labor organization and prescribing the appropriate remedy where vacation of the award is warranted, we grant the petition for a writ of certiorari and reverse. The motions for leave to file briefs *amicus curiae* of the National Academy of Arbitrators and the Office of the Commissioner of Baseball are granted.

In the late 1980's, petitioner Major League Baseball Players Association (Association) filed grievances against the Major League Baseball Clubs (Clubs), claiming the Clubs had colluded in the market for free-agent services after the 1985, 1986 and 1987 baseball seasons, in violation of the industry's collective-bargaining agreement. A free agent is a player who may contract with any Club, rather than one whose right to contract is restricted to a particular Club. In a series of decisions, arbitrators found collusion by the Clubs and damage to the players. The Association and Clubs subsequently entered into a Global Settlement Agreement (Agreement), pursuant to which the Clubs established a $280 million fund to be distributed to injured players. The Association also designed a "Framework" to evaluate the individual player's claims, and, applying that Framework, recommended distribution plans for claims relating to a particular season or seasons.

The Framework provided that players could seek an arbitrator's review of the distribution plan. The arbitrator would determine "only whether the approved Framework and the criteria set forth therein have been properly applied in the proposed Distribution Plan." *Garvey v. Roberts,* 203 F.3d 580, 583 (C.A.9 2000) *(Garvey I).* The Framework set forth factors to be considered in evaluating players' claims, as well as specific requirements for lost contract-extension claims. Such claims were cognizable " 'only in those cases where evidence exists that a specific offer of an extension was made by a club prior to collusion only to thereafter be withdrawn when the collusion scheme was initiated.' " *Id.,* at 584.

Respondent Steve Garvey, a retired, highly regarded first baseman, submitted a claim for damages of approximately $3 million. He alleged that his contract with the San Diego Padres was not extended to the 1988 and 1989 seasons due to collusion. The Association rejected Garvey's claim in February 1996, because he presented no evidence that the Padres actually offered to extend his contract. Garvey objected, and an arbitration hearing was held. He testified that the Padres offered to extend his contract for the 1988 and 1989 seasons and then withdrew the offer after they began colluding with other teams. He presented a June 1996 letter from Ballard Smith, Padres' President and CEO from 1979 to 1987, stating that, before the end of the 1985 season, Smith offered to extend Garvey's contract through the 1989 season, but that the Padres refused to negotiate with Garvey thereafter due to collusion.

The arbitrator denied Garvey's claim, after seeking additional documentation from the parties. In his award, he explained that " '[t]here exists . . . substantial doubt as to the credibility of the statements in the Smith letter.' " *Id.,* at 586. He noted the "stark contradictions" between the 1996 letter and Smith's testimony in the earlier arbitration proceedings regarding collusion, where Smith, like other owners, denied collusion and stated that the Padres simply were not interested in extending Garvey's contract. *Ibid.* The arbitrator determined that, due to these contradictions, he " 'must reject [Smith's] more recent assertion that Garvey did not receive [a contract] extension' " due to collusion, and found that Garvey had not shown a specific offer of extension. *Ibid.* He concluded that:

> [t]he shadow cast over the credibility of the Smith testimony coupled with the absence of any other corroboration of the claim submitted by Garvey compels a finding that the Padres declined to extend his contract not because of the constraints of the collusion effort of the clubs but rather as a baseball judgment founded upon [Garvey's] age and recent injury history. *Ibid.*

Garvey moved in Federal District Court to vacate the arbitrator's award, alleging that the arbitrator violated the Framework by denying his claim. The District Court denied the motion. The Court of Appeals for the Ninth Circuit reversed by a divided vote. The court acknowledged that judicial review of an arbitrator's decision in a labor dispute is extremely limited. But it held that review of the merits of the arbitrator's award was warranted in this case, because the arbitrator " 'dispensed his own brand of industrial justice.' " *Id.,* at 589. The court recognized that Smith's prior testimony with respect to collusion conflicted with the statements in his 1996 letter. But in the court's view, the arbitrator's refusal to credit

Smith's letter was "inexplicable" and "border[ed] on the irrational," because a panel of arbitrators, chaired by the arbitrator involved here, had previously concluded that the owners' prior testimony was false. *Id.,* at 590. The court rejected the arbitrator's reliance on the absence of other corroborating evidence, attributing that fact to Smith and Garvey's direct negotiations. The court also found that the record provided "strong support" for the truthfulness of Smith's 1996 letter. *Id.,* at 591–592. The Court of Appeals reversed and remanded with directions to vacate the award.

The District Court then remanded the case to the arbitration panel for further hearings, and Garvey appealed. The Court of Appeals, again by a divided vote, explained that *Garvey I* established that "the conclusion that Smith made Garvey an offer and subsequently withdrew it because of the collusion scheme was the only conclusion that the arbitrator could draw from the record in the proceedings." No. 00–56080, 2000 WL 1801383, at *1 (Dec. 7, 2000), judgt. order to be reported at 243 F.3d 547. *(Garvey II).* Noting that its prior instructions might have been unclear, the Court clarified that *Garvey I* "left only one possible result—the result our holding contemplated—an award in Garvey's favor." *Ibid.* The Court of Appeals reversed the District Court and directed that it remand the case to the arbitration panel with instructions to enter an award for Garvey in the amount he claimed.

The parties do not dispute that this case arises under § 301 of the Labor Management Relations Act, 1947, 61 Stat. 156, 29 U.S.C. § 185(a), as the controversy involves an assertion of rights under an agreement between an employer and a labor organization. Although Garvey's specific allegation is that the arbitrator violated the Framework for resolving players' claims for damages, that Framework was designed to facilitate payments to remedy the Clubs' breach of the collective-bargaining agreement. Garvey's right to be made whole is founded on that agreement.

Judicial review of a labor-arbitration decision pursuant to such an agreement is very limited. Courts are not authorized to review the arbitrator's decision on the merits despite allegations that the decision rests on factual errors or misinterprets the parties' agreement. *Paperworkers v. Misco, Inc.,* 484 U.S. 29, 36, 108 S.Ct. 364, 98 L.Ed.2d 286 (1987). We recently reiterated that if an " 'arbitrator is even arguably construing or applying the contract and acting within the scope of his authority,' the fact that 'a court is convinced he committed serious error does not suffice to overturn his decision.' " *Eastern Associated Coal Corp. v. Mine Workers,* 531 U.S. 57, 62, 121 S.Ct. 462, 148 L.Ed.2d 354 (2000) (quoting *Misco, supra,* at 38, 108 S.Ct. 364). It is only when the arbitrator strays from interpretation and application of the agreement and effectively "dispense[s] his own brand of industrial justice" that his decision may be unenforceable. *Steelworkers v. Enterprise Wheel & Car Corp.,* 363 U.S. 593, 597, 80 S.Ct. 1358, 4 L.Ed.2d 1424 (1960). When an arbitrator resolves disputes regarding the application of a contract, and no dishonesty is alleged, the arbitrator's "improvident, even silly, factfinding" does not provide a basis for a reviewing court to refuse to enforce the award. *Misco,* 484 U.S., at 39, 108 S.Ct. 364.

In discussing the courts' limited role in reviewing the merits of arbitration awards, we have stated that " 'courts ... have no business weighing the merits of the grievance [or] considering whether there is equity in a particular claim.' " *Id.,* at 37, 108 S.Ct. 364 (quoting *Steelworkers v. American Mfg. Co.,* 363 U.S. 564, 568, 80 S.Ct. 1343, 4 L.Ed.2d 1403 (1960)). When the judiciary does so, "it usurps a function which ... is entrusted to the arbitration tribunal." *Id.,* at 569, 80 S.Ct. 1343; see also *Enterprise Wheel & Car Corp., supra,* at 599, 80 S.Ct. 1358 ("It is the arbitrator's construction [of the agreement] which was bargained for ..."). Consistent with this limited role, we said in *Misco* that "[e]ven in the very rare instances when an arbitrator's procedural aberrations rise to the level of affirmative misconduct, as a rule the court must not foreclose further proceedings by settling the merits according to its own judgment of the appropriate result." 484 U.S. at 40–41, n. 10, 108 S.Ct. 364. That step, we explained, "would improperly substitute a judicial determination for the arbitrator's decision that the parties bargained for" in their agreement. *Ibid.* Instead, the court should "simply vacate the award, thus leaving open the possibility of further proceedings if they are permitted under the terms of the agreement." *Ibid.*

To be sure, the Court of Appeals here recited these principles, but its application of them is nothing short of baffling. The substance of the Court's discussion reveals that it overturned the arbitrator's decision because it disagreed with the arbitrator's factual findings, particularly those with respect to credibility. The Court of Appeals, it appears, would have credited Smith's 1996 letter, and found the arbitrator's refusal to do so at worst "irrational" and at best "bizarre." *Garvey I,* 203 F.3d, at 590–591. But even "serious error" on the arbitrator's part does not justify overturning his decision, where, as here, he is construing a contract and acting within the scope of his authority. *Misco, supra,* at 38, 108 S.Ct. 364.

In *Garvey II,* the court clarified that *Garvey I* both rejected the arbitrator's findings and went further, resolving the merits of the parties' dispute based on the court's assessment of the record before the arbitrator. For that reason, the court found further arbitration proceedings inappropriate. But again, established law ordinarily precludes a court from resolving the merits of the parties' dispute on the basis of its own factual determinations, no matter how erroneous the arbitrator's decision. *Misco, supra,* at 40, n. 10, 108 S.Ct. 364; see also *American Mfg. Co.,* 363 U.S. at 568, 80 S.Ct. 1343. Even when the arbitrator's award may properly be vacated, the appropriate remedy is to remand the case for further arbitration proceedings. *Misco, supra,* at 40, n. 10, 108 S.Ct. 364. The dissent suggests that the remedy described in *Misco* is limited to cases where the arbitrator's errors are procedural. *Post,* at 1729 (opinion of Stevens, J.) *Misco* did involve procedural issues, but our discussion regarding the appropriate remedy was not so limited. If a remand is appropriate *even* when the arbitrator's award has been set aside for "procedural aberrations" that constitute "affirmative misconduct," it follows that a remand ordinarily will be appropriate when the arbitrator simply made factual findings that the reviewing court perceives as "irrational." The Court of Appeals usurped the arbitrator's role by resolving the dispute and barring further proceedings, a result at odds with this governing law.[2]

For the foregoing reasons, the Court of Appeals erred in reversing the order of the District Court denying the motion to vacate the arbitrator's award, and it erred further in directing that judgment be entered in Garvey's favor. The judgment of the Court of Appeals is reversed, and the case is remanded for further proceedings consistent with this opinion.

It is so ordered.

[The concurring opinion of JUSTICE GINSBURG *has been omitted.]*

■ JUSTICE STEVENS, dissenting.

It is well settled that an arbitrator "does not sit to dispense his own brand of industrial justice." *Steelworkers v. Enterprise Wheel & Car Corp.,* 363 U.S. 593, 597, 80 S.Ct. 1358, 4 L.Ed.2d 1424 (1960). We have also said fairly definitively, albeit in dicta, that a court should remedy an arbitrator's "procedural aberrations" by vacating the award and remanding for further proceedings. *Paperworkers v. Misco, Inc.,* 484 U.S. 29, 40–41, n. 10, 108 S.Ct. 364, 98 L.Ed.2d 286 (1987). Our cases, however, do not provide significant guidance as to what standards a federal court should use in assessing whether an arbitrator's behavior is so untethered to either the agreement of the parties or the factual record so as to constitute an attempt to "dispense his own brand of industrial justice." . . .

Without the benefit of briefing or argument, today the Court resolves two difficult questions. First, it decides that even if the Court of Appeals' appraisal of the merits is correct—that is to say, even if the arbitrator did dispense his own brand of justice untethered to the agreement of the parties, and even if the correct disposition of the matter is perfectly clear—the only course open to a reviewing court is to remand the matter for another arbitration. That conclusion is not compelled by any of our cases, nor by any analysis offered by the Court. As the issue is subject to serious arguments on both sides, the Court should have set this case for argument if it wanted to answer this remedial question.

Second, without reviewing the record or soliciting briefing, the Court concludes that, in any event, "no serious error on the arbitrator's part is apparent in this case." *Ante,* at 1729, n. 2. At this stage in the proceedings, I simply cannot endorse that conclusion. After examining the record, obtaining briefing, and hearing oral argument, the Court of Appeals offered

2. In any event, no serious error on the arbitrator's part is apparent in this case . . . The arbitrator's explanation for his decision indicates that he simply found Smith an unreliable witness and that, in the absence of corroborating evidence, he could only conclude that Garvey failed to show that the Padres had offered to extend his contract. The arbitrator's analysis may have been unpersuasive to the Court of Appeals, but his decision hardly qualifies as serious error, let alone irrational or inexplicable error. And, as we have said, any such error would not justify the actions taken by the court.

a reasoned explanation of its conclusion. See 203 F.3d, at 589–592; see also *id.*, at 593–594 (Hawkins, J., concurring). Whether or not I would ultimately agree with the Ninth Circuit's analysis, I find the Court's willingness to reverse a factbound determination of the Court of Appeals without engaging that court's reasoning a troubling departure from our normal practice.[1]

Accordingly, I respectfully dissent.

* * *

Questions

1. Did the Court give serious consideration to the argument that the arbitrator had rendered a decision that was untethered to the parties' agreement? Note that *Garvey* is a per curiam decision. Note also that the Court accepted the amici brief of the National Academy of Arbitrators. Consider this explanation of what happened in *Garvey*:

> In petitioning for certiorari, lawyers for the Players Association said that the Ninth Circuit's decision in *Garvey* was so clearly erroneous that it warranted a summary reversal. 2001 WL 34091962. Counsel for Garvey contended that the Ninth Circuit's decision was consistent with Supreme Court precedent and, in any case, so dependent upon its unique facts that Supreme Court review was unwarranted. 2001 WL 34090262. An amicus brief by Professor David Feller, on behalf of the National Academy of Arbitrators, told the Court that, although the case did have its unique facts, it was an example of an egregious pattern in the lower federal courts. As he wrote:
>
>> Many of the lower federal courts have adopted a simple formula when faced with a decision with which they disagree: First set out the correct rule that a court has no business vacating an arbitration award simply because it believes it to be wrong. Cite *Enterprise* and *Misco*. Then, go ahead and find some reason why the particular award involved nevertheless has to be set aside because it is wrong.
>
> 2001 WL 34091989. Professor Feller agreed with the Players Association that oral argument was unnecessary, but, unlike the Association, he suggested that the lower courts needed stronger chastisement than a summary reversal would provide. He encouraged the Supreme Court to remind the lower courts at least every decade of the degree of deference required by *Misco*. He therefore urged the Court to do what

1. The Court's opinion is somewhat ambiguous as to its reasons for overturning the portion of the Court of Appeals' decision setting aside the arbitration. It is unclear whether the majority is saying that a court may never set aside an arbitration because of a factual error, no matter how perverse, or whether the Court merely holds that the error in this case was not sufficiently severe to allow a court to take that step. If it is the latter, the Court offers no explanation of what standards it is using or of its reasons for reaching that conclusion.

it ended up doing in *Garvey*, that is, dispensing with further briefing and oral argument and issuing an explanatory per curiam opinion.

Laura J. Cooper et al., ADR in the Workplace 97–98 (2d ed. 2005).

2. Which opinion in the *Garvey* case—the majority or the dissent—better applies the "essence test" from *Enterprise* and *Misco*?

3. How should a court review an arbitral award to determine whether the arbitrator acted within the scope of his authority and "dispense[s] his own brand of industrial justice" instead? Is the court permitted to review the record that was presented to the arbitrator? Is it compelled to do so? How deeply should a court delve into the underlying facts of the case to determine whether the arbitrator properly construed and applied the contract and acted within the scope of his authority? At what point does a review of the underlying factual record become a review of the merits of the dispute?

* * *

B. JUDICIAL REVIEW UNDER THE FEDERAL ARBITRATION ACT

1. JURISDICTION TO REVIEW ARBITRAL AWARDS

Although the Federal Arbitration Act is a federal statute, the Supreme Court has interpreted the statute as not itself bestowing jurisdiction on the federal district courts. Southland Corp. v. Keating, 465 U.S. 1, 16 n. 9 (1984) (The FAA "creates federal substantive law requiring the parties to honor arbitration agreements, [but] ... does not create any independent federal question ..."); Moses H. Cone Mem'l Hosp. v. Mercury Constr. Corp., 460 U.S. 1, 25 n. 32 (1983) ("The Arbitration Act is something of an anomaly in the field of federal-court jurisdiction. It creates a body of federal substantive law establishing and regulating the duty to honor an agreement to arbitrate, yet it does not create any independent federal-question jurisdiction").

A suit to confirm or vacate an arbitration award therefore belongs in state court unless there is either federal question jurisdiction or diversity jurisdiction. Case law concerning the application of both types of jurisdiction to suits to confirm or vacate arbitration awards is an awful mess.

a. FEDERAL QUESTION JURISDICTION

Prior to 2009, there was widespread agreement among the circuits that a federal court could not "look through" a suit to confirm or vacate to the underlying dispute to find jurisdiction. If, for example, the underlying dispute was a federal employment discrimination claim, that by itself would not suffice to confer federal jurisdiction—federal jurisdiction would exist, if at all, only if the suit to confirm or vacate *itself* created federal jurisdiction.

In 2009, however, the Supreme Court decided Vaden v. Discover Bank, ___ U.S. ___, 129 S.Ct. 1262, discussed in Chapter 1.3. In *Vaden*, the Court held that federal courts could "look through" a suit to compel arbitration to establish federal jurisdiction. Presumably, the same reasoning will apply to suits to confirm or vacate, though courts had not ruled on the issue prior to the date of this book's publication.

Adding further to the confusion is the conclusion of several circuits that suits to vacate arbitration awards on the ground that the arbitrator "manifestly disregarded the law" automatically confer federal question jurisdiction, whereas suits to vacate based on other grounds do not. The Second Circuit has explained:

> In contrast to grounds of review that concern the arbitration process itself—such as corruption or abuse of power—review for manifest disregard of federal law necessarily requires the reviewing court to do two things: first, determine what the federal law is, and second, determine whether the arbitrator's decision manifestly disregarded that law. This process so immerses the federal court in questions of federal law and their proper application that federal question subject matter jurisdiction is present.

Greenberg v. Bear, Stearns & Co., 220 F.3d 22, 27 (2d Cir. 2000); see also Luong v. Circuit City Stores, Inc., 368 F.3d 1109, 1112 (9th Cir. 2004). But this distinction may be invalid after the Supreme Court's decision in Hall Street Associates, L.L.C. v. Mattel, Inc., ___ U.S. ___, 128 S.Ct. 1396 (2008), which arguably held that manifest disregard is not a valid standard for judicial review. *Hall Street* will be discussed at length later in this chapter.

b. DIVERSITY JURISDICTION

Diversity jurisdiction exists when a case is between citizens of different states and the amount in controversy exceeds $75,000. The federal courts are divided over how to calculate the amount in controversy in a suit to confirm or vacate. For example, in Theis Research, Inc. v. Brown & Bain, 400 F.3d 659 (9th Cir. 2005), a client brought a $200 million malpractice arbitration claim against a law firm that previously had represented the client in an unsuccessful patent litigation suit. The arbitration resulted in a zero dollar award for each party. The client then sued in federal court to vacate, and sought to litigate the same $200 million claim that it had lost in arbitration. Before the court could reach the merits of the motion to vacate, it had to ascertain whether it had jurisdiction:

> If we measure the amount in controversy for purposes of [diversity jurisdiction] by the amount of the arbitration award, the district court lacked subject matter jurisdiction. If we measure the amount in controversy by the amount in dispute in the underlying litigation, the district court had subject matter jurisdiction.

The federal circuit courts have taken three different approaches to the issue.[1] One group of courts has held that the amount in controversy is

1. See generally Christopher L. Frost, *Welcome to the Jungle: Rethinking the Amount in Controversy in a Petition to Vacate an Arbitration Award Under the Federal Arbitration Act*, 32 Pepp. L. Rev. 227 (2005).

equal to the amount of the award regardless of how much was sought at the beginning of the arbitration proceeding.[2] In *Theis*, this would have yielded an amount in controversy of $0, and the federal court would have lacked jurisdiction.

Another group of courts has measured the amount in controversy by examining the amount sought in arbitration, as opposed to the actual amount awarded. This is the approach the *Theis* court took. By this calculation, the amount in controversy was $200 million, and the court had jurisdiction.

A third group of courts calculates the amount in controversy by reference to the amount sought in arbitration, but only if the suit to vacate asks the court to reopen the arbitration.[3] By this calculation, the amount in controversy is the amount awarded in arbitration plus the amount that would be at play if arbitration were reopened. A variation on this theme occurred in Choice Hotels Intern., Inc. v. Shiv Hospitality, L.L.C. 491 F.3d 171 (4th Cir. 2007), where one party sued, the other party successfully moved for a stay pending arbitration, and the arbitral loser then sought to re-open the original court case.

---

2. THE STATUTORY STANDARDS

The Federal Arbitration Act, Section 10, provides for vacating an award:

(1) where the award was procured by corruption, fraud, or undue means.

(2) where there was evident partiality or corruption in the arbitrators, or either of them.

(3) where the arbitrators were guilty of misconduct in refusing to postpone the hearing, upon sufficient cause shown, or in refusing to hear evidence pertinent and material the controversy; or of any other misbehavior by which the rights of any party have been prejudiced.

(4) where the arbitrators exceeded their powers, or so imperfectly executed them that a mutual, final, and definite award upon the subject matter submitted was not made.

The first three grounds do not go to the merits of the arbitral award, but rather to the nature of the arbitral process. Although the first phrase in subsection (4) suggests that an award can be overturned if the arbitrators

2. See Baltin v. Alaron Trading Corp., 128 F.3d 1466, 1472 (11th Cir. 1997) (holding that because the amount sought to be vacated was only $36,284.69, there was a "legal certainty" that the amount in controversy could not be met).

3. Peebles v. Merrill Lynch, Pierce, Fenner & Smith Inc., 431 F.3d 1320, 1325–26 (11th Cir. 2005); Sirotzky v. N.Y. Stock Exchange, 347 F.3d 985, 989 (7th Cir. 2003).

exceeded their powers, the remainder of the subsection refers to judicial review for process defects rather than a substantive review of the merits.

* * *

Merrill Lynch, Pierce, Fenner & Smith, Inc. v. Clemente

272 Fed. Appx. 174 (3d Cir. 2008).

■ FISHER, CIRCUIT JUDGE.

Michael Clemente and Geraldine Waszkiewicz ("the plaintiffs") appeal the District Court's order, which denied their motion to vacate an arbitration award, and instead confirmed the award. The arbitration award dismissed the plaintiffs' claims against Kevin Nohilly, Gustav Albert Fingado, and Merrill Lynch, Pierce, Fenner & Smith, Inc. ("the defendants"), and denied them any relief. For the reasons set forth below, we will affirm the order of the District Court.

I.

... The plaintiffs held accounts with Merrill Lynch at its Freehold, New Jersey office. Kevin Nohilly, a Financial Advisor for Merrill Lynch, initially advised both of the plaintiffs. However, after the plaintiffs divorced in 2000, they split their assets and Clemente sought the advice of Gus Fingado, the Resident Manager of the Freehold office, while Waszkiewicz continued to use Nohilly's services.

On January 29, 2004, the plaintiffs filed a Statement of Claim with the National Association of Securities Dealers, Inc. ("NASD"), alleging that the defendants had violated tort law, contract law, and New Jersey criminal law, in their dealings with the plaintiffs. These claims stem from an alleged "stop-loss order" that would have bound Nohilly, and later Fingado, to either liquidate or convert the plaintiffs' investments if the value of the investments dropped by a certain percentage.

The parties agreed to resolve the matter in an arbitration proceeding under the NASD using a panel of three arbitrators. Between May and August 2006, the panel conducted a fourteen-day arbitration hearing. On August 7, 2006, the panel issued their [sic] award, dismissing the plaintiffs' claims, denying all relief to the plaintiffs, and assessing the fees each party must pay. The defendants filed a motion with the United States District Court for the District of New Jersey, seeking to confirm the award. The plaintiffs filed a cross motion, seeking to vacate the award. The District Court granted the defendants' motion to confirm the award, and denied the plaintiffs' motion to vacate the award. This timely appeal followed.

II.

The District Court had jurisdiction under 9 U.S.C. § 9, and we have jurisdiction under 9 U.S.C. § 16(a)(1)(D). We exercise de novo review over the District Court's denial of a motion to vacate an arbitration award. *Dluhos v. Strasberg,* 321 F.3d 365, 369 (3d Cir. 2003). Our review of the arbitrator's decision, however, is "extremely deferential." *Id.* at 370. "The net result . . . is generally to affirm easily the arbitration award." *Id.*

III.

A.

The plaintiffs argue that the District Court erred in denying the motion to vacate the arbitration award because the panel of arbitrators were corrupt and biased in violation of the Federal Arbitration Act ("FAA"). The FAA permits a court to vacate the award "(1) where the award was procured by corruption, fraud, or undue means; [or] (2) where there was evident partiality or corruption in the arbitrators, or either of them[.]" 9 U.S.C. § 10(a). Thus, "[v]acatur is appropriate only in 'exceedingly narrow' circumstances[.]" *Metromedia Energy, Inc. v. Enserch Energy Servs.*, 409 F.3d 574, 578 (3d Cir. 2005).

In demonstrating bias, we require a showing of "evident partiality," meaning that "the challenging party must show a reasonable person would have to conclude that the arbitrator was partial to the other party to the arbitration." *Kaplan v. First Options of Chicago, Inc.*, 19 F.3d 1503, 1523 n. 30 (3d Cir. 1994) (internal quotation marks and citation omitted). Moreover, "evident partiality is strong language and requires proof of circumstances powerfully suggestive of bias." *Id.* (internal quotation marks and citation omitted).

The instances that the plaintiffs cite as demonstrating the arbitrator's bias do not rise to the level of demonstrating "evident partiality." First, the plaintiffs argue that the defendants' counsel and one of the arbitrators had an exchange in which counsel gave the arbitrator an empty binder, and the two joked that cash was inside the binder. The joke, while not in the best judgment of either the arbitrator or counsel, does not "powerfully suggest [ ]" that the arbitrator was so biased that he could not render a fair decision, especially considering that it was clearly a joke that was heard by everyone at the hearing. Second, the plaintiffs allege that the same arbitrator and Merrill Lynch personnel had ex parte communications, and argue that the arbitrator "likely determined . . . that they were really 'a bunch of nice guys,' " passed these sentiments on to the fellow panelists, and the three panelists decided to find in the defendants' favor as a result. This argument is, at best, speculative, and is far too tenuous for a reasonable person to conclude that the three panelists were biased in favor of the defendants. Finally, the plaintiffs allege that the same arbitrator possibly communicated with a Smith Barney executive regarding this arbitration because, when the plaintiffs contacted the executive, he stated that he was aware that the arbitrator was on this panel. They argue that this alleged communication constituted witness tampering. However, the plaintiffs have offered no proof as to how the executive knew the identity of the arbitrator; thus, any theory is once again speculative, and even if it were true, the contact involved one arbitrator, not the panel. Moreover, Mr. Clemente testified that the executive's reason for not serving as a witness for the plaintiffs was because he served on other arbitration panels, not because of any contact with the arbitrator, thus negating any suggestion of witness tampering.

Based on the foregoing, we cannot "conclude that the [panel of] arbitrator[s] w[ere] partial to the other party to the arbitration." *Kaplan,* 19 F.3d at 1523 n. 30. Therefore, we cannot vacate the arbitration award because the evidence does not demonstrate that the arbitrators were corrupt or biased.[5]

The plaintiffs also argue that the District Court erred in denying the motion to vacate the arbitration award because the panel of arbitrators "manifestly disregarded the law." We have stated that one of the "exceedingly narrow circumstances" in which vacatur is appropriate includes "where an arbitration panel manifestly disregards, rather than merely erroneously interprets, the law." *Metromedia Energy,* 409 F.3d at 578.

The plaintiffs argue that they presented the panel with a document that was "the equivalent of a smoking gun," and as a result, any decision other than one in favor of the plaintiffs demonstrated a "manifest disregard" of the laws of negligence and fraud. However, the authenticity of this document, which was a fax on Merrill Lynch's letterhead discussing the plaintiffs' instructions regarding their "stop-loss" order, was a contested issue during the arbitration proceedings. Thus, the panel's decision did not demonstrate that it made a choice to manifestly disregard the law, but instead only that it made a choice not to credit a document as authentic. This question was one of fact, not of law, and therefore, we cannot find that the panel manifestly disregarded the applicable laws of negligence and fraud. . . .

IV.

We have considered the parties' remaining arguments and find them without merit. For these reasons, we will affirm the order of the District Court.

* * *

Lunsford v. RBC Dain Rauscher, Inc.

590 F.Supp.2d 1153, 1158 (D. Minn. 2008).

■ DAVID S. DOTY, DISTRICT JUDGE.

This matter is before the court on cross-petitions by pro se petitioners to vacate the arbitration award and by respondents to confirm the award

5. The plaintiffs further argue that the District Court erred in denying the plaintiffs' request to conduct discovery on these matters. We review the District Court's denial of discovery for an abuse of discretion. *Brumfield v. Sanders,* 232 F.3d 376, 380 (3d Cir. 2000). In the present case, plaintiffs' counsel admitted to the District Court that he thought it was "highly unlikely" that the arbitrator engaged in misconduct, but argued that because it was not "impossible," he should be allowed to conduct discovery. The District Court concluded that the plaintiffs' assertions of misconduct were unsupported, and there was no appearance of impartiality on the part of the arbitrators. We cannot conclude that the District Court abused its discretion in choosing not to permit discovery, particularly considering that plaintiffs' counsel even admitted that it was "highly unlikely" that an impropriety actually occurred.

and dismiss all remaining claims. Based upon a review of the file, record and proceedings herein, and for the following reasons, the court denies the petition to vacate, confirms the arbitration award and dismisses the remaining claims.

BACKGROUND

Defendant RBC Dain Correspondent Services ("RBC") is a securities clearing house that helps brokerage firms establish securities accounts. Defendant Nations Financial Group, Inc. ("Nations Financial") is a brokerage firm assisted by RBC and employs defendants Scott Bennett, Tom Leechin ("Leechin") and Lori LeBarge. Plaintiffs are prisoners, or former prisoners, at the Federal Correctional Institute in Edgeville, South Carolina who established securities accounts in 2003 and 2004 at Nations Financial through Leechin, their broker-representative.

On March 27, 2006, plaintiffs filed an amended complaint against defendants, asserting seven claims arising from defendants' disputed decision to no longer maintain plaintiffs' financial accounts. . . .

Defendants moved to stay the litigation and compel arbitration on April 11, 2006 [pursuant to a predispute arbitration agreement contained in the plaintiffs' Customer Agreement with defendants]. On September 28, 2006, the court [granted the motion].

On February 20, 2007, [plaintiffs] initiated a Financial Industry Regulatory Authority ("FINRA") arbitration proceeding against RBC, Nations Financial and Leechin asserting the securities claims and violation of the Equal Credit Opportunity Act. In November 2007, plaintiffs demanded an evidentiary hearing before the Panel. A telephonic hearing was held on March 13, 2008, during which the Panel considered the pleadings, testimony and evidence presented.[5] During this hearing, plaintiffs did not cross-examine defendants, the Panel denied plaintiffs' requests to subpoena recordings of their phone conversations with Leechin and the Panel did not consider Nations Financial's compliance manuals. The Panel rejected plaintiffs' claims on March 19, 2008 in a written order. Plaintiffs then moved in this court to vacate the award and rule on the merits of their claims for omission or misstatements of material facts pursuant to 15 U.S.C. § 78j(b) and control person liability under 15 U.S.C. § 78(t). Defendants moved to confirm the arbitration award and dismiss all remaining claims on July 30, 2008.

DISCUSSION

Plaintiffs argue that the Panel's failure to consider certain evidence requires vacation of the arbitration award. Judicial review of an arbitration

5. The record does not identify the evidence presented at the hearing or relied on by the Panel in making its final decision.

award is "extremely limited." *Kiernan v. Piper Jaffray Cos.,* 137 F.3d 588, 594 (8th Cir. 1998). The underlying award is entitled to an "extraordinary level of deference." *Stark v. Sandberg, Phoenix & von Gontard, P.C.,* 381 F.3d 793, 798 (8th Cir. 2004). The court may not substitute judicial resolution of disputed issues for an arbitrator's decision. *United Paperworkers Int'l Union v. Misco, Inc.,* 484 U.S. 29, 40–41 n. 10, 108 S.Ct. 364, 98 L.Ed.2d 286 (1987); *Gas Aggregation Servs., Inc. v. Howard Avista Energy, LLC,* 319 F.3d 1060, 1064 (8th Cir. 2003). Once parties submit a dispute to arbitration, the merits of the resulting arbitration award simply are not within the purview of the court. *Gas Aggregation,* 319 F.3d at 1064. The court must confirm an award so long as an arbitrator "even arguably" construes or applies the underlying contract. *Stark,* 381 F.3d at 798.

Arbitration awards, however, are not inviolate, and the court need not merely rubber stamp the arbitrators' interpretations and decisions. *Id.* The court can vacate the award under one of a limited number of statutorily or judicially recognized grounds. *See* 9 U.S.C. § 10. One such ground is where the arbitrators refused to hear evidence pertinent and material to the controversy. *Id.* § 10(a). To warrant vacation of an award, an arbitrator's refusal to hear evidence must either be in "bad faith or so gross as to amount to affirmative misconduct." *Misco, Inc.,* 484 U.S. at 40, 108 S.Ct. 364.

Plaintiffs first argue that they should have been allowed to cross-examine the defendants in-person at the evidentiary hearing. Arbitrators generally exercise broad discretion to limit cross-examination. *See Dow Corning Corp. v. Safety Nat'l Cas. Corp.,* 335 F.3d 742, 752 (8th Cir. 2003) (arbitration panel properly limited cross-examination). Here, the Panel's pre-hearing order did not contemplate cross-examination but plaintiffs could have requested that the Panel subpoena defendants for examination. *See* FINRA Code of Arb. Rule 10322(b) (describing procedure for issuance of subpoenas to parties). Without such a request, the Panel's failure to permit cross-examination does not reflect bad faith or amount to affirmative misconduct. Further, the arbitration agreement gave the Panel the ultimate authority to determine the location of the evidentiary hearing and plaintiffs were not prejudiced by testifying telephonically. *See* FINRA Code of Arb. R. 10315(a); *see also Gedatus v. RBC Dain Rauscher, Inc.,* No. 07–1750, 2008 WL 216297, at *4 (D. Minn. Jan. 23, 2008) (petitioner not prejudiced by presentation of telephonic testimony); *cf. Thornton v. Snyder,* 428 F.3d 690, 698 (7th Cir. 2005) (Federal Rule of Civil Procedure 43 allows testimony to be taken "by contemporaneous transmission from a different location"). Therefore, the Panel's decision to conduct a telephonic hearing does not require vacation of the arbitration award.

Second, plaintiffs argue that the Panel should have considered their alleged phone conversations with Leechin. The Panel denied several requests by plaintiffs to subpoena recordings of the conversations but allowed plaintiffs to testify about the conversations during the telephonic hearing. *See* FINRA Code of Arb. R. 10322(c) (arbitrator decides whether to issue subpoena). After considering plaintiffs' testimony, the Panel concluded that the recordings were immaterial to its award. *See* FINRA Code of Arb. R. 10323 (arbitrators determine relevance of evidence). Based upon the Panel's conduct, the court determines that its decision not to subpoena the recordings does not reflect bad faith or amount to affirmative misconduct. *See Marshall v. Green Giant Co.,* 942 F.2d 539, 550–51 (8th Cir. 1991) (plaintiff not prejudiced by inability to present evidence when arbitrator determined evidence to be irrelevant).

Lastly, plaintiffs argue that the Panel improperly refused to consider Nations Financial's compliance manuals, which plaintiffs allege contained information related to the taped phone recordings between plaintiffs and Leechin. On July 6, 2007, the arbitration panel ordered defendants to produce the manuals. (Pls.' Ex. C.) Plaintiffs indicate that they never received the documents and argue that they were denied the opportunity to address the issue because the Panel cancelled a pre-hearing conference scheduled for November 13, 2007. However, a pre-hearing conference was held on December 6, 2007, and there is no evidence that plaintiffs raised the issue at that time. Further, plaintiffs offer no arguments in support of the materiality of the manuals in light of the Panel's finding that the phone conversations between plaintiffs and Leechin were irrelevant. Consequently, the court determines that the Panel did not engage in affirmative misconduct or act in bad faith by failing to address plaintiffs' concerns regarding the compliance manuals. Accordingly, the court confirms the Panel's award. . . .

CONCLUSION

Accordingly, based upon the file, record and proceedings herein, IT IS HEREBY ORDERED that:

1. Plaintiffs' petition to vacate the arbitration award is denied; [and]

2. Defendants' petition to confirm the arbitration award is granted . . .

* * *

Questions

1. As *Clemente* and *Lunsford* illustrate, judicial deference under the statutory standards to arbitration awards is high and the likelihood of a successful challenge is low. Why, then, do so many arbitral losers appeal?

2. Recall from Chapter 3 that arbitrators are not bound by the rules of civil procedure or evidence. The effect of this is to further insulate arbitral awards from judicial review.

3. In *Clemente*, if the plaintiff's counsel had not admitted that it was "highly unlikely" that the arbitrator had engaged in misconduct, should the court have ordered discovery?

4. Note the attempt of the *Clemente* plaintiffs to frame their challenge under "manifest disregard." Many courts have re-framed the statutory bases for review as review under the "manifest disregard" standard. This extra-statutory ground for challenging an arbitral award will be discussed in Chapter 4.1.B.4 below.

* * *

3. BARGAINED–FOR REVIEW STANDARDS

Hall Street Associates, L.L.C. v. Mattel, Inc.

___ U.S. ___, 128 S.Ct. 1396 (2008).

■ JUSTICE SOUTER delivered the opinion of the Court.*

The Federal Arbitration Act (FAA or Act), 9 U.S.C. § 1 *et seq.*, provides for expedited judicial review to confirm, vacate, or modify arbitration awards. §§ 9–11 (2000 ed. and Supp. V). The question here is whether statutory grounds for prompt vacatur and modification may be supplemented by contract. We hold that the statutory grounds are exclusive.

I

This case began as a lease dispute between landlord, petitioner Hall Street Associates, L.L.C., and tenant, respondent Mattel, Inc. The property was used for many years as a manufacturing site, and the leases provided that the tenant would indemnify the landlord for any costs resulting from the failure of the tenant or its predecessor lessees to follow environmental laws while using the premises. App. 88–89.

Tests of the property's well water in 1998 showed high levels of trichloroethylene (TCE), the apparent residue of manufacturing discharges by Mattel's predecessors between 1951 and 1980. After the Oregon Department of Environmental Quality (DEQ) discovered even more pollutants, Mattel stopped drawing from the well and, along with one of its predecessors, signed a consent order with the DEQ providing for cleanup of the site.

After Mattel gave notice of intent to terminate the lease in 2001, Hall Street filed this suit, contesting Mattel's right to vacate on the date it gave, and claiming that the lease obliged Mattel to indemnify Hall Street for costs of cleaning up the TCE, among other things. Following a bench trial before the United States District Court for the District of Oregon, Mattel won on the termination issue, and after an unsuccessful try at mediating the indemnification claim, the parties proposed to submit to arbitration. The District Court was amenable, and the parties drew up an arbitration agreement, which the court approved and entered as an order. One paragraph of the agreement provided that

> [t]he United States District Court for the District of Oregon may enter judgment upon any award, either by confirming the award or by

* Justice Scalia joins all but footnote 7 of this opinion.

> vacating, modifying or correcting the award. The Court shall vacate, modify or correct any award: (i) where the arbitrator's findings of facts are not supported by substantial evidence, or (ii) where the arbitrator's conclusions of law are erroneous. App. to Pet. for Cert. 16a.

Arbitration took place, and the arbitrator decided for Mattel. In particular, he held that no indemnification was due, because the lease obligation to follow all applicable federal, state, and local environmental laws did not require compliance with the testing requirements of the Oregon Drinking Water Quality Act (Oregon Act); that Act the arbitrator characterized as dealing with human health as distinct from environmental contamination.

Hall Street then filed a District Court Motion for Order Vacating, Modifying And/Or Correcting the arbitration decision, App. 4, on the ground that failing to treat the Oregon Act as an applicable environmental law under the terms of the lease was legal error. The District Court agreed, vacated the award, and remanded for further consideration by the arbitrator. The court expressly invoked the standard of review chosen by the parties in the arbitration agreement, which included review for legal error, and cited *LaPine Technology Corp. v. Kyocera Corp.*, 130 F.3d 884, 889 (C.A.9 1997), for the proposition that the FAA leaves the parties "free . . . to draft a contract that sets rules for arbitration and dictates an alternative standard of review." App. to Pet. for Cert. 46a.

On remand, the arbitrator followed the District Court's ruling that the Oregon Act was an applicable environmental law and amended the decision to favor Hall Street. This time, each party sought modification, and again the District Court applied the parties' stipulated standard of review for legal error, correcting the arbitrator's calculation of interest but otherwise upholding the award. Each party then appealed to the Court of Appeals for the Ninth Circuit, where Mattel switched horses and contended that . . . the arbitration agreement's provision for judicial review of legal error unenforceable. Hall Street countered that . . . the agreement's judicial review provision was not severable from the submission to arbitration.

The Ninth Circuit reversed in favor of Mattel . . . The Circuit instructed the District Court on remand to

> return to the application to confirm the original arbitration award (not the subsequent award revised after reversal), and . . . confirm that award, unless . . . the award should be vacated on the grounds allowable under 9 U.S.C. § 10, or modified or corrected under the grounds allowable under 9 U.S.C. § 11. *Id.*, at 273.

After the District Court again held for Hall Street and the Ninth Circuit again reversed, we granted certiorari to decide whether the grounds for vacatur and modification provided by §§ 10 and 11 of the FAA are exclusive. 550 U.S. 968, 127 S.Ct. 2875, 167 L.Ed.2d 1151 (2007). We agree with the Ninth Circuit that they are, but vacate and remand for consideration of independent issues.

II

Congress enacted the FAA to replace judicial indisposition to arbitration with a "national policy favoring [it] and plac[ing] arbitration agreements on equal footing with all other contracts." *Buckeye Check Cashing, Inc. v. Cardegna,* 546 U.S. 440, 443, 126 S.Ct. 1204, 163 L.Ed.2d 1038 (2006).... The Act also supplies mechanisms for enforcing arbitration awards: a judicial decree confirming an award, an order vacating it, or an order modifying or correcting it. §§ 9–11. An application for any of these orders will get streamlined treatment as a motion, obviating the separate contract action that would usually be necessary to enforce or tinker with an arbitral award in court. § 6. Under the terms of § 9, a court "must" confirm an arbitration award "unless" it is vacated, modified, or corrected "as prescribed" in §§ 10 and 11. Section 10 lists grounds for vacating an award, while § 11 names those for modifying or correcting one.

The Courts of Appeals have split over the exclusiveness of these statutory grounds when parties take the FAA shortcut to confirm, vacate, or modify an award, with some saying the recitations are exclusive, and others regarding them as mere threshold provisions open to expansion by agreement.... We now hold that §§ 10 and 11 respectively provide the FAA's exclusive grounds for expedited vacatur and modification.

III

Hall Street makes two main efforts to show that the grounds set out for vacating or modifying an award are not exclusive, taking the position, first, that expandable judicial review authority has been accepted as the law since *Wilko v. Swan,* 346 U.S. 427, 74 S.Ct. 182, 98 L.Ed. 168 (1953). This, however, was not what *Wilko* decided, which was that § 14 of the Securities Act of 1933 voided any agreement to arbitrate claims of violations of that Act, see *id.,* at 437–438, 74 S.Ct. 182, a holding since overruled by *Rodriguez de Quijas v. Shearson/American Express, Inc.*, 490 U.S. 477, 484, 109 S.Ct. 1917, 104 L.Ed.2d 526 (1989). Although it is true that the Court's discussion includes some language arguably favoring Hall Street's position, arguable is as far as it goes.

The *Wilko* Court was explaining that arbitration would undercut the Securities Act's buyer protections when it remarked (citing FAA § 10) that "[p]ower to vacate an [arbitration] award is limited," 346 U.S., at 436, 74 S.Ct. 182, and went on to say that "the interpretations of the law by the arbitrators in contrast to manifest disregard [of the law] are not subject, in the federal courts, to judicial review for error in interpretation," *id.,* at 436–437, 74 S.Ct. 182. Hall Street reads this statement as recognizing "manifest disregard of the law" as a further ground for vacatur on top of those listed in § 10, and some Circuits have read it the same way [citations omitted]. Hall Street sees this supposed addition to § 10 as the camel's nose: if judges can add grounds to vacate (or modify), so can contracting parties.

But this is too much for *Wilko* to bear. Quite apart from its leap from a supposed judicial expansion by interpretation to a private expansion by contract, Hall Street overlooks the fact that the statement it relies on expressly rejects just what Hall Street asks for here, general review for an arbitrator's legal errors. Then there is the vagueness of *Wilko*'s phrasing. Maybe the term "manifest disregard" was meant to name a new ground for review, but maybe it merely referred to the § 10 grounds collectively, rather than adding to them. See, *e.g., Mitsubishi Motors Corp. v. Soler Chrysler–Plymouth, Inc.,* 473 U.S. 614, 656, 105 S.Ct. 3346, 87 L.Ed.2d 444 (1985) (STEVENS, J., dissenting) ("Arbitration awards are only reviewable for manifest disregard of the law, 9 U.S.C. §§ 10, 207"); *I/S Stavborg v. National Metal Converters, Inc.,* 500 F.2d 424, 431 (C.A.2 1974). Or, as some courts have thought, "manifest disregard" may have been shorthand for § 10(a)(3) or § 10(a)(4), the subsections authorizing vacatur when the arbitrators were "guilty of misconduct" or "exceeded their powers." See, *e.g., Kyocera, supra,* at 997. We, when speaking as a Court, have merely taken the *Wilko* language as we found it, without embellishment, see *First Options of Chicago, Inc. v. Kaplan,* 514 U.S. 938, 942, 115 S.Ct. 1920, 131 L.Ed.2d 985 (1995), and now that its meaning is implicated, we see no reason to accord it the significance that Hall Street urges.

Second, Hall Street says that the agreement to review for legal error ought to prevail simply because arbitration is a creature of contract, and the FAA is "motivated, first and foremost, by a congressional desire to enforce agreements into which parties ha[ve] entered." *Dean Witter Reynolds Inc. v. Byrd,* 470 U.S. 213, 220, 105 S.Ct. 1238, 84 L.Ed.2d 158 (1985). But, again, we think the argument comes up short. Hall Street is certainly right that the FAA lets parties tailor some, even many features of arbitration by contract, including the way arbitrators are chosen, what their qualifications should be, which issues are arbitrable, along with procedure and choice of substantive law. But to rest this case on the general policy of treating arbitration agreements as enforceable as such would be to beg the question, which is whether the FAA has textual features at odds with enforcing a contract to expand judicial review following the arbitration.

To that particular question we think the answer is yes, that the text compels a reading of the §§ 10 and 11 categories as exclusive. To begin with, even if we assumed §§ 10 and 11 could be supplemented to some extent, it would stretch basic interpretive principles to expand the stated grounds to the point of evidentiary and legal review generally. Sections 10 and 11, after all, address egregious departures from the parties' agreed-upon arbitration: "corruption," "fraud," "evident partiality," "misconduct," "misbehavior," "exceed[ing] ... powers," "evident material miscalculation," "evident material mistake," "award[s] upon a matter not submitted;" the only ground with any softer focus is "imperfect[ions]," and a court may correct those only if they go to "[a] matter of form not affecting the merits." Given this emphasis on extreme arbitral conduct, the old rule of *ejusdem generis* has an implicit lesson to teach here. Under that rule, when a statute sets out a series of specific items ending with a general term, that general term is confined to covering subjects comparable to the specifics it follows. Since a general term included in the text is normally so limited, then surely a statute with no textual hook for expansion cannot authorize contracting parties to supplement review for specific instances of outrageous conduct with review for just any legal error. "Fraud" and a mistake of law are not cut from the same cloth.

That aside, expanding the detailed categories would rub too much against the grain of the § 9 language, where provision for judicial confirmation carries no hint of flexibility. On application for an order confirming the arbitration award, the court "must grant" the order "unless the award is vacated, modified, or corrected as prescribed in sections 10 and 11 of this title." There is nothing malleable about "must grant," which unequivocally tells courts to grant confirmation in all cases, except when one of the "prescribed" exceptions applies. This does not sound remotely like a provision meant to tell a court what to do just in case the parties say nothing else.

In fact, anyone who thinks Congress might have understood § 9 as a default provision should turn back to § 5 for an example of what Congress thought a default provision would look like:

> "[I]f in the agreement provision be made for a method of naming or appointing an arbitrator ... such method shall be followed; but if no method be provided therein, or if a method be provided and any party thereto shall fail to avail himself of such method, ... then upon the application of either party to the controversy the court shall designate and appoint an arbitrator...."

"[I]f no method be provided" is a far cry from "must grant ... unless" in § 9.

Instead of fighting the text, it makes more sense to see the three provisions, §§ 9–11, as substantiating a national policy favoring arbitration with just the limited review needed to maintain arbitration's essential virtue of resolving disputes straightaway. Any other reading opens the door to the full-bore legal and evidentiary appeals that can "rende[r] informal arbitration merely a prelude to a more cumbersome and time-consuming judicial review process," *Kyocera,* 341 F.3d, at 998; cf. *Ethyl Corp. v. United Steelworkers of America,* 768 F.2d 180, 184 (C.A.7 1985), and bring arbitration theory to grief in post-arbitration process....

When all these arguments based on prior legal authority are done with, Hall Street and Mattel remain at odds over what happens next. Hall Street and its *amici* say parties will flee from arbitration if expanded review is not open to them. See, *e.g.,* Brief for Petitioner 39; Brief for New England Legal Foundation et al. as *Amici Curiae* 15. One of Mattel's *amici* foresees flight from the courts if it is. See Brief for U.S. Council for Int'l Business as *Amicus Curiae* 29–30. We do not know who, if anyone, is right, and so cannot say whether the exclusivity reading of the statute is more of a threat to the popularity of arbitrators or to that of courts. But whatever the consequences of our holding, the statutory text gives us no business to expand the statutory grounds.[7]

7. The [legislative] history of the FAA is consistent with our conclusion....

IV

In holding that §§ 10 and 11 provide exclusive regimes for the review provided by the statute, we do not purport to say that they exclude more searching review based on authority outside the statute as well. The FAA is not the only way into court for parties wanting review of arbitration awards: they may contemplate enforcement under state statutory or common law, for example, where judicial review of different scope is arguable. But here we speak only to the scope of the expeditious judicial review under §§ 9, 10, and 11, deciding nothing about other possible avenues for judicial enforcement of arbitration awards....

One unusual feature, however, prompted some of us to question whether the case should be approached another way. The arbitration agreement was entered into in the course of district-court litigation, was submitted to the District Court as a request to deviate from the standard sequence of trial procedure, and was adopted by the District Court as an order. See App. 46–47; App. to Pet. for Cert. 4a–8a. Hence a question raised by this Court at oral argument: should the agreement be treated as an exercise of the District Court's authority to manage its cases under Federal Rules of Civil Procedure 16? See, *e.g.,* Tr. of Oral Arg. 11–12. Supplemental briefing at the Court's behest joined issue on the question, and it appears that Hall Street suggested something along these lines in the Court of Appeals, which did not address the suggestion.

We are, however, in no position to address the question now, beyond noting the claim of relevant case management authority independent of the FAA. The parties' supplemental arguments on the subject in this Court implicate issues of waiver and the relation of the FAA both to Rule 16 and the Alternative Dispute Resolution Act of 1998, 28 U.S.C. § 651 *et seq.*, none of which has been considered previously in this litigation, or could be well addressed for the first time here. We express no opinion on these matters beyond leaving them open for Hall Street to press on remand. If the Court of Appeals finds they are open, the court may consider whether the District Court's authority to manage litigation independently warranted that court's order on the mode of resolving the indemnification issues remaining in this case....

Although we agree with the Ninth Circuit that the FAA confines its expedited judicial review to the grounds listed in 9 U.S.C. §§ 10 and 11, we vacate the judgment and remand the case for proceedings consistent with this opinion.

It is so ordered.

■ JUSTICE STEVENS, with whom JUSTICE KENNEDY joins, dissenting.

May parties to an ongoing lawsuit agree to submit their dispute to arbitration subject to the caveat that the trial judge should refuse to enforce an award that rests on an erroneous conclusion of law? Prior to Congress' enactment of the Federal Arbitration Act (FAA or Act) in 1925, the answer to that question would surely have been "Yes."[1] Today, however, the Court holds that the FAA does not merely authorize the vacation or enforcement of awards on specified grounds, but also forbids enforcement of perfectly reasonable judicial review provisions in arbitration agreements fairly negotiated by the parties and approved by the district court. Because this result conflicts with the primary purpose of the FAA and ignores the historical context in which the Act was passed, I respectfully dissent.

Section 2 . . ., which is the centerpiece of the FAA, reflects Congress' main goal in passing the legislation: "to abrogate the general common-law rule against specific enforcement of arbitration agreements," *Southland Corp. v. Keating,* 465 U.S. 1, 18, 104 S.Ct. 852, 79 L.Ed.2d 1 (1984) (Stevens, J., concurring in part and dissenting in part), and to "ensur[e] that private arbitration agreements are enforced according to their terms," *Volt Information Sciences, Inc. v. Board of Trustees of Leland Stanford Junior Univ.,* 489 U.S. 468, 478, 109 S.Ct. 1248, 103 L.Ed.2d 488 (1989). Given this settled understanding of the core purpose of the FAA, the interests favoring enforceability of parties' arbitration agreements are stronger today than before the FAA was enacted. As such, there is more—and certainly not less—reason to give effect to parties' fairly negotiated decisions to provide for judicial review of arbitration awards for errors of law.

. . . As I read the Court's opinion, it identifies two possible reasons for [interpreting the FAA as setting forth the exclusive grounds for modification or vacation of an arbitration award]: (1) a supposed *quid pro quo* bargain between Congress and litigants that conditions expedited federal enforcement of arbitration awards on acceptance of a statutory limit on the scope of judicial review of such awards; and (2) an assumption that Congress intended to include the words "and no other" in the grounds specified in §§ 10 and 11 for the vacatur and modification of awards. Neither reason is persuasive.

While § 9 of the FAA imposes a 1-year limit on the time in which any party to an arbitration may apply for confirmation of an award, the statute does not require that the application be given expedited treatment. Of course, the premise of the entire statute is an assumption that the arbitration process may be more expeditious and less costly than ordinary litigation, but that is a reason for interpreting the statute liberally to favor the parties' use of arbitration. An unnecessary refusal to enforce a perfectly reasonable category of arbitration agreements defeats the primary purpose of the statute.

That purpose also provides a sufficient response to the Court's reliance on statutory text. It is true that a wooden application of "the old rule of *ejusdem generis,*" *ante,* at 1404, might support an inference that the categories listed in §§ 10 and 11 are exclusive, but the literal text does not compel that reading—a reading that is flatly inconsistent with the over-

1. See *Klein v. Catara,* 14 F. Cas. 732, 735 (C.C.D.Mass. 1814) ("If the parties wish to reserve the law for the decision of the court, they may stipulate to that effect in the submission; they may restrain or enlarge its operation as they please") (Story, J.). . . .

riding interest in effectuating the clearly expressed intent of the contracting parties. A listing of grounds that must always be available to contracting parties simply does not speak to the question whether they may agree to additional grounds for judicial review.

Moreover, in light of the historical context and the broader purpose of the FAA, §§ 10 and 11 are best understood as a shield meant to protect parties from hostile courts, not a sword with which to cut down parties' "valid, irrevocable and enforceable" agreements to arbitrate their disputes subject to judicial review for errors of law. § 2.

Even if I thought the narrow issue presented in this case were as debatable as the conflict among the courts of appeals suggests, I would rely on a presumption of overriding importance to resolve the debate and rule in favor of petitioner's position that the FAA permits the statutory grounds for vacatur and modification of an award to be supplemented by contract. A decision "*not to regulate*" the terms of an agreement that does not even arguably offend any public policy whatsoever, "is adequately justified by a presumption in favor of freedom." *FCC v. Beach Communications, Inc.*, 508 U.S. 307, 320, 113 S.Ct. 2096, 124 L.Ed.2d 211 (1993) (Stevens, J., concurring in judgment).

Accordingly, while I agree that the judgment of the Court of Appeals must be set aside, and that there may be additional avenues available for judicial enforcement of parties' fairly negotiated review provisions, see, *ante,* at 1406—1408, I respectfully dissent from the Court's interpretation of the FAA, and would direct the Court of Appeals to affirm the judgment of the District Court enforcing the arbitrator's final award.

■ JUSTICE BREYER, dissenting.

The question presented in this case is whether "the Federal Arbitration Act ... *precludes* a federal court from enforcing" an arbitration agreement that gives the court the power to set aside an arbitration award that embodies an arbitrator's mistake about the law. Pet. for Cert. i. Like the majority and Justice Stevens, and primarily for the reasons they set forth, I believe that the Act does not *preclude* enforcement of such an agreement.... At the same time, I see no need to send the case back for further judicial decisionmaking. The agreement here was entered into with the consent of the parties and the approval of the District Court. Aside from the Federal Arbitration Act itself, 9 U.S.C. § 1 *et seq.*, respondent below pointed to no statute, rule, or other relevant public policy that the agreement might violate. The Court has now rejected its argument that the agreement violates the Act, and I would simply remand the case with instructions that the Court of Appeals affirm the District Court's judgment enforcing the arbitrator's final award.

* * *

Questions

1. Does *Hall Street* indicate a Supreme Court retreat from the contractualism evident in its arbitration decisions in the 1980s and 1990s?

2. Do you agree with the Court that the FAA text compels the result?

3. If you were re-drafting the FAA, would you permit parties to an arbitration agreement to specify the standard of judicial review? Would you limit their ability to do so in any way? To what extent can parties, by agreement, create jurisdiction or dictate procedures to be used in a court? For example, would you permit parties to an arbitration clause to only provide for *de novo* judicial review on issues of law and fact, but also to specify that any arbitral awards will be subject to a jury trial? Should they be able to specify what rules of evidence the court should apply?

4. Can parties, by contract, specify for less judicial review than a court otherwise would apply? For example, can parties contract for an arbitration procedure that does not permit any judicial review under any circumstances? Would such a provision be consistent with the FAA as interpreted by *Hall Street*? Would it raise a constitutional issue? See Peter B. Rutledge, *Arbitration and Article III*, 61 Vanderbilt L. Rev. 1189 (2008).

5. What, if anything, is left of *Wilko* and the "manifest disregard" standard after *Hall Street*?

6. Consider Little v. Auto Stiegler, 130 Cal.Rptr.2d 892, 63 P.3d 979 (Cal.2003). The parties had signed an arbitration agreement providing that "[a]wards exceeding $50,000.00 shall include the arbitrator's written reasoned opinion and . . . shall be subject to reversal and remand, modification, or reduction following review of the record and arguments of the parties by a second arbitrator who shall . . . proceed according to the law and procedures available to appellate review by the California Court of Appeal of a civil judgment following court trial." The California Supreme Court refused to enforce the arbitration agreement, reasoning that, as a practical matter, this provision subjected employee, but not employer, victories to the possibility of reversal.

7. What is the meaning of the first paragraph in Part IV of the majority opinion? Is the Court implying that state review standards that are broader than the FAA might be preempted?

State-law based standards for reviewing arbitral award often are broader than federal standards, making it easier to overturn cases in state court than federal court. Michael LeRoy, studying vacatur outcomes in employment cases, has found that state courts are much more likely to vacate employee wins than employer wins. His findings suggest that, counterintuitively, employees and perhaps consumers are better off when the standards for vacating awards are very narrow. See Michael H. LeRoy, *Do Courts Create Moral Hazard?: When Judges Nullify Employer Liability in Arbitrations*, 93 Minnesota Law Review 998, 1044–48, 1053–54 (2009).

8. The last several paragraphs of the majority opinion in Hall Street discuss how arbitration in this case arose as an agreed order in litigation. Court-connected arbitration will be discussed in more detail in Chapter 5.

* * *

4. "MANIFEST DISREGARD OF THE LAW"

Despite the limited textual grounds for judicial review of arbitral awards in Section 10, many courts have read an additional ground into the statute: where the arbitrators acted in "manifest disregard of the law". The "manifest disregard" standard of review was first formulated by Justice Reed in dicta in the 1953 decision of *Wilko v. Swan,* where he said, "[T]he interpretations of the law by the arbitrators in contrast to manifest disregard are not subject, in the federal courts, to judicial review for error in interpretation. The United States Arbitration Act contains no provision for judicial determination of legal issues such as is found in the English law." 346 U.S. 427 (1953). As the Second Circuit subsequently explained:

> "Manifest disregard of the law" by arbitrators is a judicially-created ground for vacating an arbitration award, which was introduced by the Supreme Court in *Wilko v. Swan,* 346 U.S. 427, 436–37, 74 S.Ct. 182, 187–88, 98 L.Ed. 168 (1953). It is not to be found in the federal arbitration law. 9 U.S.C. § 10. Although the bounds of this ground have never been defined, it clearly means more than error or misunderstanding with respect to the law. The error must have been obvious and capable of being readily and instantly perceived by the average person qualified to serve as an arbitrator. Moreover, the term "disregard" implies that the arbitrator appreciates the existence of a clearly governing legal principle but decides to ignore or pay no attention to it. To adopt a less strict standard of judicial review would be to undermine our well established deference to arbitration as a favored method of settling disputes when agreed to by the parties. . . .

Merrill Lynch, Pierce, Fenner & Smith, Inc. v. Bobker, 808 F.2d 930 (2d Cir.1986).

Since *Wilko,* the Courts of Appeals have grappled with the issue of whether to adopt the "manifest disregard" standard and if so, how to apply it. Several courts have noted the tension between reviewing arbitral awards to ensure that they did not "manifest[ly] disregard the law" while at the same time avoiding judicial review of the merits of an arbitral award. To resolve the tension, several courts have attempted to articulate a narrow understanding of "manifest disregard," while others have held that "manifest disregard" incorporates the statutory standards for review. Some of the differing approaches are presented in the following cases.

* * *

Irene Halligan, As Executrix of the Estate of Theodore H. Halligan v. Piper Jaffray, Inc.

148 F.3d 197 (2d Cir. 1998).

■ FEINBERG, CIRCUIT JUDGE:

I. Background

Halligan was hired by Piper in 1973 as a salesman of equity investments to financial institutions. As a condition of employment, Halligan was required by the industry self-regulatory organization, the National Association of Securities Dealers (NASD), to sign a standard form (U–4) containing an agreement to arbitrate any future disputes. In 1988, Tad Piper succeeded his father as CEO of Piper. Mrs. Halligan contends that thereafter Halligan was forced from his job in December 1992 by Tad Piper and Halligan's supervisor, Bruce Huber, because of his age and despite his continuing high performance.

In October 1993, Halligan submitted his ADEA claim, along with other claims, to arbitration before a panel of NASD arbitrators. Before he could complete his own re-direct testimony, however, his health deteriorated and in early 1995 the arbitrators were advised that Halligan was unable to testify further. By stipulation, the arbitrators struck his re-direct testimony from the record and continued the proceeding. Halligan's direct testimony had been subject to cross-examination and was not stricken. After his death, Mrs. Halligan continued the arbitration.

During the arbitration hearings, Halligan presented the arbitrators with very strong evidence of age-based discrimination. Piper for its part has conceded throughout that Halligan was "basically qualified." Piper principally contended that Halligan had chosen to retire; it also argued that performance and health issues justified its conduct.

Before leaving Piper in December 1992, Halligan was making nearly $500,000 per year. He ranked fifth out of 25 institutional salesmen. He was ranked first from 1987 through 1991, and had consistently been among Piper's top salesmen. He testified as to repeated discriminatory statements by Tad Piper, Huber, and Halligan's younger partner Geisness. For example, Halligan testified that at a meeting on August 27, 1992, Tad Piper told him "you're too old. Our clients are young and they want young salesmen," and Huber told him "we want you out of here quickly." Tad Piper and Huber denied making such remarks. Halligan also testified that during a telephone conversation on September 10, 1992, Huber told him that "we want you out of Piper Jaffray by the end of the year," and that "if you don't leave, we will fire you." Halligan testified that he then asked if he could stay for the remainder of the year, and that Huber agreed. Huber testified that during the conversation, Halligan asked him what he should do. He testified that he advised Halligan to resign, and that Halligan agreed "then that's what it will be." Huber admitted that Halligan had never requested his advice before. There were no witnesses to this conversation.

Halligan's evidence also included his notes of this and other conversations, a witness who testified that he had seen Halligan recording notes, and several witnesses who heard Halligan say he was being "fired." In addition, Halligan called many witnesses who testified that Piper personnel had expressed their intention to oust Halligan on account of his age. John Dockendorff, a former client and later competitor, testified that in 1989 (the year after Tad Piper became CEO) Huber attempted to recruit him (in

Dockendorff's words) to "learn as much as I could about [Halligan's] accounts," because Halligan "would get put out to pasture because he was getting old." All Piper personnel denied having made such statements, although their testimony was occasionally inconsistent or ambiguous. Halligan presented testimonials from current and former clients and colleagues who testified that Halligan was among the best in his field. Halligan refused to provide Piper with a letter of resignation. He also refused an offer of a retirement party and refused to write a letter to his clients saying he was retiring. On November 23, 1992, Halligan's lawyer sent a letter threatening suit if Halligan was terminated. In addition, Halligan testified that he approached Huber in November and asked him if he could keep his job. Huber replied that plans had already been made to close the New York office. Apparently, those plans consisted simply of termination notices to two support staff. Halligan's accounts were thereafter assigned to two younger men. Halligan testified that he unsuccessfully looked for a new job after leaving Piper.

Piper principally argued that it gave Halligan the options of retiring, agreeing to a new percentage split with Geisness or being assigned a new group of accounts, and that Halligan agreed to retire in the phone conversation on September 10, 1992. Piper also contended its conduct was justified by concerns over Halligan's performance and health. Halligan had surgery for oral cancer twice (in 1990 and 1991), but returned to work each time after approximately two weeks. Halligan conceded that the surgeries had caused slight speech impairment, but offered various witnesses who testified that Halligan was always able to perform his job. Piper discounted Halligan's objective evidence of performance, arguing that Halligan's accounts had more inherent potential and that the rankings failed to reflect the contributions that other employees had made to Halligan's success. In addition, Huber testified that he thought Halligan needed to develop accounts more effectively (although Huber was unable to identify specific accounts) and use the firm's research and other resources more efficiently. Piper submitted various memoranda related to these concerns, and offered testimony by various witnesses who, with the exception of one employee who had recently retired, were all Piper officers or major shareholders. Piper discounted the testimonials in favor of Halligan, arguing that it was not his clients and former colleagues whose expectations Halligan had to satisfy . . .

In March 1996, after extensive hearings, the arbitrators rendered a written award setting forth the claims and defenses of each party, and denying any relief to the Halligans. The award did not contain any explanation or rationale for the result.

In June 1996, Mrs. Halligan petitioned the district court to vacate the award under § 10(a) of the Federal Arbitration Act (FAA), 9 U.S.C. § 10(a). She argued, among other things, that given the very strong evidence of discrimination and the clear description of the applicable law presented to the arbitrators, the award reflected manifest disregard of the law.

Piper agreed that the law governing the claim was generally not disputed by the parties, but argued in response that it was not the function of the court to review the merits of the decision and that the arbitrators' award was supported by the evidence Piper presented. Piper cross-petitioned the district court to confirm the award.

The district judge refused to vacate the award. She stated in the order of April 14, 1997 that

> [h]ere, the determination of what constitutes "direct evidence" [of discrimination] ... is a difficult one to make. In addition, the record ... does not indicate the Panel's awareness, prior to its determinations, of the standards for burdens of proof.... [T]he Panel was faced with the task of evaluating conflicting witness testimony, and where it did not issue a written opinion, I cannot conclude that the panel did in fact disregard the parties' burdens of proof ... [C]rediting one witness over another does not constitute manifest disregard of the law [and] this Court's role is not to second-guess the fact-finding done by the Panel. Because there is factual as well as legal support for the Panel's ultimate conclusion, I determine that the Panel did not manifestly disregard the law ... (internal citations and footnote omitted).

The judge granted Piper's cross-petition to confirm the award in her order of June 10, 1997 ...

II. Analysis

Mrs. Halligan argues in this court, among other things, that the arbitrators' award reflected manifest disregard of the law. Piper argues in response, among other things, that it is not the function of this court to reassess the evidence or make judgments about witness credibility and that the district court was able to adequately review the award—even in the absence of a written explanation—by inferring from the record grounds that support the arbitrators' award. We have also received amicus briefs from the Equal Employment Opportunity Commission (EEOC) and the Securities Industry Association (SIA) ...

B. Standard of Review of Award

The parties agree that review of arbitration awards is generally governed by the FAA. The relevant statutory language [Section 10(a) of the FAA] is reproduced in the margin. In addition, relying on an observation by the Supreme Court in *Wilko v. Swan,* 346 U.S. 427, 436–37, 74 S.Ct. 182, 98 L.Ed. 168 (1953), overruled on other grounds in *Rodriguez de Quijas v. Shearson/American Express, Inc.,* 490 U.S. 477, 109 S.Ct. 1917, 104 L.Ed.2d 526 (1989), this court has also recognized that an arbitration award may be vacated if it is in "manifest disregard of the law." [Citations omitted.] We have also pointed out, however, that the reach of the doctrine is "severely limited." *Government of India v. Cargill, Inc.,* 867 F.2d 130, 133 (2d Cir. 1989). Indeed, we have cautioned that manifest disregard "clearly means more than error or misunderstanding with respect to the law." *Bobker,* 808 F.2d at 933. We have further noted that to modify or vacate an award on this ground, a court must find both that (1) the arbitrators knew of a governing legal principle yet refused to apply it or ignored it altogether, and (2) the law ignored by the arbitrators was well defined, explicit, and clearly applicable to the case . . .

C. Application of Standard of Review

We turn now to review of the district court's decision in this case. Mrs. Halligan argued in the district court and repeats to us that the arbitration award reflected manifest disregard of the law. Mrs. Halligan makes a strong case for that proposition. Quite simply, Halligan presented overwhelming evidence that Piper's conduct after Tad Piper became CEO was motivated by age discrimination. Halligan testified to repeated discriminatory statements, and offered contemporaneous notes supporting his version of events, which were in turn backed by the testimony of a witness who saw him making notes. Halligan also presented the testimony of numerous other witnesses who testified that Piper personnel admitted that the company wanted Halligan out. Halligan presented powerful evidence of his performance, in the form of quantitative sales rankings and relevant witness testimony. Notwithstanding Piper's testimony as to Halligan's performance and health, Piper conceded before the arbitrators—and continues to do so—that Halligan's continuing performance was not so unsatisfactory as to justify discharge. Indeed, its principal argument has been that Halligan retired voluntarily. Halligan also made a very strong showing that he did not choose the "option" of quitting but was fired. The strength of Halligan's showing of discriminatory motive is most probative of whether Piper took discriminatory action, i.e., fired him. In addition, the circumstantial evidence surrounding his departure, e.g., his statements to various witnesses about his being "fired," his refusal to write to his clients announcing his "resignation," his retention of counsel, is consistent only with a finding that Halligan was pushed out of his job.

Moreover, this is not a case like *Dirussa* where we refused to find "manifest disregard" because DiRussa had not sufficiently brought the governing law to the attention of the arbitrators. There is no such problem here. The record indicates that counsel for both parties generally agreed on the applicable law (and still do on appeal), and explained it to the arbitrators. It is true that the district court stated that the record "does not indicate the Panel's awareness, prior to its determinations, of the standards for burdens of proof." If this observation meant that counsel did not explain the law sufficiently to the arbitrators, it is not correct. Perhaps the district court meant that the arbitrators did not state that they were ignoring the relevant standards for burdens of proof. That is true, but we doubt whether even under a strict construction of the meaning of manifest disregard, it is necessary for arbitrators to state that they are deliberately ignoring the law. See *DeGaetano v. Smith Barney, Inc.*, 983 F.Supp. 459, 463 (S.D.N.Y. 1997).

In view of the strong evidence that Halligan was fired because of his age and the agreement of the parties that the arbitrators were correctly advised of the applicable legal principles, we are inclined to hold that they ignored the law or the evidence or both. Moreover, the arbitrators did not explain their award. It is true that we have stated repeatedly that arbitrators have no obligation to do so. [Citations omitted.] But in *Gilmer,* when the Supreme Court ruled that an employee could be forced to assert an ADEA claim in an arbitral forum, the Court did so on the assumptions that the claimant would not forgo the substantive rights afforded by the statute, that the arbitration agreement simply changed the forum for enforcement of those rights and that a claimant could effectively vindicate his or her statutory rights in the arbitration. 500 U.S. at 26, 28, 111 S.Ct. 1647. This case puts those assumptions to the test. The Court also stated in *Gilmer* that "claimed procedural inadequacies" in arbitration "are best left for resolution in specific cases," 500 U.S. at 33, 111 S.Ct. 1647. At least in the circumstances here, we believe that when a reviewing court is inclined to hold that an arbitration panel manifestly disregarded the law, the failure of the arbitrators to explain the award can be taken into account. Having done so, we are left with the firm belief that the arbitrators here manifestly disregarded the law or the evidence or both . . .

We want to make clear that we are not holding that arbitrators should write opinions in every case or even in most cases. We merely observe that where a reviewing court is inclined to find that arbitrators manifestly disregarded the law or the evidence and that an explanation, if given, would have strained credulity, the absence of explanation may reinforce the reviewing court's confidence that the arbitrators engaged in manifest disregard.

For the reasons stated above, we reverse the district court's orders of April 14, 1997 and June 10, 1997 respectively refusing to vacate and then confirming the award. We also reverse the order of June 16, 1997 dismissing the complaint filed in the district court by Mrs. Halligan because there is no enforceable award to bar the suit on res judicata principles. We remand to the district court for further proceedings consistent with this opinion.

* * *

Dawahare v. Spencer

210 F.3d 666 (6th Cir. 2000).

■ JOHN R. GIBSON, CIRCUIT JUDGE.

Woodrow Dawahare appeals from the district court's denial of his motion to vacate the arbitration award he obtained against Adam Spencer and Dean Witter Reynolds, Inc. Dawahare argues that because the damages awarded were grossly inadequate and bore no relationship to the evidence submitted, the award itself shows evident partiality. Further, he argues that the arbitrators manifestly disregarded the law of damages. We affirm the district court's confirmation of the award.

In view of the limited issues presented, many of the factual details are irrelevant to our discussion. Dawahare established a brokerage account at Shearson Lehman Brothers, Inc. after receiving a "cold call" from Spencer. Smith Barney, Inc. acquired Shearson Lehman sometime after Dawahare opened his account. In August 1994, Spencer informed Dawahare that he planned to leave Smith Barney and go to Dean Witter, and Dawahare agreed to transfer his account. Both before and after the transfer, Spencer engaged in short trading with the Dawahare account. As a result of the price increase of stocks in which Dawahare held short positions, the account declined in value by $495,322 during the last two months of 1994. After Dean Witter learned that Dawahare's son had complaints about the handling of his father's account, Spencer was fired.

Pursuant to pre-dispute arbitration agreements between the parties, Dawahare submitted the controversy to a National Association of Securities Dealers, Inc. arbitration panel in 1996. Dawahare claimed that Spencer had engaged in unsuitable and excessive trading, causing him damages in excess of $600,000. The NASD panel denied Dawahare's claims against Smith Barney, but found in his favor against Dean Witter, awarding $25,000 in compensatory damages and $24,000 in punitive damages. The arbitrators also found Spencer liable to Dawahare for $1,000. In the district court, Dawahare moved to vacate the award; the court denied his motion and granted cross motions to confirm the award.

The district court had before it the transcript of the arbitration hearing. At the hearing, Dawahare presented evidence that his health was failing and that he was unable to understand the significance of the short trading strategy pursued by Spencer because of progressive dementia. His wife testified that she thought Dawahare was in over his head. The brokerage firms maintained that Dawahare was an experienced investor, that he was happy with Spencer and with his handling of the account while it was profitable, and that they were unaware of any health or memory problems Dawahare may have had.

Smith Barney's expert witness testified that Dawahare's account increased in value while it was at Smith Barney. Dawahare's expert witness testified that a conservative investment strategy, assuming a reasonable return of six percent, would have resulted in an account value of $776,603.28 in contrast to the $258,731.97 the Dean Witter account was worth at the end of January 1995. Dawahare's expert then added interest to the difference between these two figures, arriving at a total of $604,463.06 in damages. Dean Witter argued that Dawahare had authorized the activity in his account. Neither Dawahare nor Spencer testified at the arbitration hearing.

The district court rejected Dawahare's argument that the arbitration award should be vacated because of evident partiality or manifest disregard of the law and confirmed the award. We review the confirmation of an arbitration award for clear error on findings of fact and de novo on questions of law. [Citations omitted.]

"It is well established that courts should play only a limited role in reviewing the decisions of arbitrators." *Shelby County Health Care Corp. v. A.F.S.C.M.E., Local 1733*, 967 F.2d 1091, 1094 (6th Cir. 1992). The Federal Arbitration Act presumes that arbitration awards will be confirmed. *See* 9 U.S.C. § 9 (1994); *Andersons, Inc. v. Horton Farms, Inc.*, 166 F.3d 308, 328 (6th Cir. 1998). A court may vacate an arbitration award in the following situations: (1) where the award was procured by fraud, (2) where the arbitrators were evidently partial or corrupt, (3) where the arbitrators misbehaved so that a party's rights were prejudiced, or (4) where the arbitrators exceeded their powers or executed them so that a final, definite award was not made. *See* 9 U.S.C. § 10(a) (1994). In addition, a reviewing court may vacate an award where the arbitrators have manifestly disregarded the law. *See Glennon*, 83 F.3d at 136.

Dawahare first argues that the award should be vacated under 9 U.S.C. § 10(a) because the discrepancy between the damages awarded and the damages alleged shows evident partiality. We see no basis to sustain this argument . . .

Dawahare also argues that the substantial disparity between the damages awarded and the damages evidence presented establishes a manifest disregard of the law of damages. He asserts that the common law entitles him to recover all losses proximately caused by the wrongful acts of the liable parties. Our review for manifest disregard of the law does not open the door to extensive review of arbitral awards. *See Jaros*, 70 F.3d at 421 ("This court has emphasized that manifest disregard of the law is a very narrow standard of review").

An arbitration decision "must fly in the face of established legal precedent" for us to find manifest disregard of the law. *Id.* An arbitration panel acts with manifest disregard if "(1) the applicable legal principle is clearly defined and not subject to reasonable debate; and (2) the arbitrators refused to heed that legal principle." *Id.* Thus, to find manifest disregard a court must find two things: the relevant law must be clearly defined and the arbitrator must have consciously chosen not to apply it. *See M & C Corp. v. Erwin Behr GmbH & Co.*, 87 F.3d 844, 851 n. 3 (6th Cir. 1996) (noting that if its review of an arbitral award were based on FAA standards, there was no manifest disregard since any mistake in applying the law was inadvertent and not based on a conscious decision to ignore the law). Arbitrators are not required to explain their decisions. If they choose not to do so, it is all but impossible to determine whether they acted with manifest disregard for the law. *See Jaros*, 70 F.3d at 421.

. . . The arbitrators' decision in this case outlined the parties' contentions and discussed the claims and evidence in some detail for some three-and-a-half, single-spaced pages. The monetary award simply designated the amount of damages without detailed explanation. It is difficult to say that the arbitrators refused to heed a clearly defined legal principle. Dawahare points to nothing in the record that shows the arbitrators' awareness of the common law that he alleges to be applicable. This is not a case where one of the parties clearly stated the law and the arbitrators expressly chose not to follow it.

Since Supreme Court dictum established the manifest disregard of the law standard forty-seven years ago, *see Wilko v. Swan*, 346 U.S. 427 (1953), *overruled on other grounds, Rodriguez de Quijas v. Shearson/American Express, Inc.*, 490 U.S. 477 (1989), only two federal courts of appeals have used it to vacate arbitration decisions. Dawahare understandably cites to these cases, but to no avail, as both cases are easily distinguished from the case before us.

The Second Circuit held that an arbitration panel that denied relief on an ADEA claim showed manifest disregard by ignoring "the law or the evidence or both" where the plaintiff presented strong evidence that he was fired because of his age. *Halligan v. Piper Jaffray, Inc.*, 148 F.3d 197, 204 (2d Cir. 1998), *cert. denied*, 526 U.S. 1034, 119 S.Ct. 1286, 143 L.Ed.2d 378 (1999). The court pointed out that the parties explained the applicable law to the arbitrators. *See id.* at 204. This is important because manifest disregard requires awareness of the relevant law. *See Jaros*, 70 F.3d at 421 (stating that an arbitrator must refuse to heed a clearly defined legal principle in order to manifestly disregard the law). Here, Dawahare points to nothing in the record that indicates the arbitration panel was aware of the law he alleges it ignored. Also, the *Halligan* court particularly emphasized the importance of assuring plaintiffs with employment discrimination claims a forum in which to effectively vindicate their statutory rights. *See* 148 F.3d at 201–03. [Similarly distinguishable is the 11th Circuit case of Montes v. Shearson Lehman Brothers, Inc., 128 F.3d 1456 (11th Cir. 1997).]

... Dawahare's vague assertion that the arbitrators manifestly disregarded the common law of damages falls far short of the necessary showing of the law that clearly applied in the case and of conscious disregard of that law by the arbitrators. It is possible to argue that the arbitrators misapplied the law of damages, that is, punitive damages would only be warranted for egregious conduct by Dean Witter and, in that case, a compensatory award of less than 5% of the damages alleged is likely too low. To show manifest disregard, however, a party must show more than "[a] mere error in interpretation or application of the law." *Jaros*, 70 F.3d at 421. There is simply no evidence that the arbitrators were aware of some relevant law on damages that they chose to ignore, and we question whether the damages evidence presented by Dawahare required any particular outcome.

... Dawahare's argument on manifest disregard of the law is premised on the fact that the only damages evidence was his expert's opinion that he had sustained damages in excess of $600,000. In essence, he argues that the arbitrators were compelled to accept this testimony and award that amount. We agree with the district court's observation that "[e]xpert testimony, even if uncontradicted, may be believed in its entirety, in part, or not at all." *See also Quinones–Pacheco v. American Airlines, Inc.*, 979 F.2d 1, 5 (1st Cir. 1992) (fact finder not ordinarily bound by uncontradicted expert opinion testimony, particularly where testimony "lacks great convictive force" in context of evidence as a whole); *Gregg v. U.S. Indus., Inc.*, 887 F.2d 1462, 1469–70 (11th Cir. 1989) (expert testimony is not conclusive and need not be accepted). The court also pointed out that the expert's opinion had been impeached on cross-examination and that there was evidence that Dawahare maintained substantial control over his investments. For us to hold that the arbitration panel was compelled to accept Dawahare's expert's damages evidence would be to disregard the fact finder's responsibility to evaluate testimony.

We decline to adopt Dawahare's suggestion that we engage in a more extensive review of arbitration awards. To do so would undermine the goal of the arbitration process: to resolve disputes efficiently while avoiding extended litigation. [Citations omitted.]

... For the foregoing reasons, the judgment of the district court is affirmed.

* * *

Questions

1. Under the "manifest disregard" standard, should a court engage in any review of the merits of an arbitral award? Is "disregarding" the law the same as incorrectly applying the law? Is it the same as deciding a case on the basis of an incorrect understanding of the law? What does the "manifest" requirement add to the standard?

2. Can you make a persuasive argument that the arbitrators in *Halligan* did not act in manifest disregard of the law? Is the court's accusation that the arbitrators ignored the evidence just a roundabout way of second-guessing the arbitrators' factfinding? Is manifest disregard of the *evidence* a ground for judicial review? See Success Sys. v. Maddy Petroleum Equip., Inc., 316 F.Supp.2d 93 (D. Conn. 2004).

3. Is *Dawahare* consistent with *Halligan*? How does the *Dawahare* court try to distinguish the cases? Is this distinction satisfactory? Or does the Sixth Circuit have a different approach than the Second Circuit to the meaning of "manifest disregard"?

4. Does the fact that *Halligan* involved an allegation of age discrimination play a role in the case? Should there be a different standard in discrimination cases? If so, what should that standard be? Wide deference to findings of fact but scrutinized review of issues of law? Deference similar to that given by courts to administrative agencies? Some other standard?

* * *

George Watts & Son, Inc. v. Tiffany and Company

248 F.3d 577 (7th Cir. 2001).

■ Before EASTERBROOK, DIANE P. WOOD, and WILLIAMS, CIRCUIT JUDGES.

■ EASTERBROOK, CIRCUIT JUDGE.

For many years George Watts & Son sold Tiffany's products in Wisconsin. After receiving a notice ending that arrangement, Watts filed suit, asserting that Tiffany had violated both the contract between the parties and the Wisconsin Fair Dealership Law, Wis. Stat. ch. 135. Before the case could be decided, Watts and Tiffany decided that they preferred arbitration to litigation. The parties received the principal benefit of that bargain: swift and inexpensive decision. But Watts decided in retrospect that its decision to arbitrate had been unwise, and it asked the district court to provide more relief than the arbitrator had afforded.

The arbitrator's award extended the time during which Watts could resell Tiffany's merchandise through Watts' bridal registry but permitted Tiffany to cease selling to Watts at the end of 2000; it also required Tiffany to repurchase at retail price all other Tiffany merchandise remaining in Watts' inventory. The arbitrator did not order Tiffany to pay Watts' attorneys' fees and costs. In this respect, according to Watts, the arbitrator departed from state law, requiring the court to repair the problem. An error of law is not a ground listed in 9 U.S.C. §§ 10 and 11 for vacating or modifying an award, but in dictum the Supreme Court has suggested that an arbitrator's "manifest disregard" of legal rules justifies judicial intervention. *Wilko v. Swan,* 346 U.S. 427, 436–37, 74 S.Ct. 182, 98 L.Ed. 168 (1953), overruled on other grounds by *Rodriguez de Quijas v. Shearson/American Express, Inc.*, 490 U.S. 477, 109 S.Ct. 1917, 104 L.Ed.2d 526 (1989). Often "manifest disregard of the law" would be covered by § 10(a)(4), which authorizes vacatur "Where the arbitrators exceeded their powers, or so imperfectly executed them that a mutual, final, and definite award upon the subject matter submitted was not made." If the parties specify that their dispute is to be resolved under Wisconsin law, then an arbitrator's declaration that he prefers New York law, or no law at all, would violate the terms on which the dispute was given to him for resolution, and thus justify relief under § 10(a)(4). But Watts does not contend that the arbitrator violated the arbitration agreement in such a fashion. This poses for us the question whether there is a broader, extra-statutory principle authorizing courts to review arbitrators' legal rulings, or the legal assumptions that influence their decisions even if not identified as conclusions of law.

What could it mean to say that an arbitrator manifestly disregarded the law? That the arbitrator made a legal error? This is Watts' view—that Wisconsin law entitles the prevailing party to attorneys' fees in every case under the WFDL, that it "prevailed" in the arbitration by obtaining an extension of its dealership plus exceptionally favorable terms for the repurchase of inventory, and that the law therefore required the arbitrator to award legal fees too. If "manifest disregard" means only a legal error, however, then arbitration cannot be final. Every arbitration could be followed by a suit, seeking review of legal errors, serving the same function as an appeal within a unitary judicial system. That would prevent the parties from achieving the principal objectives of arbitration: swift, inexpensive, and conclusive resolution of disputes. If "manifest disregard" means not just any legal error but rather a "clear" error (one about which there is, in Watts' language, "no reasonable debate"), again arbitration could not be final, and the post-arbitration litigation would be even more complex than a search for simple error—for how blatant a legal mistake must be to count as "clear" or "manifest" error lacks any straightforward answer. Cf. *Cooter & Gell v. Hartmarx Corp.*, 496 U.S. 384, 399–405, 110 S.Ct. 2447, 110 L.Ed.2d 359 (1990). In this case, for example, the parties dispute whether an award of fees under the WFDL is mandatory or only permissive (perhaps with a presumption in favor of an award); they dispute even whether the arbitrator's award was based on the WFDL as opposed to the contract. Running these matters to ground could be complex. Fortunately, we need not do so (and we therefore express no opinion on them).

A search for either simple or clear legal error cannot be proper. Courts often say, with respect to arbitrators' role in interpreting contracts, that error is not a ground of judicial review. "[T]he question for decision by a federal court asked to set aside an arbitration award ... is not whether the arbitrator or arbitrators erred in interpreting the contract; it is not whether they clearly erred in interpreting the contract; it is not whether they grossly erred in interpreting the contract; it is whether they interpreted the contract." *Hill v. Norfolk & Western Ry.*, 814 F.2d 1192, 1194–95 (7th Cir. 1987); see, e.g., *United Steelworkers v. Enterprise Wheel & Car Corp.*, 363 U.S. 593, 599, 80 S.Ct. 1358, 4 L.Ed.2d 1424 (1960). Yet in litigation the meaning of a contract is treated as an issue of law, when the text is clear and extrinsic evidence is either unavailable or precluded by the parol evidence rule. If manifest legal errors justified upsetting an arbitrator's decision, then the relation between judges and arbitrators established by the *Steelworkers' Trilogy* and reiterated by many later opinions would break down.

Our cases trying to apply the *Wilko* dictum demonstrate some of the difficulties. At least two decisions say that an award may be vacated when an arbitrator "disregards" the law in the sense of treating it as an obstacle to reaching a result preferred on other grounds. See *National Wrecking Co. v. Teamsters, Local 731,* 990 F.2d 957 (7th Cir. 1993); *Health Services Management Corp. v. Hughes,* 975 F.2d 1253 (7th Cir. 1992). But other panels of this court have held the opposite, that arbitrators need not cite or apply rules of law outside the parties' agreement. *Baravati v. Josephthal, Lyon & Ross,* 28 F.3d 704 (1994); *Flender Corp. v. Techna–Quip Co.*, 953 F.2d 273 (7th Cir. 1992); *Chameleon Dental Products, Inc. v. Jackson,* 925 F.2d 223 (7th Cir. 1991). These conflicting lines of precedent do not cite each other, except for *Baravati*, which concluded that the statutory list of reasons for setting aside an award is exclusive, that *Wilko* has after all been overruled, and that as a result "manifest disregard" of the law is not an independent reason to set aside an award. 28 F.3d at 706. But the next year *First Options of Chicago, Inc. v. Kaplan,* 514 U.S. 938, 942, 115 S.Ct. 1920, 131 L.Ed.2d 985 (1995), repeated the *Wilko* dictum, and in 1999 another panel of this court stated in dictum (without citing *Baravati*) that the statutory list is *not* exclusive and that "manifest disregard of the law" is one non-statutory ground for setting aside an award. *Koveleskie v. SBC Capital Markets, Inc.*, 167 F.3d 361, 366 (7th Cir. 1999). The law in other circuits is similarly confused, doubtless because the Supreme Court has been opaque. The dictum in *Wilko* and *First Options* was unexplained and unilluminated by any concrete application. Dictum in *Gilmer v. Interstate/Johnson Lane Corp.*, 500 U.S. 20, 32 n. 4, 111 S.Ct. 1647, 114 L.Ed.2d 26 (1991), is similarly unhelpful.

There is, however, a way to understand "manifest disregard of the law" that preserves the established relation between court and arbitrator and resolves the tension in the competing lines of cases. It is this: an arbitrator may not direct the parties to violate the law. In the main, an arbitrator acts as the parties' agent and as their delegate may do anything the parties may do directly. See *Eastern Associated Coal Corp. v. United Mine Workers*, 531 U.S. 57, 121 S.Ct. 462, 467, 148 L.Ed.2d 354 (2000) ("we must treat the arbitrator's award as if it represented an agreement between" the parties themselves). *Eastern Associated Coal* may at last clear up the confusion, having dealt with a related line of cases in which courts wrestled with the question whether violation of "public policy" (a form of disregard of legal constraints) justifies setting aside an award. The Court concluded that the judiciary may step in when the arbitrator has commanded the parties to violate legal norms (principally, but not exclusively, those in positive law) but that judges may not deprive arbitrators of authority to reach compromise outcomes that legal norms leave within the discretion of the parties to the arbitration agreement.

Suppose Watts and Tiffany had sat down to resolve their differences and had agreed on an extension through the end of 2000, a repurchase of remaining items at retail price, and each side bearing its own fees and costs. Could there be any legal objection? Surely not; it is a kind of settlement businesses reach all the time, each receiving part of what it wanted. [Citation omitted.] If Watts and Tiffany may resolve their differences without fees changing hands, why can't an arbitrator, as their agent, prescribe the same outcome? In *Eastern Associated Coal* an employer contended that an arbitrator exceeded his powers by ordering the reinstatement of a truck driver who had twice tested positive for marijuana. The Supreme Court held that reinstatement was within the arbitrator's power, because it was within the employer's power, and the arbitrator exercised authority delegated by the employer. If a federal statute, a federal rule, or some equivalently definite federal policy prohibited employment of a drug-using truck driver, then the employer and arbitrator alike would be bound to respect it; the arbitrator could not order the employer to depart from the federal decision. Similarly an arbitrator may not require a firm to put in the cab someone whose driver's license has been revoked for driving under the influence of drugs. But because neither a statute nor a federal agency with authority over transportation has banned repeat drug users from the road, the Court held, the arbitrator's award could not be condemned as an excess of power. Cf. *Paperworkers v. Misco, Inc.*, 484 U.S. 29, 108 S.Ct. 364, 98 L.Ed.2d 286 (1987).

After *Eastern Associated Coal* the "manifest disregard" principle is limited to two possibilities: an arbitral order requiring the parties to violate the law (as by employing unlicensed truck drivers), and an arbitral order that does not adhere to the legal principles specified by contract, and hence unenforceable under § 10(a)(4). Neither of these approaches helps Watts.

No rule of Wisconsin law prevents parties to a dealership agreement from agreeing to bear their own legal expenses when resolving their differences. The arbitrator's award thus did not require either Tiffany or Watts to violate state law, even if the WFDL has the meaning Watts sees in it. Our case is fundamentally the same as *Eastern Associated Coal*: what the parties may do, the arbitrator as their mutual agent may do. People who want their arbitrators to have fewer powers need only provide this by contract. Watts and Tiffany could have agreed to arbitrate under provisions forbidding the arbitrator to split the difference, requiring the prevailing side to receive 100% of its legal entitlements. An arbitrator's disregard of such a command would be reviewable under 9 U.S.C. § 10(a)(4). But when the parties agree to arbitrate without specifying a rule of decision, as Watts and Tiffany did, then the arbitrator has considerable leeway so long as he respects the limits the parties' contract and public law place on his discretion. This arbitrator did not disregard the parties' contract, did not direct them to violate the law, and did not otherwise overstep the terms of his engagement. The district court therefore properly enforced the award as written.

AFFIRMED

■ WILLIAMS, CIRCUIT JUDGE, concurring in the judgment.

Because the majority has effectively rejected the manifest disregard doctrine, I will briefly express my concern with that holding. It should be noted that the doctrine of manifest disregard has been substantively uniform in the federal courts, requiring that (1) the arbitrator knew of a governing legal principle yet refused to apply it or ignored it altogether, and (2) the law ignored by the arbitrator was well-defined, explicit and clearly applicable to the case. [Citation.] Every court of appeals, including our own, has held that a court may review the decision of an arbitrator for "manifest disregard of the law," and has adopted, in substance, that very definition. Moreover, the words in the doctrine itself are more in accord with such an interpretation. See *Montes v. Shearson Lehman Bros., Inc.*, 128 F.3d 1456, 1461–62 (11th Cir.1997) (defining the words of the doctrine). The majority's holding conflicts with that precedent, and leaves the doctrine internally inconsistent and effectively impotent. . . .

Eastern Associated Coal does not support the broad proposition that "an arbitrator acts as the parties' agent and as their delegate may do anything the parties may do directly," as the majority appears to contend. *Ante*, at 580. Rather, *Eastern Associated Coal* holds that because the parties authorized the arbitrator to interpret the contract and the arbitrator acted *within the scope of his authority* in interpreting the contract, we must treat the contract as one between the parties. *Id.* at 466–67. That rationale, if anything, stands contrary to the conclusion of the majority, because when an arbitrator acts in manifest disregard of the law, he acts outside the scope of his authority. When a claim arises under specific statutory law, the arbitrator is bound to follow the law in the absence of a valid and legal agreement not to do so. See *Montes*, 128 F.3d at 1459 (citing *Gilmer v. Interstate/Johnson Lane Corp.*, 500 U.S. 20, 26, 111 S.Ct. 1647, 114 L.Ed.2d 26 (1991)).

To review, the question before us in an arbitral contract interpretation case is not "whether the arbitrator or arbitrators erred in interpreting the contract; it is not whether they clearly erred in interpreting the contract; it is not whether they grossly erred in interpreting the contract; it is whether they interpreted the contract." *Hill,* 814 F.2d at 1194–95. And, when an arbitrator interprets statutory law, we require "something beyond and different from mere error in law or failure on the part of the arbitrators to understand or apply the law." *Health Servs.*, 975 F.2d at 1267. We ask whether she affirmatively disregarded what she knew to be the law. *Id.* The rules that govern review of arbitral contract interpretation and review of arbitral statutory interpretation do not create tension in the law. The standards are nearly identical, and they complement each other rather well.

... Even if we were to adopt the agency model advanced by the majority, no one expects that the parties intended to vest in that agent the power to ignore statutory law willy-nilly and decide the fate of the parties at her whim or caprice. Indeed, we do not accept an arbitrator's decision to ignore completely a contract, although under the agency model arguably we should, because the parties could rescind their contract entirely and fashion a completely new agreement. But the agency fiction falls apart. The arbitrator is not the parties, and, in truth, she is not their agent; therefore when the arbitrator acts in manifest disregard of statutory law, there is no compelling reason that we should not intervene and protect the statutory rights of the parties—otherwise the parties would be better off flipping a coin. With all deference to the majority, I would preserve this important question for a case in which it truly matters.

* * *

Questions

1. What does Judge Easterbrook say is the correct interpretation of the "manifest disregard" standard? Is the concurrence correct in its view that this approach effectively rejects the manifest disregard standard altogether? Can the opinion in *Watts* be read to say that the Seventh Circuit only permits an arbitral award to be vacated on the four grounds listed in Section 10(a) of the FAA?

2. A now-overruled Fifth Circuit decision articulated yet a different interpretation of "manifest disregard of the law." In *Williams v. Cigna Fin. Advisors, Inc.,* 197 F.3d 752, 762 (5th Cir. 1999), the court stated:

> First, where on the basis of the information available to the court it is not manifest that the arbitrators acted contrary to the applicable law, the award should be upheld. Second, where on the basis of the information available to the court it is manifest that the arbitrators acted contrary to the applicable law, the award should be upheld unless it would result in significant injustice, taking into account all the circumstances of the case, including powers of arbitrators to judge norms appropriate to the relations between the parties.

How does this differ from the meaning of "manifest disregard" as it is interpreted by the Seventh Circuit? the Second Circuit? the Sixth Circuit? Which interpretation best comports with the words of the statute? Which best fulfills the objectives of the statute? Which one best balances the competing policies of promoting private resolution of disputes while protecting substantive rights of the parties?

3. In *George Watts & Son,* Judge Easterbrook notes, in dicta, that "[p]eople who want their arbitrators to have fewer powers need only provide this by contract." Does this suggestion survive *Hall Street*?

4. *George Watts & Son* was decided before *Hall Street.* Given Judge Easterbrook's recitation of the history of the "manifest disregard" standard, how do you think he would resolve this case after *Hall Street*?

* * *

Citigroup Global Markets, Inc. v. Bacon

562 F.3d 349 (5th Cir.2009).

■ E. GRADY JOLLY, CIRCUIT JUDGE:

An arbitration panel ordered Citigroup Global Markets to pay Debra Bacon $256,000. Citigroup moved the district court to vacate the award, and the district court obliged on the basis that the arbitrators had manifestly disregarded the law. On appeal, we consider whether manifest disregard of the law remains a valid ground for vacatur of an arbitration award in the light of the Supreme Court's recent decision in *Hall Street Associates, L.L.C. v. Mattel, Inc.,* ___ U.S. ___, 128 S.Ct. 1396, 1403, 170 L.Ed.2d 254 (2008). We conclude that *Hall Street* restricts the grounds for vacatur to those set forth in § 10 of the Federal Arbitration Act (FAA or Act), 9 U.S.C. § 1 *et seq.* and consequently, manifest disregard of the law is no longer an independent ground for vacating arbitration awards under the FAA. *Hall Street* effectively overrules our previous authority to the contrary, so we must VACATE the district court's judgment and REMAND for reconsideration in accord with the exclusivity of the statutory grounds.

I.

Debra Bacon's quarrel with Citigroup began in 2002 when she discovered that her husband had withdrawn funds from her Citigroup Individual Retirement Accounts without her permission. By forging her signature, he made five withdrawals totaling $238,000. As soon as Bacon discovered the unauthorized withdrawals, she notified Citigroup.

In 2004, Bacon submitted a claim in arbitration against Citigroup seeking reimbursement for the unauthorized withdrawals. The arbitration panel granted Bacon $218,000 in damages and $38,000 in attorneys' fees. Citing § 10 of the FAA, Citigroup made an application to the district court requesting vacatur of the award.

The district granted the motion to vacate, holding that the award was made in manifest disregard of the law. The court based its holding on three grounds: 1) Bacon was not harmed by the withdrawals because her husband used the money for her benefit and subsequently promised to pay her back; 2) Bacon's claims were barred by Texas law, which permits such claims only if the customer reports the unauthorized transaction within thirty days of the withdrawal; and 3) Texas law requires apportionment among the liable parties, which, in this case, includes Bacon's husband.

Bacon appeals. We review *de novo* the vacatur of an arbitration award. *Kergosien v. Ocean Energy, Inc.,* 390 F.3d 346, 352 (5th Cir. 2004).

II.

A.

Although *Hall Street* clearly has the effect of further restricting the role of federal courts in the arbitration process, there is nothing revolutionary about its holding.

Even before the enactment of the United States Arbitration Act in 1925, courts of equity would set aside an arbitration award only in narrowly defined circumstances. *Burchell v. Marsh,* 58 U.S. 344, 349–50, 17 How. 344, 15 L.Ed. 96 (1854); *Karthaus v. Ferrer,* 26 U.S. 222, 228, 1 Pet. 222, 7 L.Ed. 121 (1828). If the arbitration award was "within the submission, and contain[ed] the honest decision of the arbitrators, after a full and fair hearing of the parties, a court of equity [would] not set it aside for error, either in law or fact." *Burchell,* 58 U.S. at 349. This deference was appropriate because a submission agreement—a document executed by both parties and presented to the arbitrators in order to outline the dispute and the desired arbitration procedures—was a valid and enforceable contract. *District of Columbia v. Bailey,* 171 U.S. 161, 171, 18 S.Ct. 868, 43 L.Ed. 118 (1898). Thus, a provision in the submission agreement requiring the parties to abide by the arbitrator's decision made the arbitration award binding. Even when a submission agreement did not contain an express agreement to adhere to the decision of the arbitrators, courts implied such an agreement and enforced the awards as binding. *See Smith v. Morse,* 9 Wall. 76, 76 U.S. 76, 82, 19 L.Ed. 597 (1869) ("The law implies an agreement to abide the result of an arbitration from the fact of submission"). Although arbitration was binding and final, awards could be set aside in the following circumstances: (1) where the arbitrators engaged in fraud, corruption, or improper conduct; (2) where the arbitrators failed to decide all of the issues submitted; (3) where the arbitrators exceeded their powers by deciding issues not submitted; and (4) where the award was not certain, final, and mutual. *See Burchell,* 58 U.S. at 351((1) and (3)); *Carnochan v. Christie,* 24 U.S. 446, 460–67, 6 L.Ed. 516 (1826) ((2), (3), and (4)). These limited grounds are akin to the provisions of § 10 of the FAA.

Importantly, awards were affirmed even if based upon error in law or fact. *Burchell,* 58 U.S. at 349. "A contrary course would be a substitution of the judgment of the chancellor in place of the judges chosen by the parties, and would make an award the commencement, not the end, of litigation." *Id. Burchell* also cautioned against assuming improper conduct from mere error: "We are all too prone, perhaps, to impute either weakness of intellect or corrupt motives to those who differ with us in opinion." *Id.* at 350. The Supreme Court has continued to emphasize the importance of respecting the arbitration process. In *Hall Street,* the Court explained: permitting vacatur and modification of arbitration awards on more expansive grounds "opens the door to the full-bore legal and evidentiary appeals that can rende[r] informal arbitration merely a prelude to a more cumbersome and time-consuming judicial review process, and bring arbitration theory to grief in post-arbitration process." 128 S.Ct. at 1405 (citations and internal quotation marks omitted) (alteration in *Hall Street*).

In short, strictly confining the perimeter of federal court review of arbitration awards is a widely accepted practice that runs throughout arbitration jurisprudence—from its early common law and equity days to the present.

B.

1.

Congress embraced this notion that arbitration awards should generally be upheld barring some sort of procedural injustice, and §§ 10 and 11 of the FAA enumerate the circumstances under which an award may be vacated, modified, or corrected when the action is one brought under the Act. . . .

[In *Hall Street*, t]he Supreme Court observed that § 9 of the FAA, which states that upon the application for an order confirming an arbitration award the court "must grant such an order unless the award is vacated, modified, or corrected as prescribed in sections 10 and 11 . . . ," suggests that judicial review is constrained by the statute. There "is nothing malleable about 'must grant,' which unequivocally tells courts to grant confirmation in all cases, except when one of the 'prescribed' exceptions applies." *Id.* at 1405. *Hall Street* also found that the Act's legislative history indicated that Congress intended the statutory grounds for vacatur and modification to be the exclusive means for setting aside or changing an arbitration award challenged under the FAA. . . .

Based both on the text and on the legislative history, *Hall Street* concluded that §§ 10 and 11 provide the exclusive regimes for review under the FAA. The Court reiterated this holding several times: "We hold that the statutory grounds are exclusive"; "We agree with the Ninth Circuit that they are [exclusive] . . ."; "We now hold that §§ 10 and 11 respectively provide the FAA's exclusive grounds for expedited vacatur and modification"; "In holding that §§ 10 and 11 provide exclusive regimes for the review provided by the statute. . . ." *Hall Street,* 128 S.Ct. at 1400, 1401, 1403, 1406. This rule, *Hall Street* determined, is consistent with the "national policy favoring arbitration with just the limited review needed to maintain arbitration's essential virtue of resolving disputes straightaway." *Id.* at 1405.

2.

Before we leave *Hall Street,* we must point out that the petitioner, citing *Wilko v. Swan,* 346 U.S. 427, 436–37, 74 S.Ct. 182, 98 L.Ed. 168 (1953), argued that the widespread judicial recognition of manifest disregard of the law as a nonstatutory ground for vacatur suggests that §§ 10 and 11 are not exclusive. *Hall Street,* 128 S.Ct. at 1403. They argued that if this judicial expansion is permissible, then the instant contractual expansion similarly should be accepted. The Supreme Court, however, questioned whether *Wilko* should even be read as creating an independent ground for vacatur. *Id.* at 1404. That issue, *Hall Street* observed, was not before the Court in *Wilko,* and *Wilko*'s language, upon which the circuit courts have based the standard, is vague. The *Hall Street* Court speculated and concluded:

> Maybe the term "manifest disregard" was meant to name a new ground for review, but maybe it merely referred to the § 10 grounds collectively, rather than adding to them. Or, as some courts have thought, "manifest disregard" may have been shorthand for § 10(a)(3) or § 10(a)(4), the subsections authorizing vacatur when the arbitrators were "guilty of misconduct" or "exceeded their powers." We, when speaking as a Court, have merely taken the *Wilko* language as we found it, without embellishment, and now that its meaning is implicated, *we see no reason to accord it the significance that [the petitioner] urges.*

*4 *Id.* (citations omitted) (emphasis added). In short, *Hall Street* rejected manifest disregard as an independent ground for vacatur, and stood by its clearly and repeatedly stated holding, as noted in the earlier paragraph, that §§ 10 and 11 provide the exclusive bases for vacatur and modification of an arbitration award under the FAA. . . .

III.

A.

The question before us now is whether, under the FAA, manifest disregard of the law remains valid, as an independent ground for vacatur, after *Hall Street.* The answer seems clear. *Hall Street* unequivocally held that the statutory grounds are the exclusive means for vacatur under the FAA. Our case law defines manifest disregard of the law as a *nonstatutory* ground for vacatur. *See Kergosien,* 390 F.3d at 353; *Prestige Ford,* 324 F.3d at 395; *Harris v. Parker Coll. of Chiropractic,* 286 F.3d 790, 792 (5th Cir.

2002). Thus, to the extent that manifest disregard of the law constitutes a nonstatutory ground for vacatur, it is no longer a basis for vacating awards under the FAA.

Four other circuits have considered this issue. The First Circuit, in dictum and with little discussion, concluded that *Hall Street* abolished manifest disregard of the law as a ground for vacatur.[4] *See Ramos–Santiago v. United Parcel Serv.,* 524 F.3d 120, 124 n. 3 (1st Cir. 2008) ("We acknowledge the Supreme Court's recent holding in *Hall Street Assocs., L.L.C. v. Mattel* that manifest disregard of the law is not a valid ground for vacating or modifying an arbitral award in cases brought under the [FAA]." (citations omitted)). The Sixth Circuit, in an unpublished opinion, reached the opposite conclusion by narrowly construing the holding of *Hall Street* to apply only to contractual expansions of the grounds for review. *Coffee Beanery, Ltd. v. WW, L.L.C.,* 300 Fed.Appx. 415, 419 (6th Cir. 2008). The Second Circuit has also held that manifest disregard survives *Hall Street. Stolt–Nielsen SA v. AnimalFeeds Int'l Corp.,* 548 F.3d 85, 93–95 (2d Cir. 2008). The court, however, recognized that *Hall Street*'s holding was in direct conflict with the application of manifest disregard as a nonstatutory ground for review, but resolved the conflict by recasting manifest disregard as a shorthand for § 10(a)(4). *Id.* Finally, the Ninth Circuit has concluded that *Hall Street* did not abolish manifest disregard because its case law defined manifest disregard as shorthand for § 10(a)(4). *See Comedy Club Inc. v. Improv West Assocs.,* 553 F.3d 1277, 1289 (9th Cir. 2009) ("*Comedy Club II*"). We now turn to discuss the opinions of the Sixth, Second, and Ninth Circuits.

1.

Coffee Beanery only briefly considered the effect of *Hall Street* on manifest disregard of the law. 300 Fed.Appx. at 419. In what we view as an understatement, the Sixth Circuit acknowledged that *Hall Street* "significantly reduced the ability of federal courts to vacate arbitration awards for reasons other than those specified in 9 U.S.C. § 10. . . ." *Id.* Citing *Hall Street*'s discussion of *Wilko,* which *Coffee Beanery* thought demonstrated a "hesitation to reject the 'manifest disregard' doctrine," and noting the acceptance of the standard by each and every court of appeals, the court concluded that it would be imprudent to cease vacating arbitration awards made in manifest disregard of the law. 2008 WL 4899478, at *4.

This decision suffers from two significant flaws. First, the opinion utterly fails to address *Hall Street*'s express holding that the grounds for vacatur found in § 10 are exclusive. Instead, the court narrowly construed *Hall Street* as applying only to contractual expansions of the grounds for vacatur. *Id.* In the light of *Hall Street*'s repeated statements that "*We hold*

4. This conclusion was dictum because the motion to vacate in *Ramos–Santiago* was not brought pursuant to the FAA. The Supreme Court in *Hall Street* was careful to limit its holding to the FAA and the scope of expeditious judicial review permitted thereunder: "we do not purport to say that [§§ 10 and 11] exclude more searching review based on authority outside the [FAA]." 128 S.Ct. at 1406.

that the statutory grounds are exclusive," we think it incorrect so narrowly to construe *Hall Street*'s holding. 128 S.Ct. at 1400 (emphasis added).

Second, we believe that *Coffee Beanery* misread *Hall Street*'s discussion of *Wilko.* We do not see hesitation by *Hall Street* to reject manifest disregard of the law as an independent ground for vacating an award under the FAA; instead, *Hall Street*'s discussion of *Wilko* demonstrates the Supreme Court's unwillingness to give any significant meaning to *Wilko*'s vague language. *Hall Street* observed that *Wilko* dealt with an entirely separate issue and, noting the vagueness of *Wilko*'s statement, concluded that: "When speaking as a Court, we have taken the *Wilko* language as we found it, without embellishment, and now that its meaning is implicated, we see no reason to accord it the significance that [the petitioner] urges." *Id.* at 1404.

2.

Unlike *Coffee Beanery,* the Second Circuit in *Stolt–Nielsen* did not shy from *Hall Street*'s holding. The court acknowledged that *Hall Street* "held that the FAA sets forth the 'exclusive' grounds for vacating an arbitration award." *Stolt–Nielsen,* 548 F.3d at 94. The court also recognized that this holding was in conflict with its own prior statements regarding manifest disregard, which the court discounted as dicta. *Id.*("[*Hall Street*'s] holding is undeniably inconsistent with some dicta by this Court treating the 'manifest disregard' standard as a ground for vacatur entirely separate from those enumerated in the FAA."). Instead of directly concluding that *Hall Street* eliminated manifest disregard as a ground for vacatur under the FAA, the court reasoned that manifest disregard of the law should be "reconceptualized as a judicial gloss on the specific grounds for vacatur enumerated in section 10 of the FAA. . . ." *Id.*

Describing its "reconceptualization," the court stated:

> We must therefore continue to bear the responsibility to vacate arbitration awards in the rare instances in which "the arbitrator knew of the relevant [legal] principle, appreciated that this principle controlled the outcome of the disputed issue, and nonetheless willfully flouted the governing law by refusing to apply it." *Westerbeke,* 304 F.3d at 217. At that point the arbitrators have "failed to interpret the contract at all," *Wise,* 450 F.3d at 269, for parties do not agree in advance to submit to arbitration that is carried out in manifest disregard of the law. Put another way, the arbitrators have thereby "exceeded their powers, or so imperfectly executed them that a mutual, final, and definite award upon the subject matter submitted was not made." 9 U.S.C § 10(a)(4).

Stolt–Nielsen, 548 F.3d at 95. Thus, the court seems to conclude that manifest disregard—as the court describes it—does not add to the statutory grounds. The court simply folds manifest disregard into § 10(a)(4). In the full context of the Second Circuit's reasoning, this analysis is not inconsistent with *Hall Street*'s speculation that manifest disregard may, among other things, "have been shorthand for § 10(a)(3) or § 10(a)(4)...." *Hall Street,* 128 S.Ct. at 1404.

We should be careful to observe, however, that this description of manifest disregard is very narrow. Because the arbitrator is fully aware of the controlling principle of law and yet does not apply it, he flouts the law in such a manner as to exceed the powers bestowed upon him. This scenario does not include an erroneous application of that principle.[6]

3.

Comedy Club II has a lengthy procedural history. In a decision issued prior to *Hall Street,* the Ninth Circuit found that the arbitration award at issue constituted a manifest disregard of the law. *Comedy Club Inc. v. Improv West Assocs.,* 514 F.3d 833 (2008) ("*Comedy Club I*"). The Supreme Court then vacated the decision in *Comedy Club I* and remanded for reconsideration in the light of its recently issued decision in *Hall Street. Improv West Assocs. v. Comedy Club, Inc.,* ___ U.S. ___, 129 S.Ct. 45, 172 L.Ed.2d 6 (2008).

On remand, the Ninth Circuit, unlike the Second Circuit, had no need to reconceptualize manifest disregard because its own case law had already defined it as a shorthand for § 10(a)(4). *Comedy Club,* 553 F.3d 1277, 1289. The court therefore held that manifest disregard of the law, as a shorthand for § 10(a)(4), survived *Hall Street. Id.* ("manifest disregard of the law remains a valid ground for vacatur because it is a part of § 10(a)(4)").

B.

In the light of the Supreme Court's clear language that, under the FAA, the statutory provisions are the exclusive grounds for vacatur, manifest disregard of the law as an independent, nonstatutory ground for setting aside an award must be abandoned and rejected. Indeed, the term itself, as a term of legal art, is no longer useful in actions to vacate arbitration awards. *Hall Street* made it plain that the statutory language means what it says: "courts *must* [confirm the award] unless the award is vacated, modified, or corrected as prescribed in sections 10 and 11 of this title," 9 U.S.C. § 9 (emphasis added), and there's nothing malleable about "must," *Hall Street,* 128 S.Ct. at 1405. Thus from this point forward, arbitration awards under the FAA may be vacated only for reasons provided in § 10.

To the extent that our previous precedent holds that nonstatutory grounds may support the vacatur of an arbitration award, it is hereby overruled.

6. *Stolt–Nielsen* cites *New York Telephone Co. v. Communications Workers of America Local 1100,* 256 F.3d 89 (2d Cir. 2001) (per curiam), as one example. In that case, the arbitrator deliberately refused to apply a legal principle that he acknowledged to be controlling. The arbitrator stated: "Perhaps it is time for a new court decision." *New York Telephone Co.,* 256 F.3d at 93.

IV.

The district court, which issued its opinion before *Hall Street,* held that the arbitrators in this case manifestly disregarded the law. The judgment of the district court is therefore VACATED. The court, however, did not consider whether the grounds asserted for vacating the award might support vacatur under any of the statutory grounds. Accordingly, we REMAND for further consideration not inconsistent with this opinion. The judgment of the district court is VACATED and the case REMANDED.

VACATED and REMANDED.

* * *

Questions

1. With which of the myriad approaches to "manifest disregard" do you agree?

2. The Fifth Circuit in *Citigroup* refers to a holding in *Hall Street* that "the grounds for vacatur found in § 10 are exclusive." Do you agree that this was *holding*? Can you argue it was dicta? For a discussion of judicial review grounds after *Hall Street*, see Richard C. Reuben, *Personal Autonomy and Vacatur After Hall Street*, 113 Penn St. L. Rev. 1103 (2009).

* * *

---

5. THE "AWARD" REQUIREMENT

Sobel v. Hertz, Warner & Co.

469 F.2d 1211 (2d Cir. 1972).

I

The arbitration that led to this appeal was first requested in November 1967 by appellee Herbert Sobel, who was a customer of appellant Hertz, Warner & Co., a stock brokerage firm and a member of the New York Stock Exchange. As a customer, Sobel had the right under Article VIII of the Constitution of the New York Stock Exchange to demand arbitration of any controversy he might have with a member firm growing out of its "business." Briefly, Sobel claimed that between December 1965 and March 1966 he had purchased 10,200 shares of the common stock of Hercules Galion Products, Inc., upon the recommendation of his long-time broker, Edward Wetzel, and Michael Geier, both then employed by Hertz, Warner, and that Wetzel and Geier had made fraudulent misstatements and omissions of material facts on which Sobel had relied to his detriment. As their employer, Hertz, Warner was, according to Sobel, liable for the damages he had suffered. Sobel continued to hold his Hercules shares until Hertz, Warner demanded, in connection with the arbitration, that they be sold to fix damages. This was done in May 1968, and Sobel thereafter claimed a direct loss of about $34,000.

In 1970, both parties signed a formal submission to arbitration pursuant to the provisions of the Stock Exchange Constitution and the rules of the Board of Governors. Under the Constitution, Sobel's claim was heard by a panel consisting of two persons "engaged in the securities business" and three not so engaged. The panel held two hearings at which it heard the testimony of three witnesses and received documentary evidence. At the hearings, of which there is a full transcript, both sides were ably represented by counsel.

In May 1971, the panel issued the following decision:

> We, the undersigned, being the arbitrators selected to hear and determine a matter in controversy between the above-mentioned claimant and respondents set forth in a submission to arbitration signed by the parties on April 6, 1970 and April 10, 1970 respectively;
>
> And having heard and considered the proofs of the parties, have decided and determined that the claim of the claimant be and hereby is in all respects dismissed;
>
> That the costs, $240.00, be and hereby are assessed against the claimant.

After an unsuccessful request to the arbitrators for reconsideration, Sobel moved in the Southern District under 9 U.S.C. § 10 to vacate the arbitration award on the grounds that it had been "procured by undue means" and "that the Award is contrary to public policy, in that the arbitrators refused to make their Award in accordance with the applicable Federal Securities laws." Judge Pollack heard argument on the motion to vacate and concluded, in an exhaustive opinion, that he could not decide the question without "an indication, now wholly lacking from the record, of the basis on which the petitioner's claim was dismissed." 338 F.Supp. at 289. Holding that "a District Court is justified in requiring some statement of the facts the arbitrators found decisive," id. at 298, the judge remanded the controversy to the arbitrators for that purpose. Thereafter, he certified as an interlocutory appeal under 28 U.S.C. § 1292(b) the question whether his action was proper, and we permitted the appeal.

II

... The district judge agreed with Sobel that unless the arbitrators in this case stated the basis of their decision, the judge could not determine whether it was in "manifest disregard" of the law ... [W]e believe that the issue before us is whether the arbitrators here are required to disclose the reasoning underlying their award.

... [T]he extent of an arbitrator's obligation to explain his award is necessarily related to the scope of judicial review of it. That issue, insofar as it leads to attempts to define "manifest disregard," is particularly troublesome ... It is a truism that an arbitration award will not be vacated for a mistaken interpretation of law . . . But if the arbitrators simply ignore the applicable law, the literal application of a "manifest disregard" standard should presumably compel vacation of the award. The problem is how a court is to be made aware of the erring conduct of the arbitrators. Obviously, a requirement that arbitrators explain their reasoning in every case would help to uncover egregious failures to apply the law to an arbitrated dispute. But such a rule would undermine the very purpose of arbitration, which is to provide a relatively quick, efficient and informal means of private dispute settlement. The sacrifice that arbitration entails in terms of legal precision is recognized, e. g., Bernhardt v. Polygraphic Co., 350 U.S. 198, 203, 76 S.Ct. 273, 100 L.Ed. 199 (1956), and is implicitly accepted in the initial assumption that certain disputes are arbitrable . . . Given that acceptance, the primary consideration for the courts must be that the system operate expeditiously as well as fairly.

Presumably based upon the foregoing considerations, the Supreme Court has made it clear that there is no general requirement that arbitrators explain the reasons for their award. In Wilko v. Swan, supra, just before the language quoted above at page 1213 the Court pointed out that an award by arbitrators "may be made without explanation of their reasons and without a complete record of their proceedings. . . ." 346 U.S. at 436, 74 S.Ct. at 187. This statement is especially significant because Mr. Justice Frankfurter in dissent made exactly the opposite point. A little over two years later, the Court observed that "Arbitrators . . . need not give their reasons for their results. . . ." Bernhardt v. Polygraphic Co., supra, 350 U.S. at 203, 76 S.Ct. at 276. These statements were, of course, known to the district judge; he even quoted them in his opinion. The argument, then, must be that there is something about this particular case that justifies the extraordinary requirement of the district court's order. We fail to see what that is. There was a complete transcript here of the arbitration proceeding. The arbitrators—and the district court—also had the benefit of an extremely detailed submission to arbitration, including Sobel's Statement of Claim and Hertz, Warner's Reply, excellent memoranda of law and summations of counsel, all of which indicate a number of theories upon which the arbitrators may have decided. [Citation omitted.] It is true that claims under the securities acts are frequently complicated, although those made here seem less so than usual. And the same public interest that led to the enactment of the securities acts makes it desirable that such claims be decided correctly. But there is also a public interest, manifested in the United States Arbitration Act, 9 U.S.C. § 1 et seq., in the proper functioning of the arbitral process. It would be destructive of that process if we approved the district judge's requirement here that the arbitrators give reasons for their decision. Arbitration may not always be the speedy and economical remedy its admirers claim it is—this case is proof enough of that. But forcing arbitrators to explain their award even when grounds for it can be gleaned from the record will unjustifiably diminish whatever efficiency the process now achieves.[7]

7. The New York Stock Exchange in an amicus brief suggests that in the context now before us such a requirement may put an end to arbitration altogether. The district court noted that the Exchange was not required to arbitrate non-member disputes. 338 F.Supp.

... In short, we believe that the district court erred in remanding the arbitration proceeding to the arbitrators. We do not agree with its conclusion that "the present state of the record is not sufficient to justify final determination of the issues petitioner has raised." 338 F.Supp. at 289. Those issues are whether the arbitration award was procured by "undue means," 9 U.S.C. § 10(a), or is void as against public policy. Both parties have urged us to decide those questions. While we are tempted to do so in order to bring this litigation to an end, orderly administration suggests that the district court should rule upon them first.

Case remanded for further proceedings consistent with this opinion.

* * *

Questions

1. Note 4 after *Halligan* asked whether you believe that expanded judicial review should be permitted in cases involving statutory claims. Is such review even possible absent a written opinion? What about a transcript?

a. If no opinion exists, should a court conduct an evidentiary hearing and elicit testimony to determine the basis for the arbitrator's award? Should it review the evidence of the case to determine whether the award has any basis in law or in the factual record? What problems would such an approach entail? Is there any other way a court can police arbitral awards?

b. If arbitration must include written opinions, transcripts, and judicial review, is it still arbitration?

* * *

6. ADDITIONAL STANDARDS OF REVIEW UNDER THE FAA

In addition to the judge-made "manifest disregard" standard of review, some courts have developed additional standards of review for arbitral awards. Thus, for example, some courts have refused to enforce awards that (1) conflict with a strong public policy, see, United Paperworkers Int'l Union v. Misco, Inc., 484 U.S. 29, 43 (1987); (2) are arbitrary and capricious, see, Manville Forest Products Corp. v. United Paperworkers Int'l Union, 831 F.2d 72, 74 (5th Cir. 1987); Safeway Stores v. American Bakery

at 296 n. 25. The implied suggestion was, as the amicus brief points out, that if the Exchange is unable to act with the formality thought desirable by the district judge, it should decline to hear such disputes. The Exchange notes that its arbitrators dispose of hundreds of disputes a year and that if written decisions were required the system would be seriously delayed. Thus, it concludes that a decision not to afford arbitration procedures "may, to some extent, outline the only practical course for the Exchange," Amicus Brief at 4, despite the encouragement by the Securities and Exchange Commission of informal procedures for settling non-member disputes. See 2 S.E.C., Reports of Special Study of Securities Markets 559–61 (1963) . . .

and Confectionery Workers, 390 F.2d 79 (5th Cir. 1968); (3) are completely irrational, see National Cash Register Co. v. Wilson, 171 N.E.2d 302 (N.Y.1960); or (4) fail to draw their essence from an underlying contract, see, Nauru Phosphate Royalties, Inc. v. Drago Daic Interests, Inc., 138 F.3d 160, 164 (5th Cir.1998). Which, if any, of these standards survive *Hall Street*? What standards are the courts using in the following cases?

* * *

Swift Industries, Inc. v. Botany Industries, Inc.

466 F.2d 1125 (3d Cir. 1972).

■ EDWARD R. BECKER, DISTRICT JUDGE.

I

This is a commercial arbitration case. It comes before us on cross appeals from the judgment of the District Court for the Western District of Pennsylvania confirming in part and vacating in part the Award of an arbitrator in a dispute concerning the contractual obligations of Botany Industries, Inc. ("Botany")[2] to Swift Industries, Inc. ("Swift"). The dispute arose out of an Agreement for Exchange of Stock and Plan of Reorganization ("Agreement") dated as of August 10, 1961, among Swift, Botany and the stockholders of Swift pursuant to which, on October 2, 1961, Botany transferred to Swift the shares of two corporations, Allegheny Mortgage Company ("Allegheny") and Lincoln Homes Company ("Lincoln") in exchange for stock in Swift. Prior to the acquisition of Allegheny and Lincoln stock by Botany, Allegheny and Lincoln had been wholly owned subsidiaries of Premier Corporation of America ("Premier"), a subsidiary of Botany.[4] During the period that Allegheny and Lincoln were owned by Premier, they were included in Premier's consolidated federal income tax return.

Among the many provisions of the Agreement were warranties from Botany to Swift to the effect that there were no income taxes due the government from Allegheny and Lincoln such as are the precipitating factor in this litigation. Section 12.02 of the Agreement also contains provisions for payment by Botany to Swift in the event of a breach of that warranty. In pertinent part, § 12.02 provides that should Lincoln, Allegheny, or Swift suffer any loss resulting from liabilities of Lincoln or Allegheny for taxes attributable to ownership of property or operation of their business for any taxable period ended prior to the closing date under the Agreement (other than as provided for in certain schedules appended to the Agreement), Botany is obligated to:

2. On April 25, 1972, Botany filed a petition for an arrangement under Chapter XI of the Bankruptcy Act. Receivers have been appointed and the affairs of Botany are presently being conducted under the aegis of the Bankruptcy Court. Moreover, virtually all of Botany's operating subsidiaries have filed similar Chapter XI petitions.

4. Premier then transferred the stock of Lincoln and Allegheny to Botany pursuant to an intercorporate arrangement.

> pay Swift in cash an amount equal to all losses, liabilities and expenses *incurred or suffered* by Lincoln, Allegheny or Swift . . .

by reason thereof (emphasis added).

On October 24, 1968, Premier notified Allegheny and Lincoln that the District Director of Internal Revenue in New York City had issued a letter and report (consisting of some 140 pages and 59 schedules) adjusting the income tax liability of Premier and its subsidiaries for the years 1959–62 and determining that there were deficiencies which, with interest to September 15, 1971, totaled some $8,402,670. Premier also advised Lincoln and Allegheny that under the applicable tax regulations, Premier and each of its subsidiaries were jointly and severally liable for the entire consolidated tax liability for each year that they were included in the consolidated return. The potential liability of Allegheny and Lincoln (including interest) for the years 1960 and 1961 was calculated to be $6,033,480. Swift viewed this situation with alarm, since the potential claim exceeded the combined net worth of Allegheny and Lincoln and approximated the consolidated net worth of Swift itself. Prior to the receipt of notification of the Premier tax letter and report, Swift had embarked upon a program of corporate growth through mergers and other transactions, but the balance sheet notation required by its auditors of the possible tax liability impaired its growth program and Swift's ability to borrow.

The claims asserted by the Internal Revenue Service ("IRS") were at once disputed by Premier and Botany. On November 4, 1968, Swift notified Botany that it deemed Botany responsible for taxes or liabilities together with all expenses incurred or suffered by Allegheny, Lincoln, or Swift in connection therewith. However, on December 5, 1968, Botany, through counsel, disclaimed liability. In another development, on November 26, 1968, seven former subsidiaries of Premier (which by this time was insolvent) entered into an agreement to apportion among themselves any ultimate income tax liability and the costs of the tax litigation ("Sharing Agreement"). On February 6, 1970, the District Director in New York issued to Premier a so-called 90–day letter, or statutory notice of deficiency. This notice was contested by Premier and the parties to the Sharing Agreement by appeal to the Tax Court of the United States. The tax litigation is still pending in the Tax Court and it is presently uncertain as to how or when it will terminate.

The foregoing recital is obviously the stuff of which lawsuits are made. The lawsuit which emerged was shaped by the Agreement, which had provided that disputes arising therefrom be adjudicated in the forum of commercial arbitration governed by the rules of the American Arbitration Association (AAA). In accordance with those rules, Swift filed a Demand for Arbitration with the AAA. In addition to asking for a declaration that Botany was liable to pay any taxes, penalties, and interest that might be determined to be due at the conclusion of the tax deficiency proceedings, Swift also requested that Botany undertake and pay the cost of defense of the deficiency proceedings. After much preliminary skirmishing, the arbitration finally got underway. Botany zealously argued that it was not responsible for any deficiency. During the course of the arbitration proceedings, Swift advanced the contention that only the delivery by Botany to Swift of a cash or surety bond protecting Swift against the possible tax deficiency would afford complete relief to all parties.

On June 30, 1970, the arbitrator entered his award, which consisted of five lettered paragraphs. The arbitrator's first finding (Paragraph A) was that Botany was liable to Swift for the federal tax deficiencies of Lincoln and Allegheny for the years 1960 and 1961. That finding is no longer a subject of dispute between the parties and the judgment of the District Court confirming it is not before us. Paragraph B of the award provided that Botany should deliver to Swift the sum of $6,000,000 or, in lieu thereof, a surety bond, to protect Allegheny, Lincoln, and Swift against the tax liability as finally determined. Paragraph C required Botany to reimburse Swift in the sum of approximately $100,000 for its counsel fees and expenses to that date. This sum included fees and expenses incurred in connection with both the tax deficiency proceedings and the commercial arbitration proceedings.

The provisions of paragraphs B and C of the Award, providing for payment of $6 million cash or the surety bond and for the payment of all counsel fees, are in bitter dispute and constitute the sinews of this appeal. On January 21, 1971, the District Court, acting on Swift's petition to confirm the Award and Botany's motion to vacate it, entered its judgment in which it confirmed paragraph C (as to fees) but vacated paragraph B in its entirety on the grounds that the award of a bond was improper because: (1) relief was not specifically requested in the prayer of the original arbitration demand; and (2) the Agreement did not specify that a bond could be awarded for a breach of warranty. Swift's motion to amend the Opinion, Order and Judgment was denied.

While we will perforce come to grips with the questions raised by the appeal from the award of counsel fees, the preeminent question before us relates to the propriety of the award of the bond, viewed in either of its aspects: (1) as a $6 million cash bond; or (2) as a surety bond. Swift maintains that even though award of a bond was not expressly contemplated in the Agreement, it was authorized by Rule 42 of the Commercial Arbitration Rules which the parties adopted by virtue of the arbitration clause of the Agreement. Rule 42 authorizes the arbitrator to grant "any remedy or relief which he deems just and equitable and within the scope of the agreement of the parties." Botany, on the other hand, argues that the award failed to draw its essence from the Agreement and went beyond the scope of the submission; Botany also contends that the award was completely irrational.

The conflicting contentions of the parties require us to apply to the commercial arbitration field those principles enunciated in a labor arbitration context by the Supreme Court in the case of United Steelworkers of America v. Enterprise Wheel & Car Corp., 363 U.S. 593, 80 S.Ct. 1358, 4 L.Ed.2d 1424 (1960), and by this Court in Ludwig Honold Mfg. Co. v.

Fletcher, 405 F.2d 1123 (3d Cir.1969). Although we decide the case on a different basis than the District Court, we affirm.

II

[The court summarized the "essence test" for judicial review of an arbitral award enunciated by the Supreme Court in *Enterprise Wheel and Car,* a Section 301 case. It then quoted a section of the *Honold* opinion, in which Judge Aldisert described the scope of judicial review for labor arbitration as follows:]

> [A] labor arbitrator's award does "draw its essence from the collective bargaining agreement" if the interpretation can in any rational way be derived from the agreement, viewed in the light of its language, its context, and any other indicia of the parties' intention; only where there is a manifest disregard of the agreement, totally unsupported by principles of contract construction and the law of the shop, may a reviewing court disturb the award.

A careful reading of Honold indicates that the principles governing labor and commercial arbitration cases are similar, and we therefore consider the principles of Honold with respect to the authority of the arbitrator to fashion an award and the scope of judicial review to be applicable in commercial arbitration cases as well. However, even though the principles are similar, there are differences in the rigor of judicial review, depending upon whether we are dealing with a labor or commercial arbitration case . . .

The facts of this case require that we highlight one additional principle of review that emanates from Honold. For, in holding that an arbitrator's award does not draw its essence from the agreement if the arbitrator's interpretation cannot be rationally derived therefrom, Honold has, in addition to limiting the arbitrator's authority to fashion relief, also established that an award may not stand if it does not meet the test of fundamental rationality. The New York Court of Appeals, whose opinions are the source of much instruction in this field, has held that an award of an arbitrator is not subject to judicial revision unless it is "completely irrational," Lentine v. Fundaro, 29 N.Y.2d 382, 328 N.Y.S.2d 418, 278 N.E.2d 633 (1972). We consider this formulation to be a fair rendering of Honold. In any event, it is an accurate statement of the law.

At this juncture, we must turn to the application of the principles of Honold to the facts at bar, keeping in mind that while our scope of review is limited, it is not as limited as in a labor arbitration case. We will first examine the question of the authority of the arbitrator to award a cash or surety bond as a form of relief, then the question of the inherent rationality or irrationality of the terms of the award, and finally, the appropriateness of the award of counsel fees.

III

As we have already noted, the threshold question in the case is the extent of the arbitrator's authority to fashion relief. It is, of course, fundamental that the authority of the arbitrator springs from the agreement to arbitrate. The arbitration clause in the Agreement in question (§ 14.08) is the standard AAA arbitration clause:

> Section 14.08. Arbitration. Any controversy or dispute arising under this Agreement shall be settled by arbitration in accordance with the rules of the American Arbitration Association . . .

This clause in turn invokes § 42 of the AAA rules which provides:

> SCOPE OF AWARD–The Arbitrator may grant any remedy or relief which he deems just and equitable and within the scope of the agreement of the parties, including, but not limited to, specific performance of a contract . . .

In our preliminary statement, we summarized the provisions of the Agreement providing for Botany's obligations to Swift in the event it owes federal taxes or has certain liabilities or commits breaches of covenant. Neither in those provisions nor elsewhere in the Agreement is there mention of a bond as a form of remedy in the event of breach. It is apparent that the parties never contemplated a bond as the means of making an aggrieved party whole. Swift, nonetheless, submits that, far from limiting the power of the arbitrator to consider the question of a bond, the adoption in the Agreement of the AAA rules, thereby invoking Rule 42, constitutes an articulation of the power of the arbitrator to award "any remedy or relief" including a bond. Swift also notes that § 14.04 of the Agreement provides:

> It is not intended that the rights of Swift under . . . § 12.02 . . . shall be its exclusive remedy for the breach of any . . . warranties,

and argues that the presence of this section reinforces a conclusion as to the efficacy of Rule 42 in this case. At this juncture, reversing the coin, as it were, Swift adds that, in any event, the Agreement contains no provision excluding the consideration of the bond from arbitration and that, since the AAA clause is a so-called "broad" arbitration clause under the umbrella of which every controversy or dispute is included unless, by express language, the particular dispute is excluded, see Boston & Maine Corp. v. Illinois Central RR, 396 F.2d 425 (2d Cir. 1968), the arbitrator's award of the bond was proper.

Needless to reiterate, Botany dissents from these propositions; hence it is necessary to discuss those aspects of the Agreement which shed light on the question of the authority of the arbitrator to award a bond. Before doing so, it is important to place the nature of the arbitrator's award in perspective. In our view, the arbitrator's alternative award is tantamount to a $6 million cash bond. At oral argument, Swift placed heavy accent on that portion of the arbitrator's award that provided for the posting of a surety bond in lieu of cash, intimating that a bond premium (of approximately $17,800 per year) was the full extent of Botany's liability. However, under interrogation by the Court, Swift conceded that surety companies do not idly issue six million dollar bonds upon the mere payment of premium, but indeed require in addition a demonstration of immaculate credit standing or else the encumbering of viable assets (perhaps to the extent of $6 million). At that juncture in the case it was apparent that the award was in fact tantamount to a $6 million cash bond. Although it does not influence our decision, Botany's recently acquired status as a Chapter XI debtor (see n. 2) underscores this conclusion.

The Agreement provides that, in the event of a breach of warranty, Botany will pay to Swift in cash an amount equal to "all losses, liabilities and expenses incurred or suffered by Lincoln, Allegheny or Swift by reason of any of the events specified...." Botany asserts that no party, including Lincoln, Allegheny, or Swift, has yet, within the meaning of the Agreement, incurred or suffered any liability, expense, or loss as the result of the asserted tax deficiencies. We agree. The pending tax claim is clearly not an expense or loss. The question then is whether it is a liability in the legal sense. Within the 90-day period following issuance of the Statutory Notice of Deficiency, the matter was appealed to the Tax Court, where it now resides as an open matter to be determined by that court. The Statutory Notice of Deficiency does not constitute an assessment of liability; it constitutes the assertion of the government's claim. While responsible auditors may deem it necessary to note the issuance of the Statutory Notice on a financial statement, what they do is to note it, not list it as a legal liability, which it is not. This conclusion is unaltered by the fact that the Commissioner's determination is considered to be presumptively correct, for the burden of proof is still upon the government. See Psaty v. United States, 442 F.2d 1154 (3d Cir. 1971).

Swift and Botany have always concurred that the Agreement conferred upon the arbitrator the power to declare whether or not Botany might be liable to Swift for any tax deficiency with which Lincoln and Allegheny might ultimately be charged. What Botany has questioned is whether there may be drawn from the Agreement the authority to award what is tantamount to a six million dollar cash bond to cover a liability which has not only not yet been "incurred or suffered," but which may or may not ever accrue (or which may accrue only in part). Botany points to the absence from the Agreement of any provisions which would secure either party against breaches of warranty by the other. Such provisions are frequent in agreements of this type, and we cannot assume that their absence was accidental. Botany contends that the absence of security provisions means that the parties were relying on each other's general credit with respect to repairing any breach, and certainly we cannot gainsay that this is so.

We have sought to distill from the Agreement the essence of the arbitrator's authority. Whatever that authority may be, it is clear to us that it does not include the authority to award a six million dollar cash bond to cover a liability which contrary to the requirements of the applicable breach of warranty clause, has not yet been (and may not be) "incurred or suffered," in a situation where the parties did not provide for such security in their agreement, although they might have done so. In our view, to award, as an adjunct to declaratory relief, a form of prejudgment execution which the Agreement by its lack of reference to security seems to exclude rather than to intend, is to eclipse the framework of the agreement and to venture onto unprotected ground. We subscribe to the observations of the Enterprise court that the draftsmen may be unable to perceive in advance what specific remedy should be awarded to meet a particular contingency and that in arbitration flexibility is important. But the principle of flexibility of relief cannot be permitted to obscure or to effect a metamorphosis of the claim itself. That untoward event would occur if we were to permit the arbitrator's award to stand in this case . . .

Having reviewed the Agreement in the light of its language, its context, and the parties' apparent intent, and in terms of the question of the arbitrator's authority to fashion relief, we conclude that the arbitrator's award of a six million dollar cash surety bond does not draw its essence therefrom and that it is in manifest disregard thereof and must be set aside.

IV

Assuming, arguendo, that the arbitrator had authority to award a bond, Botany nonetheless attacks the award on a second basis: that its terms are completely irrational. We approach this allegation cautiously, for, although the complete irrationality of an award is a basis for setting it aside, the irrationality principle must be applied with a view to the narrow scope of review in arbitration cases. The basis of Botany's "irrationality" attack is the Sharing Agreement.

The Sharing Agreement was executed by the then solvent former subsidiaries of Premier after receipt of the 30 day letter. Its purpose was to provide for the orderly prosecution of the Premier tax controversy, to arrange in advance a fair allocation of and a fund for defraying its costs, and to determine in advance a fair allocation of the deficiencies finally determined to be due . . .

The tax deficiency asserted by the government was $1,019,619.60 for the year 1960 and $2,783,698.17 for the year 1961. Thus, under the sharing agreement, the maximum tax liability of Lincoln and Allegheny exclusive of interest would be $98,658.04 for 1960 and $930,979.65 for 1961 for a total of $1,029,637.69. With interest, the maximum tax liability of Lincoln and Allegheny would be approximately $1.5 million, and then only if Premier were unsuccessful in all of its contentions before the Tax Court. Can a $6 million cash bond award be deemed rational in view of a maximum $1.5 million liability under the Sharing Agreement? We think not . . .

We therefore hold that there is a second ground supporting Judge Weber's action in setting aside paragraph B of the Award—its complete lack of rationality.

* * *

Questions

1. Why does the court in *Swift Industries* invoke *Honold*, a Section 301 case, as authority on the scope of judicial review of arbitration awards?

What proposition does it derive from *Honold* for FAA cases? Why does the court conclude that it should impose more scrutiny on arbitral awards under the FAA than it does under Section 301?

2. Where does the court get the proposition that it should scrutinize arbitral awards for fundamental rationality? Does the court consider fundamental rationality an alternative formulation of the manifest disregard standard, a substitute for the manifest disregard standard, or an additional standard of review? Does the court consider the manifest disregard standard identical to the essence test from Section 301 cases?

3. Could you argue that the arbitral award of a bond in this case was within the arbitrator's authority to devise flexible remedies? Did the arbitrator manifestly disregard the law? Did he manifestly disregard the contract? If not, then what was the basis for the court's decision to vacate the award?

4. What led the court to find that the award was lacking in fundamental rationality? To what extent did it review the merits of the case to reach this conclusion? What evidence did it use? Does the fundamental rationality standard of review invite a court to retry arbitration cases on the merits? Can the standard be applied without a *de novo* trial of the case?

5. When should a court look to public policy to overturn an arbitral award? If public policy is embodied in legislation or common law, do courts have an obligation to ensure that such policies are not evaded by arbitral awards? If not, can parties always use arbitration as a means to enforce an otherwise illegal transaction?

6. Should a court have an independent obligation to review arbitral awards to avoid substantial injustice?

7. Michael LeRoy has listed thirteen different arguments for vacating arbitration awards:

> (1) [M]anifest disregard of the law (non-Steelworkers Trilogy common law standard);
>
> (2) exceed powers or imperfectly execute award (9 U.S.C. § 10(a)(4) (2006) or state UAA equivalent);
>
> (3) partiality (9 U.S.C. § 10(a)(2) or state UAA equivalent);
>
> (4) award violated a public policy (Steelworkers Trilogy common law);
>
> (5) misconduct (9 U.S.C. § 10(a)(3) or state UAA equivalent);
>
> (6) lacks jurisdiction due to timeliness requirements (9 U.S.C. § 12 or state equivalent);
>
> (7) arbitrator committed a fact-finding error (Steelworkers Trilogy common law);
>
> (8) arbitrary and capricious, irrational, or gross error (non-Steelworkers Trilogy common law standard);
>
> (9) arbitrator exceeded authority (Steelworkers Trilogy common law);

(10) award procured by corruption, fraud, or undue means (9 U.S.C. § 10(a)(1) or state UAA equivalent);

(11) award did not draw its essence from the agreement (Steelworkers Trilogy common law);

(12) remedy was punitive, excessive, or unauthorized (non-Steelworkers Trilogy common law standard); and

(13) unconstitutional or due process challenge (non-Steelworkers Trilogy common law standard).

Michael H. LeRoy, *Do Courts Create Moral Hazard?: When Judges Nullify Employer Liability in Arbitrations*, 93 Minnesota Law Review 998 (2009). Which of these survive *Hall Street*?

8. What would be the consequences of expanding the scope of judicial review of arbitral awards? Are parties likely to agree to arbitration if arbitration becomes merely a preliminary step in a prolonged dispute resolution process? See Michael H. LeRoy & Peter Feuille, *Happily Never After: When Final and Binding Arbitration Has No Fairy Tale Ending*, 13 Harv. Negot. L. Rev. 167 (2008).

* * *

Quick & Reilly, Inc. v. Jacobson

126 F.R.D. 24 (S.D.N.Y. 1989).

■ SAND, DISTRICT JUDGE.

Quick & Reilly, Inc. ("Quick & Reilly") commenced a special proceeding in state court to vacate an arbitration award, which action was removed by defendant to this Court. Defendant by way of counterclaim seeks to confirm the award and to recover costs and sanctions pursuant to Fed. R.Civ.P. 11. Both parties have moved for summary judgment.

Richard O. Jacobson maintained a sizeable brokerage account at Quick & Reilly's San Diego brokerage office, which was liquidated after a margin call on October 20, 1987. Prior to liquidation, the branch manager of this Quick & Reilly office had a conversation with Mr. Jacobson concerning what action would satisfy the maintenance call and result in the account not being liquidated. The branch manager testified at the arbitration proceeding as to this conversation and also testified that Mr. Jacobson in fact complied with the Quick & Reilly request although there was testimony that Jacobson sought to withdraw this compliance. On the afternoon of October 20, 1987, Mr. Jacobson's portfolio was liquidated on the order of Leo C. Quick, Jr., Chairman of the Board and Chief Executive Officer of Quick & Reilly. Jacobson's subsequent demands for reinstatement of the account went unheeded and on November 24, 1987, Mr. Jacobson initiated arbitration proceedings pursuant to the rules of the New York Stock Exchange.

The arbitration was held after the parties had engaged in depositions and an exchange of documents. Two days of hearings were held during which time the panel heard expert testimony as well as fact witnesses. Following the hearing, the panel requested and received memoranda concerning damages. The record of the arbitration proceedings reflects that a knowledgeable and experienced panel, including two members of the securities industry and three attorneys, meticulously examined the evidence and the claims of the parties.

The arbitration panel awarded Jacobson $1,850,170.30 plus interest. The panel wrote no opinion and did not make detailed findings.

Quick & Reilly seeks to vitiate the arbitration award urging that it was entitled to liquidate the margin account at its discretion. Quick & Reilly also contends that the panel's damage award indicates that the panel construed the Margin Agreement to give the client a ten-day grace period not intended by or contained in that agreement and that such a determination exceeded the arbitrators' authority.

We note that N.Y.Civ.Prac.L. & R. § 7511(b)(1)(iii), pursuant to which Quick & Reilly seeks to vacate the award, and § 10(d) of the Federal Arbitration Act, 9 U.S.C. § 10(d) (1970), contain virtually identical provisions, so that no significant choice of law question is presented. The New York statute provides that an arbitration award may be vacated if "an arbitrator, or agency or person making the award exceeded his power or so imperfectly executed it that a final and definite award upon the subject matter submitted was not made." It is Quick & Reilly's claim that the panel exceeded its authority by interpreting the margin agreement in a manner that did not give it "the right at any point in time with or without notice to liquidate the account." Tr. at 6 (Apr. 19, 1989) (argument on motion for summary judgment).

Although Quick & Reilly of necessity frames its contention in terms of arbitrators having exceeded their authority, the claim is in fact nothing more than a claim that the arbitrators reached an erroneous decision. Mr. Quick testified before the arbitrators as to his belief that he had the right to liquidate the account during the tumultuous hours of the October 1987 crash. The panel, having been fully briefed on this issue by counsel and having heard the testimony concerning the agreements reached by Mr. Jacobson and the Quick & Reilly branch manager, concluded otherwise.

If Quick & Reilly is correct that arbitrators are not free to conclude that an account was liquidated improperly in light of evidence such as was adduced here of an explicit agreement not to do so if certain conditions were met, then the entire force of New York Stock Exchange and similar arbitration proceedings is undermined significantly.

... In sum, this Court concludes that Quick & Reilly had a full and fair determination of its claims before a New York Stock Exchange arbitration panel. No challenge—other than vague and unfortunate aspersions as to the lack of sophistication of Iowans and their inability to appreciate the chaotic state of the market during the October 1987 crash—is made to the composition of the panel or to the manner in which the proceedings were conducted. Quick & Reilly's claim, although couched in the statutory language of an excess of authority, is simply a challenge to the correctness of the panel's determination. The law is clear that such a challenge will not lie and indeed is antithetical to the very nature and purpose of arbitration—to obtain an expeditious, efficient and definitive resolution of controversies. Shearson/American Express v. McMahon, 482 U.S. 220, 107 S.Ct. 2332, 96 L.Ed.2d 185 (1987).

The motion of Quick & Reilly to set aside the arbitration award is denied and the motion by Jacobson to confirm the award is granted.

Rule 11 Sanctions

More troublesome than the decision on the motions to vacate or confirm the arbitration award is Jacobson's application for costs and sanctions pursuant to Rule 11. "Of all the duties of the judge, imposing sanctions on lawyers is perhaps the most unpleasant." Schwarzer, Sanctions Under the New Federal Rule 11—A Closer Look, 104 F.R.D. 181, 205 (1985).

There are two components to this application. [The first component concerned Jacobson's claim of lost income due to a difference on the interest rates for margin accounts and for arbitration awards. The Court rejected that claim on the grounds that Jacobson "has not shown that the delay in collection of the arbitration award in fact caused him to incur greater interest costs."]

The second aspect of Jacobson's application relates to legal fees. Jacobson's counsel asserts:

> A cursory reading of the Petition demonstrates that this action has been filed for an improper purpose and that, after reasonable inquiry, a competent attorney could not form a reasonable belief as a matter of law that the pleading is well grounded in fact and is warranted by existing law or a good faith argument for the extension, modification, or reversal of existing law. See Eastway Construction Corp. v. City of New York, 762 F.2d 243 (2d Cir.1985), cert. denied, (484 U.S. 918) 108 S.Ct. 269 (98 L.Ed.2d 226) (1987). There is no existing law ... that could possibly warrant the relief sought by Quick and Reilly.

Memorandum of Law in Support of Respondent's Motion for Sanctions at 2 ...

In response, counsel for Quick & Reilly renews its protestations that the arbitration award was indeed subject to attack because it "deviate[d] from the parties' agreement either by rewriting it, and fostering a result inconsistent with public policy, or departing from the 'essence' of their agreement." Q & R Supp. Memo. at 5–6. Moreover, Quick & Reilly's counsel asserts that, even if erroneous, the position it took was colorable and was not intended to harass, cause delay or needlessly increase the cost of litigation.

Counsel for Quick & Reilly [further asserts that because] arbitration awards are not self-executing, Jacobson would have to go to court—as he, in fact, did in Iowa—to confirm the arbitration award and convert it to a judgment. Jacobson thus necessarily would have to deal with Quick & Reilly's objections to the award, and resolve their dispute through judicial intervention.

We reject this reasoning insofar as it assumes that judicial intervention is inevitable. When an arbitration award is not subject to valid legal challenge, it should be honored without the need for either party to resort to the courts.

We find that Jacobson is entitled to recover a portion of the reasonable attorneys' fees incurred directly as a result of this proceeding. Recognizing that Rule 11 was not intended to abrogate the general American rule that each party is to bear its own legal expenses, we believe that the claims advanced by Quick & Reilly were so totally devoid of merit as to warrant imposition of Rule 11 sanctions. Perhaps counsel acted in subjective good faith; we have no reason to believe that this is not so, but this is no longer the criterion for Rule 11 determinations.

The zeal of an attorney who lost the arbitration proceeding cannot overcome the lack of merit in the claims and the fact that objective counsel should have recognized the futility of the challenge . . .

Conclusion

We are mindful of the admonition of the Court of Appeals for the Second Circuit that

> Rule 11 sanctions should be applied only where "after reasonable inquiry, a competent attorney could not form a reasonable belief that the pleading is well grounded in fact and is warranted by existing law or a good faith argument for the extension, modification or reversal of existing law." Eastway Construction Corp. v. City of New York, 762 F.2d 243, 254 (2d Cir. 1985).

Mercado v. U.S. Customs Service, 873 F.2d 641, 646 (2d Cir. 1989).

We believe that pursuant to this standard, Rule 11 sanctions in the amount stated above are appropriate in this proceeding.

* * *

Questions

1. In *Quick & Reilly v. Jacobson,* the arbitrator rendered an award that arguably suffered from defects similar to those in the arbitral award the court vacated in *Swift v. Botany.* In both cases, the losing party complains that the arbitrator implied terms into the agreement that had no basis in the agreement itself. Why isn't this award overturned? Can the cases be distinguished? Can we distinguish a claim that an arbitral award is in excess of the arbitrator's powers under an agreement from a claim that an award that is an erroneous interpretation of an agreement?

2. How does the court justify the imposition of Rule 11 sanctions? Was the claim in fact "totally devoid of merit" as the court says? Is the imposition of Rule 11 sanctions another means courts can use to limit judicial review of arbitral awards?

* * *

2. Remedies in Arbitration

A. Provisional Remedies

In disputes that are scheduled for arbitration, as with disputes pending in a court, one party may be concerned that while the case is pending an intervening event, such as the dissipation of the respondent's assents, may render any award in their favor ineffectual. Although some arbitration procedures permit arbitrators to issue interim remedies, assets still may be dissipated before an arbitrator can be appointed. One response to this concern has been for parties to an arbitration to apply to a court to obtain preliminary relief such as an injunction or other provisional remedy pending the arbitration. Typically parties ask the court for an injunction to maintain the *status quo* pending the ultimate outcome of the dispute at arbitration. Courts are divided over the question of whether such an injunction may issue under the Federal Arbitration Act, as the cases below illustrate.

Merrill Lynch, Pierce, Fenner & Smith, Inc. v. Hovey

726 F.2d 1286 (8th Cir. 1984).

■ Lay, Chief Judge.

Merrill Lynch, Pierce, Fenner & Smith, Inc. sought injunctive relief against five former employees to prevent their use of Merrill Lynch's records and their solicitation of Merrill Lynch clients. The employees counterclaimed seeking to compel arbitration under the Federal Arbitration Act, 9 U.S.C. §§ 1–4 (1982). The district court granted injunctive relief and refused to submit the dispute to arbitration. The employees have appealed.

As former account executives with Merrill Lynch, Ivan Hovey, Mary Wichmann, Bruce Markey, and Richard Kadry each signed employment agreements. The agreement provides, inter alia, that certain records "shall remain the property of Merrill Lynch at all times during my employment with Merrill Lynch and after termination of my employment ... with Merrill Lynch" and prohibits former account executives from removing or retaining copies thereof; and it purports to prohibit these employees from "soliciting" clients of Merrill Lynch for one year after the termination of employment. The employees subsequently resigned from Merrill Lynch and joined E.F. Hutton, a competitor. The employees admit that they have retained some limited information entrusted to them by clients whom they had serviced while at Merrill Lynch. Moreover, the employees admit that they have solicited these customers while at E.F. Hutton. (Appellant's Brief at 4). On appeal, we are not addressing whether this constitutes a breach of the employment agreement nor do we address the validity of the clauses that purport to prohibit this conduct. The issue presented on appeal is whether the dispute is subject to arbitration or whether Merrill Lynch may properly proceed in the federal district court.

I. Arbitrability

We initially address three issues: (1) whether there exists a valid agreement to arbitrate; (2) whether the subject matter of this dispute is covered by the agreement; and if so, (3) whether there has been a breach of the agreement....

Merrill Lynch and Hovey, Markey, and Wichmann are members of the NYSE. As members of the NYSE, they have agreed to comply with the NYSE rules, including the dispute resolution procedures detailed in Rule 347. The employees seek arbitration under the Federal Arbitration Act, 9 U.S.C. §§ 3, 4 based on NYSE Rule 347. Rule 347 provides:

> Any controversy between a registered representative and any member or member organization arising out of the employment or termination of employment of such registered representative by and with such member or member organization shall be settled by arbitration, at the instance of any such party, in accordance with the arbitration procedure described elsewhere in these rules.

It is readily apparent that this rule is binding on its signatories and is part of the employment agreement between the employees and Merrill Lynch.... Moreover, we find that Rule 347 constitutes a valid written agreement to arbitrate which is governed by the Federal Arbitration Act. 9 U.S.C. § 1–4 ...

On the other hand, Kadry and Erickson are not members of the NYSE, nor do their employment contracts contain an arbitration agreement. Kadry and Erickson rely primarily on Article VIII of the NYSE Constitution to support their claim for arbitration. Article VIII allows nonmembers to compel arbitration of any controversy "arising out of the business" of a member.[1] Merrill Lynch contends that the employees' reliance on Article VIII is misplaced. Merrill Lynch urges that Article VIII's reference to "business" reflects that the provision's intention is to allow *customers*, not employees, to compel arbitration. We find, however, that the provision is not so limited. The article of the Constitution reflects the self-regulation of the securities industry, as well as the effort to provide an integrated

1. "Any controversy between parties who are members, ... member firms ... and any controversy between a non-member and a member ... arising out of the business of such member, ... shall at the instance of any such party, be submitted for arbitration, in accordance with the provisions of the Constitution and the Rules of the Board of Directors." NYSE Const. art. VIII, § 1.

method of resolving disputes involving the affairs of the NYSE. We find that Article VIII constitutes an agreement to arbitrate, upon which Kadry and Erickson may rely.

In accordance with the Federal Arbitration Act we also find that all of the employees have timely and properly requested arbitration. The remaining issue is whether the arbitration agreement reaches the subject matter of the dispute here. . . .

The district court found that the solicitation and record duplication took place *after* the employment relationship between the parties had been terminated. Employing essentially a temporal analysis, the court concluded that the violations, therefore, could not have "aris[en] out of the employment or termination of employment." On appeal, Merrill Lynch reasserts the contention that only those disputes which occurred during the employment relationship are arbitrable. On the other hand, the employees contend that, although the dispute occurred after their termination, it is still within the scope of the arbitration agreement. Upon analysis of the applicability of the Federal Arbitration Act and the Rules and Constitution of the NYSE, along with a plain reading of the arbitration agreement, we find that the dispute is arbitrable.

Under the Federal Arbitration Act, 9 U.S.C. §§ 1–4 (1982), where the parties have agreed to seek dispute resolution by arbitration, the courts are asked to stay their hand. Moses H. Cone Memorial Hospital v. Mercury Construction Corp., 460 U.S. 1, 103 S.Ct. 927, 74 L.Ed.2d 765 (1983). The scope of the arbitration agreement will be interpreted liberally and "any doubts concerning the scope of arbitrable issues should be resolved in favor of arbitration." Moses H. Cone, 103 S.Ct. at 941 & n. 27; Johnson Controls, 713 F.2d at 373. "[T]he court's function in an action to compel arbitration may not extend beyond ascertaining whether the party seeking arbitration has made a claim which *on its face* is governed by the contract." National R.R. Passenger Corp., 501 F.2d at 427 (emphasis in original). The presumption of arbitrability, however, is tempered by the caveat that parties cannot be forced to arbitrate controversies that they have not agreed to submit to arbitration. United Steelworkers of America v. Warrior & Gulf Navigation Co., 363 U.S. 574, 582, 80 S.Ct. 1347, 1352, 4 L.Ed.2d 1409 (1960).

To support its argument that the present dispute is not arbitrable, Merrill Lynch relies primarily on Coudert v. Paine Webber Jackson & Curtis, 705 F.2d 78 (2d Cir. 1983) and the district court opinion in Downey v. Merrill Lynch, Pierce, Fenner & Smith, Inc., No. 83 Civ. 4312 (S.D.N.Y. Aug. 18, 1983), in which the appeal was pending. In Coudert, a divided panel of the Second Circuit held that a dispute involving a defamation claim of a former account executive was not arbitrable where the alleged defamation took place after the account executive had resigned. In Downing, a district court extended this holding to a dispute involving a violation of the solicitation clause after the employee had resigned and joined a competing firm. On appeal, however, the Second Circuit reversed the district court's extension, finding that "a dispute over such a contract term would clearly be arbitrable notwithstanding the time at which the dispute arose.'' Downing v. Merrill Lynch, Pierce, Fenner & Smith, No. 83–7710 slip op. at 5 (2d Cir. 1984) (remanded to determine whether there was an agreement to arbitrate).

The sole issue in Coudert was the arbitrability under the Rules of the NYSE of a grievance arising out of an employer's allegedly tortious conduct. The majority in Coudert distinguished "grievance[s] arising after the termination of the agreement to arbitrate'' from grievances that are based on conditions that arise during the term of the agreement to arbitrate. 705 F.2d at 81. The former are not arbitrable; the latter, however, are arbitrable regardless of whether the agreement to arbitrate has since ceased. In Coudert, the majority found that the basis of the grievance was the employer's conduct after the termination of the employment relationship and therefore also after the termination of the agreement to arbitrate. Id. at 82. Accordingly, the dispute was not found to be subject to the arbitration agreement. Id. Our case is distinguishable from Coudert and we decline to extend a rigid temporal approach to the determination of arbitrability in the situation before us.

To interpret the arbitration agreement in the manner asserted by Merrill Lynch would require reading the words "arising out of'' as synonymous with "during.'' This interpretation is inconsistent with the words chosen and the intent of the parties. The language of the agreement is broad and the term "arising out of'' contemplates that for some controversies the arbitration agreement will survive the employment relationship . . .

For the reasons discussed, we hold that the present controversy "arise[s] out of the employment or termination of employment.'' At least as to the construction and applicability of these conditions, we conclude that the arbitration agreement remains viable beyond the employment relationship of the parties.

II. Preliminary Injunction

In addition to determining that the controversy was nonarbitrable, the district court granted a preliminary injunction. We consistently have held that the grant of preliminary relief is within the district court's discretion. Dataphase Systems, Inc. v. C L Systems, Inc., 640 F.2d 109, 114 (8th Cir. 1981); Planned Parenthood of Minnesota, Inc. v. Citizens for Community Action, 558 F.2d 861, 866 (8th Cir. 1977). In light of our determination that the controversy is arbitrable, however, we find that the issuance of injunctive relief abrogates the intent of the Federal Arbitration Act and consequently was an abuse of discretion. Cf. Merrill Lynch, Pierce, Fenner & Smith, Inc. v. Scott, No. 83–1480 (10th Cir. May 12, 1983) (summary order staying the injunction pending arbitration).

Merrill Lynch urges this court to continue the preliminary injunction during the arbitration procedures. Merrill Lynch asserts that the continuance of the injunction is necessary to avoid irreparable harm and to assure the viability of an adequate remedy at law. The cases cited by Merrill Lynch support the contention that injunctions can be granted to preserve the status quo.[2] However, in view of our determination that the Federal Arbitration Act applies, we decline to pass on these contentions. The parties have not alleged that the contract provides for or contemplates injunctive relief along the lines granted. Accordingly, the Act directs the court to stay the judicial action. 9 U.S.C. § 3.

The congressional intent revealed in the Arbitration Act is to facilitate quick, expeditious arbitration ... Here, the judicial inquiry requisite to determine the propriety of injunctive relief necessarily would inject the court into the merits of issues more appropriately left to the arbitrator. See Prima Paint Corp. v. Flood & Conklin Manufacturing Co., 388 U.S. 395, 87 S.Ct. 1801, 18 L.Ed.2d 1270 (1967) (issue of fraud in inducement of contract was for arbitrator); see also Buffalo Forge Co. v. United Steelworkers of America, AFL–CIO, 428 U.S. 397, 412, 96 S.Ct. 3141, 3149, 49 L.Ed.2d 1022 (1976). In Buffalo Forge, the Court refused to enjoin a strike pending arbitration of the validity of the strike. The Court recognized that sanctioning judicial intervention at this preliminary stage would eviscerate the intent of arbitration agreements. Id. at 412, 96 S.Ct. at 3149.

We find this compelling authority to hold that, where the Arbitration Act is applicable and no qualifying contractual language has been alleged, the district court errs in granting injunctive relief. In doing so, we sustain not only "the plain meaning of the statute but also the unmistakably clear congressional purpose that the arbitration procedure, when selected by the parties to a contract, be speedy and not subject to delay and obstruction in the courts." Prima Paint Corp., 388 U.S. at 404, 87 S.Ct. at 1806.

For the reasons stated above, we reverse and remand to the district court for proceedings consistent with the determinations here.

* * *

Merrill Lynch, Pierce, Fenner & Smith, Inc. v. Bradley

756 F.2d 1048 (4th Cir. 1985).

■ CHAPMAN, CIRCUIT JUDGE:

This expedited appeal involves a dispute between Merrill Lynch, Pierce, Fenner and Smith, Inc. (Merrill Lynch) and one of its former

2. To support its claim for injunctive relief Merrill Lynch relies on Erving v. Virginia Squires Basketball Club, 468 F.2d 1064 (2d Cir.1972). In Erving, the Second Circuit found that the dispute was arbitrable; however, it also granted injunctive relief for the purpose of maintaining the status quo. Id. at 1067. Although Erving does provide some support for Merrill Lynch, the case is distinguishable. First, the employee's contract stipulated that his services were exceptional and unique and that the loss of them to the Squires would be unestimatable and not compensable by damages. In light of these stipulations, the contract expressly provided for injunctive relief, pending completion of the arbitration process. Id. at 1006 n. 1. Second, the issues addressed by the court to determine the propriety of injunctive relief were not the same ones that would ultimately be determinative of the merits of the dispute. In contrast, in our case we do not have such a contract provision and, moreover, the evidentiary foray necessary to satisfy the Dataphase criteria are essentially the same that we have determined are more properly left to arbitration.

account executives, Kenneth D. Bradley. Merrill Lynch brought this action against Bradley seeking damages as well as injunctive relief to prevent him from using Merrill Lynch's records and soliciting Merrill Lynch's clients. On July 26, 1984, the district court held a hearing on Merrill Lynch's motion for a temporary restraining order and Bradley's motion to stay the trial and compel arbitration pursuant to the Federal Arbitration Act, 9 U.S.C. §§ 1–14 (1982). At the conclusion of the hearing, the district court granted Merrill Lynch a preliminary injunction, denied Bradley's motion to stay the injunction, and ordered expedited arbitration of the parties' dispute. Bradley appeals from the district court's order granting Merrill Lynch a preliminary injunction pending arbitration. 28 U.S.C. § 1292(a)(1). We affirm.

I

On December 16, 1981, Merrill Lynch hired Bradley to serve as an account executive at its office in Newport News, Virginia. At that time Merrill Lynch and Bradley entered into an Account Executive Agreement which provides, inter alia, the following:

> 1. All records of Merrill Lynch, including the names and addresses of its clients, are and shall remain the property of Merrill Lynch at all times during my employment with Merrill Lynch and after termination for any reason of my employment with Merrill Lynch, and that none of such records or any part of them is to be removed from the premises of Merrill Lynch either in original form or in duplicated or copied form, and that the names, addresses, and other facts in such records are not to be transmitted verbally except in the ordinary course of conducting business for Merrill Lynch.
>
> 2. In the event of termination of my services with Merrill Lynch for any reason, I will not solicit any of the clients of Merrill Lynch whom I served or whose names became known to me while in the employ of Merrill Lynch in any community or city served by the office of Merrill Lynch, or any subsidiary thereof, at which I was employed at any time for a period of one year from the date of termination of my employment. In the event that any of the provisions contained in this paragraph and/or paragraph (1) above are violated I understand that I will be liable to Merrill Lynch for any damage caused thereby.

The Account Executive Agreement also provides that "any controversy between myself [Bradley] and Merrill Lynch arising out of my employment, or the termination of my employment with Merrill Lynch for any reason whatsoever shall be settled by arbitration...." In addition, Bradley was required to sign New York Stock Exchange Form U–4 when he registered with the Exchange and began his employment at Merrill Lynch. Like his employment agreement, this form requires that any controversy between Bradley and any member organization of the New York Stock Exchange shall be settled by arbitration. Finally, both Rule 347 of the Rules of the

New York Stock Exchange and Article VIII, Section One of the Exchange Constitution provide that all controversies between members of the Exchange arising out of the business of the members shall be settled by arbitration in accordance with the Rules of the New York Stock Exchange.

At approximately 4:00 p.m. on Friday, July 20, 1984, Bradley tendered his resignation to Merrill Lynch and announced that he had accepted a position with Prudential–Bache Securities, Inc. at its office in Virginia Beach, Virginia. Merrill Lynch alleges that as early as the day following his resignation Bradley telephoned most or all of his Merrill Lynch customers and urged them to transfer their accounts from Merrill Lynch to Prudential–Bache. Merrill Lynch learned of Bradley's actions and filed suit on Monday, July 23, 1984, alleging breach of contract, breach of fiduciary duty, and violation of Va.Code § 18.2–499.

. . . The district court's preliminary injunction prohibits Bradley from soliciting any customers whom he had serviced or learned about while employed by Merrill Lynch. The injunction further prohibits Bradley from participating in the servicing of these customers by Prudential–Bache, including any referrals to other personnel of Prudential–Bache. At the request of Bradley's counsel, however, the district court's order was modified to delete the requirement that the New York Stock Exchange conduct arbitration in an expedited fashion.

II

Merrill Lynch and Bradley both agree that the dispute between them is subject to mandatory arbitration and that Bradley is not in default in proceeding with arbitration. Thus, the principal issue on appeal is whether § 3 of the Federal Arbitration Act, 9 U.S.C. § 3 (1982), absolutely precludes a district court from granting one party a preliminary injunction to preserve the status quo pending the arbitration of the parties' dispute.

Bradley argues that the district court abused its discretion in granting Merrill Lynch a preliminary injunction because § 3 precludes a court from considering the merits of a controversy when the dispute is subject to mandatory arbitration. Bradley cites two recent decisions to support his argument. Merrill Lynch, Pierce, Fenner & Smith, Inc. v. Hovey, 726 F.2d 1286 (8th Cir. 1984); Merrill Lynch, Pierce, Fenner & Smith, Inc. v. Scott, No. 83–1480 (10th Cir. May 12, 1983). . . .

In Hovey the Eighth Circuit held that § 3 precludes a court from granting Merrill Lynch a preliminary injunction against its former account executives pending arbitration. The court stated that "where the Arbitration Act is applicable and no qualifying contractual language has been alleged, the district court errs in granting injunctive relief." 726 F.2d at 1292. In Scott the Tenth Circuit vacated, by order and without formal written opinion, a preliminary injunction which the district court had granted pending arbitration. Nevertheless, for the reasons that follow, we decline to follow Hovey and Scott and instead hold that, under certain circumstances, a district court has the discretion to grant one party a preliminary injunction to preserve the status quo pending the arbitration of the parties' dispute.

The starting point for our inquiry, of course, is the language of § 3:

> If any suit or proceeding be brought in any of the courts of the United States upon any issue referable to arbitration under an agreement in writing for such arbitration, the court in which such suit is pending, upon being satisfied that the issue involved in such suit or proceeding is referable to arbitration under such an agreement, shall on application of one of the parties stay the trial of the action until such arbitration has been had in accordance with the terms of the agreement, providing the applicant for the stay is not in default in proceeding with such arbitration.

9 U.S.C. § 3 (emphasis added). Section 3 does not contain a clear command abrogating the equitable power of district courts to enter preliminary injunctions to preserve the status quo pending arbitration. Instead, § 3 states only that the court shall stay the "trial of the action"; it does not mention preliminary injunctions or other pre-trial proceedings. Certainly Congress knows how to draft a statute which addresses all actions within the judicial power.[3] Furthermore, nothing in the statute's legislative history suggests that the word "trial" should be given a meaning other than its common and ordinary usage: the ultimate resolution of the dispute on the merits. See Senate Rep. No. 536, 68th Cong., 1st Sess. (1924); H.R.Rep. No. 96, 68th Cong., 1st Sess. (1924).

We do not believe that Congress would have enacted a statute intended to have the sweeping effect of stripping the federal judiciary of its equitable powers in all arbitrable commercial disputes without undertaking a comprehensive discussion and evaluation of the statute's effect. Accordingly, we conclude that the language of § 3 does not preclude a district court from granting one party a preliminary injunction to preserve the status quo pending arbitration.

Our interpretation of § 3 is not inconsistent with this Court's decision in In re Mercury Construction Corp., 656 F.2d 933 (4th Cir. 1981) (en banc), aff'd sub nom. Moses H. Cone Memorial Hospital v. Mercury Construction Corp., 460 U.S. 1, 103 S.Ct. 927, 74 L.Ed.2d 765 (1983). Bradley relies upon an isolated phrase in In re Mercury Construction Corp. to support his argument that § 3 requires the stay of "all proceedings" pending arbitration. See 656 F.2d at 939 ("Section 3 requires a stay of all proceedings until such arbitration has been had in accordance with the terms of the agreement . . ."). This reliance is misplaced, however, because

3. For example, 28 U.S.C. § 2283 provides:

> A court of the United States may not grant an injunction to stay proceedings in a State court except as expressly authorized by Act of Congress, or where necessary in aid of its jurisdiction, or to protect or effectuate its judgments.

(Emphasis added.) See also 11 U.S.C. § 362(a)(1) (filing of bankruptcy petition operates as a stay of any "judicial, administrative, or other proceeding against the debtor").

that decision did not turn in any way on the meaning of the term "trial" as used in § 3. Rather, In re Mercury Construction Corp. involved the unrelated question of whether a federal court may compel arbitration under § 4 even though one of the parties has instituted a state court action. 656 F.2d at 938. Thus, the "all proceedings" language is dicta ...

This Court's decisions in Lever Brothers Co. v. International Chemical Workers Union, Local 217, 554 F.2d 115 (4th Cir.1976), and Drivers, Chauffeurs, Warehousemen & Helpers Teamsters Local Union No. 71 v. Akers Motor Lines, Inc., 582 F.2d 1336 (4th Cir. 1978), provide additional support for our decision here ...

In Lever Brothers this court adopted the following standard for preliminary injunctions of labor disputes subject to mandatory arbitration:

> An injunction to preserve the status quo pending arbitration may be issued either against a company or against a union in an appropriate Boys Markets case where it is necessary to prevent conduct by the party enjoined from rendering the arbitral process a hollow formality in those instances where, as here, the arbitral award when rendered could not return the parties substantially to the status quo ante.

554 F.2d at 123. Similarly, in Akers Motor Lines we stated that if the enjoined conduct would render the arbitration process a "hollow formality," the clear language of the Norris–LaGuardia Act must give way to the congressional policy favoring arbitration. 582 F.2d at 1341.

We think the Lever Brothers–Akers Motor Lines standard represents a sound approach for determining whether a district court has abused its discretion in granting a preliminary injunction pending arbitration. Accordingly, we hold that where a dispute is subject to mandatory arbitration under the Federal Arbitration Act, a district court has the discretion to grant a preliminary injunction to preserve the status quo pending the arbitration of the parties' dispute if the enjoined conduct would render that process a "hollow formality." The arbitration process would be a hollow formality where "the arbitral award when rendered could not return the parties substantially to the status quo ante." Lever Brothers, 554 F.2d at 123. The instant case is just such a case.

We think that our decision will further, not frustrate, the policies underlying the Federal Arbitration Act. In this case preliminary injunctive relief pending arbitration furthers congressional policy by ensuring that the dispute resolution would be a meaningful process because, without such an injunction, Bradley's conduct might irreversibly alter the status quo. When an account executive breaches his employment contract by soliciting his former employer's customers, a nonsolicitation clause requires immediate application to have any effect. An injunction even a few days after solicitation has begun is unsatisfactory because the damage is done. The customers cannot be "unsolicited." It may be impossible for the arbitral award to return the parties substantially to the status quo ante because the prevailing party's damages may be too speculative.

We cannot accept Bradley's argument that preliminary injunctions support the congressional policy favoring arbitration of labor disputes but undermine the congressional policy favoring arbitration of commercial and maritime matters. Nor can we accept Bradley's argument that the district court's preliminary injunction will prejudice the arbitrator's subsequent decision on the merits. The arbitrators are sworn to render a decision based solely upon the evidence presented to them. We must assume that the arbitrators will perform their task conscientiously. Furthermore, we do not believe that Congress intended § 3 to tie a district court's hands while one party, pending the arbitration of the parties' dispute, deliberately and irreversibly altered the status quo and thereby deprived the other party of a meaningful arbitration process . . .

III

The final issue is whether the district court abused its discretion in granting the injunction. Under the balance of hardship test the district court must consider, in "flexible interplay," the following four factors in determining whether to issue a preliminary injunction: (1) the likelihood of irreparable harm to the plaintiff without the injunction; (2) the likelihood of harm to the defendant with an injunction; (3) the plaintiff's likelihood of success on the merits; and (4) the public interest. Blackwelder Furniture Co. v. Seilig Manufacturing Co., 550 F.2d 189, 193–96 (4th Cir. 1977). Under this test the district court must first compare the likelihood of irreparable harm to the plaintiff with the potential harm the defendant will experience from the grant of preliminary injunctive relief. If the balance of hardship tips decidedly in the plaintiff's favor, then the district court may grant a preliminary injunction if it determines that the dispute presents a serious issue for litigation and that the injunction will serve the public interest. Id. at 194–95. Accord, North Carolina State Ports Authority v. Dart Containerline Co., 592 F.2d 749, 750 (4th Cir. 1979). Because these determinations involve findings of fact, a district court's order granting preliminary injunctive relief may be reversed only if an abuse of discretion is shown. West Virginia Highlands Conservancy v. Island Creek Coal Co., 441 F.2d 232, 235 (4th Cir. 1971); Singleton v. Anson County Board of Education, 387 F.2d 349, 350 (4th Cir. 1967).

We are unable to conclude that the district court abused its discretion in granting a preliminary injunction pending arbitration. We think that the district court was within its discretion in concluding that the balance of hardship test tips decidedly in Merrill Lynch's favor because Bradley did not establish that the preliminary injunction pending expedited arbitration would cause him harm and because Merrill Lynch faced irreparable, non-compensable harm in the loss of its customers. This court has recognized that "irreparability of harm includes the 'impossibility of ascertaining with any accuracy the extent of the loss.' " Blackwelder Furniture Co., 550 2d at 197 (quoting Foundry Services Inc. v. Beneflux Corp., 206 F.2d 214, 216 (2d Cir. 1953)). Thus, the district court implicitly found that arbitration of this dispute would be a hollow formality absent preliminary relief. Accordingly, the order of the district court is AFFIRMED.

* * *

Note on Criteria for Imposing Provisional Remedies Pending Arbitration

The Fourth Circuit's position in *Merrill Lynch, et al. v. Bradley*, has subsequently been adopted by the First, Second, Third, Seventh, Ninth, and Tenth Circuits. In the circuits that have held that district courts can grant preliminary injunctions to maintain the *status quo* pending arbitration, the courts must determine what criteria justify the granting of such an injunction. The conventional factors a court considers in ruling on an application for a preliminary injunction include probability of success on the merits, irreparable harm, a balance of equities favoring the moving party, and the impact of the injunction on the public interest. Often these factors are formulated somewhat differently, or assigned different weights by different courts. For example, the Fifth Circuit has a four factor test in which the movant must show:

> (1) a substantial likelihood of success on the merits, (2) a substantial threat that plaintiffs will suffer irreparable harm if the injunction is not granted, (3) that the threatened injury outweighs any damage that the injunction might cause the defendant, and (4) that the injunction will not disserve the public interest.

Nichols v. Alcatel USA, Inc., 532 F.3d 364, 372 (5th Cir. 2008). In the Ninth Circuit, by contrast, a district court may grant a preliminary injunction under two sets of circumstances:

> In the first case, a plaintiff must show (1) a strong likelihood of success on the merits, (2) the possibility of irreparable injury to plaintiff if preliminary relief is not granted, (3) a balance of hardships favoring the plaintiff, and (4) advancement of the public interest (in certain cases). In the second case, a court may grant the injunction if the plaintiff demonstrates either a combination of probable success on the merits and the possibility of irreparable injury or that serious questions are raised and the balance of hardships tips sharply in his favor.

Guzman v. Shewry, 552 F.3d 941, 948 (9th Cir. 2009) (citations omitted).

The Second Circuit departs significantly from the other circuits. It applies a two-prong test alternative test to determine whether to issue a preliminary injunction:

> A party seeking a preliminary injunction ordinarily must show: (1) a likelihood of irreparable harm in the absence of the injunction; and (2) either a likelihood of success on the merits or sufficiently serious questions going to the merits to make them a fair ground for litigation, with a balance of hardships tipping decidedly in the movant's favor.

New York State Restaurant Ass'n v. New York City Bd. of Health, 556 F.3d 114, 122 (2d Cir. 2009).

Several problems emerge when courts attempt to adapt the conventional factors governing preliminary injunctions to an injunction that is sought prior to an arbitration. One is that it is often difficult for a court to determine whether an injunction should issue without inquiring into the merits of the case (especially when the "likelihood of success on the merits" is an explicit prerequisite for an injunction). Another is that there is a danger that a court will introduce a degree of delay and formality into the proceedings that the choice of the arbitral forum was designed to avoid. An even more troubling question is whether it is possible for a court to make such a determination without substituting a judicial decision on the merits for the arbitral decision that the parties have contracted for. The difficulties involved in deciding whether to grant a preliminary injunction are illustrated in the following case.

* * *

Performance Unlimited, Inc. v. Questar Publishers, Inc.

52 F.3d 1373 (6th Cir. 1995).

■ MILBURN, CIRCUIT JUDGE.

This is a case of first impression in this circuit involving the question of whether a district court can issue a preliminary injunction under § 3 of the Federal Arbitration Act, 9 U.S.C. § 3 (1982), when the parties to this action have agreed that arbitration "shall be the sole and exclusive remedy for resolving any disputes between the parties arising out of or involving [the] Agreement" sued upon. Plaintiff Performance Unlimited, Inc. ("Performance") appeals the district court's order denying its motion for a preliminary injunction, filed pursuant to 28 U.S.C. §§ 1332(a)(1), 2201, and 2202, which would have required defendant Questar Publishers, Inc. ("Questar") to pay royalties to Performance while their contract dispute was resolved in arbitration. On appeal, the issues are (1) whether the district court erred in finding that it was precluded from issuing a preliminary injunction because of the mandatory arbitration provision in the parties' licensing agreement and (2) whether the district court erred in finding that Performance did not satisfy the four factors considered in its decision to grant or deny a preliminary injunction. For the reasons that follow, we reverse and remand.

I

A.

This is an action for breach of contract, for a declaration of the parties' contractual rights, and for a preliminary injunction arising from the nonpayment of royalties pursuant to a licensing agreement between Performance and Questar. The royalties which are at the core of the parties dispute stem from the publication of The Beginner's Bible, a compilation of children's bible stories.

Don Wise, the president of Performance, developed the idea of publishing a series of children's bible stories, illustrated with drawings that would appeal to small children and aimed toward beginning readers. This concept was developed into a series of bible story books which were written by Karyn Henley and were sold under the name Dovetales. James R. Leininger invested in Performance in order to develop and promote the Dovetales books.

Eventually, however, Wise and Leininger agreed to separate their activities. As a result, Leininger received ownership of the copyrights and trademarks in the Dovetales product. Leininger licensed the rights to publish the Dovetales stories to Performance. In turn, Wise entered into a license agreement, a sublicense, with Questar to publish a book containing all of the original Dovetales stories along with some additional stories written by Karyn Henley, titled The Beginner's Bible. The license agreement between Performance and Questar is dated June 22, 1989, and is the subject of this action.

Pursuant to the license agreement, Questar published and began to sell The Beginner's Bible. Further, the license agreement obligated Questar to make semi-annual royalty payments to Performance based upon the sales of The Beginner's Bible. Questar regularly made the royalty payments to Performance until July of 1994. However, in a letter, dated July 28, 1994, Questar informed Performance that Performance had breached the license agreement. Furthermore, Questar refused to pay the accrued royalties to Performance, indicating in its letter that it wished to initiate a "mediation/arbitration process pursuant to paragraph 11 of the [license] agreement." J.A. 20. Instead, on July 29, 1994, Questar opened an account, the "Beginner's Bible Royalty Escrow Account," at the United States National Bank of Oregon in Sisters, Oregon, and deposited $184,484.94, the accrued royalties, into that account. J.A. 65.

The license agreement between Questar and Performance includes a provision for resolution of disputes. Paragraph 11 of the agreement provides in relevant part:

> The Licensor [Performance] and the Publisher [Questar] agree that God, In His Word, forbids Christians to bring lawsuits against other Christians in secular courts of law . . . and that God desires Christians to be reconciled to one another when disputes of any nature arise between them . . .
>
> [I]n their resolution of any disputes that may arise under this Agreement, each party agrees that the provisions for mediation and arbitration set forth below shall be the sole and exclusive remedy for resolving any disputes between the parties arising out of or involving this Agreement.
>
> It is further agreed that the Licensor and the Publisher hereby waive whatever right they might otherwise have to maintain a lawsuit against the other in a secular court of law, on any disputes arising out of or involving this Agreement.

> In the event of such a dispute, the Licensor and the Publisher agree to take the following steps, in the order indicated, until such a dispute is resolved:
>
> (1) the Licensor and the Publisher shall meet together, pray together, and purpose to be reconciled . . .
>
> (2) The Licensor and the Publisher shall invite other witnesses, who may have knowledge of the actual facts of the dispute or whose knowledge would be helpful in resolving the dispute, to meet together with both parties, to pray together, and to purpose to be reconciled . . .
>
> (3) Both the Licensor and the Publisher shall each appoint one person as a Mediator; these two persons chosen shall then appoint a third Mediator. The three Mediators shall together determine the process of mediation, to which the Licensor and the Publisher agree to comply, and shall be free to act as Arbitrators, to whose authority the Licensor and the Publisher agree to submit. The three Mediators shall also determine to what degree the Licensor and the Publisher shall be liable for all costs related to the mediation process . . .

B.

On August 10, 1994, Performance filed a complaint in district court, asserting a claim of breach of contract based upon Questar's refusal to pay accrued royalties due and owing to Performance pursuant to the licensing agreement between the parties and seeking a declaration of the parties' rights under the agreement. At the same time that it filed its complaint, Performance filed a motion for a preliminary injunction, seeking to enjoin Questar from refusing to pay the royalties due and owing to Performance under the license agreement and directing that Questar pay the royalties to Performance as provided in the agreement. Questar filed a brief in opposition to the motion for a preliminary injunction on August 24, 1994.

Pursuant to the agreement of the parties, the motion for a preliminary injunction was submitted to the district court based upon the documentary evidence in the record. Oral argument on the motion was held before the district court on August 25, 1994; however, the parties presented no testimonial evidence to the district court at that time.

On September 2, 1992, the district court denied Performance's motion for a preliminary injunction. Specifically, in denying Performance's motion, the district court found that it need not address the issue of whether Performance was likely to succeed on the merits of its claim that Questar breached the license agreement, "because the agreement has a mandatory arbitration provision." J.A. 26. The district court further concluded that

> it should not involve itself in the merits of a dispute when the parties, in their agreement, have clearly provided that arbitration is the sole and exclusive means to remedy disputes. . . .
>
> In summary, the Court does not feel that Performance is likely to succeed on the merits given the mandatory arbitration provision in the agreement.

J.A. 27–28.

Furthermore, the district court stated that while it

> realize[d] that the royalties [provided for in the licensing agreement] are necessary for the operation of Performance's business, . . . because Performance has come to the Court with "unclean hands," the Court concludes it should not grant Performance's request for equitable relief even though Performance's business might suffer irreparable harm.

J.A. 28–29. This timely appeal followed.

II

A.

Performance argues that the district court erred in finding that it could not issue injunctive relief because of the mandatory mediation/arbitration provision in the agreement between the parties. Performance asserts that the district court's refusal to grant injunctive relief because of the mandatory arbitration provision is contrary to the rule adopted by the majority of the United States Circuit Courts of Appeals. Performance further asserts that injunctive relief is appropriate in this case to preserve the status quo pending the arbitration of the parties' dispute, because absent injunctive relief Performance will suffer irreparable harm; namely, the collapse of its business, which will render the process of arbitration a hollow and meaningless formality.

In its opinion, the district court acknowledged that this issue was one of first impression in the Sixth Circuit. The district court further acknowledged that a number of other Circuits have held that district courts may issue injunctive relief under appropriate circumstances pending arbitration. Nevertheless, the district court rejected that approach, concluding instead "that it should not involve itself in the merits of a dispute when the parties, in their agreement, have clearly provided that arbitration is the sole and exclusive means to remedy disputes." J.A. 27–18.

. . . The issue of whether a district court has subject matter jurisdiction to entertain a motion for preliminary injunctive relief in an arbitrable dispute is an issue of first impression in this circuit. Moreover, the issue of "[w]hether the Arbitration Act deprives the district court of subject matter jurisdiction to enter preliminary injunctive relief is an issue of law subject to plenary review." Ortho Pharmaceutical Corp. v. Amgen, Inc., 882 F.2d 806, 812 n. 6 (3d Cir. 1989).

. . . After a thorough review of the relevant case law, we adopt the reasoning of the First, Second, Third, Fourth, Seventh, and arguably the Ninth, Circuits and hold that in a dispute subject to mandatory arbitration under the Federal Arbitration Act, a district court has subject matter jurisdiction under § 3 of the Act to grant preliminary injunctive relief provided that the party seeking the relief satisfies the four criteria which are prerequisites to the grant of such relief. We further conclude that a grant of preliminary injunctive relief pending arbitration is particularly appropriate and furthers the Congressional purpose behind the Federal

Arbitration Act, where the withholding of injunctive relief would render the process of arbitration meaningless or a hollow formality because an arbitral award, at the time it was rendered, " 'could not return the parties substantially to the status quo ante.' " Bradley, 756 F.2d at 1053 (quoting Lever Bros. Co. v. International Chemical Workers Union, Local 217, 554 F.2d 115, 123 (4th Cir. 1976)).

Accordingly, we hold that the district court erred as a matter of law when it found that it could not enter preliminary injunctive relief in this case because the dispute between the parties was the subject of mandatory arbitration.

B.

Performance next argues that the district court erred in finding that it did not satisfy the four factors necessary for the grant of a preliminary injunction. The four factors are: (1) the likelihood of the plaintiff's success on the merits; (2) whether the injunction will save the plaintiff from irreparable injury; (3) whether the injunction would harm others; and (4) whether the public interest would be served.... "A district court is required to make specific findings concerning each of the four factors, unless fewer are dispositive of the issue." Id. Moreover, the four factors are not prerequisites to be met, but rather must be balanced as part of a decision to grant or deny injunctive relief. In re DeLorean, 755 F.2d at 1229.

As was noted above, our review of this issue is limited to determining if the district court abused its discretion in denying preliminary relief. Gaston Drugs, 823 F.2d at 988. " 'A district court abuses its discretion when it relies on clearly erroneous findings of fact, or when it improperly applies the law or uses an erroneous legal standard.' " Id. (quoting Christian Schmidt Brewing Co, 753 F.2d at 1356). We review the district court's factual findings under a clearly erroneous standard, and its legal conclusions de novo. City of Mansfield, 866 F.2d at 166. Furthermore, in a case such a this, where "the district court's decision was made on the basis of a paper record, without a evidentiary hearing, we are in as good a position as the district judge to determine the propriety of granting a preliminary injunction." Roso–Lino, 749 F.2d at 125.

First, Performance argues that it has established that it would suffer irreparable injury in the absence of injunctive relief; namely, that it has shown that in the absence of royalty payments from Questar, its business would be destroyed or driven into insolvency. Performance further argues that this irreparable injury is the type of irreparable injury which would render the arbitration process either meaningless or a hollow formality because a decision from the arbitrator ordering Questar to pay the accrued royalties from The Beginner's Bible to Performance could not return Performance to the status quo ante if its business were destroyed.

In that regard, the record contains the affidavit of Jerry Wise, Performance's president dated August 9, 1994, in which Wise states that "[t]he license agreement between Performance Unlimited and Questar is by far the single most significant royalty-producing license agreement that Performance Unlimited has, and royalties received from the license constitute the single largest amount of royalty income received by Performance Unlimited yearly." J.A. 38. Wise further stated that "[i]f Questar does not pay its accrued royalties, Performance Unlimited will not be able to meet payroll, pay federal withholding taxes, pay vendors, pay royalties owed to licensees, or indeed continue to operate more than another two to three weeks." J.A. 40. The record also contains the affidavit of Richard Hilicki, Performance's Vice President of Finance, dated August 9, 1994, in which Hilicki stated that the accrued royalties of $184,000 that Questar had declined to pay to Performance, "constitute[d] in excess of 60% of the total projected revenues of Performance Unlimited for the second half of 1994." J.A. 42. Hilicki also stated that "[b]ecause of Questar's refusal to pay its royalties, Performance Unlimited has been unable to pay many of its vendors in a timely fashion . . ." and that "Performance Unlimited will be unable to secure additional supplies and materials from its vendors." J.A. 43. Finally, Hilicki stated that Questar was holding approximately $45,000 in accrued royalties in addition to the $184,000 which it had deposited into the escrow account, and that royalties on The Beginner's Bible were accruing at a rate of about $30,000 to $35,000 per month. J.A. 44.

Although Questar asserts that Performance's claims of irreparable injury are pretextual, the statements of Wise and Hilicki are the only evidence of record concerning the financial condition of Performance. Accordingly, we conclude that the uncontradicted statements of Wise and Hilicki dated August 4, 1994 establish that in the absence of injunctive relief, i.e., without the payment of royalties by Questar, Performance will be unable to operate its business and the business will suffer economic collapse or insolvency . . .

Moreover, the district court acknowledged as much in its opinion when it stated:

> Performance notes that the $184,000 in royalties is its largest source of revenue and without the royalties, in cannot continue to operate its business . . .
>
> [T]he Court realizes that the royalties are necessary for the operation of Performance's business . . .

J.A. 28.

The impending loss or financial ruin of Performance's business constitutes irreparable injury. "An injury is irreparable if it cannot be undone through monetary remedies." Interox Am. v. PPG, Indus., Inc., 736 F.2d 194, 202 (5th Cir. 1984). "As a general rule, a movant has not established irreparable harm where damages would adequately compensate the movant for the asserted harm. Yet, irreparable injury has been characterized as loss of a movant's enterprise." Ryko Mfg. Corp. v. Delta Servs., Inc., 625 F.Supp. 1247, 1248 (S.D. Iowa 1985) (citation omitted). See also Roso–Lino, 749 F.2d at 125–26 ("The loss of [plaintiff's] distributorship, an ongoing business ... constitutes irreparable harm. What plaintiff stands to lose cannot be fully compensated by subsequent money damages")....

Second, Performance argues that the district court erred in finding that Performance was not entitled to equitable relief because Performance had "unclean hands." The district court stated that it

> realizes that the royalties are necessary for the operation of Performance's business, [but was] ... concerned that Performance has come to it for equitable relief with unclean hands.

J.A. 28. The district court then stated the reasons why it believed that Performance had unclean hands:

> First, there appears to be an ongoing dispute between Performance and Mr. Leininger, in that Leininger has made claims to Performance for unpaid royalties. Thus, there is a possibility that Performance has breached its license agreement with Leininger. Second, there is also the possibility that Performance has breached their sublicense agreement with Questar by allowing a third party publisher, David C. Cook Company, to publish *The Beginner's Bible* [Curriculum], even though Questar has exclusive publishing rights under the agreement. Finally, there are other claims on the very same royalties Performance seeks. Of the $184,000, Mr. Leininger is due approximately $4,300 and the Henleys, writers of the *Dovetales* stories, are due $79,000.

J.A. 28–29.

... In this case, there is no evidence of record that Performance is guilty of any misconduct that rises to the level of fraud, deceit, unconscionability, or bad faith. The disputes between Performance and Questar, and Performance and Leininger are bona fide commercial disputes. The dispute between Performance and Questar centers around the issue of whether Performance could license David C. Cook Publishers to publish *The Beginner's Bible New Testament* as part of its *The Beginner's Bible Curriculum*. Further, the dispute between Performance and Leininger centers around the question as to whether Performance could deduct legal fees from its royalty payments to Leininger. In this case, the district court made no findings as to the merits of the disputes between Performance and Questar and Performance and Leininger. Thus, the district court found that Performance had unclean hands based upon nothing more than the "possibility" that the arbitrator could determine that Performance had breached its license agreement with Questar, or that Performance had breached its license agreement with Leininger, or that Performance had breached both license agreements. This is not the required finding that Performance's actions rose to the level of fraud, deceit, unconscionability, or bad faith....

Third, Performance argues that the district court erred in finding that the public interest would be served by denying Performance's motion for injunctive relief. The district court stated that it

> finds that public policy dictates that the arbitration provision in the agreement between Performance and Questar be enforced. The agreement provides for arbitration and explicitly states that the parties shall

> not bring their disputes to "secular courts." The parties should work out their disputes as provided in the agreement they both freely signed.

J.A. 29.

However, we believe that in this case the public interest would be served by granting injunctive relief to Performance "because there is a strong policy in favor of carrying out commercial arbitration when a contract contains an arbitration clause. Arbitration lightens courts' workloads, and it usually results in a speedier resolution of controversies." Sauer–Getriebe, 715 F.2d at 352. As was discussed above, we believe that in the absence of injunctive relief, Performance faces its destruction as an ongoing enterprise, and, consequently, without injunctive relief, the arbitration process agreed to by Performance and Questar in their licensing agreement will become a hollow formality. In light of the strong public policy encouraging parties in commercial disputes to submit their disagreements to the speedier resolution of arbitration where the parties have agreed to a contract containing an arbitration clause, we believe that preliminary injunctive relief is in the public interest in this case. Performance and Questar agreed to a contract containing an arbitration clause; however, in the absence of preliminary injunctive relief Performance may well lose its business. Thus, were we to reach the same conclusion as did the district court, private commercial parties will have little incentive to agree to contracts containing provisions for arbitration of their disputes, if by agreeing to arbitration of their disputes they are unable to obtain injunctive relief even when they face destruction. Therefore, the district court's finding that the denial of preliminary injunctive relief in this case would serve the public interest is clearly erroneous. Rather, the public interest is best served by the granting of preliminary injunctive relief in this case because it will foster agreements to arbitrate as a means of resolving disputes between private parties.

Fourth, Performance argues that the district court erred in finding that others, particularly Questar, would be harmed by the grant of preliminary injunctive relief. The district court found that

> [i]f the Court were to grant the preliminary injunction, and Performance still does not rectify the outstanding dispute with Leininger, then Leininger could terminate his license agreement with Performance. As a consequence, Questar's sublicense with Performance would be void. On the other hand, if the Court were to deny the preliminary injunction, and the parties continue to refuse to submit their disputes to arbitration, as provided in their agreement, then Performance will likely be forced to close its doors. As a consequence, Questar's sublicense with Performance would still be void.

J.A. 30.

We conclude that the district court's finding that Questar would be harmed by the grant of injunctive relief is clearly erroneous. The evidence shows that in the absence of injunctive relief Performance will likely collapse, thereby voiding the license agreement between Performance and Questar.

However, the district court concluded that if Performance does not rectify its dispute with Leininger, Leininger could terminate his licensing agreement with Performance, thereby also voiding Performance's license agreement with Questar. Performance and Leininger have disagreed as to whether Performance could properly deduct legal fees from its royalty payments to Leininger. However, "a bona fide dispute concerning royalty payments does not, as a matter of law, establish a material breach justifying recision of the contract absent an express provision in the contract." Arthur Guinness & Sons, PLC v. Sterling Pub. Co., 732 F.2d 1095, 1101 (2d Cir. 1984). Thus, it is not at all clear that the dispute between Performance and Leininger will result in the recision of the licensing agreement between Performance and Leininger. Furthermore, there is no indication in the record that Leininger has sought arbitration or has filed a lawsuit against Performance over their dispute, much less any evidence that Leininger has sought to terminate his license agreement with Performance. Thus, the evidence shows that Questar is likely to suffer harm in the absence of preliminary injunctive relief, regardless of the outcome of the dispute between Performance and Leininger.

Finally, Performance argues that the district court erred in finding that it had little likelihood of success on the merits. As noted above, the district court concluded that it would not address the issue of the likelihood of Performance's success on the merits because this is an arbitrable dispute. The district court then stated that it did "not feel that Performance [was] likely to succeed on the merits given the mandatory arbitration provision in the agreement." J.A. 28.

" '[W]e do not consider the merits of [a] case further than to determine whether the District Judge abused his discretion in denying the preliminary injunction.' " Mason County Medical Ass'n v. Knebel, 563 F.2d 256, 261 (6th Cir. 1977) . . . Moreover, "it is improper for a court to decide a contractual dispute relegated to arbitration." Sauer–Getriebe, 715 F.2d at 352. Nevertheless, Performance "has demonstrated enough probable success on the merits to warrant relief." Id.

In balancing the four factors for injunctive relief, "[t]he moving party must show a strong likelihood of success on the merits if all other factors militate against granting a preliminary injunction. Similarly, the moving party need show less likelihood of success on the merits if the other facts indicate that the Court should issue a preliminary injunction." Merrill Lynch, Pierce, Fenner & Smith, Inc. v. Grall, 836 F.Supp. 428, 432 (W.D.Mich. 1993) (citing In re DeLorean, 755 F.2d at 1229). As was discussed above, the other three factors in this case weigh strongly in favor of granting the preliminary injunction requested by Performance. Thus, Performance need show less likelihood of success on the merits to obtain injunctive relief.

In this case it is undisputed that if the arbitrator finds that Performance has not breached the license agreement with Questar, Performance is entitled to the entire amount of money which Questar has placed in escrow. Further, the evidence shows that Questar has placed a substantial amount of money, approximately $185,000 in escrow, and that additional royalties due and owing to Performance under the license agreement are accruing at a significant rate, approximately $30,000 to $35,000 monthly. Thus, even if the arbitrator determines that Performance has breached the contract and awards damages to Questar, given the amount of royalties in escrow, there is every likelihood that Performance will be entitled to at least some portion of the royalties being held in escrow. Consequently, because Performance will, as the result of the arbitration, most likely receive some portion, if not all, of the funds in the escrow account, Performance has a likelihood of success on the merits.

Furthermore, we believe that the district court can, and must, tailor any injunctive relief it grants in this case both to preserve Performance as an ongoing enterprise and to preserve Questar's right to damages, if any, out of the funds now held in escrow if it prevails on its claim of breach of damages. In Grall, the court noted that a "district court's authority to issue [preliminary] injunctive relief extends only until the arbitrators can determine the temporary injunctive relief necessary to maintain the status quo." Grall, 836 F.Supp. at 430 (citing Merrill Lynch, Pierce, Fenner & Smith, Inc. v. Salvano, 999 F.2d 211, 215 (7th Cir. 1993). "Once assembled, an arbitration panel can enter whatever temporary injunctive relief it deems necessary to maintain the status quo . . . '[C]ourts are ill-advised to extend the injunction once arbitration proceeds.' " Id. at 431 (quoting Salvano, 999 F.2d at 215)). Likewise, because the ultimate decision on the merits of this contractual dispute is for the arbitrators, the district court in its grant of preliminary injunctive relief should order Questar to pay only that amount of royalties necessary to ensure that Performance is not driven out of business prior to the time the arbitration proceeds. Furthermore, once the arbitration begins, it is for the arbitrators to decide how to maintain the status quo during the pendency of the arbitration process. This approach will both minimize the district court's involvement in the merits of this contractual dispute, and it will preserve the ability of the arbitration panel to fully address the merits of the dispute.

Accordingly, we hold that the district court erred in denying Performance's motion for a preliminary injunction. Therefore, the district court should grant preliminary injunctive relief to Performance pending arbitration within the parameters we have discussed above.

III.

For the reasons stated, the district court's judgment denying Performance's motion for a preliminary injunction is REVERSED and the case is REMANDED to the district court for the issuance of a preliminary injunction consistent with this opinion.

* * *

Questions

1. Who should decide requests for provisional relief—an arbitrator or a judge? If such requests are decided by a judge, what factors should a court use to determine whether a provisional remedy may issue? Can a court hold a hearing to determine whether these factors require the relief? *Must* a court hold a hearing? What problems are posed for the authority of the arbitrator when a court makes such a determination?

2. If a request for provisional relief is directed to an arbitrator and the arbitration agreement is silent on the power to grant such relief, can an arbitrator grant the relief or not? If an arbitrator grants provisional relief in such a situation, could a court set the arbitral award aside on the ground that it is exceeds the arbitrator's powers? Or should the power to grant provisional relief be implied in all arbitration clauses that do not explicitly deny an arbitrator that power?

3. On what basis should an arbitrator determine whether to issue a provisional remedy? Should she apply the same standard a court would apply? If so, must there be a preliminary hearing comparable to a hearing on a preliminary injunction, followed by a final arbitral hearing on the merits? Would such a two-part process undermine the rationale for using arbitration rather than a court?

4. If an arbitrator awards a provisional remedy, can the movant go to court to enforce it? What test should a court apply to determine whether to enforce such a provisional award? Is it the same standard that the court would itself apply when determining whether to issue preliminary relief? Is it the same standard a court would apply to a final arbitral award? Is there some intermediate standard that would be more appropriate?

* * *

B. FINAL REMEDIES

In Subsection A, above, we saw that the availability of provisional remedies in support of arbitration implicates a delicate balancing of authority between a court and an arbitration. There is a separate issue concerning what types of final remedies an arbitrator can issue. Courts have the power to award many types of remedies, including compensatory damages, consequential damages, punitive damages, attorney fees, and interest in appropriate cases. The remedy power of arbitrators is not as well established. In particular, a question arises when a parties' contract is silent as to what types of remedies an arbitrator can award. Should the court impose a limitation on the remedy power of the arbitrator, or should the court presume that the parties intended to vest the arbitrator with unlimited discretion over remedies?

For example, can an arbitrator impose a remedy such as attorney's fees in a case in which a court would not have the power to do so?. Most courts hold that an arbitrator may not award attorney fees to a prevailing party unless the parties' agreement specifically authorized an arbitral award of attorney fees,[1] or unless the party prevailed on an issue that would entitle her to fees under existing statutory law.[2] However, some courts permit an arbitrator to grant attorney fees under the general proposition that an arbitrator has wide control of remedies.[3] Further, courts have held that the failure of an arbitrator to grant attorney fees to a prevailing party on a statutory claim for which fees would have been awardable by a court is not grounds to vacate an award.[4]

One remedy that has generated considerable controversy in the field of arbitration is punitive damages. The cases that follow illustrate the conflicting views in this area.

* * *

Garrity v. Lyle Stuart, Inc.

353 N.E.2d 793 (N.Y.1976).

■ BREITEL, CHIEF JUDGE.

Plaintiff author brought this proceeding under CPLR 7510 to confirm an arbitration award granting her $45,000 in compensatory damages and $7,500 in punitive damages against defendant publishing company. Supreme Court confirmed the award. The Appellate Division affirmed, one Justice dissenting, and defendant appeals.

The issue is whether an arbitrator has the power to award punitive damages.

The order of the Appellate Division should be modified to vacate the award of punitive damages and otherwise affirmed. An arbitrator has no power to award punitive damages, even if agreed upon by the parties (Matter of Publishers' Ass'n of N.Y. City [Newspaper Union], 280 App.Div. 500, 504–506, 114 N.Y.S.2d 401, 404–406). Punitive damages is a sanction reserved to the State, a public policy of such magnitude as to call for judicial intrusion to prevent its contravention. Since enforcement of an award of punitive damages as a purely private remedy would violate strong public policy, an arbitrator's award which imposes punitive damages should be vacated.

Plaintiff is the author of two books published by defendant. While the publishing agreements between the parties contained broad arbitration clauses, neither of the agreements provided for the imposition of punitive damages in the event of breach.

A dispute arose between the parties and in December, 1971 plaintiff author brought an action for damages alleging fraudulent inducement,

1. See, e.g., *Compton v. Lemon Ranches, Ltd.*, 972 P.2d 1078 (Colo.App. 1999); *Nucor v. General Bearing Corp.*, 423 S.E.2d 747 (N.C.1992).

2. See, *Raymond, James & Associates v. Wieneke*, 591 So.2d 956 (Fla.App. 1991).

3. See *Prudential–Bache Securities, Inc. v. Tanner, et al.*, 72 F.3d 234 (1st Cir. 1995); *Gibbs v. PFS Investments, Inc.*, 209 F.Supp.2d 620 (E.D.Va. 2002).

4. *DiRussa v. Dean Witter Reynolds Inc.*, 121 F.3d 818 (2d Cir. 1997).

"gross" underpayment of royalties, and various "malicious" acts designed to harass her. That action is still pending.

In March, 1974, plaintiff brought a new action alleging that defendant had wrongfully withheld an additional $45,000 in royalties. Defendant moved for a stay pending arbitration, which was granted, and plaintiff demanded arbitration. The demand requested the $45,000 withheld royalties and punitive damages for defendant's alleged "malicious" withholding of royalties, which plaintiff contended was done to coerce her into withdrawing the 1971 action.

Defendant appeared at the arbitration hearing and raised objections concerning plaintiff's standing and the conduct of the arbitration hearing. Upon rejection of these objections by the arbitrators, defendant walked out.

After hearing testimony, and considering an "informal memorandum" on punitive damages submitted by plaintiff at their request, the arbitrators awarded plaintiff both compensatory and punitive damages. On plaintiff's motion to confirm the award, defendant objected upon the ground that the award of punitive damages was beyond the scope of the arbitrators' authority.

Arbitrators generally are not bound by principles of substantive law or rules of evidence, and thus error of law or fact will not justify vacatur of an award.... It is also true that arbitrators generally are free to fashion the remedy appropriate to the wrong, if they find one, but an authentic remedy is compensatory and measured by the harm caused and how it may be corrected ... These broad principles are tolerable so long as arbitrators are not thereby empowered to ride roughshod over strong policies in the law which control coercive private conduct and confine to the State and its courts the infliction of punitive sanctions on wrongdoers.

The court will vacate an award enforcing an illegal agreement or one violative of public policy ... Since enforcement of an award of punitive damages as a purely private remedy would violate public policy, an arbitrator's award which imposes punitive damages, even though agreed upon by the parties, should be vacated ...

Matter of Associated Gen. Contrs., N.Y. State Chapter (Savin Bros.), 36 N.Y.2d 957 is inapposite. That case did not involve an award of punitive damages. Instead, the court permitted enforcement of an arbitration award of treble liquidated damages, amounting to a penalty, assessed however in accordance with the express terms of a trade association membership agreement. The court held that the public policy against permitting the awarding of penalties was not of "such magnitude as to call for judicial intrusion" (p. 959). In the instant case, however, there was no provision in the agreements permitting arbitrators to award liquidated damages or penalties. Indeed, the subject apparently had never ever been considered.

The prohibition against an arbitrator awarding punitive damages is based on strong public policy indeed. At law, on the civil side, in the absence of statute, punitive damages are available only in a limited number of instances ... As was stated in Walker v. Sheldon (supra): "[p]unitive or exemplary damages have been allowed in cases where the wrong complained of is morally culpable, or is actuated by evil and reprehensible motives, not only to punish the defendant but to deter him, as well as others who might otherwise be so prompted, from indulging in similar conduct in the future." It is a social exemplary "remedy", not a private compensatory remedy.

It has always been held that punitive damages are not available for mere breach of contract, for in such a case only a private wrong, and not a public right, is involved....

Even if the so-called "malicious" breach here involved would permit of the imposition of punitive damages by a court or jury, it was not the province of arbitrators to do so. Punitive sanctions are reserved to the State, surely a public policy "of such magnitude as to call for judicial intrusion" (Matter of Associated Gen. Contrs., N.Y. State Chapter [Savin Bros.], 36 N.Y.2d 957, 959). The evil of permitting an arbitrator whose selection is often restricted or manipulatable by the party in a superior bargaining position, to award punitive damages is that it displaces the court and the jury, and therefore the State, as the engine for imposing a social sanction. As was so wisely observed by Judge, then Mr. Justice, Bergan in Matter of Publishers' Ass'n of N.Y. City (Newspaper Union), 280 App.Div. 500, 503, supra:

> The trouble with an arbitration admitting a power to grant unlimited damages by way of punishment is that if the court treated such an award in the way arbitration awards are usually treated, and followed the award to the letter, it would amount to an unlimited draft upon judicial power. In the usual case, the court stops only to inquire if the award is authorized by the contract; is complete and final on its face; and if the proceeding was fairly conducted.
>
> Actual damage is measurable against some objective standard-the number of pounds, or days, or gallons or yards; but punitive damages take their shape from the subjective criteria involved in attitudes toward correction and reform, and courts do not accept readily the delegation of that kind of power. Where punitive damages have been allowed for those torts which are still regarded somewhat as public penal wrongs as well as actionable private wrongs, they have had rather close judicial supervision. If the usual rules were followed there would be no effective judicial supervision over punitive awards in arbitration.

The dissent appears to have recognized the danger in permitting an arbitrator in his discretion to award unlimited punitive damages. Thus, it notes that the award made here was neither "irrational" nor "unjust" ... Standards such as these are subjective and afford no practical guidelines for the arbitrator and little protection against abuse, and would, on the other hand, contrary to the sound development of arbitration law, permit the courts to supervise awards for their justness (cf. Lentine v. Fundaro, 29 N.Y.2d 382, 386).

Parties to arbitration agree to the substitution of a private tribunal for purposes of deciding their disputes without the expense, delay and rigidities of traditional courts. If arbitrators were allowed to impose punitive damages, the usefulness of arbitration would be destroyed. It would become a trap for the unwary given the eminently desirable freedom from judicial overview of law and facts. It would mean that the scope of determination by arbitrators, by the license to award punitive damages, would be both unpredictable and uncontrollable. It would lead to a Shylock principle of doing business without a Portia-like escape from the vise of a logic foreign to arbitration law.

In imposing penal sanctions in private arrangements, a tradition of the rule of law in organized society is violated. One purpose of the rule of law is to require that the use of coercion be controlled by the State (Kelsen, General Theory of Law and State, p. 21). In a highly developed commercial and economic society the use of private force is not the danger, but the uncontrolled use of coercive economic sanctions in private arrangements. For centuries the power to punish has been a monopoly of the State, and not that of any private individual (Kelsen, loc. cit., supra). The day is long past since barbaric man achieved redress by private punitive measures.

The parties never agreed or, for that matter, even considered punitive damages as a possible sanction for breach of the agreement (see dissenting opn. below by Mr. Justice Capozzoli, 48 A.D.2d 814, 370 N.Y.S.2d 6). Here there is no pretense of agreement, although plaintiff author argues feebly that the issue of punitive damages was "waived" by failure to object originally to the demands for punitive damages, but only later to the award. The law does not and should not permit private persons to submit themselves to punitive sanctions of the order reserved to the State. The freedom of contract does not embrace the freedom to punish, even by contract. On this view, there was no power to waive the limitations on privately assessed punitive damages and, of course, no power to agree to them by the failure to object to the demand for arbitration (cf. Brooklyn Sav. Bank v. O'Neil, 324 U.S. 697, 704, 65 S.Ct. 895, 900, 89 L.Ed. 1296, affg., 293 N.Y. 666, 56 N.E.2d 259) ["waiver" of right "charged or colored with the public interest" is ineffective] . . .

Under common-law principles, there is eventual supervision of jury awards of punitive damages, in the singularly rare cases where it is permitted, by the trial court's power to change awards and by the Appellate Division's power to modify such awards [see Walker v. Sheldon, 10 N.Y.2d 401, 405, n. 3, 223 N.Y.S.2d 488, 491, 179 N.E.2d 497, 499, supra]. That the award of punitive damages in this case was quite modest is immaterial. Such a happenstance is not one on which to base a rule.

Accordingly, the order of the Appellate Division should be modified, without costs, to vacate so much of the award which imposes punitive damages, and otherwise affirmed.

■ GABRIELLI, JUDGE (dissenting).

... The basic issue presented for our determination is whether, in an arbitration proceeding brought pursuant to a contract containing a broad arbitration clause, an award of punitive damages is violative of public policy.

[In this case], the arbitrators awarded plaintiff $45,000 on her claim for royalties and $7,500 in punitive damages plus interest and fees. When plaintiff moved to confirm the award, defendant objected, for the first time, that an award of punitive damages is violative of public policy and beyond the scope of the authority of the arbitrators. Special Term confirmed the award and the Appellate Division upheld that determination. I would affirm.

In doing so, I would reject the notion that this award of punitive damages is violative of public policy. We have only recently treated with a somewhat similar argument in Matter of Associated Gen. Contrs., N.Y. State Chapter (Savin Bros.), 36 N.Y.2d 957. There we considered the effect of a public policy argument against penalty awards with respect to an arbitration commenced by a national trade association in the construction industry against one of its employer-members pursuant to the provisions of a broad arbitration clause contained in the association agreement. Specifically at issue was whether an arbitration award of treble liquidated damages, assessed in accordance with the express terms of the agreement, was enforceable. We held that since the arbitration was in consequence of a broad arbitration clause and concerned no third-party interests which could be said to transcend the concerns of the parties to the arbitration, there was present ... "no question involving public policy of such magnitude as to call for judicial intrusion" ...

The case at bar falls within the rationale and rule of the Associated Gen. Contrs. case. Controlling here, as there, is the fact that the arbitration clause is broad indeed; there are no third-party interests involved; and the public policy against punitive damages is not so commanding that the Legislature has found it necessary to embody that policy into law, especially one that would apply to all cases involving such damages irrespective of the amount sought, the relative size of the award, or the punishable actions of the parties. Or, put another way, the public policy which "favors the peaceful resolutions of disputes through arbitration" (Associated Gen. Contrs., supra, at p. 959, 373 N.Y.S.2d at p. 556, 335 N.E.2d at p. 859) outweighs the public policy disfavoring the assessment of punitive damages in this instance, where the unjustifiable conduct complained of is found to be with malice. I would conclude, therefore, that any public policy limiting punitive damage awards does not rise to that level of significance in this case as to require judicial intervention.

The majority would distinguish the Associated Gen. Contrs. case (supra) upon the thin ground that the enforcement of a treble liquidated damages clause which was applicable to numerous nationwide contracts that conceivably could have amounted to astronomical sums is not the equivalent of the enforcement of an award of penalty damages. However, as Mr. Justice Greenblott specifically stated for the majority below in that case, and in an opinion expressly approved by this court, the amount of damages therein computed in the arbitration bore "*no reasonable relationship to the amount of damages which may be sustained*" (emphasis added; 45 A.D.2d 136, 140, 356 N.Y.S.2d 374, 378); and a contract clause which is grossly disproportionate to the presumable damage or readily ascertainable loss is a penalty clause, irrespective of its label [Equitable Lbr. Corp. v. IPA Land Development Corp., 38 N.Y.2d 516, 521–522, 381 N.Y.S.2d 459, 462–463, 344 N.E.2d 391, 395–396] . . .

An affirmance here would do no violence to precedents in this court. In at least two varied circumstances we have held that although public policy would bar a civil suit for relief, that same public policy was not of such overriding import as to preclude confirmation of an arbitration award (Matter of Staklinski [Pyramid Elec. Co.], 6 N.Y.2d 159, 188 N.Y.S.2d 541, 160 N.E.2d 78; Matter of Ruppert [Egelhofer], 3 N.Y.2d 576, 170 N.Y.S.2d 785, 148 N.E.2d 129). In Ruppert was permitted the enjoining of a work stoppage in a labor dispute by arbitration despite the fact that the issuance of such relief by a court was prohibited by statute (then Civil Practice Act, § 876(a)). Similarly, in Staklinski, citing Ruppert, we upheld an arbitration award of specific performance of an employment contract in the face of the public policy against compelling a corporation to continue the services of an officer whose services were unsatisfactory to the board of directors. The rule to be distilled these cases, therefore, is that only where the public interest clearly supersedes the concerns of the parties should courts intervene and assert exclusive dominion over disputes in arbitration . . .

Nor can we hold, as defendant also urges, that the arbitrators exceeded their authority in awarding punitive damages to plaintiff. Arbitrators are entitled to "do justice." It has been said that, short of "complete irrationality," "they may fashion the law to fit the facts before them" (Lentine v. Fundaro, 29 N.Y.2d 382, 386, 328 N.Y.S.2d 418, 422, 278 N.E.2d 633, 636) . . . The award made here was neither irrational nor unjust. Indeed, defendant has not denied that its actions were designed to harass and intimidate plaintiff, as she claimed and the arbitrators obviously concluded. Hence, the award was within the power vested in the arbitrator.

As we have noted, plaintiff sought punitive damages as listed and set forth in the demand for arbitration, presenting of course a threshold question to which defendant failed to respond and, in fact, summarily refused to address himself. In effect, therefore, defendant's failure to act, respond or contest the claim is tantamount to a waiver of any objection thereto and, indeed, is equivalent to an agreement to arbitrate the allegation now complained of.

Accordingly, the order of the Appellate Division should be affirmed.

■ JASEN, FUCHSBERG and COOKE, JJ., concur with BREITEL, C.J, GABRIELLI, J., dissents and votes to affirm in a separate opinion in which JONES and WACHTLER, JJ., concur.

* * *

Mastrobuono v. Shearson Lehman Hutton, Inc.

514 U.S. 52 (1995).

■ JUSTICE STEVENS delivered the opinion of the Court.

New York law allows courts, but not arbitrators, to award punitive damages. In a dispute arising out of a standard-form contract that expressly provides that it "shall be governed by the laws of the State of New York," a panel of arbitrators awarded punitive damages. The District Court and Court of Appeals disallowed that award. The question presented is whether the arbitrators' award is consistent with the central purpose of the Federal Arbitration Act to ensure "that private agreements to arbitrate are enforced according to their terms." Volt Information Sciences, Inc. v. Board of Trustees of Leland Stanford Junior Univ., 489 U.S. 468, 479, 109 S.Ct. 1248, 1256, 103 L.Ed.2d 488 (1989).

I

In 1985 petitioners, Antonio Mastrobuono, then an assistant professor of medieval literature, and his wife Diana Mastrobuono, an artist, opened a securities trading account with respondent Shearson Lehman Hutton, Inc. (Shearson), by executing Shearson's standard-form Client's Agreement. Respondent Nick DiMinico, a vice president of Shearson, managed the Mastrobuonos' account until they closed it in 1987. In 1989, petitioners filed this action in the United States District Court for the Northern District of Illinois, alleging that respondents had mishandled their account and claiming damages on a variety of state and federal law theories.

Paragraph 13 of the parties' agreement contains an arbitration provision and a choice-of-law provision. Relying on the arbitration provision and on §§ 3 and 4 of the Federal Arbitration Act (FAA), 9 U.S.C. §§ 3, 4, respondents filed a motion to stay the court proceedings and to compel arbitration pursuant to the rules of the National Association of Securities Dealers. The District Court granted that motion, and a panel of three arbitrators was convened. After conducting hearings in Illinois, the panel ruled in favor of petitioners.

In the arbitration proceedings, respondents argued that the arbitrators had no authority to award punitive damages. Nevertheless, the panel's award included punitive damages of $400,000, in addition to compensatory damages of $159,327. Respondents paid the compensatory portion of the award but filed a motion in the District Court to vacate the award of punitive damages. The District Court granted the motion, 812 F.Supp. 845 (N.D.Ill. 1993), and the Court of Appeals for the Seventh Circuit affirmed. 20 F.3d 713 (1994). Both courts relied on the choice-of-law provision in paragraph 13 of the parties' agreement, which specifies that the contract shall be governed by New York law. Because the New York Court of Appeals has decided that in New York the power to award punitive damages is limited to judicial tribunals and may not be exercised by arbitrators, Garrity v. Lyle Stuart, Inc., 40 N.Y.2d 354, 386 N.Y.S.2d 831,

353 N.E.2d 793 (1976), the District Court and the Seventh Circuit held that the panel of arbitrators had no power to award punitive damages in this case.

We granted certiorari, 513 U.S. 921, 115 S.Ct. 305, 130 L.Ed.2d 218 (1994), because the Courts of Appeals have expressed differing views on whether a contractual choice-of-law provision may preclude an arbitral award of punitive damages that otherwise would be proper ... We now reverse.

II

Earlier this Term, we upheld the enforceability of a predispute arbitration agreement governed by Alabama law, even though an Alabama statute provides that arbitration agreements are unenforceable. Allied–Bruce Terminix Cos. v. Dobson, 513 U.S. 265, 115 S.Ct. 834, 130 L.Ed.2d 753 (1995). Writing for the Court, Justice Breyer observed that Congress passed the FAA "to overcome courts' refusals to enforce agreements to arbitrate." Id., at 270, 115 S.Ct. at 838. See also Volt Information Sciences, Inc. v. Board of Trustees of Leland Stanford Junior Univ., 489 U.S. at 474, 109 S.Ct. at 1253; Dean Witter Reynolds Inc. v. Byrd, 470 U.S. 213, 220, 105 S.Ct. 1238, 1242, 84 L.Ed.2d 158 (1985). After determining that the FAA applied to the parties' arbitration agreement, we readily concluded that the federal statute pre-empted Alabama's statutory prohibition. Allied–Bruce, 513 U.S., at 272–73 & 281–82, 115 S.Ct. at 839, 843.

Petitioners seek a similar disposition of the case before us today. Here, the Seventh Circuit interpreted the contract to incorporate New York law, including the Garrity rule that arbitrators may not award punitive damages. Petitioners ask us to hold that the FAA pre-empts New York's prohibition against arbitral awards of punitive damages because this state law is a vestige of the "ancient" judicial hostility to arbitration. See Allied–Bruce, 513 U.S., at 270, 115 S.Ct. at 838, quoting Bernhardt v. Polygraphic Co. of America, Inc., 350 U.S. 198, 211, n. 5, 76 S.Ct. 273, 281, n. 5, 100 L.Ed. 199 (1956) (Frankfurter, J., concurring). Petitioners rely on Southland Corp. v. Keating, 465 U.S. 1, 104 S.Ct. 852, 79 L.Ed.2d 1 (1984), and Perry v. Thomas, 482 U.S. 483, 107 S.Ct. 2520, 96 L.Ed.2d 426 (1987), in which we held that the FAA pre-empted two California statutes that purported to require judicial resolution of certain disputes. In Southland, we explained that the FAA not only "declared a national policy favoring arbitration," but actually "withdrew the power of the states to require a judicial forum for the resolution of claims which the contracting parties agreed to resolve by arbitration." 465 U.S., at 10, 104 S.Ct. at 858.

Respondents answer that the choice-of-law provision in their contract evidences the parties' express agreement that punitive damages should not be awarded in the arbitration of any dispute arising under their contract. Thus, they claim, this case is distinguishable from Southland and Perry, in which the parties presumably desired unlimited arbitration but state law stood in their way. Regardless of whether the FAA pre-empts the Garrity decision in contracts not expressly incorporating New York law, respondents argue that the parties may themselves agree to be bound by Garrity, just as they may agree to forgo arbitration altogether. In other words, if the contract says "no punitive damages," that is the end of the matter, for courts are bound to interpret contracts in accordance with the expressed intentions of the parties—even if the effect of those intentions is to limit arbitration.

We have previously held that the FAA's pro-arbitration policy does not operate without regard to the wishes of the contracting parties. In Volt Information Sciences, Inc. v. Board of Trustees of Leland Stanford Junior Univ., 489 U.S. 468, 109 S.Ct., 1248, 103 L.Ed.2d 488 (1989), the California Court of Appeal had construed a contractual provision to mean that the parties intended the California rules of arbitration, rather than the FAA's rules, to govern the resolution of their dispute. Id., at 472, 109 S.Ct., at 1252. Noting that the California rules were "manifestly designed to encourage resort to the arbitral process," id., at 476, 109 S.Ct., at 1254, and that they "generally foster[ed] the federal policy favoring arbitration," id., at 476, n. 5, 109 S.Ct., at 1254 n. 5, we concluded that such an interpretation was entirely consistent with the federal policy "to ensure the enforceability, according to their terms, of private agreements to arbitrate." Id., at 476, 109 S.Ct., at 1254. After referring to the holdings in Southland and Perry, which struck down state laws limiting agreed-upon arbitrability, we added:

> But it does not follow that the FAA prevents the enforcement of agreements to arbitrate under different rules than those set forth in the Act itself. Indeed, such a result would be quite inimical to the FAA's primary purpose of ensuring that private agreements to arbitrate are enforced according to their terms. Arbitration under the Act is a matter of consent, not coercion, and parties are generally free to structure their arbitration agreements as they see fit. Just as they may limit by contract the issues which they will arbitrate, see Mitsubishi [v. Soler Chrysler–Plymouth, 473 U.S. 614, 628, 105 S.Ct. 3346, 3354–55, 87 L.Ed.2d 444 (1985)], so too may they specify by contract the rules under which that arbitration will be conducted. Volt, 489 U.S., at 479, 109 S.Ct., at 1256.

Relying on our reasoning in Volt, respondents thus argue that the parties to a contract may lawfully agree to limit the issues to be arbitrated by waiving any claim for punitive damages. On the other hand, we think our decisions in Allied–Bruce, Southland, and Perry make clear that if contracting parties agree to include claims for punitive damages within the issues to be arbitrated, the FAA ensures that their agreement will be enforced according to its terms even if a rule of state law would otherwise exclude such claims from arbitration. Thus, the case before us comes down to what the contract has to say about the arbitrability of petitioners' claim for punitive damages.

III

Shearson's standard-form "Client Agreement," which petitioners executed, contains 18 paragraphs. The two relevant provisions of the agreement are found in paragraph 13.[2] The first sentence of that paragraph provides, in part, that the entire agreement "shall be governed by the laws of the State of New York." App. to Pet. for Cert. 44. The second sentence provides that "any controversy" arising out of the transactions between the parties "shall be settled by arbitration" in accordance with the rules of the National Association of Securities Dealers (NASD), or the Boards of Directors of the New York Stock Exchange and/or the American Stock Exchange. Ibid. The agreement contains no express reference to claims for punitive damages. To ascertain whether Paragraph 13 expresses an intent to include or exclude such claims, we first address the impact of each of the two relevant provisions, considered separately. We then move on to the more important inquiry: the meaning of the two provisions taken together. See Restatement (Second) of Contracts § 202(2) (1979) ("A writing is interpreted as a whole").

The choice-of-law provision, when viewed in isolation, may reasonably be read as merely a substitute for the conflict-of-laws analysis that otherwise would determine what law to apply to disputes arising out of the contractual relationship. Thus, if a similar contract, without a choice-of-law provision, had been signed in New York and was to be performed in New York, presumably "the laws of the State of New York" would apply, even though the contract did not expressly so state. In such event, there would be nothing in the contract that could possibly constitute evidence of an intent to exclude punitive damages claims. Accordingly, punitive damages would be allowed because, in the absence of contractual intent to the contrary, the FAA would pre-empt the Garrity rule. See supra, at 4.

Even if the reference to "the laws of the State of New York" is more than a substitute for ordinary conflict-of-laws analysis and, as respondents urge, includes the caveat, "detached from otherwise-applicable federal law," the provision might not preclude the award of punitive damages because New York allows its courts, though not its arbitrators, to enter such awards. See Garrity, 40 N.Y.2d, at 358, 386 N.Y.S.2d at 834, 353 N.E.2d, at 796. In other words, the provision might include only New York's substantive rights and obligations, and not the State's allocation of power between alternative tribunals. Respondents' argument is persuasive only if "New York law" means "New York decisional law, including that State's allocation of power between courts and arbitrators, notwithstanding otherwise-applicable federal law." But, as we have demonstrated, the

2. Paragraph 13 of the Client's Agreement provides: "This agreement shall inure to the benefit of your [Shearson's] successors and assigns[,] shall be binding on the undersigned, my [petitioners'] heirs, executors, administrators and assigns, and shall be governed by the laws of the State of New York. Unless unenforceable due to federal or state law, any controversy arising out of or relating to [my] accounts, to transactions with you, your officers, directors, agents and/or employees for me or to this agreement or the breach thereof, shall be settled by arbitration in accordance with the rules then in effect, of the National Association of Securities Dealers, Inc. or the Boards of Directors of the New York Stock Exchange, Inc. and/or the American Stock Exchange Inc. as I may elect ... Judgment upon any award rendered by the arbitrators may be entered in any court have jurisdiction thereof ..."

provision need not be read so broadly. It is not, in itself, an unequivocal exclusion of punitive damages claims.[4]

The arbitration provision (the second sentence of Paragraph 13) does not improve respondents' argument. On the contrary, when read separately this clause strongly implies that an arbitral award of punitive damages is appropriate. It explicitly authorizes arbitration in accordance with NASD rules;[5] the panel of arbitrators in fact proceeded under that set of rules. The NASD's Code of Arbitration Procedure indicates that arbitrators may award "damages and other relief." NASD Code of Arbitration Procedure P 3741(e) (1993). While not a clear authorization of punitive damages, this provision appears broad enough at least to contemplate such a remedy. Moreover, as the Seventh Circuit noted, a manual provided to NASD arbitrators contains this provision:

B. Punitive Damages

"The issue of punitive damages may arise with great frequency in arbitrations. Parties to arbitration are informed that arbitrators can consider punitive damages as a remedy." 20 F.3d, at 717. Thus, the text of the arbitration clause itself surely does not support—indeed, it contradicts—the conclusion that the parties agreed to foreclose claims for punitive damages.[7]

4. The dissent makes much of the similarity between this choice-of-law clause and the one in Volt, which we took to incorporate a California statute allowing a court to stay arbitration pending resolution of related litigation. In Volt, however, we did not interpret the contract de novo. Instead, we deferred to the California court's construction of its own state's law. 489 U.S., at 474, 109 S.Ct., at 1253 ("[T]he interpretation of private contracts is ordinarily a question of state law, which this Court does not sit to review"). In the present case, by contrast, we review a *federal* court's interpretation of this contract, and our interpretation accords with that of the only decision-maker arguably entitled to deference—the arbitrator. See n. 1, *supra*.

5. The contract also authorizes (at petitioners' election) that the arbitration be governed by the rules of the New York Stock Exchange or the American Stock Exchange, instead of those of the NASD. App. to Pet. for Cert. 44. Neither set of alternative rules purports to limit an arbitrator's discretion to award punitive damages. Moreover, even if there were any doubt as to the ability of an arbitrator to award punitive damages under the Exchanges' rules, the contract expressly allows petitioners, the claimants in this case, to choose NASD rules; and the panel of arbitrators in this case in fact proceeded under NASD rules.

7. "Were we to confine our analysis to the plain language of the arbitration clause, we would have little trouble concluding that a contract clause which bound the parties to 'settle' 'all disputes' through arbitration conducted according to rules which allow any form of 'just and equitable' 'remedy of relief' was sufficiently broad to encompass the award of punitive damages. Inasmuch as agreements to arbitrate are 'generously construed,' Mitsubishi Motors Corp. v. Soler Chrysler–Plymouth, [473 U.S. 614, 626, 105 S.Ct. 3346, 3353–54, 87 L.Ed.2d 444 (1985)], it would seem sensible to interpret the 'all disputes' and 'any remedy or relief' phrases to indicate, at a minimum, an intention to resolve through arbitration any dispute that would otherwise be settled in a court, and to allow the chosen dispute resolvers to award the same varieties and forms of damages or relief as a court would be empowered to award. Since courts are empowered to award punitive damages with respect to certain types of claims, the Raytheon–Automated arbitrators would be equally empowered." Raytheon Co. v. Automated Business Systems, Inc., 882 F.2d 6, 10 (C.A.1 1989).

Although neither the choice-of-law clause nor the arbitration clause, separately considered, expresses an intent to preclude an award of punitive damages, respondents argue that a fair reading of the entire Paragraph 13 leads to that conclusion. On this theory, even if "New York law" is ambiguous, and even if "arbitration in accordance with NASD rules" indicates that punitive damages are permissible, the juxtaposition of the two clauses suggests that the contract incorporates "New York law relating to arbitration." We disagree. At most, the choice-of-law clause introduces an ambiguity into an arbitration agreement that would otherwise allow punitive damages awards. As we pointed out in Volt, when a court interprets such provisions in an agreement covered by the FAA, "due regard must be given to the federal policy favoring arbitration, and ambiguities as to the scope of the arbitration clause itself resolved in favor of arbitration." 489 U.S., at 476, 109 S.Ct., at 1254 . . .

Moreover, respondents cannot overcome the common-law rule of contract interpretation that a court should construe ambiguous language against the interest of the party that drafted it . . . Respondents drafted an ambiguous document, and they cannot now claim the benefit of the doubt. The reason for this rule is to protect the party who did not choose the language from an unintended or unfair result. That rationale is well-suited to the facts of this case. As a practical matter, it seems unlikely that petitioners were actually aware of New York's bifurcated approach to punitive damages, or that they had any idea that by signing a standard-form agreement to arbitrate disputes they might be giving up an important substantive right. In the face of such doubt, we are unwilling to impute this intent to petitioners.

Finally the respondents' reading of the two clauses violates another cardinal principle of contract construction: that a document should be read to give effect to all its provisions and to render them consistent with each other . . . Restatement (Second) of Contracts § 203(a) and Comment b § 202(5). We think the best way to harmonize the choice-of-law provision with the arbitration provision is to read "the laws of the State of New York" to encompass substantive principles that New York courts would apply, but not to include special rules limiting the authority of arbitrators. Thus, the choice-of-law provision covers the rights and duties of the parties, while the arbitration clause covers arbitration; neither sentence intrudes upon the other. In contrast, respondents' reading sets up the two clauses in conflict with one another: one foreclosing punitive damages, the other allowing them. This interpretation is untenable.

We hold that the Court of Appeals misinterpreted the parties' agreement. The arbitral award should have been enforced as within the scope of the contract. The judgment of the Court of Appeals is, therefore, reversed.

It is so ordered.

■ JUSTICE THOMAS, dissenting.

In Volt Information Sciences, Inc. v. Board of Trustees of Leland Stanford Junior University, 489 U.S. 468, 478, 109 S.Ct. 1248, 1255, 103

L.Ed.2d 488 (1989), we held that the Federal Arbitration Act (FAA) simply requires courts to enforce private contracts to arbitrate as they would normal contracts—according to their terms. This holding led us to enforce a choice-of-law provision that incorporated a state procedural rule concerning arbitration proceedings. Because the choice-of-law provision here cannot reasonably be distinguished from the one in Volt, I dissent.

I

A

In Volt, Stanford University had entered into a construction contract under which Volt Information Sciences, Inc. was to install certain electrical systems on the Stanford campus. The contract contained an agreement to arbitrate all disputes arising out of the contract. A choice-of-law clause in the contract provided that "[t]he Contract shall be governed by the law of the place where the Project is located," 489 U.S., at 470, 109 S.Ct., at 1254, which happened to be California. When a dispute arose regarding compensation, Volt invoked arbitration. Stanford filed an action in state court, however, and moved to stay arbitration pursuant to California rules of civil procedure. Cal.Civ.Proc.Code Ann. § 1281.2(c) (West 1982). Opposing the stay, Volt argued that the relevant state statute authorizing the stay was pre-empted by the FAA, 9 U.S.C. § 1 et seq.

We concluded that even if the FAA preempted the state statute as applied to other parties, the choice-of-law clause in the contract at issue demonstrated that the parties had agreed to be governed by the statute . . .

We so held in Volt because we concluded that the FAA does not force arbitration on parties who enter into contracts involving interstate commerce. Instead, the FAA requires only that "arbitration proceed in the manner provided for in [the parties'] agreement." 9 U.S.C. § 4 . . .

B

In this case, as in Volt, the parties agreed to mandatory arbitration of all disputes. As in Volt, the contract at issue here includes a choice-of-law clause. Indeed, the language of the two clauses is functionally equivalent: whereas the choice-of-law clause in Volt provided that "[t]he Contract shall be governed by the law of [the State of California]," . . . the one before us today states, in Paragraph 13 of the Client's Agreement, that "[t]his agreement . . . shall be governed by the laws of the State of New York." New York law forbids arbitrators from awarding punitive damages, Garrity v. Lyle Stuart, Inc., 40 N.Y.2d 354, 386 N.Y.S.2d 831, 353 N.E.2d 793 (1976), and permits only courts to award such damages. As in Volt, petitioners here argue that the New York rule is "anti-arbitration," and hence is pre-empted by the FAA. In concluding that the choice-of-law clause is ambiguous, the majority essentially accepts petitioners' argument. Volt itself found precisely the same argument irrelevant, however, and the majority identifies no reason to think that the state law governing the interpretation of the parties' choice-of-law clause supports a different result.

The majority claims that the incorporation of New York law "need not be read so broadly" as to include both substantive and procedural law, and that the choice of New York law "is not, in itself, an unequivocal exclusion of punitive damages claims." Ante, at 1217. But we rejected these same arguments the conduct of arbitration" that Volt requires federal courts to enforce. 489 U.S., at 476, 109 S.Ct., at 1254. "Just as [the parties] may limit by contract the issues which they will arbitrate, so too may they specify by contract the rules under which that arbitration will be conducted." Id., at 479, 109 S.Ct., at 1256 (citation omitted). To be sure, the majority might be correct that Garrity is a rule concerning the State's allocation of power between "alternative tribunals," ante, at 1217, although Garrity appears to describe itself as substantive New York law. Nonetheless, Volt makes no distinction between rules that serve only to distribute authority between courts and arbitrators (which the majority finds unenforceable) and other types of rules (which the majority finds enforceable). Indeed, the California rule in Volt could be considered to be one that allocates authority between arbitrators and courts, for it permits California courts to stay arbitration pending resolution of related litigation. See Volt, 489 U.S., at 471, 109 S.Ct., at 125–152.

II

... My examination of the Client Agreement, the choice-of-law provision, the NASD Code of Procedure, and the SICA manual demonstrates that the parties made their intent clear, but not in the way divined by the majority. New York law specifically precludes arbitrators from awarding punitive damages, and it should be clear that there is no "conflict," as the majority puts it, between the New York law and the NASD rules. The choice-of-law provision speaks directly to the issue, while the NASD Code is silent. Giving effect to every provision of the contract requires us to honor the parties' intent, as indicated in the text of the agreement, to preclude the award of punitive damages by arbitrators ...

* * *

Questions

1. Should arbitrators have the power to award punitive damages? What are the arguments for and against such a result?

2. The underlying claim in *Garrity* was based on contract law, and as the *Garrity* court points out, punitive damages generally are not available in such cases. Are cases based on tort law distinguishable? What about statutory cases, where the statute expressly permits punitive damage awards?

3. What if, in a case brought under a statute expressly permitting punitive damages, the arbitrator cites to *Garrity* and refuses to award punitive damages. Should a prevailing plaintiff then be free to seek punitive damages in court? Would allowing the plaintiff to do so be consistent with the agreement to arbitrate all disputes between the parties? Would not allowing the plaintiff to do so be consistent with the statute on which the underlying claim is based?

4. What if, under similar circumstances, the arbitrator refuses to award punitive damages but does not explain why?

5. How convincingly does the majority in *Mastrobuono* distinguish *Volt*? What weight should a court give to a choice of law clause? Can a court limit the application of a choice of law clause to the chosen forum's "substantive principles" and not include "special rules limiting the authority of arbitrators"? How can it know which is which? Or, should the court presume that the parties have chosen every aspect of the law of the selected forum?

6. Suppose parties have a contract that includes a choice of law clause naming a state that permits punitive damages in arbitration, and the contract also incorporates by reference a trade association arbitration procedure that specifies that there shall be no punitive damages in arbitration. If an arbitrator then awards punitive damages in a dispute arising from the contract, should a federal court vacate or affirm the award?

7. To what extent does the Supreme Court's reasoning in *Mastrobuono* turn on the contracting parties' lack of foresight and knowledge? Is this approach consistent with the Court's approach in *First Options*? Is it consistent with the approach in *Allied–Bruce Terminix*? Would such an approach change the result in the cases concerning the presence or absence of consent to arbitration clauses?

8. An empirical study of punitive damage awards in labor and employment arbitrations found:

> (1) Express provisions for punitive awards are rare but since 1995 they appear to be ordered and enforced more frequently.
>
> (2) Punitive awards are much higher in non-union employment arbitrations compared to labor arbitrations.
>
> (3) Judges enforce less than half of the labor arbitration awards but nearly all individual employment arbitration awards.
>
> (4) In a very small number of employment cases, the ratio of punitive to compensatory damages exceeds due process limits that apply to similar jury awards.

Michael H. LeRoy & Peter Feuille, *Reinventing the Enterprise Wheel: Court Review of Punitive Awards in Labor and Employment Arbitrations*, 11 Harv. Negot. L. Rev. 199, 202 (2006). Can these findings be explained by the different standards of review for collective bargaining arbitration than in FAA arbitration?

* * *

C. CONTRACTUAL CONTROL OVER REMEDIES

Sometimes an arbitration agreement will specify limitations on the remedies an arbitrator can award. For example, some arbitration agreements prohibit the arbitrator from awarding punitive damages or attorney fees. However, if one party uses predominant economic power to deprive the other of statutory remedies that might be available, it is an open question as to whether that arbitration award will be enforced. Although arbitration is a creature of contract and parties are free to fashion arbitration agreements to suit their needs, the Supreme Court in *Mitsubishi* and *Shearson/American Express* held that it was permissible for an arbitrator to decide cases involving federal statutory rights only "so long as the arbitral forum is adequate to protect the substantive rights at issue," and that arbitration represents a change in forum only and not a waiver of substantive rights. When an arbitration agreement limits the remedies a party can obtain for a statutory violation, courts must decide whether the agreement is adequate to protect the substantive rights safeguarded by the statute. The following cases address this issue.

* * *

Graham Oil Co. v. ARCO Products Co.

43 F.3d 1244 (9th Cir. 1994).

■ REINHARDT, CIRCUIT JUDGE:

I. INTRODUCTION

Graham Oil Co. ("Graham Oil") appeals the judgment of the district court, which dismissed, with prejudice, all of its claims against ARCO Products Co. ("ARCO"). The claims were dismissed because Graham Oil refused to submit to arbitration as required by an arbitration clause in its distributorship agreement with ARCO.

Graham Oil contends that the arbitration clause is invalid because it requires the surrender of certain rights provided under the Petroleum Marketing Practices Act ("PMPA"), 15 U.S.C. §§ 2801–2806. Accordingly, it argues that the district court—not an arbitrator—must decide the merits of its claims under the PMPA. We agree.

II. FACTS

For nearly forty years, Graham Oil was a branded distributor of ARCO gasoline in Coos Bay, Oregon. On October 2, 1990, Graham Oil and ARCO entered into a Branded Distributor Gasoline Agreement ("Agreement"), which was effective from January 1, 1991, to December 31, 1993. Among other things, the parties agreed that Graham Oil would purchase a minimum amount of gasoline each month during the two-year period of the Agreement.

On November 10, 1991, ARCO notified Graham Oil that it intended to terminate the Agreement as of October 31, 1991, because Graham Oil had not been purchasing the required minimum amount of gasoline as specified in the Agreement. On November 27, 1991, Graham Oil filed a motion for a preliminary injunction against ARCO in federal district court. Graham Oil argued that ARCO had violated the PMPA by deliberately raising its prices so that Graham Oil would be unable to meet the minimum gasoline requirements. Accordingly, Graham Oil argued that ARCO should not be allowed to terminate the Agreement.

On December 3, 1991, the district court issued a preliminary injunction that prohibited ARCO from terminating the Agreement for 90 days. Instead of reaching the merits of Graham Oil's claims under the PMPA, however, the court found that arbitration was Graham Oil's exclusive remedy. The court required the parties to complete the arbitration within 90 days.

Graham Oil appealed the district court's order and refused to submit to arbitration. Upon the expiration of the 90 days, ARCO moved for summary judgment. Graham Oil filed a cross-motion to keep the court's preliminary injunction in force pending the resolution of its appeal. The court denied Graham Oil's cross-motion and granted summary judgment in favor of ARCO. On appeal, Graham Oil argues that the arbitration clause in the Agreement is invalid and that the court must determine the merits of its claims under the PMPA.

III. ANALYSIS

This case involves the validity of an arbitration clause that, in addition to specifying arbitration as the means by which disputes are to be resolved, purports to waive certain statutory rights conferred upon petroleum franchisees by the PMPA. We conclude that the clause is invalid. As a result, we strike it and remand for further proceedings.

A. Validity of the Clause.

1. Purpose of the PMPA. In determining the validity of the arbitration clause, we first review the purpose of the PMPA. Congress enacted the PMPA with the primary goal of "protecting franchisees." *See Khorenian v. Union Oil Co.,* 761 F.2d 533, 535 (9th Cir. 1985) (internal quotes omitted). Such protection was needed in order to correct the great "disparity of bargaining power" between petroleum franchisors and franchisees. *See* S.Rep. No. 731, 95th Cong., 2d Sess., *in* 1978 U.S.C.C.A.N. 873, 876 [hereinafter *Legislative History*]. According to the legislative history of the PMPA, petroleum franchise agreements generally are nothing more than "contracts of adhesion" that perpetuate the "continuing vulnerability of the franchisee to the demands and actions of the franchisor." *Id.*

In order to correct some of the effects of this disparity in bargaining power, Congress enacted certain protections for franchisees like Graham Oil. Essentially, the Act affords franchisees statutory remedies for the arbitrary or discriminatory termination (or non-renewal) of franchises by their franchisors. *Id.* Among other things, these protections include exemplary damages, reasonable attorney's fees, and a one-year statute of limitations. *See* 15 U.S.C. § 2805; *Legislative History* at 899. These rights and benefits are, of course, not only designed to compensate for injury, but also to deter unfair conduct.

2. *Arbitration Clause.* Turning to the arbitration clause, we note as an initial matter that arbitration is a form of dispute resolution that finds favor in the courts. In a number of instances, the Supreme Court has upheld agreements to submit statutory claims to arbitration, *see, e.g., Gilmer v. Interstate/Johnson Lane Corporation,* 500 U.S. 20 . . . including claims involving unfair business practices. Among the claims in that category are those arising under the Sherman Act, the Securities Exchange Act of 1934, and the Securities Act of 1933. [Citations omitted.] Some of the arbitration provisions—like the provisions here—have been contained in form agreements executed before the dispute arose. [Citations.]

3. *Analysis.* Nothing in the PMPA suggests that Congress intended to change the general presumption in favor of upholding agreements to submit statutory claims to arbitration. A simple agreement for arbitration of disputes is valid, whether or not contained in a franchise agreement. Such a provision constitutes nothing more than an agreement to substitute one legitimate dispute resolution *forum* for another and involves no surrender of statutory protections or benefits.

However, the fact that franchisees may agree to an arbitral forum for the resolution of statutory disputes in no way suggests that they may be forced by those with dominant economic power to surrender the statutorily-mandated rights and benefits that Congress intended them to possess. This is certainly true in cases arising under the PMPA, which was enacted to shield franchisees from the gross "disparity of bargaining power" that exists between them and franchisors. If franchisees could be compelled to surrender their statutorily-mandated protections as a condition of obtaining franchise agreements, then franchisors could use their superior bargaining power to deprive franchisees of the PMPA's protections. In effect, the franchisors could simply continue their earlier practice of presenting prospective franchisees with contracts of adhesion that deny them the rights and benefits afforded by Congress. In that way, the PMPA would quickly be nullified.

Here, the arbitration clause purports to forfeit certain important statutorily-mandated rights or benefits afforded to Graham Oil and other franchisees by the PMPA. First, the arbitration clause expressly forfeits Graham Oil's statutorily-mandated right to recover exemplary damages from ARCO if Graham Oil prevails on certain claims. The clause provides that neither party can be awarded exemplary damages. *Compare* 15 U.S.C. § 2805(d)(1)(B) ("If the franchisee prevails in [certain] action[s] . . . such franchisee shall be entitled . . . *to exemplary damages,* where appropriate . . ." (emphasis added)) *with* Agreement § 22(b) ("The arbitrator(s) *may not assess* punitive or *exemplary damages* . . . ." (emphasis added)).

Second, the arbitration clause expressly forfeits Graham Oil's statutorily-mandated right to recover reasonable attorney's fees from ARCO if

Graham Oil prevails on certain claims. The clause provides that each party will bear its own attorney's fees. *Compare* 15 U.S.C. § 2805(d)(1)(C) ("If the franchisee prevails in [certain] action[s] ... such franchisee shall be entitled ... to *reasonable attorney* and expert witness *fees* to be paid by the franchisor ..." (emphasis added)) *with* Agreement 22(a) ("*Each party shall pay its own costs and expenses, including attorneys' fees related to such arbitration* ..." (emphasis added)).

Third, the arbitration clause expressly forfeits Graham Oil's statutorily-mandated right to a one-year statute of limitations on its claims against ARCO. The clause reduces the time in which a claim can be brought from one year to 90 days, or in some cases six months. *Compare* 15 U.S.C. § 2805(a) ("[N]o such action may be maintained unless commenced *within 1 year* after ... the date the franchisor fails to comply with [certain] requirements ... of this title.") *with* Appendix, EXHIBIT E § A ("The party waives the right to seek any relief or pursue any claim not included in an arbitration demand filed ... *within 90 days* following the date the party knew or should have known of the facts giving rise to the claim [and in no event more than six months after the occurrence of the facts giving rise to the claim]" (emphasis added)).

Each of the three statutory rights is important to the effectuation of the PMPA's policies. The purpose of exemplary damages is to deter franchisors from engaging in improper terminations of franchise agreements. The purpose of attorney's fees is to deter franchisors from improperly contesting meritorious claims. Finally, the purpose of a one-year statute of limitations is to afford franchisees a reasonable period of time in which to seek relief for improper terminations and other abuses by petroleum franchisors. In attempting to strip franchisees of these statutory rights and benefits by means of an arbitration clause included in the franchise agreement, ARCO violated the purpose as well as the specific terms of the PMPA.

Because the arbitration clause employed by ARCO compels Graham Oil to surrender important statutorily-mandated rights afforded franchisees by the PMPA, we hold that the clause contravenes the Act.

[The court then considered whether the arbitration clause should be severed from the contract.]

... The more difficult question is whether the *entire* arbitration clause should be severed, or simply the provisions pertaining to exemplary damages, attorney's fees, and the statute of limitations. Relying on principles that are analogous to those we use in determining whether a particular clause is severable from an entire contract, we conclude that in this case the *entire* clause must be eliminated.

It is a well-known principle in contract law that a clause cannot be severed from a contract when it is an integrated part of the contract. As one leading treatise has noted, "a contract should be treated as entire when by consideration of its terms, nature and purposes each and all of the parts appear to be interdependent and common to one another." Joseph D. Calamari & Joseph M. Perillo, *Contracts* 478 n. 76 (3d ed. 1987) . . .

Here, the offending parts of the arbitration clause do not merely involve a single, isolated provision; the arbitration clause in this case is a highly integrated unit containing three different illegal provisions. Unlike the other clauses, the arbitration clause here includes a survival provision that expressly preserves the entire clause in the event the contract is declared invalid. Moreover, it establishes a unified procedure for handling all disputes, and its various unlawful provisions are all a part of that overall procedure. Thus, we conclude that the clause must be treated as a whole and that its various provisions are not severable.

Our decision to strike the entire clause rests in part upon the fact that the offensive provisions clearly represent an attempt by ARCO to achieve through arbitration what Congress has expressly forbidden. Congress enacted the PMPA precisely to prevent the type of agreement that ARCO included in the arbitration clause of its franchise contract. ARCO attempted to use an arbitration clause to achieve its unlawful ends. Such a blatant misuse of the arbitration procedure serves to taint the entire clause. As a leading treatise notes, severance is inappropriate when the entire clause represents an "integrated scheme to contravene public policy." *See* E. Allan Farnsworth, *Farnsworth on Contracts* § 5.8, at 70 (1990). For the above reasons, we conclude that the entire arbitration clause, and not merely the offensive provisions, must be stricken from the contract. We remand to the district court, which is the proper forum for the resolution of this underlying dispute.

REVERSED and REMANDED.

[The Appendix, and the dissenting opinion of Judge Fernandez is omitted.]

* * *

Larry's United Super, Inc. v. Dean Werries et al.

253 F.3d 1083 (8th Cir. 2001).

■ HANSEN, CIRCUIT JUDGE.

After being sued by a group of independent retail grocers with whom it held supply agreements, the Fleming Companies, Inc. (Fleming) and two of Fleming's former officers moved to compel arbitration of the dispute. The district court denied the motion as to all of the plaintiffs but two. Fleming and the former officers appeal. We reverse and remand for an order compelling arbitration of the entire dispute.

I.

The plaintiffs in the underlying diversity law suit are a group of independent retail grocers incorporated in Missouri and Kansas. They filed suit against their wholesale grocery supplier, Fleming, an Oklahoma corporation; Fleming's former chief executive officer and chairman, Dean Werries; and the former president of Fleming's Kansas City division, Byron Duffield. The grocers allege that they are each party to a supply agreement with Fleming, whereby Fleming contracted to sell them grocery and related products at actual cost plus a specified fee and freight, and promised to pass all vendor deals, discounts, and allowances on to the retail grocers. The grocers brought suit, asserting that for several years Fleming has been charging them in excess of the amounts authorized by their supply agreements, in violation of various state law provisions and the Racketeer Influenced and Corrupt Organizations Act (RICO), 18 U.S.C. §§ 1961–1968 (1994 & Supp. IV 1998). Their complaint alleged seven state law-based claims and the single federal RICO claim.

Each of the appellee grocers' supply agreements contains an arbitration clause providing that the parties agree to resolve by arbitration all disputes relating to the agreement and to waive all rights to punitive damages. Relying on the agreement to arbitrate, Fleming and its former officers (hereinafter collectively called "Fleming") filed a motion to compel arbitration and to stay the underlying district court proceedings pending completion of arbitration in accordance with the Federal Arbitration Act (FAA), 9 U.S.C. §§ 3, 4 (1994). The grocers resisted the motion, asserting fraudulent inducement of the arbitration provisions and asserting that the arbitration clauses are unenforceable because they preclude an award of punitive damages in violation of the public policy underlying RICO's treble damages provision. *See* 18 U.S.C. § 1964(c) (Supp. IV 1998).

Relevant to this appeal, the district court denied the motion to compel arbitration as to the appellee grocers. While it denied the motion to compel arbitration, the court did conclude that the arbitration provisions in the supply agreements are broad enough to cover the entire dispute between the parties (including the seven counts based on state law claims) and were not fraudulently induced. Nevertheless, the court agreed with the grocers that the damages limitation provisions contained in the agreements to arbitrate defeat the purposes of RICO and prevent the grocers from obtaining adequate relief in arbitration. Fleming and its former officers appeal, arguing initially that the limitation of damages is not illegal, and alternatively, that the severability provisions of the supply agreements should be applied to salvage the agreements to arbitrate. Under the alternative argument, Fleming says all the counts can and should be sent to arbitration but without the damage limitation on the RICO claim.

II.

We review de novo a district court's decision regarding the validity and scope of an arbitration clause. We bear in mind that the FAA's "provisions manifest a 'liberal federal policy favoring arbitration agreements.' " *Gilmer v. Interstate/Johnson Lane Corp.,* 500 U.S. 20, 25, 111 S.Ct. 1647, 114 L.Ed.2d 26 (1991) (quoting *Moses H. Cone Mem'l Hosp. v. Mercury Constr. Corp.,* 460 U.S. 1, 24, 103 S.Ct. 927, 74 L.Ed.2d 765 (1983)) . . .

The supply agreements each contained an arbitration clause broadly declaring that the parties agree to arbitrate "all disputes between them relating to this Agreement." (Appellants' Adden. at A–16.) While not all controversies implicating federal statutory rights may be suitable for arbitration, the Supreme Court has held that RICO claims are arbitrable. *See Shearson/American Express Inc. v. McMahon,* 482 U.S. 220, 242, 107 S.Ct. 2332, 96 L.Ed.2d 185 (1987) ... The RICO claim at issue relates to the supply agreements because the grocers assert that Fleming has been overcharging them in amounts greater than bargained for under the supply agreements. The parties do not dispute that the contract's arbitration language in the supply agreements is broad enough to include the RICO dispute at issue, and we agree that the language covers this dispute. We conclude that the district court correctly determined that the parties agreed to arbitrate all the claims including the RICO claim.

Fleming contends that the district court erred by determining that the arbitration agreement is invalid due to a limitation on punitive damages. The district court concluded that this limitation violated the public policy of RICO, and thus held the entire arbitration agreement unenforceable. We agree with Fleming that the damages limitation does not render unenforceable the entire agreement to arbitrate.

"[A] court compelling arbitration should decide only such issues as are essential to defining the nature of the forum in which a dispute will be decided." *Great Western Mtg. Corp. v. Peacock,* 110 F.3d 222, 230 (3d Cir.), *cert. denied,* 522 U.S. 915, 118 S.Ct. 299, 139 L.Ed.2d 230 (1997). In *Peacock,* the Third Circuit held that "[a]ny argument that the provisions of the Arbitration Agreement involve a waiver of substantive rights afforded by the state statute may be presented in the arbitral forum." *Id.* at 231. We conclude that this statement is equally applicable to explicit waivers of substantive rights under federal statutes. Whether federal public policy prohibits an individual from waiving certain statutory remedies is an issue that may be raised when challenging an arbitrator's award. Given the limited scope of our authority on a motion to compel arbitration, we agree with the Third Circuit that "[o]nce a dispute is determined to be validly arbitrable, all other issues are to be decided at arbitration." *Peacock,* 110 F.3d at 230.

We respectfully decline at this time to follow the lead of the circuit cases which the district court found supported its decision to deny arbitration on the grounds of public policy. *See Paladino v. Avnet Computer Techs., Inc.,* 134 F.3d 1054, 1062 (11th Cir. 1998); *Graham Oil Co. v. ARCO Prods. Co.,* 43 F.3d 1244, 1248–49 (9th Cir.), *cert. denied,* 516 U.S. 907, 116 S.Ct. 275, 133 L.Ed.2d 195 (1995). In large part, those cases are distinguishable, and to the extent they are not distinguishable, we choose not to follow them now.

At this juncture, our jurisdiction extends only to determine whether a valid agreement to arbitrate exists, not to determine whether public policy conflicts with the remedies provided in the arbitration clause. There exists a valid agreement to arbitrate the RICO claim in this case, and the Supreme Court in *McMahon* has already determined that RICO claims are arbitrable, 482 U.S. at 242, 107 S.Ct. 2332; thus, there exists no "legal constraints external to the parties' agreement foreclos[ing] the arbitration" of this RICO dispute. *Mitsubishi Motors Corp. v. Soler Chrysler–Plymouth, Inc.*, 473 U.S. 614, 628, 105 S.Ct. 3346, 87 L.Ed.2d 444 (1985). Whether a prospective waiver of punitive damages violates the public policy underlying RICO's treble damages provision is a matter for the arbitrators in the first instance when fashioning an appropriate remedy if a RICO claim is proven to the arbitrators' satisfaction, and we express no views on the issue at this time. We are limited to determining whether the matter is arbitrable. We hold that it is.

[The court also rejected retail grocers' claim that the arbitration clause is invalid because it was fraudulently induced by misrepresentations of Fleming.]

III.

Accordingly, we reverse and remand this case to the district court with instructions to enter an order compelling arbitration of the entire dispute, and we leave to the arbitrators what effect, if any, to give to the damage limitation language if indeed damages are awarded by them for any claim.

* * *

Questions

1. The court in *Larry's United Super* stated that "whether a prospective waiver of punitive damages violates the public policy underlying RICO's treble damages provision is a matter for the arbitrators in the first instance." If an arbitrator determines that the waiver does not violate the public policy of RICO and proceeds to enforce the arbitration clause's limitation on punitive damages, would that determination be subject to judicial review? What standard of review would a court apply?

2. The court in *Larry's United Super* suggested that *Graham Oil Co. v. ARCO Prods. Co.* is distinguishable. Do you agree?

3. To what extent does the result in *Graham Oil Co.* depend upon a finding that one party exploited its superior bargaining power in the framing of the arbitration clause? Does the case stand for the more general proposition that arbitration clauses restricting otherwise available statutory remedies are unenforceable?

4. Should parties be permitted to negotiate arbitration provisions with restrictions on statutory remedies? Should they be able to negotiate restrictions on common law remedies? Should they be able to negotiate arbitration provisions with remedies that are greater than whatever a court could impose, such as double or even treble damages? Might such a provision be treated as a penalty clause and thus unenforceable?

* * *

Morrison v. Circuit City Stores

317 F.3d 646 (6th Cir. 2003), en banc.

■ MOORE, J.

[The facts of *Morrison* are described in Chapter 2.7. Circuit City fired Lillian Morrison, and she sued for race and sex discrimination. Circuit City moved to compel arbitration pursuant to a predispute arbitration agreement. Rule 14 of that arbitration agreement listed the remedies that the arbitrator could award, including injunctive relief, back pay, front pay, compensatory damages, and punitive damages. Rule 14 also limited the amount of monetary damages the arbitrator could award, allowing for twelve months of back pay, starting "from the point at which the Associate knew or should have known of the events giving rise to the alleged violation," and allowing any back pay award to be "reduced by interim earnings, public or private benefits received, and amounts that could have been received with reasonable diligence." Additionally, Rule 14 stated that an arbitrator could award only up to twenty-four months of front pay, and limited any award of punitive damages to the greater of $5,000 or an amount equal to the sum of the front and back pay awards.]

We ... conclude that the limitations that the Circuit City arbitration agreement places on the damages a claimant may recover from arbitration are unenforceable. It is well-established that "a party does not forgo the substantive rights afforded by [a] statute [when she agrees to arbitrate a statutory claim but] only submits to their resolution in an arbitral, rather than a judicial, forum." *Gilmer,* 500 U.S. at 26, 111 S.Ct. 1647 (quotation omitted). In this case, however, the enforcement of the arbitration agreement would require Morrison to forego her substantive rights to the full panoply of remedies under Title VII and would thereby contravene Congress's intent to utilize certain damages as a tool for compensating victims of discrimination and for deterring employment discrimination more broadly. The critical question is not whether a claimant may obtain *some* amount of the entire range of remedies under Title VII, but whether the limitation on remedies at issue undermines the rights protected by the statute. *See Gilmer,* 500 U.S. at 26–27, 111 S.Ct. 1647 ...

The limitation on remedies provision at issue in Morrison's case undermines both the remedial and deterrent principles of Title VII. The arbitration agreement's limitation on remedies clearly impedes Title VII's remedial goal of "making persons whole for injuries suffered through past discrimination." *Albemarle Paper Co. v. Moody,* 422 U.S. 405, 421, 95 S.Ct. 2362, 45 L.Ed.2d 280 (1975). The Supreme Court has consistently recognized that one of the objects of Title VII is "[c]ompensation for injuries caused by the prohibited discrimination." *See, e.g., McKennon v. Nashville Banner Publ'g Co.,* 513 U.S. 352, 358, 115 S.Ct. 879, 130 L.Ed.2d 852 (1995). In this case, the remedies potentially available to make Morrison whole were significantly limited under the arbitration agreement, which allows only injunctive relief, including reinstatement; one year of backpay and reimbursement for lost fringe benefits (which may be further reduced by interim earnings or public/private benefits received); two years of front pay if reinstatement is not possible; compensatory damages in accordance with applicable law; and punitive damages up to $5,000 or the sum of a claimant's backpay and front pay awards, whichever is greater.

Circuit City argues, somewhat counter-intuitively, that such limits do not undermine the purposes of Title VII because Morrison could potentially receive a greater sum of damages under its agreement than she could receive under Title VII. As we read the terms of the arbitration agreement, however, Circuit City's argument is flawed for a number of reasons. First, under Circuit City's arbitration agreement, Morrison could not collect a potential compensatory and punitive damages award of $538,000, Appellee's Br. at 10 n. 4, but only $462,000. To calculate this, we suppose that an arbitrator were to award Morrison the full amount of compensatory damages that the arbitration agreement allows. Because the agreement's Rule 14(5) allows compensatory damages "in accordance with applicable law," we suppose an award of $300,000, the maximum figure allowed under Title VII. We then suppose that the arbitrator were to award Morrison punitive damages under Rule 14(6), which the agreement caps at amount "equal to the monetary award, if any, rendered pursuant to Subsections 3 and/or 4" of Rule 14. Supposing that the arbitrator were to award punitive damages equal to the maximum allowed under Rules 14(3) and 14(4), Morrison would receive punitive damages equal to Rule 14(3)'s maximum of one year of backpay, or $54,000, and Rule 14(4)'s maximum of two years of front pay, or $108,000. The sum of these figures—the agreement's maximum compensatory damages and the maximum punitive damages—is $462,000.

Second, federal law does not limit Morrison's total damages but rather only limits the sum of her compensatory and punitive damages; furthermore, it places no limits on the amount of backpay or front pay that Morrison may receive. Indeed, 42 U.S.C. § 1981a explicitly states that "[c]ompensatory damages awarded under this section *shall not include backpay,* interest on backpay, or any other type of relief authorized under section 706(g) of the Civil Rights Act of 1964." 42 U.S.C. § 1981a(b)(2) (emphasis added). Additionally, federal law does not require that a claimant's front pay award must be limited to only two years of her salary. *See Pollard v. E.I. du Pont de Nemours & Co.,* 532 U.S. 843, 848, 121 S.Ct. 1946, 150 L.Ed.2d 62 (2001). Therefore, in addition to the $300,000 in compensatory and punitive damages that Morrison could receive under Title VII, she could also collect an award of backpay from the date of her termination[13] to the date on which she receives a judgment in this case, which may consist of many years of backpay, and she could also receive a front pay award in excess of the mere two years allowed under the arbitration agreement. In other words, if Morrison had received a favorable

13. Section 2000e–5(g)(1) allows for an award of backpay "from a date [no] more than two years prior to the filing of [her] charge with the Commission." As Morrison filed her charge with the EEOC within a few months after her termination, under Title VII, she would be eligible for a backpay award starting from the date of her termination.

judgment in court, in theory she could have collected a backpay award equal to three times her salary, as opposed to one, and a front pay award, which if given in lieu of reinstatement could have equaled as much as the amount of pay she would have received from the date of her judgment to the date of her retirement. *See, e.g., Passantino v. Johnson & Johnson Consumer Prods.,* 212 F.3d 493, 511 (9th Cir. 2000) (upholding front pay award based on twenty-two years of future earnings); *Padilla v. Metro–North Commuter R.R.,* 92 F.3d 117, 125–26 (2d Cir. 1996) (upholding front pay award based on twenty years of future earnings). Given this analysis, Circuit City is simply incorrect in asserting that Morrison could have recovered more under the terms of the limitations found in the arbitration agreement than she could have under Title VII.

In sum, the Circuit City arbitration agreement does more than limit Morrison's potential monetary remedy for discrimination by limiting any backpay and front pay awards. In addition, it also prevents the remedial principles of Title VII from being effectuated because it does not allow Morrison to be fully compensated for any harms caused by wrongful discrimination.[14] Similarly, Circuit City's arbitration agreement undermines the deterrent purposes of Title VII by placing stringent limits on punitive damages available to Morrison and other claimants under the arbitration agreement. The Supreme Court has repeatedly acknowledged that monetary awards for claimants who bring discrimination claims often serve as an incentive for employers to eliminate their discriminatory practices. [Citation omitted.]

Circuit City's arbitration agreement, which limits punitive damages to the greater of $5,000 or the sum of a claimant's backpay and front pay awards, eviscerates Congress's intent to utilize punitive damages as a tool for combating discrimination, particularly in cases where no backpay or front pay is awarded. Even if Morrison were to receive the maximum amount of backpay and front pay available to her under Circuit City's arbitration agreement, she could receive only $162,000 in punitive damages, less than sixty percent of the $300,000 she could potentially obtain under Title VII. Furthermore, whereas Title VII would allow Morrison to collect a total compensatory and punitive damages award of $300,000, even if no backpay or front pay award had been given, Circuit City's arbitration agreement would allow only a $5,000 punitive damages award in such a case. Likewise, whereas Title VII would allow Morrison to collect up to $300,000 in punitive damages, even if only nominal damages were awarded, Circuit City's arbitration agreement would limit any such an award to

14. Moreover, Circuit City's arbitration agreement further undercuts Congress's intent in providing backpay awards because it allows deductions to made from such awards due to interim private and public benefits received by the claimant, a rule that directly contravenes Sixth Circuit precedent providing that backpay awards may not reduced by any public or private benefits a claimant has received between the date of her termination and the judgment. *EEOC v. Ky. State Police Dep't,* 80 F.3d 1086, 1100 (6th Cir.), *cert. denied,* 519 U.S. 963, 117 S.Ct. 385, 136 L.Ed.2d 302 (1996); *Rasimas v. Mich. Dep't of Mental Health,* 714 F.2d 614, 627 (6th Cir.1983), *cert. denied,* 466 U.S. 950, 104 S.Ct. 2151, 80 L.Ed.2d 537 (1984).

$5,000. *See Timm v. Progressive Steel Treating, Inc.*, 137 F.3d 1008, 1010 (7th Cir. 1998) (holding that punitive damages are available in an intentional discrimination action even if the jury does not assess compensatory damages); *Beauford v. Sisters of Mercy–Province of Detroit, Inc.*, 816 F.2d 1104, 1108 (6th Cir.) (holding that "a plaintiff who proves a cause of action under § 1981 may recover punitive damages where the plaintiff is entitled to an award of compensatory damages, even if nominal"), *cert. denied*, 484 U.S. 913, 108 S.Ct. 259, 98 L.Ed.2d 217 (1987).[15]

Because the limitation on remedies found in the Circuit City arbitration agreement significantly undermines Title VII's remedial purpose of making victims of discrimination whole and its deterrent purposes of forcing employers to eliminate and prevent discriminatory practices in the workplace, we hold that the provision at issue in this case was not enforceable.... Our conclusion on this point finds support in the decisions of other courts considering the same arbitration agreement....

* * *

Questions

1. When confronted with a damage-stripping clause in an arbitration agreement, should courts treat statutory claims differently from nonstatutory claims? Should they treat claims by employees and consumers differently from claims brought by commercial entities? On what authority? Should they treat cram-down agreements differently from bargained-for agreements?

2. Courts have taken a variety of approaches to damage-stripping clauses in arbitration agreements. The *Morrison* court severed the offending provision and allowed the arbitrator to offer the full statutory remedy despite the contract. Judges Posner and Easterbook, of the Seventh Circuit, are inclined to enforce damage-stripping clauses. See, e.g., *Baravati v. Josephthal, Lyon, and Ross, Inc.*, 28 F.3d 704, 709 (7th Cir. 1994). Other courts have struck the entire arbitration clause and allowed the claim to go to

15. The attorney fees provision found in Rule 13 could also be read as limiting a Title VII plaintiff's remedies in an important sense. Although the rule in effect at the time Morrison brought her claims granted the arbitrator the discretion to award the claimant attorney fees, it did not state that the arbitrator should grant attorney fees "in accordance with applicable law." Under Title VII, it is clear that "a prevailing *plaintiff* ordinarily is to be awarded attorney's fees in all but special circumstances." *Christiansburg Garment Co. v. EEOC*, 434 U.S. 412, 417, 98 S.Ct. 694, 54 L.Ed.2d 648 (1978). The wording of the arbitration agreement, however, is very similar to the statutory provision in question, § 706(k) of Title VII, 42 U.S.C. § 2000e–5(k), which authorizes the court, "in its discretion," to award the prevailing party attorney fees. For this reason, we do not hold that the attorney fees provision in the Circuit City arbitration agreement is unenforceable. The provision at issue in the present case is thus distinguishable from that at issue in *McCaskill v. SCI Management Corp.*, 285 F.3d 623, 625 (7th Cir. 2002), which required each party to pay its own fees, "regardless of the outcome of the arbitration." If arbitration is to offer claimants the full scope of remedies available under Title VII, arbitrators in Title VII cases, just like courts, must be guided by *Christiansburg* and must ordinarily grant attorney fees to prevailing claimants.

court. *See, e.g.*, *Alexander v. Anthony Int'l L.P.*, 341 F.3d 256, 267 (3d Cir. 2003). Still other courts have held that a plaintiff can take to court a request for any legally-available remedy that the arbitrator is not contractually permitted to hear. See, e.g., *DiCrisci v. Lyndon Guar. Bank of N.Y.*, 807 F.Supp. 947, 953–54 (W.D.N.Y. 1992). Which approach is more consistent with *Mitsubishi* and the rationale for permitting arbitrators to decide statutory claims?

3. Footnote 15 of *Morrison* raises the issue of attorney-fee waivers. The Civil Rights Act of 1991 permits courts in employment discrimination cases to award attorney fees to prevailing parties. In *Christiansburg Garment Co. v. EEOC*, 434 U.S. 412 (1978), the Supreme Court held that a prevailing employer may be awarded attorney fees only where the employee's lawsuit was "frivolous"; allowing the routine award of attorney fees to prevailing employers would undermine Title VII by deterring employees from bringing claims. Under what circumstances should arbitrators award such fees? Should they do so regularly or selectively? Should a court refuse to enforce an arbitration agreement in which an employee waives the right to recover attorney fees? Should a court refuse to enforce an arbitration award that denies attorney fees to a prevailing claimant, or that awards attorney fees to a losing claimant? See *Perez v. Globe Airport Security Services, Inc.*, 253 F.3d 1280, 1287 (11th Cir. 2001) (denying enforcement of arbitration agreement that contained clause requiring fee-splitting between the parties; clause impermissibly limited the employee's remedies contrary to the Title VII provision that provides fee-shifting to prevailing plaintiffs); *George Watts & Son, Inc. v. Tiffany & Co.*, 248 F.3d 577 (7th Cir. 2001) (supra Chapter 4.B.4) (an arbitrator's refusal to award attorney fees to the prevailing party as authorized by state law cannot be vacated or modified for "manifest disregard" of the law).

Should courts enforce arbitration agreements with "loser pays" provisions in cases involving statutory disputes? Several courts have. See, e.g., *Musnick v. King Motor Co.*, 325 F.3d 1255 (11th Cir. 2003); *Manuel v. Honda R & D Ams., Inc.*, 175 F.Supp.2d 987 (S.D. Ohio 2001).

* * *

3. FINALITY OF ARBITRAL AWARDS

A. MODIFICATION OF ARBITRAL AWARDS

Occasionally an arbitrator issues an award that is ambiguous, contains an error of calculation, or fails to address a matter that has been submitted. The party disadvantaged by the error or omission likely will ask the arbitrator to clarify, correct, or complete the award. If the arbitrator does so and issues a revised award, the other side may object, on grounds of *functus officio*, to enforcing the revised award.

Functus officio is Latin for "a task performed." Black's Law Dictionary defines the term as "having fulfilled the function, discharged the office, or accomplished the purpose, and therefore [having] no further force or authority." As applied to arbitrators, *functus officio* means that once an arbitral panel has issued an award, it becomes "*functus officio* and lacks any further power to act."[1] The doctrine is usually justified on the grounds that arbitrators are merely ad hoc judges, so that once the case is decided and an award issued, their decision-making power ceases. In practical terms, the doctrine reflects the policy of arbitral finality. Without the doctrine, it is feared, parties would try to pressure arbitrators to modify decisions.

Some commentators oppose the doctrine of *functus officio*, and argue that it is a vestige of the old days of judicial hostility to arbitration and should be abandoned. As a result, the doctrine has been relaxed in recent years. At present, most courts have recognized exceptions to the doctrine in the following situations:

1. An arbitrator can correct a mistake that is apparent on the face of the award;
2. An arbitrator may subsequently decide issues that were submitted but not decided in the earlier award;
3. The arbitrator may clarify an ambiguity in an award.

These exceptions are often interpreted expansively so that they can seem to swallow the *functus officio* doctrine altogether. The following cases demonstrate how courts are reaching to find exceptions to the doctrine and thereby permit arbitrators to modify their awards.

In *Colonial Penn Insurance Co. v. Omaha Indemnity Co.*, 943 F.2d 327 (3d Cir. 1991), an arbitration panel heard a case concerning indemnification under a reinsurance agreement. The panel awarded Colonial Penn $10 million in cash plus $8 million in the form of directing Omaha to release its claim to $8 million of Colonial Penn's reserves. Upon receipt of the award, counsel for Colonial Penn informed the arbitrator and the opposing counsel that the award contained a mistake. The award assumed that Colonial Penn held $8 million in reserve to which Omaha had a claim, when in fact there were no such reserves. The arbitrator agreed that the matter should be clarified, but opposing counsel responded that the award was clear and unambiguous as written. Despite Omaha's objection, the panel issued a revised award that deleted mention of the reserves and ordered Omaha to pay the additional $8 million outright. It also sent both parties a letter explaining that the original award was based on a mistaken assumption that Colonial Penn was holding some of Omaha's assets in reserves.

When Colonial Penn attempted to enforce the revised award, Omaha objected on grounds of *functus officio* and cross-motioned to enforce the initial award. The district court ruled for Colonial Penn. On appeal, the Third Circuit held that it was improper for an arbitration panel to impeach its own award. Further, it held that if there had been a mistake, it was not

1. *Ottley v. Schwartzberg*, 819 F.2d 373, 376 (2d Cir. 1987).

a "mistake on the face of the award," so that the mistake exception to the *functus officio* doctrine did not apply. It said:

> The exception for mistakes apparent on the face of the award is applied to clerical mistakes or obvious errors in arithmetic computation. Possibly, it could also be applied in a situation where the award on its face is contrary to a fact so well known as to be subject to judicial notice, but we take no position on that here.
>
> In this case, it was not possible to tell from the face of the award either that Colonial Penn held no reserves to which Omaha might have a claim or that Omaha had not submitted a claim for any reserves allegedly held by Colonial Penn . . . In extending the limited exception for mistakes apparent on the face of the award to a situation where extraneous facts must be considered, the district court opened a Pandora's box . . . Parties could, under the guise of a mistake in fact, seek recourse directly from the arbitrators in an attempt to overturn an adverse award.

Id. at 333.

After rejecting the application of the mistake exception to the *functus officio* doctrine, the appeals court nonetheless remanded the issue to the arbitrators. The court made an analogy to Sec. 11 of the FAA, which permits a court to modify or correct an award under certain narrowly defined circumstances. The court explained:

> Although there is no explicit provision in the Act for such a remand, courts have uniformly stated that a remand to the arbitration panel is appropriate in cases where the award is ambiguous . . . [While] a remand that allows a court to reconsider the merits is not permissible, . . . when the remedy awarded by the arbitrators is ambiguous, a remand for clarification of the intended meaning of an arbitration award is appropriate . . . Such a remand avoids the court's misinterpretation of the award and is therefore more likely to give the parties the award for which they bargained . . .
>
> Unlike the exception to the *functus officio* doctrine which confines the arbitrators to correcting mistakes apparent on the face of the award, an ambiguity in the award for which the court may remand to the arbitrators may be shown not only from the face of the award but from an extraneous but objectively ascertainable fact.

Id. at 334.

In *Clarendon National Insurance Co. v. TIG Reinsurance Co.*, 183 F.R.D. 112 (S.D.N.Y. 1998), the court took a different approach to the mistake exception to the *functus officio* doctrine. In a dispute between two insurance companies, an arbitration panel ruled for the plaintiff. However, the panel made an arithmetic error in its calculation of the award. The arbitrators subsequently corrected the error at the urging of Clarendon National Insurance, the party that was harmed by the error. TIG objected to the modification and moved to vacate it on the grounds of *functus officio*.

The court found that the exception to the doctrine of *functus officio* for correcting a mistake of fact did not apply. It said:

> the exemption to the *functus officio* doctrine must be stretched beyond the mistake category, since although there was an obvious mathematical error that they intended to take into account but failed to do so in their original award, . . . the error was not obvious on the face of the award.

Id. at 116. Nor did the court find that the arbitrators' revision of this award completed an incomplete award or clarified an ambiguous award. Nonetheless, the court enforced the modified award, stating that the arbitrators had simply corrected a mathematical error. "The spirit and basic effect of the award was not modified." It stated:

> In cases like this one, the *functus officio* doctrine may simply have outlived its usefulness. Arbitrators should simply be permitted to correct errorsbut only errors . . . This holding in no way gives arbitrators carte blanche to alter any decision previously rendered.

Id. at 117.

* * *

Stack v. Karavan Trailers, Inc.

864 A.2d 551 (Pa. Super. 2004).

■ McCAFFERY, J.

In this appeal, we must determine whether the trial court properly vacated the Corrected and Clarified Arbitration Decision and Award (hereinafter "Clarified Award") under the *functus officio* doctrine which prevents arbitrators from taking any further action once an arbitration award has been issued. Specifically, we are asked to decide whether any of the exceptions to this doctrine are applicable herein. We hold that the initial Arbitration Decision and Award (hereinafter "Initial Award") in this case contained a clear error which was apparent on the face of the award. Therefore, under the "mistake apparent on the face of the award" exception, we conclude that the Clarified Award was properly entered. Accordingly, after careful review, we reverse the trial court's order vacating the Clarified Award in favor of the Initial Award, and we reinstate the Clarified Award.

. . . David Stack (hereinafter "Stack") was involved in an accident in which he fell off a boat, which was then situated on a trailer, and suffered severe injuries. He proceeded to sue Karavan Trailers, Inc. (hereinafter "Karavan") (which had manufactured and sold the trailer), and Appellee, Highway Marine, Inc. (hereinafter "Highway Marine") (which had sold the trailer along with the boat), alleging negligence in the design, manufacture and sale of the trailer and the boat. Instead of a trial, the parties[1] agreed to

1. Just prior to the start of the arbitration, Stack settled with Karavan, leaving Highway Marine as the sole remaining defendant, which is a critical factor in the instant disposition.

submit to binding High/Low arbitration[2] to be governed by common law principles, before Thomas B. Rutter, Esquire ("Arbitrator Rutter") through ADR Options, Inc. (Arbitration Agreement and Stipulation, dated July 25, 2002). The arbitration at issue took place on October 4, 2002, with S. Richard Klinges, III, Esquire, representing Stack and Andrew Keenan, Esquire, representing Highway Marine.

Arbitrator Rutter issued the Initial Award on October 7, 2002. In Section C of that document, Arbitrator Rutter awarded Stack the gross sum of $2,500,000, with a total *molded* award of $1,000,000 as per the High/Low agreement of the parties. However, in Section A of that document, it appeared that 25% causal negligence had been attributed to Highway Marine, 50% had been attributed to Karavan (not a party to the arbitration) and 25% had been attributed to Stack. This was a mistake. In fact, Arbitrator Rutter's actual decision had attributed 50% causal negligence to Highway Marine, and 25% to Karavan. The award reflected in Section A was the result of a clerical error in the transcription of Arbitrator Rutter's notes detailing his decision and award.

Three days later via a letter dated October 10, 2002, Highway Marine tendered to Stack a release in the amount of only $625,000 (representing 25% of the $2,500,000 *unmolded* award). Because this amount made no sense given the parties' molding agreement, Mr. Klinges, Stack's attorney, refused to execute the release. Instead, he had his assistant place a call to Michael Carney, President of ADR Options, Inc., seeking clarification of the exact amount of damages which Arbitrator Rutter intended Stack to receive from Highway Marine. According to Arbitrator Rutter's testimony, when he was apprised of this message, he had his secretary retrieve the relevant file, as was his normal custom when questions arose about arbitration awards. Upon review of the file, he immediately discovered that the Initial Award did not, in fact, reflect the *actual findings* which he had set forth in his handwritten notes, made right after the end of the arbitration proceeding. Apparently, according to Mr. Carney's subsequent deposition, Mr. Carney had inadvertently transposed the amounts of liability attributable to each defendant when he prepared the Initial Award document. Arbitrator Rutter's notes clearly and unequivocally attributed 50% causal negligence to Highway Marine, 25% to Karavan and 25% to Stack.[5]

After discovering the mistake in the Initial Award document, Arbitrator Rutter placed an *ex parte* call to Mr. Klinges on October 15, 2002, and

2. Stack and Highway Marine entered into a High/Low Agreement which stipulated to a low of $50,000 and a high of $1,000,000.

5. Mr. Carney testified that under ADR Options' normal practice, arbitrators' awards were routinely forwarded to him for processing and preparation of the dispositional documents. Mr. Carney frequently transcribed Arbitrator Rutter's findings into his own handwriting, as Mr. Carney's secretary was unable to understand Arbitrator Rutter's handwriting. Mr. Carney realized and acknowledged that he had, in fact, crossed out the percentages of liability which Arbitrator Rutter had assessed and had replaced them with incorrect ones, but he could not recall why he had done so.

advised him that the percentages of liability had been inadvertently transposed. Following this conversation, Mr. Klinges wrote a formal letter to Arbitrator Rutter requesting clarification of the Initial Award as to each defendant. [This letter, like the phone call, was *ex parte*.]

In an effort to correct the Initial Award to reflect what his actual decision had been, Arbitrator Rutter issued a Corrected and Clarified Arbitration Award on October 15, 2002. This Clarified Award accurately reflected the percentages of liability which Arbitrator Rutter had assessed and set forth in his handwritten notes made right after the arbitration. Highway Marine filed a petition to vacate the Clarified Award and for the entry of judgment in accordance with the Initial Award, since the Clarified Award required Highway Marine to pay substantially more than the Initial Award required. Both parties then took deposition testimony. Subsequently, the trial court granted Highway Marine's motion, entered judgment in favor of Stack in the amount of $625,000, and reinstated Arbitrator Rutter's Initial Award. This appeal followed.

Stack raises the following issues for our review:

> 1. Whether the trial court abused its discretion or committed error of law in finding that Arbitrator Rutter did not have authority to correct a clerical error appearing on his award by issuing the corrected and clarified arbitration decision and award.
>
> 2. Whether the trial court abused its discretion or committed error of law in failing to correct the arbitration decision and award pursuant to 42 C.S.A. [sic] § 7315 or remand the matter to arbitrator rutter to clarify the award since the arbitration decision and award is clearly ambiguous.
>
> 3. Whether the trial court abused its discretion or committed error of law in finding that an irregularity caused the rendition of an unjust, inequitable or unconscionable award.

. . . Stack contends that the trial court abused its discretion by vacating Arbitrator Rutter's Clarified Award where the requisite "irregularity" upon which the trial court relied was not proven by clear, precise, and indubitable evidence. He contends that the trial court erred by not applying the "mistake apparent on the face of the award" exception to the *functus officio* doctrine in this particular case. We agree.

The *functus officio* doctrine is a well-settled common law principle:

> The general principle in a common law arbitration is that the arbitrators are the final judges of both the facts and the law and their decision will not be disturbed for a mistake of fact or of law. *P G Metals Co. v. Hofkin,* 420 Pa. 620, 218 A.2d 238 (1966). . . .
>
> It is an equally fundamental common law principle that once an arbitrator has made and published a final award his authority is exhausted and he is functus officio and can do nothing more in regard to the subject matter of the arbitration. The policy which lies behind this is an unwillingness to permit one who is not a judicial officer and

> who acts informally and sporadically, to re-examine a final decision which he has already rendered, because of the potential evil of outside communication and unilateral influence which might affect a new conclusion.

La Vale Plaza, Inc. v. R.S. Noonan, Inc., 378 F.2d 569, 572–73 (3d. Cir. 1967) (citing *Hartley v. Henderson,* 189 Pa. 277, 42 A. 198 (1899)).

However, three specific exceptions to the *functus officio* doctrine have been recognized:

> (1) an arbitrator can correct a mistake which is apparent on the face of his award;
>
> (2) where the award does not adjudicate an issue which has been submitted, then as to such issue the arbitrator has not exhausted his function and it remains open to him for subsequent determination; and
>
> (3) where the award, although seemingly complete, leaves doubt whether the submission has been fully executed, an ambiguity arises which the arbitrator is entitled to clarify.

Colonial Penn Insurance Company v. Omaha Indemnity Company, 943 F.2d 327, 332 (3d. Cir. 1991) (citations omitted).

Instantly, the trial court found that the Clarified Award had been improperly entered as the *functus officio* doctrine rendered Arbitrator Rutter without authority to issue the Clarified Award, once the Initial Award had been issued. As a result, the trial court concluded that the issuance of the Clarified Award constituted an "irregularity" significant enough to warrant its vacating and the reinstatement of the Initial Award.

Further, the trial court specifically found that the exception for "mistakes apparent on the face of an award" did not apply in this case, as "the percentages of liability assessed, without more, does [sic] not on its [sic] face suggest that a mistake was made." (*See* Trial Court Opinion, dated July 30, 2003, at 7). The trial court also cited *Colonial Penn* to emphasize how chary courts should be in extending the limited exception for "mistakes apparent on the face of an award" when considering allowing the introduction and consideration of extraneous facts. We disagree with the trial court's determination, and, after a thorough review of the record, we conclude that the Arbitrator's Clarified Award was properly entered because the Initial Award does fall under the first exception to the *functus officio* doctrine—here, due to a clerical error.

In this case, viewed from the perspective of those involved in the arbitration, there is a clear and obvious mistake present on the face of the Initial Award—the incongruity between Section A and Section C. In Section A (Liability Findings), the document indicates that Highway Marine, the only remaining defendant in the arbitration, was 25% liable. This would have meant that Highway Marine owed Stack $625,000 (25% of $2,500,000), which is exactly what Highway Marine rushed to tender to Stack. However, in Section C, the document indicates that Stack was awarded *molded* damages of $1,000,000 based upon a total award of

$2,500,000. Reading these two sections together, as one must, the mistake is clear and apparent, as the Initial Award makes no mathematical sense *on its face.* Because Highway Marine was the only defendant who was a party to the High/Low agreement (which capped any damages awarded to Stack at $1,000,000), the molded award of $1,000,000 could only be assessed against Highway Marine. However, clearly, 25% of $2,500,000 is not $1,000,000, it is $625,000. Indeed, if Highway Marine were only 25% liable and therefore owed Stack only $625,000, there would have been no need to mold the award at all, as the damages assessed against Highway Marine would not have exceeded $1,000,000. Therefore, Arbitrator Rutter did have the authority, under the "mistake apparent on the award's face" exception, to issue a corrected award.

Further, a careful review of the relevant case law reveals that the theoretical underpinnings of the "mistake apparent on the face of the award" exception are strongly rooted in the context of arbitrators acknowledging and correcting their own clerical mistakes. In the seminal case, *La Vale Plaza, supra,* cited in *Colonial Penn,* the Third Circuit Court of Appeals provided a comprehensive review of the *functus officio* doctrine, and set forth three specific exceptions thereto, including the instantly relevant exception for "mistakes apparent on the face of an award": "The principle that an award once rendered is final contains its own limitation, however, and it therefore has been recognized in common law arbitration that the arbitrator can correct a mistake which is apparent on the face of his award." *Id.* at 573, n. 16. *La Vale Plaza* relies on, *inter alia, The First National Bank of Clarion v. Brenneman's Executors,* 114 Pa. 315, 7 A. 910 (1886) in support of this proposition.

In *First National Bank,* the Pennsylvania Supreme Court focused upon a clerical mistake made in the appraisal of stock, an error discovered and corrected by the appraisers themselves. Our high court emphasized that arbitrators *must* be permitted to correct their own mistakes: "It is unnecessary to cite any of the numerous authorities in which it has been held that mistakes of arbitrators and referees may be corrected either by themselves or by the court." *Id.* at 320, 7 A. 910. Moreover, the Court emphasized the dichotomy between mistakes of fact and mere clerical errors:

> [R]eferring to mistakes in computation and clerical errors ... they are not mistakes in the decision itself, *but blunders in writing out the decision....* The decision may be final, *while the expression may be open to correction.* To say that a court could not correct such 'blunders,' *especially when acknowledged by the arbitrator,* would, at least from a common-sense point of view, seem absurd.

Id. at 320, 7 A. 910 (quotation omitted, emphasis added).

In addition, although there is an unfortunate dearth of case law regarding the "mistake apparent on the face of the award exception", we find the discussion set forth in *Cadillac Uniform & Linen Supply, Inc. v. Union de Tronquistas de Puerto Rico,* 920 F.Supp. 19 (D.Puerto Rico 1996), to be persuasive. In that case, the court was asked to determine whether an arbitrator could correct his award where he mistakenly reinstated an employee "without pay" instead of "with pay" due to a clerical error. In response, that court provided the following, thoughtful analysis regarding the "mistake apparent on the face of the award" exception:

> [T]he case [ ] law clearly differentiates between correcting an award because it was based on a mistaken view of fact or law and correcting an award to mend an error apparent from the face of the award. *See, Burton v. Johnson,* 975 F.2d 690, 694 (10th Cir.1992), *cert. denied* 507 U.S. 1043, 113 S.Ct. 1879, 123 L.Ed.2d 497. In the first instance, the arbitrator is clearly *functus officio* because it is correcting the substance of the award and because extraneous facts must be taken into consideration. Thus, the policies upon which the application of the doctrine to arbitral decisions stands could be subverted. *See, Colonial Penn Ins. Co. v. Omaha Indem. Co., supra,* and cases cited.
>
> However, in the second situation, courts have recognized a valid exception to the rule and granted the arbitrator [a] green light to proceed, because the substance of the award is not being compromised. On the contrary, it is being *clarified as to express the adjudicators ever present intention.* This is so, because these type of errors are perceived as *mere blunders in writing out the decision, which, if acknowledge[d] by the own arbitrator must be corrected by him. To hold otherwise, "would, at least from the common-sense point of view, seem absurd."* First Nat. Bank of Clarion v. Breneman, 114 Pa. 315, 319, 7 A. 910 (1886).

Cadillac Uniform at 22 (emphasis added and in original). We strongly agree with the distinction drawn in *Cadillac Uniform* between mistakes of fact and clerical mistakes made in the course of "writing out" arbitration awards. The former often requires an arbitrator to consider extraneous facts in order to recognize the mistake. However, an arbitrator can certainly identify clerical errors without the consideration of extraneous facts. Indeed, to prohibit an arbitrator from correcting his own acknowledged clerical blunder would contravene not only long-standing Pennsylvania jurisprudence but also common-sense. *See First National Bank, supra.*

Further, the trial court's reliance upon the *Colonial Penn* case is misplaced. In *Colonial Penn,* the Third Circuit declined to find a clear mistake on the face of an instrument, but it was under a very different fact scenario. There, the award mentioned "reserves" which Colonial Penn did not actually have. However, there was no way for the arbitrator to know that these reserves did not exist without reference to extraneous testimony. *Id.* at 332–333. Instantly, no such "mistake of fact" exists. Instead, there is an obvious clerical error apparent on the face of the award which requires no additional testimony to identify, and should, therefore, fall under the "obvious mistake" exception to the *functus officio* doctrine. Indeed, as discussed above, it is precisely this type of "blunder" made in the "writing out" of the award that the "mistake apparent on the face of the award" exception was intended to remedy. Hence, Arbitrator Rutter had the proper authority to issue the Clarified Award.

In his third issue, Stack asserts that the trial court erred by finding that the *ex parte* communication at issue in this case was significant enough to have constituted an irregularity which necessitated the vacating of the Clarified Award and the reinstatement of the Initial Award. We agree.

The trial court cites *Government Employees Insurance Company v. Lane,* 264 Pa.Super. 615, 401 A.2d 765 (1979), for the proposition that any *ex parte* communication constitutes a serious irregularity sufficient to reverse an arbitrator's award. In *Government Employees,* this Court took the extraordinary step, *sua sponte,* to reverse a second, clarified award and remand for re-arbitration where an attorney had contacted an arbitrator to express confusion over the first award which had been issued. *Id.* at 768–769. However, that case is distinguishable, because there was no clear mistake on the face on the first award—the award clearly granted damages of $20,000. Rather, the confusing element was whether *both* plaintiffs were to share the $20,000, or whether *each* was to receive $20,000 individually. In that case, we emphasized that the *ex parte* communication violated the applicable arbitration guidelines,[8] which precluded *any* communication between arbitrators and attorneys. Here, no such guidelines were in place under ADR Options. In fact, the cover letter transmitted with the Initial Award encouraged the parties to call with any questions.

It is also important to note that Mr. Klinges originally contacted the President, Mr. Carney, not Arbitrator Rutter, to clarify the apparent inconsistency on the face of the award. Indeed, Mr. Klinges was instructed by ADR Options to call Mr. Carney with any questions he might have via the cover letter, dated October 7, 2002, which he received with the Initial Award. Further, according to the deposition testimony of both Mr. Klinges and Arbitrator Rutter, the one short phone call between Arbitrator Rutter and Mr. Klinges was initiated by the Arbitrator specifically in order to let Stack know that a clerical mistake had been made, and the underlying merits of the case were not implicated or discussed. This one short phone call does not rise to the level of an irregularity serious enough to warrant the reversal of Arbitrator Rutter's Clarified Award where a clear inconsistency was present on the face of the Initial Award and the parties were in fact directed to call with any questions.

Based on the foregoing reasons, we conclude that Arbitrator Rutter had the authority to enter and acted properly in entering the Clarified Award. Therefore, we reverse and vacate the June 19, 2003 order of the Bucks County Court of Common Pleas which had vacated the Clarified Award and had entered judgment in accordance with the Initial Award. In addition, we reinstate the Clarified Award and direct the parties to comply therewith.

8. In *Government Employees,* the parties were subject to the American Arbitration Association guidelines. *Id.* at 768–769.

Order reversed and vacated. Clarified Award reinstated. Jurisdiction relinquished.

* * *

Questions

1. In "high/low" or "bounded" arbitration, the parties agree to a maximum and minimum damage award. The arbitrator may be informed of this and required to issue an award between the boundaries, or the parties may simply agree that an award higher than the boundary will be reduced to the "high" and an award below the boundary will be reduced to the "low". A variation on this theme is "final offer" arbitration, in which each party submits its final offer to the arbitrator and the arbitrator must choose one or the other. This is often called "baseball arbitration" because Major League Baseball uses it to resolve disputes over player salaries. Does bounded arbitration alter the principle that the arbitrator has control over arbitration procedure? Does it alter the dynamics of the parties' presentation of the case?

2. Why are courts generally resistant to permitting one party to attempt to convince an arbitrator to modify an award after it has been issued?

3. Without strict application of *functus officio*, how can a court determine whether one side has improperly pressured an arbitrator to modify an award? What kinds of evidence could the party opposing the modification proffer to establish that the arbitrator was improperly pressured? Can the opposing party subpoena the arbitrator to testify? What other kinds of evidence might be relevant?

4. Why is the mistake exception, in its original form, limited to mistakes evident from the face of the award? What problems arise once courts expand the exception to mistakes that require further evidence to discern?

5. It is sometimes the practice in labor arbitration for an arbitration panel to circulate a draft award to the parties before issuing a final one. This process is intended to enable parties to determine whether there are serious errors, omissions, or ambiguities in the award that need to be corrected. Could this practice obviate the problem posed by the preceding cases? What additional dangers might such an approach create?

6. In *Colonial Penn*, the court states that it has the power to order an arbitrator to reconsider an award on the grounds of mistake or ambiguity, even when the arbitration panel does not have the power to do so on its own initiative. Does the possibility of a court-ordered modification of an award create the same dangers that the *functus officio* doctrine attempts to address?

7. Should a court ever permit an arbitrator to modify an award for mistake over the objection of one of the parties? Under what circumstances? Which approach is the preferable means of determining whether to enforce such a modification?

* * *

B. CLAIM PRECLUSION

Riverdale Development Co., LLC v. Ruffin Bldg. Systems, Inc.

146 S.W.3d 852 (Ark. 2004).

■ TOM GLAZE, JUSTICE.

This appeal requires us to determine the preclusive effect of an arbitration award with respect to one who was not a party to the arbitration....

On August 30, 1996, appellant Riverdale Development Company ("Riverdale") entered into a contract with May Construction Company ("May") for construction of a commercial office building located at 2102 Brookwood Drive in Little Rock. Included in the project was May's erection of a pre-engineered metal building manufactured by appellee Ruffin Building Systems, Inc. ("Ruffin"), a Louisiana company from which May purchased the materials for construction.

Disputes began arising between May and Riverdale regarding the completion of the project. The contract between May and Riverdale contained a provision requiring arbitration of contract disputes between the parties, and on May 13, 1999, May initiated arbitration with Riverdale pursuant to the construction contract. However, on May 25, 1999, Riverdale filed suit against May in Pulaski County Circuit Court, and one year later, on May 19, 2000, Riverdale filed an amended complaint that also named Ruffin as a defendant. The complaint raised claims of negligence, breach of implied warranties, defective product, and fraud and constructive fraud.

Although Riverdale initially contested arbitration, Riverdale and May eventually arbitrated their dispute in a hearing that lasted from July 22–26, 2002. The arbitrator ultimately ruled in May's favor, finding that May did not materially breach the contract between the parties, and was excused from further performance by Riverdale's wrongful exclusion of May from the project site. Although the arbitrator noted some conflicts in the testimony regarding the alleged defects in the building and the design of the building and its mechanical and structural components, the arbitrator found that May's witnesses were more credible. All of Riverdale's claims were denied in their entirety, and Riverdale was ordered to pay May the balance owing on the contract, plus attorney's fees. The arbitrator's findings were issued on August 8, 2002.

Just prior to the arbitrator's decision, May filed a motion in the circuit court case to dismiss Riverdale's claims against it, arguing that the pleadings in the arbitration case and the circuit court case mirrored each other, and that Riverdale's circuit court claims were barred under *res judicata* and collateral estoppel; the trial court agreed and granted the motion on August 16, 2002. On August 14, 2002, after the arbitrator's decision was issued on August 8, Ruffin filed a motion for summary judgment, contending that there were no genuine issues of material fact, because Riverdale's claims were "barred under the doctrine of collateral estoppel, since all issues material to this case have been fully presented and determined ... before the American Arbitration Association."

Following a hearing on October 22, 2002, the trial court entered its order granting Ruffin's motion for summary judgment, holding that "a third party such as Ruffin is entitled to rely upon an arbitration award such as [the one] here under the doctrines of collateral estoppel or *res judicata,* even though not a party to the contract providing for arbitration and even though [Riverdale] did not agree to bind itself to an arbitration award with regard to other parties." From this order, Riverdale brings this appeal, raising as its sole point the argument that the trial court erred in granting summary judgment in favor of Ruffin on the grounds of collateral estoppel based on a finding in an arbitration proceeding to which Ruffin was not a party....

The questions to be answered in this case are (1) whether collateral estoppel will apply to bar Riverdale's suit against Ruffin, a third party who was not involved in the arbitration, and (2) whether, if collateral estoppel does apply, the elements have been established. Collateral estoppel, or issue preclusion, bars relitigation of issues, law, or fact actually litigated in the first suit. *Crockett & Brown, P.A. v. Wilson,* 314 Ark. 578, 864 S.W.2d 244 (1993); *John Cheeseman Trucking, Inc. v. Pinson,* 313 Ark. 632, 855 S.W.2d 941 (1993). For collateral estoppel to apply, the following four elements must be met: 1) the issue sought to be precluded must be the same as that involved in the prior litigation; 2) that issue must have been actually litigated; 3) the issue must have been determined by a valid and final judgment; and 4) the determination must have been essential to the judgment. *Crockett & Brown, supra; Fisher v. Jones,* 311 Ark. 450, 844 S.W.2d 954 (1993). Unlike *res judicata,* collateral estoppel does not require mutuality of parties before the doctrine is applicable. *Id.* (citing *Fisher v. Jones, supra*).

Ordinarily, collateral estoppel is relied upon by a defendant to preclude a plaintiff from relitigating an issue that has previously been decided adversely to the plaintiff. *Johnson v. Union Pacific Railroad,* 352 Ark. 534, 104 S.W.3d 745 (2003). This "defensive collateral estoppel" is the manner in which the doctrine is sought to be applied in the present case. Another form of collateral estoppel, "offensive collateral estoppel," is more controversial, although it has been specifically approved by this court. *See Johnson v. Union Pacific, supra.* Offensive collateral estoppel occurs when a plaintiff seeks to foreclose the defendant from litigating an issue the defendant has previously litigated unsuccessfully in an action with another party. *Johnson,* 352 Ark. at 545, 104 S.W.3d 745 (citing *Parklane Hosiery*

Co., Inc. v. Shore, 439 U.S. 322, 99 S.Ct. 645, 58 L.Ed.2d 552 (1979)). The *Johnson* court concluded that this rule should be available only in limited cases, and that the trial court should be given broad discretion to determine if it should be applied. The present case, however, does not involve the use of offensive collateral estoppel; instead, the court is only concerned with the defensive application of the doctrine.

On appeal, Riverdale argues that a private arbitration decision should have no collateral estoppel effect in favor of third parties, and that to hold otherwise would defeat principles of fairness and equity and produce unjust results. In making its argument, Riverdale relies primarily on four cases: *Federal Folding Wall Corp. v. National Folding Wall Corp.,* 340 F.Supp. 141 (S.D.N.Y. 1971); *Young v. Metropolitan Prop. & Cas. Ins. Co.,* 60 Conn.App. 107, 758 A.2d 452 (2000); *Pace v. Kuchinsky,* 347 N.J.Super. 202, 789 A.2d 162 (2002); and *Vandenberg v. Superior Court,* 21 Cal.4th 815, 982 P.2d 229, 88 Cal.Rptr.2d 366 (1999).

However, these cases are neither instructive nor applicable here. The first two—*Federal Folding Wall* and *Young*—involve the use of *offensive* collateral estoppel. In *Federal Folding Wall,* National Folding Wall lost a case in arbitration, wherein an arbitrator had determined that National had lost the right to use the trade name "Fairhurst." Subsequent to that decision, Federal sued National, alleging that National had infringed upon Federal's right to use the "Fairhurst" name. In its lawsuit, Federal sought a summary judgment on the basis of the arbitrator's award, but the trial court denied the motion, stating without explanation that "[t]he award of the arbitrators ... is not *res judicata* as to any issues before the court." *Federal Folding Wall Corp.,* 340 F.Supp. at 146.

In the case of *Young v. Metropolitan Property & Casualty, supra,* the Connecticut court of appeals declined to apply offensive collateral estoppel to bind a non-party to an arbitration to the results of the arbitration. In that case, the plaintiff, Young, was involved in a car accident. The car he was driving belonged to his employer, and was insured through defendant Metropolitan. Young's own insurance carrier was Continental. Young and Continental engaged in arbitration regarding the amount and availability of underinsured motorist coverage; although the two parties invited Metropolitan to participate in the arbitration, Metropolitan declined. The arbitration proceeding resulted in an award of damages for Young. Following the decision of the arbitrator, Young filed a motion for summary judgment against Metropolitan, arguing that Metropolitan was collaterally estopped from contesting the arbitration award as to damages. The trial court denied his motion. *Young,* 758 A.2d at 454.

On appeal, the Connecticut court of appeals affirmed the trial court, holding that there was insufficient privity between Metropolitan and Continental. Specifically, the court noted that, "although both Continental and [Metropolitan] are interested in the same question and in proving or disproving the same set of facts, each has, by separate and distinct contracts, chosen the process to determine those facts using its own preferred method." *Id.* at 456. In addition, the court emphasized the contractual nature of arbitration. The court pointed out that Continental had included an arbitration provision in its insurance contract, but Metropolitan had not; in addition, Metropolitan had also declined to be included in the arbitration between Continental and Young. Finally, the court noted that the interests of the two insurers were different, as were their respective incentives to fully participate in the arbitration proceedings. The court further held that "[a] trial in which one party contests a claim against another should be held to estop a third person only when it is realistic to say that the third person was fully protected in the first trial." *Id.* at 457. Accordingly, the court held that, because Metropolitan had not participated in the prior proceeding, it would be foreclosed from challenging facts already decided against it; thus, Metropolitan did not have a full and fair opportunity to litigate its claim. *Id.* at 458. The *Young* court relied on two factors: 1) Young was seeking to apply collateral estoppel *offensively* in an unfair manner; and 2) there was no privity between Continental and Metropolitan, and Metropolitan was therefore denied the opportunity to litigate the issue of liability in the prior proceeding. However, this case provides no help to Riverdale for two reasons: first, *Young* involves an offensive use of collateral estoppel, while the present case involves the *defensive* application of the doctrine; and second, unlike Metropolitan in the *Young* case, Riverdale had an opportunity to litigate the issues raised in its proceeding before the arbitrator.

Next, Riverdale relies on *Pace v. Kuchinsky, supra.* In *Pace,* the New Jersey court declined to give preclusive effect to a prior arbitration decision. There, plaintiff/appellant Pace had sustained spinal injuries in a car wreck. Pace sued both the driver of the other car, Kuchinsky, and Pace's own insurer, State Farm, alleging that State Farm had failed to provide certain "personal injury protection" ("PIP") benefits under his policy. Pace eventually dismissed the action against State Farm after State Farm confirmed that there were no medical bills outstanding. Some months later, one of Pace's doctors filed a PIP arbitration claim against State Farm, seeking payment of outstanding medical bills. Pace testified at the arbitration hearing, but did not consider himself as being present "as a party." The arbitrator determined that Pace had failed to prove that his back problems were the result of the accident (as opposed to degenerative changes), and concluded that any medical expenses incurred by Pace after April of 1999 were not State Farm's responsibility. *Pace,* 789 A.2d at 167.

A month or so later, Kuchinsky moved to dismiss Pace's claims for back injury, arguing that the issue had been decided in the arbitration proceedings. Although the trial court granted Kuchinsky's motion, the New Jersey Superior Court reversed. In concluding that the trial court erred, the superior court pointed out that Pace had never been informed that the outcome of the arbitration hearing could have a potential effect on his right to have a trial by jury. *Id.* at 169. Further, the court noted that Pace had never had his "day in court" on the specific issue in question. "Unless expressly waived, a full and fair hearing requires representation by the party's own counsel, thereby insuring presentation of the specific issue to be decided in the very manner that the party chooses. [Citation omitted.]

This is especially so where the party sought to be precluded was not the identical party in the prior proceeding." *Id.* at 172. Therefore, the New Jersey court held that the scope of the PIP arbitration between the doctor and State Farm was limited to the doctor's claims for payment, and the scope of the issue as presented "neither afforded [Pace] an adequate opportunity to be heard nor an incentive to demand a full and fair adjudication concerning his lumbar injuries and whether his resulting surgery and disability, if any, were causally related to the accident." *Id.* at 173. Again, however, this case is not helpful to Riverdale, primarily because the issues litigated before the arbitrator are the same as those raised in Riverdale's circuit court complaint, and Riverdale *did* have the opportunity to fully and fairly adjudicate its case before the arbitrator.

Finally, Riverdale relies extensively on the California case of *Vandenberg v. Superior Court, supra.* Briefly, the facts of that case were that Vandenberg leased a parcel of property from Boyd and used the land for a car dealership. In 1988, Vandenberg discontinued the leases and returned the property to Boyd. To prepare the property for sale, Boyd removed three underground waste oil storage tanks; in the process, he discovered contamination of soils and groundwater underneath the property. Boyd sued Vandenberg, alleging numerous causes of action including breach of contract, negligence, waste, trespass, and other claims. Vandenberg tendered defense of the suit to his insurers, but many of the policies contained pollution exclusions, under which property damage caused by a pollutant or contaminant was not covered except for a "sudden and accidental" discharge. *Vandenberg,* 88 Cal.Rptr.2d 366, 982 P.2d at 235.

Of Vandenberg's insurers, only USF & G agreed to provide a defense. During settlement proceedings, Vandenberg, Boyd, and USF & G reached an agreement to resolve the Boyd litigation. Boyd released all claims against Vandenberg except those based on the theory that the contamination constituted a breach of the lease agreement. Boyd and Vandenberg agreed to resolve the breach of lease issues through arbitration or trial. USF & G agreed to defend Vandenberg, but the ultimate issues of coverage and indemnity obligations were specifically reserved for future resolution. *Id.* Following arbitration, the arbitrator ruled for Boyd, finding that the contamination was not a "sudden and accidental" discharge. Vandenberg's insurers rejected Vandenberg's request for indemnification, and he then sued his insurers for failure to defend. *Id.* USF & G responded, arguing that it had no duty to defend because the discharges were not sudden and accidental; USF & G further contended that further litigation regarding the "sudden and accidental" issue was precluded by principles of collateral estoppel. The trial court granted USF & G's motion for summary judgment, but the California court of appeals reversed. *Id.* at 236.

Upon review by the Supreme Court of California, the court held that a private arbitration award cannot have nonmutual collateral estoppel effect unless the arbitral parties so agree. In reaching this decision, the court considered all the attendant public policy arguments on both sides of the issue, and concluded that fairness mandated that collateral estoppel could not be invoked by a nonparty to the prior litigation. The court noted that California's statutory scheme, while favoring arbitration in some instances, "nowhere specifies that, despite the arbitral parties' failure to so agree, a private arbitration award may be binding in favor of *nonparties* in litigation involving *different* causes of action." *Id.* at 239 (emphasis in original). Notably, the California court said, arbitrators, "unless specifically required to act in conformity with rules of law, may base their decision upon broad principles of justice and equity, and in doing so may expressly or impliedly reject a claim *that a party might successfully have asserted in a judicial action.*" *Id.* (emphasis in original). The "informal and imprecise nature of arbitration," although an advantage in some instances, "can be [a] serious, unexpected disadvantage[ ] if issues decided by the arbitrator are given leveraged effect in favor of strangers to the arbitration." *Id.* The court also noted that investing an arbitration decision with collateral estoppel effect does not serve the policy reasons for applying the principles of estoppel:

> [T]he primary purposes of collateral estoppel are to preserve the integrity of the judicial system, promote judicial economy, and protect litigants from harassment by vexatious litigation. But because a private arbitrator's award is *outside* the judicial system, denying the award collateral estoppel effect has no adverse impact on judicial integrity. Moreover, because private arbitration does not involve the use of a judge and a courtroom, later relitigation does not undermine judicial economy by requiring duplication of judicial resources to decide the same issue. Finally, when collateral estoppel is invoked by a *nonparty* to the private arbitration, the doctrine does not serve the policy against harassment by vexatious litigation. In such cases, the doctrine is asserted not to protect one who has already once prevailed against the same opponent on the same cause of action, but simply to gain vicarious advantage from a litigation victory *won by another.*

Id. at 240 (citations omitted; emphasis in original).

The California court did recognize, however, that "most other courts addressing the issue, have taken a contrary approach." *Id.* The court wrote that the predominant view is as follows:

> [U]nless the arbitral parties agreed otherwise, *a judicially confirmed private arbitration award will have collateral estoppel effect, even in favor of nonparties to the arbitration,* if the arbitrator actually and necessarily decided the issue sought to be foreclosed and the party against whom estoppel is invoked has full incentive and opportunity to litigate the matter.

Id. (emphasis added). The court ultimately concluded, however, that it would not adopt this approach.

Riverdale, both before this court and in the trial court, relies heavily on the policy arguments addressed by the California court. However, the trial court here recognized that the California approach is the minority view, and declined to follow it. We do the same. Arkansas has recognized and approved the defensive application of collateral estoppel, even where there is no mutuality of parties. *See Fisher v. Jones, supra.* Further, it is settled that, except in certain limited situations, "a valid and final award by arbitration has the same effects under the rules of *res judicata,* subject to the same exceptions and qualifications, as a judgment of a court." Restatement (Second) of Judgments § 84 (1982). The comments to § 84 of the Restatement indicate that "there is good reason to treat the determination of the issues in an arbitration proceeding as conclusive in a subsequent proceeding, just as determinations of a court would be so treated." *Id.,* cmt. c. The comment explains as follows:

> When arbitration affords opportunity for presentation of evidence and argument substantially similar in form and scope to judicial proceedings, the award should have the same effect on issues necessarily determined as a judgment has. Economies of time and effort are thereby achieved for the prevailing party and for the tribunal in which the issue subsequently arises.

Id.

Other jurisdictions have adopted and followed this reasoning. In *Ray v. Continental Western Ins. Co.,* 920 F.Supp. 1094 (D.Nev. 1996), the district court held that, where the party to be estopped had an opportunity to, and did, fully and fairly litigate the issue before the arbitrator, the decision of the arbitrator should be given preclusive effect in a subsequent judicial proceeding. There, the Rays were covered by a policy of automobile insurance issued by Continental. Mrs. Ray was involved in a car accident with Regina Elliff. The Rays sued Elliff for negligence in state court, but the parties agreed to submit the case to binding arbitration. After an adversarial hearing, the arbitrator found that Elliff was liable for the accident, and awarded the Rays a total of $17,123 in damages. *Ray,* 920 F.Supp. at 1097. The Rays subsequently sued Continental for underinsured motorist benefits, claiming a total of $135,260 in damages. Continental moved for summary judgment, arguing that the arbitrator's decision as to the Rays' damages was conclusive, and the Rays were not entitled to any underinsured benefits under the policy. *Id.*

The federal district court agreed, stating that it was evident that the Rays had an opportunity to fully litigate their claims before the arbitrator. The parties presented witnesses, deposition testimony, medical reports, and other exhibits, and they contested damages as well as liability. Further, the court noted that the arbitrator had considered the Rays' arguments regarding the amount of their damages, and had awarded damages for medical expenses, pain and suffering, and loss of consortium. *Id.* at 1098. Because the same issues had already been fully and fairly litigated, the court granted the arbitrator's decision preclusive effect, and granted Continental's motion for summary judgment. *Id.*

Likewise, in *Bailey v. Metropolitan Property & Liability Ins. Co.,* 24 Mass.App.Ct. 34, 505 N.E.2d 908 (1987), the Appeals Court of Massachusetts relied on § 84 of the Restatement and held that the plaintiff was barred from recovery under principles of issue preclusion. The plaintiff in that case, Bailey, was a passenger in a car when he was injured in a wreck, and he received the limits of the car owner's personal injury protection, medical payment coverage, and optional bodily injury coverage. The insurer, Allstate, refused to pay Bailey any of the $10,000 available under the owner's underinsurance coverage. Bailey and Allstate went to arbitration on the issue, and the arbitrator awarded Bailey $7,500. *Bailey,* 505 N.E.2d at 909.

Later, Bailey sued Metropolitan (which insured Bailey's own vehicle), seeking payment under the underinsurance provisions in the Metropolitan policy. Metropolitan denied the claims on the grounds that the arbitrator's award precluded Bailey from further pursuing the issue of damages. Although the trial court ruled in Metropolitan's favor on another issue, the Massachusetts appellate court affirmed on the basis of issue preclusion, noting first the following:

> A fundamental precept of common-law adjudication, embodied in the related doctrines of collateral estoppel and *res judicata,* is that a right, question or fact distinctly put in issue and directly determined by a court of competent jurisdiction ... cannot be disputed in a subsequent suit between the same parties or their privies.

Id. at 910 (citing *Montana v. United States,* 440 U.S. 147, 99 S.Ct. 970, 59 L.Ed.2d 210 (1979)).

Like Arkansas, Massachusetts does not require an identity of defendants for issue preclusion to operate. *Id.* Thus, the *Bailey* court noted, the inquiry was simply "whether the issue on which preclusion is sought has been the product of full litigation and careful decision." *Id.* Citing Restatement § 84 and its comment, the Massachusetts court further stated that it saw "no reason why the rule should not extend as well to a defendant who was not a party to the earlier arbitration if the plaintiff had a full and fair opportunity in the arbitration to litigate the issue, and if equitable considerations otherwise warrant precluding relitigation." *Id.* (internal brackets and quotation marks omitted).

We are persuaded by the reasoning of the Massachusetts court, and we hold that a party not involved in a prior arbitration may use the award in that arbitration to bind his opponent if the party to be bound, or a privy, was before the arbitrator, had a full and fair opportunity to litigate the issue, and the issue was actually decided by the arbitrator or was necessary to his decision.

Thus, we must now determine whether these elements have been satisfied in the case before us. Clearly, Riverdale, as the party to be bound, was before the arbitrator. The hearing before the arbitrator lasted for five days, during which time both Riverdale and May put on extensive testimony and other evidence. The issues raised and addressed in the arbitration proceedings were the same as those alleged in the circuit court complaint. In its lawsuit against May and Ruffin, Riverdale made numerous allegations against both defendants. Notably, Riverdale listed seventeen specific structural deficiencies and defects that it had noted and reported "to the defendants May *and* Ruffin." In addition, as noted above, the complaint asserted causes of action in negligence, breach of implied warranties, defective product, and fraud against both May and Ruffin. Further, the arbitrator's award itself stated that there was conflicting evidence and testimony about the design of the building and its mechanical and structural components. The arbitrator resolved these conflicts in the testimony and evidence in May's favor, and concluded that there was "no credible evidence of Riverdale's damages for repairs or for the cost of correcting defects. As a result, Riverdale [was] not entitled to an award of ... damages." Thus, it is apparent that Riverdale was before the arbitrator, had a full and fair opportunity to litigate the issues it raised, and those issues were actually decided by the arbitrator and were necessary to the decision. Therefore, we have no hesitancy in holding that the trial court properly concluded that Riverdale was collaterally estopped from further litigating these same issues against Ruffin.

Affirmed.

* * *

Note on McDonald v. City of West Branch

In *McDonald v. City of West Branch, Michigan*, 466 U.S. 284 (1984), the Supreme Court considered whether a federal court may accord preclusive effect to an arbitration award that was not appealed. The City of West Branch fired plaintiff, a police officer. He grieved pursuant to a collective bargaining agreement, contending that there was "no proper cause" for his discharge. The grievance went to arbitration. The arbitrator ruled against McDonald, finding just cause.

McDonald did not appeal the arbitrator's decision. Instead, he filed a § 1983 action against the city of West Branch and certain of its officials, alleging he had been discharged for exercising his First Amendment rights of freedom of speech, freedom of association, and freedom to petition the government for redress of grievances. The case was tried before a jury which returned a verdict in favor of all but one of the defendants, Chief of Police Longstreet.

On appeal, the Court of Appeals for the Sixth Circuit reversed the judgment against Longstreet. 709 F.2d 1505 (6th Cir. 1983). The court reasoned that the parties had agreed to settle their disputes through arbitration and that the arbitrator had considered the reasons for McDonald's discharge. Finding that the arbitration process had not been abused, the Court of Appeals concluded that McDonald's First Amendment claims were barred by res judicata and collateral estoppel.

The Supreme Court reversed, stating:

> At the outset, we must consider whether federal courts are obligated by statute to accord res judicata or collateral-estoppel effect to the arbitrator's decision. Respondents contend that the Federal Full Faith and Credit Statute, 28 U.S.C. § 1738, requires that we give preclusive effect to the arbitration award.

Our cases establish that § 1738 obliges federal courts to give the same preclusive effect to a state-court judgment as would the courts of the State rendering the judgment ... As we explained in Kremer, however, "*[a]rbitration* decisions ... are not subject to the mandate of § 1738." Id., at 477, 102 S.Ct., at 1894. This conclusion follows from the plain language of § 1738 which provides in pertinent part that the "*judicial proceedings* [of any court of any State] shall have the same full faith and credit in every court within the United States and its Territories and Possessions as they have by law or usage in the courts of such State ... from which they are taken." (Emphasis added.) Arbitration is not a "judicial proceeding" and, therefore, § 1738 does not apply to arbitration awards.

Because federal courts are not required by statute to give res judicata or collateral-estoppel effect to an unappealed arbitration award, any rule of preclusion would necessarily be judicially fashioned. We therefore consider the question whether it was appropriate for the Court of Appeals to fashion such a rule.

On two previous occasions this Court has considered the contention that an award in an arbitration proceeding brought pursuant to a collective-bargaining agreement should preclude a subsequent suit in federal court. In both instances we rejected the claim.

Alexander v. Gardner–Denver Co., 415 U.S. 36, 94 S.Ct. 1011, 39 L.Ed.2d 147 (1974), was an action under Title VII of the Civil Rights Act of 1964 brought by an employee who had unsuccessfully claimed in an arbitration proceeding that his discharge was racially motivated. Although Alexander protested the same discharge in the Title VII action, we held that his Title VII claim was not foreclosed by the arbitral decision against him. In addition, we declined to adopt a rule that would have required federal courts to defer to an arbitrator's decision on a discrimination claim when "(i) the claim was before the arbitrator; (ii) the collective-bargaining agreement prohibited the form of discrimination charged in the suit under Title VII; and (iii) the arbitrator has authority to rule on the claim and to fashion a remedy." Id., at 55–56, 94 S.Ct., at 1023.

Similarly, in *Barrentine v. Arkansas–Best Freight System, Inc.*, 450 U.S. 728, 101 S.Ct. 1437, 67 L.Ed.2d 641 (1981), Barrentine and a fellow employee had unsuccessfully submitted wage claims to arbitration. Nevertheless, we rejected the contention that the arbitration award precluded a subsequent suit based on the same underlying facts alleging a violation of the minimum wage provisions of the Fair Labor Standards Act. Id., at 745–746, 101 S.Ct., at 1447.

Our rejection of a rule of preclusion in *Barrentine* and our rejection of a rule of deferral in *Gardner–Denver* were based in large part on our conclusion that Congress intended the statutes at issue in those cases to be judicially enforceable and that arbitration could not provide an adequate substitute for judicial proceedings in adjudicating claims under those statutes. 450 U.S., at 740–746, 101 S.Ct., at 1444–1447;

415 U.S., at 56–60, 94 S.Ct., at 1023–25. These considerations similarly require that we find the doctrines of res judicata and collateral estoppel inapplicable in this § 1983 action.

[A]lthough arbitration is well suited to resolving contractual disputes, our decisions in *Barrentine* and *Gardner–Denver* compel the conclusion that it cannot provide an adequate substitute for a judicial proceeding in protecting the federal statutory and constitutional rights that § 1983 is designed to safeguard. As a result, according preclusive effect to an arbitration award in a subsequent § 1983 action would undermine that statute's efficacy in protecting federal rights.

* * *

Questions

1. Under what circumstances will an arbitral award be given collateral estoppel effect? Are *Riverdale* and *McDonald* distinguishable?

2. In *14 Penn Plaza LLC v. Pyett*, ___ U.S. ___, 129 S.Ct. 1456 (2009), the Supreme Court in a 5–4 decision significantly narrowed the scope of *McDonald*, *Gardner–Denver*, and *Barrentine*. See Chapter 1.6. The issue in *14 Penn Plaza* was the enforceability of an arbitration provision in a collective bargaining agreement that explicitly covered statutory claims. The Court stated:

> The facts underlying *Gardner–Denver*, *Barrentine*, and *McDonald* reveal the narrow scope of the legal rule arising from that trilogy of decisions. Summarizing those opinions in *Gilmer*, this Court made clear that the *Gardner–Denver* line of cases "did not involve the issue of the enforceability of an agreement to arbitrate statutory claims." 500 U.S., at 35, 111 S.Ct. 1647. Those decisions instead "involved the quite different issue whether arbitration of contract-based claims precluded subsequent judicial resolution of statutory claims. Since the employees there had not agreed to arbitrate their statutory claims, and the labor arbitrators were not authorized to resolve such claims, the arbitration in those cases understandably was held not to preclude subsequent statutory actions." Ibid.... *Gardner–Denver* and its progeny thus do not control the outcome where, as is the case here, the collective-bargaining agreement's arbitration provision expressly covers both statutory and contractual discrimination claims.

The Court then stated that

> *Gardner–Denver* is a direct descendant of the Court's decision in *Wilko v. Swan,* 346 U.S. 427, 74 S.Ct. 182, 98 L.Ed. 168 (1953), which held that an agreement to arbitrate claims under the Securities Act of 1933 was unenforceable. See *id.,* at 438, 74 S.Ct. 182. The Court subsequently overruled *Wilko* and, in so doing, characterized the decision as "pervaded by ... 'the old judicial hostility to arbitration.' " *Rodriguez de Quijas v. Shearson/American Express, Inc.,* 490 U.S. 477, 480, 109 S.Ct. 1917, 104 L.Ed.2d 526 (1989). The Court added: "To the

> extent that *Wilko* rested on suspicion of arbitration as a method of weakening the protections afforded in the substantive law to would-be complainants, it has fallen far out of step with our current strong endorsement of the federal statutes favoring this method of resolving disputes." *Id.,* at 481, 109 S.Ct. 1917; see also *Mitsubishi Motors Corp., supra,* at 626–627, 105 S.Ct. 3346 ("[W]e are well past the time when judicial suspicion of the desirability of arbitration and of the competence of arbitral tribunals inhibited the development of arbitration as an alternative means of dispute resolution"). The timeworn "mistrust of the arbitral process" harbored by the Court in *Gardner–Denver* thus weighs against reliance on anything more than its core holding. *Shearson/American Express Inc. v. McMahon,* 482 U.S. 220, 231–232, 107 S.Ct. 2332, 96 L.Ed.2d 185 (1987); see also *Gilmer,* 500 U.S., at 34, n. 5, 111 S.Ct. 1647 (reiterating that *Gardner–Denver*'s view of arbitration "has been undermined by [the Court's] recent arbitration decisions"). Indeed, in light of the "radical change, over two decades, in the Court's receptivity to arbitration," *Wright,* 525 U.S., at 77, 119 S.Ct. 391, reliance on any judicial decision similarly littered with *Wilko*'s overt hostility to the enforcement of arbitration agreements would be ill advised.

Does the Court's denigration of *Gardner–Denver* apply equally to *McDonald,* whether or not you agree with that denigration? If so, does *McDonald* survive *14 Penn Plaza*? Even if it does, has its scope been narrowly confined to a subset of collective bargaining cases?

* * *

CHAPTER FIVE

ARBITRATION IN THE STATE AND FEDERAL COURTS

1. INTRODUCTION

In recent decades, many state legislatures and some federal courts have introduced alternative dispute resolution programs into their judicial systems. Some of these programs began as experimental efforts to reduce court congestion. Others were efforts to provide a mechanism for resolving small stakes disputes between neighbors or between landlords and tenants—disputes for which litigation had become too expensive, too time consuming, and too rigid in its remedies.

Court-connected ADR programs take a variety of forms. They include mandatory pre-trial conferences in the presence of a judge to explore settlement options, and systems of early neutral evaluation, in which a neutral is assigned to evaluate the merits of a dispute prior to discovery or motion practice. Some states went even further in the direction of incorporating ADR techniques developed in the private sector. In 1958, Pennsylvania became the first state to require parties in cases involving small sums to submit their disputes to a court-appointed arbitrator before permitting the case to be heard at trial. In 1970, New York and Ohio enacted similar legislation. By 1995, twenty-five states had adopted court-ordered arbitration programs.[1] In the 1990s, several federal district courts followed suit, and since then the practice has spread in both state and federal courts.

Court-ordered arbitration is sometimes, but not always, a prominent part of court-connected ADR. In addition to court-ordered arbitration, some state courts have begun requiring parties in certain types of cases to meet with a court-appointed mediator prior to coming to trial. And recently some state and federal courts have experimented with other forms of alternative dispute resolution, such as summary jury trials, private judging, and other such techniques.

The use of court-ordered ADR is usually justified on the basis of efficiency. Supporters claim that it promotes settlement of pending cases, and thus it relieves over-crowded dockets and conserves judicial resources for the cases where they are needed most. Some also claim that parties themselves are more satisfied with results obtained with ADR than with a conventional trial.[2]

1. See John P. McIver & Susan Keilitz, *Court–Annexed Arbitration: An Introduction*, 14 The Justice System Journal 123 (1991).

2. See, e.g., Wayne D. Brazil, *A Close Look at Three Court–Sponsored ADR Programs: Why They Exist, How They Operate, What They Deliver, and Whether They*

These empirical claims, however, have not been validated. Some scholars have challenged the implicit assumption that court-ordered ADR leads to more settlements, or better settlements, than the normal civil justice system. Kim Dayton analyzed empirical data comparing federal districts that used mandatory arbitration with those that did not, and found that "ADR districts are not more efficient or effective in addressing their caseloads as a result of using ADR when compared with peer districts." Lisa Bernstein used a simulated model of litigation processes with and without court-ordered arbitration and concluded that "when both parties are overly optimistic, the most common cause of failure to settle, court-annexed arbitration programs may actually reduce the likelihood of pre-trial settlement." Roselle Wissler and Bob Dauber studied the use of arbitration in Arizona's general-jurisdiction civil trial courts and found the arbitration program did not substantially improve the effectiveness and efficiency of dispute resolution. A recent New Jersey Bar study found that parties rejected awards in 75% of court-ordered arbitrations, and recommended that that state's arbitration program be scrapped.[3]

In the 1980s and 1990s, court-ordered ADR (including arbitration) expanded significantly.[4] Since then, however, court-ordered arbitration has declined dramatically in the federal courts—of the ten courts authorized to use mandatory arbitration, seven have dropped their programs or have made arbitration voluntary. The same thing appears to be happening in state courts, but there is no empirical data to confirm it.

Court-ordered ADR programs require courts to balance the systemic efficiency-enhancing goals of ADR against the rights of parties to receive a fair hearing for their legal claims. The cases and materials that follow discuss many of the legal issues that have arisen in relation to the use of compulsory, or court-connected, alternative dispute resolution.

Threaten Important Values, 1990 U. Chicago Legal Forum 303; John L. Barkai & Gene Kassebaum, *Using Court-Annexed Arbitration to Reduce Litigant Costs and to Increase the Pace of Litigation*, 16 Pepperdine L. Rev. S43 (1989).

3. See Kim Dayton, *The Myth of Alternative Dispute Resolution in the Federal Courts*, 76 Iowa L. Rev. 889, 924 (1991); Lisa Bernstein, *Understanding the Limits of Court-Connected ADR: A Critique of Federal Court-Annexed Arbitration Programs*, 141 Penn. L. Rev. 2169, 2176 (1993); Roselle L. Wissler & Bob Dauber, *Court-Connected Arbitration in the Superior Court of Arizona: A Study of Its Performance and Proposed Rule Changes*, 2007 J. Disp. Resol. 65; Rebecca Porter, *New Jersey Bar Disavows Court-Annexed Arbitration*, 40 Trial 82 (2004). For a thorough critique of mandatory, nonbinding, court-annexed arbitration, see Amy J. Schmitz, *Nonconsensual + Nonbinding = Nonsensical? Reconsidering Court-Connected Arbitration Programs*, 10 Cardozo J. Conflict Resolution 587 (2009).

4. See James F. Henry, *No Longer a Rarity, Judicial ADR is Preparing for Great Growth—But Much Care is Needed*, 9 Alternatives 95, 95 (1991).

2. DESCRIPTION OF COURT-ANNEXED ARBITRATION

Understanding the Limits of Court–Connected ADR: A Critique of Federal Court–Annexed Arbitration Programs

Lisa Bernstein.
141 Penn. L. Rev. 2169, 2172–73, 2177–85 (1993).

In recent years the availability of private dispute resolution providers, ranging from expert mediators to rent-a-judge programs complete with black robes and model courtrooms, has increased dramatically. The alternative dispute resolution ("ADR") movement has received extensive press attention and has been hailed as a solution to crowded dockets and an inexpensive panacea for the ills of an overly litigious society. Pointing to the rapid growth of private ADR providers and studies purporting to show a high level of lawyer and client satisfaction with these alternative processes, states, joined recently by the federal government, began passing laws requiring parties to participate in an ADR process as a precondition to judicial resolution of their dispute.

In 1978, Congress authorized the creation of the first three federal district court-annexed arbitration programs. The programs required parties to participate in a mandatory non-binding court-annexed arbitration ("CAA") hearing as a precondition to obtaining a trial. The programs received strong support from then Attorney General Griffin Bell, who believed that compulsory court-annexed arbitration programs would "broaden access for the American people to their justice system and . . . provide mechanisms that will permit the expeditious resolution of disputes at a reasonable cost." In 1985, Congress funded eight additional CAA pilot programs. In 1988, it authorized continued experimentation with mandatory CAA and provided funding for ten voluntary CAA pilot programs.

The trend towards publicly sponsored or mandated ADR shows no signs of abating. One of the six "cornerstone principles" of the Civil Justice Reform Act of 1990 was "expanding and enhancing the use of alternative dispute resolution." The Act directed each federal district court to complete a cost and delay reduction plan and to specifically consider the possibility of instituting court-connected ADR programs. As of February 1992, thirty-two of the thirty-four federal courts that had completed these plans either endorsed or adopted some type of court-connected ADR. . . .

I. THE BASIC FEATURES OF COURT–ANNEXED ARBITRATION PROGRAMS

The Judicial Improvements and Access to Justice Act sets out the basic structure of federal CAA programs, but gives each district the authority to adopt local rules specifying important program features.

Suits for predominantly money damages that fall below a particular amount in controversy, which, depending on the district, ranges from $50,000 to $150,000 and do not involve federal constitutional claims or conspiracies to interfere with civil rights, must be submitted to non-binding arbitration before a trial can be requested. In some districts, the parties or the trial judge may make a motion to exempt the case from arbitration where "the objectives of arbitration would not be realized (1) because the case involves complex or novel legal issues, (2) because legal issues predominate over factual issues, or (3) for other good cause. In most districts the maximum amount in controversy is a jurisdictional limit, not a cap on the damages an arbitrator can award."

Hearings are conducted by either a single arbitrator or a panel of three arbitrators chosen from a volunteer pool of lawyers. Hearings take place 80 to 180 days after the filing of the answer and decisions are rendered shortly thereafter. In some districts, hearings are open to the public, in others, they are closed. The amount of pre-arbitration discovery permitted and the types of pre-trial motions decided prior to the hearing are governed by local rule, subject to certain constraints imposed by Congress.

At the arbitration hearing, the Federal Rules of Evidence do not apply. Arbitrators may permit the introduction of any credible non-privileged evidence, including hearsay. The arbitrators are not required to issue written or oral findings of fact or conclusions of law, and at least one district prohibits them from doing so. A few districts encourage live testimony, while others discourage it, providing by local rule that the presentation of testimony shall be kept to a minimum, and that cases shall be presented to the arbitrators primarily through the statements and arguments of Counsel. One district bans live testimony altogether and requires that "[a]ll evidence shall be presented through counsel who may incorporate argument on such evidence in his or her presentation." Some programs limit the length of the hearing.

Good faith participation in the arbitration hearing is required of both the parties and their counsel. Most districts require parties to be present at the hearing, and some districts require the presence of a person with full settlement authority. Although the authority of the court to order a person with settlement authority to be present at an arbitration hearing has yet to be definitively established, an en banc panel of the Seventh Circuit has upheld a district judge's authority to order a person with full settlement authority to be present at a settlement conference. In some districts, if either the nonattendance of a party or the preparation and presentation of counsel is deemed not to constitute "participation in a meaningful way" in the arbitration process, the court can impose monetary sanctions and/or strike a party's demand for a trial de novo ("trial"). The court's authority to strike a party's demand for a trial has been upheld by several district courts, but has not yet been considered by any court of appeals.

After the arbitrator has rendered an award, which may, depending on the local rule, include costs, each party has thirty days to request a trial. When a party requests a trial, the case is restored to its original place on the docket and treated as if it had never been arbitrated; neither the record of the hearing, if made, nor the arbitrators' decision are admissible at trial. In the pilot districts, trial de novo request rates range from forty-six to seventy-four percent of arbitrated cases.

Some districts have disincentives to requesting a trial. Most districts require the party requesting a trial to post a bond with the court in the amount of the arbitrators' fees and costs which, depending on the district and the number of arbitrators, can range from $125 to $450 for the typical case. Although complex cases often cost substantially more to arbitrate, most districts put a cap on the amount of the bond a party can be required to post in order to obtain a trial. If the party requesting the trial improves his position at trial, this bond is returned to him; if he fails to do so, it is retained by the court.

In the past, some districts had a rule requiring the party requesting a trial to pay his opponent's post-arbitration attorneys' fees and/or costs if he failed to improve his position at trial. The authority of courts to enact such local rules absent congressional authorization was a question of some dispute. In 1988, Congress decided that pending further study by the Federal Courts Study Committee, such provisions should not be part of the pilot programs. However, in its 1990 report, the Committee recommended that Congress authorize the pilot districts to experiment with fee and cost-shifting provisions, common features of many state CAA programs.

If a trial is not requested within thirty days of the arbitration decision, the decision is entered as the judgment of the court and has the same force and effect as a trial judgment. It cannot, however, be appealed.

* * *

3. Constitutionality

Firelock Incorporated v. District Court in the State of Colorado

776 P.2d 1090 (Colo. 1989).

■ Rovira, Justice.

This case requires us to determine whether the Colorado Mandatory Arbitration Act (Act), §§ 13–22–401 to 13–22–409, 6A C.R.S. (1987), violates the Colorado Constitution and the due process and equal protection clauses of the fourteenth amendment to the United States Constitution.

The Boulder County District Court held that the Act was constitutional and denied the petitioner's request to refrain from assigning the case for arbitration. We issued a rule to show cause pursuant to C.A.R. 21, and we now discharge the rule.

I

In 1988, McGhee Communications, Inc. (McGhee) commenced an action in the Boulder County District Court, which is located in the Twentieth Judicial District, against the petitioner, Firelock Incorporated (Firelock). McGhee claimed that it rendered advertising services to Firelock for which Firelock did not pay. In its complaint, McGhee certified that the probable recovery would not exceed $50,000, exclusive of interest and costs, and that the case was not exempt from mandatory arbitration. See C.R.C.P. 109.1.

Firelock filed an answer denying that the requested amount was owed, asserted several affirmative defenses, and demanded a jury trial. Firelock also filed a motion to refrain from assignment for mandatory arbitration under the Act. In support of its motion, Firelock claimed that the Act violated article II, sections 3, 6, 23, and 25; article III; article VI, sections 1 and 9; and article XVIII, section 3, of the Colorado Constitution; the fourteenth amendment to the United States Constitution; and C.R.C.P. 38. McGhee resisted the motion and requested that the trial court find the Act constitutional and order arbitration to be commenced promptly.

The trial court denied the motion, and Firelock then filed a petition pursuant to C.A.R. 21. In its petition, Firelock requested that this court issue an order to show cause why the respondent district court should not be restrained from referring the case for arbitration. Firelock also requested that we make the rule absolute and declare the Act unconstitutional.

II

The Act was approved on May 28, 1987, and became effective on January 1, 1988. The Act is scheduled to terminate on July 1, 1990. See § 13–22–402(1), 6A C.R.S. (1987). Beginning on January 1, 1989, and on each January 1 thereafter, the judicial department must submit to the General Assembly an annual report evaluating the mandatory arbitration pilot project. See § 13–22–408, 6A C.R.S. (1987).

The Act provides a framework of mandatory arbitration in eight pilot judicial districts of which the twentieth, where the Boulder District Court is located, is one. See § 13–22–402(1), 6A C.R.S. (1987). In these eight pilot districts, any civil action filed in any court of record except the county court and small claims court after January 1, 1988, and before July 1, 1990, seeking money damages in the sum of $50,000 or less, excluding costs and interest, is to be assigned to mandatory arbitration once the action is at issue. See § 13–22–402(2), 6A C.R.S. (1987).

Pursuant to the Act, the complaint and any applicable counterclaim or cross-claim governed by the Act must contain a certification that the probable amount of recovery exceeds or does not exceed $50,000, the limit imposed for mandatory arbitration. The Act establishes procedures for the selection and compensation of arbitrators, see § 13–22–403, and sets forth an outline of procedures for the arbitration hearing, see § 13–22–404. Arbitrators must be "qualified" and must file a consent to act as an arbitrator in the district in which the court is located, but an arbitrator need not be an attorney. See § 13–22–403(3). Section 13–22–405 provides for a trial de novo for any party dissatisfied with the decision of the arbitrators. The demand for a trial de novo must be filed with the court within thirty days after the filing of the arbitrators' decision. See § 13–22–405(1). The Act also provides that, unless the trial de novo results in "an improvement of the position of the demanding party by more than ten percent," the demanding party must pay the costs of the arbitration proceeding including arbitrator fees, but not exceeding $1,000. See § 13–22–405(3).

Section 13–22–406 provides that the supreme court, pursuant to its authority under article VI, section 21, of the Colorado Constitution, is empowered to promulgate rules governing the arbitration proceedings established in the Act. Pursuant to this authority, we adopted C.R.C.P. 109.1. C.R.C.P. 109.1 establishes the procedure for certification of the probable amount of recovery and the basis for any exemption from the Act, see C.R.C.P. 109.1(b), sets forth sanctions for failure to comply with the certification procedures, see C.R.C.P. 109.1(c), and provides for a detailed procedure for the selection of arbitrators, see C.R.C.P. 109.1(d). C.R.C.P. 109.1 also provides for the filing of a pre-arbitration "Disclosure Statement," see C.R.C.P. 109.1(h), sets forth limited rules for discovery, see C.R.C.P. 109.1(i), and establishes the details of the arbitration hearing and the powers of the arbitrators, see C.R.C.P. 109.1(l). C.R.C.P. 109.1(q) provides that if neither party demands a trial de novo within thirty days after the filing of the arbitrators' award, then the award becomes final and the trial court must enter judgment on the award in accordance with C.R.C.P. 58(a).

III

On appeal, Firelock presents several reasons for finding that the Act is unconstitutional. Firelock argues that the Act violates article III and article VI, sections 1 and 9, of the Colorado Constitution, which provide for the separation of powers; article II, sections 3 and 6, of the Colorado Constitution, which provide for the right of access to courts; article II, section 23, of the Colorado Constitution and C.R.C.P. 38, which provide for the right to trial by jury; article II, section 25, of the Colorado Constitution and the equal protection and due process clauses of the United States Constitution; and article XVIII, section 3, of the Colorado Constitution, which provides the General Assembly with authority over consensual arbitration. We will address each of these arguments in turn.

A.

Firelock asserts that the Act violates the separation of powers provision of the Colorado Constitution because section 13–22–402(2) requires "that the pilot district courts must refrain from exercising their general jurisdiction pending arbitration." Firelock also asserts that the Act "is an unconstitutional delegation of judicial power to unqualified private citizens" because it allows arbitration to be "conducted by persons who are not only not members of the judiciary, but indeed who do not even have to be licensed attorneys."

Article III of the Colorado Constitution provides:

> The powers of the government of this state are divided into three distinct departments,—the legislative, executive and judicial; and no person or collection of persons charged with the exercise of powers properly belonging to one of these departments shall exercise any power properly belonging to either of the others, except as in this constitution expressly directed or permitted.

"The fundamental meaning of the separation of powers doctrine is that the three branches of government are separate, coordinate, and equal." Pena v. District Court, 681 P.2d 953, 955–56 (Colo.1984). The purpose of article III is to prevent one branch of government from exercising any power that is constitutionally vested in another branch of government. Van Kleeck v. Ramer, 62 Colo. 4, 156 P. 1108 (1916).

According to article VI, section 1, the judicial power of the state is vested

> in a supreme court, district courts, a probate court in the city and county of Denver, a juvenile court in the city and county of Denver, county courts, and such other courts or judicial officers with jurisdiction inferior to the supreme court, as the general assembly may, from time to time establish.

With respect to the authority vested in district courts, article VI, section 9, states that "[t]he district courts shall be trial courts of record with general jurisdiction, and shall have original jurisdiction in all civil, probate, and criminal cases, except as otherwise provided herein."

We must decide, therefore, whether the General Assembly can constitutionally require a district court to refrain from exercising its original jurisdiction in some civil cases while arbitration is proceeding. To answer this question, we must examine the nature of the judicial function and determine whether the arbitration panels provided in the Act exercise judicial authority.

In Mizar v. Jones, 157 Colo. 535, 537, 403 P.2d 767, 769 (1965), we noted "that courts do exist primarily to afford a forum to settle litigable matters between disputing parties." A "court" consists of " 'persons officially assembled, under authority of law, at the appropriate time and place, for the administration of justice.' " In re Allison, 13 Colo. 525, 528, 22 P. 820, 821 (1889). In Union Colony v. Elliott, 5 Colo. 371, 381 (1880), we quoted Blackstone's definition of a court:

> A court is defined to be a place where justice is judicially administered.... In every court there must be at least three constituent parts; the *actor, reus* and judex; the *actor* or plaintiff who complains of an injury done; the reus or defendant, who is called upon to make satisfaction for it; and the judex or judicial power which is to examine the truth of the fact, to determine the law arising upon that fact, and if

any injury appears to be done, to ascertain, and by its officers to apply the remedy.

It is significant that, in Blackstone's definition of a court, a court must have the authority to apply the remedy.

Many courts have said that the essence of judicial power is the final authority to render and enforce a judgment or remedy. E.g., Cedar Rapids Human Rights Comm'n v. Cedar Rapids Community School Dist., 222 N.W.2d 391, 396 (Iowa 1974); Attorney General v. Johnson, 282 Md. 274, 385 A.2d 57, 64 (1978); Breimhorst v. Beckman, 35 N.W.2d 719, 733 (Minn. 1949). " 'It is not enough to make a function judicial that it requires discretion, deliberation, thought, and judgment. It must be the exercise of discretion and judgment within the subdivision of the sovereign power which belongs to the judiciary. . . .' " Solvuca v. Ryan & Reilly Co., 101 A. 710, 715 (Md. 1917).

It is clear that, under the Act, the arbitrators' decision is not an exercise of the sovereign power of the state because the decision is non-binding, and the arbitrators do not perform a judicial function because they do not possess the final authority to render and enforce a judgment. See Attorney General v. Johnson, 385 A.2d at 65 (because either party can reject the decision of the arbitration panel and because the panel cannot enforce its decision even if the parties accept it, the panels do not exercise the judicial power of the state in the constitutional sense).

According to the Act, the arbitration panel must file its decision with the district court, and if neither party demands a trial de novo within thirty days after the filing, only then will the decision be enforceable. Thus, neither party need be bound by the arbitrators' decision because either party can demand a full and complete trial on the facts and the law by the district court with no effect given to the arbitrators' decision. Furthermore, the district court, not the arbitration panel, enters the judgment in accordance with C.R.C.P. 58(a). See C.R.C.P. 109.1(q).

Therefore, we conclude that the arbitration process created by the Act does not vest judicial authority in another branch of government in violation of article III of the Colorado Constitution because the arbitration panels do not perform "a judicial function."

Firelock relies on Wright v. Central Du Page Hospital Association, 63 Ill.2d 313, 347 N.E.2d 736 (Ill. 1976), where the Illinois Supreme Court struck down provisions relating to the establishment of medical review panels in medical malpractice cases. The Illinois statute provided for a three member arbitration panel consisting of one circuit judge, one practicing physician, and one practicing attorney. The circuit judge was to preside over the proceeding and decide procedural and evidentiary issues, but as to other issues, both legal and factual, the power and function of the lawyer and physician member of the panel were the same as that of the judge. The determinations of the panel were to be made in a written opinion stating its conclusions of fact and conclusions of law with a dissenting member filing a separate opinion. Either party could reject the panel's decision and proceed to trial as in any other civil case. The expenses of the panel were to be apportioned among the parties equally, except that a party who rejected a unanimous decision of the panel and who failed to prevail at trial could be taxed with the reasonable attorney's fees of the prevailing party, the costs of the panel, and the costs of the trial.

The Illinois Supreme Court held the statute to be unconstitutional because, among other things,

> the physician and lawyer member of the medical review panel are empowered to make conclusions of law and fact "according to the applicable substantive law" over the dissent of the circuit judge. This, we hold, empowers the nonjudicial members of the medical review panel to exercise a judicial function in violation of [the Illinois] Constitution.

Id. 347 N.E.2d at 739–40 (citation omitted).

We find this case to be inapposite because, here, the Act does not provide for a member of the judiciary in the arbitration panel with equal authority in the decision. Thus, there is no provision allowing two nonjudicial members of the panel to make conclusions of law and fact over the dissent of a member of the judiciary. Because the Act does not provide a mixed panel of judicial and nonjudicial members whereby the authority of the judiciary is diluted by the presence of laymen, we find Wright to be inapposite.

B.

Firelock claims that the Act unconstitutionally impedes the right of access to courts guaranteed by article II, sections 3 and 6, by forcing litigants to arbitrate their claims before access is given to the district court and by requiring a party who requests a trial de novo to pay the arbitration costs up to $1,000 if he does not improve his position by at least 10%.

Article II of the Colorado Constitution is entitled "Bill of Rights." Article II, section 3, provides that "[a]ll persons have certain natural, essential and inalienable rights," including, among others, the right of "enjoying and defending their lives and liberties." Section 6 of article II provides that: "Courts of justice shall be open to every person, and a speedy remedy afforded for every injury to person, property or character; and right and justice should be administered without sale, denial or delay."

Generally, a burden on a party's right of access to the courts will be upheld as long as it is reasonable. "In a proper case . . . the right of free access to our courts must yield to the rights of others and the efficient administration of justice." People v. Spencer, 185 Colo. 377, 381–82, 524 P.2d 1084, 1086 (1974) (enjoining a *pro se* plaintiff who filed numerous unfounded lawsuits from proceeding *pro se* as plaintiff in the courts of this state) . . . (citations omitted).

Many other reasonable burdens similar to the one imposed by the Act are present within our system of justice. For example, section 13–32–101, 6A C.R.S. (1987), requires the payment of a docket fee at the time of first appearance in all civil actions and special proceedings in all courts of record. C.R.C.P. 54(d) provides that "[e]xcept when express provision therefor is made either in a statute of this state or in these rules, costs shall be allowed as of course to the prevailing party unless the court otherwise directs." In disputes between landlords and tenants over the return of a security deposit, the willful retention of a security deposit renders the landlord liable for, among other things, reasonable attorney fees and court costs. See § 38–12–103(3)(a), 16A C.R.S. (1982). Finally, C.R.C.P. 68 requires a prevailing party to pay costs incurred after the receipt of an offer of settlement when the judgment obtained by the prevailing party is not more favorable than the offer. Although this list is not all inclusive, it is demonstrative of the extent of a permissible burden on the right of access to the courts.

We conclude that the litigants are not denied their right of access to the courts because the Act provides for de novo review of the decision of the arbitration panel. Furthermore, the requirement that a prevailing party pay the costs of arbitration up to $1,000 if the party does not increase his position by at least 10% at trial does not place an unreasonable burden on the right of access to the courts. Therefore, we hold that the Act does not violate article II, section 6, of the Colorado Constitution.

C.

Firelock next asserts that article II, section 23, of the Colorado Constitution establishes a constitutional right to a jury trial in civil actions and the Act impermissibly infringes on this right. Firestone also argues that this court created the right to a jury trial in civil cases when we adopted C.R.C.P. 38 and that the Act violates that right.

The United States Constitution's guarantee of a civil jury trial provided for in the seventh amendment does not apply to the states. Edwards v. Elliott, 88 U.S. 532, 557, 22 L.Ed. 487 (1874). Article II, section 23, provides that "[t]he right of trial by jury shall remain inviolate in criminal cases; but a jury in civil cases in all courts, or in criminal cases in courts not of record, may consist of less than twelve persons, as may be prescribed by law." ... Although we have held that trial by a jury in a civil action is not a matter of right under the Colorado Constitution, see Setchell v. Dellacroce, 169 Colo. 212, 215, 454 P.2d 804, 806 (1969), this action falls within a category of cases for which C.R.C.P. 38 allows a jury trial as of right because the action is for "money claimed as due on contract." The Act, however, does not deprive a party of the right to a jury trial.

The Act provides for de novo review by the district court thereby giving either party the opportunity for a jury trial, and the provision for the payment of the costs of arbitration if the party does not increase its position by 10% is not an unreasonable burden on the availability of a jury trial. Reasonable prerequisites to the availability of a jury trial are not unusual. For example, section 13–70–103, 6A C.R.S. (1987), requires the payment of a jury fee "in each cause tried by jury."

We hold that the Act does not violate article II, section 23, of the Colorado Constitution because there is no constitutional right to a jury trial in civil cases and the Act does not violate C.R.C.P. 38 because it does not preclude either party from rejecting the result of the arbitration and proceeding to the district court for a de novo jury trial.

D.

Firelock next argues that the Act violates article II, section 25, of the Colorado Constitution and the equal protection clause of the United States Constitution. According to Firelock, the Act creates two classifications which violate the right to equal protection. First, the Act treats litigants in the pilot districts differently than litigants outside the pilot districts. Second, within the pilot districts, the Act treats litigants differently based on the monetary amount of the claim.

The fourteenth amendment to the United States Constitution provides that no state shall "deprive any person of life, liberty or property without due process of law, nor deny to any person within its jurisdiction the equal protection of the laws." U.S. Const. amend. XIV, § 1. The due process clause of article II, section 25, of the Colorado Constitution guarantees the right of equal protection to the citizens of Colorado. See, e.g., Heninger v. Charnes, 200 Colo. 194, 197 n. 3, 613 P.2d 884, 886 n. 3 (1980). In interpreting the equal protection guarantee under the Colorado Constitution, we have followed the analytical mode developed by the United States Supreme Court in construing the equal protection clause of the fourteenth amendment. Tassian v. People, 731 P.2d 672, 674 (Colo.1987). The equal protection clause guarantees that all persons who are similarly situated will receive like treatment by the law. See J.T. v. O'Rourke, 651 P.2d 407, 413 (Colo. 1982).

Statutes facing a constitutional challenge are presumed to be constitutional, and the party challenging the statute bears the burden of proving it to be unconstitutional beyond a reasonable doubt. High Gear and Toke Shop v. Beacom, 689 P.2d 624, 630 (Colo. 1984). We must first decide which standard of review applies to a challenge to the Act, and then we must apply that standard.

Firelock argues that a standard of strict judicial scrutiny must be applied in resolving its equal protection challenge because the Act infringes on Firelock's fundamental rights, namely, the right of access to court and the right to a trial by jury. To pass strict scrutiny, the government must establish that the statutory classification is necessarily related to a compelling governmental interest. See Parrish v. Lamm, 758 P.2d 1356, 1370 (Colo. 1988). "In the absence of a statutory infringement on a fundamental right or the creation of a suspect class, ... equal protection of the laws is satisfied if the statutory classification has a reasonable basis in fact and bears a reasonable relationship to a legitimate governmental interest." Lee v. Colorado Dep't of Health, 718 P.2d 221, 227 (Colo. 1986). "When a statutory classification significantly interferes with the exercise of a fundamental right, it cannot be upheld unless it is supported by sufficiently important state interests and is closely tailored to effectuate only those interests." Zablocki v. Redhail, 434 U.S. 374, 388, 98 S.Ct. 673, 682, 54 L.Ed.2d 618 (1978); see also MacGuire v. Houston, 717 P.2d 948, 952–53 (Colo. 1986) (Although a restriction on eligibility to serve as an election judge affects the fundamental right of association for political purposes, the injury to the right "is not of such character and magnitude to require strict scrutiny.").

As discussed in part III.B. regarding the right of access to courts and part III.C. regarding the right to trial by jury, the Act does not unreasonably infringe upon or "significantly interfere with" any fundamental right. Furthermore, neither of the classifications creates a suspect class, such as one based on race or national origin. Therefore, the strict scrutiny standard is not the correct standard to apply. Because the strict scrutiny standard is not appropriate and because there is no classification triggering an intermediate standard of review, see, e.g., Kadrmas v. Dickinson Public Schools, 487 U.S. 450, 461, 108 S.Ct. 2481, 2487, 101 L.Ed.2d 399 (1988); Tassian, 731 P.2d at 675, the rational basis standard is the applicable standard of review.

We next examine the classifications advanced by Firelock to determine whether they are rationally related to a legitimate governmental interest. First, the General Assembly's decision to examine the success or failure of the Act in eight pilot districts is not a violation of equal protection.

"The Fourteenth Amendment does not prohibit legislation merely because it is special, or limited in its application to a particular geographical or political subdivision of the state." Rather, the Equal Protection Clause is offended only if the statute's classification "rests on grounds wholly irrelevant to the achievement of the State's objective."

Holt Civic Club v. City of Tuscaloosa, 439 U.S. 60, 70–71, 99 S.Ct. 383, 389–90, 58 L.Ed.2d 292 (1978) (citations omitted); accord Kadrmas v. Dickinson Public Schools, 487 U.S. 450, 461, 108 S.Ct. 2481, 2489, 101 L.Ed.2d 399 (1988).

Here, the General Assembly chose to examine the success or failure of the Act by implementing its provisions in several judicial districts for a limited period of time during which evidence could be gathered to determine whether the Act would be beneficial on a statewide basis. The purpose of the General Assembly is evident from the Act's provision for an annual report from the judicial department to the General Assembly evaluating the management of the pilot project, the training of arbitrators, and the availability of arbitrators. See § 13–22–408, 6A C.R.S. (1987).

Second, it is not unreasonable for the General Assembly to determine that claims below $50,000 should be subject to arbitration while claims above $50,000 are not. In Bushnell v. Sapp, 194 Colo. 273, 571 P.2d 1100 (1977), we addressed a similar argument with respect to the Colorado Auto Accident Reparations Act or "No-fault statute," sections 10–4–701 to 10–4–723, 4A C.R.S. (1987). In that case, the appellant argued that the $500 medical expense threshold created an arbitrary classification and thereby denied him equal protection of the laws. We rejected this argument, stating:

> Where and how to draw the line between major and minor claims of this nature is for the legislature to determine, and not the courts.... We do not find those criteria here to be unreasonable. Nor do we find the resulting classifications to be arbitrary or irrational. Perfection in classifications has never been constitutionally required and the fact that some inequity may result is not enough to invalidate a legislative classification based on rational distinctions.

Id. at 1106 (citations omitted). Here, the General Assembly's choice that the Act apply to claims of $50,000 and below is not irrational. Other examples of reasonable monetary classifications include a $5,000 limitation in county court, § 13–6–104(1), 6A C.R.S. (1987), a $2,000 limitation in the small claims division of county court, § 13–6–403, 6A C.R.S. (1988 Supp.), and a $50,000 limitation for diversity jurisdiction in federal court, 28 U.S.C.A. § 1332 (West Supp. 1989).

Arbitration is favored by the law in Colorado ... Arbitration promotes quicker resolution of disputes by providing an expedited opportunity for the parties to present their cases before an unbiased third party. See Norris, National Trends in Mandatory Arbitration, 17 Colo. Law. 1313 (1988); Littlefield, Court–Annexed Arbitration Comes to Colorado, 16 Colo. Law. 1941 (1987). By expediting the adversary process, arbitration promotes quicker settlement of cases thereby speeding up access to the courts and decreasing the costs to the parties ...

Although administrative convenience is not a legitimate governmental purpose, see Tassian, 731 P.2d at 676, we believe that the governmental interest advanced by arbitration is more than mere administrative convenience. When the governmental interest served by arbitration is considered in light of the burden placed on the parties, we have no trouble concluding that the Act promotes a legitimate governmental interest and the procedures created by the Act are reasonably related to that interest.

Accordingly, we hold that the Act does not violate the equal protection guarantee of the United States and Colorado Constitutions.

E.

[W]e conclude that the Mandatory Arbitration Act, §§ 13–22–401 to 13–22–409, 6A C.R.S. (1987), does not violate the Colorado Constitution or the United States Constitution. Therefore, we discharge the rule to show cause and direct the district court to proceed with the assignment of the case to arbitration....

■ ERICKSON, JUSTICE, specially concurring:

While I acknowledge that the right of access to the courts is an important one, Colo. Const. art. II, § 6, the burgeoning case load in our courts has itself caused delay and increased costs. Access to the courts for all litigants may be improved by different alternatives for dispute resolution, such as arbitration and mediation. See McKay, The Many Uses of Alternative Dispute Resolution, 40 Arb.J. 12 (Sept. 1985).

In my view, the mandatory arbitration pilot project in issue was a legislative method of reducing delay and providing access to the courts by winnowing out those cases that can be resolved by simpler and less costly methods. It is certainly not obvious to me that the method selected by the legislature will prevent some litigants from obtaining access to the courts. Since a number of cases may be satisfactorily resolved before trial, it would appear that arbitration will actually improve access to the courts. See Levin, Court Annexed Arbitration, 16 J. Law Reform 542 (Spring 1983). Accordingly, I concur in the majority's decision to discharge the rule.

■ LOHR, JUSTICE, dissenting:

I respectfully dissent. The majority holds that the Mandatory Arbitration Act, §§ 13–22–401 to 13–22–409, 6A C.R.S. (1987), violates neither the Colorado Constitution nor the due process or equal protection clauses of the fourteenth amendment to the United States Constitution. Unlike the majority, I am persuaded that the Mandatory Arbitration Act violates the right of every person to obtain access to the courts as guaranteed by article II, section 6, of the Colorado Constitution. I would therefore make the rule issued in this case absolute. Because I would resolve the case on right of access grounds, I would not reach the other constitutional arguments raised by the defendant, Firelock Incorporated.

Article II, section 6, of the Colorado Constitution states:

> Courts of justice shall be open to every person, and a speedy remedy afforded for every injury to person, property or character; and right and justice should be administered without sale, denial or delay.

We have previously recognized that this provision "guarantees to every person the right of access to courts of justice in this state." Board of County Comm'rs v. Barday, 197 Colo. 519, 522, 594 P.2d 1057, 1059 (1979) . . . The constitutional right of access to the courts means "that for any act of another *which constitutes an injurious invasion of any right of the individual which is recognized by or founded upon any applicable principle of law*, statutory or common, the courts shall be open to him and he 'shall have remedy, by due course of law.' " Goldberg v. Musim, 162 Colo. 461, 469, 427 P.2d 698, 702 (1967) (quoting Cason v. Baskin, 20 So.2d 243, 250 (Fla.1944)) (emphasis in original). Article II, section 6, "limits very stringently the power to exclude resident plaintiffs from our court system where jurisdiction has otherwise been properly established." McDonnell–Douglas v. Lohn, 192 Colo. 200, 201, 557 P.2d 373, 374 (1976) (because of article II, section 6, the doctrine of forum non conveniens has only the most limited application in Colorado courts) . . . The lesson of McDonnell–Douglas is that we must carefully scrutinize any innovative procedure, however well intended, that interferes with the fundamental right of every person to obtain access to the courts to obtain redress for their legally cognizable grievances.

[T]he procedure by which a litigant must submit his claim for mandatory arbitration as a condition precedent to trying his case in a court restricts access to the courts in two important ways. First, the litigant may not present his claim to a court until he has undergone the delay[2] and expense attendant to an arbitration proceeding. § 13–22–402(2). Second, in order to obtain access to a court after arbitration has been completed, the litigant must accept the consequence that he will be required to pay the costs of the arbitration proceeding, including arbitrator fees, up to a maximum of $1,000 should he fail to improve his position by more than ten percent. § 13–22–405(3). These burdens of time and expense are considerable and will likely have the practical effect of preventing litigants with smaller claims from ever obtaining access to the courts to assert them. In short, for some litigants these barriers to access to the courts will not simply burden such access but as a practical matter will bar entry into a judicial forum. The majority does not explain why these obviously important limitations on a litigant's fundamental right of access to the courts are permissible except to analogize them to the collection of docket fees, the award of costs to a prevailing party, and the imposition of certain other incidental costs of litigation applicable in special situations. See maj. op. at 1096. The majority simply offers the conclusion that the burdens are reasonable. I cannot agree that it is constitutionally permissible to burden the fundamental right of access to the courts in these significant ways.

In sum, I regard the mandatory arbitration process at issue in this case as limiting access to the courts in a manner that conflicts with both the spirit and the letter of article II, section 6, of the Colorado Constitution. See Aldana v. Holub, 381 So.2d 231, 238 (Fla. 1980) (medical mediation statute violated due process because application of its rigid jurisdictional periods proved arbitrary and capricious, and enlargement of these periods would effectively deprive claimants of access to the courts); People ex rel. Christiansen v. Connell, 2 Ill.2d 332, 118 N.E.2d 262, 265–69 (1954) (statute that imposed mandatory waiting period before divorce action could be filed held to obstruct litigants' constitutional right of access to the courts without delay); State ex rel. Cardinal Glennon Memorial Hosp. v. Gaertner, 583 S.W.2d 107, 110 (Mo. 1979) (statute requiring that medical malpractice claims be referred to medical malpractice review panel before being filed in court held unconstitutional based on fact that it "imposes a procedure" as a precondition to constitutionally established right of access to the courts); Jiron v. Mahlab, 99 N.M. 425, 659 P.2d 311, 313 (1983) (statute requiring medical malpractice claimant to appear before a review commission prior to filing suit deprives plaintiffs of their constitutional right of access to the courts if the review requirement "causes undue delay prejudicing a plaintiff by the loss of witnesses or parties"); cf. Mattos v.

2. The arbitration proceeding "shall be held within ninety days of the date on which the case is at issue between the parties." § 13–22–404(1). "The arbitrators shall file their decision with the court within ten days of the hearing...." § 13–22–404(7). Each party has thirty days after the arbitrators' decision is filed to demand a trial de novo. §§ 13–22–404(8), 13–22–405(1). Thus, the arbitration process is designed to defer resort to the courts for up to 130 days, exclusive of the time required for the hearing itself.

Thompson, 491 Pa. 385, 421 A.2d 190, 195–96 (1980) (striking as unconstitutional a statute giving arbitration panel original jurisdiction over medical malpractice claims where delays involved in statutory procedures oppressively burdened the right to a jury trial so as to "make the right practically unavailable").

In reaching the conclusion that the Mandatory Arbitration Act cannot be squared with the constitutional right of access to the courts, I do not mean to imply that all efforts and methods to resolve disputes outside of the judicial forum violate that constitutional right. I would hold only that the particular mandatory procedure involved in this case imposes constitutionally impermissible burdens on that right. I would therefore make the rule absolute.

* * *

Questions

1. The *Firelock* court distinguished the *Wright* case in which the Illinois Supreme Court found that the medical review procedure empowered nonjudicial members to "exercise a judicial function." Yet under the Illinois procedure at issue in *Wright*, the losing party was entitled to a trial de novo, just as they are under the Colorado procedure. Under the Colorado procedure, do the arbitrators also exercise "judicial functions"? Are there other differences between the Illinois and Colorado procedure that could explain the different results in the two cases?

2. Courts in many states have held that compulsory court-annexed arbitration is only constitutional where the procedures permit a party who had a right to a jury trial to reject the arbitral award and proceed to a de novo trial. See, e.g., Valler v. Lee and Hensley, 949 P.2d 51 (Ariz. App. Div.2 1997); Barazzotto v. Intelligent Systems, Inc., 532 N.E.2d 148 (Ohio App. 1987). Does this mean that parties have an absolute right to a jury trial notwithstanding the existence of a compulsory court-ordered arbitration system, or are there circumstances in which a party can lose that right? For example, would it be constitutional for a court-ordered arbitration procedure to provide that a party who failed to appear in an arbitration forfeited its right to a trial de novo? See, *Williams v. Dorsey*, 652 N.E.2d 1286 (Ill.App., 1st Dist. 1995). Would it be constitutional for a court-ordered arbitration procedure to deny a trial de novo to a party who refused to cooperate in discovery? See Casino Properties, Inc. v. Andrews, 911 P.2d 1181 (Nev.1996).

3. Most state compulsory arbitration procedures specify that the parties must participate in the arbitration in "good faith" or participate in a "meaningful fashion." See, e.g., Illinois Supreme Court Rule 91(b), 145 Ill. 2d R. 91(b) (requiring parties to participate in court-ordered arbitration "in good faith and in a meaningful manner"); Nevada Appellate Rule 22(a) (requiring party to participate in court-ordered arbitration "in good faith."). And most state courts have held that a party who fails to engage in good faith or meaningful participation can be barred from rejecting an award and thereby precluded from a trial de novo. See Middleton v. Baskin, 618 A.2d 1263 (R.I. 1992). Does the possibility of a party being barred from a trial de novo weaken the constitutional basis for such systems?

4. Who decides whether a party participates in "good faith"? Can an arbitrator make that determination? The Illinois statute requires arbitrators to make a finding as to lack of good faith in the first instance, and requires courts to accord that finding presumptive validity. For example, in Allstate Insurance Co. v. Avelares, 693 N.E.2d 1233 (Ill.App. 1st Dist. 1998), the court denied the defendant's motion for de novo review of an adverse arbitral award because the arbitrators had found that the defendant did not appear at the arbitration hearing, and that the appearance by defendant's attorney did not constitute participation in a meaningful manner. Does such a procedure delegate excessive authority to an arbitrator, who can not only decide a case on its merits, but also prevent judicial review by finding the defendant's participation to fall short of good faith?

5. If the issue of good faith participation is determined by a court, on what can a court base its determination? How could a court determine, after the fact, whether a party participated in good faith? Must there be a transcript for a court to find lack of good faith? What kinds of evidence would it need to make such a determination? Can the arbitrator be required to testify about the conduct of the parties? Similarly, if the arbitrator makes the lack of good faith determination in the first instance, how can a court review it if there is no record made of the arbitration proceedings? See West Bend Mutual Insurance Co. v. Herrera, 686 N.E.2d 645 (Ill.App. 1st Dist. 1997). For a discussion of the similar issues that can arise in mediation, see Michael Patrick Dickey, *ADR Gone Wild: Is it Time for a Federal Mediation Exclusionary Rule?* (forthcoming 2010).

6. Both the Illinois and the Colorado court-annexed arbitration statutes involve some degree of fee-shifting for parties who lose at arbitration, request a trial de novo, and then fail to improve their position significantly at trial. Does the additional burden on a party that fee-shifting imposes act as a serious impediment to their right to a judicial resolution of their dispute? Are there other features of the mandatory arbitration procedure that might impede a party's access to the courts?

7. Can a party who lost at court-ordered arbitration obtain a trial de novo on some counts of a complaint but not others? Can the court sever the issues in dispute? Does the grant of a trial de novo vacate the arbitral decision in its entirety, or does it constitute an appeal of the specific issues on which the losing party seeks review? See Action Orthopedics, Inc. v. Techmedica, Inc., 775 F.Supp. 390 (M.D.Fla. 1991); Bridges v. City of Troy, 447 N.Y.S.2d 124 (Sup.Ct. Rensselaer Co. 1982). Would a rule that permits partial appeals operate to undermine the effectiveness of a court-ordered arbitration system? See Watkins v. K–Mart Corp., 1997 WL 597913 (E.D.Pa. 1997).

8. Consider the following hypothetical: As a result of a three-party automobile accident, an injured passenger sued both the driver of the vehicle she was riding in (the "host vehicle") and the driver of the other vehicle (the "stranger vehicle") for negligence. Under a state mandatory court-annexed arbitration procedure, the case was sent to arbitration and the arbitrator found that the driver of the stranger vehicle was negligent and the driver of the host vehicle was not. If the driver of the stranger vehicle rejected the arbitral award and sought a trial de novo, can the driver of the host vehicle, who was exonerated by the arbitration award, move to have the arbitral award in her favor declared final? Stated differently, does the de novo trial have the effect of eliminating the host vehicle's favorable ruling and make her once again potentially liable to the plaintiff? See Valler v. Lee and Hensley, 949 P.2d 51 (Ariz. App.Div.2, 1997).

* * *

4. GOOD FAITH PARTICIPATION

Employer's Consortium, Inc. v. Aaron

698 N.E.2d 189 (Ill.App. 2 Dist. 1998).

■ DOYLE, JUSTICE.

Plaintiffs, Employer's Consortium, Inc., and Cory & Associates, Inc., sued to recover on promissory notes made by defendant, Carrie A. Aaron. The case was referred to mandatory arbitration. The arbitrators found the plaintiffs had not participated in good faith and in a meaningful way pursuant to Supreme Court Rule 91(b) (145 Ill.2d R. 91(b)). Based on this finding, the trial court debarred the plaintiffs from rejecting the arbitrator's award. Plaintiffs appealed the trial court's ruling. We affirm.

Plaintiffs' amended complaint alleged defendant owed approximately $33,000 on 11 separate promissory notes. Defendant's answer admitted making the notes but denied defaulting and asserted several affirmative defenses. Defendant was present with her attorney at the arbitration hearing on January 14, 1997. Plaintiffs were represented by counsel.

Plaintiffs' attorney made an opening statement but did not call any witnesses. The chairperson for the arbitrators offered plaintiffs' attorney the opportunity to contact any potential witnesses. Plaintiffs' attorney declined to call any witnesses and did not request a continuance. Plaintiffs' attorney then rested the case and submitted the unverified complaint along with the attached copies of the promissory notes to the arbitration panel. The arbitration panel made an award in favor of defendant. The arbitration panel also entered a unanimous Rule 91(b) finding that plaintiffs failed to participate in good faith and in a meaningful manner and listed as the factual basis therefore "failure to present any evidence."

On January 31, 1997, defendant filed a motion to bar rejection of arbitration. Defendant attached the affidavit of her attorney in support of the motion. Plaintiffs filed a written response including affidavits from plaintiffs' counsel and Andrew Cory. Plaintiffs' first affidavit stated inter alia that their counsel was informed the night before the arbitration hearing that Andrew Cory, president of the plaintiff corporations, would be unable to attend. The affidavit of Andrew Cory stated that he "was outside the State of Illinois and was unable to attend the arbitration." Defendant's motion to bar rejection was granted on March 11, 1997. Following denial of their motion for reconsideration, plaintiffs appealed.

Plaintiffs present a single issue for review, namely, whether the trial court properly debarred plaintiffs from rejecting the arbitration award based on the panel's finding that the plaintiffs failed to participate in good faith and in a meaningful manner as is required by Rule 91(b).

This issue requires a two-part analysis. First, we must consider whether the trial court's finding that plaintiffs failed to participate in good faith and in a meaningful manner was against the manifest weight of the evidence. Martinez v. Gaimari, 271 Ill.App.3d 879, 883, 208 Ill.Dec. 262, 649 N.E.2d 94 (1995). Second, we must consider whether debarring plaintiffs from rejecting the award was an abuse of discretion. Williams v. Dorsey, 273 Ill.App.3d 893, 901, 210 Ill.Dec. 310, 652 N.E.2d 1286 (1995).

The supreme court adopted Rule 91(b), requiring good-faith participation at mandatory arbitration hearings. That rule provides in pertinent part:

> (b) Good–Faith Participation. All parties to the arbitration hearing must participate in the hearing in good faith and in a meaningful manner. If a panel of arbitrators unanimously finds that a party has failed to participate in the hearing in good faith and in a meaningful manner, the panel's finding and factual basis therefor shall be stated on the award. Such award shall be prima facie evidence that the party failed to participate in the arbitration hearing in good faith and in a meaningful manner and a court, when presented with a petition for sanctions or remedy therefor, may order sanctions as provided in Rule 219(c), including, but not limited to, an order debarring that party from rejecting the award, and costs and attorney fees incurred for the arbitration hearing and in the prosecution of the petition for sanctions, against that party. 145 Ill.2d R. 91(b).

The committee comments to this rule indicate the intent of the rule was to prevent parties and lawyers from abusing the arbitration process by refusing to participate. 145 Ill.2d R. 91, Committee Comments. Arbitration is not to be considered simply a hurdle to cross on the way to trial. 145 Ill.2d R. 91, Committee Comments. The purpose of mandatory arbitration is to subject a case to the type of adversarial testing that would be expected at trial. Martinez, 271 Ill.App.3d at 883–84, 208 Ill.Dec. 262, 649 N.E.2d 94.

Supreme Court Rule 91(b) provides that the finding of an arbitration panel that a party did not participate in good faith is prima facie evidence of that fact. 145 Ill.2d R. 91(b). The party subject to sanctions of Rule 91(b) has the burden of presenting evidence sufficient to rebut the prima facie evidence. Martinez, 271 Ill.App.3d at 883, 208 Ill.Dec. 262, 649 N.E.2d 94 . . .

Here, the record does not provide sufficient evidence to rebut this prima facie finding. On the date of the hearing, plaintiffs' counsel appeared before the arbitration panel. She made a brief opening statement and submitted a copy of the unverified complaint along with the attached exhibits to the arbitrators. The chairperson of the arbitrators then offered plaintiffs' counsel the opportunity to contact any witnesses. Plaintiffs' counsel did not call any witnesses, nor did she request a continuance. The panel then entered an award in favor of defendant and made the unanimous finding that the plaintiffs had failed to participate in good faith and in a meaningful manner as required by Rule 91(b).

Plaintiffs concede that their counsel's performance before the panel was ineffective. Plaintiffs admit in their brief that "[p]laintiffs' counsel may have been unprepared or even inept" and that plaintiffs' presentation "may have been considered sloppy and unprepared participation." Plaintiffs' counsel had several options. For example, she could have requested a continuance to allow witnesses to appear. She could also have examined the defendant, who was present, regarding the notes. Plaintiffs' counsel, however, did nothing and rested her case solely on the complaint.

Plaintiffs did not present evidence to provide the arbitrators with the basis for an award. Even if the unverified complaint and attached exhibits had been accepted by the arbitration panel as evidence, plaintiffs would not have presented a prima facie case. The making of the notes was undisputed. The issues in dispute centered around payment and other affirmative defenses raised by defendant. Plaintiffs presented no evidence regarding payment of the notes and did not address the affirmative defenses. It is highly unlikely that plaintiffs would have proceeded in this manner at trial. This was not the adversarial testing necessary to maintain the integrity of the arbitration process. Martinez, 271 Ill.App.3d at 883–84, 208 Ill.Dec. 262, 649 N.E.2d 94.

Plaintiffs also argue that their participation in the arbitration process was in good faith regardless of its quality. To prevent imposition of a sanction, plaintiffs have the burden of demonstrating that their actions were reasonable or justified by extenuating circumstances. Kubian v. Labinsky, 178 Ill.App.3d 191, 197, 127 Ill.Dec. 404, 533 N.E.2d 22 (1988). The only evidence of extenuating circumstances presented to the trial court was the affidavit of Andrew Cory. The affidavit stated simply that Cory could not attend the arbitration hearing because he was outside the state. Plaintiffs presented no evidence that this was reasonable or the result of extenuating circumstances. Plaintiffs also provided no explanation for counsel's failure to request a continuance when confronted with the absence of plaintiffs' primary witness. Plaintiffs argue that a sanction under Rule 91(b) was inappropriate because although "counsel may have been unprepared or even inept" she did not refuse to participate. We disagree. Rule 91(b) requires parties to participate "in good faith and in a meaningful manner." (Emphasis added.) 145 Ill.2d R. 91(b). A trial court need not find intentional obstruction of the arbitration proceeding. The purposes of Rule 91(b) are defeated whether a party's conduct is the result of inept preparation or intentional disregard for the process. See Martinez, 271 Ill.App.3d at 883, 208 Ill.Dec. 262, 649 N.E.2d 94 (validity of excuse held less important than failure to present evidence).

Finally, plaintiffs argue that the Rule 91(b) finding was deficient because the panel stated as a basis for its findings only the "failure to present any evidence." Without citation to authority plaintiffs argue that the panel's finding failed to provide a sufficient explanation and reasoning. We disagree. Given these facts, the panel's explanation is sufficiently clear to inform plaintiffs of the basis for its finding.

Therefore, after a thorough review of the record, we cannot conclude that the trial court's finding that plaintiffs did not participate in good faith was against the manifest weight of the evidence.

[The court next considered whether the trial court had abused its discretion in debarring plaintiffs from rejecting the award. The court found that it did not, stating:]

It is essential to the integrity of the mandatory arbitration process that the parties proceed at the arbitration hearing in good faith and subject their claims to the sort of adversarial testing that would be expected at trial. Martinez, 271 Ill.App.3d at 883–84, 208 Ill.Dec. 262, 649 N.E.2d 94. A trial court has discretion to enforce supreme court rules and impose sanctions on the parties as appropriate and necessary to promote the unimpeded flow of litigation and maintain the integrity of our court system. Sander v. Dow Chemical Co., 166 Ill.2d 48, 68, 209 Ill.Dec. 623, 651 N.E.2d 1071 (1995). More importantly, Rule 91 specifically allows for an order debarring a party from rejecting the award as a sanction for failure to participate in good faith and in a meaningful manner. Here, having presented no evidence, the plaintiffs failed to participate in the hearing in good faith and in a meaningful manner. It is immaterial whether plaintiffs' failure to participate was the result of lack of preparation or an intentional disregard for the process. The trial court concluded that plaintiffs' actions warranted debarment from rejecting the award as a sanction. We cannot conclude that this was an abuse of the trial court's discretion.

For the foregoing reasons, the judgment of the circuit court of Du Page County is affirmed.

* * *

Questions

1. Does the court in *Employer's Consortium* impose the same test for determining good faith participation in arbitration as it would use for determining whether there was attorney malpractice? Or, does it impose a more demanding test for good faith participation? If it is more demanding, how demanding is it? Does the requirement that parties participate in arbitration in a "meaningful manner" mean that an attorney for a party must be prepared for the hearing? Must she be *well* prepared? How is a court to determine whether there adequate preparation? How is an arbitrator to make such a determination?

2. In *Employer's Consortium*, the Illinois Court of Appeals held, in part, that the statutory requirement of good-faith participation in court-ordered arbitration would be violated by an attorney's intentional disregard of the process *or* "inept preparation." Subsequently, another district of the Illinois Court of Appeals, the 1st District, disagreed with *Employer's Consortium's* "inept preparation" standard and refused to adopt it. Nationwide Mut. Ins. Co. ex rel. Mika v. Kogut, 819 N.E.2d 127 (Ill.App. 2004) (finding "no basis in Illinois law" for the "inept preparation" standard). Why do you think the latter court rejected the "inept preparation standard?"

3. Is attorney negligence a reason to deny a party a right to a trial de novo after an arbitral award? If so, what redress would the party have against the attorney? Could an arbitral finding of lack of meaningful participation constitute evidence of attorney malpractice?

4. Must a party's attorney be an expert in the subject matter of the dispute in order to satisfy the criteria for good faith presentation of the case? Must he be a specialist in the substantive area of law? What if the arbitrator is not an attorney himself, and thus incorrectly adjudges the attorney to be inept? Would such a finding be amenable to judicial review?

5. Suppose it is well-established under the law of a state that a plaintiff in an action to collect on a promissory note need only to produce the note itself and allege nonpayment in order to make out a prima facie case. If such a dispute were sent to a court-ordered arbitration and the plaintiff, through its attorney, makes out a legally sufficient prima facie case in this fashion, can the arbitrator find that the plaintiff did not participate in good faith? Must the party attempt to rebut the defendant's affirmative defense in order to be in good faith? What if the affirmative defense is so lacking in credibility that the plaintiff's attorney decides not to offer a rebuttal? If the arbitrator finds that party did not participate in a meaningful manner, should a court use the arbitral finding as a basis for barring that party from obtaining a trial de novo? How do the facts of *Employer's Consortium* differ from this hypothetical?

* * *

State Farm Insurance Co. v. Kazakova

702 N.E.2d 254 (Ill.App. 2 Dist. 1998).

■ JUSTICE CERDA delivered the opinion of the court:

The issue on appeal is whether a non-English-speaking defendant failed to participate in good faith and in a meaningful manner at a mandatory-arbitration hearing and violated the notice to appear by failing to provide a foreign-language interpreter so she could testify. Defendant, Stella Kazakova, appeals from the orders of the circuit court of Cook County (1) finding that she did not participate in good faith and in a meaningful manner at the mandatory-arbitration hearing and that she violated the notice to appear by not appearing with a foreign-language interpreter; (2) sanctioning her by debarring her from rejecting the arbitration award in favor of plaintiff, State Farm Insurance Company, as subrogee of Robin Depender; and (3) denying her motion to vacate the sanction. We reverse.

Facts

In 1995, plaintiff filed a negligence complaint arising out an automobile collision between the vehicles of Depender and defendant. Defendant filed an answer, denying the allegations of negligence. Defendant also filed a jury demand.

The case was assigned to mandatory arbitration. The hearing was held on September 4, 1996, but the proceedings were not transcribed. The arbitrators entered an award finding in favor of plaintiff and awarding damages. The award stated in part:

> We note for the record that defendant personally appeared pursuant to a proper Rule 237 request but was unable to testify due to her inability to speak and understand English. In addition, we unanimously find that defendant failed to participate in the arbitration hearing in good faith for the following reasons: 1) Failed to produce a witness who was competent to testify; 2) Failed to present any evidence to counter the evidence presented by plaintiff on the issues of liability and damages; 3) Failed to present any evidence whatsoever in defense of the claim.

Defendant filed a notice of rejection of the arbitration award. Plaintiff moved the court to debar defendant from rejecting the mandatory-arbitration award and to enter judgment on the award. The motion was based in part on defendant's failure to testify at the arbitration hearing due to her inability to speak English, her failure to bring an interpreter, and her failure to introduce any evidence in defense. Plaintiff also sought sanctions under Supreme Court Rule 137 (155 Ill.2d R. 137) for filing an answer in bad faith. Defendant opposed the motion, arguing in part that she was not required to bring an interpreter.

On December 30, 1996, the trial court made a finding that, because defendant "fail[ed] to appear" at the arbitration hearing "prepared to testify," she failed to participate in good faith and in a meaningful manner and violated plaintiff's notice to appear. The trial court barred defendant from rejecting the arbitration award, entered judgment on the award in favor of plaintiff, struck defendant's rejection of the arbitration award, and denied plaintiff's motion for Supreme Court Rule 137 sanctions.

Defendant filed a motion to vacate judgment, which was denied. Defendant appealed.

DISCUSSION

Defendant argues that (1) defendant's failure to speak English was not a failure to participate in good faith and in a meaningful manner and was not a violation of the notice to appear at the arbitration[, and] (2) it was an excessive sanction to debar defendant from rejecting the arbitration award . . .

The arbitration in this case was scheduled pursuant to supreme court rules establishing a nonbinding, court-annexed arbitration system to resolve certain civil actions. 134 Ill.2d Rs. 86 through 95; Introductory Comments, at 86. Applicable to mandatory-arbitration hearings is Supreme Court Rule 237, which provides that the appearance at the trial of a party may be required by serving her with a notice. 166 Ill.2d Rs. 90(g), 237. Supreme Court Rule 90(g) provides as follows:

> The provisions of Rule 237, herein, shall be equally applicable to arbitration hearings as they are to trials.... Remedies upon a party's failure to comply with notice pursuant to Rule 237(b) may include an order debarring that party from rejecting the award. 166 Ill.2d R. 90(g).

Supreme Court Rule 91(b) provides a standard for parties' conduct at the arbitration hearings:

> All parties to the arbitration hearing must participate in the hearing in good faith and in a meaningful manner. If a panel of arbitrators unanimously finds that a party has failed to participate in the hearing in good faith and in a meaningful manner, the panel's finding and factual basis therefor shall be stated on the award. Such award shall be prima facie evidence that the party failed to participate in the arbitration hearing in good faith and in a meaningful manner and a court, when presented with a petition for sanctions or remedy therefor, may order sanctions as provided in Rule 219(c), including, but not limited to, an order debarring that party from rejecting the award, and costs and attorney fees incurred for the arbitration hearing and in the prosecution of the petition for sanctions, against that party. 145 Ill.2d R. 91(b).

A party can reject the arbitration award and proceed to trial. 174 Ill.2d R. 93(a) . . .

The express concerns behind Supreme Court Rule 91(b) are to prevent the abuse of the arbitration process and to uphold the integrity of the arbitration process. 145 Ill.2d R. 91(b), Committee Comments, at lxx. Defendant did not choose not to participate; she was not able to participate without an interpreter. In order to meet the standard of good-faith and meaningful participation, a defendant does not have to hire an interpreter to assist plaintiff's efforts to prove its case. If a defendant does not provide an interpreter and a plaintiff desires to examine defendant as an adverse witness, plaintiff should bear the cost of an interpreter. We hold that defendant did not violate Supreme Court Rule 91(b) by not providing an interpreter . . .

If a defendant does not notify plaintiff that defendant will not be able to testify in English and that defendant will not provide an interpreter at the arbitration hearing, plaintiff would not be made aware of the need to arrange its own interpreter to be present, if desired. Certainly that lack of notification would be a breach of civility; it might be successfully argued in a future case that such conduct also could form the basis for Supreme Court Rule 91(b) sanctions. We do not know on this record if plaintiff was aware prior to the hearing of defendant's inability to testify in English. We do not decide today whether the failure to notify would violate Supreme Court Rule 91(b).

Even if we held that defendant should have provided an interpreter as part of her good-faith and meaningful participation in arbitration, we would reverse on the basis that debarring defendant from rejecting the arbitration award was harsh and unjustified. The arbitration proceedings could have been stayed until defendant provided an interpreter, and plaintiff could have been awarded attorney fees and costs incurred for the arbitration hearing. 145 Ill.2d R. 91(b); see 166 Ill.2d R. 219(c)(i) (one possible remedy is to stay further proceedings until the party complies with the supreme court rule).

In addition, we believe that the standard to be applied in deciding whether to bar defendant from rejecting the award is whether her conduct was characterized by a deliberate and pronounced disregard for rules and the court. Walton v. Throgmorton, 273 Ill.App.3d 353, 359, 210 Ill.Dec. 1, 652 N.E.2d 803 (1995); Valdivia v. Chicago & North Western Transportation Co., 87 Ill.App.3d 1123, 1125, 42 Ill.Dec. 842, 409 N.E.2d 457 (1980). Defendant was present and available to testify at the arbitration hearing. She could have been examined by plaintiff if a Russian-language interpreter had been present . . .

As defendant did not violate Supreme Court Rule 91(b) or 237, the trial court erred in barring her from rejecting the arbitration award. The judgment of the trial court is reversed, and the cause is remanded with directions to permit defendant to reject the arbitration award.

Reversed with directions.

* * *

Questions

1. In *Employer's Consortium*, the mere presence of a party or its attorney at a court-ordered arbitration hearing was not sufficient to constitute good faith. Rather, the court held that the party or its attorney must actually participate "in a meaningful way." Why then is the mere presence of the defendant sufficient to satisfy the requirement of good faith in *State Farm Insurance?*

2. In *State Farm Insurance,* the court found that it was not incumbent upon the non-English-speaking defendant to provide an interpreter, even though an interpreter was necessary to permit her to participate in the hearing. Without an interpreter, such a party can neither present her own case, nor be subject to cross-examination. If the plaintiff in *State Farm Insurance* had appeared alone and had not had a English-speaking lawyer to present her case on her behalf, would the arbitrators have been justified in finding a lack of meaningful participation? Should it be grounds to debar her from seeking a trial de novo? What other problems might follow from such a result?

3. The court in *State Farm Insurance* stated that the standard to be applied in deciding whether to bar defendant from rejecting the award is "whether her conduct was characterized by a deliberate and pronounced disregard for rules and the court." Is this standard consistent with the standard that the court applied in *Employer's Consortium*?

4. Are parties are likely to behave differently in court-annexed arbitration than they are in binding arbitration proceedings? How, and why? See Christopher R. Drahozal, *Arbitration Costs and Forum Accessibility: Empirical Evidence*, 41 U. Mich. J.L. Reform 813, 841 (2008).

* * *

5. FINALITY OF AWARDS

Flynn v. Gorton

255 Cal.Rptr. 768 (Cal.App. 4th Dist., Div. 3 1989).

■ SCOVILLE, PRESIDING JUSTICE.

The trial court sustained a demurrer to John Flynn's cross-complaint without leave to amend after determining that a prior judicial arbitration award against Flynn was res judicata. Because we hold a judicial arbitration award has no conclusive effect on issues raised in a subsequent proceeding on a different cause of action, we reverse the judgment. As we shall explain, Flynn's action was not barred by res judicata because his cross-complaint stated a different cause of action than that involved in the judicial arbitration proceeding. Nor was Flynn barred under the doctrine of collateral estoppel from relitigating issues already resolved in the arbitration. Since we believe the monetary limits on judicial arbitration, along with the option of trial de novo, combine to dampen a defendant's incentive to litigate the issues, application of collateral estoppel to such a proceeding would be unfair and unexpected by the parties. More importantly, it could impair the efficiency and impede the purpose of the judicial arbitration system.

Facts

John Flynn and Achilda Gorton were involved in an automobile accident in 1983. Flynn was turning left and Gorton was entering the intersection when their cars collided. Kim Blackburn was a passenger in Gorton's car.

Gorton brought a personal injury suit against Flynn, alleging his negligence caused the collision. Flynn generally denied the allegation and claimed Gorton's negligence contributed to the accident.

Gorton elected to submit the case to arbitration and agreed that any award would not exceed $25,000. The arbitrator awarded her $20,281.08 in full settlement of her claims. The award became a final judgment which Flynn satisfied in full.

Blackburn then filed a personal injury complaint against Flynn and Gorton, alleging both were negligent. Flynn cross-complained against Gorton for implied indemnity, contribution and declaratory relief. He alleged Blackburn's injuries resulted from Gorton's negligence in causing the accident and he was entitled to a determination of each party's comparative negligence and an apportionment of damages.

Gorton demurred to Flynn's cross-complaint, arguing it was barred under the doctrine of res judicata because it presented the same claim decided in the judicial arbitration action. She asked the court to take judicial notice of the court files, the arbitrator's award, and his cover letter explaining the award. The award was silent as to the arbitrator's reasons for the decision. However, in the arbitrator's cover letter, he stated: "[O]nce I had completed the application of very basic accident reconstruction principals [sic] . . ., it became very clear that the issue of liability was no issue at all, and very clearly in favor of the plaintiff."

Flynn opposed the demurrer, arguing his cross-complaint for indemnity raised a new issue. The trial court sustained Gorton's demurrer without leave to amend.

On appeal Flynn argues the issue raised in his cross-complaint, i.e. whether Gorton was partially responsible for her passenger's injuries, was not addressed in the arbitration action. He contends the arbitration award did not resolve whether: (1) under comparative fault principles, Gorton was responsible in part for the collision and thus for Blackburn's injuries; and (2) whether Gorton otherwise contributed to her passenger's injuries, e.g. by failing to have seat belts or by somehow aggravating Blackburn's injuries after the collision. Flynn asserts the arbitration award and court file are silent on the issue of the parties' comparative fault in causing the collision, and it may be that the approximately $20,000 award to Gorton reflected an offset for her contributory negligence. He argues under these circumstances his action was not barred by res judicata.

Discussion

The doctrine of res judicata is composed of two parts: claim preclusion and issue preclusion. Claim preclusion prohibits a party from relitigating a previously adjudicated cause of action; thus, a new lawsuit on the same cause of action is entirely barred. (Frommhagen v. Board of Supervisors (1987) 197 Cal.App.3d 1292, 1299–1300, 243 Cal.Rptr. 390.) Issue preclusion, or collateral estoppel, applies to a subsequent suit between the parties on a different cause of action. Collateral estoppel prevents the parties from relitigating any *issue* which was actually litigated and finally decided in the earlier action. (Carroll v. Puritan Leasing Co. (1978) 77 Cal.App.3d 481, 490, 143 Cal.Rptr. 772.) The issue decided in the earlier proceeding must be identical to the one presented in the subsequent action. If there is any doubt, collateral estoppel will not apply. (Southwell v. Mallery, Stern & Warford (1987) 194 Cal.App.3d 140, 144, 239 Cal.Rptr. 371.)

Res judicata and collateral estoppel share common goals. Both prevent inconsistent results and promote finality and judicial economy by bringing an end to litigation.

Judicial arbitration was enacted by the Legislature in 1978 to serve similar ends. Due to the cost, complexity and delay involved in court adjudication, the Legislature declared that arbitration should be encouraged or required as "an efficient and equitable method for resolving small claims." (Code Civ.Proc., § 1141.10, subd. (a).) Under the statute, court-ordered arbitration is mandatory in certain courts for civil actions in which the amount in controversy does not exceed a specified amount. (Code Civ.Proc., § 1141.11.) Such arbitration can also be elected by stipulation of the parties or by the unilateral decision of the plaintiff if he or she agrees that any award will not exceed the statutory amount. (Code Civ.Proc., § 1141.12.)

Unlike commercial or true arbitration, judicial arbitration is not binding, since any party dissatisfied with an award may elect trial de novo.[2] (Code Civ.Proc., § 1141.20.) The Legislature, however, seeking to encourage finality of judicial arbitration awards, enacted disincentives to trial de novo. (See Demirgian v. Superior Court (1986) 187 Cal.App.3d 372, 376, 231 Cal.Rptr. 698.) For example, if a party requesting trial de novo does not obtain a more favorable judgment, he or she is liable for significant costs and fees. (Code Civ.Proc., § 1141.21.)

Discouraging trial de novo is essential to the proper functioning of the judicial arbitration system. Along with its goal of resolving small claims efficiently and affordably, judicial arbitration is intended to ease court caseloads. (Kanowitz, Alternative Dispute Resolution and the Public Interest: The Arbitration Experience (1987) 38 Hastings L.J. 239, 292.) The success of judicial arbitration in achieving these goals is dependent on a small incidence of trial de novo election. (Id. at p. 293.)

If trial de novo is not requested within the statutory period, a judicial arbitration award becomes final and is not subject to appeal. (Code Civ. Proc., § 1141.23.) There is no question the Legislature intended the award, once final, to be a binding resolution of the particular cause of action. Code of Civil Procedure section 1141.23 provides that a final award shall have "the same force and effect as a judgment in any civil action or proceeding,"

2. As was said by this court in Dodd v. Ford (1984) 153 Cal.App.3d 426, 432, fn. 7, 200 Cal.Rptr. 256, " 'Judicial Arbitration' is obviously an inapt term, for the system it describes is neither judicial nor arbitration. The hearing is not [necessarily] conducted by a judge, and the right to a trial de novo removes the finality of true arbitration. 'Extrajudicial mediation' would be closer to correct."

except that it shall not be subject to appeal and generally may not be attacked or set aside. Accordingly, a final judicial arbitration award, if clear and unambiguous, is res judicata in any subsequent proceeding on the same cause of action.

In the instant case, Flynn's indemnity action would have been barred if it had stated the same cause of action as Gorton's arbitrated negligence claim. The two proceedings, however, did not involve the same cause of action. Gorton's negligence claim involved her primary right to be free of personal injury, whereas this action concerns Flynn's right to equitable indemnity against third party damages. (See Slater v. Blackwood (1975) 15 Cal.3d 791, 795, 126 Cal.Rptr. 225, 543 P.2d 593; Busick v. Workmen's Comp. Appeals Bd. (1972) 7 Cal.3d 967, 975, 104 Cal.Rptr. 42, 500 P.2d 1386.) Thus, Flynn's action was not barred under the cause preclusion aspect of res judicata.

Collateral estoppel is equally inapplicable here, but for different reasons. It would be unfair and unwise to give collateral estoppel effect to judicially arbitrated resolutions of issues. To begin with, as this case well illustrates, there are practical difficulties. No record is made of arbitration proceedings and generally no findings of fact or conclusions of law are required. (Cal.Rules of Court, rules 1614, 1615.) Thus, it is difficult to determine from the award alone what issues were actually litigated and how they were resolved.

Even if this difficulty could be surmounted, it is unfair to bind the parties to judicially arbitrated resolutions of issues. The doctrine of collateral estoppel is based on the premise that a thorough fact-finding process was completed in the first proceeding. (Shell, Res Judicata and Collateral Estoppel Effects of Commercial Arbitration (1988) 35 UCLA L.Rev. 623, 648.) However, in judicial arbitration, the low monetary amount in controversy and the option of trial de novo can leave parties without a serious incentive to litigate. Because the stakes involved are low, the parties may be willing to accept a compromise position without much of a fight. (See Mahon v. Safeco Title Ins. Co. (1988) 199 Cal.App.3d 616, 622, 245 Cal.Rptr. 103.)

Moreover, it is unlikely parties would expect a judicial arbitration award to have collateral estoppel effect in other proceedings where the stakes may be higher than they were in the arbitration proceeding. If they did, the result might be intensified litigation, delays and costs, as well as an increased rate of trial de novo election. Such a development would be directly contrary to the purposes underlying judicial arbitration legislation.

In summary, we hold that judicial arbitration awards should be accorded claim preclusion, but not issue preclusion, effect.

Accordingly, we reverse the trial court's judgment and remand this matter for further proceedings in light of the views expressed herein.

* * *

Questions

1. Why does the court say there is a different standard for collateral estoppel in court-ordered arbitration than in private arbitration? To what extent does the court rely on alleged deficiencies in the arbitration process to reach its conclusion? To what extent does it rely on the expectations of the parties? How could these concerns be answered?

2. Shortly after *Gorton* was decided, another district of the California Court of Appeals held that issues decided in judicial/court-ordered arbitration *can* have collateral estoppel effect. *State Farm Mut. Auto. Ins. Co. v. Superior Court,* 259 Cal.Rptr. 50 (Cal.App. 2 Dist. 1989) (holding that issues decided in judicial arbitration/court-ordered arbitration are entitled to collateral estoppel effect as long as the award "actually, necessarily and finally" resolved the issue on which collateral estoppel is sought). Which is the better approach?

* * *

Habick v. Liberty Mutual Fire Insurance Co.

320 N.J.Super. 244, 727 A.2d 51 (App.Div. 1999).

■ WECKER, J.A.D.

Plaintiff, Rosemarie Habick, appeals from Law Division orders denying her application to vacate or modify a PIP arbitrator's determination that certain medical treatment was not required as a result of accident-related injuries, see N.J.S.A. 39:6A–4, and declaring that plaintiff would be bound by that ruling in her pending UM [Uninsured Motorist] arbitration arising out of the same accident. We conclude that the Law Division Judge erred only in denying modification of the award to exclude issues not before the arbitrator, and we otherwise affirm the orders appealed from.

After plaintiff's 1992 automobile accident, her PIP carrier, Liberty Mutual Fire Insurance Company, paid for treatment of a knee injury and a TMJ condition through 1995 and approved arthroscopic surgery on her right knee. When plaintiff's treating physician later recommended knee replacement in lieu of the arthroscopic procedure, Liberty denied payment on the basis of its own medical examiner's report. Plaintiff then filed for arbitration of her PIP claim, as permitted by N.J.S.A. 39:6A–5h. Because the other driver was uninsured, plaintiff also filed for uninsured motorist coverage, and her UM arbitration was pending at the time she sought relief from the PIP arbitrator's decision. The UM arbitrators adjourned any hearing pending the final outcome of the PIP arbitration.

The PIP arbitrator denied plaintiff's claim for further TMJ treatment as well as the knee replacement surgery, finding that neither treatment was warranted by a condition caused by the accident . . .

[T]he PIP arbitrator's award does not refer to the pending UM arbitration.

Habick, obviously recognizing the potentially binding effect of the PIP arbitration upon her UM claim, filed a verified complaint in the Law Division seeking a judgment either vacating the award or, in the alternative, modifying the award to limit its scope to the issues submitted, and "to reflect that it be without prejudice to any claim plaintiff may have outside the scope of the PIP arbitration proceedings."

There is no dispute that plaintiff suffered from osteoarthritis of both knees prior to the accident. Two factual issues were submitted to and decided by the PIP arbitrator, each of which is potentially before the UM arbitrators. The first is whether the accident aggravated the condition of plaintiff's right knee, thereby necessitating knee replacement surgery, or whether the deterioration of plaintiff's osteoarthritic knee instead reflected the natural progression of the disease and was unrelated to the accident. The second factual issue decided by the PIP arbitrator that is potentially before the UM arbitrator(s) is whether this accident was a proximate cause of Habick's continuing TMJ symptoms. The PIP arbitrator ruled that it was not.

In denying relief to Habick from the PIP arbitration award, the Law Division Judge wrote:

> [T]he arbitrator found that Liberty was not responsible for any *additional* treatment.... [T]he arbitrator gave a factual basis for reaching his conclusion. It is based on those findings that the plaintiff seeks to overturn the arbitrator's award. The court has reviewed the submissions of counsel and the findings of the arbitrator and can find no evidence that this arbitrator in the instant case exceeded his power. There is nothing in the record before the court to reflect that [the arbitrator], who had the benefit of the testimony of the plaintiff and her witnesses as well as all relevant medical evidence, made a finding that was with a gross, unmistakable or manifest disregard to the applicable law of this state.

The judge also denied plaintiff's motion for reconsideration, writing with respect to the binding effect of the PIP arbitration:

> As to whether the findings of [the PIP arbitrator] are binding on the U.M. arbitrator, the court finds in the affirmative. The plaintiff in her P.I.P. arbitration submitted all facets of her case most favorable to her position for the arbitrator's consideration. A finding was made by the arbitrator and since there are no new facts to be considered by the U.M. arbitrator, the decision of [the arbitrator] is binding on all issues he ruled on in presenting his findings.

I

There are two separate questions before us. The first question is whether the judge erred in refusing to vacate or modify the arbitration award. We are aware of no reported case addressing the standard of review applicable to a motion to vacate a PIP arbitration award (or opposition to confirming that award).

There can be little doubt that arbitration is a favored means of dispute resolution. See, e.g., United Services Auto. Ass'n v. Turck, 156 N.J. 480, 486, 721 A.2d 1 (1998). The Arbitration Act, N.J.S.A. 2A:24–1 et seq., enacted in 1923, provides narrow grounds for vacating an arbitration award:

> The court shall vacate the award in any of the following cases:
>
> a. Where the award was procured by corruption, fraud or undue means;
>
> b. Where there was either evident partiality or corruption in the arbitrators, or any thereof;
>
> c. Where the arbitrators were guilty of misconduct in refusing to postpone the hearing, upon sufficient cause being shown therefor, or in refusing to hear evidence, pertinent and material to the controversy, or of any other misbehaviors prejudicial to the rights of any party;
>
> d. Where the arbitrators exceeded or so imperfectly executed their powers that a mutual, final and definite award upon the subject matter submitted was not made.

[N.J.S.A. 2A:24–8]

Neither party to this appeal suggests that the Act is inapplicable to PIP arbitration, which was enacted as part of the 1983 amendments to the New Jersey Automobile Reparation Reform Act, N.J.S.A. 39:6A–1 et seq.

Permissible grounds for modifying an arbitration award are set forth in N.J.S.A. 2A:24–9. They include circumstances "Where the arbitrators awarded upon a matter not submitted to them unless it affects the merit of the decision upon the matter submitted ..." Id., § b. In that event, "The court shall modify and correct the award, to effect the intent thereof and promote justice between the parties." Id.

A majority of the Supreme Court further narrowed the scope of review under the Arbitration Act with respect to an award reached by voluntary contractual arbitration among private parties. Tretina Printing, Inc. v. Fitzpatrick and Assoc., Inc., 135 N.J. 349, 358, 640 A.2d 788 (1994) (4–3 decision) (quoting Perini Corp. v. Greate Bay Hotel & Casino Inc., 129 N.J. 479, 548–49, 610 A.2d 364 (1992) (Wilentz, J. concurring)):

> Basically, arbitration awards may be vacated only for fraud, corruption, or similar wrongdoing on the part of the arbitrators. [They] can be corrected or modified only for very specifically defined mistakes as set forth in [N.J.S.A. 2A:24–9]. *If the arbitrators decide a matter not even submitted to them, that matter can be excluded from the award.* [Emphasis added.]

There is no allegation of "fraud, corruption, or similar wrongdoing on the part of" this arbitrator. Later in this opinion we will address the matter not submitted to the arbitrator.

The Tretina majority carefully circumscribed the exceptions on policy grounds that would permit a broader review of private, voluntary arbitration:

> Finally, . . . we add our recognition that in rare circumstances a court may vacate an arbitration award for public-policy reasons. For example, in Faherty v. Faherty, 97 N.J. 99, 477 A.2d 1257 (1984), we held that "whenever the validity of an arbitration award affecting child support is questioned on the grounds that it does not provide adequate protection for the child, the trial court should conduct a special review of the award." Id. at 109, 477 A.2d 1257. That heightened judicial scrutiny is required because of the courts' traditional role as *parens patria*. Id. at 111, 477 A.2d 1257.

[135 N.J. at 364, 640 A.2d at 788.]

PIP arbitration justifies neither a public policy exception nor one based on the courts' *parens patria* responsibility . . .

[P]laintiff seeks a review standard comparable to the substantial-credible-evidence test applicable to judicial or to administrative agency fact findings . . .

Plaintiff's reliance upon a comparison between PIP arbitration and public sector arbitration of any kind is misplaced. Parties may be subject to mandatory public-sector arbitration either to reach a collective bargaining agreement involving a public entity—so-called "interest arbitration," e.g., Division 540, supra, 76 N.J. 245, 386 A.2d 1290—or to resolve certain labor disputes arising under such a collective bargaining agreement—"grievance arbitration," e.g., Scotch Plains–Fanwood Bd. of Educ. v. Scotch Plains–Fanwood Educ. Ass'n, 139 N.J. 141, 651 A.2d 1018 (1995).[4] The substantial-credible-evidence standard of review, applicable only to interest arbitration, has its rationale in entirely different circumstances than those underlying PIP arbitration. See Division 540 supra, 76 N.J. at 253–54, 386 A.2d 1290:

> The statute subjects the development Authority to compulsory and binding arbitration. Because it is compulsory, principles of fairness, perhaps even due process, require that judicial review be available to ensure that the award is not arbitrary or capricious and that the arbitrator has not abused the power and authority delegated to him . . .
>
> We conclude that when, as here, the arbitration process is compulsory, the judicial review should extend to consideration of whether the

4. "Interest" arbitration . . . involves the submission of a dispute concerning the terms of a new contract to an arbitrator, who selects those terms and thus in effect writes the parties' collective agreement. It is to be distinguished from "grievance" arbitration, which is a method of resolving differences concerning the interpretation, application, or violation of an already existing contract. [New Jersey State P.B.A., Local 29, 80 N.J. at 284, 403 A.2d 473 (citations omitted) (explaining history and scope of public sector interest arbitration).]

award is supported by substantial credible evidence present in the record . . .

The rationale for the broader public sector standards of review is essentially bottomed on fairness to the parties, for whom arbitration of collective bargaining agreements is compulsory, e.g., New Jersey State P.B.A., Local 29, 80 N.J. at 294, 403 A.2d 473; the public's interest in avoiding violations of law or public policy; and protection of the public welfare . . . [Citations omitted.] Plaintiff would have us conclude that the same rationale requires a broader standard of review when an insuror seeks to vacate or modify a PIP arbitration award.

Plaintiff reasons that because only the insured, and not the insuror, can choose to arbitrate a PIP claim, the insuror should not be limited by the Tretina standard. From that proposition, plaintiff argues that it would be unfair and contrary to the policy of encouraging PIP arbitration to apply a stricter standard of review to the insured than to the insuror; therefore a broader standard of review should apply to all PIP arbitration.

We assume that the same standard of review should apply irrespective of which party is dissatisfied with a PIP arbitration's outcome, cf. Division 540, supra, 76 N.J. at 253 n. 4, 386 A.2d 1290. Because PIP arbitration elected by the insured becomes mandatory for the carrier, plaintiff would have us view the carrier's challenge to an arbitration award as if it were the result of mandatory public sector arbitration. While that contention may have some facial validity, closer examination leads us to a different view. We reject plaintiff's premise that it would be unfair to subject the insuror to the limited Tretina standard of review.

Although the terms of PIP coverage, including the insured's right to elect arbitration, are mandated by statute, the carrier's participation in this market, circumscribed as it is by state law, is nevertheless voluntary. The PIP carrier has entered into a contract with its insured. Moreover, unlike the insured, whose interest lies in the outcome of a single PIP arbitration, the carrier's interest lies more in a predictable, consistent procedure and scope of review applicable across the board to all of the PIP arbitrations it faces. While a broader standard might allow the carrier to prevail in vacating certain arbitration awards it deems erroneous, such a standard would also jeopardize the finality of those awards the carrier deems favorable.

Additionally, to allow a substantial-credible-evidence test of a PIP award would require a verbatim record, with the attendant expense and delay that PIP arbitration is intended to avoid. The net result would be to defeat the overall purpose of, and public policy behind, PIP arbitration: to provide a prompt, efficient, and inexpensive means of dispute resolution that will minimize and not maximize resort to the courts. We therefore see no fundamental unfairness in holding both sides to the limited scope of review mandated by Tretina. We are satisfied that PIP arbitration warrants no different standard. Thus to the extent that plaintiff's contention is that the arbitrator was wrong because he believed the wrong expert, her appeal from the confirmed award is without merit.

However, we agree with plaintiff that the Law Division Judge erred in failing to recognize that the arbitrator's award went beyond the scope of his authority and therefore warrants modification . . . [The court concluded that the arbitrators decided certain medical issues that had not been presented.]

Therefore, to the extent the arbitrator's award purported to make findings with respect to issues other than the total knee replacement procedure and continued TMJ treatment after the cut-off date, the award must be modified to exclude those findings as beyond the scope of the arbitrator's authority.

II

Because we affirm the order effectively confirming the arbitration award as modified, we address the second issue raised by this appeal: whether the PIP award bars relitigation of medical causation in plaintiff's anticipated UM arbitration. Had plaintiff sought a determination of PIP benefits in a non-jury proceeding before the court, as permitted by N.J.S.A. 39:6A–5(c), rather than opting for PIP arbitration, she would be bound in a subsequent suit against a third-party tortfeasor by a final judgment dismissing her claim for failure to prove that injuries caused by the accident warranted the treatment requested. See Kozlowski v. Smith, 193 N.J.Super. 672, 674–75, 475 A.2d 663 (App.Div.1984) (prior PIP litigation denying benefits after finding no medical causation bars relitigation of causation in subsequent personal injury action.) We see no reason why prior PIP litigation should be any less binding in a subsequent UM arbitration than it would be in a subsequent personal injury lawsuit . . .

We look to the underlying principles of collateral estoppel, which the motion judge invoked to declare that the PIP arbitrator's determination with respect to causation would bind plaintiff in her anticipated UM arbitration. As Habick correctly contends, New Jersey follows the Restatement (Second) of Judgments respecting collateral estoppel . . .

Section 27 of the Restatement sets forth the basic rule of collateral estoppel:

> When an issue of fact or law is actually litigated and determined by a valid and final judgment, and the determination is essential to the judgment, the determination is conclusive in a subsequent action between the parties, whether on the same or a different claim.

The guiding principle is that the party to be bound had a "full and fair opportunity to litigate the issue" in the earlier proceeding. There can be no question that plaintiff had the opportunity in a PIP arbitration to present all of the evidence respecting causation that she could bring in a UM arbitration. Moreover, plaintiff chose to resolve her PIP claim in the arbitration forum and not in court. Although plaintiff's PIP and UM claims seek different remedies, the parties are identical, and several issues of medical causation that will arise in the UM arbitration were decided in the PIP arbitration. In considering the preclusive effect of an arbitration, we are guided largely by fairness and by the Restatement. Nogue, supra, 224

N.J.Super. at 386, 540 A.2d 889. There is nothing inherently unfair in giving that arbitration decision, once final, preclusive effect.

In other contexts, an arbitration award has been given preclusive effect in a subsequent judicial proceeding, so long as the party to be bound had the opportunity to make its case in the arbitration. See, e.g., Konieczny v. Micciche, 305 N.J.Super. 375, 384–87, 702 A.2d 831 (App.Div. 1997) (new home purchaser suing home inspector in negligence is bound by facts previously found in arbitration against the builder under New Home Warranty & Builders' Registration Act, N.J.S.A. 46:3B–1 et seq.) . . .

Section 84 of the Restatement specifically addresses the preclusive effect of an arbitration award:

> (1) Except as stated in Subsection (2), (3), and (4), a valid and final award by arbitration has the same effects under the rules of res judicata, subject to the same exceptions and qualifications, as a judgment of a court.
>
> (2) An award by arbitration with respect to a claim does not preclude relitigation of the same or a related claim based on the same transaction if a scheme of remedies permits assertion of the second claim notwithstanding the award regarding the first claim.
>
> (3) A determination of an issue in arbitration does not preclude relitigation of that issue if:
>
> (a) According preclusive effect to determination of the issue would be incompatible with a legal policy or contractual provision that the tribunal in which the issue subsequently arises be free to make an independent determination of the issue in question, or with a purpose of the arbitration agreement that the arbitration be specially expeditious; or
>
> (b) The procedure leading to the award lacked the elements of adjudicatory procedure prescribed in § 83(2).
>
> (4) If the terms of an agreement to arbitrate limit the binding effect of the award in another adjudication or arbitration proceeding, the extent to which the award has conclusive effect is determined in accordance with that limitation.

Habick does not suggest that "a scheme of [auto insurance] remedies" permits her to relitigate causation. The questions raised by her arguments are whether "a legal policy or contractual provision" specific to the UM arbitration, or the "purpose . . . that the [PIP] arbitration be especially expeditious," or an absence of procedural safeguards in the PIP arbitration warrant an exception to the general rule of preclusion.

Plaintiff cites the legislative intent to provide speedy resolution of medical claims for injured parties as a public interest policy basis for excepting PIP awards from the preclusive effect of collateral estoppel, apparently relying on Restatement § 84(3)(a). Habick also contends that the PIP and UM arbitration procedures are significantly different, and that PIP arbitration therefore does not warrant preclusive effect under § 84(3)(b). The procedures in each case are governed by a set of rules promulgated by the American Arbitration Association. Whereas § 8 of the

PIP rules provides for a single arbitrator in all cases, § 8 of the UM rules permits either party to request a panel of three arbitrators if both "the amount claimed and available coverage limits exceed" the statutory minimum. Whereas review of a PIP arbitration award is limited by statute and case law, as discussed in Part I of this opinion, UM arbitration review, governed by the insurance generally provides for de novo proceedings in the Law Division when the award exceeds the statutory minimum and either partly rejects the award. See Craig and Pomeroy, New Jersey Auto Insurance Law, § 23:3–3 (1998).

We are not persuaded that these differences are material. We find no legal policies implicated by UM arbitration that would be infringed or hindered by giving the PIP arbitration preclusive effect. Nor does plaintiff provide us with any basis in the UM provision of plaintiff's insurance contract to warrant an exception . . .

The PIP arbitration challenged here reasonably met the standards set forth in the Restatement, §§ 27, 28, and 84 to warrant preclusion. The policies behind the doctrine of collateral estoppel—fairness, finality, and judicial economy—are all served by giving preclusive effect to the confirmed PIP arbitrator's decision (as modified) that neither Habick's claimed need for knee replacement nor her TMJ syndrome were a proximate result of this automobile accident.

III

In light of our conclusion that Habick is bound by the judgment confirming the PIP arbitrator's decision, the scope of that decision must be clear. Habick is barred in the UM arbitration (or any personal injury litigation arising out of this accident) from alleging future pain and suffering, or loss of enjoyment or earnings, due to projected knee replacement surgery. She is not, however, foreclosed from offering evidence of aggravation of the preexisting arthritic condition of her right knee, and pain and suffering related to treatment for that aggravation, short of total knee replacement surgery . . .

As modified, we affirm the orders appealed from.

* * *

Questions

1. Does the *Habick* court disagree with the *Flynn v. Gorton* court about the relevant factors to use in determining whether to give an arbitral award collateral estoppel effect? Or is the difference in the two approaches a result of the two courts' different assessments of the values and due process protections available in arbitration?

2. Why does the *Habick* court reject the plaintiff's argument that there should be a higher level of judicial review for court-ordered arbitration than for private arbitration? What other arguments might the plaintiff have made to support her position?

* * *

Appendix A

The Federal Arbitration Act

9 U.S.C. Title 9, 61 STAT. 669, 9 USC § 1 et. seq.

Sec. 1. "Maritime transactions" and "commerce" defined; exceptions to operation of title

"Maritime transactions", as herein defined, means charter parties, bills of lading of water carriers, agreements relating to wharfage, supplies furnished vessels or repairs to vessels, collisions, or any other matters in foreign commerce which, if the subject of controversy, would be embraced within admiralty jurisdiction; "commerce", as herein defined, means commerce among the several States or with foreign nations, or in any Territory of the United States or in the District of Columbia, or between any such Territory and another, or between any such Territory and any State or foreign nation, or between the District of Columbia and any State or Territory or foreign nation, but nothing herein contained shall apply to contracts of employment of seamen, railroad employees, or any other class of workers engaged in foreign or interstate commerce.

Sec. 2. Validity, irrevocability, and enforcement of agreements to arbitrate

A written provision in any maritime transaction or a contract evidencing a transaction involving commerce to settle by arbitration a controversy thereafter arising out of such contract or transaction, or the refusal to perform the whole or any part thereof, or an agreement in writing to submit to arbitration an existing controversy arising out of such a contract, transaction, or refusal, shall be valid, irrevocable, and enforceable, save upon such grounds as exist at law or in equity for the revocation of any contract.

Sec. 3. Stay of proceedings where issue therein referable to arbitration

If any suit or proceeding be brought in any of the courts of the United States upon any issue referable to arbitration under an agreement in writing for such arbitration, the court in which such suit is pending, upon being satisfied that the issue involved in such suit or proceeding is referable to arbitration under such an agreement, shall on application of one of the parties stay the trial of the action until such arbitration has been had in accordance with the terms of the agreement, providing the applicant for the stay is not in default in proceeding with such arbitration.

Sec. 4. Failure to arbitrate under agreement; petition to United States court having jurisdiction for order to compel arbitration; notice and service thereof; hearing and determination

A party aggrieved by the alleged failure, neglect, or refusal of another to arbitrate under a written agreement for arbitration may petition any United States district court which, save for such agreement, would have jurisdiction under title 28, in a civil action or in admiralty of the subject matter of a suit arising out of the controversy between the parties, for an order directing that such arbitration proceed in the manner provided for in such agreement. Five days' notice in writing of such application shall be served upon the party in default. Service thereof shall be made in the manner provided by the Federal Rules of Civil Procedure. The court shall hear the parties, and upon being satisfied that the making of the agreement for arbitration or the failure to comply therewith is not in issue, the court shall make an order directing the parties to proceed to arbitration in accordance with the terms of the agreement. The hearing and proceedings, under such agreement, shall be within the district in which the petition for an order directing such arbitration is filed. If the making of the arbitration agreement or the failure, neglect, or refusal to perform the same be in issue, the court shall proceed summarily to the trial thereof. If no jury trial be demanded by the party alleged to be in default, or if the matter in dispute is within admiralty jurisdiction, the court shall hear and determine such issue. Where such an issue is raised, the party alleged to be in default may, except in cases of admiralty, on or before the return day of the notice of application, demand a jury trial of such issue, and upon such demand the court shall make an order referring the issue or issues to a jury in the manner provided by the Federal Rules of Civil Procedure, or may specially call a jury for that purpose. If the jury find that no agreement in writing for arbitration was made or that there is no default in proceeding thereunder, the proceeding shall be dismissed. If the jury find that an agreement for arbitration was made in writing and that there is a default in proceeding thereunder, the court shall make an order summarily directing the parties to proceed with the arbitration in accordance with the terms thereof.

Sec. 5. Appointment of arbitrators or umpire

If in the agreement provision be made for a method of naming or appointing an arbitrator or arbitrators or an umpire, such method shall be followed; but if no method be provided therein, or if a method be provided and any party thereto shall fail to avail himself of such method, or if for any other reason there shall be a lapse in the naming of an arbitrator or arbitrators or umpire, or in filling a vacancy, then upon the application of either party to the controversy the court shall designate and appoint an arbitrator or arbitrators or umpire, as the case may require, who shall act under the said agreement with the same force and effect as if he or they had been specifically named therein; and unless otherwise provided in the agreement the arbitration shall be by a single arbitrator.

Sec. 6. Application heard as motion

Any application to the court hereunder shall be made and heard in the manner provided by law for the making and hearing of motions, except as otherwise herein expressly provided.

Sec. 7. Witnesses before arbitrators; fees; compelling attendance

The arbitrators selected either as prescribed in this title or otherwise, or a majority of them, may summon in writing any person to attend before them or any of them as a witness and in a proper case to bring with him or them any book, record, document, or paper which may be deemed material as evidence in the case. The fees for such attendance shall be the same as the fees of witnesses before masters of the United States courts. Said summons shall issue in the name of the arbitrator or arbitrators, or a majority of them, and shall be signed by the arbitrators, or a majority of them, and shall be directed to the said person and shall be served in the same manner as subpoenas to appear and testify before the court; if any person or persons so summoned to testify shall refuse or neglect to obey said summons, upon petition the United States district court for the district in which such arbitrators, or a majority of them, are sitting may compel the attendance of such person or persons before said arbitrator or arbitrators, or punish said person or persons for contempt in the same manner provided by law for securing the attendance of witnesses or their punishment for neglect or refusal to attend in the courts of the United States.

Sec. 8. Proceedings begun by libel in admiralty and seizure of vessel or property

If the basis of jurisdiction be a cause of action otherwise justiciable in admiralty, then, notwithstanding anything herein to the contrary, the party claiming to be aggrieved may begin his proceeding hereunder by libel and seizure of the vessel or other property of the other party according to the usual course of admiralty proceedings, and the court shall then have jurisdiction to direct the parties to proceed with the arbitration and shall retain jurisdiction to enter its decree upon the award.

Sec. 9. Award of arbitrators; confirmation; jurisdiction; procedure

If the parties in their agreement have agreed that a judgment of the court shall be entered upon the award made pursuant to the arbitration, and shall specify the court, then at any time within one year after the award is made any party to the arbitration may apply to the court so specified for an order confirming the award, and thereupon the court must grant such an order unless the award is vacated, modified, or corrected as prescribed in sections 10 and 11 of this title. If no court is specified in the agreement of the parties, then such application may be made to the United States court in and for the district within which such award was made. Notice of the application shall be served upon the adverse party, and thereupon the court shall have jurisdiction of such party as though he had appeared generally in the proceeding. If the adverse party is a resident of the district within which the award was made, such service shall be made upon the adverse party or his attorney as prescribed by law for service of notice of motion in an action in the same court. If the adverse party shall be a nonresident, then the notice of the application shall be served by the marshal of any district within which the adverse party may be found in like manner as other process of the court.

Sec. 10. Same; vacation; grounds; rehearing

(a) In any of the following cases the United States court in and for the district wherein the award was made may make an order vacating the award upon the application of any party to the arbitration—

(1) Where the award was procured by corruption, fraud, or undue means.

(2) Where there was evident partiality or corruption in the arbitrators, or either of them.

(3) Where the arbitrators were guilty of misconduct in refusing to postpone the hearing, upon sufficient cause shown, or in refusing to hear evidence pertinent and material to the controversy; or of any other misbehavior by which the rights of any party have been prejudiced.

(4) Where the arbitrators exceeded their powers, or so imperfectly executed them that a mutual, final, and definite award upon the subject matter submitted was not made.

(b) If an award is vacated and the time within which the agreement required the award to be made has not expired, the court may, in its discretion, direct a rehearing by the arbitrators.

(c) The United States district court for the district wherein an award was made that was issued pursuant to section 580 of title 5 may make an order vacating the award upon the application of a person, other than a party to the arbitration, who is adversely affected or aggrieved by the award, if the use of arbitration or the award is clearly inconsistent with the factors set forth in section 572 of title 5.

Sec. 11. Same; modification or correction; grounds; order

In either of the following cases the United States court in and for the district wherein the award was made may make an order modifying or correcting the award upon the application of any party to the arbitration—

(a) Where there was an evident material miscalculation of figures or an evident material mistake in the description of any person, thing, or property referred to in the award.

(b) Where the arbitrators have awarded upon a matter not submitted to them, unless it is a matter not affecting the merits of the decision upon the matter submitted.

(c) Where the award is imperfect in matter of form not affecting the merits of the controversy.

The order may modify and correct the award, so as to effect the intent thereof and promote justice between the parties.

Sec. 12. Notice of motions to vacate or modify; service; stay of proceedings

Notice of a motion to vacate, modify, or correct an award must be served upon the adverse party or his attorney within three months after the award is filed or delivered. If the adverse party is a resident of the district within which the award was made, such service shall be made upon the adverse party or his attorney as prescribed by law for service of notice of motion in an action in the same court. If the adverse party shall be a nonresident then the notice of the application shall be served by the marshal of any district within which the adverse party may be found in like manner as other process of the court. For the purposes of the motion any judge who might make an order to stay the proceedings in an action brought in the same court may make an order, to be served with the notice of motion, staying the proceedings of the adverse party to enforce the award.

Sec. 13. Papers filed with order on motions; judgment; docketing; force and effect; enforcement

The party moving for an order confirming, modifying, or correcting an award shall, at the time such order is filed with the clerk for the entry of judgment thereon, also file the following papers with the clerk:

(a) The agreement; the selection or appointment, if any, of an additional arbitrator or umpire; and each written extension of the time, if any, within which to make the award.

(b) The award.

(c) Each notice, affidavit, or other paper used upon an application to confirm, modify, or correct the award, and a copy of each order of the court upon such an application.

The judgment shall be docketed as if it was rendered in an action. The judgment so entered shall have the same force and effect, in all respects, as, and be subject to all the provisions of law relating to, a judgment in an action; and it may be enforced as if it had been rendered in an action in the court in which it is entered.

Sec. 14. Contracts not affected

This title shall not apply to contracts made prior to January 1, 1926.

Sec. 15. Inapplicability of the Act of State doctrine

Enforcement of arbitral agreements, confirmation of arbitral awards, and execution upon judgments based on orders confirming such awards shall not be refused on the basis of the Act of State doctrine.

Sec. 16. Appeals

(a) An appeal may be taken from—

(1) an order—

(A) refusing a stay of any action under section 3 of this title,

(B) denying a petition under section 4 of this title to order arbitration to proceed,

(C) denying an application under section 206 of this title to compel arbitration,

(D) confirming or denying confirmation of an award or partial award, or

(E) modifying, correcting, or vacating an award;

(2) an interlocutory order granting, continuing, or modifying an injunction against an arbitration that is subject to this title; or

(3) a final decision with respect to an arbitration that is subject to this title.

(b) Except as otherwise provided in section 1292(b) of title 28, an appeal may not be taken from an interlocutory order-

(1) granting a stay of any action under section 3 of this title;

(2) directing arbitration to proceed under section 4 of this title;

(3) compelling arbitration under section 206 of this title; or

(4) refusing to enjoin an arbitration that is subject to this title.

Appendix B

Labor Management Relations Act

§ 301 (a), 29 U.S.C.A. § 185 (a)

Suits for violation of contracts between an employer and a labor organization representing employees in an industry affecting commerce as defined in this chapter, or between any such labor organizations, may be brought in any district court of the United States having jurisdiction of the parties, without respect to the amount in controversy or without regard to the citizenship of the parties.

Appendix C

American Arbitration Association Commercial Arbitration Rules*

R–1. Agreement of Parties**†

(a) The parties shall be deemed to have made these rules a part of their arbitration agreement whenever they have provided for arbitration by the American Arbitration Association (hereinafter AAA) under its Commercial Arbitration Rules or for arbitration by the AAA of a domestic commercial dispute without specifying particular rules. These rules and any amendment of them shall apply in the form in effect at the time the administrative requirements are met for a demand for arbitration or submission agreement received by the AAA. The parties, by written agreement, may vary the procedures set forth in these rules. After appointment of the arbitrator, such modifications may be made only with the consent of the arbitrator.

(b) Unless the parties or the AAA determines otherwise, the Expedited Procedures shall apply in any case in which no disclosed claim or counterclaim exceeds $75,000, exclusive of interest and arbitration fees and costs. Parties may also agree to use these procedures in larger cases. Unless the parties agree otherwise, these procedures will not apply in cases involving more than two parties. The Expedited Procedures shall be applied as described in Sections E–1 through E–10 of these rules, in addition to any other portion of these rules that is not in conflict with the Expedited Procedures.

(c) Unless the parties agree otherwise, the Procedures for Large, Complex Commercial Disputes shall apply to all cases in which the disclosed claim or counterclaim of any party is at least $500,000, exclusive of claimed interest, arbitration fees and costs. Parties may also agree to use the Procedures in cases involving claims or counterclaims under $500,000, or in nonmonetary cases. The Procedures for Large, Complex Commercial Disputes shall be applied as described in Sections L–1 through L–4 of these

** The AAA applies the *Supplementary Procedures for Consumer–Related Disputes* to arbitration clauses in agreements between individual consumers and businesses where the business has a standardized, systematic application of arbitration clauses with customers and where the terms and conditions of the purchase of standardized, consumable goods or services are nonnegotiable or primarily non-negotiable in most or all of its terms, conditions, features, or choices. The product or service must be for personal or household use. The AAA will have the discretion to apply or not to apply the Supplementary Procedures and the parties will be able to bring any disputes concerning the application or non-application to the attention of the arbitrator. Consumers are not prohibited from seeking relief in a small claims court for disputes or claims within the scope of its jurisdiction, even in consumer arbitration cases filed by the business.

† A dispute arising out of an employer promulgated plan will be administered under the AAA's National Rules for the Resolution of Employment Disputes.

rules, in addition to any other portion of these rules that is not in conflict with the Procedures for Large, Complex Commercial Disputes.

(d) All other cases shall be administered in accordance with Sections R–1 through R–54 of these rules.

R–2. AAA and Delegation of Duties

When parties agree to arbitrate under these rules, or when they provide for arbitration by the AAA and an arbitration is initiated under these rules, they thereby authorize the AAA to administer the arbitration. The authority and duties of the AAA are prescribed in the agreement of the parties and in these rules, and may be carried out through such of the AAA's representatives as it may direct. The AAA may, in its discretion, assign the administration of an arbitration to any of its offices.

R–3. National Roster of Arbitrators

The AAA shall establish and maintain a National Roster of Commercial Arbitrators ("National Roster") and shall appoint arbitrators as provided in these rules. The term "arbitrator" in these rules refers to the arbitration panel, constituted for a particular case, whether composed of one or more arbitrators, or to an individual arbitrator, as the context requires.

R–4. Initiation under an Arbitration Provision in a Contract

(a) Arbitration under an arbitration provision in a contract shall be initiated in the following manner:

(i) The initiating party (the "claimant") shall, within the time period, if any, specified in the contract(s), give to the other party (the "respondent") written notice of its intention to arbitrate (the "demand"), which demand shall contain a statement setting forth the nature of the dispute, the names and addresses of all other parties, the amount involved, if any, the remedy sought, and the hearing locale requested.

(ii) The claimant shall file at any office of the AAA two copies of the demand and two copies of the arbitration provisions of the contract, together with the appropriate filing fee as provided in the schedule included with these rules.

(iii) The AAA shall confirm notice of such filing to the parties.

(b) A respondent may file an answering statement in duplicate with the AAA within 15 days after confirmation of notice of filing of the demand is sent by the AAA. The respondent shall, at the time of any such filing, send a copy of the answering statement to the claimant. If a counterclaim is asserted, it shall contain a statement setting forth the nature of the counterclaim, the amount involved, if any, and the remedy sought. If a counterclaim is made, the party making the counterclaim shall forward to the AAA with the answering statement the appropriate fee provided in the schedule included with these rules.

(c) If no answering statement is filed within the stated time, respondent will be deemed to deny the claim. Failure to file an answering statement shall not operate to delay the arbitration.

(d) When filing any statement pursuant to this section, the parties are encouraged to provide descriptions of their claims in sufficient detail to make the circumstances of the dispute clear to the arbitrator.

R–5. Initiation under a Submission

Parties to any existing dispute may commence an arbitration under these rules by filing at any office of the AAA two copies of a written submission to arbitrate under these rules, signed by the parties. It shall contain a statement of the nature of the dispute, the names and addresses of all parties, any claims and counterclaims, the amount involved, if any, the remedy sought, and the hearing locale requested, together with the appropriate filing fee as provided in the schedule included with these rules. Unless the parties state otherwise in the submission, all claims and counterclaims will be deemed to be denied by the other party.

R–6. Changes of Claim

After filing of a claim, if either party desires to make any new or different claim or counterclaim, it shall be made in writing and filed with the AAA. The party asserting such a claim or counterclaim shall provide a copy to the other party, who shall have 15 days from the date of such transmission within which to file an answering statement with the AAA. After the arbitrator is appointed, however, no new or different claim may be submitted except with the arbitrator's consent.

R–7. Applicable Procedures

(a) The arbitrator shall have the power to rule on his or her own jurisdiction, including any objections with respect to the existence, scope or validity of the arbitration agreement.

(b) The arbitrator shall have the power to determine the existence or validity of a contract of which an arbitration clause forms a part. Such an arbitration clause shall be treated as an agreement independent of the other terms of the contract. A decision by the arbitrator that the contract is null and void shall not for that reason alone render invalid the arbitration clause.

(c) A party must object to the jurisdiction of the arbitrator or to the arbitrability of a claim or counterclaim no later than the filing of the answering statement to the claim or counterclaim that gives rise to the objection. The arbitrator may rule on such objections as a preliminary matter or as part of the final award.

R–8. Mediation

At any stage of the proceedings, the parties may agree to conduct a mediation conference under the Commercial Mediation Procedures in order to facilitate settlement. The mediator shall not be an arbitrator appointed to the case. Where the parties to a pending arbitration agree to mediate under the AAA's rules, no additional administrative fee is required to initiate the mediation.

R–9. Administrative Conference

At the request of any party or upon the AAA's own initiative, the AAA may conduct an administrative conference, in person or by telephone, with the parties and/or their representatives. The conference may address such issues as arbitrator selection, potential mediation of the dispute, potential exchange of information, a timetable for hearings and any other administrative matters.

R–10. Fixing of Locale

The parties may mutually agree on the locale where the arbitration is to be held. If any party requests that the hearing be held in a specific locale and the other party files no objection thereto within 15 days after notice of the request has been sent to it by the AAA, the locale shall be the one requested. If a party objects to the locale requested by the other party, the AAA shall have the power to determine the locale, and its decision shall be final and binding.

R–11. Appointment from National Roster

(a) If the parties have not appointed an arbitrator and have not provided any other method of appointment, the arbitrator shall be appointed in the following manner: The AAA shall send simultaneously to each party to the dispute an identical list of 10 (unless the AAA decides that a different number is appropriate) names of persons chosen from the National Roster. The parties are encouraged to agree to an arbitrator from the submitted list and to advise the AAA of their agreement.

(b) If the parties are unable to agree upon an arbitrator, each party to the dispute shall have 15 days from the transmittal date in which to strike names objected to, number the remaining names in order of preference, and return the list to the AAA. If a party does not return the list within the time specified, all persons named therein shall be deemed acceptable. From among the persons who have been approved on both lists, and in accordance with the designated order of mutual preference, the AAA shall invite the acceptance of an arbitrator to serve. If the parties fail to agree on any of the persons named, or if acceptable arbitrators are unable to act, or if for any other reason the appointment cannot be made from the submitted lists, the AAA shall have the power to make the appointment from among other members of the National Roster without the submission of additional lists.

(c) Unless the parties agree otherwise when there are two or more claimants or two or more respondents, the AAA may appoint all the arbitrators.

R–12. Direct Appointment by a Party

(a) If the agreement of the parties names an arbitrator or specifies a method of appointing an arbitrator, that designation or method shall be followed. The notice of appointment, with the name and address of the arbitrator, shall be filed with the AAA by the appointing party. Upon the request of any appointing party, the AAA shall submit a list of members of the National Roster from which the party may, if it so desires, make the appointment.

(b) Where the parties have agreed that each party is to name one arbitrator, the arbitrators so named must meet the standards of Section R–17 with respect to impartiality and independence unless the parties have specifically agreed pursuant to Section R–17(a) that the party-appointed arbitrators are to be non-neutral and need not meet those standards.

(c) If the agreement specifies a period of time within which an arbitrator shall be appointed and any party fails to make the appointment within that period, the AAA shall make the appointment.

(d) If no period of time is specified in the agreement, the AAA shall notify the party to make the appointment. If within 15 days after such notice has been sent, an arbitrator has not been appointed by a party, the AAA shall make the appointment.

R–13. Appointment of Chairperson by Party–Appointed Arbitrators or Parties

(a) If, pursuant to Section R–12, either the parties have directly appointed arbitrators, or the arbitrators have been appointed by the AAA, and the parties have authorized them to appoint a chairperson within a specified time and no appointment is made within that time or any agreed extension, the AAA may appoint the chairperson.

(b) If no period of time is specified for appointment of the chairperson and the party-appointed arbitrators or the parties do not make the appointment within 15 days from the date of the appointment of the last party-appointed arbitrator, the AAA may appoint the chairperson.

(c) If the parties have agreed that their party-appointed arbitrators shall appoint the chairperson from the National Roster, the AAA shall furnish to the party-appointed arbitrators, in the manner provided in Section R–11, a list selected from the National Roster, and the appointment of the chairperson shall be made as provided in that Section.

R–14. Nationality of Arbitrator

Where the parties are nationals of different countries, the AAA, at the request of any party or on its own initiative, may appoint as arbitrator a national of a country other than that of any of the parties. The request must be made before the time set for the appointment of the arbitrator as agreed by the parties or set by these rules

R–15. Number of Arbitrators

If the arbitration agreement does not specify the number of arbitrators, the dispute shall be heard and determined by one arbitrator, unless the AAA, in its discretion, directs that three arbitrators be appointed. A party may request three arbitrators in the demand or answer, which request the AAA will consider in exercising its discretion regarding the number of arbitrators appointed to the dispute.

R–16. Disclosure

(a) Any person appointed or to be appointed as an arbitrator shall disclose to the AAA any circumstance likely to give rise to justifiable doubt as to the arbitrator's impartiality or independence, including any bias or any financial or personal interest in the result of the arbitration or any past or present relationship with the parties or their representatives. Such obligation shall remain in effect throughout the arbitration.

(b) Upon receipt of such information from the arbitrator or another source, the AAA shall communicate the information to the parties and, if it deems it appropriate to do so, to the arbitrator and others.

(c) In order to encourage disclosure by arbitrators, disclosure of information pursuant to this Section R–16 is not to be construed as an indication that the arbitrator considers that the disclosed circumstance is likely to affect impartiality or independence.

R–17. Disqualification of Arbitrator

(a) Any arbitrator shall be impartial and independent and shall perform his or her duties with diligence and in good faith, and shall be subject to disqualification for

(i) partiality or lack of independence,

(ii) inability or refusal to perform his or her duties with diligence and in good faith, and

(iii) any grounds for disqualification provided by applicable law. The parties may agree in writing, however, that arbitrators directly appointed by a party pursuant to Section R–12 shall be nonneutral, in which case such arbitrators need not be impartial or independent and shall not be subject to disqualification for partiality or lack of independence.

(b) Upon objection of a party to the continued service of an arbitrator, or on its own initiative, the AAA shall determine whether the arbitrator should be disqualified under the grounds set out above, and shall inform the parties of its decision, which decision shall be conclusive.

R–18. Communication with Arbitrator

(a) No party and no one acting on behalf of any party shall communicate ex parte with an arbitrator or a candidate for arbitrator concerning the arbitration, except that a party, or someone acting on behalf of a party, may communicate ex parte with a candidate for direct appointment pursuant to Section R–12 in order to advise the candidate of the general nature of the controversy and of the anticipated proceedings and to discuss the candidate's qualifications, availability, or independence in relation to the parties or to discuss the suitability of candidates for selection as a third arbitrator where the parties or party-designated arbitrators are to participate in that selection.

(b) Section R–18(a) does not apply to arbitrators directly appointed by the parties who, pursuant to Section R–17(a), the parties have agreed in writing are non-neutral. Where the parties have so agreed under Section R–17(a), the AAA shall as an administrative practice suggest to the parties that they agree further that Section R–18(a) should nonetheless apply prospectively.

R–19. Vacancies

(a) If for any reason an arbitrator is unable to perform the duties of the office, the AAA may, on proof satisfactory to it, declare the office vacant. Vacancies shall be filled in accordance with the applicable provisions of these rules.

(b) In the event of a vacancy in a panel of neutral arbitrators after the hearings have commenced, the remaining arbitrator or arbitrators may continue with the hearing and determination of the controversy, unless the parties agree otherwise.

(c) In the event of the appointment of a substitute arbitrator, the panel of arbitrators shall determine in its sole discretion whether it is necessary to repeat all or part of any prior hearings.

R–20. Preliminary Hearing

(a) At the request of any party or at the discretion of the arbitrator or the AAA, the arbitrator may schedule as soon as practicable a preliminary hearing with the parties and/or their representatives. The preliminary hearing may be conducted by telephone at the arbitrator's discretion.

(b) During the preliminary hearing, the parties and the arbitrator should discuss the future conduct of the case, including clarification of the issues and claims, a schedule for the hearings and any other preliminary matters.

R–21. Exchange of Information

(a) At the request of any party or at the discretion of the arbitrator, consistent with the expedited nature of arbitration, the arbitrator may direct

(i) the production of documents and other information, and

(ii) the identification of any witnesses to be called.

(b) At least five business days prior to the hearing, the parties shall exchange copies of all exhibits they intend to submit at the hearing.

(c) The arbitrator is authorized to resolve any disputes concerning the exchange of information.

R–22. Date, Time, and Place of Hearing

The arbitrator shall set the date, time, and place for each hearing. The parties shall respond to requests for hearing dates in a timely manner, be cooperative in scheduling the earliest practicable date, and adhere to the established hearing schedule. The AAA shall send a notice of hearing to the parties at least 10 days in advance of the hearing date, unless otherwise agreed by the parties.

R–23. Attendance at Hearings

The arbitrator and the AAA shall maintain the privacy of the hearings unless the law provides to the contrary. Any person having a direct interest in the arbitration is entitled to attend hearings. The arbitrator shall otherwise have the power to require the exclusion of any witness, other than a party or other essential person, during the testimony of any other witness. It shall be discretionary with the arbitrator to determine the propriety of the attendance of any other person other than a party and its representatives.

R–24. Representation

Any party may be represented by counsel or other authorized representative. A party intending to be so represented shall notify the other party and the AAA of the name and address of the representative at least three days prior to the date set for the hearing at which that person is first to appear. When such a representative initiates an arbitration or responds for a party, notice is deemed to have been given.

R–25. Oaths

Before proceeding with the first hearing, each arbitrator may take an oath of office and, if required by law, shall do so. The arbitrator may require witnesses to testify under oath administered by any duly qualified person and, if it is required by law or requested by any party, shall do so.

R–26. Stenographic Record

Any party desiring a stenographic record shall make arrangements directly with a stenographer and shall notify the other parties of these arrangements at least three days in advance of the hearing. The requesting party or parties shall pay the cost of the record. If the transcript is agreed by the parties, or determined by the arbitrator to be the official record of the proceeding, it must be provided to the arbitrator and made available to the other parties for inspection, at a date, time, and place determined by the arbitrator.

R–27. Interpreters

Any party wishing an interpreter shall make all arrangements directly with the interpreter and shall assume the costs of the service.

R–28. Postponements

The arbitrator may postpone any hearing upon agreement of the parties, upon request of a party for good cause shown, or upon the arbitrator's own initiative.

R–29. Arbitration in the Absence of a Party or Representative

Unless the law provides to the contrary, the arbitration may proceed in the absence of any party or representative who, after due notice, fails to be present or fails to obtain a postponement. An award shall not be made solely on the default of a party. The arbitrator shall require the party who is present to submit such evidence as the arbitrator may require for the making of an award.

R–30. Conduct of Proceedings

(a) The claimant shall present evidence to support its claim. The respondent shall then present evidence to support its defense. Witnesses for each party shall also submit to questions from the arbitrator and the adverse party. The arbitrator has the discretion to vary this procedure, provided that the parties are treated with equality and that each party has the right to be heard and is given a fair opportunity to present its case.

(b) The arbitrator, exercising his or her discretion, shall conduct the proceedings with a view to expediting the resolution of the dispute and may direct the order of proof, bifurcate proceedings and direct the parties to focus their presentations on issues the decision of which could dispose of all or part of the case.

(c) The parties may agree to waive oral hearings in any case.

R–31. Evidence

(a) The parties may offer such evidence as is relevant and material to the dispute and shall produce such evidence as the arbitrator may deem necessary to an understanding and determination of the dispute. Conformity to legal rules of evidence shall not be necessary. All evidence shall be taken in the presence of all of the arbitrators and all of the parties, except where any of the parties is absent, in default or has waived the right to be present.

(b) The arbitrator shall determine the admissibility, relevance, and materiality of the evidence offered and may exclude evidence deemed by the arbitrator to be cumulative or irrelevant.

(c) The arbitrator shall take into account applicable principles of legal privilege, such as those involving the confidentiality of communications between a lawyer and client.

(d) An arbitrator or other person authorized by law to subpoena witnesses or documents may do so upon the request of any party or independently.

R–32. Evidence by Affidavit and Post-hearing Filing of Documents or Other Evidence

(a) The arbitrator may receive and consider the evidence of witnesses by declaration or affidavit, but shall give it only such weight as the arbitrator deems it entitled to after consideration of any objection made to its admission.

(b) If the parties agree or the arbitrator directs that documents or other evidence be submitted to the arbitrator after the hearing, the documents or other evidence shall be filed with the AAA for transmission to the arbitrator. All parties shall be afforded an opportunity to examine and respond to such documents or other evidence.

R–33. Inspection or Investigation

An arbitrator finding it necessary to make an inspection or investigation in connection with the arbitration shall direct the AAA to so advise the parties. The arbitrator shall set the date and time and the AAA shall notify the parties. Any party who so desires may be present at such an inspection or investigation. In the event that one or all parties are not present at the inspection or investigation, the arbitrator shall make an oral or written report to the parties and afford them an opportunity to comment.

R–34. Interim Measures**

(a) The arbitrator may take whatever interim measures he or she deems necessary, including injunctive relief and measures for the protection or conservation of property and disposition of perishable goods.

(b) Such interim measures may take the form of an interim award, and the arbitrator may require security for the costs of such measures.

(c) A request for interim measures addressed by a party to a judicial authority shall not be deemed incompatible with the agreement to arbitrate or a waiver of the right to arbitrate.

R–35. Closing of Hearing

The arbitrator shall specifically inquire of all parties whether they have any further proofs to offer or witnesses to be heard. Upon receiving negative replies or if satisfied that the record is complete, the arbitrator shall declare the hearing closed. If briefs are to be filed, the hearing shall b e declared closed as of the final date set by the arbitrator for the receipt of briefs. If documents are to be filed as provided in Section R–32 and the date set for their receipt is later than that set for the receipt of briefs, the later date shall be the closing date of the hearing. The time limit within which the arbitrator is required to make the award shall commence, in the absence of other agreements by the parties, upon the closing of the hearing.

** The Optional Rules may be found at the end of this document.

R–36. Reopening of Hearing

The hearing may be reopened on the arbitrator's initiative, or upon application of a party, at any time before the award is made. If reopening the hearing would prevent the making of the award within the specific time agreed on by the parties in the contract(s) out of which the controversy has arisen, the matter may not be reopened unless the parties agree on an extension of time. When no specific date is fixed in the contract, the arbitrator may reopen the hearing and shall have 30 days from the closing of the reopened hearing within which to make an award.

R–37. Waiver of Rules

Any party who proceeds with the arbitration after knowledge that any provision or requirement of these rules has not been complied with and who fails to state an objection in writing shall be deemed to have waived the right to object.

R–38. Extensions of Time

The parties may modify any period of time by mutual agreement. The AAA or the arbitrator may for good cause extend any period of time established by these rules, except the time for making the award. The AAA shall notify the parties of any extension.

R–39. Serving of Notice

(a) Any papers, notices, or process necessary or proper for the initiation or continuation of an arbitration under these rules, for any court action in connection therewith, or for the entry of judgment on any award made under these rules may be served on a party by mail addressed to the party, or its representative at the last known address or by personal service, in or outside the state where the arbitration is to be held, provided that reasonable opportunity to be heard with regard to the dispute is or has been granted to the party.

(b) The AAA, the arbitrator and the parties may also use overnight delivery or electronic facsimile transmission (fax), to give the notices required by these rules. Where all parties and the arbitrator agree, notices may be transmitted by electronic mail (E-mail), or other methods of communication.

(c) Unless otherwise instructed by the AAA or by the arbitrator, any documents submitted by any party to the AAA or to the arbitrator shall simultaneously be provided to the other party or parties to the arbitration.

R–40. Majority Decision

When the panel consists of more than one arbitrator, unless required by law or by the arbitration agreement, a majority of the arbitrators must make all decisions.

R–41. Time of Award

The award shall be made promptly by the arbitrator and, unless otherwise agreed by the parties or specified by law, no later than 30 days from the date of closing the hearing, or, if oral hearings have been waived, from the date of the AAA's transmittal of the final statements and proofs to the arbitrator.

R–42. Form of Award

(a) Any award shall be in writing and signed by a majority of the arbitrators. It shall be executed in the manner required by law.

(b) The arbitrator need not render a reasoned award unless the parties request such an award in writing prior to appointment of the arbitrator or unless the arbitrator determines that a reasoned award is appropriate.

R–43. Scope of Award

(a) The arbitrator may grant any remedy or relief that the arbitrator deems just and equitable and within the scope of the agreement of the parties, including, but not limited to, specific performance of a contract.

(b) In addition to a final award, the arbitrator may make other decisions, including interim, interlocutory, or partial rulings, orders, and awards. In any interim, interlocutory, or partial award, the arbitrator may assess and apportion the fees, expenses, and compensation related to such award as the arbitrator determines is appropriate.

(c) In the final award, the arbitrator shall assess the fees, expenses, and compensation provided in Sections R–49, R–50, and R–51. The arbitrator may apportion such fees, expenses, and compensation among the parties in such amounts as the arbitrator determines is appropriate.

(d) The award of the arbitrator(s) may include:

(i) interest at such rate and from such date as the arbitrator(s) may deem appropriate; and

(ii) an award of attorneys' fees if all parties have requested such an award or it is authorized by law or their arbitration agreement.

R–44. Award upon Settlement

If the parties settle their dispute during the course of the arbitration and if the parties so request, the arbitrator may set forth the terms of the settlement in a "consent award." A consent award must include an allocation of arbitration costs, including administrative fees and expenses as well as arbitrator fees and expenses.

R–45. Delivery of Award to Parties

Parties shall accept as notice and delivery of the award the placing of the award or a true copy thereof in the mail addressed to the parties or their representatives at the last known addresses, personal or electronic service of the award, or the filing of the award in any other manner that is permitted by law.

R–46. Modification of Award

Within 20 days after the transmittal of an award, any party, upon notice to the other parties, may request the arbitrator, through the AAA, to correct any clerical, typographical, or computational errors in the award. The arbitrator is not empowered to redetermine the merits of any claim already decided. The other parties shall be given 10 days to respond to the request. The arbitrator shall dispose of the request within 20 days after transmittal by the AAA to the arbitrator of the request and any response thereto.

R–47. Release of Documents for Judicial Proceedings

The AAA shall, upon the written request of a party, furnish to the party, at the party's expense, certified copies of any papers in the AAA's possession that may be required in judicial proceedings relating to the arbitration.

R–48. Applications to Court and Exclusion of Liability

(a) No judicial proceeding by a party relating to the subject matter of the arbitration shall be deemed a waiver of the party's right to arbitrate.

(b) Neither the AAA nor any arbitrator in a proceeding under these rules is a necessary or proper party in judicial proceedings relating to the arbitration.

(c) Parties to an arbitration under these rules shall be deemed to have consented that judgment upon the arbitration award may be entered in any federal or state court having jurisdiction thereof.

(d) Parties to an arbitration under these rules shall be deemed to have consented that neither the AAA nor any arbitrator shall be liable to any party in any action for damages or injunctive relief for any act or omission in connection with any arbitration under these rules.

R–49. Administrative Fees

As a not-for-profit organization, the AAA shall prescribe an initial filing fee and a case service fee to compensate it for the cost of providing administrative services. The fees in effect when the fee or charge is incurred shall be applicable. The filing fee shall be advanced by the party or parties making a claim or counterclaim, subject to final apportionment by the arbitrator in the award. The AAA may, in the event of extreme hardship on the part of any party, defer or reduce the administrative fees.

R–50. Expenses

The expenses of witnesses for either side shall be paid by the party producing such witnesses. All other expenses of the arbitration, including required travel and other expenses of the arbitrator, AAA representatives, and any witness and the cost of any proof produced at the direct request of the arbitrator, shall be borne equally by the parties, unless they agree otherwise or unless the arbitrator in the award assesses such expenses or any part thereof against any specified party or parties.

R–51. Neutral Arbitrator's Compensation

(a) Arbitrators shall be compensated at a rate consistent with the arbitrator's stated rate of compensation.

(b) If there is disagreement concerning the terms of compensation, an appropriate rate shall be established with the arbitrator by the AAA and confirmed to the parties.

(c) Any arrangement for the compensation of a neutral arbitrator shall be made through the AAA and not directly between the parties and the arbitrator.

R–52. Deposits

The AAA may require the parties to deposit in advance of any hearings such sums of money as it deems necessary to cover the expense of the arbitration, including the arbitrator's fee, if any, and shall render an accounting to the parties and return any unexpended balance at the conclusion of the case.

R–53. Interpretation and Application of Rules

The arbitrator shall interpret and apply these rules insofar as they relate to the arbitrator's powers and duties. When there is more than one arbitrator and a difference arises among them concerning the meaning or application of these rules, it shall be decided by a majority vote. If that is not possible, either an arbitrator or a party may refer the question to the AAA for final decision. All other rules shall be interpreted and applied by the AAA.

R–54. Suspension for Nonpayment

If arbitrator compensation or administrative charges have not been paid in full, the AAA may so inform the parties in order that one of them may advance the required payment. If such payments are not made, the arbitrator may order the suspension or termination of the proceedings. If no arbitrator has yet been appointed, the AAA may suspend the proceedings.

(a) The arbitrator may grant any remedy or relief that the arbitrator deems just and equitable and within the scope of the agreement of the parties, including, but not limited to, specific performance of a contract.

(b) In addition to a final award, the arbitrator may make other decisions, including interim, interlocutory, or partial rulings, orders, and awards. In any interim, interlocutory, or partial award, the arbitrator may assess and apportion the fees, expenses, and compensation related to such award as the arbitrator determines is appropriate.

(c) In the final award, the arbitrator shall assess the fees, expenses, and compensation provided in Sections R–51, R–52, and R–53. The arbitrator may apportion such fees, expenses, and compensation among the parties in such amounts as the arbitrator determines is appropriate.

(d) The award of the arbitrator(s) may include: (a) interest at such rate and from such date as the arbitrator(s) may deem appropriate; and (b) an award of attorneys' fees if all parties have requested such an award or it is authorized by law or their arbitration agreement.

Expedited Procedures

E–1. Limitation on Extensions

Except in extraordinary circumstances, the AAA or the arbitrator may grant a party no more than one seven-day extension of time to respond to the demand for arbitration or counterclaim as provided in Section R–4.

E–2. Changes of Claim or Counterclaim

A claim or counterclaim may be increased in amount, or a new or different claim or counterclaim added, upon the agreement of the other party, or the consent of the arbitrator. After the arbitrator is appointed, however, no new or different claim or counterclaim may be submitted except with the arbitrator's consent. If an increased claim or counterclaim exceeds $75,000, the case will be administered under the regular procedures unless all parties and the arbitrator agree that the case may continue to be processed under the Expedited Procedures.

E–3. Serving of Notices

In addition to notice provided by Section R–39(b), the parties shall also accept notice by telephone. Telephonic notices by the AAA shall subsequently be confirmed in writing to the parties. Should there be a failure to confirm in writing any such oral notice, the proceeding shall nevertheless be valid if notice has, in fact, been given by telephone.

E–4. Appointment and Qualifications of Arbitrator

(a) The AAA shall simultaneously submit to each party an identical list of five proposed arbitrators drawn from its National Roster from which one arbitrator shall be appointed.

(b) The parties are encouraged to agree to an arbitrator from this list and to advise the AAA of their agreement. If the parties are unable to agree upon an arbitrator, each party may strike two names from the list and return it to the AAA within seven days from the date of the AAA's mailing to the parties. If for any reason the appointment of an arbitrator cannot be made from the list, the AAA may make the appointment from other members of the panel without the submission of additional lists.

(c) The parties will be given notice by the AAA of the appointment of the arbitrator, who shall be subject to disqualification for the reasons specified in Section R–17. The parties shall notify the AAA within seven days of any objection to the arbitrator appointed. Any such objection shall be for cause and shall be confirmed in writing to the AAA with a copy to the other party or parties.

E–5. Exchange of Exhibits

At least two business days prior to the hearing, the parties shall exchange copies of all exhibits they intend to submit at the hearing. The arbitrator shall resolve disputes concerning the exchange of exhibits.

E–6. Proceedings on Documents

Where no party's claim exceeds $10,000, exclusive of interest and arbitration costs, and other cases in which the parties agree, the dispute shall be resolved by submission of documents, unless any party requests an oral hearing, or the arbitrator determines that an oral hearing is necessary. The arbitrator shall establish a fair and equitable procedure for the submission of documents.

E–7. Date, Time, and Place of Hearing

In cases in which a hearing is to be held, the arbitrator shall set the date, time, and place of the hearing, to be scheduled to take place within 30 days of confirmation of the arbitrator's appointment. The AAA will notify the parties in advance of the hearing date.

E–8. The Hearing

(a) Generally, the hearing shall not exceed one day. Each party shall have equal opportunity to submit its proofs and complete its case. The arbitrator shall determine the order of the hearing, and may require further submission of documents within two days after the hearing. For good cause shown, the arbitrator may schedule additional hearings within seven business days after the initial day of hearings.

(b) Generally, there will be no stenographic record. Any party desiring a stenographic record may arrange for one pursuant to the provisions of Section R–26.

E–9. Time of Award

Unless otherwise agreed by the parties, the award shall be rendered not later than 14 days from the date of the closing of the hearing or, if oral hearings have been waived, from the date of the AAA's transmittal of the final statements and proofs to the arbitrator.

E–10. Arbitrator's Compensation

Arbitrators will receive compensation at a rate to be suggested by the AAA regional office.

Appendix D

THE REVISED UNIFORM ARBITRATION ACT

Prefatory Note

The Uniform Arbitration Act (UAA), promulgated in 1955, has been one of the most successful Acts of the National Conference of Commissioners on Uniform State Laws. Forty-nine jurisdictions have arbitration statutes; 35 of these have adopted the UAA and 14 have adopted this Act in substantially similar form. A primary purpose of the 1955 Act was to insure the enforceability of agreements to arbitrate in the face of oftentimes hostile state law. That goal has been accomplished. Today arbitration is a primary mechanism favored by courts and parties to resolve disputes in many areas of the law. This growth in arbitration caused the Conference to appoint a Drafting Committee to consider revising the Act in light of increasing use of arbitration, the greater complexity of many disputes resolved by arbitration, and the developments of the law in this area....

SECTION 1. DEFINITIONS

In this [Act]:

(1) "Arbitration organization" means an association, agency, board, commission, or other entity that is neutral and initiates, sponsors, or administers an arbitration proceeding or is involved in the appointment of an arbitrator.

(2) "Arbitrator" means an individual appointed to render an award, alone or with others, in a controversy that is subject to an agreement to arbitrate.

(3) "Court" means [a court of competent jurisdiction in this State].

(4) "Knowledge" means actual knowledge.

(5) "Person" means an individual, corporation, business trust, estate, trust, partnership, limited liability company, association, joint venture, government; governmental subdivision, agency, or instrumentality; public corporation; or any other legal or commercial entity.

(6) "Record" means information that is inscribed on a tangible medium or that is stored in an electronic or other medium and is retrievable in perceivable form.

SECTION 2. NOTICE

(a) Except as otherwise provided in this [Act], a person gives notice to another person by taking action that is reasonably necessary to inform the other person in ordinary course, whether or not the other person acquires knowledge of the notice.

(b) A person has notice if the person has knowledge of the notice or has received notice.

(c) A person receives notice when it comes to the person's attention or the notice is delivered at the person's place of residence or place of business, or at another location held out by the person as a place of delivery of such communications.

SECTION 3. WHEN ACT APPLIES

(a) This [Act] governs an agreement to arbitrate made on or after [the effective date of this [Act]].

(b) This [Act] governs an agreement to arbitrate made before [the effective date of this [Act]] if all the parties to the agreement or to the arbitration proceeding so agree in a record.

(c) On or after [a delayed date], this [Act] governs an agreement to arbitrate whenever made.

SECTION 4. EFFECT OF AGREEMENT TO ARBITRATE; NON-WAIVABLE PROVISIONS

(a) Except as otherwise provided in subsections (b) and (c), a party to an agreement to arbitrate or to an arbitration proceeding may waive or, the parties may vary the effect of, the requirements of this [Act] to the extent permitted by law.

(b) Before a controversy arises that is subject to an agreement to arbitrate, a party to the agreement may not:

(1) waive or agree to vary the effect of the requirements of Section 5(a), 6(a), 8, 17(a), 17(b), 26, or 28;

(2) agree to unreasonably restrict the right under Section 9 to notice of the initiation of an arbitration proceeding;

(3) agree to unreasonably restrict the right under Section 12 to disclosure of any facts by a neutral arbitrator; or

(4) waive the right under Section 16 of a party to an agreement to arbitrate to be represented by a lawyer at any proceeding or hearing under this [Act], but an employer and a labor organization may waive the right to representation by a lawyer in a labor arbitration.

(c) A party to an agreement to arbitrate or arbitration proceeding may not waive, or the parties may not vary the effect of, the requirements of this section or Section 3(a) or (c), 7, 14, 18, 20(d) or (e), 22, 23, 24, 25(a) or (b), 29, 30, 31, or 32.

SECTION 5. APPLICATIONS TO COURT

(a) Except as otherwise provided in Section 28, an [application] for judicial relief under this [Act] must be made by [motion] to the court and heard in the manner provided by law or rule of court for making and hearing [motions].

(b) Unless a civil action involving the agreement to arbitrate is pending, notice of an initial [motion] to the court under this [Act] must be served in the manner provided by law for the service of a summons in a civil action. Otherwise, notice of the motion must be given in the manner provided by law or rule of court for serving [motions] in pending cases.

SECTION 6. VALIDITY OF AGREEMENT TO ARBITRATE

(a) An agreement contained in a record to submit to arbitration any existing or subsequent controversy arising between the parties to the agreement is valid, enforceable, and irrevocable except upon a ground that exists at law or in equity for the revocation of a contract.

(b) The court shall decide whether an agreement to arbitrate exists or a controversy is subject to an agreement to arbitrate.

(c) An arbitrator shall decide whether a condition precedent to arbitrability has been fulfilled and whether a contract containing a valid agreement to arbitrate is enforceable.

(d) If a party to a judicial proceeding challenges the existence of, or claims that a controversy is not subject to, an agreement to arbitrate, the arbitration proceeding may continue pending final resolution of the issue by the court, unless the court otherwise orders.

SECTION 7. MOTION TO COMPEL OR STAY ARBITRATION

(a) On [motion] of a person showing an agreement to arbitrate and alleging another person's refusal to arbitrate pursuant to the agreement:

(1) if the refusing party does not appear or does not oppose the [motion], the court shall order the parties to arbitrate; and

(2) if the refusing party opposes the [motion], the court shall proceed summarily to decide the issue and order the parties to arbitrate unless it finds that there is no enforceable agreement to arbitrate.

(b) On [motion] of a person alleging that an arbitration proceeding has been initiated or threatened but that there is no agreement to arbitrate, the court shall proceed summarily to decide the issue. If the court finds that there is an enforceable agreement to arbitrate, it shall order the parties to arbitrate.

(c) If the court finds that there is no enforceable agreement, it may not pursuant to subsection (a) or (b) order the parties to arbitrate.

(d) The court may not refuse to order arbitration because the claim subject to arbitration lacks merit or grounds for the claim have not been established.

(e) If a proceeding involving a claim referable to arbitration under an alleged agreement to arbitrate is pending in court, a [motion] under this section must be made in that court. Otherwise a [motion] under this section may be made in any court as provided in Section 27.

(f) If a party makes a [motion] to the court to order arbitration, the court on just terms shall stay any judicial proceeding that involves a claim alleged to be subject to the arbitration until the court renders a final decision under this section.

(g) If the court orders arbitration, the court on just terms shall stay any judicial proceeding that involves a claim subject to the arbitration. If a claim subject to the arbitration is severable, the court may limit the stay to that claim.

SECTION 8. PROVISIONAL REMEDIES

(a) Before an arbitrator is appointed and is authorized and able to act, the court, upon [motion] of a party to an arbitration proceeding and for good cause shown, may enter an order for provisional remedies to protect the effectiveness of the arbitration proceeding to the same extent and under the same conditions as if the controversy were the subject of a civil action.

(b) After an arbitrator is appointed and is authorized and able to act:

(1) the arbitrator may issue such orders for provisional remedies, including interim awards, as the arbitrator finds necessary to protect the effectiveness of the arbitration proceeding and to promote the fair and expeditious resolution of the controversy, to the same extent and under the same conditions as if the controversy were the subject of a civil action and

(2) a party to an arbitration proceeding may move the court for a provisional remedy only if the matter is urgent and the arbitrator is not able to act timely or the arbitrator cannot provide an adequate remedy.

(c) A party does not waive a right of arbitration by making a [motion] under subsection (a) or (b).

SECTION 9. INITIATION OF ARBITRATION

(a) A person initiates an arbitration proceeding by giving notice in a record to the other parties to the agreement to arbitrate in the agreed manner between the parties or, in the absence of agreement, by certified or registered mail, return receipt requested and obtained, or by service as authorized for the commencement of a civil action. The notice must describe the nature of the controversy and the remedy sought.

(b) Unless a person objects for lack or insufficiency of notice under Section 15(c) not later than the beginning of the arbitration hearing, the person by appearing at the hearing waives any objection to lack of or insufficiency of notice.

SECTION 10. CONSOLIDATION OF SEPARATE ARBITRATION PROCEEDINGS

(a) Except as otherwise provided in subsection (c), upon [motion] of a party to an agreement to arbitrate or to an arbitration proceeding, the court may order consolidation of separate arbitration proceedings as to all or some of the claims if:

(1) there are separate agreements to arbitrate or separate arbitration proceedings between the same persons or one of them is a party to

a separate agreement to arbitrate or a separate arbitration proceeding with a third person;

(2) the claims subject to the agreements to arbitrate arise in substantial part from the same transaction or series of related transactions;

(3) the existence of a common issue of law or fact creates the possibility of conflicting decisions in the separate arbitration proceedings; and

(4) prejudice resulting from a failure to consolidate is not outweighed by the risk of undue delay or prejudice to the rights of or hardship to parties opposing consolidation.

(b) The court may order consolidation of separate arbitration proceedings as to some claims and allow other claims to be resolved in separate arbitration proceedings.

(c) The court may not order consolidation of the claims of a party to an agreement to arbitrate if the agreement prohibits consolidation.

SECTION 11. APPOINTMENT OF ARBITRATOR

(a) If the parties to an agreement to arbitrate agree on a method for appointing an arbitrator, that method must be followed, unless the method fails. If the parties have not agreed on a method, the agreed method fails, or an arbitrator appointed fails or is unable to act and a successor has not been appointed, the court, on [motion] of a party to the arbitration proceeding, shall appoint the arbitrator. An arbitrator so appointed has all the powers of an arbitrator designated in the agreement to arbitrate or appointed pursuant to the agreed method.

(b) An individual who has a known, direct, and material interest in the outcome of the arbitration proceeding or a known, existing, and substantial relationship with a party may not serve as an arbitrator required by an agreement to be neutral.

SECTION 12. DISCLOSURE BY ARBITRATOR

(a) Before accepting appointment, an individual who is requested to serve as an arbitrator, after making a reasonable inquiry, shall disclose to all parties to the agreement to arbitrate and arbitration proceeding and to any other arbitrators any known facts that a reasonable person would consider likely to affect the impartiality of the arbitrator in the arbitration proceeding, including:

(1) a financial or personal interest in the outcome of the arbitration proceeding; and

(2) an existing or past relationship with any of the parties to the agreement to arbitrate or the arbitration proceeding, their counsel or representatives, a witness, or another arbitrators.

(b) An arbitrator has a continuing obligation to disclose to all parties to the agreement to arbitrate and arbitration proceeding and to any other arbitrators any facts that the arbitrator learns after accepting appointment which a reasonable person would consider likely to affect the impartiality of the arbitrator.

(c) If an arbitrator discloses a fact required by subsection (a) or (b) to be disclosed and a party timely objects to the appointment or continued service of the arbitrator based upon the fact disclosed, the objection may be a ground under Section 23(a)(2) for vacating an award made by the arbitrator.

(d) If the arbitrator did not disclose a fact as required by subsection (a) or (b), upon timely objection by a party, the court under Section 23(a)(2) may vacate an award.

(e) An arbitrator appointed as a neutral arbitrator who does not disclose a known, direct, and material interest in the outcome of the arbitration proceeding or a known, existing, and substantial relationship with a party is presumed to act with evident partiality under Section 23(a)(2).

(f) If the parties to an arbitration proceeding agree to the procedures of an arbitration organization or any other procedures for challenges to arbitrators before an award is made, substantial compliance with those procedures is a condition precedent to a [motion] to vacate an award on that ground under Section 23(a)(2).

SECTION 13. MAJORITY ACTION BY ARBITRATORS

If there is more than one arbitrator, the powers of an arbitrator must be exercised by a majority of the arbitrators, but all of them shall conduct the hearing under Section 15(c).

SECTION 14. IMMUNITY OF ARBITRATOR; COMPETENCY TO TESTIFY; ATTORNEY'S FEES AND COSTS

(a) An arbitrator or an arbitration organization acting in that capacity is immune from civil liability to the same extent as a judge of a court of this State acting in a judicial capacity.

(b) The immunity afforded by this section supplements any immunity under other law.

(c) The failure of an arbitrator to make a disclosure required by Section 12 does not cause any loss of immunity under this section.

(d) In a judicial, administrative, or similar proceeding, an arbitrator or representative of an arbitration organization is not competent to testify, and may not be required to produce records as to any statement, conduct, decision, or ruling occurring during the arbitration proceeding, to the same extent as a judge of a court of this State acting in a judicial capacity. This subsection does not apply:

(1) to the extent necessary to determine the claim of an arbitrator, arbitration organization, or representative of the arbitration organization against a party to the arbitration proceeding; or

(2) to a hearing on a [motion] to vacate an award under Section 23(a)(1) or (2) if the [movant] establishes prima facie that a ground for vacating the award exists.

(e) If a person commences a civil action against an arbitrator, arbitration organization, or representative of an arbitration organization arising from the services of the arbitrator, organization, or representative or if a person seeks to compel an arbitrator or a representative of an arbitration organization to testify or produce records in violation of subsection (d), and the court decides that the arbitrator, arbitration organization, or representative of an arbitration organization is immune from civil liability or that the arbitrator or representative of the organization is not competent to testify, the court shall award to the arbitrator, organization, or representative reasonable attorney's fees and other reasonable expenses of litigation.

SECTION 15. ARBITRATION PROCESS.

(a) An arbitrator may conduct an arbitration in such manner as the arbitrator considers appropriate for a fair and expeditious disposition of the proceeding. The authority conferred upon the arbitrator includes the power to hold conferences with the parties to the arbitration proceeding before the hearing and, among other matters, determine the admissibility, relevance, materiality and weight of any evidence.

(b) An arbitrator may decide a request for summary disposition of a claim or particular issue:

(1) if all interested parties agree; or

(2) upon request of one party to the arbitration proceeding if that party gives notice to all other parties to the proceeding, and the other parties have a reasonable opportunity to respond.

(c) If an arbitrator orders a hearing, the arbitrator shall set a time and place and give notice of the hearing not less than five days before the hearing begins. Unless a party to the arbitration proceeding makes an objection to lack or insufficiency of notice not later than the beginning of the hearing, the party's appearance at the hearing waives the objection. Upon request of a party to the arbitration proceeding and for good cause shown, or upon the arbitrator's own initiative, the arbitrator may adjourn the hearing from time to time as necessary but may not postpone the hearing to a time later than that fixed by the agreement to arbitrate for making the award unless the parties to the arbitration proceeding consent to a later date. The arbitrator may hear and decide the controversy upon the evidence produced although a party who was duly notified of the arbitration proceeding did not appear. The court, on request, may direct the arbitrator to conduct the hearing promptly and render a timely decision.

(d) At a hearing under subsection (c), a party to the arbitration proceeding has a right to be heard, to present evidence material to the controversy, and to cross-examine witnesses appearing at the hearing.

(e) If an arbitrator ceases or is unable to act during the arbitration proceeding, a replacement arbitrator must be appointed in accordance with Section 11 to continue the proceeding and to resolve the controversy.

SECTION 16. REPRESENTATION BY ATTORNEY

A party to an arbitration proceeding may be represented by a lawyer.

SECTION 17. WITNESSES; SUBPOENAS; DEPOSITIONS; DISCOVERY

(a) An arbitrator may issue a subpoena for the attendance of a witness and for the production of records and other evidence at any hearing and may administer oaths. A subpoena must be served in the manner for service of subpoenas in a civil action and, upon [motion] to the court by a party to the arbitration proceeding or the arbitrator, enforced in the manner for enforcement of subpoenas in a civil action.

(b) In order to make the proceedings fair, expeditious, and cost effective, upon request of a party to or a witness in an arbitration proceeding, an arbitrator may permit a deposition of any witness to be taken for use as evidence at the hearing, including a witness who cannot be subpoenaed for or is unable to attend a hearing. The arbitrator shall determine the conditions under which the deposition is taken.

(c) An arbitrator may permit such discovery as the arbitrator decides is appropriate in the circumstances, taking into account the needs of the parties to the arbitration proceeding and other affected persons and the desirability of making the proceeding fair, expeditious, and cost effective.

(d) If an arbitrator permits discovery under subsection (c), the arbitrator may order a party to the arbitration proceeding to comply with the arbitrator's discovery-related orders, issue subpoenas for the attendance of a witness and for the production of records and other evidence at a discovery proceeding, and take action against a noncomplying party to the extent a court could if the controversy were the subject of a civil action in this State.

(e) An arbitrator may issue a protective order to prevent the disclosure of privileged information, confidential information, trade secrets, and other information protected from disclosure to the extent a court could if the controversy were the subject of a civil action in this State.

(f) All laws compelling a person under subpoena to testify and all fees for attending a judicial proceeding, a deposition, or a discovery proceeding as a witness apply to an arbitration proceeding as if the controversy were the subject of a civil action in this State.

(g) The court may enforce a subpoena or discovery-related order for the attendance of a witness within this State and for the production of records and other evidence issued by an arbitrator in connection with an arbitration proceeding in another State upon conditions determined by the court so as to make the arbitration proceeding fair, expeditious, and cost effective. A subpoena or discovery-related order issued by an arbitrator in another State must be served in the manner provided by law for service of subpoenas in a civil action in this State and, upon [motion] to the court by a party to the arbitration proceeding or the arbitrator, enforced in the manner provided by law for enforcement of subpoenas in a civil action in this State.

SECTION 18. COURT ENFORCEMENT OF PRE-AWARD RULING BY ARBITRATOR

If an arbitrator makes a preaward ruling in favor of a party to the arbitration proceeding, the party may request the arbitrator to incorporate the ruling into an award under Section 19. A prevailing party may make a [motion] to the court for an expedited order to confirm the award under Section 22, in which case the court shall summarily decide the [motion]. The court shall issue an order to confirm the award unless the court vacates, modifies, or corrects the award under Section 23 or 24.

SECTION 19. AWARD

(a) An arbitrator shall make a record of an award. The record must be signed or otherwise authenticated by any arbitrator who concurs with the award. The arbitrator or the arbitration organization shall give notice of the award, including a copy of the award, to each party to the arbitration proceeding.

(b) An award must be made within the time specified by the agreement to arbitrate or, if not specified therein, within the time ordered by the court. The court may extend or the parties to the arbitration proceeding may agree in a record to extend the time. The court or the parties may do so within or after the time specified or ordered. A party waives any objection that an award was not timely made unless the party gives notice of the objection to the arbitrator before receiving notice of the award.

SECTION 20. CHANGE OF AWARD BY ARBITRATOR

(a) On [motion] to an arbitrator by a party to an arbitration proceeding, the arbitrator may modify or correct an award:

(1) upon a ground stated in Section 24(a)(1) or (3);

(2) because the arbitrator has not made a final and definite award upon a claim submitted by the parties to the arbitration proceeding; or

(3) to clarify the award.

(b) A [motion] under subsection (a) must be made and notice given to all parties within 20 days after the movant receives notice of the award.

(c) A party to the arbitration proceeding must give notice of any objection to the [motion] within 10 days after receipt of the notice.

(d) If a [motion] to the court is pending under Section 22, 23, or 24, the court may submit the claim to the arbitrator to consider whether to modify or correct the award:

(1) upon a ground stated in Section 24(a)(1) or (3);

(2) because the arbitrator has not made a final and definite award upon a claim submitted by the parties to the arbitration proceeding; or

(3) to clarify the award.

(e) An award modified or corrected pursuant to this section is subject to Sections 19(a), 22, 23, and 24.

SECTION 21. REMEDIES; FEES AND EXPENSES OF ARBITRATION PROCEEDING

(a) An arbitrator may award punitive damages or other exemplary relief if such an award is authorized by law in a civil action involving the same claim and the evidence produced at the hearing justifies the award under the legal standards otherwise applicable to the claim.

(b) An arbitrator may award reasonable attorney's fees and other reasonable expenses of arbitration if such an award is authorized by law in a civil action involving the same claim or by the agreement of the parties to the arbitration proceeding.

(c) As to all remedies other than those authorized by subsections (a) and (b), an arbitrator may order such remedies as the arbitrator considers just and appropriate under the circumstances of the arbitration proceeding. The fact that such a remedy could not or would not be granted by the court is not a ground for refusing to confirm an award under Section 22 or for vacating an award under Section 23.

(d) An arbitrator's expenses and fees, together with other expenses, must be paid as provided in the award.

(e) If an arbitrator awards punitive damages or other exemplary relief under subsection (a), the arbitrator shall specify in the award the basis in fact justifying and the basis in law authorizing the award and state separately the amount of the punitive damages or other exemplary relief.

SECTION 22. CONFIRMATION OF AWARD

After a party to an arbitration proceeding receives notice of an award, the party may make a [motion] to the court for an order confirming the award at which time the court shall issue a confirming order unless the award is modified or corrected pursuant to Section 20 or 24 or is vacated pursuant to Section 23.

SECTION 23. VACATING AN AWARD

(a) Upon [motion] to the court by a party to an arbitration proceeding, the court shall vacate an award made in the arbitration proceeding if:

(1) the award was procured by corruption, fraud, or other undue means;

(2) there was:

(A) evident partiality by an arbitrator appointed as a neutral arbitrator;

(B) corruption by an arbitrator; or

(C) misconduct by an arbitrator prejudicing the rights of a party to the arbitration proceeding;

(3) an arbitrator refused to postpone the hearing upon showing of sufficient cause for postponement, refused to consider evidence material to the controversy, or otherwise conducted the hearing contrary to Section 15, so as to prejudice substantially the rights of a party to the arbitration proceeding;

(4) an arbitrator exceeded the arbitrator's powers;

(5) there was no agreement to arbitrate, unless the person participated in the arbitration proceeding without raising the objection under Section 15(c) not later than the beginning of the arbitration hearing; or

(6) the arbitration was conducted without proper notice of the initiation of an arbitration as required in Section 9 so as to prejudice substantially the rights of a party to the arbitration proceeding.

(b) A [motion] under this section must be filed within 90 days after the [movant] receives notice of the award pursuant to Section 19 or within 90 days after the [movant] receives notice of a modified or corrected award pursuant to Section 20, unless the [movant] alleges that the award was procured by corruption, fraud, or other undue means, in which case the [motion] must be made within 90 days after the ground is known or by the exercise of reasonable care would have been known by the [movant].

(c) If the court vacates an award on a ground other than that set forth in subsection (a)(5), it may order a rehearing. If the award is vacated on a ground stated in subsection (a)(1) or (2), the rehearing must be before a new arbitrator. If the award is vacated on a ground stated in subsection (a)(3), (4), or (6), the rehearing may be before the arbitrator who made the award or the arbitrator's successor. The arbitrator must render the decision in the rehearing within the same time as that provided in Section 19(b) for an award.

(d) If the court denies a [motion] to vacate an award, it shall confirm the award unless a [motion] to modify or correct the award is pending.

SECTION 24. MODIFICATION OR CORRECTION OF AWARD

(a) Upon [motion] made within 90 days after the [movant] receives notice of the award pursuant to Section 19 or within 90 days after the [movant] receives notice of a modified or corrected award pursuant to Section 20, the court shall modify or correct the award if:

(1) there was an evident mathematical miscalculation or an evident mistake in the description of a person, thing, or property referred to in the award;

(2) the arbitrator has made an award on a claim not submitted to the arbitrator and the award may be corrected without affecting the merits of the decision upon the claims submitted; or

(3) the award is imperfect in a matter of form not affecting the merits of the decision on the claims submitted.

(b) If a [motion] made under subsection (a) is granted, the court shall modify or correct and confirm the award as modified or corrected. Otherwise, unless a motion to vacate is pending, the court shall confirm the award.

(c) A [motion] to modify or correct an award pursuant to this section may be joined with a [motion] to vacate the award.

SECTION 25. JUDGMENT ON AWARD; ATTORNEY'S FEES AND LITIGATION EXPENSES

(a) Upon granting an order confirming, vacating without directing a rehearing, modifying, or correcting an award, the court shall enter a judgment in conformity therewith. The judgment may be recorded, docketed, and enforced as any other judgment in a civil action.

(b) A court may allow reasonable costs of the [motion] and subsequent judicial proceedings.

(c) On [application] of a prevailing party to a contested judicial proceeding under Section 22, 23, or 24, the court may add reasonable attorney's fees and other reasonable expenses of litigation incurred in a judicial proceeding after the award is made to a judgment confirming, vacating without directing a rehearing, modifying, or correcting an award.

SECTION 26. JURISDICTION

(a) A court of this State having jurisdiction over the controversy and the parties may enforce an agreement to arbitrate.

(b) An agreement to arbitrate providing for arbitration in this State confers exclusive jurisdiction on the court to enter judgment on an award under this [Act].

SECTION 27. VENUE

A [motion] pursuant to Section 5 must be made in the court of the [county] in which the agreement to arbitrate specifies the arbitration hearing is to be held or, if the hearing has been held, in the court of the [county] in which it was held. Otherwise, the [motion] may be made in the court of any [county] in which an adverse party resides or has a place of business or, if no adverse party has a residence or place of business in this State, in the court of any [county] in this State. All subsequent [motions] must be made in the court hearing the initial [motion] unless the court otherwise directs.

SECTION 28. APPEALS

(a) An appeal may be taken from:

(1) an order denying a [motion] to compel arbitration;

(2) an order granting a [motion] to stay arbitration;

(3) an order confirming or denying confirmation of an award;

(4) an order modifying or correcting an award;

(5) an order vacating an award without directing a rehearing; or

(6) a final judgment entered pursuant to this [Act].

(b) An appeal under this section must be taken as from an order or a judgment in a civil action.

SECTION 29. UNIFORMITY OF APPLICATION AND CONSTRUCTION

In applying and construing this uniform act, consideration must be given to the need to promote uniformity of the law with respect to its subject matter among States that enact it.

SECTION 30. RELATIONSHIP TO ELECTRONIC SIGNATURES IN GLOBAL AND NATIONAL COMMERCE ACT

The provisions of this Act governing the legal effect, validity, and enforceability of electronic records or electronic signatures, and of contracts performed with the use of such records or signatures conform to the requirements of Section 102 of the Electronic Signatures in Global and National Commerce Act.

INDEX

References are to pages

†